BOOKS BY DOUGLAS SOUTHALL FREEMAN

LEE'S LIEUTENANTS

THE SOUTH TO POSTERITY

R.E. LEE

LEE'S DISPATCHES

LEE'S LIEUTENANTS

A Study in Command

DOUGLAS SOUTHALL FREEMAN

ABRIDGED IN ONE VOLUME BY
STEPHEN W. SEARS

INTRODUCTION BY
JAMES M. McPHERSON

SCRIBNER

SCRIBNER
1230 Avenue of the Americas
New York, NY 10020

DESIGNED BY ERICH HOBBING

Set in Adobe Caslon

Manufactured in the United States of America

1   3   5   7   9   10   8   6   4   2

Library of Congress Cataloging-in-Publication Data
Freeman, Douglas Southall, 1886–1953.
Lee's lieutenants : a study in command / Douglas Southall Freeman ; abridged in
one volume by Stephen W. Sears ; introduction by James M. McPherson.
p.   cm.
Includes bibliographical references and index.
1. United States—History—Civil War, 1861–1865—Campaigns.
2. Confederate States of America. Army—Biography. 3. United States—
History—Civil War, 1861–1865—Biography. 4. United States—
History—Civil War, 1861–1865—Regimental histories.
5. Confederate States of America. Army of Northern Virginia.
I. Sears, Stephen W. II. Title.
E470.2.F7   1998
973.7′3—dc21   98-15416
CIP

ISBN 0-684-83309-3

This is an abridged edition of the following works:
Lee's Lieutenants Volume One copyright 1942 by Charles Scribner's Sons;
copyright renewed © 1970 by Inez Goddin Freeman.
Lee's Lieutenants Volume Two copyright 1943 by Charles Scribner's Sons;
copyright renewed © 1971 by Inez Goddin Freeman.
Lee's Lieutenants Volume Three copyright 1944 by Charles Scribner's Sons;
copyright renewed © 1973 by Inez Goddin Freeman.

To
JOHN STEWART BRYAN
who has kept the faith

Contents

Maps

Introduction

JAMES M. McPHERSON

In his four-volume *R. E. Lee* (1934–35) and three-volume *Lee's Lieutenants* (1942–44), Douglas Southall Freeman wrote two million words about the Army of Northern Virginia and its commanders. These volumes were bestsellers in their time and achieved enormous influence on the writing of Civil War military history. *R. E. Lee* won a Pulitzer Prize. *Lee's Lieutenant's* was required reading for many years in British as well as American military schools. In recognition of these achievements, Freeman received twenty-five honorary degrees—not only from Southern institutions but also from leading Northern universities including Princeton, Yale, and Harvard.

Not all the influence of these volumes was salutary. So great was Freeman's impact on the field that many readers gained the impression that almost the whole Civil War was fought in the Eastern theater between the Army of Northern Virginia and the Army of the Potomac. Freeman's masterful volumes strengthened the dominance of the "Virginia school" in Confederate historiography. They also set a standard for Civil War military history that focused on command and strategy rather than on the experience of men in the ranks.

Both the Virginia bias and top-down military history have undergone considerable revision in recent decades. The Western theaters of the Civil War have received their due, and most recent studies of Civil War campaigns and battles combine the view from headquarters with the view from the ranks. Nevertheless, Freeman's studies of Lee and his lieutenants retain their extraordinary value. Nothing written since equals them for insights into the problems and techniques of Civil War command, strategy, and evaluation of intelligence. These volumes remain today the best top-down accounts of the Army of Northern Virginia and the best guide to primary sources for a student wishing to pursue further any of hundreds of subjects or individuals treated by Freeman.

Most readers of Civil War history, however, have neither time nor inclination to wade through a million words on Lee or another million on his subordinates. In 1961, therefore, Richard Harwell published a one-volume abridgment of *R. E. Lee*, in time to meet the increased demand for Civil War books during the centennial observations of the war. But until now *Lee's Lieutenants* has remained a daunting prospect for many readers. Stephen W. Sears, one of the foremost military historians of the Civil War, has performed a service of inestimable value (not to mention skillful, painstaking labor) in producing this abridgment of a classic in Civil War literature. In compressing the material into one-third of its original length, Sears has sacrificed none of the crucial narrative and interpretation of events as they pertained to command decisions and execution, and little of importance pertaining to the personalities of Lee's lieutenants. He has achieved this goal by eliminating Freeman's numerous appendices and most of the footnotes and by paring away all but essential details and quotations. What is left is more than a skeleton; it is a lean, muscular narrative.

Freeman would surely have approved. He was lean and muscular in his youth, a star track athlete in high school and college. Born in 1886 at Lynchburg, Virginia, Douglas was the youngest of four sons of Walker Burford Freeman, a veteran of four years' Civil War service in the 4th Virginia Battery of field artillery. General Jubal A. Early lived just down the street from the Freemans in Lynchburg. Douglas's older brothers amused themselves by telling the five-year-old Douglas that General Early ate little boys for breakfast. "Later in life," wrote Douglas's daughter wryly in 1985, "Father won medals in running because he had learned to sprint past the General's house when he was still very small. Respect for a Confederate officer was one of his strong concepts." Whatever the truth of this anecdote, Freeman did describe Early in *Lee's Lieutenants* as "caustic . . . snarling and stooped, respected as a soldier but never widely popular as a man."

It was not Early, however, but Freeman's own father who first inspired his passion for Confederate history. Like most veterans who had served under Lee, Walker Freeman revered the memory of Marse Robert. He inculcated the same feelings in Douglas with countless old-soldier stories of his wartime experiences. The Freemans moved to Richmond in 1892, where the very atmosphere was filled with Confederate ghosts. Young Freeman attended a private school whose headmaster, also a Confederate veteran, gave the boys a weekly talk on moral conduct illustrated by anecdotes from the lives of Lee, Stonewall Jackson, and other Southern heroes. At the age of seventeen, Douglas attended with is father a reenactment by 2,500 Confederate veterans of the Battle of the Crater at Petersburg. Young Freeman there resolved, as he later recalled, "to preserve from immolating time some of the heroic figures of the Confederacy. . . . The memory of the tattered old ranks, the worn old heroes who charged up Crater Hill will ever be fresh in my memory." Throughout his life (he died in 1955), Freeman never doubted that Confederate leaders and soldiers were "men of principles unimpeachable, of valour indescribable."

After graduating from Richmond College (now Richmond University) in 1904, Freeman entered the graduate program at the Johns Hopkins University. He obtained his Ph.D. in 1908 at the age of twenty-two. Freeman wrote his doctoral dissertation on Virginia's secession convention. We will never know how he interpreted this fateful moment in his beloved state's history, for the sole copy of the dissertation burned in a fire that destroyed the downtown campus of Hopkins in 1908. But Freeman had already published his first book, *A Calendar of Confederate Papers*, a survey and classification of the resources of the Virginia State Library and the Confederate Museum for the study of Confederate history. Despite this accomplishment, Freeman did not pursue a traditional academic career. In 1909 he joined the staff of the *Richmond Times-Dispatch*; within six years he became editor at the age of twenty-nine of the afternoon *Richmond News Leader*, a position he held for the next thirty-four years.

In 1911, Freeman had one of those serendipitous experiences that most historians can only dream of. Out of the blue he received a telephone call from an acquaintance in Savannah, who invited Freeman to lunch. It proved to be a power lunch long before that term was invented. The acquaintance turned over to Freeman two leather-bound volumes containing Robert E. Lee's confidential wartime messages to Jefferson Davis. Long thought to be lost, these dispatches filled a large gap in Confederate military history. Freeman edited and published them in 1915, accomplishing the task with such skill and writing such a brilliant introduction that he became overnight one of the most prominent historians of the Confederacy.

Lee's Confidential Dispatches caught the eye of the chief editor at Charles Scribner's Sons, who commissioned Freeman to write a 75,000-word biography of Lee. Freeman expected to complete the book in two years. Eight times two years went by, the editor died, and still no manuscript was forthcoming. The cause was not Freeman's failure to work on the book. Quite the contrary; he worked too hard, digging into every available source, mining archives and libraries for sources no previous biographer had used, spending at least fourteen and sometimes as many as twenty-five hours a week on the project and accumulating thousands of color-coded note-cards, carefully organized notebooks, and detailed chapter outlines. Freeman did all this in addition to putting in at least a fifty-hour week at the newspaper where he set editorial policy, wrote editorials, edited copy, and prepared twice-daily (at 8:00 A.M. and 12 noon) radio broadcasts that he delivered from 1925 onward. Freeman awoke each day at 2:30 A.M., worked at the *News Leader* office until the paper went to press, then returned home or to a library to work on the Lee biography.

Freeman flourished on this schedule that would have burned out a lesser man, while maintaining an active social life, enjoying a happy marriage, and raising three children. He also served on several boards and delivered dozens of lectures every year. In the fall of 1934, volumes 1 and 2 of *R. E. Lee* were published, followed in the spring of 1935 by volumes 3 and 4. The biography won superlative reviews as well as the Pulitzer Prize. But Freeman did not rest on his laurels. He immediate began work on a biography of another Virginia general, George Washington.

But Freeman's wife detected a certain restlessness, even depression in his manner. He could not let his preoccupation with the Army of Northern Virginia go. He had gathered much more material on Lee's principal subordinate than he had been able to put into the biography. In 1936, Freeman set aside the Washington project (he would eventually complete a seven-volume biography, which won a second Pulitzer Prize) and turned to *Lee's Lieutenants*. During the next six years Freeman, now in his fifties, cheerfully maintained the same punishing schedule as formerly. In 1937, for example, in addition to the newspaper, his radio broadcast, and fifteen or twenty hours of work each week on *Lee's Lieutenants*, he gave eighty-three public speeches and delivered ninety lectures as a visiting professor of journalism at Columbia University. He held this professorship for seven years, commuting twice a week between Richmond and New York.

When *Lee's Lieutenants* appeared one volume at a time during another war from 1942 to 1944, they won an even wider readership than *R. E. Lee*. Freeman was also prouder of these volumes than of his other books because, as he explains in the Foreword, the problem of writing multiple military mini-biographies while keeping the narrative driving forward presented a difficult challenge, which he solved by bringing his actors into and out of the story where relevant without interrupting the flow of events. The result is a tour de force akin to a juggler keeping a half dozen balls in the air without missing a beat of the tune to which he is dancing. By the end of the story, at Appomattox, the reader has learned much about the personalities and qualifications for command, the strengths and weaknesses, successes and failures of the 47 men who served under Lee with the rank of lieutenant general or major general and the 146 who served as brigadier general.

Freeman pulls few punches in his evaluations of these men. Just as Lee himself did not hesitate to get rid of subordinates (usually by exiling them to a Western command) who did not measure up to the stern demands of his offensive-defensive strategy and tactics, so Freeman does not hesitate to detail the weaknesses and mistakes of many of these 193 generals. At the same time, however, Freeman remained true to his vow nearly four decades earlier to preserve the memory of "the heroic figures of the Confederacy . . . men of principles unimpeachable, of valour indescribable."

The subordinate who most closely fit this description was Stonewall Jackson. This doughty warrior dominates volumes 1 and 2, which end with Jackson's death and the resultant reorganization of the army's command structure after Chancellorsville. James Longstreet dominates volume 3 until, in an ironic parallel with Jackson's fate, Longstreet is mistakenly shot by his own men a year and four days later and four miles distant from where the same tragedy had befallen Jackson. Longstreet survived, but was out of the war for five months while he recuperated. In *R. E. Lee*, Freeman had been sharply critical of Longstreet for sluggishness and occasional mulish insubordination, especially at Gettysburg. Freeman revised some of these negative judgments of Longstreet in *Lee's Lieutenants*, though echoes of them remain.

The tone of volume 3 (and of the last one-third of this abridgment) changes from the tone of volumes 1 and 2. There the mood is one of optimism and anticipation of final victory as Lee's predecessors win the first Battle of Manassas and Lee himself leads the army to one triumph after another from the day he takes command on June 1, 1862, through the incredible victory at Chancellorsville. These two years are covered in the first two volumes; Lee's first year of command alone takes up half of the whole three volumes, leaving only one volume for the final two years of the war. The abridgment faithfully preserves these proportions as well as the poignant tone of decline toward defeat that began with the retreat from Gettysburg.

In *Lee's Lieutenants*, Freeman employed the fog-of-war technique that he had perfected in *R. E. Lee*. He reveals to the reader only such information, often uncertain or ambiguous, as was available through the fog of war to Lee and/or his subordinate at the times they needed to make decisions or take actions. This technique has both disadvantages and advantages in comparison with the usual "omniscient author" approach. For the reader who is a beginner in military history, a clear description of the whole picture would make a campaign or battle easier to understand. Yet the fog-of-war technique is truer to the confusing reality of military operations and enables the reader to appreciate the commander's problems as he picks his way through contradictory or inadequate information—or misinformation.

As the astute literary critic Allen Tate also noted in his review of *Lee's Lieutenants*, Freeman's method focuses only on Lee and his army, with scant attention to the enemy or to the society for which the Army of Northern

Virginia was fighting: "If Lee and his subordinates are not fighting anybody, they are equally not fighting for anybody." But Freeman did not conceive his task to be the study of the Union army or of the Civil War as a whole. Other historians took up that duty. Freeman was writing about Lee and his lieutenants, and nobody has done it better. In this one-volume abridgment, the defects (if that is what they are) of the fog-of-war technique are less salient than in the original, for the paring away of many quotations and details of lesser importance causes the narrative to move at a brisker pace, action to follow thought more quickly, and the fog to dissolve as events and results follow hard upon information and decision. This one-volume distillation of the essence of *Lee's Lieutenants* is the best place to start for anyone who wants to understand the story of the Army of Northern Virginia.

Foreword

Douglas Southall Freeman

After completing in 1934 a life of General R. E. Lee, the writer found that mentally it was not easy to leave the struggle about which one had been writing for twenty years and more. A question plagued and pursued: In holding the light exclusively on Lee, had one put in undeserved shadow the many excellent officers of his army? It did not seem permissible to pass on until that company of gallant gentlemen had been placed in proper relationship to their chief.

It was assumed that this work could begin with a brief review of the status and personnel of the Confederate command on June 1, 1862, the date when General Lee opened the headquarters of the Army of Northern Virginia. It soon became apparent that many of Lee's problems of personnel were set for him in advance. His hopes and plans were circumscribed by appointments and by organization, good and bad, that went back to the spring of 1861. Command was not created but was inherited by Lee. Most of his assigned lieutenants had been Johnston's. The failures of the Seven Days could be explained in no other way than by tracing the men through whom Lee undertook his first major offensive.

The officers Lee used in his first campaign in eastern Virginia had acquired their combat experience in one or more of Johnston's three engagements or in Jackson's Valley campaign. To understand why some men were entrusted confidently with field command in June 1862, while others were regarded as excitable or timid, it became necessary to make a detailed study of the battles of First Manassas, Williamsburg, and Seven Pines. Equally imperative was an examination of the operations from Kernstown to Port Republic.

The choice of a method of presenting these sketches of individuals was a continuing puzzle. It sometimes would be necessary to write of as many as a dozen soldiers who had a conspicuous part in the same battle. If in

17

separate studies of these men a reader was confronted with essentially the same details of, say, Sharpsburg, he would damn the battle, the soldiers, the method, and the writer. What alternative was there to this traditional method of treatment? That question prompted another: What had these Confederates in common; what bound together their lives in all the similarities and contrasts? Obviously the nexus was their service in the same army and, for three years of the war, under the same commander. It was in this connection that a letter of General Lee's came to mind. The men of his army, Lee wrote in 1863, "will go anywhere and do anything if properly led. But there is the difficulty—proper commanders—where can they be obtained?" It was clear that Lee constantly was seeking "proper commanders." Was not that a possible basis for a study of Lee's lieutenants? Might not the work be a review of the command of the Army of Northern Virginia, rather than a history of the army itself?

As this approach was examined, it was apparent that the high command of the Army of Northern Virginia was subject to a constant and heavy attrition—by death, by disabling wounds, by intemperance, by incompetence. The army always was being built up and torn down. Aside from manpower, no aspect of the whole tragedy meant more than "proper commanders—where can they be obtained?" The connecting thread of this work well might be that of the effort to create and maintain competent senior officers. As they emerged in battle or in administration of the army, the various leaders could be introduced. If they rose, the scene of their new successes would be the proper setting for their reappearance. In the event they fell, they could be appraised and committed to posterity. All the while, the army would be marching and fighting under such leaders as it had at a given moment. In describing battles, the viewpoint would not be that of Lee but that of the men executing his orders or making decisions for themselves.

In sketching persons in this manner, they will appear and disappear, speak or hold their peace, according to their share in particular scenes. The case of Dorsey Pender is typical. He appears first, casually, in a Richmond hotel lobby, where he asks a question of Johnston. He is seen again in the Seven Days and at Second Manassas, but it is not until Chancellorsville that he becomes a major character in the drama. On the road to Gettysburg, for the final scene in Pender's life, the reader spends a night or two in the camp of the North Carolinian and, over his shoulder, reads some of the last letters written to the young wife at Salem.

Equal to the challenge of finding a suitable method of presentation has been a second, that of making a few score of men stand out as distinguishable individuals where hundreds of actors, literally, crowd the stage. Animation and reality inhere in Stonewall Jackson and Dick Ewell, because of their eccentricities, though there is always danger of historical distortion in overstressing peculiarities. Some more than others have personalities that can be caught, as it were, and held. The frequent eulogies in the *Richmond Examiner* and the details of the quarrel with Jackson may fix, in some measure, the elusive personality of A. P. Hill. One may not say even that much of that modest gentleman, the easy-going, generous Dick Anderson. Certain of Lee's lieutenants were unsensational in behavior or had emotional control so complete that they seemed colorless or even stolid. For the painting of other portraits, the pigments were scanty and dim. Nothing remains but the monochrome of formal, impersonal reports with which to paint a personality. To help visualize all these men, there follows a Dramatis Personæ. It may be consulted if, from the *mise-en-scène,* some man of remembered name but forgotten qualities steps out.

In order to adhere to the realities of a war in which old idols fell fast and new demigods rose overnight, few have been characterized upon their first appearance. Such a man as Beauregard showed his essential ego at a glance. Nothing ever was disclosed that was not plain after one day's association with him, except such a peculiarity as his mastery of his tongue and his utter lack of control over his pen. Jackson, on the other hand, had a nature not shown in all its contrasting lights until one had been with him for months. Presentation of Jackson must be by a process of color printing, where each impression brings out something different. Longstreet presents the same problem. His was not a nature to flash or flame. He talked little, but his silence should not be assumed to cover some deep mystery. A day would come when the flash of the guns in the Peach Orchard made every line of his face stand out. Consequently, the actors in the drama are not presented as definite personalities until they attract some attention by their performance. Jeb Stuart, for example, is treated as one of many promising but not pre-eminent officers of the army until, in June 1862, he made his "ride around McClellan."

After method had been determined and a gradual introduction of the actors arranged, the third question was: Who of Lee's many companions in arms should be presented? No arbitrary standard has been applied. It was apparent that some of the chiefs of division in 1862 were not historically important, and that some who never attained to the coveted rank of major general, or even to that of brigadier general, had a place in the history of the army command or of the army morale. Joseph E. Johnston and P. G. T. Beauregard stood in another category. Was it proper to list them among Lee's lieutenants when he had no command over Beauregard until June 1864, and none over Johnston until January 1865, when Lee became general in chief? On the other hand, both Beauregard and Johnston bulked large—perhaps out of proportion to their true military stature—in the history of the army command in Virginia. General Johnston, in particular, did much to shape the military outlook and esprit de corps of many of the higher officers who served under Lee. Were Johnston and Beauregard omitted, molding influences would be disregarded. In the main, it may be said that each man treated here won his own place, as it were, and determined by his deeds the extent of the treatment he received.

When the relevant facts, somber and sunny, concerning Lee's principal lieutenants had been examined, four surprises were encountered. First among them was the disregard in the Confederacy of officers' training. Prior to secession, much reliance was placed on the leadership of those Southerners who had or previously had held commissions in the United States army. Former officers of volunteers in the Mexican War and the graduates of Southern military schools were expected to supplement the regulars. Virginia listed more men in each of these categories than any other Confederate state, but the total was low—at the most, trained officers for the equivalent of fourteen regiments only. Small as was this number, virtually nothing was done in any organized way to train the required hundreds of new officers. These had to acquire the elements of tactics on the drill ground, with troops, and in the tent at night with copies of Hardee's *Tactics*. Reports of early battles contain grim admission that some officers had to direct troops in action before they themselves knew even the simple evolutions of the line.

The rapid improvement of the troops in drill and discipline would be inexplicable were two facts overlooked. One was the immense service rendered by graduates of the Virginia Military Institute and the South Carolina Military Academy as drillmasters and then as company and regimental officers. Second was the success of the few professional soldiers of the Confederacy in having their government accept and support the standards of discipline and of military usage that had prevailed in the "old army." They administered the army as if there always had been and always would be a Confederacy. One never gets the impression, after the first few months of war, that one is reading of a revolutionary, haphazard organization.

The second surprise in studying the command of the Army of Northern Virginia was the unhappy sharpness of the contrasts of character in the portrayals following the war. If any veteran went over to the Republican party or consorted with Negroes, that never was forgiven him. It canceled his military record, no matter how fine that had been. Apart from such distinctions, there was democracy in defeat. A certain sacredness that attached early to the name of General Lee came in time to embrace the high command generally. Bickering and rivalries were forgotten. Criticism was disloyalty. To mock was to betray.

On cold reappraisal, after the passage of decades, some generals have diminished in stature. The failure of two or three of them is found to have been due to definite and discoverable peculiarities of mind. There is, for example, no mystery about the unwillingness of President Davis to give Beauregard or D. H. Hill a post commensurate with their rank. Beauregard never could be rid of his Napoleonic complex or be induced to shape his strategical plans in terms of available force and practical logistics. Hill, a fine combat officer, would not accept the responsibilities of departmental command. Other men, in unpleasant number, were boastful and willing to warp the historical verities in order to glorify themselves or to extenuate error. Some of Lee's lieutenants were jealous and some were stupid; some were self-seeking and many were vaingloriously ambitious. In two or three cases, the evidence is all too explicit that men of honored name were physical cowards. Several military blunders and no little of chronic inefficiency had their source in the bottle.

In contrast with this dissipation, this smallness, this indiscipline, and this selfishness stand gloriously the character and the fortitude of Lee and of other morally unshakable leaders. In case after case, Lee patiently assuaged the victims of hurt pride, stimulated the discouraged, appealed to the better nature of wavering men, and by force of his own righteousness more than by the exercise of his authority, reconciled bitter differences or induced personal enemies to work together. The seeming absence from the Army of Northern Virginia of such rivalries and animosities as hampered nearly all the other large forces, Confederate and Union, was not in reality absence but control. In the hearts of Lee's subordinates were all the explosive qualities that existed elsewhere, but Lee himself possessed the combination of tact, understanding, prestige, firmness, and personal character necessary to prevent the explosion.

It may be remarked, also, that details of Jackson's ceaseless controversies with his subordinates, and review of his failure to maintain efficient divisional and brigade leadership, are an all-sufficient answer to the question whether Jackson, separated from Lee, would have been a great army commander. Strategically he would have been; administratively, he could not have been. Longstreet's case is similar. His corps was conspicuously free of disputes when he was with Lee. No sooner was Longstreet in semi-independent command in Tennessee than trouble began. As an army commander, Longstreet scarcely would have been able to make his proud, ambitious subordinates pull together as a team.

The next surprise was the discovery that skill in the administration of a command had an even closer relationship to morale than had been supposed. Army morale does not depend exclusively, or even primarily, on the commander-in-chief. He can do little more than give the dynamic of his personality, the stamp of his character, to that which his subordinates have achieved. Insofar as it reflects the command, morale is the mirror of the faith, the administrative skill, and the leadership in training and in combat displayed by the average officer. What is shown in battle is created in camp.

The final surprise came in the study of the third major reorganization of the Army of Northern Virginia. Those successive periods of large-scale promotion form an essential part of the history of the command. When the army was organized in 1861, few responsible leaders foresaw difficulty in procuring qualified commanders. The South was thought to be opulent in leadership. Arms were as readily the avocation of the gentleman as the profession of the soldier. In terms of confident ambitions, the material for a corps of officers seemed abundant. Joseph E. Johnston felt, in the winter of 1861–62, that he had numerous officers qualified for brigade command at the least. By the summer of 1862, General Lee, who was more cautious in his judgment of leadership, was not so sure that colonels in large number could be promoted to the grade of general officer. He was hampered then and increasingly thereafter by the necessity of maintaining a rough balance of commissions among the generals from the different states. Still more was he hindered in the upbuilding of command by the rules of seniority, which, at least in theory, prescribed that the senior colonel or, in any event, a colonel within a given brigade, should be elevated to its command if the general were slain.

Despite these rules, which are among the inherited abominations of military service, little difficulty was experienced in maintaining at a promising level the quality of general officers in the first major reorganization, which followed the campaign of the Seven Days, and in the second, which was necessitated by the losses at Cedar Mountain, at Second Manassas, and in the Maryland expedition. In the study of the third reorganization, that of May 1863, undertaken after the death of Stonewall Jackson, the evidence quickly proved that the Army of Northern Virginia did not then have a sufficient number of qualified colonels of the line to fill vacancies. The school of combat did not graduate men enough to make good the casualties of instruction. Stated explicitly, after the second year of hostilities, in an army of 9 infantry divisions, roughly 150 regiments, two officers only, John B. Gordon and William Mahone, added materially to the vigor of the high command. A few others suggest the possibility of development; at least three who might have become noteworthy commanders—

Dorsey Pender, Dodson Ramseur, and Robert Rodes—were killed in action. The remaining new general officers scarcely attained to the standard of performance established prior to Gettysburg.

This raises a question of continuing importance. The necessary qualities of high military command manifestly are administrative skill and diligence, strategical and logistical sense, military imagination, initiative, resourcefulness, boldness coupled with a grasp of practicality, ability to elicit the best of men, and the more personal qualities of character, endurance, courage, and nervous control. Are these essential qualities possessed, or may they be developed, by more than a minute fraction of those who can perform well the lesser military duties? Ere the Army of Northern Virginia passed the high noon of Chancellorsville, it was plain that a good general had been a good officer from the time of his first commission. No less was it plain that a man would not of necessity be a good general because he had been an excellent captain or had a creditable record as a colonel.

On the basis of that established truth of command in one great American army, it perhaps is a mistake to assume that when a small nation wages a long war it trains in the exacting but instructive school of battle an inexhaustible supply of competent general officers. Instead, where capable officers rise fast, their deaths or invalidism may mean that less competent men will succeed them. Whether the necessary standard of command can be sustained, in the face of heavy casualties in the corps of officers, may depend less on training and combat experience than on the size of the population. A martial tradition, public respect for the profession of arms, and the long-continued service of a well-trained general staff may be ponderable factors, but unless there is vast manpower from which to sift and develop good soldiers, mere experience may not be enough to assure continuing good field command above the grade of colonel.

A writer of biography can ask for nothing more interesting than to begin with a score of names in printed military dispatches and then to work over historical materials of many sorts until names become personalities, characteristics emerge, and reports take on the sound of a voice. At first, one had the feeling that these Confederates had ridden so far toward oblivion that one could not discern the figures or hope to overtake them before they had passed over the horizon of time. In the end, there was the sensation of reaching their camp, of watching the firelight on their faces, of hearing their brave and genial conversation.

The product of selection, training, combat, and survival was not a composite or a "typical" officer. Lee's lieutenants named in these pages interest by reason of their differences, not of their similarities. When one is able, at last, to forget the poignancy of the ninth of April and to look back over the four years, the throng and the clash of personality, in an age of individualism, puts talk of "type" out of place.

Were ever men more consistently themselves? Beauregard, with a Napoleonic complex and a reputation to maintain; Joe Johnston, who had a grievance, a scorn of detail, and an amazing ability to make men believe in him; Magruder, the ever-galloping giant; Gustavus Smith, possessed of a sensitive pomposity that offset his administrative ability and colored curiously his unwillingness to assume responsibility; Harvey Hill, whom combat stimulated and routine paralyzed; the political generals, similar only in their self-confidence and in their flow of fiery eloquence; Powell Hill, who was full of contradictions, able and negligent, cooperative with his subordinates and both punctilious and contentious in his dealings with his corps chief; Old Pete Longstreet, brusque but self-contained, always at his best in battle, a reliable lieutenant but beyond his depth in autonomous command; Jeb Stuart, a praise-loving exhibitionist, as colorful as his uniform, a superb intelligence officer, and an instructor who always trained a sufficient number of capable men to make good his losses; Dick Anderson, too much of a gentleman to assert himself; Wade Hampton, the grand seigneur and huntsman who developed with each new responsibility but never, like Stuart, looked on war as a sport; the ramrod John B. Gordon, whose attack was sharp though his sentences might be florid; diminutive Billy Mahone, growing up as soon as he got a division; John B. Hood, with capacities as a combat officer that were matched by the valor of his troops; William N. Pendleton, able as an organizer and always explaining something at great length and in labyrinthine sentences; Fitz Lee, the laughing cavalier, and Tom Rosser, the daring Lochinvar; Pelham and Pegram, seldom together but always in spirit the Castor and Pollox of the guns; Heth the ill-fortuned and Wilcox the observant; Pender the diligent and Ramseur the hard-hitting; the caustic Early and the Nordic Rodes—the list lengthens but all stand out as individuals. Devotion and that same quality of individualism are all they have in common. Beside this score, a hundred in memory ride past, to be recognized, greeted, and perhaps forgotten again. When the rear file passes, one is regretful that more of them could not be sketched, but one is grateful for the privilege of hearing so many of them talk and of watching them fight.

Editorial Note

STEPHEN W. SEARS

I have long regarded *Lee's Lieutenants* as the most important single work of Confederate historiography ever published. Exceedingly close association with Douglas Southall Freeman's masterwork, in the fashioning of this abridgment, has served only to confirm that opinion. The encomium "most important" can of course be applied just as well to Freeman's *R.E. Lee.* Yet before the four-volume *Lee* was published, in 1934–35, General Lee was hardly unknown to students of the Civil War. By contrast, before *Lee's Lieutenants* was published, in 1942–44, almost all the Confederate officers depicted in these pages were virtual strangers. Adequate biographies had been published of only two of them, Jackson and Jeb Stuart. In his Foreword, Freeman recalls that when he began his work he was concerned that these lieutenants of Lee's might have "ridden so far toward oblivion that one could not discern the figures or hope to overtake them before they had passed over the horizon of time." It was a labor of six years, but Freeman captured them all, for all time.

In abridging the original three volumes of *Lee's Lieutenants* into one volume, the focus has been steadfast on the subtitle of the work—"A Study in Command." The watchword here is *command.* Of necessity much has been pared from the original work, but everything of substance—everything—relevant to the command structure of the Army of Northern Virginia and how it operated has been retained. This made up the unique quality of *Lee's Lieutenants,* and that uniqueness is the same whether it is between two covers or between six.

Freeman's concern for what he called "the hurried reader" led him to put peripheral material into fourteen appendices. These have been deleted from this abridgment. The other large saving has been found in the detail of the battle accounts; that, after all, comprises the one thing collectively that can be found elsewhere. What cannot be found elsewhere, what cannot be duplicated, is Douglas Southall Freeman's interpretations of the officers who made up the high command of the Army of Northern Virginia through four years of war. Those interpretations remain, intact and unchanged and as valid now as they were more than a half century ago.

While the pace of the narrative here inevitably is faster, the voice is still Freeman's. Wherever bridging and paraphrases are required, they are constructed from Freeman's words and phrases. Documents in many cases are extracted or summarized. The footnotes of course required recasting. They serve now simply as source notes and are found in the back of the book. Anything in the footnotes essential to the narrative has been worked into the text.

In the Notes and the Bibliography, certain manuscripts put into print since *Lee's Lieutenants* was published are cited in their printed form. Two examples are the journal of Jedediah Hotchkiss and the letters of Dorsey Pender. The narrative has been corrected to reflect C. Van Woodward's definitive edition of Mary Chesnut's diary. Where practicable, the present ownership and location of cited manuscripts is indicated. It is hoped these alterations will make the work and its sources more accessible to students of the war and of the Confederacy.

Dramatis Personæ

Listed in substantially the order of their appearance in the narrative. Ages are those of the birthday nearest the outbreak of hostilities, April 1861.

PIERRE GUSTAVE TOUTANT BEAUREGARD

Professional soldier, "Hero of Sumter," he comes to Virginia with high reputation easily won during the initial hostilities at Charleston. He is forty-three, an admirable actor in a martial role, and he displays great self-confidence on the basis of limited experience with troops. From the outset he shows a lack of the sense of logistics and grossly overestimates the strategical combinations possible with green troops and inexperienced staff, but he has the good fortune to rout the enemy at Manassas, July 21, 1861. The aftermath of this victory brings to light some curious mental qualities and a singular infelicity in writing. All these combine to get him into trouble with the President and the War Department. Latin in look, he is of medium height and middle weight. His soldiers call him "Old Bory" and say he has the eye of a bloodhound. Lettered admirers insist he might have been the reincarnation of one of Napoleon's marshals.

JOHN BANKHEAD MAGRUDER

"Prince John" he is to all his acquaintances, fifty-one, a professional soldier with some antebellum experience as an artillerist. He is handsome, perfectly uniformed, insistent, impatient, and theatrical, and he always appears at a gallop. Despite a slight lisp, he loves to talk and he writes ceaselessly to his superiors. A certain aptitude for independent command he possesses, and with it ability to bluff an adversary. After winning much applause for the first Confederate victory in Virginia, he gradually becomes entangled in a large military organization, which irks him unreasonably. In the end, when his great opportunity comes in the defense of Richmond, he shows a weakness not uncommon in war—an excited, overzealous desire to do all his work in person.

DANIEL HARVEY HILL

Former professional soldier, educator, textbook author, and distinguished Presbyterian layman, age forty, Hill has an accidental spine injury and an exceedingly sharp tongue. In looks he is cadaverous and has haunting eyes. He is in combat as capable as in camp he is critical. Off duty he is unpretending. His judgment of men always runs to an extreme. In the days after Malvern Hill there are indications that he lacks some quality of leadership. It is not so much a lack of control of his critical and sometimes gloomy temperament as it is a disgust for routine administrative duty and a singular unwillingness to make important decisions off the field. He increases his reputation as a combat officer but barely escapes disaster at South Mountain in Maryland, where the full responsibility rests on him. It is his fate—not unusual in war—to be denied the service he magnificently performed and to be assigned unwelcome duty for which he has no aptitude. He leaves the scene of his Virginia successes and returns once and briefly in 1864.

ROBERT SELDEN GARNETT

A solitary, professional soldier, age forty-one, of intellectual stock, wholly devoted to his profession, frozen by grief to seeming austerity, but regarded as a leader of great capacity and high promise, he passes from the stage early in the first act of this tragedy.

JOSEPH EGGLESTON JOHNSTON

He considers himself the ranking officer of the United States army who joins the Confederacy and he resolves that he shall be so accepted. About him, at fifty-four years of age, are some magnetic and winning qualities which make his friends and most of his subordinates devoted to him. He has, also, unmistakable strategical sense, though doubts concerning his administrative capacity and his attention to detail gradually accumulate. Early he acquires a grievance which embitters all his dealings with the administration. Johnston is alarmed, also, to discover how readily secrets of military importance leak out, and probably for this reason he is excessively reserved in dealing with the President and the War Department. His peculiarities clash with those of the commander-in-chief until his acts are hampered and his response to orders or to suggestions is unpredictable. A difficult and touchy subordinate he is, though a generous and kindly superior—in sum, a military contradiction and a temperamental enigma. In appearance he is small, soldierly, and graying, with a certain gamecock jauntiness.

NATHAN GEORGE EVANS

Of the devil-may-care type of soldier, he is age thirty-seven, bold, reckless, schooled in Indian fighting. Savage in appearance until he smiles, he has one fine scene and then leaves the stage, to return for a time in the late summer of 1862. His nickname is "Shanks."

GUSTAVUS WOODSON SMITH

Street commissioner of New York City, former army engineer and private engineering contractor, age thirty-nine, Smith was a somewhat late arrival on the battlefield. Bulky, occasionally frowning, and always determined to impress, he is an assured administrator who maintains suavely pleasant relations with his superiors and subordinates and enjoys high rank and reputation though he is little experienced with troops. To his intimates he is "G.W." There is a suggestion of politics in his eminence. Somewhat pompously he proceeds to his first great hour of responsibility, at Seven Pines, and then collapses mysteriously. Upon his recovery it is soon apparent that the administration has lost faith in his abilities and intends to assign him to quiet sectors. He resents this. Although he does not meet the requirements of even a minor mission in North Carolina, he raises a storm because he is not made a lieutenant general. When he is put off with assuaging words, he is provoked to tender his resignation, which President Davis gratefully and caustically accepts. Smith is seen no more in the Army of Northern Virginia.

THOMAS JONATHAN JACKSON

A mediocre teacher at the Virginia Military Institute and a former professional soldier, age thirty-seven, profoundly and, some say, fanatically religious, Jackson had a precise regard for discipline and army regulations. A man of contrasts so complete, he appears one day a Presbyterian deacon who delights in theological discussion and, the next, a reincarnated Joshua. He lives by the New Testament and fights by the Old. Almost six feet in height and weighing about 175 pounds, he has blue eyes, a brown beard, and a commonplace, somewhat rusty appearance. His students called him "Tom Fool Jackson." To his soldiers he is "Stonewall" or "Old Blue Light" and then "Old Jack." From the first scene he grows in importance until he becomes the hero of the drama, and then, abruptly, he fails in a climactic hour and raises a question as to whether he can work in harness. After moving against Pope in semi-independent command, Lee joins him and he develops incredibly and gives by his brilliant obedience to orders the unqualified answer to the ugly questions asked after the Seven Days. His are the most shining of the army's achievements during the period of its greatest prowess. He wins first place professionally among Lee's lieutenants and in popular reputation exceeds his chief; but in army administration he is not uniformly successful. Perhaps because of his stern conceptions of duty, he is exacting of his subordinates. The result is a continuing bitter quarrel with A. P. Hill and inability to find men who fulfill his standards of command. Although he always is marching or winning a battle or preparing for another, he cannot forget the home he has not visited in two years or the baby he has never seen. In the spring of 1863 he does not attempt to conceal his satisfaction at having his family visit him. After that comes what the Greeks would have termed *apotheosis.*

JAMES LONGSTREET

He first seeks staff appointment as paymaster, the position he had held in the United States army, though he is a graduate of West Point. He receives line commission and soon displays administrative capacity, power to win the respect of his subordinates, and a calm imperturbability in battle. Until an epidemic kills three of his children, he is a somewhat gay comrade; thereafter he is absorbed in his duty. Blunt and roughly bantering, he is not ill-natured. In height he is about 5 feet 10½ inches, age forty. He is slightly deaf, but a dignified, impressive man, known to his soldiers as "Old Pete." If he is not brilliant in strategy or in conversation, he is solid and systematic. Ambitious he is, also, but not disposed to pick quarrels. The secret of his power is his incredible nervous control. He never gets tired. As the senior lieutenant general and commander of the First Corps, his opportunities are not so numerous nor so dazzling as Jackson's. During a period of ten months, except for one afternoon near Manassas, he does not have to fight an offensive battle. This experience may have spoiled him, may have led him to think that if he chooses a good position and remains there, an impatient enemy will attack and give him all the advantage of the defensive. Nobody seems aware of this at the time. In Lee's eyes, Longstreet remains what he called his stout lieutenant after Sharpsburg—my "war horse." Longstreet is dependable, solid, an excellent tactician. Stonewall Jackson's death then leaves him first in reputation among Lee's lieutenants. He is beguiled by circumstances into thinking himself a strategist as well as an executive officer. His failure at Gettysburg is one result of his mistake concerning his aptitudes. Sent to the Army of Tennessee, he is disillusioned and embittered. Slowly he loses faith in victory, but he unflinchingly returns to his corps after a wound received in his great hour. At the end he stands by his chief and says, "General, unless he offers us honorable terms, come back and let us fight it out!"

RICHARD STODDERT EWELL

From graduation at the Military Academy a trooper, and for most of his career as a soldier, an Indian fighter, at forty-four years old he is, at his quarters, an unsoldierly person, bald, pop-eyed, and long-beaked, with a piping voice that seems to fit his appearance as a strange, unlovely bird; he probably has stomach ulcers and chronically complains of headaches, sleepless nights, and indigestion; but he quickly shows that he has a chivalrous, fighting spirit along with a sharp tongue and an odd sense of humor. He acquires friends unnumbered. They are not quite so irreverent as the soldiers who style him "Old Bald Head." For three weeks of brilliant performance he is the character *sui generis* of Lee's army. Then he loses a leg. For months he is an impatient invalid. His career has a curious sequence— wound, promotion, marriage. When he, as notorious a bachelor as Jubal Early, returns to the army with a wife, he is cheered and she is welcomed. Soon there is a suspicion that he is changed and not altogether for the better. It may be difficult for even a lieutenant general to have two commanders. He dazzles and then dismays the army during the advance into Pennsylvania. After exploits that would have added to the fame of Stonewall himself, he loses the power of decision. He cannot exercise the discretion allotted him, though he often has displayed sound judgment when operating alone or under Old Jack, who always said, "Do this." Dick Ewell's decline is of the body and of the intellect. His spirit is as firm as ever.

TURNER ASHBY

Farmer, noted horseman, age thirty, with little formal education, though born of good stock, he shows himself so bold and resourceful a leader, so flawlessly courageous in the presence of the enemy, that he attracts to him every boy in the Shenandoah Valley who loves horses and craves adventure. Soon Ashby gets more soldiers than he can direct well, but he performs some amazing feats before a certain day in June 1862. In appearance he is strange, almost mysterious—of the darkest olive complexion, "an Arab type" some insist, small but agile and of great strength. About him, while he is still living, myths gather.

RICHARD TAYLOR

Son of a President of the United States, he is a wealthy sugar-plantation owner, sometime student at Edinburgh and Harvard and graduate of Yale. At thirty-five he accepts election as colonel of a Louisiana regiment and comes to Virginia, where he has little fighting to do until he gets a brigade under Ewell and marches to join Stonewall Jackson in the Shenandoah. There a multitude of adventures befall him. Observant, he has a fine sense of the dramatic. He is absolutely self-reliant and indisposed to accept any judgment as sound merely because it is authoritative. This does not cost him either his admiration or affection for other men, nor, before he leaves the army for the western theater, does it deny him their friendship.

WILLIAM HENRY CHASE WHITING

Son of a lieutenant colonel in the United States army, he had a higher rating at West Point than any cadet ever had won prior to his time. Thereafter, until 1861, he had been a conspicuous younger officer in the Corps of Engineers. He is forty-seven, thoroughly conscious of his position, and somewhat disposed, perhaps, to lord it over men like Jackson, who had no distinction among his contemporaries at the Military Academy. Quite soon Whiting clashes with the President, on whose black books his name is entered. Somehow—none knows exactly how—he does not quite fulfill expectations. He is below middle height but handsome, martial, and aristocratic in appearance. His troops call him "Little Billy."

Thomas Jonathan Jackson

JAMES LONGSTREET

RICHARD STODDERT EWELL

DANIEL HARVEY HILL

JUBAL ANDERSON EARLY

James Ewell Brown Stuart

AMBROSE POWELL HILL

FITZHUGH LEE

WADE HAMPTON

RICHARD HERON ANDERSON

JOHN BELL HOOD

Robert Emmett Rodes

JOHN BROWN GORDON

GEORGE EDWARD PICKETT

WILLIAM DORSEY PENDER

William Mahone

ROBERDEAU CHATHAM WHEAT

Clergyman's son, thirty-five, lawyer, soldier of fortune in Mexico and in Italy under Garibaldi, he has the dubious distinction of commanding the toughest battalion in the army and, ere his end, he shares in three of the most dramatic scenes in the drama.

JUBAL ANDERSON EARLY

Lawyer, prosecuting attorney of Franklin County, Virginia, West Point graduate, at age forty-four Early was notoriously a bachelor and at heart a lonely man. He comes from an unrenowned region, has no powerful family connections, and by a somewhat bitter tongue and rasping wit has isolated himself. He is about six feet in height, thin and stooped by arthritis. His eyes, his hair and beard are black. Amused by his odd name, soldiers call him "Old Jube," or "Old Jubilee." In the opening of the Confederate drama he has two scenes only. In one he distinguishes himself; in the other he raises a question of impetuosity: Is he too reckless to be entrusted with command he otherwise is qualified to discharge? Soon, however, he shows rapid development as a soldier. Stubbornness in combat takes the place of impetuosity. If he knew or cared a little more about the art of ingratiation, he would be something of a hero. Certainly, as an executive officer, his fighting record from Cedar Mountain to Salem Church is second only to that of Jackson himself. Fires of ambition burn behind those black eyes. He finds it easy to impress on generous Dick Ewell the views he never even thought of suggesting to the austere Stonewall. Perhaps, as he observes how Ewell is failing, he dreams of a corps command of his own. The next summer he receives the Second Corps and leads it in the very country where Jackson fought in '62. Much that is bold and soldierly is credited to Old Jube, but he has a prejudice against the cavalry, whom he does not understand, and in a campaign against a Union cavalryman who has overwhelming superiority of force, he suffers defeat worse than his worst enemies could have wished for him. His sharp tongue is so critical of others that men refuse to see his excellences as a soldier.

JAMES EWELL BROWN STUART

By training and by preference a cavalryman, though not without an affection for artillery, Stuart at twenty-eight years of age, with an excellent army record, is still a good deal of a boy, with a loud, exhibitionist manner, a fondness for spectacular uniforms and theatrical appearance, and a vast love of praise. Soon he shows, also, that he is disposed to somewhat reckless adventure, but he has remarkable powers of observation, great physical strength, and immense endurance. He is about five feet nine inches, massive and nearly square. His troopers call him "Jeb." As chief of cavalry he has only one large opportunity between Malvern Hill and the end of April 1863. He makes the most of that in a fast, horse-killing raid. Spectacular raids, in fact, are becoming his specialty, but he continues to learn the arts of reconnaissance, observation, and military intelligence. Unexpectedly, at midnight, he is called to the largest command he ever has exercised, and over infantry, not cavalry. While he fulfills the expectations of his friends, somehow he does not get quite the measure of praise he seems to have expected. That remains one of his peculiarities—that love of praise, and it does not diminish as his solid fame increases. At heart, this noisy, ostentatious young man fears God and loves country. He may be a courtier; his most depreciative critic never denies he is a fighter. He also develops a new distinction—he becomes a remarkable instructor of cavalrymen. In the cavalry there are always more men capable of leading brigades than there are brigades to lead. It is fortunately so, because Jeb's days of shining success are over. The blue cavalry knows how to fight now. It counts too many sabers. One humiliation leads Stuart to a reckless adventure in Pennsylvania and then to a long verbal defense. He is absent on the day of all days when he could reconnoiter the Federal position. He continues to be an unexcelled reconnaissance officer with a vast aptitude for analyzing intelligence reports. His end is hard, though it is curiously like that of his friend Jackson.

AMBROSE POWELL HILL

Almost five years of Powell Hill's career as a professional soldier have been spent in the office of the United States Coastal Survey. That has given him a certain knowledge of the inner workings of the machinery of government but it has not improved his temper. At thirty-five years of age, and a Confederate colonel of the line, he trains what proves to be an excellent regiment and in his first battle he shows good brigade leading. He then wins promotion to the grade of major general and almost immediately shows certain explosive qualities. In person he is thin, of average height and frail health, with heavy beard and hair of an auburn brown. He dresses picturesquely but not so conspicuously as Jeb Stuart. Proud and sensitive, he displeases Jackson and until the end is at odds with his chief. He harbors his feeling of injustice but is as quick to demand fair play for his subordinates as for himself; perhaps there is something of the army politician in him. None of this affects Hill's division, which under his intelligent administration probably is the best in the army. At Second Manassas, Sharpsburg, and Chancellorsville he has three great days. At the close of the third of them, a trivial injury cheats him of his rightful part in the glory of the army's high noon. As commander of the new Third Corps he holds the affection of his staff and the admiration of his men. After Jackson's death, Hill engages in no more controversies, but he is not the same man who impetuously led the fighting Light Division. He does not fail beyond excuse or explanation; he does not succeed. Although few say it in plain words, he is not fulfilling the hopes of the army. It may be because of ill health or a sense of larger, overburdening responsibility.

WILLIAM NELSON PENDLETON

A clergyman of the Protestant Episcopal Church, he is fifty-two years of age and is on friendly footing with the President and with Generals Lee and Johnston because he was at West Point with them. Circumstance and a certain aptitude for organization give him advancement to the post of chief of artillery, but he does not appear prominently until the last scene on the Peninsula. Then he makes the younger men of the artillery wonder if he has the basic qualities of command. Pendleton looks and dresses like the commanding general, for whom he is sometimes mistaken. He suffers from a curious form of that unhappy disease cacoëthes scribendi, which produces some remarkable distortions. After Sharpsburg, some ridicule and contempt are visited on him for mishandling an operation that might have had disastrous consequences. Then he earns solid credit for sound reasoning, hard work, and the tactful adjustment of posts and personalities in an admirable reorganization of the artillery. Before he can expand in the satisfaction he deserves, doubtful disposition of his guns on a difficult day at Chancellorsville brings new humiliation. His is a curious fate: While young professional artillerists and infantrymen laugh at him, most of them have high admiration and proudly admitted affection for his son, Sandie Pendleton.

CHARLES S. WINDER

Somewhat belatedly, this Marylander and professional soldier, age thirty-three, is beginning, by August 1862, to be credited with the abilities he had demonstrated in the Valley campaign the previous spring; but Fate outruns Fame. At Cedar Mountain, before he wins formal command of Jackson's old division, he fights his last battle. Like Robert Garnett, he seemed to have the mold and the hallmark of the true soldier.

FITZHUGH LEE

This rollicking nephew of the commanding general is twenty-five and a West Pointer with some experience as a lieutenant in the United States cavalry. He begins his Confederate service as a captain and rises steadily until in July 1862 he wears the wreath and three stars of a brigadier general. Florid, after the manner of the Lees, he is strong and already too fat; but he is active, cheerful, and on terms of companionable intimacy with Stuart. Those in the army who do not enviously attribute to "family influences" his rapid rise say he is a typical cavalryman. He has some dazzling adventures, and in the serious business of covering the rear of a retreating army he wins many plaudits. If there were a Confederate Frans Hals, he would paint Fitz Lee, but would ask this laughing cavalier of the South to trim that patriarchal beard. Fitz would laugh more boisterously than ever, but would say, "No." That beard conceals his youth. A man who is named a major general before he is twenty-eight needs to look old to be the companion of Jeb Stuart and the rival of Wade Hampton, the only two men who outrank him. Although arthritis hampers him, he fights hard and learns much of the art of command. Lack of mounts weakens the cavalry during the last winter of the war, but circumstance places him honorably at the head of the corps. From the final scene he rides off in the hope of fighting in North Carolina.

WADE HAMPTON

Probably the richest planter in the entire South, forty-two years of age, he has had no previous military education but possesses high intelligence, superb physique, and the training of a thorough sportsman. He is fighting from a sense of duty, not from love of combat, but by the time the smoke clears from Malvern Hill, he shows distinct promise as a cavalry commander. By standards of the youthful cavalry, the grand seigneur of South Carolina is mature, almost old. He shares in most of Stuart's raids and proudly conducts two of his own without the help, thank you, of any of those Virginians who act as if they discovered horsemanship. He receives some ugly wounds at Gettysburg, where the rivalry between himself and Fitz Lee almost leads to an open quarrel. Hampton's defiant physique and his unconquerable spirit bring him back to field duty with a major general's commission and a new responsibility when his senior falls. There is hesitation at headquarters about assigning Hampton to command the cavalry corps, because he is not a professional soldier; but he directs victories so shining that the old troopers are proud to call him Jeb Stuart's successor. His men say he is a "born soldier." They do not know that he thinks more often of the fallen, one of his own sons among them, than of command and power and glory. This much his troopers realize—that he believes in superior force and that he does not ask the impossible of hungry men on feeble horses.

RICHARD HERON ANDERSON

Like Hampton, he is a South Carolinian of high station. Age forty and a West Pointer, he proves himself capable of handling troops in battle and of hitting hard; but he is of a kindly, generous, and easy-going nature and, though he receives promotion to the grade of major general after the Seven Days, he has no inclination to advertise or to advance himself. At Sharpsburg he receives a wound which is not altogether misfortune because it demonstrates how much of the efficiency of his division is due to his personal influence and leadership. He has no subsequent opportunity till Chancellorsville. Then he shows himself willing that Stuart shall have the glory and he the sense of duty done; but Lee has seen what happened and, in the list of those who may lead a corps if need be, the name of Anderson is entered. He does not thrive in the Third Corps to which he is assigned in the reorganization after Chancellorsville. Perhaps he misses the guiding hand of Longstreet. It may be that Powell Hill does not know how to deal with the South Carolinian at Gettysburg. Ten sterile months follow. Then, by a simple decision, promptly executed, Anderson thrills the army and probably saves it from a defeat at Spotsylvania. His reward is promotion and continuing command of the First Corps until the return of the wounded Longstreet in the autumn of 1864. Lee sees to it that he retains his temporary rank of lieutenant general, but the corps assigned him is little more than a division. Part of it loses heart. So does Anderson. Among the hills that run down to Sayler's Creek most of his men are captured. That last scene would be blackest tragedy if the memory of Chancellorsville and Spotsylvania did not linger.

Lafayette McLaws

Stout, short, and more intense than his round face would indicate, this Georgian, age forty, had a good record as an officer in the "old army" and he shows administrative capacity as a soldier of the Confederacy. By the summer of 1862 he is entrusted with divisional command, but is not yet appraised finally because his opportunities in combat are few. He encounters bad luck on Maryland Heights and drags slowly along on the road to Sharpsburg when he should be demanding the last energies of weary men. At Fredericksburg he easily holds a strong position with ample force, but in the spring, when he has a chance to deliver a hammerstroke at Chancellorsville, he hesitates. McLaws does not progress. He has no luster in the red glare of Gettysburg, though the fault is scarcely his. He goes with Longstreet to Tennessee and there, he avers, he comes under the wrath of his chief because he will not share in an attempt to oust Braxton Bragg. An unhappy story of bitterness and court-martial is shaped with difficulty to Longstreet's purpose in this particular: McLaws never commands a First Corps division again.

John Bell Hood

By birth a Kentuckian and by choice a Texan, he appears as a somewhat ungainly lieutenant of cavalry, age thirty, but he develops amazingly as a commander and as an individual. There is reason to believe his magnificent personality, his blond, towering, blue-eyed, and handsome good looks, will advance him as surely as his fighting will. He is altogether promising as a combat officer; as an administrator and a strategist, he is inexperienced. In divisional command, his soldiers are, man for man, perhaps the best combat troops in the army, though in numbers they never approach and in fame do not equal, as yet, Powell Hill's Light Division. Hood is conspicuous in the Seven Days, at Second Manassas, and at Sharpsburg. Later, on a quiet front, he has only one ambition: to get back to the fight. As the fighting quality of his troops is, in a measure, of his making, he appears to have a brilliant future. With a wound received in a great hour at Gettysburg he passes from the scene to return no more, but his old comrades in the Army of Northern Virginia read with pride of his feats at Chickamauga and of his appointment to command the Army of Tennessee. His new responsibility is beyond the resources of a crippled general. He has a winter of catastrophe. Perhaps he never should have been assigned an army. At heart he is an executive officer, not a strategist.

ROBERT EMMETT RODES

A graduate of the Virginia Military Institute, a teacher there, and a former civil engineer for an Alabama railroad, Rodes is thirty-two years old, more than six feet in height, blond, with a drooping sandy mustache and a fiery, imperious manner on the field of battle. As if he stepped from the pages of *Beowulf,* Rodes stalks through the camps and fights always as if his battle were to decide a great cause. He has alternating fortune, now good, now bad, in the Maryland expedition, but at Chancellorsville he wins in an afternoon fame that brings him the closest approach the army can offer to promotion for valor on the field. He is the personification of the new type of Confederate leader, but he does not retain as division commander the consistent distinction that had been his as a brigadier. Perhaps on July 1 at Gettysburg—the first day he ever had led his own division in battle—he tries too hard with feeble instruments. The next day he halts his advance before it attempts to scale Cemetery Hill. Doubtless he is right, but it is not like the Rodes of Chancellorsville. When he gets back to the Wilderness in 1864, he has the furious old-time dash, and at the Bloody Angle he rivals his comrades Gordon and Ramseur. With them, under Jube Early, he goes to the Shenandoah Valley, and there, at a moment when he did not know the battle was lost, he leaves unanswered the question whether he would have realized fully his promise as a soldier.

SAMUEL GARLAND

A lawyer of wide literary taste and cultural interests, a graduate of the Virginia Military Institute, and, at thirty, a man of recognized standing. With more of the look of a scholar than of a soldier, he does admirably in all the battles he shares and ahead of him appears to lie a career of great distinction. Perhaps he scarcely cares for fame, though he will do his full duty. He has lost both wife and child and finds himself the last of his line. He goes on a difficult mission down the ridge of South Mountain, where he lacks adequate support, and he does not come back.

ROBERT TOOMBS

This well-known Georgia politician, former United States senator, and first Confederate secretary of state, age fifty-one, is a furious, fascinating person who believes that the war will be brief but that participation in it will give him more prestige than can be had in civil life during the sectional quarrel. He is ambitious, insubordinate, and quarrelsome, the impersonation of the "political general." A few of his friends hold loyally to him and share his belief that he is a great man. His hatred of President Davis develops apace. Toombs is no sooner out of a row with Harvey Hill than he is in another with Longstreet. Momentarily the thunderous Georgian is silenced, but soon, by an ironical twist, along the banks of the Antietam, he is presented with such an opportunity as he coveted. He does well enough but he somewhat overpraises himself. The promotion he feels he deserves but does not expect to get from Davis he fails to receive. He resigns with a roar and subsequently shouts in the shadows.

JOHN ROGERS COOKE

Army-born and Harvard-schooled, this twenty-nine-year-old son of General Philip St. George Cooke, U.S.A., is a brother-in-law of Jeb Stuart. When he resigned from the "old army" he was a first lieutenant. He becomes an excellent, careful colonel, and at Sharpsburg, almost before his panting men have caught their breath, he has the entire army talking of him. Promotion comes quickly and, after that, on Marye's Heights, comes a ball that hits him in the forehead but, happily, does not kill him. The Wilderness brings him his fourth wound. Steadfast, he is still leading his North Carolina brigade on its last day.

MICAH JENKINS

After he was graduated from the South Carolina Military Academy, he was one of the organizers of the King's Mountain Military School. As colonel he is bold and ambitious and, as the battles multiply starting with Seven Pines, he throws himself more furiously into them. He is full of promise—clear-eyed, with dark wavy hair and a firm, determined, but not unfriendly mouth. He becomes a brigadier before he is twenty-seven and is distinguished at Second Manassas, but he is wounded there and after his recovery he is on the unexciting line of the Blackwater. Longstreet appreciates him; fortune does not smile. Soon there arises a vindictive rivalry with Evander Law, another young South Carolinian. Jenkins's return with Longstreet to battle ends in the Wilderness.

John Brown Gordon

Mining promoter and lawyer, age twenty-nine, he has risen from captain to colonel and soon has opportunity of leading Rodes's brigade. With a fine head and penetrating eyes, Gordon is so thin and so straight that he resembles a ramrod. Although he has had no military experience before the war, he quickly learns the art of procuring the full obedience of his men and possesses an oratorical power which inspires his troops to undertake anything. His men adore him, but they wish he would not loose his eloquence on them just before they go into a battle—he makes them feel as if they can charge hell itself! He accumulates a notable collection of wounds, and after a succession of legislative mishaps, receives his deserved commission as brigadier general at the beginning of May 1864. Before the month is out Gordon has a division. By the late winter he is commanding Early's corps, and is next to Longstreet in confidential discussions with the commanding general. A certain freshness, a boldness, a freedom, an originality in sound military design are Gordon's. Character makes chivalry an instinct with John Gordon. No wonder an admiring soldier says of him, "He's most the prettiest thing you ever did see on a field of fight. It'ud put fight into a whipped chicken just to look at him!"

Isaac Ridgeway Trimble

Railroad executive, engineer, and old-time West Pointer, Trimble, at fifty-nine, leaves ease in Maryland to share the fortunes of the South. At first he shows awkwardness in handling troops but he learns fast. He is a dark, handsome man with a flaming eye and deep ambition—perhaps disposed to be contentious and certainly a dandy in dress, but of the most conspicuous courage and a furious, insatiable fighter. A bad leg wound at Second Manassas, erysipelas, and osteomyelitis in turn assail but cannot subdue him. He fulfills his ambition and heads for the enemy's country, where he had built and operated railroads and had quarreled over them. His part in the drama ends in front of Cemetery Ridge, where he falls, wounded, into enemy hands.

Maxcy Gregg

A savant and lawyer is Gregg, a rich South Carolina bachelor of wide literary and scientific interests, who has counted politics among his avocations. He had a commission, though he saw no active service, in the Mexican War, and he appears first with the army as a colonel and then a brigadier. In station, in influence, in bearing, and in entourage he is a considerable person, whose ability to adapt himself to command is of some interest to his friends. He is dignified, unfailingly courteous, forty-seven years of age, and slightly deaf. He is allotted a glorious day on Groveton Heights, and then he has a narrow escape at Sharpsburg. After that, at Fredericksburg, there is a wound, an affecting interview with Stonewall Jackson, and the long, long silence. The command loses a certain measure of gentility when he dies.

THOMAS REED ROOTES COBB

A brigade is entrusted to this hard-working colonel of thirty-nine, who is a younger brother of Howell Cobb. By his management of his men, Tom Cobb soon restores the family prestige, which had been impaired by Howell Cobb's mishandling of his troops at Crampton's Gap. As fine a fortune in the field as at the bar seems to await Tom Cobb, but at Fredericksburg, in his first battle as a general officer, he is killed.

JOHN PELHAM

A West Pointer of the class of 1861, he resigned on the secession of Alabama and prior to his graduation. He is twenty and commands as captain the Stuart Horse Artillery, which he organized. Of all the young artillerists, none is braver, more promising, or physically more magnificent. He is a tall, clear blond, who blushes red when he is praised. In camp he is quiet, and is without a touch of exhibitionism —a glorious boy in the estimation of both sexes. He goes on from splendor to splendor, makes peculiarly his own the title "gallant," and on a March day in '63, shouting "Forward!" and smiling at troopers in a charge, he falls from his horse with a fatal wound. Three girls in nearby towns put on mourning for him.

WILLIAM JOHNSON PEGRAM

Until secession he was a student of the University of Virginia, and was regarded merely as an intelligent, retiring boy of high character. At twenty he appears in this drama as a tireless captain of artillery whose tactics seem to be summed up in three orders: get close to the enemy, stay there, fire fast and accurately. He is a small young man, so near-sighted that he always wears spectacles, but he is of the type that battle develops. In less than a year he is a major in command of an artillery battalion that is marked, by the fact of his leadership, for hard fighting and for fame. He finds his sport in battle, and it seems incredible, after all his exposure to action, that he is still alive. After Gettysburg, with the Third Corps seldom fighting, he is not conspicuous for ten months. Later, the stench and stagnation of the Petersburg trenches are repulsive to him. When the caissons begin to roll and the teams tug at the traces, he is himself again. There is talk of making him a brigadier general of infantry, but Lee is unwilling to have Pegram leave the artillery though he esteems him as among the best of his soldiers. Pegram would have preferred that his end should be similar to that of his brother John, in the roar of action; but, as it befell, he dies lingeringly a few days from the end, at twenty-three and still a colonel of artillery.

THOMAS LAFAYETTE ROSSER

Like John Pelham, he is a West Point cadet of the class of 1861 who resigns before he is graduated. He procures a commission as first lieutenant and, before the Seven Days, rises to be a colonel of cavalry. Not yet twenty-five, he is six feet two inches tall, powerful, brown-eyed, and handsome. He fights hard and rises fast, and at the time of Gettysburg he has the prospect of a general's commission. It is given him in September 1863. After it come heartbreaks and hard battles. He almost loses the good opinion of Jube Early because he wants his young wife to be near the front. A valorous exploit at Moorefield restores him in his commander's eyes, but, for the attainment of larger fame, it is getting late in the life of the Confederacy. Cedar Creek and Tom's Brook cancel Trevilian. It is bitter; it is bewildering; it does not break his spirit. Nothing, apparently, could do that to Tom Rosser.

GEORGE EDWARD PICKETT

Slow recuperation from the wound received at Gaines' Mill is the fate of Longstreet's younger brother in spirit. Longstreet looks after his interests and sees that, when the major generals are named in the reorganization of the autumn of 1862, Pickett is one of them. The next spring, when Pickett goes to Southside Virginia, he is thirty-eight years old but has the good fortune of being near the home of a vivacious young girl, not half his age, who thinks him the greatest of cavaliers. She sees nothing but romance in those long ringlets of his that his brother officers consider odd. When Longstreet tells him that the Virginia division is to share in the final charge on the Union position at Gettysburg, Pickett looks and acts as if great military fortune has come to him. By midafternoon that third of July 1863, when the charge has been repulsed, George Pickett's tale is told. Neither he nor his division ever is the same again. For more than a year and a half he is a garrison general. Under the strain of a sudden responsibility, his health fails him. At Five Forks, where the enemy rolls up his flank force, whispers spread that he is attending a shad bake when he should have been with his men. In the death-spasm of the army he is relieved of command, but he is with his troops to the last hour. Fortune does not mock him without honor. "As valiant as Pickett's charge" has become a supreme martial metaphor.

Edward Porter Alexander

By the spring of 1863, Porter Alexander has a part of the recognition his consistent service since First Manassas has deserved. He is approaching twenty-eight, is erect and thin, and has more the look of the scholar than of the soldier. Those who know the artillery officers say this Georgian is among the most scientific and resourceful of them all. He is the sort of man on whom a busy commander safely may rely—and they do so notably at Chancellorsville and at Gettysburg. His reward is chief of artillery for Longstreet's corps.

Robert Frederick Hoke

A dependable line officer since Bethel, Hoke is twenty-five when, at Fredericksburg, in the absence of Trimble, he leads an excellent brigade with so much fury that men who did not know him begin to ask, Who is Hoke? His father had been a North Carolina politician of station who died when the boy was seven. Robert Hoke had not attended West Point but had received some professional training at the Kentucky Military Institute. Manifestly he has the true-born soldier's sense of combat. In appearance he is handsome, tall, strong, with a long face and deep-set eyes. A wound received at Salem Church keeps him from sharing the honors and the anguish of Gettysburg. His chance comes the next year in his native state and it brings him promotion and acclaim. The rest may have been circumstance; it may have been a desire to preserve his new reputation. It is unpleasant but it is the fact: Subsequent to that success at Plymouth, if he is fighting beside another division, there nearly always is a failure of cooperation. Neither his state nor his command loses faith in him.

WILLIAM DORSEY PENDER

Seasoned and much scarred is this hard-hitting, realistic North Carolinian who becomes twenty-nine in the winter of 1862–63. More than ever he hates a war that keeps him from his family, but if he must fight he wants to be at the front in rank and in service. He is distinctly the partisan of Powell Hill in the controversy with Jackson, and he has bitter thoughts for those who dispute the pre-eminence of the Light Division. He is efficient in campaign and is responsible for the good behavior of what he regards as the best brigade of the best division. In battle he forgets all else in persistent, flaming combat. He retains the habit of getting wounded in almost every fight. As the army enters Pennsylvania, this new major general tries to relieve the concern of his young wife that the Lord will not bless the Southern cause if the Confederacy does more than defend its own territory. He knows, as a trained soldier, that a whole-hearted offensive often is the most prudent defensive. The campaign must be fought. So run his letters. Then, abruptly, they stop. He fights successfully another battle with all his stubborn energy, and is awaiting action at Gettysburg when he is wounded once again. This time he cannot laugh it off. They miss him on the third of July when part of his division is deployed wrongly.

STEPHEN DODSON RAMSEUR

Always Dodson to his intimates, Ramseur was graduated at West Point in 1860 and, at twenty-five, becomes colonel of a fine North Carolina regiment. Seven months later he is a brigadier general. He does not behave as if he can get enough of fighting. Although he bristles with a brigand's beard, he is small, slight of frame, alert. His speech is direct and brisk, his dark prominent eyes do not flicker. He has all the ambitions and all the sensitiveness of a boy, but he handles a brigade as easily as he would have drilled a squad. In a desperate hour at Spotsylvania, when the front is almost severed by a shrewd thrust, he counterattacks with wild daring. A division is his reward, a veteran division, the day after he is twenty-seven. With these troops he shares in a spectacular campaign in the Valley under Jube Early and wins new honors, though he suffers one reversal that almost breaks his heart. Ramseur has the promise of something dearer than military distinction. One day, when a battle is in prospect, he hears that the crisis is past and that the baby is born. More than that he never learns.

CADMUS MARCELLUS WILCOX

No happy career in the army is Wilcox's from August 1862 to May 1863. In his thirty-ninth year, he is older than most of the other professional soldiers who command brigades. At West Point he was in the class with T. J. Jackson, with David Jones, with George Pickett. In the next class was Powell Hill. All these now outrank him. He is restless, sore, and disposed to go to another Confederate army where he will have a chance. Then, at an unwanted post, while a battle that will bring fame to others is raging a few miles away, his great hour comes. He meets it in a manner to make Salem Church a model of what an observant commander of a detached brigade sometimes can accomplish. Advancement and the leadership of a stalwart division bring no further praise. Again denied transfer to another front, he meets hard duty with courage, though never with inspiration. More than once his division loses heavily, but negligence never is linked with defeat. If he gains no new prestige, he forfeits no good opinion for character and steadiness. Through the last black winter of the war his men give an honorable account of themselves.

HENRY HETH

Of Virginia stock long distinguished in war and in fortune, he is thirty-seven, a West Pointer, and a former captain in the "old army." He has a high reputation, personally and professionally, and he is as devoted a soldier as he is an attractive individual. In western Virginia his small command once was seized with panic through no dereliction on his part. Now that he is a brigadier in the Army of Northern Virginia, he is called within two months to lead a famous division on a field of victory at Chancellorsville, and soon after is promoted major general. This seems good fortune, but it is to prove a continuance of the ill fortune experienced in western Virginia. As yet, nobody realizes that Harry Heth, as he is called by his friends, is doomed to be one of those good soldiers, unhappily numerous in military history, who consistently have bad luck. For a time it seems as if he has canceled his ill fortune. At Gettysburg his direction of his troops is sound, and a few folds of paper inside his hat save him from a fatal wound. Two days later, though he is not in field command, he sees his weakened division wrecked. On the retreat he has to pay the price often exacted of the rear guard. Still again, that autumn, his troops are the victims of his corps commander's impetuosity. Another time, in the Wilderness, when he wants to withdraw his men from an exposed position, Powell Hill says, "The men shall not be disturbed." Rout follows. Heth's seems to be the fate of living to exemplify the maxim that a soldier, to be good, must have good luck.

RALEIGH EDWARD COLSTON

An unusual, puzzling person is Raleigh Colston. He was born in France of wealthy Virginia parents long resident there, and in youth was sent to Lexington, Virginia, where he was entered and duly was graduated at the Virginia Military Institute. He remained there, became professor of French, and bore himself as became a faculty-colleague of T. J. Jackson and Robert Rodes. Because of Jackson's high opinion of him, Colston is called to brigade command in the Second Corps at a time when attrition has worn the corps of officers. War is not kind to "Old Parlez," as his former cadets nicknamed him, but precisely why and wherein he fails on his day of great opportunity at Chancellorsville is a mystery not easily resolved. Quiet exile from the Army of Northern Virginia follows.

EDWARD JOHNSON

By a wound received at McDowell, May 8, 1862, "Old Allegheny" was invalided for almost a year in Richmond. As he had means as well as station, he enjoyed the best company in the Confederate capital, though his proclivity of proclaiming love at the top of his voice caused young ladies to be a bit cautious in his presence. They may laugh at his social oddities and say that his head is in three tiers, like the papal tiara, but after he receives a division of the Second Corps and leads it in battle, no soldier ever laughs at Old Allegheny. He comes on with a roar and a limp which he eases with a long staff; wherefore the boys sometimes call him "Old Club." He is a powerful, bulky man of forty-seven, a soundly schooled professional soldier. He does well in nearly all his fights, hits hard, and wins the confidence of his men. A great career might have been his if certain guns had not been withdrawn that rainy night in '64 in the Bloody Angle. The result is honorable even if Johnson is captured along with most of his famous command.

WILLIAM MAHONE

"Billy" Mahone's is as strange a rise to fame as the army witnesses in devastating 1864. After the war, when his ambitions soar, his henchmen will say he had been a great soldier from the start. The reports do not show it. As a brigadier he is not lacking in diligence but he is without special distinction. A dozen of his rank might be named before him. Promotion transforms him. Dispute and caution give place to fierce action. His men become the most renowned shock troops of the army. In the last phase of the war, when he boasts the age of thirty-eight, he is the most conspicuous division commander. Small and as lean as a starvation year, he lives in unconcealed comfort and does not hesitate to question even the commanding general. Men do not always like him or take him at his own estimate, but they have to admit that he knows how to fight.

WILLIAM HENRY FITZHUGH LEE

Sometimes the careless confuse Fitz Lee and his cousin of the longer, kindred name. On occasion, the unadvanced colonels and the stranded captains of cavalry ask how many more Lees must be promoted before other men have a chance. William Henry Fitzhugh, "Rooney" for short, is not of a nature to seek promotion because of his name. Nor is he so unmindful of his name and obligation as the commanding general's son that he fails to earn promotion. He does not scintillate in conversation or in planning. At twenty-seven, when he becomes a major general, he is bulky and perhaps appears slow; but if he possessed what he wholly lacks, the stomach for self-advertisement, he could say in truth that he has distinguished himself in every battle he has fought. Perhaps his deepest, most secret pride is that he has not failed his father in any of a score of battles. "Marse Robert" is secretly proud, too, that he never calls in vain on his son.

CHARLES WILLIAM FIELD

Old Pete Longstreet does not relish the assignment of this convalescent officer to the command of Hood's division, which the lieutenant general desired for Micah Jenkins. Consequently, Charles Field, thirty-six years of age, has no warmth of welcome when he reports to the First Corps. In his first battle after that, in the Wilderness, he does well, and by the time Longstreet recovers from a wound, Field is a fixture. He sometimes fails, but he possesses unmistakable, if indefinable, military sense. When the final muster roll is made, Field's is the strongest, stoutest division of them all.

JOSEPH BREVARD KERSHAW

This South Carolina lawyer, forty-one in 1863, continues to display aptitude in command and, at a time when the First Corps is strife-riven, he keeps his poise and the good opinion of his comrades. The fatal spring of 1864, which finds him a major general, brings him many hours of high hazard. Kershaw passes through them all as if they were the unvexing incidents of a quiet life. Even toward the last, in the hour when his troops are surrounded, he loses none of his dignity. Behind that dignity is character, in the molding of which religion has first place.

CHAPTER 1

Opening Guns

1. "Old Bory's Come!"

He would go at once. The request from the President that he come to Richmond offered an opportunity as surely as it conveyed an order. Federal troops had crossed the Potomac. A battle that would assure the triumph of the new Confederacy would be fought ere long in Virginia. At the same time, departure from South Carolina would be regrettable. From the hour of his arrival there, March 6, 1861, the patriots of Charleston had welcomed him. After he forced the surrender of Fort Sumter on April 14, without the loss of a man, they had acclaimed and adopted him. Some of them seemed to find a certain Huguenot kinship in his name—Pierre Gustave Toutant Beauregard—and all of them united to do him honor.[1]

General and staff left on May 29 for Richmond, the newly selected capital of the Confederate States. Multitudes gathered at every station to have a look at the "Hero of Sumter." The journey confirmed everything Beauregard had been told of the incredible popularity he had won by his success in Charleston Harbor. How quickly fame had come to him! When he had resigned from the United States army, February 20, 1861, he had been fifth-ranking captain in the Corps of Engineers and had a brevet as major for gallant conduct in the Mexican War.[2] In his profession he was esteemed; outside of it he was little known till hostilities had been opened at Charleston. Now, seven weeks after the fall of Sumter, he had received the thanks of Congress and the laudation of the Southern press as one of the greatest soldiers in the world. Napoleonic myths had grown up about him. He was said to have warned President Lincoln to remove all noncombatants from Washington by a given date, as if he were determined forthwith to take the city.[3] Not one doubt of his military genius was admitted.

On May 30, ere his train puffed importantly into the station, hundreds of townfolk had gathered there. A carriage and four were waiting to carry the general to the Spotswood Hotel, where a suite had been reserved for him. All the honors that had been paid President Davis upon arrival two days previously were to be repeated for General Beauregard. He was most grateful when he stepped from the car; but, if the committee would permit, he would take a simpler carriage and go quietly to the hotel. Quickly he was wheeled up the hill to the Spotswood. Music and cheers and appeals for a speech were in vain. His mission was war. He must waste no time in needless words.[4]

The next day he conferred with the President and with General R. E. Lee who, in an ill-defined manner, was responsible for military operations in Virginia. Old friends they were, old and admiring. Davis as United States secretary of war had known Beauregard well and, in March 1861, had commended the general to Governor Pickens of South Carolina as "full of talent and of much military experience."[5] In planning immediate steps to combat the fast-developing Federal threat against Virginia, Jefferson Davis felt that he could rely on Beauregard.

No less did the President have self-reliance. He had hurried to Richmond in answer to earnest representations that he and he only could direct aright the defense of the frontier. Montgomery newspapers had reported that Mr. Davis was having his old Mexican War sword sharpened at a gunsmith's in Market Street. A man having his blade made ready of course intended using it. Little doubt was expressed that the President would take the field in person. With others the soldiers would fight and perhaps would win, said the *Richmond Examiner*, but "with him, the victory would be certain, and chance would become certainty."[6]

The new President felt, as he sat down with Beauregard and Lee, that he had been trained as a soldier and as a commander he had been tried. To his four years of administrative experience as secretary of war he had added that of chairman of the Military Committee of the Senate. Who had so diversified an equipment, who a better reason for self-reliance? He was confident he could discharge in more than a perfunctory sense his prerogative as commander-in-chief of the military forces of the Confederacy.

The third man at the council of May 31 was in public estimation the least distinguished of the three. Robert Lee was the son of a renowned Revolutionary soldier and had enjoyed the high admiration of Winfield Scott. In the Mexican War, Lee's work as an engineer had been brilliant, and when he resigned from the old army he had reached the rank of colonel of cavalry; but he had no such reputation as Beauregard had won at Sumter and no prestige, other than social, that compared with that of Davis.

Inasmuch as Lee had just returned from Manassas, he was asked by the President to explain what had been done to prepare that important railroad junction against the Federals, who, on the night of May 23–24, had crossed the Potomac and seized Alexandria. When Lee explained the situation in northern Virginia, Davis decided that Beauregard should have the post of instant danger, that of the Alexandria line.[7] Beauregard exhibited neither concern nor satisfaction. If that was the post the President wished him to have, he would proceed immediately to Manassas. By way of Hanover Junction, Gordonsville, Orange, and Rappahannock Station, names destined to be written red, he traveled on June 1 to Manassas and assumed command. "Old Bory's Come!" cried the South Carolina troops who had served under him at Charleston. The Virginia recruits, hearing the cheers, sought this first opportunity of observing him.[8]

If they expected a theatrical personality, they were disappointed. What they saw was a small man, forty-three years of age and five feet seven inches in height. He weighed about 150 pounds and had much strength in his slight frame, though often he fell sick. With graying hair, cropped mustache, a good brow, high cheekbones, a belligerent chin, and sallow olive complexion, he was as surely French in appearance as in blood. Imaginative Southern writers already pictured him as the reincarnation of one of Napoleon's marshals, but they said that his eyes, which were his most pronounced physical characteristic, were those of a bloodhound, large, dark, and melancholy. In manner he was quiet but cordial. Privately talkative, he was officially uncommunicative. His tongue manifestly was his ally; it was not equally apparent that his pen was his enemy.[9]

Beauregard proceeded to inspect his troops. In command was Milledge L. Bonham, who had fought the Seminoles and the Mexicans as a citizen-soldier and had resigned his seat in Congress to defend his native South Carolina. Under Bonham were two fine regiments, more than 1,500 of the best young men of the Palmetto State. A regiment of Virginians was being organized by Colonel J. F. Preston, another was being recruited rapidly by Colonel R. S. Ewell, and a third by Colonel Samuel Garland, a graduate of the Virginia Military Institute. From Alexandria had arrived in retreat a few companies under Colonel G. H. Terrett. At Culpeper, collecting men as rapidly as possible, was Colonel Philip St. George Cocke, a rich planter who had been graduated from West Point in 1832 and had been for two years a lieutenant in the United States army.[10]

The smallness of this force alarmed Beauregard. His position, he explained to the President, his troops, and his service of supply alike were inadequate. "I must therefore," he said, "either be re-enforced at once . . . or I must be prepared to retire, on the approach of the enemy, in the direction of Richmond. . . ."[11] It would not suffice, Beauregard concluded, merely to exhort the President. The populace must be aroused. To that end, he issued on June 5 a proclamation: "A reckless and unprincipled tyrant has invaded your soil. Abraham Lincoln, regardless of all moral, legal, and constitutional restraints, has thrown his abolition hosts among you, who are murdering and imprisoning your citizens, confiscating and destroying your property, and committing other acts of violence and outrage too shocking and revolting to humanity to be enumerated." Beauregard urged the farmers "to drive back and expel the invaders from your land. . . . I desire to assure you that the utmost protection in my power will be extended to you all."[12]

In their complete reliance upon Davis and Beauregard and the valor of their own sons, Virginians did not understand, in those first furious days of half-organized war, how difficult it was to muster and equip enough men to meet the four offensives that were being forged against their state. Virginia was singularly vulnerable. From the northwest, the north, and the east she could be assailed. The Federals held Fort Monroe on Hampton Roads and commanded the deep water everywhere. In particular, there was danger of joint land-and-water operations against the Peninsula between the James and York rivers. That operation would be no particular threat to Beauregard. Nor was there immediate danger to his front from an expedition in process of organization around Grafton on the Baltimore and Ohio Railroad, about 120 miles west of Harper's Ferry. Much nearer to Beauregard's line was the prospect of a Federal attack from Pennsylvania and Maryland on Harper's Ferry, where the Shenandoah flows into the Potomac. Loss of Harper's Ferry would endanger Beauregard's position at Manassas. Conversely, if Beauregard's position at Manassas were taken, an adversary might turn westward and cut the line of retreat of the forces at Harper's Ferry.

The Virginia authorities had seized Harper's Ferry and its valuable arms machinery on the night of April 18. In command there was Colonel Thomas J. Jackson, Virginia volunteers. Beauregard probably remembered Jackson, who had been a young artillerist during the Mexican War and been breveted major for gallantry at Chapultepec. Whether or not he recalled the major of the gallant days of '47, Beauregard soon heard of the work Jackson was doing at Harper's Ferry.

The colonel had been professor of physics and instructor in artillery at the Virginia Military Institute. Serious-minded persons at Lexington, the seat of the Institute, respected Jackson's piety, his diligence as a Presbyterian deacon, and his zeal in the religious instruction of the Negroes; the irreverent said he was a "curiosity," a dull teacher who hewed to the line of the text and showed much embarrassment when forced to depart from it. At Harper's Ferry he had been a different, infinitely more competent man. Terse, clear in direction, positive in orders, he was declared to be every inch the soldier. He diligently had been drilling his raw volunteers, and was fast developing to competent performance some of the 8,000 men who had been assembled.[13]

A large invading force might shut up the Confederate troops in the angle made at the Ferry by the rivers, but, for the time, Jackson seemed reasonably safe. The cavalry would give him warning. When Colonel George Deas—an old inspector of the United States army—made an official visit to Harper's Ferry, he had noted the alertness of a handsome, spirited young cavalryman, small but vigorous, who was commanding Jackson's mounted outposts. "I am quite confident," Deas reported, "that with the vigilance . . . exercised by Captain Ashby, no enemy can pass the point which he is directed to observe."[14] Besides, all five of the companies of cavalry, which included Turner Ashby's two, were "in very good condition and quite effective." Their commander was the stocky, broad-shouldered Lieutenant Colonel James E. B. Stuart: "Beauty" Stuart, the boys at West Point had called him, in tactful tribute to his notorious lack of good looks. Stuart had arrived in Richmond from the West on May 7, and, after being assigned to Harper's Ferry, had set out to organize the cavalry.[15]

Beauregard was well acquainted with the officer who had arrived at Harper's Ferry on May 24 and in somewhat unusual circumstances had assumed command. Joseph E. Johnston had been promptly commissioned brigadier general in the Confederate army after declining like rank in the service of Virginia. On reaching the Ferry, where he found Jackson exercising authority under a Virginia commission, Johnston requested Jackson to distribute an order that announced the change of command. Jackson politely but promptly declined to do so. "Until I receive further instructions from Governor Letcher or General Lee," said the former professor, "I do not feel at liberty to transfer my command to another. . . ." General Johnston was not offended by Jackson's refusal. He simply looked among his papers for one that would show he had been assigned to the post. The search was brief. On an application sent him from Richmond the general found this endorsement: "Referred to General J. E. Johnston, commanding officer at Harper's Ferry. By order of Major-General Lee." Shown to Jackson, this was accepted instantly by him as evidence of Johnston's authority. Harper's Ferry formally became a Confederate post.[16]

The correspondence was a trivial incident, but it might have been read even then as an indication of the precise military standard of Colonel Jackson: Authority was bestowed to be exercised; responsibility was not lightly to be shifted; orders were to be obeyed. If this meant that Jackson for the moment had no command, he would await one.

Soon Beauregard heard that Jackson's successor was having difficulties similar to those encountered at Manassas. Neither Johnston's position nor his troops pleased him. As an engineer he saw that Harper's Ferry could be turned, in his words, "easily and effectively from above and below." The

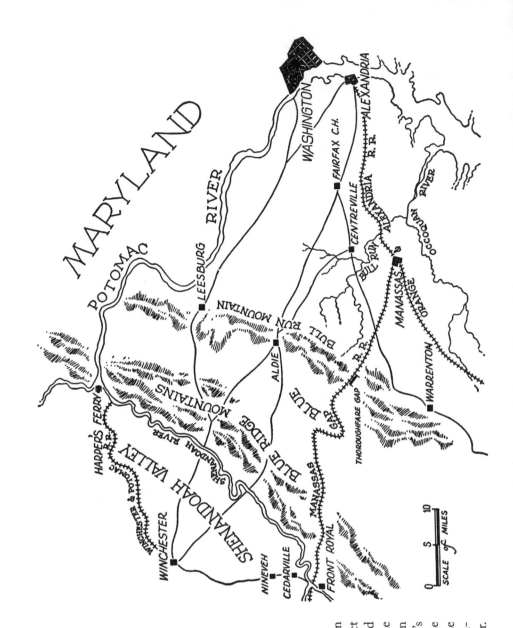

Strategic areas of northern Virginia—the district between Warrenton and Washington, and the Shenandoah Valley from Front Royal to Harper's Ferry—to illustrate how the occupation of one by the enemy threatened the security of the other.

volunteers, in his opinion, were utterly lacking in "discipline and instruction." Within a week after assuming command he asked whether it would not be better to withdraw altogether from Harper's Ferry.[17]

Of all this and of much that followed, Beauregard was informed. He listened; he pondered; he planned. French he was . . . French strategy he would employ, Napoleonic strategy.

2. MAGRUDER AND D. H. HILL EMERGE

Before the ranks of Beauregard began to swell or his strategy to take form, the actors between the James and York rivers commanded the stage. The Federals were concentrating at Fort Monroe, which apparently they intended to use as a base for operations up the Peninsula. If, simultaneously, the mouth of either the James or the York could be opened, vessels of the United States navy might pass the hastily built forts and might land troops close to Richmond. Thus the commanding officer at the mouth of the York River became from the hour of his assignment a conspicuous figure.[18] Indeed, he long had been that in the old army, not because of rank but because of personality.

John Bankhead Magruder, No. 15 in the somewhat undistinguished class of 1830 at West Point, had procured transfer from the 7th Infantry to the 1st Artillery in 1831, had earned his brevet as lieutenant colonel during the Mexican War, and thereafter held some of the choicest posts in the artillery. At Fort Adams, Newport, Rhode Island, he had won a great name as a *bon vivant* and as an obliging host. Whenever celebrities were to be entertained, Colonel Magruder—"Prince John"—would tender a dress parade, with full trappings of gold-braided pomp, and this he would follow with a flawless dinner. From Fort Adams he had been transferred to far-off Fort Leavenworth, but there, too, he had held dress parades and reviews, though the spectators might be only Indians or frontiersmen. In the serious work of his profession he directed the new artillery school at Leavenworth and convinced interested juniors that he knew his ranges as thoroughly as his vintages.[19]

The winter of 1860–61 found Magruder and his battery in Washington. When he resigned, rumor had it that he galloped off to the defense of Virginia with his men and his guns. Nothing would have delighted Magruder more, for he loved the dramatic and when occasion offered he would majestically tread the creaking boards of a garrison theater. Nor did he make a casual entrance on the stage of Virginia's tragedy. He gained an immediate audience with the governor's Advisory Council. To that serious, burdened group of devoted men, Colonel Magruder said with frowning fervor: "I have just crossed the Long Bridge, which is guarded by my old Battery. The men recognized me by moonlight and would have cheered me but I repressed them. Give me 5,000 men and if I don't take Washington, you may take not only my sword but my life!" On so bold a proposal the Council sought the judgment of General Lee. Lee shook his head. "We have not the men," said he—that and no more.[20]

Prince John was too well-disciplined a soldier to be disappointed at this. He was commissioned colonel of Virginia volunteers, and on May 21 was sent to command operations on the lower Peninsula, with headquarters at Yorktown. There he found no cavalry, little infantry, and scant equipment. Naval officers scarcely had gear for mounting the guns that were to keep the enemy's fleet at a distance. With furious energy Magruder went to work to improve his troops and his position, but like Johnston at Harper's Ferry and Beauregard at Manassas he felt his first need was of a larger force. To guard a line that extended from the James to the York, he must have, he said, 8,000 to 10,000 men. Without them he would be compelled to fall back. In opening correspondence on this subject he was detailed and insistent. Like many another professional soldier who long had dealt with the War Department, he believed with all his heart that the importunate widow who wearied the unjust judge till he avenged her was the model to be followed by the commander in seeking what was required. His early dispatches doubtless were read with eagerness. Soon the sight of one of them was to evoke groans.[21]

Fortune smiled on diligence. Prince John had the opportunity of directing the South's first land "battle" and of winning the intoxicating first victory. At the very time of Magruder's arrival, one of the regiments needed to bring up his force to the required minimum had landed at Yorktown, 1,100 enthusiastic young men of the 1st North Carolina volunteers. Their colonel, Daniel Harvey Hill, and their lieutenant colonel, C. C. Lee, were West Pointers; their major, James H. Lane, was a graduate of the Virginia Military Institute.

So well trained was the 1st North Carolina that on June 6, Magruder sent it, with four guns and a few other troops, to an advanced position at Big Bethel Church, thirteen miles below Yorktown and eight from Hampton. The enemy was at Hampton and Newport News and seemed inclined to advance. Four days later Hill received notice that the enemy was approaching. The very prospect set every heart to beating fast. Hill moved out his troops, ascertained by what roads the Federals were moving, and then withdrew in the face of superior force to his prepared position. With Magruder directing a few changes in his dispositions, Hill met and repulsed at Big Bethel some feeble, poorly handled assaults by Federals who already had sustained casualties by firing wildly into one another.

It was a small battle, to be sure. Not more than 300 of the 1,400 Confederates had been engaged simultaneously and then for no longer than twenty minutes. Three years later such a clash would have been accounted a skirmish and perhaps been the subject of a two-line dispatch. It was different on June 10, 1861. Green troops had stood, had fought, had sustained eleven casualties, had driven the enemy back to his starting point! At Yorktown headquarters there was excitement, felicitation, and exultation. The Federal casualties Hill put at 300, though actually the figure was 76.[22]

When news of this victory reached Richmond and spread across the South, there was immense satisfaction over what was proclaimed to be the demonstrated, indisputable superiority of the Confederate soldier in combat. No detail of the engagement was too trivial for mention, none was incredible.[23] Swift promotion to the rank of brigadier general was demanded for Magruder and was granted. He took his place among the foremost of Southern celebrities, a hero second only to Beauregard. Magruder accepted his new honors gratefully. In mien and dignity he lived up to his role. At fifty years of age he was tall, erect, and handsome, and was impressive despite a curious lisp. Usually he dressed in full uniform— looking "every inch a King," one newspaper insisted—and with his staff in attendance he daily made the rounds of his slowly mounting fortifications. He was a fighter, the South joyfully asserted, a personal fighter, too. Was it not rumored that he had challenged the Federal commander, General Ben Butler, to mortal combat?[24]

Harvey Hill, who had been in direct command at Big Bethel, did not appeal to the eye or to the imagination in the measure his chief did, but he had his full share of honor. He came of fighting stock. His paternal grandfather had made cannon for the Continental army and had been one of Thomas Sumter's colonels. On the maternal side Harvey Hill had as grandparent that wily scout Thomas Cabeen, who Sumter often said was the bravest man he ever commanded. Not unnaturally, with that inheritance, Harvey Hill had gone to West Point, where, despite poor health, he had been graduated No. 28 in the excellent class of 1842. Five years later, by the unhesitating display of the most reckless valor, he had won promotion from first lieutenant to brevet major during the Mexican War; but as he found army life unstimulating in time of peace he had resigned in February 1849, had taught mathematics for five years at Washington College, and then had become professor of mathematics and civil engineering at Davidson College, North Carolina.

While there Hill developed a marked interest in theology and, at the same time, a most vehement hatred of Northerners. His *Consideration of the Sermon on the Mount* (1856) had been followed by a "Southern Series" of mathematical works in which he based many of his problems on "Yankee cunning." For example, "A Yankee mixes a certain quantity of wooden nutmegs, which cost him one-fourth cent apiece, with a quantity of real nutmegs, worth four cents apiece"; again, "the year in which the Governors of Massachusetts and Connecticut sent treasonable messages to their respective legislatures, is expressed in four digits. . . ." In 1859, Hill decided that war with the fictitious masters of this alleged cunning was probable, and he accepted the superintendency of the North Carolina Military Institute. In 1861 he was called to command the camp of instruction for the North Carolina volunteers, and as a reward for diligent service was elected colonel of the 1st Regiment. He was then nearing his fortieth birthday.[25]

In person he was inconspicuous—five feet ten, thin, critical of eye, slightly bent from a spinal affliction and cursed with an odd humor; he was stiff and sharp when on duty and was wholly unpretending when not in command. Hill observed the Sabbath as diligently as did his brother-in-law, Colonel Thomas J. Jackson, then at Harper's Ferry, and he always gave God the credit for victory. Upon the expansion of the Confederate force on the Peninsula after the fight at Big Bethel, Magruder gave him the post at Yorktown. On July 10, in recognition of his achievements, Hill was commissioned brigadier general.[26]

How fast and how far would he rise? What service would he render? Intense he was in his admiration, bitter in his antagonism. He could hate as hard as he could pray: Would that make him a better soldier or a worse? An applauding country did not know enough about him to make the inquiry, nor would it have looked otherwise than with suspicion on anyone who raised that or any other question about any Confederate leader. Old Bory, Prince John Magruder, pious Harvey Hill—these three at the beginning of the summer of 1861 were men to be trusted, to be followed. They were great soldiers. Of that the South was satisfied. No less were all Southerners convinced that new military genius would blaze on every battlefield.

3. First Loss of a Leader

Exultant praise of Magruder, D. H. Hill, and the other victors at Big Bethel was interrupted by news of another sort, from western Virginia. There, from the very hour of secession, the Federals realized that the Baltimore and Ohio Railroad between Washington and Parkersburg was at once the most important and the most exposed link in the iron chain that bound together the East and the Midwest. They determined to organize at Grafton an army that would protect the line in the surest manner—by clearing all Confederate troops from northwestern Virginia.

Soon Richmond was aware of these formidable preparations. On May 20 the advance of a strong Union column compelled a small Confederate force to evacuate Grafton. Four days later the Federals surprised at Philippi the units withdrawn from Grafton, and the undisciplined, bewildered troops had to hasten thirty miles farther south to Beverly, and thence twelve miles in the same direction to Huttonsville. As Beverly was the junction of the Staunton-Parkersburg road with the turnpike to Grafton, the Confederates could not permit the enemy to penetrate farther.[27] Such troops as were available must, then, be hurried to Staunton and over the mountains to reoccupy Beverly. Because every other qualified officer already was assigned to field duty, Colonel Robert Selden Garnett, adjutant general at Lee's headquarters, though he was irreplaceable, was detached and ordered to proceed to western Virginia.

Garnett was forty-two years of age, the eldest son of R. S. Garnett, for twelve years a member of Congress from Virginia, and a representative of one of the most intellectual families of the Old Dominion. After Robert Garnett was graduated midway in the class of 1841 at West Point, he was given virtually every post a young officer could desire—assistant instructor of tactics at West Point, aide to Generals Wool and Taylor during the Mexican War. Garnett measured up to his opportunities and won his brevet as major for gallantry at Buena Vista. In 1857, while on duty at Fort Simcoe, Washington Territory, he returned from an expedition to find that both his wife and child had died in his absence. From the time he lost his family his entire interest had been fixed on his profession. It was his escape, his passion, his life. With his native austerity deepened by grief, he seemed "frozen and stern and isolated." With secession he resigned promptly and was appointed Lee's adjutant general. Now, promoted brigadier general, he had challenge, opportunity, and—more than either— the difficulties of a strange country and a raw command.[28]

Garnett left Huttonsville on June 15 and pushed straight for Rich Mountain. Over this mountain, by Buckhannon Pass, crossed the Staunton-Parkersburg road. Around the north end of Rich Mountain, under Laurel Hill, was the Grafton-Beverly road. Not content with halfway measures, Garnett occupied both Laurel Hill and Buckhannon Pass and felt, as he put it, that he held "the gates to the northwestern country."[29]

Most of his officers were as inexperienced as his troops, but some of them were unusual men. Most conspicuous among them was Lieutenant

Colonel John Pegram of the 20th Virginia, twenty-nine, a West Pointer of the class of 1854 and a former lieutenant of the 2nd Dragoons. Pegram had spent two years in Europe and had many fine social qualities, but he was a recent comer to western Virginia and had scant acquaintance with the tangled country. On July 7 he went with his regiment to a post called Camp Garnett, eight miles west of Beverly.

A second interesting officer among Garnett's subordinates was Captain Julius A. de Lagnel, a native of New Jersey but long a resident of Virginia and for fourteen years a lieutenant in the old army. De Lagnel was chief of artillery for Garnett's little command and was stationed with Pegram on the western flank of Rich Mountain.[30]

At that camp also reported for duty a man destined to have a place in Confederate service almost unique. Jedediah Hotchkiss, descendant of an old and distinguished Connecticut family, had been born in Windsor, New York, in 1828 and been educated in academies there. When nineteen he had come to Virginia on a walking tour. Soon he acquired so deep an attachment to the state that he decided to settle in Augusta County. He established Mossy Creek Academy, which soon was successful. Busy though he was as a teacher, and active in religion, he found time to learn, unhelped, the principles of engineering, and as his avocation he made maps. "Professor Hotchkiss," as he first was called in the army—he had no rank at the time—could sketch an area with substantial accuracy after riding over it once, and as he was a swift and indefatigable worker, he was to supply an incredible number of much-needed maps.[31]

Garnett soon learned something of the men entrusted to him. City-dwellers he had who had never seen mountains, and with them he had mountaineers who had never seen cities. Two things only did these soldiers possess in common—vast zeal and military inexperience. To them Garnett gave such slight instruction as time permitted. He also improved rapidly his position on Laurel Hill and at Buckhannon Pass. He occupied his fortifications, unassailed by the enemy, until July 6. Then skirmishing began. By July 8, the day Pegram took command at Buckhannon Pass, the enemy was active in that quarter.

On the morning of the eleventh, from a captured Union sergeant, Pegram learned that the Federals were endeavoring to turn one of his flanks. He concluded that the attack was to be against his right, and he sent word to Colonel William C. Scott to hold his 44th Virginia one and a half miles west of Beverly. Although Pegram believed the approach to his left-rear almost impracticable for the enemy, he sent back Captain de Lagnel with one gun and five thin companies of infantry to Hart's house at the highest point in the gap. As of July 11, the situation, in summary, was this: Garnett

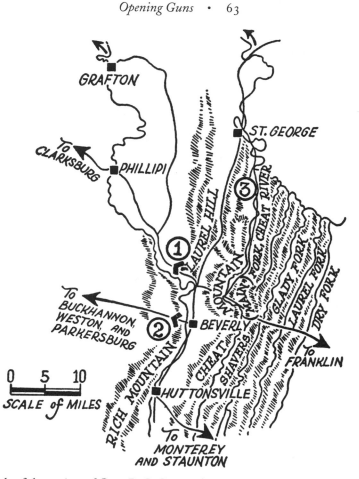

Sketch of the region of Gen. R. S. Garnett's operations in western Virginia.
Positions are: (1) Garnett's line on Laurel Hill; (2) Pegram's line on Rich
Mountain; (3) Carrick's Ford on fork of Cheat River.

at Laurel Hill, northeast of Pegram's position, had no intimation of attack,
though Union troops were known to be close at hand. In front of Camp Garnett the Federals were visible but gave no evidence of any purpose to come
directly up the mountain. At the camp, Pegram was on the alert and was
expecting an attempt to turn his right. About one and a half miles in his rear,
at the Hart house, were de Lagnel, his gun, and 310 men. Across the
mountain to the eastward, Colonel Scott was posting his 44th Virginia.[32]

At 11:00 A.M. there came an unhappy surprise: With a shout and a dash,
the Federals drove in the Confederate pickets at the pass and swarmed
from the laurel thickets for an assault on de Lagnel's little command. The
enemy came from the left and not, as anticipated, from the right. Captain

de Lagnel made the utmost of his scant numbers and his single gun. When most of his artillerists were shot down, he served the piece himself. Presently he fell with a serious wound. Colonel Pegram arrived from Camp Garnett, and by example and plea tried to get his soldiers to drive off the enemy and hold the road. His shouts and commands were in vain. The troops broke; the enemy seized the road and the gap. Pegram rode back down the hill to camp. A grim plight was his. The Unionists were squarely across his only line of retreat.

What was to be done? Pegram decided to try the one expedient open to him: He would leave half his force to hold Camp Garnett and, with the other half, he would go back up the mountain and try to clear the enemy from the road. At last his volunteers reached an elevation that appeared to be on a line with the flank of the enemy, but the pull up the mountain had exhausted them. Pegram realized that if they were thrown forward they would be slaughtered. The sole hope of escape was to go on over the crest and try to reach Beverly. Pegram entrusted this difficult mission to Major Nat Tyler of the 20th Virginia, and started back to Camp Garnett—his second descent of the day. It was 11:30 P.M. when he and his mount staggered into the camp.

The 600 men who remained there were awake and miserable. Pegram decided that an effort must be made to cross the mountain and join Garnett at Laurel Hill. He was so exhausted that he did not believe he could attempt another ascent. A column was formed, the head of which was assigned to Professor Hotchkiss. With his singular sense of direction, Hotchkiss started confidently upward. Pegram, by that time, had decided that he would make the effort, come what might, and he passed word for the troops to halt until he could reach the front. This order never reached the lead company, which continued to follow Hotchkiss.[33]

These hours had been an anxious time for General Garnett at Laurel Hill. On his own front, as the Federals shelled his position, he prepared to repel attack. All day he had watched, and waited for word from Pegram. After nightfall a panting messenger brought news that Pegram was cut off and that the enemy commanded the road through the gap. This meant that Garnett's own line of retreat was endangered. One of the "gates to the northwestern country" had been stormed. The other would not hold. As he did not know in what direction Pegram would retire, he did what a man of his temper and training most regretted to do: He abandoned his detached force, left his tents in place to deceive the enemy, and marched eastward with his regiments.

Daylight on the twelfth of July found the army of Garnett in five retreating fragments. Colonel Scott had abandoned his futile watch on the eastern side of Rich Mountain and was on the road to Huttonsville. Jed Hotchkiss was two thirds of the way to the top of the mountain, on the western side, and was disgusted to find that only one company was following him. Major Nat Tyler of the 20th Virginia, having crossed the mountain, was at Beverly. Pegram's wet and hungry men were on a high ridge whence, after sunrise, they could look down on Beverly. Garnett's hurried march was under way without pursuit by the enemy.[34]

The *dénouement* came quickly. Scott, Tyler, and Hotchkiss were able to get away in safety. Pegram lost his opportunity of reaching Beverly before the Federals, and, after wandering all day in search of food, sent at midnight an offer to surrender the troops with him. On the thirteenth his 555 officers and men laid down their arms. All except Pegram were paroled. He was held as a prisoner of undetermined status because of his previous service in the United States army.[35]

Garnett's march on the twelfth carried him to Kaler's Ford on the Cheat River, where the men bivouacked in a heavy rain. The next morning he continued his retreat over a heavy road and through a difficult country. Ford after ford lay ahead. The cavalry brought the grim news that the enemy was near at hand. By successive halts and withdrawals, the infantry covered the wagon train until Carrick's Ford was reached. At that swift, deep crossing some of the wagons stalled. The 23rd Virginia crossed and took up a defensive position, and after the 1st Georgia secured the train and passed through their line, the Virginians held off the Federals long enough for the wagons to get a good lead.

When the 23rd reached the next ford, Garnett was waiting on the farther bank with a single junior aide. The general directed Colonel William B. Taliaferro to halt beyond a near turn in the road. Would Taliaferro send back ten good marksmen? In a few minutes the Federals came in sight and encountered the fire of the sharpshooters. As only Garnett and his aide Sam M. Gaines were visible, the Federals directed their fire at them. The missiles flew past. Young Gaines ducked. Garnett, erect and calm, reproved the youth. "When I told him I had felt on my face the wind from several bullets, and that I could not help but stoop," Gaines wrote years later, "he changed his tone and talked to me in a fatherly way as to the proper bearing of a soldier under fire."

The enemy by this time was only fifty yards distant. Garnett turned his horse to see if the support he had ordered was coming up. At that instant a bullet hit him in the back. He fell from his horse. Gaines dismounted and tried to lift the general to his own saddle. The younger man struggled at the task until the Federals were close to the ford. Then he caught Garnett's horse, jumped to the back of his own animal, and galloped off unscathed.[36]

After long and wearing marches the tattered and exhausted force escaped to Monterey. The South was relieved that so many had escaped, but was grieved and humiliated that more than 700 had been killed, wounded, or taken prisoner.[37] After some hesitation, the Federals decided to hold Pegram as a prisoner of war and not as an army officer in rebellion. He was much criticized in the South for what the barroom strategists pronounced a poor deployment. Garnett's fate and the abandonment of the western approaches to the Shenandoah Valley were lamented equally. The general was dying when he fell, and as the Federals arrived he drew his last breath. His body, with all his belongings, was returned to his family by old friends in the Union army. From the list of those to whom the South looked hopefully, his high name had to be stricken—the first officer of his rank on either side to be killed in action.[38]

Although his grim defeat humiliated the South, the troops opposed to him were numerically superior and far better equipped. Their leader was Major General George B. McClellan. The attack against Pegram at Rich Mountain was delivered by McClellan's ablest subordinate, Brigadier General W. S. Rosecrans. Good Federal management, the weakness of the Confederate force, and McClellan's telegraphic reports of his success made the campaign appear on one side an example of incompetence and, on the other, of military brilliance. Garnett was buried and forgotten by the public; McClellan was the hope of the North.

CHAPTER 2

Beauregard's Battlefield

1. Beauregard Essays Grand Strategy

The tragedy of Rich Mountain and Carrick's Ford was effaced quickly by events around Manassas. Beauregard's little army increased steadily during the early summer. Most of the troops sent to him were of the very first type of volunteers, men of intelligence, courage, and good physique. Their company officers varied much, but their field officers, though in some cases without previous military experience, had station and capacity that won the respect of the men in the ranks. Training proceeded without break. "My troops," said Beauregard, "are in fine spirits and anxious for a fight." He added: "They seem to have the most unbounded confidence in me."[1]

Spurred by that confidence and by the prospect of an early advance, Beauregard prepared, on June 12, a plan of action which he sent to the President. He assumed Johnston, at Harper's Ferry, was about to be attacked. If that commander "were ordered to abandon forthwith his present position and concentrate suddenly his forces with mine . . . we could by a bold and rapid movement, retake Arlington Heights and Alexandria. . . ." Otherwise Johnston should retreat to Richmond, and he would do the same thing. Then, "acting on interior lines from Richmond as a center . . . we would crush successively and in detail the several columns of the enemy, which I have supposed will move on three or four different lines of operations. With 35,000 men properly handled on our part, I have not the least doubt that we could annihilate 50,000 of the enemy."

The President replied to this promptly and moderately. He did not dwell on the uncertainty of the assumption that the Federals first would attack Johnston, nor did he raise any question concerning the ability of an army that had little ordnance and feeble transportation to storm the approaches to Washington. In the matter of a general withdrawal on Richmond, the President withheld the obvious criticism that the enemy might not be obliging enough to advance, as Beauregard assumed, "on three or four different lines." Mr. Davis stressed only the fact that the Confederacy did not have sufficient transportation for a simultaneous withdrawal. There was not a hint in his letter that he regarded Beauregard's plan as grandiose. Nor did rejection of this proposal discourage Beauregard from formulating another.[2]

The day Prince John Magruder got his promotion, June 17, Mr. Davis appointed ten other brigadier generals. Among them were two officers already at Manassas—Richard S. Ewell of Virginia and David R. Jones, a South Carolinian. Included also were three officers with Joe Johnston in the Valley. These were Bernard E. Bee of South Carolina, E. Kirby Smith of Florida, and Thomas J. Jackson of Virginia. All five were graduates of the Military Academy and all except Jackson had been in the regular army until approximately the time their states had seceded.

Beauregard by this time had nineteen infantry regiments which, on June 20, he organized into six brigades. Milledge Bonham, whom he had found at Manassas, formally received the First Brigade, of South Carolina troops. To "Dick" Ewell were assigned two Alabama regiments and one from Louisiana. David Jones had one South Carolina and two Mississippi regiments. As these brigades exhausted Beauregard's general officers, he had to place one brigade of three Virginia regiments under Colonel G. H. Terrett. A brigade of like composition was entrusted to the great planter, Colonel P. St. George Cocke. The Sixth Brigade, of two Virginia and one South Carolina regiments, was placed under Colonel Jubal A. Early, who, like Cocke, was a retired West Pointer. Thus four of Old Bory's brigades had one-time professional soldiers at their head. Terrett was an old officer of marines, and Bonham had held a commission in the Mexican War. The regimental colonels swept a wide range of abilities—politicians, old militiamen, lawyers, teachers—but in most instances they were men who had been among the first to raise regiments and to enter the service of their states.[3]

With these troops Beauregard took an advanced position to cover Manassas and, if opportunity offered, to begin an offensive. Before he completed a new design he had discouragement. The North was as war-mad as the South and was arming furiously. Sumter was a spur, not a curb. Troops to drive Johnston up the Shenandoah Valley were being collected under General Robert Patterson, a veteran of the war with Mexico. General Irwin McDowell, who was commanding opposite Beauregard, was believed to be ready to sound the advance. Beauregard, not unnaturally, lost some of his appetite for an offensive. "If I could only get the enemy to attack me, as I am trying to have him do," he wrote, "I would stake my reputation on the handsomest victory that could be hoped for."[4]

In writing the President on July 11, Beauregard put the strength of

McDowell's army at 35,000 and credited the Federal commander with a reserve of 15,000. "In view of the odds against me," he said, ". . . I shall act with extreme caution." Then, almost overnight, he changed his mind again and dispatched Colonel James Chesnut to Mr. Davis with a new design: Johnston would join Beauregard and together they would advance and place themselves between the two lines of McDowell's army. They were to attack the Federals "separately with larger masses, and thus exterminate them or drive them into the Potomac." Johnston thereupon was to return to the Valley with his own army and 10,000 of Beauregard's troops and destroy the invading Union force under Patterson. Johnston, having wiped out Patterson, was to send part of his army to Robert Garnett, who was then facing McClellan in western Virginia. Having disposed of McClellan, Garnett would join Johnston and with him would move into Maryland and attack Washington from the rear. Beauregard himself simultaneously would attack the capital in front.

In Richmond this extraordinary plan presented by Colonel Chesnut was heard by President Davis, General Lee, and Adjutant General Samuel Cooper, but, being verbal, it was considered merely a broad suggestion. As such, it was held to be hopelessly impractical for a multitude of reasons. The details of Beauregard's proposal, in fact, made so slight an impression that the members of Colonel Chesnut's little audience were to have difficulty, a few months later, in recalling what actually had been proposed.[5]

Action now was immediately in prospect. The battle which each side expected to end the conflict between North and South was about to be joined. By July 17 it became certain that McDowell was advancing toward Manassas. Beauregard urged that Johnston move to his support, but even then he could not refrain from suggesting a touch of grand strategy: Johnston, said Beauregard, should advance in two columns. One should travel by way of the Manassas Gap Railroad. The other should cross the mountains north of the railroad and strike the enemy in flank and rear near Centreville at the moment Beauregard attacked in front.

Johnston had evacuated Harper's Ferry on June 15 and withdrawn to Winchester. If he had to reinforce Beauregard, the troops at Winchester could march twenty miles southeast and there strike a direct railroad to Manassas, thirty-five miles eastward. The one thing Johnston could not do at the time was to adopt Beauregard's suggestion and move on Manassas in two widely separated columns. "I preferred," Johnston later explained, "the junction of the two armies at the earliest time possible. . . ."[6]

This was not the end of Beauregard's strategy. Other proposals, as dazzling in detail and holding out ever richer prizes, were to be fashioned. The beginning was not promising. All Beauregard's plans from June 12 to July

17 had been rejected—all of them! He might not have even the command of the field. If the two Confederate forces were united at Manassas before McDowell attacked, Johnston would direct operations. He was the senior and might get the glory.

2. BEAUREGARD PLANS A BATTLE

Against the superior force marching to attack him, Beauregard fell back to Bull Run, took position on the south bank, and advised the President that, if the Federals were overwhelming, he would retire to the Rappahannock, "saving my command for defence there and future operations." Davis was requested to notify Johnston and Theophilus H. Holmes, who had a small force on the Potomac about twenty-five miles south of Manassas. "Send forward any reinforcements," Beauregard concluded, "at the earliest possible instant, and by every possible means."[7]

A brush had occurred at the outposts before Beauregard forwarded this telegram. On the eighteenth the Federals felt out the Confederate position at Blackburn's Ford on Bull Run. There they were smartly repulsed with some loss by Virginia troops. The commander of the defending forces was a Georgian, James Longstreet, who had been a paymaster in the old army and, in the promotions of June 17, had been made a brigadier general. Although only assuming command of his Virginia volunteers on July 2, replacing Colonel Terrett, he had advanced their training remarkably in a fortnight. Longstreet's calm and soldierly bearing in this skirmish made him a reality to many officers who previously had known him as a name only.[8]

On July 20, Johnston and part of his troops arrived at Manassas under authority received from Richmond. Johnston's supposition was that the Federal army under Patterson would not attempt to march up the Valley but would parallel his movement and proceed to Manassas. Johnston marched to Piedmont Station, whence trains were to carry his entire force to a junction with Beauregard. The first troops to reach Manassas in this manner were T. J. Jackson's brigade.[9]

Beauregard welcomed these troops and described to Johnston what had happened. The enemy was at Centreville, two and a half miles north of Bull Run. Beauregard proposed using Johnston's troops in an elaborate concentration. He had a plan ready: The new senior commander would keep his forces "united within the lines of Bull Run, and thence advance to the attack of the enemy." Johnston interpreted this proposal in terms of Patterson's response when he discovered that the Confederates had left Winchester; surely he would move his columns to the support of McDowell. They would arrive, Johnston computed, on the twenty-second. If McDowell was to be attacked before he was reinforced decisively, he must be struck on the twenty-first. Perforce, and without hesitation, he approved Beauregard's plan and directed him to undertake its execution. This was wholly in accordance with Beauregard's wishes, and perhaps was what he had been angling to effect. He ordered Johnston's and Holmes's troops into position as they arrived, and before nightfall he had in prospect the dispositions shown on the appended sketch.[10]

Beauregard's defended front, as the course of Bull Run twisted its way eastward, was approximately eight miles in length. For an advance by his right on Centreville, he placed his troops as advantageously as the roads permitted. On three miles of the right center he concentrated one half of the entire army.[11] Offensively, he was ready; defensively, he was exposed to

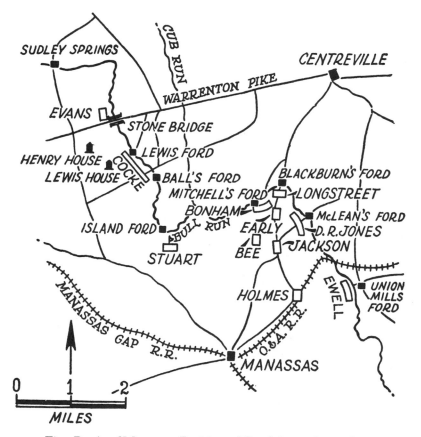

First Battle of Manassas. Position of Confederate forces along
Bull Run, July 21, 1861, sunrise.

any movement other than a direct drive on his base at Manassas. On two and a half miles of his left, where Beauregard later said he anticipated attack, he placed less than 5,000 men. Their closest support was the general reserve, almost four miles from the expected point of attack, namely, the vicinity of the Stone Bridge on the Warrenton Turnpike. Beauregard, in brief, was most heavily concentrated where his position was strongest, and was weakest numerically behind those Bull Run fords where crossing was easiest. The disproportion of force was startling. Of all this Beauregard must have been aware. He had studied the ground and had shaped the plan; obviously he based all his dispositions on offensive strategy.[12]

As Johnston entrusted the drafting of the combat order to the man who had fashioned the design, Beauregard set about that task late in the night of July 20–21. At 4:30 A.M. on the twenty-first he submitted the paper to General Johnston. It was a confused document, and in retrospect it is a gloomy instance of the manner in which, during the first stage of hostilities, the ignorance of the commanding officer may be as gross as that of the men and infinitely more expensive in blood and misery. Throughout the order its language was vague. At its end the various cooperating brigades were divided into two groups. One was assigned to General T. H. Holmes, though he was not so notified, and the other to an undesignated "second in command." Whether these officers were to direct their forces throughout the operation or only during the pursuit of the enemy could be subject to different interpretations. Such obscurities were paralyzing. Regardless of them, execution of the plan called for much staff work, prompt and complicated, which Beauregard's inexperienced staff by no possibility could perform.[13]

Before anything could be done to execute the plan, the unanticipated realities of developing action began to upset Beauregard's grand strategy. Shortly after 5 o'clock on the morning of July 21 a messenger arrived from Bonham at Mitchell's Ford, the center of the line, with a disconcerting report that the Federals had appeared in force on his left front. Did this mean that the enemy had seized the initiative and was attacking, instead of waiting obligingly to be assailed? There was no mistaking the direction of the sound of firing that now was audible. It was coming from the Confederate left, in the vicinity of the Stone Bridge, the crossing of Bull Run on the Warrenton Turnpike.[14]

Beauregard heard this bad news without evidence of chagrin. Unpleasant as was the prospect, he had to conclude that an attack was about to be made on Bonham, and probably also at Stone Bridge. In that event, of course, an immediate general offensive by the Confederates would be impossible. Even so, Beauregard's devotion to the Napoleonic strategy would not permit abandonment of all hope of an offensive. Beauregard told himself it was possible to undertake on his extreme right a diversion to confuse the enemy's attack on his center and left. At 5:30 A.M. he accordingly dispatched instructions to Dick Ewell, who commanded at Union Mills Ford, the crossing farthest downstream, to "hold yourself in readiness to take the offensive on Centreville at a moment's notice. . . ."[15]

Beauregard's attention was divided; his aides were confused; as his orders multiplied he lost his grip on his widely spread brigades. A slow cannonade now was ranging the entire left wing. Enemy forces were known to be moving down the Warrenton Pike toward Stone Bridge. That was all that actually had happened, but it shook to chaos the Confederate plan of action.

As Beauregard's orders had been issued to 6:00 A.M., or were interpreted by each of the affected officers, they provided: (1) that Longstreet should cross Bull Run and attack; (2) that Ewell should await word to launch a diversion toward Centreville; (3) that Holmes should support Ewell, though orders had not reached Holmes; (4) that David Jones should follow Ewell; (5) that Cocke and N. G. Evans should stand to the last in defense of the left-center and left; and (6) that Early should take position to support either Jones or Longstreet.[16] Involved as all this was, it might have been simplified if it had been understood. It was not. At Beauregard's headquarters nobody knew either the scope or recognized the conflict of orders.

About 7 o'clock Beauregard took his first step to reinforce his threatened left. He ordered a shift to Stone Bridge by General Bernard E. Bee, who commanded one of the brigades Johnston had brought from Winchester. With Bee went a Georgia contingent under Colonel Francis S. Bartow. Almost at the same hour, Jackson was directed to take his brigade and nine guns to fill the gap between Cocke and Bonham. In this manner, before the enemy's point of attack was discovered, all Beauregard's reserves had been ordered to move from their first positions of the morning.[17]

To be nearer the front, Johnston and Beauregard rode out to a high hill—to be known as Lookout Hill—at the rear of Bonham's position at Mitchell's Ford and established field headquarters. No sooner had they arrived than Beauregard underwent another change of mind. He had strengthened his left; he had prepared a demonstration on the right; he would turn that demonstration into an offensive against Centreville. He would hurl Ewell, Holmes, Jones, Longstreet, and Bonham across Bull Run while the Federals were preoccupied with their developing attack on the Confederate left. The commanding general approved. Whether he did so enthusiastically or after hesitation the record does not show.

For perhaps fifteen minutes Beauregard nursed this hope of a Napoleonic counterstroke. Then, about 9 o'clock, from a young captain of engineers, E. Porter Alexander by name, who was acting as signal officer, came this message: "I see a body of troops crossing Bull Run about two miles above the Stone Bridge. The head of the column is in the woods on this side. The rear of the column is in the woods on the other side. About a half-mile of its length is visible in the open ground between. I can see both infantry and artillery."[18]

The enemy, in short, already had crossed Bull Run far beyond the Confederate left and was fast taking position to turn that flank! While Beauregard was moving to strike the Federals' left, they were playing precisely the same game, and were playing it more swiftly, from their side of the Run.

The demands of the new situation were clear. With all speed the left must be strengthened further. Bee was marching for Stone Bridge—send him above it. Jackson was to take position below the bridge—let him, too, advance to meet the Federals who had crossed the stream. Colonel Wade Hampton of South Carolina had just arrived from Richmond with 600 infantry—speed them to the exposed flank. In excitement over the imperiled left, nobody seems to have considered whether new instructions were needed for the brigades on the right, where they were utterly at cross-purposes.

Sound of firing, artillery and musketry, now rolled down the Run. In swelling volume it seemed to come from the left of Stone Bridge. Worse still, Captain Alexander sent a courier to call to the attention of headquarters the rise of a cloud in the northwest. It was raised by dust, apparently, and was judged to be distant about ten miles. Johnston concluded immediately that the dust cloud marked the advance from the Valley of Patterson's Federal army. Patterson was believed by Johnston to have 30,000 men.[19]

If the van of that army was within three or four hours' march of the flank already being assailed, the afternoon might bring an overwhelming force against the Confederate left. Turning that flank and doubling it up, the Federals might seize Manassas and cut off the army from its line of supply. If Jackson, Bee, Evans, and Hampton succeeded in concentrating to resist the enemy, they could count a bare 6,650 muskets, or only a little more than 20 per cent of the effective strength of the Confederate forces. Although this would be an exceedingly thin line with which to confront a powerful adversary, Beauregard was so confident of the strategy of a counterstroke delivered from his right that he did not attempt to change his confused dispositions, or to give further reinforcement to the left. Nor did he go there himself to see what was happening. An hour passed. Beauregard kept his station on Lookout Hill. With him, puzzled and increasingly concerned, waited Johnston.

Not long before 10:30, from the extreme right at Union Mills, a messenger of Dick Ewell arrived at field headquarters: Ewell, he said, had been waiting since early morning for orders to advance; receiving none, he had sent to inquire of David Jones, next on his left, if Jones had any news or orders; Jones, north of the Run and deployed, said that he had understood Ewell also was to cross and attack. Ewell now wished Beauregard to know that he had never received such orders as Jones mentioned.

That was the doom of hope for an offensive on the right! Upon reflection and with the approval of Johnston, Beauregard directed that the brigades north of the Run recross to the south bank. "I thus," Beauregard wrote in 1863, "had suddenly or on the spur of the moment to change my whole plan of battle, with troops which had never yet fought and could scarcely maneuver. My heart for a moment failed me! . . . But I soon rallied, and I then solemnly pledged my life that I would that day conquer or die!"[20]

Johnston, who meticulously had respected his assignment to Beauregard of the conduct of the battle, became more restless. He wanted information from the left. He saw the dust clouds spread, he heard a louder fire. At length he broke over his self-imposed restraint and urged Beauregard to strengthen to the limit of the army's resources the troops on the left. "The battle is there," he said. "I am going!"[21]

3. BEAUREGARD'S STAR AT ZENITH

Beauregard hurriedly issued orders to carry out Johnston's wishes. Holmes was directed to proceed to the sound of the firing. Early, in reserve, was ordered to follow. Bonham was told to send two regiments to the left. After dispatching these orders, he set off to overtake Johnston. As the two generals approached the scene of action, they encountered stragglers, wounded men, disorganized fragments of regiments. Past these soldiers they spurred until they came to an eminence from which was visible a wide range of smoke-covered landscape. In front was a long, curving Federal line, ablaze with musketry fire and artillery. To their right, on an adjoining ridge, a short, thin line of Confederate infantry was in action. Behind this line were hundreds of confused Southern troops. To the left of the generals, admirably placed behind the crest of the hill, was a waiting Confederate brigade, near the center of which six field guns were barking viciously at the enemy. Streaming backward over the shoulder of the ridge to the right were broken units from the fight; one battered regiment without officers stood at order arms.[22]

What had happened? How fared the battle? The answer was given the generals in snatches and by different individuals, for no officer was in command of the field. Colonel N. G. Evans, at Stone Bridge, had seen early in the morning the movement of the Federals to the left and had thrown his 1,100 men directly in front of the approaching enemy column. General Bernard Bee, who had started for Stone Bridge about 7:00 A.M., had taken his two regiments and two from Colonel Francis Bartow's force and marched to Evans's support. These three commands had made a splendid fight. At a critical moment they had been reinforced by Wade Hampton's 600 South Carolinians. In the face of stiff odds and heavy fire, Evans, Bee, Bartow, and Hampton had been compelled at length to withdraw to the hill where lived the widow Judith Henry. While they were retiring, T. J. Jackson's brigade had arrived in support. When he learned of the attack on the left, Jackson, like Bee, had marched in that direction at once.

The troops that had been driven back must be identified, reorganized, and put back into the fight. Those in the stubborn line on the ridge to the right, Beauregard and Johnston soon learned, were Hampton's South Carolinians; those in confusion in the rear were the survivors of Evans's, Bee's, and Bartow's commands—all of them shattered except for the regiment that stood, unofficered and waiting. That was the 4th Alabama. The waiting brigade in a grim gray line to the left was Jackson's Virginians.

Johnston and Beauregard and their staffs made their way among the scattered fugitives. When they reached the 4th Alabama, Johnston found its flag bearer, put the boy by his side, and called to the soldiers and rode forward. With alacrity and ready cheers the men followed. Johnston placed them in line with Jackson; around these steady soldiers and the Virginians others quickly gathered. Soon the line was restored in the face of the Federals who were moving up the slope in front and on the right for another assault.[23]

Beauregard, with polite firmness, now made a startling request of Johnston: Would the commanding general please retire from the front and leave to him the direction of the fighting there?

To Johnston's surprised ear he explained that one or the other of them had to supervise the entire field and, in particular, see that reinforcements were hurried forward. If one must do this, Johnston as senior should. As the junior, said Beauregard, it was his right and his duty to handle the engaged wing of the army. Johnston at first refused. Beauregard persisted: It must be done. At length, with manifest reluctance, Johnston acquiesced and rode back to Portici, the Lewis house. This proved to be a well-chosen post of command. Close by ran the roads that any reinforcements would use.[24]

It was now after 1:00 P.M. Until that hour the initiative and the advantage had been altogether on the side of the Federals. From the Confederate side, the Unionists did not appear to have made a single mistake or to have presented even one opening. Beauregard's elaborate plan of battle had been thrice changed and in each instance had been frustrated. Only the stubborn fighting of those first Southerners on the scene had saved the army from disaster.

Disposing revived regiments on either side of Jackson's steadfast brigade, Beauregard, wherever he thought he could rally the men, made them a brief speech. He summarized it afterward in his formal report: "I informed them that re-enforcements would rapidly come to their support, and that we must at all hazards hold our posts until re-enforced. I reminded them that we fought for our homes, our firesides, and for the independence of our country. I urged them to the resolution of victory or death on that field." Said he, "These sentiments were loudly, eagerly cheered. . . ."[25]

At that moment those traitorous war gods, Chance and Blunder, who had fought all morning against the Southerners, turned on the Federals. Through the smoke there galloped recklessly up the hill of the Henry house two batteries, which opened fire immediately against the Confederate artillery. The Union infantry support was slow in coming up, and then was disorganized by a short cavalry charge which Colonel J. E. B. Stuart led. The 33rd Virginia was shouted to the charge. A roar and a volley—the Virginians were upon the Federals. Farther along the front Jackson's men fired fast. The artillerists were cut down. Both batteries were silenced.[26]

At 2:00 P.M. Beauregard boldly ordered an advance along the right of his line. Swiftly the plateau was swept clear of the enemy. The gain was momentary. Ere long the enemy quickened his fire. Bluecoats showed once again over the rim of the hill. Soon the defenders began to give ground; once the line wavered, it yielded. In fifteen minutes the Federals recovered nearly the whole of the advance positions they had lost.[27]

Five hours of fighting since Evans had challenged the Federal advance. Five hours and the question was the same: Would the Federals outflank the Confederate left? Steadily the Union line was being extended toward the southwest. Johnston, at Portici, already had seen the danger and had been hurrying forward all the troops within marching distance. But for a counterstroke there must be strong reinforcements. Beauregard believed the needed troops would come up, and without waiting for them he renewed his attack. Again he swept across the plateau and cleared it, though at heavy cost. General Bee fell. Colonel Bartow went down. This time the ground recovered by the Confederates was held.[28]

Then, as it subsequently appeared to an amazed army, a miracle occurred. The two South Carolina regiments from Bonham's brigade, panting through the dust across the July fields, hurried to the endangered left. The

28th Virginia found its way to the position of the South Carolinians and extended the left. Three good regiments of Johnston's army, who had detrained that noon at Manassas, moved under Johnston's orders straight to the sound of the firing. The left was long now and curved to the west. Opposite it the enemy front was being extended for another attempt. Another brigade on the flank was needed immediately—would it come up?[29]

As Beauregard looked anxiously to the southwest he saw a marching column. At its head was its flag. Eagerly he turned his glass on the standard: Was it the flag of the Union or of the South? For all his effort he could not tell. Now a courier brought him a dispatch from the signal corps. A large force, approaching from the very quarter to which Beauregard was looking, was believed to be Patterson's Federals. Beauregard's heart sank. Once again he focused his glass on the approaching column. There was an anxious heart-thumping delay. Then a breeze swept across the hill and set the summer leaves to rustling. It struck the column, it stirred the bunting, it spread the colors—Confederate. The needed brigade had arrived to save the day! It was Early's.[30]

Beauregard pointed it out to the near-by troops. They cheered its appearance. Up and down the front spread the news of reinforcement. Weary men were strengthened to speed their fire. The weird cry of the Southern foxhunters swelled at the prospect of such a chase as none of them had known before. Another pause, intolerable minutes of expectancy and confusion. Then, suddenly, all along the front, the Confederates rushed forward. The Federal front of attack collapsed. Before the fire of advancing Southerners collapse soon became rout, the oft-described rout of Bull Run.[31]

CHAPTER 3

Beauregard's Star Wanes

1. PURSUIT AND A CONFUSED COUNCIL

The battle was won—could there be pursuit? Three full hours of daylight remained. Bonham had fresh regiments at Mitchell's Ford. Longstreet's brigade was at Blackburn's. From these crossings the distance to Centreville was three miles. The Federals, retreating madly toward the same village, had four miles to go. If Bonham and Longstreet moved quickly they might cut them off. From the left, meantime, Colonel Stuart was spurring his small cavalry command in the direction of Sudley Ford. Early's infantry were pursuing. Other regiments were following the enemy up the turnpike toward Stone Bridge. Beauregard directed these dispositions and then galloped to the Lewis house for a brief, exultant meeting with Johnston. The senior ordered him to continue the chase.[1]

Little was accomplished. Stuart ere long was burdened with many prisoners and deprived of virtually all power to strike. Early found his men so wearied by their march that he had to rest them for a time. Before the other pursuing regiments the Federal infantry fled too rapidly for the Southerners to re-establish contact. Abandoned artillery, demoralized stragglers, and the plunder of the field were the only rewards on the left.[2]

On the right center, Longstreet advanced steadily along the Manassas-Centreville highway, but soon found Bonham's men coming into the road from the left. Bonham rode up and as senior insisted on marching his regiments ahead of Longstreet's. More minutes of waning daylight passed while Bonham formed his troops and took the lead. They did not pause again until there came from the north the challenge of artillery fire. It was reported that the Federals had a line manned with infantry and artillery. Bonham pondered. The sun was almost down. Should he risk an attack in gathering twilight against a foe that might have rallied? At that moment Major W. H. C. Whiting, Johnston's chief engineer, appeared. Whiting had heard rumors that the Federals were attacking at Union Mills and striking for Manassas.

Longstreet listened in amusement and ridiculed the possibility of a countermovement. He knew a retreat when he saw one, he said; the Federals were beaten and must be attacked at once. Let the batteries open!

Whiting rose in his stirrups. "In the name of General Johnston," said he, "I order that the batteries shall *not* open!" Longstreet maintained that he had the responsibility of the field and would engage the enemy. But Bonham intervened with a request that action not be joined. That was tantamount to orders of a direct superior, and Longstreet said no more. Bonham directed a withdrawal to the Confederate side of Bull Run. The rumor that had halted them in front of Centreville had spread widely and prompted Beauregard to order a concentration in the vicinity of Union Mills. This prevented Ewell and Holmes from striking the enemy.[3]

The evil wrought by false report (the rumor originated with one of D. R. Jones's staff, who mistook the blue uniforms of some of his own men, recrossing the Run, for those of the enemy) was forgotten amid rejoicing over the victory. In the first great test—the decisive test, many averred—the South had won. Of the manner in which their adversaries had fought that morning the victors had nothing to say; they could talk only of the mad flight of their foe in the afternoon. Surely, after that experience, the Federals would not again attempt to invade the South. Independence was won; the war was over.

The elation of the men in the ranks was shared by their officers and by Mr. Davis himself. The President had been unable to endure in Richmond the suspense of the approaching battle. On the morning of the twenty-first he had taken a special train for Manassas. In the village he had taken horse and hurried to the field. He procured from Johnston such information as the general possessed and then, after supper, sat down to enjoy the soldier's greatest delight, the writing of the first announcement of a victory.

While the President was drafting this dispatch to the War Department, General Beauregard came in. Jubilant congratulations were exchanged. New details of the triumph were explained. Just then Major R. C. Hill reached headquarters to report that he had been to Centreville, where he found the deserted street jammed with abandoned artillery. Mr. Davis observed that such a situation constituted the best of reasons for following the Federals furiously and in maximum force. At that, someone observed that Major Hill had been known in the old army as "Crazy Hill" because of his manner, which always suggested excitability. Further inquiry elicited the fact that Hill had been deceived concerning the ground and had not in fact penetrated to Centreville. This altered the outlook. Davis, Johnston, and Beauregard agreed that an advance on Centreville in the darkness would be imprudent. They would send Bonham forward the next morning.[4]

Before dawn rain began to fall and continued throughout eastern Virginia all the twenty-second. By none of the roads was mass pursuit possible. Loud was the lament, because everywhere Confederate detachments penetrated that day they found evidence that many of the Federals had become panic-stricken and abandoned all equipment that impeded flight. Public property recovered on the field or in the wake of the retreating army included 28 excellent field guns, 37 caissons, half a million rounds of small-arms ammunition, 4,500 sets of accouterments, 500 muskets, and 9 flags. The prisoners, wounded and unhurt, numbered approximately 1,460, or only about 500 less than gross Confederate casualties.[5]

Credit for these captures and for the victory itself was given immediately, without stint or scrutiny, to General Beauregard. When Johnston suggested before breakfast on the twenty-second that Beauregard's services be recognized by promotion, the President assured him that this already had been arranged. While the three were eating, Mr. Davis handed Beauregard a note in his autograph explaining: "you are appointed to be 'General' in the army of the Confederate States of America. . . ."[6]

The honor thus bestowed by the President and speedily confirmed by the Senate was followed by public acclamation. Incidents of Beauregard's valor on the field, some of them apocryphal, were read and repeated. There was praise for Johnston, to be sure. His name, by reason of his seniority, was listed first in the congressional vote of thanks, but the concentration of the two armies, not less than the victory itself, was assumed to be the work of Beauregard. The momentary, almost universal belief that the Battle of Manassas would end the war gave place to a belief that Beauregard would invade the North for a desperate struggle. Then impatience was voiced that the advance was delayed.[7]

2. SUBORDINATES OF PROMISE

So exultant was the South that it made no effort and, indeed, had no occasion to appraise critically the generalship of Beauregard. Few inquired whether the victory might not have been due as much to chance and to the valor of his subordinates as to the design and discernment of the commander. In those first intoxicating days there was general praise for all, but little of specific commendation for any except Beauregard, Johnston, and the fallen officers. The bodies of General Bernard S. Bee and Colonel Francis S. Bartow were brought to Richmond and laid in state, with a guard of honor, before they were returned for burial in native soil.

Through the circulation of stories of the death of General Bee the

South formed its first admiring estimate of General T. J. Jackson. The *Charleston Mercury* described how Bee's brigade "dwindled to a mere handful. . . . He rode up to Gen. Jackson and said, 'General, they are beating us back.' The reply was, 'Sir, we'll give them the bayonet.' General Bee immediately rallied the remnant of his brigade, and his last words to them were: 'There is Jackson standing like a stone wall. Let us determine to die here, and we will conquer. Follow me.'" This made instant appeal to the public imagination. The next day a Charleston correspondent of *Punch* wrote that he drank "two 'stone walls' and a 'General Jackson' before breakfast."[8]

Although the sober Jackson would have disapproved the medium of its expression, he deserved this tribute. At a critical point of the battle he had advanced straight to the point of danger, had held his ground through the hardest fighting, and, as became an instructor in artillery, had massed his guns to play upon the enemy in front of his compact, unyielding line. Jackson's horse had been wounded under him, and a bullet had broken the bone of the middle finger of his left hand. To reduce the bleeding and to ease the pain, he had carried his arm upraised through the remainder of the action. Observing this, some of his men thought he was invoking the blessing of Heaven.

He believed that he had received that blessing. He wrote his wife: "Whilst great credit is due to other parts of our gallant army, God made my brigade more instrumental than any other in repulsing the main attack. . . . I am thankful to my ever-kind Heavenly Father that He makes me content to await His own good time and pleasure for commendation—knowing that all things work together for my good." He was "content to await," but not to be denied "commendation." Did he mean "fame"? Was ambition burning under the faded blue coat he had brought to Manassas from V.M.I.? Beneath his cadet cap his large blue eyes had blazed with a strange light during the battle; what did that portend? His soldiers did not know, but they confirmed the tribute implied in Bee's shouted words. From that day Professor Jackson was "Stonewall" Jackson.[9]

Along with the service of Bee and Jackson on the left General Johnston ranked that of E. Kirby Smith. The Florida brigadier who had been his chief of staff at Harper's Ferry had been left behind to bring up the rear brigade. His men detrained at Manassas station about 1:00 P.M., threw off their knapsacks, and formed into line. With the back of his hand raised in front of his cap, Smith cried, "This is the signal, men, the watchword is 'Sumter'!" He begged Johnston to let him throw them into the battle, then moved his column at the double-quick to the left. Almost immediately he received a minié ball, which grazed his spinal column, plowed through the muscles of his neck, and passed out near the collar-bone.[10]

As Smith fell, he turned over the command to his senior colonel, a stout-hearted officer of the old army, Arnold Elzey. Listed in first reports as dead, Smith was to recover speedily. His future, all men saw, was to be large, nor did that of his second in command promise to be small. Elzey handled the troops admirably, giving a fine example of soldierly enthusiasm. The judgment of his leading soon won for him a commission as brigadier general.[11]

Elzey had a bluff and hearty manner and on occasion did not disdain what the soldiers called "a dram." One evening, when he and some of his comrades were in expansive mood, the general called in the sentinel on the post and gave him a drink, for which the man was pathetically grateful. Later in the night, when the party was over and Elzey was asleep, the same man was walking his post. Without abashment he put his head inside Elzey's tent and woke him with the loud query, "General, General, ain't it about time for us to take another drink?" The wrathful Elzey had the man put under arrest, but the soldier had the gratitude of the army for inspiring a question that echoed every day in all the camps.[12]

Colonel Jubal A. Early, who had extended the left flank beyond the line of Smith and Elzey, received praise on the field and later in the reports, but in smaller measure than his comrades to the right. His arrival was decisive because it showed the Federals they were outflanked, but his share in the actual fighting had been small. The personality of the colonel, even more, kept him from being a popular hero. Born in the Blue Ridge Mountains of Virginia, he went to West Point, where he was graduated No. 18 in the class of 1837, but after two years in the army he resigned to become an attorney in his native county. As lawyer, Whig legislator, and prosecuting attorney he labored until 1861, except for a period of uneventful service as a major of volunteers during the Mexican War. Early was forty-four, about six feet tall and weighed under 170 pounds; but as a result of rheumatism contracted in Mexico he stooped badly and seemed so much older than his years that his soldiers promptly dubbed him "Old Jube" or "Old Jubilee." His long beard; his keen, flashing black eyes; his satirical smile; his avowed irreligion; and his rasping, mordant wit made him appear almost saturnine. He was stern in his discipline and was charged with a snarling harshness toward his subordinates. That he was able many believed, and that he was coldly brave all who saw him on the field admitted. What he would become as a commander none knew and few cared. When the caustic colonel was promoted to brigadier from the day of the battle, there probably was scant enthusiasm.[13]

Applause was allotted also to Colonel Nathan George Evans for his first challenge of the advancing enemy. He had put up as stout resistance as could have been offered in the face of such odds. His casualties, 12 per cent of his engaged force, were entailed in heavy fighting and not in mere delaying action. Promotion was not to follow immediately, for reasons as personal as those that denied popularity to Early. "Shanks" Evans—his thinnest members received stoutest acclaim—had won some repute in the Indian fighting that had followed his graduation from West Point in the class of 1848. He was thirty-seven, of medium height, slightly bald, with the fiercest of black mustachios and small restless eyes to match. His look was quick, cunning, and contentious, as if he always were suspecting a Comanche ambush. There was no question of his capacity, but he was the devil-may-care type and was accused—falsely, it would appear—of excessive fondness of the bottle.[14]

Much of the heaviest fighting under Evans had been done by a Louisiana battalion of Zouaves from New Orleans, one company of which, styled "The Tigers," had given its name and evil reputation to the whole. In whatever cities these troops had halted on their way to the front there had been undisciplined rioting and whispers, at the least, of theft and pillage. Their major, fortunately, knew how to deal with them. Roberdeau C. Wheat he was, son of an Episcopal clergyman and inheritor of Huguenot tradition and Maryland blue blood. Physically superb, over six feet in height, with manners that bespoke his uprearing, he volunteered for service in Mexico and, on the conclusion of peace, went to New Orleans and entered politics and practiced law. He would have risen high, perhaps as a criminal lawyer, had he not become absorbed in those Latin-American adventures of the 1850s in which Gulf State ideals of political freedom were combined paradoxically with the extension of slavery.

As Wheat had fought alongside hard men of alien tongues, he had been wholly at ease when he led his Tigers into action at Manassas. In a charge he had been shot down. The surgeon who examined him shook a sage professional head: A bullet wound of that nature, through both lungs, was necessarily fatal. "I don't feel like dying yet," Wheat avowed. He was desperate; perhaps in battle he had been foolhardy, but he had accumulated more combat experience than any other Confederate officer at Manassas. Would he survive his wound to use that experience?[15]

From his brigade headquarters at Portici, Colonel Philip St. George Cocke had directed the earliest reinforcements to reach the flank. It was he who had informed first Bee and Bartow, then Hampton, and then Jackson of Evans's advance and of the progress of the action. Without Cocke's guidance, based on his thorough knowledge of the terrain, the order of battle could not have been established so readily or so soon. What seemed in retrospect a marvel of distant control by Beauregard was, in reality, the work of Colonel Cocke.

Cocke was ambitious for military rank and fame, but for neither did he have need. Born in 1808 to one of the oldest and wealthiest families in the state, he had been schooled in arms at West Point, but after less than two years' garrison duty he resigned to devote himself to the care of his estates. Virginia had no planter more renowned that St. George Cocke. Through the years he had kept his interest in military affairs. Now that the first contest was over and Cocke had shown what he was capable of doing, the press had praise of him. By brother officers he was recognized as "a high-minded and gallant soldier, a devoted patriot, and a gentleman of cultivation and refinement." Would he and men like him, the middle-aged aristocrats and the proprietors of the great estates, measure up, as a class, to the requirements of command, and could they endure the hardships and exactions of prolonged field service?[16]

South Carolina colonel Wade Hampton, of a social station as high as that of Cocke, gave on the field of Manassas a hopeful, if incomplete, answer to that question. He did more. In his antecedents and in his own career he represented the rise and the attainments, the strength and the weakness, of the economic system which the war would vindicate or destroy.

When his grandfather, the first Wade Hampton, died in 1835 he had 3,000 slaves and ranked as the richest planter in the United States. The second Wade Hampton (1791–1858) was of a fortunate generation that could spend its maturity in an era of peace and plentitude. His mansion, Millwood, was almost as much the political capital of South Carolina as was near-by Columbia. In his great library, one of the best-stocked private collections in the nation, he ruled as the "Great Warwick of South Carolina." When he died, Millwood, a fortune, and the leadership of the family passed to the third Wade Hampton, who had been born in Charleston in 1818. By the time he was in his middle thirties he came to doubt the economy of slave labor and on that account dissented from the politics of the dominant element of his state. In the legislature, which he entered so that he might counteract some of the policies of the "fire-eaters," he served diligently and without any shadow of selfish ambition.[17]

Until 1861, in short, his was the ideal life of the society in which he was reared. Standing just under six feet, he had the balance of the horseman and the smooth muscles of the athlete. His courage, personal, moral, and political, was in keeping with his physique. Once South Carolina seceded he put all argument behind him and placed at the command of the state his wealth and his services. He set about the enlistment of a "Legion," six companies of infantry, four of cavalry, and a battery of artillery. Some of the best-born young men of the Palmetto State were proud to be privates in Hampton's Legion. Colonel Hampton was then forty-three, older than many officers of like or higher rank, and he had the manner of one to whom war was not a frolic or an adventure but a grim, bitter business to be discharged as quickly as might be with determination and without relish.[18]

Hampton and his 600 infantry detrained at Manassas when the guns were already roaring. Although he had never been in action and never had been given even the rudimentary training of a militiaman before 1861, he led his men straight into the heat of the battle. He held his position until he was enfiladed, then led his men back. The Federals advanced again, to the right and to the left, surrounding Hampton on three sides. Still his men fought furiously. In their pride they might have remained on the hillside till the last of them was killed had not Bee and Bartow urged Hampton to retire. In the final advance Hampton fell leading a charge against a battery. Fortunately his wound was slight, but among his 600 men the casualties reached 121, or 20 per cent. Although in dispatches he merely was commended for "soldierly ability," everything expected of him he had done, and he had displayed inspiring courage and persistence. There was more of potential military excellence about him than his superiors at the moment realized.[19]

These, then, were the surviving officers who had most distinguished themselves in actual combat under Johnston and Beauregard: Stonewall Jackson, a former brevet major in the regular army and then a professor in a state military institute; a tall Floridian of thirty-seven, E. Kirby Smith, who only two months and a half previously had resigned a major's commission; Jubal A. Early, one-time lieutenant and for almost thirty years a lawyer and a politician; an Indian fighter, Shanks Evans; a young soldier of fortune who commanded a notoriously tough battalion, Rob Wheat; a successful planter and distinguished host, P. St. George Cocke, who had not borne arms for nearly thirty years; and a Carolina millionaire sportsman of no previous military training. Had Fate, blindfolded, drawn their names at random they scarcely could have been those of men more diverse in temperament or in training.

Others had done well. The lawyer-colonel J. B. Kershaw, 2nd South Carolina, was a man who seemed to have military aptitude. Arnold Elzey had handled his brigade most intelligently after Kirby Smith fell. All three of Early's colonels had behaved like veterans—James L. Kemper, Harry Hays, and William Barksdale. Colonel Eppa Hunton of the 8th Virginia had borne himself gallantly. Brigadier General Holmes had marched fast from the right.

Those who had been denied a hand in the fray had chafed or had cursed. There was James Longstreet, who counted among his colonels a restless man named Samuel Garland. Dick Ewell had with him a young acting assistant adjutant general named Fitzhugh Lee, and also a stalwart colonel of the fine 5th Alabama, a soldierly figure with sandy mustache and penetrating eyes, Robert E. Rodes, who had been a teacher and a civil engineer in railway employ. In D. R. Jones's brigade, ill content to play so small a role in so exciting a drama, was Micah Jenkins, colonel of the 5th South Carolina. Arriving late from the Shenandoah, Colonel A.P. Hill moved to the right with his 13th Virginia but could not fire a single shot.

The cavalry had been led with dash by Colonel James E. B. Stuart, but the mounted men had been too few to sweep the field. Many artillerists had won praise. Notable among them had been Reverend W. N. Pendleton, an old West Pointer and an Episcopal clergyman. With Jackson's guns Captain John D. Imboden had challenged every eye. A gigantic young lieutenant, Thomas L. Rosser, had command of four howitzers of the Washington Artillery. Staff officers had commendation. Beauregard saw to it that his chief of artillery and ordnance, Colonel Samuel Jones, was promoted to brigadier general. Johnston mentioned first among staff officers his chief engineer, Major W. H. C. Whiting. Whiting, like Jones, was made a brigadier as of July 21. Young Captain E. P. Alexander, signal officer, had praise but no immediate promotion.

That some of these men would acquit themselves valiantly any observer safely could predict; but none could foresee that from the 30,000 of the small Army of the Potomac (as Beauregard styled it) were to come, in a long war, so large a number of general officers. Ten men held that rank at Manassas on the day of battle. One of them, Bee, was mortally wounded. Another, Bonham, would resign at the rank he then held. A third, Johnston, already had the highest grade in the army. Of the others, Beauregard and Kirby Smith became generals; Longstreet, Jackson, Holmes, and Ewell rose to be lieutenant generals; and D. R. Jones died as a major general. Of the colonels at Manassas, A. P. Hill, Early, and Hampton ended their service as lieutenant generals, and Stuart, Elzey, William Smith, Samuel Jones, Rodes, Kershaw, and Kemper were to be major generals. Fourteen other colonels were to lead brigades, and eighteen of lesser rank at Manassas would in time become general officers.

In short, to the nine general officers who survived Manassas, forty-two were to be added from men in the army along Bull Run that July day. Of the fifty-one, ten were doomed to lose their lives during the war. Eight, and no more than eight, were to prove plainly unqualified for the final grade they reached; nine were to show themselves of low capacity to command; seventeen could be regarded as average soldiers. The remaining seventeen were to be renowned.

3. THE FAME OF BEAUREGARD IS BECLOUDED

Before the fame of any of these men of Manassas had been acclaimed, that of Beauregard was beclouded by a succession of controversies, the first of which arose over rations. During the days immediately following the battle of July 21, the poorly equipped commissaries and quartermasters were unable to supply promptly the larger army assembled at the Manassas railhead. Food ran low. Transportation was overtaxed. On July 29, Beauregard appealed directly to two congressmen who had served him as volunteer aides, revealing the fact that some regiments had been without food for more than twenty-four hours. "The want of food and transportation has made us lose all the fruits of our victory," he wrote.

This startling letter was not marked "Confidential," and the recipients felt it their duty to read it to Congress in secret session. The disclosure shocked the lawmakers. They inquired of the President "information going to show a want of sufficient and regular supply of food" for the army. Davis replied that he considered the condition of the commissariat "quite as good as was reasonable to expect," and then, on August 4, he wrote Beauregard a friendly, well-reasoned letter. The substance of it was that the emergent needs of the army had not been known, that they had been met when ascertained, and that Beauregard did himself injustice in "putting your failure to pursue the enemy to Washington to the account of short supplies of subsistence and transportation."

To this communication Beauregard made a somewhat apologetic reply. He had written "only for the purpose of expediting matters," and he regretted that his letter had been read to Congress. He added that after his task of repelling the Northern invaders was accomplished, "I shall retire to my home . . . never again to leave it, unless called upon again to repel the same or another invader." That final sentence evidently was written to assure Mr. Davis that General Beauregard did not intend to heed those urging him to be a candidate in the election of November 5 for the office of President under the "permanent" constitution of the Confederacy. Davis dropped the discussion, desiring, apparently, nothing more than to clear his own skirts. He was not seeking to besmirch Beauregard's.[20]

Had the facts been otherwise, the President could not have wished a sworn enemy to play more completely into his hands than Beauregard did by the blunders he proceeded to make. First, contrary to the plain limitations of existing military law, he did his utmost to have his troops regarded as a separate and autonomous corps. His aim seems to have been to perpetuate the conditions that existed on the day of the Battle of Manassas. Correspondence and diplomacy alike failed to reconcile him otherwise.[21]

On October 15, while controversy over this vexatious matter still was polite, Beauregard forwarded to the War Department his official account of the battle of July 21. In the amplitude of 9,000 words he presented full details and occasional excursus. After the report reached the War Department someone carelessly failed to forward it to the President. The first Mr. Davis knew either of its arrival or its content was when his attention was called to the *Richmond Dispatch* of October 23, which contained a digest of parts of the document, introduced by a reporter as follows: ". . . General Beauregard opens with a statement of his position antecedent to the battle, and of a plan proposed by him to the Government of a junction of the armies of the Shenandoah and Potomac, with a view to the relief of Maryland and the capture of the city of Washington, which plan was rejected by the President. . . ."

Mr. Davis sent at once for the report and read it. He found that the opening 600 words were an epitome of Beauregard's scheme of a great strategical combination, as communicated by Colonel Chesnut and rejected as impracticable. The whole introduction, in his opinion, was an effort on the part of the general to depreciate the work of others and to portray himself as the sole designer and executant of the Manassas triumph. Davis, accordingly, on October 30 sent a stiff protest to Beauregard. It began with a chilly "Sir" and ended "Very respectfully, yours, &c.," in pointed contrast to the "My dear General" and the "Very truly, your friend" employed in the letter concerning subsistence. "With much surprise," the President wrote, "I found that the newspaper statements were sustained by the text of your report. I was surprised, because, if we did differ in opinion as to the measures and purposes of contemplated campaigns, such fact could have no appropriate place in the report of a battle. Further, because it seemed to be an attempt to exalt yourself at my expense, and especially because no such plan as that described was submitted to me."[22]

The President wrote to Colonel Chesnut for a statement of what he had said when he came to Richmond with Beauregard's plan. He asked similar reports from General Lee and General Cooper, who had been present at the conference. Before answers to these inquiries were received, there appeared in the *Richmond Whig* for November 7 a letter in which General Beauregard acquainted the country with the fact that sharp differences had arisen between himself and the administration. He expressed his regret at the publication of the synopsis of his report, and urged his friends not to worry "about the slanders and calumnies aimed at me. . . . If certain minds cannot understand the difference between *patriotism,* the highest civic virtue, and *office-seeking,* the lowest civil occupation, I pity them from the bottom of my heart. Suffice it to say, that I prefer the respect and esteem of my countrymen, to the admiration and envy of the world. I hope . . . to answer my calumniators with new victories over our national enemies. . . ."[23]

The letter was published two days after the presidential election. For reasons that presently will appear, Beauregard's language probably was directed at Secretary of War Judah P. Benjamin rather than at the hief executive; but the general's words could be interpreted by the friends of Mr. Davis as an effort to becloud and embarrass the new administration. Even admirers of the "Hero of Sumter and Manassas" considered the letter ill-advised. "There was a theatrical circumstance and tone about it, that displeased many people." The *Examiner* called it a "very remarkable" document that would "hardly add to the General's reputation."[24]

Davis thought the communication worse than that. Letters from General Lee and General Cooper fortified him in his contention that what Beauregard had described as a "plan of operations," submitted on July 14, was "a message from General Beauregard, but . . . no plan of battle or of campaign." As for the embarrassed Colonel Chesnut, he tried to reconcile the assertions of the President with those of Beauregard. In doing so, he disclosed the fact that on his return to Manassas from Richmond he had submitted to the general a written report on the conference. "I regret," Davis told Chesnut, "that . . . I was not permitted the see the report of the interview before it became a public document."[25]

Of these unhappy exchanges, nothing at the time was made public after the appearance of Beauregard's letter to the *Whig*, but that communication itself had been sufficient to pique curiosity concerning his official account of the battle. At length, after considerable wrangling in secret session, the Congress decided to publish the report without its strategical prologue and without the correspondence it had engendered. This halted the controversy between Beauregard and the administration.[26]

Almost simultaneously, the command of General Beauregard in northern Virginia was terminated. This was not solely—perhaps not even primarily—because of Beauregard's injudicious correspondence. As will be plain in the next chapter, his relations with General Johnston, marked on the surface by comradeship, had a deeper aspect of jealousy that threatened the efficient handling of the army. Nor was that all. Differences between Beauregard and Secretary Benjamin had become irreconcilable. During one of their disputes Beauregard told the President that his "motives must not be called into question" by Benjamin, and that he was being "put into the strait jacket of the law." Davis replied in the sternest terms: ". . . you surely did not intend to inform me that your army and yourself are outside the limits of the laws. . . . I cannot recognize the pretension of any one that their restraint is too narrow for him."

There had been, also, revival of the dispute whether Beauregard commanded a semi-independent corps or was second in command of the entire army. On the last day of 1861 the general telegraphed the President: "Please state definitely what I am to command, if I do not command a corps. . . ." To this the President made no reply, but the War Department ascertained that Beauregard was willing to accept service in Kentucky under Albert Sidney Johnston and, on January 26, 1862, ordered him thither.[27]

Very different was his departure from his arrival in Virginia. No less different was his place in the respect of the President and in the admiration of a large element in the South. His star had waned. Many still looked at Beauregard in the afterglow of Sumter and Manassas, but the South, perplexed by his egotistical writings, no longer believed unanimously that in him it had found its Napoleon. The search for a leader had to be directed elsewhere and, naturally, first to Beauregard's colleague, Joe Johnston.

CHAPTER 4

Johnston Passes a Dark Winter

1. Conflict with the Administration

During the weeks of Beauregard's controversy with the administration, Joseph E. Johnston had been exercising uninterrupted, if not undisputed, command of the army around Centreville. It had few skirmishes and no major battles to fight. On October 21 there was a handsome affair at Ball's Bluff, which ended in the rout by Shanks Evans's troops of a Federal force that had ventured across the Potomac. Otherwise little occurred to divert Johnston from what he considered his main task, that of "preparing our troops for active service by diligent instruction."[1]

As Johnston rode daily through their camps, his men soon came to know a figure which, once seen, was recognized always. Johnston was of erect, trim figure and of middle height. His head was well molded, his hair was grizzled; his short side whiskers of kindred color set off his florid complexion. In his glance there was more of questioning than of suspicion; his thin lips were as capable of smiling as of sneering. If Beauregard was likened by his admirers to an eagle, Joe Johnston seemed a gamecock.[2]

His essential quality, which was not disclosed at first, was contradiction. Those of his subordinates who had demonstrated their faith in him and had won his confidence found him warm-hearted, affectionate, and loyal. In his dealings with his military peers and his civil superiors Johnston was unpredictable. Ere long Jefferson Davis was to find that any letter from Joe Johnston might smoke with wrath as it lay on the executive desk. Love was not easily destroyed in his heart; hate once inflamed always was cherished.

Toward the President, at the outset, Johnston's manner had been friendly. While the general's withdrawal from Harper's Ferry had been regretted, nothing occurred during the early summer to indicate any scorn on his part of fixed positions, any weakness as a military administrator. Scarcely a shadow had fallen across the council table when Johnston and Davis met at Manassas after the battle. Until August 31, 1861, all went well between the two. On that date Mr. Davis sent to the Senate for confirmation the names of the five officers who, under the act of May 16, were to be given the rank of full general. First on the submitted list, to rank from May 16, was the adjutant general, Samuel Cooper; second was Albert Sidney Johnston, as of May 30; third came R. E. Lee, ranking as of June 14; fourth stood Joseph E. Johnston, with the grade of general from July 4; fifth was P. G. T. Beauregard, to date from July 21, Manassas Day.[3]

This order of nominations, which was confirmed at once by the Senate, outraged Joseph E. Johnston. From that day forward he never was the same man in his dealings with the President. Vehemently, as if rank were the most important factor in his service to the South, Johnston argued his case. He held that he was the senior officer of the United States army to resign and join the Confederacy, that he was guaranteed this seniority under Confederate law, and that the act for the appointment of generals of full rank was simply a measure to raise the grade of those who had been brigadiers in the regular army of the Confederacy. In Johnston's eyes the correct order should have been: himself, Cooper, A. S. Johnston, Lee, Beauregard.[4]

In his wrath at what he considered a violation both of law and of justice, Johnston wrote the President a protest. The communication, some 1,800 words in length, stated Johnston's contention clearly enough, but much that was intemperate it added. "If the action against which I have protested be legal," said he in closing, "it is not for me to question the expediency of degrading one who has served laboriously from the commencement of the war on this frontier and borne a prominent part in the only great event of that war, for the benefit of persons"—that is, A. S. Johnston and R. E. Lee—"neither of whom has yet struck a blow for this Confederacy."

This letter Davis read with rising wrath of his own, not only as an insulting reflection on him but also as a display of ill temper and unreason. Further, Johnston's complaint was, in Davis's eyes, without basis in law or in fact. But instead of engaging, after his habit, in a long verbal controversy, he decided to rebuke Johnston in a few sharp sentences: "I have just received and read your letter of the 12th instant. Its language is, as you say, unusual; its arguments and statements utterly one-sided, and its insinuations as unfounded as they are unbecoming."[5]

Johnston made no reply to this. The issue passed, for the time, into the realm of those resentments that in private are remembered but in public are ignored. It might have remained, in Johnston's mind, an isolated if gross example of personal injustice had not a change of large consequences in the administration of the War Department brought into office a man with whom Johnston was doomed to clash ceaselessly.

On September 16, Secretary of War L. Pope Walker resigned and Mr.

Davis named the attorney general, Judah P. Benjamin, to his place. This brilliant son of English Jews had been born in St. Croix in 1811, reared in Louisiana, and schooled at Yale. When a leader of the bar, though only forty-two, he had been elected to the United States Senate from the state of his adoption, soon becoming one of the most distinguished members of that body. Short, round, rosy, and well groomed, he wore a smile that frowning disaster could dim for a moment only. He always looked as if he had just risen at the end of an enjoyed dinner to greet a friend with pleasant news.

His optimism was equalled by his industry. Benjamin exhibited a mind that was sure both of its penetration and of its quickness. Perhaps it was a mind too quick. With his confidence in himself he combined a large conception of the scope of his duties and a loyalty to the President so complete that no argument by generals in the field could weigh against the wishes of Mr. Davis, declared or anticipated. Great were Benjamin's powers of verbal persuasion, though in correspondence he was not so successful. His written paragraphs bristled with a palisade of "I's." Often he angered other men by making them seem clumsy. Most of all he maddened and baffled Joseph E. Johnston. It was not difficult to get the better of the general; Johnston's irascibility and his lack of skill in dialectics made him appear generally in the wrong.[6]

Until January the situation was embarrassed further by the fact that Beauregard, though devoted to Johnston personally, could not bring himself to regard his own command otherwise than as a separate corps. At the very time Johnston was protesting against being overslaughed, he had to notify the President that Beauregard appeared dissatisfied with a subordinate position. At that juncture Secretary Benjamin took his fellow Louisianian in hand and by a succession of flawlessly reasoned letters he so routed Beauregard that the general became willing to accept command in the West.[7]

Johnston gained nothing by this, though his authority was sustained. He had accumulated woes and humiliations of his own. Whenever he erred in administration, he brought down on himself a sharp letter from the President or Secretary Benjamin. In particular, his failure to undertake promptly a partial reorganization of the army led to unpleasantness, deep and prolonged.

Davis had directed General Johnston to brigade together troops from the same state, in the belief that this would create wholesome rivalry. For transfer of the regiments he gave time and discretion to Johnston, who, while not averse to the reorganization, considered it dangerous to undertake in the presence of the enemy. He accordingly took no step to break up old brigades, which had been formed casually as regiments from different states reported for duty at Manassas. Mr. Davis grew particularly impa-

tient to see the troops of his native Mississippi brigaded together; that
state's earlier volunteers the President himself had led in the Mexican War.
One such brigade was to go to a Mississippi native, W. H. C. Whiting, but
Whiting imprudently declared against it. He said he considered regimen-
tation by states "a policy as suicidal as foolish," and in any case he did not
wish any of his regiments taken from him. "They are used to me and I to
them, and accustomed to act together."[8]

This was not the first time Whiting had made himself conspicuous.
Son of an army officer, he had been graduated No. 1 in the class of 1845 at
West Point, with marks which were said to have been the highest ever
made at the Academy to that date. A handsome man of intellectual coun-
tenance, he was not unmindful of his social position and professional
standing, and was somewhat brusque in his dealings with the War Office.

At the instance of the offended Davis, the secretary of war administered
Whiting a stern rebuke. It was coupled with a reminder to his commanding general: "The President," Benjamin concluded his letter, "requests me
to say that he trusts you will hereafter decline to forward to him communications of your subordinates having so obvious a tendency to excite a
mutinous and disorganizing spirit in the Army." This language brought to
light one of the most peculiar contradictions of Johnston's nature—a sudden cooling of his temper, sometimes, when a controversy grew hot. Johnston apologized, interceded, and saved Whiting's pride and service to the
army by having that officer withdraw his offending letter for a "modifica-
tion" that never was made.[9]

Other tests of the temper of the commanding general were at hand,
tests that must have seemed to him to threaten the life of the army. In September, Johnston had received as major generals, to direct divisions then in
the making, Gustavus W. Smith, former street commissioner of New York
City, whose career was to form a singular chapter in the history of the
Confederacy, and Earl Van Dorn, who had been junior major of the 2nd
United States Cavalry. The diminutive Van Dorn was a man of some reputation, whose arrival in Virginia had been chronicled with much
applause. Now, on January 10, 1862, Van Dorn was relieved and ordered to
the Trans-Mississippi. As Beauregard was then about to leave the army,
Johnston felt that he would not have left with him a sufficient number of
subordinates capable of handling large bodies of men.[10]

While he was attempting to adjust himself to the loss of Van Dorn and
pleading for trained men, there came on February 3 a most disquieting
paper from Stonewall Jackson. Jackson, a major general as of October 7,
had been assigned to the Shenandoah Valley when Johnston's department
was divided into three districts, and had established headquarters at Win-

chester. To the general satisfaction of the population of the Valley, he had gone to work with great energy to improve his troops, who were few and poor. Soon he developed a well-considered plan for an advance on Romney. In acceptance of the maxims of Napoleon, he believed that "an active winter's campaign is less liable to produce disease than a sedentary life by camp-fires in winter-quarters."[11]

On January 1, 1862, his march on Romney had begun. Jackson's old brigade was under Brigadier General Richard B. Garnett, one-time captain of the 6th Infantry and a veteran Indian fighter. Three brigades were commanded by Brigadier General W. W. Loring, former colonel of the Mounted Rifles. When Jackson had cleared the Federals from a large area, he left Loring at Romney, to go into winter quarters, and returned Garnett to Winchester. In none of this had Jackson impressed Loring or his soldiers. Some of the men protested that Jackson was crazy, and they jeeringly insisted that his old brigade was as mad as he because it had cheered him whenever it had seen him. In the wintry isolation at Romney discontent had deepened demoralization. An eminent politician in Richmond received complaint; a round robin by eleven officers asking for the withdrawal of the command to Winchester was seconded by Loring. The administration became alarmed. On January 30, at the President's instance, Secretary Benjamin telegraphed Jackson: "Our news indicates that a movement is being made to cut off General Loring's command. Order him back to Winchester immediately."[12]

The paper that lay before Johnston on February 3 was a letter from Jackson, to be forwarded through channels to the secretary of war. Jackson acknowledged Benjamin's orders, and then wrote: "With such interference in my command I cannot expect to be of much service in the field, and accordingly respectfully request to be ordered to report for duty to the superintendent of the Virginia Military Institute. . . . Should this application not be granted, I respectfully request that the President will accept my resignation from the Army."[13]

Johnston read this with dismay. Beauregard and Van Dorn were gone; there was no assurance that Whiting would be retained in command; two brigadier generals were in Congress; one was absent sick. Now Johnston was to lose Jackson as a result of mandatory orders from Benjamin that had not been communicated through army headquarters. Johnston held his temper in the face of this disregard of his authority and, in a letter that showed his best qualities, urged Jackson to withdraw his resignation. "Let me beg you to reconsider this matter. . . . Is not that as great an official wrong to me as the order itself to you? Let us dispassionately reason with the Government on this subject of command. . . ." Then he sent to the President, through his friend Adjutant General Cooper, a request to be relieved of responsibility for the Valley District: "A collision of the authority of the honorable Secretary of War with mine might occur at a critical moment." He threw back on Secretary Benjamin all responsibility for the situation in the Valley. "Let me suggest," he said coldly, "that, having broken up the dispositions of the military commander, you give whatever other orders may be necessary." For good measure, forwarding Jackon's letter to Richmond, he endorsed it: "I don't know how the loss of this officer can be supplied."[14]

Fortunately, an impasse was avoided. On the day Jackson sent in his resignation he wrote to his friend Governor John Letcher a full account of what had happened. The governor went immediately to the War Department and found Benjamin entirely disposed to listen to reason. Agreement was reached that the resignation would be disregarded until Letcher had time to write Jackson. He entrusted the letter to the hands of his friend, and Jackson's, Congressman A. R. Boteler. At first Jackson showed no inclination to yield. Boteler hung on and, searching about for all arguments, insisted that Virginia's defense called for the service of all her sons. Jackson, he said, had no right to withhold his. This argument made a manifest impression. Boteler pressed with a contention from Letcher that Jackson's abandonment of his post would have a discouraging effect on the country. Shaken by this argument, Jackson yielded. He sent Letcher a candid note in which he said: "If my retiring from the Army would produce the effect upon our country that you have named . . . I of course would not desire to leave the service. . . ."

Jackson's letter of resignation was returned to him, and Loring, against whom Jackson had preferred charges for neglect of duty, was transferred to another theater of operations. But neither Jackson nor Johnston escaped without rebuke. Jackson's charges against Loring were not entertained. Johnston's punishment was a stiff reprimand from the President for his conduct in the whole affair. At the same time, Johnston received word from the War Department that Major General E. Kirby Smith, one of Johnston's best officers, must be relieved from command in order that he might be assigned to duty elsewhere.[15]

All this came at a time when his army, soon to meet the test of battle, was being disorganized by the "Furlough and Bounty Act." This extraordinary law had been passed in December as a means of assuring the re-enlistment of the twelve months' volunteers whose terms expired in the late winter or early spring. A bounty of fifty dollars and a furlough of sixty days were promised all who agreed to serve for the duration of the war to a maximum of three years. Soldiers desirous of changing company, or even their arm of service, were to be allowed to do so. After the reorganization the men could elect their own company and field officers, regardless of previous law. Johnston became convinced that the law was unenforceable and ineffective. If furloughs were not given in large numbers, the twelve-months' volunteers would not re-enlist; should furloughs be granted with prompt liberality, the army would be weakened dangerously in the face of the enemy.

Not unnaturally in these circumstances, Johnston sought to place on the War Department the responsibility of applying the act. To this the suave Benjamin was ready with a prompt reply. He urged that Johnston go to the "extreme verge of prudence in tempting" the twelve-months' men to re-enlist, but insisted that the department "could not undertake to determine when and in what numbers the furloughs could be safely granted. . . . The rest I must leave to your own judgment." The perplexed and angry Johnston, by limiting the furloughs issued in each command, hoped to maintain the army at defensive strength. All the while he had to do battle with the war secretary to prevent additional furloughs, details, and transfers from one arm of the service to another.[16]

Thus did controversy shift, continue, and accumulate. Another month, or six weeks at most, might bring sunshine that would dry the roads and start the march of the great army which General McClellan, successor to General McDowell, was known to be organizing for an offensive. Against that amply equipped and numerically superior army Johnston believed it impossible to hold his lines in northern Virginia. There was no likelihood that all the regiments organized in April and May 1861 could be induced to enlist anew before the expiration of their term of service. Daily, as the men agreed to continue in service, they would elect new officers. Any officer who had discharged his sworn duty to instill discipline might be succeeded by some popular incompetent; all that had been done in ten months to develop a competent corps of officers might be set at naught. The Southern cause might collapse.

This situation was at its blackest when, on February 19, Johnston was summoned to Richmond. The city and the government he found in gloom. Disasters had swept the Confederacy. Fort Henry on the Tennessee River had been taken. Near-by Fort Donelson, with 14,000 Southern soldiers, had been surrendered. Nashville was expected at any hour to fall. All western Tennessee was overrun, and Albert Sidney Johnston was in retreat to Murfreesboro. On the east coast of North Carolina, Roanoke Island had been captured, with more than 2,500 men. Secretary Benjamin was being assailed for incompetency. The tone of the press was nervous, critical, or bitter. Rumors of impending changes in the Cabinet were afloat. The shortage of arms and of powder was worse than the government dared to admit.[17]

In this atmosphere of concern close to despair Johnston at 10:00 A.M. called on the President and found him with the Cabinet. Greetings, apparently without restraint, were exchanged. Mr. Davis stated that Johnston had been summoned to confer on the withdrawal of his army from its exposed position: Should it be done, and if so, when and how?

Johnston stated his view. McClellan, he reasoned, could advance in such force on Richmond and by so many routes that the Confederate forces should not attempt to maintain themselves on Bull Run and Occoquan. The army must take up a line farther south, but was hampered by deep mud on the roads and embarrassed by much baggage. Withdrawals should not be undertaken until the end of winter. The council shifted to a long, long discussion of the cannon, intended for the defense of Richmond, that had been sent to advanced positions and could not be replaced; the President was most solicitous that they be saved. Johnston received no specific orders, other than that he should lead the army southward to a more secure position as soon as practicable.[18]

No sooner was Johnston out of Mr. Davis's offices than he had one experience after another that startled and alarmed him. At his hotel he met Colonel W. Dorsey Pender, 6th North Carolina, who with a soldier's zest for news asked if Johnston had heard the report, then circulating in the lobby, that the Cabinet had been discussing whether the army should be withdrawn from Manassas. An accurate report of what had been considered in the utmost secrecy, behind guarded doors, had reached the hotel almost as soon as Johnston had! Soon afterward, on the train en route to Manassas, a friend confided to General Johnston that ominous news had been heard in Richmond the previous evening: The Cabinet was considering the removal of the Confederate forces from Manassas. It was enough to make a commander despair! What hope could there be of concealing from the enemy a movement vital to the very existence of the army—if everyone from Richmond knew all about it?[19]

2. JOHNSTON'S WITHDRAWAL FROM MANASSAS

On this unhappy return from Richmond, Johnston found the roads of northern Virginia even worse than when he left. So deep was the mud around Dumfries that men on good horses took six hours and a half to cover twelve miles. Removal of the heavy ordnance from fixed positions seemed impossible.

With all the adverse conditions that would attend his withdrawal Johnston was determined that the government should be acquainted. His dispatches to Richmond became a chronicle of calamities, impending and instant. "The army is crippled and its discipline greatly impaired by the want of general officers," he wrote. ". . . The accumulation of subsistence stores at Manassas is now a great evil. . . . A very extensive meat-packing establishment at Thoroughfare is also a great encumbrance. The great quantity of personal property in our camps is a still greater one."[20]

In the eyes of the depressed general, every movement of the enemy now was designed to maneuver him out of his position before he was ready to retreat. No sooner had he learned of the appearance of a Federal force at Harper's Ferry on February 24 than he reasoned that the advance of these troops would so threaten his left as to compel without further delay the withdrawal which, he took pains to remind the President, "you have ordered." Johnston's chief concern was for his right, which extended down the Bull Run–Occoquan to the Potomac and covered the terminus of the Richmond, Fredericksburg, and Potomac Railroad on Aquia Creek. Federals in considerable number were known to be on the Maryland shore of the Potomac and might be ferried to the Virginia shore. This route, he told himself, assuredly would be McClellan's principal advance.[21]

In the expectation that he might at any hour receive news of a Federal onmarch which would force his columns back to the Rappahannock and Rapidan, Johnston expedited the removal of supplies and fumed because the overloaded Orange and Alexandria Railroad did not haul them off more quickly. Serious as this task was, busy as Johnston should have been, he took time to pursue the controversy with Benjamin and to protest against that official's grant of furloughs, of details, and of authorization to raise new companies from old regiments.

With relations at this unhappy pass, Johnston on March 5 was informed by General Whiting of "unusual activity" among the Federals across the Potomac in Maryland, opposite Dumfries. This news was decisive with Johnston. He issued directions for all the forces east of the Blue Ridge to fall back to the line of the Rappahannock River.[22]

The orders, which were issued piecemeal, were wretchedly drawn. In some instances clarity was lacking. Neither Davis nor Benjamin was advised when the movement would begin or what the lines of retreat would be. The flank columns got away promptly and plodded slowly southward through the mud. On the Manassas line Johnston held the central divisions until the evening of March 9 to cover the last-minute removal of supplies. The following morning the cavalry fired the depots and all the property left along the railroad track. The loss was heavy. At Thoroughfare Gap, where the commissary general rashly had established the meat-packing plant, more than one million pounds were destroyed or given to local farmers. As for personal baggage, "the pile of trunks along the railroad was appalling to behold." Virtually all the heavy ordnance in fixed position, except that close to Manassas, was left behind.[23]

The destruction was rendered the more depressing to the South and the more provoking to Davis because the slowness of the Federals in moving forward led Johnston's critics to aver later that he would have had ample time to remove the last pound of provisions and the newest trunk of the most recent volunteer. A Union detachment sent across the Potomac to destroy the abandoned Confederate ordnance was recalled as soon as its work was done. The main Federal army made a practice march to Centreville, but it did not start from Alexandria until sure the Confederates had withdrawn, and it did not reach Bull Run until March 11.

Among officials acquainted with the facts of his retreat, Johnston was put in the unhappy attitude of fleeing when no man pursued; publicly, in the press, his action was defended as strategically sound. Fortunately, too, the mind of the Southern people, depressed by a succession of disasters, was diverted and stimulated by the exploits of the ironclad *Virginia-Merrimack*. On March 8 this clumsy craft had steamed out from Norfolk and disposed of two wooden men-of-war, *Congress* and *Cumberland*. Despite the challenge offered next day by the *Monitor*, the Confederate people believed that their ironclad would clear Virginia waters of the enemy.[24]

Johnston did not inform the administration where he was or what he planned. From the time he left Manassas, without notifying the authorities in Richmond of his departure, he did not send a single report to the War Department until he was safely on the line of the Rappahannock. On March 13, from Rappahannock Bridge, he forwarded to the President a brief report of his position. Then he reviewed the loss of property, which he blamed on the "wretched" management of the Orange and Alexandria, on the accumulation of supplies at Manassas, and on the vast quantity of private property there. "This army," he concluded with disgust, "had accumulated a supply of baggage like that of Xerxes' myriads."

Whether the President was provoked because Johnston did not await reinforcement, whether he was incensed by the burning of stores, or whether he was angered by the general's prolonged silence, the answer he made was stiffly discouraging: ". . . before the receipt of yours of the 13th," said the President, "I was as much in the dark as to your purposes, condition, and necessities as at the time of our conversation on the subject about a month since." True, he had heard alarming reports of great destruction, "but, having heard of no cause for such a sudden movement, I was at a loss to believe it."[25]

From Richmond came further inquiries not from Secretary Benjamin but from General R. E. Lee, whom, to placate a discontented and alarmed Congress, the President had brought back from command in South Carolina and placed in general charge of military operations under his own direction. This appointment, at a period of dangerous misunderstanding, gave Johnston the assurance, at the least, that military experience and admitted abilities were to be available in Richmond whenever the President chose to employ them in dealing with Johnston's army. And Benjamin no longer was secretary of war. Mr. Davis, who was as constant in his loyalties as in the maintenance of his prerogatives, had yielded at last to the clamor against Benjamin by the somewhat unusual expedient of promoting him from the War Office to the first position in the Cabinet, that of secretary of state.

No more was Johnston to receive irritating directions from a secretary who had sprinkled his letters with too many an "I" and often had ignored official forms, but who had been singularly successful in prevailing on a Congress which did not like him to accept his recommendations. In Benjamin's stead the President named George W. Randolph, forty-three years of age, grandson of Thomas Jefferson, former midshipman in the United States navy, lawyer, and artillerist distinguished at Big Bethel. This choice, Johnston subsequently said, in terse eulogium that was the more eloquent because of its restraint, "enabled the military officers to re-establish the discipline of the army." The effect of the change was immediate, and in nothing more remarkable than in the state of mind of Johnston. Secretary Randolph confined himself to administrative duties, utilized the machinery of the department, and employed General Lee substantially as chief of staff. Lee wrote Johnston on behalf of the President, as Benjamin had done, but in a tone so different and in a military knowledge so much wider that little friction was created.[26]

Ample reason was at hand for a movement from the second line, on the Rapidan, that Johnston occupied after he withdrew from Manassas. Evidence had accumulated rapidly on March 24 that a new Federal plan of advance was taking form. Enemy troops in large numbers were being concentrated around Fortress Monroe at the tip of the Peninsula between the James and York rivers. Suspicion soon grew into certainty that General McClellan, instead of marching southward from Manassas to confront Johnston on the Rapidan, was to utilize Federal sea power in overwhelming Prince John Magruder at Yorktown, or Benjamin Huger at Norfolk. If McClellan could accomplish this, the assumption was that he would advance on Richmond from the east. To confront him and to protect Richmond, would it not be essential to dispatch Johnston's army to the lower Peninsula or to the Norfolk area?

In the decision of this cardinal question Johnston had no part. The strategy and the manner of its execution were Lee's. With the approval of the President, he directed when and in what number troops should be sent from the Rapidan to Richmond and thence eastward. On April 12, while his strongest divisions were on the march, Johnston reached Richmond and conferred again with the President. Nothing that had happened in the strained correspondence between the two seems to have been revived at the meeting. As usual when they met face-to-face, the demands of common courtesy and of a common cause outbalanced personal differences.

Immediately, by order of the President, promulgated through Lee, the departments of Norfolk and the Peninsula were "embraced for the present within the limits of operations" of Johnston's army. Although he had not been recognized in his contention that he was the senior general of the Confederacy, he had now by far the most responsible command and the largest army.[27]

CHAPTER 5

Challenge on the Peninsula

1. JOHNSTON RETREATS AGAIN

As Johnston hastened, that twelfth of April 1862, through the budding countryside and down the placid York to study the situation on the lower Peninsula, it might have seemed that the winter of his discontent was passing. It was not to be so. He was fated to pass from storm to storm, from one displeasing necessity to another unpopular decision.

After a rapid but critical inspection of the position held by Magruder, he hurried back to Richmond with a gloomy, grim report: The line was too long for the force that occupied it; engineering had been poor; superior Federal ordnance, outranging the antiquated smoothbore guns of the Confederates, could destroy the works at Yorktown and across the river at Gloucester Point. That done, the Federals could escort their transports up the York to easily land an army in rear of Yorktown or to press on toward Richmond.[1]

Davis heard Johnston's report calmly and remarked that a situation of so much importance should be discussed fully: Would Johnston return at a later hour, when Secretary Randolph and General Lee could be present? Johnston asked if he might bring Generals Gustavus W. Smith and James Longstreet with him. This was acceptable to the President. Shortly before 11:00 A.M., April 14, the six men sat down in the President's office.

Davis asked Johnston to report on his inspection, and the general repeated what he had said earlier—McClellan undoubtedly could force a passage of the James, of the York, or of both, and thereby turn the Yorktown line. That front had to be abandoned. Then he produced a memorandum which, he explained, Smith had handed him a few minutes before the conference opened. It endorsed Johnston's contention that the Yorktown line was indefensible, and proposed the early abandonment both of that position and of Norfolk. Forces should be concentrated in front of Richmond and be reinforced from the Carolinas and Georgia. One of two courses then should be followed: Either the enlarged army should attack McClellan where he

105

could not utilize his sea power; or else Richmond should be garrisoned to resist a siege while the greater part of the army marched on Washington and Baltimore, perhaps on Philadelphia and New York.

Johnston introduced his own plan, which was to draw the enemy inland, collect all available forces at Richmond, and give battle there. Smith clung to his preference for an offensive across the Potomac. With scant attention to Smith's proposal, the conference turned to a scrutiny of Johnston's plan to evacuate the lower Peninsula and Norfolk and concentrate forces at Richmond for a decisive blow at McClellan. Secretary Randolph insisted that the Confederacy could not afford to abandon the Norfolk navy yard, with its dry docks, its shipways, its shops and materials for building war vessels. General Lee maintained quietly that the Peninsula offered numerous defensive positions which could and should be utilized. The army, in his opinion, could not count on early reinforcements from the states to the south. Johnston and Smith did not attempt so much to meet these objections as they did to prove the impossibility of standing on the Yorktown line.

The argument continued all day, with the President sitting as if he were a judge. At 6 o'clock he ordered a recess for an hour, when the discussion was renewed. Both sides continued to canvass the issues, with diminishing vigor, until 1:00 A.M. Then Mr. Davis announced that Johnston's entire army would be united with Magruder's on the lower Peninsula and that both Yorktown and Norfolk would be held. Johnston's later comment curiously and not creditably revealed the man: "The belief that events on the Peninsula would soon compel the Confederate Government to adopt my method of opposing the Federal army, reconciled me somewhat to the necessity of obeying the President's order."[2]

In this mood Johnston returned to Yorktown and took command on that front. This involved the relinquishment by Magruder of his leading role in the drama of the Peninsula. This was hard fate for an officer who had remained conspicuous in the news throughout the ten months since the action at Big Bethel. A public discussion of his alleged intemperance had produced formal evidence of a war-time sobriety that a Puritan might have envied. All the South had chuckled over a hot exchange of letters with General Ben Butler, whom Magruder had worsted verbally and, it was still currently believed, had challenged to mortal combat. Now, outwardly, all this had changed. Magruder, if disappointed, was game. As new commander of the extensive right wing, he retired to watch his lines—and to employ his pen. In calm disdain of the fact that he had drawn the lines now entrusted to him, Magruder became instantly critical of their location and their armament. It was almost as if he were quarrelling with himself.[3]

Johnston probably did not see the humor in Magruder's correspondence. He certainly found no humor in the military situation. On April 22 he protested to Lee: "Labor enough has been expended here to make a very strong position, but it has been wretchedly misapplied by the young engineer officers. No one but McClellan could have hesitated to attack." By the twenty-fourth he was asking that supplies be sent to meet him on the road from Richmond "in the event of our being compelled to fall back from this point." After the twenty-seventh he interpreted the enemy's movements as an indication that he soon would be compelled to retreat, and he warned General Huger to prepare to evacuate Norfolk. More explicitly, on the twenty-ninth, he announced to Lee: "The fight for Yorktown, as I said in Richmond, must be one of artillery, in which we cannot win. The result is certain; the time only doubtful. . . . I shall therefore move as soon as can be done conveniently, looking to the condition of the roads and the time necessary for the corresponding movement from Norfolk."[4]

His one alternative proposal was an adaptation of Smith's and was made on April 30. Said Johnston then: "We are engaged in a species of warfare at which we can never win. It is plain that General McClellan will . . . depend for success upon artillery and engineering. We can compete with him in neither. We must therefore change our course, take the offensive, collect all the troops we have in the East and cross the Potomac with them, while Beauregard, with all we have in the West, invades Ohio." His proposal did not elicit support in Richmond. Lee so advised Johnston.[5]

Without regard to the development or rejection of this broad plan, Johnston gave the order for the retreat. On the night of May 3, after forty-eight hours of confusion and counter orders, the army left its position. The general effected the removal of the field pieces that had been in the works, but he left all fifty-six of his heavy guns. In this respect the withdrawal from Manassas was duplicated. So was the criticism of the commander. Johnston was again blamed for a premature retreat, but he had not miscalculated substantially the time of the impending Federal attack. McClellan reported that he would have been ready to open with all his heavy artillery on the morning of May 6 at latest. The fire of these guns "would have compelled the enemy to surrender or abandon his works in less than twelve hours."[6]

2. THE ARMY THAT LEFT YORKTOWN

The army of 56,500 men that filed out of the Yorktown lines on the night of May 3, 1862, had sustained few battle casualties since Manassas, but already its command had suffered at the hands of the foe that was to pur-

sue it to the end, the resistless foe of attrition. Besides Beauregard, who
had won no new laurels at Shiloh, the army had lost three of the early
brigade commanders. Kirby Smith had taken command in East Tennessee. On December 26, 1861, nervously shattered by eight months' anxious service, the chivalrous Philip St. George Cocke had ended his life.
Milledge Bonham had resigned January 29, 1862, because he felt himself
overslaughed, probably by the promotion of Dick Ewell to major general.
Shanks Evans also was gone from the army; at the instance of the governor
of South Carolina, he had been sent to that state.

   Not one of the brigades that had fought at Manassas remained in its
entirety under the man who had led it there. Whiting, saved from Coven-
try, had Bee's old command; J. B. Kershaw, promoted brigadier, had Bonham's; D. R. Jones had Bartow's. The three Manassas brigades that
retained their regimental organization under new commanders were
headed now by two former captains and a former first lieutenant of the
United States army. Oldest and most experienced of this trio was Richard
H. Anderson, aged forty, who had been graduated from West Point in the
class of 1842. "Dick" Anderson had served as a lieutenant in the war with
Mexico, and had spent most of his subsequent career with the Second
Dragoons in the West. As he had been a captain for six years before his
resignation, he could be regarded as a seasoned soldier by the standard that
had to prevail in the Confederate army. Tall, strong, and of fine background, Anderson never was disposed to quibble over authority or to
indulge in any sort of boastfulness. Already he was beloved in the army for
his kindness, amiability, and unselfishness. Whispers that he was overfond
of a social glass seem to have had no foundation.[7]

   One of Anderson's associates in Longstreet's division, entrusted with
the direction of Cocke's old brigade, was ex-Captain George E. Pickett of
the 9th Infantry. Although this young Virginian had been graduated at the
absolute bottom of the class of 1846 at West Point, he had been a gallant
figure in Scott's Mexican expedition, and after Chapultepec he had been
awarded his brevet as captain. Later orders had carried him to Texas and
thence to Washington Territory. He was commissioned brigadier general
in February 1862 and assignment to Longstreet's division followed soon—
an association destined to be long and renowned. Pickett and Longstreet
had served together at Fort Bliss in 1854–55, and between them the ties
were close and binding. At the moment Pickett's men knew little of him
except that he was dapper and alert, that he looked all of his thirty-seven
years, and that he wore his dark hair in long perfumed ringlets that fell to
his shoulders. Even his curling beard was anointed.[8]

   The third of the West Point brigadiers in Longstreet's division was a few months younger than Pickett and, like him, a Virginian. His name was Ambrose Powell Hill, of stock long honored and influential in the state. Young Hill had been admitted to the Military Academy in 1842, but because of bad health had not been graduated until 1847, just in time to have a small part in the closing operations in Mexico. He had resigned before secession, received his commission as colonel, and soon trained one of the best of Johnston's regiments in the Valley. In February 1862 he had been advanced to brigadier general. His men esteemed him as diligent and mindful of their wants. Beyond that, he was, as yet, merely a figure.

This was true also of another West Point brigadier, Cadmus M. Wilcox, who had entered the Academy with A. P. Hill and Pickett. He was a North Carolinian by birth, had received his appointment from Tennessee, and had served as aide to General Quitman in Mexico. After Manassas he had joined Johnston with an excellent Alabama regiment. Perhaps the better-read officers were familiar with his published *Rifles and Rifle Practice* and his translation of *Austrian Infantry Evolutions of the Line.* This was the extent of the army's acquaintance with his capabilities, though his commission as brigadier antedated that of Pickett and A. P. Hill. (Two other graduates of West Point, Lafayette McLaws and G. J. Rains, rode with the long columns away from Yorktown and will appear in the hour of combat.)

The remaining commanders of the twenty-three retreating brigades were, in the main, politicians whom the President, now mindful and now disdainful of professional training, had commissioned as general officers. Georgia had sent her two most eminent public men. One was Howell Cobb, forty-six years of age, former governor of Georgia, secretary of the treasury under Buchanan, ex-speaker of the House of Representatives, and present speaker of the House of the Provisional Congress—altogether one of the most distinguished of Southerners. By mid-February Cobb was a brigadier general, and by the end of April he had one of the largest of brigades—nearly 3,800 men. The other noted Georgian was Robert Toombs, fifty-one, former United States senator and first secretary of state in the new Confederacy, whose odd experiences will be related in a subsequent connection.

While none of the other "political generals" could compare in public reputation with these Georgians, several had distinction. From Tennessee came former congressman Robert Hatton, not yet a brigadier. The treasurer of Mississippi, Richard Griffith, commanded a brigade predominantly from that state; W. S. Featherston, for two terms a representative of Mississippi, had similar rank. Roger A. Pryor of Virginia, editor, fire-eating secessionist and congressman, wore the fresh stars and wreath of a brigadier general. As in the case of the others, he had no military training, though he was perhaps the most notorious duellist of his day.

To recapitulate, eleven of the twenty-three brigades were under men who had been officers in the United States army, three were in charge of graduates of the Virginia Military Institute, six were entrusted to politicians, one had as its head the great patrician Wade Hampton, and two were led by lawyers.

None of these men, from the nature of army organization, theoretically meant so much in wise leadership as did Johnston's four division commanders. The most conspicuous of these was Magruder. He was publicly the best known as he was in panoply the most dazzling of the major generals.

To the soldiers from northern Virginia the most familiar of the divisional commanders was the senior Gustavus W. Smith. This Kentuckian, forty years of age, had unique position among Confederate officers in Virginia. He had been graduated No. 8 in the class of 1842 at West Point. With aptitude for construction engineering, he had erected batteries, built roads, and discharged such a variety of other useful duties in Mexico that he had received brevet as captain. It had been in 1858 that he became street commissioner of New York City. Only when he was satisfied, in September 1861, that a majority of the people of his native state were on the side of the South, had he gone to Richmond, where he had been nominated almost immediately as a major general. No other man, with the exception of Albert Sidney Johnston and Leonidas Polk, previously had received so high a first commission. Smith's prestige at that time had been extraordinary and, in a sense, puzzling, because his career had included nothing that justified great reputation as a field commander.

Smith was altogether self-confident in camp and at council table. Johnston was "Joe" to Smith; their relations were cordial and intimate. Toward the other general officers Smith's feeling was one of bluff camaraderie, touched, perhaps, with a shade of superiority. In appearance he was tall and of powerful build, with massive, rough-hewn features. The line of his lips was proud, perhaps pompous. His manner was rapid and energetic and had the spirit of conscious command. Despite his assured bearing, he never had commanded troops in his life. His inexperience was not distrusted. There was doubt concerning his health. For the rest, he had prevailed upon the army and the country to take him at his own valuation of himself.[9]

Next in seniority to Smith was Major General James Longstreet. Many things had happened to Longstreet since Bonham had forbidden him to fire on the Federals in the twilight of Manassas Day. He had obeyed the order that evening and ridden off. In a grove of young pines he had dismounted—and exploded in his wrath. He had pulled off his hat, thrown it on the ground, and, with bitter words for Bonham, had stamped in a white rage.¹⁰ Since then Longstreet had discharged with soldierly diligence, but not with content, the duties of brigade and division command.

Despite the fact that he had left the line in 1858 and had become a paymaster, Longstreet placed no low estimate on what he described as the "hard service" he had rendered in Mexico and in the old army. Moreover, he considered himself the senior officer from Alabama who had left United States service, and as such he was determined that his rank should be respected. When, therefore, Gustavus W. Smith was made major general, after no previous labors for the Confederacy, Longstreet had been outraged. He had written a vigorous protest, which concluded: "The placing of persons above me whom I have always ranked and who have just joined this service I regard as great injustice. I therefore request that an officer be detailed to relieve me of this command." This had its effect. Longstreet had been made a major general on October 7, to rank as of that date. This still left him junior to Smith, but apparently it had satisfied him.¹¹

Although a slight deafness probably contributed to make his slow and unimaginative conversation largely a laconic and reluctant succession of "Yes" and "No," he had seemed to enjoy a social glass. In poker he had acquired some renown. With Mrs. Longstreet spending the winter in Richmond, he had appeared at the President's levees—a powerful figure, nearly six feet tall, broad of shoulder, with cold gray-blue eyes, thin sandy-brown hair, and a heavy beard that almost concealed his mouth. In January Longstreet had answered a hurried summons from his wife, rushed to the capital, and returned a changed, unhappy man. Scarlet fever had been raging in the city. Two of his children succumbed to it and were buried the same day; a third, a boy of twelve, died a week later. There was for Longstreet no more gaiety, no more poker, and, certainly for the time, no more liquor. Essentially, from that tragic January, he was a soldier and little besides.¹²

Proud, martial ambition remained in Longstreet's heart, and grew with the larger responsibilities that came after the withdrawal from Manassas and then from Yorktown. Now that the army was on the move, Johnston put six brigades in Longstreet's care. These included the commands of A. P. Hill, Pickett, and Anderson, all of them "Manassas brigades," with Cadmus Wilcox's Alabama and Mississippi regiments from Smith's division, R. E. Colston's small command from Huger's division south of the James, and Roger A. Pryor's troops of Magruder's Army of the Peninsula. The size of this division reflected the confidence of Johnston in its commander.

As Longstreet rode out for the long succession of battles that lay ahead, any appraisal of him would have taken into account the scantiness of his previous opportunities. He had done little and had proposed nothing that had the stamp of genius. On the other hand, his administration had been excellent and his discipline firm but not harsh. He never was tired. Days and nights of exposure he might endure and, at the end, be the same clear-headed, imperturbable soldier. His silence, his self-confidence, and his success in creating manifest morale among his troops had given him a reputation that was solid. Had those who most thoroughly knew the army been asked to describe in one word Longstreet and his command in that fateful spring of 1862, they probably would have agreed on the same soldierly term: *dependable*. Brilliance there might not be; reliability there undoubtedly was.

On that third of May the fourth and last division of the army followed the old route from Yorktown to Williamsburg. Its commander was D. Harvey Hill, who had seen much service, of large interest and of small, after his days as Magruder's lieutenant on the Yorktown front. In September 1861, Hill had been transferred to North Carolina, where he had shown great energy in organizing the defenses between Fort Macon and the Virginia line. Midway this task he had been ordered, on November 16, to report to Johnston. The change had caused much regret in North Carolina, but it had given Hill a North Carolina brigade under Longstreet. Soon it brought him semi-autonomous command at Leesburg on the Potomac, and promotion to the grade of major general.[13]

Now, as his division was leaving Yorktown, D. H. Hill was to confront the enemy with troops that never had been in action together. Four permanent and one temporary brigade (Crump's) were his, together with a mixed command (Ward's). One brigade, Jubal Early's, included that general's original 24th Virginia, which had fought at Manassas. In Robert Rodes's brigade were two of Ewell's regiments of July 1861, the 5th and 6th Alabama. Hill's third brigade, Featherston's, was the former garrison of the works at Manassas. Rains's and Crump's brigades, as well as Ward's command, were of Magruder's army. It was a division of unequal parts, to be sure, but it could be developed.

As much might have been said of the men in the ranks of all four of the divisions. Although the troops came from every station of life and included the weak along with the healthy, the illiterate by the side of the educated, they were military material in which the South had full faith from the hour of enlistment. Although that faith persisted, it was widely admitted that the army had been demoralized, perhaps dangerously, by the unwise Furlough and Bounty Act. Even when offered the bounty of fifty dollars, the furlough of sixty days, the privilege of changing from one arm of the service to another, and the opportunity of getting rid of unpopular officers by a new election, a majority of the men had declined to enter the service for three additional years. After this became apparent, the demand for general conscription grew. At length, under acts of April 16 and 23, conscription of all able-bodied white males between eighteen and thirty-five was prescribed for three years or the duration of the war. This meant, among other things, that if men of prescribed age who already were in the army did not voluntarily re-enlist, they would be mustered out and immediately conscripted.[14]

The command of the army was further impaired by the inclusion in the new statute of the provision in the old law which permitted companies and regiments, when re-enlisting, to elect their officers. Objection to this principle had been voiced earlier, but President Davis held steadfastly to it. The result was that many officers, including West Point graduates, were rejected because of the strictness of their discipline, and in their places corporals or even men from the ranks were elected. In Colonel J. C. Haskell's discerning words, "some did not re-enlist at all, others did much later. Many of the regiments reorganized with new officers. The general effect was to break up very much the organization of the army."[15]

Many of the regiments had new officers when they left Yorktown, many others were in the midst of their electoral campaigns, and in at least one case a regiment chose its commanders while bivouacked on the retreat from the Peninsula. "The troops," Johnston reported on May 9, "in addition to the lax discipline of volunteers, are partially discontented at the conscription act and demoralized by their recent elections."[16]

3. WILLIAMSBURG

It was past midnight, May 3–4, when the last division left Yorktown on the retreat to Williamsburg. To delay the troops, deep mud, that ancestral foe and eternal concomitant of war, did its worst. Roads made heavy by recent rains became almost impassable. Guns, wagons, and marching men were rammed together like a charge in a musket. Shivering troops would move on for a minute or two—to be stopped again and again in the darkness. The rear units did not cover more than a mile per hour.[17]

At length, during the late morning and early afternoon of the fourth, the struggling columns reached the line of works that Magruder had constructed across the low ridge that separated the watershed of the James River from that of the York. It was a feeble line. At the junction of the Hampton and Yorktown roads was Fort Magruder, an earthwork of bastion front. On either side were small redoubts and epaulements, twelve in all. At these entrenchments probably few of the weary officers and men cast more than a glance. They expected to rest at Williamsburg, not to fight there. The road to the west stretched out before the army as a river of mud, but otherwise the situation was no more adverse than a retreat usually is. Johnston appeared to have a chance of getting away untouched.

Then, at 1 o'clock, the outlook changed. The Confederate cavalry were driven in. Federal infantry were believed to be in close support of their skirmishing mounted units. The obvious thing to do at the moment was to occupy Fort Magruder and the near-by line of redoubts to permit Johnston to put distance between the pursuers and the main Confederate force. He personally led the nearest brigade, that of Paul Semmes, into Fort Magruder. When General Lafayette McLaws rode up, Johnston ordered him to take charge of the defense. McLaws's service with Magruder had given him some familiarity with the ground, and he quickly called up another brigade and two batteries of artillery to hold the line. He delivered a volume of fire that made the enemy recoil. By promptly erecting an adequate, if temporary, barrier, McLaws received a credit in the mind of the commanding general. The Georgian could be trusted.[18]

Because Johnston had determined that Magruder's division should head the retreat that evening, the two brigades under McLaws were recalled after sunset. Longstreet was ordered to take their place, and he sent two brigades, R. H. Anderson's and Pryor's. Anderson carefully advanced his pickets beyond the fort, but more than that, as the rain beat down in the black night, he did not attempt. His was an uncomfortable position for an officer who, while experienced, had never before occupied so responsible a field position or commanded so many men directly in the face of the enemy.[19]

After daylight on May 5, Dick Anderson could see the immediate approaches to Fort Magruder, via the Yorktown and Hampton roads. He saw, too, what he could of his own defenses through the rain, which had diminished to a cold drizzle, but visibility was low. Of fortifications on the right Anderson could discern only four redoubts, and on the left, two. These six he promptly occupied.[20] About 6:00 A.M. the Federals opened with their skirmishers and artillery. Steadily the front of action widened. The fire became more intense. Evidently they either were making a strong demonstration or else they were seeking to storm the rear guard and force a general engagement with the retreating army. In this uncertainty Longstreet felt it desirable to reinforce Anderson. As coolly as if he had fought a score of battles, Longstreet ordered first Cadmus Wilcox and then A. P. Hill to take their brigades back to Fort Magruder. Thence, as he saw the fighting extended, he ordered the reserve of his division, Pickett's and Colston's brigades, to advance for employment in any emergency.

This reinforcement emboldened Anderson. He or Longstreet or both of them decided to take the offensive. Orders were given. Ardently the

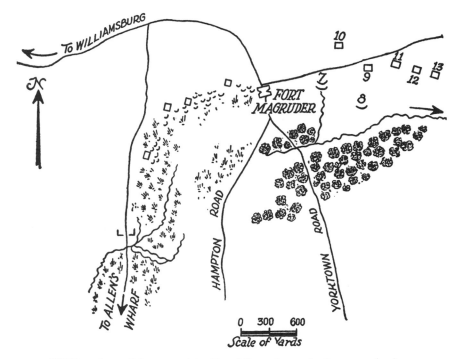

Williamsburg, May 4–5, 1862. Fort Magruder and adjacent redoubts, woods, and abatis.

men began to push forward and slowly to drive the stubborn, hard-hitting enemy back toward the woods. Guns, prisoners, and flags were taken. Casualties were not excessive, though later in the day two colonels of great promise were killed—C. H. Mott of the 19th Mississippi and G. T. Ward of the 2nd Florida. Untried soldiers bore themselves well. The field appeared to be theirs.

The rear guard action was not to end so easily. Trouble was in the making. Between 3 and 4 o'clock the Federals seized a redoubt far to the left, a redoubt that either had not been seen by Anderson or else had been assumed to be under the care of other troops. From this work the enemy began to pour artillery fire into Fort Magruder. This created much confusion and concern for the safety of the fort. Even before this occurred Longstreet had sensed danger on the left and had dispatched to D. H. Hill a request to send back a brigade to strengthen the left wing in case of necessity. Johnston himself went to the scene, alarmed by the volume of fire, but found the dispositions satisfactory and did not assume command.[21]

The brigade Hill sent was Jubal A. Early's. The men splashed their way back through the mud and drizzle and halted on the campus of the College of William and Mary. One of the four regiments was the 24th Virginia, Early's original command, which had distinguished itself at Manassas. The others were the 5th and 23rd North Carolina and the 38th Virginia; none of these had any combat experience. A muddy courier arrived with a brief order: "Move quickly to the support of Longstreet." As the fire from the front was plainly audible and to inexperienced ears was heavy, the men formed quickly and marched eastward with vigorous step. They numbered close to 2,300 rank and file.

As they pressed on Longstreet overtook Early and pointed out ground to the left and rear of Fort Magruder where he was to post his brigade and await orders. It was a ridge overlooking a wheat field and a woods, beyond which came the loud echo of furiously firing artillery. Early felt sure the guns were Federal and were firing on Fort Magruder. While he was waiting there, burning with a desire to storm the invisible battery, D. H. Hill rode up. Hill explained that on Longstreet's order he had brought up the three remaining brigades of his division. These he now was disposing in rear of Early, but he was not content to do that and no more. Hill, like Early, was full of the confident ardor of attack. If only he could throw his men forward and storm those guns![22]

Hill made a brief reconnaissance of the woods and agreed with Early that an attack could be made which would take the Federal artillery in the rear. For such an attack the consent of Johnston, who urged caution, was procured. Approval also was had from Longstreet, who directed Hill to accompany the column. Eagerly, if nervously, the men took their places. Hill directed that the advance should be in a single line on brigade front. The 24th Virginia was placed on the left. On its right was the 38th Virginia, next the 23rd North Carolina, then the 5th North Carolina. The two Carolina regiments were to be led by Hill in person; the Virginia units were to be under the brigade commander.

The 24th Virginia started off briskly across the wheat field and into the woods, but the less experienced 38th was slow in getting under way. Soon it was fifty yards behind, and in the woods contact between the two regiments was lost almost immediately. On the right the units under the guidance of Hill started together and kept their formation until they encountered a tangle so thick that Hill could see nothing of the regiments on his left. He halted the two Carolina regiments and sent to determine if the 24th and 38th Virginia were ready to attack. It was a vain precaution. Early had not waited to see whether the troops on his right were aligned. Soon he was at the edge of the woods closest the enemy. "Follow me," he shouted and plunged into the open.[23]

The general's eyes and those of his old regiment were drawn instantly to a spectacle: To their left, near some farm buildings, facing them on a line almost at a right angle to theirs, was the object of the Confederate advance—the battery that had been heard beyond the woods. Eight or nine Federal guns were in action, with infantry support near at hand. This display of strength did not deter the 24th or the general. Early pivoted the regiment roughly on its left. Quickly, furiously, it started for the artillery. The surprised Federals fired a few rounds, then limbered up and dragged their pieces over the wet ground to cover. The 24th began pursuit, but it found the field so heavy from the rain that the men were well-nigh bogged. At this moment Early received a minié ball in his shoulder. He tried to remain with the regiment, but the flow of blood and the wounding of his horse compelled him to turn back.[24]

Meanwhile, Colonel D. K. McRae of the 5th North Carolina, on the extreme right of the brigade, had emerged from the woods and was engrossed with the puzzling situation he found. His regiment was under fire from Federal guns distant some 800 or 900 yards opposite his left. Was this the battery which Hill had told him, ere the advance began, he was to charge? In doubt, McRae halted and sent to Hill for orders. Hill regretted that any of the troops had gone into the open, but now he had to tell McRae to attack the battery that was firing on the 5th and to do it quickly. Execution of this movement involved a wide oblique and the Carolinians advanced with great gallantry under a heavy fire. Moreover, to form a continuous line with the 24th Virginia, they had a long distance to go. The reason for this was that the 23rd North Carolina and the 38th Virginia, forming the center of the brigade's line, had not come out of the woods.[25]

D. H. Hill went to look for the two missing regiments. He found the 38th Virginia, to use his own words, "huddled up and in considerable confusion." Its colonel had lost direction. He then beat his way through the underbrush to find the 23rd North Carolina. At length he came upon it and ordered it to form up with the 38th Virginia, but the 23rd was poorly drilled and, in the tangle, was slow to get in line. Without waiting for them to follow, he returned to the open field.

There he found the 24th Virginia and 5th North Carolina still struggling over the heavy ground toward the enemy. The men were falling fast. The 24th and 5th came then to a stout rail fence where they paused a moment before they climbed over to a final grapple with the enemy. Perhaps Colonel McRae, as senior officer, then realized for the first time how many of his officers had fallen; perhaps he saw how scant was the force that lined the fence. In any event, he ordered his men to take such cover as they could behind the fence, and, as they were doing so, he got word from Hill to retire.

The 24th Virginia quickly obliqued into the woods on their left with little further loss, but the North Carolinians had to recross the field under fire. In doing so the regiment was shattered. The futile, bungling action ended. Early's men bivouacked where they had been when the engagement began.[26]

Casualties in Early's brigade were at least 600, and may have been higher. Of 1,560 Confederate losses that day, this adventure on the left accounted for more than 38 per cent. For the troops engaged that was excessive. There was much praise for the gallant attack, which was as fine as anything the war had witnessed, but there was no compensatory gain. The repulse of the Unionists on the Confederate center and right had been so complete, and the Northern casualties there so heavy in comparison with those of Longstreet's command—approximately 2,110 against 1,024—that the Confederates laid their emphasis on the success in front of Fort Magruder and on the right. Conversely, the Federals talked only of their accomplishments on the Confederate left, where Union losses were less than a fourth those sustained by Early.[27]

Johnston, who in his report treated the battle at Williamsburg in five brief paragraphs, did not mention the fight on the left. He had praise for Magruder's "forethought" in constructing the works there, and he commended two officers, McLaws and Longstreet, warmly. Longstreet wrote a casual, almost complacent report: "My part in the battle was comparatively simple and easy, that of placing the troops in proper positions at proper times." He distributed compliments broadly. Early's part in the battle was handled with reticence in the reports. Longstreet explained that when "a diversion," as he styled Early's attack, was made against the left, D. H. Hill was "ordered to watch it." That was all he had to say of Early, except that he "was severely wounded through the body, while leading an impetuous assault on the enemy's position."[28]

While this language was considerate, the reports and subsequent publications showed a purpose on the part of both Early and Hill to disclaim responsibility for ordering the attack on the left. Early stated in his official account that D. H. Hill expressed a wish to capture the Federal battery with Early's brigade, but first he "must see General Longstreet upon the subject." In Hill's report he stated that Early went to Longstreet, told of the battery in his front, and "asked leave to take it with his brigade...." To that account Hill adhered, though he subsequently wrote that he never thought of the attack "without horror." Longstreet, late in life, maintained that the charge was suggested by Hill to Johnston. Johnston's recollection was that Early—not Hill—sent his request to Longstreet, who passed it on to the commanding general: "I authorized the attempt, but enjoined caution in it."[29]

However this conflict of testimony may be resolved by present-day readers, contemporary opinion in the army seems to have acquitted D. H. Hill of blame and to have raised concerning the brigade commander no question save one of impetuosity. Beyond doubt, the absence of detailed critique was due in large part to the controversies over bloodier battles that soon were fought. Williamsburg dwindled, by comparison, to a small affair, a practice battle in which commanders learned what they should not do. Had there been an appraisal of those who had been most conspicuous in the largest action in Virginia after that of Manassas, the result would have been about as follows:

Joseph E. Johnston—intent on his major plan, contemptuous of mere loss of ground, disposed to leave the tactical direction of combat to subordinates.

James Longstreet—composed, almost "jolly" in battle, subjected as yet to no test of strategical ability, but tactically master of his position and able to retain a grip on his brigades.

Lafayette McLaws—undeniably able to handle at least a small force with skill and an accurate understanding of his mission.

R. H. Anderson—perhaps not altogether careful in reconnaissance, but steady and capable of handling more than one brigade with none of a beginner's uncertainty; possibly a bit negligent in watching small details.

A. P. Hill—capable, hard-hitting, and skillful in control of his men; the most conspicuous brigadier, save Anderson, on the right.

D. H. Hill—ambitious; tenacious and wholly master of himself in battle; perhaps too much disposed to the offensive and too little conscious of the tactical limitations of new troops.

George E. Pickett—distinctly promising.

Cadmus M. Wilcox—definitely capable in brigade command.

J. A. Early—brave, ambitious to win renown, impetuous, and possibly reckless.

J. E. B. Stuart—cooperative and useful, even when his own troops were not engaged.

In addition to these general officers, Colonel Micah Jenkins of the Palmetto Sharpshooters had handled Anderson's brigade and the artillery in Fort Magruder with a fiery zeal and a military judgment that won many plaudits. On the right, in an open field, a young captain of twenty-three, with gunners who had been drilling only three weeks, had commanded a battery with a gallant daring that made men ask his name. It was John Pelham. He and Jenkins were men worth watching.

4. ELTHAM INTRODUCES JOHN B. HOOD

Johnston could not be easy of mind while the danger remained of an attack on his flank or rear by a force that might land from the York. On the evening of the fourth he had ordered Magruder to resume the withdrawal toward Richmond. Smith had been started in the same direction at dawn on the fifth, the day of the rear guard action. By evening Magruder had reached Diascund Bridge. Smith camped that night at Barhamsville.

As Barhamsville was particularly vulnerable to attack from the river, Johnston reasoned that his wagon train would be exposed, and he ordered Smith to remain at the village until the column was closed by the arrival of the rear divisions. Word came on the afternoon of May 6 that Federal transports, under the protection of gunboats, had arrived, precisely as Johnston had anticipated they might, at the head of the York River and were landing troops below Eltham plantation, opposite Smith's flank. Johnston prepared for the worst. Magruder's troops were diverted, and Longstreet and D. H. Hill instructed to advance in support of Smith. By the morning of May 7 the entire army was concentrated around Barhamsville.[30]

Smith had refrained from contesting the debarkation of Federals because the heavy ordnance of the gunboats cast its shadow over the heads of the infantry. When the morning of the seventh brought no Federal advance, other than of skirmishers in woods that faced the Confederate lines, Smith changed his plan. He decided to advance the division of Brigadier General W. H. C. Whiting—the same Whiting whose official neck Johnston had saved the previous winter—to clear the woods and then, if practicable, to move up field artillery to where it could bombard the landing place and the transports.

Whiting easily drove the skirmishers back a mile and a half through the woods, between 10 o'clock and noon; but the gunnery officers reported the ships out of range. The Federal infantry meanwhile had taken shelter under a protecting bluff. With the loss of 48 of their own men, the capture of 46 prisoners, and the usual overestimate of Federal casualties, the Confederates returned in high satisfaction. Trivial as was this clash at Eltham's compared with the struggle Johnston had anticipated, the steady, well-organized advance through the woods and the ease with which the enemy had been driven under the bluff confirmed Johnston's high opinion of Gustavus Smith and of Whiting.[31]

The action, moreover, brought anew to the attention of Johnston the military qualifications of Colonel Wade Hampton. During the winter, Hampton had worked zealously to recruit and enlarge his command. He had won the professional respect and personal friendship of Johnston, who in January had given Hampton a provisional brigade. Now, after Hampton led his men successfully through Eltham Forest, Whiting had official praise for his "conspicuous gallantry." Johnston wrote of his "high merit," in the same bracket with Whiting's, and asked his promotion.[32]

At Eltham a fourth man, previously little known, made his first bid for fame. John B. Hood, son of a Kentucky physician, had served in the 2nd United States Cavalry under Albert Sidney Johnston and R. E. Lee. As his sympathies had been wholly with the South, Hood had resigned in April 1861, gone to Montgomery to receive commission as a first lieutenant, and reported to General Lee in Richmond. Lee had assigned him to Magruder, who welcomed joyfully the young, well-trained trooper and put him in charge of the cavalry companies on the lower Peninsula. As the temporary Rupert of Prince John's horse, Hood had one brush with the enemy before a colonel was sent to form the cavalry into a regiment.

Hood was not left long without like rank. He previously had decided that he would make Texas his home and accounted himself a citizen of the Lone Star State. This led the War Department, which could put its hand on few Texas officers so far away from home as Virginia, to select Hood to organize companies into the 4th Texas infantry. Hood had drilled these troops for some months at Richmond, and later had taken his regiment to northern Virginia to join a Texas brigade under ex-Senator Louis T. Wigfall.[33]

Just twenty-nine years of age, Hood stood six feet, two inches and had a powerful chest and a giant's shoulders. His hair and beard were a light brown, almost blond; his penetrating, expressive, kindly eyes were blue. When he spoke it was with a booming, musical richness of tone. On his arrival at Manassas he looked "like a raw backwoodsman, dressed up in an ill-fitting uniform," but physically he filled out rapidly and socially he learned fast. By the autumn of 1862 he was to be one of the most magnificent men in Confederate service. For the admiration of the lettered he might have stepped out of the pages of Malory; to the untutored boy in the ranks, Hood was what every hero-worshipping lad wished his big brother to be.

So quickly had Hood brought his regiment to high efficiency that, on the eve of the retreat from Manassas, he had been made brigadier general. On March 7 he had been assigned to the leadership of Wigfall's Texas Brigade. That command, which then consisted of the 1st, 4th, and 5th Texas and the 18th Georgia, was a part of Whiting's division and as such had no part in the action at Williamsburg; but now at Eltham's Landing it showed its mettle.[34]

Hood saw, ere the advance began, that there was danger of confused firing in the woods, and determined not to permit his men to load their guns until they reached the Confederate cavalry picket. With Hood in the lead, they ran squarely into a heavy Federal skirmish line. "Forward into line," he cried. "Load!" One coolheaded Union corporal picked out the figure of Hood and deliberately drew down his rifle on the general. A military career of high promise seemed at its end. At that instant a single shot was fired, but it was the Federal corporal, not Hood, who was killed. One strong-minded individualist of the 4th Texas, John Deal, had surreptitiously loaded his piece before starting and, by instant aim, saved Hood's life. The general scarcely knew whether to bless his deliverer or reprimand him for violation of orders. Naturally, after this experience, Hood's name was on many a lip.[35]

Thus, in a brief action, did Smith vindicate Johnston's confidence in him, while Whiting and Hampton added to their reputation and Hood first held the gaze of admiring eyes. The aftermath was undramatic. Smith was content to continue his retreat as far as New Kent Court House. Johnston decided to send the entire army farther toward Richmond. "The want of provision," he wrote General Lee, "and of any mode of obtaining it here . . . makes it impossible to wait. . . . The sight of the iron-clads makes me apprehensive for Richmond, too. . . ."[36]

CHAPTER 6

Seven Pines

1. TWENTY-FOUR UNHAPPY DAYS

The safety of Richmond now became a concern in itself and the symbol of the multiplying vexations of the anxious mind of General Johnston. He was fated to encounter and to display the carping and the crimination that always attend the gloom of a darkening cause. Between May 8 and May 31, more than any other time in the Virginia campaign, were the strain and misunderstanding of retreat and inactive defense exhibited.

Johnston saw his problem in this form: An army superior to his in numbers and equipment was pursuing him. Hostile forces of undetermined size faced Stonewall Jackson, who was in the Shenandoah Valley with about 8,400 infantry and perhaps 1,000 cavalry. Dick Ewell's division, 6,500, not immediately involved, was on the eastern slope of the Blue Ridge. Developments in that quarter were unpredictable.

Developments at the opposite end of Johnston's large department were all too plainly forecast. Major General Benjamin Huger, in charge at Norfolk, would be compelled to abandon his position immediately. Otherwise he might be cut off. Quite apart from this unhappy prospect, the evacuation of Norfolk would entail the loss of the invaluable Gosport navy yard. The ironclad *Virginia-Merrimack* would have no port. She drew too much water to ascend the James to Richmond.

To make a dark picture black, the 10,000 men under Brigadier General Joseph R. Anderson, defending the R.F. & P. Railroad south of the Rappahannock, were far outnumbered by a Federal column under General Irvin McDowell. This Union force probably would advance on Richmond from the north to form a junction with McClellan's Army of the Potomac. McClellan could be stopped on the York because his gunboats and transports were near the head of navigation there, but he could not be prevented from landing troops for a march on Richmond from the east. Similarly, he might attempt to send his fleet up the James. The only substantial barriers in his way were the homeless *Virginia-Merrimack* and the uncompleted batteries and obstructions at Drewry's Bluff, seven miles downstream from Richmond. If the obstacles were passed McClellan might get to Richmond before Johnston could.

What, then, should Johnston do? Here was his solution: Concentrate close to Richmond, in rear of his retreating army, all the forces that could be gathered from other parts of the Confederacy; give these forces unified command; retreat and maneuver as necessity and the enemy's movements demanded; when opportunity offered itself at the proper stage of concentration—strike.

With the broad principles behind this policy President Davis was in accord. The principles, in fact, were not debatable. He disagreed concerning details and application. Although the lives of soldiers and the independence of the South were at stake, the peculiarities of two strange men weighed more heavily on the scales of decision. Fundamentally, though never set forth explicitly, Johnston was expected to demonstrate to a somewhat skeptical President, fully satisfied of his own military knowledge, that he was as competent to administer the army as he was to command it, and that the plan of operations would be as well executed as it was soundly conceived. Johnston doubted Davis's confidence in him; Davis doubted whether Johnston was of a temperament to justify him in trusting to the general without reservation the entire conduct of a campaign on which the fate of the Confederacy depended.

President and commanding general first were to have a bristling correspondence over unity of command. Johnston attempted to direct his own field army and, at the same time, to cover Richmond and supervise the operations of Jackson, Ewell, Anderson, and Huger. All of this he undertook with a small, mediocre staff. Distance, poor communications, and, perhaps, Johnston's distaste for details soon produced misunderstanding and confusion. In Richmond Lee sought as tactfully as he could to respect Johnston's authority and yet to meet emergencies that confronted the minor forces with which Johnston lost touch.

The first of a succession of unpleasant exchanges involved orders to Huger's command at Norfolk. Johnston was ruffled by what he termed a "countermanding" of his orders to the troops south of the James. When Lee explained that this had been an emergency, without time to wait on ceremony, Johnston dropped that discussion in favor of one about the request by the President on May 1 for the assignment of Longstreet or Smith to command the force south of Fredericksburg: "This army cannot be commanded without these two officers; indeed, several more major-generals like them are required to make this an army." Johnston proceeded: "The best mode of arranging this matter will be to unite the two armies. . . . It is necessary to unite all our forces now."[1]

Thus Johnston was upheld on one essential of his plan—unity of command. The need of competent subordinate leadership seemed to be supplied, in part, by word from Lee that the near approach of the army to Richmond rendered the transfer of Longstreet or Smith to the Rappahannock less important than previously it had been. In expressing the President's view, Lee spoke with his usual consideration for Johnston's sensibilities, but Mr. Davis himself, seldom dropping controversy, took this occasion for an inopportune return to his demand that troops from the same state be brigaded together. In terms that might not unjustly be described as scolding, the President insisted on action, regardless of the situation of the army at the time. Upon receipt of the letter Johnston might well have asked, as he had of one of Benjamin's orders, whether such an order ever had been given before—at least in such circumstances.[2]

Those circumstances soon were of a character to call for a cessation of controversy. Apprehension for the security of Richmond had prompted Johnston to order withdrawal from Barhamsville. On May 9, Longstreet was ordered to concentrate near Long Bridge on the Chickahominy; Smith was moved to Baltimore Crossroads. By these moves Johnston had the bridges of the Chickahominy conveniently to the rear. Supplies now could be brought from Richmond by the York River Railroad. Improved as was this position, Johnston could not breathe easily there. The very day he took up his new line he received the disconcerting information that only three guns were in position at Drewry's Bluff. While work was progressing furiously to strengthen the defenses at the bluff, it remained obvious that the presence of the *Virginia-Merrimack* at the mouth of the James was the only means of keeping the Federal fleet from ascending the river. Once the ironclad was scuttled or lost, it was more certainly apparent than ever that the enemy would be hammering at Drewry's Bluff. Panic spread in the capital. The government packed up the archives. Belief in the invincibility of Southern leaders was shaken where it was not destroyed.[3]

One disaster precipitated another. On the eleventh the *Virginia-Merrimack* was blown up to keep her from falling into Federal hands. In Richmond, on receipt of this news, there was bewilderment, consternation, and resentment; at Johnston's headquarters there was grave fear that the enemy might pass the fortifications at Drewry's Bluff. Simultaneously, from the direction of West Point on the York, General McClellan seemed to be preparing to advance against the Confederate left.

Concerning all aspects of his defensive plan he wrote nothing to the President or to General Lee. He virtually suspended correspondence when an engagement or a movement was impending. Perhaps his memory of the quick spread of the report that Manassas was to be evacuated in March tightened his lips. Justified as was his reticence, Johnston carried it too far at this time in dealing with the President. On May 12 the chief executive and General Lee rode out to confer with him. The three talked so long that Lee and Davis could not return to Richmond that night, but the conversation did not satisfy the President. Johnston explained that he had drawn in his left to clear it of deep water, whence it could be turned, that he did not have strength to take the offensive, and that he would await attack. That was all he confided.[4]

On May 15 the Federal gunboats made the anticipated attempt to pass the fortifications at Drewry's. To the delight, and scarcely less to the surprise, of the Confederates the obstructions proved impassable. Guns of the batteries bore down almost on the decks of the warships. After three hours and twenty minutes of mauling from the heavy ordnance on the bluff, the Federals were glad to drop downstream out of range.

While this repulse was to Richmond a relief past reckoning, the enemy's attempt showed the possibility of joint operations on the James River by the Federal army and navy. Johnston reasoned that he should draw still nearer Richmond and should put himself in position to cope with an attack from the river, from the Southside, and from the direction of West Point. Accordingly, on the day of the attack on Drewry's Bluff, he abandoned the middle and lower stretches of the Chickahominy and drew his forces back to a line about seven miles below Richmond. On the seventeenth, finding this line weak and the supply of water inadequate, he fell back again until he was at some points within three miles of the city.[5]

On May 20, McClellan crossed troops over the Chickahominy at Bottom's Bridge and began a cautious advance. Soon it was suspected that he was moving up the left bank of the river also, working his way to the north of Richmond. This was interpreted in the capital as preliminary to attempted junction with the army under McDowell, which was known to be mustering in strength on the Rappahannock. The President believed that Johnston would do battle for Richmond, but he felt dissatisfaction with Johnston's preparations and redoubled his efforts to ascertain what plan the general proposed to follow. On the twenty-first he directed Lee to write specifically and imperatively for the desired information. Lee, as usual, did this with consideration: "Your plan of operations . . . may not be so easily explained, nor may it be prudent to commit it to paper. I would therefore respectfully suggest that you communicate your views on this subject personally to the President, which perhaps would be more convenient to you and satisfactory to him."[6]

Johnston readily enough supplied a desired statement of the strength of his forces, but he made no immediate reply to the invitation. It was the twenty-fourth before he came to Richmond for conference. Even then, if he disclosed anything to the President, Davis did not regard it, apparently, as detailed or adequate. Two days later, in a renewed effort to procure information, General Lee appeared again at Johnston's headquarters. Johnston by that time had ascertained that the Federals were across the Chickahominy and were not more than ten miles east of Richmond. He knew, also, that Federal cavalry had occupied Mechanicsville, five miles north of the city, and he had word that McDowell was moving southward from Fredericksburg. McClellan and McDowell, then, evidently were planning an early junction. Furthermore, Johnston had summoned to him J. R. Anderson's force on the R.F. & P. and L. O'B. Branch's brigade from Gordonsville. In addition, Huger, who had reached Petersburg, had been ordered to hold himself in readiness to repulse an attack on Drewry's Bluff or to move to Richmond.

With these reinforcements at hand Johnston felt that he could and must strike McClellan before McDowell joined the Army of the Potomac. In short, now that Johnston saw a possibility of doing more than defending himself, he could formulate a plan for an offensive. The details he promptly confided to Lee. The plan, commendably simple, was this: With part of his forces Johnston would attack north of the Chickahominy and clear that bank of Federals; then, while the Union forces were confused, he would strike with his right against the troops south of the Chickahominy and east of Richmond. The operations were set for May 29.[7]

Statement of this plan of campaign temporarily satisfied President Davis. Although the official relations between him and Johnston continued cool and formal, their sharper differences were put aside in the excited preparations for the battle. Long-sought promotions were made. The only direct vacancy created by the battle at Williamsburg had been that due to the wounding of Jubal Early. To the command of his troops Brigadier General Samuel Garland was assigned. He had served as colonel of the 11th Virginia, had the endorsement of Johnston as worthy of promotion, and had distinguished himself in leading his fine regiment in the fighting on the right at Williamsburg. He was a man who could be trusted. Colonel Wade Hampton was tendered a brigadier's commission, and like honor came to Robert Hatton, who already commanded the Tennessee regiments.

Much more necessary than the promotion of these men was, in Johnston's opinion, the appointment of at least two additional major generals. He did not have sufficient officers of that grade to handle large bodies of troops. Davis's reluctance to increase the number of high-ranking generals might confuse the coming battle and certainly would hamper Johnston in directing it. Whiting was at the head of a division though he still ranked as a brigadier. Johnston had urged his promotion but without success. The President had not forgotten that Whiting had rejected command of a Mississippi brigade; Whiting, in short, was persona non grata. Of men acceptable to Davis, D. R. Jones of South Carolina already was slated to be major general, and his nomination was pending before the Senate. As Johnston continued earnestly to ask for additional officers to command divisions, Davis at last appointed two men who had distinguished themselves at Williamsburg—Lafayette McLaws and A. P. Hill. To McLaws a division of Magruder's large force was assigned. A. P. Hill—Powell Hill to his intimates—was put in charge of Branch's brigade and J. R. Anderson's command.[8]

All five of these promotions were made between May 23 and May 26, when a major battle was imminent. Johnston's appeals for the assignment of generals of division had been frequent and pointed, and to an unfriendly mind it might have appeared that the President had waited as long as he dared before yielding to Johnston in this, the last of their current differences.

The day that A. P. Hill assumed command, May 27, was an important one in the preliminaries of the battle. General Branch, brought down from Gordonsville, had been left by Johnston to protect the Virginia Central Railroad. In the exercise of this discretion Branch moved his brigade from Hanover Court House southward about four miles, where, on the twenty-seventh, he was attacked by a heavy Federal column. Although his troops put up a stiff fight, they were driven back to Ashland, where he reported to his new commander, Hill. The affair was in no sense discreditable to Branch, but it was a somber induction of the new division.[9]

Even more serious than casualties and humiliation was the evidence offered by this clash that McClellan apparently was extending northward a strong hand of welcome to McDowell. Their junction of force was the one development above all others that Johnston had best reason to dread. He wrote Smith, "We must get ready to fight."[10] On the afternoon of the twenty-seventh battle plans were formulated. Circumstance, more than choice, shaped them. McClellan's troops north of the Chickahominy would be those who first united with McDowell. Smith and his three divisions must attack and break the link the Federals were soon to weld.

By the evening of May 28, Smith reported to a council of war at army headquarters that his preparations were complete. The enemy had a strong position about a mile east of Mechanicsville, but he had confidence that an assault by his three divisions would clear the ground of Federals. Johnston listened and then announced—with more inward relief than his manner disclosed—that an important change in the situation had occurred: "Jeb" Stuart reported that McDowell had halted his advance to join McClellan. That was not all. McDowell had returned to Fredericksburg, according to Stuart's information, and seemed to be planning to move even farther north.

What had happened to McDowell? Johnston knew that Stonewall Jackson was on the move in the Shenandoah Valley. Perhaps, even probably, McDowell's countermarch was related to Jackson's advance, but of the details nothing was clear. If McDowell was withdrawing, should the Confederates attack McClellan, and if so, where? Smith did not believe that McDowell's column was permanently off the stage of the Richmond theater of war, but he at once withdrew his plan for an attack north of the Chickahominy. It would be easier now, Smith said, to beat that part of the Federal army south of the river, where the ground was less unfavorable for an offensive. Longstreet disagreed and expressed himself in favor of the execution of Smith's original plan.

A long discussion followed. Longstreet continued to argue his point, but when overruled by his chief, urged then an attack be delivered the very next morning in the vicinity of Seven Pines, directly east of Richmond. Again Johnston shook his head. If it proved true, he said, that McDowell was not marching to join McClellan, he would strike at the first large force of Federals that came within easy reach on the south side of the river; but the next day? No! Too many of the troops were concentrated on the left in anticipation of McDowell's advance. Moreover, Huger was soon to arrive. The army could afford to await him.[11]

The twenty-ninth passed without execution of "Longstreet's scheme," but on May 30, D. H. Hill made a reconnaissance in force on the Williamsburg Road and found the enemy advanced to the west of Seven Pines. No enemy was found on the Charles City Road, which, opposite Seven Pines, was about two and a half miles south of and approximately parallel to the Williamsburg Road. The presence of the Federals on one of these roads and not the other was somewhat puzzling. Either the Federal left flank, facing west, was refused, or else it rested on low, boggy ground between the roads. Furthermore, Hill's information was that the whole of the IV Corps, Keyes's, was south of the Chickahominy.[12]

When this intelligence reached Johnston about noon, he knew that Huger was in the outskirts of Richmond and would be available the next day. Johnston accordingly decided to attack at Seven Pines on the thirty-first. In a long conference with Longstreet he worked out the detailed plan. Longstreet was told to take command of the right—his own, Harvey

Hill's, and Huger's divisions—and for his march and dispositions was given verbal orders. Those of the other division commanders were in the form of letters from Johnston.

All these messages were sent, and all preparations for the battle were made in the midst of a deluge of rain. The storm would slow the Confederate march and perhaps delay the action, but it would flood the Chickahominy and probably prevent the movement of Federal troops from the north of that stream to strengthen the drenched divisions that were to be assailed. For the great day of Johnston's life, for the first major battle he was exclusively to direct, the prospect seemed as fair as the night was black.[13]

2. A BATTLE OF STRANGE ERRORS

Johnston's aim in the battle of May 31 was to overwhelm the Federal IV Corps at Seven Pines before it could be reinforced. His concentration and deployment were based on the three highways that led to the enemy's position. The first of these was the Nine Mile Road. This left the suburbs of Richmond and ran east and southeast to Fair Oaks Station, on the York River Railroad, and on to Seven Pines. Next, to the southward, was the Williamsburg Road, which followed a course almost due east from Richmond to Seven Pines and thence to the Chickahominy at Bottom's Bridge. At no point west of Seven Pines were the Nine Mile and Williamsburg roads more than 2.25 miles apart. The third line of Johnston's advance was the Charles City Road. This forked from the Williamsburg Road 2.3 miles east of Richmond and ran thereafter southeast. Opposite Seven Pines the upper stretches of troublesome White Oak Swamp separated the two thoroughfares, and the ground between was difficult in the best of conditions and impassable after heavy rains. Except for this fact, the location of the roads seemed ideal for a swift convergence on Seven Pines.

To facilitate that convergence, D. H. Hill already had three brigades of his division on the Williamsburg Road; there seemed no reason why he could not bring his fourth brigade, Rodes's, across from the Charles City Road and lead the attack down the Williamsburg Road. Longstreet was in camp on the Nine Mile Road; simply by moving down that road he could form on Hill's left and attack the right flank of the Federals when Hill assailed their center and left. To reinforce Longstreet, in all contingencies, use could be made of Whiting's division. The remainder of Smith's command could guard the south bank of the upper Chickahominy against attack from north of that stream. Magruder could be in general reserve.

To complete a sound plan of operations, the only other essential requirement seemed to be to cover D. H. Hill's right flank against the Federal left, whose exact position north of White Oak Swamp was not known. For securing the Confederate right Johnston would use Huger's division of three brigades. No intimation was given Huger that he was to be under the direction of anyone save the commanding general. The full plan of action was not communicated to him, though the time for the opening of the battle was to be set by his movements in this essential respect: As soon as Huger's column reached Rodes, that officer was to start his brigade from the Charles City Road to join the remainder of D. H. Hill's division on the Williamsburg Road. When Rodes came up, a signal gun was to be fired. Hill was immediately to attack. Longstreet was to go into action on hearing Hill's fire. In this manner the complicated arrangements for opening the battle depended, first of all, upon the time one of Huger's brigades reached Rodes.

The one participating divisional commander of whose cooperation in battle Johnston knew nothing was General Huger. His high South Carolina birth, the reputation he had won as Scott's chief of ordnance in the Mexican War, and his former position in the old army as fourth-ranking major of the Ordnance Department had raised high expectations, which he fulfilled by his administration in Norfolk, though somewhat slowly and in the face of many difficulties. On his unopposed evacuation he had been under the close direction of General Lee. Now Huger waited west of Gillies Creek. At fifty-six years of age—medium in height, thick-set, stout, ruddy, with gray hair, gray eyes, and heavy mustache, slow of speech and of motion but bearing unmistakably the stamp of the proud and martial aristocrat—he was to lead troops into action for the first time in his life. Would he succeed? Did he know what was expected of him?[14]

At 6 o'clock the leading brigade of Whiting's division was ready to start its march out Nine Mile Road. At the mouth of the road and moving across it, Whiting found Longstreet's division. The prospect of having to wait to execute his orders until Longstreet cleared the road made Whiting nervous and impatient. He was not entirely relieved by the assurance from headquarters that Longstreet was to proceed him. He went to Johnston's headquarters, whither Smith had previously ridden; would Smith ask Longstreet to put an end to the delay? Captain R. F. Beckham of Smith's staff made off at once with a message to Longstreet. In about an hour Beckham sent back a courier to report that Longstreet was not on the Nine Mile Road. Beckham himself had ridden across country to see if he could find the general on the highway to the south.

Johnston was skeptical of this report that Longstreet was not on the designated road; one of his own staff officers would go down the Nine Mile Road to search out Longstreet. The aide Johnston designated for the

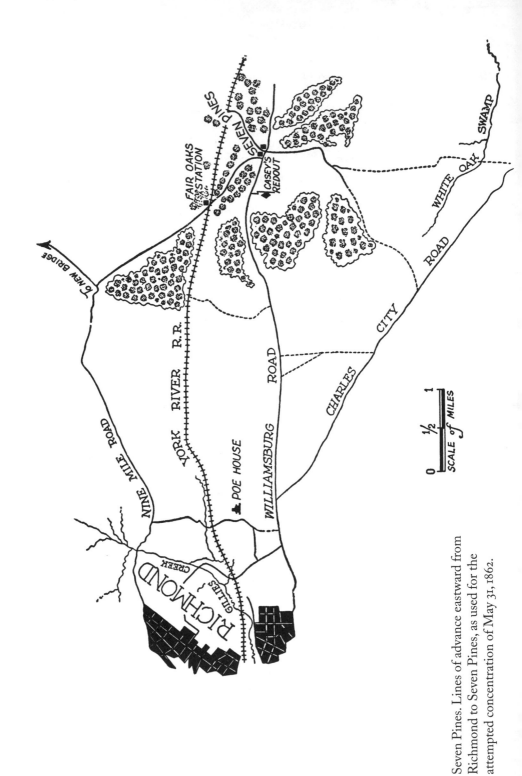

Seven Pines. Lines of advance eastward from
Richmond to Seven Pines, as used for the
attempted concentration of May 31, 1862.

mission did not return—he unwittingly rode into the Federal picket line and had to surrender—but Beckham, sometime after 10 o'clock, reported back that he had found Longstreet—on the Williamsburg Road opposite the point where the Charles City Road forked. Longstreet was waiting for D. H. Hill to pass down the Williamsburg Road in order to open the action.[15]

This meant that Longstreet was at the one point where congestion and resulting delay were most apt to occur. By perverse misfortune he was on D. H. Hill's road. Unless Huger previously had passed, his division, too, might be on the Williamsburg Road west of the turnout into the Charles City Road. With three roads available for four divisions, three of the four were, or might be, on a single mile of one road. Gone was all prospect of an early beginning of the battle!

How had such a mix-up occurred? One of two things had happened. Either Longstreet had understood that he should move down the Nine Mile Road and then across to the Williamsburg Road in rear of D. H. Hill, or else Longstreet had concluded that, as he had been placed in command of the right wing, he could modify as he saw fit the lines of advance of that wing. Whatever the reason, he had confused the advance frightfully.

Worse, his approach march had brought his whole division to a stream known as Gillies Creek, and after the storm of the previous evening the creek was raging. Confronted by this barrier, Longstreet decided that he would save time by bridging the creek instead of seeking a different route along muddy, overflowed roads. Before the leading regiment had begun to cross the makeshift bridge there, another complication developed: Huger's division came down the hillside to cross the rebellious creek to reach the Charles City Road. The fact that the movement of Huger's front brigade was to fix the time for opening the battle, by relieving Rodes, should have assured Huger the right of way, but apparently nobody at the crossing knew that the latecomers should be the first over. Longstreet insisted on the right of prior crossing because of earlier arrival. In an atmosphere of some unpleasantness, the two commanders waited for their respective troops to cross the creek. By 9 o'clock Longstreet's division had reached the position opposite the mouth of the Charles City Road where Captain Beckham found the general.[16]

The commanding general manfully told Smith that the misunderstanding over the line of advance might be his fault, not Longstreet's. Without further discussion, Johnston proceeded to revise his dispositions on the left. He chose to march Whiting forward to take the place assigned Longstreet on the Nine Mile Road. By 11 o'clock Johnston knew that D. H. Hill had cleared Longstreet's columns and was making ready to attack; by 1 o'clock

Whiting's line was across the Nine Mile Road close to headquarters. Now came a long period of suspense. From the direction of Longstreet's proposed attack not a sound was audible. No report arrived of progress or repulse. Perplexed by this silence, though outwardly calm, Johnston confided to one of his staff that he wished all the troops were back in their camps. To General Lee, who had ridden quietly out to headquarters, Johnston had little to say.[17]

As heavy minutes dragged to 2 o'clock the commander waited. What could be delaying Longstreet? Had anything gone amiss on the right? Another staff officer, Major Jasper Whiting, was sent galloping off to the Williamsburg Road; 3 o'clock came and went. Ten hours of daylight had been consumed. Was it possible that the Federals still remained without information of troop movements in their front? Had the advantage of surprise been lost? What *had* happened to Longstreet? Why did he not report?

At last, from the south, rolled the echo of artillery fire. Lee thought he heard, also, as a vague undertone, the sound of distant musketry. Johnston would not allow it. An artillery duel was in progress; that was all. The irregular, broken growl of field guns, the mysterious accompaniment of something subdued and sinister, continued until 4 o'clock was drawing near. Then the mutter swelled definitely and unmistakably into furious small-arms fire—volleys and the grim rattle of engaged columns. Major Whiting rode up; Longstreet, he said, was in the midst of heavy fighting and was gaining ground. On the heels of the major's horse dashed a courier with a note from Longstreet. This reported progress in driving the enemy, but voiced disappointment that no help had come from the left. At once Johnston ordered Smith to send Whiting's division down the Nine Mile Road to engage the troops that confronted Longstreet. Thereupon, almost before Whiting's men could fall in, Johnston mounted and rode across the fields toward the Federal position. As he hurried away, Jefferson Davis came up the lane to headquarters. Some who saw the quick departure of the commanding general thought that he hastened off to avoid a meeting with the President.[18]

Within an hour Whiting's brigades were attacking in the tangled forest around Fair Oaks Station. Strong Federal artillery and confident infantry easily repulsed Whiting's assaults. When night closed the confused action, 1,283 of his men had been killed, wounded, or captured, and the division was back on the line from which the attack had been launched. It was soon established that Whiting had encountered troops sent across the Chickahominy from the north bank to reinforce those whom Longstreet had assailed.[19]

Not until late in the night of May 31–June 1 were the details of Longstreet's battle on the right known at headquarters. A strange story

there was to tell. After Beckham's report that D. H. Hill's column had
cleared the intersection, Longstreet had kept his division waiting by the side
of the Williamsburg Road until Huger completed his crossing of Gillies
Creek. Then he directed Huger to pass him. Longstreet's orders to Huger
were to march down the Charles City Road with his division and three of
Longstreet's brigades and await further instructions. Pickett's brigade then
was detached to march north and cover the nearby York River Railroad.
Having sent off four of his brigades, Longstreet ordered the remaining two,
Kemper's and R. H. Anderson's, to move down the Williamsburg Road and
be ready to support D. H. Hill's four in the main assault. That is to say, with
thirteen brigades at his disposal, Longstreet intended to open with only five
the attack on the entrenched position of the enemy.[20]

The attack, indeed, already had opened. D. H. Hill, impatient and
ardent, sent orders for Rodes to move across to the Williamsburg Road.
About 1:00 P.M., while Rodes was still fifteen minutes' march behind the
troops on the left of the highway, Garland's and G. B. Anderson's brigades,
Hill ordered the signal gun fired for opening the attack. On initial contact
these two brigades received the full fire of the enemy, but Rodes soon
caught up. His support, Rains's brigade, cleverly flanked the main Federal
earthwork, known as Casey's Redout. Soon, by furious onrush, now here,
now there, the Federal front line was swept back. Eight guns and all the
equipment and supplies of a brigade camp were captured.

The enemy rallied in the woods behind a strong abatis, and from this
position Rodes determined to drive them. Around his martial figure—six
feet tall, clear-eyed, thin, with a drooping tawny mustache—his men
dressed their line for a second charge. Then a Federal column appeared at
an angle across the road to assail their left. Up dashed Captain Thomas H.
Carter's King William Artillery at the gallop, unlimbered, and opened fire
at the very nick. It was done magnificently. Under Carter's rapid and accurate fire the Federals on the flank soon broke and retired. Hill saw all this,
thrilled with the joy of battle, and to the end of his days averred that war
never had witnessed anything finer.

Rodes's left was safe. His center then plunged recklessly forward. His
wild-eyed, panting men reached the open space in front of the woods. The
Federals opened furiously. No pause, scarcely a wincing was there as the
first volley was received. On went the writhing, uneven, but persistent line.
Wounded men fell in water above their knees. Some drowned before they
could be succored. At length Kemper's brigade came up in support, and
together Kemper and Rodes untangled the line. Rodes received an ugly
wound in the arm, but kept the field until sunset. On Hill's order his men
were drawn out of the wood.[21]

On the other side of the Williamsburg Road, Garland and G. B. Anderson had, if possible, even worse conditions to face. Regiments were confused. Lines overlapped. Officers fell and organization was lost, but by the volume of their fire the Confederates steadily weakened the resistance of the enemy. Then, with a crash, R. H. Anderson's brigade came forward and took the lead. Anderson coolly divided his command, conducting one column and entrusting the other to Colonel Micah Jenkins of the Palmetto Sharpshooters. The South Carolinians attacked like demons possessed, swept through the abatis, stormed two gun positions, and at nightfall held the most advanced position on the entire field. The other brigades of Longstreet's division touched only the fringes of the battle or else arrived on the scene after dark.

This, in incomplete outline, was the story that reached headquarters during the night of May 31–June 1. The next morning an opportunity seemed to be offered on the Confederate right to drive the enemy further, but because of vacillation, overcaution, and conflicting orders on the part of G. W. Smith, the only results were more casualties, confusion, and recrimination. That night the Confederate army, unpursued, fell back to the position from which it had launched the attack.[22]

3. GRIM FRUITS OF ANNIVERSARY

What, then, had been achieved by the attack at Seven Pines? The Confederate left had made little progress. Five brigades on the right, despite confusion and difficult ground, had driven one Federal brigade in rout and shaken Casey's division but had not overwhelmed it before the arrival of reinforcements. In exchange for the temporary occupation of a square mile or so of woodland, two abandoned lines, ten guns, some 6,000 small arms, and a handful of prisoners, Confederate losses had been excessive. The fine brigade of Rodes had been shattered. He went into action with about 2,000 men. Of these, 1,094 were killed or wounded. John B. Gordon's 6th Alabama sacrificed 60 per cent of its effective strength. Garland's brigade lost 740. R. H. Anderson's losses were not separately reported but doubtless were as high as G. B. Anderson's 866. For the entire army the butcher's bill was 6,134.[23]

Among the fallen was Brigadier General Robert Hatton, of Whiting's division. Johnston Pettigrew, a magnificent man who commanded another of Whiting's brigades, had been shot down far to the front. Because he believed his wound mortal, he had refused to permit his men to leave the ranks to carry him to the rear. Whether he lived or died none knew until

June 4, when he sent a letter through the lines. "I was picked up by the first party which came along," he wrote, "which proved to be the enemy." Wade Hampton also was wounded but kept the field and insisted that the bullet be extracted from his foot while he sat his horse under fire. Besides this toll on the right and the wounding of Rodes, three colonels lost their lives— John R. R. Giles of the 5th South Carolina, Tennent Lomax of the 3rd Alabama, and R. T. Jones of the 12th Alabama.[24]

Despite losses and failure to achieve any substantial result, Confederate victory was proclaimed in every key. The public was assured that McClellan had been defeated with immense slaughter. Exultant praise was given, first of all, to the men in the ranks. It was deserved. They were the real heroes of the battle. Most of D. H. Hill's troops had never been in action until May 31, but where they were well led they acquitted themselves admirably. Those of Longstreet's men who got into action sustained their reputation. No fault could be found with Whiting's division. It had not beaten the enemy but it had not failed to try.

When the reports were published praise literally was poured on most of the high-ranking officers. General Johnston mentioned Longstreet first, for operations "worthy of the highest praise." In the next sentence he commended Harvey Hill; then the "skill, energy, and resolution" of G. W. Smith. Longstreet, in his turn, said of D. H. Hill: "The entire success of the affair is sufficient evidence of his ability, courage, and skill." All the brigadier generals of his division, together with the colonels commanding brigades, Longstreet wrote down as "distinguished for their usual gallantry and ability."[25]

Hill had high praise for his brigadiers, with the exception of General Rains, who after his first flank operation against Casey's Redout "did not advance farther in that direction." In sketching the operations of June 1, Hill reported that Armistead's brigade of Huger's division "fled early in the action...." Mahone, said Hill bluntly, "withdrew his brigade without any orders," while Colston "did not engage the Yankees, as I expected him to do." General Smith refrained from detailed praise of Whiting because, as he said, Whiting acted more immediately under Johnston. When the commanding general filed his report he renewed his familiar recommendation that Whiting be promoted.[26]

Some among those "mentioned in dispatches" did not deserve what was said of them; but when the account was balanced the assets of army leadership, in terms of fulfillment or of promise, had been increased by the performance of seven men:

1. D. H. Hill, though displaying the same impatience and precipitancy that had caused him to rush forward at Williamsburg, had conducted the

operation in other particulars with cold calculation, vigor, and sensitive feel of action. He acted as if the command of a division was an art he had mastered so long previously that he negligently could have disdained half he knew and still could have won.

2. R. E. Rodes emerged with reputation as a hard-hitting brigadier whom losses or difficult ground could not deter. A native of Lynchburg, Virginia, he had been graduated at the Virginia Military Institute in 1848. Thereafter he had served as civil engineer for various railroads, married in Alabama, and just before the outbreak of the war accepted a professorship at his alma mater. He left V.M.I. almost at once to organize a company in Alabama and soon received commission as colonel of the 5th Regiment. With his command he had come promptly to Virginia. On October 21, 1861, he was promoted brigadier general and assigned the 5th, 6th, and 12th Alabama and the 12th Mississippi. Until that day at Seven Pines he never had opportunity of leading them into action. Once on the field he had shone. "Coolness, ability, and determination," the qualities that Longstreet praised, most justly characterized him. He was now thirty-three. Given time he would rise.

3. Samuel Garland had justified his promotion to the command of Early's brigade. Like Rodes, he was a native of Lynchburg, Virginia, and a graduate of V.M.I. His father was a lawyer of distinction, and at the University of Virginia he had studied his father's profession and had practiced it in Lynchburg. He was one of the most studious and well-read men of his city. From a captaincy in the 11th Virginia he had been promoted speedily and, at Williamsburg, had been distinguished in A. P. Hill's brigade and been wounded. Now that he had fought his first battle as a brigade commander he had shown the unmistakable qualities of the soldier. In the thickest of the struggle Garland, though much exposed, escaped unhurt. Perhaps there was a deliberate recklessness in his conspicuous disregard of fire: He was the last of his direct line. His wife and his only son had died since the war began.

4. Richard H. Anderson had confirmed all that had been said of him in his battle on the right at Williamsburg. Through abatis and forest at Seven Pines, dripping and miry, he had led part of his own command forward and had directed the operations of two other brigades. No performance on the field had been more difficult or more admirably executed. D. H. Hill and Longstreet praised him; Johnston suggested his promotion.

5. Colonel Micah Jenkins of the Palmetto Sharpshooters, a youngster of twenty-six years, had received command of one column when R. H. Anderson divided the brigade. His conduct had been above all praise. Hill estimated that Jenkins had gone more than a mile beyond the main Federal works at

Seven Pines. Jenkins had prepared himself for that day and for the honors that awaited him. Born of high blood on Edisto Island, South Carolina, in 1835, he had been graduated at the head of his class at the South Carolina Military College. His 5th regiment was one of the best as well as one of the first to volunteer in South Carolina. During the operations of First Manassas and through the winter, Micah Jenkins had given every promise of the qualities he displayed at Williamsburg and Seven Pines. "He is highly educated in military matters," remarked an observer after the battle, "and far surpasses many of those political generals who are incessantly blundering."[27]

6. George E. Pickett, with his Virginia brigade, merited all that Harvey Hill said of his bearing. During the action of June 1, when Pickett detected Federal preparations for a heavy attack on his front, he rode rapidly to D. H. Hill to state his situation. Hill asked Pickett if he could not retire. Pickett answered that he could, but that he did not desire to do so, and that if he did he would have to leave his wounded. Hill thereupon reinforced Pickett, who beat off the attack. It was a staunch performance. "Pickett," said Hill in his report, "held his ground against the odds of ten to one . . . and only retired when the Yankees had ceased to annoy him."[28] Here, evidently, was a stubborn fighter with a mind of his own.

7. Colonel John B. Gordon of the 6th Alabama, Rodes's brigade, had attracted attention for the first time by his daring leadership. He was a Georgian of thirty, trained for the bar but engaged on the outbreak of hostilities in the development of coal mines. The admiring mountaineers of the coal district promptly chose Gordon their captain, from which rank, though he had no previous military experience, he rose quickly to colonel. Although the combination was not demonstrated until that day in the woods east of Richmond, Gordon had the natural instincts of a soldier and the persuasive power of an orator who knew his auditors perfectly. By the honest exercise of these qualities he had inculcated a superior and intelligent discipline. At Seven Pines his regiment went swiftly forward as brigade skirmishers, and a little later formed the right element in the charge on the enemy's front line. Before they were recalled, the Alabamians pushed straight on into the Federal camp. After a breathing spell, Rodes's message was received for an attack on the second line. "They moved at double-quick with such impetuosity that the enemy fled from his hiding places before us," Gordon reported.[29] Bullets pierced his coat. His horse was killed. At the end of the action he was untouched, unshaken, and in charge of what was left of Rodes's brigade.

To these seven most distinguished at Seven Pines—D. H. Hill, R. E. Rodes, Samuel Garland, R. H. Anderson, Micah Jenkins, George E. Pickett, and John B. Gordon—three captains of artillery might have been added. They were Thomas H. Carter, J. W. Bondurant, and James Dearing, who had given the infantry such support as it received in the tangle of forest-felled trees and water-covered fields.

The conduct of these officers, the indisputable valor of the troops, and all the rejoicing of the public did not alter the stubborn fact that Johnston's plan had not been executed, and that the casualties were almost 50 per cent larger than publicly they were admitted to be. President Davis had not been deceived. Before he left the field on the evening of May 31 he asked whether it would not be possible to keep the troops in their positions so that, if the enemy withdrew during the night, a victory might be asserted. Others in high position knew that plans had miscarried and they proceeded immediately to place the blame.[30]

In fairness, that blame scarcely could be put on Johnston. His orders had been drawn carelessly and had not been circulated promptly, but his general plan had been sound and his assumptions valid, except that the Federals had been able to send reinforcements from the north bank of the Chickahominy, which he had hoped high water would prevent. This error would not have deprived him of the advantage of surprise had the Confederate attack been delivered as early as Johnston's conservative logistics had led him to anticipate. The delay of two divisions at Gillies Creek and the wait on the Williamsburg Road had not been Johnston's fault. Even with that delay he still might have won a victory had he been informed when Longstreet went into action. Prompt reports would have offset failure to hear the sound of battle. The "acoustic shadow" which disguised the rattle of Hill's muskets was the chief reason for the late launching of the attack by the Confederate left.

If Johnston was not to blame for failure, who was? As early as the evening of June 1 it was alleged on the streets of Richmond that "the failure of General Huger to lead his division into action at the time appointed [was] the only reason . . . the left wing of the enemy was not completely destroyed." By his report Longstreet confirmed rumor: "I have reason to believe that the affair would have been a complete success had the troops upon the right been put in position within eight hours of the proper time." General Johnston merely rephrased Longstreet's accusation. Huger, in answer, exposed the unreason of the charge that he was eight hours late: Longstreet himself, Huger pointed out, was not in position to commence operations at that hour. The other criticisms in the reports Huger disputed, and made efforts to have a court-martial or a court of inquiry investigate the circumstances, but in this he did not succeed.[31]

Again, then, the question, whose *was* the fault? Huger's record was as follows:

1. Johnston's orders to him on the day of battle read, "As our main force will be on your left, it will be necessary for your progress to the front to conform at first to that of General Hill. If you find no strong body in your front, it will be well to aid General Hill; but then a strong reserve should be retained to cover our right."[32] These were orders for a cautious action. Aid of Hill was not made mandatory.

2. Huger received no information concerning the general plan of action prior to the time he started from his bivouac, and he had no notice that Longstreet was in general command on the right.

3. At 3:00 A.M., May 31, Huger notified D. H. Hill that he would start a brigade for the Charles City Road "as soon as possible," its commander to report to Rodes, whom he was to relieve.[33]

4. When Huger's troops reached Gillies Creek they found Longstreet's division there. Huger's leading brigade, intended to relieve Rodes, was not allowed priority over Longstreet in crossing the creek. Thereafter Longstreet, who asserted seniority, instructed Huger to march past and to go down the Charles City Road.

5. As to objective, Huger stated that "[Longstreet] directed me to proceed down the Charles City Road to a designated position, and sent three brigades of his division . . . with the three of my division, and there await orders." The time of his arrival at the "designated position" was stated by Huger to have been "before 4 o'clock."[34]

6. "Soon after getting into position," Huger wrote, "General Longstreet sent for the three brigades of his division, and in a short time afterwards sent for General Armistead's Brigade of my division. . . . If these troops could be engaged the rest of my division could have been engaged also, had I received orders." In official protest Huger said if his division "did not go into action by 4 o'clock it was because General Longstreet did not require it, as it was in position and awaiting his orders."[35]

What, in contrast, was Longstreet's record that day?

1. Whether the fault was his or his commander's, there was a misunderstanding of orders concerning his line of march. The plan undoubtedly was for Longstreet to advance down the Nine Mile Road, but this was not stated in the official reports of Johnston or of Longstreet. Smith's report gave the details of the search for Longstreet, and Longstreet's message, about 4:00 P.M., stating his disappointment in not receiving assistance from the left. Johnston sent back the report with a request that Smith eliminate all references to these incidents; he considered them as essentially matters between Longstreet and himself. Smith acquiesced, and only made the full text public twenty-two years later.[36]

2. Having started for the Williamsburg Road, Longstreet chose the

route that put Gillies Creek in his way. Had he moved by his left instead of by his right, he could have come out near the entrance to the Charles City Road, and would have had to cross only one small branch of Gillies Creek.

3. At Gillies Creek Longstreet's troops insisted on crossing before Huger. There is no evidence one way or the other that Longstreet sent anyone to expedite the march of Huger's brigade intended for the relief of Rodes.

4. After his troops reached the turn-out into the Charles City Road, Longstreet delayed them at that point for the passage down that road of the division that his own men had insisted on preceding at Gillies Creek.

5. Thereafter, for reasons that were not explained officially, Longstreet dispatched three of his brigades down the Charles City Road and left only three brigades to reinforce D. H. Hill on the Williamsburg Road and to maintain liaison with Smith on the left.

6. Longstreet's subsequent orders to Wilcox, who commanded the three brigades sent down the Charles City Road, called on him to advance, then to countermarch, then to face about again, and finally, Wilcox reported, "to move across to the Williamsburg road. . . ." When Longstreet complained of the delay, Wilcox added, "I reported the order and counter-orders, marches and counter-marches he had given, and that I had made in obedience to his orders."[37]

The record speaks for itself, but as neither Huger nor any of his brigadiers filed any official reports, the facts were not known for many years after the battle. Johnston prepared his report on the basis of what Longstreet narrated and, as a result, he accepted the charges against Huger without knowledge of all the circumstances. At the same time, Johnston's sense of honor and his affection for Longstreet led him to assume responsibility for a possible misunderstanding over Longstreet's line of advance. It is possible also that Johnston and the division commanders from the Manassas line had a *camaraderie* that made them defend one another and assume a certain sense of superiority to the Army of the Peninsula and to Huger's command from Norfolk.

Be that as it may, the Battle of Seven Pines left in widespread distrust the abilities of Huger. On the other hand, Longstreet, whose conduct at Seven Pines was most subject to question, emerged not only without blame but also with prestige increased. Now that after-discovered evidence suggests a reversal, there is danger that judgment of Longstreet, in all save one respect, may be too severe. It scarcely is reasonable to say that he marched over to the Williamsburg Road to get rid of Johnston and Smith, and to fight his own battle in his own way. The probability is that he moved southward through honest mistake in the issuance or interpretation of orders. Staff work at general headquarters on May 30–31 was about as bad is it could have been. If

Longstreet's orders were equivocal, his subsequent confusion was the result of inexperience in the logistics of a far larger command than ever he had handled in the field. The inexcusable part of Longstreet's conduct was his successful effort to make Huger the scapegoat.

The main battle of Seven Pines was fought on the anniversary of Beauregard's official assignment to the command at Manassas. One year of the army's history was written. It was a story of preparation rather than of action, a prologue to the red drama that was to begin in another month. From June 1861 to the end of May 1862 the army had grown vastly in numbers but unequally in experience. The cavalry was as yet an arm undeveloped. In the artillery service not one officer had risen to eminence. The infantry, on the other hand, had earned in marches, in charges, and in casualties the confidence of every commander. So valiant, so willing was it that the tactics of the army were based on infantry assaults. Some of the general officers were too readily disposed to employ the infantry in the discharge of tasks that should have devolved on the artillery.

Although there had been but two major battles, in neither of which the entire army had been engaged, attrition and transfer had removed in twelve months many of the leaders to whom the South, at the time of secession, had looked with confidence. Brilliant Robert Selden Garnett, aggressive Bernard Bee, chivalrous Francis Bartow, and courtly Philip St. George Cocke were dead. Bonham had resigned. Beauregard, Van Dorn, and Kirby Smith had been sent to other scenes of action. Huger had lost much of his reputation. Shanks Evans was in South Carolina. Jackson and Ewell were detached and were fighting a dramatic campaign in the Shenandoah Valley. Jubal Early, Wade Hampton, and Robert Rodes were suffering from wounds. Johnston Pettigrew was a prisoner of war. Hatton was newly fallen. Seven colonels of the line had been killed in action. Of the twelve brigade commanders of the troops that Johnston and Beauregard had sought to concentrate at Manassas on July 21, 1861, only two were now with the army in front of Richmond—Longstreet and D. R. Jones. If Jackson and Ewell were included, four of the twelve—and no more than four—remained in command of troops in Virginia on the anniversary of the first step in the organization of Beauregard's "Army of the Potomac."

Still more convulsionary changes had come. In the twilight of the battle of May 31 around Fair Oaks Station, Joseph E. Johnston had been twice wounded—once in the right shoulder by a musket ball and, a few moments later, in the chest by a heavy fragment of shell. The next day, G. W. Smith had made fumbling and overcautious efforts to continue the battle and, on June 2, had suffered an illness which he described as paralysis. In action he was one of the most unconcerned of soldiers and while under fire did not even change the pitch of his voice. Consequently no question of his personal courage could be raised by anyone who had seen him battle. Responsibility it was that shattered his nerves, responsibility and, perhaps, the fear that if he failed his reputation was gone.[38]

The commanding general indefinitely on the list of the wounded, if indeed he survived; the commander of the left wing, second in command, broken by excitement and responsibility. It was a grim price to add to the toll of the mismanaged battle. A birthday present of ill omen to the army, men might say it was, but there was another gift: To the command that Johnston laid down, to resume no more, the President on June 1 named General Robert E. Lee.

CHAPTER 7

To Defend Richmond

1. Old Snarls Are Untangled

The loss to the army of Johnston and Gustavus Smith had results far less disconcerting than might have been anticipated. Johnston's admirers among the officers of the "Manassas troops" believed the South had none like him in strategic ability, but the commanders of the Army of the Peninsula and the Department of Norfolk had been with him for so brief a time that he was to them little more than a distinguished name. Smith was scarcely that. After his wounding, moreover, Johnston played a manful and honorable part in maintaining the morale of the corps of officers. When a friend lamented his wounds as a calamity to the South, Johnston instantly objected. Said he: "No, Sir! The shot that struck me down was the best ever fired for the Southern Confederacy, for I possessed in no degree the confidence of this Government, and now a man who does enjoy it will succeed me."[1]

Although a few senior officers somewhat distrusted an "outsider" whose reputation primarily was that of an engineer, they soon began to drop their misgivings. They saw ere long that Lee had a sound knowledge of the army. To one large and useful advantage that Lee enjoyed observant colonels and generals learned in time to give proper valuation: Lee understood the President thoroughly, and he employed his knowledge to remove misunderstandings and to assure cooperation. In one of the first letters he wrote from the field, he told Davis of troubles in D. H. Hill's division and added: "I thought you ought to know it. Our position requires you should know everything & you must excuse my troubling you."[2]

One complaint the army made against Lee: He made white men do Negroes' work—wield picks, throw up parapets, build fortifications. The grumbling army did not understand that the construction of earthworks was part of Lee's preparations for an offensive. He reasoned that if he permitted McClellan to remain in front of Richmond, the superior Federal artillery soon would blast its way into the city. A defensive behind temporary fortifications was necessary until the Confederate army could be disposed and, if possible, reinforced. Then it must assume the offensive.

Vacancies were the first of several immediate problems of command. A. P. Hill's brigade of Longstreet's division had gone into action at Seven Pines under its senior colonel, James L. Kemper. Because of Albert G. Blanchard's resignation, his brigade of Huger's division had been led by Colonel A. R. Wright. If the brigade of Robert Hatton was to remain efficient, a successor to that fallen general must be selected. Until the fate of Johnston Pettigrew was known, temporary provision, at the least, had to be made for the command of his fine North Carolina regiments. On June 2, Lee wrote President Davis of this situation and asked for immediate appointments. In contrast to the delay that so often had attended similar requests from Johnston, came instant action by the President. Kemper and Wright were made brigadiers; Colonel J. J. Archer, a Marylander who had commanded the 5th Texas in Hood's brigade, received promotion and Hatton's brigade. Davis authorized the assignment of Colonel W. Dorsey Pender to the command of Pettigrew's troops with temporary rank as brigadier general. In the cases of Kemper and Pender, their quick advancement was almost equivalent to promotion on the field for valor.

General Huger presented a second problem. Lee doubtless had heard the charges against Huger for failure on May 31 and had not seen any of the evidence that absolved that officer of blame. Not unnaturally, a doubt concerning Huger's diligence was raised in Lee's mind. Twice during the three weeks that followed the commanding general suggested the possibility of transferring Huger to other stations. Soon the impression became general that he was an "old army type" who could not adjust to new conditions—that he was living in the atmosphere of the Pikesville Arsenal, not of the Battle for Richmond.

A third immediate problem of command was presented in the division of D. H. Hill. That officer promptly reported to General Lee his dissatisfaction with two of his brigade commanders—G. J. Rains and W. S. Featherston. This was the most marked display Hill yet had given of his peculiar tendency to run to extremes of opinion. If he admired conduct on the field no compliment was too extravagant; where he distrusted or disapproved, condemnation was complete. Hill's complaint against Rains apparently was his failure to deliver a second flank attack after the assault on Casey's Redout.[3]

The object of Hill's wrath was a North Carolinian, fifty-nine years of age, a graduate of West Point in the class of 1827, and former lieutenant colonel of the 4th Infantry. A man of fine appearance and pronounced patriotism, Gabriel Rains was at heart a scientist, more interested in explo-

sives than in field command. In 1840, while campaigning against the Semi-
nole Indians, he first had experimented with booby-traps. On the retreat
from Yorktown he had planted several of these in the way of the Federals.
Some of his superiors were convinced that these "land torpedoes" were not
"a proper or effective method of war." Rains consequently was forbidden to
use more of them, and a suggestion previously made by Secretary of War
Randolph was adopted. Under orders of June 18, Rains was assigned to
the river defenses, where the use of torpedoes was "clearly admissible." A
time was to come when his "subterra shells" were a welcome adjunct of the
Richmond defenses.[4]

The ground of Hill's grievance against W. S. Featherston does not
appear from the records. Presumably the reason was the frequent absence
from his post of this officer, whose health was not of the best. Featherston
was tall, clean-shaven, and eagle-faced, blunt of manner and careless of dress
but with a reputation for hard drill. In his forty-first year, he was without
formal military education beyond that which he had acquired as a young
volunteer in the Creek War. The course of justice to Featherston and of def-
erence to D. H. Hill seemed to be to transfer Featherston to Longstreet's
division and to give him troops from his own state of Mississippi.

In providing these troops, the old vexing question arose again of brigad-
ing units according to the states from which they came. General Lee's view
of the question was not materially different from that of General Johnston, but his approach was more conciliatory. Within a few days after he
took command, he wrote the chief executive: "I have . . . sent a circular to
Division Commanders to see what can be done about reorganizing
brigades by states. . . . As it is your wish & may be in conformity to the
spirit of the land, I will attempt what can be done. It must necessarily be
slow & will require much time. All new brigades I will endeavor so to
arrange." As this was acceptable to the President, a controversy that had
much vexed Johnston came to an end.[5]

There was too the issue presented by Gustavus W. Smith's division.
What should be done about it? Smith's physical condition showed no
improvement. Months might pass before he could return to the field, if
ever he could. Of his five brigades, only Hood's had at its head a man experienced in all his duties. Hampton was absent, wounded; Pettigrew was a
prisoner of war; Archer had just succeeded Hatton; Whiting had to leave
his brigade in charge of its senior colonel while he acted as divisional commander. Logically the restoration of the morale of these fine troops during
Smith's invalidism seemed a proper assignment for Whiting. The one
weakness thus far disclosed in the brilliant Whiting was his extreme pessimism. This was irritating, if not demoralizing. Whiting did not believe

that Richmond could be held or that the army could maintain itself north of the James, and on this he expatiated. The new commanding general left to time the final decision in Whiting's case. No attempt was made to get Whiting promoted forthwith or to overcome Davis's antagonism to that officer.[6]

Additional general officers, strangers to the army, arrived during the first weeks of Lee's command. Every new brigade raised hopes that the army would become strong enough to assume the offensive. One of General T. H. Holmes's brigades from North Carolina, under John G. Walker, had been brought to Petersburg, whence it soon was moved to Drewry's Bluff. Robert Ransom's brigade from the same department followed. From South Carolina, early in June, came Roswell S. Ripley, who was assigned to D. H. Hill's division.

All three of these men had been professional soldiers. Walker, a Missourian, just forty, had been a captain in the 1st Mounted Rifles; Ransom, a West Pointer of the class of 1850, had been a captain of the 1st Cavalry and was an esteemed young soldier of thirty-two, though cursed with ill health. Roswell S. Ripley, thirty-nine, had been graduated from the Military Academy in 1843. In the Mexican War Ripley had won his brevet as major, and in 1853 he had resigned from the army to enter business. He had resided in Charleston, the home of his wife, and in the operations against Sumter he had displayed skill as an artillerist. His prime defect was his contentiousness. For Lee, during the winter of 1861–62, he had acquired a contemptuous dislike. Doubtless Ripley would persist in backing his judgment against that of all men, but he cheerfully was accepted for the sake of the stout troops he brought to Richmond.

Might not others come as Ripley had? In the face of some muttering from Georgia politicians, who opposed its removal, the large brigade of General A. R. Lawton came to Petersburg. Finally, overflowing freight cars brought northward most of the remaining troops of T. H. Holmes, whose department was extended from Cape Fear River to the James. Holmes was entrusted with supervision of Drewry's Bluff.

As a result of these arrivals and of the transfers and promotions after Seven Pines, the army that defended Richmond had a command perceptibly different from that of the troops who had marched through the mud from Yorktown only six weeks previously. The infantry did not have an adequate corps of officers; but, when regarded as a revolutionary force organized hurriedly, it was remarkably well led. All Confederates had faith in mid-June 1862 that the infantry would triumph. Now, overnight, by an adventure that made every chest swell, the cavalry were to test their leadership and to prove their quality.

2. STUART JUSTIFIES HIS PLUME

The general strategic plan that rapidly was taking form in the mind of Lee contemplated an offensive against that part of McClellan's force north of the Chickahominy River. Little was known of the position of the right wing of the Army of the Potomac. Presumably it had been placed where it was for the twofold purpose of forming a junction with McDowell and of protecting the line of supply from White House on the Pamunkey. How far had the Federal flank been extended? Did it guard the ridge between the Chickahominy and the next stream to the northeast, Totopotomoy Creek? For a most particular reason, known only to a few, General Lee desired these questions answered. A reconnaissance in force was the means of ascertaining the facts—a reconnaissance by cavalry.

On June 10, Brigadier General J. E. B. Stuart, twenty-nine and in command of all the cavalry, was called to army headquarters at the Dabb house, High Meadows, on the Nine Mile Road. Stuart's zest, his vigilance, his skill in reconnaissance had won Johnston's admiration. "He is a rare man," he wrote to Davis of Stuart, "wonderfully endowed by nature with the qualities necessary for an officer of light cavalry. . . . If you add to this army a real brigade of cavalry, you can find no better brigadier-general to command it."[7]

The new brigadier had soon become one of the shining figures at Manassas. All the advanced outposts were placed under him. On December 20, 1861, he had a clash with the Federals at Dranesville, where he lost 194 men, foot and horse. Although he could not then bring himself to admit defeat—it was characteristic of him never to do so—he had distinctly the worse of the encounter.[8] Thereafter his service was routine. He covered well the retreat from Manassas; at Williamsburg he aided in putting troops in position when his own forces were unoccupied; at Seven Pines, where woods immobilized the cavalry, he acted virtually as an aide to Longstreet. In none of these events had he gratified measurably his martial ambition or won the loud plaudits he craved.

Stuart did not lack self-confidence or self-opinion. On the fourth day of Lee's command he felt that he should suggest a strategical plan to the commanding general. The young cavalryman argued that the Federals would not advance until they had perfected their works and armament on the south side of the Chickahominy. The proper course was to hold the Confederate left with a heavy concentration of artillery and to attack south of the stream. The youthful instructor of his chief concluded: "We have an army far better adapted to attack than defense. Let us fight at advantage before we are forced to fight at disadvantage."[9]

The earnestness and naiveté of this offset the defects of the strategy suggested, which essentially was that of throwing a numerically inferior force on a long front against an entrenched foe who had greatly superior artillery. Now, on June 10, Stuart was not summoned to discuss strategy but execution. Quietly he was told by General Lee of the design for an offensive north of the Chickahominy, and of the importance of ascertaining how far the enemy's outposts extended on the ridge. As the purpose of the reconnaissance was revealed, Stuart's imagination took fire: He could do more than ascertain the position of the Federal right; if the commanding general permitted, he would ride entirely around McClellan's army.[10] Lee probably shook his head at so rash a proposal, but Stuart would not dismiss it from mind. In high expectancy he rode back to his headquarters. What luck for a trooper who fifteen months previously had been a captain!

The next day, June 11, a courier handed Stuart his instructions in Lee's autograph. Caution was enjoined: "You will return as soon as the object of your expedition is accomplished, and you must bear constantly in mind, while endeavoring to execute the general purpose of your mission, not to hazard unnecessarily your command. . . . Remember that one of the chief objects of your expedition is to gain intelligence for the guidance of future operations."[11]

Stuart read, pondered, and proceeded at once with his plans. Whom should he choose to go with him? Fitz Lee, the general's nephew, was now colonel of the 1st Virginia cavalry. He must lead his regiment on the expedition, along with four companies of the 4th Virginia. The second son of General Lee, the quiet, handsome, capable "Rooney" Lee, who had just celebrated his twenty-fifth birthday, must take part of his 9th Virginia cavalry with him, and two squadrons of the 4th. Lieutenant Colonel Will Martin, of the Jeff Davis Legion, must pick 250 of the best men of his command and of the South Carolina Boykin Rangers. The Stuart Horse Artillery could supply a 12-pounder howitzer and a rifle gun, under Lieutenant Jim Breathed. That young physician, just twenty-two, had been serving as a private in the 1st Virginia cavalry when Stuart urged him to transfer to the horse artillery and arranged his election as first lieutenant. The grateful young Breathed could be relied upon to requite kindness with valor.[12]

The members of Stuart's staff must go, of course, and with them Heros von Borcke, a Prussian officer on leave who had joined headquarters as a volunteer aide and had shown joyous intrepidity on the field of Seven Pines. John S. Mosby likewise must accompany the expedition. He had volunteered in "Grumble" Jones's company from southwest Virginia, a company that Jones deliberately had garbed in homespun. Named adjutant and at length procuring a uniform, Mosby defied regulations by wearing the red facings of the artillery instead of the buff. Regimental gossip had it that he found the uniform offered cheaply in Richmond and bought it as a bargain. Mosby had good social station and had attended the University of Virginia until arrested and imprisoned for wounding a fellow student. In jail, his prosecutor had taught him some law which, after his release, Mosby practiced in Bristol. In the spring election of officers he had been defeated, but Stuart by that time sensed his daring and initiative and had retained him at headquarters. Yes, there would be use on the expedition for the gaunt, thin-lipped Mosby with his satirical smile, his stooped neck, and his strange, roving eyes.

Another scout who must accompany the expedition was the alert and tireless Redmond Burke, who seemed to have been born for outpost service. Still a third scout was William Downes Farley. This high-born South Carolina boy, a former student of the University of Virginia, was a devotee of Shakespeare and of the early English poets. One of the handsomest young men in the army, with hair a deep brown and eyebrows and lashes so dark they seemed to cast a shadow over his gray eyes, he had a soft voice, a quick smile, and a modest grace. In his veins flowed blood that fairly lusted for adventure. Farley's bold spirit had led him to undertake scouting in the enemy's country. Alone or with a few companions he would spend days in the woods on the flank of Federal columns. When he and Stuart met, an instant attachment was formed. "Farley the Scout," as everyone styled him, was soon a fixture at cavalry headquarters.[13]

These, then, were among the men Stuart selected—Fitz Lee, his cousin Rooney, Will Martin, Jim Breathed, von Borcke, John S. Mosby, Redmond Burke, William Farley—these and the best 1,200 troopers that the cavalry had. Stuart chose them quietly on the eleventh but did not notify them. All the cavalry heard was a vague rumor that something was afoot.[14]

At 2:00 A.M. on June 12, Stuart himself, in the cheeriest of moods, awakened his staff. "Gentlemen, in ten minutes," he announced, "every man must be in the saddle." Quietly and with no sounding of the bugle, the long column presently was in motion. Its route was toward Louisa Court House, as if it were bound for the Valley of Virginia, whence reports had come of a dazzling victory by Jackson. Reinforcement of Stonewall presumably was the mission of the cavalry, though nothing was confided by Stuart.

Along empty roads, past farms where the women waved handkerchiefs or aprons and the old men stared admiringly at the display of so much horseflesh, the troopers rode all day. Twenty-two miles they covered and then they went into camp near Taylorsville, close to the South Anna River. Before day Stuart had a few rockets sent up as signal for the start, but again he permitted no reveille. He had, by that time, reports from his scouts that residents said the enemy was not in any of the country to the southeastward as far as Old Church, twenty miles distant by the shortest road. The moment the column turned toward the east, a stir went down the files: Some had suspected that McClellan's flank was their objective, and now they knew it. The day for which they had waited so long had come at last. They were to measure swords with the enemy.[15]

Stuart ere long left the road and called the field officers in council. Every eye was fixed expectantly on him as he sat with careless rein on his horse. Not more that five feet ten in height, wide of shoulder, and manifestly of great physical strength, he had a broad and lofty forehead and a large, prominent nose with conspicuous nostrils. His face was florid; his thick, curled mustache and his huge wide-spreading beard were a reddish brown. Brilliant and penetrating blue eyes, now calm, now burning, made one forget the homeliness of his other features and his "loud" apparel. The army boasted nothing to excel that conspicuous uniform—a short gray jacket covered with buttons and braid, a gray cavalry cape over his shoulder, a broad hat looped with a gold star and adorned with a plume, high jack boots and gold spurs, an ornate and tasseled yellow sash, gauntlets that climbed almost to his elbows. His weapons were a light French saber and a pistol, which he carried in a black holster. When he gave commands it was in a clear voice that could reach the farthest squadron of a regiment in line. On this particular morning of the thirteenth of June—a Friday at that—his instructions for the next stage of the reconnaissance aroused among his young companions no less enthusiasm than he exhibited.[16]

On moved the column, through the woods and past fields where the young corn was showing itself. When the force came in sight of Hanover Court House, horses and men were observed. The game was flushed, but too late. The "blue birds" took alarm and fled under cover of the dust they raised. Ill luck it was to lose the first covey! Stuart left the highway about a mile below Hanover Court House and, turning south, followed the route via Taliaferro's Mill and Enon Church. As the sun climbed toward noon, heat radiated from every field, but nobody heeded it. Only one thing mattered—to find and to drive the enemy.

Near Haw's Shop anxious eyes caught a glimpse of bluecoats. The Confederates swept forward—again to no purpose. Only a few videttes were surprised and captured. Some of the prisoners stared at Colonel Fitz Lee, then broke into grins of recognition and greeted him as "Lieutenant." They were formerly of the 2nd Cavalry, with which Lee had served as a junior officer. Inquiries were made concerning old friends; familiar jests were revived. It was difficult to believe that the disarmed, laughing troopers and the smiling young colonel represented opposing armies mustered to slaughter each other.[17]

When the van approached Totopotomoy Creek, a difficult little stream with its banks a maze of underbrush, there was every reason to assume that the Federals would contest the crossing. Perhaps the very fact that the bridge had not been destroyed was a reason for suspecting an ambush. Cautiously Stuart dismounted half a squadron and sent these men forward as skirmishers. Once again there was disappointment. The Federals had left the barrier unguarded.[18]

It was now 3:00 P.M. Old Church was distant only two and a half miles. Inasmuch as the Federal cavalry were known to be under Stuart's father-in-law, Brigadier General Philip St. George Cooke, a Virginian and a renowned trooper of the old army, it could not be that he had neglected that important crossroad.

For the first time that day military logic was vindicated. Word came back that the enemy was at a stand. Stuart did not hesitate. With a shout and a roar the leading squadron, that of Captain William Latané, dashed forward and threw itself squarely against the Federals. For a few minutes there was a mad melee, sword against pistol; then the Federals made off. When the clash was over, Captain Latané was dead, pierced by five bullets. A few Federals had been shot or slashed; others were taken prisoner. Five guidons were among the trophies.[19]

Stuart was now fourteen miles from Hanover Court House. He had established the main fact he had been directed to ascertain: There was no Federal force of any consequence on the watershed down which he had ridden. But should he return the way he had come? The enemy would expect him to do so. The Federals might burn the bridge across the Totopotomoy, or they could waylay the Confederates at or near Hanover Court House. Stuart could not strike for the South Anna and swing back to Richmond on a wide arc. The bridge across the river had been burned; the fords were impassably high.[20] So Stuart reasoned. If he turned back, danger and perhaps disaster, he concluded speedily, would be his.

Perhaps he yearned for the more exciting adventure that lay ahead. Nine miles to the southeast was Tunstall's Station on the York River Railroad, McClellan's main line of supply. A great achievement it would be to tear up that railway; how the public would praise that feat! By turning south at Tunstall's and riding eleven miles, Stuart could reach Forge Bridge on the Chickahominy. That crossing, his troopers from the neighborhood told him, had been burned but not beyond quick repair. When the expedition had been planned, Stuart had suggested that the cavalry might ride entirely around the enemy: Why not prove himself correct? It was certain the enemy would not expect him to do what he was contemplating. That was an excellent reason for doing it. Besides, there was a

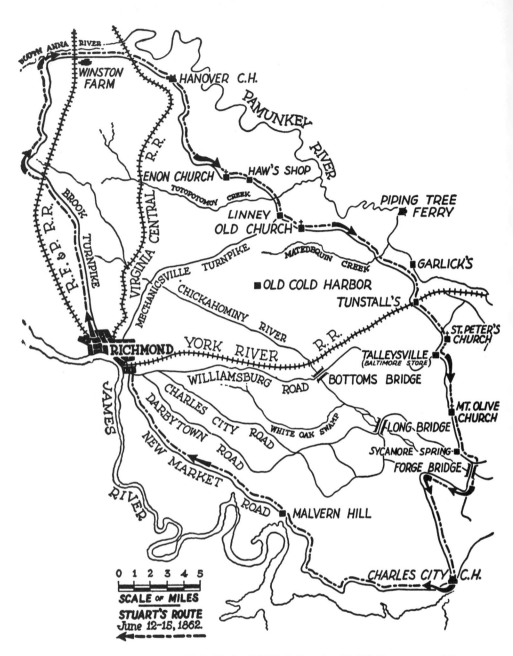

Stuart's "Ride Around McClellan" (Chickahominy Raid), June 12–15, 1862.

chance of striking terror into the heart of "a boastful and insolent foe."²¹ He would do it!

There was not a shadow of misgiving on his face. Nor, when he found that his colonels doubted the wisdom of his choice of routes, was there any hesitation. Ostentatiously he inquired of the farmers around Old Church which road he should take to Hanover Court House, and how far it was. Quietly he picked his guides from soldiers who resided in the country he was to enter.²²

The road to this adventure skirted the Pamunkey River. Southward the country was populous. Great plantations ran down to the meadows and swamps by the streamside. As the column passed, the women, girls, and old men at every house came out to greet the first gray-clad soldiers they had seen in weeks. Now and again there would be a delighted scream of recognition, whereupon some dust-covered boy would break ranks, would leap from his horse and embrace mother or sister.²³

At length the weary horses brought their tired riders to Hopewell Church, whence a road led two miles east to Garlick's Landing. Satisfied that stores were there under scant guard, Stuart detached two squadrons to swoop down on the place, to bring off any horses they might find, and to apply the torch to what could not be moved off. The main column continued on its way. The road now showed evidence of heavy travel and of vast alarm. Overturned wagons and booty of all sorts lay temptingly at hand where it had been left or thrown away by Federals who had been warned that "the rebels" were descending upon them. Perhaps at Tunstall's the enemy might be squarely across the front of the advance.

Soon it was reported that one or two companies of Federal infantry were guarding the station. Swiftly Stuart advanced the head of the column within striking distance and then ordered: "Form platoons! Draw saber! Charge!" Down swept the cavalry at a thunderous gallop. The Federals, too few to resist, scattered almost instantly. Some were captured. Others fled to the woods. Troopers began to tear up the railroad and chop down the telegraph poles nearest the station.

Now there came a shrill whistle from the westward. A train was approaching—did it bring infantry to oppose the raiders? From the boldness of the whistle blast the engineer could not know that Tunstall's was in the hands of the Confederates. Derail the train, then; shoot or capture the troops on it. Such obstructions as the men could find they hurled on the track. The troopers in ranks were hurried into ambush alongside the railway. All this was swift work, and not well done. The train came in sight and began to slow. Then, nervously, one excited trooper in ambush fired his pistol. The engineer heard it, sensed danger, and immediately put on full steam. All along the right of way Southerners' pistols rang out. Will Farley spurred his horse till it caught up with the locomotive, and, at a gallop, shot the engineer. The train continued on its way, fast and faster. A moment more and it was out of range.[24]

Stuart had to make another decision: Should he continue on his way, cross the Chickahominy and make for his own lines, or should he rush down the railroad and attempt to capture the Federal base at White House? A vast prize that was, distant a bare four miles. If it could be destroyed, McClellan would be compelled to retreat. Such a prospect was alluring, but was it not an enticement? Every moment that passed after the arrival of the train at White House would be devoted to preparation for defense. Reinforcements might close the Confederates' line of retreat. Regretfully but decisively, Stuart shut his mind to this highest adventure of all.[25]

A wagon park at the station, filled with grain and coffee, was set afire. While this was being done, the squadrons from Garlick's Landing arrived, reporting the destruction of two schooners and many wagons loaded with fodder. With that the column started at once for the Chickahominy. A bright moon now had risen, one day past the full, and lighted the bad road. The column dragged. Troopers snatched sleep, horses staggered. Midnight came before the exhausted artillery horses hauled the pieces to Talleysville. From that point the distance to Forge Bridge was less than seven miles.[26]

Long as each minute seemed, the night was almost ended. If all went well, the winding, marshy river soon would lie between the Confederates and their pursuers. Lieutenant Jonas Christian, who lived at Sycamore Springs on the bank of the Chickahominy, told Stuart that he knew a blind ford on the plantation that was nearer than Forge Bridge. The columns could slip across there and not waste precious hours rebuilding the burned Forge Bridge span. The moon was just being dimmed by a faint light in the east when Lieutenant Christian turned down the lane at Sycamore Springs. Presently young Christian halted in startled surprise. He was at the ford, but it had a different appearance from the easy crossing he had known all his life. In front of him was a wide, swift, evil-looking stream that extended far beyond its banks. The placid Chickahominy was an angry torrent, the ford perhaps a death trap.

Rooney Lee, the first officer of rank to arrive at Sycamore Springs, stripped quickly and swam into the stream to test it. Strong though he was, he had to battle to escape being drowned or swept downstream. "What do you think of the situation, Colonel?" John Esten Cooke asked when Lee pulled himself ashore. "Well, Captain," replied the half-exhausted swimmer, with all the courtesy of his stock, "I think we are caught."[27]

Stuart rode down to the ford. Carefully he surveyed the stream, then stroked his beard with a peculiar twist that his staff noticed he never employed except when he was anxious. He looked dangerous—just that. Silently he observed as the most experienced swimmers began to cross the river with their horses, but only a few of the men had enough skill in the water to breast so wrathful a stream. Trees were felled in the hope that the men might clamber over them, but they were too short to bridge the swollen stream.[28]

Time was passing. The summer sun was up. Stuart decided that his one hope of escaping was to patch together a crude bridge. He ordered his command to the site of Forge Bridge, a mile below. Here the stream was swift but the channel was narrower than at the Sycamore Springs ford. Stuart entrusted to Redmond Burke, as resourceful as dauntless, the task of building a bridge. From a large abandoned warehouse near at hand came framing timbers to span the river between the abutments of the old bridge. With much effort they were pushed across and then lifted up toward the abutments. Stuart watched all the while, and ere long the dangerous look faded from his face. He began to hum a tune. His eye told him the timbers were long enough, but even he must have held his breath when, with a final "Pull together!" the first long beam was set. It rested safely on both banks, but with few inches to spare.

A shout went up from the men. They could save the guns! Quickly the bridge was floored with siding from the warehouse. Over it, in renewed strength, the men made their way. The rifle and the howitzer lumbered across. Fitz Lee left five men to fire the bridge, and by the time the rear of the column had passed out of sight the flames were crackling. Then—as if to add the perfect dramatic touch to the climax—a little knot of Federal lancers appeared on the north bank and opened fire.[29]

When on the right bank of the Chickahominy at last, Stuart was thirty-five miles from Richmond. He turned over the command to Fitz Lee and hurried on ahead. On the morning of June 15, forty-eight hours from the time he had set out on the expedition, he reported to General Lee. The column moved more slowly and arrived in Richmond on the sixteenth, to receive a conqueror's welcome.

In the eyes of a jubilant city and an applauding South, the glamour of Stuart's exploit was not dimmed by the enemy's incredible slowness and lack of organization in pursuit. General Philip St. George Cooke, whose service Virginia had coveted a year previously, proved himself utterly incapable of grasping his military problem or of acting promptly. The Confederacy rejoiced that Stuart the son-in-law had outwitted Cooke the father-in-law. Stuart's satisfaction was as boyish as his feat had been extraordinary. Whether the raid was well conceived by Lee—whether it put McClellan on guard for the security of his right flank—is a question much disputed. That the whole was flawlessly executed none would dispute. Stuart became the hero of his troopers and one of the idols of the public. What was not less important, the cavalry was shown to be as trustworthy as the infantry.[30]

"That was a tight place at the river, General," John Esten Cooke said to Stuart when it was all over. "If the enemy had come down on us, you would have been compelled to surrender."

"No," answered Stuart, "one other course was left."

"What was that?"

"To die game."[31]

CHAPTER 8

Guarding the Valley

1. GENERAL AND DEACON JACKSON AT ODDS

"Jackson is coming!" Within a few days after Stuart had returned from his ride around McClellan, that was the rumor. "Jackson is coming to reinforce Lee." The possibility was itself enough to raise public hope and to restore to the threatened capital some of the lost confidence of 1861. Magic had become associated with the name of Jackson during the four months since his threatened resignation—magic and the victory that fervent Southerners had argued would follow a daring offensive. In February a few had appraised him as an able soldier, but some of his officers and many of this troops thought him eccentric, if not insane. Ministers and zealous church members had been those, and those only, who held him up as a model. Now, after a dazzling campaign, Stonewall was the new hero of the war.

General Jackson had not lacked resentment of Benjamin's orders for the recall of Loring from Romney, but after he agreed to permit his resignation to be withdrawn he talked no more about the episode. From his headquarters in Winchester he discharged his duties as if there had been no friction with the War Department. Drill and discipline remained his military gospel. He rode and inspected and studied ground, and when every task of the day had been performed he joined his wife, who had come to Winchester to spend the winter. Everything was agreeable. He had a place for her in the home of a minister whose sympathetic, intelligent wife had pleasant patrician friends, with handsome homes and good cooks.[1]

In this company there was little except his old uniform coat and his bronzed face to identify Jackson as the flaming "Stonewall of Manassas." His blue eyes, always direct and penetrating in gaze, seemed to soften; his voice was gentler than ever. He delighted in the company of gentle old ladies and of serious ministers. Spiritual more than martial discourse seemed to delight him. Did he not bear his full share in the exchange of religious experience and in the discussion of theology? He was not reserved of speech, either, or stumbling in expression. If the argument over religion grew complicated, he would "recur to some premise which others had overlooked," and from it proceed "by a short and convincing direction, to his own conclusion." The pleasure he found in domestic life was almost pathetic. Such a man scarcely seemed capable of doing battle. His delight was in the law of the Lord.[2]

So pleasant a life could not last long for the commander of what was, in reality, an outpost town. Of Johnston's prospective withdrawal from Manassas Jackson was kept informed, but he was loath to leave the lower Valley. He wished above all to be free to maneuver. "If," he explained to Johnston, "we cannot be successful in defeating the enemy should he advance, a kind Providence may enable us to inflict a terrible wound and effect a safe retreat in the event of having to fall back."[3] That was to be the basis of Jackson's offensive-defensive strategy.

Unwillingly, on March 11, he left Winchester and started southward. The Federal advance was under Major General Nathaniel P. Banks, and the plan of Jackson was to turn on his pursuer and deliver a swift night attack. When Jackson discovered that a blunder in logistics had sent his columns farther than he had intended that first day, he was furious. For some reason he blamed the mistake on a conference he had called to prepare for the night attack: "That is the last council of war I will ever hold!" And it was.[4]

Falling back to Mount Jackson, forty-two miles south of Winchester, Stonewall established his camps. A different man he was, in some respects, from the church-going deacon of the winter, different in apparent interest but still profoundly religious. His life in Winchester had been a New Testament sermon. In the field he was an Old Testament Joshua. God was love, but He also was Lord of Hosts and, as such, was to be followed. The Sermon on the Mount did not cancel the Book of Judges or of Kings. Soldiers began to call Jackson "Old Blue Light." Those who had read Thomas Carlyle's *Cromwell* came to wonder, perhaps, if Jackson had in him the qualities of "Old Noll."

Jackson lived in simple quarters. His fare was plain. Corn bread, milk, and butter sufficed him. Tobacco he never used. Whiskey he avoided because he thought he might come to like it. When he was attending to business in his tent, he was bolt upright on a stool and kept the toes of his boots directly in front of his legs as if that were a disciplinary exercise of mathematical precision. Sometimes he would talk freely, though never brilliantly, of general topics. Again he would remain almost wholly silent. One of his men wrote of seeing "staff officers ride up . . . and tell him something about the lines, or about something of importance, and he would calmly sit there for a few minutes, then turn his horse and ride slowly away, his staff following, without his uttering a single word." If he walked it was with the long stride of the farmer who seeks to cover ground swiftly. When he rode, his stirrups were short and his seat, though secure, was awkward. In the saddle he held his head high and his chin up, for full vision ahead, though he kept the brim of his weather-beaten cap down over his eyes. Always he wore the same ill-fitting, single-breasted major's uniform coat that had been a jest to his cadets at V.M.I. His deep-blue eyes kept their direct gaze. In height he stood close to six feet and was strong and angular, without any surplus flesh. He was slightly deaf in one ear and for that reason sometimes could not determine the direction of distant artillery fire.[5]

The commanding general was in sharp physical contrast to the next man in the esteem of the Army of the Valley—Colonel Turner Ashby, head of the cavalry. In appearance Ashby was dark, almost swarthy, suggesting the popular conception of an Arab. To romantic Southerners he looked as if he had stepped out of a Waverley novel. With fierce mustachios and a beard that a brigand would have envied, he was of middle height and of a frame not apparently robust, though wiry and of astonishing strength. Away from bugles and battle smoke Turner Ashby's mien was that of a mild, affable, and modest gentleman. Those admirers who always remembered how he looked never recalled anything he said. He spoke best with his sword.[6]

The War Department had authorized Ashby to form a company of artillery and supplied the ordnance for this battery—one long-range English Blakely gun, a smoothbore 12-pounder howitzer, a 3-inch rifle gun. Ashby had no experience in gunnery beyond that acquired in a few brushes with the enemy. Jackson, who by that time had assumed command in the Valley, doubtless knew Ashby's inexperience, but he knew also the quality of the graduates of V.M.I., his own former students, who were to command the battery. "Young men, now that you have your company, what are you going to do with it?" was the question he put them. The three addressed in this manner were Robert Preston Chew, nineteen, captain; Milton Rouse, seventeen, first lieutenant; and James Thomson, eighteen, second lieutenant. These lads had no answer at the moment to give their teacher, but Ashby was preparing one. He proposed that the thirty-three gunners who were to serve in Chew's battery should be mounted instead of being required to plod along afoot or to ride the caissons when they could. Where the cavalry went, the guns were to go. That was the substance of Ashby's proposed tactics, which were to be an all-sufficient answer to Jackson.[7]

General Banks had advanced James Shields's division to Strasburg, halfway between Winchester and Mount Jackson, and Ashby had his troopers where they could report every Federal move. The first test came quickly. On March 21, ten days after the Confederates evacuated Winchester, Ashby found that the Federals were retiring northward from Strasburg. He sent word to Jackson, and with one company of cavalry and Chew's battery started immediately in pursuit. Jackson quickly followed. Some of his troops marched twenty-one miles the next day. The rear regiments covered twenty-seven. Another rapid march, averaging sixteen miles, brought Jackson's column by 2:00 P.M. on Sunday the twenty-third to Kernstown, four miles south of Winchester.[8]

Ashby had important news. He had heard from friendly sources that only four regiments of infantry, with some cavalry and artillery, remained in Winchester. Ashby's information was that the Federal troops visible on open ground to the east of the Valley Pike, when Jackson reached Kernstown, were merely a rear guard.

Jackson probably received this intelligence with more excitement than he showed. For the first time in his career he was about to make his own decision to give battle. Not one of his subordinates did he consult; to none did he give any indication of what he was thinking. He could count a few more than 3,000 infantry, with 27 field guns. Ashby's strength was 290 cavalry and the 3-piece battery. This force seemed ample for the task in hand, which now and always, in Jackson's military code, was to smite the Northern invader and drive him from Virginia. There was one obstacle only: The day was the Lord's. Was not the commandment plain—the Lord had blessed the day and had hallowed it. That was the Law, but the fact was grim: To delay until the Sabbath was past might be a worse sin and one against his own men, because the Philistines might bring up new hosts. If the decision were wrong, might the Lord forgive a humble sinner—but the enemy must be attacked that day, aye, that hour.[9]

As Jackson saw it, his best opening was on his left. Swiftly, sharply, unhesitatingly the orders were issued. Ashby must hold the Valley Pike, with the brigade of Colonel Jesse S. Burks as support and general reserve. The Third Brigade, Colonel Samuel V. Fulkerson, and Jackson's own veterans of the First, under Brigadier General Richard B. Garnett, were to deliver on the left the attack designed to turn the enemy's right.

Jackson gave the order for the advance. Garnett moved up to support Fulkerson. The infantry pushed steadily forward. Batteries came up quickly on call. Ashby held his own. As Jackson fed in his reserves they seemed to assure victory. Then, in the center where the Stonewall Brigade was fighting, the enemy's fire swelled ominously. That of the Confederates diminished. Disheartened men, with empty cartridge boxes, began to slip to the rear. Jackson was startled but not dismayed. His eyes began to glare. He rode toward the front. He met a man with back to the enemy. "Where are you going?" he demanded. The soldier explained that he had fired all his cartridges and did not know where to get more. Jackson's face flamed. He rose in his stirrups. "Then go back and give them the bayonet!" he snapped.[10]

It was too late. Instead of a retiring rear guard the Confederates now faced onrushing regiments. Soon Dick Garnett, though as brave as the bravest, realized that the odds against him were hopeless. Before he could communicate with Jackson he might be overwhelmed. Reluctantly, Garnett ordered a withdrawal. Fulkerson's right was exposed. He, too, had to give ground.

At the sight of his own brigade in retreat Jackson put his horse at a gallop and rode to Garnett. In hoarse, commanding tones he bade the brigadier halt the withdrawal. The men must stand to their work! He was intensely excited but not despairing. Two regiments he still had in reserve. They were supposed to be advancing. With them he would remake his line and hurl back the attack. Where were they? What delayed them? Jackson soon heard the answer: The two regiments were a short distance to the rear. Garnett had told the senior colonel to halt there to cover the retreat.

That settled it! Nothing now could be done except to break off the action and get the little army out of range. But the troops must maintain their ground until every man and every musket that could be retrieved was carried to the rear. "This army stays here until the last wounded man is removed," Jackson said grimly. "Before I will leave them to the enemy I will lose many more men." This was repeated, remembered, elaborated. Thenceforward it was part of the army's creed. Wrote Dick Taylor of Jackson: "In advance, his trains were left far behind. In retreat, he would fight for a wheelbarrow."[11]

The halt that twenty-third of March was made at Newtown, four miles and a half south of Kernstown. The enemy made no immediate attempt at pursuit. In one sense Jackson had a right to be satisfied. The fault was not with his troops or his tactics but with his information and reconnaissance. Ashby had been misled by Winchester friends who themselves had been deceived. Jackson had not faced merely a rear guard. Shields's division of 9,000 men had been near Winchester on the twenty-second and had been led back quietly toward Kernstown. Reconnaissance, which had been hasty and inexperienced, had failed to disclose them. Although Jackson lost 700 men killed, wounded, and missing, he thought that the Federal casualties had been larger. He reasoned that if he had done that well with the odds three to one against him, he could afford to be satisfied with his troops, and with his cavalry and artillery no less than with his infantry.[12]

Tactics apart, there was a large strategical consideration. Jackson possibly reasoned, even at this early stage of the operations, that after so hard a blow Banks would hesitate to withdraw from the Shenandoah Valley and join the army operating against Johnston. Such a withdrawal had been considered probable, because the Confederates assumed McClellan would call to him every available man. If the fight at Kernstown held Banks's troops west of the Blue Ridge, Jackson's satisfaction would be doubled.

The possible effect of the battle and the stout defense against odds did not prevent soreness. Specifically, it did not alter the fact that General Richard Garnett had ordered the Stonewall Brigade to retire from the front of action. Jackson could not forgive that. On April 1 he relieved that general of command, put him under arrest, and drew up charges and specifications for a court-martial. Garnett was charged with neglect of duty under seven specifications.

Besides the determination Jackson thus exhibited for the maintenance of discipline and the precise execution of the letter of orders, something personally rigid was involved: He was resolved that affection for his old brigade should not induce him to spare it. "We had to pay dearly for our reputation," one private wrote years afterward. At the moment, feeling in the Army of the Valley, particularly in the Stonewall Brigade, was that Garnett did not deserve arrest and court-martial. Jackson was unyielding. He never consented to have Garnett again in his army and prepared to testify against him if a court-martial were held.[13]

Of this Jackson was convinced: The battle had been worth waging; his stand concerning Garnett was correct. Regarding one aspect of the contest he was not quite so certain. That was the violation of the Sabbath by fighting that day. The general received a letter from Mrs. Jackson wherein his beloved expressed distress and a measure of spiritual alarm that he had attacked on the Lord's Day. Deacon Jackson of the Presbyterian Church of Lexington had now to square his conduct with that of Major General T. J. Jackson in command of the Valley District. It was the deacon who wrote the apologia: "You appear much concerned at my attacking *on Sunday*. I was greatly concerned, too, but I felt it my duty to do it. . . . So far as I can see, my course was a wise one . . . though very distasteful to my feelings. . . ." Then the general had the deacon come to the point: "Arms is a profession that, if its principles are adhered to for success, requires an officer to do what he fears may be wrong, and yet, according to military experience, must be done, if success is to be attained. . . . Had I fought the battle on Monday instead of Sunday, I fear our cause would have suffered. . . ."[14]

The military argument and the religious were reconciled as well as might be: If a battle had to be fought on the Sabbath, then success was evidence of the favor of the Lord. Less clear but not to be disdained was the implication of the converse—that if a soldier unwisely delayed a Sunday battle and by so doing sustained defeat on Monday, then that was proof that the Lord disapproved poor military judgment.

In that argument the general triumphed over the deacon.

2. THE BUILDING OF A "NEW MODEL" ARMY

Stonewall's thought was centered on making ready his troops for the next move of adversaries who had followed at a discreet distance. The manner in which he went about the recruitment, training, discipline, and organization of his men brought to light some interesting personal characteristics not observed previously by his comrades. Tested also was his aptitude for army administration.

The first man he put in training was himself; his initial lessons were in geography. Jed Hotchkiss, whose skill in topographical engineering had been demonstrated in Robert Garnett's tragic expedition, had reported on March 20 as acting adjutant of the militia regiment from Augusta County. Jackson sent for him on the twenty-sixth. The general said: "I want you to make me a map of the Valley, from Harper's Ferry to Lexington, showing all the points of offence and defence in those places. Mr. Pendleton will give you orders for whatever outfit you want. Good morning, Sir." Thus, in three sentences, began the making of the maps which were to contribute to the sureness, and thereby to the speed and boldness, of all Jackson's future operations in the Valley.[15]

Recruitment was advanced by similarly direct methods. The Conscription Act had created much discontent among the peace-loving residents of the Shenandoah. Numerous Dunkards, who were an offshoot of the Mennonites, murmured much at the performance of military duty. Jackson, in the end, agreed to employ these conscientious objectors as teamsters. Although this arrangement perforce was accepted by the Dunkards, some of the Rockingham militia openly rebelled against conscription and fled to the mountains. Jackson did not hesitate for an hour. He sent four companies of infantry, some cavalry, and two guns after the insurrectionists. One was killed; twenty-four surrendered. A leader of the movement later was captured. That was the end of the insurrection.[16]

During this period the troops of Jackson's command had to elect their officers. In accordance with the rashly unwise re-enlistment acts, troops of any regiment or company could displace any man who had offended the majority. This process was democratic but it was not military. In the Stonewall Brigade it was complicated by the discontent of the colonels over the treatment of Garnett and over the severity of Jackson's attitude toward them. Colonel A. C. Cummings of the 23rd Virginia, who largely had been responsible for the most brilliant achievement of Jackson's brigade at Manassas, refused to stand for election. Cummings made no explanation, but he was supposed to have made up his mind that he would not serve under Jackson. Colonel James W. Allen of the 2nd Virginia was equally bitter toward Jackson, and his resignation was expected. Of those elevated by the suffrage, the most promising was John F. Neff of the 33rd, chosen colonel in succession to Cummings.[17]

Brigade reorganization was at least as serious a matter. To Garnett's place Brigadier General Charles Sidney Winder already had been assigned by Johnston's orders. Confederate service had few generals of a personality more military than this young Marylander, thirty-three years of age, West Point's class of 1850. Winder's thin, waving hair was combed back from a wide and towering forehead. A curling beard seemed to lengthen his sensitive, intelligent face. Restless, alert eyes, deep-set, reflected both daring and ill health. In the field he was flawlessly uniformed and always had the finest of mounts, but he did not create the impression of being a mere dress-parade officer. His reception by his brigade was distinctly cold. Because of their resentment over the arrest of Garnett, the colonels had agreed quietly that they would not call on the new commander. The men were openly hostile. All this suggested that Winder was to have a difficult assignment as head of the First Brigade.[18]

Colonel J. S. Burks, who had commanded the Second Brigade at Kernstown, was absent on an indefinite sick leave. A qualified brigadier was much wanted in his place. Colonel S. V. Fulkerson, who soon would be ripe for promotion, could be continued safely to direct the Third Brigade, formerly under Brigadier General William B. Taliaferro. On April 13, Taliaferro returned by General Johnston's order for assignment, not to the command of Burks's brigade, which might have used him, but of his old brigade, now Fulkerson's, which did not need him. Taliaferro had sided with Loring in that officer's winter squabble with Jackson, and it was surmised immediately that Jackson did not welcome him to the command of one of the Valley brigades.[19] Jackson made protest to the army's adjutant general, but in vain. General Taliaferro remained. Nothing was done in Richmond concerning a general officer for Burks's brigade.

By the middle of April the reorganization and refit of the little Army of the Valley were as far advanced as Jackson could carry them. Difficulties considered, he had been swift, decisive, and efficient in making good the losses and deficiencies of Kernstown. Jackson doubtless felt that the thanks of the Confederate Congress, published April 8, were deserved by his officers and men.[20] As for the congressional praise of himself, he gave the glory to God. His military ambition might be far greater than any of his friends knew—greater than even he realized; but always he purposed to shape it to the will of the Almighty.

The day of April 17 was a historic one. General Banks started up the Valley that day. The Federal commander was not a professional soldier, but in his rise from youthful hard labor in a Massachusetts cotton mill he had shown intelligence and persistence. A man who had been speaker of the House of Representatives and thrice governor of Massachusetts had a reputation he would do his utmost to preserve, and to increase, in campaigning against the former professor of V.M.I. All the theories Jackson had formulated of the Federal plans and all the strategy he had pondered, he now would have to put to the test.

When Johnston had quit the line of the Rapidan for his march to Richmond, he sent instructions to Jackson and also to Major General R. S. Ewell, whom he had left on the Rappahannock with a division counted now at 7,500 infantry and some 500 cavalry. Jackson was known to be facing numerically superior forces which Banks might push up the Valley to Staunton. There he would be close to a main line of supply to Richmond and, at the same time, would be master of the rich Shenandoah. Banks must be held at a distance from Staunton and, if possible, driven out of the Valley. In the event Jackson had to fall back much farther, Ewell was to retire and march to Swift Run Gap. Jackson was to withdraw to the same position. The two forces were then to unite and give battle to Banks's army near the crest of the Blue Ridge.[21]

Between Strasburg on the north and Harrisonburg on the south, a distance of forty-five miles, the Massanutton Mountains divide the Shenandoah Valley in twain. West of the Massanuttons, through a wide, open country, run the North Fork of the Shenandoah and the Valley Turnpike. East of the Massanuttons is the wooded Luray Valley, down which courses the South Fork of the Shenandoah. An inferior road leads northward to Front Royal; thence a road to the west links Front Royal with Strasburg. At the southern end of the Luray Valley, near Conrad's Store, the road from Front Royal swerves westward to Harrisonburg. Thus the Massanuttons are surrounded by a parallelogram of roads. The Massanuttons themselves are crossed only by the road that joins New Market on the Valley Pike with Luray to the east. Unless an army that was operating on the Valley Pike controlled this New Market–Luray road, it had to march north or south.

East of the Massanuttons the terrain is of high strategical interest. The road that leads across the ridge from New Market continues eastward over the Blue Ridge at Thornton's Gap to Sperryville. Another branch of the same road turns to the southeast and traverses the Blue Ridge, via Fisher's

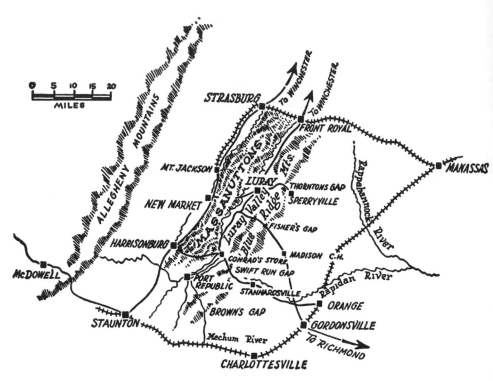

The central Shenandoah Valley in relation to the passes of the Blue Ridge
and the railroads of midland Virginia.

Gap, to Madison Court House. At the southern end of the Luray Valley,
from Conrad's Store, still a third road leads over the Blue Ridge at Swift
Run Gap and passes Stannardsville to the Virginia Central Railroad at
Gordonsville. These gaps were most useful avenues to a force operating in
the Luray Valley so long as that force was free to maneuver; in defense it
could be trapped there.

Still a third strategical value attached to the Luray Valley. If an enemy, on
the west side of the Massanuttons, moved up the Valley Pike, with his line
of communications extending northward past Strasburg, was not the Luray
Valley a perfect covered way for an attack on the rear of such an adversary?
And inasmuch as the Manassas Gap Railroad ran past Front Royal, at the
northern end of the Luray Valley, to take Front Royal was to break the line
of supply of an enemy in the main Valley. Once that line were lost to an
invader, he would be compelled to get his supplies from Winchester by
wagon; if that long and tenuous line were broken, the enemy would be compelled to retreat toward Winchester or westward over the Alleghenies.

These strategic possibilities of the Massanuttons were doubled for Jackson by his posting close to New Market. There he commanded the indispensable road over the mountains to Luray. He could oppose the Federals as they advanced up the Valley toward New Market. Should the pressure be heavy, he could move over the mountains to Luray. If Banks pursued, he either could be met in the Massanuttons or lured into the Blue Ridge. Should Banks decline to pursue and instead press on up the Valley Pike, his rear would be exposed dangerously to troops descending the Luray–New Market road. "I hope," Jackson wrote Ewell, "that Banks will be deterred from advancing much farther toward Staunton by the apprehension of my returning to New Market and thus getting in his rear."[22]

Initiative and its dynamic, which is imagination, are not for long the exclusive possession of one belligerent. What would happen if Banks should realize the importance of the New Market–Luray road, should seize it and then press on toward Staunton? Jackson had considered that question and decided that the vicinity of Swift Run Gap in the Blue Ridge was a desirable point of concentration. Swift Run Gap had much the same strategic relationship to Harrisonburg that Luray had to New Market. By placing his troops at Conrad's Store, just west of the gap, Jackson would be in position to meet any force coming south through Luray Valley. If the Federals moved toward Staunton from Harrisonburg, he would be standing on their flank and could threaten their rear.

Were Conrad's Store and Swift Run Gap a position preferable to Fisher's Gap, seventeen miles farther north? Jackson thought the junction with Ewell should be at one, then the other, then the first. Ewell obediently and uncomplainingly made successive starts and stops, but in bewilderment he began seriously to doubt whether his brother officer over the mountains, who seemed so often to change his mind, was altogether sane.

Each day brought complications justifying the caution which Ewell mistook for vacillation or for aberration. Jackson established himself on April 19 at Conrad's Store; Banks moved slowly but confidently up the Valley to New Market. Alive to the danger of an attack via the Luray–New Market road, Banks dispatched a covering force, which Jackson estimated at 1,000 men, to Luray. He did not seem disposed to adventure farther eastward toward the Blue Ridge. Altogether, he appeared to be checkmating Jackson.

Still further discouragement was presented Jackson by the situation west of Staunton. Brigadier General Edward Johnson held the crest of the Allegheny Mountains with a small contingent and had beaten off one attack with so much success that he had received the *nom de guerre* "Allegheny" Johnson. Rumor had it that now heavy Federal columns under Major General John C. Frémont were marching against Johnson from the west, thereby threatening to descend on Staunton itself and cut Jackson's rail communications with Richmond. There were indications, also, that Banks might attempt to turn Johnson's rear by a movement from Harrisonburg. Jackson sent for Allegheny—"a large and rather rough-looking man on horseback"—and from their discussion concluded that Johnson's small force would be compelled to fall back lest it be caught between one column from the north and another from the mountains. It was altogether probable that Banks could assure the fall of Staunton without material danger of an attack by Jackson and Ewell.[23]

To add to all Jackson's difficulties, part of Ashby's cavalry had become demoralized. One entire company of sixty men had been captured with their mounts. Many men on outpost duty were rendered *hors de combat* because of overindulgence in a favorite regional beverage, applejack; in a skirmish, some had run from charging Federals. Such conditions were contagious and a threat to all future operations. Manifestly, for all his prowess and brilliance in combat, Ashby was neither a disciplinarian nor an army administrator. A long personal meeting with the cavalryman revealed a new aspect of Jackson's character, a contradiction of the prevalent belief among his men that he never yielded. He apparently made the best compromise he could, keeping Ashby in command of the cavalry on that officer's promise to discipline his troopers, though left to dispose them as he saw fit. Jackson's report to General Lee faced the facts with candor: "I became well satisfied that if I persisted in my attempt to increase the efficiency of the cavalry it would produce the contrary effect, as Colonel Ashby's influence, who is very popular with his men, would be thrown against me."[24]

The cavalry commander, who meanwhile had not relaxed his vigilance, reported the enemy advancing. It was apparent Banks was moving his main army from New Market to Harrisonburg. Although still guarding the road across the Massanuttons to New Market, he was reducing force in the Luray Valley.

Either defensive or offensive demanded that the Confederate forces be concentrated. Jackson directed Ewell, on April 28, to bring his men as close as possible to Swift Run Gap. Beyond that, what was practicable? General Lee's injunctions from Richmond conformed wholly to Jackson's inclination to assume the offensive. His flaming desire was to attack Banks, whose sprawling column seemed, in Jackson's words, to present "the golden opportunity for striking a blow."[25] Such was his state of mind that twenty-eighth of April. That night must have been one of prayer and reflection. As he debated the issues, alone at his headquarters, three alternative propositions shaped themselves in his mind:

First, he might go to Allegheny Johnson's relief and assail Frémont's van, under Brigadier General Robert Milroy, which was advancing from the west.

Second, he might go northward down the Luray Valley, attack the Federals there, and, if he beat them, start across the Massanuttons toward New Market—a move that would force Banks to retreat.

Third, he might sweep down the Luray Valley, pass through Thornton's Gap to Sperryville, and so threaten the Federals' long line of communications that Banks would retire.

This last possibility had something to commend it. No great difficulty would be encountered in reaching Thornton's Gap once the small, reduced Federal force around Luray were swept aside. From Sperryville the Confederates could threaten Winchester, by way of Front Royal, or move against the enemy force holding Warrenton. The defects of this course were three: It would not protect Staunton against attack from the west; it would not involve the destruction of a single army of the Federals; and it would not prevent the junction of the Union forces scattered north of the Rappahannock. No aspect of the plan conformed to Jackson's strategy of "concentrating our forces on the enemy in his exposed positions."[26]

The difficulties of the second alternative, attacking the Federals spread out from Luray to New Market, were those of terrain. Jackson would have to cross the South Fork of the Shenandoah and then pass over the Massanuttons, where "the enemy would have decidedly the advantage of position."[27] The risks of such a move might be too great.

By elimination, then, the first alternative, the relief of Johnson, seemed preferable. If the force that threatened Johnson could be overwhelmed, Staunton might be saved. Jackson would have only Banks with whom to deal. Once Johnson was free of pressure he might join the Army of the Valley. Reinforcements by that time might come from General Lee. Banks might be assailed and routed. That done, all the Confederate troops in the Valley could cross the Blue Ridge to Warrenton, to Fredericksburg, or to any other threatened point.

The possibility was exciting; the execution obviously would depend first on the force needed by Johnson to drive the enemy from his front, and second, on the time that would be required for the operation. Banks, of course, would need watching lest he march on Staunton, but could not that be accomplished by bringing Ewell across the Blue Ridge and placing him in the strategic flank position at Conrad's Store? "I have written to General Edward Johnson," Jackson told Lee on April 29. ". . . If I receive an answer justifying a move in that direction I may leave here tomorrow via Port Republic."[28]

That afternoon of the twenty-ninth, in misty weather, Jed Hotchkiss reached headquarters and reported the results of a conference with Allegheny Johnson. The engineer described also the condition of the roads over which he had passed and furnished much topographical information of the sort his sharp eyes always observed. Jackson listened and questioned, but gave no intimation of what he intended to do. From the opening of operations he had kept his own counsel. "I think General Jackson is entirely too close about everything," his quartermaster, John A. Harman, grumbled. Even Ewell had been admonished to keep from people in the neighborhood of Madison Court House any hint of an advance to that point.

On April 30, Jackson gave terse orders and started his columns on the road to Port Republic. Only one man beside himself had any inkling of the plan. That man was Major General Ewell. Briskly that morning Ewell had come through Swift Run Gap and placed his 8,000 men in the camps Jackson evacuated. Ewell himself had scant information. All he knew was that Jackson was setting out for Staunton to aid Johnson, and that he, Ewell, was to hold Banks in check until Jackson returned.[29]

3. DICK EWELL STICKS BY A "CRAZY MAN"

Richard Stoddert Ewell had been forty-four years of age in 1861. After he had resigned his captain's commission in the 1st Dragoons and tendered his service to Virginia, he modestly asserted that in two decades of service in the cavalry he had learned all about commanding fifty dragoons and had forgotten everything else. Actually, he had been a good soldier all his life—had been graduated well at West Point, had been awarded his captain's brevet in Mexico, and in the West had been daring and diligent. Ewell was an excellent cook though a chronic dyspeptic, and, despite a lisp, was voluble. Completely bald and with bulging, bright eyes, he was likened by some to an eagle, by some to a woodcock. When he spoke he put his head to one side, and as likely as not he swore.

His oddities endeared him to officers and men. Once, when his subordinates complained of a shortage of beef, he had affirmed that he could find cattle, had gone off in person, and had returned triumphantly with a solitary, bewildered, and time-battered bull. A moment later Ewell had been crestfallen at the reminder that this venerable animal would not feed 8,000 soldiers. "Ah," he said humbly, "I was thinking of my fifty dragoons!" Ewell's peculiarities had not stood in the way of his rapid promotion. A lieutenant colonel of the Virginia service in April 1861, he was a major general before the end of January 1862. Now he occupied at Conrad's Store, on the flank of Banks's army at Harrisonburg, a position of instant strategic importance.[30]

With Ewell were three brigades of infantry. At the head of one of these was Arnold Elzey, who gallantly had handled Kirby Smith's troops at Manassas after that officer was wounded. Another of Ewell's brigades was under Isaac R. Trimble, a Virginian whose family had moved to Kentucky, from which state he had gone to West Point. Graduated there in 1822, he had served ten years in the artillery and then had resigned to embark on a distinguished career as a railroad construction engineer and superintendent. Fifty-nine when the war began, there were complaints at first that he did not know how to manage or maneuver troops, but he had persisted. During the withdrawal from Manassas he had charge of train movement, which was an assignment that would have overtaxed the ingenuity of any railroad man. He had survived that strain and rejoined his brigade. In the eyes of his fellow officers, Trimble seemed old and perhaps fussy.[31]

Ewell's third brigadier was Richard Taylor, brilliant only son of President Zachary Taylor. Schooled at Harvard and at Yale, widely traveled and even more widely read, Dick Taylor had operated a sugar plantation in Louisiana and had played a gentleman's part in politics. Although he had received no formal military training, he had studied enthusiastically the campaigns of great captains. Elected colonel of the 9th Louisiana, he had been promoted brigadier general in October and assigned five regiments from his state. At thirty-two he was absolutely self-reliant. With a "total irreverence for any man's opinion," as a comrade put it, he had deep affection for those he admired and antipathy no less marked toward those whose conduct he thought unworthy. He believed Ewell as queer as his division commander considered him odd, but the two were the staunchest of friends. When the Confederacy was no more than a memory, Taylor in his published reminiscences—among the most fascinating of military memoirs—was to present pictures of Ewell that Thackeray would not have disowned.[32]

With Taylor, and much chastened by his stern discipline, which was based on a discerning knowledge of them, were the Louisiana Tigers. They had taken all the praise lavished on them for Manassas, and along with it they had taken virtually everything else on which they could lay hands. Again they were under the eye of their daring major. Rob Wheat had survived his wound of July 21, as if to spite the surgeons. For adventures as amazing as any he had known in Mexico or in Italy, he waited in the rain of the dripping camp that Jackson had vacated and Ewell had occupied.

Ewell's instructions from Jackson were of the meagerest: He was to watch Banks and, presumably, was authorized to assail an exposed force if he could do so without great risks; but how was Ewell to determine the risks? He was a stranger to Ashby and had no intelligence system. The first plan that occurred to Ewell was to attack Banks's communications by way of the road from Luray to New Market. Accordingly Ewell wrote Jackson to ask his judgment of such an advance and to inquire how Jackson had ascertained what the enemy was doing. The answer was neither encouraging nor illuminating. Jackson barred the attack as too hazardous. For the rest, he wrote: "I have been relying on spies for my information from the enemy."[33]

This did not have a good effect on Ewell's temper. When rumor reached him, about the same time, that Banks was moving on him, he fairly seethed. Colonel James A. Walker of the 13th Virginia was calling at headquarters when Ewell saw him. "Colonel Walker," he began abruptly, "did it ever occur to you that General Jackson is crazy?" Walker, who had been one of Jackson's cadets, answered, "I don't know, General. We used to call him 'Tom Fool Jackson' at the Virginia Military Institute, but I do not suppose that he is really crazy."

"I tell you, sir," Ewell stormed, "he is as crazy as a March hare. He has gone away, I don't know where, and left me here with instructions to stay until he returns. But Banks's whole army is advancing on me, and I have not the most remote idea where to communicate with General Jackson. I tell you, sir, he is crazy, and I will just march my division away from here. I do not mean to have it cut to pieces at the behest of a crazy man." With that Ewell began furiously to pace the yard.

Glad enough to get away, Colonel Walker rode down to see his own brigade commander, General Arnold Elzey. He too was in a rage, over some order he had received from Ewell. "I tell you, sir," he roared to Walker, "General Ewell is crazy, and I have a serious notion of marching my brigade back to Gordonsville."

At that moment a raw conscript rushed into the room with a paper which he thrust before Elzey: "I want you, sir, to sign that paper at once, and give me my discharge. You have no right to keep me here, and I mean to go home!"

Elzey gasped. He stared at the man, then looked hastily around until his eyes lit on his pistols. With a bound he seized them, though not before the conscript sensed his purpose and sought safety in flight. Elzey tore open the holster as the man ran, and fired two shots while he pursued heavily. Missing his mark, he returned and glared at Walker: "I should like to know, Colonel Walker, what sort of men you keep over at that Thirteenth regiment? The idea of the rascal's demanding of me, a Brigadier-General, to sign a paper. Oh! if I could have only gotten hold of my pistols sooner."

Walker was equal to the occasion: "Well, I don't know what to do myself. I was up to see General Ewell just now, and he said that General Jackson was crazy; I come down to see you, and you say that General Ewell is crazy; and I have not the slightest doubt that my conscript, who ran from you just now, will report it all over camp that General Elzey is crazy; so it seems I have fallen into evil hands, and I reckon the best thing for me to do is to turn the conscripts loose, and march the rest of my regiment back to Richmond."[34]

Elzey's loud laugh ended the incident, but if the tale were told to Ewell he could soon have rejoined with new evidence to support his contention that "General Jackson is crazy." Indeed Ewell might have asserted that the whole military establishment of the Confederacy had gone mad. Conflicting orders rolled in. From Jackson came instructions to prevent Banks from "giving assistance to the forces in front of Johnson"; then to "do anything to call him back" should Banks himself join the Federals moving against Johnson; then to pursue Banks if, as report had it, he withdrew from Harrisonburg to Strasburg. Again, on May 6: "If you will follow Banks down the valley you will soon ascertain whether he designs going to cross the Blue Ridge."[35]

Jackson's orders were confused by proposals that General Lee made from Richmond by telegraph that the enemy's object "may be concentration at Fredericksburg. Try and ascertain. Can you cut off party at Culpeper Court-House?" Ewell pondered once more—to be interrupted by another courier from Jackson: "If the enemy go down the valley beyond the neighborhood of Mount Jackson or New Market you should follow him. . . ." To the exasperated general there came on the ninth and tenth a reiteration of orders from Jackson to watch Banks, and new suggestions from Lee that Banks might be preparing to move to Fredericksburg. Wrathful over these endless changes of plan, Ewell called for Ashby, who on his arrival was greeted with this cheerful assurance: "I've been in hell for three days, been in hell for three days, Colonel Ashby! What's the news from Jackson?"[36]

In a family letter Ewell voiced his complete disgust with the situation: "I have been keeping one eye on Banks, one on Jackson, all the time jogged up from Richmond, until I am sick and worn down. Jackson wants me to watch Banks. At Richmond, they want me everywhere and call me off, when, at the same time, I am compelled to remain until that enthusiastic fanatic comes to some conclusion. . . . The fact is there seems no head here at all, though there is room for one or two. I have a bad headache, what with the bother and folly of things. I never suffered as much with dyspepsia in my life. As an Irishman would say, 'I'm kilt entirely.' "[37]

Either from Ashby, then, or from the absent commander, in a few hours, Ewell learned that Jackson had joined Johnson and, on May 8, had given battle to General Milroy at McDowell, twenty-five miles west of Staunton. The advance had been more spectacular than the engagement.

Jackson had turned off at Port Republic and after one of the muddiest, most difficult marches of the entire war, had crossed the Blue Ridge at Brown's Gap. He reached Mechum River Station on the Virginia Central and moved his little army by train to Staunton. Thence he marched out the Parkersburg Turnpike, joined Johnson, and repulsed a Federal attack. Milroy had retreated after the action, though he sustained only 256 casualties for the 498 he inflicted on the Confederates. Jackson had started in pursuit but had been able to accomplish little. The roads were incredibly bad; his transport was feeble.

During the march and the pursuit, two of Jackson's subordinates were conspicuous. In the opening action Allegheny Johnson was wounded and rendered *hors de combat* for many months. Before the army turned back toward the Valley, Sidney Winder displayed so much enterprise and so clearly established himself as a leader that when he rode onto the field where a service of thanksgiving was to be held, men in all the regiments of the Stonewall Brigade cheered him. From that time there was lessened coldness on the part of officers and men toward Winder.[38]

Conflicting orders continued to arrive, and by May 15, Dick Ewell no longer was willing to swear over the divided counsel and wait for his superior officers to reach agreement. War was insistent. It would not wait on argument. Whatever the consequences to himself personally, Ewell had to disregard the instructions of Lee or of Jackson. The decision had to be made on the realities, not on the personalities. Ewell's latest information was that no enemy remained on the Valley Pike west of the Massanuttons and south of the New Market–Luray road. Sound strategy dictated an advance by Ewell on Luray and the movement to that town of L. O'B. Branch's force from Gordonsville. That was Ewell's decision. Jackson's instructions, not Lee's, must be followed. "On your course," Ewell wrote Jackson, "may depend the fate of Richmond." Such hope as Ewell cherished that day was for the offensive.[39]

Even this hope was dashed for Ewell on May 17 by new dispatches. Lee wrote that Joe Johnston had sent orders to Jackson, and if the two forces in the Valley could attack Banks, "it would make a happy diversion in our favor. . . ." Jackson in his turn ordered Ewell to move on New Market if Banks was not leaving the Valley; if the Federals were crossing the Blue Ridge, Ewell was to threaten them and, if he could, detain them. There followed a hint from Jackson of a plan of attack which Ewell was admonished not to "breathe . . . to any one."[40]

What were the differences the harassed Ewell had now to contrast? Lee favored an offensive subject to such orders as Johnston had sent Jackson; Jackson wanted to hold Banks and to attack him according to a plan that was taking definite form; Johnston was agreeable to this but was insistent that *if* Banks left the Valley, Ewell must follow him. That "if" was no sooner stated than it seemed to be resolved for Ewell in the manner most distasteful to him: News came that 6,000 of Banks's troops, under Shields, already were east of the Blue Ridge.[41] That gave precedence to Johnston's orders; Ewell had no discretion. No course seemed open to him other than to abandon all hope of a joint attack with Jackson on Banks, and to climb over the mountains in pursuit of Shields.

Ewell began preparations to cross Swift Run Gap, but he could not convince himself that the move was wise. What if Shields *had* left the Valley? That would leave Banks less able to beat off an attack. Jackson planned such an attack. Doubtless he was crazy, but the plan was one that might rout Banks. Must that plan of offensive action be abandoned and the forces in the Valley divided?

These questions Ewell debated. He answered them with a sharp order: Bring him his horse. He was going to ride to Jackson's headquarters.

CHAPTER 9

Jackson Launches His Offensive

1. FRONT ROYAL

When Ewell reached Jackson's field headquarters at Mount Solon, ten miles southwest of Harrisonburg, on May 18, he saw Stonewall for the first time in Confederate gray. Jackson had laid aside at Staunton on May 5 his rusty V.M.I. blue and put on the uniform required by army regulations. Not so easily had he met matters of army administration. The efficiency of Allegheny Johnson's command was crippled by the bullet that struck down its leader. Worse by far was a near mutiny in the 27th Virginia of Jackson's old brigade. Several companies asserted that to conscript them after the expiration of their term of enlistment was a breach of faith. With flashing eye Jackson had demanded: "What is this but mutiny?" He gave the men the alternative of accepting service or being shot in their tracks. The mutinous companies had yielded at once. Soon they could not be distinguished "from the rest of the regiment in their soldierly behavior."[1]

Despite such vexations, Jackson had kept his force together, closed all the roads by which Banks might communicate with Frémont, and had marched hard to get within striking distance of Banks. The plan of Jackson's attack was formulated and his ardor fired anew by a letter just received from Lee. "Whatever movement you make against Banks," Lee wrote on May 16, "do it speedily, and if successful drive him back toward the Potomac, and create the impression, as far as practicable, that you design threatening that line." This was more than an elaboration of the plan for an offensive that Jackson had long wished; just the day before he had written Johnston of his design "to try and defeat Banks." This was a suggestion of new strategic possibilities by advancing all the way to the Potomac.[2]

Sorrowfully Ewell laid before Jackson his instructions from Johnston and the report that Shields had moved east of the Blue Ridge. Was it imperative that Ewell conform? Must the whole exciting plan of an offensive against Banks be abandoned? As he reviewed the correspondence with

Lee and with Johnston, the little hope that remained to Jackson dwindled and died. Orders were orders! They must be obeyed—even though they cost the South such an opportunity as war rarely would offer. Earnestly, with his bulging eyes, Ewell stared at his commander and pondered: Although Jackson probably was insane, he was correct in thinking a unique opportunity was being thrown away. At length Ewell broke out with a bold proposal: He belonged to Johnston's army and was subject to Johnston's orders; but so long as he was in the Valley District Jackson was his immediate superior. If Jackson would say the word, he would disregard Johnston's orders and remain in the Valley until Jackson received an answer to the letter he had written Johnston the previous day.

Jackson accepted this gallant offer with eagerness and with gratitude. Regardless of the relative authority of Johnston and Lee, Jackson's May 16 letter from the military adviser to the President was of date three days subsequent to Johnston's of May 13 to Ewell. On this fact Jackson based orders to Ewell which that officer could cite, if necessary, as justification for delay in crossing the Blue Ridge to pursue Shields. Back, then, and in soldierly cheer, Ewell rode to Conrad's Store. This time he did not complain because he had once more to reverse all his preparations and to start troops, not for Stannardsville east of the mountains, but for the strategic position at New Market. Preparation now meant action.[3]

On the nineteenth the columns got in motion. On the twentieth Taylor's brigade, from Ewell's command, reached New Market. Taylor rode off to report to Jackson, whom he never had met. To quote Taylor's delightful narrative: "The mounted officer . . . pointed out a figure perched on the topmost rail of a fence overlooking the road and field, and said it was Jackson. Approaching, I saluted and declared my name and rank, then waited for a response. Before this came I had time to see a pair of cavalry boots covering feet of a gigantic size, a mangy cap with visor drawn low, a heavy, dark beard, and weary eyes—eyes I afterward saw filled with intense but never brilliant light. A low, gentle voice inquired the road and distance marched that day."

"Keezletown road, six and twenty miles," answered Taylor.

"You seem to have no stragglers," Jackson observed.

"Never allow straggling," answered the confident young brigadier.

"You must teach my people," said the senior, without a touch of satire; "they straggle badly."

At that moment one of Taylor's bands struck up a gay air. Jackson, who had no ear for music, listened attentively and took a suck at a lemon he held in his hand: "Thoughtless fellows for serious work," he concluded.[4]

That night Ewell received, like a bolt, a dispatch in which Branch announced that on the road with his brigade to join Ewell he had been recalled by Johnston's order and directed to proceed at once to Hanover Court House, on the Richmond front. Directly from Johnston there was, also, a letter to Ewell. Reflecting conditions existing in the Valley about May 12, the letter stated that Jackson must watch the enemy; Ewell must come east. Superior authority had intervened. All Ewell could do, pending execution of the orders, was to send the letter to Jackson.

Jackson received promptly this new veto on an offensive against Banks. He knew Johnston's information was days old and he felt that the course Lee had urged was the proper one. Every hour was precious. The sole way of procuring permission was to appeal to Lee. Accordingly, Jackson telegraphed Lee: "I am of opinion that an attempt should be made to defeat Banks, but under instructions just received from General Johnston I do not feel at liberty to make an attack. Please answer by telegraph at once." Then he wrote across the bottom of Johnston's letter: "Major General Ewell: Suspend the execution of order for returning to the east until I receive an answer to my telegram." The great opportunity was at its peak. It must not be lost. Shields was separated from Banks; Frémont and Banks had not formed a junction. With Lee's approval—or Johnston's, or the President's—Jackson purposed to throw the whole Confederate force against the weakened Banks and to do even more than "drive him toward the Potomac."[5]

The army that Jackson concentrated while he awaited an answer from Richmond was large enough for the task he was fashioning for it. He had added Johnson's 2,500 to his force—part under the competent direction of Arnold Elzey, the others under Colonel W. C. Scott of the 44th Virginia. Both these brigades Jackson attached to Ewell's division and thereby raised its effective strength to 10,000 muskets. Ewell's cavalry, about 500 sabers, temporarily were under Colonel Thomas S. Flournoy; but they were entrusted, ere the fighting ended, to Brigadier General George H. Steuart, a Marylander and formerly a captain of the 1st United States Cavalry. To distinguish him from the more renowned Jeb Stuart, the army always styled him "Maryland Steuart." With Ewell's two cavalry regiments to support Ashby, and Ewell's 10,000 infantry to cooperate with his own 6,000 men, Jackson was ready to set a swift pace in the offensive that hung on word from Richmond.

He had been training his men for the road. By circular he summarized regulations for the march. No soldier was to leave ranks without permission. Fifty minutes of the hour they were to march, no more, no less; after ten minutes' rest they were to start again. At midday they were to have an hour for lunch. "Brigade commanders will see that the foregoing rules are strictly adhered to. . . ."

These were to prove historic orders, not so much in any novelty of terms as in the unrelenting vigor of enforcement. When Jackson's voice no more was to say, "Close up, men, close up; push on, push on," a subordinate who had marched many days after him was to describe, half in admiration and half in awe, how Jackson had performed incredible marches: "He had no sympathy with human infirmity. He was a one-idea'd man. He looked upon broken-down men and stragglers as the same thing. He classed all who were weak and weary, who fainted by the wayside, as men wanting in patriotism. If a man's face was white as cotton and his pulse so low that you could not feel it, he merely looked upon him impatiently as an inefficient soldier and rode off, out of patience. He was the true type of all great soldiers. The successful warrior of the world, he did not value human life where he had an object to accomplish. He could order men to their death as a matter of course."[6]

There were two additions to the staff. As chief of his artillery Jackson named Colonel Stapleton Crutchfield, a young graduate of Virginia Military Institute. Crutchfield's ability was known to be high. The fact that he was entirely unfamiliar with Ewell's guns and gunners does not seem to have been regarded as of importance. The new assistant adjutant general, with rank as major, was Rev. Dr. Robert Lewis Dabney, forty-two years of age, a distinguished Presbyterian divine, a man of powerful intellect, and a professor in Union Theological Seminary, Hampden Sydney, Virginia.

Somewhat reluctantly, Dabney had joined Jackson's staff in mid-April, but he had scant liking for martial appearances. For a time he had worn his long black Prince Albert coat and his beaver hat. In preference to a sword he carried an umbrella. Thus armed and apparelled, the reverend chief of staff followed Jackson. One day, as general and staff were on the march in the rain, the sight of the major under his umbrella had provoked jeers and cheers and sarcasms: "Come out from under that umbrella! . . . Come out! I know you're under there, I see your feet a-shaking. . . . 'Fraid you're going to get your beegum spoiled?" The banter had aroused Jackson from his meditation, and he had turned off the road and trotted with his cavalcade through a nearby wood. He doubtless did this to get Dr. Dabney away from the column of mocking men, but had he desired to mar that gentleman's clerical garb he could not have found an easier way. The umbrella was a skeleton, the beaver hat a wreck. Major Dabney had to borrow a cap, and, later, buy a uniform.[7]

The day after Jackson telegraphed Lee, authorization was received from Richmond for him to retain Ewell's troops and to use them with his own against Banks.[8] Not a word of this did Jackson confide to anyone. With Taylor's brigade in front, the column would head north, he said. That was all.

The army began early on the morning of May 21 to move down the Valley Pike. Jackson rode with Taylor in the van. They had not proceeded far when he quietly turned the head of the column to the right at New Market and began to climb toward Massanutton Gap. As troops and teams toiled up the winding road to the crest and then began the descent to the South Fork of the Shenandoah, Jackson spoke scarcely at all. Toward evening the army crossed the river and headed north. When at length the troops halted, Ewell and his division were found near by. While Jackson's command and Taylor's brigade had been moving over Massanutton, Ewell had marched from Conrad's Store down the Luray Valley. For the first time Jackson now had every regiment of his infantry and all his guns with him. His officers realized what he never would have told them: Either he was going east of the Blue Ridge, or else he was moving against Front Royal, where the railroad from Manassas comes through the gap there and the two forks of the Shenandoah form their junction.

The alternatives soon were resolved by the march on the twenty-second. Front Royal was the manifest objective, and anyone who knew the country could see the three advantages Jackson's strategy offered. First, when he entered the Luray Valley and commanded the passes to the east, Jackson was between Banks and eastern Virginia, whither Lee suspected that Banks might move. Second, east of the Massanuttons Jackson was in a great covered way, secure from observation by the enemy and in position to move secretly on Front Royal. Finally, if Jackson could sweep aside the small force his scouts and spies told him was in the village, he could cut Banks's communications and probably compel his adversary to leave his fortifications at Strasburg. The rest, in Jackson's eyes, depended on God, and on his own soldiers' legs and bayonets.

In the sunshine of a fine, warm day, the army on the twenty-second continued its march down the Luray Valley. Taylor's fast-moving Louisianians set the pace. The remainder of Ewell's division followed. Then came Jackson's own men. No remembered incident marred the steady advance. Often under the shadow of the enclosing mountains, the column moved on in strict compliance with Jackson's new orders of march. Nightfall found the advance of the army within ten miles of Front Royal.[9]

The next day would bring battle. Carefully Jackson planned the details. Front Royal was as indefensible as Harper's Ferry. High ground looked down upon it from every side. The problem was not to take it, but to do so with such speed that the garrison could not escape or even send a warning to Banks. Jackson's solution to the problem was, first, to divert the attacking force from the main road to one that approached Front Royal from the shoulder of the mountain east of the South Fork and directly south of the town. There was such a road with the odd name of Gooney Manor. Second, to isolate the objective, Jackson reasoned that he need do no more than cut the telegraph line and seize the railway. The cavalry could accomplish that, closing the avenue of escape eastward. Then the enemy must surrender or retreat directly northward toward Winchester.

Six months later Jackson would have smiled in his half-apologetic way for taking so seriously the operation against Front Royal; but in the spring of 1862 he still was comparatively inexperienced in planning. He had fought two battles only. One of these, Kernstown, had not been a success. The other, McDowell, had been more Johnson's fight than his. It was prudent always to be exact in military arrangements. Besides, in this instance, full success at Front Royal would open the way to greater things.

On the morning of May 23, when Ashby arrived with his cavalry to reinforce the two regiments under Flournoy, Jackson issued these simple orders: The cavalry was to cross the South Fork and make for the Manassas Gap Railroad to cut the telegraph line and prevent a retreat from Front

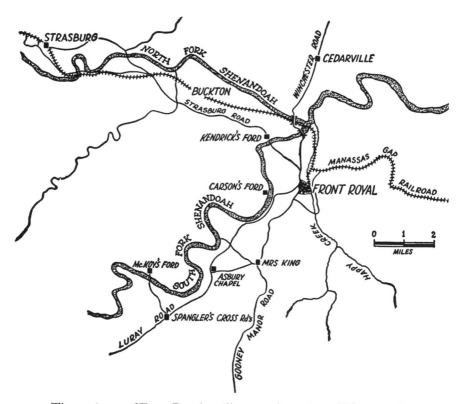

The environs of Front Royal, to illustrate the action of May 23, 1862.

Royal along the railroad or the dispatch of reinforcements from Strasburg. The infantry, with Ewell's fresh division in front, was to turn to the right to the Gooney Manor Road and move on Front Royal from the south. The enemy was to be driven and pursued. That was all: Let the march begin.

The 1st Maryland regiment of Steuart, followed by Taylor's brigade, had the lead. After the troops turned toward the Gooney Manor Road progress was slow because of a climb of 500 feet. The road itself was a succession of grades, and mire from the recent rains was deep. Jackson was alert and eager but composed. His battle blood had not risen.

Riding up to the advance, he saw the Louisiana Brigade moving at the double-quick. What had happened? Quickly he was told that a woman spy—Belle Boyd—had come out of the woods and reported the position of the enemy with so much clarity that the ambitious Taylor had determined to rush forward at once.

Jackson immediately took direction of the advance. The 1st Maryland and Rob Wheat's Tigers were diverted to the right, so that they could sweep down on the streets of Front Royal from the east. The remainder of the brigade would press forward when the attack from the east cleared the way. Everything went according to plan, to the indescribable surprise and joy of the natives of Front Royal. One girl wrote in her diary: "I could not believe our deliverers had really come, but seeing was believing and I could only sink on my knees with my face in my hands and sob for joy. Presently some one called out, 'Only see! The Yankees run!' Leaning out the back window we saw them, contrabands and Yankees together, tearing wildly by."[10]

Quickly the Marylanders and the Tigers cleared the town, but they soon discovered that the Federals were making a stand on a good position north of Front Royal, on the east side of the Winchester Road. There the Union artillery opened gallantly. Stapleton Crutchfield, Jackson's new chief of artillery, instantly ordered up Ewell's guns—only to find that the nearest battery was armed with 6-pounder smoothbores and 12-pounder howitzers, which were quite outranged. In the whole of Ewell's division, it developed, there were only three rifled guns. The infantry had, in consequence, to retain the initiative. The movement was developed steadily. After much effort Ewell's rifles were brought into action. By this time, too, Confederate horsemen were galloping over the fields on the west side of the South Fork opposite the town.

For a moment it looked as if the cavalry might reach the Pike Bridge across the North Fork and cut off the enemy's line of retreat. The Federals sensed their danger. Quickly the Union guns were limbered up and dashed through dust and smoke across the bridge over the South Fork. The Confederates started in pursuit. Jackson dashed up, his eyes ablaze now. He galloped over the South Fork bridge and toward the Pike Bridge, but on commanding ground he drew up and gazed ahead: It was too late! In plain view, the blue column was across and climbing up the road that led toward Winchester. "Oh," cried Jackson, "what an opportunity for artillery. Oh, that my guns were here! . . . Order up every rifled gun and every brigade in the army." [11]

Meantime, smoke was rising from the bridge. Jackson, dim but commanding amid the smoke, fought this new enemy. At length the flames were extinguished, but not until part of the bridge had been so damaged that passage of horsemen was hazardous. Jackson would not be balked. Colonel Flournoy was at hand with his cavalry. He must cross; he must throw himself against the Federals ere they could rally. By keeping in single file, four companies of cavalry contrived to get across the North Fork on the half-burned planks. Flournoy shouted the command, the bugle rang out, the troopers pressed up the ridge and out of sight. Jackson, too, disappeared.

Later in the afternoon cavalryman George Baxter, hurrying to catch up with Flournoy's van, shouted in annoyance at two horsemen riding ahead to get out of the way of his men. The younger of the two riders turned and motioned toward his companion. "This is General Jackson," he said. In confusion, Baxter could think of nothing better to do than to order three cheers for the general; but Jackson wheeled about for more important business. The little column was nearing Cedarville, two and a half miles north of the Pike Bridge, and the enemy had made a stand.

In a few brisk words Jackson gave his orders. Again the bugle sounded—this time the thrilling notes of the charge. The Federals gave their assailants a volley, then broke and escaped to an orchard where some of them rallied. Again Jackson ordered the charge; again Flournoy's men dashed straight at the infantry and the guns. This time the rout was complete. When the 1st Maryland Confederate infantry arrived in support of the cavalry, it had the pleasure of rounding up the Union 1st Maryland. [12]

Jackson, overjoyed, climbed to the rare state of mind in which he employed a superlative. Never, he told his staff officers, had he seen such a charge of cavalry. Jackson was satisfied. It developed that the Federals at Front Royal had numbered 1,063, of which 904 were killed, wounded, or missing. Opulent supplies had been captured; two guns, the Union wagon train, and two locomotives were in Jackson's hands. The price he paid for all this was less than 50 casualties. Gain was great, loss was small, but the reckoning was not final. That night, by Taylor's campfire, Jackson sat long and silently. His eyes were on the flames. "I took up the idea," said Taylor, "that he was inwardly praying." Perhaps Jackson was. He certainly was planning. [13]

2. CEDARVILLE TO WINCHESTER—A DREADFUL NIGHT

Until he knew the realities, Jackson had to weigh the probabilities. What was the Federal commander most apt to do? With rail communications severed at Front Royal, Banks could not remain at Strasburg longer than his supplies sufficed. Jackson's problem, then, as he shaped it in the flames of Taylor's campfire, was this: How could he dispose his troops in such a manner that he could (1) attack Strasburg if Banks stayed there; (2) thwart an attempt by Banks to slip past the rear and pass over the Blue Ridge; (3) strike in force any Federal column moving on Winchester; and (4) advance his own troops to that town swiftly? The immediate essential was to watch both lines of possible retreat and, whether Banks retreated or not, to be in position to attack him at once.

The roads offered an opportunity of doing this. From Strasburg the Valley Pike ran slightly east of north to Winchester. From Front Royal the road on which Jackson was advancing stretched almost due north to Winchester. Between these converging highways a crossroad ran from Cedarville seven miles to Middletown, which was five miles north of Strasburg. If the cavalry and part of the army were sent the next morning from Cedarville to Middletown, they might be able to strike a Federal column in motion along the Valley Pike toward Winchester. Meantime the rest of the army could start the advance from Cedarville directly on Winchester. If Banks stayed at Strasburg, the Confederate column from Front Royal could take Winchester. Should Banks decide to strike eastward from Strasburg to Front Royal, then either of the two Confederate columns could be recalled to attack him in rear.[14]

So Jackson reasoned. Before daybreak on the twenty-fourth he conferred with Ewell and explained the details of their cooperation. To make certain every saber would count, Jackson decided he would place Ewell's two cavalry regiments under Maryland Steuart. Steuart was directed to strike for Newtown, four miles north of Middletown, on the Valley Pike. Ashby's cavalry, with Chew's battery and the fine Parrott-gun section of the Rockbridge Artillery, was to start for Middletown, supported by Taylor's fast-moving brigade. Ewell, with Trimble's brigade, the 1st Maryland, and two batteries, was to advance on Winchester by the Front Royal road. The rest of the army, as it came up, was to march in Taylor's rear for the Valley Pike.

Jackson had not proceeded far with the Middletown column before a courier brought word from Maryland Steuart that all circumstances indicated Banks was preparing to leave Strasburg. Good news that! In whatever direction Banks was moving, it was far better to hit him on the march than in his works at Strasburg. The Confederate column continued on its way. If Jackson spoke at all, it was to give the command that soon was to epitomize his generalship in the minds of his soldiers: "Press on, men; press on!" Ere long there was a series of brushes with Federal cavalry— brief halts, exchanges of fire. It was not a rapid march but it was steady. At length the van came in sight of Middletown—in startled sight. Over the village and as far as vision reached to north and to south was a dust cloud raised by the hurrying feet and horses' hoofs of Banks's army. Jackson had reasoned soundly; the enemy was in full retreat down the Valley.[15]

The artillery was directed to rising ground. Rob Wheat's Tigers formed behind one of the rough stone walls in which the country abounded. Ashby hurried off cavalry to the right. A sharp order, the bark of the guns, and in a few minutes the Federal wagon train was in chaos. A considerable force of Federal cavalry was seen to the south. Crutchfield advanced his guns within canister range, opened furiously, and scattered the bluecoats in panic. When the artillery could no longer see a target, in rushed the Tigers.

Banks's column was pierced! His march was interrupted. "Good, good," Jackson might have said. What next? All that was clear at the moment, amid the slaughter and confusion, was that wagons were disappearing northward as fast as frantic drivers could force their teams down the Valley Pike. They must be captured; was not Jackson the "wagon hunter"? Ashby dashed away. Jackson and his staff sought out the residents of the bewildered village. Since early morning, they said, wagons and infantry had been pouring down the highway. Jackson's conclusion was clear: Most of the Federal column was probably between Middletown and Winchester, not between Middletown and Strasburg.

It was now 4 o'clock. The distance to Winchester was thirteen miles. For Banks's army with all its trains to reach the hills that protected the town, seven or eight hours would be required. Jackson's old brigade, under the vigilant eye of Winder, was placed in advance. Jackson, riding ahead, was as taciturn as ever, but inwardly he was confident and exultant. "From the attack at Front Royal up to the present moment," he said later, "every opposition had been borne down, and there was reason to believe, if Banks reached Winchester, it would be without a train, if not without an army."[16]

As Jackson approached Newtown, four miles north of Middletown and nine miles south of Winchester, the sound of a minor artillery duel was heard. He found Colonel Crutchfield, chief of artillery, with Poague's battery and in flaming rage. He had no troops and no cavalry to serve as support. Instead, the Tigers and Ashby's cavalry were plundering Federal wagons. Jackson was outraged at the looting and still more at the delay in the pursuit, but as he was far ahead of his infantry and the other batteries there was nothing he could do until the Federal guns were silenced by Poague or were withdrawn. It was nearly night when the Federal battery ceased its fire. Jackson ordered the pursuit resumed. He believed that Banks would seek to rally on the hills southwest of Winchester, and regardless of hunger and weariness he determined to press on through the night in order to wrest that dominating position from the Federals before they could get a firm grip on it.[7]

A hideous march it proved to be. At least one veteran would pronounce it the worst he experienced during the entire war. Past Newtown the head of the column ran into an ambuscade. Again at Bartonsville and still again at Kernstown they were delayed by skillful resistance. The tactics of this night fighting Jackson left to Sidney Winder, who handled his men with a skill that accorded with his rising reputation. Down almost every stone wall, now, a line of disputing fire would dance through the darkness. Then the Federals would stumble away to the next field. Agonizingly for men and mounts benumbed, the persecuting minutes dragged out.

About 1 o'clock Colonel Fulkerson came up to Jackson. "General," he said, "if I may be permitted to make a suggestion, I think the troops had better be rested for an hour or so. . . . Unless they are rested, I shall be able to present but a thin line tomorrow." Jackson reflected and then answered steadily: "Colonel, I yield to no man in sympathy for the gallant men under my command; but I am obliged to sweat them tonight, that I may save their blood tomorrow. The line of hills southwest of Winchester must not be occupied by the enemy's artillery. My own must be there and in position by daylight. You shall, however, have two hours' rest."

The column halted. Thousands slumped in their tracks and fell asleep on the road.[18]

3. A Victory Ends at a Manse

Jackson kept watch and, at 4 o'clock on the morning of May 25, passed word down the column for the men to be aroused and started toward Winchester. He had sent Stapleton Crutchfield across country to the Front Royal–Winchester road, and had every reason to believe Ewell would be on his right when he formed for battle. Brief instructions Jackson gave Ashby, who disappeared quickly to the left. The weather was favorable. If the column were closed and the cavalry at hand, there was promise of victory that Sabbath morning.[19]

The Federals might have been pushed so hard that they had not halted on the high ridge which shielded Winchester on the south and southwest.

Beyond that elevation there was a second, but it was commanded in part by the heights nearer the Confederates. Soon a report came back from the companies in advance that the Federals had a skirmish line, but apparently no more, on the nearer ridge. Soon Jackson saw for himself the shadowy figures against the high horizon. The sight must have revived him. Although he had not slept for twenty-four hours, he was lithe with energy.

Winder, dapper and alert, arrived and asked for orders. Jackson gave them in five words—"You must occupy that hill." Winder touched his horse and was off. Jackson rode back to Carpenter's battery and pointed out a position which he told the captain to take as soon as the infantry had cleared the ridge. Already the skirmishers were quarreling in front. From the right, also, there was the sound of fire, a welcome indication that Ewell was in position.[20]

Jackson did not have to wait long. The moment the 2nd and 27th Virginia began to mount the ridge he rode after them. By the time the Federal skirmishers had withdrawn in the face of the advancing line, Jackson was on the crest. Bullets screamed past him from a Union line 400 yards in front, on the ridge near the town. Federal artillery was plastering the position. Jackson paid no heed to the fire. At Jackson's side Colonel John A. Campbell received an ugly wound. Colonel Andrew J. Grigsby of the 27th had the sleeve of his coat cut by a bullet. The general seemed to wear magic armor. Not a bullet touched him or his garments.

Poague's two Parrott guns unlimbered squarely on the crest to challenge the Federal batteries in their front. Carpenter's battery came up. Federal infantry took shelter behind a stone wall to the left and directed a vigorous fire against the Confederate gunners, but the iron hail from the artillery was bringing down more men. Jackson would not endure this. War meant killing, but not of his own men needlessly. He wheeled his horse and went back down the hill. Three things must be done at once: Additional guns must be placed on the ridge to silence the Federal guns; second, ample infantry supports must be at hand; third, the Confederate left must be extended to drive off the infantry and guns enfilading Poague.[21]

To the first of these movements the vigilant Winder already was attending, with Cutshaw's and the rest of Poague's battery, and of the third he spoke to Jackson: The enemy must be attacked from the left. "Very well," answered Jackson, "I will send you up Taylor." His watch gave the time as a little after 6 o'clock. An early fight was at a difficult stage. Poague's battery was being overwhelmed. Carpenter was getting all he could stand. The infantry west of the Valley Pike was idle, unable to advance over the crest of the ridge. On the right, Ewell had opened at 5:40 but, as yet, seemed to be making no progress. If victory was to be won quickly, Taylor must get beyond the enemy's right and turn it. Jackson spurred toward Taylor's oncoming brigade. They had been told not to cheer, but as he rushed by, the battle light flaming in his eyes, they took off their hats. He removed his cap in acknowledgment, but not a word did he say. To Taylor one gesture and one sentence covered orders. Jackson pointed to the ridge on the left: "You must carry it."[22]

He rode with Taylor under a fire that now was quickening. It was in vain that Taylor insisted the commanding general of the army should not expose himself. Jackson paid no heed whatever. As some men fell, the Louisianians began to duck. "What the hell are you dodging for?" Taylor yelled. "If there is any more of it, you will be halted under this fire for an hour!" Taylor remembered afterward that a look of "reproachful surprise" came over Jackson's face. "He placed his hand on my shoulder, said in a gentle voice, 'I am afraid you are a wicked fellow,' turned, and rode back to the pike."[23]

Everywhere as he spurred on Jackson directed all the regiments to be ready to charge when Taylor advanced. Apparently he did not attempt to send word to Ewell to share in this movement, but that officer was maneu-

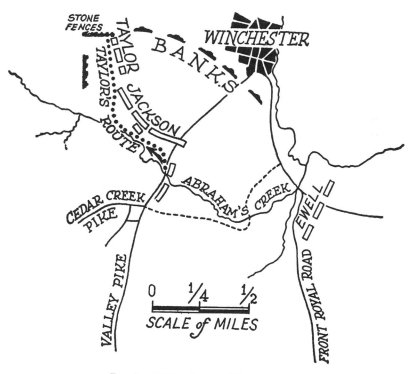

Battle of Winchester, May 25, 1862.

vering. He had taken a line of advance suggested by General Trimble and was moving around to the Federal left precisely as Taylor was to the right. The outlook was brightening. In half an hour, at most, Taylor would charge. Then the test would come! To be ready for it, Jackson headed his horse back up the hill where he had been when the Federal artillery opened. This time he did not mount the crest but stopped where he could peer over the brow of the hill.

The Louisiana Tigers under the daring Rob Wheat slipped around to a point almost directly opposite where the Federals had been firing on Poague. The regiments of the Louisiana Brigade formed in a long line to the south of Wheat. Then, about 7:30 o'clock, there was staged such a spectacle as the Army of the Valley never had witnessed before: "The enemy poured grape and musketry into Taylor's line as soon as it came in sight. General Taylor rode in front of his brigade, drawn sword in hand, turning in his saddle to see that his line was up. They marched up the hill in perfect order, not firing a shot! About halfway to the Yankees Taylor, in a loud and commanding voice . . . , gave the order: 'Charge!'" Jackson could restrain himself no longer. "Forward, after the enemy!" he cried, and bounded in full pursuit over the crest of the hill.[24]

The whole Confederate army seemed now to be pouring over the ridge and into the streets of Winchester—Ewell from the right and, from the center, the First and Second brigades of Jackson. Taylor's men were in front of them all. Jackson was among them. "Order forward the whole line," he shouted, "the battle's won"; and soon, as Taylor's men swept on, he cried, "Very good! Now let's holler!" His cap was off and in his hand; he cheered as wildly as any private. When an officer remonstrated with him, he disdained answer and commanded: "Go back and tell the whole army to press forward to the Potomac!"

Near the outskirts of the town he met Taylor. Without a word he reached over from his saddle, silently wrung the younger officer's hand, and hurried on. He found that the enemy had kept good formation for the first few hundred yards of withdrawal, but in the streets of the rejoicing city the Union columns had been broken and the regiments confused. As the Federal units crowded the approaches to the northern roads the rout had begun. When Jackson and his shouting infantry reached the open country, before them to the horizon the enemy seemed to be spread in hopeless disorder.

It was futile for Jackson to attempt swift, organized pursuit with his scattered infantry; but the situation was the traditional one for cavalry to sweep forward with pistol and saber. Jackson looked about for his squadrons. None was in sight. Ashby had gone off to the left, beyond Taylor's flank, and nothing had been seen of him after that time. Maryland Steuart had the 2nd and 6th Virginia cavalry on Ewell's right—where was Steuart now? "Never," cried Jackson as he looked vainly about him, "was there such a chance for cavalry! Oh, that my cavalry were in place!" If the troopers were not at hand, it was suggested to Jackson, advance the artillery and have the infantry follow in support. "Yes," said the general tersely, "go back and order up the nearest batteries you find!"[25]

Soon the artillery was advanced to the front, though it was plain the exhausted horses scarcely could drag the guns. Behind them staggered some of the infantry, like sick men fired to strength by some wild delirium. Jackson seemed oblivious to their plight. "Order every battery and every brigade forward to the Potomac," he cried hoarsely, and himself spurred on. It did not matter that the Potomac at Williamsport was full thirty-six miles from Winchester, and at Harper's Ferry twenty-five. The enemy was routed and must be pursued. He sent Lieutenant Sandie Pendleton back to find Maryland Steuart and order him instantly to the front. Meantime, the infantry and the artillery must keep on! They did their utmost, but men and horses were failing fast. By the time the foremost battery reached Stephenson's Depot, five miles north of Winchester, the guns were without infantry support. Reluctantly Jackson had to call a halt.[26]

An hour later Steuart came thundering up with his two regiments and went after the vanished foe. The reason for Steuart's delay, Sandie Pendleton reported indignantly, was that the cavalryman showed himself a stickler: He was under Ewell; orders to him must come through the division commander; regulations were regulations, channels were channels. Pendleton had to ride two miles farther to the headquarters of Ewell, who "seemed surprised that General Steuart had not gone immediately on receipt of the order."

Once in pursuit Steuart pressed vigorously, but the two hours that had been lost in bringing him up had sufficed for the enemy to get beyond the range of effective pursuit. Ashby was powerless to follow the Federals. When asked by Jackson why he had not reached the front sooner, Ashby explained that he had swept around to the right to cut off the Federals who moved in that direction. Jackson was not satisfied with Steuart's performance or Ashby's explanation, but there was nothing he could do. The battle was over. He gave his exhausted troops such rest as they could find, and himself rode back to Winchester. He rewarded himself with the luxury of a visit to the manse where Mrs. Jackson had spent the winter. On Monday, in gratitude for a victory on the Sabbath, he directed that religious services be held for the entire army.[27]

That day Steuart found that the enemy had evacuated Martinsburg, eight miles from the Potomac, and captured there many military stores. From Martinsburg the advance went almost to Williamsport on the river, destroying a bridge of the B. & O. Railroad. On the twenty-eighth the infantry moved to Charlestown, and on the twenty-ninth made a demonstration against Harper's Ferry. The enemy had been driven to and not merely toward the Potomac, but after the blood-stirring events at Front Royal, Middletown, and Winchester, the advance to the river was an anticlimax. Jackson's army had taken an estimated 3,030 prisoners, wounded and unwounded, 9,300 small arms, 2 field guns, many wagons, and rich commissary supplies. The captures of quartermasters' stores were valued for the thrifty Jackson at $125,185, "besides an immense amount destroyed." Confederate casualties in the entire operation had been 68 killed, 329 wounded, and 3 missing, a total of 400.[28]

This was done by Jackson in three days of fighting, but the strategical results went far beyond the impairment of a Federal corps, misstyled an army. On May 28, Jeb Stuart reported to General Johnston that the advance of McDowell's army, which had been marching southward from Fredericksburg, had turned back to that city. Both for the withdrawal of McDowell and for the resultant improvement in the prospects of holding Richmond, the credit belonged primarily to Jackson and his men.

In Washington on the twenty-fourth, when Jackson had been pursuing Banks from Middletown, Secretary Stanton had telegraphed McDowell to suspend his advance on Richmond and to send 20,000 of his men to the Shenandoah Valley. In western Virginia General Frémont was told to advance immediately to Harrisonburg in order to relieve the pressure on Banks. It was a mission more readily ordered than fulfilled. On the twenty-sixth President Lincoln was questioning whether the troops left with McDowell—less than half the original force of 40,000—should not be recalled to the defense of Washington.

Despite the reports, it was soon apparent to the President that the situation was not desperate. On the twenty-eighth he inquired of McDowell whether the suspended advance southward from Fredericksburg should not be renewed. Quickly came McDowell's answer: "I do not think, in the present state of affairs, it would be well to attempt to put through a part of that force. . . ." McDowell was immobilized. That was Jackson's reward.[29]

CHAPTER 10

Victory in the Valley

1. "FROM THE SNARE OF THE FOWLER"

By the morning of May 30, Jackson's demonstration to the line of the Potomac was developed fully. He pressed it to the utmost to give his quartermaster time to remove the supplies and equipment that had been captured. These were prizes worth some risk. In addition to the 9,300 small arms, he had taken in Winchester a rich storehouse of surgical instruments and dressings and an incredible quantity of medicines of every sort. The South needed sorely what Banks's medical director lavishly had provided for the Union troops, and quartermaster John A. Harman was hauling it toward Staunton by every conveyance he could hire, borrow, or requisition.

In making the long gamble of this demonstration, Jackson realized that the time in which he could maneuver on the Potomac was being reduced from days to hours. On the night of May 27–28 a citizen had brought a report that Shields, who had moved from the Valley to join McDowell, was hurrying toward Front Royal and was within a day's march of that town. This report was relayed to Jackson on the morning of the twenty-eighth. Now, on the thirtieth, it was confirmed by Ashby's scouts. McDowell himself was believed to be marching on Berryville. Spies from across the Potomac reported that Banks was reorganizing his defeated force at Williamsport.[1]

Jackson at Charlestown said not a word to indicate either surprise or dismay on the receipt of this news. Daily his composure was more nearly flawless. That afternoon Colonel A. R. Boteler, a former congressman and trusted friend of Jackson's, found the general stretched out asleep under a large tree. When he wakened, Boteler was busily sketching him. "Let me see what you have been doing there," Jackson said. Boteler submitted the sketch, which Jackson examined without a word of praise or of criticism. "My hardest tasks at West Point," he confessed, "were the drawing lessons, and I never could do anything in that line to satisfy myself, or indeed, anybody else." He paused for a moment and changed the subject. "But, Colonel, I have some harder work than this for you to do. I want you to go to Richmond for me. I must have reinforcements. You can explain to them down there what the situation is here. Get as many men as can be spared, and I'd like you, if you please, to go as soon as you can." Boteler expressed readiness to start at once, but said, "You must first tell me, General, what is the situation here."

Jackson answered with none of the reticence he usually exhibited. He told Boteler of the reports received that day of Federal forces marching toward the Valley. Frémont, he coolly said, would move against him also. "McDowell and Frémont are probably aiming to effect a junction at Strasburg, so as to head us off from the upper Valley, and are both nearer to it now than we are; consequently, no time is to be lost. You can say to them in Richmond that I'll send on the prisoners, secure most, if not all of the captured property, and with God's blessing will be able to baffle the enemy's plans here with my present force, but that it will have to be increased as soon thereafter as possible." Jackson then uncovered a plan which he must have pondered long: "You may tell them, too, that if my command can be gotten up to 40,000 men a movement may be made beyond the Potomac, which will soon raise the siege of Richmond and transfer this campaign from the banks of the James to those of the Susquehanna."[2]

A few minutes later Jackson left Winder to make a final thrust at Harper's Ferry. By this time troops filled the roads. The wagons were on the move. All were headed south. A retreat was on. That evening, unhurriedly, the general climbed aboard a waiting train. After the train started through a rain now falling heavily, he put his arm on the seat in front of him, leaned over, and went to sleep. He was as composed as if he were returning from a pleasant vacation. Nothing indicated that he felt any concern over the task of extracting his army from the net the enemy was spreading.[3]

Near Summit Point a courier signaled the train to stop and handed a dispatch to Jackson. The general read it, tore it up, and then said to the conductor, "Go on, sir, if you please." Without a word or even the quiver of an eyelash he resumed his position and dropped to sleep again. After the train reached Winchester the news that had reached Jackson en route was for any man's reading. The 12th Georgia had been left at Front Royal to guard the prisoners and captured stores. That morning Federals under Shields had come swiftly through the Blue Ridge and moved against the regiment, which hurriedly marched to Winchester.[4]

Grim news it was! All the captured supplies and stores at Front Royal, to the value of $300,000, had been destroyed by the retreating Confederates. Shields had closed one of Jackson's two lines of retreat up the

Shenandoah, and if he pressed rapidly westward a march of eleven miles would bring him to Strasburg. In the event that Frémont from the Alleghenies joined Shields there, the two might block the Valley Pike. From Halltown, where most of Jackson's troops had been encamped that morning, there was a long, long stretch of forty-four miles of road to Strasburg. Forty-four for the graycoats, eleven for the blue—the odds were stiff; but if Jackson had any doubt of his ability of reaching Strasburg before the enemy closed on him, he gave no indication of it.

Late in the evening, while the long columns were tramping through Winchester in the rain, Jackson summoned Colonel Boteler to his hotel room to give him some papers to take to Richmond. Ere he went to Jackson's room, Boteler ordered two whiskey toddies sent up. When he offered one to Jackson, the general drew back: "No, no, Colonel, you must excuse me; I never drink intoxicating liquors." Finally, at Boteler's urging, Jackson lifted the glass and took several sips. Then he put it down again: "Colonel, do you know why I habitually abstain from intoxicating drinks? Why, sir, because I like the taste of them, and when I discovered that to be the case I made up my mind at once to do without them altogether." Boteler remembered the conversation as an evidence of Jackson's temperance and process of reasoning. The colonel might as readily have instanced it to show the composure of Jackson in an hour of desperate danger to his army, a composure so absolute that the man and the soldier seemed to be separate personalities.[5]

At 3 o'clock on the morning of the thirty-first Jackson roused Jed Hotchkiss with orders to bring up Winder's First Brigade from Charlestown. Hotchkiss wrote in his diary that Jackson "feared that the converging columns of Frémont, Shields, McDowell and Banks might compel him to go out and fight one of them but he was in fine spirits."[6] After Hotchkiss hurried away, Jackson saw to it that the last of the wagons with captured stores started. Next the prisoners, some 2,300 in number, were put on the Valley Pike to tramp to Staunton. With his prizes and his captives ahead of him, Jackson ordered the infantry to begin the march on which the very life of the army and perhaps of the Confederacy depended. If he and his troops escaped, they might be able to go to Richmond and share the effort to drive McClellan off; but if Jackson were trapped by the converging columns and overwhelmed, what would prevent McDowell from joining McClellan and defeating Johnston's forces which, at that very hour, were deploying for the unsuccessful Battle of Seven Pines?

At 2:30 P.M., when all the infantry except Winder's brigade had cleared Winchester and only the cavalry remained to guard against a dash by the enemy, Jackson took horse and rode past his toiling men. The march proved uneventful. Regulations were followed strictly. The men rested ten minutes of every hour. Officers saw to it that the column was closed. Stragglers received no mercy. As Jackson neared his objective, he could not resist the impulse to ride ahead and see for himself whether Frémont or Shields or both of them had intercepted him. At last he came in sight of Strasburg. After the first careful gaze, he must have felt immeasurable relief. Not a Federal was in the village. The Valley Pike still was open! If it could be held until the main body reached there that evening and Winder's brigade arrived the next day, the army was safe.[7]

Jackson issued orders. The trains were to continue up the Valley. At nightfall the infantry brigades were to go into camp near Strasburg and remain the next day. Ewell's troops, who would be the last to reach there that night, would move again at daylight. Ewell's infantry were to turn westward at Strasburg and move out on the road by which Frémont was advancing eastward from Wardensburg. Jackson then went to the campfire of Dick Taylor and sat for some time. Taylor subsequently wrote that Jackson "was more communicative than I remember him before or after. He said Frémont, with a large force, was three miles west of our present camp, and must be defeated in the morning. Shields was moving up Luray Valley, and might cross Massanutton to New Market, or continue south until he turned the mountain to fall on our trains near Harrisonburg. The importance of preserving the immense trains, filled with captured stores, was great, and would engage much of his personal attention; while he relied on the army, under Ewell's direction, to deal promptly with Frémont. This he told in a low, gentle voice, and with many interruptions to afford time, as I thought and believe, for inward prayer."[8]

Reliance on Ewell was not in vain. When that officer received his orders to meet Frémont to the west, he enjoined his brigade commanders "to be in motion by the earliest dawn." Ewell was beginning to think in the very terms of the man whom, a fortnight previously, he had styled crazy. On the morning of June 1 he established contact with Frémont's vanguard several miles west of Strasburg. A lively exchange of artillery and musketry followed. Said Ewell: "I can't make out what these people are about, for my skirmish line has stopped them." The stalemate continued. About noon the fire died away, and finally Frémont put his infantry in camp. On the other flank, facing Front Royal, there was no evidence that any of Shields's infantry were close at hand. All the intelligence reports continued to indicate that, in an effort to get in rear of the Southern forces, Shields was marching up the Luray Valley.[9]

During the late afternoon of that first of June, down the road from Winchester, came the head of Winder's gallant brigade. The men were fairly staggering from weariness. The 2nd Virginia had covered thirty-six miles in a single day, and the other regiments had marched about thirty miles; but there they were, unscathed and undemoralized. Behind them was Ashby's rear guard only. The trap might snap; the army was beyond its jaws.[10]

Jackson issued prompt orders: The moment all of Winder's brigade was up, the other infantry commanders were to resume their march toward New Market. He was determined that he would not be caught west of the Massanuttons. These were hard orders for tired men, but they were necessary. To one commander Jackson had to address a biting question: "Colonel, why do you not get your brigade together, keep it together, and move on?"

"It's impossible, General. I can't do it!"

Jackson shot back: "Don't say it's impossible! Turn your command over to the next officer. If he can't do it, I'll find someone who can, if I have to take him from the ranks."[11]

Leaden clouds brought heavy rain the next day, June 2. The wagon train, moving in two columns along the Valley Pike, fell into such confusion that Jackson sent Jed Hotchkiss to untangle it. There was much straggling by exhausted soldiers. Numbers of disheartened men threw away their arms and accouterments. Under vigorous pressure by a large mounted force, the cavalry defense in the rear weakened. Maryland Steuart mismanaged his part in an affair near Woodstock and saw some of his men break in panic. Mistaken for the enemy, the 2nd Virginia cavalry was fired upon by the 27th Virginia. This fusillade was too much for Colonels Flournoy and Munford; they went to Ewell and besought him to have their regiments transferred to Ashby's command. Ewell approved his colonels' proposal and carried it at once to Jackson. Without hesitation, he assented and put Ashby in charge of all the cavalry.[12]

This unpleasant incident was offset by one bit of good news: Ashby's men had burned the White House and Columbia bridges over the South Fork near Luray, so that the Federals marching east of the Massanuttons could not cross the range to New Market to head them off. Assured of this, Jackson, with an easy mind, spent the night near Hawkinsville. There Colonel J. M. Patton came to report the final melee of the day with the Federal cavalry. He regretted, said Patton, to see the bluecoats shot down. Jackson asked quietly: "Colonel, why do you say that you saw those Federal soldiers fall with regret?" Patton answered that the Union troopers had shown so much valor that he wished their lives had been spared. "No," said Jackson in a dry tone, "shoot them all; I do not wish them to be brave."[13]

As the destruction of the South Fork bridges made it certain that Shields, who had no pontoons, could not cross the Massanuttons, it was manifest that the Federals in the Luray Valley would continue their advance to the southern end of the range. Then, almost certainly, Shields would turn west toward Harrisonburg to get in Jackson's front while Frémont assailed the rear. How could Shields be kept from doing this or, as an alternative, forming a junction with Frémont? Was there a chance one of the Federal armies could be beaten before the other came up, and in that event, where should Jackson give battle?

The immediate danger, Jackson felt, already was past. He had escaped, first, because of the speed of his march, and, second, because of the continuance of heavy rains in a region where high water favored the defensive. When on the forenoon of June 3 the last of the infantry passed over the North Fork bridge at Mount Jackson—the Valley Pike's sole crossing of that stream—Ashby's rear guard set the structure afire. With the stream already high and still rising, the destruction of the bridge would stop Frémont. He was known to have a pontoon train, but there was slight chance he could use it. Jackson consequently gave the army a rest for the day. He nearly miscalculated. Information reached headquarters that Frémont had brought up his pontoon bridge and was throwing it across the North Fork. Immediate resumption of the retreat might be necessary, but once again the rain was Southern. The North Fork rose, as a result of a widespread downpour, twelve feet in four hours. To save his pontoons, the Federal commander had to cut them loose and swing them around to the north bank. That was a boon. At least twenty-four hours would elapse before the main body of Frémont's force could take up the pursuit.[14]

Jackson was thinking more intently now of the situation that would develop when his divisions, Frémont's army, and Shields's column would be beyond the dividing ridge of the Massanuttons. Whither should the Valley army move? Its aim, of course, should be to prevent a junction of Shields and Frémont. Jackson's plan, maturing for several days, was based on terrain. The prime barrier to the junction of the two Federal forces, once they reached the southern end of the Massanuttons, was the South Fork of the Shenandoah. This was bridged at Conrad's Store. Fifteen miles farther south, at the village of Port Republic, the South and North rivers join to form the South Fork. The South River normally could be forded there with ease, but the North River could be crossed only by a bridge, beyond which the main road ran to Harrisonburg.

By sending a force to burn the crossing at Conrad's Store, Jackson reasoned, Shields would be reduced to two alternatives. First, he could go back toward Luray, rebuild the bridge near there, and cross to New Market—a slow and difficult undertaking. Second, Shields could advance up the South Fork and try to get over the stream at one of the ten fords between Conrad's Store and Port Republic, or attempt to seize the bridge at Port Republic. The river was high; which of the fords were passable, if any, Jackson did not know, but he did not gamble on the probability that none was. He directed Jed Hotchkiss to go to the Peaked Mountain at the southern end of the Massanuttons and observe Shield's movements.[15]

The van of the army Jackson sent toward Port Republic to hold the bridge there. Then he decided on dispositions in the event that Shields got across the South Fork at one of the fords between Conrad's Store and Port Republic. If part of the army were north of Port Republic and close to the Massanuttons, then Shields would be compelled to pass so close to the Confederate front that he could be struck. At that point, too, Jackson would be on Frémont's flank in the event of a Federal advance on Staunton. Still again, from Port Republic through Brown's Gap led the shortest road to the Virginia Central, the line that would transport Jackson to Richmond.[16]

Thus did Jackson's strategic sense and his eye for terrain lead him to choose a position that (1) would interpose his forces between Shields and Frémont; (2) would give him the one bridge that Shields would cross for an early junction with Frémont; (3) would limit Shields to a narrow and observed front of advance; (4) would delay any attempted advance on Staunton; (5) would afford access to the railroad which would carry the Confederate force to Richmond; (6) would at the same time leave open a

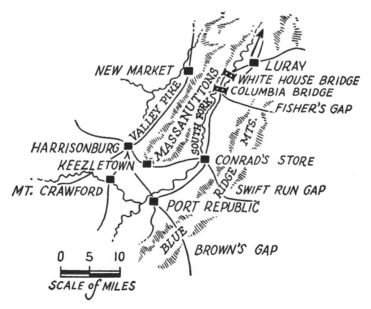

Southern end of the Massanuttons, Shenandoah Valley, to illustrate Jackson's choice of positions on his retreat before Frémont and Shields.

safe avenue of retreat were unexpected disaster to come; and (7) would make it possible for him to parallel Shields should he pass to the eastern side of the Blue Ridge.

By nightfall on June 5 some of the trains and all of the prisoners were close to Port Republic, and the advance units were near Cross Keys, but the rear brigades had been held up so long that Jackson went into camp one mile from Harrisonburg. The rain, though still falling, had slackened noticeably. There was cheering news that the force sent to burn the bridge near Conrad's Store had succeeded, somewhat narrowly, in doing so.

That evening Jed Hotchkiss came to report. From the Peaked Mountain he had been able to look across the South Fork to Shields's line of march. About 4:00 P.M. the van of the Federal army had encamped two miles beyond Conrad's Store. The roads east of the South Fork were as bad as the one Jackson was now following, and it was apparent that Shields could not reach the bridge at Port Republic before Jackson arrived there. If a battle impended, which Jackson began to doubt, there was scant prospect that it would be waged against Shields and Frémont combined.[17]

On the sixth, Jackson marched easily with the van of his army to Port Republic. There he received dispatches and newspapers from Richmond and learned of the immense sensation his operations had created. The *Charleston Mercury* had acclaimed Jackson a "true general" and predicted that the next news would be that he was "leading his unconquerable battalions through Maryland into Pennsylvania." Depressing articles in the Northern press were jubilantly republished. All this had a noticeable effect on Jackson. Ambitious as he was for military distinction, his conscience told him that the South was giving him glory that belonged to God. Those close to him observed that he ceased to read the newspapers.

The communications from Richmond were, of course, a different matter. By his own hand, President Davis wrote to congratulate Jackson on his "brilliant campaign" and to express regret that no reinforcements could be sent. This letter was based on the information Colonel Boteler had given Davis upon arrival in Richmond from Winchester. If the denial of reinforcements dampened satisfaction over the President's approval, Jackson was too disciplined a soldier to complain. Should the Army of the Valley be required at Richmond, Jackson wrote, it could march to Mechum River Station. "At present," he went on, "I do not see that I can do much more than rest my command and devote its time to drilling."[18]

About 9 o'clock that evening, at headquarters at Port Republic, Jackson received the worst news that had come to him in the entire campaign. At dusk, he was told, the rear guard fighting had sharpened, and Ewell had to send back infantry to beat off the bluecoats. The affair was over now, the danger was past; but in the first clash in the woods Ashby's horse had been shot, and Ashby himself had gone forward on foot with the cry, "Forward, my brave men"—and had fallen dead with a bullet through his body. Ashby dead? It took all Jackson's self-mastery to receive that news without paralyzing emotion. Ashby dead, the idol of his troopers, the modest gentleman, the leader whose daring seemed instinctive! Jackson had sought to discipline the troopers; Ashby had been angry and defiant, but he had been reconciled to his chief and, if possible, he had fought harder after the controversy than before.[19]

Now they were bringing Ashby's body to the town. His troopers were gathered about the body. Scout Richard Black, bravest of the brave, was delivering the soldiers' eulogy: "We shall miss you mightily, General. We shall miss you in the camp. We shall miss you as we go out on the scout. But we shall miss you most, General, when we go out to—" There he stopped. He could say no more.[20]

2. A Crowning Double Victory

On the morning of June 7 the skies smiled. The roads around Port Republic were heavy, and the streams were high, but the rain had ceased. From the west flowed the North River to meet, northeast of Port Republic, the South River; together the two passed Luray Valley as the South Fork of the Shenandoah. Port Republic lay in the angle formed by the North and South rivers. Back of the village, to the south and southwest, was a high ridge, whence ran a road to Mount Meridian and thence sixteen miles to Staunton.

Strategically, the important area was the left bank of the North River near the confluence; there commanding ground overlooked the village. Eastward and southeastward were the long, open meadows on the right bank of the South River. Still farther eastward, at a distance from one to two miles, was a heavy forest that ran up to the spurs of the Blue Ridge. The crossings were as important as the high ground that overlooked them. From the village the traveler on the road to Harrisonburg traversed the North River on a long wooden structure, but there was no bridge over the South River or over the South Fork near the junction of the two streams. Only fords were available there, and these were now dangerously high and swift.

As Shields was reported still east of the South Fork, moving south from Conrad's Store, Jackson could hope, not unreasonably, to prevent a junction between Frémont and Shields. So long as the Confederates held off Frémont to the west, Shields could continue south only along the road that led up the South Fork and under the dominating ridge. On the other hand, if Shields should venture far enough to offer battle opposite Port Republic, Jackson could not afford to disregard Frémont altogether and cross the entire army to the left bank of South River. Were Jackson to do that, Frémont could advance to the height near the bridge and with his batteries sweep the Confederates engaged with Shields east of the river.

Besides, if Jackson moved all his forces to the eastern side of South River and burned the one bridge behind him, he would have no means of dealing later with Frémont. It was reasonable to suppose that if either Frémont or Shields were defeated, the other would not venture a march on Staunton or toward the railroad that linked Staunton with eastern Virginia; but Jackson was anxious not to limit his own ability to move in any direction. His decision consequently was to tempt Frémont to battle and, meantime, to hold the ridge opposite Port Republic and the bridge linking the two positions.[21]

It was in vain, on the seventh, that Jackson rode to Ewell's lines near Cross Keys and there maneuvered in the hope of inducing Frémont to fight. The Federal commander, though he had pursued with much vigor, seemed in no mood to force events.[22] At length Jackson returned to Port Republic, and reviewed his dispositions:

Ewell was on good ground near Cross Keys with three brigades, about 5,000 effectives. Jackson on the ridge north of Port Republic had his own division and Edward Johnson's command. Taylor's brigade of Ewell's division was to come up the next morning; with it Jackson would have a total of not more than 8,000 bayonets. At the upper ford of South River, on the southeastern edge of Port Republic, was a 25-man picket under Captain Samuel J. C. Moore, 2nd Virginia. South of Port Republic and on the road to Mount Meridian was extended the army's wagon train. While the batteries were with the infantry units, the cavalry was much scattered. Most of the companies of the 6th and 7th Virginia were guarding the wagon train. The 2nd Virginia troopers were covering Ewell's right and rear. Immediately around Port Republic were a few cavalry scouting parties; in the town was J. J. Chipley's troop.[23]

Early on the morning of Sunday, June 8, a fine, cool day, news of unexpected character arrived. Federal cavalry was sighted at Lewiston, an estate some two miles east of Port Republic. This might mean much or little, but if Shields were advancing, Ewell would do well to defer action. Jackson, who was at the house of Dr. George Kemper on the outskirts of Port Republic, so advised Ewell and himself prepared to go over to the high ground on the other side of the bridge to see what was afoot on the right side of the South Fork. He felt no concern, and when Major Dabney asked if there would be any military action that day, he answered: "No, you know I always try to keep the Sabbath if the enemy will let me." The general went about his routine duties; the adjutant returned to his camp to prepare his sermon; the Sabbath calm continued.[24]

About 9 o'clock a single cavalryman rode up to the Kemper house at a gallop and went directly to the general: The Federals, he said, had crossed the lower ford of South River, with cavalry and artillery, and already were in the town! Jackson received the news quietly: "Go back and fight them," he said—that and no more. Scarcely had he spoken than firing broke out. Jackson did not wait for horse or escort. With long strides he started toward the scene of the fusillade. In a few moments he saw down the street a column of Federal cavalrymen. Had they observed the Confederates on foot? Did they recognize officers in gray? Would they dash on and capture the general? Breathless the questions, doubtful the issue, but at that moment Jackson's orderly brought up his horse. He mounted quickly and galloped off toward the bridge across North River.[25]

Just then a Union trooper rode jubilantly up to report to his colonel that the whole Confederate wagon train was "just up yonder, in full sight across that old farm—hundreds of wagons and no troops!" The Federals formed confidently in the street and started at a slow trot toward the Kemper house. As they turned toward Dr. Kemper's lawn, a brisk little volley of rifle fire greeted them. The troopers recoiled, but their colonel re-formed them and sent them forward again. This time, when they made the turn, "Bang! Bang!" went two cannon. Again the Federals galloped back; again their commander sent them forward—to be met with the same artillery fire and another infantry volley. Watching this scene in amazement was Jackson's artillerist Stapleton Crutchfield, who had not gotten away quickly enough and had fallen into the hands of the blue troopers. "Where on earth did those guns come from?" Crutchfield asked himself. "Did I not post all the batteries?" Whatever the answers might be, the Federal troopers could not again be induced to face this fire sweeping the street from end to end.[26]

Jackson had galloped across the bridge just as the Federals were closing on him. He hurried to the nearest batteries and ordered them to open on Federals who were plainly visible on the east side of South River. Taliaferro and Winder were directed to put their brigades under arms and take possession of the bridge. Taylor's brigade was called up in support. As soon as Taliaferro's Virginians came up, Jackson rode to the head of the column, ordered it to descend to the bridge, to give a volley, and then to rush the crossing with the bayonet. This said, Jackson dropped the reins on the neck of his horse and lifted both hands on high. The reply was a roar from the men, an overwhelming volley, and, in another moment or two, a dash across the bridge. In a few minutes, the village was cleared.

Crutchfield and other captured officers were recovered, and, in rejoicing and relief, the mystery of the first fire on the Federals in the village was explained. Most of Chipley's cavalry troop, which was guarding the place, had fled shamefully, but Captain Moore's infantry picket at the ford had rallied and delivered the volleys that halted the blue troopers. The artillery salvoes had been the work of just-arrived Carrington's battery, Charlottesville Artillery. Major Dabney, aroused from meditation on his sermon, had a hand in this defense. Thanks to these men, none of the wagons had been lost.[27]

Hardly had Jackson and his staff congratulated themselves on the narrowness of their escape when there drifted across the fields the sound of battle to the westward. Ewell was engaged with Frémont. Shields, of course, heard the same rumble—would he launch his attack? Was the army to be compelled to fight two actions simultaneously? Jackson decided to remain at Port Republic and leave to Ewell the handling of the action at Cross Keys.[28]

Ewell's line rested on a ridge two miles southeast of the village of Cross Keys. Woods protected both flanks. In Ewell's judgment the center, which was pierced by a road, was decidedly weak. He posted his four batteries to command the road and put Elzey's brigade in reserve behind, whence it could move in either direction. About 10:00 A.M. an artillery duel began at the center of the line that continued steadily but without decisive result of any sort. Elzey directed the gunners with fine contempt for the enemy's sharpshooters and their shell, paying no heed to the suggestion that the next shot might be his.

As Frémont made no move to follow up his cannonade on the center, it became apparent that he intended to direct his infantry attack against the Confederate right. Trimble's brigade was there, admirably placed. Slowly, conspicuously and in good order, the bluecoats mounted the hill, as if they were on a practice maneuver. Scarcely a shot greeted them until they were near the crest. Then, as if they had a single trigger, all the muskets along the Confederate line were loosed. The Federals staggered, attempted to rally, recoiled in the face of a second volley, and in a short time retired.[29]

Back, now, the action shifted to the artillery. Elzey shrewdly directed the fire for a few minutes until his horse was killed and he himself was wounded. Within fifteen minutes the battle became so dull an affair that it irked General Trimble. If the enemy would not attack him, he would take the offensive! He threw his troops forward more than a mile beyond their first position. There, when Jackson reached the field about noon, it was resting, and there Ewell reluctantly decided he must leave it. Nothing happened; the artillery fire died away; the enemy scarcely showed himself within range. Finally, after it seemed certain that no attack would develop, Ewell slowly moved up his skirmishers and at nightfall occupied the position from which the enemy had advanced in the morning.[30]

Back at Port Republic, Jackson had appeared at his strangest. Not long after noon he remarked to Dabney, his chief of staff, "Major, wouldn't it be a blessed thing if God would give us a glorious victory today?" A lieutenant who overheard him said, "I saw his face with an expression like that of a child hoping to receive some favor." Most of the time Old Jack stood in silent thought with his eyes on the ground. After some hours, confident of victory, he began shaping his plans for the morrow in the knowledge that the day's losses had been light. General Steuart had been wounded in the shoulder; General Elzey would be out of action for a fortnight or more; but the other casualties in Ewell's division had not been more than 288, of whom only 41 had been killed. The army, unimpaired, was ready for whatever might give it the largest promise of victory.[31]

How best could it be employed? Jackson's reasoning was prompt and decisive: He was nearer Shields than Frémont; he believed Shields commanded the smaller of the two Union forces. If he beat Frémont that officer would have an easy line of retreat down the Valley Pike, while Shields had a bad road to follow back to Luray. All the weight of advantage was on the side of dealing first with Shields. If Shields were beaten early, while Frémont was being held at Cross Keys, might it not be possible to return to Port Republic and cross the bridge to assail Frémont? It was worth trying! Should events preclude attacking Frémont, then the destruction of the bridge over the North River would leave Frémont powerless to force action or even attempt quick pursuit.

For the execution of the more difficult part of this daring design, Jackson issued explicit instructions. At daybreak on the ninth Ewell was to march for Port Republic, but was to leave in front of Frémont the brigade of Trimble and Patton's 42nd Virginia and 1st Virginia battalion. These troops were to put up a bold front and delay Frémont as long as possible. Should they be pressed hard, they were to retire toward Port Republic and burn behind them the bridge on North River. To make sure these orders to the rear guard were understood, Jackson sent for Colonel Patton and instructed him in detail. How long did the General expect him to delay Frémont? Patton asked. Jackson's answer was explicit: "By the blessing of Providence, I hope to be back by 10 o'clock."[32]

As the silent Jackson rode from his headquarters at daybreak he encountered General Winder, who asked for instructions. The comman-

der was cautious in his reply. Winder would take his brigade across the
South Fork of the Shenandoah. Jackson would himself go with them. He
said no more but touched his horse and, under a sky that gave promise of a
clear day, proceeded across the stream and directed Winder to march
northeastward along the line of the enemy's retreat the previous day. In the
open country that lay between the river and the rising, wooded ridges of
the mountains, the column moved slowly for nearly an hour. On the right
ahead the plantation buildings of Lewiston were visible. About 7 o'clock a
cavalry officer came back from the advance with the news that always stirs
and sickens: The enemy's picket line had been reached.

Jackson stopped and studied the position. Open ground to the northeast rose gradually from the river to the wooded shoulder of the Blue
Ridge. The profile below the mountain seemed in the form of two terraces,
on the upper one of which stood Lewiston. In rear of the house was a large
"coaling," a clear space on which charcoal was prepared, with indications of
the presence of artillery, although no guns were visible. From the coaling
down toward the river the Federal infantry could be glimpsed, its strength
unknown. Between the Confederates and the enemy the ground was
entirely open and, except for an orchard, was covered with a field of ripen-
ing wheat.[33]

A strong position the enemy held, but Jackson impetuously determined
to take it at a single blow in order not to delay his proposed march on Frémont. Without waiting for any supports to come up, he ordered Winder to
drive in the pickets and to attack the enemy. No sooner was the advance of
the infantry started than smoke billowed over the coaling near the Lewiston house. Federal shell from unseen guns there screamed down the road
and burst among the Confederate infantrymen. The cannon fire was fast,
accurate, and continuous. Quickly Jackson directed Winder to send a force
to the right through the woods to take the Federal guns; a battery was to
follow to find a position above that of the enemy. Winder assigned this
task to the 2nd Virginia, with the 4th in support, and designated Carpenter's battery to climb the ridge. The other two regiments of his brigade he
disposed on the center and left. Only the two Parrott guns of Poague's battery could reach the Federal fieldpieces at the coaling. The remaining
Confederate guns had to be held in idleness under cover. Soon it was
learned that no support was forthcoming. The brunt of the infantry action
and that killing fire from the vicinity of Lewiston must be borne by the
Stonewall Brigade alone.

Nor was this the full measure of disadvantage. When the flanking party
entered the woods on the right it ran into a tangle of mountain laurel that
proved almost impenetrable. The infantrymen crashed and cut and

dodged their way slowly forward; the battery had to give up the attempt. Captain Carpenter brought his guns back and put them into play near Poague's two Parrotts. The situation began to look serious. The Confederate fire remained defensive and inferior. If relief was to be had it must come from the 2nd Virginia reaching and overwhelming the Union battery at the coaling. He had pressed to within 100 yards of the battery, Colonel James Allen reported, when the guns "poured volley after volley of grape on us in such quick succession as to throw my men into confusion." The same fate befell the 4th Virginia. Colonel Allen had no alternative except to draw both regiments out of action.[34]

From field headquarters at the rear of the center of the line, Jackson had been watching the artillery duel and the futile attempt of Winder's men to advance along the road. His battle blood was up. He knew now that the issue was close. With reluctance he had abandoned all hope of finishing off Shields in time to attack Frémont, and couriers were spurring toward Cross Keys with orders for Trimble to hurry to Port Republic, burn the bridge over North River, and join Jackson. Soon came word from Winder that he was greatly outnumbered and must have reinforcements. Providentially there appeared Harry Hays's 7th Louisiana, coming up at the head of Taylor's brigade. Jackson immediately dispatched Hays to Winder, and in a few minutes saw Taylor riding toward him at the head of his other regiments. Jackson turned to Jed Hotchkiss and said tersely, "Take General Taylor around and take those batteries." Hotchkiss and Taylor turned at once to the approaching brigade and started it up the ridge and into the laurel thickets.[35]

Could Winder hold his position on the plain until Taylor stormed the battery? He saw his best prospect of preventing an assault was to deliver one. With a cheer the 7th Louisiana rushed forward, the 5th and 27th Virginia keeping pace. Poague's short-range guns and a section of Carpenter's battery strained through the wheat field to the rear of the infantry. The troops reached a fence and there had to halt in the face of a combined artillery and rifle fire. All they could do was precariously to hold on. Unless Taylor attacked soon, Winder would be compelled to give ground. Minutes passed. Some of Winder's men began to crawl away from the fence, and he ordered the artillery back to safety—just in time. There was a swift break. The Louisianians and the two Virginia regiments streamed back through the wheat. Their organization disappeared. Winder and the regimental officers wheeled and veered, pleaded and shouted and commanded—all was futile. To the left and front pursuing Federals now were visible, coming on fast and persistently.

Dangerous the situation was, but if it could be preserved for a few

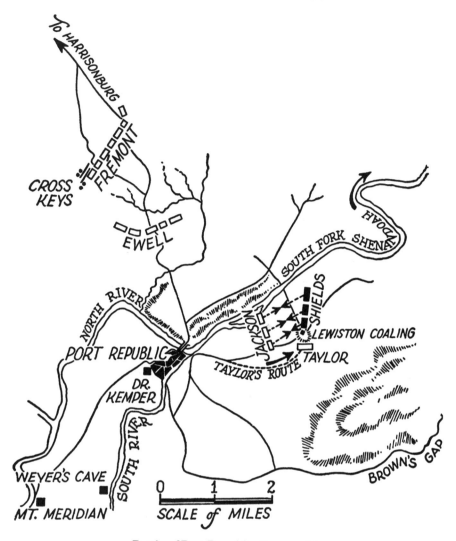

Battle of Port Republic, June 9, 1862

moments it could be redeemed. The second brigade of Ewell's division already had reached the scene of action. Ewell had started two regiments in support of Taylor, but he had always an eye for danger and a heart for a comrade in difficulties. The instant he saw the Federals pushing forward in pursuit of Winder's broken line, he unhesitatingly threw the two regiments against the Federal flank. They took the advancing enemy by surprise, they halted him, they hurled him back. But formation was not lost in the withdrawal and the Union line quickly was dressed to face Ewell. With steadiness and a hot fire the Federals advanced again and drove Ewell's men back into the wood. Poague's gunners had to leave one of their pieces and scamper for cover.

A gun abandoned, a famous brigade worsted—was the battle to be lost also? If the Federals continued to press on, and Taylor did not attack their flank, then, as the least of possible calamities, the Stonewall Brigade would be routed shamefully. Even Jackson had to admit to himself that the plight of Winder was critical.[36]

At that moment, a mile to the east, Taylor was on the edge of the tangled woodland not far from the Federal battery. To his disappointment he saw that he had not progressed far enough to take the guns from the rear; he was on the flank of the battery, and across a ravine from it. His military instinct told him he could not afford to wait. Reckless as the venture might be, he would make a dash for the coal hearth. Out the Louisianians went, more in a spring than at a dash. Before the enemy realized that a column was near, the still-smoking fieldpieces were seized. Turn them! was the order. Give the enemy his own medicine! But now the Federals were surging back, and the Louisiana boys had to run. Soon Taylor led them in a second rush for the guns. The opposing troops came to grips with bayonet, with clubbed musket, even with the ramrods of the pieces. The Federals were too strong to worst, and swearing and bloody the Confederates dropped back to the woods.

Once more, with a wild shout, the thin line rushed down the grade, over the ravine, and on to the coal hearth. The Confederates stormed the guns and then drew a line to face the woods from which the enemy twice had rushed out to repulse them. Anxious seconds dragged into minutes. No countercharge came. The guns were Taylor's! Then, to the west, a gun was rolled out within plain view, not 350 yards away, and opened on the coaling. Exposed as Taylor's men were, they could not face this fire; for the third time they tumbled over the ravine and back up the hillside.

Taylor determined that if he could not hold the battery position, he would give the force on his flank so hot a reception that it could not recover the guns. Against him the Federals skillfully threw all the strength they could muster; their approaching line appeared as a solid wall. "There seemed," said Taylor afterward, "nothing left but to set our backs to the mountain and die hard." Just then Dick Ewell came crashing on his horse through the woods. Behind him were the 44th and 58th Virginia. With this reinforcement Taylor quickly determined not to await attack but to deliver it. By happy chance his assault was delivered precisely when Winder's fire and that of his artillery began to blast the blue flank. The Federals halted uncertainly and then fell back. Taylor's men and the Virginians seized the guns on the coaling, found charges and ramrods, and in a few minutes turned them on the retreating enemy. Ewell himself, his beak shining with joy, got off his horse and served one of the fieldpieces. As the Federals disappeared, Jackson rode up to Taylor, shook his hand as at Winchester, and promised the captured guns should be attached to the Louisiana brigade.[37]

With Jackson always at the front, the pursuit pushed northward for four miles, until the woods closed in on both sides of the road so that further progress was almost impossible. The cavalry kept up the chase for another four miles. About 450 prisoners, some wagons, one field gun, and 800 muskets were the army's reward. Carefully Jackson collected this booty and marched back to Port Republic, where he found Trimble's and Patton's men. Obedient to Jackson's orders, they had left their line near Cross Keys to cross, and then burn, the North River bridge. Frémont, following fast, had found no way of crossing or of giving help to Shields.[38]

A close action this Battle of Port Republic had been, and a costly one! The Federals, it developed, comprised two small brigades, 3,000 men and 16 guns, under Brigadier General E. B. Tyler, and they had fought admirably. On the morning of the ninth Tyler had received orders from Shields to retire, but before he could do so, Jackson had been upon him. In the battle itself Tyler's killed and wounded were few. On his retreat he had lost about 20 per cent of his force as prisoners. His total casualties were 1,018. The remnant that made its way back to Luray was in sad plight. Jackson, for his part, had suffered in excess of 800 casualties, which was more than he had sustained in any other action of the campaign.[39]

On June 10 word came that Frémont had started a retreat down the Valley. To be near at hand in the event Frémont was attempting to deceive, Jackson established his camps between South River and Middle River, near Weyer's Cave and Mount Meridian. In this lush and beautiful country he rested his men, held a day of thanksgiving, and with the humblest of privates participated in brigade communion. "God has been our shield," he told Mrs. Jackson, "and to His name be all the glory."

Not all of Jackson's expressions in the aftermath of the battles were at this pitch. The day after the Battle of Port Republic he told his exhaustless quartermaster "Old John" Harman to collect the small arms scattered over the field. When Harman reported, he said, "General, a good many of them look like our own arms." Jackson exploded instantly. Shields, he said, had many similar weapons; he wanted to hear no more of such talk! Harman angrily replied that he would not be addressed in such manner, and he tendered his resignation. Jackson, explaining that he had been annoyed by frequent references to the arms his men had thrown away, would not accept the paper, and for the moment Harman was willing to leave the matter there.[40]

Less violent though no less indicative of Jackson's fighting spirit was a conversation with Ewell. It was reported that in the Port Republic fighting Ewell had so admired the gallant behavior of a Federal officer that he told his men not to kill so fine a foe. Jackson sent for Ewell and told him not to do such a thing again. Said Jackson: "The brave and gallant Federal officers are the very kind that must be killed. Shoot the brave officers and the cowards will run away and take the men with them."[41]

Still a third unpleasant incident concerned Sidney Winder. When that officer asked leave to go to Richmond for a few days on private business, Jackson brusquely refused him. Winder, already resentful over Jackson interfering with his discharge of command, became offended and tendered his resignation. Dick Taylor, convinced that so capable an officer should not be allowed to leave the army, went to Jackson, dwelt on the plenitude of the glory won during the campaign, and appealed to Jackson's magnanimity: "Observing him closely, I caught a glimpse of the man's inner nature. It was but a glimpse . . . yet in that moment I saw an ambition boundless as Cromwell's, and as merciless. . . . No reply was made to my effort for Winder." But that night, Taylor added, "a few lines came from Winder, to inform me that Jackson had called on him, and his resignation was withdrawn."[42]

Jackson's mind concentrated now on the possibilities Lee was suggesting of employing the victorious Army of the Valley in front of Richmond. Lee wrote on June 8 to propose that the troops on the Shenandoah be prepared for a movement to the capital. Before this reached Jackson, the actions at Cross Keys and Port Republic had been won and been reported to Richmond. Lee reasoned immediately that this double victory would permit Jackson to take the offensive again and that the Army of the Valley would need reinforcement. He decided to send Jackson two good brigades in addition to Alexander Lawton's brigade of Georgians and a North Carolina battalion previously ordered to the Valley. With the approval of Mr. Davis, a troop movement under W. H. C. Whiting began on the eleventh.

When he received Lee's letter of the eighth, Jackson saw one useful alternative, one only, to transferring his army to Richmond, and that was to relieve the capital by a heavy counteroffensive that would carry him into the enemy's country. If his strength could be raised to 40,000, he would cross the Blue Ridge and proceed northward until he found a convenient gap that would put him in the rear of Banks's army. Having disposed of Banks, Jackson planned to invade western Maryland and Pennsylvania. This was essentially the same plan, strategically, that he had sent Boteler to

Richmond to advocate after the Battle of Winchester. He now sent the same messenger with his report on his present situation; so doing, Boteler would suggest informally the bolder but necessarily secret design. "By this means," Jackson told his emissary, "Richmond can be relieved and the campaign transferred to Pennsylvania."[43]

For the next step Jackson had to wait on Richmond. On June 16 the first of the reinforcements under Lawton reported to him, and the next day regiments began to arrive from the Richmond front. Whiting had chosen E. M. Law's brigade and Hood's brigade, to which the Hampton Legion was attached. These were as good soldiers as the Army of Northern Virginia had. Hardly had Jackson welcomed these veterans than a decision on the proposals sent Lee by Colonel Boteler was received.

Writing on the sixteenth, Lee expressed the opinion that it would be difficult for Jackson to strike Frémont and Shields where they then were and then break off to join the Army of Northern Virginia in time for the attack that soon must be made on McClellan. "Unless McClellan can be driven out of his intrenchments," Lee explained, "he will move by positions under cover of his heavy guns within shelling distance of Richmond. I know of no surer way of thwarting him than that proposed." Nothing was said about the proposal to invade Pennsylvania. Colonel Boteler was left to state verbally to Jackson that the pressure on Richmond prevented the detachment of enough troops for a large-scale offensive.[44]

Jackson lost no time in obeying this discretionary order. With precautions to keep all early information of his withdrawal from reaching the enemy, he set the columns in motion for the Virginia Central Railroad. On the morning of June 18 he was in Staunton, and by 5:00 P.M. in Waynesboro.

3. "THE HERO OF THE SOUTH"

The next morning, in high spirits, Jackson rode on to Mechum River Station, nine miles west of Charlottesville, and there climbed aboard the postal car of a troop train bound eastward. As the wheels of the train wailed on their way toward Richmond, a candid student who wished to learn the lessons that every campaign teaches of the art of war might well have asked four questions of the silent general in the postal car. The student would not have received an answer, but he would have been prepared, in a measure, for what was soon to happen in the woods and swamps of the Chickahominy.

First among the questions raised by the Valley campaign: Was Jackson's artillery well handled on May 23 at Front Royal? Before long-range fire in any volume could be opened, the retreating Federals were gone completely. Colonel Crutchfield, frankly admitting that the Confederate guns were "badly served and did no execution," excused his lack of familiarity with Ewell's batteries on the ground that he had only recently assumed his duties.[45] Although that fact extenuates, it does not excuse. The indictment has to stand: In a situation where rifled guns might be required, no effort had been made to see that equipment of this type was close to the head of the column. Who was to blame—Jackson, or Crutchfield, or both?

The second question is more inclusive: Was or was not the cavalry efficient during the campaign? Maryland Steuart certainly made a poor showing on May 24 for the number of sabers he had at his command. The next day he refused to obey direct orders from headquarters and would not move until Ewell approved. On June 1 and 2 mismanagement led to the 2nd and 6th Virginia being taken from Steuart and placed under Ashby. More fundamentally, the campaign was marred by failure to employ in strength a force which, if united and well led, could have capitalized all the gains the infantry made by hard marching and gallant fighting.

Against this may be set down many admirable achievements. Wherever Ashby himself was engaged, there was brilliance; elsewhere, the handling of the mounted forces leaves the critic convinced that something was wrong. Certain adverse conditions could have been corrected or controlled, in large part, had the cavalry been organized properly. It was not. Ashby lacked nothing in devotion, but he was essentially a combat officer and not an administrator. How far was Jackson to be blamed for permitting the cavalry organization to become so highly personal to Ashby that it was unwieldy and ineffective? Jackson realized early that the cavalry was undisciplined and could not be handled as if it were a single regiment. He sought to change this, but when faced with Ashby's resignation he canceled the orders; he believed that if he relieved Ashby the cavalry would be even less efficient. The price he had to pay was a heavy one. At no time during the campaign, if Ashby chanced to be absent, was Jackson able to count on the cavalry as he could, for example, on Taylor's or Winder's infantry.

Of the specific shortcomings of the cavalry on the critical days of the campaign, especially May 24 and 25, the most serious was the imprudent dispersal of Ashby's command. The only possible excuse for scattering Ashby's men would be the presence with Jackson of the two cavalry regiments under Steuart. The personality of Maryland Steuart thus has bearing on these events. Of the reasons for his refusal to advance on the twenty-fifth, existing records give no hint. The natural assumption is that he was the type of soldier, after thirteen years' service in the cavalry, who was trained to the absolute letter of printed regulations, who insists, no matter how dire the emergency, that every order come "through channels." It is difficult to escape the conclusion that his experience as a captain of cavalry had not qualified him for higher command. As head of two regiments, plus part of Ashby's force, he was still a captain.

With the fullest credit for the many daring and dazzling acts of Ashby, the cavalry failed to achieve maximum results in the operations from Front Royal to Port Republic because it was organized in a manner that Jackson knew to be defective but did not feel himself justified at the moment in revising. The cavalry did less than it should because, in the second place, Ashby scattered his command too widely and thereby left to Steuart a task which that officer did not discharge with competence and cooperation.

Jackson promptly transferred the cavalry to Ashby, yet no charges were preferred against Steuart. Why was that? So many instances were there of the sternest discipline on Jackson's part that a third broad question arises: As an autonomous army commander, was Jackson wise and successful in his handling of his officers? The answer must be in the negative. Jackson sought to bring Loring to court-martial; he visited like punishment on Dick Garnett after Kernstown; he protested against the return of Taliaferro to command; he provoked the tender of Winder's resignation. That was a bad record, an indictment of many counts. Along with these examples of sternness, not to say of severity, the outcome of the clash with Ashby and Jackson's failure to take any action against Steuart appear in curious contrast.

The explanation would seem to be simple: Jackson was a stiff disciplinarian, and he always followed that bent unless he believed the Southern cause would suffer worse by the imposition of discipline than by the neglect of it. This tacit policy accounts, by his own admission, for his treatment of Ashby, and probably for his leniency toward Steuart. Jackson shared in the desire of his government to enlist Marylanders and to bring their state into the Confederacy. As a Maryland soldier of standing, Steuart was expected to have large influence, especially on recruitment. If he were arrested as a failure, Marylanders of Southern sympathy would be disillusioned and resentful. Considerations of policy outweighed personalities. Where these considerations did not appear, Jackson's rule was to hold his officers to the most rigid standards of military conduct.

In the employment of these officers and of their commands, did Jackson display in the Valley campaign any eminent tactical ability? That is the fourth question to be answered. In his first independent battle, that of Kernstown, his aim was to demonstrate on his right, hold on the center, and, on his left, turn the enemy's flank. The action at McDowell was, tactically, simple repulse and pursuit. At Front Royal, Jackson's superiority of force was so overwhelming that his principal task was expediting the chase. In the Battle of Winchester he advanced his center and then turned the Federal flank as he vainly had attempted to do at Kernstown. At Cross Keys, Ewell's position was so strong and the Federal advance so feeble that the affair was little more than a skirmish. Finally, at Port Republic, Jackson's ambition to achieve a double victory led him to attack before he had sufficient force on the field. When he discovered the strength of the Federal position on the coaling, he repeated his flank tactics and, by Taylor's successful attack, drove the enemy northward. This was, on Jackson's part, a poorly managed battle. To lose approximately 800 men in driving an enemy who had 3,000 muskets, when Jackson himself had at least 8,000 troops close at hand, was not a distinguished achievement.

Taken as a whole, Jackson's infantry tactics in the Valley campaign have to be written down as commonplace. Tactically, the battles were lifted above the level of mediocrity by nothing save an intelligent effort to coordinate the three arms of the service. That effort did not always succeed, yet Jackson cannot be denied credit for a sound theory of coordination. At a time when many other commanders were fumbling with their artillery and using their cavalry for little more than outpost duty, he was striving to weld all three arms into an effective machine.

Against these negatives must be set three superior qualities which, though perhaps not discernible at the moment or even developed, were the marks of a great captain. The first of these was Jackson's quick and sure sense of position. For military geography in its larger aspects, for fashioning an accurate mental picture of ground he had not seen, Jackson had shown no special aptitude. His insistent demand for maps may have indicated a consciousness of special personal need. Once Jackson learned the geography of an area, his interpretation of it was strategical; and when he came to a field of battle, his sense of position was sure, unhesitating, and quickly displayed. The miserable night march of May 24 he imposed on exhausted troops because he knew the ground around Winchester and determined that Banks should not be allowed to hold the key ridge there. After the battle opened, one glance at the Federal column moving for the stone wall on his left sufficed: That position must be taken immediately. At Port Republic, he saw swiftly how the Lewiston coal hearth could be turned.

Jackson demonstrated, secondly, a pronounced strategic sense, the components of which were secrecy and consequent surprise, superiority of force, and sound logistics. The interworking of the three was fascinating. First of all, he reasoned that his adversaries must not know what he intended to do. To make sure his opponents did not discover his plans, nobody must be aware of them. His lieutenants might grumble that Jackson was secretive, but the results justified the precautions. Never did he begin a march until he had stopped, as far as practicable, all communications between his lines and those of the Federals. When he started for Front Royal on May 21, Ewell was the only one beside himself who knew the objective. Jackson's plan of striking Shields and Frémont the same day was not revealed until the night before. Even Winder did not know whither he was bound on the morning of June 9 until after his van had forded South River.

Secrecy made surprise possible. In capitalizing surprise, Jackson sought always to employ superior force. Nothing suggested he relied primarily on the much-vaunted individual superiority of the Southern soldier, though he believed his men much the better fighters. The superiority Jackson sought always was that of numbers. When he took the offensive, it was in the determination that he would throw against Banks every man he could bring up. In the last phase of the operations, his maneuvers were designed, of course, to prevent the junction of Frémont and Shields in order that he might assail them separately with numbers they could not resist.

In order to strike with more men than his adversary could assemble to oppose him, Jackson relied in large part on logistics. His appreciation of swift, well-timed movement was shown before the campaign opened. His regulations for the march were familiar in content but novel in rigid application. "Close up, men, close up" was almost the epitome of his system. On June 1, when Winder had to press his men to the absolute limit in order to reach Strasburg, the 2nd Virginia made thirty-six miles; the other regiments probably averaged thirty. What once had been done by his men, under immense strain, Jackson regarded as attainable again. Although on his later marches he seldom had a macadamized Valley Pike, he always marched as if the worst road presented no more difficulties than did the thoroughfare along the Shenandoah.

This soldierly combination of secrecy, superiority of force, and excellent logistics contributed to the third notable characteristic of the campaign, namely, the employment of the initiative in such a fashion as to strip his adversary of alternatives. On unhappy May 24 it was impossible for Jackson to limit Banks to a single course that could be foreseen and countered. At every other stage of the campaign, Jackson's strategic system so completely gave him the initiative that he could impose his will and dictate his opponent's action. Jackson left Banks no alternative but to retreat and then, closely pursued, to give battle at Winchester. Even after the advantage shifted and Jackson himself had to retreat, he interposed where he could compel Frémont to attack. Shields's choice, which was fight or run, was forced upon him. In the battle at Port Republic on June 9, Jackson left Frémont as helpless as if the action had been a hundred miles away. Jackson may have known—as he subsequently demonstrated—that he was not particularly apt in guessing what his antagonist would do. He carried the problem beyond the realm of guesswork to leave his opponent only one course of action, the course for which he was already prepared.

For these three reasons—judgment of ground, a sound balance of strategy, and the employment of that strategy to impose his will on his adversary—the Valley campaign of Stonewall Jackson marked him as a soldier of the highest promise.

With a force that never had exceeded, if indeed it reached, 17,000 men of all arms, he had cleared the enemy from the greater part of the Shenandoah. What was far more important, he had used this small force so effectively that he forced President Lincoln to change the entire plan for the capture of Richmond. At a time when the junction of McDowell with McClellan would have rendered the defense of the capital almost hopeless, Jackson temporarily had paralyzed the advance of close to 40,000 Federal troops. Rarely in war had so few infantry achieved such dazzling strategic results.

Stonewall's victories had come, moreover, when they inspired a discouraged Confederacy. Press and people did not know that the larger strategic plan was Lee's, not Jackson's. What the South saw of the outcome was enough. Through a long and losing defensive, the Confederacy had seen its leaders killed and its territory overrun. Albert Sidney Johnston was dead; Beauregard's star was low in the West; Joe Johnston lay wounded in Richmond after a battle that many knew to have been mismanaged; Lee was in the public eye an administrator, an engineer, not a field commander. None of these had undertaken the offensive for which editors and politicians had been pleading until Jackson had struck. Now men's eyes lighted up when they mentioned him. He was a mystery, a phenomenon, perhaps a genius; he was the living vindication of the argument for the offensive; he was the hope of the South.

So thought the men who crowded the trains that were rumbling down the Virginia Central toward Richmond. Jackson had marched them till their legs ached; Jackson had shown them no mercy; but Jackson had won battles! The soldiers did not cease to regard him as crazy, but they looked at him with wondering eye. They called him "Old Jack" in a strange, affectionate awe. His ranking officers were less warm toward him. In colder estimation and larger knowledge of what had been done and what omitted, most of his brigadiers thought him, above all, lucky. The night before the army started for Richmond, four of Jackson's general officers were talking of the campaign. Their conclusion a staff man thus reported: ". . . all were of the opinion that Jackson could not continue to take such risks without at some time meeting with a great disaster."[46]

Some of these officers were winning the right to speak with a measure of authority. Winder had been conspicuous for sound judgment and swift, courageous leading. His advancement seemed certain, though Stonewall himself made no move to procure the nomination of another major general. Taylor's record in the campaign fully equaled Winder's. The performances of Trimble and Elzey at Cross Keys spoke for themselves. For both the generous Ewell had high praise in his report. Of Elzey he said: "I availed myself frequently during the action of that officer's counsel, profiting largely by his known military skill and judgment."[47]

He who thus bestowed praise was of all Jackson's subordinates the man who most deserved it. Next to Jackson himself, Ewell stood out. Every act of Dick Ewell's in the campaign had been at the standard of a competent, alert, and courageous lieutenant. Nor was Ewell above acknowledging his previous errors in appraising his comrades in arms. The night after Port Republic he had made the *amende honorable* in his piping voice. He reminded cavalryman Thomas Munford of a conversation of theirs one day at Conrad's Store. "I take it all back," said Ewell, "and will never prejudge another man. Old Jackson is no fool; he knows how to keep his own counsel, and does curious things; but he has method in his madness; he has disappointed me entirely."[48]

"Disappointed me entirely" . . . those were terms of high praise as Ewell jestingly used them. But as Richmond whispered "Jackson's coming" and waited expectantly for his lightning attack to flash, there was something ominous in Ewell's choice of the word "disappointed."

CHAPTER 11

Struggle for Richmond

1. JACKSON MARCHES TO A CONFUSING FIELD

Jackson had done his utmost to keep his destination a complete secret. When Whiting had ridden to Port Republic and asked for orders, Jackson merely told him to go back to Staunton—twenty miles!—where instructions would be sent him the next day. Whiting had been furious. "I believe," he stormed, "he hasn't any more sense than my horse!" Whiting found orders there to retrace his steps to Gordonsville, and he broke out: "Didn't I tell you he was a fool, and doesn't this prove it? Why, I just came through Gordonsville day before yesterday!"

Chief of staff Dabney himself had not been informed of the general's plan until the head of the column reached Mechum River. Then Jackson took the major into a room in the hotel, locked the door, and explained that he intended to go to Richmond and that Dabney must march the army down the Virginia Central toward that city. Thereupon Jackson boarded the train and started eastward. "Here, now," Dick Ewell complained bitterly, "the general has gone off on the railroad without intrusting to me, his senior major general, any order, or any hint whither we are going."[1]

Because the Virginia Central had been cut by the destruction of the long bridge over the South Anna River, Jackson had at his disposal only the rolling stock that chanced to be west of the stream when Federal raiders burned the crossing. Less than 200 small cars, most of them for freight, were available and congestion on the line was serious. The wagons, the artillery, and the cavalrymen had to make the best of the bad roads they traversed. Carelessness and inefficiency were frequent, and when Major Dabney finally caught up with Jackson at Gordonsville he was indignant. "Well, yes, these things are bad, of course, and my corps is not disciplined as I wish," Jackson admitted, "but in the urgency of the campaign I have not had time to straighten out such people. My object now must be to get the corps at the place at the time for striking the blow...."[2]

Jackson might have added that already he was losing time in accomplishing that object. Both he and much of his command had to wait at Gordonsville all of June 21 because of a rumor that a Federal force was advancing from the Rapidan. In the ranks arrival at Gordonsville fanned anew curiosity concerning their objective. From Gordonsville led the railway and the road to Rapidan, to Culpeper, and to Manassas: Did Jackson intend to follow that route and launch a movement against Washington? Was the journey to continue down the Virginia Central till within marching distance of Fredericksburg? Richmond often was ruled out as a possible objective, on the ground that there would have been no sense in dispatching Whiting to the Valley if the army were going to Richmond.[3]

Sunday morning, June 22, found Jackson at Fredericks Hall, twenty-six miles by rail east of Gordonsville. To the general it seemed proper that he and the troops remain where they were until the Sabbath was ended. He intended to apply, when circumstances permitted, the principle he had explained to Major Dabney: "The Sabbath is written in the constitution of man and horses as really as in the Bible: I can march my men farther in a week, marching six days and resting the seventh, and get through with my men and horses in better condition than if I marched them all seven days." He spent a quiet, meditative Sunday at Nathaniel Harris's home and attended religious service in Hood's brigade. That evening, when Mrs. Harris asked the general when he wished breakfast the next morning, he told her to have the meal at her usual time and to call him when it was ready. By that hour he and Major Harman and two guides were far on the way to Richmond.[4]

Hard riding for fifty-two miles brought Jackson wearily in fourteen hours to Lee's headquarters at High Meadows, the little home of the Dabb family, at the rear of the Confederate lines on the Nine Mile Road. He recognized Harvey Hill who ere long rode up the lane. Soon came also Longstreet and A. P. Hill to discuss with Jackson and the commanding general the plan for the battle. Often at Manassas Jackson had been with Longstreet; with D. H. Hill he had many ties, the closest being the fact that they were married to sisters. Jackson and Lee had not seen each other for months; Jackson and A. P. Hill had not met since Hill had become a general. Magruder and Huger were not present. Lee's only reference to their absence was the indirect one that he had chosen for the operation the divisions whose commanders sat with him.

Lee briefly explained his plan, which was shaped by the fact that McClellan's army was astride the Chickahominy on a line that ran from northwest to southeast. If the right flank, north of the river, could be turned and driven, two results could be expected: First, McClellan's line of

General line of Jackson's advance from the Shenandoah Valley to the Richmond front, June 1862.

rail supply with White House on the Pamunkey could be threatened and perhaps broken. Second, if McClellan's right were hurled back, his divisions south of the river would be compelled to retreat or to come out of their entrenchments and give battle. Excusing himself to transact some army business, Lee left his subordinates to agree on the details.

The four generals discussed first how the attack should be made. Their conclusion was that Jackson should proceed from Fredericks Hall to southeast of Ashland. Early on the morning of the day he passed Ashland, he was to notify General Branch, stationed at Half Sink on the Chickahominy and in liaison between Jackson and A. P. Hill. Branch would start south on the road paralleling the Chickahominy and east of it; Jackson was to be on the next road to the east, the second from the river. A. P. Hill would cross the Chickahominy at Meadow Bridge and proceed southeast to Mechanicsville, near which the Federal right flank was supposed to rest. The two columns, on different roads, were to make for Old Cold Harbor, whence the way was open to McClellan's line of supply. Longstreet was to cross the Chickahominy at Mechanicsville Bridge, which the march of Jackson and A. P. Hill would clear of the enemy, and support the latter; by the same route D. H. Hill was to support Jackson. All this was clear to the officers who had been around Richmond long enough to understand directions and routes. The plan readily may have been confusing to Jackson, who was not quick to grasp the geography of country he had not seen.

If the details were acceptable, when should the attack be delivered? Inasmuch as the other divisions were within striking distance, the answer depended on Jackson. After some debate, it was agreed the battle could be opened on June 26. Soon thereafter Lee re-entered the room. His lieutenants told him of their decisions, which he approved. Written orders, he said, would be dispatched to each of them. About nightfall the conference adjourned.[5]

Jackson left promptly and spent a second long and sleepless night on the road. When he reached his army during the morning of June 24 he found conditions there far from satisfactory; his faith in the versatility of ministers had not been vindicated in the case of Dr. Dabney. Not only was Dabney green at the work of directing a march, but he had been stricken with a violent intestinal malady. The column was extended over many miles of muddy roads, and prudence dictated a halt that day until it could be closed up. After two long nights in the saddle, Jackson did not possess his normal energy and probably failed to realize that he lacked drive and grasp of the situation; nothing indicates he regarded the delay as serious.[6]

Late that night a courier arrived from Lee's headquarters with the text of the order for the impending battle. It somewhat changed Jackson's role. He was directed to proceed on the twenty-fifth from Ashland and encamp for the night "at some convenient point west of the Central Railroad." Thence, at 3:00 A.M. on June 26, he was to begin his march and to communicate with Branch as previously understood. But, instead of following the second road east of the Chickahominy to the rear of Mechanicsville, he was to move farther to the east by a longer march. Then, *en échelon* with the divisions that were by that time to have crossed the Chickahominy, he was to turn at Beaver Dam Creek and to proceed, as agreed at the conference on the twenty-third, toward Old Cold Harbor.

When Jackson had been at headquarters he may or may not have learned enough about the terrain to realize that the change in orders reflected a purpose on the part of Lee to avoid a direct attack on Beaver Dam Creek, which was known to be a difficult position. The point of the orders, as they related to Jackson, was that he had a longer and perhaps more difficult march set for him on the day the battle was to open. Further, as he read, he could not have failed to reason that the time allotted him to get into position was running fast. Delay, change of orders, the prospect of long marches and hard fighting—and now, too, secrecy was lost. The Federals had wind of Jackson's approach. He could not hope for another Front Royal.[7]

2. THE NEW ORGANIZATION FAILS

The start of Jackson's march on the twenty-fifth was slow and without spirit. "The brigade commanders," Major Dabney indignantly wrote years afterward, "would not or could not get rations cooked, their own breakfasts, and their men under order earlier than an hour after sunrise, probably because their supply-trains were rarely in place, by reason of the indolence and carelessness of julep-drinking officers."[8] The "New Model" Army of the Valley, in a word, had not shaken off the habits of Old Virginia.

From the "Forward, march," mud and high water were encountered. The roads were heavy; the streams roared. Halts were frequent and long. At last, as nightfall approached, the tired, mud-covered troops had not passed Ashland, but they were so weary that Jackson had to stop and let them go into camp. He was about five miles short of the crossing of the Virginia Central, where Lee had ordered him to camp that evening. The march had been twenty miles, excellent in the circumstances. Jackson was in manifest distress that he had not reached the objective assigned him.

He decided that he would start his march at 2:30 A.M. instead of 3 o'clock. A courier brought him a dispatch from Lee, and eagerly, carefully, Jackson read the document. "By the map before me," the commanding general explained, Jackson the next day might march in two columns from the Virginia Central instead of one, following roads to Shady Grove Church and Pole Green Church, then toward Old Cold Harbor; "either of the latter routes would entirely turn Beaver Dam Creek."9

This information was supplemented by the arrival of an officer who was to become an unfailing admirer of the victor of the Valley campaign. Jeb Stuart was assigned to cover Jackson's left flank, and he had ridden out to Ashland in the hope he might assist Jackson in an unfamiliar country. Then, past midnight, Ewell and Whiting came to Jackson's quarters to ask about routes for tomorrow's march. He promised to think over the matter and communicate with them later. Said Ewell, when they were out of earshot: "Don't you know why Old Jack would not decide at once? He is going to pray over it first!" Indeed, when Ewell returned for something he had forgotten, he found the general on his knees.10

If Jackson slept at all after that, it could not have been for long. For a man who had spent two of the three preceding nights in the saddle, it was poor preparation for the coming conflict. He could not have counted for himself more than ten hours' sleep in ninety-six of anxious activity, hard riding, and vexatious administration.

Now, as if on two stages, began a grim drama. On the eastern stage, across the Chickahominy from Richmond, the gaunt figure of Jackson was to stand out as if the 18,500 men of his army were mere supernumeraries for the day. West of the river were several actors—Lee, Longstreet, D. H. Hill—but Fate was to have it that the most conspicuous, half hero, half marplot, was to be the youngest and the most recently risen of the major generals—A. P. Hill.

Jackson's camps scarcely were astir at daylight, despite his orders for the march to begin at 2:30. At 8 o'clock the columns were advancing cautiously down the Ashcake Road. At 9 o'clock the van approached the Virginia Central Railroad, five miles from Ashland. That is to say, Jackson was now six hours behind the schedule set in Lee's combat order. Jackson wrote Branch, as directed, that he was crossing the railroad. Three quarters of a mile east of the crossing Ewell turned to the right and moved south toward Shady Grove Church. Jackson went 1,200 yards farther and made a similar turn on his march in the direction of Pole Green Church.11

On the other stage, before light, D. H. Hill and Longstreet moved to the Mechanicsville Turnpike and the heights overlooking the Chickahominy. Branch marched his brigade into the open fields near the west bank of the Chickahominy, to be ready to cross when the expected message came from Jackson. A. P. Hill was concentrated opposite the Meadow Bridge. There was nothing to indicate the enemy sensed approaching danger or was preparing for it. On the front of Magruder and Huger all was quiet. At 10 o'clock Branch received Jackson's message and crossed the Chickahominy without opposition, taking the road southeast and parallel to the river.[12]

The sun was hot, the sky cloudless. At noon Jackson halted for an hour and rested his men. At 3 o'clock, which was to prove the decisive hour in the day's operations, he drove in a Federal cavalry outpost at Totopotomoy Creek. The retreating Unionists fired the bridge, but through the ingenuity of engineer officers the crossing was soon repaired. Cautiously, before advancing, Jackson shelled the woods on the opposite bank to drive out any enemy who might be lurking there.[13]

At 1 o'clock Branch approached Atlee's Station on the Virginia Central. He was not in touch with the rest of A. P. Hill's division west of the river, nor was he in liaison with Ewell or Jackson ahead of him. After a stiff skirmish he drove the Federals back toward Mechanicsville, his objective. By 3 o'clock A. P. Hill's thin patience was worn out. He had received no dispatch from Branch for several hours, and not a word directly from Jackson. Impetuously Hill determined to cross, as he later reported, "rather than hazard the failure of the whole plan by longer deferring it." Without sending word to Lee, he easily forced a crossing and started down the river toward Mechanicsville.[14]

By 4:00 P.M. Ewell had discovered Branch's column moving on a parallel road. After a brief exchange, the two resumed their march by routes that slowly diverged. Jackson's column, across the Totopotomoy, heard artillery fire and musketry at 4 o'clock, but of its significance nothing was known. Jackson passed Pole Green Church and, at 5 o'clock, reached Hundley's Corner, on the road from Shady Grove Church to Old Raleigh, as directed in Lee's orders. Ewell had meanwhile reached Shady Grove Church and turned eastward, according to the plan, to rejoin Jackson. Soon Ewell came into position on Jackson's right. Although the sound of a heavy engagement was audible, Ewell had no information of what was happening in the direction of Mechanicsville. Jackson's face showed that he was deeply disturbed. Late he was, lamentably late, but he was where Lee had told him A. P. Hill would be on his right, and D. H. Hill in support, for a general advance *en échelon.* Neither Hill was there; no notice of any change of plan—no directions of any sort—had come. Jackson decided he should move no farther. While the battle to the south still raged, he bivouacked for the night.[15]

A. P. Hill's division was across the Chickahominy by 3:30 and marching in two columns toward Mechanicsville, one of the columns on the road from Atlee's Station in advance of Branch on the same road. No courier was sent to Branch, nor was the proximity of Ewell known to Hill. About

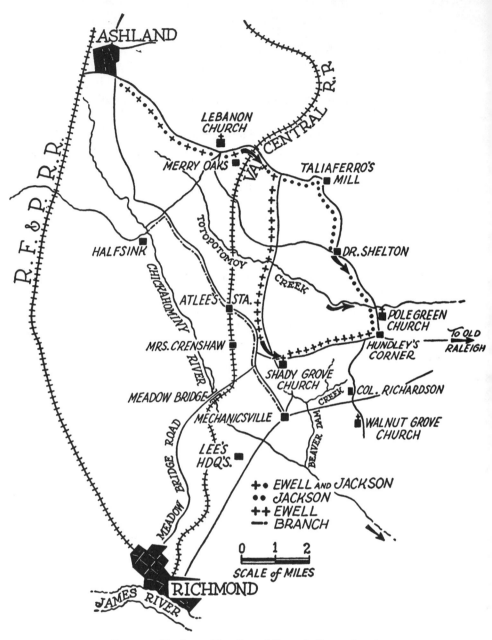

ASHLAND

LEBANON
CHURCH

MERRY OAKS

VA. CENTRAL R.R.

TALIAFERRO'S
MILL

R. F. & P. R. R.

HALFSINK

CHICKAHOMINY RIVER

TOTOPOTOMOY

CREEK

DR. SHELTON

ATLEE'S STA.

POLE GREEN
CHURCH

TO OLD
RALEIGH

MRS. CRENSHAW

HUNDLEY'S
CORNER

MEADOW BRIDGE

SHADY GROVE
CHURCH

COL. RICHARDSON

MECHANICSVILLE

BEAVER DAM CREEK

WALNUT GROVE
CHURCH

LEE'S
HDQ'S.

MEADOW BRIDGE ROAD

+• EWELL AND JACKSON
•• JACKSON
++ EWELL
—• BRANCH

0   1   2

SCALE of MILES

RICHMOND

JAMES RIVER

Routes of Jackson, Ewell, and Branch, June 26, 1862.

4 o'clock the advance of A. P. Hill's division came within artillery range of Mechanicsville, and his guns opened. This fire led Longstreet and D. H. Hill to prepare their divisions to cross the Mechanicsville Bridge. Lee's assumption was that A. P. Hill had "discovered" the movement of Branch and of Jackson opposite his front, as required by orders, and he was advancing in liaison with them. By 5 o'clock A. P. Hill was under heavy fire, but deferred assault on the Federal positions along Beaver Dam Creek because he knew this would entail heavy losses. The confusion was great. Branch would not arrive for an hour. Longstreet and D. H. Hill were delayed for want of pioneer troops to repair the Mechanicsville Bridge. A. P. Hill was waiting for the sound of Jackson's guns in the belief that Stonewall would attack at any moment, turning the creek and forcing the Federals to retreat from in front of Hill's brigades.[16]

Ere twilight came, A. P. Hill succeeded in establishing his line of battle, but he could advance his infantry no farther than the fringe of Beaver Dam Creek. D. H. Hill's and Longstreet's men crowded up behind, but in the confusion of the struggle there was little these troops could do. A. P. Hill hurled Ripley's brigade of D. H. Hill's division in support of Pender's North Carolinians against the Federal right. There the two brigades attacked, most gallantly and in vain. The repulse was complete. Infantry fire continued aimlessly until 9 o'clock; artillery disputed for an hour thereafter.[17]

Lee brought his division commanders together to review the situation. There was as yet no report of any sort from Jackson. No effort had been made to have a staff officer find him. On the field of combat it was manifest that all the Federals had been called upon to do was to wait for the Confederates to come into range and then mow them down. Already casualties were known to be heavy.[18]

Responsibility for this slaughter appeared to be divided. A. P. Hill was the conspicuous offender. Without waiting for Branch or for Jackson he had crossed Meadow Bridge in violation of orders. The defense of Hill was that he moved when he did because he believed further delay would jeopardize the whole plan. In the ranks the soldiers had done everything that could reasonably have been demanded of them. It was the high command that had failed. Hardly a detail of the plan of action had been executed on time and in accordance with the plan. A costly attack had been directed against a position the strength of which was so well known that a turning movement upstream had been regarded as the *sine qua non*. Concentration for an advance *en échelon* down the Chickahominy had not been effected. Worst of all, Jackson, the hero of the South, the unfailing Jackson who had dazzled the continent by his swift marches—Jackson had not arrived in time to have any share in the attack that was to save Richmond!

3. First Battle of the Army of Northern Virginia

When the front brigade of A. P. Hill's division renewed its attack on the line of Beaver Dam Creek in the early morning of June 27, it encountered feeble resistance. The Federals, learning of Jackson's presence, had drawn out their guns; their infantry had followed. Soon the entire Southern army was across the stream and in pursuit. Its general direction was eastward in four columns. Nearest the Chickahominy, using farm roads, was Longstreet's division. On his left A. P. Hill followed the county road toward Gaines' Mill and Old Cold Harbor. North of him marched D. H. Hill. By the same route, Jackson followed.

Of the ardor of the troops, and their determination, there could be no dispute. Whether General Lee could coordinate the attack of 56,000 men; whether the division commanders were equal to their duty; whether some of the new regimental and company officers chosen under the elective system were competent—these were the doubtful questions added to the usual uncertainties of battle. All the hazards, all the hopes, all the prowess of the thirty-five brigades of infantry seemed to be dramatized when, at Walnut Grove Church, Lee met Jackson. Scores of eyes were fixed at decent distance on Lee, who sat on a stump. As many gazed in admiration at the mysterious, bearded man from the Valley. Cap in hand, he stood by his horse opposite Lee and said little. At 11 o'clock, after a short conference, Jackson mounted and resumed the march.

A. P. Hill's Light Division (as he styled it) already had contact with the retreating Federals. The leading brigade was that of Maxcy Gregg. Forty-eight years of age was Gregg, a South Carolina lawyer, a bachelor, and culturally one of the best-furnished men of the Confederacy. Few knew the Greek dramatists or the philosophers so thoroughly. Perhaps none combined so precise a knowledge of botany, of ornithology, of astronomy. A scholar he was, a scientist and a gentleman. Was he a soldier? That day would show. He would open the battle.

Gregg's skirmishers sighted Federals behind the trees on a hill that overlooked a little north-and-south stream known as Powhite Creek. A scattered volley and then the Federal rear guard slipped away, and Gregg's men piled down the hill to the creek. There, at Gaines' Mill—a cool and pleasant place on a drowsy day—was a strong position, one where Lee had expected the Federal commander to give battle. No Federals were there, but enough and to spare in the distance! On Gregg pressed, his direction a little south of east, until he came to the crossroads of New Cold Harbor. His eager van hurled the Union skirmishers back and moved down a long hill. Suddenly and with a crash the enemy delivered a powerful volley.

Before its echo died, Union artillery opened. The enemy was flushed, was ready, was awaiting attack.[19]

Here was the position General McClellan had chosen to defend. All the cleared ground visible to the Confederates led down to a boggy little stream which natives styled Boatswain's Swamp. This was bordered widely by almost impenetrable underbrush and by large trees and small. South of the swamp, at a good elevation, most of it open farm land, the Federals had their infantry and their artillery. It was a perfectly protected position. At some points the enemy had three lines of temporary works in front of his commanding artillery. He could have searched the countryside and not have found a position easier to defend or more difficult to assail.

Powell Hill was as anxious to press the issue as he had been the previous day, but there was nothing of wild excitement about him now. Dressed in a fatigue jacket of gray flannel, with his felt hat pulled down over his eyes, he sat his horse easily and watched proudly the arrival of his other brigades. It was not easy for Hill to draw a line in the fields and fringes of woods that looked down on Boatswain's Swamp. As each of his brigades got within striking distance it drove at the enemy—only to be repulsed bloodily. Gregg did his utmost but could not shake the stubborn Federals. Branch, on Gregg's right, fought as hard as at Hanover Junction. Dorsey Pender, supporting Branch, could easily lead his men to a certain point; then even the stout North Carolinians would recoil. J.R. Anderson, Archer, and Field, in that order to the right, all had the same experience. Their men could get to the swamp; they could not penetrate it. The fire was too heavy.[20]

Longstreet's powerful command was at an angle of almost ninety degrees to the Light Division, but he had a difficult position from which to assault. "I was, in fact," said Longstreet, "in the position from which the enemy wished us to attack him."[21] Lee felt it prudent, in these circumstances, to defer Longstreet's attack until the arrival of Jackson on the extreme Confederate left forced the Federals to extend their line eastward. Then, when the force in front of Longstreet had been diminished, he would assail the Federal left.

That was a prudent, logical plan, but its success depended on the arrival of Jackson before A. P. Hill's division was wrecked. Including D. H. Hill, Jackson had under his command fourteen brigades, the largest force he ever had directed. Where was he? What delayed him? When would his men be thrown against the Federal right? Anxiously the questions were asked, but there was not the staff organization to answer them. From the time Jackson left Walnut Grove Church, no word had been heard of him.

The explanation was one of circumstances, of the trivial, unforeseen cir-

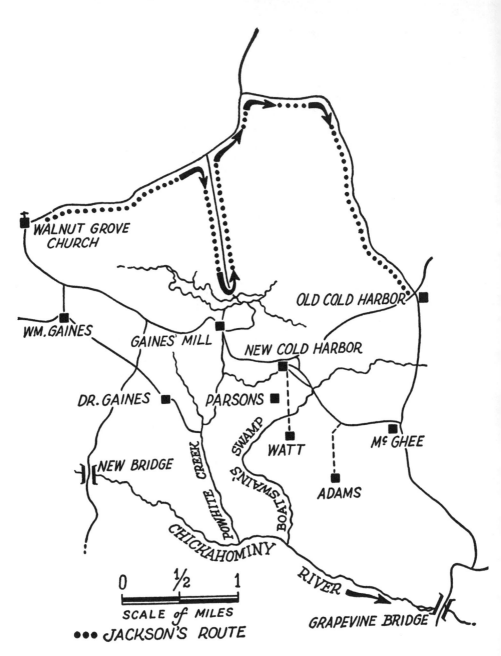

WALNUT GROVE
CHURCH

WM. GAINES

GAINES' MILL

OLD COLD HARBOR

NEW COLD HARBOR

DR. GAINES

PARSONS

Mc GHEE

WATT

NEW BRIDGE

POWHITE CREEK

SWAMP

BOATSWAIN'S

ADAMS

CHICKAHOMINY

RIVER

GRAPEVINE BRIDGE

0   ½   1
SCALE of MILES

●●● JACKSON'S ROUTE

Battlefield of Gaines' Mill, June 27, 1862, with Jackson's line of advance.

cumstances that so often wreck battle plans. D. H. Hill had taken the road ahead of Jackson and had advanced promptly to Old Cold Harbor, taking position on the upper end of Boatswain's Swamp. He found Federals there strongly posted and decided to remain until Jackson arrived. Jackson was late because his soldierly reticence, which perhaps was deepened in a strange country, had got him in trouble. To his guide he said only, in effect, Take me to Old Cold Harbor. Naturally the guide had chosen the shortest route, which struck the Cold Harbor road near Gaines' Mill. As they approached the millpond and heard firing, Jackson asked the guide where the road was leading them. Past Gaines' Mill to Old Cold Harbor, he was told. "But," Jackson broke out, "I do not wish to go to Gaines' Mill; I wish to go to Cold Harbor, leaving that place on the right." In that case, said the guide in exasperation, they should have taken the left-hand road back at the fork. It meant reversing the column and marching it about four miles to Old Cold Harbor.[22]

There Dick Ewell, at the head of the column, met Major Walter H. Taylor of Lee's staff, who had been sent to look for Jackson's troops. How far Jackson and Whiting were behind him, Ewell did not know, but he had troops at hand—Dick Taylor's, Trimble's, and Elzey's brigades—and he would use them as Lee wished. They at once were put in support of the left half of A. P. Hill's division. Ewell's seasoned troops found a task to test their staunchness. The enemy's fire shook the Louisianians. Gallant Colonel Isaac Seymour, commanding in place of the ill Dick Taylor, was killed. As Rob Wheat, leading the Tigers, cheered on his men he fell of a mortal wound. For the first time in its history the Louisiana brigade broke. Ewell had to withdraw it.

Of Trimble's brigade one regiment only and part of another got to the front on the first advance. Ewell himself could not resist the impulse to join them. He sensed the danger: If his thin line broke, the enemy might take the offensive. Trimble hurried back to bring up his other regiments, and Ewell remained near the front. Regardless of losses he must hold off the Federals. It was now past 4 o'clock. Over the field hung the smoke; dim and red shown the June sun. Close was the issue. The battle on the Confederate side clumsily had been one of divisions—first A. P. Hill's, later part of Ewell's. To the left D. H. Hill merely had occupied the enemy in his front. On the right Longstreet was ready, but still was being held for the arrival of Jackson to lead the other wing.

Now that Ewell had met such a fire that he could not advance, Longstreet got orders to make a diversion that would take some of the pressure off Hill and Ewell. He sent Pickett forward in a vigorous demonstration. The position was too strong; if Pickett's Virginians kept on they would be destroyed. Longstreet reasoned that if anything at all was to be done, a general assault had to be delivered. Notifying Lee, he began to arrange his forces for a direct thrust at the hillside in front of him.[23]

On the Confederate left the situation was no better. Jackson had arrived on D. H. Hill's front, but knew nothing of the terrain. He arranged Hill's line with open ground in advance so that, if the enemy were driven eastward, a clear field of fire would be offered. When he learned that Ewell's division was already engaged, he directed the only staff officer at hand, Major Harman, to carry orders back to Whiting and Winder. These two were to move up at once *en échelon* on the left of Ewell, and were to fill the gap between Ewell and D. H. Hill. Harman knew all about horses and wagons and little about military terms. When he reached Whiting he gave a muddled version of his instructions to that officer, who, by ill chance, was in no humor for any orders from Jackson. Whiting had been trying all the morning to tell Jackson what to do and had taken offense because Jackson paid him no heed. When the confused colloquy was ended, Whiting was left in the belief that Jackson wished him to remain where he was and to await further instructions. Whatever Winder behind him may have learned from Harman, he could not advance; the road was blocked. For an hour and more, then, the two divisions, together with Lawton's brigade, waited along the road while Ewell was wearing away his strength in the swamp.[24]

McClellan's troops were unshaken. Nothing less than an assault by the entire army, driven home at any cost, could rout the bluecoats. The outcome of the entire action might depend on Jackson. He did not realize it. Still less did Whiting and Winder. All three of them might remain idle till the hour was too late for a strong, united blow. Fortunately, Major Dabney had heard Jackson dispatch the orders Harman carried to Whiting. Ill though he was, Dabney determined to ride back up the road to the division commanders and make certain they understood the orders. Whiting confirmed in surly tones that he had seen Harman: "That man has been here with a farrago of which I could understand nothing." Dabney then explained that Jackson wished him to engage the enemy immediately. Whiting was disposed to argue, but he was prompt in moving.

With Hood's brigade in front, Whiting's division began to deploy. Lawton's brigade, at 3,500 men the largest in the army, came up and formed behind Gregg's thin but stubborn line. Dick Ewell, in the heaviest of the fighting, saw Lawton's men coming forward and, waving his sword, cried, "Hurrah for Georgia!" Far to the eastward, Harvey Hill was waiting to go forward. That left only Winder to complete Jackson's line. When he received a call to move up rapidly, Winder directed his advance to the sound of the heaviest fire, and soon found A. P. Hill, to whom he reported for orders.[25]

Five o'clock it now was. Only three hours of the long summer daylight remained. Would it be possible ere nightfall to put all those tangled brigades into position and throw them, as one man, against that fiery front on the long hill? Longstreet's deployment was complete. A. P. Hill's weary men could be expected to do little more than to follow a strong, fresh line. Ewell still was capable of hard fighting and, with Lawton's stout brigade, might share in the final gamble. Winder, rightly placed, had good firepower. D. H. Hill, ready to sweep forward, would be compelled to cross 400 yards of open ground. Was the gamble an even one? Could Jackson decide it?

The long day in a bewildering country had wearied Jackson. He needed refreshment. Out of his haversack he pulled not a bottle but a lemon. He began to suck it and, so engaged, started down the sun-scorched road toward New Cold Harbor. Dust covered him; his old cap was pulled down to his nose to shade his eyes from the glare. Not a word, not a gesture indicated his thought. Ahead he saw Lee; straight to the commander he rode.

"Ah, General," said Lee, "I am very glad to see you. I had hoped to be with you before." There was a mumbled answer, a jerk of the head—no more. "That fire is very heavy. Do you think your men can stand it?" "They can stand almost anything," came the proud answer. "They can stand that!" He listened as Lee explained how he was organizing the line. As soon as Jackson was sure he understood, he was off to the left to prepare for its execution.[26]

Delay seemed endless to those who waited for the command to advance. Slowly, almost imperceptibly, the final reinforcements felt their way across the fields. At last, close to 7 o'clock, the front was complete. Five hours it had taken to get all the brigades in position—five hours of hell for the men already engaged—but the task was done. The Army of Northern Virginia was ready for its first general assault on an enemy whose defense thus far had been superb. Lee ordered an advance by all the troops.

To Hood it was a challenge as stirring as a bugle call. Drop your knapsacks and blankets, he told his men; we are going to take that line. I am going to lead you. Whiting, too, rode along the front, and when the men cheered him he raised his hat. "Boys," he cried as he pointed toward the enemy's position, "you can take it!" The Texans and their comrades started forward across the field toward the swamp. On their right, Longstreet already was at grips with the Federal infantry. Ewell was down in the swamp in person directing his men, who were getting support from Gregg and from other of A. P. Hill's brigades. Lawton's men kept an unbroken front. Trimble was everywhere with the same cry, "Charge, men, charge!"

Winder, on Ewell's left, went forward. Back of the line Jackson was in the exaltation of conflict. His face was crimson; under his cap-brim his eyes were burning. To each division commander he sent the same message: "Sweep the field with the bayonet!"[27]

D. H. Hill, on the extreme left, moved forward swiftly to the swamp. There was confusion in the maze of underbrush. Robert Rodes, still weak from his wounds at Seven Pines, strove to untangle his brigade of Alabamians. G. B. Anderson—tall, erect, composed—found Federal infantry in the maze, but at the word of command in his magnificent voice his men drove out the enemy. Garland kept pace with Anderson. All along the left, the swamp was cleared of the enemy. Ahead was a shell-swept open field, a quarter of a mile to the crest. G. B. Anderson, Garland, and Hill gathered to study the ground, exposed but as unconcerned as if no battle were raging. Hill devised a plan to take a battery enfilading their advance. Colonel Alfred Iverson's 20th North Carolina maneuvered around the flank of the battery. The Carolinians were in full cry; then they were upon the guns. Hill unloosed every regiment on the edge of the swamp. In a long, cheering line they mounted the ridge. Soon the Federals were wavering, were breaking.[28]

Far to the west, almost at that moment, rolled the triumphant yells of Whiting's men. Hood's and Law's brigades, leaving a thousand dead and wounded behind them, had cracked the Unionist front and were clambering over the batteries that for five hours had defied A. P. Hill's attack. Longstreet was on the crest of the hill within a few minutes; Lawton and Winder and Ewell swept up. For half an hour there was spasmodic fighting, then darkness and a field of victory.

In the praise of the camps, highest honors went to Hood and his fine regiments. Said Jackson, riding over the ground of Hood's advance, "These men are soldiers indeed!" It was noticed that the Federals abandoned all resistance on that part of the field as soon as these fierce soldiers were upon them. The other brigade of Whiting, led by Colonel E. M. Law, had shared fully the advance of Hood. For his general direction of these two brigades, Whiting received the credit he deserved. Among the other general officers, Maxcy Gregg had given an unequivocal answer to the question whether he would make a soldier. Trimble and Winder had added new honors to those won in the Valley. Garland had justified everything said of him after Seven Pines. Scores of others received and deserved commendations as warm. All told, said Longstreet, "there was more individual gallantry displayed upon this field than any I have ever seen."[29]

But the casualties! Some 8,000 Confederates had fallen. Arnold Elzey had received a horrible wound of the face and neck, and Pickett had been wounded seriously. The most gruesome loss had been among the regimental commanders—eight killed or mortally wounded. With the two killed the day before at Mechanicsville, the offensive thus far had taken ten colonels, besides those wounded.

Costly, then, the victory was . . . and it was only the second engagement in what might prove a long struggle to save Richmond.

4. Magruder Stays Up Too Long

Beneath the fog of war and beyond the impenetrable woods, much had been happening to the Federals since A. P. Hill had opened the battle at Mechanicsville. General McClellan had become convinced that his army, which numbered about 105,000 officers and men, was outnumbered almost two to one. The approach of Jackson had decided him that he could not retain any force north of the Chickahominy. Accordingly, on the night of June 26, following the action on Beaver Dam Creek, he had concluded to retreat and establish a new base on the James River, where he would have the protection of the Federal gunboats. He had accepted battle at Gaines' Mill because he feared a general withdrawal on the twenty-seventh would have exposed the rear of the army and "enabled Jackson's fresh troops to interrupt the movement. . . ."

To delay the Confederate attack, McClellan had left behind at Boatswain's Swamp the V Corps of Fitz John Porter, which he reinforced to about 35,000 before the close of the action. Porter's defense, costing 6,837 casualties, confirmed McClellan's purpose to retreat or, more euphemistically, to "change his base." Any counterthrust on the south side of the river against Huger and Magruder he ruled out. His reasoning, rendered faulty by his gross overestimate of the forces opposing him, even led him to apprehend an attack on the south as well as the north bank of the river. On the night of June 27, after the Battle of Gaines' Mill, he announced his plans of withdrawal. Keyes's IV Corps was to cross White Oak Swamp on the twenty-eighth and cover the flank against attack from the direction of Richmond. Porter was to follow. As soon as the wagon trains had passed, Franklin, Sumner, and Heintzelman, commanding the other corps, were to withdraw on June 28–29 from their lines south of the Chickahominy. These troops were to hold the rear against attack and then head for the James River.[30]

To this retreat the little stream known as White Oak Swamp, forming almost a half circle of about ten miles in total length, presented both obstacle and cover. On its upper reaches the creek presented no material difficulty in dry weather, but after heavy rains it overflowed swiftly and transformed all approaches into a bog. Access to it was easy enough from McClellan's position. Numbers of roads ran down to it from the north. The principal crossing was at White Oak Swamp Bridge, about five miles southeast of Savage Station. From this crossing a decent road ascended to Long Bridge Road. Once this highway was passed, there was a slow descent to the James, distant near seven miles by road. McClellan's problem was to get quickly across the swamp without overcrowding the approaches. Then he could hope to hold the swamp against attack from the rear. As he progressed toward the James River he would have to guard his column against attack from the west only; from no other quarter did it seem likely he could be assailed.

None of this was known, on the morning of June 28, to the Confederates north of the Chickahominy or to those who faced the enemy between New Bridge and White Oak Swamp. Would the Federals remain south of the river? Might not McClellan move down southeasterly along the south bank of the Chickahominy and recross to the north bank in order to reestablish his line of supply down the Peninsula? Not until the early morning of the twenty-ninth was the answer clearly "No." Then, but not until then, was it established that McClellan was heading for the James River. It was impracticable to concentrate against the Federal rear north of White Oak Swamp before night; the distances were too great. Thus Lee did not undertake to prevent a crossing of the swamp. He planned instead to press the Federal rear north of the morass on June 29, and to move the remainder of his troops, by the roads nearer Richmond, until they could strike the Federals the next day, June 30, on the march from White Oak Swamp toward the James. This involved a difficult convergence, but against an opponent who in this terrain could steal a day's march, there was no alternative.

Early on the morning of the twenty-ninth the division commanders got their orders. Jackson was to bridge the Chickahominy and then sweep down between the river and the swamp with his own, Ewell's, Whiting's, and D. H. Hill's divisions. Magruder was instructed to push down the Williamsburg Road and have Jackson's support in attacking the enemy. Huger's orders were to proceed eastward on the Charles City Road, south of the swamp, and on the thirtieth take the Federals in flank. Longstreet and A. P. Hill were to recross the Chickahominy close to Richmond and march down the Darbytown Road to a position on Huger's right, where they, also, were to assail the flank of McClellan as he moved toward the James River. T. H. Holmes, who had crossed from the south bank of the James, was to be on the right of Longstreet and A. P. Hill, in order to head off McClellan.

Which were the more difficult tasks in this convergence? Who had the largest opportunity? How well suited for their missions were the divisional commanders? Longstreet, who ranked A. P. Hill, was given direction of their joint operations. He would have a long march, but would encounter no natural obstacle. Holmes had a clear road. Huger had to cover approximately eight and a half miles. Magruder would have rear guard action and might have to pass through some fortified positions. To Jackson, as in the opening of the campaign, the most arduous task was assigned. Troops enough he had: Was his mission too large for the time allowed him?

Magruder was to open the third act of the drama and probably was to have the largest opportunity. Thus far Magruder had taken his posting very seriously. As one of his staff put it, "we all thought that the position of holding our front lines against McClellan and thereby protecting Richmond, was the post of honor as well as of danger, because it never occurred to us that McClellan with his superior numbers could fail to attack and seek to break through. . . ."[31] The instructions to Magruder and Huger had been to demonstrate in order to ascertain what the Federals were doing. Prince John busily stirred his pickets; at frequent intervals he had his batteries challenge those of the Unionists to be sure no withdrawal was in progress. During the fighting at Mechanicsville and Gaines' Mill he had grown restless and apprehensive. What if the Federals should attack; what if they were about to do so? By the twenty-eighth all his efforts to ascertain their movements had come to nothing. Where the earthworks were visible they appeared to be fully manned; the woods were impenetrable; every road was well guarded. Magruder still remained in the deepest concern lest he be attacked.

It was now 3:30 on the morning of June 29, and General Magruder was not physically at his best for what might prove his day of days. A bad attack of indigestion was persisting, and medicine given him by the surgeon was having an exciting effect. In none of the dramas he had played as an amateur thespian had he assumed so great a role as the one that now was his, that of pursuing a vast army. His relief was immense when finally he heard that the Federals were known to be withdrawing from his front.[32]

Before Magruder made his dispositions to pursue, Colonel R. H. Chilton of Lee's staff rode up to summon him to a meeting with the commanding general. The two overtook Lee and his staff on the Nine Mile Road, and the cavalcade followed the line of the Federal retreat toward Fair Oaks. Magruder listened, perhaps abstractly, while Lee explained the plan for the reconcentration. Longstreet and A. P. Hill were to cross in rear of Magruder's position and move to the extreme right, so they could intercept McClellan en route to the James River; Huger was to proceed down the Charles City Road; Jackson was to cross—perhaps already had crossed—the Chickahominy and operate against the enemy's flank nearest the river. Magruder's mission was explicit: He was to press directly on the Federal rear and was to attack.[33]

Magruder was now in charge of the field and of the pursuit of the rear guard. Eastward, the track of the York River Railroad disappeared in a long, scarcely perceptible curve between woodland on either side. Less than a mile to the southeast, hidden by forest, was the Williamsburg Road. From the nature of the terrain, the Federal retreat had to be eastward and southeastward across White Oak Swamp toward the James River. D. R. Jones and Kershaw were coming forward. McLaws's other brigade, that of Paul Semmes, had not arrived from the line of fortifications. Magruder's own division was approaching, under Howell Cobb and Richard Griffith. Six brigades, then, approximately 11,000 infantry, could be concentrated against an enemy who, as yet, had shown no more than a skirmish line and had not halted anywhere for a stand.

As he made his dispositions, Magruder became convinced that the enemy was preparing to attack him in numbers far exceeding his own. He sent Major Joseph L. Brent, his ordnance officer, posthaste to Lee to request that Huger's division reinforce him. According to Brent, General Lee "seemed surprised and a little incredulous. He said his information was that the enemy was in rapid retreat, and he thought that his rear guard would scarcely deliver battle at the point indicated." Still, he said he would have Huger detach two brigades to report to Magruder; but if they were not engaged by 2 o'clock they must be returned to Huger.

Not content with assurance of help in that quarter, Magruder sent to the left to ascertain where Jackson was and what cooperation could be given on that flank. He was told that Jackson was rebuilding the Chickahominy bridge on his front and would not be ready to cross for two hours. Thereupon, still in the belief that he was about to be attacked, Magruder decided he would delay his advance until Huger came up on his right and Jackson on his left. When they arrived, he intended to envelop the entire Federal rear guard.[34]

Forgotten, apparently, were Magruder's orders to pursue vigorously. With six good brigades at hand, supported by artillery, he waited out of range. An hour passed, perhaps two hours. Huger rode over through the blistering heat to Magruder's field headquarters to report his two brigades were arriving and was puzzled at the lack of any indication of a Federal advance. Magruder went off to busy himself moving his troops to better defensive positions. When the bluecoats attacked him, he would give them the best battle he could! Finally a messenger from Huger reached him: General Huger presents his compliments and begs to advise that under his orders he did not think it necessary for his two brigades to remain longer, and he was withdrawing them for other service.[35]

That was not the end of the troubles for the tired and excited Magruder. D. R. Jones sent a dispatch from the left that closed, "I had hoped that Jackson would have cooperated with me on my left, but he sends me word that he cannot, as he has other important duty to perform." Huger withdrawing; Jackson unable to cooperate—what was Magruder to do? What could he do except to obey orders that had contemplated his pursuit of the enemy in the forenoon? There was no chance now of a great coup; did he reason, too, that there was small risk of defeat? "I ordered the whole to move to the front," he subsequently reported, "and each commander to attack the enemy in whatever force or works he might be found."[36]

Rhetorically the statement was fine; tactically the performance was

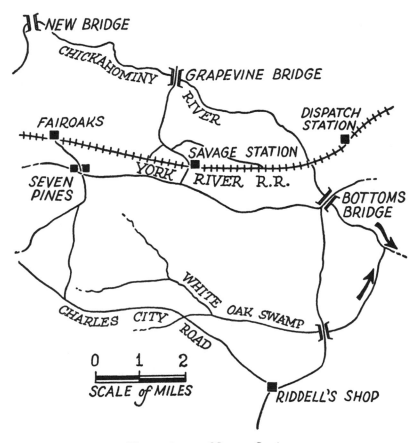

The environs of Savage Station.

timid. The "whole" was not sent forward. Of six brigades present, he used only two. The advance of Kershaw and Semmes, gallantly led and well handled, was resisted stoutly. When the two were halted by darkness and a terrific thunderstorm, after sustaining 354 casualties, they were close to the farthest point they had gained. The Battle of Savage Station was over, but Magruder was not satisfied that this meant an end to the attack of which he had been apprehensive all day. At last, about 3:30 A.M. on the thirtieth, to which hour Magruder remained anxiously awake, Jackson arrived at Magruder's post and announced that the Valley troops probably would be up by daylight. Prince John breathed freely once again. "I then slept an hour," he observed in his report, "—the first in forty-eight." His brief rest could not have been sweetened by the last note he had received from Lee. "I regret much that you have made so little progress today in the pursuit of the enemy," the commanding general wrote. ". . . We must lose no more time or he will escape us entirely."[37]

The past tense might have been employed. So far as Magruder was involved, the enemy *had* escaped already. In front of him, in the vicinity of Savage Station, had been three corps, but they had been under orders simply to hold their ground until darkness and then to continue the retreat. A sustained attack by Magruder probably would have led to a bloody repulse; when the Confederates did attack, a single brigade stopped them.[38]

Early on the morning of June 30, Magruder received orders that might have been construed as indicating that his performance on the twenty-ninth was not rated highly by G.H.Q. He was to leave to Jackson the pursuit of the enemy, retrace his steps, and move down the Darbytown Road. That is to say, he was to be taken from the rear of the enemy and placed in support of the Confederate right. The post of danger and of opportunity—if of responsibility—was taken from him and given that strange man Jackson.

CHAPTER 12

Richmond Relieved

1. THE DELAY IN THE RECONCENTRATION

While Magruder was hesitating on the afternoon of June 29 because he feared a Federal onslaught, the preparations of General Lee to attack McClellan the next morning were being developed unevenly. Longstreet and A. P. Hill were moving from the north to the south side of the Chickahominy and advancing at satisfactory speed to the Darbytown Road. There was every reason to believe they would be in position, early on the thirtieth, to assail the flank of the Federals en route to the James River. Full convergence of the Southern columns would depend, first, on the ability of Huger to come up promptly on Longstreet's left; second, on the success of Jackson in crossing White Oak Swamp to strike the rear of McClellan; and third, though less importantly, on the arrival of Holmes to the right of Longstreet.

Huger's lead brigade, on the Charles City Road, was that of William Mahone, a most unusual man. Virginia born, he physically was so short of stature and so frail that he seemed insignificant, but this Virginia Military Institute graduate had established himself as a resourceful construction engineer for railroads. When the war began he was in his thirty-fifth year, was president of the Petersburg and Norfolk Railroad, and was full of restless, driving energy. He volunteered promptly and received rapid promotion. His reputation as a swift builder had led, in the spring of 1862, to his assignment to Drewry's Bluff, where the immediate strengthening of the river defenses had been considered essential to the safety of Richmond. This work done, Mahone returned as the senior brigadier in Huger's division, and, in Huger's absence, occasionally acted as its head.

That afternoon Mahone was directing the march down the Charles City Road. At the Brightwell farm the advance encountered a cavalry outpost, which quickly disappeared. Mahone halted the troops and examined the ground. To the north a road ran to Jordan's Ford in White Oak Swamp. Might not the enemy be planning to cross at Jordan's and take this route via Brightwell's toward the James? A reconnoitering party was dispatched toward the swamp. Soon word came back that the enemy was at Jordan's and was in the very act of crossing southward. Mahone immediately threw out a heavy skirmish line. A collision followed—a spat of fire and a quick, somewhat suspicious withdrawal by the bluecoats.

General Huger now reached Brightwell's and resumed command. He was far from satisfied with the prospect. Prisoners stated that the Federals were still north of the swamp—Kearny's division of Heintzelman's III Corps. Huger learned also of the New Road that ran north of and parallel to the swamp. This road gave the Federals freedom of action to move from one ford to another; they could demonstrate at one crossing to cover the passage of another. Huger concluded that if he left Jordan's Ford unguarded, Kearny might cross in his rear as readily as in his front, and he chose to bivouac at Brightwell's. It seemed a logical or, at the least, a cau-

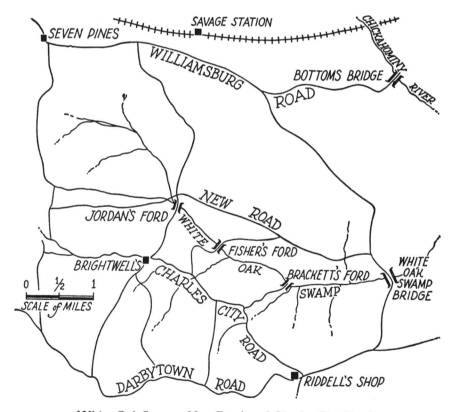

White Oak Swamp, New Road, and Charles City Road,
to illustrate Huger's advance of June 29–30, 1862.

tious course to follow. Actually, as often happens in war, Huger's information was outdated almost before it reached him. Kearny had gone down to
Jordan's but decided against crossing there, proceeded eastward on the
New Road, and already was negotiating the swamp between Huger's
bivouac and the objective Lee had set for him.[1]

While Huger was debating his proper course of action on the evening
of June 29, at the very time Magruder hesitantly was engaging the Federal
rear guard at Savage Station, Stonewall Jackson was ending two exasperating and unprofitable days. When, on the twenty-ninth, Lee became convinced that the Federal army was moving for the James River, he directed
Jackson immediately to repair the bridge the Federals had destroyed. Jackson's further orders, as Major Dabney remembered them, were "to march
eastward by the Savage Station road, parallel to . . . the Chickahominy; to
guard all the northward . . . thus forming a line of protection for the movement of Lee's other columns south of him; and not to leave that eastbound
road until he had passed the extreme northern flank of McClellan's force
and gotten in his rear."

These seemed to be clear and simple orders. To obey them, Jackson, on
the morning of June 29, directed Major Dabney to reconstruct Federal
engineer Barton Alexander's bridge (misnamed the Grapevine Bridge by
the Confederates). Dabney must have been chosen for the task because
none of the engineers was at hand; and he soon demonstrated that he was
not so good a builder as he was a preacher. Progress was discouragingly
slow. Fortunately, Captain C. R. Mason appeared with his Negro navvies.
This remarkable man was one of Jackson's "finds." Not an educated engineer, Mason had a knack for the rapid construction of rough, stout bridges
using the skilled labor of his work crew. He relieved Dabney's detachment
and began to give form to the structure.[2]

As soon as the bridge was passable at all, though still unfinished, Jackson himself went over and rode about three quarters of a mile southward to
the Trent house to examine the ground there. Then there came to him
from Colonel Chilton at headquarters a dispatch that redefined his role—
the "important duty" that he would say prevented him from supporting
Magruder as originally planned. Concerned that the enemy might yet
cross the Chickahominy downstream and escape down the Peninsula, Lee
assigned Jackson the additional task of guarding the crossings if that was
attempted. Jackson recognized no *if* in Chilton's writing; as he had not yet
crossed his divisions to the south bank, he took it as his duty to stay right
where he was. "Genl. Ewell will remain near Dispatch Station," he wrote
on the dispatch, "and myself near my present position."[3]

2. TWO COLUMNS ARE HALTED

General Lee correctly assumed that after McClellan crossed White Oak Swamp, the direction of his retreat would be toward the James River by the shortest route. This almost certainly would carry the Federals to a little settlement known as Glendale or Riddell's Shop, southeast of White Oak Swamp Bridge at the junction of the Charles City and Darbytown roads. From there McClellan would head south. The plan of the Army of Northern Virginia called for a concentration all the way southward from the fringe of the swamp to the river, and parallel to the north-south roads by which McClellan was moving. This would make the direction of the Confederate attack eastward, except for Jackson who would close in on the Federal rear from the north. Simultaneous convergence of four columns was undeniably a difficult matter, but in the situation that existed it was the only practicable maneuver, and it did not seem complicated beyond attainment—at least each of the columns was to advance by a separate road; none would cross the route of any other.

These were the specific missions of the four columns:

1. Holmes was to proceed on the River Road past New Market and engage the enemy where found. The length of his march would be about nine miles, with no material obstruction.

2. Magruder was to turn from Savage Station to the rear, cross over to the Darbytown Road, and support Longstreet. The distance was approximately eleven miles to Longstreet's bivouac.

3. Longstreet, with his own and A. P. Hill's divisions, was to continue along the Darbytown Road until he encountered the Federals. His march probably would not be more than six miles.

4. Huger was to proceed from Brightwell's for about three miles down the Charles City Road, through woodland, to the junction with the Darbytown Road and was to attack the enemy when found.

5. Jackson was to advance from the Alexander bridge and clear the enemy from the woods near the Chickahominy. Then he was to turn south when opposite McClellan's rear, pass White Oak Swamp Bridge, and press the Unionists. He had eight and a half miles to go and had to cross a stream that might be troublesome.

If all went well, the order of battle would be: extreme right, Holmes; right center and center, Longstreet and A. P. Hill, with Magruder in support; left, Huger; rear of the enemy, Jackson. Such was the plan of convergence as seen from army headquarters. Because all the generals were well instructed, the story of the day should have been one of a driving march and a straining effort by every column to reach its assigned place at the earliest moment. Instead, the events of June 30 fall into a succession of delays, of groping marches, of separate decisions as if some of the divisional commanders had no regard for time and felt more concern for their reputations than for the outcome of the battle.

Soon after daybreak, June 30, with Mahone in front, Huger started his advance from Brightwell's. Mahone proceeded with great caution. He reasoned that Kearny might wait in the swamp and get in rear of the Confederates after they had passed down the road—only to be told by residents that the Union troops had crossed at Fisher's, the next ford on the left of Huger's advance, the previous evening. Was Kearny, then, now in front, down the Charles City Road? Could the Confederate advance be pushed without further thought for the security of the left flank? Huger and Mahone concluded that this could be done. But no sooner was Fisher's passed than fire was opened from the enveloping woods. Ahead, on the road, as far as vision carried, newly felled trees lay in grim obstruction.

What was to be done now? Again Huger left the decision to Mahone, perhaps because he had the reputation of a specialist in dealing with swamp and forest. When Mahone reported that it would be easier to make a new road through the woods for the artillery than to clear the old one, Huger sent word to Lee that his march was obstructed. Mahone put his men to work felling trees, but tools were few and progress slow. The strange spectacle was presented of a battle of rival axemen. Beyond their front, McClellan's trains rumbled toward the river. It was a curious episode. In a metaphor of the woods, while the hunter fumbled, the quarry was escaping.[4]

Soon after sunrise, Lee came up and gave Magruder his orders to start for the Darbytown Road. Magruder, wrote Major Brent, "seemed to me to be under a nervous excitement that strangely affected him. He frequently interposed in minor matters, reversing previous arrangements and delaying the movement he was so anxious to hasten." Finally Brent spoke up, saying he was sorry to see that the General was not feeling well that morning. "Well, Major, you are right," admitted Magruder. "I am feeling horribly." He explained that the medicine given him for his indigestion by the surgeon contained morphine, "and the smallest quantity of it acts upon me as an irritant." He made efforts to regain his self-control, but his excitement continued.[5]

Ere Magruder started, Lee reviewed with Jackson the part that officer was to have in the operations of the day. Jackson seemed all energy. The Federals manifestly had evacuated the area, and booty was everywhere. The "wagon-hunter" could not fail to gather at least something from the abundance the enemy had left. This took time. So did the collection of hundreds of Federal stragglers from the woods. It was noon when Jackson reached the fringe of White Oak Swamp, close to the bridge over which the Federals had retreated.

A forbidding place the swamp was. Like the Chickahominy, the stream itself was shallow and little scarped. In dry weather the sole difficulty in crossing it was offered by the underbrush and briars along the banks. Of sound and beauty there was little. The kildee and the mockingbird shunned the confinement of boughs that shut out the sun. Voiceless the stream flowed over its soft bottom. No vistas opened on the variant greens. Shadows dulled the colors. Such was White Oak Swamp at its best. At its worst, the stream spread swiftly from its bed and set a barrier almost impassable, and to this condition it had been brought by the torrential downpour of the night of the twenty-ninth. The ring of the sharpshooter's rifle warned that man's weapons reinforced the swamp's resistance.

Contact was established: What was ahead? Jackson could see across the swamp to the enemy's position on the left of the road. White Oak Swamp Bridge itself manifestly was broken. Beyond it the road passed directly over a hill and disappeared. On the level crest the guns of about three batteries were visible, and behind them a long line of infantry, lying down. A heavy fringe of tall timber provokingly cut off all observation on the right. There was no way of telling in what strength the Federals occupied that side of the road.[6]

Such a situation called for the employment of Jackson's artillery. Colonel Crutchfield advanced twenty-eight guns and had them shotted under cover, and at 1:45 P.M., with a rush, he brought out these fieldpieces onto a dominating ridge and opened on the batteries across the swamp. The effect must have warmed the heart of the general who as a young man first had caught the eyes of his superiors by his handling of a gun section under the shadow of Chapultepec. The Federal artillerists limbered up their pieces and hurried off, leaving three damaged rifles. The startled infantry dashed for the rear.

It was now 2 o'clock. Along the Darbytown Road General Lee and President Davis were waiting with Longstreet's command and wondering what had delayed for hours the attacks by Huger and Jackson. On the Charles City Road Huger was chopping trees and dragging the trunks aside to clear a new road for his artillery. Late as it was, Jackson's part in the convergence did not seem beyond attainment. Let Munford's 2nd Virginia cavalry cross the swamp, charge up the hill, and secure the guns the Federals had abandoned. Jackson himself mounted to ride with the troopers.[7]

The clatter of the cavalry, a splash through the ford, and then—up the hill! The column deployed as it reached the open ground. Jackson was close in the rear. Immediately a field battery roared. Jackson turned to see whence came this challenge. One glance was enough: There were blue infantrymen opposite his right, thousands of them, in full possession of a fine position, the strength of which had been hidden by the trees that cut off vision from the north side of the swamp. As Jackson looked, more Union batteries dashed up. Regiments were forming in line of battle. What could Munford's men do? Nothing except quit the field or subject themselves to futile slaughter! Skillfully the colonel veered off to the east to escape the fire. Jackson turned back swiftly the way he had come and returned to his lines north of the swamp.[8]

The incident was a definite repulse. Those Federals on the high ground could prevent a crossing at the bridge. It was manifest; it was indisputable. Incredibly, almost mysteriously, and for the first time in his martial career, Jackson quit. His initiative died almost in the moment of his return from the south side of the swamp. The alert, vigorous Jackson of the early morning grew weary, taciturn, and drowsy. Marshy approaches, destruction of the bridge, and the fire from the new Federal position made a crossing impossible. This he concluded and then, exhausted, went to sleep under a tree.[9]

D. H. Hill was not willing to admit that nothing more could be done. As Crutchfield's guns dueled with the well-protected Federal batteries, Hill tried to get a fatigue party to the site of the broken bridge, but they could not work under the enemy's shellfire. Nothing stirred Jackson to action. When he awakened, he sat on a tree trunk, gazing at the ground, and said little. "Rans" Wright, of Huger's command, came up to report that he had traversed the length of the New Road and found no Federals north of the swamp. Jackson had no orders for him. Cavalryman Munford announced that he had found an unguarded crossing. Jackson sent him no instructions.

General Wade Hampton had also discovered a good crossing, and Jackson seemed to show somewhat more interest. Could Hampton make a bridge at the point he had described? It would be easy, Hampton answered. Build the bridge, Jackson ordered. Soon Hampton returned from his mission to report the bridge done and his brigade ready to cross; the Federals on the other side, he said, were quiet and unsuspecting. Jackson sat on the log, silent and motionless, his cap pulled down over his eyes, listening until Hampton was finished. Then, without a word of thanks or of instruction to the brigadier, he got up and walked away.

Progressively louder roared the sound of a battle from the south. Efforts to rebuild White Oak Swamp Bridge were abandoned. Eighteen thousand infantry, as good troops as wore the Confederate gray, loitered in the thickets and listened to the cannonade till the shadows fell. Night found

Jackson so weary, so confused, after almost twenty hours of profitless marching and waiting, that he was stupefied. When he sat down to eat with his staff, he nodded with food in his mouth. "Now, gentlemen," he said, arousing himself, "let us at once to bed, and rise with the dawn, and see if tomorrow we cannot *do something*."[10]

3. HOLMES ADVANCES AND MAGRUDER GALLOPS IN VAIN

Jackson's words, at the end of a futile and fateful day, might well have been echoed on the extreme Confederate right, that June thirtieth, by Major General Theophilus H. Holmes, a stiff and deaf representative of the old army. After service on Aquia Creek in the winter of 1861–62, General Holmes, fifty-seven years of age and a close friend of the President, had been sent to North Carolina. Federal pressure in Virginia compelled Lee early in June to call for troops from Holmes's department, and on the twenty-sixth Lee ordered Holmes to join him.

Directly east of New Market the road forked, the River Road continuing to parallel the James; the diverging Long Bridge Road turned to the left and put Holmes within easy supporting distance of Longstreet and A. P. Hill on the Darbytown Road. Holmes could muster not more than 6,000 infantry, most of whom had never been under fire, but he did have 6 batteries. This column manifestly was not strong enough to engage in heavy infantry action, but if it could bring its guns into play it might confuse the Federal retreat.[11]

For the coming of this or of any other opportunity, Holmes waited at New Market through the forenoon of June 30 and until about 4 o'clock. Then Major R. K. Meade of the engineers galloped up to report exciting news: The enemy was retreating in some confusion over Malvern Hill, a strong ridge two and a half miles east of Holmes's position. If Holmes would advance some of his batteries, he could sweep the line of the retreating enemy. Holmes approved, and his chief of artillery, Colonel James Deshler, selected three sections of two rifled guns each. Infantry was ordered to support the artillery. As Holmes moved forward he met the commanding general. Informed that a Union column was moving south, Lee had asked himself whether this might not indicate that McClellan was seeking to get off while Longstreet and A. P. Hill waited on Huger and Jackson. He affirmed Holmes's advance and urged him to open fire with the rifled guns the moment his infantry support was at hand.

Holmes promptly moved his division down the River Road, but the hurrying feet of the men raised so much dust that it gave the Federals warning of their approach. Soon, over the heads of the men in line, there burst a heavy shell. "We could form no idea whence it came," wrote a member of the 50th North Carolina, "but were not long kept in doubt, for in a few minutes there was a perfect shower of shells of tremendous proportion and hideous sound. . . ." The raw troops were startled and confused by this fire rushing in from Union gunboats in the river and from heavy batteries posted on Malvern Hill. The cavalry stampeded, ran into a plank fence, and crushed some infantrymen who had taken shelter behind it. The 45th North Carolina broke. A reserve battery was caught in a tangle of timber. The excited artillerists cut the traces, and left two guns and three caissons and galloped off. Everywhere, for a moment, there was chaos. General Holmes alone was calm, and he by reason of his deafness. Emerging from a little house by the roadside amid the din, he stopped abruptly and cupped his ear suspiciously. "I thought," said he, "I heard firing."[12]

As Holmes worked furiously to restore order in the ranks, Major Brent arrived and stated that his chief, General Magruder, was under orders to move over in support of Holmes; did that officer have any suggestion to make concerning their position? Holmes answered "very brusquely"—to quote Brent—that he had no suggestion. Could the General inform him where the enemy was and in what strength? "No," said Holmes. Did the General have any message for Magruder? "No"—that was all. Brent wrote, years later, that "Genl. Holmes found in some way a cause of resentment at receiving a message from Genl. Magruder. His bearing was the most singular I have ever seen, and was marked by the absence of even a simulation of ordinary courtesy."

Holmes had ordered Colonel Deshler to open on the Federals who still were crossing Malvern Hill, but Deshler's challenge was answered with a salvo. Case shot and shell crashed into the woods, and horses and men went down. The hostile bombardment became a tornado. After an hour, as night fell, Deshler's batteries, badly mauled, were withdrawn. An infantry attack, in Holmes's words, would have been "perfect madness."[13]

Prince John Magruder had suffered irritating mishaps all day. After a morning march confused by want of guides, Magruder halted at 2 o'clock when he found the Darbytown Road blocked by the rear of A. P. Hill's division. At 4:30, Longstreet, who was ranking officer during Lee's reconnaissance on the right, directed Magruder to go to the support of Holmes—apparently a design to cover Longstreet's own flank in the event that the enemy should drive Holmes. Magruder, ever galloping, started immediately in that direction, then dashed off to answer a summons from Colonel Chilton, Lee's chief of staff. After that he spurred away to locate Holmes. Finally there came orders to abandon the movement on the right to Holmes and to return to the support of Longstreet. By now exhaustion, lack of sleep, and indigestion had brought Magruder to a state of mental confusion. Not until 3:00 A.M. did he sleep an hour—his second hour of repose in seventy-two. His men were exhausted. Most of them had marched twenty miles that day and had kept the road for eighteen hours; not one of them had drawn trigger.[14]

This, then, was the result of the attempted convergence of all the infantry opposite the line of McClellan's retreat: Holmes had been stopped by superior artillery; the reserve divisions of Magruder had been worn out to no purpose; Huger had spent the day cutting a road; Jackson had not crossed White Oak Swamp. Almost 50,000 Confederate troops, for one reason or another, had done virtually nothing on the day when Lee had hoped to overwhelm his adversary.

To complete the tragedy of the army's failure, Lee had felt compelled to attack in the late afternoon, at Riddell's Shop and Glendale, with the divisions of Longstreet and A. P. Hill. A vigorous onslaught with the troops at hand seemed the one alternative to permitting McClellan to march unhindered past the Confederate front. The two divisions fought magnificently. Slowly the fluctuating lines pressed through the woods and charged with ghastly losses across clearings where the Federals had planted artillery. The Federals were forced back until, when blackness covered the field and stopped the battle, they held one small part only of their previous line.

Tactically this battle was of encouragement solely because Longstreet and Hill showed themselves capable of maintaining touch with all their troops through a maze of woodland. To Longstreet went first honors, but Hill, who commanded the field for an hour while "Old Pete" was posting a brigade, showed admirable judgment. The gain was small. All the army had to show for its effort was a causeway of dead bodies, some hard-won Federal ordnance, and a bit of shell-torn woods.[15]

4. MALVERN HILL: A TRAGEDY OF STAFF

The army that bestirred itself in the clear dawn of July 1 was weaker by 10,000 men than it had been at the beginning of the campaign. Nine of its thirty-eight brigades had changed command. After the wounding of Pickett at Gaines' Mill, Colonel John B. Strange led the brigade. To the command of Arnold Elzey was assigned Jubal Early, back from his Williamsburg wounding though unable to mount a horse without assistance. The Mississippians of the fallen Richard Griffith were under their senior colonel,

William Barksdale, a veteran of the Mexican War and a former congress-man. Wade Hampton had been assigned to temporary command of Talia-ferro's brigade. Named at the instance of Stonewall himself, Brigadier General John R. Jones now led Campbell's brigade. Taylor's Louisianians passed to Colonel L. A. Stafford. As Featherston had been wounded severely on the thirtieth, his brigade was in the care of a colonel, as was that of Joseph R. Anderson, injured at Glendale. Finally, because Robert E. Rodes found himself too weak to keep the field, Colonel John B. Gordon led a brigade that already had twice distinguished itself.

Thus under new or unfamiliar brigade commanders, more than a fifth of the army faced the next uncertain stage of the campaign. All the divisions remained in the charge of the generals who had commenced the operations, and those who came up to Lee's field headquarters showed in varying degree the strain of five days of march and combat. Lee was tired and somewhat unwell. His disappointment over the failure of his plan was manifest; his curb on his temper was not perfect, but he was calm and clear of mind. Longstreet showed no weariness, nor did A. P. Hill. The night's rest which Jackson had commended to his staff seemed to have benefited him: He was alert and ready. Huger was absent from the early conferences. Delay awaited him because, he said, "I had no one to show us what road to take."[16] Physically, Huger had no complaint. Magruder's nervous condition must have been worse than ever, although apparently he was unaware of any impairment. Holmes, down on the River Road, did not report in person at headquarters.

D. H. Hill was fit for the tests of the day, but when he met General Lee he had a warning: A chaplain who had been reared in the country through which the army was passing had described to Hill a strong position known as Malvern Hill, ahead of the line of advance. Hill repeated his description of the ground, and added: "If General McClellan is there in force, we had better let him alone." Longstreet broke in, half-banteringly: "Don't get scared, now that we have got him licked!" Hill did not like this, and said no more.[17]

Ignorant of the ground and having no alternative, Lee ordered an advance toward the James River on the road that led over the eminence Hill mentioned. Jackson and Magruder were to press after the enemy. Huger was to receive orders on arrival. Longstreet and A. P. Hill, who had borne the brunt of the fighting on June 30, were to be in reserve. Jackson took the lead. Lee's instructions to Magruder were to proceed by the Quaker Road and form on the right of Jackson. Lee intended to have Huger follow substantially the same line of march.[18]

These orders seemed simple enough, but from the time they were put in execution coordinated effort virtually ended. Although the divisional leaders were not far apart at any hour, most of them lost touch. This was due, in the first place, to the nature of the ground and to the lack of information concerning it.

Most of the divisions had to move down the narrow Quaker or Willis Church Road, and after a mile and a quarter they came to a little creek known as Western Run. This constituted near Malvern Hill a swamp almost as difficult as White Oak itself. To the right of the road, thick and nearly impassable woodland led directly into this swamp. The task of organizing a line there called for a soldier of large experience. Left of the road, beyond a shallow woodland, was the open ground of the Poindexter farm, a decent position of some strength; but for Jackson to get his three divisions deployed there consumed all the morning hours until 11 o'clock.[19]

Coordination was lost, in the second place, through a singular mistake on the part of General Magruder. The Quaker Road was to be his line of advance, but apparently the galloping Magruder did not ask to examine Lee's map—the only one available—and instead determined to find the route himself. He had three guides from the neighborhood. When these men started Magruder's division to the west, almost at a right angle to Jackson's march southward, Longstreet questioned the direction. Magruder recalled his guides and catechized them. They insisted they were correct, nor did any of them know that the road from Glendale to Malvern Hill also was styled the Quaker Road, though often called the Willis Church Road.

Thus reassured by his guides, Magruder marched westward roundabout to an obscure, little-used byway which his guides told him was the veritable Quaker Road. Longstreet, meantime, became convinced Magruder was following a divergent line of advance, probably so reported to Lee, and then overtook Prince John to argue that the virtually abandoned lane could not possibly be the Quaker Road. Further argument was ended by the arrival of one of Lee's staff with orders for Magruder to retrace his steps.[20]

While Magruder was marching and countermarching, an incomplete order of battle was drawn up with much fumbling and difficulty in the tangle along Western Run. Whiting's division formed the left of a front that faced south, with the rest of Jackson's division and most of Ewell's in reserve. Trimble's brigade was put in position next to Whiting. Astride the Quaker or Willis Church Road was D. H. Hill's division. Next was to have been Magruder, but in his absence the ground was occupied by Armistead with his and Wright's brigades of Huger's division.[21]

Malvern Hill in times of peace would have been a pleasant site. Its locust trees were breeze-swept, its grass abundant. Now, where the enemy was visible, his position was one of discouraging strength, if not of impregnability. Opposite Whiting and D. H. Hill the cleared farmland leading up to the West house did not appear too steep to be mounted, but its length concealed the full grade. It offered the Federals a perfect field of fire for 300 to 400 yards. A level crest afforded space for many batteries. On the Confederate right the Federals' advantage appeared even more disheartening. The open fields of the Crew farm occupied part of the same broad hillside that confronted the left and center. The western face of the hill was almost a bluff, affording an excellent position from which artillery could rake the approaches. Every part of this position was crowned with guns. Powerful lines of infantry were in support. The Federal position behind Boatswain's Swamp on June 27 had been strong; this front on Malvern Hill seemed a field fortress![22]

No high-ranking officer was at hand to assume responsibility for a careful examination of the terrain on the right. Brigadier General Armistead apparently did not know that he was senior officer on that flank and consequently he made no effort to extend his observations or to inform Lee of what he had seen. After posting his own and Wright's men, he decided that no advance could be made until artillery coped with the Union batteries on the hill. The same conclusion had been reached on Jackson's part of the line.[23]

At length two tenable artillery positions were found on the Confederate front. One was to the left, in a large wheat field on the Poindexter farm. The other was on the wooded rim of a hill in rear of Armistead. From them a converging fire might be opened on the Federal array. If the Union guns were silenced, or even were thrown into confusion, a general infantry assault might rout the enemy troops who were believed to be demoralized by their previous defeats. Armistead had the most favorable position; the plan was that he should start his advance when the saw the Federal line broken by the artillery, and when he went forward with a cheer, the whole line should sweep up the hill. Orders to this effect were given to all the division commanders who could be reached.[24]

To bring up the guns was the first task. Unfortunately, Stapleton Crutchfield, Jackson's wholly competent chief of artillery, was absent sick that day. Jackson himself had to order the batteries up. Available fieldpieces were not abundant. On order, D. H. Hill had sent all his artillery back for refitting and had no guns to add to the fire. He should have been supplied from the reserve, but General Pendleton, with more than twenty batteries at his disposal, was not to be found. For his station Armistead could find but two batteries, one of which had only two guns of sufficient range to reach the enemy. No divisional officer was at hand to supply more artillery.

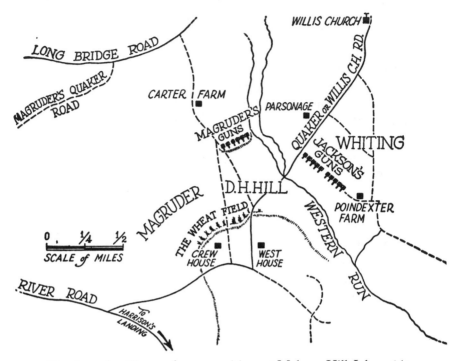

Terrain and artillery and troop positions at Malvern Hill, July 1, 1862.

As the Southern batteries came up, one after another, they received a concentrated, powerful, well-directed fire. Gun after gun was put out of action. Jackson, first and last, got eighteen only in action. The Federals soon commanded the entire front. Harvey Hill complained to Jackson that the bombardment from the Poindexter farm was of the "most farcical character." Lee himself concluded that the Confederate batteries would fail to break the Federal front, and he rode out with Longstreet beyond Jackson's extreme left to see if he could turn the Union right from that quarter.[25]

By 3:30 a few guns still were in action, though almost overwhelmed by the blasting fire from the hill. The infantry watched, listened, and wondered whether, as at Gaines' Mill, they would be commanded to charge the artillery position. Beyond D. H. Hill's right the situation remained one of confusion. Behind Armistead and Wright, Mahone and Ransom, both of Huger's command, were floundering through the woods toward the front. Armistead had no information regarding Huger's movements and now, uncounselled, had to act. Federal skirmishers were creeping forward and threatening the front. He advanced three Virginia regiments that drove them back to the hillside below the Crew house. There, in an advanced position but covered by the roll of the land, Armistead had to leave this part of his brigade.

Disappointment was general among the commanding officers scattered through the woods and over the fields. Five hours the army had waited. Nothing had happened except the uneven artillery duel, which now was drawing to a humiliating end. D. H. Hill waited at his post with his five brigadiers. Armistead and Wright held to their ground. Mahone, Cobb, and Barksdale were moving to their support. The divisions of D. R. Jones and McLaws, of Magruder's command, were being formed and directed by Longstreet.[26]

Now, suddenly, everything changed. Galloping Magruder came on the scene after his long, wasted march. He was all ardor, all excitement, altogether ignorant of the situation on his immediate front. He undertook a reconnaissance with officers supplied by Armistead. He sent back word to bring up thirty rifled pieces from the divisional artillery. Wheeling then, before any of his troops were in position, he dashed to the rear to hurry forward D. R. Jones's division. While he was attempting to speed the advance, Magruder received for the first time the circular Lee had dispatched to the division commanders, some three hours previously, for a general advance when Armistead raised a shout. In a short time there also was handed Magruder a note from a staff officer he had sent Lee. This was brief and mystifying, but behind it was a new situation.

Lee had ridden far to the left, after he had concluded that the bombardment would be a failure, and found favorable ground for launching an attack. He discussed with Longstreet how the reserve divisions could be moved up for an assault. Riding back toward the center, he had word from Whiting that heavy infantry columns were moving to the Federal left, and that wagons and troops in retreat could be seen in the Federal rear. He heard too from Magruder that Armistead had won advantage. Lee promptly abandoned his design for an attack on the left and reverted to his earlier plan for a general assault. The note he sent back with Magruder's staff officer was to the effect that, as the Federals were said to be getting off, Lee expected him to advance rapidly and follow up Armistead's success.[27]

Once more Prince John put spurs to his horse and galloped to the front, directing Armistead and Wright to prepare for the assault. Magruder's plan, as he subsequently stated in his report, was "to hurl about 15,000 men against the enemy's batteries and supporting infantry; to follow up any successes they might obtain. . . ." Because Magruder acted on assumption and did not get in touch with his support, execution fell murderously short of the plan.

When Wright was ordered to begin his advance, no other troops were in position to go forward with him. Less than 1,000 men stepped out into the open to storm the hill. Mahone suffered delay because Magruder took time to "address a few words" to the brigade. Armistead, told to move up his three rear regiments, replied that they were raw troops. In their place, Magruder sent in three regiments of Cobb's brigade. When Ransom was called on to charge, he replied that he could not move without orders from Huger, to whom he was submitting Magruder's request. Magruder thereupon rode back to Barksdale's brigade, of his own division, and undertook personally to deploy it.[28]

The result of all these orders, messages, and gallops forward and back was that now, by 6 o'clock, Magruder had put into action two of Huger's brigades besides the three regiments of Armistead on the hillside. Only one brigade and part of another had been brought to the front, and these were in support rather than in the front line of attack. Not more than 5,000 men were challenging the stronghold of the Crew House Hill, and they had little artillery behind them.

Hopeless and ill-handled as was Magruder's partial attack, it precipitated a slaughter of D. H. Hill's troops, who had been waiting for the charge of Armistead's men. When troops rushed out of the woods to the right with a shout, reported Samuel Garland, Hill exclaimed, "That must be the general advance! Bring up your brigades as soon as possible and join in it." The well-trained officers of Hill's division hurried to their commands and, between 6:30 and 7:00, led them, cheering, straight up the low, cleared hill on either side of the Willis Church Road. It was not war; it was mass murder. As in every action of the campaign, the men in the ranks did all they could to make good the blunders and delays of their leaders; but this time they were sent to achieve the impossible. Valor could not conquer those batteries on the crest, nor could fortitude long endure the fire that seemed to sweep every foot of the open ground. Some of Gordon's regiments got within 200 yards of the Federal guns, though they lost half their numbers; Ripley's troops reached level ground, where they were mown by canister. In the end, the shattered, bloody wreckage of D. H. Hill's division slipped back down the hill. Ewell gallantly attempted to lend support, but it was futile.[29]

Magruder ere this completely had lost his grip on his troops. The first attackers were pinned down almost under the mouths of the guns. Cobb and Barksdale, first in support, were beaten back with heavy casualties. D. R. Jones's division, split into three parts, had little power to strike. McLaws's two brigades were put in so far apart that one could not see the other. As night fell the opposing forces could be distinguished only by their lines of musketry. On the field and in the woods lay 5,000 dead and wounded boys.[30]

During the night General McClellan retreated, as he had after every battle of the campaign. This time he took a position at Harrison's Landing, where he was sheltered by the fire of gunboats in the James River. His weary men left more rifles and equipment along their route than on any previous march of the retreat. No pursuit was attempted.

The strategic aim of the campaign had been achieved despite bad coordination, worse tactics, and the worst imaginable staff work: Richmond had been relieved. McClellan was no longer at the city's gates. In the brief period of rest that followed, the command of the army could be appraised, the men who had failed in action could be relieved, and a reorganization, historic in all its aspects, could be effected.

CHAPTER 13

Lessons of the Seven Days

1. THE END OF MAGRUDER AND OF HUGER

First to be reckoned were the casualties. Including those of Huger's affair of June 25, on the first of the Seven Days, the final computation was 20,141 killed, wounded, and missing. These were most unevenly divided. Those of thirteen brigades, one third of the army, were 10,506, more than half the total. Eight of these thirteen were in Longstreet's and A. P. Hill's divisions. In Jackson's and Ewell's divisions, casualties numbered 1,195, less than 6 per cent of the whole; the three brigades of the old Army of the Valley, Jackson's own division, accounted for only 208 of these. Magruder's three divisions, six brigades, lost 2,491. Heaviest losses in a single brigade were those of Cadmus Wilcox, Longstreet's division—1,055. Of regiments, the worst toll in a single battle was the 335 paid at Mechanicsville by the 44th Georgia, D. H. Hill's division. Whatever the explanation of these figures, they showed that the Army of the Valley had not contributed heavily in blood to the direct defense of Richmond. Lee's men, not Jackson's, had borne the brunt.[1]

Fatalities in the high command had not been numerous. Only one brigadier general, Richard Griffith, had been killed. Of the seven who had been wounded or injured, Arnold Elzey alone was disabled permanently for field duty, though Pickett and Featherston were listed as "severely wounded." Far more numerous had been the fatalities among regimental commanders—fourteen colonels killed or mortally wounded. Two others had received hurts that were to keep them from ever serving again with their regiments.

Some of the brigades had been crippled by the loss of officers. A. P. Hill had two colonels killed, and two brigadier generals, eleven colonels, and six lieutenant colonels wounded. Hood lost eighteen officers in his brigade at Gaines' Mill; at Glendale, all of Wilcox's regimental commanders were wounded; in the fighting around Malvern Hill, Ransom had three colonels wounded and one lieutenant colonel killed. Ripley had to report three of his four colonels killed during the campaign. In some instances, the heavy casualties among both officers and enlisted men were due to bad positions, to unavoidable assaults, or to circumstances unpreventable. Other casualty lists, laden with hundreds of names, could be explained in terms of poor leading only.

All of the division commanders had escaped physical injury, but several of them had suffered in reputation. Magruder was the most conspicuous of these men, and figured in a curious dispute. He had been irked for weeks by his loss of independent command, and was most anxious to accept transfer to the Department of the Trans-Mississippi, promised him in May but suspended until the contest for Richmond was settled. The day after Malvern Hill Magruder applied for orders. Without hesitation, Lee relieved him on July 3 and broke up his cumbersome command: Jones's half division was put under Longstreet; Magruder's own division, made up of Toombs's and Barksdale's brigades, was consolidated with McLaws's.[2]

As soon as these arrangements were made, Magruder ceremoniously bade farewell to his troops and started on July 12 for his new post. Rumor, by that time, was wagging a vicious tongue concerning him. He was accused of gross recklessness, of wild excitement and intoxication at Malvern Hill. "Old Magruder," wrote Colonel T. R. R. Cobb to his wife. "made no reputation in this battle. He lost rather than gained. He was depressed, and I fear was drinking." Still darker, in the eyes of many, was the wholly unjust charge that the general had shown the white feather and had sought to screen himself from the enemy's fire. These allegations were not long in reaching the ears of the President. To ignore them was unjust alike to the army and to Magruder. While en route to his new post he was recalled to Richmond for an explanation. In his place, General Holmes temporarily was assigned to the Trans-Mississippi.[3]

Back in the capital, Magruder did not bluster publicly but took the charges seriously and undertook to meet them with meticulous regard for military usage. Two days after Malvern Hill he had written a report of some 200 words. This he proceeded to elaborate into a document of forty times that length. He assiduously collected field dispatches, and from his guides affidavits to prove that the road he had taken on July 1 was the true and only Quaker Road. To clinch his case, he included a statement by the surgeon of the 16th Georgia, who duly denied that the general was excited or drunk or showed "disposition . . . to screen himself from the enemy's fire." In certain respects his report was not altogether frank; inferentially, the enemy's retreat on the night of July 1 was attributed to the attack Magruder had delivered. He was the hero of his narrative and, apparently in his own mind, of the Battle of Malvern Hill.

When the report was finished, on August 12, he transmitted it to Lee. After setting right in seven "remarks" Magruder's "misapprehensions" concerning events of the campaign, Lee sent it to the secretary of war. His covering letter was at once candid and reserved. Magruder "had many difficulties to contend with, I know," Lee wrote. "I regretted . . . that they could not have been more readily overcome. I feel assured, however, that General Magruder intentionally omitted nothing that he could do to insure success." That was both just and generous. With it was coupled not a hint, even the faintest, that Lee desired Magruder to remain with the Army of Northern Virginia.[4]

It was not until October 10 that Magruder received orders, and then he did not get the entire Trans-Mississippi command. Instead he was given the District of Texas, New Mexico, and Arizona. He arranged at his own cost for the separate printing of his report, announcing with a flourish that his explanation of his part in the battles had been made "to the satisfaction of the War Department as well as of General Lee." New and curious adventures awaited Prince John in Texas, but with these words he verbally galloped off for the last time from the Army of Northern Virginia.[5]

General Benjamin Huger, next to Magruder, was the officer most criticized for his part in the Seven Days. To his slow march on June 30, more than to any other miscarriage of the day, was attributed the failure of Lee's plan. When Lee wrote his report of the campaign, he distinguished between Huger's failure and that of Jackson by a delicate choice of words: "Huger not coming up, and Jackson having been unable to force the passage of White Oak Swamp," Longstreet and A. P. Hill lacked support at Glendale.

Huger's own report failed to change the impression that he was what press and army styled a "do-nothing general." What he recorded and what others remarked of him then and thereafter constitute a singular exhibit of the opportunities of good and evil—by doing foolish things and of doing nothing—that an "independent" division commander may have in battle. At 3:00 A.M. on June 30 he sent the brigades of Armistead and Wright off at a right angle to his line of advance to "take the enemy in flank." He neither notified the commanding general of this decision, nor joined or attempted to direct his lieutenants' movements after they began their march. Armistead and Wright, advancing aimlessly, were eventually directed toward the front by General Lee. Ere that, at his leisure, Huger had directed Mahone and Ransom to advance, but found other troops in the way and "I had no one to show us what road to take." Although Huger, in effect, had lost his brigades during the morning, he insisted in his report that his troops had been taken from him. "As I was treated in the same manner at Seven Pines," he said, "I can only hope this course was accidental and required by the necessities of the service."[6]

Previously Lee had suggested that Huger might be sent to South Carolina. Now, quietly and without an explanatory word in newspapers or in army orders, General Huger was relieved of duty with his division and assigned as inspector of artillery and ordnance, the type of work that had been his before the war. There is no record of any protest by Huger. A singular, silent, and proud figure he dimly appears through the years. He had been too long habituated to the slow peacetime routine of the ordnance service to adjust himself to field command, for which he had no aptitude.

General Holmes, in the judgment of some critics of the campaign, had been as remiss as either Magruder or Huger. The probability is that those who criticized him knew neither the weakness of his troops nor the strength of the position against which he was sent. At the moment, resentfully they wrote him down as a failure, but they soon forgot him. He was the commander of a separate department, he did not associate long with the Army of Northern Virginia, and within a few weeks he went west to command the department previously assigned Magruder.[7]

If Holmes be regarded as scarcely an active participant in the campaign and consequently be not adjudged responsible for serious failure, there was a question concerning the performance of a fourth prominent officer—the chief of Lee's artillery, Brigadier General W. N. Pendleton, who will appear often and curiously in these pages.

At age twenty-one Pendleton had been graduated at West Point, No. 8 in the class of 1830. After three years in the artillery he had resigned, and had taught in Pennsylvania and at Delaware College. Having entered the ministry in 1837, he had accepted the rectorate of the small Episcopal church in Lexington, Virginia. In 1860 some of the young men of the community organized a battery and asked him to drill them. This he undertook. After secession the command enlisted as the Rockbridge Artillery and elected Pendleton, then fifty-one, as its captain. At Manassas, on July 21, 1861, the gunners under Pendleton did such fine service that he was commended by Jackson and mentioned in Johnston's report as the army's "one educated artillerist . . . that model of a Christian soldier."

Pendleton had acted during part of the autumn as Johnston's chief of artillery and, on March 26, 1862, had been made a brigadier general. Picturesque in person, he somewhat resembled General Lee. With gray beard and with mien half martial, half clerical, he had preached fervently when he was not drilling. At the end of April 1862 he had been listed as in command of the reserve artillery. He wrote letters as long, though not so numerous, as those of Magruder, and he had definite aptitude for organization.[8]

On June 21 he had submitted to Lee the first of many proposals for the regrouping of the batteries under an "army chief of artillery." Lee approved, but in the haste of preparation for battle it was not made operative in its entirety. The result was that General Pendleton did not enter the campaign with all his guns wisely apportioned, nor could he or any other single officer exercise authority over all the batteries scattered among the brigades and divisions. His specific charge was the reserve artillery, a fifth of all the artillery in the army. Pendleton had cooperated on the south side of the Chickahominy June 26–27, while Lee was fighting at Mechanicsville and Gaines' Mill. On the twenty-eighth he had worked to put heavy guns in position to cover Magruder's position.[9]

Thereafter, Pendleton's own curious account of his movements is a sufficient commentary on his conduct. Officially he wrote: "Fever supervening disabled me on the 29th, so that the day was necessarily passed by me as a quiet Sabbath." Privately he told his wife, "I am lying on a lounge under a shady tree in the yard of my headquarters. . . . I feel better already, and hope a day's rest, a blue pill, etc. may have me quite well again tomorrow." The next day, as he predicted, he was well enough for field duty: "On Monday, 30th, I was again able to be in the field, and employed the forenoon in ascertaining movements in progress and adjusting to them the arrangements of my own command."

"Tuesday morning, July 1"—the day of the Battle of Malvern Hill— "was spent by me in seeking for some time the commanding general, that I might get orders, and by reason of the intricacy of routes failing in this. . . . No occasion was presented for bringing up the reserve artillery— indeed, it seemed that not one-half of the division batteries were brought into action on either Monday or Tuesday. To remain near by, therefore, and await events and orders . . . was all that I could do."[10]

There was somber, costly truth in what Pendleton said about the nonemployment of divisional artillery. The tragic losses of the infantry attested the failure of the Confederates to bring up their guns through the woods. This did not alter the fact that the chief of artillery, on the final day of the operation, did not even reach general headquarters. Lee made no criticism of Pendleton in his report. Had he been dissatisfied, with whom would he have succeeded him? Who could boast even Pendleton's limited experience in directing a large number of guns? Some of the younger artillery officers were not so philosophical; they laughed at Pendleton behind his back. More mature men felt that the reserve batteries had not been handled well. Lieutenant Colonel A. S. Cutts described the day at Malvern Hill: ". . . although I am sure that more artillery could have been used with advantage in this engagement, and also that my command could have done good service, yet I received no orders. . . ."[11]

Would Pendleton learn? Outranged, the Confederate artillery was served with ammunition less good. Was it now to be outfought or better handled? Pendleton had not fulfilled his opportunities. That was the most charitable judgment. Would he justify Lee's confidence, or would he at some new crisis follow Magruder and Huger into obscurity? Of stout fabric was Lee's patience, but it might wear thin.

2. STRANGE PROBLEMS OF COMMAND

If Pendleton had not purged himself on June 29, he might have had the energy to reach headquarters on July 1. In Magruder's case, his excitement and confusion, his reckless galloping to and fro, his attempts to perform the duties of half a dozen general officers undoubtedly were attributable, in part, to inappropriate medication and a lack of sleep. Huger had the look of a man prematurely aged, and his slowness may be explained by the despairing term "arteriosclerosis." Other officers exhibited during the campaign a discontent, an arrogant or disdainful individualism, or an insubordinate spirit of criticism that raises a question: Were they physically ill or were they unsuited temperamentally for command?

Unhappily on this list of the disgruntled was Brigadier General W. H. C. Whiting. On the surface his record shone. Beneath there were ugly rumors—that he was jealous of Jackson, that he had been overcritical of the dispositions made by his superior, that he had been tipsy at Gaines' Mill, that he had not personally shared there in the charge of his division, and that he had done less than his part at Malvern Hill. Of none of these alleged derelictions was there a hint in reports, but neither was there praise for the division commander. In his own account Whiting had no admiring words for his chief. In relating the disappointing events of July 1, he made it conspicuously plain that he had acted under Jackson's direct orders. Common report had it that Whiting cried bitterly, "Great God! Won't some ranking officer come and save us from this fool?"[12]

Although the campaign developed nothing tangibly to the discredit of Whiting, he did not distinguish himself either in leadership or cooperation. Doubtless at headquarters there was speculation over the reason. Perhaps, too, there was disappointment that a man of his intellectual endowment should not have risen in reputation. What was amiss? Was it a permanent defect, enslaving habit, or temporary eclipse? Lee left Whiting at the head of the division in a semi-autonomous command, as if he did not know under whom the abilities of Whiting effectively could be employed.

In a far lower bracket of military knowledge than Whiting, but enjoying a political reputation that made his discontent a subject of much gossip, was Brigadier General Robert Toombs. When his native Georgia seceded, Senator Toombs was in his fifty-first year and was in general estimation among the half-dozen leading public men of the South. Portly but pale, with a face half-studious, half-contemptuous, he had a frowning senatorial air. Limitless confidence in the rightness of his views, skill in dramatic phrase-making, and a plausible if superficial logic made his oratorical deliverances as convincing to his followers as they were provoking to his opponents. Had he been less entrenched as a member of the ruling class, he would have been a demagogue. Had he been more patiently tolerant, he would have been a statesmen. As he was, he was neither. Nor was he politically consistent. "Bob Toombs," it was said, "disagrees with himself between meals." Howell Cobb remarked of him, "Toombs had altogether the best mind of any statesman in the United States but lacked balance." Wrote Major Raphael J. Moses, who saw him at close range, "[Toombs's] impulses were generous and noble, his faults were bluster and a vivid imagination not always hampered by facts."[13]

When the Confederate government was organized, Toombs was disappointed in not being elected to the presidency, and was not placated by the tender of the first position in the Cabinet. He accepted and labored, furiously if sullenly, for about five months. Then he resigned to accept command of a Georgia brigade. He did not believe the war would be long, and did not intend that it should stop his political career, but he felt that more of service was to be rendered and more of honor won in the field than in the forum.[14]

During his service in the winter of 1861–62, Toombs indulged in a correspondence that was a succession of growls. Johnston, he wrote, "is a poor devil, small, arbitrary and inefficient." Again of Johnston he wrote: "As he had been at West Point, tho', I suppose he necessarily knows everything about it. . . . The army is dying. . . . Set this down in your book, and set down opposite to it its epitaph, *'died of West Point.'*" Still, he enjoyed martial pomp. One observer laughed at the memory of Toombs's performance in the march through Richmond to the Peninsula: "He put himself at the head of one regiment and moved it out of sight amid hurrahs, then galloping back he brought on another, ready himself for cheers, until the brigade was down the street and near the embarkation."[15]

On the retreat from Yorktown Toombs lost the temporary rating as a divisional chief awarded him by Magruder, and he reached Richmond in deep discontent. "We had a rough time in the Peninsula," he wrote Vice President Stephens. ". . . This army will not fight until McClellan attacks it. Science will do anything but fight. It will burn, retreat, curse, swear, get drunk, strip soldiers—anything but fight." It was in that mood that

Toombs entered the battles of the Seven Days. He cheerfully promised his surgeon that during the operations he would not indulge in strong liquor, and there is no evidence that he failed to keep his pledge; but neither is there evidence that he progressed toward the military fame he coveted.[16]

His best opportunity came at Malvern Hill, but there his force, though resolute, was mishandled inexcusably. Toombs virtually lost control of it. During the confusion, D. H. Hill came upon the bewildered Toombs and hotly demanded to know why, after pretending to want to fight, Toombs had not done so, though the enemy was in plain sight. "For shame! Rally your troops! Where were you when I was riding up and down your line, rallying your troops?" Toombs's reply is not on record, but after the battle he demanded an explanation and, when it proved "unsatisfactory," he challenged Hill. Scornfully Hill rejected the demand as contrary to his religion and his duty and "the laws which we have mutually sworn to serve," and the Confederacy was not made ridiculous by a battle behind the battle line. Apparently, in short order, Hill and Toombs were reconciled.

In appraising the Seven Days' Battles, Toombs was violent: "They were fought without skill or judgment and were victorious by dint of dead hard fighting. . . . Longstreet has won more reputation, and I think deservedly, than all of our major generals put together. Stonewall Jackson and his troops did little or nothing in these battles of the Chickahominy and Lee was far below the occasion. If we had a general in command we could easily have taken McClellan's whole command. . . ." He did not seem to have considered that he had failed in any particular, but he was disgusted. He told Stephens, "I shall leave the army the instant I can do so without dishonor."[17]

These opinions on the part of a man habitually outspoken doubtless were known in the army, but nothing was done to silence or to discipline Toombs. Presumably Davis and Lee did not wish to arouse resentments among Toombs's supporters. Probably the feeling was that he would do less harm if kept closely under the eye of a vigilant division commander than he would if he became an anti-administration leader in Georgia or in the Confederate Congress.

In a category different from that of Toombs, save in one troublesome particular, stood D. H. Hill at the close of the campaign. His leadership had been courageous and skillful. General Lee, who abhorred adjectives and used adverbs sparingly, employed both in his report describing Harvey Hill's advance at Gaines' Mill. Jackson, himself scoring obstacles, was at pains to explain those Hill had overcome on June 27. For failure to drive home his attack on July 1, Hill was not and could not have been blamed by his superiors.

Personally, too, Hill had been recklessly and obstinately contemptuous of danger. Colonel John B. Gordon, at Malvern Hill, found his divisional commander busy drafting an order on the exposed side of a large tree. To Gordon's warnings he said only, "I am not going to be killed until my time comes." Almost at the sound of the word, a shell crashed close by. The concussion rolled Hill over on the ground; a fragment of the iron tore the breast of his coat. He got up without a word, shook the dirt from his uniform, and sat down again—on the far side of the tree. That was the maximum he would concede in self-protection.

Hill's strategic sense had been excellent, his tactics sound. No complaints of clumsiness or of negligence in administration are in the records. Professionally, then, at the close of the Seven Days D. H. Hill was among the first of Lee's lieutenants, but he was not generally popular. "I don't like Hill, much to my surprise," confided cavalryman Thomas Cobb, "for I was ready to love him for his Christian character." Cobb went on regretfully, "There is much bad blood among these high officers, jealousies and back-bitings."[18]

Backbiting was not the word to describe Hill's habit of mind, but critical he was, ceaselessly critical. For his dead officers he usually had laudation; the living, high or low, he seldom spared when he thought them derelict. Nor would he stop at the line of his own division. Adjoining units and their commanders, if they did what he considered to be less than their part, would receive the arrows of his wrath. More often than not, Hill was sound in his adverse military judgment, though apt to disregard practical difficulties; but his insistence on pointing out the errors of others, at the same time that he dwelt on the accomplishments of his own men, irritated some of his comrades.

There is every reason to believe that Harvey Hill's criticisms sprang from his chronic dyspepsia and not from jealousy or any sense of superiority. Whether this was recognized at the time is unclear, but at army headquarters there was no disposition to overlook the abilities of the man because his tongue was sharp. Beyond question, Hill would have remained with the Army of Northern Virginia after the Seven Days had not the transfer of Holmes to the Department of the Trans-Mississippi created a vacancy in North Carolina that seemed to demand the appointment of Hill. As he was at the time the outstanding North Carolinian in Confederate service, it seemed best to name him to command in his own state, which had been stripped of troops.

He was assigned accordingly. In his place, because of uncertainty regarding the permissible number and seniority of major generals, no successor was named. His troops continued to be known as "D. H. Hill's Division" and, in some minor operations undertaken by him south of the James after the Seven Days, were under his direction. Strange and unpredicted was the fate that awaited him.[19]

3. STUART MAKES A SECOND "RAID"

When reports of the Seven Days were filed and the service of the different arms was given its proper valuation, how stood the cavalry? Had Jeb Stuart added to the reputation he had won in the ride around McClellan?

In covering the left of Jackson's advance on June 26, Stuart executed his orders literally, but without imagination. Like Jackson, he failed to see the importance of liaison on the right. On the twenty-seventh, at Gaines' Mill, he gained no new laurels; his troopers were well-nigh helpless in the blinding underbrush and enveloping forests of the Chickahominy. On the twenty-eighth he was sent to cut the York River Railroad and thereby sever McClellan's communications with the shipping on the Pamunkey. The task was performed easily in the face of trivial opposition.

Ere the end of the day, Stuart observed immense clouds of smoke billowing upward from the direction of the Federal base at White House. Dawn of June 29 found the troopers advancing on the smoking ruins, and what soon held Stuart's gaze was a Federal gunboat at the landing. Cavalry against a navy—there was a chance for an encounter that would make the entire army talk! Stuart sent in a line of skirmishers and a howitzer, "a few shells from which," he reported with gusto, "fired with great accuracy and bursting directly over her decks, caused an instantaneous . . . and precipitate flight under full headway of steam down the river." He added that the howitzer "gave chase at a gallop," and the gunboat—she was U.S.S. *Marblehead*—never returned.

To the deserted base the cavalrymen trotted and found evidences of prodigal destruction that made them marvel at the resources of their foe. "The accumulation of commissary supplies," wrote one officer, "seemed endless." Sutlers' stores, the prize most desired by hungry soldiers, had been set out, as if a Union column had been expected. "Provisions and delicacies of every description lay in heaps," Stuart reported with a smack of his lips, "and the men regaled themselves on the fruits of the tropics as well as the substantials of the land." To feasting and to destruction of what could not be removed, Stuart devoted the day. Otherwise the Federals might return, he reasoned, and carry off anything he left.[20]

From Lee came a question on which the strategy of the campaign hung: What movements of the enemy had Stuart observed; what did he think McClellan intended to do? The answer in this instance was not difficult,

but it involved sound military reasoning from evidence a cavalry commander on outpost duty always should seek to collect. Promptly Stuart sent
back word to Lee that he saw no indications of any retreat down the
Peninsula, and that he had no doubt McClellan, having lost communication with the York, was moving toward the James.

Reveille on the morning of June 30 presented Stuart with the cavalryman's usual problem—what next? His decision was prudent if simple: The
column must proceed to the Chickahominy. If McClellan intended to
recross that river, Stuart would be in position to ascertain that fact; if the
Federals were making for the James, Stuart could pass over the Chickahominy and close on them. He found the Forge Bridge and Long Bridge
crossings picketed by the enemy. "I tried in vain," Stuart reported, "to
ascertain by scouts the force beyond, and it being now nearly dark we
bivouacked again." There had come meanwhile from the direction of
White Oak Swamp the disturbing sound of heavy fire. A battle manifestly
was on—and Stuart was not there to share its dangers and its honors!
While others were winning fame he could do nothing but wait and sleep.[21]

Next morning at 3:30 brought a courier with orders to cross the Chickahominy to cooperate with Jackson. This proved to be a day-long march.
Stuart decided that the point toward which he should direct the last stage
of his march was Haxall's Landing, south of Malvern Hill, but distance,
darkness, and the proximity of the Federals compelled him to halt before
he could join Jackson. About an hour after he bivouacked, the roar of the
battle at Malvern Hill died out. His men were then about a mile and a half
east of the Confederate left flank, and had covered forty-two miles that
day.[22]

July 2 was spent by Stuart in reconnoitering, rounding up Federal stragglers, and collecting abandoned arms. That night he reasoned that the
Federals were close to the James River and that a bit of artillery fire might
keep McClellan's tired army where it was. Young Captain John Pelham of
the horse artillery was sent off through the darkness to find a position from
which he could sweep the River Road. Before morning Pelham had in
Stuart's hands a report that the enemy was near the famous old Byrd mansion of Westover, on low ground dominated by a long ridge known as
Evelington Heights. Much might be gained, Captain Pelham suggested,
by planting artillery on those heights.

It was a prospect that appealed to Stuart. Early on July 3 his force was
hurrying eastward, then southward. The march was swift and easy. Evelington Heights was reached and a Federal squadron on guard there sent
ascampering. Below the heights the enemy's camps and wagon trains
could be seen. Pelham, who had been waiting quietly near-by, was told to

"let 'em have it." Soon the bark of his little howitzer, his one and only serviceable gun, was heard. The fall of his shell on the flats set teamsters to running and horses to rearing, but did no other damage.

While the gun kept up its fire, Stuart collected stragglers and questioned residents, and their information was all to the same effect—the whole of the Federal army was in far-spreading camps under the heights and adjacent to the river. This important news he sent forthwith to General Lee and, in reply, learned that Jackson and Longstreet were on the march eastward. Yet by 2 o'clock Stuart's game was up. Federal pressure forced back the troopers; Pelham rapidly exhausted his ammunition. Stuart learned that Longstreet, leading the advance, was then on the Charles City Road six or seven miles distant. The heights could not be held, by any possibility, long enough for the infantry to arrive. Reluctantly he fell back two miles and went into camp. The next morning, July 4, when both Longstreet and Jackson were near enough to strike, the Federal grip on Evelington Heights was too strong to be challenged.[23]

In this manner ended Stuart's part in the campaign of the Seven Days. Had it been a full part, the maximum that could have been expected of the cavalry commander in an offensive on which the life of the Confederacy depended?

There were no misgivings in Stuart's mind—certainly he admitted none—concerning the duration of his absence from the immediate flank of the army. He seems never to have asked whether the time spent at White House on the afternoon of June 29 might not have been utilized more profitably in hurrying back to share in the pursuit of McClellan. For the wasted day of the thirtieth Stuart made no apologies. Among his companions in arms were some who felt that his operations had been to no good purpose—in particular, that from sheer bravado he had flushed the game at Evelington Heights. If Stuart, said his critics, had kept to the woods after he reached the heights, exhausted Union commanders would have neglected to seize that key position that day. Then Lee, coming up, could have used his artillery to slaughter the Federals and perhaps to compel their surrender.

In long retrospect, Stuart's action was proof, as Porter Alexander put it, that "dangers lurk in excess of enterprise as well as in its deficiency." Beyond that, it is by no means certain that the half-exhausted Confederate artillery could have conducted from Evelington Heights a successful bombardment of McClellan's camp in the face of a covering fire from the gunboats in the James River. General Lee himself did not sit in judgment of the actions of Stuart. When he came to recount briefly the events of July 2–4, he omitted all reference to the affair on Evelington Heights.[24]

Stuart might be theatrical and loud, might be avid of praise, might be inclined to prolong his raids at a distance from the army; but he was alert, he was intelligent, he was possessed of many essentials of sound military judgment, and he was beginning to show uncommon aptitude in fathoming the intentions of the enemy. Lee had faith in Stuart, and now that the cavalry had increased to two brigades and required divisional command, he recommended Stuart for promotion. As of July 28, Jeb became a major general.

His assigned senior brigadier, in a wise settlement of obscure differences with President Davis, was Wade Hampton. The second cavalry brigadier, named on Stuart's recommendation, was Colonel Fitz Lee of the 1st Virginia cavalry. "In my estimation," said Stuart, "no one in the Confederacy possesses more of the elements of what a brigadier of cavalry ought to be than he."[25]

The cavalry was organized—and ready.

4. The Juniors Who Vied with Veterans

As ready as Stuart were others of less renown. In young John Pelham the trial of the Seven Days had developed leadership unmistakable. Far to the left at Gaines' Mill on June 27, wrote Stuart, "ensued one of the most gallant and heroic feats of the war"—Captain Pelham, with his single Napoleon, directing fire against two Federal batteries "with a coolness and intrepidity only equalled by his previous brilliant career." Pelham it was who cleared the way for Stuart's advance to White House, Pelham who chased the *Marblehead* down the Pamunkey, Pelham who, at Stuart's order, opened from Evelington Heights. "I feel bound to ask for his promotion," said Stuart, "with the remark that in either cavalry or artillery no field grade is too high for his merit and capacity."[26]

Among Pelham's classmates at West Point had been the young Virginian Thomas L. Rosser. Upon Virginia's secession, Rosser had sent in his resignation and hurried to Montgomery. He was physically a superb young man, well over six feet, Indian in erectness, broad-shouldered and muscular, with the indescribable quality of the soldier in his bearing and direct gaze. Assigned first to the Washington Artillery of New Orleans, he was promoted colonel two days before the opening of the Seven Days campaign and given command of the 5th Virginia cavalry. On June 30, picketing Malvern Hill, he had discovered the enemy crossing hurriedly to the river. When Longstreet and Holmes did not respond to his report, the youthful Rosser would not be balked. He sent the information directly to Lee. His reward was the early appearance of the commanding general himself at his outpost, first to observe the movement of the enemy and then to order Holmes forward. This notable service Rosser followed, the next week, by a stubborn defensive on the River Road below Westover. Stuart watched and applauded, and from that day, in a service that boasted many daring and ambitious officers, Rosser was a marked man.[27]

Opportunities for the artillerists in the Seven Days had been few because of the absences, defective organization, poor leadership, and unfavorable terrain; but where battery commanders had a fair field of fire, some of them shone. First among them was Captain William J. Pegram, a younger brother of Colonel John Pegram, who had shared in the tragedy of Rich Mountain. "Willie" Pegram, small of stature, spectacled, retiring, had been a quiet listener at the University of Virginia while fiery fellow students had debated the burning question of secession. When the hour of decision came, he left the university and reported as a member of "Company F," a *corps d'élite* of his native Richmond. In a short time he was elected lieutenant of the Purcell Battery, another Richmond command, and saw action during the First Battle of Manassas.[28]

Eleven months later, when Lee opened the offensive at Mechanicsville, Willie Pegram was captain of the Purcell Battery and was sent forward in the van of A. P. Hill's division. He soon came under the converging fire of the Federal artillery across Beaver Dam Creek. His six guns coped for a time with close to thirty of superior accuracy. When night mercifully came to cover him, Pegram had lost forty-seven of his command, with many of his horses, and had four of his guns out of action. Somehow he got his battery into condition to fight the next day, and engaged gallantly at Gaines' Mill.

At Malvern Hill Pegram answered the desperate call of Armistead for artillery support. With the fine Portsmouth Battery of Carey F. Grimes, Pegram crashed through the woods, unlimbered, and defied the blast from the ordnance that crowded the crest of the hill. "No men," wrote Armistead, "could have behaved better than Captains Pegram and Grimes; they worked their guns after their men were cut down, and only retired when entirely disabled." After the last hot fieldpiece was hauled out and the casualties of the campaign reckoned, the roll showed that Pegram had lost 7 killed and 53 wounded, a total of 60, in a battery of 80 men. A gruesome toll it was, and due in part to Pegram's belief that the largest service was to be rendered at the short range.[29]

The roll of those conspicuous in the hard service of the infantry was so long that brigade commanders had to explain that, with few exceptions, they could not attempt to name those below the rank of field officer. For the first time appeared prominently in reports the names of Robert F. Hoke, S. Dodson Ramseur, Samuel McGowan, E. L. Thomas, all of whom, then colonels or lieutenant colonels, soon were to be promoted. Colonel John B. Gordon won new admiration for his gallant leading of Rodes's brigade at Malvern Hill, where more than 400 of his Alabamians fell.

Of all the brigadiers, R. H. Anderson, in his modest way, probably had been the most definitely marked throughout the campaign by soldierly competence. At Glendale he had been in charge of Longstreet's division while Old Pete directed the field. In Longstreet's bestowal of praise, Anderson's name headed all. Jackson, too, had observed the "gallant style" of the South Carolinian's advance on the twenty-seventh in support of Whiting. It was plain that Anderson soon was to be promoted.[30]

George Pickett, he of the curling locks, had been wounded in the charge that added to Dick Anderson's reputation at Gaines' Mill, but he was not forgotten in reports. Cadmus Wilcox, another of Longstreet's brigadiers, had acquitted himself admirably in the same battle. At Glendale Wilcox had perhaps the hardest fighting of the day, in the face of two valiantly defended Federal batteries. When the day was over, his record was as good as that of any brigadier, though his loss had been ghastly.[31]

In A. P. Hill's division, Pender's attack at Mechanicsville, Gregg's at Gaines' Mill, and the final, well-organized advance of Joseph R. Anderson at Glendale probably had been the outstanding accomplishments. For a division of which three brigades had never been previously under fire, the showing of all the units was creditable and more. D. H. Hill felt that Colquitt and Ripley had done less than their part at Gaines' Mill and in his report he was to say so in plain terms. For Samuel Garland and George B. Anderson he had nothing but praise.[32]

Of all the brigadiers of Jackson's command, the most shining figure had been Hood, whose attack at Gaines' Mill was regarded as the most brilliant single achievement in the Seven Days. Winder was credited with excellent leadership, as was Lawton. Trimble, all ardor, had displayed his fighting spirit in pleading—in vain—with Jackson to launch a final assault at Malvern Hill. Magruder's command had been so overmarched and so mishandled that the competent men had not been revealed, though the worst misfits had been exposed. As for Huger's division, the commander had better reason to be proud of Armistead, Mahone, and Wright than they had to applaud his direction.

Tactical mistakes there had been, wasteful exposure under fire, and assaults that more experienced leading might have rendered unnecessary; but had all the reports been bundled together, and one word written across their jacket, that one word would have been *Promising*.

5. The Enigma of Jackson's State of Mind

More important than the promise of any of the brigadiers during the Seven Days was the performance of those divisional commanders who, despite tactical blundering and in the face of delays by others, had carried the strategical plan to success.

Dick Ewell was to be reckoned high among those who had contributed unmistakably to the defeat of the Federals. In every essential, to the limits allowed him, he had met the test. His marches had been well-ordered and prompt. At Gaines' Mill he had not only led his men admirably, but also had given all possible aid to the adjoining units. At Malvern Hill he had been held in reserve until late in the action. Then he had advanced valiantly. No officer was mentioned more often or more gratefully by others. The picture of him that takes form, in a score of reports, is that of an intelligent, trained, self-contained, and daring man, unique in personality, who had cheer and help for every fellow soldier who needed either.

In the final hours of the Seven Days' Battles, Jackson had been as diligent as his lieutenant, Ewell. Late in the evening of July 1, when Stuart's engineer came to report that the cavalry were close at hand, Jackson was in good humor and disposed to joke. "That's good! That's good!" he said in his usual formula of approval. "Changing his base, is he? Ha, ha." During the night, after some of his officers awakened him from a hard sleep with a request for orders, he answered only, "Please let me sleep; there will be no enemy here in the morning." At daylight, when it was not yet clear that he was right in his prediction, he sent a fatigue party to clean up the battlefield on his front. When asked his reason for this, he said simply, "I am going to attack here presently, as soon as the fog rises, and it won't do to march the troops over their own dead, you know; that's what I am doing it for." His complete dissent a little later from Lee's decision not to pursue McClellan that day was silent but apparent to observers.[33]

All this was in keeping with the reputation Jackson had acquired in the Valley. But what of the march of June 26, of the delay at the Chickahominy bridge, of the day-long wait on the north side of White Oak Swamp? How were these things to be explained? Were they the performance of a man who could be trusted to lead larger forces under a ranking general in a new campaign?

Many Confederates in and out of the army had unfriendly answers. Longstreet, perhaps at the time and publicly in later years, maintained that "Jackson was a very skillful man against such men as Shields, Banks, and Frémont, but when pitted against the best of the Federal commanders he did not appear so well." Among staff officers it was whispered that Old

Jack had said "he did not intend that *his* men should do all the fighting." His light casualties gave some color to the rumor. Even D. H. Hill thought that "an important factor" in Jackson's lost day at White Oak Swamp was his "pity for his own corps, worn out by . . . numerous sanguinary battles." Hill echoed the gossip of staff officers that Jackson thought the "garrison of Richmond ought now to bear the brunt of the fighting." Dr. Dabney believed Jackson mentally exhausted on the critical day. William Allan, not second even to Dabney in his admiration for his chief, could say only, when the evidence had been sifted, that "Jackson's comparative inaction" was "one of the few great mistakes of his marvelous career."[34]

Jackson himself never indicated that he thought he had failed during the Seven Days. He described his marches of June 26–27 as though they were made precisely in accordance with the plan. For his failure to advance on June 30, the marshy character of the soil, the destruction of the bridge, and the strong position of the enemy were set down as the reasons. Only once did he ever speak of White Oak Swamp. Overhearing his staff arguing whether troops from his command should have been sent across the swamp to Longstreet's assistance, Jackson said curtly, "If General Lee had wanted me, he could have sent for me." What made him give that answer? On the thirtieth had he been striving to hold rigidly to soldierly subordination in the large army to which he was a stranger; had he been so weary that he had not exerted himself beyond the letter of his orders? Did he voice justification or excuse? He gave no hint.[35]

Lee never understood why the delay occurred at White Oak Swamp, but he did not lose his high opinion of Jackson as a soldier. The commanding general may have reasoned that Jackson in an unfamiliar country, cooperating with distant columns through inexperienced staff officers, faced difficulties that could not be overcome. Chance and not lack of ability or of effort may have seemed to Lee the reason for Jackson's failure. Although Jackson had not accomplished what was expected of him, in his report Lee was content to believe he could not have done it.

Physical exhaustion and the resulting benumbment of a mind that depended much on sleep probably are the basic explanation for Jackson's inability to meet the demands of the campaign. In addition, every other circumstance was adverse: Jackson had no skill in quick mastery of terrain, though his eye for tactical use of a position was admirable. The man who could have helped him most, his topographer Jed Hotchkiss, was not with him. Whiting may have been sulking. Major Dabney, an excellent administrator in camp, was inexperienced in transportation. On the critical days' marches quartermaster Harman was absent or, like his chief, was weary. Jackson was attempting, also, to handle a much larger force than ever had been under his charge. Most of this Lee took into account. If, at the end of the campaign, he had doubts concerning Jackson, they probably were two—whether the victor of the Valley could display his full capacity in a subordinate position, and whether he could use the abilities of other men sufficiently to direct a large force.

Circumstances curiously deferred the answer. On June 26 the Federal forces in the Shenandoah Valley and those designated for the defense of the approaches to Washington had been consolidated as the Army of Virginia. To its direction was assigned Major General John Pope, who had displayed much vigor in successful operations on the upper Mississippi. Within a fortnight Pope began an advance toward the Rapidan River. His army appeared capable, at the least, of advancing to the Virginia Central Railroad at the "Gordonsville loop" and thereby severing communications between Richmond and the Shenandoah. That done, Pope, if strong, might march toward Richmond and renew the threat McDowell had made in May of a junction with McClellan.

Jackson would not state the case in defensive terms. He went to Lee and argued with vigor that the best means of dealing with McClellan and with Pope was through an offensive into the enemy's own country. When Lee reserved judgment, Jackson determined on a bold step: He would appeal over the head of the commanding general to the President. In doing this he would be proceeding close to the farthest line of military insubordination and he must, in consequence, be careful. After some reflection he sent one evening for his aide and political champion, Colonel A. R. Boteler.

Jackson laid out his appraisal: The Army of the Potomac was beaten; the Federals would not resume the offensive until they were reinforced; Richmond was safe; the offensive proposed by him in May should be launched. At this point Jackson's caution and military training prompted a disclaimer: While Boteler must tell all this to the President, he must make it plain that Jackson was not self-seeking in urging persistently this offensive. He was willing to follow any leader Davis might designate. Boteler interposed: What was the use of going to Mr. Davis; he would only refer the matter to Lee. "Why don't you yourself speak to General Lee upon the subject?"

He had already done so, Jackson admitted: "He says nothing." At Boteler's further prompting, he added: "So great is my confidence in General Lee that I am willing to follow him blindfolded. But I fear he is unable to give me a definite answer now because of influences at Richmond, where, perhaps, the matter has been mentioned by him and may be under consideration. I, therefore, want you to see the President and urge the importance of prompt action."[36]

Congressman Boteler went to the President and repeated Jackson's argument. Davis was no more prepared than was Lee to say that the Confederacy could muster immediately in northern Virginia sufficient force to assume the offensive. At the moment the task was to halt Pope. What part of Lee's forces could perform that mission so readily as the Army of the Valley? Jackson could not be allowed sufficient troops for the early invasion of the North, but he could be given again the semi-independent status in which he had shone. His aptitude fitted the strategical necessities.

Orders were issued on July 13 for entraining Jackson's and Ewell's divisions, less Taylor's brigade. Six days later Jackson reached Gordonsville and saw again the Blue Ridge. Was he glad for other reasons than those of health to be away from a "malarious region"? Had he learned while in front of Richmond to cooperate willingly, or had he chafed? Not one line did he write, not a word did he speak that disclosed his mind. Curious posterity will never know whether, in his heart of hearts, a battle was raging between ambition for independent command and a purpose to discipline his own spirit for labor with Lee and Lee's other lieutenants in the achievement of Southern independence.

With one of the division commanders in Lee's army Jackson again became associated before the end of July, in circumstances as curious as its results were to prove. Impetuous A. P. Hill had been, on June 26, in crossing the Chickahominy and opening the Battle of Mechanicsville. Impetuous Hill had been in assailing the Federals behind Boatswain's Swamp—but stubbornly determined he showed himself to be, and capable of directing men on a long, confused front. At Glendale Hill had handled his troops easily and with indisputable effectiveness. All his marches had been prompt and orderly; he had shown clear competence.

That and more could be said of Longstreet. Among the division commanders of Lee's army, Old Pete—as his men had begun to call him—now stood pre-eminent. His attack on the right at Gaines' Mill had been shrewd and not unduly expensive of life. In the woods west of Glendale Longstreet had directed his own and A. P. Hill's division with confidence and entire calm. There can be little doubt that, when the campaign ended, Lee was leaning more heavily on Longstreet than on any other of his subordinates. All Longstreet's actions had been well-reasoned and apparently free of any grasping after authority. Not a suggestion was there of the spirit he had shown at Seven Pines. Had he been conscious that he should redeem a less than credible record in the action of May 31? His new record—had it been aroused by a new commander? Was he, like Lee, learning the art of war? Or had he determined that in a campaign where divisional leadership was shared by the hero of the Valley, he would not be outdone? History cannot answer.

The fine record of cooperation between A. P. Hill and Longstreet was marred almost as soon as it was made. Among Hill's volunteer aides during the campaign had been John M. Daniel, editor of the *Richmond Examiner.* His slashing, dogmatic editorial style and sense of news made his journal much the most interesting of Richmond's wartime papers. After receiving a trifling wound at Gaines' Mill, Daniel retired forthwith to Richmond and, through the columns of the *Examiner,* glorified the general under whom he had served. A. P. Hill was credited with the "investment of Mechanicsville" against four times his numbers. Glendale, the paper proclaimed, was fought under "the immediate and sole command" of Hill. Daniel affirmed that Hill's command, consisting of his own and "one of Longstreet's two divisions," had achieved on June 30 a "success which broke the spirit of the enemy and completed the circuit of our victories."[37]

As the *Examiner* was read in all the camps, the laudation of A. P. Hill, with implied disparagement of others, stirred many jealousies and aroused no little wrath. Longstreet, in particular, was incensed. He wrote editor Daniel a stiff note stating that the articles in the *Examiner* were calculated to alarm the public, and pointed out their various deficiencies. Exaggerated statements, he concluded, might do great injury to the army both at home and abroad. Since Hill was not associated directly with the adulation voiced by the *Examiner,* Old Pete did not propose to publish this answer over his own signature. One of Longstreet's military family should sponsor the reply. Major Moxley Sorrel, assistant adjutant general of the division, was entirely agreeable to doing so.

On July 11, in the rival *Richmond Whig,* the "card" appeared. It created satisfaction among those who had resented the manner in which one division had been credited with winning the campaign, but its publication aroused wrath at Hill's headquarters. Hill wrote Lee: "I have the honor to request that I may be relieved from the command of Major-General Longstreet." The paper, transmitted through channels, was endorsed by Old Pete with deliberate unconcern. He saw "no particular reason why Maj. Gen. A. P. Hill should not be gratified." Of this, at the moment, Lee took no notice.

The dispute widened when Hill refused to obey an order of Longstreet's as delivered through Major Sorrel, and Longstreet had him placed "in arrest with orders to confine himself to limits of his camp and vicinity." A furious correspondence between the two generals followed, with one of its points of contention their relative command roles at Glendale. No adjustment could be reached. Friends were called in, and all the indications pointed to a duel.[38]

Could the perplexities of the reorganization of the Army of Northern Virginia after the Seven Days have been illustrated more dramatically than by the threat of this duel? Huger had proved "too slow"; Maguder was to leave Virginia with the assurance that he would deal with his critics; Jackson, in the eyes of many, had not fulfilled expectations; Whiting's conduct had raised a question; D. H. Hill was overcritical, though competent, and had been sent a challenge by Toombs. Of the division commanders only Ewell, A. P. Hill, and Longstreet had come through the campaign with a record for meeting creditably the opportunities that had come to them; and two of these three might seek to kill each other!

Forced now to intervene, General Lee, as Sorrel phrased it, "brought matters, through other friends, to an adjustment honorable to both." That "adjustment" grew out of urgent military necessity. Jackson, at Gordonsville, had found himself too weak to attack Pope, who was closing to within striking distance of the Virginia Central. Another division had to be sent Jackson from the Richmond front, and it must be under a competent leader. Lee reasoned that if A. P. Hill were selected for the mission, he would be satisfied to drop his demand for a duel, and Longstreet would release Hill from arrest. So it happened: Hill was returned to duty July 26, and the next day was ordered to move his division by rail to reinforce Jackson.[39]

With Hill went the Louisiana brigade, but Dick Taylor was not with it. His illness had proved serious and had produced temporary paralysis of his lower limbs. He was sent home to rest and to recruit his old regiments, and was given the well-won rank of major general. Taylor always thought this was on Jackson's recommendation for service in the Valley. The army was the poorer for Taylor's departure.[40]

6. A New Organization for New Battles

By the date of Powell Hill's departure, the first major reorganization of the Army of Northern Virginia had been completed. It had been necessitated by the failure of some leaders and, no less, by the defects of the old organization. Among a multitude of lessons in command taught by the Seven Days, the most impressive was this: Under a system that placed the direction of operations largely in the hands of division commanders too numerous to be controlled directly by the general in chief, the divisions were, in effect, distinct little armies. In a wooded country of confusing roads, the major general of a column operating even a few miles from army headquarters virtually was independent. If reckless, he could not be restrained; if determined to take no risks, he could not be brought into action. Every battle had demonstrated this. In all the Seven Days there had been one instance where two divisions had cooperated for the whole of a battle—Longstreet and Powell Hill on June 30. Elsewhere how tragic had been the record, how complete the indictment of the organization! At Mechanicsville Powell Hill had acted as if he were afraid the other divisions might snatch glory from his hands; the next day at Gaines' Mill he had plunged in eagerly before any help was at hand. Harvey Hill had outmarched Jackson that day as if determined to seize the honors of battle from his senior. Savage Station, the futile marches and long halts of June 30, the failure of Lee to get the full force of any division employed together with its neighbors against Malvern Hill— had war ever offered worse examples of dissipated strength, of might ill-used?

Along with the leaders, the law was to blame. The Confederate military acts provided no formal organization larger than a division. Legally, there was no such military body as a corps, no grade between major general and general. Now, after the disappointments and lapses of the Seven Days, a means had to be found of coordinating the independent divisions. The Confederacy could not hope to win if it had six armies, six independent commanders on one field. Scarcely a reference appears in extant correspondence to any decision to establish corps, but by the time A. P. Hill reinforced Jackson at Gordonsville, the remainder of the infantry had been placed under Longstreet. No new titles were conferred; neither "corps" nor "wing" was mentioned. The infantry around Richmond simply became "Longstreet's Command," and the troops near the Rapidan "Jackson's Command." Necessity forced Lee to anticipate the amendment of the law.

The organization now was as follows:

Jackson's Command

Jackson's Division was under the command of Charles S. Winder, of the First Brigade, who, next to Jackson, was the senior general officer. John R. Jones had the Second Brigade, William B. Taliaferro the Third, and A. R. Lawton the Fourth.

Ewell's Division had substantially the same organization as in the Valley campaign, but Jubal Early had Elzey's brigade and Harry Hays the Louisiana brigade. Trimble continued at the head of his troops.

A. P. Hill's Division was unchanged except that Joseph R. Anderson had resigned to resume direction of the important Tredegar Iron Works in Richmond; E. L. Thomas headed the brigade.

Longstreet's Command

Longstreet's Division remained intact otherwise than for the transfer of R. H. Anderson's brigade to Micah Jenkins, promoted brigadier general on Lee's strong recommendation.

D. R. Jones's Division of two brigades, under G. T. Anderson and the tempestuous Toombs, retained its organization but passed from the disbanded command of Magruder to Longstreet.

McLaws's Division of Semmes's and Kershaw's brigades was enlarged to regulation size by the inclusion of Cobb's and Barksdale's commands, which previously had been Magruder's own division.

D. H. Hill's Division was increased by the addition of a brigade under Henry A. Wise. No commander had yet been appointed in succession to Harvey Hill.

R. H. Anderson's Division was Huger's old command—Mahone's, Armistead's, and Wright's brigades. So manifestly was Anderson's promotion deserved that it created little comment.

A special case was *Whiting's Division,* kept under the direct control of Lee and not part of Longstreet's command.

The Cavalry

The cavalry now constituted a division of two brigades under Major General Stuart. One brigade was under Wade Hampton, the other was commanded by Fitz Lee.

The Artillery

Artillery organization was not improved. Each brigade had a battery assigned as substantially its own. This battery might assist another of the same division, or in theory, another division commanded by the same general. During the Seven Days Jackson alone had been able to mass the guns of more than one division.

To summarize the reorganization, it involved two promotions only to the grade of major general, those of Jeb Stuart and Dick Anderson. As brigadiers, Fitz Lee, Micah Jenkins, and Harry Hays were commissioned. To the infantry returned Jubal Early, to the cavalry went Hampton—historic assignments both. So tactfully were the changes made—especially the selection of Longstreet and of Jackson to direct all the infantry—and with such manifest regard for merit that few realized how far the army had been revolutionized.

A long list it was of the "Manassas men" who had disappeared from the army in the year past. Dead were Bartow, Bee, and Cocke; wounded, transferred, or resigned were Johnston, Beauregard, Kirby Smith, Bonham, and Shanks Evans. Robert Garnett had fallen in western Virginia; Allegheny

Johnson had been wounded at McDowell. To the list of dead Richard Griffith and Turner Ashby had to be added. Arnold Elzey had been wounded again and grievously, and Maryland Steuart had a broken bone that would not knit. Johnston had begun to recover, but he certainly would not replace Lee. That was assured. Besides Johnston, the army had lost the long-esteemed Gustavus Smith, whose nervous condition still was puzzling. Magruder, Huger, and D. H. Hill had been transferred. These five, with Longstreet and Whiting, ere the arrival of Jackson, had been the most conspicuous figures in the army that faced McClellan between White Oak Swamp and the Chickahominy. Now, of the seven, only three remained!

The explanation for all this was the one grim word, *combat*. Those forty days of bloody action from Front Royal to Malvern Hill had shattered the command. Many had fallen, but more had failed. The battle deaths the South had expected, the failures it had not. In 1861 appearance had shaped appraisal. A confident people had accepted promise before performance. Then, under test of fire, high reputations quickly had been destroyed, pretense shattered, nerves that seemed strong had been as wax, excitement cost some men their self-mastery and others it had bewildered. That same fire of battle, burning to the soul of man, had shown valor beneath a cover of uncouthness, heroic composure under a commonplace mien, steel where the surface seemed soft, ability as dazzling as unsuspected.

All the capacities of the new army would be required now. Fire-eating politicians and editors were beginning to doubt the recognition of the Confederacy by England and France and the intervention of those powers against the North. The bloody way of battle, whether it led across the Potomac or back again to the James, was lengthening, though it was promising; past belief was the transformation in the Southern cause since the dreadful days of February. Still . . . John Pope was threatening an advance down the Orange and Alexandria Railroad against Jackson. At Harrison's Landing, McClellan's army still outnumbered Lee's. A force of unknown destination was being mustered at Fort Monroe.

Could the reorganized Army of Northern Virginia cope with all these troops? Was it well led now, or had it merely been fortunate in the operations against McClellan? After a year, how much more capable, if any, would Lee show himself than Johnston? That strange man Jackson, was he a mad genius, unable, unwilling to cooperate, or would he prove himself the right arm, perhaps the successor to the commanding general? Longstreet the impassive, was he qualified, or was he another Huger, imperturbable, to be sure, but well-nigh immovable? Would the new leaders, like the old, find battle a traitor to reputation, a betrayer of the fame it brought?

CHAPTER 14

Facing a New Threat

1. NEW TROUBLES FOR OLD JACK

Was it a major change in Federal strategy with which Stonewall Jackson had to deal in mid-July 1862? Was Pope's Army of Virginia opening a "second front" in advancing on the Virginia Central? Another Federal force of unknown strength was at Fredericksburg. This column, uniting with Pope, might overwhelm Jackson. Either one might push forward, cut the railway, and sever communications between Richmond and the Shenandoah. Against this possibility, Jackson had, first of all, to protect the long stretch of rail from Hanover Junction to Charlottesville. He had also to watch for an opening and, if he found one, strike at once. In this spirit, when he was satisfied Pope was north and west of Culpeper, Jackson advanced the Army of the Valley on July 19 to Gordonsville.[1]

Jackson was conscious that his men needed a renewal of stiff discipline. Before he left Richmond, he had prescribed the tonic of three drills a day. Now, as he awaited developments, he sought to restore whatever might have been lost in soldierly qualities. It was an exacting and burdening task. If he had time for Holy Writ, that was all. Newspapers he still declined to peruse lest they destroy his Christian humility. They spoke too well of him. "Everything here seems so quiet," his aide Frank Paxton wrote cheerfully home. "The troops are drilling and ... it is very much needed. Everything has a happy, quiet appearance, such as I have not seen in the army since we were in camp this time last year after the battle of Manassas."[2]

The arrival of A. P. Hill's division did not disturb this calm. The Light Division reached Jackson on July 29 and the days immediately following. In dispatching Hill from Richmond, Lee had written the commander of the Army of the Valley, "A. P. Hill you will, I think, find a good officer, with whom you can consult, and by advising with your division commanders as to your movements much trouble will be saved you in arranging details, as they can act more intelligently. I wish to save you trouble from my increas-

ing your command."³ This was as pointed as it was tactful. The event was
to show that Lee's counsel was lost on Jackson. If Stonewall was willing, as
he told Boteler, to follow Lee blindfolded, he required no less of his subordinates. Hill said nothing and asked nothing. Doubtless he was glad
enough to be away from Longstreet.

If Hill kept the peace, others did not. Some privates of the Stonewall
Brigade had straggled badly on the march and wandered far in search of
food at private homes. Winder decided that the one way of stopping this
was to punish it severely. Thirty offenders were "bucked" for a day. Their
resentment was worse than their straggling. About half of them deserted
that night. Jackson thought it politic to direct that men not be bucked
again, thus ending that humiliating form of punishment, but it did not
cool the wrath of the sufferers. John Casler wrote that Winder "was very
severe, and very tyrannical, so much so that he was 'spotted' by some of the
brigade; and we could hear it remarked by some one near every day that
the next fight we got into would be the last for Winder."⁴ That in the
Southern Cromwell's own brigade of the Model Army!

Simultaneously with this unhappy affair in the Stonewall Brigade, Jackson's cavalry was in the turmoil of reorganization. Following the death of
Ashby, Richmond had not consulted Jackson in the search for a successor.
The President chose Colonel Beverly H. Robertson and promoted him
brigadier general. Robertson was a midland Virginian, thirty-six, a graduate of West Point in the class of 1849, a veteran of much Indian service and
in person the embodiment of the fashionable French cavalry officer of the
time. Somewhat bald, with unsmiling eyes, Robertson wore long, flowing
mustaches and whiskers in the mode of Louis Napoleon. He had entered
Confederate service as colonel of the 4th Virginia cavalry.

Because Robertson adhered sternly to the rigorous discipline of the regular army, he was defeated in the election for colonel in the reorganization
of his command. That canceled his commission but made him available for
other service. Davis's hope was that Robertson's admitted abilities as a
drillmaster could be well employed in the training of Ashby's men. The
loose, cumbersome organization of the cavalry in the Shenandoah was
conformed to army regulations. Ashby's troopers were regimented as the
7th and 12th Virginia, and the 17th Virginia battalion. With Munford's 2nd
and Flournoy's 6th, they constituted Robertson's "Laurel Brigade." The
organization was thus completed but it was not popular. Boys who had
been accustomed to the easy-going if adventuresome life under Ashby
could not be reconciled overnight to "old army" colonels and methods.⁵

Had this been all, Jackson readily could have dealt with it. Now that
Ashby's influence no longer could be exerted against him, he could have

assured support for Robertson had he himself had faith in that officer. There was the barrier. Stonewall seems from an early date to have disliked his new chief of cavalry. Perhaps this was because he was not consulted about the appointment, or because he did not believe Robertson qualified for the command. In either event, Jackson quickly concluded that Robertson lacked vigor in reconnaissance and outpost duty. On August 7 he forwarded a request that he be rid of Robertson and that William E. "Grumble" Jones, 7th Virginia cavalry, be put in command. "That subject," answered Lee, "is not so easily arranged, and . . . I fear the judgment passed upon [Robertson] may be hasty." With the frankness he always displayed in dealing with Jackson, he continued, "Neither am I sufficiently informed of the qualifications of Col. W. E. Jones . . . to say whether he is better qualified." To Mr. Davis, Lee wrote, "Probably Jackson may expect too much. . . . An undisciplined brigade of Cavl. is no trifling undertaking & requires time to regulate." There, uncertainly and unpleasantly, the matter had to rest.⁶

If Jackson could not have his way with the cavalry, he could do his full duty, as he saw it, in disciplining his infantry. He soon observed that he had so many courts-martial under way that he had been compelled to assign all his general officers to that duty. Of all these, the one that involved the largest issue of justice was that of Brigadier General Richard B. Garnett for withdrawing the Stonewall Brigade from the front of action at Kernstown. The accused officer had seen the letter in which Jackson said, "I regard Gen. Garnett as so incompetent a Brigade commander, that, instead of building up a Brigade, a good one, if turned over to him, would actually deteriorate under his command." As he was satisfied his action at Kernstown had been proper, Garnett was determined to have vindication and, no less, to renew in some capacity his military service in defense of the South. He called for a court to try him, and in due course Lee arranged for one to be held in the field with Jackson's army.⁷

On August 5 this court assembled at Ewell's headquarters near Liberty Mills and began to take testimony. Jackson had drawn with much care broad charges of neglect of duty under seven specifications. The allegation was that Garnett had divided his command at Kernstown, separated himself from his troops, permitted them to become confused, and "given the order to fall back, when he should have encouraged his command to hold its ground." To all of this Garnett had prepared a detailed answer.

On the stand Jackson gave coldly his story of what he had sought to do at Kernstown and what he believed to be Garnett's derelictions. Garnett himself cross-examined his former chief. When the examination turned to the tactical details of the advance, Jackson's memory of the circumstances was completely at variance with Garnett's. So far were they apart that at three points on his transcript of the testimony Garnett wrote opposite Jackson's answer, "Lie." When he opened his defense, he prefaced it with the assertion that, at Kernstown, "Gen'l Jackson did not communicate to me any plan of battle. . . . I was . . . entirely ignorant of his schemes and intentions." He entered denial, in detail, of each specification, and submitted reports, personal letters, and affidavits from his colonels and others who had fought at Kernstown. He cited Jackson's letter alleging unfitness for command and other complaints of Jackson's against him. "Such covert attacks," said Garnett, "are inconsistent with honors and justice, and should arouse grave doubts as to the motives and truthfulness of these secret allegations."

Before Garnett had finished presenting his case, the spies Jackson had sent to ascertain the position of Pope's forces returned with their findings. Only a part of the new Army of Virginia, it was reported, had reached Culpeper. Jackson believed that precisely such an opportunity as he had hoped to find now was offered him. Pope apparently had made a mistake. By a swift march Jackson might destroy the Federal van ere the whole army could be concentrated. No time must be lost. The court was suspended. On August 7 the columns were in motion from the camps around Gordonsville.[8]

The day's objective was Orange Court House. Thence Jackson intended to drive straight on Culpeper, twenty miles beyond. To reach Orange was an easy matter, because Jed Hotchkiss had chosen roads that scarcely would be under the observation of the enemy. The one trouble, a minor one, concerned Sidney Winder. He was sick, and his surgeon insisted he should not attempt active field command. Winder was willing to obey the surgeon if the march did not involve a battle, but if there was to be a fight he was determined to have a hand in it.

He sent Lieutenant McHenry Howard to report his condition to Jackson and to inquire whither the army was moving and whether Jackson expected an action. The lieutenant did not like the idea of putting such questions to the taciturn Jackson and said so, but Winder was insistent. Howard found Jackson in his headquarters tent and reported Winder's illness, and then rushed on: "But he sent me to ask you if there will be a battle, and if so, when and he would be up, and which way the army is going." He spoke it all in a mouthful and expected to be met with a sharp retort. Instead, Jackson reflected for some moments and then indulged in a diffident smile at young Howard's manifest confusion. "Say to General Winder I am truly sorry he is sick"—a pause and then: "that there will be a battle, but not tomorrow, and I hope he will be up; tell him the army will march to Barnett's Ford, and he can learn its further direction there."

Gratefully Howard hurried away and reported to Winder, who resolved to follow the column.⁹

At Orange Court House, during the night, Jackson issued orders for the three divisions to march at dawn. Ewell was to lead; Hill was to follow; Jackson's own division, under Winder, was to close the rear. Then, with these orders delivered, Jackson changed the plan, deciding to send Ewell by a parallel route and reunite with the other divisions at Barnett's Ford. Of this change of plan A. P. Hill was not informed. At the appointed hour, on the morning of the eighth, he had his leading brigade near the street in Orange up which he expected Ewell to move. Shortly after sunrise troops began to pass. Hill assumed they were Ewell's men. A brigade or more had tramped northward before he learned that the troops were of Jackson's division.

What was Hill to do? All his choices were poor, and he concluded it would be best to keep the Light Division where it was until all of Jackson's men had passed. After a time, up rode Jackson. Why, he asked Hill, was his command not on the march? Hill explained, perhaps too briefly, that he was waiting for Jackson's division to pass. Jackson looked down the street, saw a halted column of his men, and tersely told a staff officer to order it to move on. Then he turned his horse and rode off. When Hill finally got the Light Division into the road, the progress of his column was halting. He rode ahead to Barnett's Ford to ascertain the reason, and found part of Jackson's division waiting on Ewell's troops, whose route converged at that point. Thereupon Hill sent word to Jackson that the march was delayed. No response came. Finally he was told to return to Orange Court House and encamp there.¹⁰

A feeble, farcical performance the advance had been! On a day when sound strategy demanded maximum speed, Jackson's "foot cavalry" had crawled. Ewell's leading division had been able to do no more than eight miles. What had gone awry? Excessively hot weather was in a measure responsible, but the prime reason was a combination of poor planning, bad staff work, and unnecessary reticence on Jackson's part. Worst of all was his failure to notify A. P. Hill of the change in orders, or to acquaint him with even the essentials of the general plan. Lee's admonition to Jackson to advise with Hill had violated something deep, something almost instinctive in Stonewall. Caution, distrust, jealousy, inborn reticence—whatever it was, cost Jackson a day's march by his largest division.

For the failure of the advance Jackson blamed himself, but he blamed Hill for not preceding Jackson's division from Orange. He did not arrest the commander of the Light Division, but he became doubtful of Hill's ability to conduct a march. Seeds were sown that August day for animosities that might have a grim harvest.

2. Jackson Fumbles at Cedar Mountain

After the wretched march of August 8, Jackson began the next morning a movement that was related almost as vitally to the grand strategy of the changing campaign in Virginia as his advance on Front Royal had been to a somewhat analogous situation in May. Then, as now, McClellan was in front of Richmond; a column was waiting at Fredericksburg; in northern Virginia a third force was afield. The first difference was in the balance among these hostile armies. In the Valley campaign McClellan threatened Richmond; in August he was passive at Harrison's Landing. The force at Fredericksburg under McDowell had been powerful; in August the strength of the troops on the Rappahannock was not believed to be large. In contrast, Pope had many more troops around Culpeper than had been credited to Banks at Strasburg fifteen weeks previously.

Another and a confusing strategic difference there was. Major General A. E. Burnside, in command of a small army on the coast of North Carolina, had left that area and taken transport to Fort Monroe. Was he to reinforce McClellan, or to strengthen Pope? If he was to join Pope, what would be his line of advance? Suppose he ascended the Rappahannock and debarked at Fredericksburg: Would he move vigorously against the Virginia Central Railroad? Did the Federals hope such a movement would force Jackson to retreat so that Pope would have a clear road to Gordonsville? Was that, in turn, preliminary to a junction by Pope with McClellan in front of Richmond? If Burnside did not move against the Virginia Central, would he march westward from Fredericksburg to join Pope on the Rapidan in an effort to overwhelm Jackson?

All these possibilities had been debated anxiously in Richmond, but without sufficient information to shape an answer. On August 5, Jeb Stuart, sent to make a reconnaissance in force toward Fredericksburg, reported that he had located two brigades of Federal infantry. The enemy, Stuart thought, was preparing an advance on the railroad that linked Jackson with Richmond. John S. Mosby, returning from Fort Monroe as an exchanged prisoner of war, reported that Burnside, according to gossip at the post, had been ordered to Fredericksburg. This information was suggestive but not conclusive. At the moment Lee could not send further reinforcements to Jackson. McClellan's strength was so superior that he could not weaken the force defending Richmond. Jackson therefore had started his march northward from Gordonsville in the hope of engaging Pope before the full Army of Virginia could concentrate; but he did not know what flanking operation he might encounter, or what move might be made against the railway on which he depended.[11]

The underlying strategy and tactical dispositions of the Federals were being influenced by circumstances which no opposing general could have divined. Pope's mission had been outlined on June 26. He was to cover Washington, control the Shenandoah Valley, and "so operate upon the enemy's lines of communications in the direction of Gordonsville and Charlottesville as to draw off . . . a considerable force of the enemy from Richmond. . . ." Before Pope could undertake this, McClellan's retreat to the James had been made. In growing doubt that Pope and McClellan could work together, Mr. Lincoln now brought Major General Henry W. Halleck from the western theater to coordinate operations in Virginia, giving him the title of general-in-chief. Pope meanwhile undertook a succession of cavalry raids on the Virginia Central until Jackson reached Gordonsville and secured the railway against anything short of a general offensive. After a fortnight of hesitation, Halleck ordered McClellan on August 3 to abandon operations on the James River and to move his army by water to Aquia Creek, near Fredericksburg. Thence, it was reasoned, he could defend Washington and later participate in a new overland campaign. Burnside had already been ordered to Aquia, which he reached on the third.

This change of underlying strategy had not modified greatly the mission of General Pope. As previously, he was to demonstrate against the Confederate lines of communication in the hope of compelling Lee to detach to guard those lines; thus McClellan's prospects of an untroubled departure from the James River would be increased. Pope specifically was required to hold the line of the Rappahannock and maintain contact with Burnside on his left. Although the news of Jackson's forward movement on August 8 led Pope to canvass the possibility that his adversary had seized the initiative, he decided that Jackson more probably was undertaking a reconnaissance in force. As the hot day of Jackson's slow march burned on, Pope's principal doubt was whether the advance of the Confederates would be on Madison Court House or on Culpeper.[12]

At dawn on the ninth, Pope was satisfied that the attack, if delivered, would be on his right. His dispositions were made accordingly. On a wide front was his cavalry, supported, on Cedar Run, by Crawford's brigade of Banks's II Corps. The remainder of Banks's corps was five miles south of Culpeper, or about three miles in rear of Crawford. Ricketts's division of McDowell's III Corps was three miles behind Banks. Sigel's I Corps, formerly the command of John C. Frémont, had not yet reached Culpeper. In spite of instructions from General Halleck to be "very cautious" until more troops reached the line of the Rappahannock, Pope decided to advance the remainder of Banks's II Corps to the position occupied by Crawford's brigade; orders to that effect were sent at 9:45 A.M.[13]

In the early morning of August 9, Jackson knew only that the Federal cavalry were in his front and that infantry of unknown strength were behind the horsemen. Gloomily he wrote Lee: "I am not making much progress. . . . I fear that the expedition will, in consequence of my tardy movements, be productive of but little good." Still in the belief that no more than the advanced units of Pope's army had reached Culpeper, he determined to press on toward that town. With Robertson's cavalry in advance, Ewell moved northward from Barnett's Ford on the Rapidan.[14]

The lead brigade was that of Jubal Early, "Old Jube." It was the first time Early had shared in a new operation since that bloody charge of May 5 outside Williamsburg. He was full of fight and was to show, ere the day was done, that he had disciplined well the old brigade of the invalided Arnold Elzey. Behind him tramped the rest of Ewell's division and next, three brigades of Jackson's old division. Winder was little better than on the seventh, but insisted on taking the field. Pale and manifestly weak though he was, he soon abandoned his ambulance and rode to the head of the column. Powell Hill, smarting under the black look that Old Jack had given him the previous day, had begun his march before daylight and soon closed the rear brigades of Winder. Whatever the price, Hill was determined that the division which had fired the first shots of the Battle of Gaines' Mill should not be backward in any action the Army of the Valley might undertake.[15]

Twenty-four thousand men crossed the Robertson River in the sunshine of what promised to be a blistering day. Of the heat Jackson scarcely seemed conscious, but to the vulnerability of his train of 1,200 wagons he was sensitive. The troopers under Robertson seemed too inactive, and he halted the trains and left the brigades of Gregg and Lawton to guard them. This arranged, the column pressed its march, but still not to Jackson's satisfaction. Persistently he urged Robertson to locate the enemy; as persistently Robertson complained that his men were straggling. In a situation that called for the eyes of Ashby, the army was half-blinded.[16]

Ahead the roads constituted a capital "Y." To the northwest the route led to Madison Court House, to the northeast, the highway to Culpeper. The main features of the terrain were woods in the angle of the "Y," low ridges and cleared land to the right of the easterly highway, the low shoulders of Cedar Mountain (known also as Slaughter's Mountain) to the east and southeast, and forests to the westward. About midmorning, on a long cleared ridge to the northeast, Union cavalry could be seen. Early's guns opened on the troopers, and they withdrew. As they did so, an answering salvo came across the ridge from their rear. Enemy guns in support! Was there infantry behind the ridge also? Word was sent back to the commanding general, and Early, with skirmishers deployed, moved up the road to the "Y" and halted. He perceived at once that the Federals did not intend to give ground.[17]

Jackson by this time reached the front and rode to the house where Dick Ewell was waiting for orders. Jackson laid out his map; he and Ewell bent over it. The topographical fact which fairly smote them in the face was that the ridges of Cedar Mountain covered the Confederate right and commanded the Union left, and on that Jackson based his plan of action. Ewell was to take two brigades over the shoulder of the mountain and turn the Federal left flank; Early was to advance up the Culpeper Road; Winder was to support Early and to extend his left in such a fashion that it could sweep around the Federal right. For pressing the attack on the center and left, the Stonewall Brigade was to be in immediate reserve. A. P. Hill's division would constitute the general reserve.

Confidently, almost indolently, while he awaited the deployment of his infantry, Jackson stretched out on the porch for a rest. Ewell followed his example. Jackson probably acquainted Winder as well as Ewell with his plan, but he did not tell the other subordinates any more than they had to know. Ewell was not so reserved with Early. Old Jube was informed of all Ewell's division was to undertake, and that he would be supported by three brigades of Winder, who would notify him when the troops were at hand.[18]

At 2 o'clock Early was told Winder was less than three-quarters of a mile in rear and ready to advance. Quietly and unobserved, Early led his troops into the open ground east of the road. With his skirmishers deployed, he climbed the ridge to the northeast. The moment they showed themselves over the crest, three Union batteries opened from the left front. Early, feeling they were needlessly exposed, quickly recalled his regiments to the south slope. He was ready now for the attack he had been told to deliver. He sent back a request for Winder to move up promptly, and as he waited he studied the terrain closely.

In his front, on the right, was a clump of cedar trees on a knoll that dominated the little valley. That clump of trees, Early decided at a glance, was an excellent artillery position, and a staff officer was dispatched to bring up a battery. As Early continued to examine the ground, two things troubled him. One was the distance between his right flank and the brigades Ewell was advancing over the shoulder of Cedar Mountain. The interval was a mile, a dangerously long mile. It must be protected by more than the battery he intended to place among the cedars. A brigade should be there: Early sent Jackson a request for that reinforcement.

The second condition disturbing Early was uncertainty of what might be going on beyond a little watercourse in his front. Above the fields beyond the branch was a crest similar to the one that covered Early's line of battle. Were Union infantry waiting behind that farther ridge? It was ground that might lend itself to surprises, ground that should be watched. Early counted the Federal guns by the smoke from their fire, and kept a vigilant eye for any sign of the presence of infantry.[19]

Old Jube had not been on the lookout long when up the Culpeper Road on his left came three fieldpieces. Well enough! Put them in the grove of cedars. A few minutes more and the three pieces were blazing away. The immediate prospect on his front was for nothing more than an artillery duel. Was a different adventure ahead for Winder's men? Apparently the sick but careful Winder did not think infantry action was imminent, and he took his time with the dispositions of his brigades to the left of the Culpeper Road. He decided it would be possible to advance guns along the road, opposite Early's left, and to occupy, perhaps even to overwhelm, the Federal batteries. The prospect of this seemed the brighter because Ewell's batteries on Cedar Mountain now had added their fire to that of the three pieces in the clump of cedars. Major Snowden Andrews, Winder's chief of artillery, brought up the best guns available.[20]

The artillery duel now began in earnest. Winder kept his binoculars to his eyes, watched the fall of the Confederate projectiles, and called the correction of the range. The fire was beginning to have effect now; the Federal batteries were changing position. Winder turned to give new directions to the boys serving Poague's nearest Parrott rifle. In the din his words were inaudible; he put his hand to his mouth to repeat the order. At that instant a shell passed through his left arm and side and mangled him frightfully, mortally. With his frame in a spasmodic quiver, he fell straight back, full length.[21]

Taliaferro was notified at once that the command had devolved on him—on him who knew nothing of Jackson's plan of action beyond what he could see for himself. He may not have been informed of an ominous warning from Jubal Early, who had caught the glint of the bayonets of a Federal column moving through the woods toward the Confederate left; an attack might be launched at any time against that exposed wing of the army. A reconnaissance of his own did reveal a blue line in a cornfield opposite Early, and Taliaferro shifted some of his regiments to face the flank. He also ordered up the Stonewall Brigade from the reserve.

Thus far—it was about 4:30 P.M.—no Federal attack had developed in the quarter where Early had seen the moving enemy infantry. The action continued to be one of artillery. More guns were added now on the center, and rashly added. A. P. Hill, hearing the fire ahead, ordered forward the

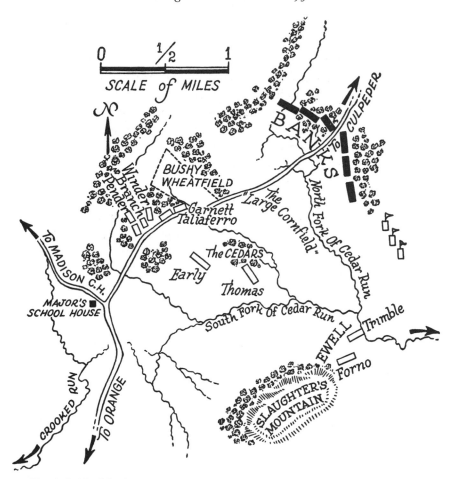

Battlefield of Cedar Mountain, or Slaughter's Mountain, August 9, 1862.

long-range guns of the division. Two batteries managed to push through the crowded roadway and into an open field on Early's left. There, quickly and defiantly, without any infantry support, the guns were unlimbered. Horrified, Early saw the Federals begin to creep forward to capture so recklessly exposed a prize. Old Jube did not hesitate. In his high penetrating voice he ordered his brigade to advance at the double-quick to the batteries. They fired, they raised a yell, they won the race. Thus delivered, the gunners redoubled their efforts.[22]

At 5:45 from the left there came the tearing sound of infantry volleys, a terrific, rolling din. Those Federals, the glint of whose bayonets Early had seen, were attacking. It was reported they had turned the left of Thomas

Garnett's brigade and were closing in on its rear. In front of Early, too, and of Taliaferro's own brigade, the enemy was advancing. An assault was being made against the center and the left; the infantry battle was on. Every commander must look to his own command, and Jackson to the whole!

Early hurried to his right to straighten his line; Taliaferro counterattacked immediately with his brigade and the right of Garnett's. Across Early's rear and toward his right—as if timed for that dramatic moment— there moved Thomas's brigade, the reinforcements Jackson had promised. Welcome they were! The right and center of Jackson's line now could be maintained, probably—if the left held.[23]

The left did not hold. Soon, through the woods, panting and begrimed Confederates began to appear. Some were bloody, many were without arms. All had the same story to tell: The 1st Virginia battalion and the 42nd Virginia had broken. No organization existed on the left. Now the enemy was taking Taliaferro in the rear. Hill's two batteries withdrew swiftly. Back went Taliaferro's brigade. His retreat exposed the left of Early. Was it a second Kernstown—or worse? That wing of the Army of the Valley appeared to be close to rout. Jackson realized it—order the rifled guns to the rear before the enemy took them; rally Taliaferro and Garnett. Where was the Stonewall Brigade? How close at hand was Hill? Could not Ewell attack?

Into the confusion on the eastern fringe of the wood Jackson spurred his horse. For the first time in the war he was seen to wave his saber. In the spirit of Joshua he cried: "Rally, brave men, and press forward! Your general will lead you. Jackson will lead you. Follow me!" Bullets were flying in three directions. No man was safe, nowhere was shelter. Taliaferro hastened to Jackson's side and insisted the commanding general should not expose himself. For a moment Jackson hesitated and then with his habitual, "Good, good!" he turned to the rear.[24]

Little by little the center began to mend. After 6 o'clock it was now, the sun blood-red in the west, the situation still at touch-and-go, but the din that came from the left was beginning to change in pitch. Through the wood there rolled the sound of a volley and snatches of a rebel yell. The Stonewall Brigade was up at last. It was driving the Federals, but its ranks were thin and its flanks were in the air. Could it press on?

Of its progress and of its danger the commanding general was unaware. After Taliaferro protested his presence at the front, Jackson had ridden in search of the leading brigade of Hill's division, the general reserve. Soon he found it—Branch's North Carolinians, in line of battle west of the road. Few words he had for Branch: The left wing was beaten and broken, Jackson said; the enemy had turned the flank. "Push forward, General, push forward!" Branch cried, "Forward, march!" and the brigade moved on the instant. Ere he had gone 100 yards he met fugitives—fugitives of the Stonewall Brigade itself! The 27th Virginia, its right assailed by the enemy, had broken and run. Ranks were opened to permit the fleeing men to pass, and Branch's regiments crashed onward in the forest. Once he threw the weight of his fresh brigade against the now exhausted Federals, he cleared them speedily from the gap between Winder's right and the shattered left of Garnett's and Taliaferro's brigades.[25]

The latter two were rallied by now. Early had reorganized his left. Slowly these troops began to fight their way northeastward along the Culpeper Road and to the right of it. As they advanced there came a roaring Federal cavalry charge. It was courageous but foolhardy. One volley from Early and Taliaferro and the flanking fire of Branch's men disposed of it. That was the last thrust of the enemy. Now was Jackson's turn. He rode along Branch's line, which had scarcely paused in its advance, and doffed his cap in tribute to them. Archer's and Pender's brigades extended the left flank. Ewell on the right advanced *en échelon*. A general attack by the Confederate left swept back in the twilight of the sultry day the last reserve units of the Federal right.[26]

Jackson was determined to make the most of the advantage he narrowly had won. In an effort to drive the enemy back to Culpeper that night, he ordered A. P. Hill to take the lead and press steadily forward. Shelling the woods ahead, Hill's vanguard advanced until it was past 11 o'clock. The moon was bright, but foreboding was in the air. Grumble Jones arrived from Madison Court House with his cavalry regiment and news that a second Federal corps had arrived on the ground. This was enough to stop even Jackson. He ordered the troops to bivouac. In a roadside grass plot he threw himself down. When someone offered him food, he muttered, "No, I want *rest*, nothing but *rest!*" Two miles to the rear lay Winder, forever asleep.[27]

Jackson awakened, on the tenth of August, to a disturbing reality—two Federal corps in front, one of them fresh! The remainder of Pope's army might be near at hand. It would be prudent to wait, to bury the dead, to get the wounded safely to the rear, and, of course, to collect all the arms and booty left on the field. Soon afterward, Jackson heard a loud, friendly voice inquiring for the commanding general. It was Jeb Stuart, and most welcome. Jackson had felt himself badly served by Robertson. On the ninth, little or nothing had been done by the cavalry with the army. Jones, not Robertson, had learned of the arrival of Federal reinforcements whose approach should have been discovered much earlier. Readily Stuart undertook to find how many Federals had joined Banks, and after reconnaissance, brought information which led Jackson to conclude that the enemy was too strong to be attacked.

That night Jackson had campfires lighted all along the front and, while they burned, he led his troops back across the Rapidan. This, he explained later, he did "in order to avoid being attacked by the vastly superior force in front of me, and with the hope that by thus falling back General Pope would be induced to follow me until I should be re-enforced." Jackson's hope was not realized. Beyond the Rapidan Pope did not venture.[28]

Jackson considered that he had won a success and, in a characteristic dispatch of August 11 to Lee he so asserted. "On the evening of the 9th instant," he said, "God blessed our arms with another victory." He had 400 prisoners, one gun, three colors, and a goodly store of small arms to justify his assertion. As for casualties, his dead numbered 229 and his wounded 1,047. This total of 1,276 was not high in terms of the number of troops engaged, but it mounted to 611 in two brigades, Thomas Garnett's and Taliaferro's. The Federal losses, in comparison, were 2,381, among whom were the 400 prisoners. Not less than 20,000 Confederate troops had been within easy striking distance on the day of the battle; Banks had on the ground less than half that number.[29]

Viewed tactically, the battle should have added nothing to Jackson's reputation. On the contrary, it might have raised doubts concerning his leadership—that with his superior numbers he should have taken larger advantage of Banks's gross recklessness. The Federal general had been convinced that a small force confronted him. An opportunity was offered, Banks apparently believed, of winning the field and of effacing the discredit of defeat by Jackson in the Shenandoah Valley. He had hurled three of his four brigades in an assault for which he had not prepared. The initial attack on the Confederate left had been made by no more than three regiments and six companies of a fourth.[30]

Why, in these circumstances, had not the assault been crushed at once? How were the two left brigades of Jackson's army thrown into wild confusion and one of them and part of the other routed? There is one answer only: The Confederate left was not protected with the measure of precaution that should have been expected of a soldier of competence. That flank had been in the air. Although the wood was so thick that surprise might have been expected, no reconnaissance had been made to the left.

Was this the fault of Jackson, or was it due to the wounding of the divisional commander before the brigades on the left had been deployed fully? Winder's previous actions make it reasonable to conclude that if he had not been wounded when he was, he would have deployed his left anew and, doubtless, more carefully. After Winder's fall, Jackson saw quickly the danger to the left, but his instructions seem to have been inadequate. Should not Jackson personally have acquainted himself with conditions on a flank that was threatened and in the air? As for Taliaferro's share of responsibility, when a senior brigadier is kept in ignorance of the part the division is to play in action, how can he be blamed if, on sudden call, he does not follow a plan he does not know? Jackson's reticence—not to say secretiveness—was responsible in part for the rout of his left wing.

Another criticism, and one of definite validity, is that Jackson's general management of the action was lacking in grasp and control. The picture one gets is wholly at variance with that of Jackson at Winchester. On May 25, Jackson seemed to have his hand on all his brigades, on all his regiments even. At Cedar Mountain, though he outnumbered his adversary two to one, he did not utilize anything like his entire force. Nor did he dominate the field. Except for a hand in rallying the center after it broke, Jackson had a small part in the critical operations of the day. Early fought his battle undirected; Taliaferro received too little counsel from the commanding general. The sole order to Hill was for the dispatch of a brigade to reinforce the center. Is this to be explained on the ground that Jackson was unable personally to direct as many as three divisions, and had not learned, as yet, to share his plans and his responsibility with any of his subordinates except Ewell? Had Lee's advice to him, when Hill was sent to Gordonsville, been based on the belief that Jackson's handling of his enlarged command during the Seven Days showed that same deficiency?

None of these questions was asked in Richmond. When Jackson announced that "God blessed our arms with another victory," Lee sent his congratulations and assured Jackson, "the country owes you and your brave officers and soldiers a deep debt of gratitude." Jackson himself ordered a day of thanksgiving in the army. Neither his thanksgiving nor the satisfaction of the Confederate government was marred by the withdrawal behind the Rapidan. Pope's assertion of victory and his publication of General Halleck's congratulations on his "hard earned but brilliant success against vastly superior numbers" were received with ridicule by the Southern people. The Battle of Cedar Mountain, rightly or not, confirmed the faith of the Southern press in the military prowess of Stonewall Jackson.[31]

The incident of the Battle of Cedar Mountain most often mentioned was the death of General Winder. He was carried to the rear past the advancing Stonewall Brigade, whose veterans sorrowfully took their last look at him. McHenry Howard recorded: "Perhaps prompted by this, he asked me how the battle was going, and seemed gratified at my reply. He became quieter presently, and as I walked beside with his hand in mine, I could feel it growing colder. . . . At sundown, with my arm around his neck and supporting his head, he expired, so quietly that I could scarcely mark the exact time of his death." Said Jackson, "I can hardly think of the fall of

Brigadier-General C. S. Winder without tearful eyes." Lee paid tribute to "the courage, capacity, and conspicuous merit of this lamented officer."[32]

If the loss of Winder deprived Jackson of the best lieutenant he had, Ewell alone excepted, the Battle of Cedar Mountain set a star opposite Early's name. Old Jube had been the most conspicuous figure on the field. His dispositions, which were as careful as those at Williamsburg had been the reverse, stood flawlessly against the tension of the struggle. Ewell singled out Early for special mention, and urged his promotion. Ewell's part in the battle, though wholly credible, had been limited by the difficulties of the ground. A. P. Hill had not been permitted to throw into the action the full weight of his division, but into the rout of Taliaferro's men he had ridden, coat off and sword bared, and had rallied some of those who were fleeing. Zealous though Hill had been, he received scant mention in Jackson's report.

If Hill and his men thought this an under-appraisal of their service, they had their secret satisfaction. Branch wrote in his diary with grim pleasure of Jackson's call for him to save the day. "I had not gone 100 yards through the woods," wrote Branch, "before we met the celebrated Stonewall Brigade, utterly routed and fleeing as fast as they could run." The young artillerist Ham Chamberlayne wrote that the Federals "fought miserably and but for a wavering on the part of two Brigades of Jackson's Division, they would have given us no trouble whatever." He added, "Several of Jackson's Regiments behaved very badly, yielding to a mere panic."[33]

What more could A. P. Hill have wished? Had Jackson counted him tardy on his march toward the battle? There could be no complaint of him after he had reached the field of action and had found some of Jackson's own men running from it.

3. JEB STUART LOSES HIS PLUME

The Battle of Cedar Mountain exposed much and decided nothing. Mr. Lincoln's advisers were not to be shaken from their belief that they must deprive the Confederates of the advantage of strategic interception. Halleck stated the case explicitly in a dispatch to McClellan: "You are 30 miles from Richmond and General Pope 80 or 90, with the enemy directly between you, ready to fall with his superior numbers upon one or the other, as he may elect. Neither can re-enforce the other in case of such an attack." It had been for this reason that Halleck had decided McClellan must abandon James River and take shipping to some point whence the Army of the Potomac could march easily to form an early junction with Pope. The Fredericksburg area seemed the most convenient point. If Pope could hold the upper Rappahannock while McClellan mustered farther downstream, Halleck hoped "to prevent any farther advance of Lee, and eventually with the combined armies to drive him back upon Richmond." The reasoning was not changed by the battle. McClellan must move, Pope must stand, the two must unite.[34]

To the Confederates, after Jackson's withdrawal from Cedar Mountain, the danger on the Rappahannock seemed more imminent than that on the James. Pope manifestly was too strong to be attacked by Jackson. The Army of Virginia might resume its advance on Gordonsville; rumor persisted that McClellan was preparing to evacuate. The wisest course, in the judgment of Lee, was to concentrate against Pope and, if possible, to dispose of him before McClellan could join him. By August 13 it was apparent that Burnside either had left or was ready to leave Fredericksburg. His objective might be either Pope's army or an attack on the Virginia Central. To protect that line Lee decided to post two brigades at Hanover Junction. In order that the blow against Pope might be heavy, reinforcements sent directly to Jackson on August 13 were formidable—ten brigades under Longstreet. Two days later Lee himself arrived at Gordonsville and opened army headquarters.[35]

All of this entailed some changes in the high command. For the general supervision of the Richmond front there returned to duty a one-time celebrity who already was being forgotten—Major General Gustavus W. Smith. That officer had recovered slowly from his collapse of June 1, but by August 10 was well enough to undertake divisional command again. To him were assigned D. H. Hill's old troops, and in addition Lee requested Smith as "senior officer with this wing of the army" to direct the operations of Dick Anderson's division at Drewry's Bluff and those of D. H. Hill's Department of North Carolina. Smith now exercised as conspicuous a command as ever had been his under Johnston. If there was any hesitation about entrusting so large a field to Smith, it does not appear in surviving records.[36]

Before Smith had undertaken his new duties, the rumors of McClellan's evacuation of his base on the James River were verified. By transport and by march, the Army of the Potomac moved to join Pope. This could not have been prevented by Lee, but the humiliation was that McClellan escaped without casualties. In the whole operation, August 7–20, he lost scarcely a wagon wheel. The failure of D. H. Hill to make any move against McClellan somewhat shocked Lee and, no doubt, the President. This unpleasant incident arose because Hill commanded directly across the James from McClellan's base and must have observed the activity of the Federals, but he neither harassed them on the river nor organized any pursuit of the rear guard.

Such negligence was worse than surprising in the light of what had happened earlier in August. On the first, Hill had been directed to bombard the Federal camps at Harrison's Landing and the shipping in the James River. The bombardment was in every respect a fiasco and had been the occasion of painful concern on Lee's part regarding Hill's fitness for departmental command. Now that he did nothing to interfere with McClellan's withdrawal, Lee had regretfully to write the President, "This induces me to say what I have had on my mind for some time. I fear General Hill is not entirely equal to his present position. An excellent executive officer, he does not appear to have much administrative ability. Left to himself he seems embarrassed and backward to act." These were not pleasant phrases to couple with the name of the soldier who had shone through the battle smoke of Seven Pines and of Gaines' Mill, but the facts could not be blinked. What should be done? Lee's decision was to recall Hill to field service when opportunity offered.[37]

Another difficulty of a personal sort, involving Beverly Robertson of the cavalry, continued to cause friction but presented no new difficulty after Lee's arrival at Gordonsville. Jackson persisted in his belief that Robertson had rendered less service than he had a right to expect, but Lee, it would seem, continued to think Jackson might have been too exacting. The simplest remedy was applied: On August 17, Robertson's brigade and the other cavalry of Jackson's command were put under Stuart, who personally supervised, for a time, Robertson's movements.

A new Federal blunder now offered an opening for swift, decisive action. When Lee took command at Gordonsville on August 15, General Pope remained incautiously in an exposed position north of the Rapidan. Behind him was the Rappahannock, and the Union army was in the "V" formed by the two rivers. If the Confederates could throw cavalry in the rear of Pope and burn the main railroad bridge across the Rappahannock, he would be cut off from his base. That done, his army might be attacked furiously and captured or slaughtered in detail. To effect this, promptness and secrecy were essential: Any discernible preparations for an offensive would send Pope's army streaming back across the Rappahannock to wider fields of maneuver. Lee believed that speed was the muzzle of secrecy, and decided to ford the Rapidan on the night of August 17 and to assail Pope on the eighteenth.[38]

A great opportunity this presented the cavalry, which, unfortunately, was not concentrated. Hampton's brigade was on the Richmond front and could not be used. Stuart, with the other brigade under Fitz Lee, was at Davenport's Bridge on the North Anna. On the morning of August 17, Stuart boarded a train for army headquarters with the understanding that

Fitz Lee would proceed that day across country to the vicinity of Raccoon Ford on the Rapidan, a march of approximately thirty-two miles. After Stuart had completed his railroad journey and reported to the commanding general, he and his staff rode to Verdiersville, a hamlet through which Fitz Lee would pass en route to Raccoon Ford.

When Stuart arrived there, late in the evening of August 17, the residents had no news of the cavalry. He was puzzled but not alarmed; doubtless Fitz would come up shortly. Meantime there could be relaxation and perhaps sleep. On the porch of the Rhodes house Stuart prepared his bivouac. He divested himself of his haversack and carefully laid to one side his plumed hat. It was a hat of which he had particular reason to be proud. During a truce to bury the dead after Cedar Mountain, he had met the Union generals Samuel Crawford and George Bayard, both of whom he had known in the old army. They had made jesting claims concerning the battle, whereupon Stuart bet Crawford a hat that the Federals would assert Cedar Mountain had been a victory for the Union. In due time, under a flag of truce, a hat had arrived at the outpost for Stuart, and with it a New York paper proclaiming a triumph for Pope in the action of August 9. This was the hat Stuart now put beside him on the porch where he spread out his cloak for a bed.

At dawn the mist of August lay heavily over the fields. As the men stirred they heard from the east the clatter of a column of cavalry. Stuart got up and walked down to the fence that fronted the property. Through the mist he could see troopers moving down the road leading to the Rapidan. The column came from the direction of Fitz Lee's delayed advance; the men must be his. Stuart directed two of his men to go up the road, halt the column, and tell its commander to report immediately. A fine if jovial rebuke there would be for Fitz Lee, twelve hours late on a march of thirty-two miles! A minute more and then pistol shots, the challenge of voices, the scamper of returning horsemen—the column was not Fitz Lee's but the enemy's!

Every man for himself! Stuart did not wait for hat and cloak. He turned; he ran to his horse; he vaulted into the saddle; he struck with his spurs. Over the garden fence, at one bold jump, went horse and rider. The others scattered. Vigorously they were pursued, but all escaped. When they assembled again, after the blue column clattered off to the river, they were chagrined, humiliated, and amused all at the same time. Stuart had lost not only his cloak, his hat, his sash, and his plumage, but also something much more serious—the haversack that contained his maps and some recent correspondence that would be informative to the enemy. When the sun mounted hotly, Stuart had to make of his handkerchief a cover for his reddish locks. Thus adorned with what seemed to be a capillose flag of truce, he was greeted everywhere with the same jibing question: "Where's your hat?"[39]

Fitz Lee did not feel he was to blame for the embarrassment of his chief. His explanation was the simple one that he never had understood his presence was required on the Rapidan at a particular time. When Stuart left him, Fitz's impression was that the advance could be leisurely. Besides, he was short both of ammunition and rations, and as his trains were at Louisa Court House, he decided to move via that town. This made his march fifty-two instead of thirty-two miles, and prevented him from joining Stuart until the night of the eighteenth. He had notified General Lee that his horses were in bad condition and would not be fit for hard service on the nineteenth. The commanding general, accordingly, deferred the advance of the army until the twentieth. By that time, Pope had taken alarm, crossed the Rappahannock, and escaped from the "V."

Stuart was outraged that the tardiness of one of his officers should have been responsible, even in part, for the escape of the Federals. His outrage was in a measure justified, but in a measure only. Although Fitz Lee manifestly should not have carried his brigade twenty miles off its march without authority for doing so, he was not solely responsible for delaying the offensive. Even had he arrived on schedule, the army's commissary was unready; Anderson's division was not at hand. At the earliest, the crossing would have been twenty-four hours later than planned. Pope would not then have been caught between the rivers, but his rear guard might have been assailed. If Fitz Lee was culpable, Stuart himself was not free of blame. Apparently his orders to his lieutenant were verbal and they may have been vague. This seems to have been overlooked at the time. Stuart blamed Fitz Lee; nobody blamed Stuart.[40]

When Fitz Lee had not appeared on the seventeenth, Longstreet, with his usual vigilance, had sent infantry to watch the roads that led up from the crossings of the river. How had the Federal cavalry passed that guard? Why were they able to reach Verdiersville and so nearly catch Stuart? Inquiry showed that Longstreet's order to cover the road from Raccoon Ford had been sent to Robert Toombs. Toombs himself was absent, but his senior colonel duly detached two regiments in accordance with instructions. On his return, Toombs found the order that the troops were to cook three days' rations in preparation for the advance. He sent a request to Longstreet to recall his regiments so they might prepare their rations. Longstreet was not to be found, whereupon Toombs on his own account ordered the men back to their brigade. It was over the road they thus left open that the Federal cavalry passed.

Toombs was put under arrest, but the next day he strapped on his sword when he went to ride, an act contrary to regulations. Further, he delivered a violent speech to his men, who cheered him. For these new offenses he was ordered back to Gordonsville and told to stay there. He did, but prepared to make a political issue of his treatment. In a letter to his confidant, Vice President Stephens, he made no reference to the fact that the enemy had penetrated the position he had vacated. In his eyes, the entire affair was persecution. Said he, "My zeal for the public service and desire to prepare my starving regt. for battle is my sole and only fault."[41]

CHAPTER 15

Return to Manassas

1. RAPPAHANNOCK: ACT ONE OF A NEW DRAMA

The infantry that crossed the Rapidan on August 20, 1862, was divided, without formal order, into Longstreet's Right and Jackson's Left Wings. This of itself was historic because it meant that the Army of the Valley ceased to exist as a separate force; Jackson's command definitely became a part of the Army of Northern Virginia after the Battle of Cedar Mountain.

To this unified army two new brigades had come. At the head of one returned Shanks Evans, who had won fame at Manassas. Shanks was full of fight and sure of the valor of his four South Carolina regiments, which were left as an independent brigade, unattached to any division. The other new brigade had been brought, as had Evans's, from South Carolina and was under the command of Thomas F. Drayton, a former classmate of President Davis's at West Point and a member of one of the leading families of the Palmetto State. In that family the tragedy of the divided nation was exemplified: While Thomas Drayton was defending the coast of South Carolina, his brother Percival commanded U.S.S. *Pocahontas* in the operations against Port Royal. General Drayton was in spirit a gentleman and in bearing a soldier. Whether he had the qualities of command had been put in some doubt. He was brigaded now with Toombs and G. T. Anderson in D. R. Jones's division, a connection not ideal. Jones's health was getting progressively worse, and he could not be expected to direct closely the administration of his command.

This division was one of four to undergo change at the beginning of the campaign. A second was Ewell's, to which was transferred Lawton's brigade from Jackson's division. The third change was in the command of Whiting's division. Whiting was on sick leave at the time and did not attempt to share in the new campaign. His old brigade, now under Colonel E. M. Law, continued to serve with Hood's in a half division that Hood commanded. Soon it became known as Hood's.[1]

307

The fourth change presented a problem of administration and, still more, of command. Longstreet's old division counted six brigades, two of which were under general officers—Pryor and Featherston—whose ability in the field was subject to question. George Pickett, reckoned among the best leaders in the division, had not yet recovered from the wound received at Gaines' Mill. Longstreet was charged with duties so numerous that he could not undertake to handle the division in action. What should be done with it? Should it be divided, and if so, under whom? The necessities of war soon dictated the informal assignment of three brigades to Cadmus Wilcox and three to James Kemper. Both arrangements were known to be temporary and both seem to have been devised by Longstreet himself. He was beginning to show excellent judgment of his subordinates, whose admiring support he was winning rapidly.

The Left Wing, Jackson's, had to undergo less reorganization. No successor to Winder had been named, and William B. Taliaferro, the senior brigadier, was acting head of the division. Taliaferro's ability to handle four brigades had not been established. He was young enough—he was not yet forty—and had abundantly the social station and acquaintance with public life that counted much in easing the way. Did he possess, besides, the essential qualities of command? In Jackson's mind Cedar Mountain had not answered the question one way or the other. Some of Stonewall's misgivings of the spring must have been relieved; otherwise he would have found a way of keeping the command out of Taliaferro's hands.

In Jackson's division William E. Starke now was serving as the head of one of the two Louisiana brigades. He was forty-eight and by birth a Virginian, but he had lived for years in Mobile and in New Orleans, where he prospered as a dealer in cotton and interested himself in politics. To him early in the war had been assigned the 60th Virginia. When the Louisiana troops in Virginia were brigaded separately, in accordance with Mr. Davis's cherished policy of organization by states, Colonel Starke's associations with the Gulf seemed to warrant appointment as a Louisiana brigadier. In the Seven Days he had earned reputation as a hard fighter; now a surprising climb awaited him.

Because of his demand for the letter and the spirit of discipline, Jackson had a new encounter with A. P. Hill. In preparing for the passage of the Rapidan, Stonewall remembered what had happened at the start of the advance to Cedar Mountain, and particularly admonished Hill to march on August 20 at moonrise, with his division taking the lead. So Jackson specified. Early on the designated morning he rode forward to see if Hill was on the move. He found to his annoyance that none of the troops of the Light Division had left their camps. Indignantly he ordered forward the first of Hill's brigades that he found ready for the road. It appears that Hill was misled by conflicting orders, or perhaps misinformed concerning the time of moonrise. In any event, wrote Jed Hotchkiss, Jackson was "much put out" at the slow start, and no doubt was convinced that whatever the military virtues of A. P. Hill, promptness was not among them.[2]

In the earliest light of what gave promise of being a hot, dry twentieth of August, the infantry clambered up the banks of the Rapidan and began a drama in three scenes. The first scene was shaped by the country in which the rival armies were operating. For most of its length the left bank of the upper Rappahannock, above where it receives the waters of the Rapidan, commands the lower right bank. Consequently, if Pope showed diligence, he could move up or down the river and dispute Lee's attempts to cross at any point. By guarding the fords, he could protect his line of supply via the Orange and Alexandria Railroad or, at the least, should receive early warning of a threat to that line. Most of the advantage seemed to be on the side of the defensive. Pope, by every applicable test, should be able to stand off Lee till McClellan arrived.

Lee, for his part, scarcely could afford to lose time or men in forcing the Rappahannock. An attempt to do so east of the railroad was ruled out by exposure to a flank attack from Fredericksburg. A crossing west of the railroad was the strategy imposed on him. He had to make an effort to outflank Pope by marching up the river—and at the same time protect the lower crossings so his adversary could not get on his flank or in his rear. The first actors in this part of the drama, which covered August 20–25, were the cavalry.

On the day the Rapidan was passed, Robertson's brigade got into a lively action with Bayard's Federal cavalry, in which most of the fighting was done by Grumble Jones. Stuart had praise for Robertson as well as for Jones—no doubt gratifying to Lee and reassuring to Jackson—but he wanted more. Stuart felt that he had lost the opportunity of burning Rappahannock Bridge and been robbed, besides, of hat and cloak. He could not recover his apparel, but he could get revenge. His eye settled on the point where the Orange and Alexandria crossed Cedar Run near Catlett's Station. If the bridge there were destroyed, Pope would perhaps be compelled to retire. In any event, there would be adventure in a raid against the railroad. On the second day after the passage of the Rapidan, Stuart's proposal was approved by headquarters.[3]

Stuart selected his stoutest lieutenants and boldest blades—Fitz and Rooney Lee, William C. Wickham and Tom Rosser among them—and with 1,500 troopers started up the Rappahannock. He found unguarded fords, and Warrenton was reached without contest. The enemy, said the residents, had not been there for days. So far, all gain and good prospects! Then, as they neared their objective, black clouds gathered and, ere evening, delivered a violent thunderstorm. While the storm raged in all its fury, Rosser, in command of the advance, captured the Union pickets before they could give the alarm, and conducted Stuart within the Federal lines. At intervals the lightning gave a glimpse of the surroundings; then, when the flash passed, the low-hanging clouds made the night drip blackness. It was, Stuart wrote, "the darkest night I ever knew."

Was it prudent to venture on? Would not the regiments become confused? But the goddess of chance, who had deserted Jeb Stuart at Verdiersville, favored him now. Someone brought him a Negro who had been captured nearby, and who recognized Stuart from the cavalry's service in Berkeley County in 1861. He said he had been impressed to wait on Pope's headquarters, and knew where General Pope's tent, staff, and horses were to be found; he could lead the Confederates to the place. To accept his tender was to gamble heavily on the man's fidelity; to go without a guide was to play against odds that might be heavier. Stuart decided to trust him.

He must act with the utmost speed. Rooney Lee would take the 9th Virginia and with their guide capture whatever and whoever was to be found at Federal headquarters; the 1st and 5th were to attack another camp near-by and obstruct the railroad; a picked contingent under Wickham and W. W. Blackford was to set the Cedar Run bridge afire; Robertson would constitute the reserve.

Through the violence of the downpour a dash was made for Pope's tent; shouts were raised; firing broke out; frightened teamsters scattered. Guided by the lightning, the Confederate cavalrymen seized prisoners by the score and picked up much booty. But against the bridge their comrades could do nothing. It was too wet to burn and too heavy to cut down. "I gave it up," said Stuart in his report, which he seldom said of anything he undertook to do. Before morning the column was on its way back.

When the prisoners could be counted and the loot examined in daylight, Stuart was satisfied. There were more than 300 prisoners, many of them officers. Of manifest importance were Pope's dispatch book and the originals of numerous letters sent him. Chief of the treasures were General Pope's hat, his military cloak, and one of his uniform frock coats. The latter was given to Stuart, as partial payment for the hat he had lost at Verdiersville. After proposing to trade it to Pope for his hat, Stuart sent it to Richmond as a present for Governor Letcher. It went on display in the Capitol. The raid on Catlett's Station created talk of the kind most pleasing to Stuart's ears, but of military value it had little.[4]

That same storm of August 22 supplied more than stage-effects for the second scene in the first act of the new drama, a scene in which General Early played a central and singular role. Jackson's advance up the Rappahannock in search of an uncontested crossing brought Ewell's division, on the afternoon of August 22, to a point opposite Warrenton Springs. Here the bridge had been destroyed, but as no enemy was on guard Jackson decided to throw troops across the Rappahannock and, if they found a favorable situation, to follow with the entire force. Lawton's brigade, with two batteries, started the passage of the river opposite Warrenton Springs; Early's brigade used an old dam a mile downstream. As Old Jube's regiments moved over the unstable crossing, the rains came, and night fell before the next brigade could attempt to use the treacherous dam.

Morning brought as much of concern as of relief. The rain was over, but what troubled Early was the stage of the river between him and the remainder of Jackson's force. Angrily the Rappahannock rushed southward, full-banked and impassable for troops. The dilapidated dam over which his brigade had passed the previous afternoon was awash and roaring. Early was cut off. Nor could he count on aid from Lawton at Warrenton Springs; Lawton reported that only his two batteries and the 13th Georgia had crossed. Early's brigade, plus those Georgians, might have to face overwhelming Federal attack.

While Early was pondering what he should do, Jackson was examining the scene from the other side of the river. He directed Early to good defensive ground near-by until the crossing could be repaired. If the Federals on his front should become too numerous, Early was to proceed upriver to Waterloo Bridge, in which event, Old Jack explained, he would advance simultaneously along the other bank to cover Early's movement. Ere the morning was far advanced, scouting Federal cavalrymen were seen, hovering around Early's front in a manner to alarm him. Anxious hours crawled around the clock-face. Infantry in large numbers began to arrive in support of the Federal cavalry. The one consolation Old Jube found, as he viewed what he styled "a critical condition," was that the bluecoats proceeded with great caution. They evidently did not know his numerical weakness and had as much fear of him as he of them.

As the afternoon dragged on, Early received welcome reinforcement from the greater part of Robertson's cavalry brigade, returning from the Catlett's Station raid. To discomfort the Federals, Robertson's two guns and two of Early's engaged in a noisy, banging artillery duel that produced little real hurt to either side. The river still was too high to be forded. Jackson was at work on a temporary bridge, but there was no ascertaining when— or even whether—it could be completed. As night came, scarcely a man in Early's regiments had tasted food in thirty hours or more. In the darkness and a baffling, obscuring mist there roared a volley from the Federals, and Early thought the end had come and his men would have to fight to the death. He ran out two Napoleons and had them open with canister. The Federals fell back in silence and made no further demonstration.

At last word reached Early that Ewell would cross over to his position and, if he found the Federals very strong, Early's and Lawton's forces would be recalled. The army command did not desire to bring on a general engagement at Warrenton Springs. At 3:00 A.M. Ewell arrived in person, listened to report of the enemy's movements, and promptly ordered the whole force back to the other bank. Hungry men lost no time in getting the guns to safety and in following, regiment by regiment, as fast as the feeble bridge would take them. Soon after daylight they were safe on Jackson's side of the stream. "My command," Early concluded, "was thus rescued from almost certain capture...."[5]

One other there was, besides Early and Stuart, to have his moment in the center of the stage during this first act of the new drama. The day that Jeb rode to Catlett's and Old Jube found himself cut off near Warrenton Springs, August 22, General Trimble was left by Ewell to guard the crossing of Hazel River while the Confederate wagon train was laboring northward. All of Jackson's other troops had passed; Trimble was to remain until the vanguard of Longstreet's command should reach the ford. To the pugnacious Trimble, a duty normally boresome proved welcome.

Soon after taking position, he received word that a Federal force had crossed the Rappahannock and captured some mules and ambulances from the train. Immediately Trimble detached a regiment in pursuit, which overtook the marauders and recaptured the property. From a prisoner he learned that one, and perhaps two, Federal brigades were on the south side of the river and intent on mischief. He reasoned that the bluecoats might be too numerous for him to assail without help, and chose to emulate the rabbit and "lay low." He ascertained the enemy's position and awaited the coming of Hood, who was in the lead for Longstreet.

Trimble was proud of what followed, and described it with gusto: "After a sharp conflict ... the enemy were driven back to the hills on the river.... Our men boldly advanced with enthusiastic cheers ... and slaughtered great numbers as they waded the river or climbed up the opposite bank.... I retired unmolested and camped one and a half miles distant, leaving General Hood, who had taken no part in the contest, to look after the enemy."

This exploit was soldierly and creditable, and was written down to Trimble's credit in the book of Jackson's long memory. The one unpleasant aspect of the affair was Trimble's casual, not to say slurring, remark that Hood "had taken no part in the contest." Hood's report did not conform to Trimble's on that score, reporting that the Texas Brigade and Law's had attacked on each side of Trimble "leading off in the center." What did this conflict of testimony indicate? Would Hood seek credit for an action he had not fought? Was Trimble disposed to ignore what others had done in the battle?[26]

2. Jackson Is Himself Again

It was August 24, Sunday, but Old Jack, for all his love of the Lord's Day, was not in a Sabbath mood. His quartermaster and commissary services were not working well. The troops were ill fed. Officers were not setting the example they should. To discourage straggling, Jackson had already staged a dramatic warning. Three deserters who had been caught were court-martialed and condemned. Blindfolded, they had been placed by open graves. The whole of Jackson's division had been marched through somber woods to see the trio fall before a firing squad, and then been filed past the dead bodies to observe how they had been riddled. Jackson insisted that officers bestir themselves to enforce the discipline without which there could be no army. Five regimental commanders—all those in Gregg's brigade—had been placed under arrest because their men, contrary to orders, had burned some fence palings.[7]

Early afternoon brought a change to Jackson's mood, a thrilling change. Lee presented him such an opportunity as never had come to him, not even on that May day when he had been told he could advance on Banks. An end was put to watching fords, to side slipping on the Rappahannock. Larger maneuver was necessary. Jackson was to move secretly up the river, cross at some convenient place, and strike in Pope's rear the Orange and Alexandria Railroad, the Federal line of supply. The remainder of the army was to occupy the enemy long enough for Jackson to get a good start. Then the troops left on the Rappahannock would march to rejoin him. On this bold move Lee had decided because he believed a threat to the Federal rear would force Pope to retreat quickly and thereby lengthen the distance between Pope and the reinforcements that soon would be arriving. Jackson was to take all three of his divisions and start as soon as arrangements could be made.[8]

The mission fired Old Jack. He knew in detail the country immediately around Manassas, but with the routes east of the Blue Ridge that led to the Orange and Alexandria he was unacquainted. His topographical engineer, J. K. Boswell, who came from that section of Virginia, was ordered to report immediately. He was instructed to ascertain the best, most covered route around Pope's right and to the Federal rear.[9] No immediate decision concerning a precise objective was attempted at the moment. The imperative task was to reach the railroad. From the very nature of the terrain and the course of the roads, the vicinity of Manassas Junction was the indicated general objective.

Arrangements had to be made, next, for the issuance and cooking of rations that evening and for the driving of beef-cattle with the column. Longstreet rode up for conference, agreeing to relieve A. P. Hill's batteries with guns from his command so that Hill's brigades would be free to start with Jackson's other divisions. All the preliminaries were smooth and encouraging, except for the fear that the commissary could not supply sufficient rations. Should meat and bread be lacking, the men would have to subsist on the corn that was nearing maturity in the fields along the roads Jackson would follow.

All baggage was to be left behind; with the columns were to move only the cattle, the ordnance train, and the ambulances. The order of march was to Ewell, A. P. Hill, Taliaferro. Doubtless this was arranged deliberately: Ewell was a fast, sure man on the road. If Hill kept Ewell's pace, there could be none of the tardiness that Jackson charged against the Light Division. The start was to be at early dawn, "with the utmost promptitude, without knapsacks."[10]

"Fall in" was shouted in the half-dawn of August 25. Quietly and swiftly the column moved northwestward five and a half miles, past the hamlet of Amissville, then turned northeast another two miles to Hedgeman's River, the larger of the two streams the united flow of which, meeting at Waterloo Bridge, made the Rappahannock. Unhindered and unopposed, Jackson was "across the Rappahannock" and headed for the rear of Pope's army. In the van rode Captain Boswell to guide the column. Well in advance, the 2nd Virginia cavalry scouted to make sure no enemy troopers lay in wait.

The order was the familiar one, "Close up, men, close up." No straggling and no delays were permitted. Those who had cooked rations devoured them soon on the soldiers' principle that food is safer in the stomach than in the haversack. Corn from the fields and apples from nearby trees were snatched and eaten as the men pushed on. Progress was excellent. Orlean was passed. Salem, eleven miles farther north on the Manassas Gap Railroad, must have been set by Jackson as his objective for the day.

Late in the afternoon, as he approached Salem, Jackson halted, got off his horse, and stood for a time by a large stone by the roadside. Bareheaded, he paused to look at the sun as it disappeared behind the mountains. In that dramatic posture he was overtaken by a marching regiment. Immediately the men forgot their weariness and began to cheer him. He made a swift, friendly gesture to silence them, and then sent an officer to explain that they must not make any noise lest the enemy hear. The word

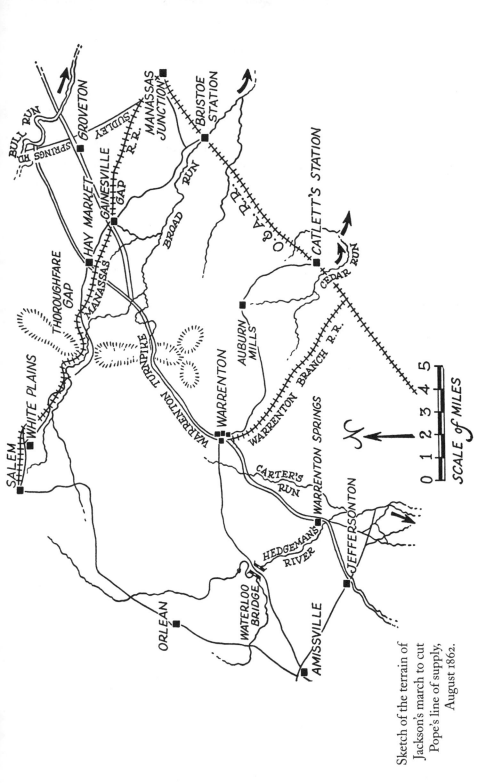

Sketch of the terrain of
Jackson's march to cut
Pope's line of supply,
August 1862.

was passed down the column—"No cheering." Obediently the men passed in silence. Their look, their smiles, their uplifted caps and raised arms were more eloquent than their shouts. Jackson was proud and pleased. "Who could not conquer," he said to his staff, "with such troops as these?"[11]

One mile south of Salem the column halted for the night. Ewell's division arrived in time for reasonable slumber. The rear guard did not reach the bivouac until late in the evening. Thousands had to stretch themselves out hungry. Jackson regretted that these men had not been fed, but otherwise he was at ease and gratified. The army had marched twenty-five miles. Ahead, on August 26, was a march equally long.[12]

One material obstacle, one only, had to be faced on the twenty-sixth. About halfway between Salem and the Orange and Alexandria was Thoroughfare Gap in the Bull Run Mountains. If it was defended by a Federal force of any size, it might be held long enough for the alarm to be sounded and for Jackson to be cheated of a surprise attack on the railway. He would make the best of the inescapable gamble—he sent his cavalry forward as soon as there was a touch of gray in the eastern sky. When the 2nd Virginia climbed to the pass and scrutinized all the approaches, it found—not one Federal. The gap was unguarded.

Upward by White Plains and through the gap the column moved and over the rolling hills that led toward Hay Market. Not until the troopers in the van reached Hay Market did they encounter any Federals. The dozen or so horsemen picked up seemed more like stragglers than videttes. Everything gave promise that the ideal military situation would be created—that the enemy would be surprised in his own rear. Hungry men plundered corn fields and orchards, but caught up again; the speed of the march was not slackened. Always Jackson's exhortation was, "Close up, men, close up; push on, push on!" Old Jack himself was dust-covered and silent. Of his thoughts, his reasoning, he said not a word. In midafternoon the main body of Stuart's cavalry overtook the laboring column, at hand and ready to cover the van and the flanks.[13]

Now the direction of the march changed. To reach the railroad, Jackson's assigned objective, the shortest route was from Gainesville to Bristoe Station, four miles below Manassas Junction. Near Bristoe Station the railway bridged Broad Run, and destruction of that crossing would make the quick repair of the railway impossible. Obediently toward Bristoe the soldiers now turned their faces. Limping and weary, they were encouraged by the absence of any Federal outposts. Residents said that only one company of infantry and one of cavalry were stationed at Bristoe. A dash on the village would result, no doubt, in the capture of this guard. Then would come the work of destroying the railroad and the bridge.

Munford readied his 2nd Virginia cavalry for a dash to Bristoe Station. As his supporting infantry waited in the sunset, he quietly advanced to within 100 yards of the station before he was seen. As his troopers rushed forward with a shout, the few Union cavalrymen at the station made off in frenzied haste. The infantry ran into a hotel and from that shelter opened a weak, nervous fire. While Munford's troopers were dealing with these Federals, the Louisiana and North Carolina infantry with them were alerted by the sound of a train whistle from the south. Some snatched up a few wooden sills which they threw across the track. Others sought frantically to unbolt a rail, but the engine was upon them. It passed, struck the sills and scattered them, and in a shower of bullets rushed off toward Manassas Junction.

The Confederates would be ready next time. They found a derailing switch which they opened, and the 21st North Carolina lined up alongside the right of way to give the train crew a volley. They had not long to wait. A whistle, and the train swept confidently nearer with no reduction in speed, came under fire, and hit the open switch. With a crash engine and half the train plunged down an embankment. Loud were the guffaws when the men saw that the locomotive was named the "President" and its steam dome bore a picture of Mr. Lincoln. Through this a Confederate rifle ball had passed. A third train soon followed, ran into the cars left on the track, and created a jungle of shattered wood and twisted iron. Still another train approached, but by this time the drama was played out. The engineer saw the wreckage ahead, put on his brakes, and quickly backed out of range. To finish the scene, Jackson had the bridge over Broad Run burned.[14]

Booty was not to be had from the smashed freight cars, but the residents of Bristoe spoke of Manassas Junction, where General Pope had accumulated enormous supplies of every sort. Rations by the hundreds of thousands were in storage. Quartermaster stores in equal quantity awaited call. Jackson listened, calculated, and concluded that he could not afford to wait till morning to start after these treasures. Lest they be spoiled or burned, they must be seized for the Confederacy, but by whom? Many of the infantry, where they were halted, had fallen into exhausted sleep. They had earned their rest; A. P. Hill computed that in the two days' march his men had covered fifty-four miles. Who, then, would march in darkness four long miles up the railroad to secure those supplies?

Trimble was the man. As soon as he heard that troops were wanted for the extra march, he offered his. Had he not been urging, ever since he joined Jackson, that all advantage be pushed to the ultimate? Now he was to have his opportunity. Jackson gratefully accepted the offer to march on Manassas.

With the 21st North Carolina and the 21st Georgia, less than 800 muskets, Trimble set out about 9 o'clock. In an afterthought, Jackson sent Stuart's cavalry. On arrival they came under fire, and Trimble disposed a regiment on either side of the railroad and advanced. In the darkness Union gunners fired wildly, and the Confederates rushed forward and took the guns before they could be reloaded. Wrote General Trimble, ". . . each of the two batteries contained four fieldpieces, horses, equipments, and ammunition, complete."[15]

These were no more than the first fruits. The base itself was incredibly rich. What loot there would be when daylight came—provided Old Jack would allow the soldiers a free hand. Would he do that? At Winchester he sternly had admonished his men that all captured supplies were the property of the Confederate government. Was he to be more moderate now? Of course he would take into account that the soldiers had received no rations since the evening of the twenty-fourth, but beyond the formal issue of bread and bacon, would he throw open the stores? After the manner of man when hungry, that question bulked larger in the dawn of August 27 than did the fact that one of the great marches of history had been made.

3. JACKSON DEFIES POPE AND THANKS GOD

Before even his usual "early dawn," Jackson advanced in support of Trimble—Hill's division, the remainder of Taliaferro's. At Bristoe, Ewell was left with three brigades, with orders to resist any Federal advance and, if hard pressed, to fall back on the main force. Jackson found the Federal property at the Junction fully as much as predicted. Two tracks for a distance of half a mile each were covered with freight cars loaded with supplies of a variety that outscaled imagination. Flour and like staples crowded warehouses. "The display of luxuries among the sutlers' stores," wrote Colonel W. W. Blackford, "was even more extensive than at the White House. . . ."

To the loot the cavalrymen helped themselves liberally, but stern Trimble had ordered his two regiments to guard the captured stores. The Stonewall Brigade, which reached Manassas soon after daylight, likewise was restrained, but imperfectly. Comrade Casler reported breaking into a commissary depot: "When we had appropriated all we could carry we found a barrel of whiskey . . . but as we had our canteens full of molasses, and our tin cups full of sugar, we had nothing to drink out of. We soon found an old funnel, however, and while one would hold his hand over the bottom of it another would draw it full. In this way it was passed around.

But the officers soon found us out and broke up that game." Hill's men, following the Stonewall Brigade, proved of irrepressible appetite.[16]

Meantime, north of the Bull Run railroad bridge, a New Jersey brigade was detrained by its general, George W. Taylor, under orders to hold the bridge. In his ardor General Taylor decided to press on to Manassas and drive off a Confederate force he evidently though small. As the inexperienced Jerseymen came on, Poague's and Carpenter's batteries opened on them. Jackson watched with admiration and felt that he should save them, if he could, from the slaughter that was beginning. He halted the firing, rode out in front, waved his handkerchief, and shouted to the enemy to surrender. In response a Federal infantryman took careful aim and fired at Jackson. The missile came close enough for a cannoneer near the general to hear the spiteful whistle. With that Confederate fire was reopened. The Federals stumbled on for a few minutes, then broke and fled, leaving 300 prisoners and 135 dead and wounded. The unequal fight was over by 11 o'clock.[17]

Back at the Junction, the stores the Southern army most lacked were being loaded into the ambulances and ordnance wagons. The remainder was offered to the men in haphazard if liberal fashion. Boylike, the members of numerous messes would stop the preparation of plain, familiar food when a new delicacy was triumphantly brought in. For better or worse they would try their hand at cooking the rare viand. After Jackson had seen to it that all discoverable liquor was dumped from barrels and every bottle not requisitioned by the surgeons was remorselessly smashed, he agreed that the men might as well enjoy what their government could not salvage. Truth was, all who could do so had been plundering on the sly ever since their arrival.

The hours that followed never were to be rivalled in the Army of Northern Virginia and never forgotten. Said John H. Worsham: "It was hard to decide what to take. Some filled their haversacks with cakes, some with candy, and others with oranges, lemons, canned goods, etc. I know one who took nothing but French mustard. . . ." The lament was that certain of the troops did not get their share. Worse still, in the view of infantrymen, was the advantage enjoyed by the mounted men. The boy on foot had his haversack and his pockets—no more; the trooper had an animal that could bear much loot. The advantage enjoyed by an officer who had two horses was scandalous. "For my part," wrote an artillery lieutenant, "I got a tooth brush, a box of candles, a quantity of lobster salad, a barrel of coffee, & other things which I forget."[18]

Delightful plundering, like affrighting battles, had to end. Long Federal columns by midafternoon were threatening Ewell at Bristoe. It was manifest that Pope's army was coming up. Ewell decided to retire, as Jackson had authorized, to Manassas. Admirably was this done, and when

Ewell's veterans arrived at the Junction and drew rations, they had earned a full share of the luxuries. What they got was prosaic meat and bread and perhaps some coffee. The delicacies were gone. Already Jackson was preparing to evacuate the place and give to the flames what he could not consume or transport and would not leave to the enemy.[19]

The first part of Jackson's mission now was performed: He had cut off the supplies of the Federal army and thereby assured its speedy withdrawal from the Rappahannock. Ahead of him was the second part of his mission, the task of preserving his force until the two wings of the army were reunited. Realistically Jackson determined to stay close to the line of Lee's advance from Thoroughfare Gap, ready to cooperate on Lee's arrival, to retreat if Lee were delayed, and, meantime, to strike a blow should the Federals give him an opening.

For this bold maintenance of his advanced position, Jackson would need strong, readily defensible ground. Reconnaissance and his own knowledge of the terrain acquired the previous year led him to select a low ridge north of the road from Warrenton to Alexandria. The ridge was styled Groveton after a nearby settlement, and as if in good augury, was just a mile west of Henry House Hill where Jackson had fought in the first battle at Manassas. Groveton was not a perfect position, but it was probably the best the nearby countryside offered for the mission Jackson had assigned himself.

That advantage of position Jackson might never have realized, had his adversaries been alert, because he got into a tangle on August 27–28 as a result of an excess of reticence. By telling his lieutenants only that a guide would direct them to their objective, the day ended with just Taliaferro's division at Groveton. Hill was misdirected to Centreville; Ewell was south of Blackburn's Ford. As one of Ewell's staff explained in disgust, their guide "had not been told where to take us, or if told, it had been in some very general terms." There was worse confusion than had prevailed on any of Jackson's marches save that of August 8 en route to Cedar Mountain.[20]

Before the scattered divisions could be concentrated on the morning of the twenty-eighth, intelligence began reaching Jackson of Federal forces concentrating on Manassas. This evidence of gathering opposition did not lead him to modify his plan of remaining where he was until Lee arrived. At first he was not convinced, even, that the enemy intended a stand; perhaps Pope was reorganizing for a retreat to unite with McClellan and then resume the offensive. As soon, therefore, as he was assured that his three scattered divisions would be reunited in the course of a few hours, he began to seek an opportunity of striking a blow. Now evidence accumulated that instead of running away from Jackson, the enemy might be preparing to give him battle. For a time he could do nothing except to watch the Federals.[21]

He waited—and not in vain. Toward sunset a blue column came up the Warrenton Turnpike, but did not follow the route of those that had turned southeastward toward Manassas. It was marching straight for the Stone Bridge. The flankers were out heavily; the column itself was compact and well closed.

What followed was witnessed by Stuart's engineer, W. W. Blackford: "Jackson rode out to examine the approaching foe, trotting backwards and forwards along the line of the handsome parade marching by, and in easy range of their skirmish line, but they did not seem to think that a single horseman was worthy of their attention—how little they thought that this single, plainly dressed horseman was the great Stonewall himself. . . . All felt sure Jackson could never resist the temptation, and that the order to attack would come soon, even if Longstreet was beyond the mountain. Presently General Jackson pulled up suddenly, wheeled and galloped towards us. 'Here he comes, by God,' said several, and Jackson rode up to the assembled group as calm as a May morning and, touching his hat in military salute, said in as soft a voice as if he had been talking to a friend in ordinary conversation, 'Bring out your men, gentlemen!'"

From the woods, said Blackford, "arose a hoarse roar like that from cages of wild beasts at the scent of blood." Taliaferro sent his cheering men forward. Ewell followed with two of his brigades. Three batteries opened. Into the open the infantry plunged, and then the advance abruptly halted; there at close quarters was begun a bitter stand-up fight. The Federals, it was later discovered, belonged to King's division of Burnside's corps. Gibbon's brigade, of one Indiana and three Wisconsin regiments, was the tough bone Jackson attempted to crack; quickly to its support came part of Doubleday's brigade. These six regiments stood off Jackson's division and half of Ewell's. For two hours and a half, until 9 o'clock, artillery and infantry banged furiously away. Then the Federals, withdrawing slowly, broke off the fight.[22]

Tactically the action taught nothing, and demonstrated nothing save the stubbornness of both forces. In casualties, for the numbers engaged, it was one of the costliest battles Jackson ever had fought. The Stonewall Brigade lost two promising officers, John F. Neff and Lawson Botts, and was left with about the personnel of a regiment of moderate strength. In the high command serious losses there were. General Taliaferro was wounded painfully, in the foot, the neck, and in the arm. Worse, far, was the case of Dick Ewell. That incorrigible had yielded once too often to his love of being in the middle of a fight. Not until the battle was over and the litter bearers searched the field did they find Ewell on the ground with a bad leg wound. When the surgeons examined him they could say one thing only—*amputate.* That would mean the absence for long months of the most generous, best disciplined, and, in many soldierly qualities, the ablest of Jackson's subordinates.[23]

To lose, within less than three weeks, Winder, Taliaferro, and the irreplaceable Ewell must have seemed, even to the believing heart of Jackson, a stern "dispensation of Providence." When Taliaferro fell, the new brigadier, William E. Starke, who had received his appointment August 6 and never had handled a brigade in action until Groveton, suddenly found himself in command of the most famous division of the army. Ewell's troops passed, by seniority, not to Early but to the devoted Alexander R. Lawton.

The enemy, said Jackson, "did not permit us to remain inactive or in doubt as to his intention to renew the conflict." Daylight of the twenty-ninth showed the Federals in major force. Pope was striving to concentrate 25,000 men east of Jackson and a like number west of him in order, he wrote, "to crush Jackson before Longstreet could by any possibility reach the scene of action." Carefully Jackson drew back his men to take full advantage of the higher ground and of the right of way of an unfinished railroad cut north of the Warrenton Turnpike. A compact front it was of not more than 3,000 yards, on which could be put as many of his forty guns as could be brought to bear. Casualties had reduced the infantry to not more than 18,000.[24]

As the morning wore on, and Union batteries shelled the woods, there were demonstrations on the right, easily repulsed. The eyes of the Confederates were less on the Federals than on the Warrenton Turnpike beyond and the distant blue silhouette of Bull Run Mountain. Thence Lee was to come. From that direction there rose a long cloud of dust. Was it raised by the hurrying feet of Longstreet's regiments? About 10:30 officers and men on the right saw a brigade boldly filing into position almost at right angles to their line. Were these confident newcomers Federals who disdained the proximity of Jackson's guns; or were they Confederates extending Jackson's flank along the high ground to the south of the Warrenton Turnpike? Quickly General Starke sent off a courier to ascertain. Soon he came flying back. "It is Longstreet!" he cried even before he reached his general. A great cry that Longstreet had come was taken up by the men all down the line.

The news was true. After a march that rivalled Jackson's, some of Longstreet's men on the night of August 28–29 had bivouacked triumphantly east of Thoroughfare Gap. Hood's division, in the van during the early morning of the twenty-ninth, had raised the dust that Jackson's division had seen. Hood greeted Stuart, who had gone out to welcome and to guide Lee, and then made contact with Early's outposts and formed the line of battle that Jackson's men admiringly had observed. Under Lee's eyes, other brigades now were spreading a long front that hinged on the right of Jackson.[25]

For the time, Pope gave no evidence that he intended to attack on that flank, or even that he was aware of Longstreet's arrival. A brief foray was undertaken against Jackson's wagon train and was repelled. Next came on Ewell's front two attacks of no great vigor. Then the heavy pressure of the enemy seemed to be shifting to the left, to A. P. Hill's part of the line. To strengthen Hill the two brigades under Early, no longer needed as a flank guard on the right, were moved eastward and placed in the rear of the Light Division.

Jackson ordered this, but he did not himself visit that flank early in the day. Had he done so, he would have condemned the position of Hill's force. Nothing had been done to clear the ground where the front passed through the woods; part of the line remained in a tangle of trees and bushes; much of it was drawn where undergrowth concealed all movement. Almost no artillery could be used. Between the brigades of Gregg and Thomas there was an interval of 125 to 175 yards. Nobody ever explained why this gap was left, or how Hill failed to observe that immediately in front of it the railroad cut was deep enough to shelter a considerable force.[26]

Here the Federals soon became the aggressors. As fast as successive lines could be formed, they were directed against Hill's left. As morning passed meridian, the Federal attacks grew heavier and centered on Thomas and Gregg, who met them with volleys as furious as their own. Ere long, from the railroad cut in front of the interval in the line, a cloud of bluecoats swept forward. A thunderous counterattack by Gregg's 14th South Carolina and Thomas's 49th Georgia restored the line, but they won only the briefest of respites. Back came the Federals to the assault. Could Gregg hold out? Anxiously Hill sent to inquire; Gregg answered that his ammunition was about expended, but he still had the bayonet.

Hill sent to Jackson that he would do his best but scarcely could hope for success. Stonewall decided to go in person to the threatened left, and on the way met Hill, who repeated the message he had sent. "General, your men have done nobly," said Jackson; "if you are attacked again you will beat the enemy back." At that moment a rattle of musketry swept the left. "Here it comes," Hill said, and without another word he galloped back toward his command. "I'll expect you to beat them," Jackson called after him.[27]

In the face of this assault, Gregg's South Carolinians gave ground slowly to the top of a knoll, whence if they were driven they would be routed. From one end of the line to the other strode Gregg. His old Revolutionary War scimitar was bare; his words were inflexible: "Let us die here, my men, let us die here!"

Hill drew on his reserves. Forno's Louisiana brigade was sent to relieve the pressure on the left. Early was thrown in, moving confidently against an enemy that had spent his strength. All the ground lost in Gregg's defensive was regained. The Federals were driven from the railroad cut. Proudly, with a relief that words could not convey, Hill sent this message to Jackson: "General Hill presents his compliments and says the attack of the enemy was repulsed." Jackson's face broke into one of his rare smiles as he answered, "Tell him I knew he would do it."

Early and Gregg and Thomas and the others waited uncertainly. A long hour of suspense passed without a further move by the Federals. Tension imperceptibly diminished. The gallant Union troops had enough! "When the sun went down," wrote a southern gunner, "their dead were heaped in front of that incomplete railway, and we sighed with relief. . . ."[28]

When darkness fell at last, Jackson's tired staff prepared to bivouac on the scene of the army's hard battle. Dr. Hunter McGuire had a long list of casualties to report. Gregg had lost more than 600 men. In his whole brigade two field officers only were unscathed. Among officers of rank the casualties had been almost as severe as on the previous day. Lamentably at the head of the list was General Trimble, badly wounded. General Field and Colonel Forno had been shot. "General," Dr. McGuire concluded his report to Jackson, "we have won this battle by the hardest kind of fighting."

"No, no," answered Jackson, "we have won it by the blessing of Almighty God."[29]

4. The Gallant Rivalry of Manassas

As Jackson gave thanks at his bivouac for the success of the bloody twenty-ninth of August, James Longstreet was completing his first tactical maneuver on the right of the long line formed that afternoon. Although Old Pete, prior to the move from the Rapidan, never had handled more than two divisions in action, he had directed admirably his part in the movement up the Rappahannock. In marching to support Jackson his infantry made as good time as had the renowned foot cavalry of the former Army of the Valley, and his dispositions for the march beyond Thoroughfare Gap had been excellent. Now he was to face a new test, the leadership of four divisions immediately and of five as soon as Dick Anderson arrived with Huger's old command. D. R. Jones was experienced and of moderate abilities. Hood, with his own and Law's brigade, could be trusted. Cadmus

Wilcox, with the three detached brigades of Longstreet's old division, was capable though not brilliant; at the head of the other three brigades was James L. Kemper, who as recently as Seven Pines had been a colonel.

Perhaps Longstreet felt that he should be cautious; he certainly hoped that he could receive attack instead of having to deliver it. Whatever the precise reasoning behind his calm mien and composed manner, he shook his head several times on the twenty-ninth when Lee asked if a forward movement was not in order. Deliberately, almost stubbornly, Longstreet delayed any action until late afternoon. Then he ordered a reconnaissance in force by Hood. Hood encountered an advancing Federal column and gained the better of the clash, but concluded that a withdrawal under cover of darkness was desirable. As he did so, he came on Dick Anderson, who had come up and, in ignorance of the ground, marched almost within the enemy's lines.[30]

At morning on August 30, with Anderson's arrival and Hood's return, Longstreet had all his troops united and under the eye of Lee himself. Their position was one of exciting military interest. They were thrown diagonally across the Warrenton Turnpike in such a way that their line, following the best elevations, formed an angle of about 160 degrees with Jackson's front. The two commands were jaws that opened widely to the southeast. Would Pope be reckless enough to thrust his infantry into those jaws? Longstreet's men waited to see; Jackson's veterans remained where they had dropped at the end of the fighting on Friday evening. Their order of battle from right to left was the same—Jackson's division under Starke, Ewell's under Lawton, and A. P. Hill's.

The morning of August 30 was hot, silent, and dry. Such activity as the Federals displayed during the early forenoon seemed to be directed against the right of Jackson, not far from the apex of the angle his flank formed with Longstreet's left. Curiosity concerning the situation opposite Longstreet led Jackson to trot over to army field headquarters. Lee was there with Longstreet and Stuart. Already the commanding general was pondering how he should stir Pope if the Federal leader permitted the day to pass without action. Of this, perhaps, the four Confederate generals talked. The curious silence persisted, a silence so complete that one would have thought the breathing of the 150,000 men lying in the fields would have been audible.

As the drowsy hours passed Jackson began to doubt whether an attack would be delivered. Then, with a suddenness that shook and startled, there crashed from his right the sound of many rifles. Old Jack knew the sound too well to be deceived. Without a word he mounted and rode off to see how his thinned regiments met the shock. He found that the enemy was streaming forward in three lines against his right, and that a similar formation was developing an attack on his center and left. The bluecoats were more numerous than they had been the previous day, and they pushed their advances farther. Jackson's division contrived to hold its own, though narrowly. Ewell's men had little to do. Farther toward the left Hill had to repair a break the Federals made.[31]

Sterner the assault became—violent, determined, and in abundant force. It was watched sharply by Old Jack. Usually he relied with pride on his own unsustained forces; this time—were the odds impossible? Would the right be overwhelmed? Assistance must be had; an officer must ride immediately to General Lee and ask for men from Longstreet to bolster the line.

On Jackson's call for help, chief responsibility for the battle shifted to Longstreet. He was alert. At the angle between his line and Jackson's he had taken his station. Already he had dispatched to commanding ground near-by the artillery battalion of Stephen D. Lee. The moment Colonel Lee's batteries were ordered into action, they could fire eastward, directly across the left flank of the Federals who were moving stubbornly northward against Jackson's right. It was an incredible opportunity, such as a gunner knows he will not have twice, an opportunity that Pope could not have allowed an adversary otherwise than through desperation or misunderstanding of the Confederate position.

When Longstreet received from Lee the request of Jackson for reinforcements, it was coupled with instructions to send a division. Old Pete looked again at the exposed Federal flank, within easy range. Far less time, he reasoned, would be required to break with gun-fire the lines assailing Jackson than to dispatch a column to the ridge. "Certainly," he said in answer to Jackson's call, "but before the division can reach him, that attack will be broken by artillery." Wisely and unhesitatingly, he determined to disregard the letter of Lee's order and to use the swifter method of relieving Jackson.[32]

The alert artillery commanders had harnessed and hitched the teams. Within minutes after Longstreet called for them, the guns had swept magnificently forward and were firing furiously. The effect was all Longstreet had expected. The fire of the battalion was overwhelming. Pope's second and third lines in front of Jackson were torn and blasted. Bewildered men turned back under the swelling fire. When the front Union line found its supports had vanished, it broke off the fight. Joyfully Jackson's men saw the enemy waver and fall back. Instinctively the gray-jackets raised their fox hunters' yell and followed their foe.

Longstreet, ere that, had seen his chance. His waiting regiments could

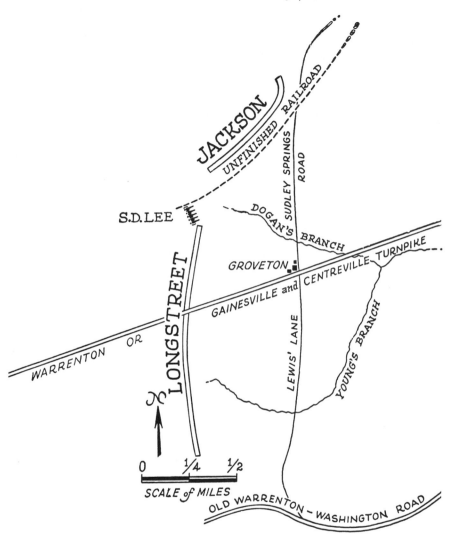

Sketch of the position of Jackson's right, Longstreet's left,
and S. D. Lee's artillery, August 30, 1862, near Manassas.

sweep forward and overwhelm the confused enemy. With perfect composure but with the joy of battle in his soul, he sent word along the line for a
general advance. One of Lee's staff officers galloped up to inform
Longstreet that the commanding general had directed just such an
advance. Old Pete must have been proud to be able to answer that the line
was in the act of throwing its full weight against the enemy.

For most of Longstreet's men, a furious, roaring attack soon became a pursuit in which valor had full play. Daring raced against the setting sun. Across the undulating fields swept the divisions of the right wing as if they were determined in that single afternoon to win as much of fame as Jackson's foot cavalry had gained from the hour Hill and Ewell and Taliaferro had left the Rappahannock. The sole lament of Longstreet's men was that heavy clouds brought early darkness. Jackson's men said the advance of the Confederates from the right was across the front of the defenders of Groveton, who were denied their part in the pursuit. Longstreet's the afternoon was, though some of Jackson's brigades were able, late in the evening, to strike a blow.[33]

Morning of August 31 found the roads heavy with mud and the streams high from a night-long rain. Attempted pursuit could be little more than floundering. Besides, the Stone Bridge over Bull Run had been destroyed. Only by roundabout roads could Pope be followed; yet orders were to strike the Federals once more before they found shelter in the defenses of Washington. Longstreet was directed to remain on the field of battle to occupy the attention of the enemy and look after the victims of the action. Jackson was instructed to put his three divisions in motion and seek the flank of Pope. The line of advance was to be across Bull Run at Sudley's Ford and thence to the Little River Turnpike. Down that road, in the direction of Fairfax Court House, Jackson might be able to reach the flank of the defeated Federal army which, the cavalry warned headquarters, was now being reinforced heavily with more of the veterans of McClellan.

Weary the Confederates were after marching or fighting for six days, but on Jackson's call they started northward through the rain. It was a time for congratulations, and it might have been a time for wiping out old scores, such, for example, as Jackson's against Powell Hill. Had Hill not redeemed all his blunders, actual or imagined, by the stubborn vigor of his fighting? If Jackson pondered this, it meant less at the time than did the fact that Hill was marching too fast. Because of the pace, the men of the Light Division were said to be straggling, and Jackson sent to admonish its commander. In his mind he made another entry against A. P. Hill as a bad marcher. Before, Hill had been slow in moving; the reverse charge was equally serious. Both, Jackson told himself, involved a definite and reprehensible neglect of duty.

The divisions bivouacked for the night at Pleasant Valley with no issue of rations; the wagons were far to the rear. By morning appetite had triumphed over discipline. "The soldiers were very bad," Jed Hotchkiss admitted in his journal, "stealing everything eatable they could lay their hands on, after trying to buy it. They were nearly famished, our wagons being still behind." They dragged hungrily down the Little River Turnpike toward Fairfax Court House. Afternoon found the van near the fine old mansion Chantilly where, under black, lowering clouds, it ran directly into the Federals. The column halted and was deployed—Hill on the right, Ewell's veterans, under Lawton, holding the center, Jackson's division under Stark guarding the left. These arrangements were made quickly because the enemy was aggressive and seemed determined to attack unless driven at once from the field.[34]

On Jackson's order Hill opened the action on the right, his men advancing under a violent thunderstorm that drove a lashing rain directly in their faces. Soon five of Hill's six brigades were engaged, but even with this force could not bring a decision. On the left, one of Lawton's brigades broke under its new and confused leader and Early's men had to beat off the attackers. With advances here and repulses there, the fire raged furiously until the two Federal commanders, Brigadier General Isaac Stevens and Major General Philip Kearny, were killed. Then, sullenly, the Federals broke off the action in the gathered darkness.

To the Federals, any action was costly that had such a toll of leadership;

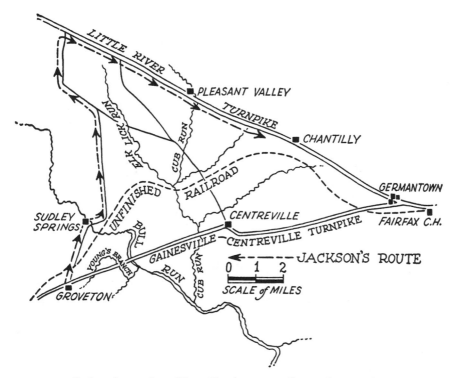

Jackson's march to Chantilly, August 31–September 1, 1862.

to the Confederates, the Battle of Chantilly was disappointing both because of the storm and because of the absence of fine performances. Most, from private to commanding general, seemed at the time to have regarded the action as a skirmish rather than as a serious meeting engagement.[35]

Chantilly ended what might be termed the Virginia phase of the campaign begun when Jackson, on July 13, was dispatched to Gordonsville. On the Federal side the first part of the operations had been entirely creditable. Pope had ventured recklessly far beyond the Rappahannock but discovered his danger, quickly put the river between him and the Confederates, and guarded the fords. It was on August 25–26 that the change came. From the hour Pope's lookouts reported Jackson on the march northward the Federal commander lost his grip on the situation. He overworked his cavalry; his infantry he was slow to concentrate. He believed Jackson's march of August 25 was a withdrawal toward the Shenandoah Valley. He held to that until he established beyond all possible self-deception the identity of the troops that had reached Manassas Junction; then he concluded that Jackson was in full, hurried retreat and that he could cut off and destroy the impudent raiders. On the twenty-ninth Pope did not know until late afternoon that Longstreet had arrived, then misjudged his posting. Until the Army of Virginia was driven from the field and in retreat on Washington, Pope insisted that the Confederates had been beaten.

Lee, for these reasons, was fortunate in his opponent, but no less was he wise in judging how far he could gamble on Pope's confusion; to the commanding general, more than to anyone else, credit for the victory was due. Lee's dispatches and his final report presented the achievements of Jackson and Longstreet with so balanced a hand that the reader suspects a deliberate purpose not to stir jealousies.[36]

The special satisfaction of Lee was in the evidence that the army at last had what every army requires, capable corps commanders. Both Longstreet and Jackson, he felt, now were qualified to handle large numbers of men and to throw the entire force simultaneously into action. Could the contrast of two months have been more nearly incredible? June 30, Glendale; August 30, Second Manassas—the dates recorded a swift revolution. If, moreover, there was in Lee's mind any suspicion that Jackson was selfishly ambitious and more interested in the furtherance of his own fame than in the advancement of the Southern cause, his behavior at Second Manassas began to remove that suspicion.

As possible doubts concerning Jackson faded, misgivings about Longstreet did not arise. It had been because he hoped Pope would assail him that Old Pete had stood out against delivering an attack on the afternoon of August 29; Lee's questions and hints were not pushed with the vigor of one who believed his lieutenant definitely in error. Nor is it easy to say how much Lee lost on the field of Manassas by delaying the attack until the thirtieth. Had a general assault been made successfully on the afternoon of the twenty-ninth, Lee would have had the whole of the next day to follow up his advantage before the rain of the thirty-first halted him.

How reasonable was the basic assumption? The commanding general himself evidently did not believe that Longstreet's unwillingness to attack that day had any serious consequences. Lee is never known to have mentioned it, or to have considered it otherwise than as an entirely permissible disagreement on an open question. The effect on Longstreet may have been definite and deplorable, though here again there can be no certainty. Did Longstreet tell himself that he could say "No" and impose his will on Lee? Was there developing in his mind a belief that, no matter what the public might say of Jackson, he and not Stonewall had the large influence on Lee? A day was coming when these questions were to be asked again and perhaps with more reason.

To the divisional commanders under Longstreet and Jackson, the word most accurately to be applied at Second Manassas was *adequate*. The new organization had succeeded under the new men. There was nothing brilliant in the performance of any of them, but there was no conspicuous shortcoming by a major general anywhere during the campaign. A. P. Hill's failure to close the gap between Gregg and Thomas on the twenty-ninth and to secure his flank the next morning were forgotten, perhaps too readily, in admiration of his superb defense. Dick Anderson might have been negligent in not having his advanced guard where it could warn him on the night of August 29 that he was stumbling almost into the enemy's lines. If he was careless then, he hit furiously the next day. John B. Hood was magnificent. He had recommended the position of Stephen Lee's guns. Hood's Texans had set the pace in pursuit with all the contempt of danger they had shown in the swamp at Gaines' Mill.

After Taliaferro was wounded, the handling of Jackson's division by the new brigadier, William E. Starke, was that of a veteran. It began to look as if the smashing brigadier from civil life was worthy to be Sidney Winder's successor. Not quite so large an opportunity as Starke's had come to James L. Kemper, but the stout-hearted Kemper had led gallantly. In keeping with the curious custom of regarding the cavalry as an ally, whose excellence it was proper to commend, and not merely as an arm of the service expected to perform its duty as the infantry did, Stuart received prominent mention in Lee's dispatches. Stuart's task had been simplified to the extent that the Federal horse had been sent galloping on one purposeless mission after another until men and mounts were worn to utter weariness. Stuart's troopers had kept their striking power to the hour of decision. It was not Lee's nature to be hasty in his judgment of men, but after Second Manassas he reasonably could feel that in the dread test of unequal battle he could count on such men as Dick Anderson and John Hood and Jeb Stuart.

There were fine performances at Second Manassas by officers of lesser rank. The details were different, but the valor was the same. Gregg brandishing his scimitar on the little knoll; Colonel Bradley Johnson shrewdly directing a brigade of Jackson's division by special assignment of Stonewall himself; Shanks Evans pursuing as hotly as he had resisted at First Manassas; old Bob Toombs released from arrest and rushing to his cheering brigade; Cadmus Wilcox unhesitatingly and swiftly moving his troops to threatened points; Beverly Robertson redeeming a late start by a gallant finish—these and many exploits no less splendid were reported.

Perhaps the most distinguished of the brigadiers was none other than the most conspicuous figure at Cedar Mountain, the sharp-tongued, keen-eyed Jubal Early. To him, in large part, belonged credit for Ewell's adroit withdrawal from Broad Run; Early it was who relieved Gregg at the critical moment on the afternoon of the twenty-ninth. Early was entirely satisfied with his performance and was convinced that he had earned promotion. Already he was hinting that if he could not get his deserts in Virginia, he would join Bragg in the western army. A shining performance among the colonels was Stephen D. Lee's. His handling of his battalion of artillery on the great day at Manassas had won the plaudits of the army at the same time that it broke the final assault on Jackson's right. When the Federals undertook to silence Colonel Lee's fire by a direct charge, he had held his ground and repulsed them, though some of them got within 200 yards of him. Praise was awarded him by both Longstreet and the commanding general.

Failures amid fine achievements were few. In Longstreet's command there was criticism of Brigadier Generals Featherston and Pryor for drifting away from their designated line of advance and for failure, later in the day, to strike the rear of Federals who were attacking Jackson. No explanation of this was satisfactory to Cadmus Wilcox, under whom the two brigades fought. Still less explicable was the failure of Thomas F. Drayton. When he was ordered to advance on the thirtieth, he was delayed by a report the enemy was attempting to flank the right wing of the army. D. R. Jones sent repeatedly for Drayton as the other brigades became heavily engaged, but he did not arrive until twilight was putting an end to the action. Lee felt that Drayton, with the best of will and of effort, was not able to get his men into battle.

These were trivial failures when set against the general excellence of the army's performance. Seven thousand prisoners, not to mention 2,000 wounded left by Pope on the field of battle, 30 guns, 20,000 small arms, and vast stores were impressive proof that the officers had learned how to lead and the troops how to fight together. Army unity, long lacking, was achieved. As always, the price had been high. Total casualties exceeded 9,100.[37]

In the high command, Ewell, losing a leg, would be absent for months. Neither Trimble nor Taliaferro appeared so badly injured, but they could not follow the army on its next move. Besides these three, Brigadier Generals William Mahone, Micah Jenkins, and Charles W. Field were wounded severely. The wounding of six of the thirty-five general officers then with the army was a serious matter. Scarcely less serious was the continued slaughter of some who were rated among the ablest of the colonels. By the time the last gun was fired at Chantilly, ten colonels had been killed or mortally wounded.

A. P. Hill in the aggregate lost three colonels and one lieutenant colonel killed, and five colonels and four lieutenant colonels wounded. Jackson's division ended the operation with no general officer besides Starke. The regiments of the Stonewall Brigade at the close of action, September 1, were commanded by captains and lieutenants. Gregg's brigade, on the twenty-ninth, had all save two of its field officers killed or wounded. For such tasks as lay ahead, the subordinate army command was suffering more from attrition than ever it had, but the high command had learned much that it was, by turn of circumstance, quickly to be called upon to apply.

CHAPTER 16

Across the Potomac

1. THE IMPONDERABLES OF INVASION

From the *Charleston Mercury* came the summons: "Our victorious troops in Virginia . . . must be led promptly into Maryland, before the enemy can rally the masses of recruits whom he is rapidly and steadily gathering together. When the Government of the North shall have fled into Pennsylvania, when the public buildings in Washington shall have been razed to the ground . . . then, at last, may we expect to see the hope of success vanish from the Northern mind, and reap the fruit of our bloody and long continued trials."[1] It was not the first demand of the year for an offensive, and it was in accord with General Lee's appraisal of the military and diplomatic situation. Before the men had time fully to rest their limbs from the strain of Manassas, or even to dry the ragged garments soaked at Chantilly, the Army of Northern Virginia headed for the Potomac.

Small the invading force was to be, and in much of its equipment deficient; but Hampton's brigade of cavalry, Pendleton's reserve artillery, and three divisions of infantry were added to the army. One of these divisions was that of D. H. Hill, his return to which had been prompted by Lee's misgivings of Hill's capacity as an administrator. A second division to rejoin the army was that of McLaws. The third, in reality a half division of two brigades only, was led by a Missouri brigadier, John G. Walker. One of his brigades was Robert Ransom's. The other, Walker's own, was commanded by its senior colonel, Van H. Manning of the 3rd Arkansas, a valiant, hard-hitting regiment. In this brigade, also, was the 27th North Carolina. Its colonel was John Rogers Cooke, known in the old army as the son of General Philip St. George Cooke and as the brother-in-law of Jeb Stuart. Of Cooke's capacities there had been little test, and of the quality of his regiment still less; it had been under fire two or three times, was well drilled, and was devoted to Cooke. This was all that could be said of

Walker's brigade. No officer, unless it was Cooke himself, could have predicted what a fortnight was to prove them capable of performing.

The accession of strength represented by Walker, McLaws, and D. H. Hill was canceled in part by the 9,000 casualties of Second Manassas and, more particularly, by the loss of commanders who could not be replaced immediately. In this appeared the first of two imponderables which, despite the care with which Lee weighed his plans for the campaign, either were overlooked or else were considered less important than they proved to be.

Through seniority, Lawton and not Early was in charge of Ewell's division. John R. Jones's return gave him, instead of Starke, the care of Jackson's old division. A. P. Hill only, of Jackson's division commanders, had the rank appropriate to his responsibilities. Of Jackson's fourteen brigades, eight were under colonels. Worst of all in this respect were the brigades that Taliaferro had directed till he fell wounded at Groveton—not one general officer, save Starke, was there in the division. The Stonewall Brigade, a stubborn fragment, was led by Colonel A. J. Grigsby. He learned that Jackson would not recommend him for promotion to brigade command, and felt himself aggrieved, though he displayed consistent courage.[2] For assignment to a leaderless brigade the one trained man available at the moment was Dick Garnett, whose court-martial had been interrupted by the preliminaries of Cedar Mountain. He was released from arrest and, as he could not be employed with the unrelenting Jackson, was assigned to Pickett's brigade, Longstreet's command.

This gave Pickett's men an experienced leader; but if one fine division of Longstreet's wing thereby was strengthened, two others equally good were weakened by arrests. On the Manassas battlefield John B. Hood had coveted and captured several new Federal ambulances. A few days later Shanks Evans, who had titular authority over Hood's troops, directed that the ambulances be given to his Carolina brigade. Hood refused, insisting Evans's brigade "was in no manner entitled to them." For this Hood was placed under arrest and ordered by Longstreet to remain at Culpeper until the case was tried. Lee overruled Longstreet to the extent that Hood was authorized to stay with his troops, though not to exercise command. Doubtless this leniency was displayed by Lee both because of the trivial nature of the alleged insubordination and because of the probable need of Hood's services. Hood's feelings were eased somewhat by Lee's action, but his men became half mutinous in their resentment.[3]

The other arrest that might weaken the army came through a renewal of Jackson's disciplining of A. P. Hill. On the night of September 3, Jackson gave instructions for the start of each division the next morning, and as usual rode out at dawn to see if his orders were being followed. They were not. Gregg's brigade was not even ready to start. In Hill's absence, Jackson asked why Gregg was not on the march, whereupon, perhaps with some resentment, the South Carolinian replied that his men were filling their canteens. Something in Jackson's manner, or some words that passed between the two, created a bitterness that did not pass with the day or the campaign. For the moment, Gregg merely obeyed orders.

Jackson kept his eye on the column, ahead of which Hill rode steadily onward. Some units were straggling badly, which Hill seemed to be making no effort to prevent. The corps commander observed this dereliction. When the hour arrived to rest the men as Jackson had directed, Hill paid no attention to the time and did not call a halt. Jackson's wrath was aroused. He accosted the commander of the leading brigade, E. L. Thomas, and ordered him to stop the column in accordance with regulations. Thomas did. In a few minutes Hill came storming back demanding to know by whose order the troops had been halted. "By General Jackson's," said Thomas. Hill turned on Stonewall, sitting silent on his horse. With some statement that if Jackson was to give orders, the general had no need of him, Hill offered his sword to Jackson. "Consider yourself under arrest for neglect of duty," Jackson answered, and summoned Branch to take command of the Light Division.[4]

So, as the army passed over the grassy hills of Loudoun, en route to the Potomac, Jackson sacrificed his only experienced divisional commander to his ideal of discipline. He could not have overlooked the fact that the troops of the Left Wing were facing new battles on hostile soil with all three divisions under brigadier generals not one of whom had received professional training. Longstreet was better circumstanced, though he would miss Hood. All this constituted the first imponderable.

The second was straggling. Some warnings had come before Second Manassas that men were leaving the ranks without proper excuse. A few executions for desertion had occurred. Officers and provost marshal guards had been sent to Lynchburg, where martial law was declared when that city was found to be something of a rendezvous for deserters. None of this prepared the army for what came en route to Maryland—straggling of a magnitude so appalling that it made Johnston's evacuation of the Peninsula appear orderly. Thousands of men fell behind or disappeared. Jackson characteristically met with sternness this ominous breakdown of discipline: His order was that men who left the ranks were to be shot without argument or ado. Lee designated Brigadier General Lewis A. Armistead as provost marshal with authority to call for guards, and sorrowfully had to admit that discipline was "defective." Exhortation, orders, threats, penalties alike failed. As the campaign progressed, the weak soldier fell away with the indifferent, until, as the indomitable Alexander Haskell wrote, "none but heroes are left."[5]

The first reason for this straggling was the obvious one of worn-out shoes. Most of the troops were being called upon to make long marches immediately after a succession of battles that had themselves been preceded by hard, steady pounding of the roads all the way from Gordonsville to Bull Run. Apparently the quartermasters had not realized that the shoes of so large a part of the army would go to pieces at the same time. After another six months of hardening, most of the troops were to find themselves possessed of feet so tough that shoes in summer were a nuisance. It was far from being so in September 1862.

Another reason for much of the straggling was the diet on which the men had to subsist. Lee realized that the commissary could not supply the army from Virginia, and he doubted whether rations could be had in Maryland. His decision, regretfully made, was that the army must live for the time being on green corn and fruit. The army did. For an average of probably ten days, during the first three weeks of September, the men had little other food. Many who ate too freely of the corn developed serious diarrhea which weakened them and inevitably caused much absence without leave. "We call this even now," adjutant W. M. Owen wrote after some twenty years, "the green corn campaign."[6]

Besides bruised feet and diarrhea, the inexperience of some acting brigade and regimental commanders was a factor in straggling. Numerous officers never previously charged with the care of a column were unable either to keep it closed or to distinguish between the skulker and the sick. This represented a weakness that was shown hourly and disastrously.

A fourth reason there was for straggling, a reason not anticipated to any degree. It was exemplified by the 25th North Carolina of Ransom's brigade. The greater number of its men came from the extreme western counties of North Carolina, and until President Lincoln called for troops in April 1861 they had been Unionist in sentiment. They enlisted for the defense of their homes against invasion, and when they learned they were to cross the Potomac they responded in varying confusion of mind. Some, in the language of their historian, "said they had volunteered to resist invasion and not to invade; some did not believe it right to invade Northern territory...." This was a feeling not to be repressed by orders or by punishment. Those of extreme conscience found opportunity of leaving the ranks for the duration of the Maryland expedition.[7]

Together these conditions were responsible for so much straggling even before the Potomac was reached that the commanding general thought it dangerous alike to the stragglers and to the Confederate cause in Maryland for thousands of hungry, scattered men to follow the army across the river. He stationed his bodyguard at the principal ford and told its commanding officer to direct all stragglers to Winchester, where they might be organized and forwarded in numbers large enough to avoid risk of capture.[8]

2. GENERALS ON DISPLAY

The passage of the Potomac on September 4–7 was to the spectators a drama of incredible contrasts, to the boys in the ranks a diverting lark, and to the commanding generals the beginning of a venture diplomatic, political, and social no less than military. Said Heros von Borcke of the cavalry's crossing: "It was . . . a magnificent sight as the long columns of many thousand horsemen stretched across this beautiful Potomac. The evening sun slanted upon its clear placid waters, and burnished them with gold, while the arms of the soldiers glittered and blazed in its radiance. There were few moments, perhaps, from the beginning to the close of the war, of excitement more intense, of exhilaration more delightful, than when we ascended the opposite bank to the . . . strangely thrilling music of 'Maryland, My Maryland.'"[9]

All the generals were determined to be agreeable to the Marylanders, to the hoped-for benefit of the South, but as ill fortune shaped it, Lee, Jackson, and Longstreet were in varying degrees incapacitated. On August 31, Lee had injured his hands in a fall and had to ride in an ambulance for a few days. Jackson's mishap was the cause of some alarm. No sooner was Stonewall on Maryland soil than he was presented with a "strong-sinewed, powerful, gray mare." He accepted thankfully because he had lost Little Sorrel temporarily. When he mounted his new gift, however, she reared instantly, lost her balance, and went over backwards. Jackson was stunned and for half an hour was compelled to lie where he fell. His pain was acute; there was momentary fear of a spinal injury. He ingloriously spent the remainder of the day in an ambulance. Longstreet's injury, the lesser of the three, was a badly rubbed heel, requiring of him the indignity of wearing a carpet slipper.

The crippled Lee and the bruised Jackson, together with the limping Longstreet, pitched their tents quite close to one another, that sixth of September, in Best's Grove, near Frederick, and soon had visitors from town and farm. Lee was busy and perhaps uncomfortable from his hurt, and excused himself from callers. Jackson kept to his tent most of the day. Longstreet had to do the honors. "Stuart," said Henry Kyd Douglas, not without a touch of envy, "was ready to see and talk with every good-looking woman."[10]

Jackson did not venture forth the next morning, though it was the Lord's Day. After as quiet a time as he could make for himself, he decided he would go to evening service. He rode in his ambulance to the Reformed Church after it was ascertained that the Presbyterians were not meeting. The occasion was not altogether a success. Courageously enough, in the presence of one of the most "notorious rebels," the minister, Dr. Daniel Zacharias, prayed for the President of the United States. Jackson, unfortunately, did not hear that petition. He fell most trustfully asleep as soon as the sermon was begun. Dr. Zacharias's most earnest periods, the flight of the peroration, the prayer of minister and the response of congregation—none of this awakened Jackson. He enjoyed a soldier's rest until the organ and the closing hymn brought him back to a world of clashing armies and divided churches.[11]

September 8 witnessed the issuance of General Lee's tactful address to the people of Maryland. Of this much was hoped, but, in an immediate social way, a dance given by the cavalry had a more practical appeal. Stuart himself had proposed the dance while inspecting a disused academy at Urbana, a village southeast of Frederick. He promised to find the music. Major von Borcke supervised the lighting and decorating and the invitations. Guests, at the stated hour, arrived in gratifying number; the band of the 18th Mississippi supplied gay music. The gray and yellow of cavalry uniforms whirled in the candlelight with the lovely girls; "the strange accompaniments of war added zest to the occasion"; from the dames on the bench, as well as from the girls in the quadrille, came exclamations that everything was "perfectly charming."

Suddenly, above the Mississippians' horns, there echoed the challenging bark of a field gun and a distant rattle which, to experienced ears, bespoke the clash of outposts. A dusty courier stamped in and announced loudly to the general that the enemy had surprised and driven in the pickets. The band crashed into discord; girls turned pale; officers bade hasty bows and ran for their sabers. In five minutes the academy was stripped of fighting men, though reassuring promises were shouted over tall shoulders that after the Federals were driven away the dance must be resumed.

About 1:00 A.M., under a full, high-riding moon, the troopers jingled back to the academy lawn and reported that the alarm had amounted to little. The band and many of the girls had remained, and soon lilting feet were answering every rhythmic beat of the drum. Two o'clock, three, four, a sinking moon and a graying east—still the dance went on. It only ended when the gory, smoke-marked, dazed boys wounded in the skirmish were brought in on stretchers. The belles became nurses in evening dress. "One handsome young fellow," wrote Captain Blackford, "as he looked up into their faces with a grateful smile, declared that he would get hit any day to have such surgeons to dress his wounds."[12]

The infantry private did not attend any dance in Maryland. "Johnny Reb," if the truth be told, was less interested in making a good impression on the people and more anxious to get something to eat. By observing accurately when the sentry made his rounds, a light-footed soldier might slip into Frederick and contrive to get a good meal. Said adjutant Worsham: "A friend and I succeeded in passing the guard. . . . We were invited into several houses and entertained handsomely at supper. We ate enough for half a dozen men." Liquor was to be procured in town and was not disdained by some, even, of Jackson's Model Army. Others had at least an opportunity of washing their persons and their clothing, and perhaps buying a few toilet articles or garments.[13]

Although lionized by Southern sympathizers, the army could not regard itself as welcome. Where hostility was not disclosed, public indifference was displayed. Supplies of flour in the country around Frederick soon ran low. Recruits from Maryland did not offer in numbers worth counting. Nowhere was there any movement to accept the help of the Confederates "in regaining the rights" of which Maryland had been "dispoiled." Removal from Frederick seemed desirable on all these accounts.[14]

A final consideration for such a move was presented at Harper's Ferry. The expectation had been that when the Confederates entered Maryland, the Federals along the south side of the Potomac would be withdrawn as a reinforcement of the main army, which newspapers reported as again under the command of General McClellan. No such evacuation of Harper's Ferry and near-by posts had occurred. As soon as he learned this, Lee asked himself whether he should divert part of his forces to capture the towns the enemy still held in Virginia, but deferred action. Now that he had to move to the vicinity of Hagerstown, he decided that a single wide-sweeping advance might compass everything. While one column marched westward, another might envelop Harper's Ferry, take it, and then rejoin at Hagerstown, whence communications with the Shenandoah Valley might be opened or, if circumstances justified, Pennsylvania could be invaded.

On September 8, Lee had summoned Jackson to his headquarters tent and outlined his plan for taking Harper's Ferry quickly. Jackson was to march with his three divisions and invest the town from the rear. Two divisions were to cooperate from Maryland Heights, which overlooked the Ferry from north of the Potomac. A sixth division was to climb Loudoun Heights, across the Shenandoah from the Ferry. Surrounded, subject to a triple fire, the arsenal town and its garrison could be captured readily.

In the midst of this conversation, Longstreet came to Lee's tent on other business, was invited to enter, and was told of the plan. The difference between his comment and Jackson's was revealing. Stonewall frankly was pleased at the prospect of aggressive, semi-independent action; he even essayed a mild joke that he had been neglectful of his "friends" in the Valley. Longstreet was not inclined to violate the established maxims of war. Dispersal of force was dangerous. If Harper's Ferry was to be taken, said Longstreet, let the whole army share in the operation. That is to say, orthodox warfare was to be preferred to daring.[15]

The next day orders for starting the operation on September 10 were prepared and sent to all the division commanders. On the march north Jackson had assumed direction of D. H. Hill, and when he read in the orders that Hill was to move with Longstreet, he thought he should advise Hill that he was cognizant of the transfer. Jackson's regard for secrecy forbade entrusting the paper to anyone for transcription, so he personally made a copy and dispatched it under seal to Hill. That officer studied it and then put it away where he was sure he would not lose it.[16]

Under these orders, Jackson on September 10 was to begin the advance. By Friday, the twelfth, he was to close in on Harper's Ferry from the rear. John G. Walker and his division were to be on Loudoun Heights the same day. The actual capture of the Ferry was to be the task of Lafayette McLaws, who was to seize Maryland Heights. Jackson would direct the final operations when the columns were within cooperating distance of one another.

By daylight on the tenth Jackson's division, under Starke, was moving. So were Ewell's men, for whom Lawton was responsible. The Light Division had Branch at its head; A. P. Hill, still under arrest, followed his six brigades. Into Frederick rode Jackson and his staff, to find the streets well filled with Marylanders who wished to see him and his terrible troops at close range. As a ruse, he had officers inquire for a map of Chambersburg, Pennsylvania. Through the town and along the road to Middletown Old Jack continued in advance of the infantry. Reaching Middletown, he was greeted by "two very pretty girls with ribbons of red, white and blue in their hair and small Union flags in their hands." They ran to the curb stone, reported Kyd Douglas, "and laughingly waved their colors defiantly in the face of the General. He bowed and lifted his cap and with a quiet smile said to his staff, 'We evidently have no friends in this town.'"[17]

From Middletown the column climbed Turner's Gap in South Mountain, and a mile east of Boonsborough Jackson called a halt in the evening. Powell Hill, all the while, had ridden at the rear of his division but had not received copies of orders. Still, he could draw his own soldierly conclusion: A battle was brewing; he must have his hand in the fighting; but how? Soon he thought of Kyd Douglas, who seemed at the moment to be closest to Jackson. Douglas agreed to present Hill's case. Jackson listened and, without argument or explanation, assented. He knew how admirably Hill led his troops in battle and, no doubt, felt a measure of relief that the most experienced on his commanders was again to be available.[18]

Jackson proceeded then to make a wide sweep in the hope of catching the Federal garrison at Martinsburg, but the bluecoats slipped through his closing net and reached the larger force that was holding Harper's Ferry. The Confederates on the twelfth entered Martinsburg. In that friendly town the soldiers consumed an incredible quantity of food and enjoyed themselves vastly, and Jackson was all but overwhelmed by the welcome of the residents.

"About 11 o'clock on the following morning (13th)," as Jackson later reported, "the head of our column came in view of the enemy drawn up in force upon Bolivar Heights." Of the success of the impending attack there could be no doubt. "Harper's Ferry," a Federal officer subsequently said in disgust, "is represented as an immense stronghold—'a Gibraltar.'" Instead, he maintained, it "was a complete slaughter-pen."[19] The sole question was the familiar one of time. That same question was about to assume for D. H. Hill, on other ground, a mien more threatening than it bore at the junction of the Potomac and the Shenandoah.

3. HARVEY HILL'S BATTLE

The day of Jackson's march through Middletown, September 10, witnessed the removal of virtually all the other Confederate infantry to the west of the Blue Ridge, which in Maryland is styled South Mountain. Lee's plan had been to hold Longstreet and D. H. Hill temporarily at Boonsborough in order to block Federal retreat in that direction from Harper's Ferry; but these dispositions had to be changed before they could be executed. Rumors came of an impending Federal advance from Pennsylvania to Hagerstown, which Lee had selected as his advance base for operations toward the Susquehanna. Precautions had to be taken. Longstreet was directed to leave D. H. Hill at Boonsborough and press on to Hagerstown with the remainder of his force. The prospect did not please Longstreet. "General," he complained to Lee, "I wish we could stand still and let the damned Yankees come to us!" It was to no purpose; the march had to be made. Then, at Hagerstown, all was quiet. Reconnaissance northward did not uncover even a vidette.[20]

At Boonsborough, where D. H. Hill had been left with the rear guard, trouble began to brew. Hill's mission was, in his own words, "to dispose of my troops so as to prevent the escape of the Yankees from Harper's Ferry . . . and also to guard the pass in the Blue Ridge near Boonsborough." The first part of these orders entailed guarding the roads that led northward from Maryland Heights on the Potomac, to which McLaws's march was directed. Dick Anderson's division was in the same column. These two were to force the surrender of Harper's Ferry, which Jackson and Walker were to assail from the south and east.

As for the second part of Hill's orders, the general plan did not contemplate any long defense of South Mountain. McClellan was east of the range, watched by the cavalry, but advancing so slowly that the capture of Harper's Ferry before the Federal army reached the mountain seemed almost certain. If Harper's Ferry were taken ere McClellan could relieve the post, did not good strategy dictate an effort to draw McClellan west of the undefended mountain? The longer his communications, the greater the advantage in dealing with him. On the basis of this reasoning Harvey Hill had been instructed. From Boonsborough, three miles west of Turner's Gap, the principal pass in South Mountain, Hill spread his outposts toward the south, whither the roads from Harper's Ferry led. To the possibility of attack from the east, to defending Turner's Gap, he gave little thought.[21]

This was not merely another familiar instance of a soldier's concentration of thought on the sector of assumed danger, to the neglect of precautions elsewhere. Harvey Hill relied on Jeb Stuart. East of South Mountain and Catoctin, a lower range between Frederick and Washington, the Confederate cavalry faced on all the roads the slowly advancing Federals. Stuart was in general command of an ample, vigilant force. Besides Fitz Lee's men and the Laurel Brigade, he now could employ Hampton, recently come up from Richmond with his troopers. On September 5, Beverly Robertson had been ordered to report to the Department of North Carolina where, the orders read, "his services are indispensably necessary for the organization and instruction of cavalry troops. . . ."[22] The Laurel Brigade passed to its senior colonel, Tom Munford.

These three cavalry brigades, by the early afternoon of September 13, were subjected to so much pressure from a heavy force of Federal infantry that they had to yield the Catoctin range and retreat to South Mountain. This gave Stuart no special concern. Through D. H. Hill he notified headquarters of his withdrawal, and he counseled Hill to watch Turner's Gap. Guard of the pass was regarded by Stuart as a precaution—and no more— because he thought that Harper's Ferry already had surrendered. He reasoned that Jackson, Walker, McLaws, and Anderson soon would be on their way to rejoin Lee, and that no bullets need be wasted defending South Mountain. On receipt of this news from Stuart, Hill ordered Colonel A. H.

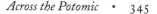

Terrain of the Confederate operations in Maryland, September 1862.

Colquitt to carry his brigade to Turner's Gap to support Stuart. As reinforcement if needed Garland's brigade was ordered to make ready. Hill himself did not ride up that evening to the gap to make reconnaissance. His eyes still were on the roads by which the Federals might retreat from Harper's Ferry.

After night had settled, Hill received a curious message from Colquitt, who was on the eastern crest of Turner's Gap. Since darkness, said Colquitt, many more fires had become visible than would have been required for the two brigades of cavalry that were, in Stuart's opinion, the only Union troops approaching the mountain. This news alarmed Hill. He forwarded to Lee all the information he had received, and about midnight had a response. Lee knew that Harper's Ferry had not yet been captured, and he could not disregard the possibility that a vigorous advance by the Federal army might sweep past McLaws and relieve the town. Then, while the Confederates were divided, McClellan might turn and attack the divisions north of the river. The one sure way of preventing this was to hold the passes of South Mountain. A defensive barrier Lee had planned to disregard, in order to lure McClellan westward, suddenly became indispensable to the plan of operations. Lee ordered Hill to cooperate with Stuart in holding the passes and, showing how seriously he regarded the situation, said that Longstreet's troops were returning from Hagerstown to join in the defense.[23]

Already, with a start, Hill had become conscious of his ignorance of the ground he was to defend, and hurriedly dispatched Ripley to Stuart for information about the passes. Stuart told Ripley that he had left Colonel Tom Rosser with a detachment of cavalry and the Stuart Horse Artillery to occupy Fox's Gap, a mile to the south of Turner's Gap. Stuart explained, also, his intention of going southward to Crampton's Gap. That pass was on the shortest route from McClellan's position to Harper's Ferry and, for that reason, was "as much threatened as any other" crossing of the mountain.[24]

During the night, Stuart received strange news from an unexpected visitor. A Southern sympathizer, residing in Frederick, reached him after a hard, hurried ride and informed him that during a visit to McClellan's headquarters that morning he had witnessed the general react exuberantly to some dispatch handed him and, subsequently, sudden activity by the Federals. McClellan, who usually proceeded most deliberately, seemed to be pushing westward fast. Stuart was not alarmed by this disclosure. Still in the belief that Harper's Ferry had been captured, he reasoned that the army would be reunited before the Federals could do great mischief; but he promptly forwarded to Lee the intelligence reported by the friendly Marylander.[25]

The truth behind this intelligence was far worse than Stuart imagined. On the morning of September 13, Corporal B. W. Mitchell of the 27th Indiana infantry had picked up along a roadside near Frederick a crude package of three cigars. Around these was wrapped a paper. When Mitchell took it off, he observed handwriting on it and, upon closer examination, saw that he had a copy of S.O. 191, Army of Northern Virginia. It was addressed to Major General D. H. Hill and was marked, "By command of Gen. R. E. Lee, R. H. Chilton, AA General." Mitchell realized his find might be important, and in company with his sergeant went immediately to his colonel, who carried the paper to corps headquarters. There, unluckily for the Confederates, the staff officer on duty recognized Chilton's name as one he knew from before the war. By noon McClellan had the authenticated paper in his hands and could act in documented assurance of what the Confederate plans had been on September 9, though he did not realize that only D. H. Hill, instead of the entire force of Longstreet, had been left at Boonsborough.

After this unhappy night, Hill rode to Turner's Gap at dawn of the fourteenth of September. It was to be his day of opportunity, his first day to direct command of an entire field where large forces were engaged. On the mountain, at the moment, he had no other troops than Colquitt's brigade, though Garland's North Carolinians were toiling up and were close to the crest. Three other brigades Hill had, G. B. Anderson's, Ripley's, and Robert Rodes's. These troops, about 3,000 in number, were disposable, but Hill was still weighing both parts of his orders: Deploy to prevent escape from Harper's Ferry *and* guard the pass near Boonsborough. Even the fact that Lee was hastening back to South Mountain with Longstreet's troops did not convince Hill that a heavy thrust might be impending.

Soon enough, in a quick succession of surprises, the seriousness of his plight was disclosed. Hill had expected to find Stuart on South Mountain; instead, he learned that the cavalryman had gone farther south to Crampton's. That was not the worst of it. When Hill and Colquitt rode along the crest to reconnoiter, they scarcely had gone three quarters of a mile before they heard the rumbling of wheels and the voices of Federal officers. The enemy was on the mountain, almost on the crest! If the Federals got much farther, they could flank Turner's Gap. South of it a road crossed at Fox's Gap, whence several trails ran along the ridge toward the main highway through Turner's Gap. North of the pass were several higher knobs, approached by several roads. "An examination of the pass," Hill later reported, ". . . satisfied me that it could only be held by a large force, and was wholly indefensible by a small one."

What was Hill to do? He decided to bring up a third brigade, G. B. Anderson's, but more than that, even when he knew that the Federals were almost atop the mountain and beyond his flank, Hill could not bring himself to do. "I felt reluctant," he wrote in his official account of the battle, "to order up Ripley and Rodes from the important positions they were holding until something definite were known of the strength and design of the Yankees." He did not state what he desired more "definite" than the evidence brought him by his own ears.[26]

Until G. B. Anderson arrived, Hill planned that Colquitt hold the ground dominating Turner's Gap, and that Garland should defend the right. Since his last battle, at Malvern Hill, new happiness had come to Samuel Garland. Social Richmond was expecting news of the engagement to him of one of the loveliest and most brilliant daughters of the city. On this day of danger he led out along one of the narrow roads on the western flank of the mountain his North Carolina regiments. His task was to hold at any cost the road that crossed at Fox's Gap and uncovered Turner's Gap. He sought, as he deployed his infantry, to place his veteran regiments where they would meet the shock and to station on ground less contested those of his men who never had been in action.

Reconnaissance established contact about 9 o'clock. In a few minutes a jumbled battle was joined. The Federals attacked vigorously and in strength;

almost from the initial clash, Garland was hard put to hold his own. Ere long the drift of the fighting indicated that the enemy was trying to turn the left flank, where Garland was standing. "General, why do you stay here?" said one of his officers. "You are in great danger." He answered casually, "I may as well be here as yourself." Moments later Garland dropped to the ground. One glance at him by the men who knelt to lift him showed that his wound was mortal. Already he was in his death spasm.[27]

When word of the fate of Garland was brought to Hill, he was contemplating the scene before him. After twenty years he wrote of it: "The marching columns extended back as far as eye could see in the distance. . . . It was a grand and glorious spectacle, and it was impossible to look at it without admiration. I had never seen so tremendous an army before, and I did not see one like it afterward." He realized that his division could be overpowered in time, but he reasoned that if he could hold the gap until Longstreet arrived, their joint resistance might allow time for the army's trains to get across the Potomac, or for Jackson to complete the capture of Harper's Ferry, or even for both these things to happen.

A few minutes later, Hill learned that Garland's brigade had been broken and pushed steadily back. He could not afford to move Colquitt to assist the remnant of Garland's command. No other troops yet had arrived at the top of the mountain. The best that Hill could do was to run out two guns and, with the flank regiment of Colquitt and a scratch contingent of "staff-officers, couriers, teamsters, and cooks," to give some semblance of support to the artillery. He recorded later his sensations of the moment: "I do not remember ever to have experienced a feeling of greater *loneliness*. It seemed as though we were deserted by 'all the world and the rest of mankind.' "[28]

If Hill, however lonely, was to prevent the turning of his flank and the loss of his position, he had to forgo continuing to guard the route from Harper's Ferry to Boonsborough. The brigades of Ripley and Rodes must be ordered to join him as soon as they could climb South Mountain. He had waited too long already in sending for them. Anderson was on his way, but probably not before 3 o'clock could Ripley and Rodes reach the crest. As for reinforcements, Longstreet had thirteen miles to cover from Hagerstown to Boonsborough, and Hill could do no more than guess the time of his arrival. His plight appeared well-nigh hopeless. Four Federal corps, he estimated, were spread to the eastward. He had, at the moment, only Colquitt, the cavalry contingent under Tom Rosser, a few guns, and the broken regiments of Garland. If the Union commanders realized how weak he was, they could destroy him.

The scattered little force waited for an overwhelming blow that did not come. On Hill's right, from the vigor of his artillery fire and from what could be seen through the underbrush, the Federals thought graycoats in heavy numbers had taken up a strong position. They decided to await the arrival of more men. On Hill's left, the Federals had not yet woven their way through the ravines and ridges that covered the approaches. An incredible, a well-nigh miraculous delay there was. For the two hours from noon onward, when Hill most nearly was helpless, he had the mercy of a general lull. Critics might have said he was luckier than he deserved to be.[29]

Before 2 o'clock stalwart G. B. Anderson had climbed to the pass and filed to the right. Rodes and his fine Alabamians then were pressing toward the crest. By Hill's order, Rodes turned to the left and made for an eminence which it was manifest the enemy was preparing to seize. Ripley followed G. B. Anderson to the right but had difficulty in reaching his position. Although his force still was feeble, Hill now had greater defensive strength than he had commanded at any time during the day. His prospect was less desperate. Word had come that Longstreet's troops were nearing Boonsborough. Hill's answer was a request that Old Pete hurry.

With Drayton in advance, D. R. Jones's division of Longstreet's command climbed up the ridge from Boonsborough. Behind him for miles spread the other brigades. Road weary they were after their all-day struggle with heat and thirst and dust. Regiments were depleted to battalions, to companies even. In the 8th Virginia of Pickett's brigade not more than thirty-four men were ready for action. In the 56th Virginia there were eighty muskets.[30]

Under Hill's orders, Drayton's brigade and G. T. ("Tige") Anderson's which followed it, were sent southward toward Fox's Gap. Hill brought Tige Anderson, Ripley, and Drayton together and explained that he wished them to attack in line with G. B. Anderson. As the senior, Ripley assumed command of the four brigades, but before the deployment was complete he unwisely ordered an advance. It collided almost at once with an advancing Federal force, which quickly penetrated a gap between Tige Anderson and Drayton. Drayton's men were driven. Ripley's brigade in some fashion was squeezed out of the line or misdirected and for a time could do nothing. G. B. Anderson, as always, fought vigorously but accomplished little against the odds he faced. The whole effort, incompetently directed, soon was in baffling confusion. Then, toward evening, intelligent and determined leadership in the person of John B. Hood drove back the enemy and restored the field.[31]

Hill had ridden back to Turner's Gap and became absorbed in the battle to the left of the highway. Robert Rodes had plunged boldly into action there. He occupied high ground, but had to extend his line until its firepower was weak. Repeatedly he repulsed the enemy, and when at length he had to fall back, it was stubbornly, slowly, and with a bold front. John B. Gordon's 6th Alabama was held together by the singular moral leadership of its colonel. Another young officer, Colonel Cullen A. Battle of the 3rd Alabama, caught many an eye by a magnificent display of valor.[32]

Harvey Hill saw all this and rejoiced in it. Precisely that type of battle was his forte—hard combat where a man might fight with all his strength and cunning and not be responsible for strategy. In close, doubtful action he was superb. No man seemed able to get more firepower from a given number of troops. If Hill were charged with the direction of a campaign or with exclusive conduct of a large field…well, he justified all that was said about him after the farcical bombardment of McClellan's camp and the unchallenged departure from the James of the Federal army he was supposed to watch.

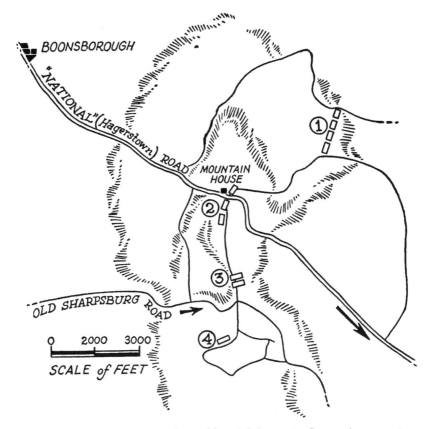

Positions on the crest and ridges of South Mountain, September 14, 1862:
(1) Rodes's advanced position; (2) Colquitt; (3) Hood in the late afternoon;
(4) Garland's morning position.

After Longstreet had come up, Hill, the doubting independent commander, became once again the sharply critical subordinate: "I had now become familiar with the ground, and knew all the vital points, and had [Longstreet's] troops reported to me, the result might have been different." In a narrow sense that strange statement may have been correct. Reinforcements thrown hastily to the right had to be recalled to the left before the Federal advance on that flank could be halted. Even so, the stiffened resistance Longstreet offered on the left and the assured conduct of Hood on the right put an end to the action if they did not redeem the field. Hill was not satisfied. Had his and Longstreet's forces never been separated, he asserted, "the Yankees would have been disastrously repulsed...." Not a word was there of self-criticism for failure to get the whole of his own division on the mountain until after midday.[33]

4. THE TEST OF LAFAYETTE McLAWS

While Harvey Hill was fighting at Turner's Gap that fourteenth of September, he heard from the south the sound of another engagement where McClellan was trying to force a gap in South Mountain. There was being tested the Georgian in command of the column sent to capture Maryland Heights and to force the surrender of Harper's Ferry.

Lafayette McLaws, forty-one years of age and a major general since May, had been denied any conspicuous part in the army's battles. At Williamsburg he had acted with decision in manning Fort Magruder, but he had not fought at Seven Pines. Magruder, rather than he, had directed most operations of his command at Savage Station and Malvern Hill. His division had not rejoined Lee in time for Second Manassas. Now McLaws had been given Dick Anderson's six brigades in addition to his own four, but, according to plan, he was to have opportunity without excessive responsibility. He was not to be so far from Lee or his immediate superior, Longstreet, that he would be called upon to make any important strategical decisions. After arrival at Harper's Ferry, if there was a change in the general plan, responsibility would not rest on McLaws but on Jackson. On the other hand, the most difficult tactical operation in the effort to capture Harper's Ferry devolved on McLaws.

The ground imposed dual obligations on McLaws: He must command Maryland Heights if he was to keep the garrison of Harper's Ferry from escaping westward into Maryland, and, at the same time, he must guard well his rear. If he neglected this second duty, McClellan might fall upon him, overwhelm him, and divide the Confederate forces north of the

Potomac from those south of the river. The importance of McLaws's mission explained the assignment to him of so large a force as ten brigades.

McLaws began his movement early on September 10. From Frederick to the foot of Maryland Heights was not more than twenty miles. His first day's march ended east of Brownsville Gap, and most of the eleventh was consumed in crossing the mountain to Pleasant Valley, between South Mountain and the upper end of Maryland Heights. The plan had been to close on Harper's Ferry on Friday, the twelfth, but nightfall on the eleventh found McLaws encamped at Brownsville, six miles from his objective.[34]

Six difficult miles they promised to be. The only way of capturing the Heights seemed to be to climb them well to the north of the Potomac and then proceed southward along the crest. Access to the ridge could be had by way of Solomon's Gap, four miles north of the Federal batteries that overlooked Harper's Ferry. McLaws's information was that these gun positions were reached by a road along the backbone of the ridge. On this basis, McLaws made his plan.

He would send to Solomon's Gap the fine South Carolina brigade of Joseph B. Kershaw, supported by Barksdale's Mississippians, another excellent command. His remaining eight brigades McLaws would dispose to meet any column that might seek to beat its way into Pleasant Valley from South Mountain or to escape from Harper's Ferry. Under McLaws's own leading, the van of the larger Confederate force by nightfall on the twelfth reached the Potomac three miles downstream from Harper's Ferry. Kershaw, for his part, climbed to the northern end of Maryland Heights and from there advanced along a mountainside so steep that the men sometimes had to pull themselves up by gripping the bushes. A mile from the southern edge of the Heights Kershaw encountered heavy abatis and perforce halted for the night.[35]

An early start by Kershaw on the morning of Saturday, September 13, carried the 7th South Carolina past the abatis to another and heavier obstacle of logs and stones. Then Barksdale's Mississippians, clinging to the rim of the heights by sheer tenacity, contrived to outflank this crude fort. Panic swept the bluecoats. They abandoned the position, plunged down the hillside, and sought to make their way to Harper's Ferry. By 4:30 the last Federal soldier was driven from Maryland Heights. McLaws occupied the little settlement of Sandy Hook, nestled under the east edge of Maryland Heights on the main line of retreat northward from Harper's Ferry. He had outstripped both Walker and Jackson, and it appeared that the honor of forcing the surrender of the Ferry would be his.[36]

Vigorously, on the morning of the fourteenth, McLaws pushed for the completion of his part of the enterprise. He cut a road to the crest of

Maryland Heights and at 2 o'clock he opened on Harper's Ferry with four guns. Then calamity threatened suddenly. Back on the twelfth, in garrisoning the exposed points in the terrain assigned him, McLaws had sent Paul Semmes, with his own and Mahone's brigade, to watch Brownsville Gap, by which the column had crossed South Mountain. Semmes, taking his duties in serious spirit, discovered that less than two miles north of Brownsville Gap was another important pass, Crampton's Gap. Accordingly, on the morning of the fourteenth, he dispatched a battery and three of Mahone's regiments, under Colonel William A. Parham, to Crampton's. Jeb Stuart, coming south from Turner's Gap and seeing the danger of an attack at Crampton's, left Munford's Laurel Brigade with Parham, and sent a warning to McLaws. Immediately McLaws directed Howell Cobb as a reinforcement.

To McLaws these arrangements seemed adequate, and he climbed Maryland Heights to direct the bombardment of Harper's Ferry. Stuart joined him there, reporting that no more than a brigade of Federals appeared to be moving against Crampton's Gap. That reassured McLaws; with three brigades at or close to the pass in addition to Stuart's cavalry, he need have no concern. Later in the afternoon, when he heard firing from the direction of Crampton's Gap, it did not alarm him at first. At length, as the firing became heavy and sustained, he decided to ride in that direction. Stuart bore him company. Before they had proceeded far, Major T. S. McIntosh came galloping down the road and brought them appalling news: The Federals had broken through Crampton's Gap; Cobb was in mad retreat; the enemy was pressing hard.[37]

It was true. At the gap Munford's cavalry and Mahone's regiments, under Colonel Parham, had been hammered by bluecoats who seemed to come up the mountain like a rain cloud. Cobb's brigade came up to cover Parham, but before the line could be rectified, its center gave way. The regiments thereupon broke wildly and ran down the western side of the mountain. The best Cobb and Semmes could do was to employ a battery to delay the pursuers and serve as a rallying point.

When Stuart and McLaws arrived, Cobb greeted them in vast distress. Said he: "That I should live to experience such a disaster! What can be done? What can save us?" Soon it was manifest that the enemy had halted temporarily, but the situation of the three brigades remained as dangerous as it could be, short of out-and-out slaughter. Might not the Federals overwhelm the remainder of McLaws's force, recover Maryland Heights, and relieve Harper's Ferry? Would not Lee and Jackson be divided and then destroyed?

In his report McLaws said only: "Fortunately, night came on and allowed a new arrangement of the troops to be made to meet the changed aspect of affairs." A line of battle, under Dick Anderson, was formed across the valley below Crampton's Gap, comprised of the brigades of Wilcox, Kershaw, and Barksdale, with the remnants of those of Cobb, Semmes, and Mahone. The enemy did not press hard in the twilight. The Federal commanders seemed to think their day's work was done when the pass was cleared. Night overtook them ere they overtook McLaws's hastily drawn line.[38]

Even so, midnight on South Mountain was doubly black for the Confederate invaders. D. H. Hill believed the army should withdraw from Turner's Gap before dawn, and so advised General Lee. The outcome of the fight at the two gaps led Lee to doubt for a few hours whether he could attempt to remain longer in Maryland. He wrote McLaws to abandon the position in front of Harper's Ferry and to recross the Potomac. Lee explained, in his dispatch to McLaws, that the forces with him would retire via Sharpsburg into Virginia. Everything indicated a hurried and divided retreat. It might have been necessary, with excessive, perhaps ruinous losses, had there not spurred through the night a courier from Jackson with a message that changed the army's plan.[39]

CHAPTER 17

Desperate Hours on the Antietam

1. THE WAGON HUNTER'S GREAT DAY

When Old Jack reached the vicinity of Harper's Ferry at 11:00 A.M. on September 13, the day before the struggle for the gaps in South Mountain, his first move was routine. He placed his troops so that he could meet any maneuver on the part of the Federal garrison, which had been reinforced, he learned, by the regiments that fled from Martinsburg. He then studied Loudoun Heights across the Shenandoah and Maryland Heights beyond the Potomac. Walker and McLaws had been ordered by Lee to take those positions by the twelfth. Jackson himself was a day late. Had the cooperating generals completed their shorter marches, or had they, too, found the logistics of Lee's plan too exacting?

Jackson scanned the picturesque eminences across the rivers but could see nothing of any Confederate troops. He instructed his signalmen to establish contact with the other commands by flag, but they worked to no purpose. Late in the afternoon the sound of Kershaw's attack down the backbone of Maryland Heights could be heard, but there was no answer to the signal flags. Despairing of signaling, Jackson turned to couriers to find where the cooperating columns were. Not long after dark a courier returned to report Walker in position on Loudoun Heights. Ere that, McLaws's approach had been verified, but Jackson was not sure when McLaws could clear Maryland Heights and open fire on Harper's Ferry.[1]

On the morning of the fourteenth, while D. H. Hill was fighting on South Mountain, Jackson proceeded deliberately with his preparations. Under his orders now were six of the nine infantry divisions of the army. This was much the largest force he ever had directed. Ere long his signal station was in touch with Walker, but it still was unable to reach McLaws. Walker reported he had six rifled guns in position on Loudoun Heights. "I do not desire any of the batteries to open until all are ready on both sides of the river. . . ," Jackson signaled Walker. "I will let you know when to open. . . ." Walker replied that McLaws reported the enemy in rear of him and said "that he can do but little more than he has done."²

Meantime, A. P. Hill's division, Lawton's, and John R. Jones's were disposed in rear of Harper's Ferry, between the Potomac and the Shenandoah. By a mere demonstration on the part of the Stonewall Brigade and one battery of artillery, commanding ground on the Federal right was carried. Dorsey Pender handled with much skill and small loss an advance to a good position opposite the Union left. There ten guns of Lawton's artillery were posted. By 8:15 P.M. Jackson felt he could make a favorable report to Lee: "Through God's blessing, the advance, which commenced this evening, has been successful thus far, and I look to Him for complete success tomorrow. The advance has been directed to be resumed at dawn tomorrow morning."³ This was the letter that prompted General Lee to cancel orders for a withdrawal across the Potomac and to direct, instead, a new concentration west of the mountains.

Before dawn on the fifteenth, Jackson had all the troops aroused and put in line of battle. Walker's artillerists, looking down from Loudoun Heights on a heavy mist that enveloped Harper's Ferry, could do no more than wait and pray for a sight of their target. The moment the other batteries had sufficient light they opened a pattern of fire Jackson had designed. Soon afterward, Lawton's guns chimed in; then Walker's set echoes rolling from Loudoun Heights. Jackson was fulfilling a dream of the officer of artillery: He had his guns precisely where he wanted them, he was firing as he desired, and he perceived ere long that he was silencing the enemy.⁴

An hour of steady hammering seemed to exhaust the Federals. Their fire became slack and discouraged and soon virtually stopped. Jackson signaled the infantry assault. Dorsey Pender began at once to move forward the brigades that were to drive home the attack. The Federals then opened again, though their fire was slow and uncertain. Pender halted. Two of Hill's batteries dashed out, unlimbered, and assailed the Federals furiously. In about five minutes a horseman was observed on the Union works, waving something. Eyes were strained; soon it was unmistakable—white, the signal of surrender! Cheers swept the front.⁵

Through the lines came Brigadier General Julius White, designated to arrange terms of surrender. As White drew rein in front of Jackson, the contrast in appearance of the two men made irreverent young staff officers grin. Kyd Douglas remembered that White "was mounted on a handsome black horse, was handsomely uniformed, with an untarnished saber, immaculate gloves and boots. . . . He must have been somewhat astonished to find in General Jackson the . . . most faded and dingy looking general he had ever seen anyone surrender to. . . ." White was told that the capitulation must be unconditional. Jackson turned him over to A. P. Hill, instructed in terms that did not lack in generosity. All officers and men were to be paroled; officers might retain their side arms and private baggage.

While these negotiations proceeded, Jackson was writing to Lee about the next vital step in the campaign, the reconcentration of the forces. "Through God's blessing, Harper's Ferry and its garrison are to be surrendered," he announced. A. P. Hill would be left in charge of the prisoners. "The other forces can move off this evening so soon as they get their rations. To what point shall they move?"[6]

When the prisoners were counted, they numbered about 11,000. The booty included some 13,000 small arms, 73 cannon, and approximately 200 wagons, together with the provisions and quartermasters' stores usually kept at a busy post. It was a noble haul, one that much gratified the "wagon hunter." "Ah," said Jackson to von Borcke, as he viewed the prisoners and the booty, "this is all very well, Major, but we have yet much hard work before us." There was to be no holiday. All the energies of all the officers must be devoted to getting the men on the road as soon as they were fed.[7]

While the essential arrangements were being made, most of the troops were given liberty to explore the sutlers' establishments at Harper's Ferry. Some of the brigades of Hill's Light Division had been denied their proper part of the loot at Manassas, and now Pender's men and Branch's and others could enjoy canned lobster or fill stomach and haversack with cake or stuff pockets with candy. When Walker's column came over the Shenandoah and McLaws's streamed across the Potomac bridge, there was much grumbling because the booty had all been devoured or appropriated. "Jackson's troops fairly swam in the delicacies, provisions, and 'drinkables,'" wrote comrade Dickert, resentful after more than thirty years, ". . . while Kershaw's and all of McLaws's and Walker's troops, who had done the hardest of the fighting, got none."[8]

Neither feasting nor complaining was for long. First Lawton's division, then Jones's, started for Sharpsburg, Maryland, which Lee had named as the point of concentration. The march by Jackson's own admission was "severe." Twenty-four hours from the time he had received the flag of truce at Harper's Ferry, he was approaching the rendezvous, distant sixteen miles by road. As the regiments one after another, during the morning of September 16, reached the little town of Sharpsburg and halted, the men dropped silently down. Jackson, dust covered and gray, rode on to report to Lee, who was waiting, with more anxiety than he exhibited, the arrival of the detached divisions to reinforce the thin line he had drawn behind Antietam Creek.[9]

Already, on the opposite ridges, east of the stream, the Federals in vast numbers seemed to be deploying for an offensive battle. Had McClellan attacked with his full strength before the arrival of Jackson, fourteen brigades of infantry would have been compelled to face six corps in a hopeless battle. Now that Jackson was up, he raised the number of Confederate brigades to twenty-two. These were not enough for successful prolonged resistance, but they might suffice to hold their ground until A. P. Hill, McLaws, Anderson, and Walker arrived with their eighteen brigades. Jackson had relieved a desperate situation by a prompt march.

That day Jackson was completing his third month in the school of the Army of Northern Virginia. He had not shone, during the Seven Days, in cooperation with others or in the swift movement of his divisions; on his first test under his new teacher he could not have been graded above "Fair." His next test, Cedar Mountain, might by lenient marking have been rated "Good," but no more than that. Then he made the superb advance of August 26 from Salem to Bristoe. By that time Jackson had mastered the essentials of the art of the executive officer. His operation against Harper's Ferry had not been perfect logistically or as an example of communication among cooperating columns, but the task had been performed. All that was marked in the improvement of Jackson, the advance from Harper's Ferry to Sharpsburg confirmed. The grade that had risen from "Fair" on July 1 to a doubtful "Good" on August 9, now had mounted from "Good" to "Excellent." An examiner might have asked himself whether that high adjective connoted quite the full measure of praise that Student Jackson, T. J., had earned.

2. THE WORST OF CRISES

Lee's withdrawal of Longstreet and D. H. Hill from South Mountain, after the news of the impending capture of Harper's Ferry, had been directed to Sharpsburg for three reasons. First, at that point Lee would be on the flank or rear of McClellan if he sought to cut off McLaws. Second, Sharpsburg was close to the Potomac across which the forces under Jackson were to move to reunite with Lee. Third, the terrain around Sharpsburg was moderately favorable for defensive action.[10]

The march of Longstreet and D. H. Hill on the fifteenth had been uneventful. Once arrived at Sharpsburg, the two divisions were disposed along the high ground to cover the Boonsborough road, by which they had marched, and the road from Hagerstown. For the protection of these roads and for the defense of the ridges, the Confederate army was alarmingly weak in comparison with an adversary who followed fast and deployed boldly. Even after Jackson arrived on the sixteenth, the army was weaker than ever it had been under Lee. A strong attack by the whole of McClellan's command manifestly would threaten not merely defeat but ruin. The worst of all the succession of crises had come. An army of liberation was an army in desperation.

Could the new McClellan be beaten? Not unless all the missing brigades could be brought up quickly and massed. Walker came up with his small force during the afternoon of the sixteenth. In Anderson's division and his own, McLaws had ten brigades, or more than half the army's reserve. His orders were to move over to Harper's Ferry and to hurry on to Sharpsburg. What delayed him? A. P. Hill was detained at Harper's Ferry to parole the prisoners and secure all the captured property. How long would that require? If emergency demanded, could he be available on the seventeenth? None of these questions found an assured answer. Battle was in the air. Sharp clashes had occurred before darkness fell. All night long restless pickets plied an intermittent fire.

With the dawn the Federal artillery opened furiously. The battle was to rise with the sun. Joe Hooker's I Corps, as the Confederates soon ascertained, was moving against their left. Jackson instantly sensed danger. Stuart and his cavalry supported well-placed artillery near the Potomac. Jackson moved Jube Early's men to serve as the flank infantry element. Next to Early, to the right, was Jackson's division under John R. Jones, and beyond, Ewell's division under Lawton. To the right of Lawton the line turned southward to cover the Hagerstown road. Here the depleted regiments facing the advancing Unionists were those of D. H. Hill.

Neither Hill nor Jackson had any reserves of his own command, but the previous night Jackson had relieved Hood, at his request, so the Texas Brigade and Law's might cook rations. Jackson prudently had exacted a promise that if he called, Hood would move immediately to his relief. Hood's division, then, might be counted as Jackson's reserve. It was all Jackson had, all the left wing had.[11] The line had no fortifications and little cover. On either side of the Hagerstown road were scattered woods which, on the west, extended southward to the rear of a whitewashed Dunker church that overlooked much of the ground of the Federal advance. East of the Hagerstown road and about 500 yards north of the church was a fine field of corn, thick and head high. To this field Jackson was moving Lawton's Georgians under Colonel Marcellus Douglass, and the Louisiana brigade to which Harry Hays had just returned.

On these troops and Jackson's division to the left of the Hagerstown road, Hooker's sunrise attack was furious, overwhelming. The fire of the blue regiments mowed down the men of Lawton and Hays, shattered Jackson's depleted division, and, almost at the first clash, carried one of Lawton's staff to Hood with a panting message: "General Lawton sends his compliments with the request that you come at once to his support." Hood did not hesitate. As "To arms" sounded, hungry privates put up their frying pans, sighed over the food they had to throw away, and fell in for what they knew from the sound of the firing would be a desperate fight.

With the élan they had shown at Gaines' Mill the two brigades of Hood's division pushed swiftly into the southern edge of the cornfield. Hardened though they were, they were appalled. Shambles, ghastly and streaming red, the Federals had created. Almost half of Lawton's and Hays's troops had been slaughtered, and Lawton himself was wounded. Colonel Douglass had been killed in front of the Georgians. A shell had exploded a little above the head of John R. Jones, and he said it stunned him so badly that he could not exercise command. W. E. Starke had taken Jackson's withdrawing division, only to fall in a few minutes with three fatal wounds. A. J. Grigsby assumed command—a colonel in charge of a division. Never in all the army's battles had so many high officers been put out of action so quickly. In the three brigades of Lawton's division all save two regimental commanders either were down or soon were to fall.[12]

In the midst of this carnage Hood deployed his men boldly. To aid him Stonewall directed Early to return from the support of Stuart on the extreme left. Early must take command of Lawton's division and give the utmost help to Hood. It was "hold or perish." In a time amazingly brief, the enemy had cut a gap on either side of the Hagerstown road. Every brigade that had occupied the ground from Early's right to D. H. Hill's left had been swept aside. No organized force of more than a few score men remained to confront the enemy.

The Federals now were close to the Dunker church. To stop them, Hood's hungry, mad Texans and their like-tempered comrades under Law could not level 2,000 muskets. If Hood knew the odds he faced he gave no sign. He must drive the enemy; he would. Gallantly his men entered the gap and pushed forward. For the moment they had the reward of daring. D. H. Hill's line contributed a steady if not a heavy fire against the Federal left. On the opposite flank Old Jube was coming up. With his own troops and some 300 of Jackson's division whom Colonel Grigsby and Colonel Stafford had rallied, Early formed on the Federals' right. If Hood seemed to have thrown himself into a gap, it now appeared that Hooker's corps had advanced into a pocket, the three sides of which were held by D. H. Hill, by Hood, and by Early.

It was not Jackson's nature to silently stand idle while his comrades

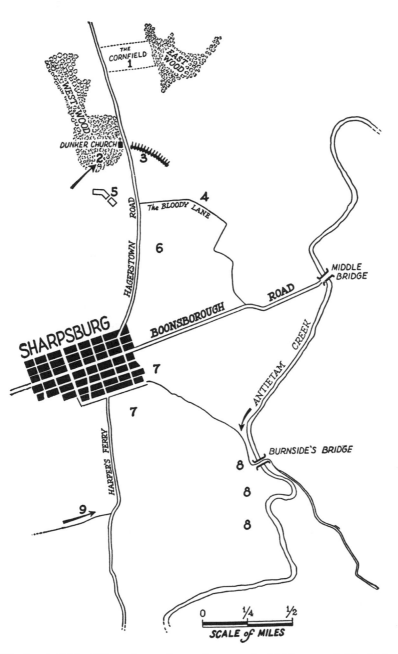

The battlefield of Sharpsburg, September 17, 1862: (1) The cornfield which first Lawton and Hays defended, and into which then Hood and subsequent reinforcements advanced; (2) McLaws's line of advance; (3) first position of S. D. Lee's artillery battalion; (4) the scene of Rodes's disaster; (5) position from which John R. Cooke charged; (6) general zone of D. H. Hill's defense; (7) main body of Longstreet's troops on the right; (8) Toombs's advanced regiments; (9) the line of A. P. Hill's advance.

fought. He had done that once—at White Oak Swamp—but he had come far since that last day of June. He must know how Hood fared. Would Sandie Pendleton ride forward and ascertain? Sandie was off at the word. Said he afterward: "Such a storm of balls I never conceived it possible for me to live through. Shot and shell shrieking and crashing, canister and bullets whistling and hissing their most fiend-like through the air until you could almost see them. In that mile's ride I never expected to come back alive." At last, unscathed, he found Hood and delivered his message.

A great moment that was for John Bell Hood, but he was too intent to be eloquent. In his reply was nothing sensational, nothing of exhibition or declamation. "Tell General Jackson," he said simply, "unless I get reinforcements I must be forced back, but I am going on while I can!"[13]

On he went, not so fast as at Gaines' Mill or at Second Manassas, but as intrepidly and in the face of a heavier fire. Ere long that fire grew fiercer, fresher, faster. Heavier resistance was being encountered. Although it was not plain at the moment, the I Corps had been repulsed but Mansfield's XII—Banks's old corps—was advancing in Hooker's stead. Hood had to halt. The best he could hope to do, with the help of D. H. Hill and a sharpening attack by Early, was to hold on till reinforcements reached him.

Jackson, ere this, had received Hood's brave message. Stonewall had not a soldier of his own to send into the cornfield. Every brigade, every regiment save one that Early had left to support Stuart's guns, was engaged or shattered or wrecked altogether. The only recourse was the army reserve: Sandie Pendleton must find General Lee, repeat to him Hood's message, and ask for help. Once more Pendleton dashed away. When he returned, it was to report that Lee had already dispatched Walker's division from the right and said, also, "I'll send McLaws."

Hood waited and, as he waited, fought. His battle raged uncertainly but not long. By supreme exertion, Mansfield's attack was repulsed. The action fell away to an artillery exchange. What was left of Hood's division slowly drew back to the Dunker church. In some regiments ammunition had been spent to the last cartridge. "For God's sake, more troops!" cried Hood. When a brother officer rode over and asked, "Where is your division?" Hood answered grimly, "Dead on the field."[14]

The forces of Tige Anderson and Walker were called into confused action, and then McLaws reached the scene. The Georgian quickly met the impact of a fresh corps, Sumner's II, but he repeated Hood's gallant feat in driving the enemy back to approximately the point where the battle had opened at sunrise. In doing this McLaws's division was scattered badly and in time forced to give ground, but it was not pursued. Jubal Early, who had done magnificently on the left, proudly held his flank position. For the first time since sunrise, Jackson's front now was free of pressure. He now could mend his worn line, carry off his wounded, and prepare to meet another attack—if it came. Three corps he had beaten off in successive assaults—the I, the XII, and the II. At Groveton only had he ever been so long or so violently assaulted.[15]

The reason for the lessened force of the hammer-strokes on Jackson was the shift of the fiercest action to the Confederate center. Of D. H. Hill's brigades, Ripley's, Colquitt's, and Garland's had been battered in the onslaughts of the morning, but Rodes's and George B. Anderson's had been damaged little. They had been placed in a sunken road that branched from the right of the Hagerstown highway about 500 yards south of the Dunker church. There they had been well protected from hostile fire. To their left, to fill the gap between Jackson and Hill, were the 27th North Carolina and the 3rd Arkansas of Walker's brigade. Of these forces—indeed, of everything to the right of Jackson—the command was vested in Longstreet, but Hill handled Longstreet's left, which was the center of the entire Confederate position. The North Carolinian was as contemptuous as ever of danger. Perhaps he was more confident, more certainly full of fight, because the responsibility of the field did not rest on him.

General Lee inspected the sunken road position, and Hill heard him exhort the men: They must hold their ground, because a break on their front would endanger the whole army. The 6th Alabama's John B. Gordon—the ramrod Georgian who had fought with glorious valor at Seven Pines, at Gaines' Mill, at Malvern Hill—cried out: "These men are going to stay here, General, till the sun goes down or victory is won!" This, Gordon wrote afterward, he said "to comfort General Lee and General Hill, and especially to make, if possible, my men still more resolute of purpose."[16]

With soldierly calm, Harvey Hill faced the coming storm. He watched the approach of the left of Sumner's corps, which continued to press vigorously after the right had been repulsed by McLaws. Toward the sunken road two blue divisions, well supported, advanced steadily if slowly. Hill beat off the first attacks without great difficulty. Learning that R. H. Anderson had arrived in support, he frugally kept Anderson behind him as a second line. Soon came word that Anderson had fallen, severely wounded, and that the command had devolved on Roger A. Prior, senior brigadier. From that moment Anderson's division ceased to act as a unit; it lacked leadership, direction, striking power. Hill realized that his division, unsupported, would have to bear the brunt of the next attack.

That attack came speedily. The Federal left, driving gallantly forward, reached a position from which the bluecoats could enfilade part of the 6th Alabama in the sunken road. Colonel Gordon was down and unconscious with his fifth wound of the day. For orders his lieutenant colonel, J. N. Lightfoot, hurried to Rodes, who was at his gallant best. Rodes was determined to hold fast to the sunken road by refusing his right. An order to that effect he gave Lightfoot, who turned at once to execute it.

Soon afterward, returning from helping a wounded aide to the rear, Rodes stared in amazement at almost the whole of his famous brigade running back in confusion. Nothing had happened, so far as he could observe, to force a retreat. The enemy was not pressing the Alabamians; artillery fire was no more destructive than it had been. Yet his veterans were breaking for shelter as if they were raw recruits. He must rally them. He shouted, he commanded, he pleaded. It was to small purpose. Aided by Major E. L. Hobson of the 5th Alabama, he managed to rally only some 150 undaunted men under the shelter of a ridge about 150 yards from his position. The other survivors scattered.

They had left the sunken road, Rodes learned, through a misunderstanding. Lightfoot had ordered the 6th to "about face and forward march." Major Hobson naturally asked if the order was meant for the entire brigade. When Lightfoot mistakenly replied that it was, Hobson had started his regiment. The other troops assumed that the position was being evacuated and had broken for cover. George Anderson on the left of Rodes fought to hold his ground, but soon the rushing enemy turned him. Anderson himself was wounded. His brigade was driven and broken.

The center now was wrecked. East of the Hagerstown road, for hundreds of yards, no organization of even a thousand men confronted the advancing Federals. "Lee's army," said Porter Alexander, "was ruined and the end of the Confederacy was in sight." One more heavy thrust by McClellan would divide beyond possible reunion the two wings of the Confederate army and would bring the Federals to the rear of both fragments.[17]

If Harvey Hill realized that the rout and ruin of the Army of Northern Virginia might come then and there, on his front, he did not exhibit new anxiety. Neither did Old Pete. Fuming in the carpet slipper his injured heel compelled him to wear, Longstreet rode or hobbled in search of men and guns to mend the gap in the line. In a cornfield Hill found Boyce's South Carolina battery, which in a few minutes was sprinkling with canister the Union troops who now had crossed the sunken road. Longstreet rushed into action Miller's battery of the Washington Artillery. Closely watching Federal gunners opened with a devastating blast. Miller's men began to fall. Longstreet's staff officers slipped off their mounts and took the stations of the stricken gunners. Old Pete himself held their horses and calmly assisted in correcting the range.[18]

At this instant, when oncoming disaster and improvised defense were balanced, Miller, Boyce, and the scattered remains of D. H. Hill's command found on their left unbending support—the 27th North Carolina and 3rd Arkansas of Walker's division. Now that the Federals had swept back the troops on either flank, these two regiments held an advanced position. They were under Colonel John R. Cooke of the 27th, whose gallantry was matched by that of Captain John W. Reedy commanding the 3rd Arkansas. From these well-handled regiments poured a volume of fire which the Federals might have credited to a strong and confident brigade. Cooke's bold fire and that of the two batteries began to tell. On Hill's center and right the blue line stopped, wavered, and slowly slipped back.

Hill sensed opportunity. A single fresh regiment, he thought, "could drive the whole of them in our front across the Antietam." He did not have a regiment—not one, fresh or blown—but would not the still unwounded soldiers attack? He would lead them. Soon he had some 200 in an uneven line. Hill seized a rifle, shouted a command, and started forward. It was fine but it was fruitless. So small a force could not get far in the face of the fire the Unionists poured into it. Hill reluctantly had to recall his volunteers.[19]

Then Cooke, unmindful of the odds, ordered his two regiments forward. On the Carolinians' front the most conspicuous figure was the color bearer, William H. Campbell. In the storm of bullets, waving the regiment's red flag, he pushed ahead of the line. Cooke had to call out to him to slacken the pace. "Colonel," protested Campbell, "I can't let that Arkansas fellow get ahead of me!" The two regiments, disdaining security for their flanks, pushed wildly on till they found the enemy in ranks behind a fence in a cornfield. With a cold prudence that matched his hot valor, Cooke decided not to assault. His position was too advanced, his numbers too few, his ammunition too low. He ordered a withdrawal. Both regiments were thinned and exhausted before they reached the position from which they had launched their attack, but they still were undaunted. "Tell General Longstreet to send me some ammunition," he said. "I have not a cartridge in my command, but will hold my position at the point of the bayonet." He would stay there, he swore, "if we must all go to hell together!"[20]

As much to the amazement as to the relief of the Confederate leaders, about 2:00 P.M. the attack on the center came to an end. It was learned subsequently that Franklin's VI Corps had arrived on the field, but that McClellan decided against employing the fresh troops. "The repulse of this, the only remaining corps available for attack," the commanding general explained, "would peril the safety of the whole army."[21]

The battle was not over; it had undergone another shift. Other actors held the stage. At 7 o'clock that morning the scene of supreme danger had been on the Confederate left, where Jackson's line had been broken. Noon had brought the crisis of Rodes's withdrawal from the center. Now the Confederate right was being threatened with ruin.

At dawn that wing of the army had been numerically weak; hourly it had become weaker. Walker had been hurried to the left. Only the troops of D. R. Jones remained—six small brigades, whose "aggregate present" was 2,460 men. From this force Tige Anderson's five Georgia regiments had been sent to help Jackson. Until A. P. Hill arrived from Harper's Ferry—if he could hope to complete his march that day—Jones could call up two regiments only. Jones, in a word, with about 2,000 infantry, had to defend more than a mile of front.[22]

This risky thinning of the right had been ordered in sound knowledge and shrewd appraisal of the terrain. The position assigned David Jones was, for the most part, on heights overlooking Antietam Creek. Artillery was posted where it could cover the infantry. A narrow bridge, which after that day was styled Burnside's, crossed the creek at the foot of the heights midway Jones's position and was so tempting an avenue of advance that the enemy was almost certain to attempt to force it. But the road leading to the bridge ran parallel to the creek for a quarter of a mile. A few hundred men on the heights to the west could make that stretch of road a slaughter pen.

Command of the small force defending the crossing of Antietam Creek was in the hands of Robert Toombs, who had been restored to duty on the field of Manassas. Toombs had written his wife of his desire to distinguish himself in some great battle. "The day after such an event, I will retire if I live through it."[23] His opportunity had come. The stage was his. If Toombs the politician was to prove himself the successful soldier, the hour was striking.

During the morning the Federals threatened to plunge over the bridge and overwhelm the two regiments Colonel Henry L. Benning had stationed where he could command both the crossing and the approaches to it. Each time the Federals advanced, they were repulsed bloodily. By noon signs had multiplied that a major attack was coming. How could these forces be resisted? The two Georgia regiments defending the stream-side opposite the bridge had almost exhausted their ammunition. David Jones designated a new position, high on the hillside, where Toombs's brigade could be positioned. Benning—"Old Rock" to his men—was redeploying his men when, about 1 o'clock, from across Antietam Creek, there came a sudden stir. Swiftly and in heavy mass, two Federal regiments dashed for the bridge. Before the Confederate artillery could be trained on them, they were over!

West of the stream, in a moment, the Stars and Stripes were floating. Wild, hoarse cheers were raised. Jones's infantry could do nothing but watch and steel their hearts for the coming charge. Moment by moment the

Union force grew stronger, the threat to Toombs more desperate. Close to 3 o'clock, slowly and ponderously, the mighty line began to move up the hill.[24]

The chief attack was to the left of Toombs and against those of Jones's brigades on the crest directly east of Sharpsburg. Small as they were, they had good artillery, and for a time it was a stand-off fight. This was encouraging, for word had come that A. P. Hill's Light Division was coming up. If the Union force could be held until Hill arrived, five veteran brigades could be thrown against the blue line creeping through the corn and across the open ground. Jones was diligent; Lee himself came to the Confederate right and brought to bear all the supporting artillery he could find.

It was not enough. The Federals moved up with a strength not to be resisted by Confederates so few. Kemper's brigade was driven back on the town.[25] Drayton's command was broken. Dick Garnett's men, when they at length gave ground, went far around to the north side of the town. Jenkins's brigade was in danger of being cut off and surrounded. By 4:00 P.M. the battle on the right was almost lost to the Confederates. The Federals had gained nearly all the high ground east and south of Sharpsburg. If they could push 1,200 yards farther westward, they would be across the line of retreat of the left wing of Lee's army.

Disaster should have been in the air, and with it the first signs of stampede. It was not so. The thrilling news had spread that A. P. Hill was coming. For fate or fame, his was to be the last scene. On that furious march from Harper's Ferry the impetuosity that had been Hill's vice was now his spur. If regiments swooned by the road, to Sharpsburg he would go in time of reinforce Lee. Soldiers were to say he urged the laggard forward with the point of his sword. Every sound of fire was a summons. Speed the march, close up, close up! The life of the Confederacy might depend on the pace of that one division.[26]

Hill rode ahead to meet Lee, who greeted him in relief: "General Hill, this is the last force we have. You must hold half in reserve, and send in the other half." Where were his troops; how soon would they arrive? The answer well might have been proud: Batteries already were arriving; not far behind were the South Carolinians of Gregg. Although sixteen miles of weary road had worn them, Gregg's men marched as became the vanguard of Gaines' Mill. Closely following Gregg was Archer.[27]

In brief conference Hill and David Jones agreed on dispositions for a joint attack on the exposed right of the Federals pressing into the very streets of Sharpsburg. "I immediately ordered a charge," wrote Robert Toombs, "which, being brilliantly and energetically executed by my whole line, the enemy broke in confusion and fled." That was as Toombs saw it in retrospect. In the red reality of the field, the repulse involved far more troops than Toombs's brigade and a part of Kemper's. A. P. Hill threw Archer's men forward in a direct charge. Gregg and Branch supported Archer and Toombs vigorously with a flank fire.[28]

On that right flank, directing the fire at the head of his brigade, L. O'B. Branch fell. Maxcy Gregg was just wheeling his injured horse when a bullet crashed near his right hip and almost knocked him out of the saddle. His first concern was a soldierly transfer of the command. Then a stretcher bearer examining the injury cried, "General, you aren't *wounded,* you are only *bruised.*" Up sprang Gregg and soon was directing his men from the back of a bony ambulance horse he stripped of its harness.[29]

By that time, the Confederates were driving the whole left wing of the Federals downhill to the banks of the Antietam. Above the din of battle could be heard the fox-hunters' call, the wild "rebel yell." Red banners were following Stars and Stripes. Yard by yard the Union line, sagging and gaping but unbroken, fell back to the shelter of the low ridges near the creek. Slowly, after sunset, the fire died away. By nightfall the ghastly action ended. To the bark of the gun succeeded the wail of the wounded.

Never had the Army of Northern Virginia fought a battle so doubtful, save at Malvern Hill. During twelve hours and more of conflict, Lee had thrown into action every organized infantry unit north of the Potomac. Within supporting distance south of the river was only Thomas's brigade, guarding the guns and stores captured at Harper's Ferry. Straggling had reduced to less than 40,000 the men who had withstood the shock of the furious assaults that rolled from left to right. Sharpsburg, indeed, was not one battle but three. Mercifully for the Confederates, the mismanagement of the battle by the Federals was such that after Jackson had been strained to the utmost and close to disaster, the Unionists left his troops panting and had attacked the division of D. H. Hill and the reinforcements sent him. For an hour or two Hill had been in danger of being overwhelmed. When it seemed that one more thrust inevitably would drive him in rout to the Potomac, the enemy had desisted. Then the thin Confederate right had been assailed.

Outside Dick Anderson's command, which had not been brought fully into the battle after the fall of its commander, every division had suffered cruelly. Retreat seemed as logical as, after so gallant a fight, it would be honorable; but Lee would not have it so. He held his ground all the next day, while his adversary hesitated, and not until the evening of the eighteenth did he begin a withdrawal to Virginia through Boteler's Ford near Shepherdstown. The price of the expedition had been 13,900 casualties or more. Of these, about 10,300 represented Sharpsburg. Federal losses were 27,767, of which Harper's Ferry accounted for 45 per cent. Twice as many men the Federals had lost as had the Confederates, but one for two was more than the South could afford to pay.

3. PENDLETON FAILS TO COUNT HIS MEN

Like many another tragedy, that of Sharpsburg did not end at its high moment. It was prolonged to an anticlimax in which the embarrassed central figure was the Reverend William Nelson Pendleton, brigadier general and chief of artillery, Army of Northern Virginia. On September 19 came what Pendleton termed "my great responsibility." Under orders from Lee to post guns to dispute the crossing of the Potomac at Boteler's Ford, he found positions for thirty-three and held eleven others out of range but within call. Scarcely had this been done than the Federals appeared on the opposite side of the river. Long-range rifles soon opened on Pendleton's batteries. While an indifferent duel went on, Lee moved southward to get the men out of range. Pendleton's orders were to hold the crossing all day and through the night unless pressure became too great. In that event, he was to evacuate his position after nightfall and follow the track of the army.

The minister-artillerist never before had commanded infantry, of which he had two battle-thinned brigades. He instructed the inexperienced colonels commanding them in their duties in the face of a long-range artillery exchange, but neglected to inquire as to how many men they had in their ranks before the forces were sent off to their various postings. Federal fire from the opposite shore quickened late in the afternoon. Sharpshooters seemed to be practicing at the expense of the Confederates. Soon the colonels of the infantry at the ford sent in their complaint. Pressure was getting too heavy, they said, to be resisted at that point by the 300 men at their command.[30]

Three hundred men? No more than that? The news that he had not more than 300 riflemen opposite the ford must have made the gray parson look grayer still. With the equivalent of a good-sized battalion he had to protect forty-four guns, thirty-three of which were where withdrawal might be difficult! It was, said Pendleton, a "critical and anxious hour" until dusk would come. The batteries began to slip off in the shadows. Suddenly infantry were hurrying past him to the rear. In answer to his inquiry they said they were sharpshooters from the ford. Their thin line had given way; the Federals had reached the south side of the river!

He sent staff officers to hurry to the rear the last batteries and the headquarters equipment. "Intending first," he explained to his wife, "to save all I could, and, secondly, not to expose myself needlessly to capture, I passed

... toward the road which some of the artillery had, I knew, already taken." Turning out of the column in the darkness to search out support, he saw no more of his guns and did not know what befell them. At last, past midnight, the alarmed Pendleton stumbled into the bivouac where Lee and his staff were sleeping. Arousing Lee, he recounted his afternoon's experience, and announced that the enemy had captured all the reserve artillery. "All?" exclaimed Lee. "Yes, General, I fear all."

A staff officer present observed that Lee "exhibited no temper, made no reproach that I could hear, either then, or even afterwards...." With Jackson it was different. Pendleton's report brought from Stonewall more show of anxiety and perhaps of disgust than he exhibited on any other occasion during the war. "He took the matter in his own hands," wrote Kyd Douglas. By 6:30 the next morning, September 20, Jackson had ordered A. P. Hill to return to the Potomac and drive the enemy back across it. Early was to move in support.[31]

The movement was rapid, the action swift and decisive. Pender and Archer, cooperating perfectly, drove the Federal party into the river and shot scores who were splashing vainly toward the northern shore. "This severe work having been accomplished," wrote the relieved Pendleton, "I found that but four of our pieces had been lost." It seemed that Major William Nelson of his staff had stayed on the previous night and labored diligently until he had nearly all the guns withdrawn safely. Nelson, in the estimation of the army, had saved the reserve artillery.[32]

The Boteler's Ford affair provoked artillery lieutenant Ham Chamberlayne to say hard things of General Pendleton, but he concluded in somewhat milder vein: "... Pendleton is Lee's weakness. He is like the elephant, we have him & we don't know what on earth to do with him, and it costs a devil of a sight to feed him."

In the end, Lee's report of the Maryland expedition dismissed Pendleton's part in the affair with two cold sentences: "General Pendleton was left to guard the ford with the reserve artillery and about 600 infantry. That night the enemy crossed the river above General Pendleton's position, and his infantry support giving way, four of his guns were taken." That was all, although it seemed to satisfy Pendleton. Rarely, after that day in September 1862, did he command any infantry. Had he done so, it is safe to say that he would, at the least, have counted them.[33]

CHAPTER 18

Rebuilding an Army

1. LONGSTREET AND JACKSON STEP UP

Driving the Federals into the Potomac at Shepherdstown greatly relieved the feeling of the army, which refused to admit that it had been worsted in Maryland. The Southern press was like-minded. The *Richmond Enquirer* assured readers that if there had been a withdrawal, it was to cope with a flanking operation against Harper's Ferry. Sharpsburg, said that authoritative journal, had witnessed "one of the most complete victories that has yet immortalized the Confederate arms." This optimistic language did not stifle rumors. In Charleston, Rhett's *Mercury* gloomily remarked that the recrossing of the Potomac to Shepherdstown was a "movement which, to the unmilitary eye, with no more subtle guide than the map, would certainly resemble a retreat."

Richmond papers still would not have it so. They continued to assert a Confederate victory and the achievement of the objects of the campaign, which were described as the capture of Harper's Ferry and "the rousing of Maryland." Not until after September 25 were they willing to concede that the entire army was back in Virginia. The maximum the *Richmond Dispatch* ever admitted was that "the victory, though not so decisive as that of Manassas, was certainly a Confederate victory."[1]

In none of the comment on Sharpsburg was reference made to the condition which was second only to the prowess of the individual fighter on that field. That condition was the success of the Confederate command in bringing every unit at hand into action. At Second Manassas that same ideal of combat had been achieved offensively. Sharpsburg was cheering proof that the full cry of pursuit on Longstreet's front at Manassas had not been the result of lucky accident.

Among other reasons, Second Manassas was won and Sharpsburg not lost because direction by two men, Longstreet and Jackson, under Lee's orders, had succeeded the system of semi-autonomous, frequently jealous, and often uncooperative divisions. That awkward system, which had proved so nearly ruinous during the Seven Days, had been forced on Johnston and then on Lee by the fact that Confederate law had not provided for any unit larger than a division. The device employed after June, of placing a number of divisions under Longstreet and Jackson, scarcely would have been possible had not those two able men been senior major generals. The restrictions of the statute had been accepted in theory and obviated in practice because the two senior divisional commanders fortunately were good soldiers.

Now the law was changed for the better. A brief amendatory act, approved by the President September 18, 1862, provided for the organization of divisions into corps, which units were to be commanded by officers of the new grade of lieutenant general. The President asked Lee's opinion concerning the men who should be promoted. Outside his own army, Lee recommended Kirby Smith. In it, he felt that two corps commanders would suffice.[2]

One of these should be Longstreet. To that conclusion Lee came so readily that when he wrote Davis on the subject he did not think it necessary to elaborate on Longstreet's merit or record. Both had been distinguished during the Maryland expedition. Longstreet's judgment in deferring attack at Second Manassas on August 29 perhaps was questionable; his mood may not have been the most cooperative when he learned of Lee's purpose to detach Jackson for operations against Harper's Ferry; but after that his counsel had been wise and his handling of his troops all that could be asked.

His A.A.G., Moxley Sorrel, did not overpraise the performance at Sharpsburg he thus described: "He seemed everywhere along his extended lines, and his tenacity and deep-set resolution, his inmost courage, which appeared to swell with the growing peril to the army, undoubtedly stimulated the troops to greater action, and held them in place despite all weakness." When the fight was over, and Longstreet was able to report to field headquarters, Lee rewarded him with words that made Old Pete's staff officers swell with pride: "Ah! Here is Longstreet; here's my old *war-horse!* Let us hear what he has to say." The next day, September 18, Old Pete concluded that the extension of the Federal right to the Potomac was in such strength that the army should return to the Virginia shore. When Lee came to his bivouac that evening and expressed his intention of withdrawing from Maryland, Longstreet was so much pleased his view coincided with Lee's that he recorded the fact in his report.[3]

If, then, Longstreet was to be one of the two new lieutenant generals of the army, was Jackson to be the other? On the basis of military performance, could there be any other choice? Stonewall's part in the operations around Manassas had been flawless. No allowance had to be made there for lack of experience in handling large bodies of men. Had Jackson done as well in Maryland? He undeniably had closed in slowly on Harper's Ferry, and had shown there a certain awkwardness in the use of signals. An exacting critic might have disputed on the seventeenth the tactical wisdom of placing Lawton's and Hays's brigades where they were at the time of Hooker's onslaught. These three matters apart, Jackson's capture of the Ferry and his tenacious battle on the left at Sharpsburg had been shrewd, vigorous, and free of mistakes. His achievement was the more remarkable because A. P. Hill, Ewell, and Trimble were absent, the trusted Winder was dead, and eight of the fourteen brigades had colonels, some of limited experience, at their head.

That the divisions on the left could be held together at Sharpsburg, even at the price of excessive casualties, evidenced not only Jackson's ability *in se,* but also his influence over his subordinates. Many of his lieutenants were developing a faith in him as a leader comparable to that which great captains of the past had aroused. Sandie Pendleton wrote, when the expedition was ended, "I have been reading Carlyle's "Cromwell." General Jackson is the exact counterpart of Oliver in every respect, as Carlyle draws him."[4]

Jackson proved himself at Sharpsburg as stubborn in conflict as "Old Nol." As soon as his front grew comparatively calm, he sought out Walker and, while he made his lunch off apples plucked from a tree, Old Jack planned a counter-stroke on the left. "We'll drive McClellan into the Antietam!" he said confidently; but he found he could not challenge the powerful batteries the Union commanders had placed to guard their flank. The next morning, September 18, he was at the front soon after daylight. When he found John B. Hood there his instant question was, "Hood, have they gone?" A negative answer brought a regretful, "I hoped they had," and he went on to see how fared his own exhausted troops. All day Jackson awaited, almost eagerly, the attack that did not come.[5]

One thing only marred Jackson's fine record during the entire operation from Cedar Mountain to Shepherdstown. That was his relations with A. P. Hill. The fiery commander of the Light Division had no intention of accepting the stigma of arrest. At the first moment the army was free of pressure after Sharpsburg, Powell Hill addressed to the commanding general an application for a court of inquiry on Jackson's charges. He was determined that Jackson should explain the public humiliation of a fellow-officer. Jackson endorsed the application with a summary statement of the facts as he saw them, and stated flatly, "I found that under his successor, General Branch, my orders were much better carried out."

General Lee faced the difficult task of maintaining Jackson's authority and of applying an emollient to the bruised sensibilities of Hill, whom he regarded as an excellent officer. Lee's immediate conclusion was that the circumstances did not justify an inquiry. In endorsing Hill's application, he mentioned "what appeared to be neglect of duty . . . but which from an officer of his character could not be intentional and I feel assured will never be repeated," and concluded, "I see no advantage to the service in further investigating this matter. . . ."[6]

For once, Lee's tact failed to relieve unpleasantness. The sensitive Hill misinterpreted Lee's reference to "what appeared to be neglect of duty" which "will never be repeated" as acceptance of Jackson's charges. Vigorously, on September 30, Hill renewed his application for a court of inquiry. "I deny the truth of every allegation made by Major General Jackson," he wrote Lee, "and am prepared to prove my denial by any number of honorable men." Nor was that all: On his own account, Hill drew up charges against Jackson and boldly forwarded them to Jackson to be sent to Lee.

The matter presented Jackson with something of a puzzle. He had no reason to find fault with Hill's conduct during the Maryland expedition. Hill had obeyed every order with promptness and with precision, and he had won the plaudits of the entire army. Jackson concluded he should accept Hill's virtual challenge to present charges and specifications, but Old Jack decided that in sending these to Lee he would state personally he did not think a hearing was necessary. The result was Jackson's charges of neglect of duty, in eight specifications. He explained he was not presenting the charges because he wished Hill brought to trial, but he could not forbear arguing the points Hill had made in the renewed application for an inquiry.

A stubborn temper there was on both sides, a temper so stubborn the patient Lee did not attempt forthwith to bend it. Instead he applied his usual philosophy and left to time what he could not himself settle: Hill's renewed application and charges against Jackson, along with those of Jackson against Hill, were put in the confidential files at headquarters and left to slumber there. Quietly Lee exercised his discretion of deciding in any given case whether charges should be brought before a court.[7]

Was this unhappy affair to be weighted against Jackson? Was he to be denied promotion to lieutenant general and corps command because he always was having difficulties with one or another of his subordinates? Apparently Lee did not take this into account at all, or if he did, he counted it for righteousness on Jackson's part that discipline was inculcated, even though the method was stern.

If Lee had felt any concern about Jackson, it had been on different ground. In his letter to the President, Lee wrote: "I can confidently recommend Generals Longstreet and Jackson, in this army." Of Longstreet he said not another word. Concerning Jackson the language of the commanding general was somewhat unusual. Was Lee revealing his own previous doubts, or was he seeking to relieve the President's misgivings? "My opinion of the merits of General Jackson," he wrote, "has been greatly enhanced during this expedition. He is true, honest, and brave; has a single eye to the good of the service, and spares no exertion to accomplish his object."[8] What was behind the "enhancement" of Lee's opinion? Why should it be in order to speak of an eye to the good of the service? The evidence does not permit an answer, but Lee's opinion was one he never changed later. From the time of these operations, Lee's trust in Jackson and his confidence in the abilities of Stonewall were absolute. Every new experience was to increase the respect of general and lieutenant each for the other.

The response of the two men themselves to their new honors was typical of the difference between them. Longstreet's reflections on his rise in military rank nowhere appear. If there was any change in him, it was an enlargement of his confidence in his own military judgment. In the close and costly fight at Sharpsburg, he had seen the vindication of his view that the army should not have been divided for the capture of Harper's Ferry. Feeling that he was right and Lee wrong, he may have considered himself the better soldier of the two.

Jackson's feeling about his promotion was one of a deliberate subordination of the soldier to the Christian. When his wife joyfully congratulated him and asked if she might have an article prepared about him, he wrote back in Cromwellian spirit: "It is gratifying to be beloved and to have our conduct approved by our fellow-men, but this is not worthy to be compared to the glory that is in reservation for us in the presence of our glorified Redeemer. . . . It appears to me that it would be better for you not to have anything written about me. Let us follow the teaching of inspiration—'Let another man praise thee, and not thine own mouth: a stranger, and not thine own lips.' "[9] Was it difficult for him to write that?

2. A CRISIS IN REORGANIZATION

Promotion of Longstreet and Jackson legalized and facilitated the system of command Lee had created after the Seven Days, but among general officers of lower rank that organization had now to be rebuilt. Cedar Mountain, Second Manassas, South Mountain, and Sharpsburg had taken exorbitant toll. The loss of Winder at Cedar Mountain and the wounding of Ewell, Taliaferro, Trimble, and Field at Second Manassas had been followed at South Mountain by the death of Garland. At Sharpsburg the number of slain general officers proved to be three. George B. Anderson, who appeared to have been wounded slightly, died on October 16. He was thirty-one and had graduated high at West Point. In command of a brigade under D. H. Hill, he had displayed qualities of stout leadership. All the physical excellencies coveted by soldiers were abundantly his—a handsome figure, fine horsemanship, a commanding presence that inspired his regiments. A soldier's death, in combat, had come to Brigadier W. E. Starke, who had succeeded to field command of Jackson's old division after John R. Jones had reported himself incapacitated. The other general who fell in the Maryland expedition was L. O'Brien Branch. "He was," A. P. Hill wrote sorrowfully, "my senior brigadier, and one to whom I could have intrusted the command of the division, with all confidence."[10]

Besides these three whose names had to be stricken permanently from the rolls, five generals had been wounded—Dick Anderson, Robert Toombs, Rans Wright, R. S. Ripley, and Alexander Lawton. Of these the man whose absence would be most seriously felt was Anderson. His brigadiers were of unequal ability. The senior of them, Roger Pryor, was by no means the most skillful in combat. If Anderson were to be incapacitated for any length of time, transfer of at least one of the brigade commanders would be necessary to assure competent handling of the division. Below brigade command the casualties had been grievous. Two colonels had been killed at South Mountain and eight at Sharpsburg. Among the lieutenant colonels the slaughter had been heavy. For the corps of officers as a whole, it never had reached such ghastly totals.

D. H. Hill, in five small brigades at South Mountain and Sharpsburg, lost one brigadier general killed, one mortally wounded, three brigade commanders wounded, four colonels slain, eight colonels wounded, one lieutenant colonel killed and seven wounded. Colquitt's brigade of that division had gone into action at Sharpsburg with ten field officers. Four of these were fatalities, five were badly wounded, and the tenth was stunned by a shell. In Lawton's brigade all save one of the regimental commanders was killed or wounded. Hays lost all his staff and all the men who led his regiments. In Trimble's brigade the colonel commanding and three of the four officers at the heads of regiments were casualties; the fourth was seriously wounded on the twentieth at Boteler's Ford. In Jackson's division the higher officers had been massacred—no less. When the battle shifted from the left that red seventeenth of September, what was left of the division was under command of a colonel, A. J. Grigsby. The famous Stonewall Brigade was commanded by a major. Taliaferro's and Starke's brigades were in the charge of colonels. Jones's brigade was in the hands of a captain who had succeeded two other captains shot down.

Summarized for the army, these frightful losses meant that for longer or shorter periods during the operations in Maryland, this situation existed: The commanders of nine divisions, instead of being nine major generals, had been four generals of that grade, four brigadiers, and, in the last hours of Sharpsburg, one colonel. The end of action on the seventeenth found fourteen general officers only in command of brigades. Colonels or officers of lower rank led the remaining twenty-six brigades. Some brigades were smaller than regiments should have been. Regiments, which long had been too thin, were in numerous instances bare companies.

This was a crisis in command. The army could not continue under temporary officers. Straggling, which so nearly had wrecked the Maryland expedition, was due in part to the inexperience or incompetence of officers who led in the absence of sick or wounded seniors. Here, again, the law was at fault. Under existing Confederate statute, the colonels, in order of seniority, exercised brigade command during the absence, however prolonged, of the brigadier general. In the higher grades the same rule applied. A major general might be incapacitated for months; seniority might make the least competent of his brigadiers acting division commander; but nothing could be done under the law to replace the incapacitated major general or to rid the division of an acting commander not qualified to discharge his duties.

The statutes required, moreover, that vacancies below the rank of general officer be filled by promotion or election. For amendment of this paralyzing law, Lee appealed to the War Department, and Secretary Randolph laid the issue before the Congress. The condition of the Army of Northern Virginia, he explained, required conferring on the President "the power of appointment, where neither promotion by seniority nor election will furnish competent officers." Randolph added, "the experience of the commanding general of that army has been unable to devise any expedient by which he may avoid the alternative of violating law or of exposing his army to ruin."[11]

Of all this President Davis was most unhappily conscious, but he also was aware of the political difficulties. First, on October 8, he asked Congress for authority to appoint from within brigade officers for any regiment of that brigade when neither election nor promotion would assure competent leadership. He spoke in strong words: "Tender consideration for worthless and incompetent officers is but another name for cruelty toward the brave men who fall sacrifices to these defects of their leaders." Two days later he sought "some provision by which brigadier and major generals may be appointed when, by the casualties of service, commanders of brigades and divisions have become temporarily disabled."[12]

The Congress proceeded to compromise between the counsel of the President and the "democratic" organization of the army. First, it set up a complicated arrangement whereby an "examining board" would pass on the competency of any officer of any grade. Upon proof of incompetency, a successor would be named from the same command, by seniority or by examination. Only in the event no qualified man could be found within the command was the President authorized to make an appointment, which had to be from the same state. The most any commanding general could hope to accomplish under this act would be to remove, by a slow, complicated, often angry proceeding, an officer manifestly, perhaps notoriously, incompetent. Even then the restrictions were so stiff that there was no assurance that the man who took his place would be any better.

A more acceptable if evasive compromise was a second law which authorized the President, with the advice and consent of the Senate, to appoint twenty general officers and "assign them to such appropriate duties as he might deem expedient." This meant that where the promotion to brigade command of the senior colonel could not be justified, the President could go outside the brigade and select a general for it. Wise selection would strengthen the shattered brigade and divisional command of the Army of Northern Virginia.[13]

With Jackson and Longstreet promoted, two new major generals had to be named to take their old commands. In addition, as Ewell's return to the field was doubtful, there was the possibility of a major general to lead Ewell's division. A fourth promotion to the same grade was being arranged. Whiting's division of two brigades, which Hood had led, now was increased to the standard of four brigades by the assignment of Tige Anderson's and Toombs's commands. Its head would be entitled to rank as a major general.

Prospects of four promotions to coveted divisional rank aroused the ambitions of perhaps half a score. Trimble and Early made no concealment of their desire to change the buttons on their coat and to lead a division. Lawton, for his part, could not see why he, the senior brigadier of the entire army and *ipso facto* the senior in Ewell's division, should not have Old Bald Head's place. Toombs felt that he deserved, though he did not expect, promotion for his conduct at Sharpsburg. Longstreet sought promotion for George Pickett, who was his senior brigadier and in spirit his younger brother. Jackson felt that John B. Hood, though not under his command, deserved promotion and he so wrote the adjutant general.

Hood's record fully justified praise. He had remained under arrest as a result of his controversy with Shanks Evans, but on the afternoon of September 14, approaching South Mountain, Lee had told him, "I will suspend your arrest until the impending battle is decided." After Hood's stubborn and persistent fighting at Sharpsburg, no more was said about arrest. Hood himself described the fighting on the Confederate left as "the most terrible . . . by far, that has occurred during the war."[14]

Of Hood's merit Lee was no less appreciative. He had approved if he had not suggested the enlargement of Hood's division. The one difficulty in the way of his promotion was to dispose of the difficult Whiting, who had now returned from sick leave. If Whiting took the division again, Hood's promotion would be blocked. Lee found a way of effecting his purpose. He knew that Whiting had exceptional ability as an engineer, and he urged on the War Department that he be sent to some other post where engineering skill was needed. Within three days Whiting was ordered to repair to Richmond and report to the secretary of war for duty.[15]

With the way cleared for Hood, who were the other new major generals to be? Jackson advocated the promotion of I. R. Trimble. Of an assault by Trimble at Second Manassas, Jackson wrote: "I regard that day's achievement as the most brilliant that has come under my observation during the present war." That was a tribute not lightly to be disregarded. "Brilliant" indeed was a feat which drew that adjective from Old Jack. Such commendation gave Trimble an advantage that his comrade in Ewell's division, the shrewd and cynical Jubal Early, scarcely would have had a chance of overcoming; but Early's achievement at Sharpsburg had been entirely comparable to that of Trimble at Manassas. Old Jubilee, in fact, was one of the heroes of September 17. He showed himself tenacious, cool, and hard-hitting, earning praise in the reports of Lee, Jeb Stuart, and Jackson himself. Early had, in short, shown himself capable of handling a division. The sole question was whether the War Department would regard Ewell as incapacitated and give his division to Early, or, failing that, could find a vacancy for Old Jube.[16]

If three or four brigadiers were to be major generals, a corresponding number of vacancies in brigade command would be created. In addition, successors to Garland, George B. Anderson, and Branch had to be named. A leader for Starke's brigade was already named: Colonel Francis T. Nicholls, of Taylor's old Louisiana brigade, who had been wounded at Winchester and later had been captured and exchanged. Roswell Ripley was to return to South Carolina at the request of Governor Pickens. No successors had been named to Gabriel Rains or Joseph R. Anderson. The brigades that David Jones and J. G. Walker had directed before they assumed divisional command should have regular commanders. With eleven, twelve, perhaps fourteen or fifteen promotions thus in prospect, there must have been extensive wire-pulling by ambitious colonels.

Old Jack wanted a brigadier's commission for his acting A.A.G., Major Frank Paxton, thirty-four years of age, God-fearing, industrious, and prior to the war a lawyer and bank president. Paxton had risen to be a major in the 27th Virginia of the Stonewall Brigade but had failed of election; he lacked the art of ingratiating himself with the men. Jackson had a good opinion of him, and wished not only to give Paxton three stars and a wreath on the collar, but also to entrust to him the Stonewall Brigade itself.

In like spirit, Longstreet must have urged the advancement of John R. Cooke, whose performance with his 23rd North Carolina and the 3rd Arkansas was commended in every report from that of his divisional chief upward to Lee himself. Longstreet used the high phrase "very gallantly" in describing the charge of the young North Carolinian. On a par with Cooke's performance, in the estimation of senior officers, was that of John B. Gordon. After receiving his fifth wound he was carried to the rear and thence across the Potomac, where he recovered under the devoted nursing of his wife. D. H. Hill styled Gordon the "Chevalier Bayard of the army" and asserted that he had excelled his feats at Seven Pines and in the later battles around Richmond. "Our language," Hill concluded, "is not capable of expressing a higher compliment."[17]

In personal valor many had shone on the hills above the Antietam. Former Governor Smith—Extra Billy—of the 49th Virginia had been conspicuous. When Early had succeeded temporarily to Ewell's division, command of Early's brigade had passed to Extra Billy, who had just observed his sixty-fifth birthday. Thrice wounded, he directed his troops till the battle was over. Jeb Stuart observed the old colonel, dripping blood but fighting gallantly, "conspicuously brave and self-possessed." Smith was rivaled in prowess by Colonel A. J. Grigsby, who late in the action led Jackson's division, and by Colonel Leroy A. Stafford, who handled Starke's brigade until a wound compelled him to leave the field.[18]

Other colonels had distinguished themselves during the Maryland expedition not only for bravery but also for intelligent leadership and for their administrative capacity, on which Lee put high valuation. All this had to be taken into account in recommendations for promotion. For some brigades, seniority could be respected without risk to the service.

Monty Corse of the 17th Virginia had been mentioned by Longstreet as "one of the most gallant and worthy officers in this army . . . distinguished in at least ten of the severest battles of the war." Lee also had a word for the "gallant colonel" of the 17th Virginia. If Pickett were promoted, Corse seemed the logical successor in brigade command. Similarly, if Trimble or the long-absent Arnold Elzey became a major general, Jim Walker of the 13th Virginia fitly could take his place. Carnot Posey of the 16th Mississippi could measure up in the event that W.S. Featherston did not return from his sick leave. Should Bob Toombs conclude that he had won enough fame to avenge himself on Davis, then Toombs's brigade could go to his fellow-Georgian, capable Tom Cobb, Howell's younger brother—a succession that Toombs could not protest.[19]

The decision at army headquarters was to fill the certain, the probable, and the hoped-for vacancies. Here, in the end, were the names Lee submitted on October 27:[20]

To be major general

George E. Pickett, for command of the larger part of Longstreet's old division.

I. R. Trimble, for assignment to the command of Jackson's division.

Jubal A. Early, for command of Ewell's division in the event that a successor to Ewell was deemed necessary.

To be brigadier general

Carnot Posey, colonel of the 16th Mississippi, to succeed W. S. Featherston of Anderson's division, who was absent sick.

M. D. Corse, colonel of the 17th Virginia, to have the brigade of George E. Pickett, promoted.

J. B. Robertson, colonel of the 5th Texas, to be in charge of the Texas Brigade.

G. T. (Tige) Anderson, to permanent command of D. R. Jones's brigade, which he had been directing as senior colonel.

T. R. R. Cobb, colonel of Cobb's Legion, in the event of a vacancy created by the wounding of Robert Toombs.

John R. Cooke, colonel of the 27th North Carolina, to command the brigade of J. G. Walker, who was directing a small division.

E. F. Paxton, major and A.A.G., to have the Stonewall Brigade.

James A. Walker, colonel of the 13th Virginia, to command Trimble's or Elzey's brigade.

William (Extra Billy) Smith of the 49th Virginia to the brigade of Ewell's division not given Walker.

George Doles, colonel of the 4th Georgia, to succeed R. S. Ripley, detached.

S. Dodson Ramseur, colonel of the 49th North Carolina, to have the brigade of George B. Anderson, mortally wounded.

John B. Gordon, colonel of the 6th Alabama, to command Rains's old brigade, which had been under Colonel A. H. Colquitt.

James H. Lane, colonel of the 28th North Carolina, to succeed L. O'B. Branch, killed in action.

Alfred Iverson, colonel of the 20th North Carolina, to take the brigade of Samuel Garland, killed at South Mountain.

E. L. Thomas, colonel of the 35th Georgia, to the permanent command of Joseph R. Anderson's brigade, which he had been leading as senior colonel.

Unfortunately, this list was marred almost as soon as it was made. General Featherston returned from sick leave and resumed command of his brigade, which Lee had planned to give to Carnot Posey. Next, Lee found that A. H. Colquitt had been promoted brigadier by the War Department, closing the vacancy to which Lee had been anxious to promote John B. Gordon. Still again, E. A. Perry of the 2nd Florida was named brigadier with a view to assigning him command of the Florida regiments. Whether or not this was engineered to remove Roger Pryor from temporary command of Anderson's division, it had that effect. It deprived the editor and ex-congressman of his troops, and Lee made no effort to keep Pryor with the army by providing another brigade for him. He suggested Pryor for the force Gustavus Smith was developing in Southside Virginia.

When Lee's recommendations had been hammered to fit these conditions and then rolled through the political mill by a President who sought to please both Lee and the Senate, they emerged with these differences: Early and Trimble were not promoted; Gordon was appointed, but immediate confirmation was not sought; Carnot Posey, James A. Walker, and Extra Billy Smith were passed over. Those promoted to divisional command thus were Pickett and Hood. The new brigadiers were Monty Corse, T. R. R. Cobb, J. B. Robertson, Tige Anderson, John R. Cooke, George Doles, S. Dodson Ramseur, Alfred Iverson, James H. Lane, E. L. Thomas, and Frank Paxton.

One of the two recorded instances of outspoken resentment of the promotions was in Jackson's cherished Stonewall Brigade, where the elevation of Frank Paxton made many faces red and loosed hot tongues. Jackson had asked the appointment because he did not think a single one of the regimental officers was as well qualified to direct the brigade as was Paxton. Within the brigade there was vehement disagreement. Jackson's judgment of men often had been disputed; some of his appointees had been failures;

his partiality for Presbyterians often had been alleged. Never had all these criticisms been so combined as now. The leader of the opposition to Paxton was the colonel of the 27th Virginia, Andrew Jackson Grigsby. He felt that he had earned promotion, and when he failed to receive it he resigned. "Colonel Grigsby was filled with resentment," McHenry Howard remembered, ". . . and told me that for the good of the service he would do nothing while the war lasted, but that as soon as it ended he would certainly challenge Jackson."[21]

The other protest was over the promotion of Monty Corse instead of Eppa Hunton, who was his senior in commission and had been in more numerous battles. Other colonels of Pickett's brigade came to Hunton and proposed that all of them resign in order to show their disapproval. Gallant Eppa Hunton would not hear of it: All of them must remain and do their duty.[22]

This spirit eased the difficult task of General Lee, who had made the best of the material he had. Some good men he had found and promoted. In some he was to be disappointed. He could not hope quickly to replace such men as Winder and Garland, or to find division commanders to measure up forthwith to the stature of the wounded Ewell and Dick Anderson. When weak were balanced against strong, the unpromising against the able, the major gain of the reorganization was the advancement of Longstreet and Jackson.

3. The Balance of the Two Corps

The reorganization of the army into two corps, the First under Longstreet, the Second under Jackson, was announced formally on November 6. Longstreet was given McLaws's, Anderson's, Walker's, Hood's, and his own division, which last, after the two brigades were given Hood, was Pickett's. To the Second Corps were apportioned Jackson's own sadly depleted division, Ewell's division, and those of A. P. Hill and D. H. Hill.

From this organization, at the outset, disappeared David R. Jones. This was because of the failure of his health, not because of the failure of his leadership. He had not been a brilliant division commander but had been capable, direct, and honorable and had won Longstreet's commendation. Lee, in his final report, had praise for his "determined and brave resistance" at Sharpsburg. Before this tribute appeared in the official accounts of the battle, Jones was to breathe his last, a victim of heart disease.[23]

John G. Walker disappeared, also, before he fairly could take his place in the new First Corps. Promoted major general, he was ordered to the Trans-Mississippi Department. His two brigades passed temporarily to their senior brigadier, Robert Ransom, Jr. Almost at the same time, the army lost the picturesque Shanks Evans as the result of a call by the War Department for the dispatch of a brigade to Weldon, North Carolina.

As the new corps took on some permanence of character, a critic might have compared their divisional and brigade commands and, in the light of the battles that had culminated at Sharpsburg, asked how well balanced they were. Was there anything in their constitution to suggest that the First might be the corps of defense and the Second of offense? Did the Second have in it men who would see that it outmarched the First?

Of Longstreet's divisional commanders, Hood could be regarded as a leader of high promise and Dick Anderson as a soldier of competence. Pickett was untried at his new rank, but he had been an excellent brigade leader and with Longstreet's full support was apt to direct with wisdom his larger force. The one division chief of the First Corps regarding whom the Maryland expedition had raised any doubts was the stout and comradely Lafayette McLaws. During the greater part of the time the army was in Maryland, McLaws had exercised semi-autonomous command without conspicuous success. He erred in not making better reconnaissance at Crampton's Gap, though he was unintentionally misled by Jeb Stuart concerning the strength of the enemy in that quarter. The second time McLaws went astray was in not picketing a road running under the flank of Maryland Heights, despite Stuart's counsel. In consequence, on the night of the fourteenth all the Federal cavalry at Harper's Ferry escaped, intercepting part of Longstreet's trains en route.[24]

More serious than this dereliction was the slowness of McLaws's march to join Lee at Sharpsburg. He received his marching orders during the early afternoon of September 15, but it was 8:00 A.M. September 16 before he bivouacked at Halltown, four miles from his starting point. Sharpsburg was distant fifteen miles, but McLaws required twenty-three hours to cover that distance. In all, some forty-one hours elapsed from the time he received his orders on Maryland Heights until he reached his objective. He attributed his slow march to the exhaustion of his men from their fighting, their loss of sleep, and their inability to get or to cook rations. This excuse was not entirely acceptable to Lee. In his report he came as close to censure of McLaws as ever he did in written comment on his officers' performances: "Owing to the condition of his troops and other circumstances, his progress was slow. . . ." What the "other circumstances" were the commanding general, with his usual reserve, did not specify. His language did not carry with it any implications that McLaws had failed; it did raise a question whether McLaws would succeed and, more particularly, whether he could make his division march.[25]

Longstreet's five newly commissioned brigadiers would have to stand the test of promotion. Some at least might exhibit the familiar tragedy of being advanced beyond the grade for which they were qualified—and of remaining colonels in ability though they were generals in title. If Toombs refused to return to an army in which he was not a major general, his brigade would be well handled by Henry Benning. In the odd circumstance that led not Robert Toombs but Howell Cobb to stand aside in order that his brother Thomas might be a brigadier there was prospect for improvement; Howell Cobb was not held responsible for the bloody reverse at Crampton's Gap, but he was not considered as able as his brother.

With the best of these men of brigade and divisional rank Longstreet could hope to make his corps strong and reliable, but none save one had displayed qualities of eminence. The exception was Hood. In battle there was about him some of the effulgence of the true captain of men. Anyone would have said, after Gaines' Mill, that of all the officers under Longstreet the most likely to be a great soldier was Hood.

In the Second Corps there was no provision for filling Ewell's place and none for supplying Jackson's division with an officer of appropriate rank. Until Ewell was able to return to duty or was retired by formal action, the law left his troops in the care of his senior brigadier. This would put the division under Lawton when that earnest but relatively inexperienced officer recovered from the wound received at Sharpsburg. In the event Lawton did not return, the division would be well used by Jube Early. Jackson's division was intended for Trimble, but that vigorous fighter could not be assigned until he was well enough to serve. There was uncertainty on that score, for he had developed camp erysipelas and a malady that probably was an osteomyelitis.

Jackson's reliance, for the autumn, had to be on Harvey Hill and Powell Hill. With the one his relations presumably were as cordial as with the other they unhappily were strained. No less sharp was the contrast between the records of "the two Hills" during the Maryland expedition. Harvey Hill's handling of the action on South Mountain seems to have been unfavorably appraised, at least among certain irreverent junior officers. Said young Ham Chamberlayne: "People up here are very generally beginning to call D. H. Hill a numskull. If Harper's Ferry had held out 24 hours longer, as it should have done, D.H. would have cost us our army, our life, our freedom."[26] At Sharpsburg Harvey Hill had been stubborn and personally courageous. He proved that day, by comparison with his performance at South Mountain, that he was at his best when he had good men on either side of him and was fighting without full responsibility for the field. In that type of combat he had no superior. Off the field, however,

Hill's disposition to find fault with his comrades helps to explain the difficulty of using to best advantage his undeniable excellencies.

Powell Hill's record had been, all in all, the best by any division commander, except perhaps Hood. Much of the burden of maneuver and preparation had fallen to the Light Division at Harper's Ferry. Hill's march to Sharpsburg had equaled the best performance of Jackson's foot cavalry. Nothing had been lacking in the fierce and well-directed attack of the division at the moment the battle almost was lost. Lee, in his report, described the attack as the decisive move of the day. Proud and sensitive the commander of the Light Division was, but diligent in camp and furious in battle. If he and Jackson could work together, his brigades might prove to be the backbone of the new Second Corps. They were well organized; together they were numerically stronger than any other division; they had fewer officers of rank absent on account of wounds.

The brigadiers of Jackson's corps were, at the moment, about on a par with those of Longstreet—five new generals, the same number as in the First Corps. The gamble on individuals was in proportion. Nothing indicated any particular doubt concerning Alfred Iverson, colonel of the 20th North Carolina, who was advanced to the command of Garland's brigade. No distress was expressed that George Doles of the 4th Georgia had replaced Roswell Ripley, ordered to service in South Carolina. The experience of Ripley at South Mountain had not been happy. D. H. Hill complained in his report that "Ripley did not draw trigger," and that night, in withdrawing, Ripley forgot altogether the 4th Georgia, which narrowly escaped capture. At Sharpsburg Ripley's personal conduct, as always, was courageous and bold. The choleric general was carried to the rear with a neck wound, but within an hour and a half he was back with his men and able to keep the field till action was concluded. Doles, who succeeded him, had been a businessman in Georgia before the war, but he had aptitude for the military life and as a colonel had shown fiber and vigor.[27]

Nothing was done immediately in the case of President Davis's close friend, Thomas F. Drayton. In Maryland the poor performance of Drayton's troops at Manassas was twice duplicated. Even the considerate commanding general had to admit to the President that the brigade "broke to pieces" at South Mountain and Sharpsburg.[28]

These were minor weaknesses in the Second Corps. A majority of the brigade commanders were capable and some of them were rich in promise. Particularly this was true of Powell Hill's subordinates. Branch would be missed, but Jim Lane, who succeeded to the brigade, was a two-fisted, vigorously human commander. Especially had Archer and Pender distinguished themselves in Maryland. On the heights above Burnside's Bridge

Archer was so ill that he scarcely could keep his saddle, but in his handling of his brigade there had been nothing feeble, nothing doubtful. At Harper's Ferry and Shepherdstown Dorsey Pender had shown himself qualified to handle more than one brigade. The forthright young general had increasingly the confidence of his chief.

The artillery had won at Sharpsburg honors that equaled those of any of these infantry commands. Outranged, outgunned, and exposed to better projectiles than they could return, the Confederates had suffered frightfully. On Jackson's wing, John Pelham held control of a dominating hill to the left with the spirit and fire the army had come to expect of him. On the center, where Boyce and Miller distinguished themselves, the most shining figure was Colonel Stephen D. Lee, who commanded a battalion of six batteries stationed near the Dunker church during much of the heaviest fighting. On the opposite flank, A. P. Hill reported his satisfaction with the service of his "splendid batteries." As always, Captain William Pegram was in the heaviest of the action and for the first time was wounded. In the reorganization following the battle, Stephen D. Lee was promoted brigadier general and ordered to Vicksburg. To his battalion was assigned another young artillerist who was to win fame both as a participant in and as a historian of the campaigns of the Army of Northern Virginia—Lieutenant Colonel E. Porter Alexander.[29]

In the cavalry, also, after Sharpsburg, praise was distributed and reorganization was undertaken. For Jeb Stuart's part in the campaign there was no stint of the applause he loved. Performance justified praise, but for the first time Stuart almost had a rival. Fitz Lee's conduct was so fine that his uncle, the commanding general, though careful never to display his deep pride of family, could not ignore what Fitz had done. He covered admirably the withdrawal from South Mountain, delayed the advance of the Federals to Sharpsburg, and held the enemy in check the morning after the infantry recrossed the Potomac into Virginia. Stuart had high words of praise for Fitz Lee, but in commendation of Hampton, who had done splendid service, he was not so warm; nor was he generous toward Colonel Tom Munford, who had defended Crampton's Gap, or Colonel Tom Rosser, who had held off the Federals atop South Mountain. Stuart's silence may have been the result of oversight; it may have been the first expression of jealousy.

Reorganization of the cavalry, dictated by the increase in the number of units, involved the creation of another brigade. To the command of this, Rooney Lee, colonel of the 9th Virginia cavalry and second son of the general-in-chief, was named. Stuart, and not the new brigadier's father, doubtless was responsible for this. By the transfer of Beverly Robertson a vacancy had been created at the head of the Laurel Brigade, which included Ashby's old command. In Maryland this brigade had been led by Colonel Tom Munford, but, contrary to Stuart's wishes, the promotion went to William E. ("Grumble") Jones, colonel of the 7th Virginia—an appointment that was to bring Jones into difficulties. This was followed by a transfer of a few regiments to give approximately equal strength to each of the four cavalry brigades.

Deserved as were most of the promotions of October and November, the real hero of the army at Sharpsburg was, once more, the army itself. Lee had said of it, soon after it had entered Maryland, ". . . the material of which it is composed is the best in the world, and, if properly disciplined and instructed, would be able successfully to resist any force that could be brought against it." When the 40,000 who remained to fight, footsore and hungry, had beaten off the attacks at Sharpsburg, Lee could have echoed the exclamation of J. R. Jones: "In this fight every officer and man was a hero. . . ." That spirit in Maryland—and not Early, or Cooke, or Hood, or Powell Hill, or even Jackson and Lee—made the Army of Northern Virginia "terrible in battle."[30]

4. HOW TO ACCOMPLISH "THE IMPOSSIBLE"

Restful weeks those of the early autumn of 1862 were for an army that had been fighting since June. Monotonous weeks they might have been, too, if Jeb Stuart had not offered one question, at least, for campfire debate. That question was whether he and his men ever should have attempted the October raid, or having undertaken it, should have escaped with whole hides.

The operation originated, so far as the records show, not with the chief of cavalry but with the army commander. Lee wished to know what McClellan was doing and where the Union forces were spread. A reconnaissance in force seemed to be justified and might be extended to a raid pushed as far as Chambersburg. North of the town the Cumberland Valley Railroad crossed a branch of Conococheague Creek. By burning the bridge there the Southern cavalry could stop the southward movement of supplies to the Federal railhead at Hagerstown, forcing McClellan to rely exclusively on the B. & O. for railway communication. That prospect was worth the risk of a brief "expedition," as Lee chose to style it.

Stuart was delighted with the assignment and gratified by the discretion his orders gave him. Any legitimate damage he could inflict on the enemy while gathering information would be in order. "Should you be led so far east as to make it better, in your opinion, to continue around to the Potomac," Lee's orders read, "you will have to cross the river in the vicinity of Leesburg." In other words, if the cautions that had preceded the raid of June 12–15 were repeated, the opportunities were duplicated. With daring and luck, a second glorious "Ride around McClellan" was ahead for those lucky enough to share in the expedition![31]

Stuart selected 1,800 of his most reliable and best-mounted cavalry and chose as the commanding officers Wade Hampton, Rooney Lee, Grumble Jones, Williams Wickham, and Calbraith Butler. Four guns of the horse artillery were to go under Pelham's charge. Stuart and his staff made their farewells at headquarters by dancing the night away with the young ladies of the neighborhood.[32] At daybreak on October 10 the column crossed the Potomac, overwhelmed a small picket at McCoy's Ford, ten miles upstream from Williamsport, and started northward.

So long as the column was in Maryland it kept in close order and turned not at all from the road for food or plunder. Crossing the Pennsylvania line and pressing on toward Mercersburg, Stuart placed a "division" of 600 troopers in front under Hampton, and 600 to cover the rear. The central unit of 600 was sent out on either side of the road to collect horses from farmers who had no warning that graycoats were north of the Potomac. Little trouble was encountered. Powerful draft horses were led off without the removal even of collars. Well was it so. No quartermaster on the Confederate side of the Potomac had any collars large enough for those animals.[33]

Before the column could reach Chambersburg darkness descended. "I deemed it prudent to demand the surrender of the town," Wade Hampton reported. ". . . In reply to this summons three citizens, on the part of the citizens at large, came forward to ask the terms proposed." These were arranged quickly. The troopers clattered in and established themselves. Stuart named Hampton "Military Governor," as if he were to spend the autumn there. It was found that the bank's funds had been carried away at the first alarm. The mission to burn the railroad bridge over Conococheague Creek was no more successful. The bridge was of iron and defied Grumble Jones's axes. A military depot and the railroad shops were left to be burned by the rear guard.[34]

The next morning, to the troopers' surprise, Stuart started eastward as if he were going to a college town of which, perhaps, few of the men ever had heard at the time—a place called Gettysburg. This choice of the longer road back to Virginia was not a display of bravado. It was application of the sound old principle of strategy that the unexpected move often is the wisest. Stuart said to Captain William Blackford, "If I should fall before reaching Virginia, I want you to vindicate my memory," and explained that every argument was for recrossing the river downstream. Every advantage would be on the side of the Confederates, except for the distance to be covered and the proximity of the large Union forces at Harper's Ferry. Quick marching and precautions against the dispatch of the news of the column's position, said the general, would overcome the two disadvantages.[35]

Stuart's choice of a return route exhibited his developing strategic sense and one quality of military character that he had displayed on the ride around McClellan in front of Richmond. He chose the bolder course in Pennsylvania as on the Chickahominy. Nor was there any question, from Lee's orders, of Stuart's authority to exercise discretion. "I started directly toward Gettysburg," Stuart related, "but, having passed the Blue Ridge, started back . . . to Maryland by Emmitsburg. . . ."

As soon as Maryland soil again was reached, the seizure of horses ended. Captured animals to the number of 1,200 remained with the central "division." These well-broken Pennsylvania draft horses shared obediently in the march. The weather was itself good fortune. Roads damp from rain the previous evening raised no dust. Small prospect there was that the remote Federal signal stations could guess the direction of the Confederate march. At that, Stuart took no chances. He halted and held temporarily all travelers the column met or overtook.[36]

Learning from a captured courier that General Pleasonton and 800 Union cavalry were four miles west of the point where Stuart then was, he veered eastward across the Monocacy to a road that paralleled the Frederick-Emmitsburg highway. He was now approximately thirty-seven miles south of Emmitsburg and a mile or two farther than that from the Potomac—about halfway to safety. Long the road stretched ahead under a high-riding moon that was nearing its last quarter. The men were hungry, nodding, numb, or asleep. Stuart could not afford to give them the rest even of an hour. They must keep the column closed and must continue southward.

Although Stuart could not have been free of anxiety, he outwardly was all confidence. So much so, indeed, that in good cheer he turned out of the column and led several of his staff and some of the couriers down a side road leading to Urbana, scene of the high festivities in September. Soon the little cavalcade made a midnight call at the hospitable household of several of their erstwhile dancing partners. In response to their knock, a frightened female voice asked who they were. "General Stuart and his staff," Jeb himself replied with his unmistakable laugh. "Come down and open the door." A frenzy of dressing, and the girls were on the stoop in the moonlight, and there was the sweet sound of feminine chatter. Half an hour of this, and then it was "Good-bye, good-bye," waving handkerchiefs and graceful figures, and soon nothing but the beat of horses' hoofs, the jingle of spurs and scabbards and mumbled soldiers' farewells.[37]

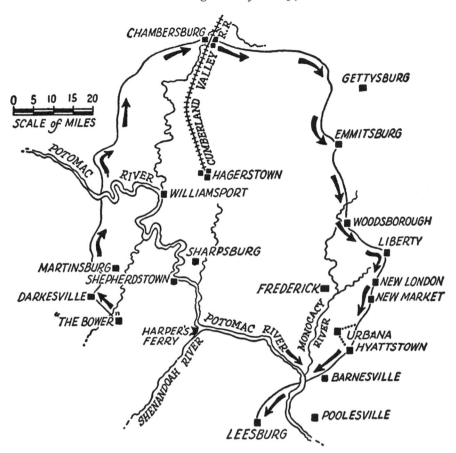

Route of Stuart's "October Raid," 1862.

Morning of the twelfth found the raiders at Hyattstown, twelve miles from Virginia soil. Rooney Lee commanded the van, Wade Hampton the rear "division," M. C. Butler the rear regiment. Two guns under Pelham were in front, two behind. Guides scouted ahead. Though the column had been trotting nearly all night, it must keep that stern pace as it neared the zone of danger. Stuart directed his command toward an eleven-mile stretch of the Potomac, between the mouth of the Monocacy and Edwards' Ferry, in which there were four crossings to choose from. On the principle of making the unexpected move, he selected little-used White's Ford.

A ruse was to be executed below Barnesville. There, said his guide, Captain B. S. White, a forest extended for well nigh two miles on the right of the highway. Through this wood an old and disused road led southwestward. If the Confederates entered the wood and followed the obscure track, White said, they would emerge just half a mile from a farm road that led down to White's Ford. Stuart took his place with the advance guard as it turned into the wood. The old road was abandoned but scarcely overgrown, and entirely practicable.

They emerged into open country and trotted on. Two miles from White's Ford there was a sudden clash with a party of Federal cavalry. With a rush the van scattered the enemy horsemen and seized a ridge which commanded the road of the Federal advance and, at the same time, covered the approaches to the ford. Under the cover of the fast, staccato fire of Pelham's guns, the exhausted troopers and their dull-eyed dragging horses pushed down the farm track toward the river. If the column was well closed and the rear guard safe, Pelham could be relied upon to hold off the enemy until it was time for him to withdraw. Escape, therefore, seemed to depend solely on whether the Federals held White's Ford in strength. If the enemy was at the ford, Rooney Lee must deal with them.[38]

Approaching the ford, Lee discovered bluecoats in a near-by quarry. No artillery was visible, nor could the probable strength of the enemy be discovered. He pondered the scene and thought it worthwhile to try a bluff. He wrote out a formal demand for the surrender of the position within a quarter of an hour; General Stuart, he said, commanded an overwhelming force but wished to avoid unnecessary bloodshed. There was no reply, and Rooney made his dispositions for an attack. Then movement was observed. Confederate officers focused their glasses, and there were smiles and delighted gestures: Undeniably, if incredibly, the Federals were filing out of their quarry fortress and withdrawing downstream!

White's Ford was abandoned and open. Danger, though reduced, was not past. Speed the crossing! First the two fieldpieces in the van, to command the approach. Now followed the gray-clad cavalrymen as fast as weary mounts could be spurred. Across the wide ford the column pushed—a cheering and picturesque sight in the October morning.

Stuart's concern now was for the rear guard. He had sent four couriers back for Butler, but none had returned. "Let me try it, General," said the young engineer William Blackford. Three miles and more Blackford spurred until at last he found the missing regiment. Butler wheeled his troopers about and got his gun under way. At the ford they prepared to cut their way through when they found the dauntless Pelham and his smoking gun. At a respectful distance, north and south, Federal troops were to be seen. Into the ford Butler's Carolinians splashed. Pelham and his men limbered up and followed. From the Virginia side, his other gun admonished the Federals to keep their distance.[39]

On with deliberation to Leesburg and thence to camp. There the booty was counted—full 1,200 horses in exchange for about sixty animals left behind as lame or broken down. Some thirty public men were brought back as hostages for Southern sympathizers in Federal hands. Public and railroad property estimated to be worth a quarter of a million dollars had been destroyed. As a price of this, not one Confederate trooper had been killed. Few had been wounded.

For his exploits Stuart had both the praise and the criticism of the army. In Channing Price's opinion, "The moral effects [were] great, teaching Pennsylvanians something of war and showing how J. E. B. Stuart can make McClellan's circuit at pleasure."⁴⁰ The chief argument was whether the results of the raid were worth the risks. Jeb and his men had marched thirty-two miles their first day out, and on October 11–12, by moving almost continuously, they had covered eighty miles in twenty-seven hours—all this close to a hostile army of 100,000. Had they been justified in an operation that involved this frightful strain of man and horse? How had Stuart contrived to do what seemed to be impossible?

The reasons could be ticked off: Picked men, spare horses, good guides, an accurate map, excellent teamwork, fortunate escape from observation. Yet all these scarcely would have sufficed if Stuart had not decided to keep moving. His night march of October 11–12, more than anything else, saved the raiders from the Federals who were set on their trails. If the Union cavalry had been diligent, prompt orders should have sufficed to snare the raiders. These essential conditions were not met; action instead was miserably slow. Even so, Stuart might have met superior force at White's Ford had he halted on the night of the eleventh-twelfth. He had learned early in the war the advantages of night marching, but he never applied his lessons better than in pushing steadily southward through that autumn night.

Captain Blackford had sharp words for the Federal cavalry: "The truth was that their cavalry were afraid to meet us and gladly availed themselves of the pretext of not being able to find us. Up to this time the cavalry of the enemy had no more confidence in themselves than the country had in them, and whenever we got a chance at them, which was rarely, they came to grief." If it was so, it was not so to remain.

General Lee did not fail to report the failure of the prime object, the destruction of the bridge across the Conococheague, but he pronounced the expedition of Stuart and his men "eminently successful. . . . To his skill and their fortitude, under the guidance of an overruling Providence, is their success due."⁴¹

That was a longer plume for Jeb.

CHAPTER 19

Battle at Fredericksburg

1. CHIEFLY PERSONAL TO JACKSON

Two weeks to the day after Stuart's return from his Chambersburg raid, the Army of the Potomac crossed the river that gave it a name. Whither was "Little Mac" bound—up the Shenandoah Valley or southward on the coastal side of the mountains? Because the answer had to wait on the march, Lee divided his forces. On October 28, Jackson was directed to retire a few miles toward Winchester with his troops; Longstreet was ordered to move over the Blue Ridge into Culpeper County. Care was to be taken to man all the passes, so that the two columns could not be assailed separately.

The cavalry, of course, had to screen this operation. A difficult task it proved. Hampton's men were at Martinsburg and could not unite with Stuart for several days. Grumble Jones's brigade had to be left to guard the rear of Jackson's command in the Valley. Fitz Lee's troopers alone were available to protect the march of Longstreet's corps, and they scarcely were able to count 1,000 sabers. A malady among the horses had left hundreds of men without mounts. Not until the grayjackets had been skirmishing for five days did the arrival of Hampton give Stuart sufficient strength to risk a general action. Even then, at Barbee's Crossroads, Jeb had to break off the engagement because of a rumored threat to his rear. Seldom had it happened previously that Stuart declined to fight to the finish. The operation as a whole, despite several fine individual performances by Pelham and command skills displayed by Williams Wickham and Tom Rosser, was not one of which Stuart subsequently spoke often.[1]

Undistinguished as was the record of the cavalry during those first days of November, Stuart's men assured an uneventful march of the First Corps. After its arrival in Culpeper, Lee made a brief visit to Richmond, during which time Longstreet administered all three arms of the service. After Lee's return, Old Pete directed the whole of the infantry around

Culpeper. He did it unostentatiously and well. Jackson, in the Shenandoah Valley, resumed virtually the semi-independent command he had exercised in the spring.

Neither Jackson nor Longstreet had done more than make the first adjustments to the new divisional and brigade commands within their corps when Northern newspapers revealed the fact that the bluecoats, too, were undergoing a reorganization. McClellan had been displaced and sent home to "await orders," which never were to be sent him. Ambrose Burnside—he who had commanded opposite Toombs at Sharpsburg—had been given command of the Army of the Potomac. The *Richmond Dispatch* commented on McClellan: "It is said that he is the best general they have, and we think it probable he is. Yet they could have fallen upon no man who could have made a more signal failure than he did in his campaign against Richmond. If he be the best, they must all be exceedingly bad."[2]

While Burnside prepared to campaign, Jackson's men were destroying railways. Every mile of track within their reach, from the Potomac to the southern terminus of the Manassas Gap Railroad, they sought to wreck beyond repair that autumn. Old Jack, one soldier grumbled, "intends us to tear up all the railroads in the state, and with no tools but our pocketknives." The general held his men strictly and severely to their tasks, yet with this was mingled admiration for them. One night while he was in his tent, the Stonewall Brigade raised the rebel yell and split the air until the brigade in the nearest camp joined in. Then another and another brigade sent echoing through the wood the fox hunter's cry. "Old Blue Light" came from his quarters, strode to a rail fence, leaned on it after his fashion of resting, and listened till the last echo died away. As he walked back, he said as if to himself, "That was the sweetest music I ever heard."[3]

His officers, like his men, found in him this odd combination of discipline and good will. Publicly Jackson said nothing of the controversy with Powell Hill. To others of his lieutenants, if the relationship were close, Jackson on occasion spoke frankly of their military shortcomings. Hotchkiss was admonished that his "great fault" was "talking too much." In another instance, there was a suspicion that Jackson was not all tears over the death of a man who had sent him many excited reports. Said Hotchkiss: "I think the general put him down as a decided sensationalist and so replied, though I know not. The general dislikes rumors, exceedingly; unless he can get substantial facts, I don't believe he likes to hear anything"—which is not a bad rule for a soldier to follow.[4]

Shifting headquarters to Winchester put Jackson in pleasant humor. Even a day there was a delight because of the Christian associations he had established there. The soul of Deacon Jackson had been stirred anew that autumn by the ministry of the eloquent Reverend Dr. Joseph C. Stiles. That eminent minister, who was unofficial chaplain general of the Confederacy, had come to the Valley and by his fervent preaching had helped fan religious feeling into the spiritual fire of the great revival that subsequently spread through the army and had historic influence on its morals and on the life of the South during drear and bitter years that were ahead. Early in the revival Jackson heard Dr. Stiles preach, and felt himself much edified. "It was a powerful exposition of the Word of God," he wrote Mrs. Jackson. "... Dr. Stiles is a great revivalist, and is laboring in a work of grace in General Ewell's division." The soldier's ambitions were forgotten in the elder's admiration of the preacher: "It is a glorious thing to be a minister of the Gospel of the Prince of Peace. There is no equal position in this world."

While he was in Winchester, Jackson made a special point of calling on the Reverend and Mrs. James Graham at the manse where Mrs. Jackson had been with him the previous winter. To Anna, who was close to the delivery of her first-born, conceived at the manse, Mrs. Graham wrote of the general: "He is looking in such perfect health—far *handsomer* than I ever saw him—and is in such fine spirits, seems so unreserved and unrestrained in his intercourse with us, that we did enjoy him to the full."⁵

The Second Corps had left Winchester before Old Jack went to call at the manse. He followed his troops the next day past the battlefield of Kernstown. On the twenty-third he rode almost to Mt. Jackson. The march of November 24, when the van reached New Market, repeated for Jackson the move he had made the preceding May from the opposite direction on the Valley Pike. He turned to the east, passed over the windswept Massanutton, and then, crossing the Shenandoah at Columbia Bridge, began to climb the Blue Ridge. Night brought him to the road to Madison Court House, from whence Dick Ewell had entered the country of the Shenandoah in the spring. Now Jackson was looking over this road of new adventure to the Rappahannock, whither Lee and Longstreet had preceded him.

In dealing with the enemy, the commanding general had continued to allow discretion and free movement to Stonewall, though gradually Lee himself had become convinced that the two corps of his army should be united. Jackson had lingered in the Valley as long as he dared. Doubtless this was because he hoped an opportunity might offer for another thrust at the rear of the Federals; but as scant prospect of a third Manassas developed, he reluctantly now was bound eastward.

He dramatized this decision in a manner somewhat unusual for him. The morning his camp was nearest the crest of the mountains, he dressed with a larger expenditure of time and care than he usually allowed himself, and when he came from his tent he wore a dazzling uniform coat Jeb Stuart had given him. Sometime before, he had put aside his old weatherbeaten cap for a tall black hat Jed Hotchkiss found for him. As he wore this with the brim turned down all around, he far outshone all previous appearance. To complete his adornment, he buckled on his sword. Before the incredulous gaze of his staff, he blushed and then smiled. "Young gentlemen," he said, with an expansiveness as rare as his fine appearance, "this is no longer the headquarters of the Army of the Valley, but of the Second Corps of the Army of Northern Virginia." They knew that this meant he was on his way to rejoin Lee.[6]

By the evening of November 25 he was at Madison Court House, and in the hope that the Lord would deliver into his hand some part of the Union host, he kept his headquarters on the Gordonsville road November 26 and 27. Perhaps a personal consideration was added to his military reasons for lingering within easy distance of Gordonsville. In the knowledge that Mrs. Jackson's pregnancy was nearing its end, he had told her when he left Winchester to address her next letter to him at Gordonsville.

His forethought had its reward in a letter postmarked Charlotte, North Carolina. "My Own Dear Father," it began. "As my mother's letter has been cut short by my arrival, I think it but justice that I should continue it. I know that you are rejoiced to hear of my coming, and I hope that God has sent me to radiate your pathway through life. I am a very tiny little thing. I weight only eight and a half pounds. . . ." It was signed, "Your dear little wee Daughter." A girl, then! He had wanted a boy, but if God had sent a girl, then he not only would accept the Divine mandate meekly but he also would prefer a daughter to a son. As for sharing the news of his happiness, well . . . keeping one's secrets was an essential rule in war and might be no less proper in respect to one's private affairs. Kyd Douglas would say that not until December 26 did he learn his general was a father.[7]

Jackson on the twenty-ninth of November started for Fredericksburg. Ahead of his infantry he travelled fast, fully forty miles. Much of his afternoon ride carried him through a gloomy, wooded, infertile district known as the "Wilderness of Spotsylvania." The trees were mixed. Fine hardwood soared close to tangles of stumps where trees had been cut to feed a nearby iron furnace. Well-clad pines were elbowed by scrub oaks and stubborn little hickories. On Jackson's mind, so far as the record shows, the Wilderness made no special impression. He merely sent back word that for the best road the wagons and artillery should proceed via Chancellorsville.

At nightfall the party reached army headquarters in the vicinity of Fredericksburg and was welcomed most heartily by the commanding general. The near-by estate home of Muscoe Garnett was thrown open to

General Jackson. "Stonewall Jackson? Is he here?" exclaimed his host. "Go and tell him to come at once; all my home is his, sir!" Jackson had a good supper, a pleasant evening, and then a warm bed in which to think of his own home and his new daughter.[8]

2. The Battle of the Pontoons

Jackson's corps had been brought to the vicinity of Fredericksburg because Burnside had decided to attempt from the mid-Rappahannock a new drive on Richmond. The Federal commanding general had arrived at Falmouth, opposite Fredericksburg, on November 19; Longstreet the same day had taken position on the hills behind the city. Lee reached the scene on the twentieth. His defensive plan was firm. He was determined, if the enemy advanced overwhelmingly, to retire toward Richmond and tear up both the R.F. & P. Railroad southward from Fredericksburg and the Orange and Alexandria to Gordonsville.[9]

Once Burnside found himself resolutely opposed, he appeared to lose all zeal for rapid movement. The Army of Northern Virginia, in consequence, had a period of rest, during which headquarters undertook to improve its organization. One change only seemed to be imperative—the removal of Thomas F. Drayton from command of his South Carolina–Georgia brigade. The division commander, Lafayette McLaws, despaired of results: Drayton's colonels were absent; he could not so much as keep his staff together. Longstreet considered that the service of potentially good soldiers was lost to the army.

The most direct procedure was to assign Drayton's regiments to other brigades and, as the general would be without command, to give him leave of absence. This course was followed. The 50th and 51st Georgia were transferred to Paul Semmes's brigade; the 15th South Carolina was placed with Kershaw; the Phillips Legion went to Cobb. Drayton left the Army of Northern Virginia to return no more. The whole unpleasant affair was handled with the least possible disturbance and publicity. Addition of the two Georgia regiments to Semmes released two Virginia regiments which, with one from Kemper and one from Cooke, were formed into a new brigade for Monty Corse. That officer thereupon was relieved of command of Pickett's old brigade, which was placed under Dick Garnett. Nothing further was done in the hearing of Jackson's charges against Garnett.[10]

Longstreet was entirely willing to have Garnett in the First Corps, which the new lieutenant general industriously was preparing for the next battles. He was active and efficient; the administration of his corps was smooth. Dick Anderson had recovered quickly from his wound at Sharpsburg and found that to his four experienced brigade commanders, a fifth of less experience had been added—E. A. Perry with a small Florida brigade. Pickett of the curly locks had reported himself cured of the wound suffered at Gaines' Mill and, for the first time, was directing a division in the field. Its five brigadiers, with the exception of Monty Corse, all were seasoned and all, without excepting Corse, were capable. As much could be said for John B. Hood and his four brigades.

The most interesting accession to Longstreet's divisional commanders was Robert Ransom, Jr. He had served in the Seven Days and at Sharpsburg, was senior brigadier under the departed John G. Walker, and now was in command of his own and John R. Cooke's North Carolina regiments. In the old army Ransom had been known as a capable junior officer in the 1st Dragoons and the 1st Cavalry. Immediately upon secession in his native North Carolina he had organized the first cavalry of that state, then, after an early introduction to combat, had transferred to infantry command.

A gallant spirit was Ransom's, but he was not altogether popular with his men. He was too much the regular, the West Pointer, in handling troops. "If he had understood volunteer soldiers," one of his veterans said of Ransom, and realized they were "as anxious for the success of the cause as he, he would have been one of the greatest generals in Lee's army...." In action he was cool, and in judging ground sure. In the heat of battle his bald pate shown above the abundant hair on his temples; his eyes flashed; every inch of him was soldier. Then, if then only, his men ceased to grumble about his discipline and told themselves that when the shells were bursting and the minié balls whining, they had rather have Robert Ransom than any other man as their commander because he knew how to move them swiftly and with minimum losses.[11]

Among the promising new brigadiers Thomas R. R. Cobb, in particular, gave fully to his new brigade the high abilities with which he was credited. Cobb was thirty-nine and had behind him in Georgia and in the Confederate Congress a reputation for legal acumen and vast industry. He left Congress to organize Cobb's Legion. Without previous military training, he learned fast. Initially he was annoyed by professional soldiers. "Let me but get away from these 'West Pointers,'" he wrote his wife. "... Never have I seen men who had so little appreciation of merit in others. Self-sufficiency and self-aggrandizement are their great controlling characteristics." From this state of mind he had been won by the tact of the commanding general, and now, as he approached the first battle in which he was to command a brigade, he wrote reassuringly to Mrs. Cobb: "Do not be uneasy about my being 'rash.' The bubble reputation cannot drag me into folly. God helping me, I will do my duty when called upon, trusting the consequences to Him."[12]

This was the spirit of the army. Lee was so confident of that spirit that he became impatient of Burnside's delays. "Gen. Lee is very anxiously waiting for a fight," Dorsey Pender wrote his wife. "He told me today he would be willing to fall back and let them cross for the sake of a fight. All accounts are to the effect that they will not fight, and their numbers are not so terrible as might be supposed." This confidence was heightened by the strength of the ground the Confederates, especially Longstreet's corps, held in rear of Fredericksburg. "We have a magnificent position, perhaps the best on the line," said Cobb. McLaws's division was upon Marye's Heights immediately behind the city; Anderson was on McLaws's left; Pickett on McLaws's right; beyond Pickett was Hood.

It scarcely seemed possible that the strong ground held by McLaws would be assaulted, but its defense represented the type of work at which Lafayette McLaws shone. He prepared pits for his batteries and strengthened some parts of his front with abatis and fire trenches. At the foot of the heights was a sunken road, protected by a stone wall, that paralleled his front. McLaws was not content with this. He had a ditch dug on the lower side of the road, and the dirt banked against the front of the wall—an ideal trench for point-blank fire. This was to be Cobb's position.[13]

Longstreet gave to McLaws, also, the more difficult task of guarding Fredericksburg's riverfront. From their side of the Rappahannock the Unionists could employ their overpowering artillery to keep the Confederate batteries at a distance and to cover their own advance. The only defense was posting infantrymen in the houses and behind any cover they could find next to the river. This assignment was given the fine Mississippi veterans of William Barksdale. They had been much diminished in number by the hard fighting of the summer, but in valor they were worthy of their stout-hearted commander. Barksdale had displayed, at Malvern Hill, what Lee styled the "highest qualities of the soldier."[14] Lesser opportunities had not made him appear smaller.

On the evening of December 10, observing stir and movement on the Federal side of the Rappahannock, Longstreet concluded that Burnside's men were about to cross the river. Old Pete shared the general opinion that nothing could keep the Federals from crossing under the cover of their superior artillery, but, as a matter of course, he wished to meet the attempt boldly, and harass and delay it to the last moment of prudence. In Fredericksburg, along the riverfront and downstream as far as a quarter of a mile below the mouth of Deep Run, Barksdale's 17th and 18th Mississippi were on the *qui vive*. Barksdale doubled his pickets, and he himself rode ceaselessly along his front of a mile and a half. In the blackness nothing could be seen, but sound carried clearly. By 4:00 A.M. Barksdale was satisfied that the Union engineers were beginning to throw their pontoons at three points—one on the site of the rope ferry in the town, one near the railroad bridge, and one opposite the mouth of Deep Run.

At 5 o'clock, at the ferry site, the excellent riflemen of the 17th Mississippi, supported by a contingent of the 8th Florida, opened on the bridge-builders. They could see nothing through the enveloping fog; their ears had to serve for their eyes. The task of holding off the enemy at the ferry landing did not prove difficult. If the bullets from the rifles of the Mississippians reached few Federals, they made many cautious. At last, as wintry dawn slowly dissipated darkness and thinned the fog, the defenders could calculate the distance of the closest pontoon as eighty feet from the west bank where they were hiding. Their first shots drove off the working party. The sharpshooters at the railroad bridge found it equally simple to keep the pontooniers at a distance. Opposite Deep Run the situation was not so favorable. Well-led, competent engineer troops worked steadily under a shielding and impenetrable fog. So well were the bridge-makers covered that the Confederates did not know that two bridges were being thrown.[15]

To the spiteful bark of the rifles along the riverfront the Federal artillery made wrathful answer. Barksdale's men in the town were not to be shaken by random cannonade. They hugged the ground or pulled close to stout brick walls and waited till the fire slackened. Then, as the pontooniers ran out on the bridges again to resume their work, Barksdale's rifles mockingly picked them off. Burnside ordered all artillery within range to open on the town in the hope of compelling Barksdale to withdraw. A furious bombardment it was. It swept the streets, shattered houses, shook the very hills; but it did not drive out Barksdale's men. They took to the cellars or found deeper ditches and at intervals they would peer out to be certain the bridge-builders had not returned to work. "Tell General Lee," Barksdale said grimly to a messenger, "that if he wants a bridge of dead Yankees, I can furnish him with one!"[16]

After the bombardment the Union bridge-builders tried again. From the eastern bank loaded bateaux of Federals put boldly out and started to row across the river. Barksdale's men challenged the enemy as before, but this time the fire was weaker. Union batteries were beginning to search out the position of the Mississippi marksmen. Barksdale stuck stubbornly to his task, but at 4:30 P.M. he had to call his men back to Caroline Street. Ere long, as Federal infantry continued to move fast across the bridges, McLaws sent orders to evacuate the town. Doubtless Barksdale would have fought joyfully to the last soldier and the last cartridge, had not his orders been repeated. He had reluctantly to obey.

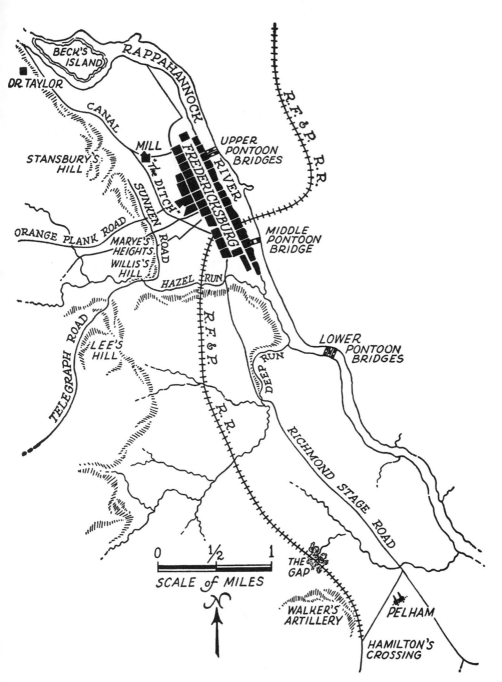

BECK'S ISLAND

DR. TAYLOR

RAPPAHANNOCK

R.F.&P. R.R.

CANAL

STANSBURY'S HILL

MILL

UPPER PONTOON BRIDGES

The DITCH

FREDERICKSBURG

RIVER

ORANGE PLANK ROAD

SUNKEN ROAD

MARYE'S HEIGHTS

WILLIS'S HILL

MIDDLE PONTOON BRIDGE

HAZEL RUN

TELEGRAPH ROAD

LEE'S HILL

R.F.&P. R.R.

DEEP RUN

LOWER PONTOON BRIDGES

RICHMOND STAGE ROAD

0   ½   1

SCALE of MILES

THE GAP

WALKER'S ARTILLERY

PELHAM

HAMILTON'S CROSSING

Sketch of the battlefield of Fredericksburg, December 1862.

The 21st Mississippi, which had not been engaged along the river, was selected by Barksdale to cover the withdrawal. At the rear of this rear regiment was a detachment under Lieutenant Lane Brandon, a graduate of the Harvard Law School. From a prisoner Brandon learned that the lead company of the 20th Massachusetts pursuing him was commanded by his chum and former classmate, Henry L. Abbott. That was enough for Brandon. Cost what it might, he would whip Abbott then and there! He halted his rear guard, turned about, and attacked the 20th Massachusetts and momentarily pressed it back. He was preparing to carry the contest back through the town when orders most peremptory were sent him to break off the fight. So mad was he, even then, to outdo his friend Abbott that he had to be put under arrest.[7]

Without further loss or incident Barksdale marched through the darkness of the winter's early night to the foot of Marye's Heights . . . across a wide, deep field, a field of execution.

3. ON THE RIGHT AT FREDERICKSBURG

The completion of four pontoon bridges by nightfall on December 11 led the Confederate commanders to conclude that Burnside was almost certain to attack somewhere near Fredericksburg. He scarcely could have afforded to put down that many pontoons as a ruse to hold the Confederates at the town while he crossed at a remote point on the Rappahannock. The hour of battle must be near. Jackson at Guiney's Station was advised of the situation; Powell Hill was ordered to move at dawn and take the position previously held by Longstreet's right division. D. H. Hill and Early, watching the lower crossings, were left where they were until the probability of an attack at Fredericksburg became a certainty.

On the morning of the twelfth the fog was widespread, shifting and uneven. Troops in large numbers evidently had crossed and bivouacked both in Fredericksburg and near the bridges opposite Deep Run. As the morning wore on, with no news of Federal activity elsewhere on the Rappahannock, the question became that of where, on the Fredericksburg front, Burnside would concentrate his attack.[18]

At first Longstreet thought the attack would be against Jackson on the right, but when he saw how heavily the Federals were massing in Fredericksburg, he concluded that the main assault would be against his right and the left of Jackson. Old Pete accordingly summoned Ransom's division from reserve and put it with the left units of McLaws's division to guard Marye's Heights. The previous night, most of Tom Cobb's brigade had been moved down to the sunken road under the heights to relieve Barksdale's tired men. On Cobb's left, Ransom placed the 24th North Carolina of his own brigade. John R. Cooke's great regiment, the 27th, was placed near the crest.[19]

Some time about noon, Jackson dispatched orders for Early and D. H. Hill to join him. No concern did he express that the distance they had to cover—eighteen to twenty-two miles—was too long a march for a December night. Other preparations Old Jack completed promptly and with his habitual care for detail and discipline. In particular he instructed his provost marshal to prevent all straggling of the sort that had so dangerously weakened the army in the Maryland operations. His orders were explicit: The provost marshal guard was to shoot, first, all stragglers who refused to go to the front; and, second, all soldiers who were said by two witnesses to be straggling for the second time. Instructions did not specify whether the straggler was to be shot in the head or in the heel.[20]

On the arrival at the front of Taliaferro, who had recovered from his wound and temporarily had charge of Jackson's old division, that veteran command had an unusual privilege. All too often, as its thinned ranks showed, the division had been in the "very front of battle." Now it was placed behind A. P. Hill, out of range of adventuresome minié balls—sure evidence that Lee, for once, had ample reserves. What a contrast to that dreadful September day at Sharpsburg, not three months previously!

One subject only was there for debate while the Confederates filed into position on the ridge: Was that strong position weakened by the bit of woodland that projected toward the river from the line of A. P. Hill? The Light Division's line ran northwestward from Hamilton's Crossing one and a half miles on a wood-covered ridge. About 1,300 yards from Hamilton's was a boggy little ravine on the border of which was a narrow triangle of woods. To avoid this bad ground the nearest units had been placed on either side. Lane's brigade had its right about 150 yards from the left of the projecting triangle. Archer's brigade was close to the right of the tangled, sodden woods. That is to say, about 500 or 600 yards of front, between Archer's left and Lane's right, was not occupied by troops. Was it safe to leave so wide a gap? With the batteries placed as they were, Powell Hill apparently thought the gap would offer no danger, especially with Gregg stationed on higher ground at the rear of the boggy wood. Jackson probably heard nothing on the twelfth about the gap in his corps front, though he rode the length of the line.[21]

The chill of that windy night of December 12 was relieved, for all save the pickets, by hundreds of campfires. Jube Early and Harvey Hill were on the march up the Rappahannock. Taliaferro had his men in the assigned reserve position behind Powell Hill. To the left of Hill, the division of Hood was moved nearer. Hood's instructions from Longstreet were to cooperate with Hill or with any other of Jackson's troops. Confidence was complete. Why not? The position was stronger than any the Army of Northern Virginia ever had occupied. Reserves would be ample. Artillery would take its toll when those tens of thousands who crowded the fields and the town undertook to assault the ridge . . . if they were foolish enough to do so.

Much the worst of the day's happenings had been in Fredericksburg itself, where numerous noncombatants had remained throughout the bombardment. The plundering to which they were subjected was described at the time by a Federal major, Francis E. Pierce: "Great three-story houses furnished magnificently were broken into and their contents scattered over the floors and trampled on by the muddy feet of the soldiers. . . . Finest cut glass ware goblets were hurled at nice plate glass windows, . . . rosewood pianos piled in the street and burned or soldiers would get on top of them and kick the key-board and internal machinery all to pieces. . . . The soldiers seemed to delight in destroying everything."[22] Well it was, perhaps, that the gray men on the gray hills behind Fredericksburg knew nothing of this. Had they been aware of the plundering and purposeless destruction, the battle of December 13 might have been marked by hot vindictiveness and not by cold, defiant repulse.

The thirteenth of December dawned cold. Spotsylvania's hills were damp with the fog that covered the river valley. At 7:17 the sun rose red and fiery behind the Federal left and promised from a cloudless sky to drive away the moisture. "Peter" Longstreet was in his battle mood—brusque but hearty, alert but perfectly composed, eager for a new adventure. Burnside's chief assault, he told Hood and Pickett, would be south of them, on Jackson's front. Their two divisions must be prepared to deliver a counterattack on the Federal flank should Jackson's line be broken. He expected to be assailed farther north, near his left center, where he felt he was strong enough to beat off the enemy without calling on Pickett or Hood. In conversation with Porter Alexander, who was about to fight his first battle as commander of a battalion of First Corps artillery, young Alexander told him with pride, of the ground in front of Marye's Heights, "General, we cover that ground now so well that we comb it as with a fine-tooth comb. A chicken could not live on that field when we open on it!" That pleased Longstreet, and sent him in high humor to the commanding eminence near the center of the line, where General Lee had established field headquarters.[23]

Thither Jackson was making his way. He had risen early and for reasons known to himself only, decided that he would wear that day the uniform coat Jeb Stuart had given him in October—the coat of resplendent gold braid—as well as the hat Hotchkiss had presented him on the march to Harper's Ferry. Thus glorified, Old Jack was dazzling to the eye if manifestly embarrassed. The remarks of his men did not lessen his discomfort. A private shouted: "Come here, boys! Stonewall has drawed his bounty and has bought himself some new clothes!" Everywhere along the line there was the same astonishment over Jackson's appearance. On his arrival at the hill—from that hour "Lee's Hill"—Jackson created no less of a sensation. Lee, of course, made no remark about the unwonted smartness of Jackson's appearance; Longstreet trained his eye but reserved his verbal fire; Jeb Stuart was delighted Jackson was using on so great a day a present from affectionate hands.[24]

When conversation turned to the battle that soon would begin, Jackson was in zealous advocacy of immediate attack. If the Confederates assailed the blue infantry while the fog hung low, the Union artillery would be useless. Stuart seconded his hero's proposal, but Lee shook his head. The odds were too great, he said. It was the course of wisdom to receive the attack, to reduce the odds, to wear down the enemy, and then to take the offensive. Jackson acquiesced in the decision of the commanding general, as he always did, heartily and without reservation, but he pondered the move he should make when the enemy's attack on his front collapsed. Would there be opportunity for a counterstroke? He would make ready.

By 10 o'clock, with a mystic majesty that made eyes brighten and cheeks flush, the scene visible from Lee's Hill began to change. Down, down the fog sank until the church steeples of the little town could be distinguished, then the mustered lines of blue, the ambulances, the ordnance wagons, the batteries. The spectacle stirred Longstreet. "Jackson, what are you going to do with all those people over there?" he inquired. Jackson doubtless answered in the spirit of his deepest impulse as a soldier, "Sir, we will give them the bayonet!"[25]

Back on the front with his corps, Jackson was greeted with a swelling Federal fire and every evidence of a brewing infantry attack. Von Borcke voiced some anxiety over the near approach of the unchallenged Federals. Jackson was more than unconcerned. He was pleased. "Major, my men sometimes fail *to take* a position, but *to defend* one, never! I am glad the Yankees are coming!" A few minutes later, he directed that the horse artillery open against the Federal left flank, which he believed he could rake.[26]

The duel that followed on the Confederate right was the most dramatic of all those in which John Pelham had been engaged. Boldly he advanced his guns—a Blakely rifle and a 12-pounder Napoleon—beyond the infantry line and opened with solid shot on a heavy column moving almost at right angles to his position. Furious Federal guns speedily were turned on him. A blast put his obstreperous Blakely out of action. Four batteries were soon trying to hit his solitary Napoleon. Undaunted, Pelham gave the only answer he could, the answer of redoubled fire. Although his men were falling fast, the loss seemed justified because the whole menacing Federal line now had halted. Evidently its commander intended to advance no more until Pelham was silenced. Not until his caissons were almost empty did Pelham limber up and, amid a pursuing blaze of shells, drive back to Hamilton's Crossing. "It is glorious to see such courage in one so young!" exclaimed an admiring General Lee.[27]

The Federal batteries now opened violently on the hill where fourteen of A. P. Hill's guns were hidden as well as the ground permitted. Jackson watched without anxiety. He believed Hill's artillery would be able to beat off the infantry who evidently were about to resume their advance. Until the proper minute arrived, all the Confederate batteries were to remain inactive. For close to an hour the Southern gunners hugged the cold earth and passively watched the shells burst over and around them.

At the end of that time, the Federals apparently concluded that the batteries on the hill had been destroyed and the position could be stormed. Those long, awe-inspiring blue ranks began to move. Onward, straight for the ridge, came thousands of Federals across the open fields. No challenge met them. Within 1,000 yards they came; 900 it was; 800 yards. Then a hoarsely shouted order was repeated by each gray battery commander. Lanyards were pulled; shells went screaming toward the blue line. The startled Federal infantry hesitated a moment but steadfastly pushed on again. Once more and still once more the artillery of Hill and Stuart tore the ranks. There was a wavering, a halt, then a slow recoil.

The blue soldiers fell back, but merely beyond effective range. Jackson and Stuart watched the enemy mend his broken lines and perfect his formation. About 1:00 P.M. across the fields the Federals advanced again in three long, massive lines. The whole front of A. P. Hill was to be assailed. On the neck of woodland—the woods that represented part of the gap in the lines of the Light Division—the first blow would fall. For a few minutes it looked as if the fire of Hill's divisional artillery would drive back the Federals again. The lines slowed, hesitated, and retired ever so little. Then instead of turning back, the Union troops pushed more furiously forward. Northern blood was up. The front line entered the apex of the triangle of boggy woods. Lane's men were at grips with the enemy.[28]

A rise of ground here served to deflect the Federal attack toward Lane's right and directly into the gap between him and Archer. Before any precautions could be taken, the Federals were crashing their way through the wood and assailing the two regiments on Lane's right and the two on Archer's left. In his first hour of combat as a general officer, Lane was having a test that might have shaken steel nerves. The sick Archer had a well man's task and more. As the defenders on both sides of the gap fought stubbornly, both Lane and Archer sent back word that they were hard-pressed. The Federals pressed into Lane's weakened front and threatened envelopment. His North Carolinians had to give ground.

Through the gap the enemy now could pour thousands of men, but precisely what the Federals were doing, amid the smoke and confusion, Hill's subordinates could not ascertain. Of divisional staff work there was none. Except as the brigade commanders informed one another, they were in the dark. In Gregg's brigade, in rear of the gap, arms had been stacked and the men told to lie down to protect themselves from the Federal artillery. Of a sudden, without so much as a shout of warning, Orr's Rifles, Gregg's right regiment, found the Federals upon them. Before the Confederates could load their rifles, or even grab them, common sense demanded flight. Away ran as many of Orr's men as could escape. Gregg, directly between his retreating soldiers and the pursuing Federals, was shot from his horse.

Gallantly the Unionists had thrust, but now they could not push farther the spearhead of their attack. The 1st South Carolina stopped the infiltration; from either side of the gap the Confederates began to close in. Field's brigade sent aid to Archer. Thomas hurried forward to relieve Lane. Farther to the rear, Old Jube was resolving a doubt. A courier told him of Archer's plight; a staff man arrived from Jackson with orders to hold himself in readiness to move to the right, where the enemy was making a demonstration. Early chewed and spat and inwardly debated. Then word came of an "awful gap" between Archer and Lane, and that the batteries on the right would be lost. That decided the question for Early, and he ordered forward his own, Lawton's, and Trimble's brigades.

As Early's veterans overtook those of Hill's regiments driven from the front, there were jests: "Here comes old Jubal; let old Jubal straighten that fence!" Early launched his counterattack furiously. He pushed down the ridge and drove every Federal regiment out of the gap. Officers would remember seeing a man pull himself painfully up by the side of a little tree, and wave them onward. It was Maxcy Gregg.[29]

The battle on the Confederate right did not end with Early's counterattack. Southern artillery had put a heavy price on the advance of the Federals and now it exacted a toll on the retreating bluecoats. John Pelham had nothing but compliments for Poague's 20-pounder Parrotts in an extended duel with the Federal artillery. "Well," said Pelham, "you men stand killing better than any I ever saw." As an old gunner, Jackson observed the bombardment with keen eye. His spirits were high. During a lull, he rode out to the extreme right and, dismounting, went forward with no companion except his aide, James Power Smith. As Jackson and Smith were walking forward to reconnoiter, a bullet whizzed past between their heads. Said Jackson in calm delight: "Mr. Smith, had you not better go to the rear? They may shoot you!"

Other leaders had escapes as narrow. Jeb Stuart galloped up and down the right wing and reconnoitered several times beyond it. Once he rode within 200 yards of some Federal sharpshooters hidden behind a hedge. That square, stout figure of his on a tall horse was an ideal mark. The Federal marksmen strained over their sights and sent two bullets through his clothes, but did not injure him.[30]

On Jackson's left, whither the fight seemed to be drifting, action was not close. Spitefully the Federal artillery explored the position before which the infantry hesitated. In support of a battery Dorsey Pender, as usual, was wounded—this time by a bullet that passed between the bones of his left arm. He had to go to the rear to have his wound attended, but he soon was back on the field. He found little to do defensively on the lines of the Second Corps.[31] Burnside had shifted his battle to Longstreet's front in one of the most ghastly and dramatic assaults of American war.

4. LONGSTREET WINS AN EASY VICTORY

On the edge of the town nearest the heights, the Federals visibly were massing in great numbers for an assault. Nothing could have been more acceptable to Longstreet. He had abundant infantry on strong ground; ample reserves were nearby; the Confederate batteries had been located admirably. Old Pete had simply to wait for the oncoming wave to break itself in daunting loss against the heights. He did feel some concern for the somewhat exposed position of Dick Anderson's left brigade. Were it driven back, Cobb's brigade in the sunken road would be enfiladed. When Cobb read Longstreet's warning to this effect, he could not repress one proud assurance: "Well, if they wait for me to fall back, they will wait a long time!"[32]

The Federals at that moment made the first move toward an attack. They manifestly proposed to drive straight to the sunken road and to attempt to storm the heights. It seemed inconceivable that an effort would be made, but there before Southern eyes was the evidence of their preparation and, about noon, the reality of their advance. As the blue line pushed forward, it crumpled a board fence across its path as if it had been paper. This élan availed nothing. Once the fire of the batteries on the heights blasted the line, it faltered, it halted, it fell back in bloody confusion. Cobb's brigade in the sunken road and Cooke's on the crest had opportunity of firing one volley and no more.

From the Confederate side, when the smoke lifted, only three stands of Union colors planted at the point of deployment, and the dead or writhing victims on the ground, showed where the attack had been delivered. The repulse was as well directed as it was easy. Longstreet's First Corps was vindicating the record the separate divisions had achieved. McLaws was at his best. Ransom was measuring up to every requirement. Cooke on the hilltop was as gallant a figure as at Sharpsburg.[33]

Down in the sunken road, Tom Cobb was cool and self-possessed and was holding perfectly in hand his confident troops. He was moving among the men, preparing them for a second test, when with a gasp he dropped to the ground. A bullet from the rifle of a sharpshooter had shattered his thigh. Blood poured from severed arteries. The first surgeon who reached Cobb did what he could to staunch the flow, but he looked grim. They brought him whiskey and poured it down his throat, but he was past stimulation. Suddenly he became insensible. Soon his heart ceased to beat.

Almost at the moment of Cobb's fall, John R. Cooke had been hit in the forehead while he was atop Willis's Hill, as that part of the heights was styled. An ugly wound Cooke had, and one that manifestly had fractured the skull. Whether it would be fatal, none could say. Odds were that his end had come, like that of Tom Cobb, in the first battle he had fought as a general officer. The two brigades that apparently were to be hammered hardest that day on the anvil of attack were now to be commanded by their senior colonels present.[34]

Before Longstreet could reflect whether this would make any difference in the defense, the Federal attack was renewed. Did McLaws have enough men in the sunken road to beat back the bluecoats? He was not sure. Kershaw had better send two of his regiments to help Cobb. The reserve regiment of Cobb's should move down to the sunken road. Thither, also, Ransom hurried two regiments of Cooke's brigade. These North Carolinians, being the nearest, got to the sunken road in time to share in beating off with small effort the second Federal attack. Not long did the Confederates have to wait for another. Before rifles began to cool in the December air the enemy was coming up again. Along the sunken road the volleys flashed; down the hillside roared the echo of the guns. The repulse was swift, easy, ghastly.

McLaws reasoned that reinforcements and the firm voice of a leader who had nerves of steel would steady the Georgians if they were shaken by the loss of Cobb. The man to replace him was Kershaw. Two of that excellent soldier's regiments were on their way to the sunken road. Let Kershaw go there in person; let his remaining troops follow him. Joe Kershaw now became the central figure on the smoke-swept stage. His men must march fast behind him, he said, and he rode into the fire with no more hesitation than he would have shown on his way to a political barbecue in his native South Carolina. When he emerged on the crest of Willis's Hill, a conspicuous and defiant target, men said afterward that the Federals withheld their fire as if in admiration, and that he took off his cap in acknowledgment ere he disappeared on his way to the sunken road. An army myth this may have been, but a tribute it was to bravery that thousands had seen and admired.

When the volleys of Kershaw's regiments were added to those of the men in the sunken road, the enemy faced an impenetrable front of fire. Never had Lee presented so many muskets on so narrow a front. Said Kershaw afterward: "I found, on my arrival, that Cobb's brigade . . . occupied our entire front, and my troops could only get into position by doubling on them. This was accordingly done, and the formation along most of the line during the engagement was consequently four deep." Firepower, then as always, bred confidence. The Federals could continue their assaults. They would get more than they could stand![35]

So thought the men, so their corps commander. Old Pete observed everything, kept his eye on everything. The sole difference that anyone could have noted in him, as he sat and smoked and watched the enemy through his field-glasses, was an increased heartiness, an added forthrightness of manner. When Lee expressed some concern lest repeated Federal assaults break the front of the First Corps, Longstreet answered proudly, almost bluntly: "General, if you put every man now on the other side of the Potomac on that field to approach me over the same line, and give me plenty of ammunition, I will kill them all before they reach my line. Look to your right; you are in some danger there, but not on my line."[36]

By 2:45 P.M. it was evident that the front-line units had to settle down to an afternoon of slaughter. Attacks seemed to come at intervals of scarcely more than a quarter of an hour. Behind each assault was the might of all the guns the Federals could bring to bear. Stafford Heights blazed ceaselessly. Many guns were firing from the town. The Confederate batteries answered defiantly when the infantry advanced but at other times husbanded their fast-dwindling ammunition.

The Washington Artillery on the heights bore the heaviest burden of defense. Finally, its caissons empty, it had to leave the post of honor. In its place came a part of the battalion that had been Stephen Lee's and now was Porter Alexander's. Into the zone of furious bombardment dashed Alexander's column, up the hill, then raced at a gallop along the face of the ridge—a sight so stirring that watchers caught their breath. Still at the gallop, the guns were brought to the earthworks where they were unlimbered and put into action as smartly as if they had been at practice for a dress review.

The welcome opening of these guns was to the infantry under the hill music as sweet as the sound of the swelling rebel yell to the ears of Old Jack, but so far as the Confederates could ascertain, the appearance of fresh artillery on the hill did not deter or even discourage the Federals. Union batteries boldly took position within little more than 300 yards of the sunken road and attempted to cover the advance of the infantry. Alexander divided his fire scrupulously between the infantry and the batteries.[37]

Repulsed, slaughtered, the Federals appeared indomitable. Again they came, again, again, till Confederates lost count of the advances. The sun set not so late, nor seemed to sink so slowly as at Sharpsburg, but the bravely mad assaults continued till twilight. Gallant they had been, their repulse the most costly the war had brought. Much truth appeared in the dispatch of a Northern newspaper correspondent: "It can hardly be in human nature for men to show more valor, or generals to manifest less judgment. . . ."[38]

Nothing touching that indictment of the Federals could be said of Longstreet. Every phase of the fighting he had watched. After his brief exchange with Lee concerning the security of his position, Old Pete did not receive a single suggestion from the commanding general. Confidently he left the defense of the heights to McLaws, to Ransom, and to their men. Easy his bearing had been, easy his handling of his corps. A great day for Longstreet that thirteenth of December was, a day that confirmed his faith in the tactical defensive.

5. The Night of the Northern Lights

At twilight and from a position so much exposed to the Federal artillery, a counterstroke by Longstreet was not to be considered. On his front, Jackson had waited to repulse a renewed attack, but all the while he burned with a desire to throw his veterans against the troops in the plain. For once he spoke openly of his plans. "I want to move forward," he said, "to attack them—to drive them into the river yonder!" and he threw out his arm as he spoke.[39]

Jackson's military judgment challenged his impulse. On the one hand, the foe was weakened and discouraged by the vain assault. At the enemy's back was a wide, deep river. As inviting a situation this was as any apostle of the offensive could ask. On the other hand, the Federal artillery was undiminished in strength and admirably placed to mow down infantry that descended from the ridge. If the Second Corps could reach the Northerners, it could drive them; but how was it to get at them? Jackson thought of a solution: A counterstroke delayed until nearly sundown, then launched after a heavy, close-range bombardment. If this demoralized the enemy for a few minutes, the Confederates might reach the masses of blue soldiery. If their thrust were repelled, Jackson's men would have darkness to cover their return to their own lines.[40]

Jackson decided that this plan was not unreasonably hazardous. Batteries were called up that had not been engaged. Quickly they prepared for the advance, which was to be followed in a few minutes by that of the infantry. Four divisions of infantry, no less, Jackson intended to use on the sound principle that if the attack was worth anything, it was worth maximum effort. To this point everything went smoothly, but abruptly, like a wagon that lost a wheel, Jackson's staff work broke down. Sandie Pendleton, his A.A.G., was hit and stunned. Without Sandie, the transmission of Jackson's orders was slow, confused, and wholly incompetent.

D. H. Hill received word promptly, but no instructions reached A. P. Hill until about dusk. Then he was directed, in few words, to advance his whole line and drive the enemy. Hood's orders, received as the sun was setting, bade him join in the movement on his right as soon as Powell Hill advanced. No intimation did Early receive during the afternoon of any plan to attack. The instructions that finally reached him only left him puzzled and confused.[41]

In due course Jackson recovered grip on the movement he had ordered. He knew where his units were and he could control the field. Through fast-gathering twilight he gave the word for the artillery to emerge and deliver what he hoped would be a surprise bombardment. Speed the advance, speed it! Whatever was done at all must be done quickly. December twilight would not linger.

Intently Jackson listened; anxiously he waited. The leading battery was out of the woods. It advanced 100 yards. Soon it would be within range. . . . Then the Federals opened. At first a few shots, then a dozen, a score, a hundred guns joined in. On a wide arc they flashed and roared. Over the field that Jackson's line would have to cross swept a scythe of fire. The Southern gunners answered, but Jackson stopped them. They were wasting ammunition. The advance could not succeed. Halt all forward movement. When Jackson returned to his quarters he did not seem especially disappointed that he had lost the twilight gamble on the plain. Although the glare of battle faded from his eyes, he did not abandon hope that God on the morrow would deliver the enemy into his hands.[42]

Darkness fell, but not for the undisputed reign of the long December night. Soon from beyond the Confederate left, far up the Rappahannock, there rose a glow. The sky flushed and grew dark again. Now shining white, it reddened and dimmed and blazed once more till it lighted the faces of the marveling soldiers—"northern lights" it must be, the fantastic sky-painting of the aurora borealis. The spectacle awed but it flattered. Wrote one Confederate: "Of course, we enthusiastic young fellows felt that the heavens were hanging out banners and streamers and setting off fireworks in honor of our victory."[43]

Of all the wounded that night the man most on the minds of Lee's lieutenants was Maxcy Gregg. He had been carried to the Yerby house and there, fully conscious, he dictated a proud dispatch to the governor of his state. "I am severely wounded," he wrote, "but the troops under my command have acted as they always have done, and I hope we have gained a glorious victory. If I am to die now, I give my life cheerfully for the independence of South Carolina, and I trust you will live to see our cause triumph completely." This was in the spirit characteristic of Gregg. Politeness and courtesy were his second nature. Did not men say that not long before Gregg was shot down, Sandie Pendleton had shouted to him that the enemy was firing at him; and Gregg had answered, "Yes, sir, thank you, they have been doing so all day." Now that the surgeons examined more carefully his injured spine, they had to conclude that his hurt was mortal. He received the death sentence without a tremor.[44]

Ere dawn, into the Yerby house, stalked Jackson—a Jackson very different from the stern-jawed, sharp-lipped general who once had put all of Gregg's colonels under arrest by a single order. The voice that greeted Gregg was low and husky and scarcely to be identified as that of the man who on the fourth of September harshly had told Gregg to take the road. Gently the Southern Cromwell slipped his hand into that of the dying officer. "The doctors tell me that you have not long to live," he said with deep emotion. "Let me ask you to dismiss this matter from your mind and turn your thoughts to God and to the world to which you go." Tears were in Gregg's eyes. Deep patrician courtesy triumphed over pain. "I thank you," he murmured, "I thank you very much." Jackson said farewell and went out. "Silently we rode away," his companion reported, "and as the sun rose, General Jackson was again on the hill near Hamilton's Crossing."[45]

Long before that, the northern lights had died away.

CHAPTER 20

In Winter Quarters

1. AFTER FREDERICKSBURG—LAMENT AND LAURELS

From Prospect Hill on the morning of December 14, Jackson could see the blue troops spread line on line for a front of one mile, but he could discern no activity. A little later, when he reconnoitered with Lee and Hood, not one Federal flag was visible. All the standards had been lowered—a circumstance that led Hood to assert that the Unionists would not give battle that day. Occasionally the sharpshooters skirmished. At intervals the Union batteries opened. To Jackson, as he rode up and down the lines, the enemy appeared to be awaiting attack instead of preparing for it.

On Longstreet's sector that fourteenth of December there was some spitting of the indignant batteries at one another, and some outburst of the chronic contention between pickets. The most gruesome scene on the front of the First Corps was the field across which the assaults of the previous afternoon had been made. The sweep of ground was covered with distorted corpses and with wounded men who writhed in misery or dragged themselves inch by inch toward the rear. "Water, water," they were calling as always the wounded do. Amid discordant screams and groans and oaths and the strange, mournful mutter of the battlefield that pathetic cry ceaselessly was audible.[1]

That night word was passed that the enemy was preparing a great assault for the next day, December 15. D. H. Hill's division was brought up to the front line by Jackson to replace Early and Taliaferro. The second line was put in Powell Hill's care. Longstreet kept a detail at work steadily on gun pits. Ransom was instructed to strengthen his position with rifle trenches. Expectancy was high everywhere. But no attack was there on the fifteenth, right, center, or left. During the afternoon the Federals asked a truce on Jackson's front for the removal of the dead who lay unburied nearer the Confederate lines than the Federal burial squads had been willing to venture at night. Jackson granted the truce. For a few hours, butternut and bluecoats were mingled on the field. Still the Confederates could not believe the Federals would abandon the offensive; still Lee refused to throw away his defensive advantage and launch an attack where his troops would come under the fire of those powerful batteries on the farther side of the Rappahannock.[2]

Late, blusterous dawn on the sixteenth disclosed the retreat of the Federals. Covered by a nighttime storm and muffled by the wind, the movement had been completed without the knowledge of the Confederates. Even the pontoon bridges had been removed or, when first seen that morning, were swinging inshore on the Federal side of the river. A more complete and humiliating failure the Army of the Potomac had not made since First Manassas.

Quickly the facts came to light at the demand of an indignant North. Burnside had planned a swift drive on Richmond, but the pontoon train he had ordered from Washington arrived too late for a surprise crossing at Fredericksburg or at any other point. A singular and unsubstantial plan of action finally was adopted and reluctantly accepted by the commanders of the three "Grand Divisions" into which he had divided his army. He had been brought by some process of reasoning to conclude that the Southerners would be more surprised by his crossing at Fredericksburg than elsewhere. Tactical arrangements were not quite so vague as the strategic plan. Enough troops had been put on the Federal left, Burnside believed, to have pressed home the attack of George Gordon Meade, whose division entered the gap between Lane and Archer. The fault, in Burnside's judgment, was with William B. Franklin, commanding the left Grand Division, who did not support vigorously the attack of Meade.

The costly attack on Longstreet's front had been ordered by Burnside in the belief that Franklin already had attacked heavily on the Confederate right and had caused Lee to weaken his left to support the right. Mistaken in this, Burnside had continued the attack on Longstreet because, apparently, he could not think of anything else to do, and would not break off the fight. He intended to renew the action the next morning, but suspended the attack when his generals expressed unanimous opposition to it. "I felt that I could not take the responsibility of ordering the attack," General Burnside wrote, "notwithstanding my own belief at the time that the works of the enemy could be carried."[3]

Although the Confederate commanders were chagrined that the enemy had escaped with no more punishment than that of a costly repulse, the South was jubilant. The *Richmond Examiner* proclaimed the battle a "stunning defeat to the invader, a splendid victory to the defender of the sacred soil." In the eyes of the *Richmond Dispatch* Fredericksburg was the greatest battle ever waged on this continent and a complete Confederate victory. The *Charleston Mercury* reflected confidently, "General Lee knows his business and that army has yet known no such word as fail." Burnside's return to the left bank of the Rappahannock spiced the newspaper rejoicing with somewhat confused speculation, but ended in the declaration that the Federal commander had admitted defeat and could do little further harm during the winter. In the whole of this discussion there was no shadow of disappointment that Lee had not been able to follow up his success.[4]

Along with celebration was lament. Total casualties were 4,201, though the dead numbered 458 only. Many who were reported "wounded" were seeking a Christmas holiday. A remarkable fact—unique in the major battles of the Army of Northern Virginia—was that not a single colonel was killed. Sorrow was widespread for Maxcy Gregg—Gregg remembered now as the soldier, not as the extremist of state's rights, the advocate of a re-opened slave trade. South Carolina and all the South mourned him. Of Gregg and Tom Cobb, Lee wrote, "the Confederacy has lost two of its noblest citizens, and the army two of its bravest and most distinguished officers. The country consents to the sacrifice of such men as these, and the gallant soldiers who fell with them, only to secure the inestimable blessing they died to obtain." Although Tom Cobb's name was linked with Maxcy Gregg's in many like tributes, the Georgian did not lack distinctive honors of his own. Longstreet wrote, ". . . we have lost one of our most promising officers and statesmen." McLaws added, "Our country has lost a pure and able defender of her rights both in council and the field."[5]

Laurels followed laments. Officers most praised in official reports were Barksdale for his defense of the waterfront on the eleventh, Pelham for his artillery duel on the right in the first stage of the battle, Alexander for his dash under fire to the crest of Marye's Heights, and Archer for his quick change of front after the breakthrough on his left. Most of the men from whom the South had become accustomed to expect fine service sustained at Fredericksburg their reputation. Lee did no more than equal justice when he said in his final report: "To Generals Longstreet and Jackson great praise is due for the disposition and management of their respective corps." This was tribute to the new organization as surely as to the men who directed it. Staff organization had not been perfect, to be sure, but the authority of the lieutenant generals had been adequate. The contrast with conditions during the Seven Days had been marked at Second Manassas and Sharpsburg. Now that the system of corps command was legalized as well as tested, it was vindicated. One question only, in this connection, began to trouble Lee: Were the corps too large?[6]

Had Lee's tribute to his corps commanders been reduced to comparisons, Longstreet would have been entitled to somewhat more distinction at Fredericksburg than Jackson. During the whole of the day of battle Old Pete kept his hand on every unit of his corps. Though he had no tasks of especial difficulty, he did not make a faulty move. Jackson had done nothing amiss and had done several things admirably; but there remains a question concerning the vigilance of his examination of his front before the battle opened. Stonewall himself was far from satisfied with the outcome. As he looked glumly across the fields on the morning of the sixteenth, he spoke gravely, almost bitterly: "I did not think that a little red earth would have frightened them. I am sorry that they are gone. I am sorry I fortified."[7]

If the most notable of Lee's lieutenants vindicated at Fredericksburg the reputation won by wise administration and hard fighting, at least one divisional commander regained standing that had been impaired. This man was Lafayette McLaws. In contrast to his course during the Maryland campaign, McLaws's handling of his troops had been sagacious. Reports both of his corps commander and of the commanding general praised him. Privately he wrote his wounded friend Dick Ewell a letter that reveals the fineness of his character. Said McLaws: "Three brigades of my division were active participants and I can say with perfect conviction that never in the world has there been more determined devotion and dauntless courage than they exhibited."[8]

Some of the new brigade commanders had been distinguished. General Lee's report made plain the substantial service rendered by Robert Ransom in the defense of Willis's Hill. John R. Cooke's serious wound in the head—from which he would make recovery—had not been received until he had shown that he could handle a brigade with ability. Jim Lane had the misfortune to lose more than 500 men in this, his first fight as a general officer, but he was not held responsible for the gap on his right, and officially was praised by A. P. Hill for his firm defense.[9]

Several colonels attracted the notice that usually marked a man for promotion. In the absence of A. R. Lawton, who still was suffering from wounds, his brigade had been under its senior colonel, E. N. Atkinson of the 26th Georgia. When Atkinson fell, Colonel Clement A. Evans of the 31st Georgia had taken command and done admirably. Trimble's brigade, in the same manner, had been under a tall, magnificent North Carolinian, Colonel Robert F. Hoke of the 21st, who had fought gallantly in every battle of his regiment. Hoke had perfect self-confidence and a certain ferocious quality of leadership, which was tempered with discretion. Sent forward by Early to help mend the gap between Lane and Archer, he aided in driving out the Federals and rushed on headlong; but he soon saw his danger and carefully withdrew and established a strong outpost. This was the work of a man who manifestly knew how to fight.

As much was to be said of James A. Walker of the 13th Virginia, who was commanding Early's brigade while Old Jube was acting for Ewell. The difference was that Walker had been tried frequently enough to make it clear that he was qualified already for brigade command. Still another colonel who had his first opportunity, though a brief one, in brigade command was Alfred M. Scales of the 13th North Carolina, whose career from the Peninsula campaign onward had been one of consistent stout service in Pender's hard-fighting brigade. During the short time Pender required to go to the rear and have his wound dressed, Scales was in command of the brigade. He met the test.[10]

The improved morale of the army and the absence of straggling were commended in numerous reports. Lee for the first time was able to say that "the calmness and steadiness with which orders were obeyed and maneuvers executed in the midst of battle, evinced the discipline of a veteran army."[11] Those final words represented the ideal toward which Johnston before him, and then he and Jackson and Longstreet and Stuart and the Hills and others less renowned, had been working.

"A veteran army"—twenty months had been required to make it that, but now all the arms of the service had earned the title. The infantry spoke for itself through its volleys and its movements; the cavalry had caught the spirit of Stuart. At Fredericksburg the artillery, though still outgunned and outranged by the Federals, gave a good account of itself. After Pelham and his men, the greatest honor went with the worst danger on Jackson's right, where Colonel R. Lindsay Walker kept A. P. Hill's artillery calm and resolute under concentrated fire for a long time before it could reply. As usual, where the fire was furious, there was Willie Pegram. By his side fought David McIntosh.

The men with the long-range guns had a hard if not an encouraging day. At army headquarters two 30-pounder Parrotts exploded, though without injuring anyone. Artillerists were dissatisfied with the performance of their 20-pounder Parrotts. The only long-range gun that won special praise was an English Whitworth, which was under the command of Captain R. A. Hardaway, a marksman of special skill. Harvey Hill, who always found artillery very good or very bad, credited Hardaway and this Whitworth with killing Brigadier General George D. Bayard, because Hill did not believe any other Confederate gun could reach Franklin's field headquarters, where Bayard was struck fatally by a fragment of shell. Similarly, General Lee was pleased to observe that Colonel Armistead L. Long of his staff, who had been trained as an artillerist, had forgotten none of his art. Before and during the battle, Lee stated, Colonel Long was "particularly useful . . . in posting and securing the artillery."[12]

The long, ugly quarrel between Jackson and A. P. Hill probably explained the tone of part of the discussion of responsibility for the gap between Archer and Lane. In Hill's report he mentioned an "interval" there, but he spoke of Gregg, in reserve, as "crossing the interval." There was no inaccuracy in anything Hill said about the gap, but there was no statement of the distances involved, nor was there any admission of negligence or error in permitting the gap to remain. In Lee's report there was no praise for Hill or for any other division commander; consequently there was no implication of censure for Hill even by Lee's usual device of omitting reference to those he could not commend.

Jackson's handling of the episode was different. Nothing directly was said of the interval until he described the main assault of the Federals: "they continued . . . ," he wrote, "still to press forward and before General A. P. Hill closed the interval which he had left between Archer and Lane, it was penetrated, and the enemy, pressing forward in overwhelming numbers through that interval, turned Lane's right and Archer's left." That was all, but it was unmistakable censure and deserved censure. Hill had left a somewhat similar gap in his front at Groveton. A second offense of the same character was not to be overlooked by Hill's corps commander. Jackson did not stop to ask the reasons for not occupying the gap. The gap was there; Hill was responsible for it; that was the fact set down—that and no more. Who can say whether Jackson introduced this censure of Hill merely because he felt it was his duty to do so, or because, in their continuing controversy, he intended to add new evidence of Hill's carelessness?[13]

2. CAVALRY RAIDS AND QUARRELS

In the mind of the soldier, the winter of 1862–63 was dull and purposeless; in the history of the army the season was one of anxiety and alarms. It was marked by six developments. First came a series of cavalry raids that culminated, March 17, in the sharp and costly action at Kelly's Ford. Second were two sets of promotions and a marked change in the status of Gustavus W. Smith. Third, the army acquired a better knowledge of its components, and more particularly of its staff, during the closer relationship of winter quarters. Fourth, a basic and vital reorganization of the artillery was effected. Fifth was a period of semi-independent command for James Longstreet. Last of all was the climax of the quarrel between Jackson and Powell Hill at a time when Jackson was being prepared spiritually for his supreme achievement.

Through all this were the cohesives of sustained morale of the men in the ranks and the leadership of Lee. Usually, if the soldier despaired, it was because he did not get letters from home. When, as more often happened, he endured cold without compliant and short rations without grumbling, he had in his pocket a courageous message from wife or mother or sweetheart. While the women kept high the spirit of the men who carried the rifles, the commanding general resolved the problems and smoothed the ruffled sensibilities and settled the contention of those who bore the insignia of rank.

Of this care on the part of Lee, the cavalry needed little. Stuart was abundantly able to direct operations. At the instance of Lee, even before the Battle of Fredericksburg, Stuart had bedeviled Burnside by raids north of the Rappahannock. Virtually all the supplies and munitions for the Union army were dispatched by water to the base on Aquia Creek; but cavalry reinforcements, sutlers' wagons, and occasional supply trains used the Telegraph Road. That old highway ran south from Alexandria and parallel to the Potomac. Along the road were two small towns only that the Confederates could hope to reach—Dumfries and Occoquan. Guards of some proportion were known to be at both places, and these troops and their provisions and stores, together with the telegraph line from Burnside's headquarters to Washington, were avowed objects of the raids Stuart ordered. He must be credited also with a desire to keep his regiments alert by field exercises. Stuart must be suspected, moreover, of cherishing the troopers' familiar hope of picking up a well-furnished sutlers' train.

Not one raid was there, but four, and in rising strength or deeper objective. On November 27, Wade Hampton took 158 men from the Carolina and Georgia mounted units and crossed the Rappahannock. Under the very noses of nodding Federals he captured about 100 horses and 92 officers and men. This affair of Hartwood Church, as it was styled in reports, won high praise for the men and their leader, and started an angry hue-and-cry among the Federals. So successful was the foray that Stuart permitted Hampton on December 10 to march on Dumfries. This time with 520 troopers, Hampton readily enough captured the guard of some 50 men at Dumfries, caught a wagon train, and cut the telegraph line. When he turned back, along with his prisoners he brought 17 wagons across the Rappahannock, and for his raid he did not have to pay with so much as a scratch to any of his men. Three nights in the snow did not daunt them.[14]

As soon as his adventurers were rested, Hampton tried on December 17–18 to reach Occoquan. He ran into a green New Jersey cavalry regiment which put up some show of a fight, but managed to get off with about 150 prisoners and 20 wagons. The finest feat of this raid was the capture of all 41 of the pickets on eight miles of guarded road. To take each picket post without alarming the next was a tribute to the stalking skill of the troopers. Extensive sutlers' supplies were captured though nothing was said of them in official reports. The booty included 300 pairs of excellent boots, numerous baskets of champagne and claret, and some toothsome cheeses.[15]

The fourth raid was conducted by Stuart himself and was the most ambitious of the series. With 1,800 men and four guns, Stuart rode up the south bank of the Rappahannock the day after Christmas, crossed to Morrisville, and prepared, as he reported, "to take possession of the Telegraph Road, to capture all the trains that might be passing." The plan was to descend on the road in three columns, under Fitz Lee, Wade Hampton, and Rooney Lee. For once Jeb, traveling with Rooney Lee, picked for himself the wrong road of adventure. Fitz Lee and his troopers had the good fortune to overtake nine sutlers' wagons, while all Rooney caught were a few pickets and army wagons. Dumfries proved too well defended a position to risk storming, and regretfully Stuart led Rooney and Fitz Lee's columns to an untroubled bivouac nine miles northwest of Dumfries. He met there Hampton, whose assault on Occoquan had misfired to the extent of capturing seven wagons only and ten or fifteen prisoners.[16]

So small was the recompense that Stuart was at first of a mind to end the raid, but he determined instead to cross the Occoquan and raid north of that stream. In the event the enemy tried to cut him off, he felt he could make a long detour in the direction of the Orange and Alexandria Railroad and rejoin the army on the Fredericksburg front. The column had ridden some five miles through the chill December morning when Union cavalry were reported ahead in a wood. Hasty reconnaissance disclosed two regiments and, so far as Stuart could see, no more. He decided promptly that his men could ride over this force. Let Fitz Lee charge. Put the 1st Virginia in front. Clear the woods and pursue.

Forward roared the 1st Virginia. It met scattered pistol fire and brief resistance and then it had the target of fleeing men. Some of the Federals were killed. Approximately 100 were captured. The pursuit continued across the Occoquan, where they found the Federal cavalry's camps deserted and comfortably furnished, though reports mention no sutlers' establishments. Everything of value that could not be carried off was burned.[17]

Stuart did not propose to take the desperate gamble of returning as he had come, by a route on which hostile troops might be collecting fast. As on the Chickahominy and Chambersburg raids, the bolder course seemed more prudent, the longer road the safer. So the column turned westward and pressed rapidly on and, after dark, approached Burke's Station on the Orange and Alexandria Railroad. There Jeb was deeper than ever in the Federal lines, but he was unshaken in his confidence that surprise and

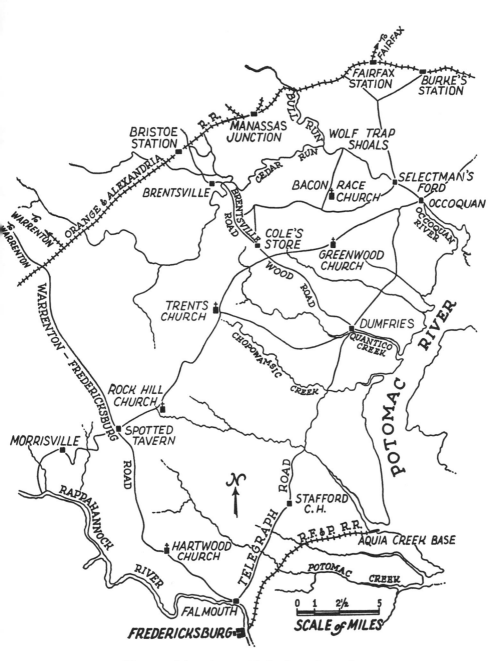

Terrain of the winter raids by Stuart's cavalry.

swift movement would get him safely out of any net the Union commanders might spread.

He sent men ahead to pounce on the telegraph office before an alarm could be sent over the wire, then his own operator sat down at the sounder and read off the messages that excited Federal commanders were transmitting about ways and means of catching "the rebel raiders." Thereupon Stuart drafted a telegram to the quartermaster general of the United States army and his operator sent it to Washington. A protest and remonstrance it was concerning the poor quality of the mules being supplied the Federal army. They were so inferior, said Stuart, that when put to captured wagons they scarcely could pull the vehicles within the Confederate lines. To this message Stuart attached his signature.

Approaching Fairfax Court House they encountered sharp fire from securely posted Federals. To this they sent not a shot in answer, and a flag of truce was sent out to inquire if they were friend or foe. A Southerner replied that the flag would be answered in the morning. The Confederates lighted enormous campfires to deceive the enemy and by morning were on their way to Frying Pan—which was neither warm nor full—and Middleburg. Stuart and his troopers made their leisurely way back to the Rappahannock, stopping where hospitality offered, and reached Fredericksburg on New Year's Day.

Losses had not been large—one killed, thirteen wounded and the same number missing. To these casualties Major H. B. McClellan added, "The captured sutlers' wagons proved capable of inflicting nearly as much damage as the rifles of the enemy." Stuart, with high delight, counted about 200 prisoners, an equal number of horses, 20 wagons, 100 arms or more, and much miscellaneous loot. Of these gains Stuart made the utmost, reporting that he had destroyed Burnside's direct line of communication with Washington and scattered the Union cavalry on the Occoquan.[18]

In the relaxing leisure of winter quarters Stuart cemented old friends and made new enemies. It always was that way with him. Women uniformly liked him. Men thought him an ideal soldier or an exhibitionist. There was no middle ground of opinion concerning him, no indifference to him. Of all his admirers, none was more fascinated than was Jackson. The affection of the Southern Cromwell was returned by the young Rupert in overflowing measure. Few dared joke with Jackson; Stuart did often and never received a rebuke. He had won the right to laugh sometimes because he supported always.

Jackson's staff and his admirers were quite ready to admit what Stuart maintained in praise of their chief. Others doubtless rallied the more heartily to Lee because Stuart was a "Jackson man." Lafayette McLaws, for example, himself honest, sincere, and not overcritical, had undisguised contempt for Stuart's showmanship. The Georgian wrote Dick Ewell, "Stuart carries around with him a banjo player and a special correspondent. This claptrap is noticed and lauded as a peculiarity of genius when, in fact, it is nothing else but the act of a buffoon to attract attention."[19]

Still other officers disliked Stuart without reference to any division into Jackson or Lee factions. No Stuart foe could match the flaming hatred of Grumble Jones. That strange man had become a more conspicuous figure because of his promotion in the autumn at Jackson's instance to the rank of brigadier. At year's end Jones had been assigned, again on Jackson's recommendation, to command the Valley District. It is possible that one reason for the assignment was the wish of General Lee to utilize Jones's capacity for command to a more effective degree than was possible when Jones was under Stuart.

The differences between Grumble and Jeb ran back to the beginning of the war. Jones, who was thirty-seven at the time of the secession of Virginia, had graduated from West Point in 1848 and afterward served in the Mounted Rifles. In 1852, in a shipwreck, his young bride was swept from his arms and drowned. Jones never recovered in spirit. Embittered, complaining, suspicious, he resigned from the army. In 1861, answering the call to Virginia's service, he was assigned to Jeb Stuart's regiment. Although promoted colonel when Stuart became brigadier, Jones, in the judgment of Jeb's friends, was jealous from the first of Stuart. This feeling, W. W. Blackford wrote, "ripened afterwards into as genuine a hatred as I ever remember to have seen." Jones widened his animosity to include his lieutenant colonel, Fitz Lee, one of Stuart's closest friends. As Jones was unpopular with the regiment and Fitz much admired, an ugly situation developed. In the spring elections of 1862, Jones was displaced, but then was assigned to the 7th Virginia.[20]

The Laurel Brigade, placed under him later, had as its nucleus Ashby's famous command, which lacked nothing in valor though its discipline out of action was defiantly low. Grumble had gone to work to correct this. He kept his men as busy as he could on raids, and in camp drilled them daily and made them obey the letter of regulations. In his reports he described all his trials in a manner to justify his *nomme de guerre*. Lee commended and encouraged him, but the people of the Valley emulated him in grumbling. Ere long the secretary of war went so far as to ask Lee to replace Jones with Fitz Lee. In answer the patient commanding general defended Jones, and continued to support him. But Jones's state of mind respecting Stuart and Fitz Lee, and the state of mind of the Valley people concerning him, promised trouble for the spring of 1863.[21]

With division in the ranks of the cavalry, with horses dying and fodder scarce, pessimists might question whether the mounted arm could keep safe the wings of the army, guard the outposts, and bring back promptly accurate news of the enemy's movements. The grayjackets themselves never doubted. Nor did Lee, nor Stuart nor Hampton. When the time for field operations approached in the spring of 1863, they sought more cavalry but they did not lack faith in what they had.

3. PROMOTION AND A FIERY RESIGNATION

One question endlessly was asked in camps around Fredericksburg: Would Burnside renew the attack? Against the background of the wintry sky his campfires seemed to cover Stafford Heights and to gleam northward, division by division, mile on mile. It seemed so improbable that the commander of that great army would be content with a single blow that the cavalry were spread on a wide front to watch for any secret march. The infantry fortified heavily the Fredericksburg heights. If the numerically superior Federals made a feint there while preparing to attack at another point, a small Confederate force could hold the key position near the town. The remainder of the army could start after the enemy.

Burnside's next move was not the sole strategical perplexity. At the time of his attack in December, the Federals took the offensive in North Carolina and pushed from New Bern to Kinston and Goldsborough. The government and the people of the North State were much alarmed. Reinforcements had to be snatched up wherever they could be found in lower Virginia and South Carolina and hurried to the threatened quarter. The competence of the command there was brought into question and forthwith was entangled with rank and promotion in the Army of Northern Virginia. The odd personalities involved generated controversies and vexations, and illustrated the difficulties of organizing effective army command in an individualistic democracy. Grimly amusing, too, at least in retrospect, some of the complications appear.

Much that Lee had planned for command in the army in October was set at naught by the President's strict construction of military law. Mr. Davis would not promote officers who were unable physically to exercise immediate command, and, at the same time, he refused to retire some of those who seemed to be invalided. In application, this meant deferment of the promotion of I. R. Trimble because he still was crippled by the wound received at Groveton. Conversely, it postponed the advancement of Jube Early because Ewell might resume command.

Neither Ewell nor Trimble had been doing any too well. Trimble had been dogged by camp erysipelas and later by what probably was osteomyelitis of the leg bone that had sustained a compound fracture. His temper was not one of sweet reasonableness. Dick Ewell was in a healthier state of mind but not of body. In November 1862 the great marcher had been moved to Richmond to the home of Dr. F. W. Hancock. Despite the care Dr. Hancock had given, Old Bald Head had lost his temper because he had not recovered faster, and then one day had lost his balance, too, and had fallen. His amputated leg hemorrhaged badly and put Ewell flat on his back for weeks. Still chivalrous he showed himself to be in answer to a letter Jubal Early wrote in complaint over delayed promotion: ". . . what ought to be most gratifying to you is that the injustice in your case is almost universally recognized. An officer of high rank in your division"—Ewell did not say *my*—"told me the other day they had just discovered they had a trump and the country is fast arriving at the same conclusion."[22]

This was not flattery on the part of Ewell. Although Early had won no popularity, he had earned increasing respect as a soldier. Trimble had affection as well as respect. The promotion of these two to permanent divisional command seems to have been regarded as a continuing probability. In addition, General Lee had been watching Harry Heth. Nor had the commanding general forgotten Arnold Elzey, who had been wounded in the head at Gaines' Mill, and Allegheny Johnson, still limping badly from the bullet he had received at McDowell. Doubtless on Jackson's endorsement, when Allegheny began to recover Lee recommended a major general's commission.

Of these five men marked for promotion to the grade of major general—Early, Trimble, Heth, Elzey, and Johnson—circumstance gave the first step-up to Arnold Elzey. Although the injury to his face and tongue was such that he scarcely could speak, he was thought physically able to administer a district. On December 4 he was commissioned at the new rank, and on December 12 placed in command of the Richmond defenses and adjacent areas to the south.

This assignment infuriated Trimble. He believed Elzey had discredited him, and he suspected also that he missed promotion because Jackson, in endorsing him, had stated, "I do not regard him as a good disciplinarian." In a raging letter to Adjutant General Cooper, whom he knew well, Trimble spoke bluntly of Elzey's love of liquor. In his own behalf Trimble defended himself against Jackson's charge. Said he, ". . . the General knew but little of any brigade, but his *old one*. It is well known to all, that I was most particular in my enforcement of discipline. My brigade had fewer stragglers; burnt no rails, committed no thefts in the country, was more often drilled . . . than any other in the Army of Jackson. . . . If I am to have promotion I want it *at once* and I particularly request, that my date may be from 26th August, the date of the capture of Manassas—which General Jackson was pleased to say he considered 'the most brilliant exploit of the war.'"

Although Jackson inquired whether Trimble was well enough to direct a division in camp and Lee did his utmost to smooth ruffled feelings, the Marylander did not improve rapidly. He did find one outlet for his energies and imagination in planning a paper campaign against the Federal advanced base at Aquia Creek, a plan the ever-patient Lee examined and praised but could not apply. Trimble's promotion was not delayed as long as he feared it would be. On January 19, 1863, Lee announced the promotion of Trimble and Early to the coveted rank of major general. The only recorded opposition came from W. B. Taliaferro. As senior brigadier in Jackson's division, he felt he should have had the divisional command, and when he did not get it, he told friends he would seek transfer to some other theater of operations.[23]

The vacancies at the grade of brigadier general were not difficult to fill. The man to lead Gregg's famous command was Colonel Samuel McGowan of the 14th North Carolina, who already was distinguished for quick perception and prompt, energetic action. For Tom Cobb's brigade the choice manifestly should be Colonel W. T. Wofford of the 18th Georgia, able and experienced. As Trimble was to be promoted, his regiments well might go to the hard-hitting Colonel R. F. Hoke of the 21st North Carolina, who had ably commanded the brigade at Fredericksburg. To succeed Paul Semmes temporarily at the head of Georgia troops no colonel was so well qualified or so well known to the army as "Old Rock" Benning, who had won fame with Toombs's brigade and most notably at Sharpsburg. Finally, as W. S. Featherston decided he would prefer duty in the Gulf States, he was relieved. The delayed appointment of Colonel Carnot Posey became effective.

Such, then, were the promotions and changes in January—Trimble to take Jackson's division when strong enough to do so, Early to continue in temporary command of Ewell's division at appropriate grade, McGowan to have Gregg's men, Wofford to lead Cobb's, Hoke to take Trimble's former brigade, Benning temporarily to have Semmes's, and Posey to be assigned Featherston's.

As these changes came little more than two months after the reorganization necessitated by the losses of the late summer, an optimist might have hoped that the army would have stable command in the spring of 1863. It was not to be. Resignations as well as casualties were in prospect. For the future as in the past the two dominant jealousies were to complicate and mar the promotions: Some of the officers who had entered the army from civil life carped always at the West Pointers; others maintained that Virginians always were preferred.

It was over competence in command, however, that a situation of gravity was developing in North Carolina. Gustavus W. Smith had been able in August to report for duty after the so-called paralysis that had overwhelmed him on the second day at Seven Pines. Lee tactfully assigned to Smith the "right wing of the army," which included Richmond and departmental command as far south as the Cape Fear River. His duties were chiefly those of watching an inactive enemy along the Virginia and North Carolina coast.

Nothing of large moment had arisen to disturb Smith until the seven lieutenant generals were appointed under the act of September 18, 1862. As all those officers, with the exception of Leonidas Polk, had been Smith's juniors at the grade of major general, the offended officer promptly inquired of the secretary of war why he had been passed over. Secretary Randolph told Smith that the departmental command he was then exercising was not considered one that rated the high grade within the intent of the law. This explanation did not satisfy Smith. On October 21 he wrote a long protest at being overslaughed and closed with formal tender of his resignation, but at Randolph's instance he agreed to continue in a post the secretary said he did not then know how to fill.[24]

In December Federal forces under John G. Foster made the raid on Kinston and Goldsborough in North Carolina. With scarcely more than 2,000 Confederates at the outset, Shanks Evans put up the best fight he could, but he lost by capture over 400 of his men and six of his guns. During the closing days of this affair Smith was on the scene and in general command. Beverly Robertson with his cavalry, Samuel G. French from the Suffolk-Petersburg district, Johnston Pettigrew—all these had some part in the affair. In the end, the Federals burned the main bridge on the Weldon-Wilmington Railroad, paroled 496 Confederates, and carried off the captured guns. "Our troops," wrote French, "were not properly handled at Goldsborough." That was a moderate statement of the fact.[25]

So serious was the prospect of a renewed Federal invasion that North Carolina manifestly must be reinforced substantially and at once. On January 3, General Lee started Ransom's demi-division southward. Consideration had also to be given to command in North Carolina. Harvey Hill, the most conspicuous soldier from the state in the Army of Northern Virginia, was sick and depressed: Would it help him and North Carolina also, to detach him for service there? Despite misgivings of Hill's administrative capacity, Lee put the question to the President and the now secretary of war, James A. Seddon. Both of them concluded that the suggestion was worth canvassing, and on January 14, Harvey Hill was ordered to proceed to Richmond and to report to the adjutant general. Hill by that time must have been in serious plight physically. He sought relief from all service and talked of resigning, though he agreed, at length, to go home to Charlotte and to withhold formal resignation. There the matter rested. In the meantime, circumstances forced a decision of another sort.[26]

Robert Ransom had reached North Carolina with his half-division and had observed something of General Smith's handling of the command, and he was much disturbed by what he saw. In accordance with the usage of the old army he determined to write unofficially what he could not transmit to army headquarters without insubordination. In a personal letter to General R. H. Chilton of Lee's staff he set forth his unhappiness and enumerated some of the faults he saw in the defense of the state. Essentially it appears that he felt Smith lacking in energy and inclined to dodge matters that involved excitement.

This state of affairs Chilton informally described to Lee, as Ransom doubtless had intended. Lee considered the situation so serious that he at once forwarded Ransom's letter to President Davis. If, the commanding general explained, Smith's health was impaired, it was more than ever to be desired that Kirby Smith, who had been under consideration, should take the command in North Carolina. Should that not be possible, then, said Lee, it might be better for Elzey to take the field in North Carolina and for Gustavus Smith to assume command of the Richmond district. Action came quickly. As Kirby Smith was not immediately available, the President recalled Gustavus Smith to Richmond, sent French temporarily to North Carolina, and had Secretary Seddon telegraph to inquire whether D. H. Hill would accept the command of his own state. Hill hesitated to accept responsibility of that magnitude and answered Seddon that he would prefer to serve under Smith.[27]

In Richmond Smith became restless and unhappy. In a personal interview with the President he was given no instructions. This fired new discontent. For ten days Smith fumed and kicked his heels and then, February 7, he forwarded as a formal resignation a copy of his letter of October 21 to the previous secretary of war. With this he coupled a new explanation and protest. He concluded it, "I cannot consent to remain here and be responsible at this time for operations in North Carolina. Neither am I willing to serve under the orders of those who were recently my juniors. There is no alternative left me but to resign my commission in the army."

The letter of resignation was returned with a stinging endorsement by Davis of what he termed "this remarkable paper." After sparing no sarcasm or acid in dismissing point by point Smith's grievances, the President endorsed Smith's second and final resignation thus: "Secretary of War—If the alternative of resignation or appointment as Lieutenant-General be presented as a claim founded on former relative rank as a Major-General it will only be proper to accept the resignation, as to admit the claim would be in derogation of the legal power of the Executive and in disregard of the consideration due to services rendered in battle and campaign."[28]

As a soldier who had been a politician and was as quick to draw pen as sword, Smith would not permit the President's endorsement to pass unchallenged. He took his time, and on February 23 completed a letter of some 2,400 words in which he reviewed again his grievances, answered the President's points, and no doubt satisfied himself that he had demolished Mr. Davis's argument. The gravamen of Smith's letter was that he had been "overslaughed by wholesale," that he had in effect commanded a corps at Manassas during the winter of 1861–62, and that, when his juniors were promoted over him, he became convinced that he was not "respected, supported and confided in by the government to an extent sufficient" to authorize his remaining in service. It was the kind of letter a man writes in order to read aloud to his friends at a club-table, where he pauses at the impressive flourishes as if to say, "I got him there, did I not?"[29]

All this Smith wrote with care and forwarded to the President, but he got no answer. He went to Charleston as a volunteer aide to Beauregard, who was of a temper to welcome any Confederate hostile to Mr. Davis. Besides, Beauregard personally was fond of Smith. So were many of the officers and politicians who knew him intimately. Harvey Hill was among those who lamented the departure of Smith from the service. In a letter to him, the North Carolinian confirmed in a few words all General Lee had written the President about Hill's unwillingness to assume exclusive responsibility. Said Hill: "At present I feel at a loss what to do. I have not yet assumed command and do not wish to do so. I came here with the understanding that I was to serve under you. Honestly and truly I prefer that position and shrink from the other."[30]

CHAPTER 21

Facing a New Campaign

1. THE DEVELOPING STAFF

With more of eagerness than of anxiety, the question asked so often during December was repeated in the New Year—When will Burnside advance; where will he strike? Scouts' reports on January 20, a blustery, threatening day, indicated a Federal offensive was to be undertaken, and that the crossing would be in the vicinity of Banks' and United States fords. Preliminary dispositions were made to cope with the advance. It did not come. On the evening of the twentieth a violent storm began and continued all night and for two days thereafter. Patriotic Virginia roads on the north side of the Rappahannock swam in defiant mud. Federal infantry could do no more than creep forward, artillery had to double teams, pontoon trains could not be moved at all. This "Mud March" simply stalled. A second storm began early on the twenty-seventh and did not halt its attack until the twenty-ninth. By that time, six inches of snow covered the ground. Said Lee, ". . . the probabilities are that the roads will be impractical for some time." That was not the only promise of a respite. Burnside on January 25 was relieved of command. A new commander was given the Army of the Potomac in the person of "Fighting Joe" Hooker, who had led one of the Grand Divisions and had been one of the most vigorous of Burnside's critics.[1]

As mud and the preparation of a new plan would preclude another advance for weeks, Lee's lieutenants at last could expect days and days of inactivity. The army settled down in winter quarters for the first prolonged period of quiet the whole command had spent together. Many of the units encamped back of Fredericksburg had not joined until after the winter of 1861–62. Jackson in that first wintry season had been on detached service in the Valley. Lee was in South Carolina. Now the Manassas army, Magruder's men, Huger's Norfolk garrison, Jackson's Army of the Valley, Loring's men—all these, as the Army of Northern Virginia, shared the same camps and enjoyed the same period of rest.

435

A satirist only could have styled it a period of content. Although it was not a severe winter in the estimation of natives, it seemed to men from farther south intolerably frigid. Some of the soldiers built log huts, and some dug themselves holes which they covered with tent flies. Chimneys of many patterns rose. Often the soldiers were close to hunger. They would have fared miserably worse had not parents and kinsmen stripped the pantries of Southern homes to provide the boys boxes of provisions. Consolation and perhaps even a measure of reconciliation to the miseries of war came through religious meetings. The revival, begun in the Valley during the autumn, deepened during the winter. Despite their various trials, most of the men maintained their morale, and found amusement in dramas, minstrel shows, and snowball battles.[2]

Jackson, as will be set forth, spent the bleak months amid comforts that might have shocked some of the admirers of the ascetic leader of the New Model Army. Lee lived simply in a tent near Hamilton's Crossing till illness compelled him to go to Yerby's. Stuart was not far distant. The other generals of division found such comfort or bore such hardship as the location of their posts of command offered. It was in liaison among these commanders that some of the staff officers first became familiar to all of their seniors. Most of the generals, of course, knew Jackson's assistant adjutant general, Sandie Pendleton, and as many of them had cordial comradeship with Moxley Sorrel, the A.A.G. of Longstreet. All officers above the grade of colonel at one time or another had met General R. H. Chilton, senior staff officer to Lee. Other officers of the staff who scarcely were known outside brigades in December became familiar to many of the generals by May.

Staff organization at the beginning of the war barely deserved the name. A crude distinction was made between the so-called staff departments such as those of the quartermaster and the commissary, and the personal staff of a commanding officer; but the modern conception of a general staff was not applied. Some generals appeared to think they were privileged to have in addition to the staff provided by army regulations as many volunteer aides as they might desire. Beauregard before Manassas had the usual heads of the staff departments, two assistant adjutants general, and no less than six volunteer aides, several of whom were powerful South Carolina politicians—a total of fifteen.[3]

Confederate law did nothing to keep officeholders from acquiring martial titles. The President, at discretion, on the application of a general officer, was authorized "to appoint from civil life persons to the staff of such officer."[4] This opened wide the door to personal and political appointments and, what often was worse, to the designation of sons, nephews, cousins, or brothers-in-law to positions for which they had neither training nor aptitude. Personal staff appointments were regarded all too often as personal patronage. Where nepotism was unabashed, a staff almost without exception might bear one family name.

The manifest defects of organization were laid before Congress that winter of 1862–63. The influence of Lee was exerted in behalf of the adoption of the French staff organization. Lee urged also a reduction in the number of aides and more adequate provision for adjutants and inspectors. Of the staff as a whole, he told President Davis, "If you can fill these positions with proper officers not the relatives and social friends of the commanders, who, however agreeable their company, are not always the most useful, you might hope to have the finest army in the world."[5]

Although that ideal never was approximated, many men who began the war with no experience had become by the winter of 1862–63 qualified staff officers, and they still were developing. At army headquarters most of the officers were older than the youthful average of the corps and divisional staffs. Colonel Charles S. Venable—approaching thirty-six years of age and a professor of mathematics besides—in fact was considered of an age and dignity that equipped him, when necessary, to present staff grievances to the commanding general. In extreme instances he was expected to beard the general and to point out the lapses of the "Great Tycoon," as the staff sometimes among themselves made bold to style Lee.

Of all the personal staff at army headquarters, the man best known to visitors and on most intimate terms with the aides of other general officers was Walter Taylor. He was the youngest of Lee's official family and served as "inside man" because of his skill and accuracy in handling the official correspondence that Lee detested. Of unassuming personality was Taylor but magnetic from youth, friendly, and understanding. Possessed of a memory as notable as his industry, his one weakness was an impulse to steal off during a battle and participate in a charge. Fortunately he was never caught by Lee while thus indulging his love of martial excitement.[6]

Jackson's staff was regarded by the army as most unequal in merit. When Major the Reverend Dr. R. L. Dabney had been chief of staff he commanded respect for his intelligence and, in camp, for his activity; but on the march and in battle he had been wholly lacking in experience. Opinion was expressed, *sotto voce,* that Jackson overestimated the value of Presbyterian clergy in the army. James Power Smith, a Jackson aide after Sharpsburg, was an exception to the army's low estimate of the soldierly value of Old Jack's Presbyterian coterie. This sober-faced youngster, often teased by Lee and even by Jackson, was of fighting fiber and as tireless as brave.

In sharp contrast to the clerical element of the staff, Major John A. Harmon was the incomparable quartermaster whose profanity exercised a mysterious influence on the pulling power of mules. The major never professed to understand Jackson and perhaps never withdrew mentally his threat to quit so crazy and secretive a chief. Jackson, for his part, probably could not excuse the major's oaths, inability to keep a secret, and general skepticism regarding the commander of the Second Corps. But Jackson knew that the major could get a wagon ahead when nobody else could, and for that virtue he was willing to overlook talkativeness and reports of shocking language.

During his eight months of service on Jackson's staff, Kyd Douglas gave to it virtually all the style and swagger it ever had, because he was one of the handsomest young men in the army, rode superbly, and had a dramatic appearance. When he resigned in November to accept a captaincy in the hard-bitten 2nd Virginia, he did not sever his social relations with the staff, but, of course, could not be its representative on parades, reviews, or formal missions.

Less colorful than Douglas but popular, vigorous, and exceptionally competent was Jackson's topographical engineer, Captain J. K. Boswell. His other topographical engineer, the indispensable Jed Hotchkiss, was not commissioned because of limitations on the lawful number of topographical engineers. Although in every sense a member of the staff, Hotchkiss was at this time a civilian employee. Rated very high in ability, and almost unique in charm, was the medical director of the Second Corps, Dr. Hunter McGuire, then in his twenty-seventh year. McGuire was an ardent Confederate who, after the John Brown raid, had led a hegira of Southern medical students from Philadelphia. Young McGuire was as good a story-teller as he was a surgeon and by the fireside was as charming as he was encouraging at the bedside.

The bulwark of Jackson's staff, its core, its driving force, was the lantern-jawed Sandie Pendleton who, though not yet twenty-three, was one of the most promising staff officers in the Army of Northern Virginia. He was the son of the chief of artillery, Brigadier General W. N. Pendleton. All his life, it was said, Sandie Pendleton had waked up in a good humor. He had been the medallist of his class at Washington College and had been graduated Master of Arts at the University of Virginia in 1861. About him there was a charming courtesy of manner, a cordiality, a magnetism that made every acquaintance regard him as a friend.

His mental endowment was in keeping. Judgment was as discerning as memory was retentive. Jackson was wont to say, when asked about an unfamiliar officer or a regiment concerning which he was in doubt, "Ask Captain Pendleton; if he doesn't know, nobody does." The skill, the mature wisdom, the promptness and the system with which this boy ran Jackson's headquarters were, perhaps, the best refutation of the oft-repeated assertion that Jackson lacked judgment in the choice of officers. Pendleton had never missed a battle except that of Second Manassas, which was fought while he was ill. It was the injury to him at Fredricksburg—"I was struck by a musket-ball," he explained, "which went through both my over- and under-coats, and was stopped by striking the knife in my pants pocket"— that threw the staff work of the Second Corps entirely out of gear that afternoon.[7] As for risk, exposure, and danger, he met them without thought. Jackson was as quick to seek the recognition of rank for his proven lieutenants as he was slow to praise them, and Sandie was promoted major before the Battle of Fredericksburg.

Peter Longstreet's staff was as different from Old Jack's as were the two corps commanders themselves. No ministers were there on Longstreet's staff. Perhaps the essential quality distinguishing Longstreet's headquarters from Jackson's was a lack of austerity. Longstreet was efficient and administered army business promptly and with no noisy grinding of gears; but when his staff officers had finished their work and gathered in Major John Fairfax's tent for a nip, Old Pete said nothing. Nor did he frown and lecture them the next morning.

Foremost among Longstreet's staff officers was G. Moxley Sorrel, a tall, trim Georgian whose Gallic grace, dark eyes, and dash displayed the blood of a grandfather who had been a colonel of engineers in the French army. Moxley Sorrel was a clerk in the banking division of the Central Georgia Railroad at the outbreak of hostilities, and came to Virginia and found a place as a volunteer aide to Longstreet. So much aptitude did he display that Old Pete quickly procured his commission and thereafter relied increasingly on him. Socially, Sorrel was charming; as a rider he was the envy of many a cavalryman; at work in Longstreet's headquarters tent he need not have feared comparisons with any staff officer of the army.

Major Osman Latrobe, physically and mentally a powerful representative of the Maryland family of that name, was Longstreet's A.A.G. and inspector. Similar rank and title were those of John W. Fairfax, a Virginian of ancient line and positive habits. He was "fond of his bottle, his Bible and his bath; always in front when danger pressed, but a fine-looking fellow very much given to show." More than once, to his high satisfaction, on entering a strange town he was mistaken for General Longstreet, whom he regarded with affectionate loyalty as the foremost Southern soldier. Wherever the corps went, Fairfax carried a bath tub that bore an odd resemblance to a tin hat, and unless battle broke with the dawn, he had his bath and his toddy before he ate. On Sunday he gave himself the refreshment of Holy Writ without neglecting his dram.

Major Raphael Moses was the wit and story-teller of the staff. A lawyer of high distinction in Georgia, he sought combatant duty in 1861, but General Toombs prevailed upon him to undertake the thankless but essential work of commissary. So admirably did Moses victual Toombs's brigade that he soon had charge of the commissary of D. R. Jones's division and, in due time, of Longstreet's corps. Moses was probably the best commissary of like rank in the Confederate service. His stories were endless; his narrative flawless. The darkest, dullest night at headquarters he could enliven.

One other of Longstreet's staff officers must have mention—Dr. J. S. Dorsey Cullen, medical director of the Second Corps. Dorsey Cullen, who was thirty, had been born in Richmond and schooled at the University of Virginia and in the medical department of the University of Pennsylvania. So promising was he that one of the most renowned of Southern surgeons, Dr. Charles Bell Gibson, took him into partnership. When war came, Cullen went to the front as surgeon of the 1st Virginia and soon attracted Longstreet's attention. Soon he was as secure in the affection of Longstreet as Hunter McGuire was welcome in Jackson's tent.

Because the cavalry under the energetic Stuart ranged far, his staff officers were widely known. For that matter, Stuart saw to it that everything connected with the cavalry was known. One of his staff officers, Heros von Borcke, lent himself admirably and willingly as an exhibit. Von Borcke was of vast bulk and appropriate height and had to ride a tall and powerful horse. He dressed in a fashion that emphasized his size at the same time it suggested the rainbow. Unquestioned valor was von Borcke's, a contempt for danger and an unfeigned delight in combat. He possessed polish and much experience. His most provoking quality was not revealed till the struggle was over. Then, in his published *Memoirs,* where none of his service lost weight in the telling, he calmly credited himself with many feats that had been performed by other members of the staff.

The honor and the burden of Stuart's chief of staff again were Major Norman FitzHugh's. He had been exchanged at length after he fell into Federal hands at Verdiersville, and had been prompt to return to active duty. John Esten Cooke, the novelist, was ordnance officer and was sharing observantly, though not happily, all that Stuart was doing.

Two other of Stuart's staff officers had qualities worthy of note. W. W. Blackford, chief engineer of the cavalry division, was one of four brothers in the Confederate army, all of them excellent soldiers. He had received sound, disciplinary training as a civil engineer, and as he helped to raise a volunteer cavalry company after the John Brown raid, he adhered to that arm and in 1861 rode off with this command. One of the obligations Blackford imposed upon himself was that of going over every battlefield he

could examine after the battle closed. He explained that "... nothing culti-
vates the judgment of topography, in relation to the strategic strength of
position, so well as to ride over the ground while the dead and wounded
still remain as they fell. You see exactly where the best effects were produced, and what arm of the service produced them, for there lies the harvest they have reaped, each sheaf distinctly labeled with the name of the
reaper in the wound received." This was the viewpoint of a scientific but
not of a cold-blooded soldier.[8]

Best loved of Stuart's staff was the remarkable young A.A.G. that Jeb
had found in his distant cousin R. Channing Price of Richmond. Channing Price had entered the war as a private in the Richmond Howitzers. In
the summer of 1862, Stuart gave him a place on the staff, and as Channing
quickly learned his duties, Jeb never had occasion to regret the appointment or to apologize for the selection of a kinsman. An exacting chief was
Stuart. His aides had to justify their title at any hour and had always to be
close at hand. Channing met the strain. At the "inside" work he was facile
and unfailing. When he was acting as A.A.G. in the field he had no superior in the army. He would listen as Stuart dictated orders, said Blackford,
"and without asking him to repeat a single thing, or taking a single note, he
would ride out to one side of the road, dismount, take his little portfolio
out of his haversack, and write the letters ready for the General's signature;
and it was rarely the case that any alteration was made...." This was attributed to Price's development of a retentive memory by acting as secretary to
his father who, in late life, lost his vision and carried on his correspondence
by dictating to his son.[9]

Taylor for Lee, Pendleton for Jackson, Sorrel for Longstreet, Price for
Stuart—these were not the only staff officers of outstanding capacity. Nor
by any means did they carry all the burden of detailed staff work in winter
quarters. Others of industry as great and ability almost as high labored
patriotically, but these four, different in background though not in uprearing, were typical of the best of the army and of the South.

2. Artillerists Get Their Stars

Along with the developing young staff officers, some of the ablest of the
artillerists received one star or two during the months the army was in
winter quarters. The reorganization of the "long arm" had been undertaken immediately after Sharpsburg. Small and inefficient batteries then
were demanding far more horses than the quartermasters were able to supply. On the roster were batteries that had won the plaudits of the entire

army, and certain others that were an encumbrance of road and camp and battlefield. Eighteen of the latter were stricken from the list. Their personnel was divided among other units; their guns were given to better batteries or were turned back to the army chief of ordnance.[10] In the process, where so many sensibilities were exposed, not a few were bruised; among ambitions so numerous some were trodden upon.

This reduction in the number of batteries was followed in February 1863 by a historic, long-needed change in the organization of the artillery as a combat arm. From the time the brigades and divisions had been formed in 1861, designated batteries had been assigned to each of these units. A brigade had one battery; normally a division had four. Soon the batteries were so habituated to service with particular brigades that any attempt to send the guns elsewhere was regarded as the darkest injustice to the gunners and to the brigade—an act far worse than the detachment of an infantry regiment for temporary service with another brigade.

By the autumn of 1862 the artillery of most divisions had come under the command of a divisional chief of artillery, who exercised a measure of discretion, but the permanence of the relations between certain batteries and one specific division continued to be taken for granted. If a massing of guns or the reinforcement of an artillery position was necessary, the added units were expected to come from the general reserve, which consisted of fifteen or twenty batteries, rather than from the adjoining division, even though that division might be idle.

This system patently was bad beyond defense. The employment of large forces of artillery was almost impossible. Field officers of artillery had little practice training. Batteries in isolated camps behind the lines often were neglected by supply officers who could not, to quote General Pendleton, "devote to one or more batteries the time and attention they imperatively needed." Lee and Pendleton both had concluded that battalions of four batteries, a total of sixteen guns, each battalion with two field officers, would be an organization far preferable. The chief of artillery went over with Porter Alexander and Stapleton Crutchfield the details of a plan of this character and, on February 11, 1863, presented it, complete even to the assignment of batteries, for the consideration of Lee.[11]

When Lee sent to the corps commanders the proposed organization and the contemplated assignments for their commands, Longstreet made no objection. The shifting of batteries and the few necessary advancements in rank seem to have been satisfactory to him. His old friend Colonel J. B. Walton of the Washington Artillery battalion was to be retained. Porter Alexander was to be made a full colonel. The other promoted officers were meritorious and acceptable.

Jackson was not so ready to accept the men Pendleton proposed for him. He had objections of principle to the assignment to his artillery of field officers who had not served with it, when he had good men of his own batteries whom he felt worthy of promotion. In addition, Crutchfield felt that one major of artillery did not deserve promotion. Besides, Captain David G. McIntosh, whom Crutchfield considered one of the best of his artillerists, was not assigned a battalion. These considerations Old Jack set forth earnestly in a letter to Lee, and in so doing advanced the claims of one of his "boys" of the old Army of the Valley, Captain R. P. Chew, who had commanded the famous battery that always was barking where Ashby was slashing. Complaint Jackson also made, probably at the instance of Crutchfield, on the subject of the comparative armament of the two corps.

Lee satisfied Jackson quickly regarding guns, but Old Jack's other arguments did not pass unscrutinized. Lee did not think it right, he said, "at any time to pass over worthy men who have done good service, unless you can get better." As for Chew, was he not with the artillery of the cavalry rather than of the Second Corps? Jackson did not take any of this in good part, and the conclusion of his reply lacked little of being rude. Said Jackson: "I have had much trouble resulting from incompetent officers having been assigned to duty with me regardless of my wishes. Those who have assigned them have never taken the responsibility of incurring the odium which results from such incompetency." With his lieutenant in this temper, Lee argued no more, but sought, as best he could, to reconcile Pendleton's suggestions and Jackson's objections to them.[12]

The assignments were announced on April 16. Four battalions were attached directly to each corps. In a deliberate effort to provide greater mobility and increased firepower, the two best battalions of Longstreet's command—the Washington Artillery and Alexander's battalion—were designated as corps reserve for the First Corps. Two battalions that included some batteries not quite of the same level of distinction constituted the reserve of the Second Corps. The general reserve was reduced to two battalions.[13] Jackson got all he had asked except in two cases: Chew was not assigned a battalion; the major whose promotion had been disapproved by Crutchfield was advanced to the rank of lieutenant colonel.

Although it disappointed these and other ambitions, the battalion organization was to justify itself many times over. Whatever objection there was to the new system in February was to disappear on the third of May. Some superb young men were given higher rank because of heavier responsibility. Tom Carter became a colonel—he who had equaled on many fields, though he never could excel, his performance at Seven Pines. Snowden Andrews, though still unfit for active duty because of a wound received at Cedar Mountain, had the stimulus of promotion to lieutenant colonel. Willie Pegram, promoted major, was made second in command of Lindsay Walker's battalion. David McIntosh stepped up to major and head of a battalion that was thereafter to bear his name. W. T. Poague became a major and second in command to McIntosh. In the Second Corps Major J. W. Latimer, who had handled Ewell's artillery with much skill at Cedar Mountain, was named as the junior field officer of Snowden Andrews's battalion. Second in command to Porter Alexander was Major Frank Huger, son of General Benjamin Huger and an officer whose judgment matched his heroism.

Older men of higher rank and of outstanding service there already were in the artillery; but as it chanced, most of the young men who appeared as battalion field officers for the first time in the order of April 16, 1863, were those who added most to the luster of the long arm. Alexander, Huger, Tom Carter, Latimer, Pegram, McIntosh, Poague—take these from the roll of Lee's artillery and half its glory is gone. They won their new rank by merit and they had the endorsement of Longstreet and Jackson. Perhaps some of the aggressive battalion commanders would have been loath to admit it, but they owed something, also, to General Pendleton. Individual performance he had observed faithfully and, with a few exceptions, had appraised soundly.

On a footing different from any of the artillerists who fought with the infantry units was the recognition of John Pelham. His performance on the right at Fredericksburg had underscored all his achievements from First Manassas onward. In an army that did not lack brave men, he was "the gallant Pelham." It was asked if he were not something of a military genius who was developing new artillery tactics. It might not be daring or sheer combativeness that inspired Pelham to dash with his guns ahead of all infantry support, to pursue as if he led cavalry, to withdraw swiftly but with so many halts on good ground that he delayed pursuit. Together these might be tactical devices that would give a new function to artillery.[14]

No praise seemed in any way to affect Pelham. His manner remained simple and unspoiled; he never spoke of himself or his exploits. If he was commended, he blushed. Apparently he gave no thought to death. He told John Esten Cooke once that he had never felt he was destined to be killed in the war. His friends ranged from the humblest to the most exalted. A man's man he was by every act and impulse; yet he drew many a sigh and gentle glance from the young ladies of every town where he halted. How could it be otherwise? He was blond enough to match his dazzling blue eyes, and was "tall, slender, beautifully proportioned and very graceful." He was, one of his closest friends had to admit, "as grand a flirt as ever lived," though scandal never touched his name. Stuart had for his chief of artillery the same sort of older-brother affection that Longstreet had for Pickett, and Pelham consequently lived with the cavalry staff and, to all intents, was one of them.[15]

With either of "the Lees," Fitz or Rooney, with almost anyone else, and above all with the chief of cavalry, Pelham wished to ride on every raid, but during the worst mud of the wintry months the horse artillerist had to content himself officially with inspections. At length came March, the month of mystery in Virginia. Often when the air is cold, the wind is searching, and the whole aspect of nature is blusterous. On the highways, deep in mud when they are not snow-covered, winter seems unrelenting. In the woods the buds are swelling confidently. Spring was coming for John Pelham; spring and, his friends predicted, advancement to a lieutenant colonelcy.

It was in mid-March that Pelham contrived a scheme to confound the boredom of camp by slipping away to call on a young lady in Orange. His visit was interrupted by sudden news of the enemy advancing in some force. Before night on the sixteenth Pelham had hastened to Culpeper and found Stuart there as a witness at a court-martial. The next morning, March 17, on borrowed horses, Stuart and Pelham began a hurried ride toward the quarters of Fitz Lee, who by that time had received fairly accurate and somewhat alarming intelligence of the enemy's movements. Scouts reported the arrival of the Federals at Morrisville, in the southeastern part of Fauquier County, about nine miles east of the familiar crossing of the Rappahannock at Kelly's Ford. Whatever their intentions, should they strike for any point south of the Rappahannock they probably would cross at Kelly's. Fitz had reinforced the picket post there. His brigade was placed to the north of Culpeper. By these dispositions he seemed to be protected against surprise and in position to meet a Federal advance on either side of the river.[16]

At 7:30 on the morning of March 17, Fitz Lee was confronted with news that Union cavalry had forced the crossing at Kelly's Ford. The bluecoats might be riding straight for the Orange and Alexandria Railroad south of the Rappahannock. They must be met and defeated before they could reach the track. His regiments—1st, 2nd, 3rd, 4th, and 5th Virginia— moved out promptly. Eagerly Pelham rode with Stuart till they reached the cavalry's field headquarters. There Pelham had to wait. James Breathed's battery, attached to Fitz Lee's service, had not yet come up. If an onslaught came before the artillery arrived, Pelham could carry messages, perhaps, or he might have a hand in the clash of horses and the crossing of sabers.

This Kelly's Ford country was familiar to Pelham from the campaigning in the summer and autumn of 1862. At that time he already had shared the actions at First Manassas and Williamsburg, the ride around McClellan, the bloody battle of Gaines' Mill, the raid on White House, and the amusing chase of the gunboat. Then, in August, began the pulse-raising days around Groveton, the Maryland expedition, Sharpsburg, the Chambersburg raid, and Fredericksburg when the eyes of the army had been home. Yes, this Kelly's Ford country had been the halfway bivouac in the rise of John Pelham. Ahead of him now, as in August, was . . . the promise of an exciting battle.

The advance guard located the enemy. Fitz Lee turned to Stuart: "Hadn't we better take the bulge on them at once?" Stuart was always agreeable to a fight that held any promise of advantage. Pelham watched as the 3rd Virginia, in a column of fours, charged straight for a stone fence sheltering the Federals. The men were firing at the blue line behind the fence, but had not been able to get over the barrier. Now they were making for farm buildings on the left where, surely, there would be a gate or a gap in the fence. This at a glance was plain to Pelham. Instantly he drew saber and put spurs to his horse. He would share that charge, help as he could. The joy of battle was in the boy's shining eyes. As he waved his sword, he smiled and shouted "Forward!"

"Forward!" he continued to shout as he reached the farm buildings where the troopers were streaming through an opening in the fence. Pelham drew rein at the gate and yelled encouragement to the men as they passed. In the high ecstasy of conflict he stood in his stirrups, sword uplifted, battle shout on his lips. Overhead a roar, a flash, the loud explosion of a shell. The horse leaped. Pelham fell. He lay on his back. His eyes remained open; his face was not marred. He looked as if at the next moment he would rise and shake off the dirt and shout again, "Forward!"; but in the back of his head, just at the hair-line, there was a small bleeding wound where a fragment of shell had entered. Comrades got the wounded boy across the withers of a horse and carried him to the rear.[17]

Almost from the time of Pelham's fall the action lost its menacing character. Soon it degenerated into demonstrations. At nightfall it ended in the withdrawal of the Federals by the road of their advance. Confederate casualties numbered 133, those of the Federals little more than half as numerous.

Most of all was there lament for the famous young artillerist. Surgeons examining Pelham found that the fragment of shell, no larger than the tip of the little finger, had crashed through the back of the skull for two inches. The steel had done fatal hurt to nerves. About 1:00 P.M. Pelham opened his eyes, drew a long breath, and, without so much as a whisper, died. When Stuart heard this he bowed his head on his horse's neck and wept. "Our loss is irreparable," he said.[18]

The corpse was borne to Richmond where it lay in state in the Capitol. Then, with a guard of honor to the railroad station and with mourning dignitaries in procession, John Pelham's body began its long, last journey home to Alabama. "The gallant Pelham," said Stuart, "—so noble, so true—will be mourned by the nation." Lee wrote the President: "I mourn the loss of Major Pelham. I had hoped that a long career of usefulness and honor was still before him. . . . I hope there will be no impropriety in presenting his name to the Senate. . . ." It was as a lieutenant colonel that John Pelham went home.[19]

3. LONGSTREET TRIES INDEPENDENT COMMAND

Early in January General Lee had thought it probable that if Burnside went into winter quarters on the Rappahannock, part of his army would be transferred south of the James for operations there. A considerable Union force already occupied Suffolk. After reinforcing that command, the Federals might undertake an advance against the Petersburg and Weldon Railroad, which was for the Army of Northern Virginia the sole rail supply line east of the Blue Ridge. Southside Virginia and the corresponding part of North Carolina was, moreover, a country of hogs and corn—an easy country in which to subsist forces and not a difficult one to occupy.

For the remainder of January nothing of any consequence occurred between the James and Cape Fear, though there was vast speculation over the probable objective of the Federal flotilla now believed to be moving down the coast. At length, February 14, Lee's headquarters heard that Burnside's old corps, the IX, had taken transports for Hampton Roads. Scouts reported Federal camp gossip that the corps was going to Suffolk. General Lee anticipated it might, but remembered that the corps had done well in North Carolina and he counted among the possibilities a return there.

Regardless of ultimate objective, the presence in Hampton Roads of a corps of veteran reinforcements placed heavy striking power in the hands of an adversary who commanded the deeper waterways. A swift voyage up the James and a surprise expedition against Richmond might be contemplated. Precautions had to be taken. Pickett's division was started for the Confederate capital. Hood was directed to hold himself in readiness. If these first-line troops were to be sent from the First Corps, Longstreet himself should command them. On February 18 orders were issued accordingly. There was the implication here of an independent command for Old Pete. Several times, during the absence of Lee, he had commanded the Army of Northern Virginia for a few days. It appeared that the taste of power beyond the camps of the First Corps had not been unpleasant to Longstreet. Now, in a new field, he was to have more than a taste.

Longstreet formally was appointed on February 25 commander of the Department of Virginia and North Carolina, which extended from Richmond to the Cape Fear River. The department was in reality three—the Department of Richmond, over which Arnold Elzey presided; the Department of Southern Virginia, under Samuel G. French; and the Department of North Carolina, which Harvey Hill reluctantly was taking in charge. The personnel of these departments was not all that could be desired. Officers who had been tried in Virginia and then shunted southward were so numerous that Old Pete must almost have thought he was back in the old Confederate Army of the Potomac as it existed before the coming of Lee.

At Charleston was Beauregard, somewhat repressed perhaps in his Napoleonic ambitions, but otherwise the same as after Manassas. Wilmington on the Cape Fear, with its elaborate defenses, was under command of W. H. C. Whiting, comrade of Centreville days. Harvey Hill, of course, was bound to Longstreet by all the ties of Seven Pines. Shanks Evans, another companion of First and Second Manassas, was at Kinston, North Carolina. Other officers were known to Longstreet from later association. Robert Ransom had gone to North Carolina with his own brigade and John R. Cooke's. Johnston Pettigrew had been restored to health and assigned a brigade of some 2,500 men in the North State.

Along with varied excellencies, some of the best of these new lieutenants of Longstreet had more than their share of temperamental peculiarities. Doubtless because of his health Harvey Hill was in his most nervous, critical mood. He had more separate responsibility than he cared to assume, and he had permitted his prejudices to sour him. In an extraordinary address to his command he urged his infantry to "cut down to 6 feet by 2 the dimensions of the farms which these [Northern] plunderers propose to appropriate." To artillerists he said: "It is glorious to lose guns by fighting them to the last; it is disgraceful to save them by retiring early from the fight." Hill opened the sluices of his favorite prejudice—that against the cavalry—by announcing that any troopers "who permit themselves to be surprised deserve to die."[20]

It developed that Harvey Hill's particular sarcasms were directed against "the wonderfully inefficient" cavalry brigade of Beverly Robertson, the same Robertson who had provoked Jackson the previous August. One of Longstreet's first letters to the adjutant general, after assuming command, was an effort to have Robertson superseded. On the Blackwater was Roger A. Pryor, and for a short time the ex-editor was retained, but he soon was in a fair way of being deprived of his brigade by the same expedient used earlier—transferring his troops to other stations or to different commands. Longstreet managed this as suavely as if he had been Lee himself, and soon Pryor once more was a brigadier without a soldier. As for Chase Whiting, some of his peculiarities doubtless were familiar to Longstreet, but as departmental commander he had yet to learn of the endless apprehension, the persistence, and the prolixity of Whiting as a correspondent. Nor could Longstreet be expected to know at the outset the depth of Whiting's ambition to be an independent commander.

The last of the ranking commanders in the sprawling department was one of whom Longstreet knew little. Samuel G. French was a West Pointer who served thirteen years in the regular army after graduation in 1843. In 1861, though a New Jersey man, he unhesitatingly threw in his lot with the Confederacy. In command of the Department of Southern Virginia, he had directed operations all the way from Drewry's Bluff on the James River to the Cape Fear. Personally French was sociable and blessed with more than a spark of humor. As an "old army man" he knew thoroughly his duties and his rights, and was of a disposition to maintain his rights while discharging his duties.

These were a few of the men with whom and through whom Longstreet had to work. In ability they were about of the average of the army. Temperamentally, they may have been somewhat more difficult than the average. That probability ought to be remembered in weighing the events that followed as a first test of Longstreet in separate command.

Was "separate" to be synonymous with independent, in the sense that Longstreet no longer was under Lee's orders? Longstreet himself does not appear to have been quite sure during March. In so far as acts explained equivocations, he proceeded to order offensive operations without reference to Lee. Two days after assuming command, he suggested to D. H. Hill an enterprise which was to open Longstreet's eyes concerning some of his subordinates.

In North Carolina the Federals had been occupying New Bern on the Neuse River, using it as an excellent base from which to raid inland. In December 1862 the Federals under General J. G. Foster had made exactly such a raid against Goldsborough. In the face of slow and clumsy defense by some of Gustavus Smith's troops, Foster had burned the important railroad bridge over the Neuse. A repetition of this Longstreet sought to prevent by the direct and soldierly expedient of nipping off New Bern. That done, he could hope to forage extensively in a district long closed to the Confederate commissaries.[21]

He proposed vigorously that Hill take the offensive against New Bern.

For the attack Longstreet reasoned that he could spare one long-range Whitworth field gun, and Whiting could send up another of these rifles from the Wilmington defenses. Of troops, Longstreet estimated that Hill would have 14,000 or 15,000 men, provided 4,000 from Whiting's command cooperated. It was over this proviso that Longstreet's calculations went astray. His letter on the subject had on Whiting as exciting an effect as if it had been warning that the entire Federal navy was concentrating for an attack on Wilmington. "So far from considering myself able to spare troops from here," Whiting explained, he had applied for another brigade to be sent him immediately. Concerning the Whitworth gun he was unyielding.

It was in the face of Whiting's manifest reluctance to cooperate that the expedition against New Bern was prepared. Hill as usual was weighted down by his responsibility and discouraged by his failure to get a brigade from Whiting. His attack scarcely deserved to be called anything more than a reconnaissance in force. No exaggeration appeared in the report of General Foster: "The whole affair, meant to be effective and strong, was ineffective and weak." Said Hill, "The spirit manifested by Whiting has spoiled everything. . . . If I am to be cut down to two brigades I will not submit to the swindle." Longstreet was philosophical in dealing with the failure, and with Hill's bitter report: "I presume that this was not intended as an official communication and have not forwarded it. I hope that you will send up another account of your trip."[22]

Complications now developed rapidly. From Hampton Roads to the Savannah every Confederate garrison was on the lookout for Federal ironclads and for the appearance of the troops that had left the Army of the Potomac. Where was the blow to fall? Lee thought the major offensive was apt to be on the Rappahannock, and instructed Longstreet to keep Hood and Pickett close enough to the railroad for their quick return. At the time of the raid on Kelly's Ford he ordered the two divisions to rejoin, but canceled these instructions as soon as he discovered that the movement was of no importance. Longstreet, for his part, explained that he could not keep two divisions ready to move back to the Rappahannock and, at the same time, collect from eastern North Carolina the large supplies of salt fish and meat known to be there.

Increasingly the stores of that region were assuming importance in many minds. To aid in getting the herring and much-needed bacon, Longstreet and Hill were considering plans for demonstrations against Suffolk, against Washington, North Carolina, and against New Bern once more. At the least, it was reasoned, the Federals could be held at the threatened points while the Confederate commissaries scoured the country, which for a year they had not been able to enter. Major Raphael Moses, Longstreet's corps commissary, learned of the dangerous depletion of the reserve rations of the troops in Virginia at the same time he ascertained there were tons of bacon and unreckoned barrels of fish in the counties east of the Chowan River. He laid these facts before his chief. In forwarding Moses's report to General Lee, Longstreet wrote: "We can occupy that country and draw the supplies out with another division of my old corps, but I do not think it would be prudent to attempt such a move with a less force."[23]

While this and other possibilities were being considered, preparations were made for the investment of Washington, North Carolina, the western gate to a region from which the Confederacy was drawing no supplies. Whiting most reluctantly sent Ransom's brigade from Wilmington. To add further strength to the expedition, Longstreet lent Hill the brigade of Kemper and continued the loan of Garnett's brigade. Of the capture of Washington Longstreet cherished small hope, but he believed its investment would pin down the Federals to such an extent that his agents would be unhampered in purchasing provisions in the region north of the town. The "siege of Washington," as it was styled by the Federals, was begun on March 30 and was regarded by Hill one day as promising and the next as futile.[24]

Longstreet had more than the fluctuating moods of Hill to puzzle him. Should he attempt to drive the Federals from Suffolk? Had he force enough to invest the town? Could he at least occupy the Federals by a protracted feint while he brought out supplies from the district to the east and southeast? Longstreet argued these questions in correspondence with Lee. That Longstreet was coming to regard himself as a strategist who without abashment could dissent from the opinions of his chief, the exchange of opinions plainly shows. Beyond that, if one is looking for a lieutenant who considered himself the superior of his chief and was anxious to advance his campaign at the expense of the main army, one can interpret Longstreet's language to confirm that view. With equal show of logic, one may read Longstreet's dispatches as the frank expression of a plain-spoken and somewhat cautious man anxious to have adequate force for his mission, but was not insubordinate or unreasonable.[25]

Lee felt there was no military justification for making further detachment from the Army of Northern Virginia. For the rest, he was willing to trust Longstreet's judgment of what could be effected in front of Suffolk. If Longstreet was too heavily committed when Hooker attacked, Lee was willing to retreat from the Rappahannock to the North Anna. Longstreet, for his part, remained doubtful of the results that could be obtained at Suffolk without a larger force than he had. Lee could defend the Rappahannock, Longstreet boldly maintained, with Jackson's troops and safely could detach to Southside Virginia the remaining two divisions of the First Corps.

At length Longstreet decided the provisions of eastern North Carolina were worth the risks of a heavy demonstration against Suffolk. The advance was to be in the department of Major General French. Longstreet would be compelled to use French's division, but he was not disposed to employ French's services. Micah Jenkins had been transferred to French's division, where he was senior officer, after French himself, and Old Pete probably felt that the South Carolinian could handle French's troops better than their regular commander could. "The next thing I knew"—French is speaking—"[Longstreet] . . . put his command in motion and took from me a division and a number of batteries, and was on his way to Suffolk without informing me in any way of his designs, or of his wishes."

Immediately French concluded that the reason for Longstreet's secrecy was a desire to transfer the division to Micah Jenkins. Was he to acquiesce quietly and remain behind in Petersburg? Not Sam French! He had too much zeal for the cause and knew too well his rights to let himself be supplanted in this fashion. "The next day," he wrote, "I . . . rode to Suffolk and took command of my own troops. . . ." That was all there was to it. Samuel G. French, major general, blandly presented his compliments and awaited the orders of the lieutenant general.

Longstreet showed no impatience when French rode up and reported in front of Suffolk, but he determined to use French otherwise than with infantry. Knowing French's reputation as an artillerist, Old Pete issued orders for all the artillery with the forces on the Blackwater to report to General French. French, in turn, promptly reassigned most of the batteries to the chiefs of artillery of Pickett's and Hood's divisions. To French the whole incident appeared as an effort on Longstreet's part to get rid of him as division commander by assigning him artillery duties he was entirely justified in evading. He was suave in this; Longstreet was not awkward. Both proceeded so skillfully that many officers of less experience did not know what was afoot.[26]

Out of French's anomalous position developed a sensation that might have been termed a scandal. As the Confederate lines were drawn facing Suffolk, on the left stood Fort Huger, an open work that had been constructed in 1861 to protect Suffolk. Opposite it was the channel used by the Federal gunboats that patrolled the Nansemond. Fieldpieces in Fort Huger might close the river to the gunboats, and Longstreet accordingly directed French to put a heavy battery here. French sent in five of Stribling's guns—two 24-pounder brass howitzers and three 12-pounder Napoleons—and decided to put in pits at the rear of the fort's two 32-pounders.

For infantry support French appointed part of Colonel J.K. Connally's 55th North Carolina. General E. M. Law, commanding one of Hood's brigades downstream, sent into the fort as support two companies of the 44th Alabama, approximately fifty men. These troops, Law understood, were to be relieved by some of Connally's regiment. French understood, apparently, that it was Law who was to garrison the fort and that Connally's sole duty was to guard the two 32-pounders at the rear of the fort and serve as general reserve.

As always may happen when responsibility is not fixed, there came a surprise. About 6 o'clock on the evening of April 19, some 270 Federals landed above the fort. They encountered no opposition in getting a foothold. Neither Connally nor Law had picketed the riverbank at that point, because each thought the other would or had. With a rush the Federals broke into the fort and forced its surrender. Five guns, 7 officers, and 130 soldiers were captured and carried across the river.[27]

The "capture of Stribling's battery," as the affair was styled in the Confederate army, created a tremendous stir. French in his report blamed the garrison of the fort for negligence, and in his diary expressed himself "tired of volunteering against gunboats." He resolved to confine himself to the immediate command of his own division and to "take no more interest in Hood's line." Longstreet was altogether moderate in his judgment. There seemed to have been "a general lack of vigilance and prompt attention to duties," he said. ". . . This lesson, it is hoped, will be of service to us all."[28]

George Pickett was giving Longstreet trouble of an entirely different sort. The gentleman with the perfumed ringlets was desperately in love with LaSalle Corbell. That interesting romance would have been exclusively his affair had not "the charming Sally," as he styled her, lived in the very county where Pickett's lines were now drawn. The miles from his headquarters to her home at Chuckatuck were not too long to deter a lover on a good horse; but double that distance between the end of one day's duty and the labors of another was a heavy strain on man and mount. Longstreet would deny Pickett nothing that a chief honorably could grant a lieutenant and, again and again, he gave assent for Pickett to rush to Chuckatuck to make his avowals. At length Longstreet must have sworn that for so many days he would not authorize Pickett to leave camp. The gallant lover did not despair. He pleaded with Moxley Sorrel, the corps A.A.G., to give him authority to go. No, Sorrel insisted, he must go to the lieutenant general. "But he is tired of it, and will refuse . . . ," said Pickett. "I swear, Sorrel, I'll be back before anything can happen in the morning." Sorrel stood his ground, and wrote afterward, "Pickett went all the same, nothing could hold him back from that pursuit. . . . I don't think his division benefited by such carpet-knight doings in the field."[29]

To the other major general on the Suffolk front, John B. Hood, little of interest happened. Hood was a bachelor and was becoming a social lion in Richmond, but he had no love affair on the banks of the Nansemond. He was bored, in fact, by the conduct of what had become a make-believe siege. He wrote Lee a boyish letter: "I presume we will leave here so soon as we gather all the bacon in the country. When we leave here it is my desire to return to you. If any troops come to the Rappahannock, please don't forget me."[30] That was his temper; if there was to be a fight, he wished to share it.

Vexation there was, finally, for Longstreet in the situation in the Carolinas. In Charleston, over which Longstreet had no control, Beauregard was expecting attack; Whiting in Wilmington apprehended every day that on the next tide the Federal fleet would arrive off his sand forts. Harvey Hill in front of Washington insisted that he must have more troops if he was to recover the town. Then the Federals ran in two vessels and replenished the supplies of the little garrison. That resolved all lingering uncertainty. Confinement of a small Federal force was not worth the effort and cost. The siege was abandoned. As an offensive it would have been rated close to the bottom of military effort, but as a demonstration it served a purpose. The Federal commander, General Foster, wrote Washington "that heavy operations will be necessary in this state. . . ."[31]

Longstreet's fruitless first experience in semi-independent command was drawing to a close. Had there been any real justification for an attack on the Federals at Suffolk, the time to have delivered it was immediately after Longstreet crossed the Blackwater. Then he had something over 19,000 men in French's, Pickett's, and Hood's commands. The Federals at the outset were of approximately equal strength, but from the twelfth of April onward Union reinforcements arrived almost daily. The end of the month was to find about 9,000 more bluecoats around Suffolk than had been there when the month opened. Longstreet had to forgo any tenuous hope he ever cherished of assuming the offensive. All he could say of his situation on April 29 was, "I am of the opinion . . . that I can hold my position against any attack from the front."[32]

The day he wrote that letter, Longstreet received notice that the Federals were crossing the Rappahannock in the drama that was to represent the supreme achievement of his comrade Jackson.

4. OLD JACK PREPARES FOR SPRING

Jackson spent the winter in preparation for the call that came to him and to Longstreet the twenty-ninth of April 1863. After Burnside evacuated the right bank of the Rappahannock the night of December 15–16, word came on the sixteenth that Federals were recrossing downstream, at Port Royal. Jackson put the Second Corps on the road to meet the new threat. They had marched some ten miles when Stuart announced that the report of a Federal crossing was untrue. Jackson promptly called a halt and ordered the column into bivouac for the night. He had the staff make a chill, cheerless camp in the woods. Eventually the cold, hunger, and a pulsing earache persuaded even the stubborn Jackson to yield. "Pendleton and myself rode forward in search of Corbin's place," Jed Hotchkiss entered in his journal, "and . . . secured an invitation to come to 'Moss Neck,' the palatial home of Corbin, and Hd. Qrs. were established there late in the night."[33]

Old Jack went to spend the night and stayed for three months. That protraction was not deliberate. It was due, primarily, to the insistence of the Corbins. When they breakfasted with the general and his staff the next morning, he was offered a wing of the mansion as headquarters. He declined promptly with the argument that the house was "too luxurious for a soldier, who should sleep in a tent." After about a week in the open, however, Jackson again developed an earache. Dr. McGuire insisted that Jackson go indoors, and the Corbin family prevailed on him to utilize the office on the lawn—a separate building of three rooms.

Both Lee and Stuart professed to be scandalized by such self-indulgence on the part of the Southern Cromwell. Unabashed, Jackson gave his chief and his beloved Jeb Stuart a Christmas dinner at Moss Neck from the abundant food sent him for the holiday. Turkeys he had, a ham, oysters from down the river, unlimited white bread, pickles, even a bottle of wine that had come in a box from Staunton ladies. The general's body servant, Jim, prepared all the dishes; the mess-boy, John, put on a white apron. Because of this flourish, Lee protested that Jackson and his staff were playing soldier. To see how plain soldiers live, they must come to Lee's own headquarters. Stuart was even more shocked. Look at the print of butter on the table. Observe its adornment—it was a rooster, doubtless a game-cock. Jackson might protest that the print had been so made by the person who gave him the butter, but who could believe that? It must be Jackson's coat of arms![34]

Jackson remained at Moss Neck despite this and much similar banter and, in the main, enjoyed himself. He met the large number of callers at his office pleasantly and entertained them courteously, though with no wealth of small talk or of large. Over one peculiarity of his, irreverent young staff officers would smile privately: Whenever a guest came, Jackson would say, "Let me take your hat, sir," and after he took it he would look around in some bewilderment for a place to put it. Finding none, he would deposit it on the floor. Apart from such trifles, there was no denying the expansion of Deacon Jackson. He was dressing much better, although the staff averred, in tribute to Jackson's thrift, that most of his adornment represented gifts to him.[35]

Old Jack displayed small oddities of manner that soldiers loved to exaggerate when they spoke of him. He was not merely another general officer; he was not a corps commander only, though the army had no more than two. A personality he was, whose mannerisms plus his victories made thousands of boys believe that he had a mysterious genius, a special relationship to the Almighty. When he was not Cromwell, he was Joshua. Sometimes he was both.

In either role he watched ceaselessly the discipline of his corps. When six men of the Stonewall Brigade were tried by court-martial for desertion, the penalty for the three worst offenders was death. Paxton protested. No more than one of the three, he said, need be shot, and that one should be chosen by lot. Old Jack rebuked sternly his subordinate: "With the exception of this application, General Paxton's management of his brigade has given me great satisfaction. . . . It appears to me that when a Court Martial faithfully discharges its duty that its decisions should be sustained. If this is not done, lax administration of justice and corresponding disregard for law must be the consequence." Lee upheld Jackson; the President overrode both in the cases that involved the death penalty; but in these or in similar instances floggings occurred.[36]

In another dark matter of discipline that winter, Jackson stood firm. Charges were filed against Brigadier General J. R. Jones of Jackson's old division for the offense of which no general in Lee's army ever before had been accused formally—cowardice. Jackson was troubled and humiliated because he had himself selected Jones for promotion. He told Chaplain Tucker Lacy that he had almost lost confidence in man, for when he thought he had found just such a man as he needed and was about to rest satisfied in him he "found something lacking in him." Jackson added, "I suppose it is to teach me to put my trust only in God." In this spirit he had to face the prospect of a court-martial of the assailed officer.[37]

Amid these continuing daily demands for the enforcement of discipline, which was his prime duty that winter, Jackson had to prepare the reports of his battles. As he wrote slowly and painfully, with endless cancellation and revision, he manifestly needed literary assistance. To procure it he turned to Charles J. Faulkner, for eight years a member of Congress and, in 1859–61, United States minister to France. Faulkner held a lieutenant colonel's commission in the adjutant general's department and had the necessary skill in letters, but he knew nothing of the battles he was to assist in reporting. This required him to collect the material from subordinate reports and to settle controverted points by interviews with the participants.

Three months Faulkner spent on the reports, and then, with relief if not with full satisfaction, he submitted the last of them to Jackson for final changes and approval. Faulker himself felt that Jackson had prescribed a "severe Roman simplicity." In particular, he was disappointed because Jackson eliminated much that had been written with great care to show the reason for some moves. On this Jackson was unyielding. He did not wish to publish to the enemy, he said, why he did certain things, and thus enable them "to learn [our] mode of doing." Jackson realized how difficult it was to prepare accurate reports after a long interval. Said he to Faulkner, half seriously, half jestingly, "Now, Colonel Faulkner, when a battle happens . . . I want you to get where you can see all that is going on, and, with paper and pencil in hand, write it down, so we may not have so much labor and so many conflicitng statements, and then write up the Report at once after the battle."[38]

In Jackson's corps there was the endless question of vacancies to be filled and ambitions to be gratified or denied. From January 19 to April 30 these vacancies had to be filled: First, and far most important, as there was every reason to assume that D. H. Hill would remain in North Carolina, his division must have a permanent commander. Next, there was scant prospect that A. R. Lawton would return to command his brigade of Ewell's, now Early's, division. Third, Charles Field was still bed-ridden with the wound received at Manassas; his brigade needed a leader who would pull it together again as an effective unit of A. P. Hill's division.

Besides these three, a definite vacancy now existed in Toombs's brigade. At last Toombs had concluded he could not "remain in the service with any advantage to the public or with honor" to himself.[39] The question of "honor," so far as one could observe, simply was the honor of promotion. On March 5 he formally bade farewell to his brigade. There may have been more relief at having him out of the army than concern over the prospect of having him in Congress. A year before, the reverse would have been the feeling. Yet another vacancy of the spring was due to the fulfillment of William B. Taliaferro's threat that if he were not named to command Jackson's old division, he would seek transfer. The continued denial of a major general's commission was an affront to Taliaferro's station as a landed aristocrat and a gentleman politician. He asked transfer, received it, and never fought again in the Army of Northern Virginia.

To succeed Taliaferro, the choice of Jackson fell on Brigadier General Raleigh E. Colston, who had been in command under French on the Blackwater and then had been transferred temporarily to Pickett's division. Colston was graduated from the Virginia Military Institute in 1846, and in that year was added to the faculty of V.M.I., where he taught

French and later Military History and Strategy. To the students he was "Old Polly" in an obvious pun on the *parlez* he required of the cadets. Colston had been mildly commended for his part at Williamsburg, but had been a subject of some contention in the operations of June 1 at Seven Pines. After that battle he had been stricken with a long and obscure illness. He was brought now to the Army of Northern Virginia because Jackson, who had been his colleague at V.M.I., had a high opinion of him.

Apparently Jackson had no concern because of Colston's limited combat experience, or the fact that he was senior brigadier of Jackson's old division, now Trimble's. If Trimble's recovery were again delayed, the division in the next action might be under a man who had two battles only to his credit as a brigade commander, and those two not at their hottest where he fought. There is no record of any reflection by Jackson on the seriousness of such a risk.

Charlie Field's brigade of A. P. Hill's division went to Harry Heth. This was as definitely Lee's choice as Colston was Jackson's. Heth was thirty-seven, a cousin of George Pickett's, and a graduate of West Point in the class of 1847. In the old army he had followed the usual career of an infantry officer with something more than average credit. The good opinion of Lee he won while serving as acting quartermaster of the Virginia forces. He served in the Department of East Tennessee whence Lee asked his transfer to the Army of Northern Virginia. Tradition is that Heth was the one general officer whom Lee called by his first name; certain it is that Lee interested himself in Heth's advancement as in no other instance of record. Heth was truthful, he was socially charming, and he had the finest elements of character, but in war he was to prove himself of a type not uncommon—the type that is capable but unlucky. Taking Field's brigade, he became the senior brigadier in the Light Division. Was this just to such men as Archer and Pender?

Toombs's brigade went to Old Rock Benning, who had been temporarily in command of Semmes's troops. Early's famous brigade passed temporarily into the devoted if unskilled hands of Extra Billy Smith. An appointment destined to mean far more to the army than either of these brought John B. Gordon at last to the head of Lawton's brigade. Lawton, recovering from the wound received at Sharpsburg, had many calls and many opportunities in Richmond and in Georgia, and Lee doubted he would come back to the Army of Northern Virginia. If Lawton was not to return during the spring, then a vacancy existed among Georgia troops, a vacancy that Gordon could best fill. The commission that could not be used in the autumn, because there was no brigade for him, might be delivered him now.

Who was to receive the most coveted of the promotions, that of major general to head D. H. Hill's division? Jackson was clear in his mind: He wanted Edward Johnson, "Old Allegheny." Johnson, said the commander of the Second Corps, "was with me at McDowell and so distinguished himself as to make me very desirous of having him as one of my division commanders." Lee was entirely agreeable to the promotion.

The sole question was whether Johnson was able to discharge field command. His ankle bones had not knit satisfactorily, nor had his leg lost its stiffness, from the wound received at McDowell. Johnson went to Richmond and there, chafing at his slow mending, made the best of misfortune. If he could not pursue the field of Mars, he enjoyed the domain of Venus. It was said that his thunderous voice had been heard in a loud proposal of matrimony to one belle of the city, and that, not a week later, he admitted "paying attention" to one of his cousins, whom he pronounced a "lovely girl." A curious, somewhat uncouth, strangely fascinating man was Old Allegheny. He winked ceaselessly because of an effection of one eye, and sometimes by this shocked newly met ladies who thought him overconfident if not impertinent. "His head," reported Mrs. Chesnut, "is so strangely shaped—like a cone, an old fashioned beehive. . . ."[40]

If and when his ankle mended, whether or not his suit had ended, Allegheny Johnson would join the Army of Northern Virginia as a division commander. He would come solely on the basis of Jackson's estimate of him, and he would be among soldiers who knew him by reputation only. Never had he fought with any part of that army save with the few regiments of his old command and with the troops Jackson had moved to McDowell almost a year previously. This, manifestly, was as long a chance as Lee took with Heth.

Curious it was that Jackson, who insisted so often on the right of subordinates to the promotion he so seldom gave them, should in two instances have entrusted so large a part of his corps to men of combat experience so limited. As Lee sponsored one of these assignments, that of Heth, and approved those of Johnson and Colston, much of the responsibility was his. The aim of Lee and Jackson was to bring to the army the most capable men available, but that had an ominous implication: The supply of men ripe and qualified for promotion within the army was, in the judgment of the commanders, at the moment exhausted. Good colonels there were; but none who had the required seniority, or could get it readily by transfer, was suited to brigade command. The attrition of two years, particularly in Jackson's corps, now had offset the development of new men in the hard school of battle.

Among those in line for the next major generalship, Dorsey Pender did not believe he could win promotion while he was under A. P. Hill. Reports that he had been commended to Jackson as the best brigadier in the corps did not make his pulse beat faster. Said Pender: "I do not believe Gen. Jackson will have me promoted because I have been recommended by Gen. Hill."[41] Pender's pessimism was deepened, in all probability, by the knowledge that the quarrel between Jackson and Powell Hill had been renewed with more violence than before.

In January Hill asked General Lee for a trial on the charges preferred against him by Jackson. Lee explained patiently, "Upon examining the charges in question, I am of opinion that the interests of the service do not require that they should be tried, and have, therefore, returned them to General Jackson with an indorsement to that effect. I hope you will concur with me that their further prosecution is unnecessary. . . ." Hill did not concur. He argued that while the return of the charges to Jackson was a rebuke to that officer, it was "not as public as was General Jackson's exercise of power toward me." If the charges against him were true, "I do not deserve to command a division in this army; if they were untrue, then General Jackson deserves a rebuke as notorious as the arrest."

As Lee did not answer, nothing developed until, in March, Hill wrote his report of Cedar Mountain. In that document he set forth his version of the disputed day's events that had been the beginning of the quarrel between him and Jackson. This was the sort of challenge Jackson never failed to take up. He responded with a detailed endorsement of the report; Hill pressed anew for a hearing. Painstakingly Jackson revised his charges and specifications, and on April 17 had them ready for presentation to a court.

Before any action was taken by Lee, who was anxious to bury the whole affair, an entirely new controversy arose. Hill was a stickler. He insisted that all orders to his subordinates, from even officers of the general staff, pass through him. While that matter was being adjudicated—General Lee disapproved the practice—a dispute boiled up over an order Jackson sent directly to Hill's signal officer. Hill said defiantly that the order need not be obeyed; it was not passed through him. This moved Jackson to a startling climax: "When an officer orders in his command such disregard for the orders of his superior, I am of the opinion that he should be relieved from duty with his command, and I respectfully request that Genl. Hill be relieved from duty in my corps." To that the long quarrel had come: Jackson asking that the commander of his strongest division—many thought, the best division in the army—be relieved of command when a great battle manifestly was in the making![42]

Strange, strange the spirit of all this was in contrast to what had been happening at Jackson's quarters. Old Jack long had been planning to emulate the officers who got their wives through Richmond and found quarters for them in the spacious country homes around Fredericksburg. With Mrs. Jackson, of course, must come the baby he had never seen. Till his own baby visited him, he found such comfort as he could in Janie Corbin. She was the five-year-old daughter of his hostess at Moss Neck, and she came every day to his office, after work was done, and chatted with him. He grew proficient at cutting out paper dolls for her, many figures with hands joined, which always had the same name in their conversations—the Stonewall Brigade. Janie's hair was long and golden and sometimes it tumbled into her blue eyes. One day with a smile he cut loose the gilt band of his gray cap, a present from his wife, and bound it around her hair. "Janie," he said, "it suits a little girl like you better than it does an old soldier like me." She was delighted, and thereafter, for any special event, she always wore her shining fillet.

As pleasant as life had been at Moss Neck, Jackson's military conscience began to prod him. The office afforded him too much worldly comfort; with the coming of spring he would move to a tented campsite not far from Lee's near Hamilton's Crossing. Before he left, Janie was stricken with scarlet fever. When he went to thank Mrs. Corbin for her kindness and to inquire after Janie, his little friend was better. Two days later, however, to the grief and dismay of Jackson, word was brought to him that Janie was dead. He who had gazed dry-eyed on the battlefield of Sharpsburg sat down and wept unabashed.[43]

The thought of coming conflict and the surge of religious enthusiasm through the army made the days of early spring a season of prayer for Jackson. He shared the daily morning devotions that Chaplain Tucker Lacy held at headquarters, and unless army business demanded, never absented himself from the somewhat longer prayer service Mr. Lacy conducted on Wednesday and Sunday evenings. The members of Jackson's military household were encouraged on Sunday afternoon to assemble and sing hymns. If he could not "raise the tune" or even join in the refrain, Jackson could "pray in public," and when called upon, or when Chaplain Lacy was absent, he did so. At a prayer meeting on Sunday, March 29, Old Jack prayed fervently for peace and invoked the blessing of the Lord on his country's enemy "in everything but the war."[44]

There Jackson drew the line, because he was seeking Divine guidance and favor for the South and for himself in defeating the enemy. In February he had told Jed Hotchkiss to make a map of the Shenandoah Valley and to extend it into Pennsylvania—proof enough of the direction of his military thought. The difficulties that lay ahead he did not minimize, yet he awaited avidly the next move of Hooker, and made ready to meet it.

Never did he work harder to have the corps at its keenest fighting edge. Any day now the long roll might be sounded, the wagons started for the rear, and the lean gray infantry headed for the advancing enemy. A great battle was coming soon. Of that Jackson was confident. "We must do more than defeat their armies," he told his staff; "we must destroy them."[45]

Instead of a new army, calm descended on the Rappahannock for the leafing of the trees. "I have hardly ever known the army so quiet as now," said Frank Paxton. Through a soft, enriching rain Jackson rode on the twentieth of April to Guiney's Station. It was his great hour, the hour for which he had been waiting since he had the first news of the baby's birth: Mrs. Jackson and the little girl were coming, coming on the very train that was whistling now. No sooner had it stopped than he was on the crowded car. There she was and there the baby. He spoke to his wife and then, turning ever so little, for the first time gazed at his child. "She was at the lovely, smiling age; and catching his eager look of supreme interest in her, she beamed her brightest and sweetest smiles upon him."

A blissful season it was for the Southern Cromwell. He installed wife and child at William Yerby's. While not neglecting any of his duties as a corps administrator, he spent every moment he could with them. For hours daily he studied with fascinated eyes the child's face. While she slept he often would kneel by the cradle and tell Mrs. Jackson that the baby looked almost as if she were . . . well, yes, honestly, an angel! He found time to show his wife the presents given him. Among them was a new horse. She praised the steed, and he smiled and wheeled and galloped, because there was enough of the cavalier in this Cromwell to make him wish to exhibit his horsemanship.

On the fourth day of the visit, Jackson arranged for Mr. Lacy to baptize the child, and in an expansive mood, invited the staff to attend. So, in their gray coats and with their youthful, strangely grim faces, the staff officers arrived at Yerby's for the baptism. They could not fail to observe that when there was some delay in bringing the child into the room for the ordinance, the father suddenly became the impatient general. He stalked out of the room, made short settlement of what had held Mrs. Jackson, and came back with the infant in his arms. That was Stonewall Jackson's way—there must be punctuality!

Perhaps the greatest event of all was the service of Sunday, April 26—an outdoor religious assembly with a full-length discourse in the noblest style of Chaplain Lacy. Mrs. Jackson rode in an ambulance to the meeting place and went to the tent that had been spread to shade the pulpit and the general officers and their guests. General Lee was there and greeted her with flawless courtesy; Jubal Early, looking not at all out of place at church, paid her homage. In front of the tent were some 1,500 to 2,000 of her husband's soldiers. They sang the songs of Zion lustily; with reverence they listened as Chaplain Lacy expounded the parable of the rich man and Lazarus.[46]

That Sunday afternoon the general and his beloved spent together, without interruption or reception of guests. Wrote Mrs. Jackson later: "... his conversation was more spiritual than I had ever observed before. He seemed to be giving utterance to those religious meditations in which he so much delighted." Several times that winter he had opened his heart in much the same way. "Nothing earthly can mar my happiness," he told a friend. "I know that heaven is in store for me; and I should rejoice in the prospect of going there tomorrow. . . . And I would not agree to the slightest diminution of one shade of my glory there—no, not for all the fame I have acquired or shall ever win in this world." In that same spirit he talked to her till the Sabbath shadows fell.

The twenty-seventh and twenty-eighth, Monday and Tuesday, he was with her every hour he was not at headquarters. Reports had come that the enemy on the other side of the Rappahannock had brought up troops from the rear; Stuart placed Stoneman and the Federal cavalry at Warrenton Springs. Lee had called on Longstreet to expedite the commissary operations in North Carolina because the two detached divisions of the First Corps might be recalled at any moment.

Dawn on the twenty-ninth of April in the great bedroom at William Yerby's. Suddenly a stamping on the stairs, a knock at the door: "General Early's adjutant wishes to see General Jackson." Jackson got out of bed. "That looks as if Hooker is crossing," he said to Mrs. Jackson, and then tumbled quickly into his clothes. Down the steps he went to hear what the waiting officer had to say.

After a few minutes he came hurriedly back—the general now. It was as he had expected. Hooker had launched the spring offensive. A battle would be fought. Mrs. Jackson must prepare at once to start for Richmond. If Jackson could, he would return to see her off; if not, he would send her brother Joseph Morrison to escort her to the train at Guiney's. One last kiss; a long, long look at the baby. . . . Good-bye, good-bye![47]

CHAPTER 22

Jackson Gets His Greatest Orders

1. "How Can We Get at These People?"

A mild and cloudy morning it was, that twenty-ninth of April, but rich in the promise of spring. The leaves of the oaks were beginning to open; the peach and cherry trees were in full bloom. In the woods and on the hillsides the anemone could be seen; the houstonia added its color. But Old Jack's eyes were toward the Rappahannock, whence battery-smoke already was rising. He found that Jubal Early had deployed the veterans of Ewell's division, now Early's own, along the R.F. & P. Railroad and forward to the old Stage Road. Under the bank of the river were the Federals, who had crossed in pontoon boats and were laying bridges but as yet showed no disposition to attack.[1]

Jackson could ascertain little concerning their numbers or their disposition, but he concluded a fight was certain and that Mrs. Jackson and the baby must leave at once. He wrote his wife a little note to that effect and summoned his brother-in-law, Lieutenant Joseph Morrison. Would Morrison take an ambulance and go immediately to Yerby's, get Mrs. Jackson and the child, and put them aboard the cars? Morrison was disciplined and not disposed to argue with a lieutenant general, but he could talk plainly to his sister's husband. The general, said Morrison, would have need of all the staff officers. He would prefer to remain on duty and send Chaplain Lacy in his place. Jackson acquiesced; Lacy got the summons and went forthwith to Yerby's. He hurried Mrs. Jackson and her maid and the baby to Guiney's in time for the southbound morning train. Their safe departure he duly reported to his chief.[2]

Jackson ere that had seen the commanding general and learned of reports that indicated the Federals might be crossing the Rappahannock west of Fredericksburg either for a movement against Lee's rear or for a drive against Gordonsville and the Virginia Central Railroad. Upon Lee, not upon Jackson, rested the burden of sifting these reports and of deciding whether to start a column immediately up the river or to await further development of the situation. Jackson's task was to watch the enemy in his front and to bring up his other divisions. Rodes was putting D. H. Hill's division into position on the extreme right. A. P. Hill was ordered to place his brigades on the military road above the railway and on the ridge where Maxcy Gregg had fallen. Trimble's division, at Moss Neck and Skinker's Neck, was called up to Hamilton's Crossing.[3]

One circumstance might have disturbed a man less resolute than Jackson: Neither Allegheny Johnson, who was to take Harvey Hill's division, nor Trimble, who was to lead Jackson's old division, was with the troops. In place of Johnson, who had not yet reported for duty, Robert Rodes, the senior brigadier, well might act. He had experience and in every battle he had fought, from Seven Pines onward, he had distinguished himself. In Jackson's own division, which Trimble still was too crippled to direct in the field, the senior of the brigadiers, the man who now must assume responsibility for the command, was Raleigh Colston. He had been with the division less than a month and never had fought in it.

While Colston was marching up the Rappahannock, the Federals threw another pontoon bridge opposite Smithfield, the Pratt homestead, but they did not move from the riverbank. Every hour deepened Lee's belief that the major effort of the enemy would be elsewhere. By evening he was so well persuaded the principal attack would be directed against his left, upstream, that he started in that direction Dick Anderson, who already had four of his brigades widely extended on that flank. Anderson was to bring up the fifth, Wright's, and take command. On the Fredericksburg front remained Jackson's entire corps, McLaws's division of Longstreet, and part of the reserve artillery.[4]

Dawn of April 30 found Jackson awake early and from the first hour full of fight. Together with Lee he observed the Federal dispositions and discussed proper tactics. The commanding general was quite clear in his own mind: It was better to await the enemy's attack, if one was to be delivered. The artillery on Stafford Heights imposed the same conditions that had prevailed in December. The Confederates would find it difficult to get at the enemy and still harder to get back across the flats after driving the Federals. Jackson had abundant reason for knowing this, in the light of what had happened to his batteries on the evening of December 13, but he could not bring himself to forgo the chance of striking an enemy who was hugging the riverbank. As he stood unconvinced, Lee spoke again: "If you think it can be done, I will give orders for it."

That put the onus on Jackson. Willing as always he was to make decisions, he was loath to go against the judgment of the man, as he had told Boteler, he was "willing to follow blindfolded." Jackson asked for more time in which to examine the terrain. At length and most regretfully he had to own to himself that an advance would be costly and that withdrawal would have to be under a devastating fire. Back he rode to army headquarters. Lee was correct, he said: "It would be inexpedient to attack here." What should he do instead? Lee was waiting with the answer. He was entirely convinced that the Federals below Fredericksburg were no more than a holding force, and that Hooker was striking through the Wilderness of Spotsylvania to turn the Confederate left. "Move then," said Lee to Jackson, "at dawn tomorrow up to Anderson." He went on to explain that McLaws with three brigades would precede Jackson and that Early, with his division, Barksdale's brigade, and part of the reserve artillery would be left to face the Federals on the river.[5]

For these instructions Jackson was not unprepared. During the afternoon he had called Jed Hotchkiss to him and told the topographical engineer to strike off eight maps of the country between the Rappahannock and the Rapidan. His own copy, said Jackson, should be extended westward to Stevensburg. He gave no explanation, but the fact was, Jackson had crossed the Rapidan on the road to Stevensburg the previous August en route to meet Pope, and he knew what a trap to a retreating army was the famous "V" between the Rappahannock and the Rapidan. Perhaps Hooker might be caught where Pope had escaped.[6]

Soon after midnight Jackson ordered the troops awakened. Rodes must proceed to the Orange Plank Road and head westward. Hill would follow; Colston, with Trimble's division, which had marched all day on the twenty-ninth, would close the rear. As the men confidently tramped on, the setting moon was lost in a dense mist at dawn; but the morning proved pleasant—a "genuine May day," wrote Jed Hotchkiss.

Jackson rode ahead of the infantry and, at 8 o'clock, about five and a half miles from Fredericksburg, came upon Anderson's division entrenching on a front more than a mile in length. Anderson had a report to make of vigilant and prompt action. He told it modestly, because that was his nature, but it was a report to belie the persistent yarn that he was indolent and that only under the spur of Longstreet could he be made to exert himself. On the twenty-ninth, as directed by Lee, Anderson had advanced to the crossroads where, in the gloomy tangle of the Wilderness of Spotsylvania, stood the Chancellor house, a large brick structure used often as a tavern. At the crossroads, which bore the pretentious name Chancellorsville, were the brigades of Billy Mahone and Carnot Posey. These officers had withdrawn from United States Ford on the Rappahannock on receipt of news that the Federals in large numbers were at Germanna and Ely's fords, on the Rapidan to the west.

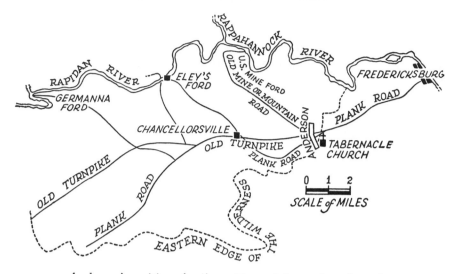

Anderson's position, April 30, 1863, and the roads and terrain
on the Fredericksburg-Chancellorsville front.

To oppose the Union army converging on Chancellorsville Anderson would have but three brigades when Rans Wright overtook him on the morning of the thirtieth. With that small force it would be foolish and worse to make a stand in that thickly wooded country where they might be surrounded before they were aware of the proximity of the bluecoats. Anderson decided that he would get out of the Wilderness, withdraw toward Fredericksburg, and take as strong and open a defensive position as he could find there. Near Tabernacle Church he found Lieutenant Colonel William P. Smith, Lee's acting chief engineer, who had been sent out to run a line of entrenchments on the best ground thereabouts. At this point the old Turnpike and the Orange Plank Road were not more than 1,300 yards apart and could be covered by even so small a command as Anderson's. In front and on both flanks was forest, but the elevation was sufficient to afford a fair field of fire.[7]

In the afternoon the 3rd Virginia cavalry arrived and threw out pickets. Their reconnaissance gave abundant evidence that a mighty force was moving through the Wilderness toward Anderson's front. What was Anderson to do? When someone asked him, his answer was as firm as brief—"Fight, General Lee says so." He kept detachments laboring on field fortifications all night. Shortly before sunrise on May 1 he had the satisfaction of welcoming Lafayette McLaws, who arrived from Fredericksburg with three of his brigades. Wright, Mahone, and Posey of Anderson's division, then, and Kershaw, Wofford, and Semmes of McLaws's—these six brigades were in a defensible position at 8:00 A.M. when Jackson arrived. As soon as he studied the ground and got word that his own corps was approaching from Fredericksburg, Old Jack began in his convinced, staccato manner to issue his orders.[8]

Stop work on the entrenchments. The column was going to advance on the enemy. Send for Wilcox and Perry, still on the river, to rejoin Anderson at once. Start Mahone toward Chancellorsville over the old Turnpike; he knew the road. Give him a battery. Behind him could move McLaws. On the Plank Road, which Posey and Wright had traversed the previous day, Wright could lead the way. Let part of Alexander's battalion go with him. When the Second Corps arrived it must take the Plank Road behind Anderson. There was room for maneuver on that flank; the other was too close to the Rappahannock. Nothing was to be gained by standing on the defensive. Instead of waiting for Hooker to strike, hit him.

At 11 o'clock, May 1, the Confederate advance began. In about fifteen minutes, from the direction of the old Turnpike, came the challenging pop-pop of picket fire and then the boom of field guns. Evidently McLaws, commanding on that road, had encountered the Federals almost as soon as he set his column in motion. In a few moments, in his own front on the Plank Road, Jackson heard the dispute of pickets. A heavy Federal force was discovered in the act of deploying. Word came from McLaws that Unionists in large numbers were advancing on him. Behind them, a mile or more in the Wilderness, many troops could be seen on higher ground. The better opportunity, McLaws went on, seemed to be offered for a flank attack from the direction of the Plank Road.

Hooker, then, was ready for a fight on both roads and, if left alone, might attack. Jackson did not intend on this account to surrender the initiative. If McLaws could hold his ground, Jackson would try the effect of Alexander's guns on the Federals who were deploying, then try to turn their flank and get in their rear. Rodes was directed to send forward one brigade to help Anderson. A courier brought a note in which Jeb Stuart announced that he was coming up on the left and that Fitz Lee was still farther west and in position to observe troops movements in that quarter. Jackson turned over the sheet from Stuart and said much in fourteen words: "I trust that God will grant us a great victory. Keep closed on Chancellorsville."[9]

Now Lee arrived to see how the battle was developing on the flank where he expected the heavier bolt of the Federals to be hurled. The commanding general had remained at Fredericksburg during the morning to counsel Jube Early, Barksdale, and Pendleton in the defense they might be called upon to make. Jackson reported no serious opposition yet had been encountered; the ground to the south, said he, was favorable for a turning operation. In that direction, past the cheering line of Second Corps veterans, Jackson rode some distance with his senior. Lee had no suggestions to make, and soon started for the right to see whether any Federal attack was developing between the Rappahannock and the flank of McLaws.[10]

Word came from the Turnpike that Semmes's brigade, with some help from Billy Mahone's men, had beaten off the attack. A rumor was spreading through the advancing ranks that Hooker was withdrawing. Harry Heth, fighting his first battle with the Army of Northern Virginia, had been told by A. P. Hill to take three brigades—his own, Lane's, and McGowan's—and hurry over to the Turnpike. Thence Heth was to push straight for Chancellorsville. On the Plank Road Jackson urged Anderson's men forward, and at 2:30 he sent McLaws similar instructions to press the enemy. Now leading the advance on the Plank Road was the brigade sent from Rodes's division, under its new brigadier, S. Dodson Ramseur. Rans Wright was to the south of Ramseur; northward was Carnot Posey with the Mississippi brigade formerly the charge of W. S. Featherston. Whenever the advance reached a point where the enemy might have set an ambush or formed an invisible line, Jackson had the artillery "feel" the woods. Always his word to the regimental commander was the same—"Press them, Colonel."

As the enemy appeared now at a stand, Anderson did not wait for Jackson to order the Federal flank turned. He directed Wright's brigade to sideslip to the left until it reached the line of an unfinished railroad. Then the Georgians were to march westward along the right of way. This was done swiftly and successfully, the Federals giving ground rapidly. The Confederate advance was resumed on both roads. It was now about 4:00 P.M.

Jackson decided to see how Rans Wright was progressing and what the nature of the ground was to the left front. He rode quickly to the vicinity of Catharine Furnace, about a mile and three quarters south and west of Chancellorsville. There he found Stuart with the 1st Virginia cavalry and some of the horse artillery. Wright already was deploying to sweep a woodland to the northward. Jackson asked Stuart to ride with him to some higher ground whither Beckham was moving several of Stuart's guns to clear the way for Wright. Beckham's opening salvo brought a furious and well-directed answer from two batteries of masked guns. Jackson and Stuart and their cavalcade had to turn about and make for safety. Major Channing Price was hit with a bit of shell but proudly refused to think the hurt serious. With fine pluck he kept his seat until the little company was out of range and then, with scarcely a sound, he fainted and dropped from his saddle. It was found that the iron had severed an artery and that the major had lost much blood.[11]

Jackson went back to the Plank Road where he met A. P. Hill and Anderson. They told him regretfully that the advance had been halted in the face of a stubborn stand by the enemy. Everything indicated that Hooker was in great strength about Chancellorsville. Jackson then bade Hill ride with him to the Turnpike, whence was rolling the sound of a brisk skirmish. McLaws, it was found, was halted on the Turnpike, and half a mile in advance was Harry Heth with the three brigades Powell Hill had sent to that road. As a newcomer, Heth was determined not to be found wanting in dash. When he ascertained he was facing determined resistance, he sent to McLaws to inquire whether he would support him in attacking. McLaws had no words for such nonsense at that time of day.

Even in the face of that implied rebuke, Heth had not abandoned his mission. McLaws or no McLaws, support or no support, he would go on to Chancellorsville. Captain Alex Haskell, quick-witted as always, said he would go forward with two regiments: "If the enemy have gone, we can sweep through as your advance guard; and if they are there, the rest of your command will be saved for the general fight." Haskell had thrown forward two famous regiments, Orr's Rifles and the 14th South Carolina, McGowan's old command. A blasting fire had greeted them. When Jackson and Hill rode up, Haskell came to meet them. "Captain Haskell, what is it?" Jackson said quietly. "Ride up here, General," said the South Carolinian, "and you will see it all." Jackson rode up and took out his field-glasses. Ahead, plainly visible, were three lines of battle and crude but strong earthworks. McLaws had reported before noon that Hooker occupied a strong position. Here was the proof of it. Would Hooker stay there?[12]

Back to Heth's line and across to the Plank Road Jackson galloped. Near the junction of the Plank and Furnace roads Old Jack halted and there, before darkness fell, he saluted General Lee, who rode up to investigate the report that Hooker had been brought to bay. With few words, the Confederate chieftains went back into the woods in order to get out of range of a Federal sharpshooter who could not be driven from his perch.

Among the pines Lee sat on a fallen log and asked Jackson to take a place beside him. What, Jackson was asked, had he found on the left? Briefly the corps commander told of Wright's attack near Catharine Furnace and of the strength the Federals had displayed there. It was Lee's belief that Hooker's main effort was to be on that flank. What they were witnessing on the fringe of the Wilderness was no feint. Hooker had planned to give battle there and would not abandon the attempt so lightly. If the Unionists remained in position the next day, they must be attacked. Where could that be done successfully? Lee's reconnaissance on the right had convinced him that an effective blow could not be delivered between the old Turnpike and the Rappahannock. The Wilderness was too thick. Was the situation immediately in front of the Chancellorsville line equally discouraging? Apparently it was; but before the possibility was discarded, a careful reconnaissance ought to be made. Talcott of Lee's staff and Boswell of Jackson's were named for that task.

Till the two engineers returned, Lee and Jackson canvassed the alternative that was shaping itself by elimination: If an attack on the Confederate right were ruled out, and the reconnaissance on the center revealed no opening, what could be done on the left? Beyond Catharine Furnace, where Wright and Beckham had fought, what were the prospects? Where was the Federal right? How securely was it anchored?

Jeb Stuart rode up and jubilantly announced that Fitz Lee had been reconnoitering to the west and had satisfied himself that the Federal right was "in the air." That news gave more importance than ever to the location of a route that extended beyond Hooker's exposed flank. It must be a concealed route, but it should not be overlong if the infantry were to cover it in time to give battle the next day. Hooker most obligingly had given the Confederates a boon by sending virtually the whole of his cavalry on a raid to the southward. He had shown little cavalry in front of Stuart and he might have few squadrons elsewhere to watch Confederate movements. A turning operation that would roll up his right seemed entirely practicable, if any decent adjacent roads out of sight of the Federal pickets could be found.

Talcott and Boswell came back from their reconnaissance and were of one mind: The Federal line in the Wilderness was too strong to be assailed. It was being fortified steadily; it was located where little artillery could be brought to bear on it. The whole country in front of the Confederates was a maze of mixed timber of all heights. Much of the "original growth" had been felled years before for charcoal and had been replaced with stubborn young hardwood. A Wilderness in truth that terrain was!

The chain of thought this report suggested moved Lee to ask, "How can we get at these people?" Jackson did not assume the commanding general was asking advice. He knew that Lee often asked just such a question when he really was addressing it to himself. The answer then was as loyal as it was understanding. "You know best," said Jackson, in effect; "show me what to do, and we will try to do it."

Lee's was the responsibility, Lee's the decision. On the map, in a few moments, he traced the approximate direction of an advance that should put the Confederates beyond the right flank and in rear of Hooker. Then Jackson had the pleasure of hearing Lee entrust the ascertainment of the exact line of march and the execution of the operation to him. "General Stuart

will cover your movement with his cavalry," he added. The assignment
brought a smile to Jackson's face. Lee doubtless never had any other idea
than that of committing the operation to Jackson, but until that moment
had not said so. Now the task and all the tactical arrangement were Jackson's. He rose quickly and saluted: "My troops will move at four o'clock."

Quietly Jackson went back a little farther into the woods and spread out
his saddle blanket on the ground. He gratefully accepted Sandie Pendleton's proffer of a cape to protect himself from the chill of the night and
stretched out. Staff officers and couriers came and went. Around nearby
campfires was slow conversation and now and again a laugh, but the
mournful whip-po'-wills in the thickets almost drowned the voices.
Moonlight outshone the flickering fires and gave sleeping soldiers a
strange look . . . as if they were dead already. What mattered ghastly faces?
Tomorrow would bring Jackson as great an opportunity as ever Winchester had offered . . . or Port Republic . . . or Groveton, or . . .[13]

2. "YOU CAN GO FORWARD THEN"

The chill of the damp earth and the scantiness of his cover caused Jackson
to awaken before daylight on the second of May. He was shivering and felt
the first symptoms of a cold. He went to a little fire a waiting courier had
kept alive. With his rubber coat around him the general sat on a cracker
box the Federals had left there and bent over the fire as if he were hungry
for heat.

Presently Tucker Lacy, the chaplain, came to the fire. He had arrived
during the night, after Jackson had gone to sleep, and told General Lee
what he knew of the roads in the district, in which his family had large
holdings of land. Jackson greeted him, "Come, sit down; I wish to talk to
you." Was there, he asked, any road by which either flank of the enemy
could be turned? On the Confederate left, Lacy answered, there was a succession of roads, good and bad, that led around to the Turnpike west of
Chancellorsville. Jackson showed him a rough map of the area and said,
"Mark it down for me."

Lacy sketched the road, but Jackson was not satisfied. "That is too near.
It goes within the line of the enemy's pickets. I wish to get around *well* to
his rear, without being observed. Do you know of no other road?" He did
not, Lacy replied, but someone who doubtless would know was the propri-
etor of Catharine Furnace, Charles C. Wellford. This fired Jackson. He
woke up Jed Hotchkiss and explained to the topographical engineer what
he wanted—a concealed route, not too long, from Catharine Furnace to

the Plank Road west of the point where the Federal right was "in the air." Hotchkiss and Lacy were to find out from Mr. Wellford whether such a route existed, if so what its length was, whether it was practicable for artillery, and if a guide could be procured.[14]

Hotchkiss and the chaplain got their horses and rode down the Furnace Road to consult Mr. Wellford. Soon to Jackson's side came the commanding general. Day was breaking; it gave promise of warmth and pleasantness. Refreshed and alert—always at his vigorous best in the early morning—Lee sat down by his lieutenant. Jackson told of dispatching Hotchkiss and Lacy to the Furnace. The conclusion already reached by the two generals was that the flank of Hooker must be turned. What now was to be decided was whether a march to the Federal right was practicable within the time that Hooker might be expected to remain on the defensive.

Jackson had determined what he would propose to increase the prospect of success in a furious offensive that would hurl one Federal wing back on Chancellorsville and the fords of the Rappahannock. Everything was contingent on the report Hotchkiss would make on the roads. Up from the Furnace Hotchkiss soon rode, and with good news. Mr. Wellford said there *was* a way! Hotchkiss picked up another of the cracker boxes the Federals had left behind and placed it between Lee and Jackson. On it he spread a map across which he traced the route Mr. Wellford recommended: From Catharine Furnace you follow a newly opened road south and west to the Brock Road, which runs north. You do not turn north because you may come within sight of the enemy. Instead, you move south about 600 yards and then make a sharp right turn and go back north again past the Trigg and Stephens houses. You keep on parallel to the Brock Road to the place of a free Negro named Cook. There you get back into the Brock Road and follow it to the Orange Plank Road.

When Hotchkiss finished there was a moment of silence. Lee looked at Jackson, whose head probably was still bent over the map. "General Jackson," he said quietly, "what do you propose to do?" The question was superfluous in view of the previous understanding, but it was polite. Jackson put his forefinger on the map and followed the line that Hotchkiss had traced. "Go around here," he answered.

"What do you propose to make this movement with?" Undramatic the question was, and spoken in a conversational tone, but it presented on the instant a supreme test of both generals. If Jackson asked for little he could do little, but if he asked for much, would he be fair to Lee? The answer had to be in terms of opportunities, not of sensibilities. Hooker's army must be overwhelmed, hurled back to United States Ford, destroyed. Sufficient force to do this must be provided. So, without hesitation or preliminary,

Jackson gave the answer he probably had been fashioning for hours. With what did he propose to make the movement?—"With my whole corps."

"What will you leave me?" the commanding general asked. Without so much as an apologetic inflection to acknowledge that he was putting upon Lee the burden of facing perhaps 50,000 men with 14,000, Jackson replied, "The divisions of Anderson and McLaws."

Why not? Lee had not forgotten that Jackson had started one flank march the previous August and found his way, swiftly and surely, to the rear of Pope. In September had not Jackson left Frederick with just such a column as he now wished to put on the road, and had not the reward been 11,000 prisoners at Harper's Ferry and more than 70 guns? Second Manassas, Harper's Ferry, Chancellorsville—retreat, surrender, destruction—might not that be the ascending order of Jackson's achievements? "Well," said Lee calmly, "go on," and he took pencil and paper to make notes for the orders he would issue.[15]

Quickly Jackson left the bivouac to prepare for the advance of his corps. Already the blue of his eyes was beginning to burn, the line of his thin lips was sterner, his words were clipped. Although he made his dispositions rapidly, much time was consumed in getting even the well-disciplined men of Rodes's division to cook and eat their breakfast and to move out to the road. After Rodes was to march Colston, with Trimble's division, which had been Jackson's own. Powell Hill was to close the rear. A long, long column it would be—15 brigades, 29,000 bayonets—with artillery, ambulances, and wagons, on those narrow trails through the Wilderness.

It was about 8 o'clock when the head of the column crossed the Plank Road on the way down the Furnace Road toward Wellford's. Jackson was alert but not impatient. At the crossroads he saw the commanding general. Few words Jackson had, because all was in order, and those few he uttered tersely. His sole gesture, wholly characteristic, was to point ahead. Lee nodded; Jackson rode on. Under the brim of his cap his eyes were shining fiercely now.[16]

Jackson sought to keep the column at his standard—a mile in 25 minutes with 10 minutes' rest every 2 miles. Fortunately the dirt roads were "just wet enough to be easy to the feet and free from dust." The only discomfort that developed as the sun rose higher was lack of water. Few streams or farm wells were passed.[17] The first danger point was where the road crossed an open elevation close to Catharine Furnace. Not long after the van started the descent to the Furnace, a shell from the direction of the Turnpike made an inquisitive flight over the heads of the Confederates. Another followed, and another. As the fire continued, Jackson directed the troops to double-quick across the open space. Reconnaissance showed a woods road by which the corps train could detour and escape a pounding on the exposed stretch. Happily there was no increase in the volume of fire, but Jackson did not overlook the possibility that a Federal column might descend on the Furnace to ascertain the meaning of the movement. Rodes was directed to detach a regiment to guard a trail that entered the Furnace Road from the north.[18]

Neither the steadiness of the march nor the absence of any new threat led Jackson to relax. "Permit no straggling!" was his continued exhortation or, terser still, "Press on, press on!" Only one circumstance showed that he was satisfied with the advance: He talked somewhat freely. Conversing about the Federals and their reported great strength, Old Jack remarked in his quiet, half-muffled voice: "I hear it said that General Hooker has more men than he can handle. I should like to have half as many more men as I have today, and I should hurl him in the river!"[19]

By 1:00 P.M., after the men had eaten and rested briefly, the advance became more exciting. Not far ahead was the Orange Plank Road. Was it guarded? The 2nd Virginia cavalry had turned eastward into that road. Did the enemy's flank rest there? Would battle be joined there?

Down the Brock Road toward the head of the column galloped Fitz Lee to meet Jackson. "General," he said, "if you will ride with me, halting your column here, out of sight, I will show you the enemy's right." Into the Plank Road rode Jackson and the cavalryman, followed by a single courier. Fitz turned off to the north to follow a path through the woods, then climbed a hill to a cleared crest. There he drew rein and, with a broad gesture, bade Jackson see for himself. Spread out, near enough for the movement of individuals to be observed, were long lines of Federals. Arms were stacked. The men were at ease. The smoke of campfires already was rising. A few cannon were in position; some earthworks had been thrown up, but the enemy manifestly was not expecting attack.

Eagerly, carefully, Jackson measured the Federal line, trying to find exactly where, in the forest to his left, the right flank might be. On the left was open ground around a farmhouse near the Turnpike. Talley's farm this was. Half a mile eastward was another farm-clearing, with some earthworks facing southward. This place was Melzi Chancellor's. All the while Fitz Lee was talking, pointing out his observations. Jackson made no answer and scarcely seemed to regard what the cavalryman was saying. "In the air" the flank was, precisely as the Confederates had hoped, and vulnerable; but where stood the flank guards? How much farther must the Second Corps proceed before it would be beyond the Federal right?

Not five minutes after he had reached the hilltop, Jackson had seen enough to justify decision. Abruptly he turned to the courier. His words snapped like a drover's whip: "Tell General Rodes to move across the old Plank Road, halt when he gets to the old Turnpike, and I will join him there." The man touched his horse and rode off. Jackson's eye swept once more the wide arc before him and then, without a word to Lee, he started down the hill. Said Fitz Lee afterward, in amusing candor: "I expected to be told I had made a valuable personal reconnaissance—saving the lives of many soldiers, and that Jackson was indebted to me to that amount at least."[20]

Was Rodes moving northward to the intersection of the Turnpike? He was—rapidly. A brigade must be sent to guard the Plank Road eastward; if this was secured and the Confederate cavalry was vigilant, the deployment of Jackson's infantry could be masked. Send Paxton, then, with the Stonewall Brigade. As for the Confederate left, Munford of the 2nd Virginia cavalry was instructed to "seize the Ely's Ford Road and hold it and keep me posted on that flank." Now to notify the commanding general! Timing his dispatch "Near 3 p.m.," he scrawled: "The enemy has made a stand at Chancellor's which is about 2 miles from Chancellorsville. I hope as soon as practicable to attack. I trust that an ever kind Providence will bless us with great success." In a postscript he added: "The leading division is up & the next two appear to be well closed."[21]

Rodes's brigades tramped northward through the brilliant May sunshine, and when they reached the Turnpike they headed eastward. Unopposed, unobserved even, Rodes led them almost a mile to a long, low ridge. His skirmishers under Major Eugene Blackford were advanced 400 yards. The division quietly was deployed. Jackson's instructions to Rodes were that when the bugles sounded the advance, the whole line was to sweep forward. The road was to be the guide. Talley's farm was the first objective. If it found the Federals strong at Melzi Chancellor's, the division was to

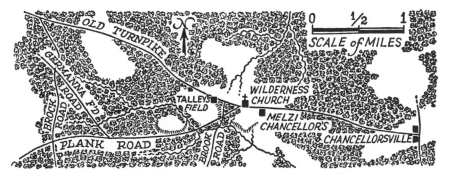

Talley's and Melzi Chancellor farms, battleground of Chancellorsville.

seek shelter until the Confederate artillery got into action. Otherwise the line was to pursue the enemy as far as he could be driven.

While Rodes was instructing his brigadiers, Colston was forming Trimble's division. Colston's orders were to follow Rodes and support him. A commander in the front line who needed help would send back to the officer of the second line, who would move up without waiting to refer the call to his division chief. Heth and Pender of Hill's division were placed on the left of the road as a third line. Lane and McGowen, in column, were instructed to move forward by the flank, on the Turnpike, as the lines advanced.[22]

About this time Jackson learned that Archer and Thomas had turned back to repulse an attack on the wagon train. Their absence would not be fatal to the plan. In the three lines were ten brigades. Jim Lane and Sam McGowan would be a reserve. Frank Paxton could advance the Stonewall Brigade when his front was cleared. Moorman's battery of the horse artillery was waiting on the Turnpike, and other batteries would come up quickly. The Federals still had given no evidence that they even dimly apprehended danger. Every command that could be glimpsed from any lookout seemed to have concluded that the day would end in a good supper by the campfire, a leisured smoke, gossip and banter, and then the warmth of a blanket and the quiet companionship of the stars.

Amid the underbrush and in the thick woods the Confederate deployment was slow. Five o'clock it was now. By 7:30 darkness would fall. What was done that afternoon had to be done with the speed and force of a hurricane. Jackson was in the high excitement of conflict. Under his cap brim his eyes were blazing. Robert Rodes, as full of fight as Jackson, rode up and drew rein. With a bugler, Major Blackford followed presently to report the skirmish line waiting to go forward. Jackson could look left and right to veteran regiments. With these troops ready, their morale perfect and their ears straining for the first notes of the advance, what man worthy of the name of leader would fail that day to destroy the Amelekites? From his pocket Jackson took his watch and opened it. The hands were at 5:15. "Are you ready, General Rodes?" the commander asked.

"Yes, sir!" answered Rodes decisively.

"You can go forward then," Jackson said in even tones.[23]

Rodes with his long blond mustache and his penetrating blue eyes looked as if he were Wotan still young. A glance and a nod to Blackford were all the orders he need give. Through the forest rang the notes that set every soldier's heart to racing. To right and left from each brigade sounded the advance. Now—forward all and no stop, no pause! The gray line crashed through the woods. Ahead, terrorized, dashed deer and rabbits.

Challenging shots came presently from the Federals, next some pretense of a volley, a few cannon shots. Instantly, as excited graycoats realized that they had flushed the enemy, they raised the rebel yell. It rose and swelled and echoed through the forest. Soon a break was visible in the Federal front. It widened. Within ten minutes the Federals were being driven back toward Talley's.

Vigorously Doles pursued on the right center. North of the road the other brigades pressed on. Trimble's men were on their heels. Only on the extreme right did the line lag. There, in confusion, Colquitt thought his right was threatened. In defiance of orders he halted. That blocked Ramseur and immobilized the Stonewall Brigade on the Plank Road. Furious, Dodson Ramseur reconnoitered and found nothing. To Colquitt he crashed his way: Go on, continue the advance; leave to us any Federal forces on the flank! Colquitt caught his breath and, at length, ordered his brigade to push on. Few who made the assault knew the right was lagging and that the three divisions had in the column of attack no more than half their strength. Old Jack's boys were fighting, not ciphering![24]

Now for the pursuit to Melzi Chancellor's. Boldly, immediately, Rodes pressed on. With a fiendish yell that froze blood in the gathering twilight, the Second Corps stormed up the elevation. A wild volley was all the resistance encountered. As Rodes's brigadiers straightened their line for the

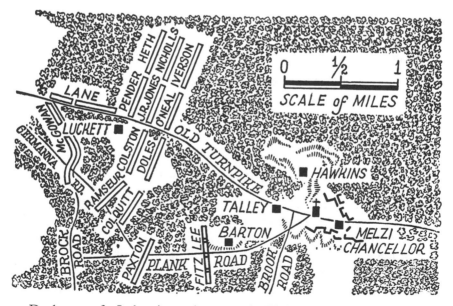

Deployment for Jackson's attack against the XI Corps flank, May 2, 1863.

next onslaught, Trimble's troops came rolling into the works behind them. With two lines now united and the enemy on the run, Rodes hurriedly prepared to push on toward Chancellorsville.

Close to the front Jackson had ridden; again and again he shouted, "Press on, press on!" The ecstasy of conflict appeared to have seized him. Never had he been so transformed—never in such sure reliance upon the God of Battle. Every time the wild yell of victory swept across the fields or through the wood, he would lift his head and give thanks. Said Jackson's principal companion on the advance, "I have never seen him so well pleased with the progress and results of a fight."

Beyond Melzi Chancellor's, which was on open ground, the advance units entered a thick wood where, in an instant, they seemed to pass from twilight to night. That changed everything. The right of the line became entangled in an abatis. Officers lost touch with their men. To Jackson came a report from Rodes that he had been compelled to call a halt but he begged the general to throw Hill ahead of him so that the original first line could re-form. Powell Hill was anticipating Rodes's wishes. Pender was in support of Colston's left; Heth's men were directly behind J. R. Jones's brigade. McGowan and Lane had their brigades in the road, behind the third line. The full moon was rising, as yet a dim red orb through the low-hanging smoke. A kindly Providence seemed to be lifting that lantern in the sky to light the Confederacy on its way to independence.

Jackson resolved that Hill should deploy and drive the enemy back to Chancellorsville. Perhaps more could be done. It might be possible to get between the Federals and United States Ford, to force the Federals to attack him there—and to slaughter them. Jackson touched his horse to ride still nearer to the front and see for himself what the field promised. Hill overtook him and Jackson turned abruptly. His order to his lieutenant sounded like picket fire: "Press them! Cut them off from the United States Ford, Hill! Press them!"[25]

3. A NIGHT IN THE WILDERNESS

Jackson, tense and resolute, resumed his ride eastward along the Plank Road.[26] He drew rein by an old schoolhouse and ascertained from officers there the little they knew of conditions ahead. With a touch of the heel he set Little Sorrel toward the front again, riding through shadows and the uncertain light of a moon still low in the east. He passed Heth's brigade and then Lane's. In the belief that he could organize quickly a night attack, he sent one staff officer after another to assist in the deployment. The spirit of his speech, the sharpness of his commands, was that of a battle still raging. Every detail of preparation he directed. Lane came up to ask whether he should begin his advance. Would Jackson give the order? "Push right ahead, Lane," the general answered earnestly, and extended his hand as if he were bodily pushing the Federals. Without another word he rode on. It was then about 9:00 P.M.[27]

His signal officer, Captain R. E. Wilbourn, came up and began to describe Hill's deployment. Lieutenant Morrison returned from a mission. Captain Boswell was nearby. Jackson himself, impatient, excited, anxious to strike the final blow, determined to ride out to the skirmish line to get some further understanding, if he could, of the terrain. With staff officers and couriers and signalmen he now had a small cavalcade. Some of his companions began now to be solicitous for his safety. "General," said one of his staff, "don't you think this is the wrong place for you?"

"The danger is all over—the enemy is routed!—go back and tell A. P. Hill to press right on!"[28]

Except where the moonlight reached the empty road, nothing could be seen ahead. There was darkness, but ahead was the sound of axes, of trees being felled, of voices. Jackson listened. Was the enemy too strong to assail? Was a night attack too hazardous? Was it possible to follow impulse and boldly, instantly, drive the confused enemy? Jackson held to his plan. The attack must be pressed.

Suddenly from south of the dark road there was a shot. Several others were fired. A volley roared through the woods. "Cease firing, cease firing!" Powell Hill's voice rang out. Jackson felt the sorrel swerve suddenly toward the north and dash into the woods. With his left hand he checked the horse. His right hand he lifted to hold his cap and protect his face from the low-hanging boughs. "Cease firing!" Morrison yelled as he ran toward the lines. "You are firing into your own men!" A voice shouted back, "Who gave that order? It's a lie! Pour it into them, boys!"[29]

There was a long flash in front of Jackson—a volley by a kneeling line. His left arm fell limp; his grip on his bridle rein was lost; a bullet struck his uplifted right hand. Dazed, Jackson felt on his head a sudden blow from a bough that threw him back and almost off his horse. Somehow he contrived to find the bridle rein with his right hand and desperately began to pull in the frightened horse. A moment later he felt a strong hand jerk the rein. Captain Wilbourn had come to his aid. On the other side, signalman W. T. Wynn dashed up and together the two halted Little Sorrel and steadied the rider. Quickly Wilbourn sprang to the ground. "They certainly must be our troops," he exclaimed.

Jackson nodded but said nothing. He was looking up the road, toward his own line, as if he scarcely could realize that his soldiers had fired on him. "How do you feel, General?" asked Wilbourn. "Can you move your fingers?" The general replied weakly that he could not; the arm was broken. "You had better take me down." He nearly fainted as Wilbourn and Wynn eased him to the ground and laid him under a small tree by the roadside. Wynn was sent to find Dr. McGuire, the corps medical director, or some other skillful surgeon. As Wilbourn examined the wounded left arm, Jackson heard the voice of Powell Hill. "I have been trying to make the men cease firing," cried Hill and, with words of deep regret, he knelt by Jackson. "Is the wound painful?" he inquired. "Very painful," answered Jackson, "my arm is broken."

Gently Hill took off Jackson's blood-filled gauntlets and assisted Wilbourn and Lieutenant James Power Smith with a tourniquet and a sling for the general's arm. Fortunately, the blood had begun to clot by this time. The assistant surgeon of Pender's brigade now arrived with a litter and examined the major wound. Jackson whispered to Hill to inquire whether the surgeon was competent. Receiving a reassuring answer, he said, "Very good, very good." Surgeon and attendants had to decide what next should be done. To move Jackson might be to start the flow of blood again; to leave him where he was, between the lines, would be to risk capture or death from new projectiles.[30]

Before a decision could be taken, a new alarm sent Powell Hill hurrying off to form the troops to meet an attack. Thoughtfully he added that he would do his utmost to keep from the men the fact that Jackson was wounded. "Thank you," said Jackson faintly. Back at the lines, Hill with furious words prepared Lane's men to repulse the expected assault. A sudden burst of fire, and a moment later Hill felt a sharp and stunning blow across his boot tops. A fragment of shell left both legs numbed and bruised. He found he could not walk otherwise than with an agonizing limp. So great did the pain become that Hill could not hope to ride a horse or to exercise command.

If Hill was disabled, who should command? In the whole of the Second Corps not another major general was present on the field. Rodes was the senior brigadier then with the corps. He must assume command. Should he keep it? That day for the first time he had exercised authority over a division. Hill debated the question and probably discussed it with Sandie Pendleton. The conclusion was to notify Rodes and, at the same time, to send for Jeb Stuart. To be sure, Stuart was not an infantryman, but he was known to the army as a leader. Rodes's abilities, though high, had not yet been recognized outside the division he was leading. General Lee, of course, was to be notified as soon as he could be reached.

Rodes assumed temporary command of the corps. Neither he, Hill, nor anyone else believed that the tired troops, without Jackson's leadership, could press farther that night. All that Rodes could do was to direct Colston, who kept command of Trimble's men, and Heth, who now succeeded to Powell Hill's division, to prepare for a resumption of the attack when daylight returned.[31]

During these hours of confusion, of abrupt bursts of fire and of sudden silence, Jackson was having an experience that never had been his before on a field of battle—evading an enemy he could not combat. At the time of the alarm that sent Hill hurrying back to his command, Lieutenant Morrison had thought to reconnoiter the road ahead of them. In a few minutes he was back, on the run and in immense excitement. Jackson heard him shout, "The enemy is within fifty yards and is advancing; let us take the General away!" They debated carrying him, but Jackson said faintly, "No, if you can help me up, I can walk."

Painfully, with help on either side, Jackson got on his legs and started slowly walking toward the line. The staff tried to shield him from inquisitive passing soldiers. One man, dodging among the horses, got close enough to stare at the pale, bearded man who was walking with uncertain step along the road. "Great God," he cried in an agonized voice, "that is General Jackson!" Given a deceptive reply, he looked again at Jackson and turned away in silence.

Before Jackson had walked more than twenty paces he was exhausted. He was prevailed upon to let the litter bearers carry him. Hardly had they started when the road was swept with a new hurricane of fire. Quickly he was lowered to the ground. His lieutenants lay down alongside, forming an embankment of flesh around the general. Jackson struggled for a moment to get up. "Sir," said Lieutenant Smith, "you must lie still; it will cost you your life if you rise!" Overhead the projectiles were shrieking; severed branches and smitten saplings tumbled to the ground. They could see again and again the spark of the canister that hit the stones of the road.[32]

Presently the Federal battery widened the range and opened with shell. The slow march to the rear resumed. Dorsey Pender came up and recognized Jackson. "Ah, General, I am sorry to see you have been wounded. The lines here are so much broken that I fear we will have to fall back." Instantly Jackson was the corps commander and raised his head to answer with flashing eye: "You must hold your ground, General Pender; you must hold your ground, sir!"[33]

The staff officers decided there would be less danger and they would make better time if they turned off into the trees by the roadside. For half a mile, on willing shoulders, the general was carried through the woods. He was weak but conscious. Then, without warning, one of the litter bearers caught his foot in a trailing vine and went down. As the litter slipped from the man's shoulder the general fell heavily and landed on his shattered arm. A groan of pain, the first he had uttered, escaped his lips, but he struggled hard with his nerves and soon recovered his composure.

At last the party was rewarded by the sight of Hunter McGuire, Jackson's medical director and friend. Although the doctor was eleven years his junior, Jackson had for him not merely respect as a professional man but affection as an individual. On none of the officers of the general staff did Jackson lean so heavily. With relief he saw McGuire kneel by his litter and heard the warm inquiry, "I hope you are not badly hurt, General."

"I am badly injured, Doctor; I fear I am dying." The words were faint, but the tone was calm. A moment later he added, "I am glad you have come. I think the wound in my shoulder is still bleeding." Said Dr. McGuire: "His suffering at this time was intense; his hands were cold, his skin clammy, his face pale, and his lips compressed and bloodless." As soon as the bleeding was stanched, Jackson received from McGuire some whiskey and a dose of morphia. These had prompt effect. In a few minutes he was so much relieved of pain that he could be started by ambulance to the field hospital, nearly four miles to the rear.

En route, beyond the range of fire and within the Southern lines, torches were used to reveal the chuck holes in the road and save the general from jolts. McGuire sat with him, his finger on the severed artery in his arm should the tourniquet slip. The other passenger in the ambulance was Jackson's chief of artillery, Stapleton Crutchfield, in agony with a shattered leg. "Is Crutchfield dangerously wounded?" Jackson whispered. "No," McGuire answered, "only painfully hurt." Presently, in much the same way, Crutchfield inquired about Jackson. When he heard that the general was seriously wounded, the younger man could not restrain his emotion: "Oh, my God," he cried with a groan.[34]

Back to Talley's Jackson rode slowly in the rumbling vehicle, back to the ridge where the troops had deployed, back to the crossing of the Brock Road. Shortly after 11 o'clock the ambulance reached Wilderness Tavern and turned into a field where the Second Corps hospital had been established. The surgeon in charge, Dr. Harvey Black, had received news of Jackson's wounding and had prepared and warmed a tent into which the general was immediately carried. More whiskey Jackson received, and then slowly, under protective canvas and abundant blankets, he seemed to come back to life. His pulse became stronger; warmth returned to his body. Over him Dr. McGuire and Lieutenant Smith watched quietly.

Midnight came and went. Except for the forlorn call of the whip-po'-will, there was quiet over the field. From the front there floated not an echo of conflict. One o'clock—still Dr. McGuire waited for a stronger pulse and a clearer mind. Then, at 2:00 A.M., with three other surgeons at his side, McGuire explained to Jackson that chloroform would be administered to permit the painless examination of the wounds. This might show the bone of the upper arm so badly broken that the surgeons would consider amputation necessary. Did Jackson wish them to proceed with the operation immediately? The answer was weakly spoken but firm and instant: "Yes, certainly, Dr. McGuire, do for me whatever you think best."

The chloroform was administered and in a few minutes Jackson began to feel the effects. "What an infinite blessing!" he exclaimed. The same word, "blessing, blessing" came often but more slowly. Then he was relaxed and insensible. The wound in his right hand was examined first by Dr. McGuire. A round ball had entered the palm, broken two bones, and lodged under the skin at the back of the hand. McGuire took it out and, from his wide experience, could say that it had been fired from a smooth-bore Springfield musket. That weapon was much used by the Confederates but had been discarded by the Federals. This mute evidence answered the question the army already was beginning to ask: Had Stonewall Jackson been wounded by his own men, who mistook him and his companions for Federal cavalry?

McGuire laid bare the general's left arm. An ugly wound was disclosed. A ball had entered about three inches below the joint of the shoulder, divided the main artery, shattered the bone, and passed out. A third bullet had struck the forearm and come out on the inside of the arm just above the wrist. McGuire shook his head as he looked: Conditions were as he had feared they would be. It was not possible to save a member so badly damaged. The arm should be amputated at once. The other surgeons were of the same mind. It was an operation each of them had performed scores of times. Dr. McGuire swiftly made a circular incision and sawed off the bone. With so many experienced hands at work, little blood was lost. After McGuire had applied the dressings, the anesthetic was withdrawn.[35]

After half an hour Jackson was conscious and took a cup of coffee. An hour later Dr. McGuire entered with Sandie Pendleton, who had come with an important message. "Well, Major," Jackson greeted him, "I am glad to see you; I thought you were killed." Sandie reported that Hill had been disabled, and told of the decision to send for Stuart. The cavalryman had arrived at the front, he said, but knew little of the situation and sent to Jackson for instructions. The general struggled visibly to find a solution that would help Stuart. For a moment, McGuire wrote, "his eye flashed its old fire, but it was only for a moment; his face relaxed again, and presently he answered very feebly and sadly, 'I don't know—I can't tell; say to General Stuart he must do what he thinks best.' "[36]

With this message Pendleton rode back to Stuart, who by this time had received the transfer of command from Powell Hill. In the finest spirit, Robert Rodes acquiesced—good augury for a situation that had no parallel in the history of the army. Tired though the troops were, and confused in organization, they represented three fifths of the army, and they must push the offensive on which the outcome of the battle, perhaps of the campaign, would depend. For their direction there was a cavalryman who never had conducted an infantry action. To execute his orders he had not a general officer who, till that second of May, ever had led a division in action.

Jeb was not daunted by this, by lack of information, or by the absence of all Jackson's staff officers except Pendleton. Calmly and cheerfully he made the best of his plight. The guns of the Second Corps must be made ready, he reasoned. Crutchfield wounded? Who was next in artillery command? Porter Alexander? A capable man! Send for him to locate and occupy the best positions that could be found. Stuart himself would ride along the tangled line, impose silence on the troops, and prepare to attack with the dawn.

CHAPTER 23

Victory and Tragedy
at Chancellorsville

1. THE YOUNG COMMANDERS' DAY

When the first light of a warm and pleasant day began to filter into the Wilderness on May 3, Powell Hill's division was widely deployed in the front line. Harry Heth, though still a stranger to most of the officers and men, was undertaking manfully and intelligently to direct the force Hill was too badly bruised to command. The division was in two lines across the Plank Road, almost exactly one mile west of Chancellorsville. On the extreme right of the first line was Archer. On Archer's left was McGowan. Next him, with left flank on the Plank Road, was Lane; on Lane's left, north of the road, Heth's own brigade, now under Colonel J. M. Brockenbrough, formed a short second line. The division of Trimble, now led by Raleigh Colston, was from 300 to 500 yards in rear of Heth. The third line, Rodes's, was across the highway at Melzi Chancellor's. The troops had slept a few hours and were able to give battle, though manifestly they could not be expected to show the fighting edge they had displayed the previous afternoon.

The artillery was in somewhat better condition. Porter Alexander's reconnaissance had shown that some guns could be employed advantageously in and near the Plank Road. Besides this, he had found one other place—on the right, an opening about 25 yards wide that led for 200 yards to what had seemed in the moonlight to be a cleared eminence where the Federals already had guns. Alexander brought up several batteries before daylight and concealed them close to the clearance. At dawn this high ground was hidden by mist, but as the sun drove away this screen the hill appeared to be what Alexander thought it was—an admirable position from which to assail the Federals. Guides said the elevation was called Hazel Grove. Its strategical importance Jeb Stuart realized, and the tem-

487

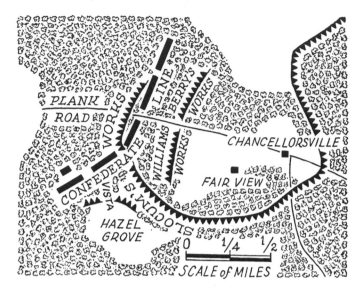

Terrain and Federal works west and southwest of Chancellorsville,
about 5:00 A.M., May 3.

porary commander of the corps would devote a large share of his personal
attention to its occupation.[1]

From the moment Stuart gained his first knowledge of the situation, he
determined to attack as soon as possible and with his full force. In his code
of war, where the offensive was not too hazardous it always was the best of
any or many courses. He delayed now only as long as the sun demanded
time to rout the shadows. Confidently he gave his first orders to Archer
and McGowan on the right. Archer began his movement at sunrise and
almost immediately lost touch with McGowan on his left—but at the
same time established contact with the enemy. Archer drove this force
through the woods and into the open, taking four guns and 100 men.
Without knowing that he had seized the strategic position of Hazel
Grove, he pressed on. As soon as Stuart got word of this advance, he
ordered more of the Confederate batteries to Hazel Grove.[2]

By this time Stuart had sent forward the other brigades of Hill's division. These experienced troops had no difficulty in storming a crude Federal work of logs and brush. With a yell the men of the Light Division
pressed immediately toward the second Federal line, but they soon
received on both flanks the challenge of angry fire. North of the Plank
Road, Thomas's Georgians and the left units of Pender's brigade struck for
the third Union line, but Thomas's own left soon became encumbered.

On the right of the road, McGowan pushed 100 yards beyond the first line, only to find a gap opening between his right and Archer's left, which the Federals began to exploit. In heavy fighting the old brigade of Maxcy Gregg went back, almost step by step, to the first Federal line, which it reoccupied and held. McGowan's withdrawal in turn uncovered the right of Lane, whose consequent retirement forced back all of Pender's regiments save the 13th North Carolina. That regiment, under the admirable leading of Colonel Alfred Scales, continued its advance and ere long captured a Federal brigadier, William Hays.[3]

By 7:00 A.M., then, Stuart had this situation before him: The right and center of the corps had been repulsed from the second Federal line and were being re-formed on the line captured in the first rush; the left of the corps was precariously advanced. This phase of Stuart's advance represented a gain scarcely worth counting. The one substantial success was Archer's. The valuable ground of Hazel Grove was firmly in Confederate hands, and Major Pegram now was opening there with three batteries. Captain R. C. M. Page followed immediately with his fine battery of Napoleons. When Stuart saw the Stars and Bars at Hazel Grove, he may have sensed the possibility of defeating the Federal infantry by the fire of artillery massed there, but he did not rely exclusively on the long arm. He would try the rifle and the bayonet and wrest Chancellorsville from the enemy. Move guns to Hazel Grove; tell Colston and Rodes to bring up every man in support of Hill's division. Press the assault straight to Chancellorsville.

Gloriously the first part of Stuart's orders was obeyed. Thanks primarily to the new battalion organization of the artillery, one battery after another climbed to Hazel Grove and wheeled into position. Never in the annals of the Army of Northern Virginia had so great a concentration of guns been effected so quickly or with comparable ease.

The infantry were not so fortunate. The old division of Jackson was poorly led. Colston did not have experience in handling so many men, and one only of his four brigades had at its head a general officer. The result of this lack of command was lack of confidence. The utmost endeavors of perplexed officers failed to get the line moving. While Pender and Thomas, on the left of the road, at heavy loss, were driving the enemy, the veterans of Jackson refused to face the fire. In Colston's own brigade, three commanders quickly were shot down; two of Colston's brigades on the right of the road were "somewhat broken and disorganized." To their shame, officers had to admit themselves powerless. The assault must await the arrival of Rodes's division.[4]

This was not the full measure of disgrace: It began to look as if the enemy, who now was advancing menacingly, might throw Jackson's men out of the shallow trenches. So bewildered were these veteran soldiers, so completely without leadership, that they were not even keeping up a fire against the approaching enemy. In this balance 'twixt death and doom, Colston decided he would bring the veteran Stonewall Brigade from north of the Plank Road and throw it and Garnett's brigade against the Federals. Unless Paxton stiffened the right, or Rodes arrived quickly, Stuart might lose his first infantry battle.

Paxton crossed the road and with Garnett on his right, prepared to advance. At the works, McGowan's proud South Carolina officers were striving vainly to get the men to press forward and repel the enemy. Some even of the tried old soldiers who gained lasting fame at Gaines' Mill and Groveton refused to budge. Now, through them, the first volunteers of the Palmetto State, pushed Paxton's Virginians of the Valley. "The Stonewall Brigade passed over us," wrote the historian of McGowan's brigade, "some of them saying, with no very pleasant levity, that they would show us how to clear away a Federal line." It was a valiant effort. Garnett's men supported them with equal bravery. Although both Paxton and Garnett were shot down, their men met the Federals in the spirit of the Valley campaign. They pushed on until they were within seventy yards of the Union line. There they faced precisely such a whirlwind of fire as they had thrown against their foe. Back to the log works, broken and decimated, they had to go. Not without a certain cold satisfaction did the same historian write, ". . . their reckoning was not accurate. They were forced back into the works with us."[5]

It was now about 8:15. On the left as on the right, Stuart's attack had been beaten back. Thomas and Pender, north of the road, had withdrawn from their advanced positions. Rodes was close behind Heth and Colston, though he could not command his full strength. One brigade, Colquitt's, had been sent to the extreme left because of reports of the enemy demonstrating there, and in advancing through the thick undergrowth some regiments were separated. Rodes, in consequence, was not yet ready to push through Heth and Colston to deliver his assault. The battle lagged.[6]

Even the buoyant Jeb might have been discouraged had he not perceived that from Hazel Grove gunners of the Second Corps, moment by moment, were increasing the weight of the metal they were throwing against the flank of the Federal line. To the guns of Pegram, those of Alexander's battalion under Frank Huger had been added. Tom Carter and David McIntosh sent some of their pieces. Before the morning was out, all of these and numbers from Poague, Hardaway, Hilary Jones, and Lindsay Walker were to be used.

At Hazel Grove, in short, the finest artillerists of the Army of Northern Virginia were having their greatest day. For once they were fighting on equal terms against an adversary who on fields unnumbered had enjoyed indisputable superiority in weapons. With the fire of battle shining through his spectacles, William Pegram rejoiced. "A glorious day, Colonel," he said to Porter Alexander, "a glorious day!" There was an uncertainty, a nervous irregularity in the Federal return fire. Here and there—the sight made the heart beat higher!—Federal infantry were beginning to recoil under the shells of the Southern batteries. The right of Stuart might suffer heavily in gaining the ground necessary to form a junction with Lee, who was moving up from the south; there might be much more of hard fighting and of costly assault; but if those gray batteries could continue to sweep the field, the Federals must yield![7]

Rodes's division was now deployed for the advance, and as courageously as on the ridge by Jackson's side, Rodes gave the order. Almost from the moment the first men clutched their guns and crashed through the bushes, the baffling tangle of woods confused his line. Doles's brigade split. Colonel E. A. O'Neal, commanding Rodes's brigade, went down, and his troops divided. From Iverson's line in the maze of woodland north of the Plank Road, Colonel H. D. Christie of the 23rd North Carolina started an attack all his own. To Rodes, this sundering of his division meant that he could handle those troops only that were close to the center of the line.

Rodes's embarrassment was Dodson Ramseur's opportunity. Until May 1 the North Carolinian never had led in action the fine brigade of George Anderson that had been committed to him. Now Ramseur went forward with a fury that had not been shown on the field that morning. Doles on the right was to have a gallant adventure, and Iverson and Christie on the left were to have high moments, but for the next hour the battle was to be Ramseur's.

His line moved into the crowded works and sternly Ramseur ordered the troops of John R. Jones's brigade who were crouching there to advance with him. In his own indignant words, "Not a man moved." Ramseur was as puzzled as he was wrathful. He assumed that General Jones was on the field and he must have known that charges had been preferred against that officer, but as Jones's junior could Ramseur order the men forward? He decided to send back to Stuart for instructions. Word came back promptly for Ramseur to assume command and force the shirkers to advance. Again Ramseur gave the order; again the men in the works ignored it. Then, for the first time, he learned that Jones had left the field and that Garnett had been killed. Apparently he could not find Colonel A. S. Vandeventer, who was now in command of Jones's brigade.

Undeterred, Ramseur exhorted and pleaded and denounced, to no purpose. Present he stalked back to Stuart, and in brief, angry explanation of what had happened, asked if he might "run over the troops" in his front. Cheerful and approving permission instantly was granted. Ramseur hurried back to his waiting line. Loudly he commanded, "Forward, march!" Without hesitation his North Carolinians broke through the mob, climbed over the entrenchments, and pushed forward. As Bryan Grimes went over the works, he heard a gloomy voice shout, "You may double-quick, but you'll come back faster than you go!"[8]

At the same time, two other parts of Rodes's division were advancing with equal dash. On the left of the Plank Road, Iverson swept ahead, and Colonel Christie, with his 23rd North Carolina, crashed around the rear of an enemy command and made a drive for Fairview, the dominant Federal artillery position nearest Chancellorsville. He failed to get there, but held what he had gained. This advance had the strong, gallant support of Pender and Thomas. On Ramseur's right, Doles broke loose furiously, with his 4th and 44th Georgia pushing to the south of Fairview and for a time assailing the flank and rear of a strong adversary. Soon Doles had to withdraw, but Christie and Pender and Thomas, with part of Rodes's own brigade, fought to retain the advanced position near Fairview.

Ramseur pushed his left across the log works of the second Federal line, but met a furious fire. The young North Carolinian had a clear understanding of his position and realized that he must strengthen his right or fall back. If only the troops in the works behind them would sweep out and fill a gap of some 500 or 600 yards between his right and Hazel Grove, all would be well! Several times Ramseur sent back to Colonel Vandeventer to move out Jones's brigade, and twice he went back in person through a fiery hail. Jones's men insisted they would not move except on the orders of their own division commander, Colston, who was then on the other flank. In hot wrath, Ramseur had to notify Rodes that unless troops were sent up, his brigade would have to withdraw. Even Rodes, always a commanding figure in battle, could move none of the troops behind the log works.

Happily for the honor of Jackson's old division, Stuart learned of the sorry state of affairs and galloped up to the Stonewall Brigade. By a combination of authority and showmanship—by exhorting the men to avenge Jackson and by singing, "Old Joe Hooker, won't you come out of the Wilderness"—Stuart got the troops in motion.

They advanced to the right of Ramseur, where they were most needed, and made possible the orderly withdrawal of his regiments that had exhausted their ammunition. Once started, the men who had fought with Jackson in all his battles continued to press on until they were assailing Fairview. By that time they were alone in their attack. Christie and Doles and all the others who had sought to break the Federal front had done their best but had withdrawn. Colonel John Funk, who had succeeded Paxton at the head of the brigade, found he had lost a third of his troops and that no support seemed forthcoming. His men got the order to withdraw and slowly, unpursued by the enemy, as became veterans, they fell back to the log works.[9]

All the units of the Second Corps, save Colquitt on the extreme left, now seemed "fought out." Stuart was forming a new line, issuing rations, replenishing ammunition. He would try again, but he had mustered all the might of seasoned troops and appeared to have failed in his offensive. Then, abruptly—almost miraculously—the last of the Federal artillery, which had been leaving Fairview since 9 o'clock, evacuated that position. At Chancellorsville, where guns were massed, there was a perceptible decline in the volume of fire. Had their ammunition supply failed? It had, but something equally important had happened.

With the intelligent cooperation of Anderson and McLaws, General Lee had extended to the west the left of the First Corps. Lee rode up to Archer's brigade at Hazel Grove and ordered Archer to attack in the direction of Fairview. Junction of Dick Anderson's left and Stuart's right was effected. The united forces now could drive on a concave front against Chancellorsville. Jubilant gunners raced from Hazel Grove to Fairview; yelling infantry poured northward through the woods and eastward on both sides of the Plank Road. By 10:30 or a little later, Lee was at Chancellorsville amid wild scenes of rejoicing. The price of victory had not been unduly high; if only Jackson had been there![10]

Jackson had awakened about 9 o'clock that pleasant Sabbath morning. Calm the scene was at the hospital, but rolling and rising and ebbing and echoing was the sound of the guns from Hazel Grove and Fairview. Their bark was the best of tonics for the wounded man. He took some nourishment and displayed a cheering resilience. The prognosis was favorable. None of the surgeons seemed to have any fear for his recovery. He sent all but two of his staff to assist Stuart on the battlefield. Lieutenant Smith was to stay as nurse and companion. Morrison was to go to Richmond to bring Mrs. Jackson and the baby to the general's bedside.

By 10 o'clock Jackson felt so much pain in his right side that he asked Dr. McGuire to make an examination. It was probable, the general said, that in the fall of the litter he had struck a stone or the stump of a sapling. McGuire could discover no bruise; there was nothing to indicate a broken rib; breathing seemed to be normal. The surgeon ordered some local applications and felt no special concern.

Chaplain Lacy, on entering the tent, exclaimed, "Oh, General, what a calamity!" Jackson reassured him. The loss of the arm, he said, was by the will of God. He proceeded, almost eagerly, to recount the circumstances of his wounding. He confided that when a bearer tripped and the litter fell, he thought he would die on the field, and gave himself into the hands of his Creator. Perfect peace, said Jackson, had been his—a precious experience."

Lieutenant Smith then recounted for him news of the battle. The death of Paxton and other well-known officers of the Second Corps Smith announced as gently as he could shape his words. The general was grieved and shaken, but he was even more stirred when Smith gave an account of the charge of the Stonewall Brigade in answer to an exhortation by Stuart. "It was just like them to do so," Jackson exclaimed; "just like them! They are a noble body of men!"

In early afternoon a courier brought a reply to the dispatch Jackson had sent Lee, announcing his wounding and the transfer of command. By permission, Smith opened it and read: "I have just received your note, informing me that you were wounded. I cannot express my regret at the occurrence. Could I have directed events, I should have chosen for the good of the country to be disabled in your stead. I congratulate you upon the victory, which is due to your skill and energy."

When Smith stopped reading, Jackson paused for a moment and then—was it from modesty or from a desire that his aide should not see his pleasure over praise from such a source?—he turned his face away. "General Lee," he said in his quiet, half-muffled voice, "is very kind, but he should give the praise to God."[12]

2. JUBE EARLY HAS A RIGHT TO SWEAR

While Jackson affirmed that the commanding general should give the thanks to God, Jube Early was wondering what perverse devil had placed him where he was. In the army's strangest battle, Early had the most incredible part to play. On the afternoon of April 30 he had received notice from Second Corps headquarters that he was to remain on the ridge of the Rappahannock, and with his own division and Barksdale's brigade of McLaws's division was to observe the foe. With him were a corps artillery battalion, part of Pendleton's reserve guns, and two units of a battalion attached to McLaws's division. Early's conclusion was that his infantry and this artillery were to be employed as a containing force while Lee moved with three divisions of Jackson's Second Corps and three brigades of McLaws to support Anderson and take the offensive against Hooker. For coping with what was manifestly a superior Federal force, Early had about 9,000 men and 56 guns, but he was resolute.

Early had his division posted south of Lee's Hill, where he believed the attack would be delivered. All four of the brigade commanders were present—John B. Gordon, R. F Hoke, Harry Hays, and Extra Billy Smith. The bold Snowden Andrews was back after partial recovery from the frightful wound received at Cedar Mountain and was in command of his artillery battalion. Early saw to it that Andrews took full charge of the batteries on the right and General Pendleton confined his energies to the guns on the left. The front extended for no less than six miles.[13]

Lee's instructions were explicit: (1) Early was to observe and, if he could, hold the enemy in the vicinity of Fredericksburg, concealing the weakness of his force. (2) If compelled to retreat, Early was to withdraw in the direction of Guiney's Station and protect the army's supplies and the railroad. (3) On the morning of May 2 he was to feel the Unionists with his artillery. In the event that the enemy had disappeared or reduced force, Early was to post at Fredericksburg troops sufficient to hold whatever the enemy left and with the remainder of his command march to join Lee.[14]

The third of these orders involved of necessity a discretion that Lee did not hesitate to entrust or Early to accept. Had not Old Jubilee fought for a time unaided and alone in the van at Cedar Mountain? At Sharpsburg had there not been a critical hour when Early saved from a shattering blow the left flank of Jackson? Surely now, if someone had to remain at Fredericksburg, and Jackson had to go and Longstreet was absent, Early, all in all, was the division commander best qualified to guard the heights and protect the rear of the Confederate forces moving against Hooker.

Early had to decide where he would dispose his few troops on his line of six miles. His judgment was that the main assault would be on his right, and consequently he determined to leave his entire division between Hamilton's Crossing and Deep Run. The stretch of a mile and a half between Deep Run and Lee's Hill on the left Early thought he could protect with a thin picket-line, because he could cover that part of the front with a crossfire of artillery. Barksdale and the greater part of the artillery must watch Lee's Hill and Marye's Heights. On May 1 the battalion of the Washington Artillery came up; the guns of the New Orleans men, added to those already in position, should make the heights impregnable.

In the clear dawn of May 2, Early was prepared and hopeful: If the answer of the Federals to his test bombardment was feeble or perfunctory, he intended to start two of his brigades to join Lee. The answer to his "feeling-out fire" was listless, and the Unionists on his right were observed withdrawing behind the protecting bank of the river. Before he could act on this, Barksdale and Pendleton reported a concentration of Federal troops at Falmouth, opposite the upper end of Fredericksburg. The two expressed the opinion that the enemy might be preparing to throw pontoons in that vicinity to assail the Confederate left.

They had joined Early on Lee's Hill to speculate on the Federals' plan when, about 11:00 A.M., straight from army headquarters, arrived Colonel R. H. Chilton, chief of staff. He communicated what he described as verbal orders from Lee: Early was to march toward Chancellorsville with his entire force, except Pendleton's artillery and one brigade of infantry. The bulk of the artillery, especially the heavy pieces, must be started for a place of safety down the R.F. & P. Railroad.

The parson-gunner and, even more, Old Jube, were stunned by these instructions. It was impossible, Early argued, to withdraw his force in daylight without being observed by the Federals. As soon as he abandoned the position the Unionists would occupy Fredericksburg and Marye's Heights. Chilton replied that General Lee presumably had decided that the advantage of having Early with him outweighed the loss of Fredericksburg, which could be recovered easily after Hooker had been defeated. Early still could not bring himself to believe that Lee had set aside the plain orders given him earlier. Was it possible Chilton had misinterpreted the verbal orders? Chilton was sure there could be no mistake. "This," Early afterward wrote, "was very astounding to us...."[15]

It was now between 11 and 12 o'clock on the second of May. Jackson at that hour was well advanced on his march to the left of Hooker. Lee was playing a fine game of bluff with Anderson's and McLaws's divisions, trying to make the Unionists believe he was preparing to attack in that sector. Early was nonplussed. He could not see the logic of his orders, but the chief of staff insisted they were explicit and positive. Foolish as abandonment of the Fredericksburg front appeared to be, orders were orders; Lee must know more about the operation than Early could.

Early devoted himself to getting off his foot troops covertly. As Barksdale's 21st Mississippi could not be withdrawn from Fredericksburg without attracting attention, it must stay where it was. Harry Hays's brigade most conveniently could be left in the lines. The rest of the infantry was made ready to start, and by late afternoon the last of them were in motion toward the Plank Road. Now, abruptly, came another disconcerting messenger. He brought a dispatch from Lee, written after Chilton had returned and reported on the orders given to Early. Those orders, Lee wrote, reflected a misunderstanding by Colonel Chilton. It had not been intended that Early withdraw from Fredericksburg unless this could be done with safety. The discretion given Early still was to be exercised.

How profusely Old Jube swore the records do not show. He was in a quandary. The enemy, he assumed, had occupied—or was in the act of seizing—his abandoned works. These he could not hope with his small force to recapture. If he went back and made the effort and failed, he would deprive Lee of any use of his division. The start, under misapprehension of orders, had been foolish; an attempt to go back might be equally so. Let the column go on!

A mile the exasperated Early rode with his men along the Plank Road and then—another messenger. This one had a note from Barksdale, whose brigade was following Early's division. The enemy was reported to be advancing against the heights in great strength, and Pendleton and Hays had informed Barksdale that without immediate relief all the artillery left behind would be captured. The courier added that Barksdale was hurrying back to help Hays. Early had to make a decision on the changed basis: The enemy might not yet have occupied the heights. What was to be done? Old Jube debated the question with himself and decided he had a sufficient chance of success to justify him in securing his old positions—and thereby of protecting Lee's rear. A courier was hurried off to Lee with a report of what was being done, and on the Plank Road the troops and the trains were turned around and started back to the ridge of the Rappahannock.

On arrival, to his relief, Early found that the Federals had not advanced at Fredericksburg and, on the Confederate right, had not proceeded beyond the Richmond Stage Road. Warm was the welcome given the returned column by Hays and Pendleton. A singular episode appeared to have been closed with more of good luck than the Confederates could have hoped to enjoy. Exasperating and nerve-wearing had been the result of Colonel Chilton's curious and never-explained misunderstanding of orders, but it had involved no loss of life or of ground.[16]

Before daylight on May 3, Early was aroused by Barksdale, who was not in a placid mood. Earlier, when a lieutenant had come to his quarters and asked if he was asleep, Barksdale had barked: "No, sir! Who could sleep with a million of armed Yankees around him?" Now he told Early that the Federals had laid a pontoon bridge at Fredericksburg and were moving over. The attack would be delivered in rear of the town, the Mississippian predicted; reinforcements were needed there. Old Jube meditated and then told Barksdale that Hays's Louisiana brigade would be ordered to the left. Barksdale could place it where his judgment of the ground told him it would be most useful. One brigade seemed the maximum that Early could afford to shift to the left, if the main Federal attack was to be on the right; but the reinforcement was the minimum with which Barksdale could hope to offer successful resistance. At the moment, with somewhat formidable artillery but no more than 1,500 infantry, he was occupying a front of about three miles.[17]

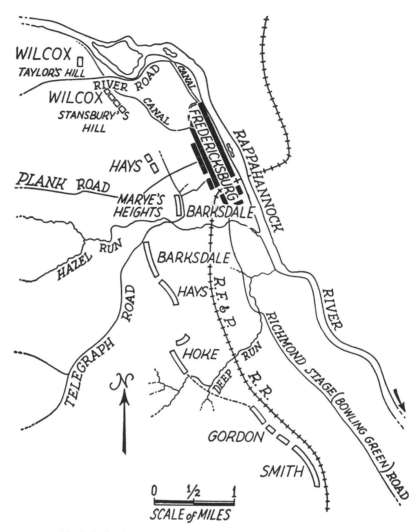

Early's deployment, Fredericksburg, morning of May 3.

Almost before Early had sufficient daylight for reconnaissance, a rattle of picket fire and then infantry volleys and the roar of awakened cannon announced an attack on Marye's Heights. Ten taut minutes sufficed to show that this assault was premature. It was beaten off readily. The success was a bracer for the Confederates. Still better was the stimulant of news Early now received—that the main army had won a victory the previous evening and hoped on the third to complete a triumph. Early ordered announcement of this made to his troops.

The attack assuredly was coming, Early told himself, and it probably was going to be on his right which, in December, all the Confederate commanders had known to be vulnerable. Hooker, it was reasonable to assume, would not repeat Burnside's costly blunder of an attack on the heights. Early felt that he must make ready for a stubborn defense of Jackson's old lines. For a time, Barksdale and Pendleton reported frequently that all was well on the left. Their batteries were keeping the enemy at a distance. Ere long, Barksdale sent word that a Union column had moved out of Fredericksburg to turn the Confederate flank. Hays's men had arrived, filed into the trenches, and repulsed the enemy. Barksdale and Pendleton, who had their post of command on Lee's Hill, assured Early that they could hold their ground.[18]

Time slipped on. The hands of Early's watch were climbing toward 11:00 A.M. Six hours of skirmishing and demonstrations had passed. Everything seemed favorable . . . except that no further reports had come to Early from Barksdale. Northward, in front of Marye's Heights, the Federals still were banging away, but they had been doing that all morning. Was anything amiss? Early began to fume, perhaps to swear, and at length he determined to ride toward Lee's Hill and see the situation for himself. As he started, a courier arrived from General Pendleton: The enemy had been repulsed; the position could be held. Almost before Early could draw a deep breath of relief, W. G. Callaway, one of his staff he had sent to the left, rode up with a rush. He had just left Lee's Hill, he said, and had seen the enemy mounting Marye's Heights and he knew the position was lost!

The Federals on Marye's Heights—that stirred instantly the combativeness of Jube Early's soul! By God, he would not retreat without a fight. He galloped to the Telegraph Road to rally any troops that might be making off. Down the road, toward the rear, were rushing Pendleton's reserve batteries. "Halt! Halt!"—with added words, perhaps, not found in the manual of arms. Furiously Early galloped on until he came upon Barksdale. The Mississippian was untouched by panic. Twice, he said, the bluecoats had been beaten back from the stone wall at the foot of Marye's Heights. In a few minutes more the Union line had advanced irresistibly, and his men who held the road under the wall had been overwhelmed. Some field pieces of the Washington Artillery and of Parker's battery had been captured.

Early found the Washington Artillery angry and humiliated at the loss of some of their famous weapons. One of the defenders broke out wrathfully, "I reckon now the people of the Southern Confederacy are satisfied that Barksdale's brigade and the Washington Artillery can't whip the whole damned Yankee army!" Barksdale himself did not put it that strongly. "Our center has been pierced, that's all," he said; "we will be all right in a little while."

Quickly Early and Barksdale formed a line along the plateau in rear of Lee's Hill. They fell back at intervals until, at Cox's house, on defensible ground, Early determined to make a stand. He drew Smith and Hoke back to the new line. Gordon and Hays found their place in this new order of battle. By 3:00 P.M., though his strong position overlooking the Rappahannock had been snatched from him, Early could say that he had his force in hand, ready to fight, and that the infantry losses had not been excessive. Artillery commands had not been so fortunate. The guns taken from the Washington Artillery proved to be six. Parker's battery lost two.[19]

If the balance of the morning's account was slightly, though no more than that, to the credit of Early, he had that afternoon remarkable good fortune, which he had not anticipated and, for that matter, did not deserve. Three and a quarter miles above Fredericksburg, Cadmus Wilcox had been stationed with his Alabama brigade. Banks' Ford, of much strategical importance, was his post. His instructions were to hold the position at all costs if it was assailed. In the event it was not, he was to detach a guard to watch the crossing and with the remainder of his brigade march via the Plank Road toward Chancellorsville. Since his fine conduct at Second Manassas, Wilcox had been denied a conspicuous part in operations. He had wished to leave the Army of Northern Virginia in the belief that he would have better prospects elsewhere. Lee had declined to permit this, but efforts to procure a major general's commission for Wilcox had been futile. Was he now merely to watch a ford while his division and his army won another victory that would bring praise and promotion to those who led their men wisely?

The whole of the war brought few instances to demonstrate more dramatically that vigilance often makes great the small opportunity. On the morning of May 3, Cadmus Marcellus Wilcox was—as soldiers always should be—early astir. He observed with critical eye everything he saw of the enemy across the river. As there was not the slightest sign of any attempted crossing at Banks' Ford, all the circumstances, Wilcox later explained, "induced me to believe that much of the force at Banks' Ford had been sent to Chancellorsville." He directed that fifty men, with two pieces of artillery, be detached to watch the ford and that the remainder of the command proceed toward Chancellorsville in the manner contemplated by orders.[20]

This plan was interrupted by the Federal assault on Marye's Heights, and Wilcox positioned his brigade to cooperate with Harry Hays. Soon a courier from Barksdale brought Wilcox news of the lost fight on Marye's Heights and the suggestion that Wilcox, like Hays, proceed to the new line Early was forming on the Telegraph Road. The suggestion was both polite and permissible, but as Wilcox ranked Barksdale, he had no obligation to follow the plan of the gentleman from Mississippi. Wilcox determined to follow his own judgment in the application of his orders from army headquarters. In doing so, he made the finest of his several wise decisions on this, his greatest day. His nearest avenue for the execution of his contingent orders to join Lee was the Plank Road; down that same road it seemed reasonable to assume that the enemy, whose heavy lines were in plain sight, would be certain to advance. He said afterward, "I felt it a duty to delay the enemy as much as possible. . . ."

Wilcox drew his line parallel to the Plank Road on the best near-by ground he could find, held off the enemy for a time, then side-slipped to his right to see what the Federals would do. They seemed to be puzzled and hesitant. From this he felt confident that if he had to retire along the Plank Road, "ample time could be given for re-enforcements to reach us from Chancellorsville; and . . . should the enemy pursue, he could be attacked in rear by General Early, re-enforced by Generals Hays and Barksdale." That seemed irrefragable logic after the event. At the time, it represented risk as well as daring—a combination that must be balanced on the beam of judgment.[21]

Wilcox moved over to the Plank Road, threw his command squarely across the line of the enemy's advance, and boldly offered shell for shell. He did not suffer unduly from the attacks of a cautious adversary; but he must have been pleased, in the early afternoon, to learn that three brigades from McLaws's division were on their way to reinforce the Alabamians. Wilcox did not know it at the time, but reinforcements for him and for Early had cost Lee dearly. In the hour of victory that morning, while Anderson's men were mingling with Stuart's at Chancellorsville, Lee had received word that Early had been driven from the heights of Fredericksburg. Further pursuit of Hooker had to be deferred that day. By no other course was Lee able to detach sufficient troops to deal with the Federals who were marching against his rear.

After the arrival of McLaws's men, the work of the afternoon was simple for Wilcox. Federal commanders at about 5:15 threw their regiments against the Confederate position at Salem Church. The repulse by the four waiting brigades was bloody. Wilcox then took the initiative and, with the support of Paul Semmes's Georgians, drove the column of attack back upon strong reserves. Darkness ended the action. Wilcox could tell himself without vainglory that he had protected the rear of Lee and had made it possible for Early to reconcentrate scattered forces. Daring and devotion had their reward. Cadmus Wilcox that day gave military history an example far outliving his time of the manner in which one brigade, courageously led, can change the course of a battle and retrieve a lost day.[22]

Early owed more to Wilcox than he acknowledged then or thereafter, but as senior officer of the sector nearest Fredericksburg, he received, on the evening of May 3, Lee's instructions. Lee's dispatch was an expression of regret at the loss of Fredericksburg and an appeal for Early to unite with McLaws in an attack: "I think you ought to be more than a match for the enemy." At the same time, a dispatch from McLaws inquired naively what Early proposed. The Georgian was in term of service the oldest major general with the army, and the Virginian the most recently appointed; but that circumstance neither deterred McLaws from asking for suggestions, nor led Old Jube to hesitate in giving them.

Early determined to recover the high ground at Fredericksburg in the morning. When this was accomplished, he would have secured himself against an attack from the direction of the town and separated the Federals there from the units on the Plank Road. He believed he could deliver successfully this first stroke with part of his forces, and with the remainder extend their left to unite with McLaws's right. It would be easy, after that, for Early and McLaws to close in and overwhelm the brigades cut off on the Plank Road. It was a practical operation, Early thought, provided McLaws would cooperate heartily. McLaws forwarded the outlined plan of action to Lee, who thought the plan good but had some doubt whether it was practicable. Lee realized that McLaws's active aid was necessary, and he particularly enjoined that officer to press the Federals "so as to prevent their concentrating on General Early."[23]

Nothing in Early's action indicated any misgiving. He was self-reliant, if not self-confident, and was not oppressed by his responsibility. Old Jube was growing as a soldier. McLaws's mental approach to the battle is more difficult to ascertain. If he was apprehensive, it was on three counts: First, he did not feel that he knew the ground of probable action. He undoubtedly was troubled, also, because he thought the enemy was in superior force. Third, he had been much impressed by the Federal bombardment on the afternoon of the third, when the enemy batteries "were admirably served and played over the whole ground." It is possible, in addition, that McLaws missed Longstreet and felt overwhelmed by his responsibility, but of this there is no positive evidence. Uneasy he was, and unconvinced that he should or could carry the burden of the fighting the next day. That seems to have been his state of mind.[24]

Daylight on May 4 found Early's entire division astir. The general himself intended to march with John B. Gordon's brigade, which he had selected to recover the heights and cut off the Federals from the town. Snowden Andrews was to follow with his battalion of artillery. Smith's and Barksdale's brigades would be in support. When Early had all these troops ready to advance, he rode off to show Hoke and Hays where to take position on the right of McLaws. Hurrying back to the Telegraph Road where he had left Gordon's brigade, Early found that the Georgians were not there. Neither were Andrews's guns. A moment's inquiry elicited the disconcerting fact that instead of waiting for Early to direct him, Gordon already was moving toward Lee's Hill, with Andrews following.

Early did not delay to ask why this had been done. If Gordon launched the attack prematurely, it must be supported. Let Smith and Barksdale proceed to join Gordon with the least possible delay! Fortune laughed—as Fortune rarely does—at a misunderstanding of orders. Gordon had an unopposed march to an invaluable objective. He found that Lee's Hill was not occupied by the enemy—nor was Marye's Heights. Early, arriving quickly, gave Gordon the support of Smith and ordered Barksdale to resume the familiar position under the heights and, if possible, reoccupy Fredericksburg. The Mississippian reported seeing in Fredericksburg what appeared to be a heavy force, and Early had to content himself with ordering him to maintain position and keep the Federals from advancing.[25]

If Early's eyes, all the while, had been on the ridge, his ears had been straining for the sound of McLaws's guns. No echo had rolled down Hazel Run; no message had come. Had the plan for a joint attack gone awry? Was McLaws waiting on Early? He hurried off a staff officer, Lieutenant A. L. Pitzer, to explain his situation to McLaws. The Georgian was to be informed that Hoke and Hays were in position on the left and ready to cooperate with McLaws. As soon as these troops and McLaws's own engaged the enemy, Early would throw in Gordon and Smith against the Federal left.

McLaws received in some puzzlement the report that Pitzer brought. The terrain confused McLaws; the strength of the enemy in his front made him doubtful of success. He was willing to help Early, but should not Early open the attack? Moreover, Lee had sent word that Dick Anderson was marching from Chancellorsville to reinforce the troops around Salem Church. Was it not prudent to wait until Anderson arrived and then strike with a stronger force? So reasoning, McLaws bade Pitzer take back this message to Early: The advance would not be made until Anderson was in position; then three guns fired in rapid succession would signal the general attack.

About 11:00 A.M. Anderson arrived in the vicinity of Salem Church, but before McLaws could decide where to put his troops, the commanding general reached the ground and assumed direction of affairs. This was a deliberate and not a chance appearance of Lee. Preferably, if he could have mustered the men, he would have struck Hooker's main army that day north of Chancellorsville. Instead he came personally to deal with the

Federals on the Plank Road because he seems to have felt that McLaws was proceeding with too much caution and deliberation. Lee began, with manifest if unusual impatience, to get into position Anderson's brigades.[76]

Even under the eyes of "Marse Robert" himself, progress was slow. Tired men did not show their old alacrity. At length, in the afternoon, Lee rode out and met Early. Apparently the commanding general had concluded that he could expect little of McLaws, and that the attack must be committed to the other divisions. He sent this message: McLaws was to occupy the enemy in his front and, after Early and Anderson opened the attack, was to throw in Kershaw and Wofford. It was close to 6 o'clock when McLaws received word that Anderson and Early were about ready to attack.

In a few minutes all along the line was heard the signal of three guns fired in swift succession. On the right, Gordon started ahead; Hoke and Hays immediately were set in motion by Early; on the left of Hoke, Anderson ordered forward Wright's Georgians; beyond them, Posey's orders were to advance. Gordon encountered scant opposition at first; Hays, Hoke, and Wright started magnificently out. Old Jube's pulse beat up and his sharp eyes shone more brightly than ever. The onset was thrilling, the next stage was expectancy, the third was suspense. After that, gallantry did not suffice. Nothing went well. Hays's lines of advance converged with Hoke's; the two

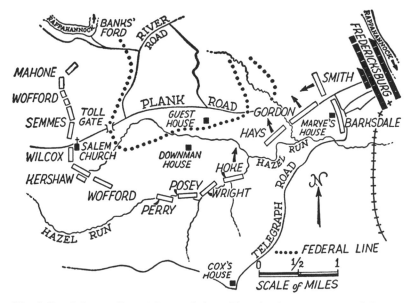

Final Confederate disposition at Salem Church, about 6:00 P.M., May 4.

brigades mingled and between them some mistaken fire tragically was exchanged. When Hoke fell with a shattered arm, none of his colonels knew under what orders the brigade was acting. Just as Early reached the Plank Road, the two brigades fell back to it. Neither Wright nor Posey crossed the Plank Road, according to Early, until nightfall.

As for McLaws, his report was a chronicle of confusion: "Alexander opened his batteries, and Generals Kershaw and Wofford advanced to the front through a dense woods. Night now came rapidly on, and nothing could be observed of our operations." Commanders scarcely knew where they were or what they were expected to do. Amid this confusion came the sound of troops moving across the pontoon bridge above Banks' Ford, a tremendous clatter as if giants were beating the long roll on the pontoons. Protected by night, all the Federals in the vicinity of Banks' Ford got safely off.

As a considerable force still was believed to be in Fredericksburg, Early was ordered back there during the night with two of his brigades to strengthen Barksdale. Early predicted that the enemy would quit the right bank of the Rappahannock before morning, and fact bore him out. By daylight on May 5 the whole force of the Union's General Sedgwick, from Fredericksburg to Banks' Ford, had the river between him and the Confederates.[27]

Of these events Stonewall Jackson heard with a pleasure he was physically strong enough to express. "Good, good," he would say at the recountal of some gallant deed, and with glistening eye he warmly would praise some officer to whom, had he been present on the field, he might have given at most a glance of approval. Late on the evening of May 3 had come a message from army headquarters: Lee sent word that the military situation demanded the removal of Jackson to a place less exposed. Dr. McGuire was instructed to turn over all other duties to the senior surgeon, and was himself to attend the general and remain with him. As the commanding general left to the patient the choice of a nearby haven, Jackson promptly said that if it was agreeable to the family, he would go to Fairfield, the home near Guiney's of Mr. and Mrs. Thomas Coleman Chandler, who had shown him many courtesies. Whether the journey should be made the next day was left to be determined by Jackson's condition, which hourly seemed better.[28]

Jackson slept well and, in the judgment of his surgeons, he now could look forward to normal convalescence. Dr. McGuire told him the orders of General Lee could be executed without excessive risk. The weather on the fourth was favorable, a fair and pleasant morning. Preparations to take the road already were being made. In Jackson's mind, that road to recovery did not end at Guiney's. From it, when his wounds began to heal, he would go to a pleasant village, such as Ashland, conveniently near Richmond but free of the bustle and excitement of the capital. Finally, he would complete his recovery at Lexington, in the home he had not seen for more than two years. Then, in the mercy of God, with one hand he would smite the invader more heavily than ever he had with two![29]

At length the ambulance was ready. On the flooring a mattress had been placed. His young chief of artillery, Stapleton Crutchfield, again was to accompany him as a fellow patient. Jed Hotchkiss was to choose the route and clear the road; Smith and Lacy were to remain at the general's side; Dr. McGuire was to direct everything. The safest road was one of the shortest— by way of Todd's Tavern to Spotsylvania Court House and thence southward and eastward to the R.F. & P. at Guiney's. It would be an all-day journey.

Before long they overtook lightly wounded men walking toward the railroad. These Second Corps veterans shouted friendly messages to the wounded man. Over and over, soldiers cried out that they wished they could have been wounded instead of their general. Rough teamsters they encountered stood bareheaded and in tears as the ambulance passed. When word spread that Old Jack was coming, residents came out to welcome the general and to offer him the few delicacies they had—their bread, their milk, a little butter, a handful of eggs. At Spotsylvania Court House refugees and residents crowded sympathetically around the ambulance.

The journey was rendered less tedious by conversation in which Jackson shared freely. When he was asked for his opinion of Hooker's plan of campaign, Jackson did not hesitate: "It was, in the main, a good conception, sir; an excellent plan. But he should not have sent away his cavalry; that was his great blunder. It was that which enabled me to turn him. . . ." In answer to tactful questions, Jackson confided that he had hoped to press forward on the night of May 2 and seize a position between Hooker and United States Ford, where the Federals would have been compelled to attack him. He spoke in unclouded memory of the attack on Hooker's right, and in glowing words of those officers who had most distinguished themselves. First in his praise was Robert Rodes. He expressed high admiration for the man who had directed the advance of Harvey Hill's old division. Rodes, said Jackson, should be promoted; promotion for valor, especially promotion on the field, was the greatest possible incentive to gallantry on the part of others.

In these replies and exchanges, Jackson showed no confusion of mind and no fatigue. He had no symptoms of distress until, late in the day, he became slightly nauseated. For this malady and for sundry other ills Jackson previously had used the "water cure," and with Dr. McGuire's consent, wet towels were applied to his abdomen. The result, whether psychological or physiological, was entirely to Jackson's satisfaction.

The long journey of twenty-four miles came to its end at 8:00 P.M. At

Guiney's he had accorded him a martial reception. The pleasant May skies became overcast. Clouds banked high. The rumble of thunder grew louder, and nearer. Lightning swept the forest. Salvo followed salvo as overwhelmingly sounded the artillery of the firmament. Was it the challenge of battles to be fought, or was it salute to the victor of Chancellorsville?[30]

At Fairfield it was found that the hospitable Chandlers already were entertaining a large company of refugees and sick and wounded soldiers. A less noisy place might be desirable. Dr. McGuire concurred with emphasis because he was told that a case or two of erysipelas had occurred in the main house. Instantly Mr. and Mrs. Chandler placed at the general's exclusive disposal the office in the yard, a building quite similar to that which Jackson had occupied during the winter at Moss Neck. This was ideal! Jackson was conveyed in the ambulance to the door of the office and then carefully moved inside. He was placed on a bed in one of the two rear chambers. In this setting Jackson immediately was comfortable and relaxed. He ate some bread, drank a cup of tea, and ere long he quietly fell into normal sleep.

The cool morning of May 5, Jackson awoke in good condition. Dr. McGuire examined the wounds. The one in the right hand was giving little pain but McGuire thought the hand should be splinted to keep the fragments of bone at rest. No serious infection was discovered. The stump of the left arm was doing equally well. Some parts of it seemed to be healing by first intention. Granulation elsewhere was observable. Jackson ate with heartiness and began to speculate on the length of time he would be absent from duty. He was altogether cheerful. "Many," he said to Smith, "would regard [these injuries] as a great misfortune; I regard them as one of the blessings of my life."

" 'All things work together for good to them that love God,' " Smith quoted.

"Yes, that's it, that's it."[31]

3. Promotion for Rodes and for Jackson

After Anderson and McLaws rejoined the three divisions under Stuart, preparations were made for a renewal of the general offensive on the morning of the sixth. Wasted effort it was. During the night of May 5–6, Hooker recalled the last of his troops from the right bank of the river. Another "On to Richmond" had ended—as McDowell's and McClellan's and Pope's and Burnside's had—in retreat. The cost had been 17,304 Federal casualties. Lee's had been 13,460, of which 6,039 had been in A. P. Hill's and Rodes's divisions.

Although Hooker proclaimed in general orders that "the events of the last week may swell with pride the heart of every officer and soldier of the army," he personally had little of which to be proud. Strategically, his plan of containing a part of the Southern army at Fredericksburg, while turning Lee's left up the Rappahannock, was as sound as it was simple. Tactically, the whole operation was discreditable to commanders who previously had done well. For the failure of his offensive, five major reasons may be cited.

First, Hooker did not have a staff organization capable of conducting simultaneously an attack in the Wilderness and another at Fredericksburg. The general attempted to clear all communications through his chief of staff, Daniel Butterfield, at Falmouth. Butterfield failed to maintain liaison, but not because of any lack of effort or understanding; it was not the men but the equipment that failed. On so long a front, the wires and the instruments were not equal to the demands made on them. As Hooker's own difficulties increased in the Wilderness, he made, in the second place, enlarged and perhaps excessive demands on Sedgwick, who during this campaign was much below the level of best performances. Next, the Federal command erred in its singular misapprehension of the strategic importance of Banks' Ford, which if used to the fullest would have permitted Hooker to separate Early and Lee and kept them apart.

A fourth important factor in defeat was the feeble employment of Hooker's artillery. Never had the strongest arm of the Federal service been so weak. This was due to the fact that Hooker limited Henry J. Hunt, his chief of artillery, to administrative duty. There was no unified control of the artillery. Misuse and nonuse of the guns was one indication only of the fifth principal failure of the Federal army, namely, a singular lack of coordination of the forces in the Wilderness. In the main, they fought separately as corps and more often as divisions. Hooker lacked the power to elicit that confident, whole-hearted cooperation of his lieutenants which is the cohesive of command.

All five of these failings were aggravated by two mistakes on Hooker's part that were capitalized fully by his opponents. His initial blunder was in sending off virtually all his cavalry for operations against Lee's lines of communication. The absence of the cavalry simplified the march of the Second Corps to the Federal right. Hooker could say in his defense that if the cavalry had done their full duty, they could have destroyed Lee's lines of supply and compelled the Army of Northern Virginia to retreat or to attack Hooker on ground selected by him. Such an argument, of course, prepared the way for blaming the cavalry for the failure of the campaign.

Hooker's second blunder is full of instruction. On May 1, the day Jackson arrived from Fredericksburg to reinforce Anderson, Hooker about 1:00 P.M. suspended his advance and soon afterward ordered a retirement into the tangled Wilderness. Why he did this he never explained fully, only that "as the passage-way through the forest was narrow, I was satisfied that I could not throw troops through it fast enough to resist the advance of General Lee, and was apprehensive of being whipped in detail." All the vast preparations of the Federal army and all the advantages that had been won by a surprise crossing of the Rappahannock were thrown away in that single decision. From that hour, the initiative in the Wilderness was with Lee.[32]

Notable the victory was, if not overwhelming, but it was no surprise to the people of the Confederacy. "A Glorious Confederate Victory" the *Richmond Dispatch* blazoned its editorial. Some surprise was voiced that the North was not stampeded: The South must work to make the most of what the army had gained; a blow must be struck again before the enemy had time to recover. The most discerning appraisal of Chancellorsville was the *Richmond Whig*'s, pointing out that it was "a battle of maneuver in which we beat the enemy utterly in strategy." In addition, the *Whig* summarized, "there was no straggling or disorganization" and "our artillery is at last perfected"—a most intelligent observation.[33]

Satisfaction was dampened from the first by the news of the wounding of Jackson, but of other casualties, though they were many, little was said. The most distinguished of those killed in action was Franklin Paxton, who fell on the morning of May 3. Five colonels had been slain and a larger number of other field officers. Besides Jackson, six general officers were wounded: The new Louisiana brigadier, Francis T. Nicholls, lost a leg; Samuel McGowan was injured seriously; Ramseur, Heth, Pender, and Hoke were hit but not dangerously. Most of the men in Jackson's party when it came under fire were killed or wounded. Among the dead was the chief topographical engineer of the Second Corps, J. K. Boswell. Dead, also, was Channing Price, who never rallied from the loss of blood suffered in the reconnaissance of May 1. Stapleton Crutchfield survived the wound that cost him a leg, but from his post as Second Corps chief of artillery he would be absent for months.

Crippled was the mildest word to describe the condition of the command of the Second Corps. In D. H. Hill's (Rodes's) division, 30 officers were killed, 148 wounded, and 59 missing—a total of 237. Ere the battle ended A. P. Hill's division had four successive commanders—Hill, Heth, Pender, and Archer. The brigade of McGowan, formerly Gregg's, finished the action of May 3 under its third colonel. Colston's brigade entered the fight under its senior colonel and emerged under its fifth-ranking officer, a lieutenant colonel. Lane's regimental leadership was almost destroyed.

The 26th Alabama of Rodes's old brigade was led, during the final hours, by a lieutenant.

Like losses in command had been met and endured by the Army of Northern Virginia: Was there a point beyond which competent successors to fallen officers could not be found? If that question occurred to any besides General Lee himself, an optimistic answer was taken for granted. Neither the civil authorities nor the press said anything to indicate that they considered attrition of command in terms of crippling cumulative loss of the bravest from Williamsburg to Chancellorsville, over a period of precisely one year.

The same grim process of attrition was wearing to feebleness some of the most reliable units of the army. The Stonewall Brigade never was itself in full might after Chancellorsville. The 22nd Virginia battalion lost 45 of its 102 men and, as the next engagement was to prove, lost its fighting edge also. In Lane's brigade, nearly one third of the entire command was put out of action during the first assault on the morning of May 3. These casualties, men might say, could be made good by bringing into the army the thousands who were evading military duty. The veterans would shame the conscripts into fighting. Perhaps it would be so. Was there not also a possibility that the best men were in the ranks already and, as they fell, would be irreplaceable from the small white population of the South?

Nor could the balance sheet of command be drawn immediately after Chancellorsville entirely in terms of killed and wounded. The battle had created certain doubts at the same time it had confirmed judgments. Competence as well as attrition had to be taken into account.

First might be written down the principal credit entries. At the head of the list, next to the commanding general himself, stood Jackson, of course. His performance had not been flawless. The start on May 2 had been late; the march had not been brilliant; Jackson had not maintained regular communication between van and rear; into the attack he had been able to throw no more than six of his twelve brigades. All of this was defective technically; but the wisdom of the plan, the vigor of the conception, and the fury of the attack were superlative. At the time, the secrecy of the march, the surprise of the enemy, and the climax of the wounding of Jackson had an imaginative appeal that made men ignore minor shortcomings which today are plain and instructive. Anyone who criticized Jackson's leadership at Chancellorsville would have raised in Southern minds a question concerning his own sanity and patriotism.

For the manner in which Jeb Stuart assumed and exercised command of the Second Corps he was most elaborately complimented by Lee and Powell Hill. Within limits, this was deserved. Stuart had taken courageously at midnight the direction of a situation so confused that staff officers could not have explained it to a newcomer even had those officers been at hand. From daylight on the third Stuart pressed the attack. To be sure, his forces soon were piled up, immobile, on his right; but was that his fault? The advance from the south facilitated the last successful stage of his attack, an advance directed by Lee and executed by Dick Anderson. Neither of those modest men was of a nature to dispute any assertion by Stuart, who never failed, in his reports, to make the most of his achievements. The main consideration in just appraisal of Stuart's service is the difficult one of ascertaining his responsibility for the decisive concentration of artillery at Hazel Grove. At least as much credit belonged to Porter Alexander as to Stuart, but the entry at the time was made on the account of the cavalryman. Even then, as will develop, Stuart was not satisfied with the praise given him.

Next after Stuart, reports seconded Jackson in applauding the soldierly performance of Robert Rodes. The handling by him of D. H. Hill's fine division was in keeping with the quality of the troops. On the field, astride his black, froth-covered horse, Rodes was a superb figure. His "eyes were everywhere, and every now and then he would stop to attend to some detail of the arrangement of his line or his troops, and then ride on again, humming to himself and catching the ends of his long, tawny mustache between his lips." All in all, Rodes's leadership had about it something Jacksonian. As Lee wished both to reward Rodes and to please Jackson, he asked immediately for Rodes's promotion, with assignment to the division he had led against the flank of Hooker. The President appointed Rodes a major general on May 7 to rank from May 2—the nearest approach the army had known to promotion on the field for valor.[34]

It would have been easy, even at the time, to have raised many questions concerning Jubal Early's handling of the situation at Fredericksburg. Did he make proper dispositions, or did he concentrate too heavily on the right and leave too great a defensive task to Barksdale? How much of the credit due Early for operations on the afternoon of May 3 belonged to Cadmus Wilcox? Was Early's plan of operations for May 4 too elaborate? In describing events of May 4, did Early assert too much for Gordon and did he thereby depreciate Barksdale? The last only of these matters came under review. Barksdale heard a report that Early said Gordon's troops "had recaptured Marye's Hill on the 4th that Barksdale lost on the 3rd." This aroused the Mississippian. He adduced proof that one of his scouts had gone to the heights before Gordon arrived, and found there only a group of ladies from the town looking after the wounded; and, further, that two of his lieutenants had already secured the heights when Gordon "stormed" them.[35]

This brief controversy served to show that Early's achievements lost nothing in his recountal of them, but the achievements themselves were solid enough. He was subjected at a post of danger and difficulty to the impact of misstated orders and the uncertainties of attack by an overpowering foe. In the face of this, and of a doubtfully efficient handling of part of his artillery, Old Jube had kept his head. Without excessive loss of men or ground, he, with Wilcox, had frustrated an essential part of the Federal plan, that of an attack by Sedgwick on the rear of Lee's army.

In Lee's report Dick Anderson received commendation he honestly had earned. He fought admirably at Chancellorsville and did much to hold the Confederate right while Jackson struck on the left. The South Carolinian, said Lee, was "distinguished for the promptness, courage, and skill with which he and his division executed every order."[36] Always it was Anderson's nature to take the largest blame and the least praise. At Chancellorsville, as previously, he merited far more than ever he would have thought of claiming. He never seemed to realize that his side-slipping to the left and his subsequent attack to the northward at the climax of the fighting on May 3 exhibited tactics of the first order.

Cadmus Wilcox, said Lee, was "entitled to especial praise for the judgment and bravery displayed" in impeding Sedgwick "and for the gallant and successful stand at Salem Church."[37] A memorable example Wilcox afforded of the manner in which emergency and responsibility on occasion lift men of certain types far above their average performance. On May 3 he reasoned intelligently and promptly when he should leave Banks' Ford. Then, instead of joining Early, he took his chance of being destroyed in order that he might delay the advance of the enemy on the Plank Road. Never before had such an opportunity come to Cadmus Wilcox; never again was he to have another such; but it could be said that of the one supreme day he had made the most.

Others there were who had done well. Heth had not failed the expectations of Lee, his sponsor. Dodson Ramseur had given a fine example of what a fighting brigadier should be. Said Dorsey Pender in full knowledge of what the words meant, "Ramseur covered himself and Brigade with glory." George Doles had proved himself the peer of Ramseur. Gordon's quick movement on the morning of May 4 was commended, though Early had to say that if Gordon had not been successful, he would have been forced to court-martial the Georgian for starting before the other brigades were prepared to move.[38]

As always, the impersonal army itself deserved more praise than any person. Company officers and men in the ranks of the infantry had distinguished themselves so greatly that few officers were disposed to dwell on the unhappy morning hours of May 3 when hundreds of veteran soldiers had huddled under the breastworks south of the Plank Road. Instead, there were valiant deeds beyond counting to report. Like commendation now could be given the artillery as a whole. This was Lee's language: "To the skillful and efficient management of the artillery the successful issue of the contest is in great measure due." Jackson, from his bed, credited the new power of the artillery arm, as did Stuart, to the recently established battalion system. Porter Alexander's account of the ease with which guns were concentrated at Hazel Grove confirmed all that his superiors said.[39]

Fine as much of this conduct was at Chancellorsville, a few men had failed or, at best appraisal, had not fulfilled their opportunities and had made doubtful or dangerous their retention in command. Raleigh Colston, in particular, was not commended in Lee's report. In the commanding general's official narrative, where there had been so much to approve in the conduct of so many, failure to include a word of praise for the commander of one of the three divisions that delivered the attack on Hooker's right could not be regarded otherwise than as censure.

What was the nature of Colston's failure? The records are vague, but when silences are probed and obscure references are traced down, it would appear, in the first instance, that Colston lost his grip on his troops during the early morning hours of May 3 and did not recover it that day. This was not surprising, if it be recalled that Colston had led men in battle only twice before—once briefly at Williamsburg, and again at Seven Pines. In neither instance had his responsibility gone beyond his brigade. At Chancellorsville he had a division with which he had little acquaintance, a division in which only one brigade went into the action of May 3 under a brigadier general; the three others were led by colonels. During the battle the different brigades of his division fought under twelve and lost eight commanders. Three of these were killed, five wounded. In these circumstances, surely, it was not surprising that the division became, in Powell Hill's phrase, "somewhat broken and disordered."

This could not have been the full measure of Colston's failure. Had it been he would have escaped criticism, if for no other reason than that other commands, with a less depleted corps of officers, had done scarcely better. A black entry must have followed an occurrence on the afternoon of May 3. After the seizure of Chancellorsville, Colston was ordered to undertake an advance up the road to United States Ford. His engineer, directed to make a reconnaissance, reported the Federals' position stronger than could be taken by Colston's weakened division. Colston thereupon told Stuart that "my division was not able to attack with any prospect of success the position of the enemy." Stuart evidently was disgusted that an officer of rank should say, in effect, that he could not. The acting corps commander ordered Colston to shelter his men in some abandoned Federal entrenchments, and placed him and his division under the general direction of Rodes. This episode may have been judged to mean that Colston did not have and could not hope to gain the confidence of his men. Lee's conclusion was that Raleigh Colston was not suited to active field leadership. By May 20 he was relieved of command—a course of action Lee seldom took. Even to the President no explanation was given by Lee. He wrote only, "I think it better to relieve Colston from duty." It was a curious case.[40]

The next man of rank who came through the campaign with diminished reputation was McLaws. He, like Colston, received no praise in Lee's report. References to the Georgian's actions on May 4 were stiff and formal. This cold treatment could mean only that Lee was disappointed in McLaws's performance, which he must have considered below the opportunities and requirements of the situation. Ignorant of the ground and doubtful of his strength, as compared with the enemy's, McLaws had not been aggressive. Nothing had he risked that more he might gain. Again the question: Was it overcaution, or hesitation in dealing with Early; or was it that McLaws missed the cool direction of Peter Longstreet, his absent corps commander? The record is silent.

That Brigadier General Pendleton was considered the third failure of the campaign is plain from the manner in which he, like Colston and McLaws, was denied Lee's commendation. Early, who directed Pendleton's operations part of the time in the fighting at Fredericksburg, mentioned him casually and without a syllable of approbation. Unofficial criticism of Pendleton included the charge that he made faulty dispositions and then did not recall any of the reserve batteries hurried to the rear at the time Chilton told Early to evacuate the heights. Amid rejoicing over the efficiency of the new battalion organization, nothing derogatory of Pendleton seems to have been said publicly. He had not shone; he had not disgraced himself; it was doubtful whether the best of artillery employment would have prevented on May 3 the capture of the hills behind Fredericksburg. The worst that could be said of him was that he had seemed more interested in saving than in serving his guns.

After Colston, McLaws, and Pendleton, the man who had to be written down next as of doubtful achievement was Alfred H. Colquitt. Concerning him the question fundamentally was one of judgment. Had he lessened the victory of the evening of the second by his halt on the right, in the belief that cavalry was threatening his flank? Colquitt not only deprived

Jackson of hundreds of good Georgia rifles but also blocked Ramseur, whose fine brigade showed the next day what it was capable of doing. The Georgian may be said to have redeemed himself on the third, but apparently he did not clear himself in the estimation of his superiors. At first opportunity, as will appear, his brigade was exchanged for one then in North Carolina.

Appraising Chancellorsville produces substantially this estimate of change and of stabilization:

Second Corps command

Jackson—at his superlative best in the dash and the dramatic success of his march to Hooker's right.

Divisional command of the Second Corps

Early—resourceful, unafraid, manifestly capable of acting on his own.
    Rodes—full of fire and drive; amply qualified for divisional command.
    Colston—disappointing.
    Hill—disabled but cooperative and courageous.
    Heth—not brilliant as a second to Hill, but steady and reliable.

Among Second Corps brigade commanders

Paxton—dead and difficult to replace.
    J. R. Jones—probably had written himself off the army roster by leaving the field because of an ulcerated leg.
    Ramseur—full of promise in the spirit of Jackson and Rodes.
    Doles—of the same mold as Ramseur.
    Pender—as always, valiant and hard-hitting.
    Gordon—daring, quick, courageous, with a singular grip on his command by reason of his personality and eloquence.
    Nicholls—justifying his commission but probably invalided permanently by loss of a leg; no successor among his colonels.

First Corps division commanders

Anderson—admirably efficient, despite the tradition that Longstreet only could elicit his full powers.
    McLaws—shown to be hesitant and unaggressive.

Among First Corps brigade commanders

Wilcox—one of the most conspicuous and useful officers in the campaign; promotion almost imperative.

Wright—In the spirit of Malvern Hill, the first to reach Chancellorsville in Anderson's fine advance from the south.

Posey—like Nicholls, justifying promotion, and of the same hard-hitting indomitable spirit as Ramseur and Doles.

Artillery and staff

Pendleton—all the misgivings of Malvern Hill and Shepherdstown deepened, but nothing of a positive nature to warrant displacement.

Artillery battalion commanders—almost without exception qualified for their new rank and able to use their battalion organization most effectively. Alexander especially distinguished.

Crutchfield—outstanding but now incapacitated for months; none of his battalion commanders pre-eminently marked to act in his stead.

Boswell, of Jackson's staff—dead and deplored but survived by his capable comrade Jed Hotchkiss, who could succeed him.

Price, of Stuart's staff—the most useful cavalry staff officer; an able man required to fill the place made vacant by his death.

Longstreet, of course, had been missed greatly. It was difficult to think of any part of the First Corps in battle without his calm direction. With Old Pete and his generals returning ere long, then, in corps and divisional command Chancellorsville had wrought no harm beyond repair. Rodes could be trusted with D. H. Hill's division; someone—most probably Edward Johnson or Arnold Elzey—would take Trimble's division if its commander remained a cripple. New brigadiers would be needed. They always were. To procure qualified men in any considerable number might be more difficult now than to get one or two new major generals. Reorganization might be vexatious and troublesome, but it would entail no impossible task, provided, of course, Jackson soon were back in the field.

Tuesday morning, May 5, Old Jack welcomed Chaplain Lacy, who arrived at 10 o'clock to conduct bedside worship and to give the general the satisfaction of discussing religion. Jackson asked that Lacy come every morning at the same hour; meantime he could enjoy to the limit of his strength the privilege of Lieutenant Smith, who was of his same Presbyterian faith and was minded to the ministry. Jackson took occasion to expound one of his favorite views—that the Bible supplied rules for every action of life. He asked Smith with a smile, "Can you tell me where the Bible gives generals a model for their official reports of battles?" When Smith answered that he never had consulted Holy Writ to find examples of battle reports, Jackson gave as an example the narrative of Joshua's battle with the Amalekites: "There you have one. It has clearness, brevity, fairness, modesty; and it traces the victory to its right source, the blessing of God." Lee's battle, as well as Joshua's, came in for discussion, with Jackson expressing no doubt of the outcome.

The general passed the next day, Wednesday, as he had spent Tuesday with no symptoms of other involvement, and with additional delectable discourse on theology. This helped to make a day of consistent and encouraging gain. Ere its close, Chaplain Lacy went to army headquarters to request the detail of Dr. Samuel B. Morrison of Early's division, who had been the general's family physician and was, besides, a kinsman of Mrs. Jackson's. He would be an excellent medical counselor and a relief chief nurse in place of Dr. McGuire, who could not endure much longer his vigils at the bedside. Lacy returned with a thoughtful message for Jackson from General Lee: "Give him my affectionate regards, and tell him to make haste and get well, and come back to me as soon as he can. He has lost his left arm; but I have lost my right arm."[41]

That night, Wednesday, May 6, Dr. McGuire was so weary that he decided he would sleep on a couch in Jackson's room and leave the patient in the care of Jim Lewis, the general's body servant. With Dr. McGuire on the couch and Jim silent in the chair, Jackson went to sleep without difficulty. About 1:00 A.M. he was awakened with nausea and quietly told Jim to get a wet towel and apply it to his stomach. Vaguely conscious that this was the wrong thing to do, Jim asked if he might wake Dr. McGuire and ask him. Jackson refused: The doctor had been very tired; let him sleep; get the towel.

The cold compress did no good. Paroxysms in the right side were added to the nausea. Moment by moment, pain increased until it almost passed endurance. The general's frame was shaken but his resolution was firm: He would not waken the sleeping surgeon if he could endure till morning. Soon he observed, though without panic, that the pain was sharpened every time he drew breath. He held out until the gray of dawn, then permitted Jim to awaken McGuire. The young physician listened intently to the general's breathing and examined the painful area of the chest. All too readily, McGuire became convinced of what the patient himself may have suspected: Jackson was developing pneumonia.

Hope and planning and confident expectation were halted. There must instead be a stern battle here in the cottage at the Chandlers'. If it was won, Chancellorsville was a double victory. Were the battle lost—were it possible, even, to think that Jackson might not recover—then the North would be repaid for all the boys who had been slain or maimed there in the Wilderness of Spotsylvania, where the burnt forest still smoked and the dead lay unburied.

Jackson was not afraid. He did not believe pneumonia would kill him. Judgment, confidence, faith, ambition—something had convinced him that he had more work to do. Attack, then, the disease that was assailing him! Preliminary to cupping, which would bring more blood to the affected member, Jackson was given morphia. This of course made him less sensitive to his pain but it threw him quickly into a stupor. From that hour the personality of Jackson, as his officers knew it, seemed in a haze, obscured, uncertain. In the first offthrust of reason, he seemed to be carried back again to the attack on Hooker's right. "Major Pendleton," he exclaimed, "send in and see if there is higher ground back of Chancellorsville."

That afternoon he became aware of another presence in the room. There, by his bed, white-faced but composed, was his wife. He stirred himself to greet her, but so deeply was he under his opiate that he dropped off again quickly. At length, when she ministered to him he was able to show by smile or glance that he knew her. Looking steadfastly at her he observed the emotion she was trying to conceal. With an effort, but seemingly in full command of his faculties, he said, "My darling, you must cheer up and not wear a long face. . . . Do not be sad; I hope I may yet recover. Pray for me, but always remember in your prayers to use the petition, 'Thy will be done.' "[42]

Dr. Morrison now arrived and came at once to the general. As the surgeon leaned over him, Jackson opened his eyes, recognized Morrison, smiled and said simply, "That's an old, familiar face." Morrison and McGuire now held a consultation and decided they should call from Richmond its most distinguished authority on pneumonia, Dr. David Tucker. Lieutenant Smith was sent to the city on the next train. Jackson all the while seemed half asleep, half delirious. His mind turned to the battlefield. More than once he seemed to be thinking of his troops as weary at the end of a long conflict. He wanted the commissary at hand, wanted the soldiers fed. "Tell Major Hawks to send forward provisions to the men." The name stuck in his mind . . . "Major Hawks . . . Major Hawks" he muttered.

Despite his delirium, the doctors did not feel discouraged. When the cool Thursday evening closed in rain, they could not dispute the nature and progress of the malady, but they believed he was holding his own against it. There were some reasons for thinking him better, though these may have been nothing more than the effect of the opiates the surgeons continued to administer. At bedtime Dr. Morrison took his seat by Jackson to watch and to give the medicines. The doctor had little to do. Jackson lay in stupor but kept a grip on himself. Once, during the night when Morrison offered him a draught, Jackson seemed almost to reprimand with a terse answer—"Do your duty!"[43]

Friday, May 8, was the anniversary of the Battle of McDowell. Among the camps there was profound concern. Men were asking: Was Old Jack in danger? How could the army do without him? For a year, a rounded year that very day, his name had been the symbol of victory. Many who had seen him in battle, those blue eyes ablaze, had shared Dick Taylor's belief that the bullet which could kill Stonewall never had been molded. The enemy had not struck him down; his own troops had; and if they, even they, had not been able to slay him, could pneumonia? In the name of all of them General Lee was to speak when he said, "Surely, General Jackson must recover; God will not take him from us, now that we need him so much."

In the cottage at the Chandlers', that Friday, some of the surgeons were not so sure. The ominous condition was his difficult breathing and his great exhaustion. Later in the day, Dr. Morrison had to express a fear that the disease might not be overcome. To this Jackson listened without emotion, and then, rallying his mind and tongue, said deliberately, "I am not afraid to die; I am willing to abide by the will of my Heavenly Father. But I do not believe that I shall die at this time; I am persuaded the Almighty has yet a work for me to perform." Even after Dr. McGuire, his own medical director, admitted doubt concerning the outcome, Jackson still insisted that he would recover. He had a restless night, but he did not appear to be shaken in his confidence that he would beat his new adversary.

Out of doors, the brightest day of a changeable May week was Saturday, the ninth. It found Jackson's breathing apparently less difficult and his pain diminished. His weakness manifestly was worse. David Tucker, the Richmond authority on pneumonia, at length had arrived. Later in the day Jackson said slowly to McGuire: "I see from the number of physicians that you think my condition dangerous, but I thank God, if it is His will, that I am ready to go." In the afternoon he asked for Chaplain Lacy. At the time, his lungs were so nearly filled that his breathing was difficult again, and his respiration was shallow and cruelly fast, but he would not be balked from conversing with Lacy. He wanted to know if the chaplain was working to promote Sunday observance by the army in the manner previously enjoined on him. Lacy was able to report that he was. When at length

Lacy rose to go, he offered to be with the general on the Sabbath Day; but Jackson insisted that he go to Second Corps headquarters and preach, as usual, to the soldiers.

Evening came, clear and warm. The general talked more of battle than anything else and he commanded and exhorted—"Order A. P. Hill to prepare for action.... Pass the infantry to the front." Most of his other words were confused or unintelligible. Mrs. Jackson read to him from the Psalms, and then she and her brother, Lieutenant Morrison of the staff, sang the most spiritual of the hymns that he favored. "The singing," Mrs. Jackson said afterward, "had a quieting effect, and he seemed to rest in perfect peace." Later the spirit of the soldier asserted itself once more. "I think I will be better by morning," he said. Determined as he was to fight on, he lost ground as the night passed.[44]

The soft spring night ended at last in warmth and promise of sunshine. It was the tenth of May. It was Sunday; was this the day to witness the last battle in the long list of Jackson's battles? Presently, as the morning light grew brighter, Mrs. Jackson sat by him and the others left the chamber. Long before, he had told her that he did not fear to die but that he hoped he would "have a few hours' preparation before entering into the presence of his Maker and Redeemer." Her voice came to him on the border of the far country: "Do you know the doctors say, you must soon be in Heaven?" Then, "Do you not feel willing to acquiesce in God's allotment, if He wills you to go today?"

He opened his eyes and looked at her. "I prefer it," he said slowly and with much difficulty. "I prefer it." She said, "Well, before this day closes, you will be with the blessed Saviour in His glory." He steadied himself for the effort of speech and said deliberately, "I will be an infinite gainer to be translated." She talked with him further and asked his wishes about many things, but could not hold his attention.

Toward noon full consciousness seemed to return, and he called for Dr. McGuire. "Doctor," said Jackson distinctly, "Anna informs me that you have told her that I am to die today; is it so?" Gently McGuire replied that medicine had done its utmost. Jackson seemed to ponder, gazing upward for a few moments. Then, as if he thought the orders of Higher Command had been given, his response was strong: "Very good; very good; it is all right."

In accordance with the custom of the day, it seemed proper that he say farewell to his child. Jackson recognized her at once. The baby smiled back and did not seem in any way frightened. Through the fog of morphia and weakness he played with her and called her endearing names until he sank back into the unconscious. When next he aroused, Sandie Pendleton was standing by his bed. The presence of the young soldier brought Jackson back for an instant to a world of camps and sinning soldiers. "Who is preaching at headquarters today?" he asked, and was gratified when told that Lacy was. Still more was Jackson pleased when Sandie told him the whole army was praying for him. "Thank God," he murmured, "they are very kind. . . ." Presently he spoke again. "It is the Lord's Day. . . . My wish is fulfilled. I have always desired to die on Sunday."[45]

Sandie went out to weep and not to weep alone. Everyone was in tears. The faithful Jim was overwhelmed. Dr. McGuire thought he should stimulate Jackson with some brandy. Jackson shook his head. "I want to preserve my mind, if possible, to the last." Once more he slipped back into the land of far and near. He murmured again, gave orders, sat at mess with his staff, was back in Lexington with his little family, was fighting, was praying.

More there was in the same mutter—Hill, Hawks, orders to the infantry—and then a long, long silence. Now . . . the clock striking three, the spring sunshine in the room, the rustle of new leaves in the breeze, peace and the end of a Sabbath Day's journey. Fifteen minutes more; breathing now was in the very throat; and then from the bed, clearly, quietly, cheerfully, "Let us cross over the river, and rest under the shade of the trees."[46]

CHAPTER 24

Renewal and Reorganization

1. "HAVE NO FEAR WE SHALL NOT BEAT THEM!"

A wail went up everywhere in the South. From the time the first news of the wounding of Jackson had reached the Confederate people, they had felt a concern that hopeful professional assurances had not relieved. That Jackson would not die, the *Whig* assured its readers: "We need have no fears for Jackson. . . . He came not by chance in this day and to this generation. He was born for a purpose, and not until that purpose is fulfilled will his great soul take flight."[1] Now that hope was disappointed and faith was challenged, there was an emotional outlet in such ceremonies as a battling people could provide. The decision was to transport the body to Richmond and send it thence to Lexington for burial.

All the pomp the grieving capital could command it displayed for the body of the fallen soldier. The few church bells that had not been molded into cannon were tolled. All business stopped. Arnold Elzey led the procession down Broad Street and to the entrance to Capitol Square. Thence between lines of troops at present arms the casket was borne to the governor's mansion. Over the coffin, by the President's order, a handsome new "national flag," the first of a modified white design, was draped. The next day, in order that thousands might see, a new procession carried the body to the Capitol, where it was laid in state in the Confederate House of Representatives. To the hall now were admitted all who could file past during the day and a long evening.

On May 13, with added tributes, the body was placed aboard a Virginia Central train and carried to Gordonsville, whence by the Orange and Alexandria it was transported to Lynchburg. From that city, on a canal boat, it was sent to Lexington. Everywhere along the route there was repetition, more distressed, of the scenes on the road from Wilderness Tavern to Guiney's. Then it had been food and drink brought out for him; now it was spring flowers. Covered with these blossoms, the casket lay for the night of the fourteenth in Jackson's old classroom. On May 15, Friday, after a funeral in the church of which he had been a deacon, the body was committed to the earth. Among the escort was the V.M.I. cadet battalion and convalescents and invalided veterans of the Stonewall Brigade.[2]

The President telegraphed General Lee: "A great national calamity has befallen us." In general orders of May 11, Lee spoke of "the daring, skill, and energy of this great and good soldier." So deeply was Lee moved by the loss that he scarcely could speak of Jackson without tears, and to the end of his days he never mentioned his greatest lieutenant otherwise than with deep, affectionate admiration. "Such an executive officer," he said, "the sun never shone on." Any disparagement of Jackson was an offense to him. In the press lament was universal. As the *Examiner* saw him, "There was the stuff of Cromwell in Jackson. Hannibal might have been proud of his campaign in the Valley, and the shades of the mightiest warriors should rise to welcome his stern ghost."[3]

From the moment that the death of Jackson had seemed probable, the same question had concluded every lament—Where was his successor to be found; what would be the effect on the Southern cause of a loss so dire? Mingling resignation and deep perplexity were the words of the commanding general: "I know not how to replace him. God's will be done. I trust He will raise up someone in his place. . . ."[4]

Most often mentioned was Dick Ewell. In the judgment of some, the sole question concerning Ewell was whether, after the loss of his leg at Groveton, he could be sufficiently active to exercise field command. Ewell's own attitude was flawlessly generous. He was convinced that Early had earned command of the division Jube had led during his long absence from the field. "What is very certain," he had written Early, "is that I won't ask for any particular duty or station, but let them do as they see proper with me." Ewell could now walk readily on his wooden leg with the help of a stick and he showed himself acrobat enough to mount his horse from the ground and to keep his seat when mounted. Did his physique match his record? Would Davis and Lee conclude that he could endure the strains of long marches, of cold bivouacs, of far-spread battlefields?[5]

Was Powell Hill better qualified? In the autumn of 1862, Lee had esteemed him, after Longstreet and Jackson, the best commander then with the army. Lee had intimated, even, that if a third lieutenant general had been needed, Hill would have been qualified. Nothing had happened after that time, despite Hill's quarrel with Jackson, to lower Lee's estimate. On May 6, as soon as Hill was sufficiently recovered from his bruises to ride, Lee had restored him to temporary command of the Second Corps and returned Stuart to the direction of the cavalry. That bespoke his confidence in Hill. Powell Hill's brigadiers enjoyed his hospitality, admired him as a leader, and liked his fiery spirit. Outside his division, due to the quarrel, feeling against Hill may have existed among a few of Jackson's more emotional friends.[6]

Some of Hill's supporters were both jealous and suspicious of Stuart. The chief of cavalry is not known to have hoped for the command of the Second Corps, or even to have desired it. Stuart himself was more concerned to receive full credit for what he had accomplished May 3. Failure to receive prompt praise was not Stuart's only distress. He mourned for Jackson, he mourned for Channing Price. The work of that invaluable staff officer Stuart entrusted, with uncommon discernment, to the former adjutant of the 3rd Virginia cavalry, Henry B. McClellan. Fortunately for Stuart, when he lost his fine young cousin he could lean almost from the start on McClellan.

Besides Ewell, Powell Hill, and Jeb Stuart, no other officers of Lee's army appear to have been mentioned widely as immediate successor to Jackson. By seniority, Harvey Hill was next to Ewell among Lee's major generals; both Harvey Hill and Lafayette McLaws held older commissions at that grade than did the commander of the Light Division or the chief of cavalry. McLaws had ruled himself out of promotion by what he had not done at Maryland Heights and Salem Church; Harvey Hill was at the moment engaged in another painful exchange of notes that led the commanding general to believe more firmly than ever that Hill would not assume responsibility. If Harvey Hill and Lafayette McLaws were not considered when perhaps they expected to be, two others who probably did not anticipate that honor so soon were regarded as of the stature of future lieutenant generals. These men were John B. Hood and Dick Anderson. They were rated "capital officers" by General Lee who added: "They are improving, too, and will make good corps commanders, if necessary."[7]

Around hundreds of mess tables, Stuart, Powell Hill, and Ewell were discussed as the three among whom a choice would be made. Nothing was certain until May 23. Then, almost a fortnight after the death of Jackson, notice was sent to Dick Ewell in Richmond that he was promoted lieutenant general. Formal orders directed him to proceed without delay to Fredericksburg and to report to Lee for assignment to duty.

Ewell received the news, so far as the records show, with no undue elation. Before he left Richmond, he allowed himself time to fulfill one ambition that he probably had cherished long: He married his widowed cousin, Lizinka Campbell Brown, daughter of George W. Campbell, former senator from Tennessee, secretary of the treasury, and minister to Russia. She was an able, strong-minded woman and had the complete, unquestioning affection of her soldier cousin, whom she probably rated far higher as a soldier than Ewell himself ever dreamed of doing. Surrender of he who was regarded as incurably the bachelor had been unconditional. She was his; but not in his mind so completely his that he could introduce her as such. For a time she was, to bowing generals, "my wife, Mrs. Brown."[8]

In part, the appointment of Dick Ewell was made because of sentimental association of his name with Jackson, and in part because of admiration for his unique, picturesque, and wholly lovable personality. Of his ability to lead a corps nothing was known. Ewell had never handled more than a division and he had served directly with Lee for less than a month. When he was advanced to corps command, nothing was said of his brief connection with Lee. So closely was his name linked with Jackson's, and so justly popular was Old Bald Head for his gallant generosity that none questioned, apparently, either the appointment or his ability to fill it.

Perhaps Ewell's reserved commanding general should be excepted from this statement. Lee may have wished to divide risks at the same time that he recognized merit. On the morning of May 24, the day after Ewell was promoted and before the news of his advancement reached the men on the Rappahannock, Powell Hill received a call to army headquarters. He was admitted to Lee's tent and in a few friendly sentences was told that the two existing corps were unwieldy for operation in a wooded country, that the President had consented to the establishment of a Third Corps, that it would consist of Hill's old division, of Anderson's transferred from Longstreet, and of a third division still to be formed, and that this new Third Corps was to be commanded by . . . Ambrose Powell Hill, lieutenant general.

As in October Lee had recommended the promotion of both Jackson and Longstreet, so now he advocated to the President, who heartily approved, the elevation of both Ewell and Powell Hill. Ewell, Lee told the President, "is an honest, brave soldier, who has always done his duty well." Hill was recommended as "upon the whole . . . the best soldier of his grade with me." Lee justified in sound words the advancement of the two men: "I wish to take advantage of every circumstance to inspire and encourage . . . the officers and men to believe that their labors are appreciated, and when vacancies occur that they will receive the advantages of promotion. . . . I do not know where to get better men than those I have named."[9]

There was little open grumbling at these promotions. Longstreet in later years wrote that Ewell deserved promotion, but Old Pete pointed out that both Harvey Hill and McLaws were Powell Hill's seniors. At the time the promotions were made, he voiced no objection and, except for his waning personal dislike of Powell Hill, probably felt none. If anyone complained, it may have been Lafayette McLaws, who could affirm that he was overslaughed by the advancement of Powell Hill; but if McLaws said anything, it simply was to inquire why he was passed over.[10]

Hill's elevation meant that some officer would be named to head the Light Division and would be made a major general. Hill knew that his advancement had been expected, and that Harry Heth and Dorsey Pender had been regarded as open, rival candidates to succeed him. As soon as he left the commanding general's tent on the day he was told of his promotion, Hill took the first opportunity of writing Lee a letter, which he delivered in person that afternoon. The new chief of the Third Corps explained that he ascribed the Light Division's good conduct "to its esprit de corps, to its pride in its *name,* and to its uniform 'shoulder to shoulder feeling,' and good feeling between the different brigades. If a judicious appointment of major general is not made, I fear that all this will be lost."

Concerning the two candidates, Hill went on: "Of Gen. Heth, I have but to say that I consider him a most excellent officer, and gallant soldier." Of Pender, he "has been four times wounded and *never* left the *field,* . . . has the best drilled and disciplined brigade in the division, and more than all, possesses the unbounded confidence of the division. . . . Hence, as much as I admire and respect Gen. Heth, I am conscientiously of opinion that in the opening campaign, my division under him, will not be *half* as effective as under Gen. Pender." Wherefore, Hill suggested what Lee already had decided to recommend—that two brigades of Hill's command be united with two other brigades, so that, if Heth were promoted, he might have this command, while Pender became a major general to head his own brigade, McGowan's, Thomas's, and Lane's.

This plan was submitted to the President. Higher rank for Heth was put in some doubt by the fact that he had been nominated by Davis in October 1862 and been refused confirmation by the Senate, but in view of the need for a qualified man for a new ninth division, the commanding general and the President had decided to proceed. One other obstacle stood in the way—a third candidate for early promotion in the person of Robert Ransom, Jr., who came from the same state, North Carolina, as Pender. Political ties might be twisted and friendships taxed by preferring one to the other. A choice was avoided by sending Samuel G. French to Mississippi and advancing Ransom to take French's place and thereby clearing the way for Pender.[11]

Heth had so many old friends and bound new acquaintances to him so readily by his social charm that few begrudged what manifestly he had desired. Ransom was pleased. Dorsey Pender, after Chancellorsville, wrote his wife: "If not before, I won promotion last Sunday and if it can be done

I think I shall get it." Once he had the advancement he coveted, he ceased to record his feelings. It was his nature to desire, to strive, to achieve, and having reached his goal, to minimize what he had gained.

Difficulty was faced in procuring the troops assigned Pender. Two of the four brigades were in the Carolinas, and some unpleasantness with Harvey Hill and sharp misunderstanding occurred before an accord was reached on their departure. This bargain confirmed Lee's belief that Harvey Hill would not exercise discretionary powers and that, ipso facto, he was not suited to the type of command Lee exercised. That was the end of Hill's place in Lee's esteem as a departmental commander, though he did not lose the personal good will of his chief. Nor did he lose then or thereafter his merited reputation as a superb combat officer.[12]

Ransom would remain south of the James, but the new major generals, Harry Heth and Dorsey Pender, would take their places in the new Third Corps. Rodes would command the former division of Harvey Hill. The fourth vacancy had been filled at the peak of the emergency that followed the discovery that Colston was unsuited to lead a division. Scarcely had Trimble begun to conquer his osteomyelitis than he fell sick again. As always, his spirit was free; his flesh held him captive. He could not take the division that Jackson long had saved for him. In Trimble's stead, Allegheny Johnson, who had been slated for D. H. Hill's division—now assigned Rodes—was called from Richmond on hurried orders. Trimble, for his part, was given charge of the Valley District, which Grumble Jones had not directed to public satisfaction. Although the assignment was not one that a man of Trimble's fighting impulse desired, it was accepted cheerfully and with a certain satisfaction because of Jackson's service on that famous battleground.[13]

So much for the major generals, all of whom seemed competent. Cadmus Wilcox was deeply and not unreasonably disappointed that he was passed over. If the selections were a bitter cup for anyone else, no taste of it lingers in the records. As for the brigadiers, Paul Semmes was back; but the promotion of Rodes, Heth, and Pender, the death of Paxton, the retirement of J. R. Jones, the absence of Lawton, the disabling of Nicholls, and the relief of Colston necessitated the promotion of eight men to the grade of brigadier general.

Was there sufficient qualified material from which to draw? One promotion was a matter of course. Difficult as Pender's place would be for any man to fill, Colonel Alfred M. Scales of the 13th North Carolina had led the brigade several times and had demonstrated his capacity. Similarly, John B. Gordon was fitted logically for command of Rodes's old brigade. But Gordon had been assigned temporarily to Lawton's brigade of Early's division, and so completely had Gordon won the hearts of his fellow-Georgians that their officers unanimously petitioned that he remain their chief. Lee thought it wise to accede to this request.

Aside from Scales and Gordon, trouble immediately was encountered in finding competent men. The grim truth was that in six brigades that lacked generals, not one of the senior colonels was ripe for promotion. Perhaps Lee was expecting more of brigadier generals and was setting higher standards for them, but for the first time attrition at the level of brigade command was threatening dangerously the organization of the army. Some of the most reliable, veteran regiments might be rendered ineffective because they would not be well led.

What was to be done? For a time, Rodes's brigade could be left under Colonel E.A. O'Neal of the 26th Alabama. Again, though Colonel J. M. Brockenbrough of the 40th Virginia was not suited for promotion to the command of Field's brigade, he could be counted upon to keep together a command sadly reduced in numbers. This temporary arrangement left four brigade vacancies, all of them unfortunately in the famous Jackson-Trimble-Colston-Johnson division. Who could take the Stonewall Brigade? J. R. Jones's brigade readily might have been given to Colonel T. S. Garnett of the 48th Virginia, but Garnett had been killed on May 3. Colston's brigade—who was to handle it? Three of its regiments were from Virginia, two from North Carolina. Unpleasant state rivalries had shown themselves; how were they to be resolved? Lastly, could anything be done with Nicholls's Louisiana brigade that had lost its most promising chief? Was it to be admitted that this excellent brigade could not be supplied with a qualified officer of appropriate rank?

That must not be! To support and assist the new divisional commander, Allegheny Johnson, competent brigadiers must be provided, but from what source? The answer given was itself evidence of the army's strait. In the first place, it was decided that Maryland Steuart, who had recovered from his Cross Keys wound, would be utilized as an old regular army man to take the Virginia–North Carolina brigade of Colston. Experience had indicated that where an officer well-schooled in the "old army" took a brigade that had regiments from more than one state, rivalries might be ended.

Paxton's brigade presented a second and more vexing problem. So famous a command deserved the best unattached brigadier who could be found. That man, in the judgment of Lee, was Colonel James A. Walker of the 13th Virginia, Early's old brigade. During the Maryland operations Walker had been "loaned" to Trimble's brigade, at the head of which he had done well, and he had been distinguished anew at Fredericksburg where he had been in charge of Early's brigade. Qualified Walker was.

Although he had no connection with the brigade or the division, he was made commander of the Stonewall Brigade.

This was a choice doubly sensational because of previous relations between Walker and Jackson. In 1852, at the Virginia Military Institute, Walker, who was a senior, professed himself insulted by a remark made to him by Professor Jackson. The belligerent young Walker challenged the teacher to a duel. The matter was closed by the court-martial and dismissal of Walker from the institute. With the coming of war, each acquired respect for the other. Walker laid down his grievance; Jackson did what he could to advance Walker. Now the colonel of the 13th Virginia was to have the unusual honor of transfer to Jackson's brigade, and of promotion over the heads of the senior officers of five of the most famous regiments in the army. A strident, echoing outcry was made by the field officers of the Stonewall Brigade. They were outraged, and in protest tendered their resignations. They named three whom they said they would have accepted cheerfully. The resignations were declined so quietly and with so much tact that no trace of the incident appears in the official records.[14]

For J. R. Jones's brigade, as for Paxton's, choice of a new commander had to go beyond the brigade and the division. The man promoted was Lieutenant Colonel John M. Jones, inspector general of Early's division. Jones was a West Point graduate of the class of 1841 and had served at the academy for seven years as assistant instructor of infantry tactics. When he resigned to defend Virginia, Jones was a captain of six years' standing. McLaws also had been a captain, Cadmus Wilcox a lieutenant. McLaws had risen to divisional command and Wilcox long had been a brigadier; why Jones had mounted no further was suggested vaguely in Lee's letter to Davis at the time of the appointment: "Should [Jones] fail in his duty, he will instantly resign." If this meant that Jones's enemy was strong drink, the new brigadier met and overcame that adversary.[15]

Steuart for Colston's brigade, Jim Walker for Paxton's, John M. Jones for J. R. Jones's command—this left the Louisiana brigade, but there, even when Lee looked through the other divisions, a suitable man could not be found at once. In the end, Nicholls's brigade, as well as Rodes's and Heth's, had to be left without commanding officers of proper grade—an ominous admission that superior, developed material of high command had been exhausted temporarily.

Such was the reorganization necessitated by the loss of Jackson, whom the army felt to be irreplaceable, and by the establishment of a Third Corps, which prudence, good organization, and justice to Ewell and A. P. Hill demanded. How those two officers would handle their enlarged commands it was impossible to foretell. The preliminaries were auspicious.

When Ewell arrived with his bride on May 29, after an absence from the army of nine months, his and Jackson's old divisions met him at the cars and gave him a cheering salute. "General Ewell is in fine health and fine spirits," wrote Sandie Pendleton. ". . . I look for great things from him, and am glad to say that our troops have for him a good deal of the same feeling they had towards General Jackson."

Old Bald Head was glad to take over Jackson's competent staff, and he was overjoyed to be again with his troops. On June 1, 1863, Ewell assumed direction of a reconstituted Second Corps—his old division under Early, Jackson's former division under Edward Johnson, and Harvey Hill's under Rodes. Simultaneously, Ambrose Powell Hill became the first commander of a new Third Corps. In it were part of his own division with Dorsey Pender as its chief, Heth's division, half of which had been Hill's own division, and third, Dick Anderson's brigades transferred from the First Corps.[16]

The adjustment of the artillery to this organization of three infantry corps proved a matter of no difficulty. To each of the corps three battalions were assigned. Instead of a general reserve, provision was made for a reserve of two battalions for each corps. To suffice for this organization, a fifteenth battalion was created, with Major William T. Poague, long-time captain of Jackson's own Rockbridge Artillery, as its head. In these assignments Longstreet's artillery organization remained intact. That of the Second Corps was unchanged except that Nelson's Battalion, previously of the general reserve, became one of its corps reserve battalions. The new Third Corps was not stinted. Every one of its five battalions was good. Quick as Hill was to take offense at any alleged slight, he seems to have been entirely satisfied with the batteries allotted to him.

Under this organization Pendleton ceased to be chief of the reserve artillery, for the reason that there no longer was any general reserve. He reverted to his one-time status as chief of artillery for the army. His corps chiefs of artillery—who were they to be? Colonel J. B. Walton was the titular and undisputed chief of the First Corps' guns, as for months he had been. This was a proper assignment. Walton embodied the spirit of the Washington Artillery, but he was no longer young nor alertly active. Much as Longstreet admired and respected Walton, he soon was to look to the sober-faced and scientific Porter Alexander to handle the artillery in the field.

The Second Corps inevitably would suffer much from the absence of Stapleton Crutchfield during the long months he would require to adjust himself to the loss of a leg. In his stead would serve the senior battalion commander—J. Thompson Brown, an able and conscientious soldier, patient and diligent in administration but not brilliant. For the Third Corps, Powell Hill nominated and Lee approved Colonel R. Lindsay

Walker. This officer, thirty-six years of age and a Virginian of high connections, had been graduated from V.M.I. in 1845. First as commander of the Purcell Battery of Richmond and then as chief of artillery of Hill's division, he had shared, always with honor, the fortunes of Hill's men on nearly all their fields of battle after the Seven Days. Walker was not the theatrical type whom soldiers cheer on the road and deride affectionately around the campfire, but he was the skillful leader that men are glad to have in battle. Careful and free of recklessness, he knew when the artillerist could afford to be bold.

Reorganization of the cavalry was another part of the endless task of promoting the worthy, replacing the incompetent, and making good the losses due to attrition. After Chancellorsville the need was, first, to increase the mounted troops for offensive operations. In southwest Virginia was a large force under Brigadier General A. G. Jenkins. These troops had not been well schooled in cavalry tactics or in hard fighting at close quarters. Some had the complex of home guards, and some preferred the life of a guerrilla to that of a trooper, but many were good raw material. They were badly needed by Stuart. After much diplomatic correspondence, Lee procured three regiments and one battalion. With that force Jenkins himself came, a man of oft-proved daring and gallantry but of untested administrative qualities.

Besides Jenkins's men, there was the prospect of getting from North Carolina some of the curious brigade of Beverly Robertson, who had quietly been transferred after Lee's army entered Maryland in September 1862. Inasmuch as Harvey Hill in the North State had denounced Robertson's men in every tone of vehemence, he could not object to ridding himself of them. Hill agreed to send Lee two of Robertson's regiments, and Robertson offered to return to Virginia with them. This was acceptable to Lee, who never had lost his good opinion of Robertson as an organizer and instructor. Stuart's judgment in not recorded, but before the end of May his roster included Robertson and the 4th and 5th North Carolina.

W. E. Jones and his regiments that had been in the Shenandoah Valley were also added to Stuart's immediate command. Jeb had been anxious not to have Grumble Jones with him again and was active in trying to get him transferred to the command of the Stonewall Brigade after Paxton's death. In this he had met with no encouragement from headquarters. Said Lee: "I am perfectly willing to transfer [Jones] to Paxton's brigade if he desires it; but if he does not, I know of no act of his to justify my doing so. Do not let your judgment be warped."[17] That, of course, silenced Jeb but it did not satisfy him. The commanding general could make the two men work together. He could not make them like each other.

When the opportunity of another offensive came, there was still another prospect of adding to the cavalry of the army. John D. Imboden and his mounted units had been campaigning in western Virginia and now might assist Stuart temporarily, but whether they would help stoutly was another question. Imboden had lost by desertion 200 men from a single battalion after he had forbidden them to seize citizens' horses for private use. A command that would do this scarcely would respond with the spur to Stuart's bugles, but undisciplined as were Imboden's rangers, they could ride, they could shoot, they could drive cattle, and they could guard a countryside. They must be employed.

While this third major reorganization of the army was being effected, the First Corps was reunited by the return of Longstreet from the Blackwater. The corps did not seem quite itself without Dick Anderson's men, but its other divisions had undergone no change in leadership and were little diminished in number.

Besides these returning veterans, the army received during May three new brigades. The first of these was Julius Daniel's large if raw North Carolina brigade, which Harvey Hill exchanged for Colquitt's depleted command. Daniel was unknown to most officers of the Army of Northern Virginia, but he was of high standing in North Carolina. His brigade was assigned to Rodes's division, which Colquitt had left. The other accessions, which went to Heth's division, were the North Carolina brigade of Johnston Pettigrew and the Mississippi brigade of Joseph R. Davis. Pettigrew had the good will of many officers who had known him on the Peninsula in 1862. Joe Davis, a nephew of the President, on whose staff he had served for some months, was entirely without combat experience.

The bargaining that produced these latter troops would have appeared more appropriate among jealously cautious allies than among the officials of a Confederacy engaged in a life-and-death revolution. In the end, Pettigrew and Davis were sent to northern Virginia on condition that, temporarily, Micah Jenkins's and Robert Ransom's brigades were left in southern Virginia and North Carolina. This exchange, like that involving Daniel, was not wholly acceptable, and for the same reason: In the place of tested veterans it gave the Army of Northern Virginia troops of little experience in combat, and some officers whom Lee tactfully styled "uninstructed."

The Army of Northern Virginia now made ready to embark on the adventure of operating without Stonewall Jackson. The First Corps, though reduced to three divisions, had its command well organized. Its divisional and brigade leadership was more uniform and seasoned than that of either of the other corps. Ewell was the greatest question mark of the Second Corps. Under him, Early had able brigade commanders with the possible exception of the valiant but unmilitary Extra Billy Smith. The famous division of Jackson had a new chief in Allegheny Johnson and four new brigade leaders, three of whom were strangers to the men. Rodes's division, less sharply organized, was under a man whose recent promotion had come after a clear demonstration of his capacity for command. The weakness of Second Corps command could be stated explicitly: Of the seventeen corps positions of rank, seven only were filled by men who, at the rank prescribed by regulations, had led the same or corresponding units at Chancellorsville.

In Hill's Third Corps there was a new lieutenant general, one major general, Pender, whose insignia was fresh, and one, Heth, whose divisional experience was of the shortest. Of thirteen brigades, eight were under experienced general officers of appropriate rank, two were led by brigadiers without combat experience at their grade, and three were in the care of senior colonels.

To summarize the army as a whole, as of June 6, two of the three corps commanders, Ewell and Hill, had to prove their ability to handle the larger forces entrusted to them. Of the nine divisional chiefs, four could be counted as definitely experienced—McLaws, Anderson, Hood, and Early. Two, Johnson and Pender, were new in their posts; two, Rodes and Heth, had been briefly in acting command of divisions; and one, Pickett, though administering a division for some months, had never led it in combat. Among the thirty-seven brigadier generals of infantry, twenty-five had a measure of experience at their grade, though neither in experience nor in ability were they uniform. Six brigades had new leaders; six others were in charge of colonels. Even with these men of inexperience or doubtful capacity, it was an army command of much prowess under a superlative general-in-chief . . . but it lacked Jackson.

The troops were pleased with the prospect of maneuver. They had enjoyed their weeks of rest after Chancellorsville, and believed themselves stronger than before battle. They had defeated Hooker at his strongest when two of their divisions under Longstreet were absent. Even though the fighting in the tangled Wilderness had cost them Jackson, they had added so spectacular a victory to so long a record of success that they now considered themselves invincible. Their commanding general, appreciative of valor but usually conservative, was of his soldiers' sanguine mind.

All the spring there had been talk of another offensive north of the Potomac to feed the army and to wrest the initiative from the Federals. The strategical problem was difficult, but nearly all the Confederates were convinced that Lee would find a way of carrying the war into the enemy's country. Said the new major general, Dorsey Pender: "All feel that something is brewing and that Gen. Lee is not going to wait all the time for them to come to him."[18]

The first days of June brought confirmation of these predictions. On the morning of June 3, McLaws's division quietly left its camps and started for Culpeper; that night, Heth's men got orders to take the place of Rodes's pickets; by mid-morning of the fourth, Rodes's camps were deserted; then on the fifth, Early and Johnson started up the Rappahannock. Soon the new Third Corps alone was left. Culpeper, men whispered, was the immediate objective, and after that—Maryland? Pennsylvania? A victory that would decide the war? Another and worse Sharpsburg? Dorsey Pender answered for the army—"Have no fear we shall not beat them . . . !"[19]

2. Much Pomp Ends in Humiliation

Jeb Stuart was to blame. All his enemies said that. The advance of the Army of Northern Virginia in June would not have met that humiliating initial check if the chief of cavalry had not been so intent on displaying his increased force. He now had five cavalry brigades of 9,536 officers and men—more than ever he had commanded. Lee must see them, Lee and all the young ladies of the Piedmont region of Virginia.

When Stuart moved his headquarters from Orange to Culpeper, he set his staff to work on plans for such a pageant as the continent never had witnessed. The stage for it fairly thrust itself upon him: It was a long wide field in the vicinity of Brandy Station, between Culpeper and the Rappahannock. A hillock would excel as a reviewing stand. The field was so close to the Orange and Alexandria Railroad that a halted train would offer seats for spectators. Stuart pitched his tents on Fleetwood Hill, overlooking Brandy Station, and set June 5 as the date. Each staff officer must provide himself a new uniform and must see to it that mounts were flawless. A ball must be arranged in Culpeper the night before the review and, perhaps, another after the cavalry had shown its magnificence.[20]

From Charlottesville and nearer towns on the O. & A. came streams of guests. Wagons and ambulances distributed beauty at every hospitable gate. All preliminaries were auspicious; the ball on the evening of the fourth was praised by a newspaper reporter as a "gay and dazzling scene." One disappointment there was, one only, but it was serious: The commanding general of the army was concerned with some difficult matters of logistics and would not be present for the grand review.

On the bright morning of June 5, Stuart and his staff started for Brandy Station. Heralded by buglers and welcomed by throngs, the cavalcade rode triumphantly upon the field and started down the front of a line of horses that extended for a mile and a half. On its flank were twenty-four of Beckham's guns. As the reviewing party reached each brigadier, he and his staff fell in behind. The cavalcade swept to the left flank and then, in regulation manner, rode the length of the line in rear. Stuart then took his position on the knoll, beneath a gallantly flying Confederate flag. Again the bugles sounded, and the troopers moved out in columns of squadrons. During the second "march past," a hundred yards from the reviewing stand the men spurred to a gallop, drew sabers, raised the "rebel yell," and dashed by the admiring Jeb at a furious gait. Beckham opened with blank charges as if to repel attack. For the ladies the gallop, the excitement, the foxhunters' call from nearly 10,000 throats were overwhelming. Everyone went home to praise the cavalry and its commander. That night there was another ball, danced on the greensward to the crackling of great fires.

Stuart's orders on June 7: Prepare for review tomorrow by the commanding general on the same field at Brandy Station. Lee had arrived and wished to see in what condition were officers and men for the next hard adventure across the Potomac. Stuart now had the satisfaction of welcoming formally the notables he had missed at the first review. General Lee rode magnificently on the field. After him came Longstreet and the other leading figures of the First and Second corps. The review went well enough as far as it went. Stuart could see that Lee observed keenly and proudly the marching squadrons, but there was no gallop, no yelling, no service of the guns. Lee forbade that. The horses needed their flesh, the gunners their powder. Let the march past be at a walk. If tame in comparison with the display of the fifth, it was still a vast show of strength.[21]

With the review over, equipage was packed for an early move on the morning of June 9. Lee was about to start Ewell and Longstreet for the Potomac; the cavalry were to cross the Rappahannock to cover the march. On the night of the eighth, at his headquarters on Fleetwood Hill, Stuart made final preparations. Across the Rappahannock not a campfire was visible to suggest that the enemy's cavalry had sensed the movement of Lee's army and begun reconnaissance. Postings for the night, in anticipation of the morning march, placed Grumble Jones's pickets at Beverly Ford, a major crossing of the Rappahannock about a mile and a half above the O. & A. railroad bridge. Kelly's Ford, four miles down the Rappahannock from the railroad crossing, was in the care of Beverly Robertson's pickets. The dispositions of Stuart's five brigades were made in the belief that the front was safe and the enemy remote.

Just at the cool, hazy dawn of June 9, Stuart on Fleetwood Hill heard the sound of firing from the direction of Beverly Ford. The enemy must be crossing. There could be no other explanation. Soon a dashing courier on a panting horse brought the news from Grumble Jones: The Federals were on the south side of the Rappahannock at Beverly Ford and were advancing in strength. Jeb immediately directed that the wagon trains be started for Culpeper and prepared to reinforce Grumble.[22]

The Federals began to deploy, but before they opened an attack Stuart received two messages that the enemy was crossing at Kelly's Ford, four miles downstream. He sent reinforcements in that direction and summoned all his other troopers to the front and upstream flank of the Federals who had moved toward Brandy Station by way of Beverly Ford. The situation seemed entirely in hand when Grumble Jones sent word of a threatened attack on the right flank by troops that had crossed below Beverly Ford. Stuart's pride and his dislike of Grumble probably shaped his answer: "Tell General Jones to attend to the Yankees in his front, and I'll watch the flanks." Jones's reply was: "So he thinks they ain't coming, does he? Well, let him alone; he'll damn soon see for himself."[23]

About noon a courier spurred to Stuart from Major McClellan, who had been left at Fleetwood: Hostile cavalry in strength, the staff officer reported, was almost at Brandy! Stuart had confidence in Henry McClellan, but he was incredulous. He told an aide to "ride back there and see what this foolishness is about!" The man had hardly gone when a headquarters clerk, Frank Deane, galloped up. "General," cried Deane, "the Yankees are at Brandy!"

In mocking confirmation, there rolled down from the hill the sound of rapid fire. Stuart immediately ordered two regiments of Jones's brigade back to Fleetwood, and started after them himself. As soon as he got out of the woods his mood must have become grim. A long column was in sight, mounting Fleetwood Hill boldly. Stuart snapped out orders for one and then a second of Wade Hampton's regiments to ride at a gallop for the heights—a superfluous order, as it proved, because the South Carolinian had seen the Union troopers and already was withdrawing to meet them.[24]

A fine situation, surely, this was for the day after a review. The most distinguished regiments of the cavalry division caught in the rear while engaged heavily in front! Nothing but hard, stand-up combat would win the field now. Stuart saw that all his cavalry and all his artillery must be massed on Fleetwood if he was to hold it against an adversary who, most incredibly, had assumed the offensive. Repulse of a sharp attack by the 6th Virginia demonstrated that the Federals were in strength and, prisoners said, were of the division of David Gregg, who had crossed at Kelly's Ford.

As the Federals surged forward, Confederates who looked from Fleetwood saw a sight that made veterans catch their breath and lift their hats

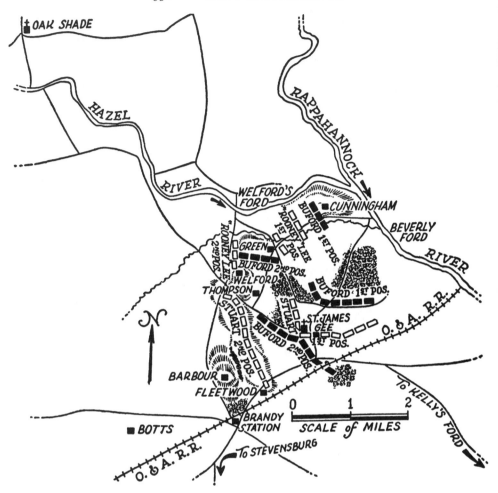

The battlefield of Brandy Station.

in admiration. Hampton's regiments were coming up in magnificent order. On the right was Cobb's Legion under Pierce Young; in support was Black's 1st South Carolina; on the left were the 1st North Carolina and the Jeff Davis Legion. Sweeping in splendor across the field abreast of Hampton's column was Hart's horse artillery. The enemy threw themselves at the column and almost immediately there was a rolling melee, confused by smoke and dust; but when this cleared, Hampton still was advancing. The enemy was falling back toward Brandy Station. To clear the ground adjoining the station became the next task of Stuart. This was undertaken in a charge by the 11th Virginia of Jones's brigade.

This charge would have removed Stuart's last concern had not a new development come. All day he had been on the lookout for Federal infantry, assigning Captain Blackford the special duty of watching for any evidence of their presence. "It was not long," said Blackford, "before I found them with my powerful field glasses deployed as skirmishers. . . ." On Stuart's orders, Blackford rode six miles to Longstreet's headquarters, whence the intelligence was communicated to Lee. Rodes's division was started for Brandy.[25]

While Rodes was marching, Stuart's position on Fleetwood was being consolidated. Hampton, Jones, and all the horse artillery were deploying on the ridge. Rooney Lee held position on the left of Jones. Against the front of these three brigades, increased to four by the late arrival of Fitz Lee's brigade, the Federal under Gregg were wise enough not to shatter their weary squadrons. Before Rodes got to Brandy, the enemy was withdrawing toward Beverly Ford. The Battle of Brandy Station was over. A mellow glow after sunset, a "burnished and glowing horizon," ended in splendor an ugly day. Stuart's casualties had been 523. Those of the Federals subsequently were ascertained to be 936, of whom 486 were prisoners of war, and three guns lost.[26]

By his campfire, Stuart had to ask how Gregg had eluded Beverly Robertson, who had been sent toward Kelly's Ford for the very purpose of blocking an advance from that direction. The facts, as finally developed, were that when Robertson learned that the Federals were moving toward Brandy and the railroad by roads to the south of him, he made what Stuart subsequently pronounced the wrong decision. Had he sent part of his force southward with promptness, he might have caught Gregg on the flank. Instead, Robertson reasoned that he could not divide his small brigade or abandon the road he was covering. He remained where he was, and was not at any time actively engaged.[27]

A report more distressing than Robertson's was made by the 2nd South Carolina and 4th Virginia, which had been sent to Stevensburg, five and a half miles south of Brandy Station. In a confused, far-spreading fight, their 500 men had held off a column under Colonel Alfred N. Duffié, but they had paid with the loss of valuable officers. Lieutenant Colonel Frank Hampton of the 2nd South Carolina, Wade Hampton's brother, was mortally wounded. Captain Will Farley, Stuart's legendary chief scout, had a leg severed by the shot of a Federal fieldpiece. "He called me to him," wrote a comrade, "and pointing to the leg that had been cut off by the ball, . . . asked me to bring it to him. I did so. He took it, pressed it to his bosom as one would a child, and said, smiling—'It is an old friend, gentlemen, and I do not wish to part from it'. . . . Courteously, even smilingly, he nodded his head to us as the men bore him away. He died within a few hours." Other reliable scouts Stuart had and still others he developed, but there never was in the cavalry division another scout who in every quality was the peer of Farley.[28]

Jeb Stuart was humiliated more deeply than ever he had been in his campaigning, humiliated and, if not disillusioned, disconcerted. The Federal cavalry never had battled so hard and never had stood up so stubbornly. Most of the day they had held the offensive and had given as good as they had taken. Stuart had fought his heaviest battle after thunderous, demonstrative reviews of more troops than ever had been under his command. Instead of a thrilling victory that every man in the army would have to acclaim, there was sarcastic talk of an exposed rear and of a surprise!

The commanding general understood. Stuart was sure of that. Fairminded men took into account the final victory though they did not ignore the surprise. Stuart never saw what his West Point classmate, Dorsey Pender, wrote, but he must have heard echoes of similar comment. Said Pender: "I suppose it is all right that Stuart should get all the blame, for when anything handsome is done he gets all the credit. A bad rule either way. He however retrieved the surprise by whipping them in the end."[29]

The *Examiner* in Richmond harped on "the late affair at Brandy Station." Its words stuck in Stuart's mind and rankled: "tournament . . . vain and weak-headed officers . . . surprise . . . reorganization . . . more earnestness on the part of officers." Jeb would show whether the criticism was justified![30]

CHAPTER 25

Across the Potomac Again

1. As If a Second Jackson Had Come

Stuart's humiliation in the Battle of Brandy Station did not delay the advance of the Army of Northern Virginia toward the Potomac. On June 10, Ewell's Second Corps set the pace at a brisk staccato, and the divisions of Allegheny Johnson and Early reached the vicinity of Winchester on the thirteenth. Their prey was a Federal force of an estimated 6,000 to 8,000 men under Major General Robert H. Milroy. The division of Rodes was directed to Berryville, where it was hoped he could capture an outpost of 1,800. With Rodes moved the 1,500 cavalry of Albert G. Jenkins, newcomers from western Virginia.

Reconnaissance by Ewell on the morning of June 14 showed no Federal troops anywhere near except west of Winchester, on ground from which Ewell had planned to launch his attack against the known fortified positions to the north and northwest. Old Bald Head did not swear at this discovery. He had broken that bad habit, of which Mrs. Ewell had disapproved. Oaths did not become a professed Christian, successor to the sainted Jackson. So, instead of oaths, the crippled Ewell drove to Early's position.

Old Jube had fight in his black eyes. He had seen the Federals, damn 'em, on that high ground he coveted. Their chain of fortifications was strong, *but,* he explained, it was vulnerable! He pointed to Little North Mountain. From its cover, said Early, he believed he could silence the guns in the westernmost of the forts; and that commanded the main defense, what the Confederates called the Flag Fort. He would run out his guns, capture the west fort, then drive the Federals out of the Flag Fort.[1]

Old Bald Head listened, surveyed the ground, pondered, assented promptly. He saw to it that Johnson occupied the enemy while Jube marched by a concealed, circuitous route to Little North Mountain. All this was done as briskly and with as much decision as if Jackson himself were directing the movement. By six o'clock Dick Ewell was awaiting the attack and jumping about more impatiently than ever. Early snapped a command. His artillerists bent their backs to the gun wheels. Out into the open rolled twenty pieces. Almost at the same instant, all twenty guns roared, to the amazement of the startled Federals in the west fort. But there was scant delay in meeting the challenge of Early's guns. Sixteen shells to the minute the Federals soon were sending.

It was a gallant but not too long a duel. In forty-five minutes the Federal fire died away. Now, Hays! In a few minutes Hays was through the abatis, his cheering men were leaping over the parapet, they had the guns, they were turning them. The fort was Hays's! The bluecoats were running, taking refuge in the Flag Fort. Dick Ewell, his field-glasses glued to his eyes, thought he saw Jube among the first to mount the parapet. "Hurrah for the Louisiana boys! There's Early! I hope the old fellow won't be hurt!" As he spoke he felt a thud, a shock. He had been hit squarely in the chest, but by a spent ball, which inflicted no worse hurt than a bruise.[2]

It troubled Ewell not at all. His mind was on the probable effect of the capture of the west fort. It might induce Milroy to retreat under protecting darkness. Then, by the bones of the mighty Stonewall, the enemy must be pursued! Milroy would have to leave Winchester via the turnpike to the north. Johnson must march in the night with his division and get across the enemy's line of withdrawal. If Milroy did not retreat, Johnson must be sufficiently close to Winchester to have a hand at dawn in supporting Early.

By 3:30 A.M. on the fifteenth the head of Allegheny Johnson's column was near Stephenson's Depot on the Winchester and Potomac Railway, close by the turnpike. Johnson with his staff pushed on to reconnoiter. In a moment they heard the neighing of horses and the mumble of voices, then pistol shots from a dim file encountered in the road. Milroy it must be—he must be bagged! Maryland Steuart should go to the right, Nicholls's Louisianians should extend to the left. Dement's battery would be in support. Quick the deployment was, but none too quick, because now, with a cheer and heavy volleys, the Federals determined to cut their way through to the Harper's Ferry road. Such an attack was gore and glory for Old Allegheny. He waved his long walking stick and shouted encouragement to his troops.

Milroy gave thought to changing his tactics and trying to envelop the flanks, but his chance vanished when Walker came up on the right. The commander of the Stonewall Brigade had not received notice of the division's march, and had not started from Winchester till midnight. Hastening forward, he formed on Steuart's flank. Two regiments of Nicholls's brigade in reserve were brought up simultaneously. The timing and the placing of these reinforcements were as perfect as a textbook example. Milroy with 200 or 300 cavalry got away. The other Federal troops, confused by the swirling melee, began to surrender. Soon the prisoners numbered more than 2,300. Old Allegheny himself could not refrain from the pursuit, and asserted afterward that he had taken thirty prisoners "with his opera glass."³

Back in Winchester, almost in the words of Jackson, Ewell called on the troops to "unite . . . in returning thanks to our Heavenly Father for the signal success which has crowned the valor of this command." Chaplains were directed to hold religious services, but as the day was Monday, Ewell thriftily enjoined that thanks be returned "at such times as may be most convenient." He lingered long enough in Winchester to attend a celebration on the afternoon of the sixteenth, when rejoicing soldiers ran up at the main fort, proudly renamed Fort Jackson, a flag made from captured Stars and Stripes. The provost marshals had corralled by that hour a total of 3,358 prisoners. Ordnance officers had the whole of Milroy's artillery—four 20-pounder Parrotts, seventeen 3-inch rifles, two 24-pounder howitzers. More than that scarcely could have been asked in compensation for Confederate losses that did not exceed 269. "This," said Jed Hotchkiss, "has been one of the most complete successes of the war; our men behaved splendidly." Honors were equally divided. The general plan had been that of Ewell, who knew the ground thoroughly; the execution Early's and Johnson's.⁴

Enough of flag-raising and yelling and felicitation! The mission of the Second Corps was not in Winchester but across the Potomac. Rodes already was there with his division. He had started for Berryville on June 13 in hopes of capturing that post, but his cavalry commander, Jenkins, was unaccustomed to operating with infantry that marched as fast as Rodes's men did. Through poor cooperation the Federals escaped from Berryville. Much the same thing happened at Martinsburg, except for the capture of five guns. Jenkins pushed boldly across the Potomac and headed for Pennsylvania. Rodes followed on the sixteenth as far as Williamsport on the Maryland side of the river, where he was to remain till the other divisions overtook him.

Ewell did not keep Rodes waiting long. Sunset on June 19 found the van of the Second Corps near Hagerstown and the rear on the southern shore of the Potomac. Jackson himself would not have been ashamed of that advance in June weather. Through all of this Ewell was brisk and diligent. Lee told him if food could be found, the army might follow him into the enemy's country: "If Harrisburg comes within your means, capture it." The strategy behind these orders was Lee's, not Ewell's, but the aim of the operations was plain: Lee was hoping to lure the Army of the Potomac out of Virginia and to subsist his own forces during the summer on the rich abundance of Pennsylvania. He also sought an opportunity of striking a blow and of compelling the Federal administration to retain in the East, or to recall, troops designated for operations elsewhere. By a vigorous campaign of maneuver, the enemy's plans for the hot months might be disarranged. Virginia might be free of an enemy who destroyed what he did not consume.[5]

Ewell's part in this was understood, from the outset, to be essentially that of collecting horses and cattle and flour. As it concerned him, the enterprise was primarily an offensive for the benefit of the commissary. Later instructions were more soldierly, and the suggestion that he might be able to capture Harrisburg became in Ewell's eager mind orders to do so. On the lines of advance the troops encountered no organized enemy, but as they moved deeper into the enemy's country and took sleek horses and fat cattle, faces grew sullen and words were sharp. Ewell himself noted the acid in the air and wrote teasingly to a cousin whose mother had been born in York, Pennsylvania: "It is like a renewal of Mexican times to enter a captured town. The people look as sour as vinegar and, I have no doubt, would gladly send us all to Kingdom come if they could." The fatness of the land amazed the Confederates. Said Jed Hotchkiss: "The land is full of everything and we have an abundance." General needs were met by forced purchase or by formal requisition on the towns.[6]

Daily as the columns advanced, Old Bald Head studied how to scour the country for the supplies Lee expected him to collect. He was instructed to keep one division east of the mountains, to deter the Federal army, if it crossed the Potomac, from moving westward before Lee could concentrate. These troops were to undertake to destroy the bridge across the Susquehanna at Wrightsville, a short distance northeast of York. While this was in process of execution, Ewell reached Carlisle on June 27. Early, with the easternmost of the columns, proceeded to Gettysburg, where he stampeded a regiment of raw Pennsylvania militia, and the next morning advanced toward York.

Extra Billy Smith had his "tooting fellows," as he called his bandsmen, play "Yankee Doodle" as he proceeded in his triumph through the streets of York on June 28. He bowed, he smiled, he displayed so genial and courteous a mien that by the time he reached the center of town he had elicited some cheers. He halted the column and directed the men to stack arms, and loosed a bantering, half-joking flow of eloquence to the effect that warm weather in Virginia had led his men to "take an outing" in Pennsylvania. He was in the flood of this when a volley of oaths roared down the street as Jube Early sought wrathfully to make his way through the ranks that Smith's deliverance had halted. At last, with many weird explosions of unpremeditated profanity, Old Jube reached the still-declaiming Smith. "General Smith," Early demanded, "what the devil are you about, stopping the head of the column in this cursed town?" Smith's answer was naive and unruffled: "Having a little fun, General, which is good for all of us, and at

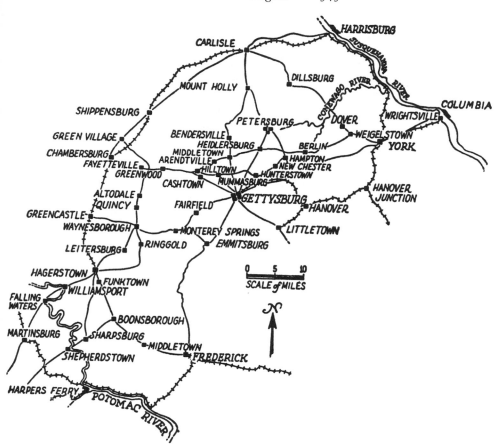

Routes from the Potomac to Carlisle, Harrisburg, Gettysburg, and York.

the same time teaching these people something that will be good for them and won't do us any harm."

There was no quarreling with a man who talked in that manner. Early got the column moving, made requisition of cash in the sum of $28,000, and, before night, rode on to the Wrightsville bridge over the Susquehanna. But before he could seize both ends of the long bridge the enemy set it afire. Early was disappointed. He had been planning ambitiously to cross the river there, cut the Pennsylvania Central Railroad, and assail Harrisburg from the rear while Ewell attacked from the south.[7]

Ewell's adventure, too, was approaching a climax far different from that which Old Bald Head had planned or wished. As he had approached Carlisle he continued to collect cattle. The number sent back for the subsistence of the two corps following him totaled 3,000. Ewell was pleased, but he was more interested in reaching the state capital. The day he entered Carlisle, he sent Jenkins and the corps engineer to reconnoiter the defenses of Harrisburg. While he awaited their report, he took part in the raising of the Stars and Bars over the famous old Carlisle Barracks, where so many cavalrymen had served. Ewell even spoke a few words on the occasion—he was no orator—but his mind remained on Harrisburg. If Jenkins's reconnaissance was favorable, he was resolved to start his infantry the next day for the Susquehanna. The new month must yield a new prize, the handsomest the Confederacy yet had won. Jenkins's report on June 29 was encouraging. Orders were given Rodes to start for Harrisburg during the afternoon.[8]

Expectation in Carlisle was mounting to excitement when, from the south, there arrived a headquarters courier. He brought a letter written in haste at Lee's order: The Federal army, said the commanding general, was reported to have crossed the Potomac and reached Frederick, Maryland. Ewell must move southward and rejoin the other corps. The married and converted Ewell did not swear, but he did not pretend to conceal his displeasure at being compelled to forgo an advance on Harrisburg. He started Johnson for Chambersburg and dispatched orders for Rodes and Early.

After Johnson had gone some miles, there came new orders from Lee: Instead of concentrating at Chambersburg, the army should assemble around Gettysburg. There, east of the mountains, it seemed preferable to challenge the enemy. This change of unpleasant orders upset Ewell still further. Lee put on him a responsibility of choice concerning a matter regarding which he was ignorant. Lee said: "When you come to Heidlersburg, you can either move directly on Gettysburg or turn down to Cashtown." Ewell was disturbed that Lee should have made that discretionary. Hotchkiss had to write in his diary: "The General was quite testy and hard to please, because disappointed, and had every one flying around. I got up in the night to answer questions and make him a map."

Ewell inflicted no hardships on the townspeople of Carlisle before departing. The worst that was done was what Johnson might have termed a work of necessity. Many of Old Allegheny's men were barefoot; his prisoners were well-shod. Johnson had lined up his captured Pennsylvania militiamen in their new Federal uniforms and relieved them of their shoes and socks for the benefit of his soldiers. "Johnson said they were going home," John Casler recalled, "and could get other shoes quicker than he could, as he had work for his men to do." Ed Moore found the prisoners "greatly crestfallen" at the prospect of returning to "wives and little ones at home, after having sallied forth so valiantly in their defense. How embarrassing bare feet would be instead of the expected trophies of war!"[9]

To Heidlersburg, on the road to Gettysburg, Dick Ewell made his way before sundown on June 30. This march had a disconcerting end. In a note delivered by another headquarters courier, Ewell was told again by Lee to move to Cashtown or to Gettysburg, as circumstances might dictate. Ewell received also a message from A. P. Hill, who said that he was at Cashtown and that the enemy's cavalry and probably other troops in undetermined strength had been observed that day at Gettysburg. Ewell was perplexed. Rodes, Early, and Isaac Trimble, who was newly arrived as a volunteer aide, were called to informal council.

Lee's orders were read again and again. On them Ewell commented sharply. He was as caustic as he had been in the spring of 1862 in his criticism of Jackson's mysterious orders. The more he talked, the more did he confuse the issue. Trimble alone had a suggestion based on the realities. He had seen Lee on the twenty-seventh and discussed with him the geography of that part of Pennsylvania. Lee intended, said Trimble, to assail the advance of the enemy. If Federals were in Gettysburg, Lee would want Ewell there. Ewell fumed and protested, but decided nothing that night.[10]

If Ewell was disturbed, his chief was not. Nor were Old Bald Head's division commanders. They were more than satisfied with their new leader. After three weeks of high distinction and well-nigh flawless performance, his first period of semi-independent service as head of the Second Corps was about to end. Twenty-eight guns and close to 4,000 prisoners had been captured. Besides all the food, mounts, and quartermasters' supplies seized and issued to Ewell's own men, some 5,000 barrels of flour, in addition to the 3,000 cattle, had been located for the chief commissary of the army. A trainload of ordnance and medical stores had been dispatched from Chambersburg. All this had been achieved with losses that scarcely exceeded 300 and with straggling so limited that it found no mention in reports. "I never before or afterward saw the men so buoyant," one young soldier testified. Without storming or scolding Ewell had directed wisely and executed promptly. His first operations as corps commander seemed to duplicate, if not to outdo, the cherished accomplishments of the dead Stonewall. Except for his grumbling over discretionary orders, he at no time during the campaign had given the least evidence of any lack of decision. As Dick Ewell approached Gettysburg, almost every Confederate soldier would have asserted that a fitting successor to Jackson had been found.[11]

2. Longstreet Develops a Theory

The second of Lee's lieutenants whose state of mind was to influence the operations in Pennsylvania had shared two victories and one drawn battle after the army in August 1862 left Richmond. In all three of these contests, Second Manassas, Sharpsburg, and Fredericksburg, James Longstreet had been most fortunate. He had been able to take a defensive position and to receive the enemy's assaults. At Second Manassas the attack had been on Jackson, but Longstreet's counterstroke had been demolishing. Narrowly the following month, on the heights above the Antietam, Old Pete had beaten back the onslaught of the enemy and had recrossed the Potomac with all his guns and most of his wounded. Fredericksburg, from his position, had been a triumph of the defensive.

On this foundation of experience, Longstreet reared a tactical theory that if the Confederates could be maneuvered to commanding ground, close to their adversaries, the Federals always could be induced to attack. Longstreet built up, also, a conviction that a small Southern force, comparatively, could repulse any charge the Union army could deliver. Most fully he subscribed to Jackson's observation: "My men sometimes fail to take a position, but to defend one, never!"

While he was developing this theory of a superior tactical defensive, Longstreet watched intently the operations in Tennessee and the Gulf States. He followed the reports of Braxton Bragg's withdrawal to Tullahoma after the battle at Stone's River, and he doubtless wondered where the Confederacy could find the reinforcements for Pemberton at Vicksburg. In speculating on the future employment of the divided forces of Pemberton and Bragg, who were under Joseph E. Johnston's titular command, Longstreet made his first-known venture in grand strategy.

There was nothing sensational about the plan he evolved. It simply was to rely boldly upon the defensive power of the Army of Northern Virginia, and to utilize the inner lines of the Confederacy. He concluded that half of Lee's forces could remain defiantly on the line of the Rappahannock, and the other half could reinforce Bragg and help in destroying Rosecrans. Then all the strength the Confederacy commanded in a wide region could be turned against the Federal divisions mustering to capture the strategic town of Vicksburg. A part, at least, of this plan its author communicated to Lee on the twenty-third of January. One implication of this theory was that in March Lee could afford to dispatch the two remaining divisions of the First Corps to Southside Virginia where Longstreet was operating with Pickett and Hood. Lee could not agree to march additional troops to the vicinity of Suffolk and leave no more than one corps of infantry, with some cavalry, between Richmond and the enemy. Longstreet was not offended; nor was he shaken in his conviction that he had a sound plan.[12]

When Longstreet was summoned to evacuate the Suffolk front and return to the Rappahannock, there was time for a stopover in Richmond.

That brief halt at the Confederate capital set another stone of conviction on the path of James Longstreet. The secretary of war, James A. Seddon, was a man who had great art in making his guests feel that their opinions were desired on public questions. When Longstreet called on him, the secretary welcomed him and, among other things, spoke of the difficulty of collecting troops and supplies in Mississippi for the relief of Vicksburg.

The conversation led Longstreet to present the theory he had been cherishing since January: Rather than attempting the direct relief of Vicksburg, he said, Johnston might take his force at Jackson, Mississippi, and advance to Tullahoma, where Bragg's army was awaiting a move by Rosecrans. Simultaneously, Longstreet could take his corps or the two divisions of it then returning to Lee and proceed by rail to Tullahoma. These two converging columns would make Johnston strong enough to crush Rosecrans and then would permit a march for Ohio. As soon as the North faced the prospect of invasion, Longstreet continued, Grant would be recalled from Vicksburg to defend Ohio. The whole operation, Longstreet concluded, simply meant the employment of inner lines, which were the sole means by which the South could "equalize the contest." Seddon mildly suggested that the objection to the plan was the manifest one that it weakened too heavily the army defending Richmond. In any event, gratifying it was to Longstreet to be asked for counsel by the secretary on what was the most fateful question of strategy the government faced in the summer of 1863.[13]

On the ninth of May Longstreet came back in satisfaction of spirit to Fredericksburg heights. His mind was full of his plan for a defensive in the East and an offensive from Tennessee with Joe Johnston, whom he regarded as the greatest soldier of the Confederacy. Longstreet believed in this strategy but had no immediate opportunity of presenting it. He found his chief in acutest distress because of the illness of Jackson. The next afternoon Jackson died, and by this tragedy Longstreet became the most conspicuous of Lee's surviving lieutenants. None so surely could present all his views to the commanding general.

While Lee mourned over Jackson, weighed the merits of possible successors, and considered the reorganization of the army into three corps, Longstreet had time for an examination of the tactics and strategy of Chancellorsville. To the contest he applied the theory he had advocated in dispatches to Lee—"to stand behind our intrenched lines and await the return of my troops from Suffolk." So considered, Longstreet did not approve Lee's operation. The point to be stressed is not that Longstreet was correct or incorrect in his appraisal, but that in making it he showed himself an unqualified advocate of a tactical defensive by the Army of Northern Virginia. Its strategy might be offensive, but not its tactics.[14]

In this state of mind, when he found Lee free to hear him, Longstreet submitted his plan for the reinforcement of Bragg, an offensive against Rosecrans, and the attempted invasion of Ohio as a means of forcing the recall of Grant from Vicksburg. The proposal was given unbiased consideration by Lee. In the end, it was rejected. Face-to-face with Hooker's army, which numerically was much superior, Lee did not feel that he safely could divide his forces. The alternative, so far as it concerned Vicksburg, was for Johnston to reinforce Pemberton instead of sending help to Bragg for an advance against Rosecrans. As for the Army of Northern Virginia, what better service could it render the other Confederate armies and their common cause than to invade the North and threaten Washington?

Longstreet frankly opposed such an offensive. He argued; he restated the case for his own plan; he pointed out the difficulties of an advance in the enemy's country. When he saw that Lee had reached a final decision on the larger question of strategy, the argument was turned to tactics. In detail, Longstreet reviewed the theory he had formulated. He recorded later: "I suggested that, after piercing Pennsylvania and menacing Washington, we should choose a strong position, and force the Federals to attack us. . . . I recalled to [Lee] the battle of Fredericksburg . . . when, with a few thousand men, we hurled the whole Federal army back, crippling and demoralizing it, with trifling loss to our own troops. . . ."

To this argument, as he subsequently admitted, Longstreet held with "great persistency." He did not find his chief in opposition. Lee agreed with the principle, though he never had any thought of committing himself to a tactical policy that was to be applied regardless of circumstances. To Lee's mind, any such commitment would have been a negation of strategy. Longstreet mistook courtesy for consent and believed that Lee had pledged himself to defensive tactics though the strategy might be offensive. The Battle of Fredericksburg, Longstreet kept saying, was an example of what he hoped to achieve in Pennsylvania.[15]

After the advance of the army began, Longstreet had in mind the possibility that Lee might attack the enemy should an opening appear. Stuart's battle at Brandy Station made him especially apprehensive that Lee might follow up the advantage by attacking with heavy force this detachment of Federals. When Lee refrained from pursuing the Union cavalry, Longstreet told himself that Lee "had determined to make a defensive battle, and would not allow any casual advantage to precipitate a general engagement."

Cheerfully, then, on a flawlessly arranged march behind the Second Corps, Longstreet moved his troops toward the Potomac. His advance was without sensation, and on June 27 reached Chambersburg, Pennsylvania. The Third Corps was with the First; Ewell was at Carlisle. Stuart was detached, but as nothing had been heard from him, it was supposed that the Federal army still was in Virginia and that the Confederate cavalry was watching it. The troopers of Imboden had operated on the left of Ewell as he advanced toward the Susquehanna, but they, too, had disappeared. They were, in reality, resting idly at Hancock, Maryland, more than fifty miles southwest of Chambersburg. When this became known it was to provoke the wrath of Lee as did few events of the war. On June 27–28 it was assumed that the mounted forces were doing their full duty and that all was well; but there was uneasiness, almost exasperation, over the failure of the cavalry to send in any information of the enemy's movements.[16]

In this disagreeable state, when the army was in the dark, Longstreet put the Confederacy in his debt. While Old Pete had been at Suffolk, Secretary Seddon had dispatched to his headquarters a Mississippian of adventurous spirit named Henry T. Harrison, who offered to serve as a spy. All spies were suspected of being double traitors and giving the enemy as much information as they got from him; but Longstreet employed Harrison and found the man both active and trustworthy. Before the army left Culpeper, Longstreet directed him to go to Washington and glean intelligence. When Harrison asked where he should report on his return, Longstreet remarked evasively that headquarters of the First Corps were large enough for any intelligent man to find. Staff officer Sorrel noted that Longstreet "was very far from giving even to his trusted scout information as to his movements. But Harrison knew all the same; he knew pretty much everything that was going on."

Harrison disappeared; the army moved northward; on the night of June 28 the spy appeared at a Confederate outpost and was taken to headquarters, recognized, and escorted to Longstreet's tent. Harrison had news of first importance: The Federal army had left Virginia and moved north of the Potomac; at least two corps were close to Frederick; once more the command had been transferred. This time the new leader of the Army of the Potomac was Major General George Meade. In the absence of Stuart's cavalry, none of this information had reached army headquarters. Even if the cavalry had been at hand, some of the facts unearthed by Harrison might not have been discovered. Credit, then, was due Harrison and, indirectly, Longstreet. Corps commanders seldom employed spies, but Longstreet, with his usual care for detail, saw to it that his spies were well-chosen and diligent.

Harrison's report produced an immediate change in the dispositions of the army. In order to keep the enemy at maximum distance from the lines of supply, A. P. Hill was directed to move his corps east of the mountains. Longstreet was to follow. Pickett's division should be left on guard at

Chambersburg. On the thirtieth Hood and McLaws moved to Greenwood, where they remained for the night. Lee established his headquarters near Longstreet's. An English military observer wrote in his diary that June 30: "The relations between Lee and Longstreet are quite touching—they are almost always together. . . . I believe these two generals to be as little ambitious and as thoroughly unselfish as any men in the world."[17]

There was no difference between them as they approached the crisis of their cause. No difference there was, but—to repeat a fact soon to make history—each misunderstood the other's view of the course they were to follow: In Longstreet's mind, Lee was committed morally to a tactical defensive, which was Longstreet's own conception and, to his way of thinking, an essential of Confederate success. Lee never had intended to commit himself to that tactical policy and he did not know that Longstreet considered him so pledged.

3. THE PRICE OF 125 WAGONS

Different far from Longstreet's state of mind and different no less from Ewell's was that in which Jeb Stuart looked forward to a second invasion of the North. Ewell entered Pennsylvania with reputation much heightened, Stuart with fame impaired. Longstreet was resolved to justify a tactical theory, Stuart to vindicate his name as a leader. The slurs on Jeb in the press stung. The *Richmond Sentinel,* which spoke with some authority on military affairs, had cried: "Vigilance, vigilance, more vigilance, is the lesson taught us by the Brandy surprise. . . . Let all learn from it, from the major general down to the picket." It was said openly in the city that "Stuart's headquarters had been fired into before the enemy's presence was known," and that Stuart had been outgeneralled. The indignant whisper was that the surprise had occurred because Stuart and his officers were "rollicking, frolicking and running after girls." Surveying all this, the *Richmond Whig* concluded an editorial defense of the Beau Sabreur, "We shall be surprised if the gallant Stuart does not, before many days, make the enemy repent sorely the temerity that led them to undertake as bold and insulting a feat [as the advance on Brandy]."[18]

Stuart read, raged, and doubtless resolved that the *Whig's* prediction should be fulfilled. First must come opportunity. His immediate duty, though difficult, was the unspectacular one of screening Hill and Longstreet while they were moving toward the Potomac. He had to keep the enemy east of the Blue Ridge so that the northward march of the Confederate infantry down the Shenandoah Valley would not be interrupted. Clashes were frequent and furious though they usually were on a small scale. The bluecoated troopers under Alfred Pleasonton, David Gregg, and John Buford demonstrated that the vigor of the attack at Brandy Station was not accidental. They now were an experienced, confident, and well-led corps, scarcely resembling in anything but uniform the clumsy horsemen over whom Stuart's men had ridden in 1862. The day of easy Confederate cavalry triumphs was gone. All Stuart's men possessed of courage, resourcefulness, and endurance they needed in these fights around Aldie, Middleburg, and Upperville.

Stuart, fighting defensively, planned offensively. Now that all the infantry were west of the Blue Ridge, he reasoned that it would be possible to leave one or two brigades of cavalry to defend the gaps and with the remaining three to descend on the enemy and harass Hooker in any advance the Federals might make to parallel Lee's own. If Hooker crossed the Potomac, Stuart could do the same thing or could rejoin the army on its advance into Pennsylvania. This expedition could be started as soon as the Union cavalry withdrew from their inquisitive and persistent daily attacks.[19]

Jeb suggested such an operation to Lee and gained approval of the general idea. Longstreet, also, was favorable. The one basic stipulation made by Lee was that as soon as Stuart found that the Federals were moving into Maryland, the Confederate cavalry, too, must pass the Potomac and must cover the flank of the advancing Southern infantry. By the night of June 21 this much of the plan was accepted. On the twenty-second the Federals did not return to contest the roads to the mountain gaps. The country between Aldie and the Blue Ridge was secure; the task of screening the infantry was nearing completion.

That evening a courier brought Stuart a note from Longstreet, who enclosed a letter from the commanding general. Lee expressed concern lest the retirement of the Federal cavalry might mean that Hooker was stealing a march on the Confederate army and might get into Maryland before it did. Then Stuart read, "If you find that he is moving northward, and that two brigades can guard the Blue Ridge and take care of your rear, you can move with the other three into Maryland, and take position on General Ewell's right. . . ." Longstreet's covering note approved, if Stuart thought the cavalry could make the move successfully. The prospect, Longstreet went on, was that Stuart would be less apt to disclose the Confederate plan to the enemy if the cavalry crossed the Potomac in rear of the Federals. It would be well, the commander of the First Corps concluded, if Stuart delayed the start until certain he could move northward into Maryland in rear of the Unionists.[20]

A gracious Providence scarcely could have shaped opportunity more to

Stuart's wishes! On the morning of June 23, Jeb had his scouts search for the enemy. Reports were encouraging. Major John S. Mosby, the boldest and most responsible of partisan rangers, wrote that the enemy was inactive east of the Blue Ridge and was encamped over so wide an area that Stuart could push his way between two of the corps. All this information Stuart promptly forwarded to Lee. The intelligence developed a possible contingency not covered by orders: Mosby thought the Federal infantry had been stationary for almost a week. If they did not start an advance, new instructions were necessary. Stuart doubtless asked for them.

Late that rainy night Major McClellan awakened Stuart with a dispatch from army headquarters. It was from Lee, written at 5:00 P.M. in answer to Stuart's messages of the morning. Said the commander, in three sentences that were to weigh in the balance of a nation's destiny: "If General Hooker's army remains inactive, you can leave two brigades to watch him, and withdraw with the three others, but should he not appear to be moving northward, I think you had better withdraw this side of the mountains tomorrow night. . . . You will, however, be able to judge whether you can pass around their army without hindrance, doing them all the damage you can, and cross the river east of the mountains. In either case, after crossing the river, you must move on and feel the right of Ewell's troops, collecting information, provisions, &c." After giving general instructions for the cavalry to be left behind, Lee added, ". . . I think the sooner you cross into Maryland, after tomorrow [June 24], the better."[21]

This was language to chew and digest. If Hooker's army remained "inactive," then three brigades and presumably Jeb himself must return to the main army. The proviso was firm, but discretion was left. Stuart was free to determine whether he could "pass around" the Federal army "without hindrance." If he could do that, he could cross the river "east of the mountains."

Taken together, then, the instructions of June 22 and June 23 coupled two conditions for a crossing west of the mountains: If Hooker remained inactive *and* Stuart could not pass around Hooker's sprawling force unhindered, then three cavalry brigades must rejoin the main army and cross via Shepherdstown. That was displeasing to Stuart not only because it robbed him of independent adventure but also because it would throw his columns on congested roads. He reasoned that he had authority to cross east of the Blue Ridge even in the rear of the enemy, if this could be done "without hindrance." Jeb knew that this term was not intended to exclude contact with the enemy. Lee's letter of June 23 enjoined him to do the Federals "all the damage you can."

What was possible was permissible. That, as Stuart saw it, was the substance of his orders. He did not define "hindrance" rigidly in terms of days and hours. He did not realize that he would be hindered most seriously were he delayed in crossing the Potomac to "feel the right of Ewell" and collect information and provisions. Stuart summed up his interpretation of his orders when he said later: ". . . it was deemed practicable to move entirely in the enemy's rear, intercepting his communications with his base (Washington), and, inflicting damage upon his rear, to rejoin the army in Pennsylvania in time to participate in its actual conflicts."[22]

In the conviction that he could shape his route as opportunity required, Stuart on the twenty-fourth made his preparations. The men were to cook three days' rations to be carried on their persons. Horses, like men, must live off the land. Six fieldpieces, their caissons, and the ambulances were to be the only wheeled vehicles. Everything must be ready to move soon after midnight of June 24–25. Lee had said, "The sooner you cross into Maryland, after tomorrow, the better." Jeb would not lose a minute.

Orders were to take three brigades and leave two. The five among which choice had to be made were Hampton's, Fitz Lee's, Rooney Lee's, Grumble Jones's, and Beverly Robertson's. Duty in the Valley surely was less exacting than a long raid in the enemy's country would be. To watch the passes and clear the Valley was, moreover, the type of duty in which Grumble Jones was proficient. He was rated the best outpost officer in the cavalry division. Besides, he was the one officer, among all subordinates, with whom Stuart could not operate on friendly terms. Let Jones and his brigade remain. With him, Beverly Robertson could maneuver or wait. Everyone knew that Robertson was entirely unpredictable in battle. He would not be suited for the work that might be awaiting the Confederates north of the Potomac. The harder duty must be assigned the strongest units. Nothing should be done to break up the combination of Hampton and the Lees. They had shared numerous raids; they were a team and knew how to fight together.[23]

By nightfall of the twenty-fourth all instructions had been given. Thousands of troopers clattered into the rendezvous at Salem. The man whom Stuart most joyfully welcomed was Fitz Lee, returning to duty after a month's absence due to inflammatory rheumatism. His cousin, Rooney Lee, was recovering from a leg wound received at Brandy Station; in temporary command of the Third Brigade was its senior colonel, John R. Chambliss, a West Pointer, retired lieutenant of the old army, and a competent man who was learning rapidly.

With these brigadiers, old and new, Stuart got the column under way about 1:00 A.M. of the twenty-fifth. Passage through Bull Run Mountain was easy and unobserved, but on the familiar Warrenton-Centreville turnpike he soon encountered Hancock's II Corps. This mass of Federal infantry was moving north on almost the line of march that Stuart intended to follow. Such information as Stuart could collect from natives indicated that Union forces were still well to the east. A report of the movement of Hancock's corps was sent to Lee, but if Stuart that night debated whether he should turn back and cross the Potomac west of the Blue Ridge, he dropped no hint of it and asked no advice. Probabilities are that he gave no thought to withdrawal. The quickest, surest route would be southeastward and then northward. If the march were rapid enough, it would put the cavalry between the Federals and Washington . . . Washington! The very name itself was an argument for the downstream crossing![24]

On June 26 the three brigades moved east past Bristoe Station and Brentsville and then on a long northerly arc to a bivouac south of Wolf Run Shoals on the Occoquan. Nowhere on the march were any Federals encountered, but nowhere was any forage found. The country had been swept bare. Halts had to be called to graze the weakened animals. Orders had been to cross the Potomac as soon as practicable after the twenty-fourth. In more than fifty hours Stuart had covered but thirty-four miles. He still was at least two score miles from the nearest ford. The fast-moving cavalry had covered less ground in two days than the most laggard infantry would have accounted respectable. None of Stuart's companions recorded that he spoke on the twenty-seventh of any tardiness. He was interested far more in the news sent by his outposts that the Federals had disappeared from Wolf Run Shoals. That opened the way.

Onward the troopers toiled to the Orange and Alexandria Railroad at Fairfax Station, then to Fairfax Court House, where, to the infinite cheer of hungry boys, several sutlers' shacks were found, fallen upon, and emptied. Perhaps it was as much for the pleasure of the men as for the grazing of the horses that Stuart allowed a halt of several hours. Word came that the Army of the Potomac was converging on Leesburg and that the local defense troops were retiring to Washington. Now the best approach to the Potomac would be via the road between Alexandria and Leesburg that paralleled the river. At Dranesville the trail of the enemy was fresh. Federal campfires still were smouldering; Sedgwick's VI Corps, said the villagers, had marched off that morning in the direction of Leesburg. After reconnaissance and delay, the troopers and the guns crossed the Potomac without loss at Rowser's Ford. Stuart had been on the road seventy-two hours and still was on the southern edge of Maryland soil. He did not know where Lee was. All the information the cavalryman got was that the Army of the Potomac was en route to Frederick. In this state of affairs, Lee's instructions to take position on Ewell's right applied. Said Stuart: "I real-

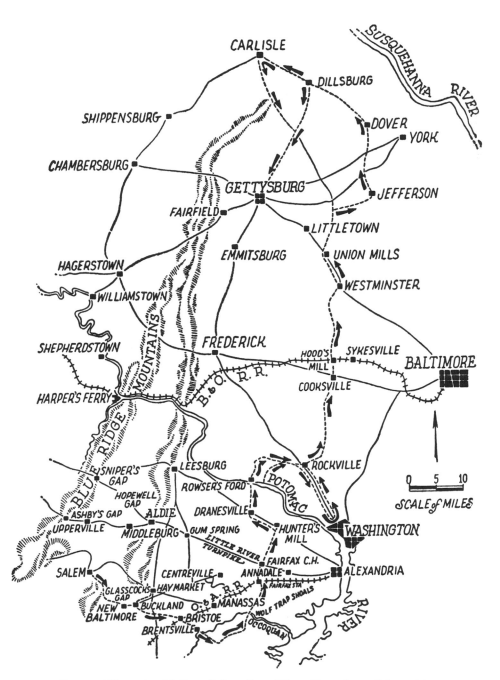

Route of Stuart's raid, from Salem, June 25, to Gettysburg, July 2, 1863.

ized the importance of joining our army in Pennsylvania, and resumed the journey northward early on the 28th."[25]

The intention was undeniable. So were three obstacles. The first was lack of information of Ewell's position. Lee had said that Ewell's right-hand column would move toward the Susquehanna by the Emmitsburg route, but with the Federals in Frederick, that road was one to be avoided. The alternative route to the Susquehanna was via Westminster, to the east. In making that movement, a second manifest obstacle to a swift march was the condition of men and mounts. They were worn and hungry and must be subsisted on what could be collected. Some delay was certain to result. The third obstacle to a prompt junction with Ewell developed almost in the hour the cavalry reached Maryland. It was the familiar one, and the most destructive foe of discipline—booty.

In Rockville the cavalrymen suddenly had the most lamentable good fortune that ever had fallen to their lot. Rockville, as it chanced, was on the direct supply line between Washington and Hooker's army, and toward the town, Stuart learned, a Federal wagon train was moving. All he had to do was to wait. Surprise was complete. In a mad chase the troopers destroyed many vehicles and captured 125 of them. Said Colonel R. L. T. Beale: "The wagons were brand new, the mules fat and sleek and the harness in use for the first time. Such a train we had never seen before and did not see again." This wagon train was Jeb's stumbling block. The length of the road and the weariness of his men might be surmounted by cheer and resolution; but a captured train of "125 best United States model wagons and splendid teams"—this must be brought back to Virginia, no matter where; meantime, it had to be carried.[26]

Stuart determined, as a minimum next exploit, to cut the enemy's second line of supply, that of the Baltimore and Ohio Railroad. After much delay collecting the captured wagons and paroling the 400 prisoners, the railroad was reached and the tracks torn up. This produced no fine, smashing train wrecks like those at Bristoe Station the previous August, and Stuart's only reward was the doubtful one of possessing for some hours a railroad that otherwise might have been employed in the service of the enemy.

Reaching Westminster about 5:00 P.M. on June 29, the troopers found forage and rations enough for the entire command as well as a good night's sleep. For his part, Stuart would have been hurt and ashamed had he known how anxiously Lee was inquiring for news of him and how faltering was the movement of the army in the absence of the cavalry. Ignorant of his chief's distress, Jeb was not concerned, apparently, over the encumbrance of his wagon train. June 30 brought the column to Hanover, east of Gettysburg, and a brisk clash with Federal cavalry.[27]

Hampered as he was by his train, Stuart could not bring himself to abandon it. Believing the column to be not far from Lee's infantry, he reasoned that he should deliver the vehicles to his chief for use in collecting provisions from rich Pennsylvania. Once again, the crux of a military solution was the choice of a line of march. To escape the Federal cavalry operating to the westward, he would detour east and north toward the Susquehanna. Newspapers told him of Early's arrival on the twenty-eighth—two days previously—in York. This indicated for the cavalry a night march to unite with Jube. Said Stuart afterwards: "Whole regiments slept in the saddle, their faithful animals keeping the road unguided."[28]

Such was the night of June 30 for Jeb Stuart, a third of the men whose state of mind was making history for America while the Confederate army converged on Gettysburg. He had gone on and on in the exercise of the discretion Lee had given. Almost six days Stuart had been on his raid. Not a single time had he heard from any of the infantry commanders with whom he was directed to cooperate. One dispatch only he had sent, and that on the twenty-fifth. Other adventure was to be his, but nothing he had achieved and nothing he could hope to accomplish with his exhausted men could offset the harm which the events of coming days were to show he already had done to his chief and his cause.

CHAPTER 26

Two Days of Battle

1. PROMISE OF ANOTHER TRIUMPH

That night of June 30, while Stuart's sleepy boys plodded along, Dick Ewell was fuming over discretionary orders. Longstreet confidently was expecting his plan of a tactical defensive to be accepted by his chief. And A. P. Hill was preparing for the advance of part of his troops from Cashtown to Gettysburg at the end of a long advance from the Rappahannock. When Lee had made ready to move toward Pennsylvania, he left Hill and the Third Corps to watch Hooker's army and to occupy it while the First and Second corps slipped away. This was the most responsible assignment, the most shining proof of Lee's confidence, that the new corps commander could have asked or received.

Just as Lee was about to strike his tent and follow the First and Second corps up the Rappahannock, the Federals began to stir on Stafford Heights. On the afternoon of June 5, protected by artillery, they laid a pontoon bridge opposite the mouth of Deep Run and crossed a strong column. After watching closely, Lee the next afternoon told Hill the force on the right bank of the river did not appear too strong for the Third Corps to handle. With good wishes to his lieutenant, he rode to overtake the troops who were to invade the Northern states. Hill was left to watch and to worst the enemy.

That proved easy. Hooker did not change his original plan, which was that of reconnaissance and demonstration, and by the morning of June 14 he had withdrawn from the right bank of the Rappahannock. Gradually during the day the thousands of vehicles and tents that had stood for months on Stafford Heights vanished. Hill correctly assumed that Hooker was abandoning the line of the Rapphannock to interpose between Lee and Washington. The duty of the Third Corps now was to follow the main army. Dick Anderson was started that day for Culpeper. Harry Heth followed on the fifteenth. Dorsey Pender was only left long enough to make quite certain the Unionists were not employing a ruse. "Thus far Gen. Lee's plans have worked admirably . . . ," Pender wrote his wife. "I do not anticipate any fight this side of the Potomac."[1]

Swiftly Pender marched toward the other divisions. The advance prospered. "We have a grand race on hand between Lee and Hooker," Pender explained. "We have the inside track, Hooker going by Washington and we by Winchester." Again from Berryville: "Everything thus far has worked admirably. . . . Keep in good spirits, honey, and hope that this summer's work will tend to shorten the war." Pender's views were far exceeded by those the newspapers were expressing. "General Lee intends something much more serious than a mere incursion into Pennsylvania . . . ," the *Richmond Dispatch* observed with discernment. "The South is, for a time, relieved, and the North is bearing the whole burden of the war." Other papers, led by the *Charleston Mercury,* clamored for reprisal and destruction.

During the marches that stirred these thoughts, Hill, Pender, and the other commanders of the Third Corps had for a time the company of Lee. Pender wrote: "The General seemed yesterday in fine spirits, but said he was going to shoot us if we did not keep our men from straggling. They marched finely coming up here." Of detailed plans Lee said little, but raised many hopes when he told Pender that if the Army of Northern Virginia met and crushed Hooker, and Vicksburg and Port Hudson did their part, "our prospects of peace are very fine."[2]

Lee had directed, on the twenty-ninth, that all the corps move east of the mountains in order to hold the enemy there and prevent interruption of his line of communications with Virginia. Hill was to advance in the direction of Cashtown. Longstreet was to follow. Ewell was to march from Carlisle. Under Hill's direction, Heth proceeded to Cashtown that day. On the thirtieth, Johnston Pettigrew, of Heth's division, advanced toward Gettysburg, where he had heard he would find some shoes for his barefooted men. Heth remained at Cashtown and, after the practice of Confederates in Northern states, undertook to do a bit of shopping. His particular need was a hat. The one that appealed to him most was too large for him. A clerk at divisional headquarters tucked several folds of paper inside the sweat band and pronounced it a fit. Heth thanked his officer and, as the event proved, had the best of reason for doing so.

Although Heth got his hat at Cashtown, Pettigrew missed the shoes at Gettysburg. Late in the afternoon of June 30 the Carolinian returned and reported that as his troops neared Gettysburg they encountered cavalry outposts. Officers thought they heard, as if on the other side of the town, the roll of infantry drums. When A. P. Hill arrived, Heth had Pettigrew repeat the story of his day's experience. "The only force at Gettysburg is cavalry," said Hill confidently—it was corroborated by his scouts and by General Lee's. "If there is no objection," Heth answered immediately, "I will take my division tomorrow and go to Gettysburg and get those shoes."

"None in the world."[3]

On those four words fate hung. At 5 o'clock the next morning, July 1, Heth started for Gettysburg. In front was the veteran brigade of Archer. Joe Davis's brigade followed under its inexperienced, pleasant, and unpretending brigadier. Pettigrew's North Carolinians and Field's Virginians, led by Colonel J. M. Brockenbrough, were behind Davis. Prudently, Hill decided to have Pender's division follow Heth immediately. Anderson's division, at Fayetteville, would start early that morning for Cashtown.

The day was warm. Water was scarce. Otherwise the march was not unpleasant. Three miles west of Gettysburg blue videttes were encountered, but they did not delay the advance. As the column descended toward Willoughby Run, about a mile and a half from the town, everything indicated the presence of the enemy, but no hostile line was observed. Heth had Archer deploy on the right and Davis on the left and sent them forward to occupy the town. As Archer crossed the little stream there were pauses, shouts, desultory fire. Federals were advancing! Davis, too, quickly met an oncoming force. The fire was instant, the clash furious. As fate would have it, Archer encountered the Iron Brigade, a command of Michigan, Wisconsin, and Indiana soldiers who deserved their name. In a few minutes they overwhelmed Archer's thin brigade. Archer himself, in pathetic exhaustion, was captured—the first general officer of the army to fall into the hands of the enemy since Lee had taken command.

On the other flank, as it happened, Davis's advancing line overlapped that of the Federals, who quickly retreated. From lack of experience, Davis permitted two of his regiments, pursuing the enemy, to enter a railroad cut at right angles to the front of attack. There they were captured by a reserve regiment of the Iron Brigade. Back, then, the wreck of Archer's brigade and the remnant of Davis's surged. Their reconnaissance had been costly. No choice remained except to renew the fight or quit the field. Neither Lee nor Hill had arrived, and Heth had to make his own decisions. He concluded the soldierly thing to do was to put his infantry in line of battle and prepare for a new advance. Pegram's and McIntosh's artillerymen found positions. Heth waited an hour, two hours. He scarcely hoped the enemy would attack him, but he desired to delay his own assault if he could until Hill arrived or Pender was in support.[4]

At length Lee rode over from Cashtown. Heth reported and learned that Lee did not wish a major battle joined before the converging Southern columns were all in position. Soon, too, word came that Pender was arriving with his division. Desultory action continued. About 2:30, from the north, came the welcome sound of Southern guns. In obedience to Lee's orders, Ewell's Second Corps was approaching Gettysburg. Rodes's division was forming almost at right angles to Heth and preparing to attack. On the road, Ewell received from army headquarters the same information given to Heth: If the Confederates encountered the enemy in large force, they were to avoid a general engagement, if practicable, until the entire army was at hand. Rodes had seen that if he continued along the high ground called Seminary Ridge to the east of Willoughby Run, he could assail in flank the Federals who were opposing Hill. He deployed on a front of three brigades.

Quickly the gunners of Carter's battalion opened fire to enfilade the Federal line that faced Hill. As Rodes watched, he thought for a moment that the Union forces were caught by surprise and might be routed. Soon he observed troops pouring out of Gettysburg as if to deploy against him. Directly southward, also, the blue regiments began to change front and draw a line across the ridge. Although Rodes could not know it, the whole of the I Corps now was being arrayed against him and Hill. Toward Rodes's left, two divisions of Howard's XI Corps—adversaries of Chancellorsville—were moving.

Rodes had been assured that Early's division of the Second Corps would arrive in a short time and take position nearer Gettysburg. Consequently, he determined to hold with his left and attack with his right. George Doles, wholly capable, was directed to place his veteran troops on the left to hold that flank. This made O'Neal's brigade, formerly Rodes's own, a major element of the column of attack. Iverson, west of O'Neal, would share the advance. Junius Daniel's brigade, which had never fought in Virginia, was supporting Iverson. In reserve was one of the brigades that had earned greatest fame at Chancellorsville, Ramseur's North Carolinians. Within the time available this deployment probably was unavoidable, but it was far from ideal. It left the well-tested brigadiers, Ramseur and Doles, out of the first attack and put the direction of the assault on O'Neal and Iverson, who had not distinguished themselves in the battles of May.[5]

It chanced, also, that from the nature of the ground a gap existed between Doles's right and O'Neal's left. To cover this gap, Rodes directed the 5th Alabama, O'Neal's left regiment, to stay where it was and await Rodes's personal orders. Further, Rodes realigned O'Neal's right regiment to a position in line with Daniel's brigade. These arrangements either angered or confused O'Neal. Soon the Federals moved boldly out to attack Rodes, whose fighting spirit rose at the sight of them. He would strike at once! He pointed out to O'Neal the line of advance. Iverson was to move simultaneously on the right of O'Neal. Daniel would support Iverson.

The advance was launched. In a few minutes it went awry. By some misunderstanding, O'Neal's front was narrowed to three regiments only. Units were mingled. Direction was faulty. The gap between O'Neal and Doles widened. Another gap appeared between O'Neal and Iverson. It was apparent that Iverson's line of advance was exposing the whole of Daniel's supporting brigade. The Alabama regiments of O'Neal opened their fire but, in their confusion, could not drive the enemy. To Rodes's surprise, he found that O'Neal had remained back with the 5th Alabama instead of going forward to direct the advancing regiments. "The result," Rodes subsequently stated, "was that the whole brigade, with the exception of the Third Alabama . . . , was repulsed quickly, and with loss."

That was not the full measure of humiliation. Word was brought to Rodes from the frantic Iverson that one of his regiments had raised the white flag and gone over to the enemy! Such a thing had never happened in the Army of Northern Virginia. For a few minutes there was chaos. Soon the ghastly truth was discovered: In Iverson's advance his line of battle had come under a decimating fire and men fell by scores. Still fighting, the left units were exposed when O'Neal was repulsed, and some of Iverson's men, realizing they were about to be surrounded and slaughtered, waved their handkerchiefs in surrender. Iverson saw this and thought the dead men in line were alive and were yielding. So unnerved was he, as his brigade scattered, that one of his staff had to assume command.[6]

To the south, Harry Heth had seen enough of this confusion to feel certain that Rodes was having a desperate fight. Heth could not find A. P. Hill, and consequently he rode to Lee, who silently was watching the battle. "Rodes is very heavily engaged," said Heth, "had I not better attack?" "No," Lee answered, "I am not prepared to bring on a general engagement today—Longstreet is not up."[7]

Over the ground to which Lee and Heth were looking, Daniel's brigade was now advancing. Daniel got astride the railroad cut where earlier many of Davis's men had been captured, but could not throw all his troops immediately into the assault. Ramseur, with the reserve brigade, was advancing to support the center, where O'Neal and Iverson had been repulsed. George Doles was fully occupied on the left. The prospect was grim. All of Rodes's troops now were engaged or soon were to be. The young divisional commander who had won plaudits at Chancellorsville was not sweeping the field. He was, on the contrary, in undeniable difficulty. His men were fighting gallantly enough, but clumsy mistakes and nervous failures of leadership had almost wrecked the division. Robert Rodes might be headed for a humiliating defeat.

Then, once again, as so often had happened to Lee's army, the most

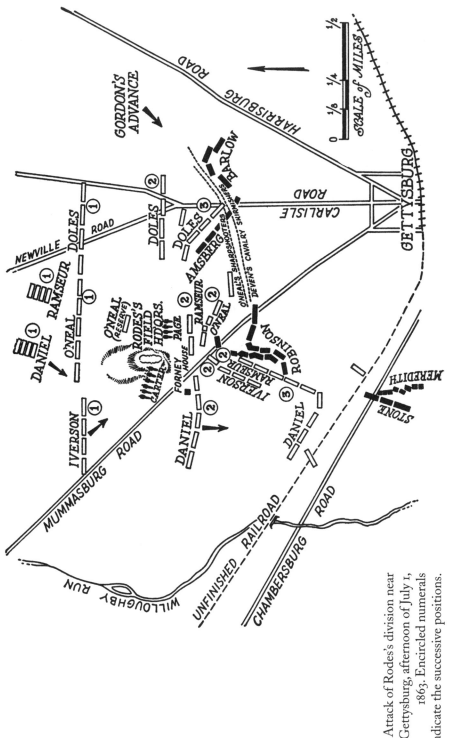

Attack of Rodes's division near Gettysburg, afternoon of July 1, 1863. Encircled numerals indicate the successive positions.

desperate moment proved the most fortunate. On the left of Rodes, where Doles was hard-pressed, Gordon's brigade of Early's division arrived from the north and rushed into action. About the same time, with Lee's consent, Hill sent Heth forward. When the division grew weary and Heth himself fell with a head wound, Hill sent Pender's division through the ranks of Heth to clear Seminary Ridge. It was done with the fierce might that always made Pender's charges terrifying. Rodes was able, meantime, to advance Daniel and Ramseur and parts of O'Neal's and Iverson's brigades. Doles now attacked as if he wished to be avenged for having to maintain an earlier defensive. Seminary Ridge was cleared, but beyond that high ground General Hill did not think it prudent to advance his exhausted and now disordered troops.

Ramseur and Doles, of Rodes's division, pursued the enemy into Gettysburg. Hays's brigade of Early's division, losing few, also fought its way into town, where Union soldiers of the I and XI corps were crowded in confusion and bewilderment. About 4,000 prisoners were captured in the town; an additional 1,000 were taken on the ridge and elsewhere. Among the Confederates an exultant spirit prevailed. Rodes's discomfiture and the earlier repulse of Archer and Davis were forgotten. Gettysburg, the soldiers felt, was Chancellorsville all over again: The enemy was being routed. Officers of the high command were no less pleased, but they had no time for rejoicing. A new decision had to be made.[8]

2. Ewell Cannot Reach a Decision

In the direction of Rodes's battle and Early's advance, Dick Ewell had small part. The fight of Rodes had been too swift, too full of change, and too confused for the corps commander to have any useful role. Ewell had the sound, soldierly sense not to interfere where he could not aid. As for Early, his dispositions had been prompt and confident. They had called for no correction. When Lee's courier had brought the message that if Ewell found the enemy "too large" the commanding general did not want an engagement brought on until the remaining divisions arrived, Ewell pondered this instruction with his blood up. He concluded that he could not break off the fight without disaster, and he had pressed it vigorously.[9]

Now that the enemy was being driven out of Gettysburg, Ewell rode toward the town and had a nearer view of the high ground to the south of it. A mile away was Cemetery Hill, about eighty feet above the level of the center of Gettysburg. Somewhat closer to the town and to the east was a second eminence, East Cemetery Hill, almost as high. Still farther east-

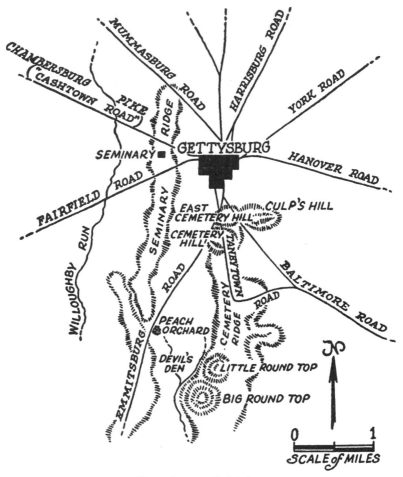

Gettysburg and vicinity.

ward, around the head of a ravine, the ground rose nearly another 100 feet to a rocky, wood-covered eminence which the natives called Culp's Hill. From the crest of Cemetery Hill to the top of Culp's Hill, as Ewell looked at them, the distance was slightly more than half a mile. These elevations dominated the town. It was manifest, also, that Cemetery Hill and an elevation south of it constituted a natural defense against attack from Seminary Ridge, the high ground where Hill's weary men were awaiting orders.

On Cemetery and East Cemetery hills, Federal infantry were visible, but in what numbers it was difficult to ascertain. The bluecoats were evidently to defend the hills. Toward them—a thrilling sight for Southern eyes—were moving the Union troops who had been driven from Seminary Ridge. Some were without formation. Others, dogged and better controlled, moved slowly in column. If these troops reached Cemetery Hill and entrenched, they might be able to hold out until they were reinforced. Many Southern officers stated the situation in reverse: If the hill were attacked at once, the Federals could be routed. It was not yet 4 o'clock. The summer sun was more than three hours above the horizon. Darkness would not fall until after 8 o'clock.

Gordon was for instant attack. He believed that a swift thrust at one Federal command after another, before they concentrated, would give the Confederates the hill and the victory. He hurried to Second Corps headquarters and found Ewell on a quiet mount, immobile. Outwardly Old Bald Head was the same man who had made swift decision three weeks previously at Winchester, the same Ewell who that very afternoon had decided that he must press the fight, even though Lee wished to avoid a general engagement. Inwardly, something had happened to the will of Richard Ewell. In place of his usual chatter there was silence. While some of the most fateful seconds in American history ticked past, he waited. Gordon waited, too, tensely expectant, but he got no orders.

Then Kyd Douglas rode up from Allegheny Johnson with the announcement that Johnson was advancing along the Chambersburg road and on arrival could go into action. Before Ewell made any reply, Gordon broke disciplinary bounds. In the ardor of battle and the magnitude of the opportunity, he disdained etiquette. He could join Johnson's attack, he said. Cemetery Hill could be taken before dark.

The old-time Dick Ewell would have piped "Yes, attack!" before the words were off Gordon's lips. This new, changed lieutenant general paid no heed to Gordon. Deliberately Ewell turned to Douglas with his answer: Johnson should continue his advance until well to the front, then halt and await orders. There was nothing more for Gordon to say; but some auditors who had been on the staff of Stonewall Jackson scarcely could believe their own ears, or credit the eyes which told them the man before them was the once-decisive Dick Ewell. Sandie Pendleton said in a low voice, with intense feeling, "Oh, for the presence and inspiration of Old Jack for just one hour!"

With Gordon still by his side, Ewell started into Gettysburg. He found, quickly enough, that some Federals remained in the town. There came a fusillade and several men fell. Gordon heard the ugly, familiar thud of a minié ball close by. Ewell had been struck. "Are you hurt, sir?" cried Gordon. Ewell was calm. "No, no, I'm not hurt. But suppose that ball had struck you: we would have had the trouble of carrying you off the field, sir.

You see how much better fixed for a fight I am than you are. It don't hurt a bit to be shot in a wooden leg." That sounded like the old Ewell . . . but still, though thousands of Federal refugees were climbing Cemetery Hill, there was no decision.[10]

In the town square Ewell seemed in no hurry. He drew rein under a tree and chatted cheerfully with those around him. It began to look as if he did not intend to make a decision on his own account. As firing persisted in the town, Ewell was prevailed upon to leave the square and go to a house on the outskirts. Gradually then his composure began to weaken. He grew restless and excited. Presently up rode General Trimble. "Well, General," Trimble began in the candor of long association, "we have had a grand success; are you not going to follow it up and push our advantage?"

Ewell replied that General Lee had instructed him not to bring on a general engagement without orders, and that he would wait for them. Trimble said that Lee's orders could not apply, that a hard battle already had been fought, and that the advantage should be developed. Ewell visibly was disturbed by this, but he made no reply. Trimble persisted. Still Ewell asserted that he should not act further without orders. In wrath, which he probably did not conceal, Trimble rode off to see for himself what opportunity offered.

Presently he was back, more than ever convinced from what he had observed that no time should be lost in occupying the high ground southeast of Gettysburg. "General," said Trimble in his emphatic manner, pointing to Culp's Hill, "*there* is an eminence of commanding position, and not now occupied . . . . I advise you to send a brigade and hold it if we are to remain here." Was he sure it commanded the town, Ewell asked. "Certainly it does, as you can see, and it ought to be held by us at once." Then, as Trimble remembered it, "General Ewell made some impatient reply, and the conversation dropped."[11]

Jubal Early had marched through Gettysburg the previous week, and Ewell had sent to him for an opinion as to where Allegheny Johnson's division might best be placed. The answer came back that Johnson, on arrival, move at once to Culp's Hill because it commanded the enemy position— precisely the counsel Trimble had given. With this came a sketchy report from Extra Billy Smith of the enemy advancing against the Confederate left and rear. This somewhat alarmed Ewell. He wanted more details and he wished Early's counsel at first-hand. A messenger was sent to bring Early to field headquarters. Until he arrived, nothing was to be done.

When Early was conducted to Ewell's post of command, he repeated that Culp's Hill, which apparently was unoccupied by the enemy, should be taken by Johnson. Further, he went on, he felt sure that Cemetery Hill could be taken readily if Ewell would advance from the north and Hill from the west. Early added that he had sent a verbal suggestion to Hill that the Third Corps make the assault. It was imperative that the high ground be taken at once by storm. Ewell accepted, though with no enthusiasm, the suggestion that he get help from his right in an attack on Cemetery Hill. Lieutenant J. P. Smith must ride to General Lee and tell him that Ewell could attack and take the hill if given support from the west.

While Smith was delivering this message to Lee, Major Walter Taylor of the headquarters staff visited Ewell. From Seminary Ridge, said Taylor, the commanding general could see the Federals retreating in great confusion. It would only be necessary to press "those people," Lee went on, to secure the heights. If possible, Lee wished Ewell to do this. Before Ewell could consider the matter, Smith was back with a supplementary message: Lee "regretted that his people were not up to support him on the right, but he wished him to take the Cemetery Hill if it were possible." He would "ride over and see him very soon." This meant that if Cemetery Hill was to be taken, Ewell must do it with his own men. More than that, whether Taylor and Smith made the fact plain or not, Lee meant that his earlier orders for the avoidance of a general engagement still applied. To quote Lee's own words, "General Ewell was ... instructed to carry the hill occupied by the enemy, if he found it practicable, but to avoid a general engagement until the arrival of the other divisions of the army...."[12]

Ewell's concerns were several. He had concern over the Union batteries on Cemetery Hill. Also, there might be truth to Extra Billy Smith's report of Federals marching down from York toward the left. Still again, the force with which Ewell could attack was small. Two brigades of Early's and the tired survivors of Rodes's confused charges—these were all he had for the assault. Nor would this force have any support from the right. Lee himself said that. If Johnson was near at hand, he soon could seize Culp's Hill and from it could dominate Cemetery Hill. So Ewell reasoned.

Soon Rodes joined them. Old Bald Head had no instructions for either of the divisional commanders. He was waiting for Johnson's arrival and also for the promised visit from Lee. Nor could he dismiss his concern regarding the situation on the left. Early continued to insist that the trouble was not a hostile advance but panic on the part of Extra Billy Smith. Ewell remained skeptical and presently chose to see for himself if the left actually was in danger of being turned. With Early and Rodes he went to high ground east of Gettysburg from which a long stretch of the highway to York was visible. Skirmishers appeared at a distance too far for their uniforms to be distinguished. "There they come now!" cried Rodes, who believed them to be Federals. Early doubtless swore. Gordon, he explained, was in the direction of the skirmishers' advance. Ewell did not profess to know whether he was looking at friend or foe, but directed his staff to ascertain. It was close to sunset now. Not a blow had been struck against the enemy on the hills south of Gettysburg. After Ewell returned from his fruitless reconnoiter, word came that the skirmishers on the left were in fact Confederate.[13]

Now, through gathering dusk, there was a stir outside Ewell's headquarters: The commanding general was dismounting. Cordially Ewell met him and escorted him to a little arbor at the rear of the house, the coolest available place that warm night. Ewell had not seen Lee since June 10. This was the first time he ever had been directly under Lee in combat. Always previously, during Lee's command, Ewell had received his orders from Jackson. Chance decided that at a time when everything forecast a great battle, the Second Corps commander was to have his introduction, as an immediate subordinate, to the mind of Lee.

The army commander asked for details of the situation on the front of the Second Corps. No reference was made to the possibility of attack that evening on Cemetery Hill. Without discussion, all four officers realized that the time for this was past. The question to be considered was that of action the next day. After Ewell, Rodes, and Early had made their explanations, Ewell heard Lee ask: "Can't you, with your corps, attack on this flank at daylight tomorrow?"

Ewell had no immediate answer, but Early did. Jube felt his reconnaissance that afternoon and his casual examination of the ground the previous week, en route to York, gave him the best understanding of the terrain. He said flatly that he did not believe an attack should be made southward from Gettysburg against Cemetery Hill the next day. Success was doubtful. Loss inevitably would be large. Ewell listened and concurred. Rodes, too, believed no attack could prudently be made against the hill from the front of the Second Corps. At length, as if convinced, Lee said questioningly: "Then perhaps I had better draw you around towards my right, as the line will be very long and thin if you remain here, and the enemy may come down and break through it?"

Again it was Early who, without a by-your-leave, spoke up before Ewell attempted to answer. Lee need have no concern, said Jube; the enemy could not break the Second Corps line. Ewell found Early's opinion and his own once more in accord. Rodes was on the same side. Unanimous as were these views, it must have been manifest to Ewell that his counsel was not altogether to Lee's liking. The commanding general, in fact, was perplexed, almost stunned, at finding a defensive state of mind among his lieutenants. In the end, before Lee rode off, this understanding was reached: Lee was to attack the next morning on the right; Ewell was to make a demonstration on the left, and convert this into an attack if opportunity offered, and was to pursue the Federals if the attack on the right drove the blue army from its position.[14]

Ewell now received the staff officers who had been reconnoitering on the York road. They had been on Culp's Hill and reported it unoccupied. As Johnson's division was then moving into position, it was reasonable to assume these veterans could seize Culp's Hill. If so, delay during the afternoon would have cost nothing. Hardly had this prospect developed when Ewell received a note from Lee. He had examined anew the situation on the right and concluded that an attack there had a good prospect of success. Unless Ewell was satisfied the Second Corps could be used to advantage where it was, said Lee, it should be moved to the right. This stirred Ewell. Now that reconnaissance showed Culp's Hill unoccupied, he felt there was good prospect of striking a heavy blow there. He must present Lee the report of the reconnaissance. The only way to do this would be to ride over to army headquarters.

Old Bald Head rode through the night to Lee's headquarters. He found the commanding general attentive and ready to consider alternatives. Lee's one reason for deciding to shift Ewell to the right had been doubt of the ability of Ewell to make up his mind to do anything. Now that Ewell had determined to attack Culp's Hill, Lee with few words agreed that the Second Corps should remain on the left. The plan that had been formulated at the council in the arbor was reaffirmed: In the morning a demonstration was to be made on the left and, if promising, was to be turned into an assault.[15]

Back Ewell rode to his own front, and hurried off an aide to tell Johnson to occupy Culp's Hill. No time must be lost in taking the ground that was, in Ewell's opinion, the key to the Federal citadel. The officer returned with startling news. A reconnaissance party sent by Johnson up Culp's Hill had encountered the Federals in superior numbers. The enemy undoubtedly was on the eminence Old Allegheny was ordered to take.

With this message Johnson enclosed a dispatch taken from a captured Federal courier. It placed George Sykes's V Corps four miles to the east of Gettysburg and almost in rear of the position Johnson was to occupy. It indicated, also, that Henry Slocum's XII Corps must be close to Gettysburg. Prisoners had said earlier that the Federals had two corps around the town, the I and the XI. A third might have arrived; a fourth was to reach Gettysburg early the next morning.

Ewell's staff officer continued his report: General Johnson had said he would not attack until Ewell was apprised of the fact that the Federals occupied Culp's Hill. Further orders would be awaited by Johnson. "Day was now breaking," Ewell wrote afterwards, "and it was too late for any change of plan."[16]

3. THE ARMY SLIPS BACK A YEAR

James Longstreet's first of July was as unsatisfactory as Ewell's. He rode toward Gettysburg in the company of the commanding general until the sound of Hill's battle prompted Lee to hurry forward. Longstreet followed with McLaws's and Hood's divisions. Pickett was left at Chambersburg; Law's brigade was held on guard at New Guilford. About 5:00 P.M. Longstreet joined Lee on Seminary Ridge whence there was a wide sweep of vision: the town ahead, a long trough-like meadow to the right front, and east of that, stone-littered Cemetery Ridge, which swept southward and gave place to the two eminences that bulked almost as if they were mountains—Little Round Top and Round Top.

Longstreet studied through his glasses the position of the enemy, studied it with an eye to the defensive tactics he thought the Confederates should employ. From the Round Tops nearly all the way to the hill just south of Gettysburg, he observed that the sides of the ridge were rough and an obstacle to a swift descent by the Federals for an attack on Seminary Ridge. A certain satisfaction there was for Longstreet in the strength of the Federal position: It discouraged a Confederate attack and invited the defensive on which his heart was set. Fortune was smiling on him! It had given him the ideal theater for another Fredericksburg, an easy repulse of a foolish assault and rich fruits of victory from the Longstreet plan!

At length he lowered his glasses and turned to Lee, and there commenced a long conference. Lee began with some observation to the effect that he felt he should attack the enemy. Longstreet immediately objected that this was not desirable. He may have added that an attack was contrary to the plan discussed before the army left Virginia. If that was part of Longstreet's remark, Lee ignored it then and did not remember it afterwards. He never had intended to commit himself to any such plan, and he may not even have understood to what Longstreet referred. In his report Lee said candidly that he had not intended to "deliver a general battle so far from our base unless attacked," but he had never contemplated a campaign without the possibility of a battle, and he certainly had made no pledge concerning that or the strategy or tactics to be employed. Whatever the language of Longstreet's objection that afternoon on Seminary Ridge, Lee answered, in effect, If the enemy is there tomorrow, we must attack him.

This remark opened a frank exchange of views. The sound general strategy, said Longstreet, was to get between Meade and Washington, to threaten the flank and rear of the Federals and force them to attack on good defensive terrain. If operations became necessary where the army then was, the troops should be shifted toward Round Top. Meade then could be threatened, if maneuver was the aim, or attacked to better advantage if battle was to be delivered. In what manner Lee answered, Longstreet did not relate. Subsequently he wrote: "[Lee] seemed under a subdued excitement, which occasionally took possession of him when 'the hunt was up,' and threatened his superb equipoise. The sharp battle fought by Hill and Ewell on that day had given him a taste of victory."[17]

Actually Lee was reasoning the larger alternatives. He could withdraw; he could remain where he was and await the next Federal move; or he could attack without delay. To retreat in the face of a strong, pursuing adversary was to take heavy risks. As for waiting, it would not be possible to remain on the defensive for any length of time. Supplies were low; the army was living off the land; the Federals could easily block the mountain passes and limit the area in which the Southern army could forage. Hunger, perhaps starvation, might be the cost of a prolonged defensive.

If, by elimination, an offensive was indicated, the army either could maneuver to the right, as Longstreet urged, or it could attack the Federals before they could concentrate. The objections to maneuvering between the enemy and Washington were manifest: In the absence of the cavalry, the position of the Federals could not be determined readily. A southward shift might involve days of delay during which the army would suffer for food precisely as it would if it remained on the defensive. So little possibility did Lee see of successful maneuver that he scarcely regarded it as a separate alternative. Immediate attack was, in his eyes, the wisest course. There was good reason to assume that Cemetery Ridge was not held, as yet, in strength. In Lee's succinct appraisal, "A battle had, therefore, became in a measure unavoidable, and the success already gained gave hope of a favorable issue."

It is not known how much of this Lee explained to Longstreet. As he was unaware of the extent to which the heart of his senior lieutenant was fixed on the defensive, he probably wasted few words and employed no diplomacy. Longstreet said little more. After Lee returned from his conference with Ewell, he told Longstreet and Hill, so Armistead Long testified, "Gentlemen, we will attack the enemy in the morning as early as practicable." When Old Pete left army headquarters late in the evening, he was sure of Lee's intention to attack, but was not sure Lee had decided where the attack would be delivered or with what force. For his part, Longstreet was determined to prevent, if he could, an attack he believed to be unwise. Better not to have fought that day, he said, than to have left the

Federals in a position from which the whole army would be needed, and then at great sacrifice, to drive the enemy.[18]

Longstreet rose at 3:00 A.M. on July 2 and found Lee on Seminary Ridge anxious to ascertain how heavily the Federals had been reinforced during the night on the opposing high ground. Engineers S. R. Johnston and J. J. Clarke were sent to reconnoiter as far as possible to the right, but without waiting for their report Longstreet renewed his argument for the defensive tactics of a maneuver around the left of the Union army. His appeal made no impression on the commanding general. Lee still believed the one practicable course was to attack the Federals on Cemetery Ridge at once, before they could complete their concentration. A. P. Hill joined the conference. Briefly, it was decided that Longstreet should deliver the attack from the extreme Confederate right. Hood's division now, about 7:30, was approaching. Behind Hood was McLaws. Longstreet heard Lee say to Hood, in a brief exchange of greetings, "The enemy is here, and if we do not whip him, he will whip us."

By the time McLaws arrived, Lee had matured the tactical plan of attack, and he summoned the Georgian to tell him what he had to do. Longstreet was walking nearby and heard Lee explain a plan for an oblique attack on Cemetery Ridge and the Emmitsburg road, which ran between Seminary and Cemetery ridges. "Can you do it?" Lee asked of McLaws. "I know nothing to prevent me," McLaws said. He wanted to go in advance and reconnoiter. Lee said Captain Johnston of his staff had been ordered to reconnoiter the ground. "I will go with him," McLaws began, but got no further. Longstreet strode up and broke in: "No, sir, I do not wish you to leave your division." Then he leaned over and drew his finger across the map. "I wish your division placed so."

"No, General," Lee replied quietly, "I wish it placed just opposite." McLaws observed that he would like, in either event, to go over the ground with Johnston. Bluntly, Longstreet forbade. He manifestly was irritated.[19]

Lee said nothing and gave no indication that he knew Longstreet was angry. With Old Pete on one side and Hill on the other, he sat on a fallen tree, map on knee, and talked of the arrangements for the action. Now Johnston and Clarke returned from their reconnaissance and Johnston reported. There was nothing in his report or in his manner to indicate that a decisive moment of the campaign had been reached. He had not attempted to mount Cemetery Ridge, Johnston said. At Little Round Top he had gone forward and climbed to a shoulder of that eminence. He found no enemy there, and he had seen no organized force anywhere. Johnston and Clarke then had ridden southward to a point opposite the southern end of Round Top. There they had turned back.

Lee was visibly interested in Johnston's report. At that time, opposite Lee's headquarters, the enemy was not seen in strength. Johnston indicated that Union forces were not on the dominating ground farther southward. The decision of Lee to attack the enemy was confirmed. If the Confederates could launch an oblique assault north of the two Round Tops, get astride Cemetery Ridge at its lowest point there, and sweep up the ridge, the Federals could be driven from it! That was Lee's conclusion. He turned to Longstreet and said, "I think you had better move on."[20]

Soon the commanding general rode off to the left for another conference with Ewell over his employment in cooperation with the attack by the First Corps. Longstreet was expected to make his preparations during Lee's absence, but the lieutenant general was less disposed than ever to deliver his attack. He had no reason to doubt Johnston's report that the lower end of the ridge was unoccupied, but he felt that the attack should not be made. If he must assault, he would delay until the entire First Corps was at hand. He said to Hood, "The General is a little nervous this morning; he wishes me to attack; I do not wish to do so without Pickett. I never like to go into battle with one boot off."

At 11 o'clock or a little later, Lee rode back up the hill to field headquarters of the First Corps. To all who had seen him on the left, it had been apparent that he had expected Longstreet to attack and was disappointed because he had not heard the guns of the First Corps. The previous evening, in discussing the desirability of an attack on the right, Lee had confessed that he hesitated to attack on that flank because Longstreet would have to deliver the blow. "Longstreet is a very good fighter when he gets into position and gets everything ready," Lee had said, "but he is so slow." Now he probably could not conceal altogether from Longstreet his disappointment that nothing had been accomplished, but his first remark was that it would not do to have Ewell open the attack. If Longstreet made any reply to this, it was perfunctory.[21]

The morning was almost past. Opposite Lee's post of command, a ridge that had appeared almost unoccupied at sunrise now was bristling with men and guns. Despite the increase in Federal strength, Lee believed he had no alternative to attacking as speedily as possible and, further, that his tactical plan would obviate the necessity of a frontal assault. Quietly, then, and in violation of long practice of merely "suggesting" movements to his lieutenants, Lee gave the explicit order: With that part of his command available, Longstreet was to attack along the Emmitsburg road in the manner explained earlier that morning to McLaws.

As a soldier, Longstreet did not think of disobeying, but he asked permission to wait until Law's brigade arrived from New Guilford. As that fine command would come up in a short time, Lee consented. Old Pete said nothing to expose his thoughts, but his every important act for the next few hours showed that he had resolved to put on Lee the entire responsibility for what happened. In plain, ugly words, he sulked. The dissent of Longstreet's mind was a brake on his energies.

About noon Longstreet had word that Law had joined Hood, and he ordered the advance to begin. He left the direction of the van entirely to S. R. Johnston, the reconnaissance officer Lee had put at his disposal. Longstreet himself remained near the middle of the column. For a time the commanding general rode with him, but of what passed between them no record survives. When Lee turned back, Longstreet was in authority as complete as he cared to have it. He had the large discretion that Lee's system of command allowed the senior lieutenants.[22]

When the van came to a point where the road was visible from the Federal position, McLaws halted, told Longstreet that the column could be seen by the enemy, and suggested that the two divisions countermarch and follow a route he had reconnoitered during the forenoon. This was done, though it put Hood's division in advance. Where the Federal left flank rested Longstreet did not know, though he had seen nothing to indicate that it extended far down the ridge toward Round Top. "How are you going in?" he asked McLaws. That would be determined when he could see what was in his front, McLaws answered. "There is nothing in your front; you will be entirely on the flank of the enemy." Then he would continue his march, said the division commander, "and after arriving on the flank as far as is necessary, will face to the left and march on the enemy."

"That suits me," replied Longstreet, and rode off.

Lee had been told of two good artillery positions, one opposite Round Top, the other in a peach orchard about 1,600 yards northwest of Little Round Top. He had concluded that good artillery preparation would make possible the oblique attack that would clear the orchard and put the Confederate right on the lowest part of Cemetery Ridge. As the attack advanced, A. P. Hill's right division, Dick Anderson's, was to cooperate. The remainder of Hill's corps was to demonstrate to hold the Federal forces that faced Hill's left. Ewell was to feint, also, as soon as he heard the sound of Longstreet's guns, and convert this into a real attack if opportunity offered.[23]

The major assumption of this plan was that the Federal line on Cemetery Ridge was short. On no other evidence than that of Johnston's and Clarke's reconnaissance, the Confederates assumed that the Federal left did not extend far and that it could be turned easily when the men of the First Corps were astride the ridge. Longstreet was of this opinion, which was Lee's also. Consequently, when Longstreet presently heard firing from the front McLaws was to occupy, he told himself McLaws must have engaged an outpost only. He reasoned that he should extend his right to be certain he outflanked the Federal left, and Hood was instructed to form on McLaws's right. After giving this order, Longstreet waited. Nothing happened. Puzzled and provoked, he sent to inquire why McLaws had not opened the attack. McLaws's answer was prompt: He would charge as soon as the division was formed, but the Federals were in great strength in his front. They held the Peach Orchard and they spread far to his right. Abundant artillery was with them. Longstreet thought the report exaggerated, or else he reasoned that Hood, going speedily into action, would get beyond the Federal flank. McLaws's instructions were renewed. He must attack at once.

McLaws replied that the Federal guns were so numerous that the Confederate batteries must be used against them; careful artillery preparation was necessary to prevent failure. He wished Longstreet would ride to the front and see for himself. Longstreet gave no heed to this. McLaws was in the position assigned by Lee for the attack Lee had ordered; McLaws must go forward. Let him understand that the order was peremptory.[24]

Scarcely had these instructions gone to McLaws than a messenger arrived from Hood with the worst news yet: The Federal line extended almost to Round Top! From the Peach Orchard southward the Union front was concave. An attack across the Emmitsburg road, in the manner contemplated by Lee's orders, was impossible. It would expose flank and rear to the enemy's fire. However, Hood reported that some of his Texas scouts had reconnoitered the southern end of Round Top and found no troops there. They believed it would be easy to get in rear of the enemy and to reach the Union wagon trains. Hood asked that the attack order be suspended and that he be allowed to move around the Federal left. Longstreet shook his head. No, "General Lee's orders are to attack up the Emmitsburg road." Tell Hood that.

None of his staff suggested that in a situation that had been misunderstood from the first and had now changed decisively, Lee should be informed. Longstreet apparently did not feel that he should delay the assault still further for a report to the commanding general. But he did conclude that McLaws must wait until Hood was deployed and ready to go forward.

Almost before the courier could spur away with this message, another officer arrived from Hood. He repeated his request: He feared that nothing could be accomplished under his orders. Would not Longstreet permit him to undertake to turn Round Top? Again the answer from Longstreet: "General Lee's orders are to attack up the Emmitsburg road." About this time the Confederate artillery opened in front of Hood and McLaws. As the salvoes shook the countryside, there arrived still another of Hood's staff officers with the same plea: The enemy's position was one of great strength; Hood thought his attack could be repelled easily, and asked permission to try the turning movement. For the third time Longstreet's answer was, "General Lee's orders are to attack up the Emmitsburg road."

To reinforce this as a final, imperative order, Longstreet rode over to the high ground on the extreme right where Hood's veterans were waiting. Earnestly Hood expressed his regret that Longstreet would not permit him to advance under the southern flank of Round Top. Longstreet varied his answer to the extent only of saying, "We must obey the orders of General Lee." Hood argued no further. He had made his request. Longstreet had seen the ground. Orders stood. He gave the word for the advance.[25]

Longstreet watched the start and then, in bitter mood, rode north to McLaws's position. In the Peach Orchard, distant less than 600 yards, Union troops were moving as if they intended to attack. This was more than could be endured by William Barksdale, he of the battle of the pontoons at Fredericksburg. "General," he kept pleading with McLaws, "let me go; General, let me charge!" When Longstreet appeared, Barksdale impetuously came up to him: "I wish you would let me go in, General!" "Wait a little," answered Longstreet, "we are all going in presently."

Hood's attack by this time was becoming confused, with Hood falling with a bad arm wound. Evander Law, assuming command of the division, pushed his own brigade over Round Top and grappled with the enemy on Little Round Top. With heavy losses the rest of the division fought its way as far as it could without support on its left. Law halted it on the best defensive line he could find and sought help from McLaws's troops.

McLaws had been awaiting word from Longstreet to launch his attack, but Old Pete was not to be hurried. When presently the signal gun fired, Joe Kershaw's South Carolinians advanced in an effort to seize the Peach Orchard and take position on the left of Hood. By some mischance, Barksdale's advance, which should have been timed to Kershaw's, was so delayed that Kershaw had to change front to cover his left. When Barksdale's Mississippians at last received their orders, they drove the enemy from the Peach Orchard but could get no farther. Semmes and then Wofford pushed forward in support. Both Longstreet's divisions now were engaged, though thrown into action piecemeal. "Then was fairly commenced," said Longstreet, "what I do not hesitate to pronounce the best three hours' fighting ever done by any troops on any battle-field."[26]

The time had come for Dick Anderson's Third Corps division to go in on Longstreet's left. The plan was to engage by brigades right to left—Wilcox, Perry, Wright, and Posey, with Mahone in reserve. Wilcox's

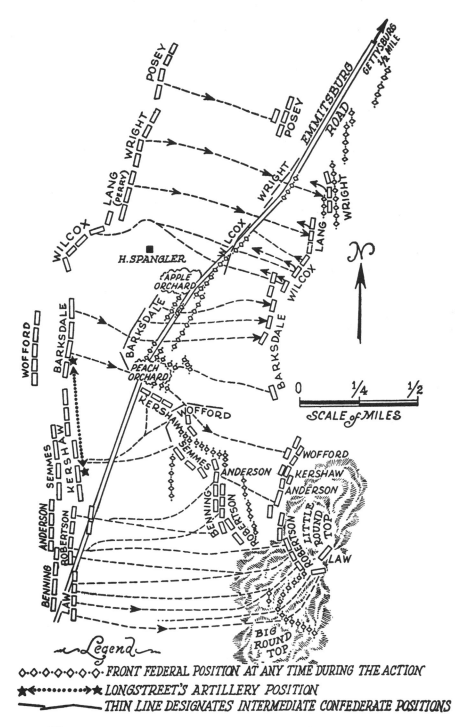

POSEY

POSEY

POSEY

WRIGHT

WRIGHT

LANG (PERRY)

WILCOX

WRIGHT

WILCOX

WRIGHT

LANG

WILCOX

H. SPANGLER

EMMITSBURG ROAD

GETTYSBURG ½ MILE

APPLE ORCHARD

N

WOFFORD

BARKSDALE

BARKSDALE

BARKSDALE

BARKSDALE

PEACH ORCHARD

KERSHAW

WOFFORD

0   ¼   ½

SCALE of MILES

SEMMES

KERSHAW

SEMMES

WOFFORD

ANDERSON

KERSHAW

ANDERSON

BENNING

ROBERTSON

ROBERTSON

LITTLE ROUND TOP

ANDERSON

LAW

BENNING

ROBERTSON

LAW

BIG ROUND TOP

~ Legend ~

◇·◇·◇·◇·◇·◇·◇· FRONT FEDERAL POSITION AT ANY TIME DURING THE ACTION

★←·············→★ LONGSTREET'S ARTILLERY POSITION

———————— THIN LINE DESIGNATES INTERMEDIATE CONFEDERATE POSITIONS

The attack of the Confederate right, south of Gettysburg, July 2, 1863.

advance was over rising ground to the Emmitsburg road, then down grade to a shallow ravine above which towered the ridge. Perry's Florida troops under Colonel David Lang advanced as far as Wilcox did and for a time, together, they drove the enemy. Wright's advance was superb. As the general himself described it, "we worked our way across that terrible field for more than a mile, under the most furious fire of artillery I had ever seen." The Georgians outran their support on either side. "Thus we were perfectly isolated from any portion of our army a *mile* in advance," said Wright, ". . . and abandoning our captured guns we rushed upon the flanking column of the enemy and *literally cut our way out.*"

When Wilcox earlier had sent back to Anderson for help, Wilcox's staff officer was dispatched to Mahone with orders to go forward. Mahone said he had instructions to hold his position and would not leave it. "But," the aide answered, "I am just from General Anderson and he orders you to advance." Mahone replied, "No, I have my orders from General Anderson himself to remain here."

The attack, in a word, had been uncoordinated. Wright fell back because Posey had not covered his left flank or Perry his right. Posey's troops were badly placed and unable to advance as a unit. Perry's men withdrew in the belief that Wilcox had done so; Wilcox felt he had support neither on the right nor the left. In the failure of these brigades of Anderson's, the experience of McLaws and Hood was duplicated. Each division fought its battle almost alone and in no case with its full strength exerted. That was not like Dick Anderson and not like James Longstreet.[27]

For the opening of Longstreet's battle, Dick Ewell had been waiting all day. Lee had visited him during the morning, and several times said with manifest point, "We did not or could not pursue our advantage of yesterday, and now the enemy are in good position." Lee impatiently waited on the left for the sound of Longstreet's guns and then had ridden off to see why the battle was delayed. Ewell was left to guard the left and to strike if he could. As soon as Longstreet's artillery began to roar, Ewell ordered the batteries of Latimer's battalion to open on Cemetery Hill. The Union batteries answered wrathfully with heavier metal. While the firing was in progress, Ewell decided to turn the demonstration into an assault. What he saw in the bombardment to think it held promise of a successful infantry attack he never explained. He sent to the nearest division of the Third Corps on his right—led now by James H. Lane after Dorsey Pender was wounded in mid-afternoon—to request its cooperation when he advanced.

Meanwhile, Latimer's battalion was being overwhelmed by the fire directed against it. Latimer was directed to cease fire and to withdraw all his guns except four, which should be left to cover the advance of the

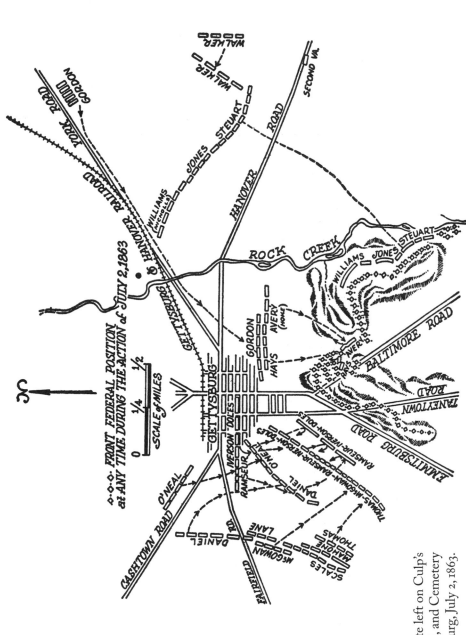

Attack of the Confederate left on Culp's
Hill, East Cemetery Hill, and Cemetery
Hill, Gettysburg, July 2, 1863.

infantry. Ewell heard the slackening of the fire and then its conclusion. He had no answer to his appeal to Lane, but determined to make the attack even though he had no assurance of help on that flank. Orders went to Johnson to begin the assault by taking Culp's Hill. Early and Rodes were to follow on their front.[28]

The sun had been near its setting when the artillery duel ended. Whatever was done by Johnson's men must be done within the hour. With the Stonewall Brigade engaged in skirmishing on the far left, Johnson had to start his assault slowly and with three brigades only. In their groping in the gathering darkness the right brigades soon met repulse. Maryland Steuart on the left got a footing on the hillside. Although his line could be traced only by the fact that the flash of his fire was upward, his men hung on. The enemy by 11:00 P.M. desisted from efforts to drive Steuart out that night.

As soon as Jube Early ascertained that Johnson's division had launched its attack, he prepared to go forward. He had three brigades to employ in the fight, and decided to keep one of these as a reserve. In his assault he would use only Hays's Louisianians and Hoke's North Carolina troops. These were directed to take East Cemetery Hill, which lies next to Cemetery Hill, the key position on the Federal front. One line they crashed easily. They climbed a stone wall and took prisoners. An abatis was passed, rifle pits were overrun, the climb was continued. At last the crest was reached—a bold rush, and guns were seized and flags captured. "At that moment," said Hays, "every piece of artillery which had been fired upon us was silenced."

For a few minutes there was quiet, but for a few minutes only. Through the shadows now, the Confederates could see heavy masses of infantry south of them on the crest of the ridge. Hays did not know whether they were Union or Confederate. He had been cautioned to watch for friends on either flank and in front. A wave of fire swept along the front of the approaching troops. Hays did not reply. Perhaps these were Confederates who mistook his troops for Federals. Another volley—still Hays would not shout an order. A third volley! It was so close that the flash of the muskets lighted the uniforms of the men: They were blue.

Hays gave them every bullet he had in the rifles of his two brigades. For a time, firing fast, he held them off. Soon he saw behind the first line a second; in the rear still another force was gathering. To these odds he could oppose only his own brigade and Hoke's. Early had held back Gordon's brigade, seeing nothing to indicate that Rodes was advancing on the right. Further resistance on the crest would be a waste of life. Hays must give up the prize of guns and commanding ground. Like Wright an hour previously, he had to retreat for lack of help at the decisive moment.[29]

When Early started forward, Rodes did as well, but moving his troops through the streets of Gettysburg consumed slow, expensive minutes. Rodes had to advance some 1,200 yards before he could open fire. Early had scarcely more than half that distance to go. When Early attacked, Rodes was still advancing. When Hays was hoping for reinforcements, Ramseur and Doles were halting their column and debating whether to storm the frowning position ahead of them. Two lines of infantry behind stone walls and breastworks were discovered, supporting well-placed batteries. The two young brigadiers had shown on many a field they did not fear adverse odds, but this time they did not think they should attack what they considered a field fortress until they had asked Rodes.

By the time their messenger reached Rodes, their question had answered itself. Rodes was informed that Early was withdrawing from East Cemetery Hill. It appeared a useless sacrifice of life to deliver an isolated attack. Accordingly, the division quietly withdrew to a position from which Rodes hoped he could spring forward with advantage the next morning.[30]

The battle of July 2 now was ending. On the extreme right, along the western slope of Little Round Top, Hood's men were building with boulders a fortification to protect the barren ground they had won. The Peach Orchard remained in Confederate hands. Far to the left, Maryland Steuart's men were holding a section of the front trenches of the enemy. These three strips of Pennsylvania soil might be, as Lee hoped, points of departure for a decisive attack the next day. But the contrast with a corresponding night two months before was worse than a humiliation. At Chancellorsville, May 2, all the troops working together to strike a joint blow; at Gettysburg, July 2, a battle of divisions, of brigades even! In tactical effort this was not the army of Chancellorsville, but the army of Malvern Hill. It had unlearned the lessons of a year. Said Walter Taylor afterward: "The whole affair was disjointed. There was an utter absence of accord in the movements of the several commands. . . ."[31]

Every division on the field had been engaged either the first day or the second. Two brigades only had escaped lightly—Extra Billy Smith's of Early's command, and Mahone's of Anderson's. The sole infantry reinforcement was Pickett's division of Longstreet's corps, which had reached the field in the afternoon. No other reinforcement of any sort would be available except Stuart's cavalry.

Jeb at last had rejoined the army. After his night march from Hanover he had reached Dover, west of York, on the morning of July 1 but had not found any Confederates there. He started the column for Carlisle, reasoning that if the Southern infantry had advanced to the Susquehanna and were not in the vicinity of York, they must be around Carlisle or Harrisburg. It was late afternoon when the van reached Carlisle and found the pleasant little town garrisoned. The weary, hungry troopers scarcely were in condition to clear the place. By report militia held the town, and when Stuart arrived he had a flag of truce sent in to demand the garrison's surrender. When this was refused, Stuart renewed the demand and gave warning that if the town was not given up he would burn it. Hoping to drive out the militia in panic, he began a slow shelling.

Happily, Stuart was saved both waste of his shells and the destruction of civilian property. Up the road from the south came one of the scouts he had sent out. The rider had found the army! It had been engaged that first of July with the enemy's advance; General Lee directed that Stuart move to Gettysburg. Jeb did not delay compliance. Exhausted troopers mounted their staggering horses. It was afternoon of July 2 when Stuart, riding ahead, reached his anxious chief on Seminary Ridge. No record of the exchange between them is known to exist. The tradition is that Lee said, "Well, General Stuart, you are here at last"—that and little besides.[32]

Stuart may have been disappointed that no applause greeted his return from his longest raid, which he was to persuade himself was his greatest; but of his thoughts he said nothing. Much the same silence covers the reflections of the two other men whose state of mind added to the dangers of the invasion. To the extent that Ewell's report may be assumed to reflect his feelings at the time of the battle, he was chagrined that Rodes had not be able to advance because of assumed lack of support on the right. Said Ewell: ". . . had it been otherwise, I have every reason to believe, from the eminent success attending the assault of Hayes and [Hoke], that the enemy's lines would have been carried."

Longstreet, the last of the trio, had lost something of his sullenness, though not of his depression. Outwardly he seemed almost philosophical. "We have not been so successful as we wished," he told an Austrian military observer, and attributed this chiefly to the fact that Barksdale had been killed and Hood wounded. Inwardly, Longstreet still was determined to argue that Meade's position could be turned and the tactical defensive recovered. After darkness offered concealment, he sent out his scouts toward the southern end of Round Top, and he did not go to army headquarters to report or to ask for orders.[33]

CHAPTER 27

Gettysburg and Its Cost

1. LONGSTREET'S BITTEREST DAY

At dawn July 3, Dick Ewell proceeded to execute his orders for a renewal of the attack against the Federal right. With six brigades at his disposal, Allegheny Johnson unhesitatingly prepared to assault Culp's Hill. Maryland Steuart's brigade alone had gained strategic ground in the twilight attack of the previous evening. Less than a mile west of him was a "little clump of trees" that was destined to be the objective that day of the decisive charge of the battle. With the dawn there swept over Steuart's troops a furious Federal bombardment. To it the Confederates could not oppose anything heavier than a rifle. Johnson moved Daniel's brigade close to that of Steuart and directed the two to deliver an attack with the support of the units on the right. Neither Steuart nor Daniel believed the attack could succeed, but they made ready to advance.

Steuart drew his saber, yelled "Charge bayonets!" and started forward with his men. The left was checked; the right became exposed; the center pressed on until the fire was overwhelming. Daniel had to halt when Steuart did. With the failure of this attack the Confederates yielded the initiative to the Federals, who, by 10:30 A.M., had recovered most of the ground occupied by the Confederates on the second. The heavy losses of those wasteful assaults was the more lamentable by reason of the fact that half an hour after Johnson attacked in accordance with orders, a courier brought a message in which Lee told Ewell that Longstreet would not advance till 10 o'clock; Ewell was directed to delay his forward movement until he could deliver it simultaneously with Longstreet.[1]

During the night of July 2–3, Longstreet had not reconciled himself to a continuance of the offensive. Although Lee wrote later that he gave Longstreet on the second orders "to attack the next morning," Longstreet either was slow or else he was resolved to oppose to the last a plan he believed dangerous. He said afterward that he never was "so depressed as upon that day," but he took grim encouragement from a report by his scouts that no enemy was found beyond the southern end of Round Top. He determined to start troops in that direction and take the eminence in reverse, and was working on the details when Lee rode up to his field headquarters.

With scant ceremony Longstreet began: "General, I have had my scouts out all night, and I find that you still have an excellent opportunity to move around to the right of Meade's army, and maneuver him into attacking us." He probably elaborated, but he could not shake Lee's conviction that the only practicable course left the Confederates was to break the Union center. Lee did not feel that his troops had been defeated. He considered that failure on the second had been due to lack of coordination, and he still believed that, if the army could throw its full strength against the enemy from the positions already gained, he could win the battle. In this belief, Lee reaffirmed his intention of attacking Cemetery Ridge. The whole of the First Corps, he said, must make the assault.[2]

The forces thus assigned for the attack, about 15,000 men, did not seem adequate to Longstreet. He later quoted himself as replying to Lee, "General, I have been a soldier all my life ... and should know, as well as anyone, what soldiers can do. It is my opinion that no 15,000 men ever arrayed for battle can take that position." Lee reiterated his purpose to attack. Soon Longstreet was back with a new objection. Hood's division and McLaws's were exposed to attack from the Round Tops and were weakened by the battle of July 2. If they were withdrawn, the enemy would turn the Confederate right. On this point Longstreet prevailed. Probably in the hope of placating him and giving him faith in the movement, Lee agreed to leave Hood and McLaws where they were. Their place would be taken by Heth's division and half of Pender's. This decision to use Heth appears to have been made quickly and without ascertaining the condition of the troops. The omission was to prove itself one of the worst of the many mistakes of Gettysburg.

Longstreet next argued that the distance, about 1,400 yards, was too great for a successful assault. He insisted that the column of attack would be enfiladed from Round Top. To this Colonel Armistead Long of Lee's staff, an artillerist of high reputation, answered that the guns on the eminence could be silenced. Tactically this assurance almost certainly was unjustified, but the state of mind of the two generals was such that neither of them disputed Long's assertion. Longstreet now had exhausted his arguments. Bitterly he wrote afterward of Lee, "He knew that I did not believe that success was possible ... and he should have put an officer in charge who had more confidence in his plan. Two thirds of the troops were of other commands, and there was no reason for putting the assaulting forces under my charge." To this, of course, the answer was that Lee, with Jackson dead, had no other subordinate of the same experience or military grasp as Longstreet.[3]

The troops designated for the assault were at hand. Pickett's division had arrived by 9 o'clock and moved to the western side of Seminary Ridge. When Pickett rode up to report, Longstreet explained the plan of operation. The plan was the simplest: When all preparations had been made, the artillery was to bombard the front and weaken or silence the Federal batteries. This fire was to center on a "little clump of trees" opposite Pender's position. After the bombardment, the line of battle, previously established by Pickett, was to come over Seminary Ridge and go forward to converge on the grove. Pickett, who had three brigades only, decided to put Garnett and Kemper in the first line and Armistead in the second. In rear and to the right, Longstreet determined to employ Wilcox as a flank guard. On Pickett's left, Johnston Pettigrew was to advance the division of the wounded Harry Heth. In support of Pettigrew were to be Scales's and Lane's brigades of Dorsey Pender's division, to the command of which Trimble belatedly was appointed. Over Trimble and Pettigrew, Longstreet was to have control for the day, and if he needed additional troops he was to call on A. P. Hill for them.

Colonel Alexander had the responsible duty of posting the batteries to deliver the preparatory bombardment. He was instructed, also, to observe the fire and determine when Pickett should charge. Besides directing these arrangements with manifest depression of spirits, Longstreet had twice to ride the length of the corps front with Lee, who was resolved that for the success of the decisive attack on the Federal center no preparation should be neglected. Longstreet was not pleased with the supervision.

Powell Hill was assumed to understand equally well the part his corps was to have in the unfolding drama. The two lieutenant generals were on speaking terms and had in some measure abandoned the antagonism that led to the transfer of Hill from Longstreet after the Seven Days, but they were not cordial and may not even have been genuinely cooperative in spirit. Lee must have taken it for granted that they would arrange between themselves the preparation of the troops of the Third Corps for the assault. Actually, each seems to have left this to the other. The sensitive Hill, always mindful of military etiquette, may have concluded that he must not interfere after his troops temporarily were transferred. Longstreet may have considered that the troops would be supervised by Hill until ordered to advance. No inquiry ascertained whether the regimental command of Pettigrew's division was adequate after the losses of

July 1. Brockenbrough's weak brigade under Colonel Robert M. Mayo and Joe Davis's shattered, inexperienced troops, almost without field officers, were to be on the extreme left. If anyone questioned the prudence of this arrangement, no hint has survived.

Lee intended that Pender's two brigades should be *en échelon* on the left of Pettigrew, as a second line; but, here again, the records do not show that either of the two corps commanders gave instruction to effect this. When Lane came to Longstreet to report for orders, Longstreet told him to form in rear of Pettigrew. Nowhere did Lane indicate in his report that he was told of any plan for *échelon*.[4]

Military remissness always is clearer in retrospect than in prospect. The man who now became the central figure for two bloody hours at Gettysburg was so depressed by his conviction of the unwisdom of an attack that he was not conscious of any failure in preparation. Longstreet was not and could not be reconciled to delivering the assault, but he and the cause he represented now were being dragged by the very ticking of his watch to the inevitable hour. During the early morning there scarcely had been a cannon shot on the Confederate right. As the warming sun rose higher, the skirmishers quieted. Over the Confederate center and right there hung a sinister silence.

Now, an hour before noon, blue skirmishers undertook to wrest from Hill's men a barn and dwelling in front of Pettigrew's right. Hill's guns became heavily engaged for over half an hour. Neither Hill nor his chief of artillery seems to have asked whether so much of the artillery ammunition of the corps should have been wasted in any unnecessary cannonade. To the right, Porter Alexander forbade his seventy-five guns to have any part in this exchange, knowing he would need every round of his short supply if he was to clear the way for Pickett and Pettigrew.

Longstreet was attentive to Alexander's preparations, and about noon sent word to the artillerist that he would himself give the signal for the opening of the bombardment. With Pickett, on Seminary Ridge, Longstreet waited. When it was reported to him that the batteries had been informed of the signal—two guns fired in succession by Miller's company of the Washington Artillery—Longstreet answered quietly, "All right, tell Colonel Walton I will send him word when to begin."[5]

The last of Pickett's infantry was in position. Dick Garnett was there with officers who had won their stars and wreath while he vainly sought to correct the injustice he felt Jackson had done him after Kernstown. Lewis Armistead was in place, Armistead of Malvern Hill. James L. Kemper had his brigade on the ridge. Wilcox was close by. To the left, only one of Heth's brigades was going into the charge under its regular commander—

that one the newest and least experienced of them all, Joe Davis. The brigade of Pettigrew would be under Colonel J. K. Marshall; Archer's would be led by Colonel B. D. Fry. Both Archer's and Davis's brigades were almost without field officers because of the tragic losses of July 1. In the most difficult charge the Army of Northern Virginia ever had made, many of these regiments would be directed by company officers.

One of the supporting brigades of Pender's division, James H. Lane's, was headed by its regular commander. The other brigade was Alfred Scales's, formerly Pender's, which had lost fifty-five officers on the first of July. This command now was to be taken into action by Colonel William Lowrance of the 34th North Carolina, an officer who never previously had exercised brigade command in the field. In a word, of six brigades to the left of Pickett, that of Lane alone was in the keeping of a brigadier of tested combat experience.

The dangerous deployment of the second line was not relieved as the hour of the attack approached. Scales and Lane were in rear of Heth's division, where Longstreet had told them to take station, but their front was by no means as long as that of Heth. The two brigades were centered, moreover, on Pettigrew's line. The result would be that the left of the broad column of attack would consist of one line only. None of the officers inquired whether this was as Longstreet desired. Isaac Trimble had arrived to take command of Pender's men after Lane had put them in position, and of the disposition of the troops Trimble knew scarcely anything. The time he might have given to an examination of the front he devoted to making a speech to his men. No question was raised concerning any shift of the second line to the extreme left, nor was Trimble told that his two brigades in support of Pettigrew were expected to advance *en échelon* to cover the left of Pettigrew. The overconfidence of Lee, the depression of Longstreet, and the probable misapprehension of A. P. Hill caused many thing to be overlooked that July day.[6]

Afternoon it now was. The bombardment must begin. Longstreet realized this but said later he was unwilling to entrust himself with the entire responsibility of ordering the guns to open. With dragging hand, he wrote Alexander, "If the artillery fire does not have the effect to drive off the enemy or greatly demoralize him so as to make our efforts pretty certain, I would prefer that you should not advise General Pickett to make the charge. I shall rely a great deal on your good judgment to determine the matter. . . ."

After this came one of the strangest incidents of a bewildering day: Longstreet went off into the woods and lay down. This was done, he explained in his old age, "to study for some new thought that might aid the assaulting column." Colonel Fremantle, the British observer who was with

Longstreet at the time, recorded that "The General then dismounted and went to sleep for a short time." Sleeping or reflecting, the general was aroused when a courier brought back from Alexander a note which showed that the young artillerist thought Longstreet had in mind some alternative to an assault. The note made it clear, also, that he did not think he should be asked to assume the responsibility of the corps commander.

"General," he wrote, "I will only be able to judge of the effect of our fire on the enemy by his return fire, for his infantry is but little exposed to view and the smoke will obscure the whole field. If, as I infer from your note, there is any alternative to this attack, it should be carefully considered before opening our fire, for it will take all the artillery ammunition we have left to test this one thoroughly, and if the result is unfavorable, we will have none left for another effort."

The depressed Longstreet evidently did not grasp the full meaning of what Alexander said about the supply of ammunition. Nor did he reflect that Alexander, like himself, was doubtful of the success of the charge now that responsibility for it was being placed on him. The point that stuck in Longstreet's mind was that Alexander apparently wanted to know how to determine when the charge should be made. Accordingly, Longstreet wrote: "The intention is to advance the infantry if the artillery has the desired effect of driving the enemy off, or having other effect such as to warrant us in making the attack. When the moment arrives advise General P." Subsequently Longstreet explained, "I still desired to save my men, and felt that if the artillery did not produce the desired effect, I would be justified in holding Pickett off."

It was now 1 o'clock. From the fields the heat was rising, but a west wind was blowing. The artillery along the entire line was silent. Skirmishing was light. Longstreet knew that all the orders had been issued and that all the troops were in position. He swept the field with his glasses to see if the guns were well placed and, at last, he wrote a note to Colonel Walton, his corps chief of artillery: "Let the batteries open; order great care and precision in firing. . . ."[7]

There was one cannon shot, then another. It was 1:17 P.M. In a few seconds battery after battery, firing salvoes, acknowledged the signal. At first the answer of the Federals was slow; then from Cemetery Ridge came the swelling bass of guns in chorus. Smoke clouds rose opposite the Peach Orchard, to the right and to the left till the whole ridge was screened. It was on! For success or failure, for the refutation of Longstreet's fears or for the vindication of his belief that the enemy's position was impregnable, the testing bombardment had begun.

Although the smoke concealed the explosion of the shells, it was manifest that the Confederate fire was shaking the enemy. For once the Southerners appeared to have more guns in action than the enemy was employing on the front of attack. Far off to the left the guns of the Second Corps opened; nearer, the batteries of the Third Corps went into action. After Longstreet had watched the exchange for some minutes, he spurred his horse through the roar of the artillery duel and entered the woods in front of Pickett's anxious men. Slowly dismounting, he waited. The ridges were shaking with the violence of the cannonade. Every battery was surrounded by smoke. The stench of battle was in the air. Shells struck and shattered limbs of trees, or ploughed up the stony earth of Cemetery Ridge, or shrieked in disappointed wrath overhead. The loudest shout of men was drowned by the ceaseless, pulsing roar of the guns.

A courier rode up to General Pickett and handed him a folded paper. Pickett read it and strode toward Longstreet. The moment had come. The note must be from Alexander. Now it was in Longstreet's hands, open: "If you are coming at all you must come immediately or I cannot give you proper support; but the enemy's fire has not slackened materially. . . ." As Longstreet read, Pickett waited. Longstreet said nothing. "General," asked Pickett, "shall I advance?" There was no reply. Pickett did not move. His eyes were on his chief. Slowly Longstreet dropped his chin on his uniform collar. That was his answer. Pickett wished only to be sure: "I shall lead my division forward, sir." Not a word was there from Longstreet. He turned from Pickett and prepared to mount. By the time he was on his horse, Pickett had walked away.[8]

In the saddle of command again, the stir of action possessed Longstreet. Near the Peach Orchard he found Alexander blazing away with his guns and watching excitedly the little clump of trees. Union fire had slackened. No fresh guns had appeared. It was now or never for the infantry! If Pickett did not start at once, Alexander repeated, the artillery could not give adequate support. Ammunition was very low. Longstreet was startled: "Go and stop Pickett right where he is," he cried, "and replenish your ammunition."

"We can't do that, sir! The train has but little. It would take an hour to distribute it, and meanwhile the enemy would improve the time." Longstreet stood irresolute for a moment. Then, in unwonted emotion, he said: "I don't want to make this charge; I don't believe it can succeed. I would stop Pickett now, but that General Lee has ordered it and expects it." He paused again. He would not ask explicitly whether the artillerist agreed with him; Alexander did not think he should express an opinion on so large a subject unless directed to do so. At length, as if the fates themselves gave the answer, down Seminary Ridge came Garnett's brigade. On his right Kemper was emerging. At length Heth's men advanced into the open. At a shouted word of command the long line was dressed. The west wind lifted the smoke. Nineteen battle flags began to flap.[9]

Kemper called out, "Armistead, hurry up! I am going to charge those heights and carry them, and I want you to support me." Armistead answered, "I'll do it! Look at my line; it never looked better on dress parade." Every soldier within hearing was stirred by Pickett's appeal: "Up, men, and to your posts! Don't forget today that you are from Old Virginia." Farther up the line Pettigrew called to one of his officers, "Now, Colonel, for the honor of the good old North State, forward!" Soon the line was passing Longstreet, whose pride rose with his concern. Salutes were exchanged. In old affection for the chief of the division he observed how jauntily Pickett went on. Garnett, too sick to walk, was wrapped in a blue overcoat, but he sat his great black horse in soldierly composure.[10]

Quietly Longstreet got down from his horse, perched his bulky form on a rail fence, and watched with sharp, professional eye as much as he could see of the attack. "The advance was made in very handsome style," he said afterward. The flawless line halted briefly in a little depression and then went steadfastly into the full fury of the enemy's fire. Most of the Confederate guns were silent by this time. If they were served any longer, no ammunition would be left for them when they followed the infantry.

An officer was directed to tell Wilcox to go forward at once; let him support the assault. Pickett's troops were charging gloriously. They were within canister range; they defied it; they kept straight on. So did the right brigades of Heth's division. On the left of Pettigrew's division, Mayo's men and Davis's brigade began to hesitate. At the first report of this, Longstreet sent to Dick Anderson with instructions to move forward in support of Heth and Pettigrew.

Pickett and Pettigrew's right brigades soon were converging on the little clump of trees. All the battle flags appeared to be running together. A Southern flag would cease to wave, would fall, would rise, would drop again. Shells cut gaps. The flanks withered under the flame. Amazingly on the right and center, the formation was retained. On the left, where Mayo had no support, discouraged soldiers were turning back or were lying down among the dead. The high quaver of the rebel yell was faintly audible through the wrathful roar of a hundred Federal guns. Pickett keeps on. Fry and Marshall do. More of Mayo's men have halted; scores have started to retreat; some are running to the rear. Davis's regiments, with untested leaders, are wavering on their left.

In support—and not *en échelon*—Scales and Lane are marching over Pettigrew's fallen. The left has melted away or has merged with the right of Pettigrew. Now, the entire line has disappeared into the dust and smoke

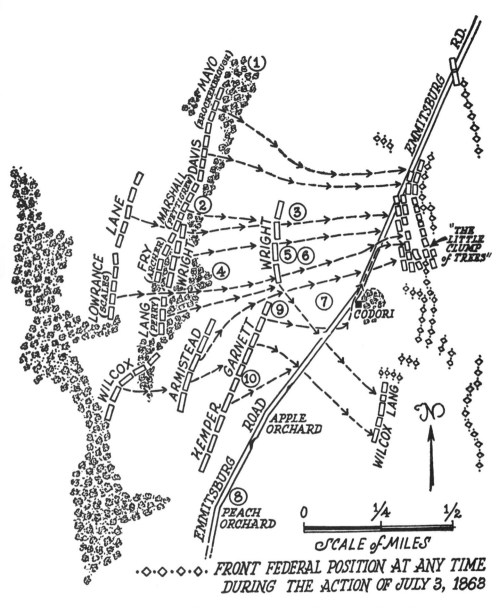

·◇·◇·◇·◇· FRONT FEDERAL POSITION AT ANY TIME
DURING THE ACTION OF JULY 3, 1863

The lines of advance of Pickett, Pettigrew, and Trimble at Gettysburg,
afternoon on July 3, 1863. The encircled numerals indicate: (1–2) position
of the massed artillery of the Third Corps; (3) advance of Poague's artillery
battalion, Third Corps; (4) position of Woolfolk's battery, First Corps;
(5) position of Wright's brigade, which went out to rally the broken assault
troops; (6) position of Cabell's artillery battalion, First Corps; (7–8) position
of the massed artillery of the First Corps; (9–10) intermediate position
of Wilcox, directly in front of Garnett before the final stage of the assault.

that overhang the ridge. The thin Southern ranks are grappling unseen beyond the stone wall. All the might of the enemy is now thrown against them. A mat of fallen red flags lies under the trees. Longstreet strains eyes and ears and knows who the victor in that unequal struggle will be. Sternly he orders an officer to halt the advance of Anderson. For a few moments there is the blank of utter suspense, then a perceptible decline in the infantry fire and then a slow trickle backward of men who do not appear to be wounded.[11]

Colonel Fremantle, joining Longstreet, cries, "I wouldn't have missed this for anything!" Longstreet on the top of the worm fence laughed grimly as he replied, "The devil you wouldn't! I would like to have missed it very much; we've attacked and been repulsed: look there!" Fremantle "then had a view of the open space between the two positions, and saw it covered with Confederates slowly and sulkily returning towards us in small broken parties under a heavy fire of artillery."

Longstreet ordered Wright to move out and collect and rally the fugitives, but, strangely, he did nothing to halt the advance of Wilcox or the little Florida brigade that was to follow Wilcox. Longstreet perhaps observed scarcely at all the advance of Wilcox because he now expected a counterattack and busied himself in preparations to meet it.[12]

The survivors of the charge were coming up the slope from the meadow. The men were in every mood of repulse. Some raged, some swore, some scarcely could believe they had been repulsed. Dazed and exhausted, some looked blankly ahead. In the face of others was the uncertainty of escape from pursuing furies. Every emotion there was of vain and costly assault, every one except a consciousness that more than a battle had been lost: The enemy had beaten them back; they could do no more. The rest of it—war's decision, America's destiny, the doom of the Confederacy—all this was read afterward into the story of their return.

Tense moments passed. The enemy continued an uncertain fire. Nobody knew what to expect next. Federal skirmishers advanced from Cemetery Ridge, with every indication that a line would follow, but in the face of artillery fire they withdrew. If the Confederates were disorganized, the enemy was irresolute. While Dick Anderson's division stood ready to repel assault, where Longstreet had halted the line, no enemy came within range.[13]

After the fire of the opposing forces died in darkness, there was no further argument over the course the army must follow. One thing only could be done. With food supplies low and artillery ammunition almost exhausted, retreat was imperative. Instructions came from G.H.Q. The wagons and the wounded were, of course, to be started before the infantry moved. Withdrawal was to be by way of the Hagerstown road and across the mountains. Hill was to lead, Longstreet to follow, Ewell to bring up the rear.

On the morning of the fourth of July Longstreet was afield early to ascertain what was the prospect of the development the army had most to fear—a heavy attack by Meade. As the forenoon passed without a single thrust from Cemetery Ridge and nothing more formidable than Federal reconnaissance, Longstreet and the other Confederate commanders permitted themselves to hope that Meade had been too heavily injured to strike. It was the Glorious Fourth, a young artillerist reminded Longstreet: "We should have a salute from the other side at noon." Noon came and passed. Not a gun was fired. Said Longstreet with satisfaction: "Their artillery was too much crippled yesterday to think of salutes. Meade is not in good spirits this morning."[14] In another hour rain began to fall. With difficulty the ambulances and the wagons were started toward the mountains through a downpour.

After darkness the infantry began to move from Seminary Ridge along the Hagerstown road. A grim but not a despairing march it was. In most hearts there was bitterness and humiliation that the columns were headed for the Potomac instead of Baltimore or Philadelphia. None realized, to repeat, that Gettysburg was more than a battle in which the army, winning two days, had been unable on the third to drive the enemy from a position of great strength. Mercifully or tragically, none could see that the afternoon of the Confederacy had come.

If any shadow of resentment still lay on the soul of James Longstreet, it was lightened at the fire of his own bivouac. There, while the rain poured down, Lee came and spoke briefly of the struggle. "It's all my fault," he said; "I thought my men were invincible." Longstreet's only recorded observations that day or the next were tactical. The mistake, he told Colonel Fremantle, was in not concentrating the army more, and failing to make the attack "with 30,000 men instead of 15,000." The troops who gave way, he explained, "were young soldiers who had never been under fire before." Not one word did Fremantle report of any contention by Longstreet that the basic tactics of battle had been defective.[15]

On the fifth of July resumed a retreat that seemed half nightmare, half mercy. Unvoiced, unadmitted, was the fear of many a leader that Meade by some miracle of march might catch the column while it was strung out on the road. On the morning of the seventh they took up a line to cover the crossings of the Potomac. The river was past fording, and Confederate detachments under the eyes of Jackson's former quartermaster, Major J. A. Harmon, had to set to work building pontoons. Until July 12 nothing occurred except cavalry clashes and occasional skirmishes. That day the

Federal infantry approached. Lee's veterans steeled themselves for another Antietam, but the enemy appeared more anxious to cover himself with entrenchments than to prepare to attack.

During the night of July 13–14 and the forenoon of the fourteenth, at Williamsport and Falling Waters, the army passed back to Virginia. Harry Heth was left under vexing conditions to cover the rear. He did so with the loss of two guns and of approximately 500 stragglers from many brigades—difficulties considered, a wholly creditable performance.[16]

2. "Jackson Is Not Here"

First reports in Southern newspapers were jubilant. "A brilliant and crushing victory"; 14,000 or 40,000 prisoners captured; Lee marching on Baltimore. When it was manifest, instead, that Lee had withdrawn to the Potomac, the public was assured that "there is nothing bad in this news beyond a disappointment." Lee had fallen back to secure his "vast train of materials," fifteen miles long. A few days later the result was declared "favorable to the South," but the success "had not been decisive" because of "the semblance of retreat." Not until July 25 could even the anti-administration *Richmond Examiner* bring itself to speak of the "repulse at Gettysburg." By July 30, having blown hot, the *Charleston Mercury* blew cold and asserted: "It is impossible for an invasion to have been more foolish and disastrous." That was an extremist's view.[17]

In the state of mind that prevailed immediately after the battle, critical discussion was considered unpatriotic. The present-day student, on the other hand, finds Gettysburg the most interesting of all the battles of the Army of Northern Virginia. It is the campaign that provokes the warmest, longest debate because it is in bewildering contrast to the operations that preceded it. The reader must be cautioned at the outset that there is no "secret" of Gettysburg, no single failure which, if ascertained and appraised justly, "explains" the outcome. A score of circumstances, working together, rather than any one, wrought a major Confederate defeat.

Many reasons for the non-success of the invasion sprang from the reorganization necessitated by the death of Jackson. These inhered in the new organization included the absence of the more efficient cavalry units, the awkward leadership of men in new and more responsible positions, the state of mind of Stuart, Longstreet, and Ewell, the overconfidence of Lee, the poor handling of the artillery, and the lack of coordination in attack.

Of exterior factors, the first was the limitation imposed on Lee's action by the factor of time. The campaign was fought while the army was living off the country. Much of the collection of supplies had to be undertaken with little cavalry. Lee stated this succinctly: ". . . we were unable to await an attack, as the country was unfavorable for collecting supplies in the presence of the enemy. . . ."[18] A second exterior factor was the extent and thinness of the line. Five miles and more in length and shaped like a great fish-hook, it made communication and concentration difficult.

Always to be considered were the skill, persistence, and might with which the Army of the Potomac defended on the second and third of July a position of natural strength. This third factor was a disillusioning reality and a gloomy warning of what the Confederacy might expect of Northern veterans under competent leadership. At Gettysburg the magnificent Federal divisions had strong ground, interior lines, the sense of fighting for home, knowledge of combat, and the intelligent, courageous leadership of Meade, Hancock, and other wholly capable captains. Vigorous and experienced as was Lee's army, it could not prevail over that adversary.

These were the larger reasons for the defeat as seen from the standpoint of the high command. It will be observed that all the Confederate errors of overconfidence, bad organization, and inept leadership were aggravated by the factors of chance and circumstance which the Federals, for the first time in the long contest of the two armies, were in position to capitalize fully.

At the beginning, the approach of the Confederates to the battlefield was incautious. From the time the army entered Pennsylvania it was blinded by the absence of Stuart. Nothing was comparable to this in preparing the way for a tragedy. On July 1, having no information beyond that collected the previous day by Pettigrew, the van of the Third Corps advanced without cavalry. Before the Confederates were aware of it, their leading divisions were engaged beyond easy conclusion. For this the greater part of the blame rested on Stuart, who should have been present to reconnoiter.

As the Second Corps advanced to the aid of the Third, that first afternoon of the battle, Rodes's line of battle was formed in a manner that put the best brigadiers where the fighting was lightest and the feeblest men in the most difficult fray. Ramseur and Doles should have formed, if possible, the column of attack. Lee would tell Rodes, "I am proud of your division,"[19] but after all the facts were known, the employment of Rodes's division must have been judged distinctly below expectations.

The final debate of the first day concerns Ewell's conduct and, particularly, the question whether he should have assaulted Cemetery Hill as soon as he reached Gettysburg. Nothing that had happened from the time the army left the Rappahannock had indicated, even to the slightest, that Ewell was lacking in power of decision as a corps commander. Everything on the march had been marked by so much promptitude, positiveness, and unhesitating action that no superior would have hesitated to allow discretion to Ewell, or would have imagined for a moment that the commander of the Second Corps would hesitate to exercise that discretion.

In the drama of July 1, it is difficult to criticize Ewell for anything he did until he entered the town, and as difficult to praise him for anything he did thereafter. The picture is of a man who could not come to a decision within the time swift action might have brought victory. In most informed opinion, an attack delivered within an hour after the defeat of the I and XI corps would have been successful; at any subsequent hour an assault would have been repulsed. The impression persists that Ewell did not display the initiative, resolution, and boldness to be expected of a good soldier.

On July 2 coordination among the corps was lacking, with the result that the battle opened late. Reconnaissance was inadequate. The Confederate high command was deceived concerning the strength of the Federal left. When action was begun, it was poorly directed on both flanks. The engagement on the right of Lee's line probably should not have been fought at all under the vague and misfounded plan of the commanding general. Errors of subordinates deprived it of whatever chance of success it might have had. This is a broad indictment, but historically, count by count, it is a "true bill."

All reasons for Longstreet's failure to attack during the forenoon are the subject of one of the most familiar controversies of Gettysburg. There can be no escaping the conclusion that his behavior was that of a man who sulked because his plan was rejected by his chief. This conclusion need not be framed from the testimony of those who hated Longstreet after the war as a political renegade. Longstreet's own A.A.G., Moxley Sorrel, is the only witness who need be called. Sorrel wrote, with all the evidence before him, "We can discover that he did not want to fight on the ground or on the plan adopted by the General-in-Chief. As Longstreet was not to be made willing and Lee refused to change or could not change, the former failed to conceal some anger. There was apparent apathy in his movements. They lacked the fire and the point of his usual bearing on the battlefield."[20]

Beyond this it is not just to go in criticizing Longstreet's conduct on the second prior to the time his march to the right was begun. His attitude was wrong but his instinct was correct. He should have obeyed orders, but the orders should not have been given. Information concerning the enemy's left was scant and inaccurate. The early-morning reconnaissance of Captain S. R. Johnston was accurate—so far as he went. No Federals were on Little Round Top when he climbed the slope there at 5:30 A.M., but he missed them on that eminence by a margin of minutes. Two brigades of the XII Corps were moving northward when Johnston was on the ridge of Round Top. He did not see them. If he had . . .

That is not the end of the curious factor of chance that fateful morning. Johnston did not attempt to climb the southern stretches of Cemetery Ridge. Had he done so he might have been captured; but if he had escaped he might have brought back information the Confederate critics of Longstreet never possessed. It was this: By 9:00 A.M. July 2 the Federals had between Ziegler's Grove and the Round Tops at least 18,200 men ready to fight. The troops thought to be moving into position on the ridge, while Longstreet loitered, actually had been there since early morning.[21]

All question of the effect of Longstreet's delay must, therefore, be limited to what might have been accomplished early in the day on the extreme Federal left, at the Round Tops or directly north of them. The tradition must be discarded that the southern stretches of Cemetery Ridge were unoccupied on the morning of the second. By the time McLaws and Hood arrived, that part of the ridge was held by strong, well-placed troops. In that fact, much of the criticism of Longstreet evaporates. There remains the consideration whether a thorough reconnaissance could have been made; and whether, in the absence of it, battle should have been joined. The chief blame is that of Stuart, absent when most needed for reconnaissance.

Obviously, when the commander of the column of attack found the plan contrary to the hard actualities of the field, he should have notified Lee. Had Longstreet been himself in temper, he would have done this. When the belated attack reluctantly was delivered by Longstreet, it lacked even an approach to unity. Hood's division was allowed to wear dull its fighting edge before McLaws went into action. McLaws's advance was not followed immediately by that of Anderson, who apparently knew little of what was planned. Scarcely at any time during the afternoon was the full strength of any division hurled against the enemy. The participation of Hill and his artillery in the operation was so slight that his name scarcely appeared in reports of the day's operations.

The mismanagement of the action during the afternoon of July 2 in front of Ewell's corps was principally in loose direction or in no direction at all. Apparently Ewell knew little of the condition of his units in the assault on Culp's Hill. Early's attack was prompt and vigorous but was delivered with only two of his brigades. Smith's brigade was treated as if that leader could not be trusted in action. Such frail liaison as existed between Early and Rodes was effected by those two officers and not by Ewell. The lieutenant general did not know what division was on the right of his corps and did not take any step to elicit its aid till the attack was about to be launched.

Ewell's semi-passive role did not destroy the initiative of all his subordinates. Early's conduct was soldierly. His attack on East Cemetery Hill followed quickly that of Johnson on Culp's Hill. Early was wise also in abandoning the assault when he did. On Early's left, Allegheny Johnson's performance on July 2, though not brilliant, was vigorous.

Rodes manifestly should not have neglected, as he did, to calculate the time required for him and for Early to deliver their attacks simultaneously. To the allegation that Rodes should have assaulted Cemetery Hill, an answer is found in the character of the men who shared his decision against delivering the attack. Ramseur and Doles were among the most daring, hardest fighters of the army. If they agreed with their militant commander that the hill could not be carried, few who knew them would maintain the contrary. It is difficult to escape the conclusion that Rodes's second of July was in disappointing contrast to his second of May. Dash was lacking.

The employment of Ewell's artillery on July 2 was as inefficient as that of Hill's guns. While Latimer was being driven from his position at the price of a wound that proved fatal, four batteries and no more were preparing for the advance of Early and Rodes. Two battalions of artillery were left idle all the while north of Gettysburg. Some of the inaction of the gunners of the Second Corps could be attributed to the absence of the wounded corps chief of artillery, Stapleton Crutchfield, but that circumstance should have made Ewell more diligent. It did not.

On the third of July the lack of coordination in attack was scarcely less than on the second. The first question, of course, is whether an attempt should have been made to break the center of the Federal position. On this, little more is to be said. Lee felt that the assault was in a measure unavoidable and that, if the full strength of the army could be brought to bear, the attack would be successful. He accepted the responsibility, and he meant precisely what he said when he told Longstreet, "It's all my fault; I thought my men were invincible."[22]

The second criticism of the Confederate operations of the third day is that the artillery preparation for the charge of Pickett and Pettigrew was inadequate, and that when the bombardment was well-handled it had to be halted because ammunition was exhausted. This criticism is justified. Gettysburg demonstrated that the reorganization of the artillery gave flexibility within a corps, but among the corps there was little cooperation. Pendleton had neither the prestige nor the authority to assure the employment of all the guns as one weapon under one leader. He appears in the campaign more as a consultant than as a commander. Porter Alexander subsequently argued convincingly that if sufficient guns had been massed on the Confederate center to silence the batteries on Cemetery Hill, the column that attacked Cemetery Ridge would not have been exposed to so heavy a flank fire. In addition, there was scant liaison. In Hill's and Ewell's corps, Alexander computed that fifty-six guns were not used, and that of the eighty-four employed, eighty were parallel to the line of the enemy, though an enfilade of part of the Union position would have been possible.[23]

So far as the records show, no check was made on the morning of July 3 to ascertain how heavily the firing of the previous days had depleted the ammunition supply. The Third Corps caissons were drawn upon heavily during the useless morning cannonade. When battalion commanders sent their caissons to the point designated by Pendleton as the position of the ordnance train, they found the wagons had disappeared—moved without notice farther to the rear. As a result, many of the guns of the Third Corps and a number of those of the First stood idle for lack of ammunition at a time when the Federals were shattering the flank of the advancing line. Fundamentally, the lack of effective general supervision of the artillery and of the ordnance supplies was responsible.[24]

The column that delivered the attack, like the cannonade that preceded it, was inadequate for the task assigned it, and tactically, in at least three respects, was not well employed. First of all, a wrong choice was made when Heth's division was chosen to join Pickett's in the final assault. Headquarters was guilty of a most serious omission in not ascertaining the condition of the command before it was designated for further action. Its loss had been worse on July 1 among officers than in the ranks. Davis's brigade on the left flank was almost without field officers. In Pettigrew's division not one of the men who led a brigade during the charge possessed experience in handling so many men. Heth himself had not resumed his duties because of the head wound received on the first. His luck then had been extraordinary. A minié ball had broken the outer coating of the skull and cracked the inner coating, but had not penetrated the brain. Heth thought this was because of the folds of paper inside the sweat band of his hat, inserted by a clerk when the hat was fitted at Cashtown.[25] His troops came under the direction of Johnston Pettigrew, a man of large intellectual capacity but of limited field service. He never had led a division in action.

It seems reasonable to suppose that Pender's division would have done better than Heth's if for no other reason than that it had suffered less in the first day's battle. Anderson might have used Mahone and Wilcox, or Mahone and Wright, to support Pender in the manner Lane and Scales supported Heth.

The column of attack, in the second place, had its supporting troops improperly placed. Rather than supporting Pettigrew's left *en échelon*, the brigades of Lane and Scales were in a foreshortened second line that was aligned on Pettigrew's right. Lane moved the two brigades into position knowing nothing of any orders to advance *en échelon*. It evidently was not the intention of Lee to permit Lane to carry the division into action, but the delay in assigning Trimble was overlong. It is doubtful if Trimble knew enough, on short notice, to see how dangerous his deployment was.

Part of the blame should be placed at Longstreet's door, yet here he was not well served. Lane was aware of the situation—he explained in his report, "there was consequently no second line in rear of [Pettigrew's] left"—but did not notify Longstreet. Trimble's account contains no reference to the fact that his line was not so long as Pettigrew's. He certainly did not report it to Longstreet. If it is fair to say that Longstreet should have been acquainted with his own order of battle, it may be answered that the officers on that flank should have seen that he was better informed.[26]

Although Hill technically was relieved of responsibility when Pettigrew's division and half of Pender's were placed under Longstreet, it would have been the part of good comradeship to send an officer to Longstreet to say that the lines were formed and the second line extended to such and such a point in rear of Pettigrew. This may have been expecting too much of a man who had disliked Longstreet, but it is by lack of cooperation in matters seemingly as small as this that battles sometimes are lost. The question of the relative responsibility of handling these Third Corps units is sharply pointed in the tragic wastage of Wilcox's brigade in a futile advance after Pickett had gone forward. Wilcox apparently was under everybody's order and nobody's.

The third tactical defect was that two weak units were put on the left flank. Brockenbrough's brigade, on the unsupported left of Pettigrew's line, had been Field's, but he had been absent for ten months. Under Harry Heth it recovered somewhat; then, at Chancellorsville, under Brockenbrough, it was greatly reduced in numbers. The troops suffered further in the action of July 1. On July 3 the brigade was commanded by Colonel Robert M. Mayo of the 47th Virginia. Successive change of leaders doubtless weakened the discipline of the brigade. Next to the right was the brigade of Joseph R. Davis—brave, inexperienced troops under an officer who matched his men. In the battle of July 1, Davis had lost all except two of his field officers and many of his company officers.

Neither Davis's brigade nor Brockenbrough's should have been placed on the exposed left, which was without help from Trimble's short line. To say that the relative strength of the various brigades of this division should have been known to Longstreet would be overcritical, but to say that the weakness on the left should have been disregarded by all the responsible officers would be to set an exceedingly low standard of command. Through negligence or overconfidence, the organization failed to provide the strongest order of battle its numbers made possible. All the contemporary accounts agree that the first wavering and then the first abandonment of the charge were in these brigades on the left. Men from nearly all the regiments pressed on and reached the ridge, but could not hold their ground. Most of the troops under Mayo and Davis started back to their own lines before they reached the ridge.

Stuart refused, as always, to admit any shortcomings on his part in the Pennsylvania campaign, but the other three men who were responsible for the chief failures at Gettysburg accepted the blame without hesitation. Next to that of Malvern Hill, the Battle of Gettysburg was the worst fought of all the engagements of General Lee. When he said "It's all my fault," he meant that his own responsibility was greater than that of any and all other officers. Ewell was no less frank. Months later he told General Hunton that "it took a dozen blunders to lose Gettysburg and he had committed a good many of them." Longstreet wrote to his uncle three weeks after the battle: "I cannot help but think that great results would have obtained had my views been thought better of; yet I am much inclined to accept the present condition as for the best. . . . As we failed, I must take my share of the responsibility. . . . As General Lee is our commander, he should have the support and influence we can give him. If the blame, if there is any, can be shifted from him to me, I shall help him and our cause by taking it."[27]

Lee never gave any intimation that he considered Longstreet's failure at Gettysburg more than the error of a good soldier. It was not until years afterward, when Gettysburg was seen as the turning point of the war, that criticism of Longstreet became, in effect, blame for the loss of the battle that lost the war. The sum of just accusation against him is that he held too tenaciously to his favorite theory of defensive tactics, that he sulked and delayed on July 2 when his tactics were rejected, that he did not use his forces in their full strength on the second, and that he did not exercise the same care in the direction of the Third Corps units that he gave to his own dispositions on the final day of the battle. To Longstreet's credit was the belief that Cemetery Ridge, on July 2–3, was too strong to be stormed successfully. If, when the balance of Longstreet's account is struck, it still is adverse to him, it does not warrant the traditional accusation that he was the villain of the piece. The mistakes of Lee and of Ewell and the long absence of Stuart were personal factors of failure as serious as Longstreet's.

3. THE PRICE OF GETTYSBURG

The Confederate casualties of the Gettysburg campaign made the hardest veteran shudder. Of the rank and file, the killed have been computed at 4,637, the wounded at 12,391, and the missing at 5,846, a total of 22,874—

virtually the same as the Federal aggregate of 22,813. Not even at Sharpsburg had bullets claimed so many general officers. Six had been killed or mortally wounded, three captured, eight wounded. Almost exactly a third of the fifty-two general officers in the campaign had become casualties. In addition to the six who had been slain, at least five had been made prisoners or been wounded so severely that their ability to take up their duties again was in doubt. By the most optimistic estimate, 20 per cent of the general officers would have to be replaced. Several others, it was apparent, ought not again be entrusted with troops.

Among the lost officers were several of established place or developing promise. The killed or mortally wounded were Lewis A. Armistead, William Barksdale, Richard B. Garnett, Dorsey Pender, Johnston Pettigrew, and Paul Semmes. The captured were Isaac R. Trimble and James L. Kemper, both badly hurt, and James J. Archer. The most seriously injured of those carried back to Virginia were John B. Hood and Wade Hampton.

Until the great charge at Gettysburg, Lewis Armistead never had such an hour as came to him at Malvern Hill, but he had been consistently a good officer. Always a leader, at the stone wall he was among the first to leap over. Beyond it he fell. William Barksdale, though not professionally trained to arms, had proved his mettle at Fredericksburg in the battle of the pontoons, and he died where he would have chosen—in battle at the head of his men. Dick Garnett had won the affection of all his officers during the months he commanded a brigade in Pickett's division. He had been sick and was almost incapacitated for duty on the third of July, but insisted on leading the charge of his brigade though he had to ride and offer a target to every marksman. Of like spirit was Paul Semmes, whose brother Raphael captained the *Alabama*. Semmes was seriously wounded in the advance of McLaws's division on the afternoon of the second. He came to his end in Virginia on July 10 with the proud assurance, "I consider it a privilege to die for my country."[28]

Johnston Pettigrew was among the most deplored of the casualties. On the night of July 13, during a dash by Federal cavalry against the rear guard, a blue trooper inflicted a grievous abdominal wound on Pettigrew. On the long, agonizing journey into Virginia he was the inspiration of his soldiers. "Boys," he said as he observed their sympathetic distress, "don't be disheartened; maybe I will fool the doctors yet." At Bunker Hill, on July 17, he expired. For none who fought so briefly in the Army of Northern Virginia was there more praise while living or more laments when dead.[29]

Curiously similar to Johnston Pettigrew's was the fate of Dorsey Pender. He passed unscathed through the hard fighting of July 1, and on the afternoon of the second, while inspecting his divisional line on Seminary

Ridge, he was struck on the leg by a fragment of shell. The wound manifestly was serious, but Pender had been hit so often that he could not believe this injury mortal. Regretfully he turned over the command to James H. Lane and undertook in an ambulance the long journey back to Virginia. At length he reached Staunton, but by that time infection had spread. Amputation became necessary on July 18. He never rallied from the operation. Pender's death deepened the disappointments of Gettysburg. General Lee was quoted as saying that Dorsey Pender was the most promising of the younger officers in the army.[30]

Hood had been hit severely in the arm by a shrapnel shot. He realized that he could not keep the field and called immediately for his senior brigadier, E. M. Law, and for his surgeon. At first there was fear he would lose the arm, but safe in a Charlottesville hospital his comrade Wade Hampton was able to write: "He is doing well, and his arm will be saved. All he needs now is good nursing, together with cheerful company and generous living. . . ." Although Hood's wounded arm was never again to have its full strength, he was not to be counted with the dead or the invalided. Nor was Hampton, though his wounds, too, were severe. He had to admit that much: ". . . I have been handled pretty roughly, having received two saber cuts on the head—one of which cut through the table of my skull—and a shrapnel shot in my body, which is there yet. But I am doing well and hope in a few days to be able to go home."[31]

If Hampton and Hood could be regarded as temporarily absent, the fate of Isaac Trimble was uncertain. In the charge on the afternoon of the third he fell with so severe a leg wound that amputation was necessary. He had to be left in the hands of enemies, some of whom had for him a vindictive hate as an alleged "bridge burner" of 1861 in Maryland.[32] None could say when, if ever, he would resume his command. The same was true of J. J. Archer, though he had fewer personal enemies than Trimble delighted to count. James L. Kemper might hope for early exchange if he survived his injury. The remaining wounded general officers—Harry Heth, A. M. Scales, A. G. Jenkins, J. B. Robertson, G. T. Anderson, and John M. Jones—would be back on duty before many weeks.

Field officers had been slaughtered. Seven of the nine colonels, lieutenant colonels, and majors of Davis's brigade were killed or wounded in the first day's battle; every field officer of Scales's brigade, save one, fell in that action along with their general. Four of Wilcox's colonels were wounded on the second day. When the charge of July 3 ended, Archer's brigade had only two unwounded field officers, Pettigrew had one, Davis had none. Regimental command of Pickett's division virtually was destroyed. Five colonels were killed, two mortally wounded, and five received injuries from which they recovered. Three lieutenant colonels were killed; four others, commanding regiments, were wounded. Of all the field officers in the fifteen regiments of Pickett's men, one only, Lieutenant Colonel Joseph C. Cabell, escaped unhurt.

Many regiments marched back to Virginia under captains. Garnett's brigade was commanded by a major, Tige Anderson's and James Archer's by lieutenant colonels. Some of these losses never were made good. As late as the autumn of 1864 regiments of the First Corps were suffering in discipline because so many field officers had been wounded and left on the field at Gettysburg.[33]

After the army rested a few days in Virginia, and the uncertainties regarding the fate of some of the missing officers was removed, a major general had to be named in succession to Dorsey Pender. It was not necessary to select another officer of like rank to take the place of Isaac Trimble because he might be exchanged, and was without a division anyway. New brigadiers had to be found, if possible, to take the places of Semmes, Barksdale, Armistead, Garnett, and Pettigrew. Decision might wait, for a time, as respected Archer and Kemper, both prisoners of war. In Extra Billy Smith's place a competent man was imperative. Otherwise a once-splendid brigade might be ruined. That made six brigadiers. As it was manifest that O'Neal could not succeed to Rodes's old brigade, a seventh brigadier was needed there. If an eighth could be found, Iverson might be given some other permanent duty. One division commander, then, and at least eight new brigadiers were needed.

Scrutiny of the record of the colonels who passed through the red fury of the battles of July showed four infantrymen only who could be promoted confidently and at once. One of these was Eppa Hunton, colonel of the 8th Virginia, Garnett's brigade. Hunton, in his fortieth year and by profession a lawyer, had been in the service since the outbreak of hostilities and, after Sharpsburg, had been recommended by the other colonels of the brigade as a successor to Pickett, in preference to Garnett, when Pickett was promoted. Now the advancement earned by Hunton could be given him without conflict or embarrassment. As of August 3 he was appointed.

Another automatic promotion, so to say, was that of Benjamin G. Humphreys, colonel of the 21st Mississippi, Barksdale's brigade. Humphreys had been Barksdale's mainstay and was well tested. He was fifty-four and therefore among the older colonels, but he had spent more than a year at West Point before he and other cadets were dismissed for pranks on Christmas Eve, 1826. As a planter and lawmaker he had shown capacity. His army record was clean. Promotion, which was as logical as it had been long delayed, was awarded him August 14.

In Rodes's old brigade, once O'Neal was passed by, the man qualified for promotion by his fine conduct at Gettysburg was Colonel Cullen A. Battle of the 3rd Alabama. He and his regiment had been detached from O'Neal's brigade before the advance of July 1, and at the crisis of the fighting he had joined Ramseur and fought fiercely. Battle's previous record being on parity with his furious advance on Seminary Ridge, he was promoted brigadier general on August 25—a vigorous, hard-hitting man of thirty-eight, a lawyer and a politician but able and self-taught in the school of war.

The only other senior colonel who could be advanced to fill a vacancy was Goode Bryan of the 16th Georgia. In his case the vacancy was not in his brigade, Wofford's, but in that of another Georgia brigade, Semmes's of the same division, McLaws's. There was apparently no complaint that the commanding general "went outside" the brigade in Bryan's advancement. No doubt the reason was the fact that he was a graduate of West Point and accounted a regular. As far as Lee could, he applied the rule that professional soldiers could be appointed to command without consideration of the state of their birth and without regard to seniority. This rule never was formulated legally but it often was invoked.

When these four—Hunton, Humphreys, Battle, and Bryan—were named, the list of eligibles was exhausted. Several colonels of late commissions were abler soldiers than the ranking field officers of their brigades, perhaps, but law and regulations forbade their promotion over their seniors. It might be assumed, optimistically, that future battles would show merit that had not previously been displayed. Some captured officers might be exchanged. Wounded veterans might return. Until one or another of these things happened, the grim truth was written on the army roster. As of August 31, two of Pickett's brigades, two of Hood's, one of Rodes's, one of Dick Anderson's, and two of Heth's, a total of eight infantry brigades, were without permanent commanders of appropriate rank.

Command of the Field-Brockenbrough-Mayo brigade was resolved by the promotion of Henry Harrison Walker, a West Pointer of the class of 1853 who as lieutenant colonel of the 40th Virginia had been wounded at Gaines' Mill. Recovering from a long illness, Walker was sent to Lee and assigned to the command of Field's, the brigade with which he was serving when wounded. The case of Alfred Iverson was handled in the most considerate manner. There must have been clamor against him in his North Carolina brigade and a demand for the appointment of a native of the state. He was transferred for a time to Nicholls's brigade. Later in the year, Iverson quietly was ordered to Georgia to organize the cavalry there.

There could be no temporizing with the command of Pender's division. None of the brigadiers of the division were available. McGowan was absent, wounded; Lane and Scales were recent appointees; Edward L. Thomas was a capable officer, but as he commanded the Georgia brigade in a division that included two North Carolina brigades and one South Carolina brigade, his advancement, said Lee, might "create dissatisfaction."[34] Trimble was wounded and a prisoner. One or another of the excellent young cavalrymen or artillerists might have been almost as vigorous as Pender, but the line between the infantry and the other arms was so sharply drawn that promotion from one to the other was rare and provocative of discontent.

In the eyes of Lee, the best man available for the vacancy was Cadmus Wilcox of Anderson's division, who was recommended a fortnight after Pender died of his wound. Davis's acceptance of the recommendation was prompt and unqualified, and on August 13, Wilcox was appointed major general. Among his associates the choice was a popular one. Every officer of rank knew of Wilcox's fight at Salem Church. He had been for twenty-one years a cadet and then an officer in the United States and Confederate armies. Off duty he was genial and informal, on duty precise and insistent on precision. He might not rise above the rank of major general; he might not be brilliant as a divisional chief; but he had earned that promotion at Salem Church. In all the army's battles he had been dependable and by every campfire he had been a gentleman.

Such was the reorganization of the infantry, best described as incomplete, partial—grim proof that attrition of command now exceeded renewal through the school of experience. The Army of Northern Virginia recrossed the Potomac one year to the day from the date of Jackson's movement toward Gordonsville after the battles around Richmond. One year earlier the great offensive in the direction of the enemy's country was beginning; now it was ending. Run the eye down the roster of the army that marched toward Second Manassas and as it came wearily back from Gettysburg:

Of Longstreet's former Right Wing, the commander now was lieutenant general and next in rank to Lee.

Dick Anderson's division: Armistead, dead; Mahone and Wright, on duty with the army.

McLaws's division: Its commander still on duty; Kershaw, present; Howell Cobb, transferred; Semmes, dead; Barksdale, dead.

David Jones's division: The division no longer in existence; Jones, dead; Toombs, resigned; Drayton, sent elsewhere; Tige Anderson, wounded.

Longstreet's own division: Wilcox, promoted; Pryor, deprived of troops; Featherston, transferred; Kemper, wounded and a prisoner; Micah Jenkins, detached; Pickett, promoted.

Whiting's division: Its commander on coast defense duty at Wilmington; Hood, promoted but wounded; Law, with his brigade; Shanks Evans, back in the Carolinas.

Of Jackson's Left Wing, the great commander dead.

Jackson's own division: Winder, dead; Taliaferro, on other duty; Colonel W. S. H. Baylor, dead; Starke, dead.

Powell Hill's division: Its leader a lieutenant general. His brigadiers: Branch, dead; Pender, dead; Gregg, dead; Archer, captured; Field, still incapacitated; Thomas, with the troops.

Harvey Hill's division: Its commander transferred to North Carolina; Ripley, returned to South Carolina; Rodes, promoted; Garland, dead; George B. Anderson, dead; Colquitt, sent elsewhere.

Ewell's division: Maimed Dick Ewell, corps commander; Lawton, transferred; senior colonel Marcellus Douglass, dead; Trimble, twice wounded, promoted, now a prisoner; Early, a major general; Harry Hays, at his usual post.

In short, of the general officers of infantry during that year, one had died of disease and ten of wounds. In addition, Tom Cobb and Franklin Paxton, promoted, had been killed before the advance into Pennsylvania. Of the ten transfers and two resignations, nine and possibly ten had been welcome to the commanding general because the men were found incompetent or mediocre or troublesome.[35] Two other promoted general officers, Iverson and Colston, had been tried and found wanting. One, John R. Jones, had left the army under charges. Another, Francis Nicholls, probably had been incapacitated permanently for duty in the field.

In July 1863 six of the nine infantry divisions were under officers who had not commanded them in July 1862. Five—five only—of the thirty-eight infantry brigades were led by men who had held the rank of brigadier general twelve months previously. The surviving commanders of Gettysburg were a new army, without a Jackson. Lee's words of May, after the death of Stonewall, had grayer, somber meaning: "We must all do more than formerly."

CHAPTER 28

Challenges for Longstreet, Hill, and Stuart

1. The Cavalry Are Reshuffled

By the third of August, all the Confederate infantry were south of the Rapidan. This withdrawal, as always, was covered by the cavalry. Their absence during the Pennsylvania campaign had been much discussed. Among those officers who realized how the army had groped in the dark while Stuart was riding to the Susquehanna there was disappointment over his conduct "and a disposition to hold him strictly to account."

To the charge that he should have been in front of the army on July 1, Stuart replied in his report that Albert Jenkins's men had been selected as the advance guard of the army and numerically were adequate for the mission. If, said Stuart, "the peculiar functions of cavalry with the army were not satisfactorily performed in the absence of my command, it should rather be attributed to the fact that Jenkins's brigade was not as efficient as it ought to have been, and as its numbers (3,800) on leaving Virginia warranted us in expecting."

In Lee's report the statement was made that Stuart's crossing of the Potomac between the Federal army and Washington was "in the exercise of the discretion given him." With equal candor, Lee recorded that Stuart was "instructed to lose no time in placing his command on the right of our column as soon as he should perceive the enemy moving northward." Lee wrote further, "The movements of the army preceding the battle of Gettysburg had been much embarrassed by the absence of the cavalry." This was the measure of official criticism visited on Stuart. The full measure of historical criticism did not come in time to hurt his pride, though it impaired his fame. Jeb's worst shortcoming, ignored at the time, was his absence on the morning of July 2 when the adoption of a sound battle plan depended on careful reconnaissance of the Federal left.[1]

Stuart was busy with a reorganization of his forces. The task was different this time. Imboden had angered Lee by remaining in Maryland. Albert Jenkins's men had shown their inexperience in fighting of the sort familiar to the veterans of Jeb's command. Beverly Robertson had been slow in moving from the positions he had been left to defend in the Blue Ridge; not until July 3 did he join Lee. During the retreat from Pennsylvania, Robertson had aroused Stuart's wrath by not holding a pass entrusted to him.

In contrast, all the brigadiers who had accompanied Stuart had done admirably. Colonel John R. Chambliss, Jr., leading the brigade of the wounded Rooney Lee, showed well enough to remain temporarily in that place. In late June, recuperating at Hickory Hill, Rooney had been swept up by a Federal raiding party and was awaiting exchange. Calbraith Butler, Williams Wickham, Tom Rosser, Pierce Young, Lawrence Baker—all these colonels deserved promotion. Lunsford L. Lomax, a West Pointer and a former officer in East Tennessee, had been brought back to Virginia and assigned to the 11th Virginia as colonel. He evidently was of the material of higher command.

When Jeb decided to get men promoted he usually found a way. He convinced the commanding general that the existing brigades were too large. Fitz Lee had five regiments and one battalion; Rooney Lee, five regiments; Hampton, three regiments and three legions; Jones, four regiments and one battalion; Jenkins, three regiments and two battalions. Lee wrote President Davis on August 1 to express his belief that three full regiments or four, if weak, were as large a cavalry command as one man could direct. On this basis, he explained, the cavalry would include seven brigades. These should be divided into two divisions, at the head of which should be major generals.

For the command of one of these newly organized divisions Lee recommended Wade Hampton, who "deserves [promotion] both from his service and his gallantry." Fitz Lee was recommended for the other division. Of him the commanding general said, "I do not know of any other officer in the cavalry who has done better service." Two vacancies would thus be created. By relieving Robertson a third man could be advanced. Reduction of the size of the brigades would make possible the selection of a fourth brigadier. Lee proposed that Calbraith Butler succeed Hampton, that Williams Wickham take Fitz Lee's command, that Lawrence Baker have a brigade built on Robertson's command, and that another of the reorganized brigades go to Lunsford Lomax. These were appointed as Lee recommended. The average age of all these men was thirty-three. Two of the brigadiers and one of the major generals were twenty-seven.[2]

The real triumph of this reshuffle was that the promotion of Hampton and Fitz Lee had been arranged in a manner that did not aggravate the rivalry that always was suspected but never was avowed. Stuart, knowing the fine qualities of both men, sought by praising them in his report to avoid offense to either. The commanding general had put their names in the same sentence proposing their promotion to major general. All this care had been repaid. Both men were satisfied.

If Stuart was not dissatisfied and Hampton and Fitz Lee were pleased, the reorganization could be judged a success; but in accordance with the history of promotion from the days of the Trojan wars, almost as many officers were offended as were pleased. Tom Rosser of the 5th Virginia might have maintained that his title to advancement was as good as that of any who were made general officers. Colonel Tom Munford of the 2nd Virginia was aggrieved. He was one of the senior colonels of cavalry in the army and had shared in almost every campaign after that of First Manassas.

Stuart was embarrassed over the unhappiness of these two officers. In January 1863 he had recommended the creation of an additional brigade of cavalry and in warm eulogium had urged that Rosser be appointed to it. From this recommendation Stuart had not withdrawn, but Rosser had fallen into disfavor with the War Department. His regiment declined in efficiency; his own morale was low. Then, in May 1863, he married a girl of great charm, and soon his bride's letters rallied him. His conscience rebuked him for drinking and for being less diligent in camp than on the field of battle. In this spirit Rosser overcame whatever objection there was to his promotion. But there was no brigade for him until the long, ugly feud between Stuart and Grumble Jones reached a climax.[3]

Stuart's decision to leave Jones to guard the Virginia mountain passes during the preliminaries of the Gettysburg campaign had fired anew the animosities between the two. All the tact and diplomacy of Lee failed to soften the feeling of either man. At length, early in September, a direct verbal clash occurred. Stuart arrested Jones for disrespect to his superior officer and brought him to court-martial. Jones swore he never would serve again under Stuart. Grumble might have saved his oath because the court found him guilty. The patient commanding general now reluctantly concluded that Jones must be sent elsewhere, and he was ordered to southwest Virginia to take charge of the cavalry there. Jones's men were reconciled by the wisdom of Stuart's choice of a new brigade commander. He recommended and Lee endorsed the promotion of Rosser, who on October 10 was commissioned brigadier general.[4]

Munford's case took a different turn. When he was told that Rosser would be recommended ahead of him, he took it manfully, but his friends appealed to General Lee. In answer to one of these admirers, Lee assured

George Wythe Munford, secretary of the Commonwealth of Virginia, that consciousness of duty, faithfully performed, "is the most certain road to honorable advancement. That such will be the action of your son, his previous conduct leads me to expect, and that the result will meet his expectations and those of his friends, I have no doubt."[5]

On August 1, Lawrence Baker was wounded so seriously that he might be invalided. To act for Baker during his incapacity the choice of Lee and Stuart was Colonel James B. Gordon of the 1st North Carolina. Gordon was forty-one years old and without professional military training, but he had been distinguished for bravery and intelligent leadership in all the battles of his brigade. It was a departure from hampering bad precedent to name a colonel to the next grade while there was a prospect that his senior would return to the field. The necessity of maintaining discipline was the reason for abandonment of a rule Lee often had reason to deplore.

Calbraith Butler was recovering slowly from the wound received at Brandy. For temporary direction of his brigade Stuart and Lee chose Pierce M. B. Young, colonel of Cobb's Legion, South Carolinian by birth and Georgian in uprearing. Young had been a cadet at West Point but resigned on the secession of Georgia. He was twenty-seven, of splendid manners and great magnetism, though considered somewhat spoiled. His record had been of the highest.

With these appointments the reorganization of the cavalry corps was complete. Hampton's division consisted of the brigades of James B. Gordon (Baker's), Pierce Young (Butler's), and Thomas L. Rosser, formerly Jones's. In Fitz Lee's division were the brigades of J. R. Chambliss (Rooney Lee's), Lomax, and Wickham. Albert Jenkins's brigade was detached. In command, this was a force entirely different from that which Stuart had carried into Pennsylvania, except for one significant fact: The two most renowned of the former brigadiers were now divisional commanders. Before them was fame.

2. THE DETACHMENT OF LONGSTREET

While the cavalry was being reorganized, the infantry command was confronted with a new problem, mass desertion. This began as soon as Gettysburg was lost. On the afternoon of July 4, when the wagon train was started for the Potomac, about 5,000 unwounded men slipped away from their posts and went with the vehicles. Many of these were captured by the enemy, many were returned to their commands, others were listed as A.W.O.L. Of the wounded or sick men who went to hospital, some quietly disappeared. The calamity threatened by these conditions was to be read from the rolls of the army. General Lee estimated the missing from all causes at the end of July at not less than 20,000. To rally the negligent and shame the cowardly, a general order for the return of absentees was issued July 26. "I do not know whether it will have much effect," Lee wrote the President, "unless accompanied by the declaration of an amnesty."[6]

The words of Lee were emphasized by events. Fifty men of Scales's shattered brigade deserted on the night of July 29. Forty-two belonged to the 22nd North Carolina, a regiment that had an honorable name. It was assumed that these men were conscripts who had been prompted to desert by seditious articles in the *Raleigh Standard,* whose editor, William Woods Holden, was proclaiming that conscription was unconstitutional. His arguments could not always be answered within Scales's command. On July 1 the brigade had lost fifty-five officers; Pender, who had held the division in his grasp, was dead; Scales, who might have exploded the absurdities of Holden and stiffened discipline, was absent wounded.[7]

These conditions, which were typical of those in many regiments, explained though they did not excuse the behavior of the North Carolina soldiers. President Davis followed Lee's advice and on August 11 offered a general pardon to deserters who would return to their commands. Amnesty was supplemented for a brief time by a system of furloughs to soldiers of meritorious conduct. Extra Billy Smith was sent on a speaking tour to supplement amnesty and furloughs and to stir the people by his eloquence. Assemblies were held in many North Carolina regiments to reaffirm their loyalty and to denounce the "factious and treasonable course" of the *Standard.*[8]

The effect of this was nil. Some men even presumed upon the amnesty to go home without leave, in the expectation that if they returned before the twenty days of mercy expired, no punishment could be inflicted. Numbers of Virginians who had wearied of the hard infantry service deserted to join companies of partisan rangers, who were supposed to combine good living and high adventure. Few commanders seem to have asked themselves whether their own shortcomings as army administrators, rather than the innate baseness of deserters, was responsible for the steady disappearance of men who previously had fought well. Lee realized some of the causes of discontent, but when amnesty and furloughs had been tried, he abandoned hope of stopping desertion otherwise than by the imposition of death sentences on men captured after leaving the ranks. The good soldier did not need this lesson, and if he belonged to the First Corps he soon demonstrated his devotion anew in operations that had their unhappy origin in events in the Far South.

The fall of Vicksburg on July 4 had been followed by General Joseph E. Johnston's retreat deep into Mississippi. Remote as these maneuvers appeared from Virginia, the government knew how closely they were related to battles on the Rapidan. If Johnston's army was considered the Confederate left, on the long front from the Mississippi to the Rapidan, the center was Braxton Bragg's Army of Tennessee. This force stood idle in front of Chattanooga, facing the Federal forces under Generals W. S. Rosecrans and A. E. Burnside. Unattached to Bragg but affecting nearly all his movements was the Confederate right, the Army of Northern Virginia, which, despite Gettysburg, still had faith in itself and in its commander.

Almost all the Southern leaders agreed that they could not maintain a strict defensive. To win, Confederate armies had to strike. The difference of opinion concerned the place—left, center, or right. Bragg proposed that he reinforce Johnston for an attack on Grant, but Johnston dismissed this with four gloomy words: "It is too late." Lee believed that if his army could recover sufficient strength, the best hope of the Confederacy lay in the renewal of the offensive against the Federals in northern Virginia. General Samuel Cooper thought the wisest course would be to strengthen Bragg from Johnston's army and attack Rosecrans. Longstreet was aggressively convinced that this was the imperative strategy but that the troops for Bragg should come from Virginia, not from Mississippi. With unwonted eagerness, he renewed the argument he had advanced at the conclusion of the Suffolk campaign. Lee's army might be reduced temporarily; one corps, at least, might be sent to Tennessee. Bragg then should be able to crush Rosecrans. Unless this was done, he feared that the Federals would follow their triumph at Vicksburg with a march through Georgia. That would wreck the Confederacy.

In this conviction, Longstreet about the middle of August wrote Secretary of War Seddon a general outline of a proposed transfer of troops from Lee's army to Bragg's. Longstreet told Seddon that he had not discussed the subject with Lee, but this secrecy did not persist. In conversation with Lee soon afterward, Longstreet argued that Bragg should be reinforced from the Army of Northern Virginia for an attack on Rosecrans.

If the decision were to strengthen Bragg at the expense of the Army of Northern Virginia, said Lee, would Longstreet care to have the command of the forces sent west? Longstreet showed that he already had been considering the possibility. He would accept, he said, on two conditions which he had framed carefully: First, he must have opportunity of winning the confidence of the forces before leading them into action; second, he must be given assurance that any success would be exploited.[9]

Late in August Lee went to Richmond and discussed with President

Davis the general strategic situation. In some fashion, word was spread during the next few days that Longstreet was going to Tennessee and, what was more, was going as Bragg's successor, not as one of Bragg's corps commanders. This was not in the mind of the President at the moment, but Longstreet did not hesitate to suggest it to Lee. The Army of Northern Virginia, he said on September 5, could maintain a safe defensive with a reduced force and, if need be, could retire to the Richmond defenses. In the event the First Corps could not be spared from Lee's army, he thought the Confederacy "might accomplish something" by giving him three brigades from the Richmond front, putting him "in Bragg's place," and transferring the commander of the Army of Tennessee to the head of the First Corps under Lee. If instead the First Corps went to Tennessee, Longstreet continued, "We could surely take no great risk in such a change and we might gain a great deal. . . . I doubt if General Bragg has confidence in his troops or himself either. He is not likely to do a great deal for us."[10] In this bid for command Longstreet was entirely confident. Nothing he wrote on the subject disclosed any doubt on his part that he could administer and lead successfully the contentious Army of Tennessee.

The President wished Lee to assume general command in the region where Johnston and Bragg were operating, but when Lee expressed belief that officers already on the ground could do better, Davis acquiesced, though perhaps reluctantly. With Lee's acquiescence, the swift, final decision was to send the greater part of Longstreet's corps to reinforce Bragg, who was to continue at the head of his army. On September 6, Lee ordered the quartermaster general to prepare the transportation. By the eighth, troops were moving toward Richmond from the camps on the Rapidan.[11]

Longstreet made no complaint that he was not to supplant Bragg, but busied himself in exchanging brigades. Simultaneously with the troop movement to Tennessee, detachment had to be made from the troops in Virginia to reinforce Charleston, which for almost two months had been under violent attack. If he had to supply two brigades from his corps for Charleston, Longstreet concluded to leave in South Carolina two weakened Georgia brigades, Bryan's and Tige Anderson's, and thereby reduce the prospect of desertion from these commands when they were on the Georgia-Tennessee boundary, close to home. He also negotiated to leave Pickett's division, weakened in numbers and dangerously lacking in officers, in the Richmond defenses, and take in its place the brigades of Micah Jenkins and Henry A. Wise, who were stationed close to the capital. In urging this, Longstreet undoubtedly was angling to have Jenkins. The South Carolinian was a splendid fighter and was anxious to reunite his excellent troops with their old comrades. In this Old Pete was partially successful. Pickett was left in the quiet Richmond sector, Tige Anderson's and Wise's brigades were sent to South Carolina, and Jenkins and Bryan went west.[12]

The time came for Longstreet to leave the Rapidan. After the friendliest of farewells, Lee's parting words were, "Now, General, you must beat those people out in the West." Immediately Longstreet answered: "If I live; but I would not give a single man of my command for a fruitless victory." Lee replied that it should be so. Plans to pursue a success already were being made.[13]

In the Confederate capital, Longstreet was disappointed by a vexatious change of route. All the logistics of the operation had been based on the dispatch of the troops directly to Chattanooga by way of the Virginia and Tennessee Railroad. The Federals prevented this. Knoxville was occupied by the Federals on September 2, and Chattanooga fell to the Unionists on the ninth. The same day Cumberland Gap was surrendered, making it certain that Federal cavalry would proceed from the Gap to the railroad. All Confederate reinforcements had now to be routed by the overloaded railway that led south from Richmond. "Never before," said Moxley Sorrel, "were so many troops moved over such worn-out railways, none first-class from the beginning." He elaborated: "Never before were such crazy cars— passenger, baggage, mail, coal, box, platform, all and every sort wabbling on the jumping strap-iron—used for hauling good soldiers."

By September 14, Longstreet had advanced the troop movement to the stage where he could schedule his own departure for the West. In a final letter to his old commander he wrote, "If I can do anything there, it shall be done promptly. If I cannot, I shall advise you to recall me. If I did not think our move a necessary one, my regrets at leaving you would be distressing to me, as it seems to be with the officers and men of my command. . . . Our affections for you are stronger, if it be possible for them to be stronger, than our admiration for you." It was bravely said, was honestly felt, and, as concerned Longstreet himself, was hopefully written in strange and unhappy contrast to the experiences that awaited him in Tennessee.[14]

3. LONGSTREET AND HILL IN DISTRESS

Old Pete reached the Chickamauga battlefield, in northern Georgia near the boundary with Tennessee, in time for the second day of fighting. To Longstreet, without hesitation, Bragg committed the whole left wing of the army. On September 20, Longstreet's veterans and their new comrades went forward magnificently. Hood headed the column of attack and equaled any of his exploits in Virginia, but fell with his thigh fractured by a rifle bullet. Longstreet established his usual grip on his men and soon had the troops violently engaged. He husbanded his forces and, with excellent judgment, threw in his last division at precisely the correct moment. At nightfall the enemy had been swept from the field.

All the early news of the Battle of Chickamauga that reached Richmond presented it as an overwhelming triumph for the Confederacy. To Longstreet went a cordial letter from Lee. "If," said the general, "it gives you as much pleasure to receive my warmest congratulations as it does me to convey them, this letter will not be written in vain."[15] The distressful part of the first reports was that of heavy casualties. Hood's wound was such that his leg had to be amputated on the field. For a few days his recovery was in doubt, but he rallied. By the end of the first week in October he was asking how long a time would elapse before he could take the field again. That field would not again be Virginia, however. In deep tragedy the fame of Hood was to wane. When he was crippled and defeated and no longer had the bright blue flame of battle in his eye, his old comrades in Virginia were to remember his boldness, his bravery, his chivalry, his magnanimity.

The letter that carried congratulations to Longstreet expressed warmly the consciousness of Lee's need for his "Old War Horse." Lee wrote, "Finish the work before you, my dear general, and return to me. I want you badly and you cannot get back too soon." The situation justified the language. On September 13, Federal cavalry crossed the Rappahannock, and for the next fortnight all the intelligence reports indicated an early advance by the Army of the Potomac. Then, overnight, the outlook in Virginia changed. Now the report was that Meade's XI and XII corps, under General Hooker, were to be dispatched to Rosecrans. Cumulative proof of the accuracy of this information reached army headquarters almost daily. By October 1, Lee was convinced that the two corps had left Meade. New plans were made immediately. Instead of awaiting attack, the Army of Northern Virginia once more was to deliver it.[16]

But while Lee believed he could give battle in the absence of Longstreet, that officer was beginning to regret, for the best of reasons, his change from Virginia to Tennessee. On the morning after the Federals were driven from the field of Chickamauga, Longstreet had urged Bragg to take the offensive. The commanding general hesitated, reflected, and did not send his columns after the defeated enemy until that afternoon. Then he moved to Missionary Ridge instead of directly against Chattanooga. In the judgment of Longstreet and the other lieutenants, their commander thus yielded to the enemy, by indecision and delay, all the fruits of the victory at Chickamauga.

Disillusionment came quickly to Old Pete. By September 25, after hardly five days with his new chief, he felt so outraged that he wrote directly to Secretary of War Seddon in galled criticism of Bragg. "To express my convictions in a few words," Longstreet wrote, "our chief has done but one thing that he ought to have done since I joined this army. That was to order the attack upon the 20th. . . . I am convinced that nothing but the hand of God can save us or help us as long as we have our present commander. . . . Can't you send us General Lee?" There was much more to this unhappy episode. A round-robin urging the President to relieve Bragg of command prompted a visit by Davis to Bragg's headquarters. On the ninth of October the grievances of all the senior officers were heard by the chief executive in the presence of Bragg. That unusual procedure produced a concurrence, as Longstreet phrased it, "that our commander could be of greater service elsewhere than at the head of the Army of Tennessee."[17]

The next day Longstreet received a summons to a private conference with Mr. Davis. It lasted nearly all day. Longstreet could see from the President's manner that a change in the army command was in contemplation, and conjectured that he was being considered as a posssible successor to Bragg. A month previously Longstreet had suggested confidently that he take Bragg's army. Now the outlook was less hopeful. In his effort to escape an undesirable assignment, he forthrightly, perhaps tactlessly, remarked to the President that Bragg's forces were in the military department of Joseph E. Johnston. In no other way could they be effectively used than in combined operations. Under Johnston, said Longstreet, he gladly would serve in any capacity.

That name, according to Longstreet's narrative, provoked Davis and led to "severe rebuke." The temper of both men must have flared. Longstreet verbally tendered his resignation, which Davis rejected. Then there was a stubborn and fruitless conversation over naming Evander Law or Micah Jenkins to lead Hood's division. When president and lieutenant general had disagreed thoroughly and ended their conference, Davis walked to the gate, shook hands cordially, "and dismissed me with his gracious smile; but a bitter look lurking about its margin, and the ground-swell, admonished me that clouds were gathering about head-quarters of the First Corps even faster than those that told the doom of the Southern cause." Longstreet evidently thought that he had put himself on Davis's black books by proclaiming his faith in Johnston. The President, in turn, perhaps concluded, with his usual sensitiveness, that Longstreet had joined the forces arrayed against the administration.

The decision of the President, maturely reached, was to retain Bragg in command. In the controversy, Longstreet's former commander in Virginia was careful not to interfere or, for that matter, even to admit that differences existed between Bragg and his subordinate commanders. During the second week in October Lee undertook his projected offensive against Meade's weakened forces, and when the operation was over, he wrote Longstreet, ". . . I missed you dreadfully, and your brave corps. Your cheerful face and strong arms would have been invaluable. I hope you will soon return to me. I trust we may soon be together again."[18]

In that brief campaign several new general officers participated. Colonel Robert M. Johnston of the 23rd North Carolina was promoted to take Iverson's brigade. To Pettigrew's brigade, W. W. Kirkland, former colonel of the 21st North Carolina, was assigned. Colonel Leroy A. Stafford, a man of conspicuous courage, was given a wreath around his three stars and placed in charge of Nicholl's brigade. In the cases of Stafford and Kirkland, promotion was from the same division but a different brigade. This was saved from being blasphemy against states' rights because they came from the same state as the troops they were to lead. As it was now manifest that Samuel McGowan would not return at an early date to lead his brigade, Colonel Abner Perrin of the 14th South Carolina was promoted to direct that famous command—to the dire offense of Colonel D. H. Hamilton, who thought he should have been advanced.

Seth M. Barton, a Virginian and a West Pointer of the class of 1849, formerly a brigadier in Stevenson's division, was exchanged after the surrender of Pemberton's army at Vicksburg and was assigned to the command of Lewis Armistead's old brigade, Pickett's division. Another general officer to join Lee's army and take command of a worn brigade was John Pegram, who last was seen as the leader of a captured column at Rich Mountain in 1861. Pegram had been exchanged and, like Barton, had been given a post in the western army. There he had won his brigadier's commission, but for reasons of the heart he had decided to come back to Virginia. He was given Extra Billy Smith's brigade in Early's division—a promising appointment. No man could have a better introduction to the Army of Northern Virginia than to be presented as the older brother of Major William J. Pegram.

It probably did not escape attention that of these six new appointments, two only—Johnston and Perrin—were by promotion within the brigades. Stafford and Kirkland had belonged to the division to which their new brigades were a part, but the two had no previous connection with those brigades. Barton and Pegram, though Virginians, were strangers to their troops. New and grim confirmation there was in all this of the ill-omened truth that the material of command was close to exhaustion.

In the next scene of the drama, in which these men made their first appearance as general officers, the central figure was A. P. Hill. He had not shone at Gettysburg, and after that defeat bore an industrious though not a conspicuous part in restoring the Third Corps to fighting competence. On the record, he proved less notable as a corps commander in June-September 1863 than he had been as head of his famous Light Division. Now Hill had a new opportunity.

Meade early in October was encamped north of Culpeper Court House, with two of his corps extended to the Rapidan. The sole inexpensive way of attacking him was to turn his position, force him to retreat, and then assail him in motion or where the ground was less readily defensible. On the ninth of October the Confederate columns began to move. Ewell and Hill proceeded with their corps to Culpeper. On the morning of October 12, on orders of the commanding general, who was trying to intercept the enemy's retreat, the Third Corps started on a wide circuitous advance toward the Orange and Alexandria Railroad. Ewell had the shorter road via Jeffersonton and Sulphur Springs in the direction of Warrenton. Hill moved by way of Sperryville, Gaines' Crossroads, and Waterloo Bridge. From the east, as Hill's men swung along, they occasionally heard the sound of artillery. On the thirteenth the steady march brought the corps near Warrenton, which Ewell also had reached.

The Third Corps resumed its march on the morning of October 14. "We all entered now fully into the spirit of the movement," wrote a brigade historian. "We were convinced that Meade was unwilling to face us, and we, therefore, anticipated a pleasant affair, if we should succeed in catching him." In a larger knowledge of the situation, Hill must have realized that the odds now were against the Confederates in the northward race between the armies. The Federals had started early and were following the direct roads up the Orange and Alexandria railway. Hill and Ewell had to use roads more remote. All the indications were that the Army of the Potomac was moving toward the Washington defenses.[19]

Five miles north of Warrenton, Hill received word that a Federal column was moving northward almost parallel to him. At Greenwich, reached about 10:00 A.M., the Third Corps was definitely on the trail of the Federals. Fires were still burning. The road toward Bristoe Station was strewn with the articles retreating soldiers throw away, knapsacks, blankets, guns even. The eyes of the Southerners brightened. It was August 1862 again! Ahead of them, at that time, had been all the delights of plundering the great base at Manassas. Memory spurred lagging feet. Like speed to Bristoe might yield like prizes. "It was," said one North Carolinian, "almost like boys chasing a hare."

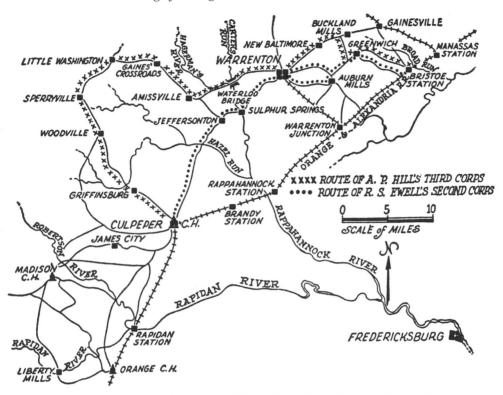

Lines of advance of the Second and Third Corps from Culpeper Court House
to Bristoe Station, October 12–14, 1863.

As the column approached Bristoe Station, Hill spurred ahead to see
whether the enemy had cleared Broad Run. He doubtless knew that the
railroad bridge across the Run could be used by infantry and that easy
fords existed on either side of the bridge. There always was a chance that a
swift pursuit might surprise an adversary who thought himself safe at the
crossing site. When Hill came to high ground in sight of Bristoe, he saw
thousands of Union soldiers on both banks of Broad Run near the fords.
They offered such a mark as the army had not seen since that May afternoon when Jackson deployed in the woods west of Chancellorsville.
Instant action was imperative. Heth with the leading division must speed
his advance. As soon as he was in striking distance he must form line of
battle. Let Poague bring up his artillery battalion immediately! Such an
opportunity might not come again![20]

Hill's eyes were on the enemy near the fords, and on them only. In his
eagerness to assail them, he sent to Heth to hurry forward with the troops

already in line of battle. To Hill it may have seemed a long, long time before Heth's line of battle came in sight. John R. Cooke's brigade was on the right; Kirkland, with Iverson's old command, was on the left. Henry Walker's Virginians had not reached the line when the order came for Heth to push forward. Now Walker was trying vainly to catch up with Kirkland and form on his left. Poague's gunners dashed into position and, at Hill's order, opened fire. A few shots sufficed to send to the north bank those Federals who had been resting on the near shore. Their flight sharpened Hill's combativeness. Heth must move by the left flank, cross the Run, and attack the fugitives.

As Heth made the shift and began his advance toward Broad Run, Hill turned to examine the ground between the fords and the advancing line of gray. He saw something he had not observed before: Federal skirmishers on the Confederate side of the stream. They were spread southward and parallel to the railroad. When Heth's line advanced, they would get on its right flank and in its rear. Hill sent back for McIntosh's battalion of artillery and hurried a messenger to Dick Anderson to advance two brigades immediately to cover Heth's right flank. Another messenger was rushed to Cooke, commanding Heth's right brigade, to watch his flank.[21]

So far as Hill could see from his command post, Cooke drove back the skirmishers. Heth sent a report that showed he was alive to the situation: On his right, he said, a heavy column of the enemy had appeared. Hill had to halt the division quickly or order it immediately across the stream in pursuit of the Federals. He reflected for a moment and decided that the movement should be suspended, but soon changed his mind. Looking to his right, Hill saw the head of Anderson's column. In a short time Anderson would be on Heth's right and could deal with any Federal force that remained on the near side of the Run. Impetuously a courier was sent to order Heth to the fords and in pursuit.

Soon a rider dashed up to Hill with another message: Heth sent word that Cooke was certain that as he moved forward, the Federals near the railroad would take him in flank. In this contingency, should Cooke advance? Hill was positive in his answer: Anderson was coming up; Cooke would be safe. That was enough for the subordinates. Orders were orders. In a short time Hill saw Cooke's line come over the crest of a hill and start forward. Kirkland was on Cooke's left.

Thus Hill hastily planned the attack, but a furious burst of fire soon showed how mistaken he had been. Anxious messages explained what smoke quickly concealed from the eyes—Federals still on the Confederate side of the stream in great numbers. They had not been observed earlier because they were concealed behind the railroad embankment, which Hill had not thought to reconnoiter. When Cooke and Kirkland advanced toward the stream, their entire right was exposed to Union fire from the embankment. Instead of making a flank attack across the Run, the two brigades became heavily engaged in front of the embankment and, to save themselves, had to try to drive the Union force from its cover.[22]

In the attempt Cooke's brigade was slaughtered. Not less than 700 of its men were killed, wounded, or captured. The 27th North Carolina, which had earned immortality at Sharpsburg, sacrificed 33 of its officers and 290 of its 416 men. Kirkland lost 602, of whom nearly half surrendered after they reached the railroad and saw that they could not escape otherwise. Total casualties in Heth's division were 1,361 and for the army during the entire operation, in killed, wounded, and missing, probably 1,900.

Both Cooke and Kirkland were badly wounded, to the dire impairment of their shattered commands. Both leaders realized the danger in which their brigades were put by Hill's instructions, but they charged boldly. Said Cooke, "Well, I will advance, and if they flank me, I will face my men about and cut my way out." In addition, a third general officer was wounded. In a futile attempt by Dick Anderson to cover Heth's flank, Carnot Posey was badly wounded in the left thigh. In Charlottesville on November 13 he was to succumb to his injuries.[23]

For these casualties no blame was placed on Harry Heth. He had acted in precise accord with his orders from Hill, and had taken pains to see that the full measure of the danger to the flank of the attacking column was made known to the corps commander. The battle was another instance of the singular ill fortune that pursued Heth, but the responsibility was Hill's, not his. The army realized this. Criticism of Hill was on every lip. In his report, Hill admitted that he did not know of the presence behind the railroad embankment of the Federals who, after repulsing the Confederates with light losses, calmly marched on.

In forwarding to the War Department Hill's confession, Lee said in his endorsement: "General Hill explains how, in his haste to attack the Third Army Corps of the enemy, he overlooked the presence of the Second, which was the cause of the disaster that ensued." President Davis wrote realistically, "There was a want of vigilance." More painful far to the proud, sensitive Hill must have been Lee's rebuke. The day after the battle, Hill conducted the commanding general over the field and explained what had happened. Lee had little to say and showed plainly in his face that he was disappointed. At last he spoke: "Well, well, General, bury these poor men and let us say no more about it."[24]

4. JEB STUART'S NEW ADVENTURES

The cavalry's part in the Bristoe campaign tested Jeb Stuart's new divisional organization but not all of his new general officers. Hampton was absent still because of his wounds; Fitz Lee had a vigorous hand in the fighting. Of all the brigadiers, only Lunsford Lomax and James Gordon were at their posts. The other brigades were led by colonels. Pierce Young headed Butler's brigade and probably did not know, until the campaign was over, that he had been promoted. Rosser, too, participated as a colonel. Grumble Jones's brigade was under Colonel O. R. Funsten. The troopers of Wickham were in the care of Colonel Thomas H. Owen of the 3rd Virginia. Colonel John R. Chambliss, Jr., again directed Rooney Lee's brigade, but he had done this so often that he was to be counted now as a seasoned brigade leader. Exercise of higher command by colonels involved, of course, the care of regiments by lieutenant colonels and majors. In short, since the Seven Days there scarcely had been a time when so large a part of Stuart's force was under men who had not been tested in the posts they now filled.

Orders from army headquarters were that one division of cavalry should be left temporarily on the Rapidan and the other should be employed on the right of the army during the attempted turning movement. Stuart of course rode with the van, in command of the three brigades of Hampton's men. This arrangement left Fitz Lee on the Rapidan. On October 11, near Culpeper, the Union cavalry was found in manifest strength between the retiring infantry and Stuart's regiments. The sensible thing to do, Jeb reasoned, was to turn the Federal position and get in the enemy's rear on the old battleground of Brandy Station. This appeared to be a course as safe as profitable, and for this cheering reason: From the east there rolled the echo of artillery, which Stuart took to be that of Fitz Lee in pursuit of Federals from the line of the Rapidan. Thus Fitz would be available with his three brigades when Stuart struck the enemy.

As Stuart approached Brandy Station his pride sank: He saw that the Federals had fathomed his plan and were moving toward Fleetwood Hill in heavy columns. Instinctively he determined to push on and charge them before they could reach the high ground he had defended on the humiliating ninth of June. He looked eastward across the Orange and Alexandria Railroad and there could see the rising smoke of Fitz Lee's guns. Fortune seemed to favor the bold. The enemy was squarely between Fitz Lee, closing on Brandy from the east, and Stuart, pushing from the west! It was a glorious opportunity to redeem the Brandy of four months previously . . . but just when Jeb was about to apply the vice, shells began to fall most unpleasantly close. Fitz Lee had seen the column of Stuart and, mistaking it for arriving Federal reinforcements, was firing on it!

The sole means of informing Fitz on his mistake was to attack the Federals, who already suspected they were in a trap. "Regiment after regiment," as it seemed to Stuart, "broke and dispersed." The reliable 12th Virginia was at the head of the column: Let it charge the scattering enemy! Without a second of hesitation, the 12th, which had fought previously at Brandy, dashed at the enemy. As Stuart looked, his blue eyes aflame, the regiment swung like a scythe in a harvester's hand and cut off many hundreds of the enemy. If only Fitz Lee would come up now and throw his column against the opposing flank, what a harvest of prisoners there would be! Fitz did not gallop forward; he still believed Stuart's men were Federals. To corral the bluecoats, Stuart must bring quickly to the front the 5th and 6th North Carolina, whose advancing troopers were spread for hundreds of yards back on the narrow road.

At that moment, a battalion of Federal cavalry bore down on the flank of the approaching Carolina regiments. Everyone who watched its approach observed that the force was small and without support. The Confederates in the road either did not see or did not comprehend. They stopped, wheeled, then made off in utter panic. Stuart himself dashed back to halt them. Gordon pleaded and shouted. Nothing availed. It was now too late to capture the Federals who had scattered in the first charge. Nor could Fitz Lee, after discovering his error, reach his chief in time to prevent the Unionists from executing a defiant withdrawal toward the Rappahannock.[25]

During the twelfth Meade ascertained that Confederate infantry were moving around his flank, and he started northward to protect his rear. Stuart had anticipated this and hoped now that he might assail shrewdly a retreating foe. On the morning of October 13 he received orders to make a reconnaissance in force toward Catlett's Station, the scene of one of his great adventures the preceding summer. By mid-afternoon Stuart had reached a point within sight of Catlett's Station and of Warrenton Junction simultaneously. What he saw was enough to make him drop his jaw and grip his sword hilt. Along the railroad, the enemy's thousands were spread northward. The greater part, perhaps the whole of Meade's army, was in retreat toward Manassas! Between Catlett's and Warrenton Junction was an immense park of wagons, such a park as cavalrymen dream about in happy sleep. Stuart looked and sensed a triumph: If Lee moved down that night from Warrenton, he could strike the Federals in motion! He dispatched Major Reid Venable to ride immediately to General Lee and tell him of the opportunity.

Until Lee knew the enemy's position and could begin his march, the cavalry must keep in the background. Stuart had seven guns and two brigades and he believed he might strike a hard blow if he could arrange a surprise; but the gain would be unreckonably greater if Lee could employ the two corps of infantry against the sprawling, exposed files that were plodding northward. So reasoned Jeb. The next development was as unexpected as that first sight of the incredible park of wagons: A courier rode up and reported that when Venable had reached Auburn Mills, en route to Warrenton, he had found the village in the hands of the Federals. Venable sent word that he was making a detour and had every confidence he could get through to Warrenton, but he wished Stuart to know that the enemy was between the Confederate cavalry and Lee. To rejoin the army, Stuart's butternut troopers must ride through or around the enemy. Instead of a night march to descend on the enemy, there might be a hard ride to evade them.

Further scouting reports indicated, in the confusion and the gathering twilight, that there were Federal troops on the retreat on roads to the east, west, north, and south. To be sure, their lines of march were not dangerously close together. From north to south, Stuart might have as many as five open miles. His range east and west was approximately that, but scarcely more. Manifestly there was no quick way of slipping from this pen. Troopers, horses, seven guns, the ambulances and ordnance wagons must be hidden until the enemy was gone or a line of escape was found.

Search for a concealed refuge began. To the east of Auburn Mills a little valley was found, with an entrance well concealed by woods. With little noise the men moved into the valley. Soon it was almost as quiet as it had been before the Confederates arrived, but from the nearby road came the groan of wagon wheels and the sound of marching men's talk. The Federal column was not more than 150 yards distant. As scores of the marching Federals had lanterns, the scene was picturesque even if the outlook was dangerous. Proposals for cutting their way out were entertained and rejected. Besides, if Major Venable had reached army headquarters, Lee might attack from the west at dawn. If the cavalry remained within striking distance of the enemy, they might do great damage. It was best, then, for Stuart to stay where he was for the night and to look to the main army to succor him by attacking the enemy. Jeb sent off six messengers, one after another, to slip through the Federal column and ride to Warrenton to inform Lee of the plight of the cavalry. This done, Stuart and his men prepared to "outwatch the stars."

The October dawn mercifully cloaked the road and the valley in thick fog. When it was light enough to see through the woods, there was a sharp skirmish with a surprised Federal command. Stuart determined that a swift movement on a wide arc might carry the two brigades out of danger. Quickly on word of command the ambulances and ordnance wagons were readied, the guns were limbered up, and the column was off. Around the flank of the Federals the graycoats dashed—and encountered scarcely a challenging shot. After that, rejoining Lee was merely a matter of keeping awake in the saddle long enough to reach field headquarters.[26]

The cavalry achieved little during the infantry's unhappy experience at Bristoe and in the days immediately following, and Lee's report of this period barely mentioned the mounted arm. Better luck came to Stuart on the withdrawal. On October 19, at Buckland Mills on Broad Run, his command and Fitz Lee's combined in an ambush of an unsuspecting column of Federal cavalry. As the Southerners dashed at them, the startled Federals drew rein, turned, and fled in confusion. Always afterward Stuart's men called their pursuit the "Buckland Races." Colonel Blackford complained that "We got only 250 prisoners and eight or ten ambulances."[27]

During the Bristoe campaign the cavalry's new divisional organization had justified itself in spite of the contretemps when Fitz Lee fired into Stuart's lines at Brandy. The new brigadiers had been competent, though none had performed any feat of special brilliance. Near the close of his report, Stuart described an ominous condition: "The matter of greatest concern to me during this short and eventful campaign was the subject of forage for the horses. Operating in a country worn out in peace, but now more desolate in war, it is remarkable how the horses were able to keep up."[28] Subsistence for the animals was failing. So was the supply of horses. A man who lost his horse might find the purchase of another almost impossible. A rising percentage of the cavalry slowly were to revert to the status of infantry. Stuart did not know it, but his organization had been expanded at a time when his mobility was beginning to decline and his ranks to thin. He might not be able to repeat the "Buckland Races."

CHAPTER 29

Tests and Trials of Winter

1. JUBE EARLY'S BAD DAYS AND GOOD

The infantry had no consolation for the disappointments of the futile march to Bristoe Station. On the contrary, as soon as the army was back on the line of the Rappahannock, it sustained a disaster unlike any experienced by the troops in all their marching and fighting. Every rank and grade from headquarters to guardhouse was humiliated.

The scene was Rappahannock Bridge, the crossing of the Orange and Alexandria Railroad. Farther down the Rappahannock, in the vicinity of Kelly's Ford, the ground on the north bank so fully commanded the southern side that Confederates posted there could not prevent the passage of the river by a strong Federal force at any time. The best that could be done at Kelly's was to hold off the enemy long enough for troops to take position in rear of the ford. Because this situation subjected the Confederate army to the danger of surprise whenever it was on the Rappahannock, the high command retained on the north bank of the river at Rappahannock Bridge a *tête-de-pont* where it could hold part of Meade's army while it concentrated against the Unionists who attacked at Kelly's. So long as this bridgehead was retained, a crossing farther down the Rappahannock was hazardous for the Federals.[1]

The position, two redoubts and a line of rifle pits, was held on November 7 by Harry Hays's brigade of Early's division, a trustworthy command of Louisiana veterans. They had access to the south bank of the river by a pontoon bridge that stretched in rear of the main redoubt. This bridge was beyond the range of any of the Federal batteries and was covered by batteries on the south side of the river. On the Confederate shore the army extended for several miles opposite the crossing. Hill was to the west, Ewell to the east. Rodes had command of the sector that included Kelly's. The bridgehead and the position opposite it were in Jubal Early's care.

About noon on the seventh of November the Federals began a demon-

633

stration at Kelly's Ford and soon pushed a considerable force of infantry to the southern side. Rodes had poor luck trying to reinforce the regiment in the rifle pits with another, but manned his main position and notified headquarters. Ewell hurried to the scene. Upstream, Early received word that the enemy in force was approaching the bridgehead. He put his troops in motion for the site, to which he hastened. En route he met and conferred briefly with Lee, and then crossed to the exposed redoubts and rifle pits. Brief reconnaissance showed Old Jubilee the enemy drawing near. Hays manifestly would need reinforcements. To aid him, Early returned to the south bank and sent the first units that arrived, the greater part of Hoke's brigade. Hoke himself was detached, but his men, under Colonel Archibald C. Godwin, marched confidently across the pontoon bridge and into the works. The dispatch of any further reinforcements seemed to Lee to be unnecessary. Early agreed.[2]

It appeared the Federals had put more guns into action and crossed their fire on part of the Confederate line. In some concern, Early sent Major Samuel Hale, Jr., across the river to ascertain what this meant. As the insistent darkness of autumn began to descend, Early could see flashes of musketry close by the rifle pits but could make out nothing decisive. Presently he and General Lee agreed that the fire was slackening. This they took to mean that the enemy had given up the attack. If so, it would not be renewed that evening. The Federals never delivered night attacks against the Army of Northern Virginia. In that belief, Lee started for his headquarters. When Major Hale returned, it was to report that he had seen both Hays and Godwin. They had faced heavy attacks but had captured most of the men in the first line thrown against them and thought their lines secure.

Hale added that coming back over the bridge he found a few of Hays's men who asserted that their line had been broken. He thought they were skulkers. With that, Early bade another staff officer, Major John Daniel, go to the pontoon bridge and get any news the fugitives brought. Daniel was soon back. Near the bridge, he said, he had met Hays, who told him the line was broken, the Louisiana brigade overwhelmed, the Federals closing in on Godwin.

Early was appalled. He could not believe Hays's veterans beaten so quickly, or Hoke's in a foredoomed fight. It was an impossible situation, but it was impossible to do anything for them! It would have been folly to attempt to cross the bridge, "and I could not open with the guns on the south side, as it was so very dark . . . we would have been as apt to fire into our own men as into the enemy." Soon the fire died away. Cheers rose above the wind. Godwin's men were prisoners. From the two brigades not more than 600 escaped.[3]

With the bridgehead lost and the enemy already on the south side of the Rappahannock at Kelly's Ford, the Southern army had to retreat. It moved that night and recrossed the Rapidan the next night. There, still smarting, the command could appraise the disaster at Rappahannock Bridge. Early had 1,674 killed, wounded, and captured. At Kelly's Ford the loss among Rodes's men was 349. For the two divisions that made 2,023, a figure that outraged the Second Corps and shocked the entire army. Said Sandie Pendleton, "It is absolutely sickening, and I feel personally disgraced by the issue of the late campaign, as does every one in the command. Oh, how every day is proving the value of General Jackson to us!"[4]

No blame could be put on the soldiers. As Lee said in his report, "The courage and good conduct of the troops engaged have been too often tried to admit of question." Hays, as always, handled his men well. After he was surrounded and a prisoner, his horse took fright and ran. When the enemy began to fire at him, Hays decided he might as well try to reach the bridge, because he could not be in greater danger there than in the midst of shouting enemies. He escaped unhurt. Colonel Godwin, resisting with a remnant of sixty or seventy of his men, was overcome with his weapons in his hands.

Early felt that he was in no way responsible for the disaster. "I am conscious of having done all in my power to defend the position," he said in his report, "but I must candidly confess that I did concur in the opinion of the commanding general that the enemy did not have enterprise enough to attempt any serious attack after dark, as such attacks are so foreign to his usual policy. . . ." He added that his troops could not have been withdrawn with safety "after the enemy had gained their immediate front." Lee accepted substantially the explanation given by Early.[5]

The real explanation of the reverse was one which, even after their experience at Gettysburg, the Confederates were unwilling to admit: At Rappahannock Bridge a sound Federal plan of attack had been executed admirably by courageous men. So well handled were the assaulting troops, numbering only 2,100, that they were able to occupy the first line of rifle pits without firing a shot. At Kelly's Ford the Federals had moved in overwhelming strength and encountered little resistance.

About three weeks after the Federals had advanced from the Rappahannock, they threatened a blow on the line of the Rapidan. On November 26, cavalry scouts reported the enemy in movement for the lower fords of the Rapidan. The possibility of such a move had been considered. Lines of defense had been chosen. Officers were on the alert. Dick Ewell was absent on account of sickness, but his corps was in Jube Early's care. At the moment it was impossible to ascertain whether Meade intended to move on Richmond or whether he merely was preparing to turn the right wing of the Southern army. An advance toward the enemy was dictated by either contingency. Early was to take the lead because the Second Corps was on the right and nearer the Federals. Hill was to follow Early.

In the early afternoon of the twenty-seventh Rodes's division and Early's, under Harry Hays, were the first to establish contact with the enemy in the vicinity of Locust Grove, a settlement about seven miles southwest of Wilderness Church. The decision of General Lee was to await the arrival of Allegheny Johnson's division before engaging the Federals. Rodes and Hays accordingly formed line of battle, and when Johnson came up the head of his column formed on Rodes's left and rear. The center and rear of his column on the road constituted virtually a refused flank for the Second Corps.[6]

The rearmost of these brigades was Maryland Steuart's, which contained some splendid troops that had not always been well led. Shortly after noon, Johnson received from Steuart a report that he was under fire from the left. Johnson started at once for Steuart's position. He followed the sound rule of the vigilant commander—when in doubt, see for yourself. He found Steuart skirmishing heavily, ordered him to redeploy to parallel the enemy's line, and as quickly as possible recalled the other brigades of the division and placed them on the right of Steuart.

A stubborn and confused action followed. At first the Confederates repulsed two attacks. Then Johnson directed that the division take the offensive. Because of the tangled terrain, this involved a somewhat complicated maneuver in which brigades and even regiments became separated. The battle line swung like a pendulum. Regiments advanced, drifted apart, and fell back. Jube Early had to confess afterward that he "could not see any portion of the troops engaged." At length, more from bewilderment than from punishment, most of the Confederates fell back a few hundred yards to a fence-line. There they repulsed all attacks till darkness put an end to the fight. This affair of Payne's Farm was costly. Maryland Steuart was wounded lightly in the arm and John M. Jones in the head. Total casualties for Johnson's division were 545. By holding the road in this meeting engagement, said Early, Old Allegheny "saved the whole corps from a very serious disaster."[7]

Skirmishing was in progress all the while on the front of the Second Corps, east of Mine Run. All the indications were of a wintry battle, a Fredericksburg fought in the forest. Early had previously examined the vicinity with an eye to its defense and knew that the west bank of Mine Run offered better positions than could be found at Locust Grove. He accordingly moved back the Second Corps and Dick Anderson's supporting division on the night of November 27. Lee directed Early on the twenty-eighth to retire a short distance farther to a line that had been selected previously as the strongest available in that district.

Rain fell all day on the twenty-eighth. When the downpour ceased, temperature dropped to extreme chill. The wind rose. Shivering graycoats steeled themselves and piled higher the parapets behind which they intended, come what might, to hold against their attacking adversary. Except for a cannonade of about an hour on the twenty-ninth, the Union troops made no move. The thirtieth passed without incident. Blue columns appeared to march now to the left and now to the right, but the forest was so thick that nothing could be seen clearly. When December 1 passed without a Federal attack, Lee decided to assume the initiative. Wilcox's and Anderson's divisions were shifted to the extreme right, whence it was thought they could turn the Federal left. An anxious night of preparation ended in a dawn of disappointment. The Federals had retreated. Nor in that tangled country could they be overtaken in their withdrawal across the Rapidan.[8]

The reasons given by Meade for the retirement were varied. Throughout the operation he had suffered disappointments and failure of logistics. Delays were frequent. General G. K. Warren told Meade that he could turn the Confederate right easily, and Meade concentrated heavily on his left for the movement. On the thirtieth, when all was prepared, a message was handed him from Warren: "I advise against making the attack here. The full light of the sun shows me that I cannot succeed." Meade was astounded. By the time he could return the troops to their former positions, he believed Lee had made the Confederate position more nearly impregnable. "It was my deliberate judgment that I ought not to attack," he confided manfully to his wife. "I acted on that judgment, and I am willing to stand or fall by it at all hazards."[9]

The Confederate commanders were disappointed at Meade's unpunished escape. In Ewell's absence, Jube Early had handled the Second Corps with apparent ease and with moderate efficiency. On November 27 the terrain was so confused and the situation so uncertain that Early's caution in leaving Johnson to fight his own battle was explicable and probably justified. There was at the time no suggestion that Early, acting as corps commander, was too much inclined to fight a battle by divisions. His admission that he "could not see any portion of the troops engaged" did suggest one of the few defects of Early as a soldier. He had a poor sense of direction. On more than one battlefield it is possible that what appeared to have been tardiness was due to his inability to grasp quickly the guiding features of the ground over which he was to operate.

Of other officers, three only had opportunity of distinguishing themselves in the Mine Run operations. Maryland Steuart fought vigorously when he was assailed on the twenty-seventh. As Steuart's superior, Allegheny Johnson was prompt in grasping the situation and vigorous in correcting it. His troop movements were intelligent. The other officer who added to his soldierly reputation was cavalryman Tom Rosser. He attacked a Federal corps ordnance train, destroying 35 or 40 wagons, and brought off 8, together with 7 ambulances, 230 animals, and 95 prisoners.[10] The vigilance of his patrol and the vigor of his onslaught were his own.

The most serious adverse entry in the Mine Run campaign was the general failure of the army to achieve any military result. That had been true of Bristoe and, most lamentably, of Rappahannock Bridge. For the five months since the return from Pennsylvania, the record had been negative, though more than 4,200 casualties had been sustained. In every operation there had been creditable performance. Each failure could be explained logically. The great difference was that before Gettysburg there had been few failures to be explained. From headquarters, where his discerning eye saw everything, Walter Taylor wrote an ominous sentence: "I only wish the general had good lieutenants; we miss Jackson and Longstreet terribly."[11]

2. LONGSTREET IS WEIGHED

After Mine Run the infantry of the Army of Northern Virginia fought no battle for five months. Promotions were few during the period because fatalities were negligible. In January 1864, John R. Chambliss, Jr., who had acted for months as commander of Rooney Lee's troopers, was made brigadier general. The next month, Colonel Nathaniel H. Harris of the 19th Mississippi, an officer of proven parts, was advanced in rank to succeed Carnot Posey, who had died in November of the wound received at Bristoe Station.

The only other promotions were in the artillery, which had not shown at Gettysburg in the Second and Third Corps a leadership equal to that of the First. In September Armistead L. Long of Lee's staff had been advanced to brigadier general and placed in charge of the guns of the Second Corps, which were not handled acceptably by the corps chief after the wounding of Stapleton Crutchfield. Before the war Long had been an artillerist of some reputation, and Lee had used him in reconnaissance and posting batteries. Long was returned regretfully from staff to line, because he was most useful at army headquarters; but Lee did not feel that a man of Long's experience should be withheld from a field service in which men of professional training were few.

Concerning other artillerists, Pendleton, at Lee's instance, reported in detail. Some were recommended for higher rank. Transfer was proposed for several who, in Pendleton's opinion, were incompetent or physically incapacitated. The principal promotion suggested by Pendleton was that of E. Porter Alexander to the rank of brigadier general and command of the artillery of the First Corps. Like advancement was not advocated for R. Lindsay Walker, chief of artillery of the Third Corps. The reason probably was that under the governing law the artillery of the army was entitled to three general officers only. As Pendleton and Long already held that rank, there was place for Alexander but not for Walker also. Pendleton reported that "some of the best officers of this corps," finding promotion slow, were seeking transfer to other arms. This was an unwelcome state of affairs because the artillery officers with the rank of company or field officers were of an average competence definitely above that of infantrymen or cavalrymen of like rank.[12]

Although battles were not fought, the winter was far from quiet. It was an alternation of excitement and misery. When the commanding general was not present to repress jealousies, they began to develop among old comrades. Ugly disputes eclipsed gallant deeds. Much the worst strife was in the absent First Corps. The new experiences of that command, in combat and controversy, did more than the previous two years of campaign to show the character, the capacities and the limitations, of James Longstreet. Any element of mystery that had clung to him by reason of habitual silence was stripped off him by his own pen.

Bragg began, in October 1863, the partial investment of Chattanooga, but he made little progress beyond that of rendering the Federal lines of supply somewhat hazardous. General George H. Thomas, who succeeded Rosecrans, proceeded to secure his supply line by placing a strong force downstream on the Tennessee at Brown's Ferry. At the sight of this operation, Longstreet's fighting blood was stirred. He gained Bragg's approval for a night attack on the Federal rear guard at Wauhatchie, three miles from the main force at the ferry. To make the assault Longstreet selected Micah Jenkins, then in temporary charge of Hood's division, and Evander Law, in command of a detached brigade. The two had been bitter rivals for Hood's position, and in their night attack, always a difficult operation, they did not work together. Law suffered lightly in the failed attack, while Jenkins sustained 356 casualties. Longstreet's report of the affair asserted that the difference in casualties showed a "want of conduct" on the part of Law. As Law's troops were veterans, their behavior had to be attributed "to a strong feeling of jealousy among the brigadier-generals."[13]

Besides Law, the commander of the Texas Brigade, Jerome B. Robertson, was blamed by Longstreet for the failure at Wauhatchie. Old Pete went to Bragg seeking Robertson's removal. The equities are not easily established in the case of Robertson or in the controversy between Law and Jenkins, but the effect was to impair a division which had been, all in all, probably the finest combat force in the Army of Northern Virginia. An absence of a month and a half from that army had sufficed to produce dissension, talk of incompetence, and a whisper of something morally worse than lack of cooperation!

The next move of Longstreet was to deepen these differences and to spread dissatisfaction to McLaws's command. For reasons that have not been clear to others, if indeed they were plain to him, Bragg decided to weaken further a weak army in the face of a strong adversary and send Longstreet to deal with General Burnside, who was guarding East Tennessee with a force of some 22,200 men based in Knoxville. Longstreet was as anxious to leave Bragg as the commanding general was to be rid of him. The force that left the Chattanooga line November 5–6 consisted of about 12,000 men of all arms. Longstreet considered it scarcely half as strong as it should be for the mission. Inefficient staff work, lame transportation, and lack of cooperation at Bragg's headquarters deepened Old Pete's discouragement. He pushed on but, in retrospect at least, considered himself persecuted. In his memoirs he wrote, "It began to look more like a campaign against Longstreet than against Burnside."[14]

On the fourteenth, approaching Knoxville, contact was made with Burnside's forces, with the prospect of battle, but the enemy slipped away. Again, as at Wauhatchie, there were rumors of a lack of concert between Law and Jenkins. At Knoxville the Federals awaited attack behind strong earthworks. Longstreet proceeded with no suggestion of haste and with some maneuvers that suggested his unfruitful operation of the previous spring against Suffolk.

On November 23 came word that the Federals at Chattanooga had moved out of their defenses and attacked Bragg. The situation suddenly became more complicated. If Bragg worsted the enemy, now under the vigilant direction of U. S. Grant, the outlook at Knoxville would be bright. Longstreet might get reinforcements and, at the least, have his rear safe from serious threat. Were Bragg defeated, Longstreet might be caught between two forces. In that event, if he were lucky enough to escape destruction, he would be compelled to retreat into East Tennessee. A different prospect, surely, this was from the picture of victory that Longstreet had painted two and a half months previously, when he had bidden farewell to Lee!

An earthwork fortification at the northwest corner of Knoxville's defenses called Fort Sanders was selected as the target. The attack was to be delivered at dawn on November 29 by two of McLaws's brigades, to be followed *en échelon* on the left by Jenkins. Intelligence gathered by Jenkins on the forbidding ditch and parapet in front of the fort was alarming, and he wrote to Longstreet in warning. Old Pete was devoted to Jenkins. Next to Pickett, perhaps, he esteemed the ambitious young South Carolinian more highly than he did any of his subordinates; but he did not like his undertone of misgiving. "Do not listen to the idea of failing and we shall not fail," he exhorted Jenkins. ". . . Let me urge you not to entertain such feelings for a moment. Do not let any one fail, or any thing."

This was not Longstreet's sole vexation. Rumors had come that Bragg had been engaged heavily at Chattanooga in a battle of undetermined result. McLaws asked whether the attack on Knoxville should not be deferred until the outcome for Bragg's army was known: "If the enemy has been beaten at Chattanooga, do we not gain by delay at this point? If we have been defeated at Chattanooga, do we not risk our entire force by an assault here?" If defeated at both places, he asked, "would we be in condition to force our way to the army in Virginia?" Longstreet replied sharply: "There is neither safety nor honor in any other course than the one I have chosen and ordered. . . . The assault must be made at the time appointed, and must be made with a determination which will insure success."[15]

After that there could be no hesitation or further argument on the part of McLaws, but it was ominous that both the division commanders, men of unquestioned courage, felt so much concern that they expressed their doubts to their chief. This never had happened before on the eve of an attack. If Longstreet observed that fact, he did not permit it to show in his action. He made no alteration in his plans.

Obediently, at the scheduled hour, the assault columns rushed forward. Soon they piled into the deep ditch, slippery with half-frozen mud, of Fort Sanders. The ditch was jammed, a trap, a grave trench. The defense was too powerful. Assault was hopeless. If the men remained there, every one of them would be killed. Longstreet ordered the recall. The attack had failed. Get out the survivors and stop the fight. That was his order.

Hardly had fire ceased when Longstreet was handed a telegram from Richmond. He read: "General Bragg has fallen back before superior forces at Ringgold and hopes to make a stand there, and . . . cooperation is necessary and the greatest promptitude is required." It was signed by Jefferson Davis.[16]

Braxton Bragg had prepared the road to ruin by permitting the Federals to open sure lines of supply at Chattanooga. The dispatch of Longstreet to Knoxville had weakened his long, concave line. Himself of doubtful military competence, Bragg had faced in Grant an able, self-reliant, aggressive adversary who had in Sherman and Thomas two lieutenants of unusual capacity. As a result of these circumstances and of incredibly bad tactics, Bragg had lost Lookout Mountain on November 24 and the next day had sustained a heavy defeat on Missionary Ridge. His casualties of 2,500 were not excessive, but his loss of 40 guns was serious, and his men's loss of confidence in him was worse. He had retreated to Ringgold and then Dalton, Georgia.

From there word was relayed to Longstreet: "General Bragg desires me to say he wishes you to fall back with your command upon Dalton if possible. If you find that impracticable, he thinks you will have to fall back toward Virginia." In perplexity of mind, Longstreet called a council of his lieutenants, whose opinion was to remain in East Tennessee. It shaped Longstreet's action. He remained in front of Knoxville, holding Burnside, until intelligence reached him that Sherman was approaching to relieve the garrison. On the night of the third of December the trains were put in motion northeastward. The infantry followed on the night of the fourth.[17]

As Longstreet turned his back on Knoxville, all informed Southerners, outside his own circle, felt that he had sustained a humiliating defeat. In that mirror of Confederate gossip, the diary of Mrs. Chesnut, the opinion of a multitude was reflected: "Detached from General Lee, what a horrible failure. What a slow old humbug is Longstreet."[18] At Chickamauga he had been the Longstreet of Second Manassas, but at Knoxville he was back in front of Suffolk. The entire war had witnessed no repulse more complete, by a force of insignificant numbers. In Fort Sanders a garrison of less than 250 men was responsible for much of the loss of 813 sustained by some of the most renowned regiments of the famous First Corps of the Army of Northern Virginia.

The advance of these veteran troops had been organized carelessly. They had converged in too narrow a zone. Supports had crowded upon them. The whole plan of action had been clumsily executed. On the day of the frustrated assault and at the council of war that evening, Longstreet said nothing, so far as the record shows, to indicate that he held McLaws responsible for the failure. When he had reflected upon the failure of the campaign, Longstreet decided that the fault was not his but that of his senior division commander. McLaws, he told himself, had not cooperated acceptably during the Knoxville campaign. He wrathfully concluded, also, that McLaws had not shown confidence in the plans of operations or in the leadership of his chief. McLaws's letter of November 29, urging that the assault on Fort Sanders wait on news from Bragg, probably was one of several such incidents that stuck in Longstreet's memory.

On December 17, in his encampment at Rogersville, Tennessee, Longstreet sprung a sensation that was to trouble him for many a day. In a few brief sentences he relieved McLaws of command, directed that officer to proceed to Augusta, Georgia, and placed the division under the senior brigadier. McLaws had no intimation that this was to happen to him, and asked the reason. Longstreet's A.A.G. replied: "I am directed to say that throughout the campaign on which we are engaged you have exhibited a want of confidence in the efforts and plans which the commanding general has thought proper to adopt, and he is apprehensive that this feeling will extend more or less to the troops under your command."

McLaws had been a major general since May 23, 1862, and had been in nearly all the principal battles of Lee's army. He was not accounted among the ablest of the division commanders, but he was respected as a man and a soldier. To relieve him of command was to startle thousands of Southerners. From Augusta he forwarded to the adjutant general the correspondence that had passed. He insisted: "I have differed in opinion with General Longstreet concerning many things, but that this difference has influenced my own conduct or that of the troops under my command I utterly deny. I therefore respectfully request that my division be restored to my command."[19]

Longstreet decided to undertake to make good his complaint against McLaws by the presentation of formal charges and specifications. McLaws's alleged general lack of cooperation during the campaign was ignored now. All three of the specifications were drawn from McLaws's failure to take precautions in the assault on Fort Sanders. McLaws struck back hard. In a letter he evidently designed to be circulated among his friends in Richmond, he said that Longstreet "attempted to make me a blind to run public inquiry off from his complete failure in the whole Tennessee campaign. . . . The difficulty with Genl. L. and myself commenced at Chickamauga when I, not believing that he was a greater man than Genl. Bragg kept aloof from the coalition which was forming against him, headed by Genl. L. . . . Genl. L. has never forgiven me my not joining that clique. . . . When it is considered that Genl. L failed to assault the enemy before reaching Knoxville, and his long delay before the place, . . . and that he has nothing to recommend him as a commander but the possession of a certain bullheadedness, it is mortifying when one feels that he is allowed to tyrannize, as he is doing."

McLaws pressed for trial before a court-martial and for restoration to his command. If held, this court-martial was not to be the only one of importance that would be convened at the instance of the lieutenant general. In the opinion of Longstreet, Jerome Robertson at the head of the Texas Brigade had indulged in pessimistic utterances which Longstreet took to be part of an effort to dodge heavy duty. With the letter that carried the charges against McLaws there was an arraignment of Robertson for specified remarks "calculated to discourage . . . the said regimental commanders . . . and weaken their confidence in the movement then in progress" and, in general, "to prevent that hearty and hopeful cooperation necessary to success."[20]

Longstreet was not unconscious of the fact that the filing of charges against two of his senior officers was almost as much a reflection on him as on them. At the moment he was in the depths. Gone was the desire to direct an army of his own; gone, too, was the confidence in which he had come to Tennessee. He wrote the adjutant general that he was cut off from communication with Bragg and desired to be "assigned as part of some other officer's command." He went on to say that if East Tennessee was to be held for future operations, he wished them to be under another commander. "I regret to say that a combination of circumstances has so operated during the campaign in East Tennessee as to prevent the complete destruction of the enemy's forces in this part of the State. It is fair to infer that the fault entirely is with me, and I desire, therefore, that some other commander be tried."

Longstreet doubtless wrote this in humiliation, but if he expected the President or the War Department to placate him with soft words and compliments he was disappointed. He was notified that it was doubtful whether he could relieve an officer from duty and send that individual beyond the limits of the command. Mr. Davis took a serious view of the charges against McLaws and deferred the question of Longstreet's request to be relieved of responsibility in East Tennessee. At length the court-martial was set for February 3, 1864, then delayed until the twelfth. First to be heard was the complaint against Jerome Robertson. If there was a verdict the record of it has not been found, though Robertson was suspended from his famous command. Much later, in June, he was ordered to take command of the "reserve forces of the State of Texas." His transfer marked his final disappearance from the First Corps. Longstreet doubtless was glad to be rid of the Texan.

It was February 13 when the trial of McLaws began. McLaws had prepared for it with much care and he had the better of it. The trial was interrupted and prolonged, and would not be adjourned finally until March 19. The court's findings were announced on May 4. McLaws was found guilty of one specification only—"failing in the details of his attack to make arrangements essential to his success" in the assault on Fort Sanders. Sentence was suspension from rank and command for sixty days, but Adjutant General Cooper overturned the verdict due to "irregularities" in the court's procedures. McLaws was ordered to be restored to command of his division. As will be seen, however, the commanding general of the Army of Northern Virginia would have a say in this matter.[21]

The case of Evander Law was equally difficult. On December 19, 1863, Law had tendered his resignation through Longstreet's headquarters. It was his purpose, Law intimated, to transfer to the cavalry and procure a command in that service. Law's subsequent explanation was that Longstreet had recommended Jenkins's promotion after promising that Hood's division should go to Law. While action on the resignation was pending, Law asked leave of absence. It is entirely probable that Old Pete granted this leave without any urging, perhaps even with alacrity, because he shared the belief that Hood's old division never would have its former value as a combat unit so long as both Jenkins and Law served with it.

After Law had departed for Richmond, it was reported to Longstreet that certain officers of Law's Alabama brigade were circulating a petition to the War Department for transfer to their native state. Law was said to have engineered the leave of absence in order to exert his influence in Richmond to have the petition granted. Longstreet was outraged, and drew up charges against Law for "conduct highly prejudicial to good order and military discipline." When Law did not present his resignation in the capital as promised, Longstreet filed new charges against the South Carolinian.[22]

The vexatious cases of Robertson, McLaws, and Law showed a weakening, if not a demoralization of Longstreet's command, but they were not the full measure of Old Pete's tribulations that winter. In February Congress passed an act to provide for the appointment of an additional general of full rank. The measure was designed solely to give adequate administrative and military powers to Kirby Smith in the Trans-Mississippi Department. In spite of this, Longstreet felt himself aggrieved that Smith, "of lower rank than mine," was appointed "to hold rank above me." Longstreet late in life wrote that he thought his resignation was proper when passed over in this manner, but he decided he should "stay and go down with faithful comrades of long and arduous service."[23]

After his period of doubt and humiliation and discontent, Longstreet swung to the other extreme. Subsequently he explained that "the disaffected"—meaning McLaws, Robertson, and Law—"were away, and with them disappeared their influence." His little army, he said, "was bright and cheerful and ready for any work to which it could be called." He returned eagerly to the same sort of planning in which he had indulged in the spring and late summer of 1863. It is futile to inquire whether this sudden activity was itself a confession of failure or the expression of his purpose to make a new record that would efface the old. This much is clear. In his planning he showed less of undisguised striving for leadership and more of regard for the cooperation of others—as if he had learned his lesson!—but he scarcely displayed more of wisdom concerning the practicality of the strategical combination he urged.[24]

Bragg had relinquished command of the Army of Tennessee on December 2. Joseph E. Johnston took Bragg's place but found himself confronted by superior force. So was Longstreet. Between them, in effect, were two Federal armies, Grant's at Nashville and Thomas's at Chattanooga. Longstreet felt that he could do nothing where he was unless the enemy obligingly came up and attacked him. The only course he could follow, as he saw the situation, was to mount the whole of his command, move into Kentucky, and seize the Louisville and Nashville Railroad. This he thought he would be able to hold long enough to force the Federals to withdraw from Tennessee, which Johnston then could occupy. "The only way to mount us," he wrote Lee, "is by sending us 5,000 mules from Virginia, 2,500 from Georgia, and 2,000 from South Carolina; I have 5,000. . . . We have no time to spare. . . ."

It was entirely beyond the resources of the Southern government to convert Longstreet's command into mounted infantry. Before he could be brought to see this, his enthusiasm for his plan led him to inquire directly of the President whether he could undertake the movement. From the War Department came back a singularly stiff snub. Old Pete continued to press for his plan until the second week in March, when he concluded that the animals and forage were unprocurable. But he would not surrender the idea of an offensive against the Louisville and Nashville Railroad. His new plan was that Beauregard should move from South Carolina to unite with him. Thence the two commands would advance against Louisville. Longstreet hoped then to hold the Federals' lines of supply long enough to compel them to retreat. Thereupon Johnston was to advance behind the retreating Federals. Junction of the three Confederate armies would give them superior force.

This plan assumed that Beauregard could take all the infantry from Charleston and march them 300 miles to Louisville. A further assumption was that the combined troops of Longstreet and Beauregard could be subsisted and foraged en route and would be strong enough to beat off attacks until Johnston arrived. Longstreet journeyed to Richmond to join Davis, Lee, Bragg, and War Department officials in a discussion on March 14. Longstreet's scheme for a triple concentration was examined carefully. When the council adjourned without announcement of Davis's decision, Longstreet was of the opinion that the President favored the return of Old Pete's command to the Army of Tennessee before anything further was attempted. The spirit of the meeting, in Longstreet's opinion, was cold, if not positively uncivil to Lee and to him, and after he left the room with

Lee he probably invoked his old commander to support his plan and to take direction of the army he hoped to see newly organized.

His plan remained uppermost in Longstreet's mind. He devoted hour after hour to letters in which he explained to Beauregard, to Davis, and to Lee what he thought the strategy of the Southern army should be in Tennessee and Kentucky. In describing all this Longstreet was explicit, but he said afterward that he believed little attention would be paid his views by Davis and Bragg, both of whom he thought hostile to him. Consequently he sent Lee a copy of his fullest letter to Davis, and he again besought Lee to sponsor the plan and to take command of the expedition when it was ready to move into Kentucky.[25]

By March 18, Longstreet was back in East Tennessee and on the down curve of his emotional crisis. Disappointment of every sort met him. Troops were on short rations. Corn arrived in such small quantities that Longstreet doubted whether he could keep his horses and mules alive. The answers to his appeals for action in Kentucky were discouraging. Davis replied in terms that Longstreet considered a rebuke. The President's preference for the union of "the two wings of the Army of Tennessee" was reiterated. Beauregard questioned the soundness of the plan Longstreet proposed. Johnston did not think an advance should be undertaken. Lee agreed that either a concentration on Johnston's line or an advance into Kentucky was feasible, but he thought the heaviest Federal blow might fall in Virginia, and he said frankly that he would not advocate an advance into Kentucky if Johnston was opposed to it.[26]

Old Pete held to his opinion with the stubbornness that made some of his comrades think of him as German in his mentality; but he soon had other and scarcely less humiliating matters to deepen his distress. He was anxious that men of his own choice be named to succeed McLaws, whom he did not wish to return, and Hood, who would be incapacitated for months. Longstreet's choice for Hood's division continued to be Micah Jenkins, whose promotion he previously had sought. If Jenkins was advanced, Longstreet wanted Joe Kershaw to succeed to McLaws's division. In the event only one vacancy occurred, Longstreet wished Jenkins to have it.

At the outset an obstacle to the execution of Longstreet's plan was presented in the person of Charles W. Field. That fine officer at length had recovered sufficiently from the wounds suffered at Second Manassas to resume field duty, though he still was crippled. The War Department on February 12 ordered Field to join Longstreet for assignment to duty with Hood's division. The same day Field was promoted major general, which automatically under his orders gave him command of the division.

At the moment Longstreet made no protest at the assignment of "an outsider" to the command of a division which the senior brigadier, Jenkins, was qualified to lead. Hopeful of doing by indirection what the promotion of Field kept him from doing directly, Longstreet tried this arrangement: With him, on temporary duty, was Major General Simon Buckner, a capable and experienced soldier whose whole career had been spent in the Mississippi Valley. There was no reason to assume that Buckner would wish to go to Virginia. Hood's division was larger than Buckner's and in need of an active commander. Field was crippled. Longstreet transferred Buckner to command Hood's division and put Field in charge of Bucker's troops. If, subsequently, Buckner was called to other duty, the direction of Hood's division would be vacated in favor of Jenkins, who was eager for promotion to regular command of that division.

Blandly Longstreet reported his action to the War Department. As soon as his letter reached Richmond, the adjutant general telegraphed disapproval. "The order from this office," said Cooper, "assigning General Field to [Hood's] division will be carried into effect." Longstreet was not to be outdone. Command of McLaws's division was vacant so long as its former head was suspended. If Field were put in McLaws's place, command of Hood's division might be retained for Jenkins. Accordingly Longstreet telegraphed Cooper, "Would it meet the views of the Department to assign Major-General Field to the division formerly commanded by Major-General McLaws?" The answer came the same day: "It does not suit the views of the President to assign Major-General Field to the division lately commanded by Major-General McLaws. He is to take the division which he was assigned in orders from this office."[27]

Longstreet said no more at the time, but as the days passed his indignation mounted. On March 20 he wrote a wrathful letter asking to be informed of "the distinguished services rendered by [Field] and the high recommendations of his commanding generals which have induced the Government to make this unusual promotion and assignment." This was a challenge of the sort Jefferson Davis never ignored. His was the constitutional right to appoint general officers; it was the duty of his military subordinates to accept his choice. The adjutant general was directed to administer a strong rebuke. "The advice you have asked [concerning Field's service] is considered highly insubordinate and demands rebuke," Cooper wrote. "It is also a reflection upon a gallant and meritorious officer . . . and is deemed unbecoming the high position and dignity of the officer who thus makes the reflection. The regulations of the Army, with which you should be familiar, prescribe that appointments of general officers are made . . . by the Executive, by whom appointments are made under the Constitution . . . and your inquiry is a direct reflection upon the Executive."[28]

This came when Longstreet's mission was nearing its end. The tone of the rebuke, which approached a reprimand, had not been the temper of all officialdom toward Longstreet. He and his men had received on February 17 the thanks of Congress. Had these thanks been specific, they might have dwelt on what Old Pete and his veterans achieved at Chickamauga. Although Longstreet had little or no part in planning that battle, he had done much to win it.

When this is stated, it covers substantially everything that can be said to Longstreet's credit in Tennessee. He had done poorly in all the actions he directed independently. His administration had been as luckless as his combat. While serving under Lee, the one serious difficulty Longstreet had with subordinate commanders involved A. P. Hill, but in Tennessee, during five months of detached service, one major general and two brigadiers were ordered before courts-martial. A famous division had been crippled because of rivalries between two of its brigade commanders. The return of Micah Jenkins was followed by strife. Concerning all this Longstreet never wrote a line to indicate that he considered himself at fault.

That was not all. With his command disorganized and his achievement in tragic contrast to the hopes he had cherished before he left Virginia, Longstreet remained confident that he could shape the soundest strategy to terminate the war successfully in 1864. To this confidence in himself as a strategist he tenaciously held. In advocating the recovery of Kentucky, without previously defeating the Federals in Tennessee, the one point of departure for an army would be southwest Virginia. The objective would be the Louisville and Nashville Railroad. This was unshakable logic, a perfect paper basis for a campaign. Practicality was lacking. The mounting of Longstreet's men on mules scarcely would have been possible at a time when the shortage of horses and mules was one of the most acute of the army's problems, and supplying forage in a country remote from the railways would have been impossible.

Longstreet's alternative plans for the convergence of all the infantry in the southeastern states of the Confederacy were by no means original with him. They were part of what might be termed the prevailing strategical theory of the South. All military men of experience accepted without argument the doctrine that the Confederate armies should be concentrated, but the administration consented to dispersion because the people of each state demanded protection from the invader. Seapower made it possible for the Union leaders to take advantage of the Confederacy's mistaken policy and immobilize a great part of the Confederate army. Where Longstreet's planning was original it was not practical, and where it was practical it was not original. He personified the familiar danger to the effective organization of an army, the danger that a competent executive officer will destroy his usefulness by regarding himself as a great strategist.

3. WINTER TESTS TEMPER

By comparison with conditions Longstreet found in Tennessee, the army command in Virginia seemed a happy fellowship, but during the months of Old Pete's absence some of Lee's other lieutenants had probably more of contention and heartburning than they had known since the spring of 1862. Of different nature, but manifestly serious was the threat, early in December 1863, that the man whose tact, courage, and character held the army together would himself be sent to Georgia to succeed Bragg. The President was frankly desirous that Lee assume command in the Mississippi Valley. It was only by definite expression of his desire to retain his old association that Lee escaped an assignment that would have placed him, not Joseph E. Johnston, in front of Sherman. Had Lee gone, the Southern government might have discovered, quickly and unhappily, the extent to which the morale not less than the strategy of the Army of Northern Virginia depended on him.

As for Bragg, after Mr. Davis reluctantly had concluded that the man who lost Lookout Mountain and Missionary Ridge was not qualified to command one army, he decided to give that unsuccessful officer command of all the armies. On February 24, 1864, Bragg, under direction of the President, was "charged with the conduct of the military operations in the armies of the Confederacy."[29] The post, which vaguely resembled that of a modern chief of the general staff, was one which Lee had found impossible in the spring of 1862. Bragg was to surprise everyone by his discharge of his new duties, which better fitted his abilities than did field command.

If the crisis of Lee's transfer and Bragg's promotion was passed without hurt, a progressive decline in the rations of the troops and the forage of the animals brought to the camps the specter of starvation. "Unless there is a change," said Lee in January, "I fear the army cannot be kept effective and probably cannot be kept together."[30] Hunger was the normal condition of man and mount. The men damned the commissaries; artillerists and troopers blamed the quartermasters. No Southerner, unless it was Colonel Northrop, would admit that the food and the fodder actually were unavailable.

In this want and suffering, the army had to recruit or re-enlist its cavalry. A proposal to bring from South Carolina some regiments that had enjoyed an easy life provoked bitter complaints on their part—something scarcely thought of a year before, and certainly not two years previously. Worse even than the task of recruiting the cavalry was that of filling the gaps in the infantry. The veterans re-enlisted, but to catch the skulkers a new conscription act had to be passed. Some state judges so captiously disputed the constitutionality of various military laws that the writ of habeas corpus had to be suspended.[31]

Certain army officers, like these jurists, began to balk. Harvey Hill, on October 15, 1863, had been relieved by Bragg from duty with the Army of Tennessee. Hill thought the reason for his removal was his participation in the round-robin against Bragg. He demanded a court of inquiry be detailed to investigate the charges, but was told that a court was not necessary. Prediction, freely made, of a duel between Hill and Bragg came to nothing. Instead of trying to kill Bragg, the aggrieved Hill sought service elsewhere.

In doing this he stipulated that the position be one equivalent to his interim rank of lieutenant general, to which he had been promoted in July 1863 but which had not yet been confirmed by the Senate. This insistence disclosed a newly developed quality of his mind. Harvey Hill had not previously expressed dissatisfaction with his commission or with any field command. Now he became jealous of his rank. Corps command, it seemed, was the only service in keeping with that rank. The adjutant general accordingly had to advise him on the sixteenth of November that there was no command to which he then could be assigned. "Until a suitable opportunity is offered for placing you on duty according to your rank, you will consider yourself authorized to dispose of your time is such manner as may best suit your convenience, reporting your address monthly to this office."[32]

While Hill waited obediently at home, the Senate assembled on December 7 and from time to time received presidential messages. None of the lists of officers submitted by Mr. Davis for confirmation included the nomination of D. H. Hill to be lieutenant general. When Beauregard called for an experienced subordinate for duty in Charleston, the President proposed to assign to the post Hill "as a major-general and explain to him that thus only could we employ him at this time and at that place." There ensued a complex exchange of orders and requests and demands and proposals and counter-proposals. At length Hill concluded he would accept a command at his old rank only if it was accompanied by a statement of the government's full confidence in him.

When the stiffness of Hill's terms was perceived, Mr. Davis was unwilling to put laudation into orders. As Cooper reminded Hill, "to express in orders 'undiminished confidence' in an officer would be unprecedented in military history." Harvey Hill therefore remained at home, and with the exception of one brief period of service, had for a long time no other duty than that of reporting monthly that he was awaiting orders. His friends shared his belief that the President held him, more than anyone else, responsible for the agitation against Bragg after the Battle of Chickamauga.[33]

Early in December 1862, Major General Samuel Jones had somewhat reluctantly assumed command of the Department of Western Virginia. Strictly speaking, Jones did not then become an officer of the Army of Northern Virginia, but as his department was under the supervision of the commander of that army, Jones was one of Lee's lieutenants. A West Pointer of the class of 1841, Jones had been Beauregard's chief of artillery at Manassas and afterward served at Pensacola and commanded a division in Kentucky and Tennessee. He was by birth and manner a gentleman and had excellent training as a professional soldier. There was every reason to hope that he would be successful in the defense of a region which included the major iron, lead, and salt mines of the Confederacy.

Expectations were not realized. Jones had to direct a department which, as he wrote subsequently, "has had the reputation of being cursed with intrigue and political plotters ever since the war commenced." He found politicians among the soldiers, but few soldiers among the politicians. The traditional shortcomings of the detached commander would have been forgiven Jones had he been successful in dealing with Federal raids into southwest Virginia. When he failed in this, even the patient Lee lost faith in his aggressiveness. A change in commanders seemed imperative. Largely at the instance of Lee, a decision was reached by February 11, 1864, to relieve Jones. His manful reply—in contrast to the usual protests of the displaced—was that "I await the orders of the President, feeling confident that he will not assign me to any duty which I will not perform cheerfully and to the best of my ability."[34]

When it was suggested that Jones's successor might come from the Army of Northern Virginia, Lee appraised some of his own lieutenants in reviewing possible appointees. He expressed "great confidence" in Early, Rodes, Edward Johnson, Wilcox, and John B. Gordon. Simon Buckner and Robert Ransom were mentioned.[35] The President's final choice was John C. Breckinridge, former vice president of the United States. Samuel Jones was sent to Savannah and then to Charleston, where he remained in command till W. J. Hardee arrived and took charge in the autumn of 1864.

The difficulties of Samuel Jones, Harvey Hill, and Longstreet were more serious than any that arose in the winter of 1863–64 among the troops immediately under Lee; but even there jealousies and unhappy differences arose. The most serious of these troubles developed around Jube Early.

On Ewell's recovery from his sickness, immediately after the Mine Run campaign, Early's relief from active field duty proved brief. The troublesome Federal commander W. W. Averell undertook on December 8 a long raid through the Allegheny Mountains to the Virginia and Tennessee Railroad. Averell reached that supply line at Salem, Virginia, destroyed a large quantity of cereals, and tore up several bridges and some miles of track. It was certain that Averell would attempt to return by roads that passed west of Staunton. If Confederate forces moved swiftly and in superior force, Averell might be captured. Early was assigned this exciting task. He hurried to Staunton, but bad weather slowed the march of this troops. Lack of correct intelligence led him to dispatch his cavalry in the wrong direction. The enemy got off unscathed. Early wrote a sour, disappointed report, which was accepted by Lee as adequate explanation of the reason nothing was accomplished.[36]

Now that Old Jube was in the Shenandoah Valley, he was directed to stay there temporarily and undertake to collect supplies. His expedition toward Moorefield and Petersburg, hampered by bad weather and icy mountain roads, was limited to the capture of a considerable ordnance train and a drove of cattle. Early was disappointed, particularly with Imboden's brigade of irregular cavalry, and professed himself much inconvenienced by the lax discipline of these forces. Then, when a lieutenant of Imboden's brigade murdered a sergeant in Staunton, Early exploded violently.

It was one of Early's vices that when an incident of this sort occurred, he would not act and forget. He would act and continue to talk. In private conversation, Old Jube asserted, frequently and vehemently, that Imboden's brigade was inefficient, disorganized, undisciplined, and unreliable. Jubal Early, in short, acquired a violent dislike of the troopers who garrisoned the Valley and probably, without being aware of it, became prejudiced against cavalry in general. Certain it is that he made no effort to acquaint himself with that arm or to study its place in tactical cooperation. For this neglect, whatever its origin, he was doomed to pay.

Imboden resented Early's remarks and asked a court of inquiry. Lee saw that nothing could be gained and much might be lost by angry exchange at a court, and found it not "advantageous" at present. There the matter rested, but it was not without value and warning. Old Jube had snarled and sneered privately from the beginning of the war; now he was careless, if not loud, in his condemnation of those he did not approve. It was not a change of character that would improve leadership in the Second Corps.[37]

A controversy between Early and Tom Rosser was avoided by curious circumstances. The recently wed Rosser had made an unauthorized visit to his bride in Staunton, to which Early took exception. While the matter was still unpleasantly fresh in Jube's mind, a new raid was undertaken against Moorefield and Petersburg in western Virginia. This time Rosser was senior officer of cavalry. He had the best of luck and captured ninety-three loaded wagons, fifty of which were removed safely. His conduct was in every way so admirable on the raid that Early forgave him and urged the confirmation of Rosser's appointment as brigadier—a wish that at length was realized. Rosser's career went on in high promise with the encouragement and sometimes with the scolding of Jeb Stuart. The morale of the brigade was excellent. All the men re-enlisted in a manner that gave Stuart a text for the exhortation of other commands. In the Valley Rosser himself began to take on some of the romance of Turner Ashby.[38]

If Early was pleased over Rosser's rise and unrepentant of his sneers at Imboden's troops, his difficulties with these two were not comparable in evil potentialities to the change that now began to take place in Early's relations with his oldest, most devoted friend in the army, Dick Ewell. Old Bald Head was not then in good physical condition. While his sickness prior to the Mine Run campaign had been brief, his general enfeeblement had given deep concern to army headquarters. During the Bristoe operations Lee was in daily fear that Ewell would wear himself out or collapse under his duties. In spite of Ewell's surprising agility on horseback, his wooden leg was of poor design and made his movements uncertain.

When it was suggested in Richmond that Ewell, instead of Lee, might be sent to succeed Bragg, Lee had to answer: "General Ewell's condition, I fear, is too feeble to undergo the fatigue and labor incident to the position." A proposal that Ewell go to Tennessee and take Longstreet's command, and that Longstreet return to direct the Second Corps, Lee disapproved on many grounds. In January Ewell had a bad fall when his horse slipped in the snow. He made light of the accident, but Lee did not. The whole undertone of Lee's counsel was one of doubt whether the chief of the Second Corps could meet the strain of open campaigning.[39]

Ewell chose to continue where he was and to give the country his best. The same choice was that of Mrs. Ewell, who had joined her husband on the Rapidan in the late autumn of 1863. In her influence over him, some of those around Ewell thought they saw another evidence of what they began frankly to consider a decline of mental as well as of physical power. Doubtless they confused the psychological effect of the loss of a leg with that of the acquisition of a wife. Once she married him, she managed him, and not him only. Said Colonel James Conner, who saw both the general and the lady at close range: "She manages everything from the General's affairs down to the courier's who carries his dispatches. All say they are under petticoat government."

Mrs. Ewell's son by her first marriage was the able Campbell Brown, one of Ewell's assistant adjutants general, and her interest in the welfare and advancement of husband and son was equal. That she was overzealous and too active at least one observer at headquarters was convinced. According to Colonel Conner, "Mrs. Ewell [has] the best intentions in the world no doubt, and the very cleverness which would at other times render her agreeable has only tended to make her more and more unpopular." Thomas T. Turner, one of Ewell's aides, spoke up on the matter: "Old Ewell told me he had never exposed Campbell but once and then was so miserable until he came back he did not know what to do: 'If anything had happened to him, I could never have looked at his mother again, sir.'" Turner added, "Hang him, he never thinks of my mother, I suppose, for he pops me around, no matter how hot the fire is." The case of Mrs. Ewell, while amusing, was not without an ominous aspect. It boded no good for the Second Corps or for the campaign of 1864 when so able and fair-minded a man as James Conner could speak of Dick Ewell as a "fond, foolish old man . . . worse in love than any eighteen-year-old you ever saw."[40]

As senior major general of the Second Corps, Early of course realized that if Ewell were disabled he would assume command temporarily, perhaps permanently. In her turn, the clever Mrs. Ewell reasoned that if her husband was thought to be incapacitated for duty, Early would supplant him, and she soon became suspicious of Jube. It is impossible to say whether she had any direct part in a curious and obscure incident that occurred some weeks after Early's return from the Valley. For reasons not now determinable, Ewell found Early so much at fault in some incident that he had to arrest him, April 26, for conduct "subversive of good order and military discipline." The controversy reached General Lee, who dismissed it with a statement that Early was at fault, and that harmony among officers was imperative. Restraint must have been shown by those involved, because no echo of it appears in the records. Inwardly, the affair did nothing to lower Early's self-opinion. He never had been more ambitious and more confident of himself, or more intolerant of others, than he was as the spring of 1864 approached.[41]

The army itself, the always-impersonal but always-observant army, was as confident as Early. What thousands believed, Dodson Ramseur wrote on April 15: "I feel so hopeful about the coming campaign. I have never felt so encouraged before."[42] He was influenced, no doubt, by the events which, in the opinion of the troops, indicated that the Army of the Potomac lacked initiative.

Mine Run had been followed in February by a curious affair at Morton's Ford on the Rapidan. On the sixth the Federals pushed a brigade across the river toward high ground in rear of the ford. A second and then a third brigade crossed in support. Ewell, arriving promptly, directed an easy defense with his old-time skill. The next dawn showed the Federals back on the left bank of the river; by the eighth they had disappeared from the ford. Lee regarded it merely as a foray "intended to see where we were," but Ewell's men were pleased, and the army felt its old sense of superiority to the enemy.[43]

At the end of February, Federal cavalry made on Richmond an attack which the Confederates styled "Dahlgren's Raid." The aim of the enterprise was to release the Federal prisoners in the Confederate capital. Boldness and a measure of skill were shown in the advance, but it was repulsed with some loss. The raid served the Confederates usefully in this respect: Those who examined the body of the slain Colonel Dahlgren reported that they found on it papers in which the raiders were instructed to burn Richmond and to kill President Davis and his Cabinet. Evidence of this purpose inflamed to new fury the fighting spirit of the South.[44]

Efforts, also, to recover some of the towns on the tidal estuaries of eastern North Carolina served to strengthen further the confidence of the army. Most noteworthy was the expedition against Plymouth, on the Roanoke River close to the point where it empties into Albemarle Sound. Braxton Bragg developed a plan for the surprise of Plymouth using troops under Brigadier General R. F. Hoke and the Confederate ram *Albemarle*. On April 20, by the shrewd use of his artillery and with the valiant employment of the new ram, Hoke forced the surrender of Plymouth and its garrison. The country was thrilled. Davis telegraphed his congratulations and promoted Hoke major general from the date of the battle. Hoke was more than ever a marked young soldier. Little or no credit was given to Bragg, who did the basic planning and collected the troops when it seemed impossible to find men enough for the expedition.[45]

Insistent appeals by Lee for the return of Hoke's brigade and of the other troops loaned for operations in southern Virginia, the Carolinas, and Tennessee were based on the certainty that the Federals would advance from the Rapidan as soon as the roads were dry. Davis and Bragg had become convinced at the beginning of April that Johnston would not assume the offensive in Tennessee, and they accordingly saw no reason for retaining Longstreet in East Tennessee. On April 7 he was ordered to Charlottesville, whence he could be advanced either to Lee on the Rapidan or to the defense of the Richmond-Petersburg area. Lee was notified the next day that Longstreet was returning. The First Corps reached Charlottesville and then camping grounds at Gordonsville. There, to all observers, the decline in the size of the corps and the depreciation of its equipment were manifest and serious. Longstreet received all the help army headquarters could give him in making good his losses.[46]

Law's brigade had been kept in Tennessee, with its commanding officer under arrest, but Lee prevailed on the War Department to order these excellent troops to unite with their division. The charges against Law, said Cooper, would not be considered further. When Longstreet learned of this, he delivered to the commanding general an ultimatum of a sort he knew his chief would support: "If my efforts to maintain discipline, spirit, and zeal in the discharge of official duty are to be set aside by the return of General Law and his restoration to duty without trial, it cannot be well for me to remain in command. . . . It is necessary, therefore, that General Law should be brought to trial upon the charges that have been preferred against him, or that I be relieved from duty with the Confederate States service." Army headquarters, of course, was not prepared to have Longstreet resign at a time when Ewell was in precarious health and the enemy was expected to launch an offensive any day. Accordingly Longstreet learned that Lee had forwarded his ultimatum to Richmond and advised that a court-martial be ordered. "I would recommend that General Law be relieved of duty until an investigation can be had."[47]

In Longstreet's case, in Early's and in Ewell's—to say nothing of Sam Jones's and Harvey Hill's—the winter had wrought curious reversals. Edward Johnson, Hoke, and Rosser had gained in reputation. In addition to these three, no less a person than the army's chief of artillery received new prestige. General Pendleton made a long tour of the South to prepare a plan for the more effective use of Johnston's artillery. Remarkably, his plan pleased both the administration and General Johnston. So favorably did he impress Davis that later in the year, after the death of Lieutenant General Leonidas Polk, the President was to ask Lee whether Pendleton would be a qualified successor. "As much as I esteem & admire Genl Pendleton," Lee replied, "I could not select him to command a corps. . . . I do not mean to say by that he is not competent, but from what I have seen of him, I do not know that he is."[48] Pendleton was destined to stay and mildly to share the adventures of his juniors, who left him little to do. With the battalion and battery chiefs, the great question mark of the campaign was not whether Pendleton went or remained, but whether the horses could survive hard work, poor shoeing, and half-feed.

The cavalry raised that same question, but, for the rest, they were the one arm of the service that approached the spring battles with least reason to be concerned over command. Stuart was in flawless health and, surely, more qualified by experience than ever he had been to direct the two divisions. They were well led and had, in the main, those brigadiers who best had earned leadership.

These, then, to summarize, had been the changes during the winter of 1863–64 in the army command:

Longstreet had failed in a semi-independent command and had failed equally to maintain peace in his corps; his interest in strategy continued despite discouragements; a bitterness toward the administration had developed in his heart. He was less the imperturbable "Old War Horse" and more the aggrieved, restive lieutenant who thought all the authorities, except Lee, arrayed against him.

Of Longstreet's three division commanders, McLaws was fighting to be restored to his post. His fate was then uncertain. Hood was promoted and transferred to another army and was succeeded not by Micah Jenkins, as Longstreet wished, but by Charles W. Field, who had never led a division in action and had not served in the field since Second Manassas. Pickett was in charge of the Department of North Carolina and was out of touch with the corps.

Ewell of the Second Corps was not in good condition physically. There was some question whether he was mentally the man he had been before his wound or, in spirit, the fighter he had been before his marriage. His senior lieutenant, Early, was in a strange, confident, perhaps overbearing state of mind. Rodes had not developed, though he had not lost the good opinion of the commanding general. Edward Johnson had done well at Mine Run and had earned the good opinion, in particular, of Lee. Suggestion had come from Richmond that Johnson was needed elsewhere, in circumstances that might have led to his promotion to lieutenant general. Regretful as Lee was to deny Old Allegheny such a post, he had to tell the President that he could not spare Johnson.

In the Third Corps, Powell Hill had sustained the humiliation of Bristoe Station, but otherwise had spent a quiet winter. All his division commanders—Anderson, Heth, and Wilcox—were present with their troops. None of the three had been given opportunity of acquiring new fame or of demonstrating higher qualities of command than were credited to them. The corps was competently directed. There was no reason to hope it would be brilliantly led in the operations about to open.

Grim these operations would be, and against an adversary more powerful than ever, more seasoned, and more belligerently led. Ulysses Grant, the man who had beaten Albert Sidney Johnston and John Pemberton and Braxton Bragg, had come east as general-in-chief of the Union forces, and had established his headquarters with the Army of the Potomac. Had he been in Hooker's place a year previously, he would have faced Jackson and Pender, the old Second Corps in its glory, and the First Corps before the frustrated Longstreet had shaken its command. Now Longstreet was changed, Ewell enfeebled, Early arrogant, and Hill, after eleven months, still not established in reputation as a corps commander.

CHAPTER 30

The Wilderness and Spotsylvania

1. The Wilderness Takes Its Toll

The recall of the First Corps was the last step that could be taken to reinforce the Army of Northern Virginia against the expected offensive of the powerful Federal forces under Grant's strategic direction. On April 29, Lee and the headquarters staff visited Gordonsville where Old Pete's veterans were awaiting them. Longstreet would have met one newcomer on the staff—Major General Martin L. Smith, sent to the army as chief engineer. Smith, a New Yorker by birth and a professional soldier, had developed the defenses of Vicksburg. He was a man of intelligence and character. How high his abilities were in field engineering events must show.

The First Corps now could muster no more than 10,000 men of all arms, but it did its dilapidated best to make itself presentable to Lee. As the reviewing party went down the ranks of the two divisions, Charles Field, thirty-six years of age, was in the place of Hood. At the head of McLaws's division was its senior brigadier and prospective new commander, Joseph W. Kershaw, who was forty-two and known to all the veterans. He had been distinguished in almost every battle he had shared. Pious, intelligent, a clear blond of high-bred, clean-cut features, Kershaw had the bearing of command and a clear voice that seemed to inspire courage when it was raised in battle. Of the brigadiers in the First Corps, the only stranger to Virginia was John Gregg, who had been assigned to command the famous Texas Brigade in succession to Jerome Robertson. Gregg had served in the Gulf States, under Johnston during the Vicksburg campaign, and under Longstreet at Chickamauga. Without professional training in arms, he had the spirit of "a born soldier."[1]

All these officers rejoiced to see their gray general on his gray horse, and they cheered him wildly as they passed in review. Longstreet, too, was happy to be with his old chief again. The next few days were tense for lieutenant and chief. From the signal station on Clark's Mountain, as the month of April drew to its close, Lee viewed the verdant valley of the Rapidan. After he studied the scene with his glass, he said what the whole army had concluded: "I think those people over there are going to make a move soon." Turning to young B. L. Wynn, in charge of the signal station, he asked, "Sergeant, do you keep a guard on watch at night?" When Wynn answered in the negative, Lee said, "Well, you must put one on."[2]

On May 2 there was smoke in unusual volume along the north bank of the Rapidan. The next day dust clouds and marching columns were visible. About 12 o'clock on the night of May 3–4 the signalmen on Clark's Mountain could catch glimpses of troops passing in front of distant campfires far across the Rapidan. Army headquarters was notified. Were the lights moving toward Germanna Ford or toward Liberty Mills? Was Grant attempting to turn the Confederate right and proceed in the direction of Fredricksburg, or was he undertaking to pass the Southern left and move on Gordonsville? The signal station could not say. Lee consequently acted on the larger probability. He had the station flash to the right: "General Ewell, have your command ready to move at daylight."[3]

Dawn ended doubt: The enemy was moving toward Germanna and Ely's fords and moving, apparently, with all his forces. From every vantage point the picture was the same—heavy columns of cavalry, endless files of infantry, wagon trains that spread their white sheets for miles on every road. Confederates looked and guessed at the strength of the moving army. It numbered, in reality, 102,000 present for duty. When reinforcements immediately at hand—Burnside's IX Corps overtook the Army of the Potomac—its effective strength would be at least 116,000. To oppose this host the Confederates had eight divisions of infantry—an effective force of all arms of approximately 64,000. These grim odds made it necessary that each musket do the service of two. The more intelligent of the men were conscious of this. If perhaps the army was not in as good spirits as it had been before Gettysburg, it was ready to fight; it sensed the most difficult of all its struggles.[4]

From the camps around Orange the infantry began their countermovement on the fourth of May. Ewell marched by the turnpike that ran from Orange to Fredericksburg. Hill conducted Heth's and Wilcox's divisions by the Orange Plank Road, and left Dick Anderson to guard the upper fords of the Rapidan until it was certain the whole of Meade's army was moving eastward. Longstreet started from Gordonsville at 4:00 P.M. toward Brock's Bridge. Thence his route was to be by way of Orange Plank Road and the Catharpin Road. The cavalry covered the advance but concentrated on the right in the hope of enveloping the enemy.

The army on the morning of May 5 resumed its march to confront an enemy now on the south side of the Rapidan and moving toward the Wilderness. Ewell's orders were to regulate his march on the Turnpike by that of Hill on the Plank Road. If practicable, a general engagement was to be avoided until Longstreet arrived—an order singularly reminiscent of the first day at Gettysburg.[5]

It was not yet apparent that the operation undertaken by Grant on the Rapidan was part of the farthest-reaching offensive the enemy ever had launched in Virginia. Word was received of the landing at West Point, May 1, of a Federal force thought be to the vanguard of an army that would move on Richmond. Soon the report was that B. F. Butler, with a large naval escort and a river full of transports, was moving up the James toward the capital. This was not to be the only expedition in support of Meade. Franz Sigel had orders to march southward up the Shenandoah Valley. The instructions of George Crook were to advance into southwest Virginia and do all possible damage to the Virginia and Tennessee Railroad. Daily, after May 5, as Lee's lieutenants grappled with the main army of the most determined Federal commander they yet had encountered, new details of the other contests were to reach them.

The first decision of the commanding general was represented by the swift advance of his army to meet the enemy. On the morning of May 5, Hill continued on the Plank Road, which curved to the northeast. Ewell held to the old Turnpike, which ran more nearly east. At 11:00 A.M. the advance of Ewell's corps, John M. Jones's brigade of Johnson's division, was ordered to halt. The message that always made hearts beat faster was passed down the files: Federals were ahead. They were moving across the Turnpike along the route that led from Germanna Ford to the Orange Plank Road. Mindful of his orders to avoid a general engagement before the arrival of Longstreet, Ewell thought it best to suspend his advance, form line of battle, report his situation to headquarters, and await further instructions. Sandie Pendleton hurried across to the Plank Road, found Lee with A. P. Hill, and brought back word that Ewell was to adhere, if feasible, to previous orders.[6]

The enemy was no respecter of such orders. The Unionists began what appeared to be merely a demonstration against John M. Jones. To his support Ewell moved up Cullen Battle. Abruptly a furious assault was made on Jones's front and right flank. It had behind it strength and impetuosity, and in a few minutes Jones's troops broke. Their commander was killed as he attempted to rally them. As they went back through the line of their support, they threw into confusion the ranks of Battle's brigade. A sudden and dangerous crisis was upon the Second Corps. The other brigades of Johnson's division were too far to the left; Rodes was half deployed. That

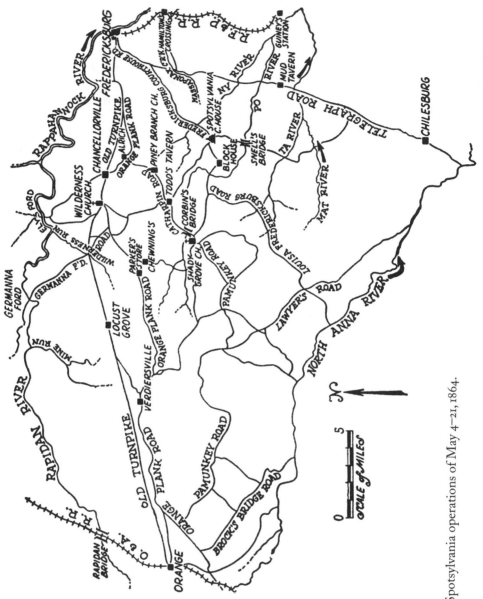

Terrain of the Wilderness-Spotsylvania operations of May 4–21, 1864.

left only Jube Early's men, the rear division on the march. Dick Ewell galloped back and drew rein by the side of John B. Gordon. "General Gordon," piped Ewell excitedly, "the fate of the day depends on you, sir!" Gordon answered boldly, "These men will save it, sir!"

Immediately Gordon wheeled a regiment into line for a counterattack. A similar thrust by Junius Daniel of Rodes's division confused the Federals. Ewell gained time enough to form a new line and recover the ground lost by Jones. In this grim work Battle's brigade, which had recovered quickly, bore a conspicuous part. The situation was eased. Meade's attack was stopped. The Confederates' heaviest loss, after that of John M. Jones, was in the mortal wounding of one of the new brigadiers, Leroy Stafford, and the serious injury of John Pegram, who was shot in the leg.[7]

As combat lost its violence on the Turnpike, it rose in wrath on the Orange Plank Road. As Hill advanced with Heth's and Wilcox's divisions, they heard on their flank the echo of Ewell's action. About 1 o'clock they began skirmishing against Federals organizing on the Brock Road a line perpendicular to the Plank Road. Little happened until about 3 o'clock. A staff officer from Lee's headquarters found Harry Heth and explained that the commanding general was anxious that Heth occupy the Brock Road if this could be done without bringing on a general engagement. Heth answered that the Federals held the road in strength. Whether he could drive them from it could be determined only by using his entire division. Before anything more could be determined, the bluecoats attacked.

Defense was stern and desperate. So heavy were the attacks on Heth and Wilcox that at one time the only troops not engaged in the wild fighting were 125 Alabamians acting as guard over the prisoners. Even this detachment had to be called to repulse the assault. In the opinion of Porter Alexander, who had seen most of the battles, none of them had been fiercer. At nightfall the enemy still was in firm possession of the Brock Road, but in the mad exchanges of the furious day he had done no more than hold his own. When weary Southern commanders could draw breath, they exchanged congratulations. Ewell sent to headquarters his special commendation of John B. Gordon and Junius Daniel. Lee had praise for Cooke and Kirkland of Heth's division. Strong as the enemy had shown himself to be, the Confederates must retain the initiative. The decision at army headquarters was to turn the left of the enemy on May 6, if it was not too far extended and, if it was, to try to cut him off from his base by enveloping his right. Indications were that the attack on the left would prove the more promising.[8]

An immediate question was whether anything should be done to untangle the front of Heth and Wilcox. Both generals were much concerned. They wanted to leave only a skirmish line where the fighting of the day had ended and form a new line to the rear. Wilcox, in his anxiety, rode at once to Lee. Anderson's division, Lee explained, had been instructed to move forward: "He and Longstreet will be up, and the two divisions that have been so actively engaged will be relieved before day." Wilcox had to content himself with this. Harry Heth went to Hill instead of Lee. Heth insisted that a skirmish line "could drive both my division and Wilcox's, situated as we now are. We shall certainly be attacked early in the morning." Hill was sick but sought to be reassuring: "Longstreet will be up in a few hours. He will form in your front. I don't propose that you shall do any fighting tomorrow." The men must be tired; let them rest. Heth was not satisfied. Twice more he came back to argue with Hill. The lieutenant general became vexed: "Damn it, Heth, I don't want to hear any more about it. The men shall not be disturbed."[9]

This was final. Heth and Wilcox awaited with gnawing, time-dragging anxiety the arrival of Longstreet; but 1 o'clock, then 2 and at last 3 o'clock passed with no word that the First Corps was approaching. In the Wilderness the east reddened and the light came, and at 5 o'clock, on the stroke, the Federals began a careful but determined advance.

Wilcox's men were slightly in advance and first received the shock. Scattered as they were, they soon were driven. They did not run fast or far, but they ran. Heth's troops, according to General Wilcox, did not wait for the onslaught. They made for the rear at once to form their line. In the eyes of brave men who kept their heads and stopped to load and fire, the break of two veteran divisions was a disgrace. Cowards simply ran till they were out of range. Wilcox hurried to General Lee and, at the instance of the commanding general, went down the Plank Road to find Longstreet.

Powell Hill was too ill to do more than share the tense anxiety. The burden fell on Lee and his staff. Toward high ground north of the Plank Road the enemy was moving steadily and almost unopposed. Farther northward, the Unionists were working their way into the space that unavoidably had been left between Hill's left and Ewell's right. The crisis was instant and desperate. Unless Longstreet came up quickly, the center of the army would be penetrated, the Third Corps rolled up, and what remained of it hurled back on Ewell toward the Rapidan. There had been no danger more acute since the day the Federals had shattered the Confederate line at Sharpsburg.

Not long did leaders have to hold their breath. Up the Plank Road in parallel columns the First Corps was moving fast. "Here they come!" cried delighted artillerists in greeting to the veterans of Hood's old division, now under Field, who formed the van on the left. Barksdale's famous old Mississippi brigade headed Kershaw's division on the right-hand side of the road. Quickly Longstreet ordered Gregg to establish the line to the north while Humphreys, Barksdale's successor, placed his regiments in line south of the road. It was John Gregg's red hour, his first great opportunity. As the Texans were forming under his eye, he saw approaching him the commanding general and several staff officers. "General," Lee called out as he drew rein, "what brigade is this?"

"The Texas Brigade!" was the proud answer. "I am glad to see it," said Lee. "When you go in there, I wish you to give those men the cold steel— they will stand and fight all day, and never move unless you charge them." Gregg drew in his breath and shouted, "Attention, Texas Brigade! The eyes of General Lee are upon you. Forward, march!" Lee lifted his hat and raised himself in his stirrups. "Texans always move them!" The men nearest began to cheer; his words were passed down the line; the cheer spread. "I would charge hell itself for that old man," cried one courier as he paused between yells. For a moment the commanding general appeared intent on leading the charge himself. The Texans cried "Lee to the rear!" and would not go forward until "Marse Robert" went to a place of safety.

In a short time Lee rode up to the knoll where Longstreet was waiting for his troops to complete their formation. The staff had never known the commanding general to be so intensely excited. Colonel Venable whispered to Longstreet that he had experienced the greatest difficulty in persuading Lee to leave the Texans; would Longstreet please prevail on him to go farther to the rear? Longstreet spoke up with affectionate bluntness, saying that if the commanding general intended to direct the First Corps, he personally would be glad to ride to a place of safety.[10]

Old Pete watched as Lee reluctantly went a few hundred yards to the rear, then turned to his task. He was at his combative best in organizing a front line. The most shaken of the withdrawing Third Corps men already had passed through Longstreet's troops amid the jeers and laughter of the veterans. "Do you belong to Lee's army?" they yelled. "You're worse than Bragg's men!" Then, without a break or waver, Field's and Kershaw's arriving regiments prepared for the shock of receiving the enemy. There was no time to trim a line, to throw out skirmishers and then counterattack. Federals were almost on the heels of every fugitive.

Longstreet's spirits and activity mounted with the danger. He rode straight to the front and shouted his commands in a voice that rose above the battle. Now on the left, now on the right, exhortation was mingled with orders. Old Pete's very presence seemed to strengthen his men. Soon he had a line from which volley after volley was poured into the enemy. Said one of his artillerists, "Longstreet, always grand in battle, never shone as he did here." Slowly but with supreme resolution Kershaw began to advance. Field moved forward on the other side of the road, with Gregg's Texans in the lead and Benning's Georgians directly behind them. Every step was contested, but back toward Heth's position of the previous night, back toward the ground occupied by Wilcox, the veterans of Longstreet pushed the Union regiments. Resistance gradually weakened. By about 9:45 A.M. the opposing forces were approximately where the day's fighting had started. A hot fire continued, but neither side attempted for the moment to drive the other.[11]

Lee was not content to have the situation remain one of wasteful exchanges of lead. Nor was Longstreet willing to end his battle in stalemate. Strategically and tactically a Confederate attack was dictated. Force for it, Dick Anderson's division of the Third Corps, was at hand. Expert reconnaissance was assured also. The army's new chief engineer, Martin Smith, had been sent out to examine the enemy's position, and he reported that the Federal left extended a short distance only to the south of the Plank Road. It would be entirely feasible to turn that flank. Longstreet listened intently and pondered. He would try it! And if he were facing a gap in the Federal line instead of its actual left, then he would find the extreme left and turn that, too. Smith was directed to reconnoiter beyond the Brock Road to find the farthest position of the Federals.

W. T. Wofford, one of the ablest of the brigadiers, suggested that the column move by the right flank until it reached the cut of an unfinished railroad from Orange to Fredericksburg. This cut, he said, would be an excellent place from which to start the attack on the enemy flank. The plan had practicality. Longstreet explained it to Lee, who had been near-by during most of the action, and he approved. Moxley Sorrel, Longstreet's A.A.G., was put in charge of collecting the troops for what Old Pete termed "a fine chance of a great attack by our right." He told Sorrel, "Hit hard when you start, but don't start until you have everything ready. I shall be waiting for your gunfire, and be on hand with fresh troops for further advance."

Off went Sorrel in full consciousness that his great opportunity had come. In about an hour he had in line and starting through the woods Tige Anderson's brigade of Field's division, Wofford's of Kershaw's command, and Mahone's of Anderson's—two brigades of the First Corps and one of the Third. Longstreet then had immediately in front of the foe only the brigades of Benning, Law, and Gregg of Field's division, but Micah Jenkins's brigade of that division and three brigades of Kershaw's division and three of Dick Anderson's were close at hand. If Mahone, leading the flanking column, turned the Federals, Longstreet would have ample force to press them in front and to prepare for the second and perhaps larger turning movement on which engineer Smith was to report. Old Pete's hopes were high.[12]

Intently, at his post of command on the Plank Road, Longstreet awaited the sound of fire from the right. At length there came the challenge of skirmish fire and then the roll of a volley. The attack had begun! Let the troops on the Plank Road redouble their fire and occupy the enemy while the flank attack developed. Send word to the commanders of the reserve to prepare to advance. Everything proceeded as perfectly as on the great day of Second Manassas or on that triumphant December afternoon at Fredericksburg. The roar from the right gave assurance that the three brigades were advancing. In front the enemy was beginning to yield ground. The fire from the right was approaching the Plank Road. Victory was in the air. The hour scarcely was past 11, though it was climbing toward Longstreet's high noon. Not many miles away, in that same Wilderness and on a May day, too, Jackson had turned the Federal right beyond the same Plank Road. Now Longstreet was to roll up their left in an action as decisive.

Back to Longstreet came Martin Smith. The engineer had located the extreme Federal left, and he suggested a route that would carry a flanking column beyond the Brock Road. Longstreet was highly pleased. He decided to repeat the maneuver of the early morning and to entrust this operation to Smith who, said he, "was a splendid tactician as well as a skillful engineer, and gallant withal." Smith was directed to take the troops that already had advanced beyond the flank and proceed to the east of the Brock Road. Kershaw was to push forward with his division; Micah Jenkins, who was chafing in reserve, was to cooperate with Kershaw.[13]

Jenkins was summoned and soon was by the side of Longstreet. Close behind Jenkins marched his men, who wore new uniforms of a gray so deep that they appeared dark blue or almost black in the forest. Jenkins was jubilant and called for a cheer for Longstreet. The Carolinians for the moment drowned the sound of the firing. Longstreet, much pleased, bade Jenkins ride forward with him toward the Brock Road. The cavalcade was joined by Kershaw and Wofford and their staffs. Longstreet explained the part Kershaw's and Jenkins's men were to have in the final operation while Smith swept northward from the far right flank. The attack was to be pressed by all available troops. Meade's army was to be pushed toward Fredericksburg. All this Longstreet made clear, and then, in his most cheerful manner of the battlefield, touched his horse and started forward again. Kershaw and Jenkins dropped back a few paces to the head of Jenkins's brigade and followed their chief.

Longstreet was now almost within musket range of the Brock Road and passing the position reached by Mahone and Tige Anderson in their earlier advance from the right flank. These Virginians and Georgians were in line of battle to the right of and parallel to the Plank Road and about sixty yards from it. At that moment, to the left of the road, Longstreet heard the sound of two or three rifles close at hand. There was an instant of uncertainty. Then came shots from the woods on the right. Longstreet did not follow the rule of caution. Instead of throwing himself from his horse on the opposite side, he instinctively turned the animal's head toward the fire and started to dash forward to stop it.

A savage volley greeted him. The impact of a heavy bullet lifted Longstreet from his saddle, into which he fell back uncertainly the next instant. Micah Jenkins and two others were struck mortally. At the flash of the volley, Jenkins's men turned to the right and lifted their rifles. Instantly Joe Kershaw dashed among them. "They are friends!" he cried in a voice that everyone heard. Jenkins's disciplined men threw themselves on the ground to escape another volley. There was none. Mahone's men, who had done the firing, quickly recognized their mistake. Some of them rushed out to voice their regret and to render such aid as they might.[14]

By this time Longstreet had been taken from his saddle and placed by the roadside. His condition manifestly was serious. A minié ball had entered near the throat and crashed into the right shoulder. Hemorrhage was severe, though the medical director of the corps soon was at hand to stanch it. So great was the vitality of Longstreet that he blew the bloody foam from his mouth and whispered instructions: "Tell General Field to take command, and move forward with the whole force and gain the Brock Road." Field was soon at his side, then Dick Anderson and the commanding general rode up. To them, as fully as his clogged throat and shaken vocal organs permitted, Longstreet explained his plan.

Lee undertook to direct the execution of it, but the troops were scattered widely. Confusion ruled the field. Time was required to draw the lines and make the deployment. The enemy meanwhile strengthened his front. Late in the afternoon, when the Confederate right wing attacked, it was repulsed almost before it got under way.

Longstreet was carried to the rear past soldiers who recognized his bulky form, though his hat was over his face. "He is dead," some of them said, "and they are telling us he is only wounded." Longstreet heard them and gamely, with his left hand, lifted his hat from his face. He said afterward that the answering cheers of the troops eased somewhat his pain. Once in an ambulance the general was quiet in his pain. One observer told himself, "He is calm and entirely master of the situation—he is both greater and more attractive than I have heretofore thought him."[15]

While Longstreet was being carried to the rear, Micah Jenkins was dying. A bullet had penetrated his brain. Half conscious, "he would cheer his men and implore them to sweep the enemy into the river, until he became too weak to talk." He died without knowing he had been hit. He was twenty-eight years of age. Others were lost that day of rank less exalted but of long service in the army. Colonel Van Manning of the famous 3rd Arkansas was wounded and captured. James D. Nance, colonel of the 3rd South Carolina, said to be "the best all round soldier" of his brigade, was killed. Dead, too, was Colonel J. Thompson Brown, who had been senior officer of the Second Corps artillery at Gettysburg. Still another excellent soldier who fell that May 6 was Colonel C. M. Avery of the 33rd North Carolina, Lane's brigade.

The thought, the talk, was of Longstreet. He, the "Old War Horse," had fallen in the Wilderness that had witnessed the mortal wounding of Jackson. The two disasters had been almost precisely a year apart. Every soldier who remembered Chancellorsville observed the similarities and wondered whether Longstreet would have the fate of Jackson. Four surgeons, including the medical director of the army, concluded that the wound was "not necessarily fatal." In relation to the command of the army, the loss of Longstreet, even temporarily, might be as serious as the fall of Stonewall, because the leadership of the other corps was shaken. Besides the illness of Powell Hill, a development that day raised anew the question whether Ewell was qualified to command in the field.[16]

It was a curious development, for which there scarcely was a parallel in the history of the army. During the night of May 5–6, John Gordon had sent out scouts to ascertain the position of the enemy near his front, which was on the extreme left of the Confederate line. About dawn the scouts returned with an astonishing story: The Federal flank, they said, was in the woods a short distance ahead. Gordon's left considerably overlapped the Union right. This seemed scarcely credible; it did not seem possible that the careful Meade had committed such a blunder. Gordon ordered another examination of the ground. The second party came back with full confirmation of the first report and with the further assurance that no supports were within several miles of the Federal flank. Gordon went forward to see for himself. A rapid ride convinced him that no Federal supports were directly ahead or within striking distance.

The sight inflamed Gordon's spirit. His great opportunity had come. An attack on that flank would overwhelm it. Gordon hurried to corps headquarters. There he found Ewell and Early, described the condition on his front, and asked permission to attack with his brigade. Early opposed. Scouts had brought him reports of Federal infantry between Gordon and the river. Another report, though of the vaguest sort, was that Burnside's IX

Corps was taking position in rear of the Federal right, the very ground that Gordon had found unoccupied. Neither Ewell nor Early had undertaken to make personal reconnaissance or even to have staff officers establish the facts. Early insisted an attack on the left might be repulsed, leaving the Second Corps no reserves if the enemy then assumed the offensive. The corps, indeed the whole army, might be involved in disaster. His argument was based on the domineering assumption that his intelligence reports were correct and those of Gordon were in error, though Gordon had verified his reports and Early had done nothing to substantiate those he received.

Ewell was puzzled. In much the same mood as at Gettysburg, he hesitated. He reported that he could not decide on the move, one way or the other, without personal examination, which he resolved to make later in the day. He was not to be brought to a more positive frame of mind, even though Gordon offered impetuously to assume all the blame in the event of failure. While on the Plank Road Longstreet fought and fell, and Lee painfully put confused lines in order for an advance against the Federal left, Ewell did little or nothing to clarify conflicting intelligence reports. Perplexed or weary or hypnotized for the moment by the confident insistence of Early, he permitted the fateful afternoon to pass without an offensive blow.[17]

Toward sunset, about 5:30, Ewell saw the commanding general draw rein at corps field headquarters. Lee had passed one of the most anxious days of his military career and now, still shaken by the narrow escape of the morning, the fall of Longstreet, and the repulse of the last attack on the Federal left, he came to ask if something could not be done by Ewell to relieve the pressure on the other Confederate flank. Gordon listened for a time while his seniors discussed the situation, and at last told Lee of the situation he had found on the Federal right during the morning and of the plan he had proposed for rolling up that flank. Immediately Old Jube renewed with vigor the objections he had raised when Gordon first reported. Gordon stood his ground squarely. Lee had confidence in Gordon and wished to know why, in the circumstances, the assault had not been delivered. The answers must have been so feeble that Lee considered silence the best rebuke. In a few words he ordered the attack.

The result was all that Gordon had promised. As soon as the Confederates were astride the Federal flank, regiment after regiment gave way. Gordon's men pronounced the advance the "finest frolic" they had enjoyed during the war. Steadily they moved along the line till darkness halted their advance. "Had the movement been made at an earlier hour," said Gordon in his report, ". . . it would have resulted in a decided disaster to the whole right wing of General Grant's army, if not in its entire disorganization."[18]

The darkness that had halted Gordon was weird and affrighting. On the right, where the battle had been most furious, there was the fantastic light of forest fires that a brisk wind was spreading fast. The reflection of the fire gave the clouds a sickening yellow cast. Louder were the frantic cries of the wounded who could not creep away as fast as the flames approached. Two hundred of them soon were suffocated or burned to charred trunks of flesh. At dawn the forest had been an impenetrable maze of greenery; now, after the fire swept on, there were long, black-bordered aisles and a smouldering floor—a hideous temple of Mars.[19]

The sacrifice had been bloody. John M. Jones and Micah Jenkins were dead. Leroy Stafford was dying. John Pegram and Harry Benning were wounded. Powell Hill was so sick that he might not be able to exercise command the next day. Ewell seemed unable to reach a decision. Longstreet, the strongest and most dependable of all the lieutenants, was the victim of a wound that might kill him and certainly would incapacitate him for the months of decisive fighting with this new and stubborn adversary, Grant.

2. The Advantage of an Early Start

To meet Grant's next attack, whenever and wherever delivered, the Confederates must have the best procurable successor to Longstreet. The senior division commander of the First Corps was Lafayette McLaws. By odd chance, the court-martial findings in this case were announced on May 4, the very day the offensive on the Rapidan commenced. So light was the judgment of his failings for so heavy an alleged offense that it was, in effect, a vindication of McLaws and a humiliation to Longstreet. The War Department, unwilling to have even that mild sentence stand, disapproved the findings on the ground of irregularity of procedure. At Bragg's instance, McLaws on May 7 was directed to rejoin his command.

Notice of this order was not telegraphed to Lee at once, nor was McLaws immediately ordered to rejoin the army. Consequently Lee did not know on the day after Longstreet's wounding that McLaws was to return and, by seniority, assume temporary command. The acting commander of McLaws's division, Joseph B. Kershaw, was not yet a major general and could not be considered for corps command. Nor could Charles W. Field, head of the other division of the First Corps, be advanced. He was of appointment too recent and of experience too limited. Pickett, second in seniority among the division commanders of the corps, apparently was not mentioned as a possibility.

First intimation of what was in the mind of the commanding general was given Moxley Sorrel. Early on the morning of the seventh the A.A.G. was summoned to headquarters and conducted by Lee to the shade of a large tree, where they would not be overheard. Sorrel was told that Dick Anderson, Edward Johnson, and Jubal Early were under consideration. Which of the three did Sorrel think best suited? Early, said the young colonel, probably was the ablest of them but would be the most unpopular with the corps. Johnson was quite unknown to the corps. "His reputation is so high that perhaps he would prove all that could be wished, but I think someone personally known to the corps would be preferred." Without weighing good qualities against bad, Sorrel took up in Anderson's behalf where he stopped in objecting to Johnson. "We know him," he said of Anderson, "and shall be satisfied with him."

From Lee's response, Sorrel went away in the conviction that the commanding general believed Early best qualified and that he would be named. Instead, later in the day, an order was issued naming Dick Anderson "to the temporary command of Longstreet's Corps." William Mahone would assume command of Anderson's division. It was welcome news to the First Corps and was entirely defensible because Anderson, next to McLaws, was the senior major general of the army. He had been transferred to the Third Corps some months before, but he was remembered and beloved. Before another twenty-four hours passed, these men had reason to be proud, for the army's sake, that Anderson was their commander.[20]

The morning of May 7 passed with scarcely an exchange of picket fire. Grant had not been so badly hit the previous day that he had to rest and lick his wounds; consequently, the assumption was that he had begun, or soon would begin, another move. From Ewell came a report that the Federal lines in front of the extreme Confederate left had been evacuated. The enemy evidently had abandoned during the night his line of supply via Germanna Ford. He could open a new supply line by way of Fredericksburg, or proceed southward in the direction of Richmond and procure supplies from the lower Rappahannock or down the R.F. & P. Railroad from Fredericksburg. If moving to Fredericksburg, he would cover both the Plank Road and the Turnpike and advance down them. In the event his objective were the railroad and the direct approach to Richmond, his road would be by way of Todd's Tavern and Spotsylvania Court House.

Without any evidence of a choice by the enemy between these routes, Lee considered the probability of a move on Spotsylvania so great that early in the day he directed General Pendleton to cut a road from the Confederate right to the main road to Spotsylvania in order that a swift flank march could be made to the Court House by the shortest route. A series of reconnaissance reports by the cavalry deepened the suspicions of the commanding general that the next move of the enemy would be toward Spotsylvania, as did observations made with a strong marine glass of the movements of what appeared to be a park of heavy artillery. By 7:00 P.M. Lee issued orders for Dick Anderson to take Kershaw's and Field's divisions and start before 3:00 A.M. for Spotsylvania.[21]

Anderson was chosen for this movement because his troops were farthest on the right and could start more readily. The whole operation, in fact, could be a swift side-slip to the right. Anderson's was an exceedingly critical pursuit. If he did not reach Spotsylvania ahead of the enemy, the Army of Northern Virginia might not be able to interpose between Richmond and the Federals. Orders gave him discretion in starting for his objective: He was to withdraw quietly from the lines after nightfall and move his troops to some point where they could rest. Before the designated hour of 3, they were to take the road for Spotsylvania that Pendleton had cut that day through the forest.

"I found the woods on fire and burning furiously in every direction," Anderson subsequently recorded, "and there was no suitable place for a rest." The new road, moreover, was narrow. Stumps remained, and some of the trunks of trees had not been removed. Progress over it would be slow. Upon ascertaining this, Anderson promptly decided that he would forgo the hours of rest authorized by headquarters. He would push on until he was close to his objective. It was a soldierly resolution that made history and it was put into execution while the air was vibrant with sound. Someone cried, "Three cheers for General Lee!" Instead of cheers there was the weird rebel yell, rendered all the more weird by the night and the burning forest. Down the line it swept from brigade to brigade. Again it was raised; again it was carried to the river and, at the last, thrown across the Rapidan to die in its echoes over the fields of Culpeper and Stafford. It was, said one chronicler, "The grandest rebel yell of the war."[22]

Through the darkness of the forest, along the wretched road, the men of Kershaw and Field had to feel their way. To them it was a long, long night broken only by the brief halt at the end of fifty minutes and by the usual vexatious starts and stops of the march. About dawn Anderson had the column turn out of the road to rest and eat breakfast. Spotsylvania Court House was then distant about three miles. The sound of firing drifted down from the north, perhaps two miles away. Jeb Stuart's men were in that vicinity. Much might depend on whether their foe was infantry or cavalry.

Haskell's battalion of artillery, which had halted in advance of the infantry, was the first to receive any information of what was occurring. Down the road there rode rapidly a courier who drew rein and called for the commanding officer. Major John Haskell stepped forward. As good luck would have it, the courier knew Haskell and in the belief that the paper called for action, gave him an unsealed dispatch addressed to "General Lee or General Longstreet." Because it was unsealed and urgent, Haskell opened and read the message. In it, Stuart asked for artillery support and said that he was hard-pressed by the enemy. Haskell returned the dispatch to the courier and immediately started his battalion on the road to Spotsylvania.

When Stuart's dispatch reached Anderson, he advanced his leading division, Kershaw's, toward the sound of the firing. Soon word came from Fitz Lee that he was fighting on the Brock Road, which ran through the Wilderness and past Todd's Tavern to Spotsylvania, and most urgently needed assistance. The call was not one that a soldier of Anderson's character would disregard or even debate. He immediately ordered his old brigade and Humphreys's to go to Fitz Lee's relief. They came in sight of piles of fence rails, thrown together to provide insecure but useful field defenses. A cavalryman rushed up to the lead regiment and shouted for it to run for the rail piles. "The Federal infantry will reach them first, if you don't run!" Kershaw's veterans sprang forward without waiting for a command. The bluecoats were only sixty yards away when the South Carolinians crouched behind the rails and opened fire.[23]

By a narrow margin, then, had Anderson won the race, if, indeed, he had won more than the first heat! The Federals pressed straight to the weak line of rails, and there for once they crossed bayonets. The repulse, which was costly to the Unionists, might not have been possible had Haskell's batteries not been at hand. At the same time, word came to Anderson that Rosser's brigade was at Spotsylvania Court House and facing an impossibly superior force of cavalry. Rosser, too, must have help! Stuart sent what he could, withdrawing some of Fitz Lee's men after the arrival of the infantry. Further assistance must come from Anderson. Again Longstreet's temporary successor acted with vigor and decision. The remaining brigades of Kershaw's division, Wofford's and Bryan's, were designated to reinforce Rosser.

Two battles, then, were to be Dick Anderson's. The Federal infantry in front of Kershaw's and Humphreys's brigades showed no inclination to break off the fight after a single repulse. They were in great strength. Prisoners said they belonged to the V Corps. The two Confederate brigades would need stout reinforcement. Field's division was coming up: Let part of it move toward Spotsylvania Court House; the remainder must extend Kershaw's line to the left and westward. Almost before Anderson's left could be strengthened, the whole line was assailed. Once again the enemy was beaten off easily. After that, as the minutes passed, it was manifest that the Federals were entrenching and steadily extending their lines opposite the Confederate left. At touch and go the situation remained—two divisions against four. A bold front, stern resistance by the infantry, stubborn artillery fire, and about the hardest fighting ever done by the cavalry kept the enemy at a distance. He must be held there till the remainder of Lee's army arrived.[24]

During early afternoon there were indications that the other Federal flank was being prolonged. This time, if the Unionists struck heavily on the Confederate right before the arrival of reinforcements, surely Grant could turn that flank. Only if the veterans of Lee's Second or Third Corps arrived in time could the army block the road to Richmond. Manifestly the outcome might hang on a few hours, on minutes even. As the hot afternoon passed slowly, the heat seemed to be a third belligerent. Ewell's men were marching to Anderson's assistance under the eyes of the commanding general himself, but they had "a very distressing march through intense heat and thick dust and smoke from burning woods."

About 5 o'clock the fire quickened. Scattered cheers were audible. The bluecoats were coming! This advance would decide the day, one way or the other. On the center the attack was half-hearted; on the right the enemy threatened to turn the flank and get in rear of Kershaw. The prospect was ominous when the Confederates had, once more, their old-time battlefield luck. Ewell arrived! Rodes was thrown forward at once to the right of Kershaw. That was enough. As soon as the Federals realized that the Southern front was stronger, they withdrew. Rodes's advance had decided the doubtful action. The enemy attacked no more that evening. Ewell put Johnson's division on obscure, night-covered ground to Rodes's right. Early's old division was held in reserve.[25]

Anderson had won his battle. It was because he had started early.

3. From Mule Shoe to Bloody Angle

Through the morning of the hot ninth of May, the Confederate soldiers around Spotsylvania kept one eye on the enemy, who seemed to be taking a day of rest, and the other eye on their earthworks, which were being strengthened hourly. Examination of prisoners had shown the Southerners where the various Federal corps had advanced and where they had fought. Grant started on May 3–4 from his camps north of the Rapidan and had moved with three corps of infantry, the II, V, and VI, and a cavalry corps of three divisions. The IX Corps was to follow the main force. Once across the Rapidan, Grant's plan was to hold the Army of Northern Virginia while General Butler's army from the lower Peninsula moved up the James River in an effort to capture Richmond. If Butler failed, Grant purposed to hammer Lee so hard and so steadily that the Confederate commander would have to retreat or, at the least, would have to keep the Southern forces together without detaching any of them for another invasion of the North.

After the failure of the attacks in the Wilderness, the movement of the Army of the Potomac toward Spotsylvania was prompted by what Grant had seen of the strength of the Confederate fieldworks on the morning of May 7. He had concluded then that Lee's army no longer would face him in the open field but would await attack. "I therefore determined," the Union chief explained later, "to push on and put my whole force between [Lee] and Richmond."[26] While few details of Grant's plan were known to the Confederates, no thoughtful officer in gray could overlook the fact that on the fifth, on the sixth, and again on the eighth, when contact had been established, the aggressor had been the Federals. This new commander, Grant, manifestly believed in the offensive.

This was by no means the full measure of Grant's aggressiveness. Although Butler's operation against Richmond was not being conducted skillfully, it involved gravest danger to the capital. Beauregard and Robert Ransom had been summoned to cope with it, but there was divided command and all the resultant confusion. From Winchester, on May 9, Franz Sigel was starting in the hope of forming a junction high up the Shenandoah Valley with troops of George Crook, who was in command of the raid against the Virginia and Tennessee Railroad. More menacing than this was a cavalry raid launched that day by Sheridan but, at the moment, unknown to the Confederates around Spotsylvania.

In the Southern infantry two men were in new positions. The circumstances of their advancement were unhappy. Powell Hill's malady had grown worse rather than better, and by the eighth he was so ill that he could not sit up. On the march that day Jubal Early was notified that he was assigned, during Hill's disability, to the command of the Third Corps. Anderson's appointment in Longstreet's place had left only Heth and Wilcox as divisional leaders of Hill's corps. Neither was sufficiently seasoned for the handling of a corps. Early appeared to be, and had done well with Ewell's command during the Mine Run operations.

Transfer of Early meant, of course, that his division had to pass to other hands. He had three brigades only, because Hoke's had not yet rejoined. Of the three commanders of brigades, John Pegram was wounded. That left Harry Hays and John B. Gordon. The commission of Hays antedated that of Gordon by more than eleven months, but Lee believed Gordon better qualified for higher command. In order that Gordon might assume command of Early's division, Hays was transferred from Early's division to Johnson's and was entrusted with Stafford's Louisiana brigade in addition to his own. This increased Hays's prestige at the same time that it assured competent leadership for the soldiers of the fallen Stafford. To take the place of Hays's brigade in Early's division, Ewell was directed to transfer to Early's division the brigade of Robert D. Johnston or some other of the five brigades of Rodes's division. Old soldiers might have asked themselves whether so many changes ever had been made by army headquarters to give a brigadier general a division.

This was a notable compliment for Gordon, but when it was taken with the other changes necessitated by four days' fighting, it disclosed a startling shift of command. The record of five days now stood: One lieutenant general wounded and another incapacitated by sickness; two divisional commanders elevated, at least temporarily, to corps command; two brigadiers entrusted with divisions; three brigadiers killed or mortally wounded; two others seriously wounded; six brigades passed into the hands of senior colonels.

So stood the command on May 9. The Third Corps arrived and took position on the right of the Second, in the immediate vicinity of Spotsylvania Court House. At the moment there were no Unionists in front of this corps, but the extension of the front opposite the Confederate right was expected. Chief engineer Martin Smith was laying out a line which, when completed, would anchor the flanks on the steep banks of the little river Po and make the most of such natural advantages as the ground offered.

On the tenth a venture of the Federal II Corps across the Po failed of surprise and was brought to a standstill by two of Early's divisions and consequently recalled. All that was accomplished by the action was the maiming and killing of good soldiers. On the Confederate side the most serious individual losses were those of Harry Hays and H. H. Walker, who had succeeded to the command of the Field-Brockenbrough-Mayo brigade. Hays would recover easily, but Walker was so badly wounded in one foot that amputation was necessary—another casualty that would require a new appointment or the consolidation of two brigades.[27]

In the Second Corps there was no sense of complacency regarding its position. When Ewell's men formed on the right of Anderson, on the afternoon and evening of May 8, they began to fortify an awkward and irregular salient to the northward. Its apex was almost a mile from the point of divergence of an east-and-west line. The extreme width was about 1,200 yards. This manifestly was a difficult position, but evacuation of it would have left to the Federals two stretches of open ground from which

Ewell thought the enemy could command the Southern line. Further, if the salient were abandoned, a stretch of road much needed for the movement of men and supplies would be exposed. The decision consequently was to hold the salient with ample artillery and infantry, but to construct a second line across the base. For reasons never satisfactorily explained, work on his line was deferred. In the salient from left to right was part of Rodes's division and the whole of Johnson's. To the right of Johnson, beyond the salient, was Wilcox's division.[28]

On the western face of the salient, George Doles's Georgia brigade of Rodes's command held an incomplete work and, 150 to 200 yards in front of it, a main line in the form of a lesser salient that looked out on 200 yards of open ground. Beyond this field was woodland. In support was the Third Company of the Richmond Howitzer battalion. On the afternoon of the tenth, when artillery fire was directed against him, Doles placed most of his men behind the front line of works. Precisely at 6 o'clock the bombardment ceased. To Doles and his men the end of the day's combat seemed at hand.

At 6:10 a wild cheer rose from the edge of the woods 200 yards away. Out from among the green trees swept one line. Close behind it was a second. A third emerged almost immediately. There scarcely was time for a volley before the Federals were at the parapet. Hundreds of bluecoats poured into the trench. A furious hand-to-hand clash followed, but not for long. The outnumbered Georgians ran back toward the second line; scores of them, surrounded, had to throw down their guns. The Howitzer battery poured in canister until the guns were overrun. Heroic Captain B. H. Smith and twenty-four of his men were captured at their pieces.

Quick action was taken by the Confederates to mend the break. Battle's Alabama brigade was put in line directly ahead of the attacking Federals. Gordon and Johnson closed on their flanks. As soon as the countercharge reached the captured battery, artillerists from Cutshaw's battalion rushed forward, manned the guns, and used them against the enemy. Other batteries opened on lines deploying farther up the salient, which withdrew out of range. This discouraged the column that had broken into Doles's lines. For a few minutes it fought to retain its ground. Then the Unionists ducked over the parapet and ran for their own lines. With them went perhaps a thousand prisoners.

This affair created much talk in both armies. Confederate commanders had praise for the valor of the defense, but some became more concerned than ever for the safety of the salient which the soldiers by this time had dubbed the "Mule Shoe." Federals commended the fine planning and vigorous assault. Colonel Emory Upton, who directed the operation, was recommended immediately by General Grant for promotion to brigadier general. There seemed a new and more stubborn spirit in the Union army. The resolution of Grant showed itself in a dispatch written the morning after Upton attacked: "I am now sending back to Belle Plain all my wagons for a fresh supply of provisions and ammunition, and propose to fight it out on this line if it takes all summer." The Confederates had seen enough by the eleventh of May to make them certain they faced the hardest campaign in their military experience.[29]

No fighting interrupted the labor on the works during the eleventh. Intelligence on Federal activities and movements was conflicting, but its substance was that the enemy seemed to be moving away from the line. In the evening Harry Heth welcomed to his headquarters near the Court House the sick Powell Hill and, a little later, the commanding general. In a free conversation some of the officers declared that Grant was slaughtering his troops by throwing them against earthworks. Lee was not of that mind. "Gentlemen," he said, "I think General Grant has managed his affairs remarkably well up to the present time." He turned to Heth: "My opinion is the enemy are preparing to retreat tonight to Fredericksburg. I wish you to have everything in readiness to pull out at a moment's notice, but do not disturb your artillery till you commence moving. We must attack these people if they retreat."

Hill spoke up: "General Lee, let them continue to attack our breastworks; we can stand that very well." Then the conversation became more general, but Lee wished to emphasize one truth: "This army cannot stand a siege. We must end this business on the battlefield, not in a fortified place."[30]

Lee rode to Ewell's headquarters in the Mule Shoe sector. It would be necessary, Ewell was told, to withdraw the advanced guns before nightfall and place them where they could be started when the direction of the enemy could be determined. As soon as Lee left, Armistead Long, Second Corps chief of artillery, began to send to the rear the exposed artillery. Of this movement Allegheny Johnson was not informed, and the first he knew of it was when he saw guns going to the rear. Only eight fieldpieces, in two of Cutshaw's batteries, remained in the Mule Shoe. Twenty-two were halted near the Court House a mile and a half in rear of the salient. Guns of the First Corps were handled differently. Porter Alexander did not relish the idea of withdrawing all artillery support from positions close to the enemy. Instead of moving the pieces back that night, he visited each of his batteries and had them place all their equipment where it could be pulled quickly to the rear with minimum noise over roads he took pains to clear.[31]

With nightfall the weather had grown worse. A cold rain fell steadily and the night air was raw and penetrating. Long before midnight, the pickets outside the right face of the salient heard sounds from the Federal front. A steady rumble was audible, though its nature could not be determined. Two of Maryland Steuart's staff at once went out toward the skirmish line. Reports were correct. The enemy must be moving. Only that could account for the slow, steady rumble. It sounded like a waterfall or the grinding of some powerful machine. Thousands of men evidently were in motion. There was no way of ascertaining, as yet, whether they were proceeding to the right or were massing for an attack on the Mule Shoe.

Steuart promptly concluded that the enemy's movement was preliminary to an assault on the salient, and so advised Johnson, whom he requested to return the artillery that had been withdrawn. John M. Jones's and Stafford's men had lost their experienced leaders and perhaps were lacking in similar vigilance. Walker's brigade was on the extreme left of the divisional front, next Doles, and may not have heard so plainly the mysterious sounds of motion. The alarmed Johnson wrote Ewell that the enemy was massing in his front and repeated Steuart's request that the artillery be returned at once. Johnson's staff officer who delivered the message did not feel that Ewell was sufficiently alive to the danger, and he prevailed on Johnson to ride in person to Ewell. By this time Ewell had started Johnson's message to artillery chief Long, and Johnson was told that the guns would be back in position not later than 2:00 A.M. Yet it was not until 3:30 that the courier reached Long. Within ten minutes his instructions for the dispatch of batteries to the salient were given to Major Richard C. M. Page, and Page got the guns under way with promptness and speed.

Fog clung close to the ground until about 4:30, when it began to lift slightly. Soon, from the northwest face of the salient, the approaching tramp of many men could be heard. A moment more and there came a mighty cheer, and then the sight of bluecoats advancing in a dense mass. Johnson had sensed the point of extreme danger and ridden up to that part of the line. He exhorted the men to fire fast. The artillery was coming to help, he said; it soon would be there. When, presently, he saw Page's guns moving up, he sent back to order a gallop straight toward the apex of the salient. As the first gun unlimbered, Captain William Carter sprang forward to help load it. One round was discharged at the advancing enemy. "Stop firing that gun!" a voice shouted. Carter turned . . . and looked into a score of rifles held by determined men in blue. The enemy already was in the salient and in rear of guns and infantry.

Federals appeared everywhere the startled Confederates looked. The Union soldiers quickly found a gap in the front of Jones's brigade, poured through, got behind the Stonewall Brigade, and captured nearly the whole of that famous command. Simultaneously, plunging ahead, they overwhelmed Jones's men and seized Allegheny Johnson himself. To the right of the salient, where a stronger resistance was offered, part of Maryland Steuart's brigade, including its commander, were made prisoners. All eight of Cutshaw's guns and twelve of Page's fourteen were taken.

After this brilliant coup de main, thousands of men pressed southward down the salient in pursuit of the Confederates who escaped. The Federals met with little resistance until they reached, midway of the salient, about 5:30 A.M. an incomplete line the existence of which they had no previous knowledge. Already they had achieved much. In three quarters of an hour they had captured 2 general officers, more than 2,000 men, and 20 guns.[32]

The Confederates who met the bluecoats at the incomplete line were men of Early's old division, now under John B. Gordon. After Johnson announced that the Federals were massing in front of the salient, Gordon had sent him Pegram's brigade. His other troops he disposed where he thought they could be most quickly available. When the attack opened, he threw Robert Johnston's brigade forward. After it was repulsed, he ordered his old brigade to deploy and demonstrate. So admirably did these troops do their part that the Federal advance was checked momentarily. Gordon meantime recalled Pegram's brigade and with this and his other troops, he undertook, in confusion approaching chaos, to form a line of battle.

Gordon thought the fate of the army was in the balance. Grant had broken the front. If he were not checked, the Confederate army would be divided. At any cost the division must charge, halt the enemy, drive him back. He touched his horse and started through the woods to dress his line. At the sight of a familiar figure on a gray mount, Gordon pulled in his animal and saluted. "What do you want me to do, General," he asked, and began to explain what he was planning. With few words, grim but calm, Lee told him to proceed. As he started away, Gordon observed the commanding general head his horse up the salient, in the direction of the advance the division was to make. He had heard, of course, that Lee wanted to join the charge of the Texans on May 6, and he suspected immediately that Lee intended to do the same thing now.

Back, swiftly, Gordon rode and confronted his chief. "General Lee, this is no place for you. Go back, General; we will drive them back!" He spoke so that his men might hear, and the troops were calling now to Lee to "go back." Lee would not move. Finally Gordon saw a sergeant take Traveller's bridle and lead the animal toward the rear. Lee said nothing but did not resist. Gordon could turn again to his troops. "Forward! Guide-right!" he shouted. Soon the line was moving steadily, irresistibly, up the salient.[33]

Gordon's line was too short to cover the width of the salient. On his left

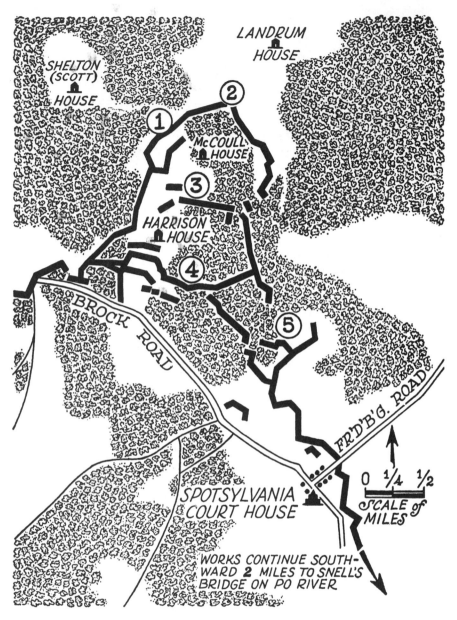

Confederate works at the Mule Shoe or Bloody Angle, Spotsylvania Court House, May 10–12, 1864. The numerals indicate: (1) immediate objective of attack by Upton, May 10; (2) "the Apex," approximate point of Federal penetration, May 12; (3) "Gordon's Line," or "Incomplete Line," May 12; (4) the line constructed May 12 and occupied that night; (5) "Heth's Salient."

Rodes came into action by changing the front of Daniel and then of Ramseur from west to north. The right of the First Corps was moved into the salient to occupy the ground left vacant by the shift of Ramseur. Rodes's North Carolinians swept up the salient, said Ewell, in a "charge of unsurpassed gallantry." To strengthen the counterattack, Nat Harris, a new brigadier, brought up his Mississippians to Ramseur's right. Mahone followed Harris; McGowan was placed in rear in support. Later, to relieve some of the exhausted troops, Bratton's and Humphreys's brigades of the First Corps were sent to the salient.

Their fire seemed merely to heighten the fury of the fight. "The rain poured heavily, and an incessant fire was kept upon us from front and flank. The enemy still held the works on the right of the angle, and fired across the traverses." Before that fire and the blast of artillery many went down. Robert Johnston had fallen early; Daniel was mortally wounded; McGowan was shot again; Ramseur received a ball through his arm; James A. Walker was removed from the field dripping blood; Abner Perrin was killed. In all the bloody fighting of the two armies there never had been such a struggle as this. "Many were shot and stabbed through crevices and holes between the logs; men mounted the works, and with muskets rapidly handed them kept up a continuous fire until they were shot down, when others would take their places and continue the deadly work."

On the right of the salient, Gordon with the help of Wilcox's division of the Third Corps drove the enemy almost to the apex. An attack by the IX Corps was repulsed with ease. An attempt to organize a counterstroke failed. By mid-afternoon many soldiers were so weary that they went through the motions of combat and scarcely knew what they were doing. To some, death seemed preferable to another hour of din and stench and blood. Veterans said afterward that the entire war had offered no scene to equal that fight at the apex of the salient. All the troops, even survivors of the first onslaught, were told they must remain at the front till a line across the base of the salient was strong enough to afford adequate defense. That order seemed a death sentence. Till darkness, till 9 o'clock, the bitter exchange of fire continued. Ten o'clock scarcely brought a slackening. At 11 word was, "Not yet." It was past midnight when the survivors, staggering and wild-eyed, fell back to the new line.[34]

They had bought at heavy cost a re-establishment of the front. Killed, wounded, and captured Confederates must have exceeded 5,000 that day. Included were some of the best troops and ablest leaders of the army. Allegheny Johnson had resisted to the last and then with good heart ate a breakfast provided by his old friend Seth Williams of Grant's staff. Maryland Steuart, refusing the courtesy of one-time friend Winfield Scott

Hancock, passed unceremoniously into the custody of the provost marshal. Steuart would be missed; even more would Johnson be. To replace the slain brigadiers Abner Perrin and Junius Daniel might not be an easy task. Many of the injuries of the day were deplorably serious. No wonder, after those ghastly hours, the Confederates spoke not of the "Mule Shoe" but of the "Bloody Angle." A division, in effect, had been destroyed. By this battle and the struggle in the Wilderness, the command of the infantry, which had been weakened at Gettysburg, now was shattered to a degree no one realized at the time. Nor was the only loss of the fatal month of May sustained in the dripping forests of Spotsylvania. News as dire as any from the salient had reached headquarters on the twelfth from Richmond.

CHAPTER 31

Richmond Threatened

1. "I Had Rather Die than Be Whipped"

Into the desperate fighting of the Wilderness and Spotsylvania, the cavalry had entered with its organization changed to conform to the return of Rooney Lee. When he was captured while recuperating from the wound received at Brandy Station, he had ranked as a brigadier general. In January John R. Chambliss, Jr., had been given Rooney's brigade. Now that the second son of the commanding general was an exchanged prisoner, provision had to be made for him. The prompt decision of the War Department was to advance him to the rank of major general and supply him a division by reducing the brigades of the divisions to two each. Exception was made in the case of Wade Hampton because he was receiving South Carolina reinforcements that could not be placed acceptably in another division; his command, therefore, was Young's, Rosser's, and Butler's brigades. Fitz Lee's division was reduced to Lomax's and Wickham's brigades. Rooney Lee had his own old command, now Chambliss's and James Gordon's North Carolina regiments.[1]

None of Stuart's brigades was now under the man who had commanded it a year previously; few of his personal staff had served with him that long. Von Borcke had not recovered sufficiently from a wound suffered in the Pennsylvania campaign to resume his duties. Channing Price was dead. Pelham was no more. Norman FitzHugh was quartermaster of the cavalry. William Blackford had resigned to become lieutenant colonel of a regiment of engineer troops. John Esten Cooke remained but was not happy. Henry McClellan was the backbone of the staff. The most useful recent addition, certainly the one closest to Stuart, was the assistant inspector general, Major Andrew Reid Venable, almost universally called Reid Venable. With these men and some young aides Jeb was content, but headquarters lacked the old hilarity, the old buoyancy of spirit even. The war was becoming too serious! Grant's new cavalry commander, Phil Sheridan, was flinty. He had novel conceptions of firepower and of the function of mounted troops, and he took excellent care of his horses. His fighting was hard and intelligent.

In the first stages of combat in the Wilderness, the Confederates met their stronger adversary with vigor. On May 5, Rosser acquitted himself with honor in a brisk fight. On the sixth and seventh the butternut cavalry again were assailed by superior force on the Confederate right. Most of the fighting was on foot. All of it was furious. The rolling character of those clashes carried the opposing mounted forces toward Spotsylvania where, on the eighth, Stuart's men stood off the Union cavalry and an increasing force of infantry until the arrival of Anderson and the First Corps. Stuart did his utmost to get the arriving First Corps into position, and at Anderson's request he directed operations on the left of the line.

Early the next day, May 9, Stuart received news that Sheridan's cavalry had proceeded to the Telegraph Road on which they had turned southward. Wickham's brigade at once undertook pursuit. Jeb already had taken Gordon from Hampton and he had to leave Rosser and the cadre of Young to cover the flanks of Lee's army. Few as were his available men, Stuart spurred toward the Telegraph Road. There he and Fitz Lee, with the brigades of Lomax and Gordon, joined Wickham. Federal strength, said residents, was immense. The column covered thirteen miles of road.

Sheridan had turned now from the Telegraph Road and taken the route to Beaver Dam on the Virginia Central Railroad. Bad news this was because Lee had his advance base at that point. That was not the worst prospect. If Sheridan merely were making a raid on Beaver Dam, he scarcely would have taken so many troops with him. He might be proceeding toward Richmond. If so, at least a part of the cavalry must interpose between him and the capital. Stuart concluded that Fitz Lee with two brigades should follow the enemy at least for a few hours, while he himself took Gordon's brigade and made for Davenport's Bridge on the North Anna, whence he could ascertain whether Sheridan was advancing on Richmond.

On the morning of the tenth Stuart pushed southward to Beaver Dam Station. There he rejoined Fitz Lee and again concentrated his men, who numbered between 4,000 and 5,000; but what he saw at Beaver Dam sickened him. Several units of Sheridan's command had reached the advanced base during the night. The few Confederate guards ignited the stores there. About 915,000 rations of meat and 504,000 of bread were consumed by fire while Southern boys lay hungry in the woods around Spotsylvania. A grievous blow this was, nor was this the full measure of loss and hardship. What the guards at Beaver Dam could not burn, Sheridan's men destroyed—the army's reserve medical supplies, more than 100 railroad cars, and two locomotives. Sheridan recovered, also, 378 Federal prisoners.[2]

Although Jeb was humiliated, of course, that an enterprising enemy had reached the advance base, nothing was to be gained now by camping amid the ashes. Sheridan had gone southward, in the direction of Richmond. The Confederates must follow and defeat him. Jeb spared himself time for a brief visit to the nearby Fontaine plantation, where Mrs. Stuart was a guest. After a few minutes' private conversation he kissed her and bade her a most affectionate good-bye. Somber thoughts pursued him as he rode away. He never expected to outlive the war, he told Reid Venable, and he did not want to survive if the South were conquered.

In this fighting spirit, Stuart continued to receive reports of the Federals' advance. He speculated on Sheridan's possible alternatives. Perhaps he was aiming at Richmond, but his route suggested also that he might strike the R.F. & P. and the Virginia Central railroads between Hanover Junction and the capital. Stuart consequently divided his forces again: Gordon must hang on the rear of the enemy; Fitz Lee with Lomax and Wickham must move by way of Hanover Junction and get across Sheridan's path. Stuart was not without hope of defeating the Federals. He reasoned that if they advanced on Richmond, he could assail their rear while the garrison of the capital contested their advance. If they contented themselves with cutting the railroads, he would press their escape.

The column reached Hanover Junction not long before 9:00 P.M. The enemy was reported on the South Anna River, within nineteen miles of Richmond. By 1 o'clock on the morning of May 11, Stuart had the troopers pushing south again on the Telegraph Road. Soon he was on the ground of the start of the first of his great adventures under Lee, the "ride around McClellan." These mounted Federals were stronger and more daring than ever they had been. They were closer to Richmond now. Stuart told himself, in his romantic way, that he must save the women and children of the city.

At Ashland Stuart learned that the enemy had raided the town during the night, destroying a locomotive and a train of cars and tearing up the track of the R.F. & P. for six miles. The issue was at hand! If some of Sheridan's troops were this close to Richmond, the others would be encountered quickly. Jeb urged the troopers forward. About 7:00 A.M. the sound of firing was heard from the direction of the South Anna. An hour later the head of the Southern column reached Yellow Tavern, where the Mountain Road from the west and the Telegraph Road from Fredericksburg joined the Brook Turnpike running to Richmond. If Sheridan was ahead of Stuart, the Federals would have moved, in all probability, by one of those roads or the other. Natives said the bluecoats had been seen on neither.[3]

Stuart examined the ground around Yellow Tavern and considered his tactical problem. As Sheridan had not preceded him, Jeb had now to aban-

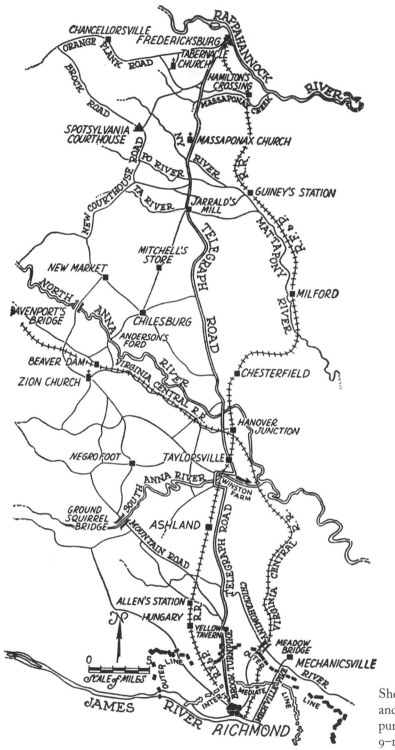

Sheridan's raid and Stuart's pursuit, May 9–11, 1864.

don the plan of attacking the Federals in the rear while the Richmond garrison stopped them in front. By 11 o'clock all the indications were that
Sheridan's main force was arriving over the Mountain Road. Stuart made
his dispositions—a compromise between a frontal and a flank position. He
placed Wickham on the right and Lomax on the left. Gordon was
assumed to be engaged with the enemy's rear guard. Two Confederate
brigades had to contend against the undetermined strength of Sheridan.

The first Federal attack against the position on the Telegraph Road was
beaten off by the 5th Virginia in a hand-to-hand grapple that stirred both
Stuart's pride and his apprehension. Henry Pate commanded the 5th, an
able man and a furious fighter. Between him and Stuart had developed a
bitterness of feeling. Stuart now rode over to Pate to commend him for his
firmness and to ask him to hold the position until reinforcements could be
sent. The colonel listened and then walked over to Jeb and held out his
hand. Gladly and cordially Stuart grasped it and, on the instant, effaced all
difference. Now at one point the enemy assailed the line in an effort to find
the weakest spot. Then the "feeling out" was shifted. This went on and on.
Southern losses mounted. Pate again beat off the hard-striking bluecoats—but in so doing yielded his life.[4]

Though he expected to be compelled to repulse more attacks, Stuart
told his chief of staff, Henry McClellan, that he would hang on Sheridan's
flank. If the troops in the Richmond defenses delivered a strong attack, he
could take the offensive and, with good fortune, cripple the blue cavalry.
There came now a lull in the fight, but nobody was deceived by it. In particular, Lomax's men on the left were on the alert; theirs was the most vulnerable position. But the first evidence of renewed attack was against the
center and right. Stuart rode to the scene and in his gay, confident manner,
encouraged the soldiers. Presently Reid Venable spoke up: The general
was exposing himself needlessly on horseback, a conspicuous target. Stuart
answered laughingly, "I don't reckon there is any danger!" Apparently there
never had been any. He had been fighting for three years and never had
been touched by a Federal missile.

Jeb told Venable to ride with him to the left. They found a broken line
and men who seemed close to the limit of organized resistance. As always,
Stuart reasoned that the best way to defend was to attack, and he told Venable to remain there and help Lomax organize a counterthrust. Alone,
Stuart rode to the extreme left. Whistling as he went, doubtless seeking to
spread confidence among the men, he drew rein at a fence in the woods
near the point where the left flank was "in the air." There he waited for the
next assault.

Soon it came. With a roar, three mounted regiments of Custer's brigade advanced. Two of the regiments kept together to assail the left center; one advanced against the extreme left. The 5th Michigan dashed by Stuart. Out of his holster Jeb jerked his pistol and began to fire at the Federals. Quickly they were past, but soon they roared back, met by a counter-charge by the 1st Virginia. "Steady, men, steady; give it to them!" Stuart called. Soon the recoiling bluecoats were gone, except for a few who had lost their horses in the advance and now were trying to get to the rear. Stu-art felt a sudden shock that almost threw him off balance. His head dropped; his hat fell off. Instantly he put his hand to his side.

"General," cried one of the boys with him, "are you hit?" They crowded around him and scarcely observed the Federal trooper, almost the last of the dismounted men, who ran off down the fence with the smoking pistol that had fired the one bullet that hit Stuart. "Are you wounded badly?" an anxious voice inquired. "I am afraid I am," said Stuart calmly, "but don't worry, boys: Fitz will do as well for you as I have done."[5]

His companions must leave him, Stuart said, must collect the men and repel the enemy. It did not matter about himself. He feared he was mor-tally wounded and past all service. Fitz Lee dashed up. He was now the senior officer on the field, the man who must direct a difficult and doubt-ful battle. Stuart did not permit him to waste time on sympathy: "Go ahead, Fitz, old fellow, I know you will do what is right." Presently an ambulance was found for him. As it crossed the field, he saw numbers of disorganized men who were making for the rear. Prostrate, Jeb wrathfully cried, as loudly as he could, "Go back, go back and do your duty. . . . Go back, go back!" Then, in complete self-revelation he shouted, "I had rather die than be whipped!"

The surgeon, Dr. J. B. Fontaine, must have realized, after examination of the wound, that Stuart had been shot through the abdomen, probably through the liver, and that the prognosis was hopeless. After some argu-ment, Jeb agreed to take some whiskey as a stimulant and, once again in command, he repeated substantially to the men gathered around him what he had said to the fugitives: "Go back to the front, I will be well taken care of. I want you to do your duty to your country as I always have through my life."

These words were his farewell to the field. The next move was in the ambulance toward Richmond. Custer's attack had made two battles of one. Part of the conflict continued north of Yellow Tavern. Another phase of the conflict was carried to the outer line of the Richmond defenses. This was a dramatic advance and one that made the pulse of the Federals beat faster because they could hear plainly the tocsin in Richmond.

The ambulance had to make wide detours over poor and unfamiliar roads, and Stuart suffered cruelly. It was long after dark when he was lifted from the vehicle in front of the home on Grace Street of his brother-in-law, Dr. Charles Brewer. By that time, official Richmond and most of Stuart's private friends knew that he had been wounded, though the seriousness of his condition was not realized by all. The night was one of misery for Jeb—the same night of foreboding that witnessed the withdrawal of the artillery from the Bloody Angle and the mysterious sounds from the Federal lines. In the same dawn with that of the battle for the salient, Jeb Stuart rallied his courageous spirits to face that "last enemy, Death."[6]

He had, as reinforcement, the best medical men of the city, but they knew he was beaten. Staff officers came to comfort him and to execute his final orders. From the direction of the Chickahominy there rolled the sullen sound of cannon fire. In moments of relief from his paroxysms of pain, Stuart asked Henry McClellan what was happening. McClellan told how the Richmond garrison and the cavalry corps were seeking to trap the enemy. "God grant that they may be successful," Stuart answered with his old eagerness. Then he checked himself and said with a sigh, "But I must be prepared for another world." To the next visitor, an anxious President Davis, he said in an even voice that he was "willing to die if God and my country think I have fulfilled my destiny and done my duty."

As the afternoon slipped by, his paroxysms grew more excruciating, his lucid intervals fewer. He roused himself to ask Dr. Brewer whether he could survive the night. The physician answered honestly that death was near. Stuart nodded as if he had received an order to go forward: "I am resigned if it be God's will. . . ." When it became apparent, after 7 o'clock, that his end was at hand, two ministers came to his bedside. At his request they prayed and then they sang the hymn he asked, "Rock of Ages, cleft for me." He turned his head toward Dr. Brewer. "I am going fast now," he whispered, "I am resigned; God's will be done." Then, in spirit, he rode off to New Adventure.[7]

Stuart had the tribute of President, of press and Cabinet, and as impressive a funeral, May 13, as the war-wrung Confederate Capital could give. More impressive still was the tribute by one of his adversaries, Brigadier General James H. Wilson. Of Yellow Tavern and the death of Stuart, Wilson wrote, "From it may be dated the permanent superiority of the national cavalry over that of the rebels." Even critical officers shared General Sedgwick's opinion that Jeb was "the greatest cavalry officer ever foaled in America."

The commanding general of the Army of Northern Virginia had looked to Stuart for service of the sort Jeb had described in a letter to John R. Chambliss, April 4, 1864. Stuart had said then: "Bear in mind that your telegrams make the whole army strike tents, and night or day, rain or shine, take up the line of march. Endeavor, therefore, to secure accurate information. . . . Above all, vigilance! vigilance! vigilance!" By Stuart's own fulfillment of that ideal of the outpost officer, more than by any other, Lee had judged him. The commanding general spoke in the fullness of grief a few unpremeditated words that showed how lofty was the estimate he put on Stuart. In the midst of the fighting for the Bloody Angle, someone placed in Lee's hands a telegram. He opened it, read it, and had to get a firm grip on his emotions before he trusted himself to speak. "Gentlemen," he said, "we have very bad news. General Stuart has been mortally wounded." Lee paused and then exclaimed: "He never brought me a piece of false information!"[8]

Reliable information of the sort that Stuart sent him Lee seldom needed more than during those baffling days around Spotsylvania. Only during the Gettysburg campaign had he been more completely in the dark. Never had the army had so few discerning eyes. Daily the grim list of fallen leaders was lengthened—Longstreet wounded, Powell Hill sick, Ewell in danger of collapse under his burdens, Edward Johnson in the hands of the enemy, nine of the brigadiers killed, wounded, or captured, some of them among the best; and now Jeb Stuart dead. The Wilderness might be the graveyard of the army command.

2. THE DEBITS AND CREDITS OF MAY

The rain of May 11–12 fortunately continued through the fifteenth and into the sixteenth. "It looked," said George Neese, "as if Heaven were trying to wash up the blood as fast as the civilized barbarians were spilling it." While the Southerners peered from muddy trenches through the dripping forest at the dim position of an enemy held captive by mud, a few appointments were made for the command of leaderless troops. John B. Gordon was promoted major general as reward for his attack on May 6 and for his service in the Bloody Angle. When Hill's recovery permitted the return of Early to his own division, Gordon's old brigade was transferred to what was left of Edward Johnson's command, at the head of which Gordon was placed. So many men in Johnson's wrecked division had been captured in the Bloody Angle that the units could not operate as brigades. Grievous as was the necessity, the Stonewall Brigade, Jones's, and Steuart's brigades had to be consolidated. Even after consolidation they remained pathetically small. John Casler's company of the 33rd Virginia consisted of the captain and three privates. One of these was a cavalryman who had lost his horse.[9]

Another matter that could not be delayed was action in the case of Lafayette McLaws. On May 4, it will be remembered, Longstreet's charges against McLaws had been dismissed, and Bragg recommended that he be ordered to rejoin his command. As it chanced, before his orders to return became effective, Bragg put the facts before General Lee. In framing a reply, Lee had to reason that if Longstreet recovered and resumed command, as there now was every reason to believe he would, he and McLaws could not work together. Moreover, Kershaw was handling McLaws's old division with skill and success. It had to be admitted, further, that McLaws's record as a divisional commander had not been one of uniform promptness and average success. To Bragg's telegram, therefore, Lee dispatched this reply: "I request that Gen. McLaws be not ordered to this army, but assigned to duty elsewhere." That settled the case. McLaws was assigned to command the District of Georgia, and there he remained till the final retreat.[10]

A second question of command that would not wait for more merciful days was that of a successor to Jeb Stuart. Hampton was the senior of the three major generals of cavalry and had more prestige. In combat he undeniably was the peer if not the superior of Fitz Lee. Fitz, on the other hand, had been closer to Stuart personally and had much of Jeb's joy of battle. The difficulty was that Hampton and Fitz Lee were secret rivals. At heart, Fitz Lee represented and Wade Hampton challenged the Virginia domination of the cavalry corps and, some would say, of the entire Army of Northern Virginia. Advancement of one man over the other might be demoralizing. Lee directed that the three divisions of cavalry "will constitute separate commands and will report directly to and receive orders from these headquarters."[11] This was a heavy burden to add to the overloaded shoulders of the commanding general. It was, moreover, a dangerous gamble in coordination, even though the chief of one division was the son and the chief of another division the nephew of the man to whom they were to report. The risk had to be taken. There appeared at the moment to be no sound alternative.

Not all the news of those mid-May days was as gloomy as the weather or as grim as that of promotion to fill dead men's saddles. Within less than a fortnight after Grant launched offensives in southwest Virginia, in the Shenandoah Valley, and up the James River, all three of these subordinate operations had been ended or frustrated. Sheridan's raid lost its momentum after the action at Yellow Tavern. His troopers hammered feebly at the Richmond defenses and then rode away down the James. This raid and all the subsidiary operations of the Federals were brought to naught without the dispatch from Lee's army of any troops besides the cavalry that Stuart had used against Sheridan.

Lee was doing everything possible to procure reinforcements from the other fronts, because he felt sure Grant's attack would be renewed as soon as the rain ceased. Promptly at 4:00 A.M. on May 18 the Federal advance began, again at the Bloody Angle. The Confederates scarcely could believe their eyes that a frontal assault on that line was to be made by the enemy. The moment the Unionists came within shrapnel range, orders were given to fire case shot and shell. Hotter grew the artillery fire; nearer raced the enemy; then orders to serve canister along with the shrapnel. The short-range artillery fire was past endurance now. The lines hesitated and broke. The attack was abandoned. General Long was justified in saying, "this attack illustrates the immense power of artillery well handled." General Meade, beyond the woods, was realistic: ". . . we found the enemy so strongly entrenched that even Grant thought it useless to knock our heads against a brick wall. . . ."[12]

Evidence accumulated that the enemy was shifting to his left again. An ominous and threatening move that might prove to be. Unless met as Grant's flank march of May 7 was, the side-slip might put the Federals between Lee's army and Richmond. Such scant intelligence as was available suggested that the Federals might be abandoning their positions opposite Ewell on the Confederate left. Ewell accordingly was ordered to demonstrate on the nineteenth to ascertain whether the Federals still were in his front.

Ewell did not relish the prospect of a frontal demonstration, and obtained leave for a flank operation as a substitute. In mid-afternoon on the nineteenth, as Ewell naively stated it, "I came on the enemy prepared to receive me." A spoiling attack by Dodson Ramseur held the initiative for a time, but presently Ramseur and then Gordon were pushed back to the ground from which the North Carolinian had started his assault. They might have been overwhelmed but for Wade Hampton's battery of horse artillery. When Ewell's confused plight was close to disaster, Hampton's guns helped to hold off the enemy until nightfall. Ewell then was able to withdraw. He had demonstrated that the Federals still occupied the right of their line, and he delayed for twenty-four hours the start of another turning movement, but he paid with 900 casualties.[13]

With this unhappy affair, the ghastly fighting around Spotsylvania Court House came to its conclusion. Grant now undertook a farther advance by his left flank. A race similar to that from the Wilderness to Spotsylvania was beginning. Insofar as this again was to challenge the command of the Army of Northern Virginia, the one encouraging circumstance was that Powell Hill had sufficiently recovered from his illness to resume direction of the Third Corps on May 20.

If the repair of the unparalleled losses had not occupied the full thought of Lee during every hour he could spare from the direction of operations, appraisal of individual performance during the campaign would have shown, as usual, much that was admirable and at least as much that was mediocre.

For Longstreet's brief part in the campaign there could be nothing but praise. Charges made subsequently that he was slow in his advance to the Wilderness rest on no sure foundation. Primarily the question is whether he was wise in allowing his men as many as five or six hours of sleep on the night of May 5–6. The probability is that the troops fought the better on the sixth because of that rest. Once Longstreet was on the field, his management of his men and his entire conduct were at his top pitch of performance. If his behavior in the Wilderness was an indication of what was to be expected of him, his recently developed penchant for strategy had not marred him as an executive officer under Lee.

Ewell's record in the Wilderness might have prompted Lee to make the same criticism he subsequently passed on that officer's action at Gettysburg—that he could not get Ewell to act with decision. The command of the Second Corps on the fifth of May was undistinguished. On the sixth, so far as Ewell was concerned, indecision cost the army the superb opportunity offered by the exposure of Grant's right. An attack on that flank, delivered while Longstreet was rolling up the left, might have involved a complete defeat of the Union forces. This was the first and only time during the campaign that both flanks were found to be vulnerable simultaneously. Ewell failed at that great hour because he could not make up his mind when his subordinates were divided in opinion.

Malady left Powell Hill unable, after the first day's fighting, to exercise field command. The one decision he made on May 6, when he already was sick, was unwise and might have been fatal. It was proper, of course, to provide for Heth's and Wilcox's men such sleep as they could get in the presence of the enemy, but on the night of May 5 his alternatives were not those of allowing the men to sleep or of forcing them to entrench. He could easily have left a strong picket in the woods and moved the divisions of Heth and Wilcox back to form a new line. Lee evidently thought Hill erred in doing nothing to protect the men from sudden onslaught. In fact, Heth believed that Lee never forgave him and Wilcox for failing to protect their front. Heth brought up the subject in a later conversation with the commanding general, explaining how he and Wilcox had sought to get Hill to act. Lee was unconvinced. "A division commander," said Lee, "should always have his division prepared to receive an attack." Heth answered, "That is certainly so, but he must also obey the positive orders of his superior." Lee said no more.[14]

The divisional command in the Wilderness had been competent but no more than that. Johnson had done well on May 5. Kershaw had fulfilled expectations and Field had exceeded them on the sixth. The other major generals had not shone. In particular, Jube Early's refusal to believe John Gordon's report concerning the Federal flank was not creditable. It was not even open-minded. Early was satisfied his intelligence reports accurately reflected the situation on the Union right and that Gordon was wholly wrong in thinking the flank unprotected. In that belief, Early would not verify either set of reports. He may have tried to browbeat both Gordon and Ewell. More than that, in later writings Early persisted in asserting that Burnside was in rear of the Federal right, though the contrary was demonstrable from the records.

Perhaps the strangest part of the whole affair was Early's statement that Gordon's attack before sunset on May 6 was suggested by Early himself. Not one word did Early say of Lee's visit to the left, which visit, according to Gordon, alone was responsible for the order to deliver the attack. Ewell, for his part, reported that "after examination" of the ground, he "ordered the attack." Lee's judgment was expressed in his prompt shuffling of commands to give Early's division temporarily to Gordon, who was promoted eight days later to the rank of major general. This was an honor due Gordon. He shared with Old Pete the laurels of the Battle of the Wilderness. In recognizing Gordon's service, Lee did not disparage or rebuke Early. On the contrary, to Jube was entrusted the Third Corps during the illness of Hill. It is difficult to escape the conclusion that Lee thought Ewell, not Early, to blame for failure to act promptly on Gordon's report of as glorious an opportunity as Jackson had found the previous year in that same treacherous Wilderness.[15]

At Spotsylvania the heroes of the first day were Dick Anderson, Jeb Stuart, Fitz Lee, and Tom Rosser. Had not the cavalry fought stubbornly and shrewdly on the eighth, the First Corps would not have been able to recover the Court House and the crossroads; but if Anderson had not started early, the cavalry would have been defeated before he could have reached the scene. The cooperation of Anderson was cool, well-balanced, and prompt, though deliberate. The modesty of his nature kept him from asserting anything more concerning his march to Spotsylvania than that he kept moving because he did not find a suitable place at which to rest. This may have been the literal fact, but behind it was the soldierly spirit which almost instinctively applies this sound principle: When on the march, the best insurance against the accidents of the road is an early start. An extra hour allowed at the beginning will compensate for an hour unexpectedly lost en route.

Anderson maintained after the eighth the excellent rating he won that day. As for Dick Ewell, it is not easy to appraise him fairly for the period from May 10 to the end of the operations around Spotsylvania. Most of the criticism of his handling of his corps spring from the existence and form of the Bloody Angle. Had the line been drawn farther southward, the difficulty of communications between the flanks would not have been comparably so serious a matter as the loss of a division was. The question as it concerns Ewell is primarily whether his part in drawing and then retaining the salient was such that he had to share the blame along with the commanding general and the chief engineer.

The principal witness is Captain W. W. Old, Johnson's aide. After describing Johnson having to take a post on Rodes's right in the darkness, without a guide, the night of the eighth, Old went on, "My recollection is that on the 9th of May the engineer officers, with General M. L. Smith at their head, went over the line and considered it safe with artillery." In that event, then, Ewell is not to be blamed for the choice or occupation of the salient. Failure to complete the support line must be charged against chief engineer Smith. For the withdrawal of artillery from the salient, the blame rests on the commanding general, not on Ewell. Lee was prompted by outpost statements of enemy shifts of ground. What the intelligence officers mistook for preliminaries of a withdrawal or a new flanking operation was, in reality, the evacuation of wounded and the dispatch of vehicles for supplies. Lee was conscious of his mistake and, as always, was instant in assuming the responsibility for it.[16]

The next question concerns the time required to bring back the guns. Johnson's request for their return was sent Ewell, endorsed by him, and transmitted to Long by courier. The courier had much trouble locating Long's headquarters, and approximately three hours and forty minutes elapsed before a most urgent request from Johnson passed through corps headquarters and reached the officer, distant two miles, who was to return the artillery. To say this is to make it virtually certain that the late return of the guns, which may have been responsible for the loss of the salient, was attributable to the slow transmission of orders. In one sense, then, a courier probably cost the Confederacy the greater part of the casualties of the Bloody Angle; in a sense more accurate, the disaster was due partly to a slow and awkward method of transmitting orders. Ewell's responsibility for this was that of any commanding officer who fails to correct what manifestly is wrong.

Ewell's mishandling of the demonstration against the Federal right on May 19 was not subject to the reservations and allowances that have to be made in any examination of his conduct at the Bloody Angle. As he procured the consent of the commanding general to attempt an elaborate turning operation, some of the blame must be put on Lee. For managing it as he did, without his own artillery, Ewell must he held accountable, but he can be charged with nothing more specific than errors of military judgment. Small though this action was, compared to the other battles of May, it must have been regarded at army headquarters as cumulative evidence that Ewell's mental powers were failing or else that the strains of the campaign were exhausting him dangerously. He was at the front daily, and he was as devoted as ever, but he was not the Ewell of 1862.

If it has to be concluded that Ewell was not equal to the demands of the campaign, it should be said that, next to Anderson, the most conspicuous figures of the operations around Spotsylvania were three of Ewell's lieutenants. In the restoration of the battle on the twelfth, wrote Colonel Charles S. Venable, "Gordon, Rodes and Ramseur were the heroes of this bloody day."[17]

Gordon, as the designated reserve, acted with sound judgment and the utmost speed. Instead of simply drawing a defensive line, Gordon threw forward offensively the first troops he met, formed a line as far to the front as he could, and immediately attacked. Whether or not he reasoned that he would find the enemy in confusion, he did so find them. Federal reports spoke of the counterattack as one before which the II Corps had to withdraw.

Rodes's conduct was flawless. In the crisis, which allowed no time for deliberate reflection, he displayed the soundest economy of force. His tactics were those of protecting his flank while the greater part of his division fought its way up the earthworks. The achievement was reassuring proof that Rodes had learned much since Gettysburg in the handling of a division.

Ramseur showed once again his remarkable leadership in offensive combat. Seldom had one brigade accomplished so much in fast, close fighting. After Ramseur was wounded, Colonel Bryan Grimes handled the brigade in a manner to mark him as ripe for promotion. Nat Harris was next in merited praise for his behavior on the twelfth. Harris was a well-educated Mississippi lawyer who had raised a company and served in every capacity with the 19th Mississippi from captain to colonel. He was steady and hard-hitting.

Encouraging as were these performances, it has to be repeated that too many of the apt pupils were being killed. The schoolmaster of the army, the commanding general, had to be ceaselessly active in seeking new students, giving instructions to those who survived, and correcting the exercises of others. He explained much of his method one day near Spotsylvania while urging Powell Hill not to be severe with a brigadier who had blundered: "I cannot do many things I could do with a trained army. The soldiers know their duties better than the general officers do, and they have fought magnificently. . . . You'll have to do what I do: When a man makes a mistake, I call him to my tent, talk to him, and use the authority of my position to make him do the right thing the next time."[18] It was a limping rule, but Lee could apply no other.

3. A NEW STRUGGLE FOR THE RAILROADS

The period of Lee's grapple with Grant in Spotsylvania County was one of exciting contest for Richmond and its railroad connections. Here Pierre Gustave Toutant Beauregard reappeared, Beauregard *Felix* as some now styled him. His consistent good luck justified the *nom de guerre*. At Shiloh, after Albert Sidney Johnston fell, Beauregard, as the officer next in rank, held the advantage at the end of the first day's fighting. He retreated at the close of the battle the second day, but escaped blame for the defeat. In the subsequent operations around Corinth he lost little reputation. After an interval of sickness he took his old command at Charleston, where in 1863 he conducted an excellent defense against an adversary who controlled the waterways.

It might have seemed, in April 1864, that Fortune was abandoning him. A worse assignment scarcely could have been devised than the one Mr. Davis gave him of protecting southern Virginia and North Carolina from an invasion the Federals openly were preparing to launch. Beauregard may have been a poseur, but he certainly was a patriot. On April 14, in answer to an inquiry whether his health permitted him to take the field, he gave assurance he was "ready to obey any order for the good of the service."[19] As it was not then certain where the blow would fall on the seaboard, he was ordered to Weldon, North Carolina. Beauregard named his new command the Department of North Carolina and Southern Virginia.

Within this large area and adjacent to it he found military jurisdiction confused. Chase Whiting commanded on Cape Fear. North of that, most of the best troops in North Carolina were being concentrated in front of New Bern, where Robert Hoke, under Bragg's direct orders, was hoping to duplicate his success at Plymouth. These operations were in the separate Department of North Carolina, the charge of George Pickett, whose headquarters were in Petersburg, Virginia. To what extent Pickett was responsible for affairs between the James and the Appomattox, Beauregard manifestly did not know. His own statement on assuming command was, in effect, that the northern boundary of his new department was "the

James and Appomattox Rivers." Beauregard's language left in doubt the control of the heavy fortifications at Drewry's Bluff on the James, the important "water gate" of Richmond. The Department of Richmond was about to be transferred from Arnold Elzey to Robert Ransom. Ransom would be independent unless he took the field in cooperation with Beauregard; in that event, as senior, Old Bory would exercise command. Beyond the Department of Richmond was the domain of General Lee, whose control of affairs, in an emergency, was recognized to the southern limit of Whiting's department. Beauregard's command, in a word, scarcely could have been more complicated or less clearly defined.

The military problem had unhappy qualities of a nature more dangerous. The War Department was anticipating Grant's offensive on the Rapidan, and an advance up the James or inward from the Peninsula or from the Southside. The objective might be Richmond, Petersburg, the railroad between the two, or the line that joined Petersburg and Weldon. Great superiority of force was known to be on the side of the Federals. The one hope of reducing these adverse odds lay in the probability that the Unionists would draw troops from the South Atlantic coast for the advance into Virginia or upper North Carolina. Were that to occur, proportionate reduction of force could be made by the Confederates. Beauregard himself already had admitted that two brigades could be withdrawn from Charleston for service in the assailed states, and the War Department would call as many additional troops as the inactivity in South Carolina, Georgia, and Florida justified. The alarming question was whether this withdrawal of men would be sufficient to hold Richmond, Petersburg, and the railroad leading from them into the Carolinas. Lee was insisting with the fullest of his polite firmness that the troops "borrowed" from the Army of Northern Virginia should be returned. Besides these, there would not be many for Beauregard.

After the universal manner of commanders who leave one post for another, Old Bory at Weldon did not think the situation at Charleston as dangerous as it had appeared from the Battery. He determined to summon the strongest of the brigades from South Carolina—Johnson Hagood's and Henry A. Wise's. With these troops and those already in his department, Beauregard believed he would be able to strike the rear of the Federal force expected to march inland. That was to be Beauregard's basic plan. Bragg was so advised. Developments came swiftly. Hoke matured his plans for the capture of New Bern. From Charleston Hagood started northward by train to reinforce Lee, and Wise prepared to follow. In Petersburg Pickett was directed to proceed to Hanover Junction and assume command there of two of his brigades.[20]

Before Pickett could pack his kit, he was notified on the morning of May 5 that the new invasion had begun. The James River below City Point was full of transports—fifty-nine by the latest count—with barges in tow. Monitors and gunboats formed an escort. Pickett read and reflected. Although ordered elsewhere, he could not leave or refuse to act. All the troops at his disposal were one regiment of infantry, the city battalion of Petersburg, the militia, and the Washington Artillery, twenty-one guns, that had been wintering near the city. His first step was to notify Beauregard, who telegraphed him to remain in command and assume direction of troops arriving from the south. As for himself, Beauregard said he was sick and unable to come to Petersburg that night. For counsel and aid from the War Department, Pickett waited in vain.

Pickett could only chafe and wonder and take such small precautions as his force permitted. At nightfall it was reported that the invaders were at Port Walthall, above the junction of the Appomattox with the James, which would indicate their immediate objective was not Petersburg but the railroad between that city and Richmond. During the night of May 5–6 new reports reached Pickett of landings by the enemy at Bermuda Hundred, on the James opposite City Point, but in the absence of directives from the War Department he could do little and plan little. It was a black night for George Pickett. The Federals, if well led, would advance the next morning. They could wreck railroads, seize Petersburg, threaten Richmond. It was a crisis as acute as any the war had brought.[21]

At the darkest hour of foreboding, about 3 o'clock on the morning of May 6, there rolled into Petersburg a train aboard which were 300 infantrymen of the 21st South Carolina, Hagood's brigade. Few as they were, they represented a troop movement which might save the city. In obedience to new orders from Richmond, Pickett had to permit the train to proceed toward the capital, but he could count on the employment of these South Carolinians against the enemy somewhere. Hope of saving Petersburg hung on the troops that would follow Hagood's van.

Tangible assistance of a second sort reached Pickett before many hours. On the morning of May 6, D. H. Hill arrived in Petersburg. He came in the odd capacity of volunteer aide to Beauregard; he had learned of the mounting danger and tendered his services. Beauregard sent him to render such help as he could. This raised hopes a little. Pickett could take counsel with an able combat officer and with the War Department, which now seemed conscious of the desperate need at Petersburg. Bragg authorized him to hold the remaining units of Hagood's brigade, as they arrived, and use them against the enemy who, Pickett thought, would that day seek to cut the Richmond and Petersburg Railroad. At the moment, Pickett could do nothing more than ask officials of the Petersburg and Weldon line when they expected more cars from the south.[22]

Before noon, as if in answer, another train arrived in Petersburg from Weldon. Its passengers were 300 more men of the 21st South Carolina, Hagood's brigade, under Colonel R. F. Graham. Pickett directed Graham to march on the enemy. A battery was sent with him. Gideon himself would have quailed in the face of such odds. Still, orders were orders. Graham and his South Carolinians must march against the host of the invader. At length, after 4:00 P.M., they reached Port Walthall Junction, a discouraged station on the main line to Richmond from which a branch ran to the lower Appomattox. A glance showed the rails intact. Another glance disclosed the presence of troops, but they wore gray, not blue, and carried the Stars and Bars. To Graham's surprise, they proved to be none other than men of his own regiment, the van that had reached Petersburg during the night. They had detrained at Drewry's Bluff and marched back to meet the anticipated attack at the Junction. The two contingents had not a moment to greet one another. The enemy was reported at hand and in great strength.

Graham cast about for cover. About 300 yards east of the railroad was a sunken road and a ravine. Into this position, with a prompt decision that would have done credit to a veteran, Colonel Graham moved his 600 men. They scarcely had time to load before the bluecoats began an advance upon them. Firing rapidly, they twice drove back the invaders. After the repulse of the second assault, the South Carolinians held their ground and anxiously watched the fields and woods. Soon there was movement. Down the road from Drewry's Bluff there marched a small brigade, 800 good Tennessee soldiers, under Brigadier General Bushrod R. Johnson.

This brigade might veritably have seemed to have dropped from heaven. Johnson and his troops had fought under Longstreet at Chickamauga and served with him in East Tennessee. Late in April they had moved from the Virginia-Tennessee border to Richmond to share in the city's defense. On the night of May 5–6, Johnson was directed to Drewry's Bluff, and about 11:00 A.M. on the sixth he was ordered to the Junction by the commander of the Department of Richmond, Robert Ransom. Said Ransom, "The railroad must not fall into the enemy's hands. Rapidity is necessary. Act at once. If the enemy be at Port Walthall Junction dislodge him." Johnson marched to the sound of the firing and assumed the command there.[23]

Nothing quite like this small concentration, in an hour of extreme danger, had occurred previously in Virginia. The vital railroad between Richmond and Petersburg, at its most vulnerable point, now was in the keeping

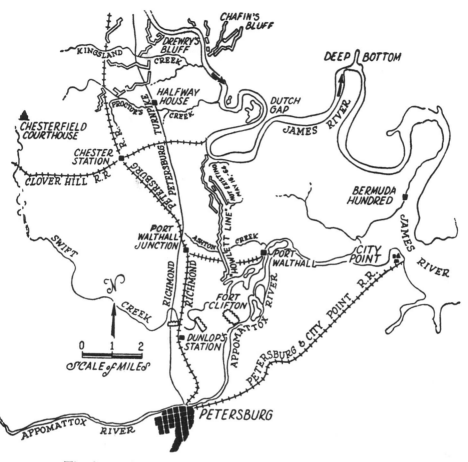

The district between Drewry's Bluff and Petersburg involved
in the operations of May 5–17, 1864.

of some 1,400 men. The astonishing fact was that none of these soldiers
ever had performed a day's field service in Virginia. All of them were
newly arrived from other states. To this narrow margin of men and time
was the Confederacy reduced.

In Petersburg Pickett had notice of yet another serious threat. Word
came that 3,000 Federal cavalry with eight guns were on the move westward from Suffolk. To Pickett it must have been apparent that these cavalrymen might be seeking to cut the railway between Petersburg and
Weldon, precisely as the force from the James was endeavoring to sever
connection between Petersburg and Richmond. No cavalry was available
to oppose these raiders. If the enemy reached the Petersburg and Weldon

tracks, then the Confederate troops hurrying northward would be detained. With no information concerning the trains then moving, it was impossible for Pickett to reach any conclusion except that the race between the cavalry and the carrier might be close.

The first heat was won by the railway. After dark on the sixth a train brought to Petersburg Johnson Hagood and the 25th South Carolina. Hagood, a forthright soldier, marched directly from the railroad track to reinforce his men at the Junction. Behind his train rolled another, aboard which was the 27th South Carolina. This regiment also started off on foot. Before daylight Hagood's command had reached the Junction and raised the defending force to 2,668 infantry under the informal command of D. H. Hill, who, at Pickett's request, had gone to the scene to advise Johnson and Hagood. With all his old spirit of combat, Harvey Hill examined the ground and suggested dispositions his less experienced juniors cheerfully made.

Although the situation was vastly better than it had been twenty-four hours previously, command remained in confusion. Pickett in Petersburg was aware of Beauregard's sickness and increasingly apprehensive of the danger to the Weldon Railroad. Beauregard himself had the President's directive to proceed to Petersburg, when his physical condition permitted, to direct operations. Old Bory replied that he hoped to leave on the seventh, but he remained at Weldon. There he did what he could to expedite the movement of Wise and Hoke. In obedience to orders, Hoke had abandoned the expedition against New Bern and was hurrying his troops to the railroad.[24]

On the afternoon of May 7 the fight was renewed at Port Walthall Junction. The bluecoats showed neither dash nor originality, and first a frontal and then a flank attack were repulsed. The one achievement of the Federals was the severance of the telegraph wires and the tearing up of more than 300 yards of railway track during the brief time they held it. The Confederates were well pleased. Johnson and Hagood both felt that the repulse was due in large degree to the leadership of Harvey Hill. The final contingent of Hagood's brigade now reached the battleground and raised the total strength of the Confederates to about 3,500. This encouraged the defenders of the railroad, but instructions from the rear began to hamper them. Pickett thought he saw indications of a direct assault on Petersburg, and he sent insistent demands for the troops at the Junction to fall back to the good defensible ground at Swift Creek. By midnight of May 7–8 they were on the road to the rear.

Early on the afternoon of the seventh telegraphic communication with Beauregard had failed. A scouting locomotive sent down the Weldon Railroad reached Stony Creek, nineteen miles south of Petersburg. There the crew found that the Federal cavalry raiders from Suffolk, under Brigadier General August V. Kautz, had burned the railway bridge. It could be rebuilt quickly but, during the critical days immediately ahead, Beauregard could not move troops by rail directly to Petersburg. The enemy had won the race. Richmond's main line of supply, up the coastal plain, was severed north and south of Petersburg. Before it could be reopened, anything might happen in the face of the adversary at Bermuda Hundred.[25]

That opponent now was known to have two corps, the X and the XVIII, opposite the Richmond and Petersburg Railroad, and was identified as Major General Benjamin F. Butler, "Beast" Butler to the more vehement Southerners. Some there were who doubted so important a command had been entrusted to a "political general" of limited experience. Whether Butler was competent or not, the Confederates still thought he had 40,000 men—the actual number was about 22,000, more than six times as many as stood in his front.

Surprisingly, the next day, May 8, Butler did not take advantage of his superior numbers. He remained idle within easy striking distance of the Richmond and Petersburg, though he readily could have destroyed several additional miles of track. By this blunder on his part the Confederate commanders gained a day in the northward movement of the troops still in the Carolinas. The expedient of the authorities was to hasten the advance of the soldiers as far north as the break in the line at Stony Creek. There the regiments were to be detrained and marched to cars being assembled north of the burned bridge. Behind this arrangement and all other aspects of the concentration to save Richmond from Butler's army, the driving power was that of Braxton Bragg. He was scouring the entire South Atlantic seaboard for reinforcements, and ceaselessly urging Whiting and Beauregard to speed traffic on the railway.

The day of inaction by Butler was not one of relief on the Petersburg and Weldon Railroad. South of Weldon, the Confederates could make the most of poor equipment and limited rolling stock; north of Weldon, bad conditions grew worse. Early on the eighth Kautz attacked the defenders of the railroad bridge across the Nottoway River, five miles south of Stony Creek, and set the structure on fire. In twenty minutes the ruined bridge fell into the river. This was a more serious blow than the destruction at Stony Creek, because the Nottoway bridge was 210 feet in length. Troops could march around the long break, but for an indefinite period all supplies sent up the Petersburg and Weldon had to be unloaded south of the Nottoway, hauled by wagon to Stony Creek, and reloaded there—an added burden on overworked quartermasters.[26]

Still another difficulty was presented now by Pickett. His military judgment began to show the effect of strain. Although he had ordered Bushrod Johnson to evacuate Port Walthall Junction and take position on Swift Creek, Pickett on the eighth directed D. H. Hill to march the troops back to the Junction. Fortunately there was good understanding between Hill and Johnson, who had become acquainted during the Chickamauga campaign. Doubtless with Hill's approval and possibly at his suggestion, Johnson retained the main body at Swift Creek and sent only detachments to reconnoiter at the Junction. He employed his men usefully on the eighth digging rifle pits south of the creek. The next day the enemy appeared in considerable strength north of Swift Creek.

The zone of action now widened. Because Butler at Bermuda Hundred was a continuous threat to the southern face of the Richmond defenses, General Ransom had sent from the city garrison the brigades of Archibald Gracie and Seth Barton to reinforce the garrison of Drewry's Bluff. Reports of a Federal advance were seen by Bragg as both a danger to Drewry's and as an opportunity for delivering a blow. About noon on May 9 he telegraphed Pickett an order to push forward all troops as fast as they arrived from the south in order that they might recover the lost position at Port Walthall Junction and reopen the line to Richmond. If Butler advanced on Drewry's Bluff, the Confederates in the Petersburg area must assail him in the rear from the Junction. At 1:10 there came new and imperative instructions from Bragg: The enemy was moving on Drewry's Bluff; all the troops at Pickett's disposal must move out immediately and attack the Federals in the rear; this admitted of no delay. Pickett acknowledged this at once, and then communicated with D. H. Hill and told that officer to advance.

Soon the troubled commander at Petersburg repented these orders. Bushrod Johnson was weak; indications were that the Federals were about to attack at Swift Creek. For the moment, in spite of Bragg's imperative, it seemed wise to hold the creek and ascertain, if possible, whether the enemy there was making a feint or a serious thrust. Johnson was so advised. About 3 o'clock Pickett received Johnson's acknowledgment of the earlier attack orders. In utmost haste Pickett replied that a countermand had been sent and Johnson was to hold the line of Swift Creek if it was true, as reported, that the Federals were advancing on that position.[27]

Johnson, it may be assumed, was as much bewildered by these changes of orders as Pickett was by Bragg's instructions and the enemy's threats. Johnson's conclusion was that Pickett wished him to make a reconnaissance in force. He undertook this with part of Hagood's brigade and sustained 137 casualties to establish the fact, almost obvious, that the enemy was strong and in his immediate front. At the other end of the exposed section of the Richmond and Petersburg Railroad, the advance on

Drewry's Bluff did not materialize. Ransom was easy in his mind and of the opinion that the enemy was seeking only to destroy the railroad. His chief concern was over the difficulty of communicating with Bushrod Johnson, whom he considered under his command.

The end of the day left Pickett the most harassed of all the commanders on the Southside. He expected to be attacked the next morning from Swift Creek, from City Point, from the south, and he could not understand why no effort seemed to be made to push northward the troops delayed by the burning of the bridges. On the night of May 8 he had sent trains to the northern end of the break in the Weldon Railroad. For eighteen hours and more they had waited, but no contingent had arrived. His appeal to Bragg was desperate: "Why do not the forces . . . below march up and drive off the enemy? This delay is criminal."[28]

4. BEAUREGARD PLANS AGAIN (STYLE OF 1861)

Before 9 o'clock on the morning of May 10—the day of the first attack on the Mule Shoe—Beauregard reached Petersburg. He brought his good luck with him. From the south, over repaired tracks and by marches around the destroyed bridges, more of the long-delayed reinforcements came that day. Hoke's brigade arrived. So did three regiments of Wise, and two of Matt Ransom. On the road, due that day, were Clingman's brigade and four regiments of brigades already on the ground. By 9:00 A.M. the accession of strength was 4,900 infantry—more men than previously had been collected, with haste and anguish, for the defense of the southern end of the Richmond and Petersburg Railroad.

These newly arrived troops Beauregard, with his old self-confidence, prepared to organize. Hoke was to have one division. Pickett was relieved of command of his military district in order to be assigned to the other division. To each division Beauregard attached an extemporized battalion of artillery. He could proceed, for the moment, without concern. After demonstrating during the morning, the Federals withdrew from Swift Creek by midday. Before the day was over Beauregard was able to telegraph Bragg, "Hope to be in position for offensive tomorrow night." For his part, Ransom at Drewry's Bluff was distinctly stronger. To the brigades of Barton and Gracie he was adding Eppa Hunton's brigade from the Richmond garrison. This would give Ransom almost 5,000 men, to which number a part of those arriving at Petersburg were to be added.[29]

During the night of May 10–11 the telegraph brought an alarming message from Secretary of War Seddon. "This city is in hot danger," it began.

Sheridan's powerful cavalry divisions had reached the Virginia Central, torn up the track, and headed in the direction of Richmond, which had been stripped of almost all its defending infantry in order to protect Drewry's Bluff and the Richmond and Petersburg Railroad. Beauregard's forces, including those at Drewry's Bluff, were the sole hope of the city. Divided, his troops could save neither Richmond nor Petersburg. Brought together, they might be able to deal successively with Sheridan or Butler. This was the military logic that shaped the secretary's telegram.

It was Beauregard's intention to form a junction with Ransom and assail Butler, and to that extent Seddon's anxious message conformed to Old Bory's strategic view; but he did not like to be tied to a specific plan. Although he started Hoke for Drewry's Bluff the next morning, May 11, he did not hasten the column's advance, and directed Hoke to make a forced reconnaissance toward the river to press Butler should he be preparing to withdraw. "Division of your forces is earnestly objected to," Seddon telegraphed. Back and forth went the telegrams, in one of which Beauregard asked to be relieved if his course was not approved. In the end, the reconnaissance toward Bermuda Hundred showed the Federals as numerous as ever. Hoke went on to join Ransom two miles below Drewry's Bluff.

Pickett did not participate in this movement. He had reported sick and on the eleventh kept to his quarters. In the belief that Pickett might not recover promptly, Beauregard telegraphed to Wilmington for Chase Whiting to command the forces at Petersburg. He was anxious to use in the field an officer for whose abilities he had high admiration. Pending Whiting's arrival, he himself would remain at Petersburg, although the harassed War Department manifestly wished him to proceed immediately to Drewry's Bluff. He lingered in part, no doubt, because of his taste for independence, for suspense, for dramatic appearance at the climax of a scene. His arrival must mean action.[30]

The day of the Bloody Angle and of Stuart's death, May 12, was one of taut anxiety along the James. Ransom and two brigades hurried across the river to man the Richmond earthworks against Sheridan. Hoke, left in command at Drewry's Bluff, faced a hesitant attack on his front. Hoke had gained vastly in self-confidence by his successful attack on Plymouth. He needed all his faith in himself. The enemy was across the Richmond-Petersburg turnpike; his orders were to hold the railroad as well as the defenses of Drewry's. Beauregard, receiving the reinforcements from the south he had been waiting for, announced that he would join Hoke the next day.

On the morning of the thirteenth the situation on all the Virginia fronts was gloomy. The defenders of the Bloody Angle had limped back to their line across its base. In the Shenandoah Valley, Sigel was moving southward in force superior to any the Confederates could hope to concentrate against him. Crook and Averell were on a raid in southwestern counties and, after a bloody little fight at Cloyd's Mountain, were destroying bridges and trackage on the Tennessee Railroad. That railway had to be added to the four already cut—the Richmond and Petersburg, the Weldon, the Virginia Central, and the R.F. & P. Kautz's troopers were even then seeking to cut the last two railways within Confederate lines, the Richmond and Danville, and the Southside.

Black as was this situation, a change was discernible on May 13 in two respects: First, Sheridan had ridden down the James and gave no evidence of resuming his attack. Second, the Confederates no longer were thinking in terms of defense. An offensive plan had taken shape in Bragg's mind. It was that Hoke should engage the Federals in his front while Beauregard moved up swiftly from Petersburg to form a junction. Beauregard was ordered to march at once. The day passed with no reply, as Kautz's raiders had cut the telegraph line. Waiting in vain for Old Bory, Hoke fought all day against an enemy who captured part of the outer line of the Drewry's Bluff defenses. Luckily, the Federals could not exert equal pressure at all points; fortunately, they undertook no twilight offensive.[31]

The time for the appearance of the principal actor in the drama had arrived. At 3:00 A.M. on May 14, in the midst of a hard rain, General Beauregard rode up to the Drewry mansion near the bluff of that name. As always in such a setting, Old Bory was cap-a-pie the soldier, all energy, altogether for action. Precisely as in the days of glory and unchallenged primacy at Manassas in 1861, he indulged himself in the fashioning of grand strategy. The pattern of three years previously was unchanged. Nothing, apparently, had widened his sense of the militarily practical, or modified his early theories of logistics. His own account was characteristic: If Mr. Davis would send him 10,000 men that day from the Richmond defenses and from Lee's army, "I w'd attack Butler's 30,000 men [and] capture or destroy them by 12 h. on the 15th. I would then move to attack Grant on his left flank & rear, while Lee attacked him in front, & I felt sure of defeating Grant & probably open the way to Washington where we might dictate *Peace!!*"

Unwilling to awaken the President at so early an hour to present this grand design, Bragg ordered his horse and rode at once to Drewry's to hear what Beauregard had to say in support of his plan. He discovered that Beauregard intended the Army of Northern Virginia to fall back to the Richmond defenses while heavy detachments from that army were sent to support the attack on the Southside. "Bragg, circumstances have thrown the fate of the Confederacy in your hands and mine, let us play our parts boldly and fearlessly!" said Old Bory. "Issue those orders and I'll carry them out to the best of my ability. I'll guarantee success!" This did not appeal to Bragg. He merely said he would lay the facts before the President. His report must have been unsparing; in a memorandum for the record, he completely riddled Beauregard's entire scheme. In a short time Davis himself came to the Bluff to listen to Beauregard. Like Bragg, the President could see nothing practical in the proposal. All he promised was that he would send back Ransom and all the troops that could be spared from the Richmond garrison.[32]

Doubtless both Davis and his military adviser were steeled by the emergency to the unceremonious rejection of a plan that was basically and irredeemably wrong in its logistics and its psychology. The crisis could not wait on theory or theatricals. A desperate moment in the life of the Confederacy had been reached. The previous night Kautz had torn up part of the track of the Richmond and Danville. On the fourteenth some of his troopers struck the Southside line and thereby severed the last railroad that connected Richmond and Petersburg with any large section of the Confederacy. Even if Butler were held, Sheridan with his powerful cavalry still lingered at Haxall's Landing below Malvern Hill. The alternative to Beauregard's grandiose scheme was clear: Butler must be destroyed and a part of the troops confronting him sent back to the north side of the James to guard against Sheridan assailing the capital.

In contrast to the excited men in Richmond, Beauregard began the duties of the fifteenth in a composed and leisured state of mind. It would be best, as he saw it, to allow Whiting the whole of the day and the greater part of the sixteenth to bring up the troops from Petersburg to join him. May 17 would be a suitable day for the battle. This caused great alarm in Richmond. Bragg telegraphed, "It is hoped you may receive him [Whiting] in time to attack tomorrow. Time is all-important to us. . . ." Beauregard now altered his plan. It would be better, he reasoned, to leave Whiting south of Butler. Then Whiting could attack the Federals in the rear while Beauregard moved against them near Drewry's Bluff. He later pictured the anticipated result: "Butler, thus environed by three walls of fire, with the defeated troops, could have no resource against substantial capture or destruction, except in an attempt at partial and hazardous escape westward, away from his base, trains, or supplies."

For the operation Beauregard reorganized his divisions into three commands, under Ransom, Hoke, and Alfred Colquitt, which varied in strength from two to four brigades that never had fought together. Colquitt was an old acquaintance, but Hoke and Ransom had not been known to the army commander until this campaign. He might have noted that, along with some able men like Hoke and Ransom, his subordinates included an undue number of brigadiers who had been tried in the Army of Northern Virginia and found wanting. One potential liability, of which he had no forewarning, was in the brain of Chase Whiting. Having solicited field command, now that he had it Whiting seemed appalled by its responsibilities. He was apprehensive of attack, and he believed that Petersburg was the actual Federal objective. He worked ceaselessly, under immense strain, day and night, to protect the city. He was able to lean heavily on D. H. Hill, who had remained to counsel Pickett's successor.[33]

At Drewry's Bluff the plan simply was to take the offensive on the Confederate left and cut off Butler's army from its base at Bermuda Hundred. While Ransom was directing this attack, Hoke was to demonstrate on the Confederate right and hold the Federals there so they could not send reinforcements to the assailed Federal right. When the Union right was broken, Hoke was to advance. Colquitt's two brigades would constitute the reserve. Whiting was to advance at daylight on the sixteenth to Port Walthall Junction and wait there until he heard the sound of the engagement. Then he was to fall on the flank or rear of the Federals.

At 4:45 A.M. on May 16, Ransom began the advance of his four brigades, only one of which was under a general officer. Fog delayed and confused, but in about an hour Ransom's men carried the first line of Federal fortifications. Five stands of colors, a brigadier general, and about 400 other prisoners fell into their hands. It was an encouraging start but it had been costly. Visibility was at zero. When Ransom heard that Hoke's left was being driven back, he started his troops ahead again. Under brigade officers who did not know how to handle them, they drifted to a halt in confusion. Hagood's brigade captured five guns and overran a section of the outer lines, but it and Hoke's other brigades, in the face of a hot fire, were soon stalemated as well.

At 8 o'clock, while the Confederate left was idle and only Hagood and Bushrod Johnson were in close action, the sound of firing was heard from the south, the direction of Whiting's expected advance. The noise continued for a time and then died away. Beauregard took this to mean that Whiting was advancing against little or no opposition. In expectation of his arrival, Beauregard decided not to order Ransom to resume the offensive on the left. In fact, the movement to cut off Butler from his base had yielded little ground, a few guns, and some hundreds of prisoners and then had come to a halt in the face of stiff resistance. Thus it developed that Whiting's cooperative movement, which had been a minor part of the plan, grew in importance with the passage of the hours until it became the contingency on which success was believed to hang.

The noon hour passed and brought no change of any importance, no news of Whiting's arrival. At 1:45, while President Davis and General Beauregard were standing on the works, the long-awaited sound of renewed firing was heard from the direction of Whiting's advance. "Ah, at last!" said Davis with a smile. They waited till hopeful seconds lengthened to doubting minutes. Not another sound came from the south or southwest. Beauregard concluded that Confederate cavalry, not Whiting's infantry, was responsible for the firing. There came heavy rain, and darkness approached. "It was deemed imprudent to attack," said Beauregard. He had to content himself with his 5 captured colors, his 5 guns, and his 1,388 prisoners as compensation for 2,506 casualties.[34]

The next morning brought to Beauregard *Felix* a measure of his old good luck. He discovered that Butler had retreated to the Bermuda Hundred lines where, it soon developed, the Federal commander was "corked" as if in a bottle. To Beauregard came also, that May 17, Whiting's two brigades from Petersburg. They arrived with ranks full and men in condition for battle, but they were under the informal command of Harvey Hill, not of Chase Whiting.

Behind the change of commanders was a strange, strange story. On the morning of the sixteenth, in obedience to orders, Wise's and Martin's brigades had assembled for the advance from Petersburg. Whiting rode with them, and had D. H. Hill at his side as counselor. When enemy pickets were flushed near Port Walthall Junction, Whiting asked Hill to take charge of the advance while he watched the right. With all his old combativeness, Hill maneuvered Wise's troops and soon had the enemy in rapid withdrawal. A few minutes later, to his amazement, he found the Confederates in a withdrawal. To his inquiry, Whiting said that he had received no message from Beauregard, that the enemy was threatening him, that the sound of firing from Drewry's Bluff was not heavy. He had been instructed to advance when the firing was heavy. This was not. Beauregard might be ending his fight. Petersburg might be in danger.

The two brigades fell back to Swift Creek in a wretched tangle of wagons and troops, artillery and ambulances. "Feeling that I could accomplish nothing more," said a disgusted Harvey Hill, "I retired to Dunlop's house. . . ." At 7:15 P.M., in reply to a message from Beauregard, Whiting said tersely, "Too late for action on my part." Subsequently he added, "My personal presence was absolutely required in Petersburg, and . . . I hoped to be able to join the general readily on the 17th." The next day, for the march to Drewry's Bluff, Whiting relinquished command to Hill after Wise and Martin expressed "dissatisfaction . . . with my movements and orders of the preceding day."

The reason, in the judgment of the army, was that Whiting was drunk. This was the conclusion of Henry A. Wise, who was near him several times during the day. Harvey Hill, on the other hand, reported that he "saw no evidence of alleged intoxication." In his own behalf, Whiting certified on his honor that he drank nothing except water and coffee. Nobody seems to have reasoned that Whiting may have given the full explanation when he said that he had not rested from the time of his arrival in Petersburg on the thirteenth. He may have been the type, wholly familiar in war, that loses through prolonged loss of sleep all grip on the mental faculties.[35]

Whiting immediately asked to be relieved and, when Harvey Hill temporarily was assigned to command his scratch division, prepared to resume his station at Wilmington. Beauregard in his report said only that Whiting's "premature halt" before obstacles that should not have deterred the column from Petersburg was one of the reasons the "more glorious results" of the victory were lost. For Whiting's failure none of the responsible leaders blamed Beauregard, but some felt that in an effort to execute a spectacular coup, he had neglected the sure way to success, which they held to be that of bringing Whiting to Drewry's Bluff early so that the united superior forces could fall on Butler and destroy the Union army. For his part, Old Bory's self-confidence did not appear to be shaken in the slightest. He was convinced now, as always, of his rightness as a tactician and as a strategist. In a swiftly changing crisis, he already had new plans for his own army and for Lee's which now was moving from the battleground of Spotsylvania.[36]

CHAPTER 32

New Fronts, New Battles

1. THE END OF THE OLD ORGANIZATION

On the bloody front where Lee's lieutenants had faced Grant for almost a fortnight it was apparent by the morning of May 21 that the Federals had undertaken another side-slip. Again they were trying to get between Richmond and the Army of Northern Virginia. The next line of defense appeared to be the North Anna River, twenty-three miles north of Richmond. On the deep bank of that river the Southerners would have good prospect of repulsing any direct attack, and from the North Anna, if the enemy sought to assail Richmond from the northeast, the Southern divisions could be shifted readily to the Pamunkey.

The departure from Spotsylvania was executed cleanly, with no loss and little straggling. The corps commanders were entitled to a credit for this, because two of them scarcely were able to discharge their duties. Powell Hill probably had reported for duty too soon after his illness. Ewell managed to ride with his men, though his collapse was apprehended by Lee. Only Anderson, the least experienced of the three, remained in good physical condition.

On the North Anna the Confederates had a few hours of rest and then, on May 23, repelled an attack on their left. The task of beating off the Federals fell on Hill's men and principally on Wilcox's division, which sustained 642 casualties. Lee had been assailed by an intestinal ailment that had the usual effect of sharpening his temper and shaking his control of it. Never, said his staff, was he so difficult as during a sickness. When he rode to the front of the corps and saw what had happened, he gave Powell Hill what was, perhaps, the stiffest rebuke ever administered to any of his general officers during the war. "Why," Lee demanded, "did you not do as Jackson would have done—thrown your whole force upon those people and driven them back?" Hill had no answer. If the question had been put by Jackson, there might have been a scene. Against Lee's judgment, no matter how unfavorable, Hill never protested.[1]

For the disappointment of this affair there were two compensations. The first was the arrival of the only reinforcements the army had received, except for Robert D. Johnston's brigade, since the opening of the campaign. Pickett's division returned and found a place temporarily with the Third Corps. Hoke's old brigade was reassigned to Early's division. John C. Breckinridge had defeated Sigel and moved to Lee from the Shenandoah Valley with two brigades. For the time being, these troops were placed directly under Lee's orders. In the aggregate, the three commands counted about 8,000 muskets. The second, if momentary, compensation was a succession of Federal maneuvers that left one wing of Grant's army more vulnerable to assault than at any time since the opening of the campaign. But Lee was too sick to direct the attack. Had Jackson been alive or Longstreet unwounded, either of them could have handled the operation. As it was, Lee did not even attempt to deputize one of his corps commanders to make the effort. All he could do was to say from his cot, "We must strike them a blow—we must never let them pass us again—we must strike them a blow."[2]

On May 27 the Union army was once more marching by its left flank in the hope of getting between Lee and Richmond. This time it was manifest that the shift would bring the Federals embarrassingly close to the defenses of the Confederate capital. If it was possible, the enemy must be defeated before warfare became stationary. The alternative Lee soon was to state in grim words to Jubal Early: "We must destroy this army of Grant's before he gets to James River. If he gets there it will become a siege, and then it will be a mere question of time."[3]

To catch a numerically superior adversary on the march or in some situation favorable to an attack, every general officer had to be ready to strike instantly. This, unhappily, was more than the stricken command could hope to be. By the worst of fortune, while Lee himself was ill, Ewell was stricken with an acute intestinal malady. On the twenty-seventh, the day the new Federal movement began, he was so ill that he had to ask Early to handle the corps. This was not unexpected at army headquarters. For months Lee had been uneasy about Ewell, who recklessly slept on the ground and exerted himself ceaselessly. In his place Early could serve, but it was dangerous business to be changing officers ceaselessly while critical operations were in progress! Ewell became so prostrated that the Second Corps had to be put formally under Early's command. Ewell was given indefinite leave that he might have the benefit of rest and medical treatment. Characteristically, he declined to avail himself of this leave. He was resolved to remain with his men and, to the limit of his strength, to discharge his duties.[4]

By May 29, with superlative care, in spite of his sickness, Lee disposed the three corps where they covered all the approaches to Richmond from the Pamunkey, which Grant was expected to cross. A forced reconnaissance that day by the cavalry, in which the green 4th and 5th South Carolina valiantly experienced their baptism of fire, revealed that Grant was crossing his infantry as well as his cavalry. Indications were, in addition, that Butler was releasing troops from his "bottle" at Bermuda Hundred and reinforcing the Army of the Potomac. The first suggestion of this transfer reached Lee's headquarters in a Northern newspaper. Butler's two corps, it was said in a Washington dispatch, would be called to service with Grant because "they are not strong enough to take Richmond, and too strong to be kept idle." Beauregard was best placed to observe any withdrawal from his front. He believed the enemy at Bermuda Hundred might have sent 4,000 troops to Grant, but he did not think the situation justified any diminution of his own command.

This opinion was contrary to Beauregard's most recent exercise in theoretical strategy. He had proposed that if the Army of Northern Virginia would retire to the Chickahominy, he would detach 15,000 men, join Breckinridge, fall on Grant's flank, and, while Lee attacked in front, destroy the Army of the Potomac. Then Butler could be overwhelmed. Until that time, he could not release more than 5,000 men to reinforce Lee's army. Lee reasoned that if the Army of Northern Virginia could not resist Grant, the forces under Beauregard and the Richmond garrison could not save the city. Cooperation, Lee thought, was demanded immediately. On the evening of May 29, Beauregard came to field headquarters to review the situation. As always graciously courteous, he maintained that his force could not be reduced further without creating more danger for Richmond than was averted. When he left, it was manifest at headquarters that the Army of Northern Virginia would have to fight without assistance from the south side of the James.[5]

On the thirtieth the crisis was heightened. All the indications were that Grant once more was extending his left. The Army of Northern Virginia had not received as reinforcements more than half as many soldiers as it had lost. Lengthening of line, therefore, meant that unless Beauregard sent aid, parts of the Confederate line would be so stripped that they could not be held safely. The one hope was to strike the enemy hard enough to halt him. An opening seemed to be offered the Second Corps near Bethesda Church. Early was given discretion to develop the opportunity. He did so, head on, without proper reconnaissance or coordination with the First Corps. The result was a bloody repulse. After Early's failure, it was safe to assume that Grant would extend his left as far as fitted his plan. Because of the roads meeting at Cold Harbor, that familiar village seemed a logical objective. In addition, there was reason to believe that a large part of Butler's troops would reach Grant's left. The Confederate front might be broken where the momentum of the attack might carry the Federals into the streets of Richmond.

Representations of Beauregard still were such that the War Department hesitated to issue an order for the detachment of part of his men to assist the Army of Northern Virginia. Lee made a direct appeal to Beauregard and was refused, leaving him no recourse except the President. At 7:30 P.M., May 30, he telegraphed Davis that "this delay" in sending him troops from Beauregard's command "will be disaster.... Hoke's division, at least, should be with me by light tomorrow." Never had such a message as that come to the President from Lee. Often the general had said that this evil *might* occur, or that he feared possible calamity from such and such a mistake. Here the language contained no reservation, no proviso. Davis lost no time. He and Bragg agreed that Hoke and his 7,000 men must be sent immediately to Lee. The order to Beauregard was peremptory: "By direction of the President," Bragg began, "you will send Hoke's division, which you reported ready, immediately...."[6]

This was the pistol shot that started Hoke's lean men in a race to overtake the troops from Butler that had been sent to Grant. By 11:30 A.M. of the twenty-ninth, four Federal divisions—nearly 16,000 infantry, with sixteen field guns—were embarked at Bermuda Hundred. Twenty-four hours later, May 30, they began to disembark at White House, sixteen miles by road from Cold Harbor. Early the next morning, May 31, Hoke received his first train and started Clingman's brigade at 5:15. By rail and road, Hoke had eighteen miles to go. The odds were against him.

To hold the crossroads of Cold Harbor until Hoke's arrival, the cavalry of Fitz Lee had been posted. Clingman with Hoke's van came, but so did the Federals and in strength sufficient to drive him and Fitz Lee's troopers from the crossroads. Lee, the senior, was not willing to leave the village to the enemy. He decided to anticipate the Federals, if he could, and roll up their flank. This decision showed characteristically his innate daring. Now that even 7,000 muskets were to be added to his force, Lee shifted at once from defense to offense. Anderson was to side-slip to the right until he touched the left of Hoke, whose division would be in position before daylight. Anderson attacked early on the morning of June 1. In the first encounter, Kershaw's old brigade was led by the inexperienced colonel of the 20th South Carolina, Lawrence M. Keitt. He was a man of high political and social distinction in his state but had seen little action. Now, in his first battle, he rode recklessly forward. His regiment broke. In an effort to rally it Keitt fell mortally wounded. The panic spread to other units of the brigade. Anderson's advance came quickly to a halt. Hoke's men did virtually nothing in what had been expected to be a general attack.[7]

After their repulse that morning, June 1, the Confederates began to put between them and the enemy every tin cup of dirt that could be scraped from the loamy soil. It was well that they sensed danger. After protracted delays—more than twenty-four hours at White House—and misdirections, the Federal troops from Bermuda Hundred at last reached Cold Harbor, and at 4:00 P.M. launched a furious attack in company with the VI Corps. They pushed the assault until they separated Anderson's right and Hoke's left; but the labor of the midday hours had piled the dirt high enough to stop the Federals before they penetrated far. Narrowly, Lee's lieutenants had saved their flank and, probably, their capital.[8]

On the second of June the center of action shifted toward Cold Harbor. Confederate troops were moved there and placed still farther to the right until, at nightfall, Wilcox's division was within half a mile of the Chickahominy. The chief distresses of an anxious day were the wounding of James H. Lane and the death of George Doles, one of the best brigadiers of Rodes's division, indeed, of the Second Corps. In these operations, with exhausting efforts and dark risks, the movements of the enemy were completely anticipated.

General Grant lost patience. He decided to lower his head, as it were, to put his full weight behind his blows, and to beat down his adversary. At dawn on the morning of June 3 he attacked along the whole line in the blind, brutal action known as Second Cold Harbor. At one point he temporarily made lodgment in Confederate lines held by some of Breckinridge's troops, but on the greater part of the front his assaults were beaten off so easily that the battle was over before some of the Confederates knew that an effort had been made to break the line. Eight minutes sufficed to show the men of three Union corps that farther advance would be suicide. At the price of not more than 1,500 casualties, the Army of Northern Virginia killed or wounded 7,000 of Grant's men. The only injury in the Confederate high command was the wounding of E. M. Law.[9]

So dispirited was the Army of the Potomac by this defeat that Grant had to give the men rest while he decided on his next step. During this pause in the fighting, time was found for another reorganization of the depleted Army of Northern Virginia. It was a necessary, an imperative reorganization. New commanders had to be provided immediately for many units. Otherwise the casualties in the high command during the bloody month of May would cost the army both discipline and leadership. The humiliating repulse of Kershaw's brigade on June 1 had shown what might be apprehended even of veteran troops if they lacked a competent brigadier.

In facing with reduced personnel the perennial task of finding qualified leaders, the commanding general fortunately had the benefit of a new act of Congress. This authorized the appointment of brigadier generals, major generals, and lieutenant generals to hold rank "for such time as the temporary exigency may require," then to revert to their regular status. The new law permitted appointments to fill vacancies that otherwise would last as long as the illness or other physical incapacity of a general officer continued.[10]

As authorized by this act, it seemed proper that Dick Anderson should be given the temporary rank of lieutenant general while commanding the First Corps during the absence of Longstreet, who now was recovering, though slowly. Anderson had won advancement by his famous march to Spotsylvania. He had fought prudently and intelligently there. Although Lee had directed him much more closely than he would have thought of doing in the case of the senior corps officers, Anderson had shown no lack of stalwart qualities for his new post. If he was not brilliant he was dependable. At Cold Harbor, June 1, his handling of the advance and subsequent defense had not been good, but the fault may have been Hoke's.

Another lieutenant general was to be named because it was manifest that Ewell could not resume safely his duties as commander of the Second Corps while the army was in a furious field campaign. He must be given an easier post until the battles of the summer were past. This did not suit Ewell and it acutely displeased Mrs. Ewell. In the end, reluctantly, Old Bald Head accepted direction of the Department of Richmond. If he had not shown uniformly, after his return to the army at the end of May 1863, the dash and decision that had marked him under Jackson, the reason was simply that he was never the same man in body or mind after the loss of his leg at Groveton. Transfer of Ewell dictated, on May 31, the promotion of Early to lieutenant general on the same temporary footing with Dick Anderson.[11]

These two promotions left vacancies in Early's and in Anderson's divisions. For these positions the decision of Lee was prompt and probably was not doubtful. Anderson's senior brigadier, William Mahone, was entirely qualified for promotion, though his opportunities in the field had been fewer than might have been assumed for a man who had been a brigadier from November 16, 1861. Early's successor was Dodson Ramseur. This might have been a surprise, because Ramseur had been a brigadier of Rodes and not of Early, but John Pegram's wounds and Gordon's promotion had left in Early's division no officer then qualified for promotion. Ramseur had won the honor by a career of consistently fine, hard fighting.

Besides these two appointments to temporary rank as major generals, Joseph B. Kershaw's command of McLaws's division was made permanent. This action strengthened the First Corps and rewarded the admirable service of one of the ablest of the South Carolina general officers. All three of these appointments were fortunate. Several times Lee had lamented that his inability to get rid of a mediocre senior had prevented the advancement of a much abler junior. In these instances, except as McLaws unhappily was involved, the three deserved promotion. None of them might prove a Jackson or a Longstreet, but none of them was apt to fail.

Permanent promotion as brigadier general went to Colonel Bryan Grimes, who was assigned to the command of the dead Junius Daniel's North Carolina troops. This advancement came because Grimes was in line of promotion, was qualified, and had been much distinguished at the Bloody Angle. The able, diligent, always courageous Colonel James Conner at last had sufficiently recovered from an old wound to take the field, and he was made brigadier general and assigned temporarily the brigade of the wounded Samuel McGowan. To Rufus Barringer, a cavalry colonel of excellent record, went the insignia of brigadier general and the fine regiments of James B. Gordon, killed at Yellow Tavern. Of temporary brigadiers, five were named: Colonel William R. Cox of the 2nd North Carolina to take Ramseur's brigade; Colonel Thomas F. Toon of the 20th North Carolina to handle the men of the injured Robert Johnston; Lieutenant Colonel William G. Lewis of the 43rd North Carolina to direct John Pegram's brigade while that officer was wounded; Colonel Zebulon York of the 14th Louisiana to lead the combined Louisiana brigades until Harry Hays recovered; and Lieutenant Colonel R. D. Lilley of the 25th Virginia to command Early's old brigade. All these were solid men of character but, with the exception of Cox, they scarcely could be termed conspicuous. They were simply the best that could be chosen quickly and without manifest unfitness from an officers' corps that had no superfluity of talent after the loss of so many able officers.

How much the army command had suffered in the Wilderness and at Spotsylvania no statistician set forth at the time. The list was longer than in any previous campaign and nothing short of terrifying. Of the fifty-eight general officers present from May 4 through June 3, 1864, eight were killed, twelve wounded, and two captured. The killed were: First Corps, Micah Jenkins; Second Corps, Junius Daniel, George Doles, John M. Jones, and Leroy A. Stafford; Third Corps, Abner Perrin; Cavalry Corps, Jeb Stuart and James B. Gordon. The following sustained wounds severe enough to incapacitate them for command, temporarily or permanently: First Corps, James Longstreet, E. M. Law, and Henry L. Benning; Second Corps, Harry Hays, Robert D. Johnston, John Pegram, and James A. Walker; Third Corps, John R. Cooke, James H. Lane, Samuel McGowan, Edward L. Perry, and Henry H. Walker. The captured generals were Edward Johnson and George H. Steuart. By rank the casualties ran in this manner: killed, one major general and seven brigadiers; wounded, one lieutenant general and eleven brigadier generals; captured, one major general and one brigadier.

In addition, the commanding general had been almost incapacitated by diarrhea for a week; one corps commander, Hill, had been too sick for almost a fortnight to direct his troops; and the other corps chief, Ewell, had been failing so steadily in vigor that he had to be relieved of duty. In the First and Second Corps, two experienced divisional leaders, R. H. Anderson and Early, had been separated from their commands and corps, for a part of the campaign, in order to direct other corps.

These changes were more far-reaching than anyone seems to have realized at the time. Faith in the army itself was so unshakable that the President, the War Department, and General Lee apparently believed the normal process of training would be reversed: Instead of the generals instructing the troops, the veterans would school their new commanders. Within the limits of the tactics of everyday combat, this might prove true, but it could not be true of discipline and morale in a time of continuing discouragement and waning hope. A new development, a stern challenge, was to be expected daily. Liaison with Beauregard and his newly arrived troops would be imperative. At a time when experience would be required to effect swift cooperation, two of the corps of Lee's army would be in the charge of men who had exercised that command less than a month. Of the nine divisions, two in the First Corps were under promising men, Kershaw and Field, though they scarcely could be regarded as fully seasoned at their higher rank. Two of the divisional leaders of the Second Corps were entirely new to that duty, Gordon and Ramseur. One of the three divisional chiefs of the Third Corps, Mahone, had never acted in that capacity for any length of time before the eighth of May. The only major generals left with the army who had led divisions as recently as Gettysburg were Pickett, who now was returning from detached service, Rodes, who had done admirably in Spotsylvania County, and Harry Heth, who carried some new odium for the events of May 6. None of these older major generals had directed as many as four brigades in any hard action before Chancellorsville.

The battles of a single month had put 37 per cent of the general officers of the Army of Northern Virginia *hors de combat*. Except as Lee himself embodied it, the old organization was gone!

2. THREE MORE FEDERAL DIVERSIONS

On other fronts in Virginia, the week after Cold Harbor brought alarms and advances. The first of these was in the Shenandoah Valley. There Franz Sigel had been relieved of command after he was defeated at New Market, May 15, by Breckinridge. The force under Breckinridge had consisted of John Echols's and Gabriel Wharton's brigades, to which in the emergency the small cadet corps of the Virginia Military Institute was added. When battle was joined near New Market, the cadets had fought with a disciplined courage and a consistent élan that added to the prestige of the remarkable school without which the Army of Northern Virginia could not have had competent regimental command in the first year of the war. Seldom did a small victory have so large an effect. Had Sigel not been driven back, the Valley of Virginia might have been occupied by the Federals before the wheat crop was harvested. Hunger would have come sooner. The prospect of losing the western end of the Virginia Central Railroad might have compelled Lee to send part of his army to the Valley while pressure at Spotsylvania was heaviest. Short as was the time saved by the Battle of New Market, it was invaluable.[12]

Now, in the first week of June, Sigel's successor, David Hunter, was moving rapidly up the Shenandoah. At Piedmont he attacked and defeated a scratch force of about 5,000 under Grumble Jones. About 1,000 Confederate prisoners were taken. In a tragic end to a tragic life, Jones himself was killed. The next day, June 6, Hunter occupied Staunton. He was joined there by George Crook, returning from his raid on the Virginia and Tennessee Railroad. The combined forces of Hunter and Crook were in position to do vast military mischief. To delay them, Breckinridge and his 2,100 men were started from Cold Harbor for Lynchburg, whence they could move to the upper Valley or dispute a crossing of the Blue Ridge.[13]

Before a decision could be reached for any larger action against Hunter, it was discovered that Sheridan had started on another raid. Reporting this movement, Wade Hampton reasoned that Sheridan would strike for Gordonsville and Charlottesville, to effect a junction with Hunter. On June 8, Hampton was ordered to proceed after the enemy with his own and Fitz Lee's division. This order was an approach to a reorganization. After Stuart's death, Lee had each cavalry division report directly to him—almost certainly to avoid a choice between Hampton and Fitz Lee as successor to the dead commander of the cavalry corps. Now that the divisions of these rivals had to operate together at a distance from Richmond, there was no safe alternative to applying the army regulation which entrusted command to the senior. This gave Hampton the greatest opportunity that had come to him during the war.[14]

While Hampton was en route on that ninth of June, a critical alarm reached army headquarters from Petersburg, through Bragg's office. A third diversion had begun—a surprise attack was being delivered on that city. Beauregard telegraphed: "Without the troops sent to General Lee I will have to elect between abandoning lines on Bermuda Neck and those of Petersburg."[15] In mid-afternoon of June 9, then, the high command of the Army of Northern Virginia faced this situation: Grant with his powerful host was directly in front; Hunter was in Staunton and preparing to march, his objective unknown; Sheridan was headed for the Virginia Central and possibly a junction with Hunter. The activity around Petersburg did not appear to Lee to be more than a reconnaissance, but there was no way of determining what adventure might follow the reconnaissance.

To cope swiftly and vigorously with these three diversions was a grim assignment for a tired, weakened army. The nearest of the three operations proved the easiest to combat. A clumsy, half-hearted attack on Petersburg was repulsed by the effort of Beauregard's troops, old civilians, boys too young for military service, and jail prisoners released on their promise to fight. After dark on June 9 the attacking force withdrew.[16]

On the ninth and tenth Hampton's troopers followed the long, hot, dusty road to Louisa Court House. Hampton's superb endurance served him well, and during the night of the tenth he collected information about the enemy's movements. He learned to his immeasurable relief that his column, on the shorter arc, had reached the Virginia Central ahead of the enemy. The railroad was intact and in operation, but its safety had been assured by the thinnest of margins. Carefully Hampton questioned the natives and studied his map. Toward the enemy at Clayton's Store led two roads, one from Louisa Court House, the other from Trevilian Station. His conclusion was to proceed with his own division from Trevilian while Fitz Lee advanced from Louisa. Their columns would be converging, with the hope to close and hurl the enemy against the North Anna. This was, for an inferior force, a plan of great boldness.

By dawn of June 11, Hampton had his troopers in the saddle. Butler and Young were made ready for the advance. Rosser was held in reserve to protect the trains and led horses. A courier brought a message from Fitz Lee that his division at Louisa was moving out. Hampton passed word to Calbraith Butler. In a few minutes, shouts and an exchange of fire showed that

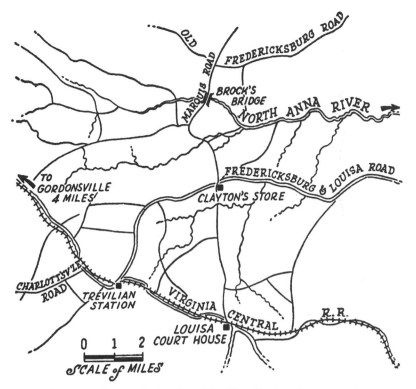

Scene of the cavalry battle at Trevilian Station, June 11, 1864.

the enemy had been encountered. Hampton then dismounted the remainder of Butler's men and sent them forward in line of battle. When the enemy made a stand, he immediately sent Young to reinforce Butler. Hampton felt confident he would effect a junction with Fitz Lee in a short time.

At that promising moment, Hampton received startling intelligence. The enemy was in his rear. From the Louisa Road Custer's Union brigade had slipped past Fitz Lee's force by a woods road and soon found itself among Hampton's wagons. Nearby were about 800 of Butler's led horses. This fine booty Custer was collecting when Hampton was told what had happened. He of course had to break away from the Federals on the Trevilian-Clayton Store road and devote his fire to Custer.

There followed as bewildering a fight as the Confederate cavalry ever had waged. At one moment Hampton's withdrawal appeared to be a rout; at another, Custer seemed in danger of destruction. Fitz Lee closed on him from the east, Rosser from the west, Butler from the north. In the end, the

Confederates recovered all their lost horses and vehicles and captured some of the Federals'; Custer contrived to hold Trevilian Station and the adjoining track. Fitz Lee was separated for the night from Hampton, but Custer had been so badly crippled and the entire Union force so roughly handled that Sheridan did not press the fight. The next afternoon several furious attacks by the bluecoats were repulsed with heavy loss. The Union commander decided it was unwise to continue his attempt to join Hunter. That night, having destroyed part of the railroad track, Sheridan abandoned the campaign and recrossed the North Anna.

Although the heavy Confederate losses at Trevilian Station included a painful wound for Tom Rosser, the operation could not be regarded otherwise than as a Southern victory. It was the most encouraging small action to that date in Virginia during 1864 and it equaled Stuart's final performance.[17]

Insofar as the Battle of Trevilian Station involved Hampton's leadership, it showed him capable and careful. He believed in superiority of force and exerted himself to concentrate all the men he could at the point of contact. A man who displayed on the field of battle highly intelligent leadership and the most unflinching courage could not fail to impress his soldiers. Increasingly Wade Hampton won favor as the best procurable successor to the lamented Stuart. If Fitz Lee cherished still the ambition to take the place of his beloved Jeb, he was too good a soldier and too honorable a patriot to withhold full support.

The larger effect of Hampton's victory was to dispose of the second diversion undertaken by Grant and to simplify the abatement of the third threat, that offered by Hunter's advance up the Shenandoah Valley. On the day of the first grapple at Trevilian Station, June 11, Hunter entered Lexington. When it became manifest that action against him had to be taken, the decision was to do this effectively. The forces sent to drive Hunter from the Valley should be strong enough to pursue him and, if possible, threaten Washington. For this large enterprise an entire corps would be required. The honor and responsibility of the mission went to Jube Early. The old "Army of the Valley" belonged to his Second Corps, and its presence on the Shenandoah would be reassuring. Furthermore, Early was a man of independent mind, entirely self-reliant, and with an aptitude for strategy. He was not a Jackson or even a Longstreet, but he had some knowledge of the Valley and he appeared to be the most available man.[18]

Before the first glint of dawn on June 13, Early's men were moving. He had scarcely more than the bone of the famous old corps. Eight thousand muskets were all he could count, with two battalions of artillery. Of the twelve brigadier generals in command at the opening of the Wilderness campaign, one only, Cullen Battle, remained in charge of the same troops.

Ramseur and Gordon had been promoted; all the others had been killed, wounded, or captured within less than six weeks.

Not until he established communication with John C. Breckinridge did Early learn of Hunter's movements. Breckinridge was at Lynchburg, organizing its defenses as best he could. Besides his two small brigades of infantry, he had the corps of cadets of the Virginia Military Institute and two badly mounted and poorly armed forces of cavalry, under John McCausland and John Imboden. As soon as Early ascertained that Breckinridge was facing odds he could not hope to beat, he requisitioned rolling stock of the adjacent railroads to move his troops to Lynchburg. Old Jube was furiously in earnest and was to balk at nothing.

At 1:00 P.M. on the seventeenth, when he reached Lynchburg with the van of Ramseur's division, Early found Breckinridge in bed recuperating from an old wound that a fall from a horse had made angry. By good chance, Harvey Hill was in the city and had helped put the troops to fortifying. Harry Hays was there, recovering from a wound received at Spotsylvania, and he tendered his services. The invalided Arnold Elzey was on his way to Lynchburg from Richmond. With these commanders and those of Ramseur's division, Early occupied the trenches against the challenge of the enemy.

On June 18, Early held to the defensive as his remaining troops came up slowly. A few small-scale attacks were made on him during the afternoon and were repulsed easily. Early made his preparations to attack on the nineteenth, only to learn, soon after midnight, that Hunter was in retreat. At dawn pursuit began. That was all Jube could do. He had saved Lynchburg and the Southside Railroad; he had ended the third Federal diversion; he had not destroyed Hunter.[19]

3. TOWARD IMMOBILIZED COMMAND

These days had witnessed a new climax in the struggle for Richmond. On June 13, as the Second Corps was beginning its long march west, the troops who remained on the line at Cold Harbor ascertained that the enemy had left their front. Grant had undertaken another shift. The probability that he might move to the south of the James River had been recognized, but his departure was into baffling, heavily wooded country. While Grant made the most of the day's march that either adversary could steal on the other in that difficult terrain, Lee searched for him. By the afternoon of June 15, but not before that time, the Confederate command knew Grant's approximate position and perceived how readily the Union army could move over the James to Petersburg.

The next day, June 15, Petersburg, not Richmond, became the theater and Beauregard's troops, rather than Lee's, the actors. On the road from City Point to Petersburg Dearing's cavalry sent word of a Federal advance. Beauregard had on the front opposite Bermuda Hundred and in front of Petersburg a force slightly in excess of 5,400. Of these, about 2,200 of all arms defended Petersburg. Wise's Virginia brigade was concentrated immediately on the Petersburg earthworks that faced the approaching Federals. Fighting opened quickly. With varying fortune and no great show of initiative on the part of the assailants, the day passed. Wise's men closed on the second line and prepared to renew the contest at dawn. To aid them, Beauregard stripped almost naked the front opposite Bermuda Hundred and appealed in loudest terms for help from Lee.[20]

As soon as it had seemed probable on the fourteenth that Grant might cross the James, Hoke's division was ordered to the pontoon bridge above Drewry's Bluff. Hoke reached the Petersburg front during the night of the fifteenth. Richmond and Petersburg, either or both, now were in acutest danger. Grant had the initiative, had superior force, and had alternatives of action. Anything might happen, and happen swiftly, once the Union army had shaken itself loose and could strike where it chose.

Beauregard and Lee faced different aspects of the same difficult problem. For Beauregard the question was whether he could retain his long lines with his small forces until larger help came from Lee. His conclusion was that if he were to hold Petersburg till relief came, it would have to be by abandoning and not merely stripping the so-called Howlett Line across Bermuda Hundred Neck. Lee, in his turn, did not feel he could reinforce Beauregard heavily at the expense of the scanty divisions defending the capital. It seemed probable, from the first intelligence reports, that those of Butler's troops sent to Grant were being returned. If they were all who faced Beauregard, he could checkmate them with moderate assistance. In the event Grant was detaching heavily from his own army to assist Butler's, then Beauregard must have larger reinforcements. The instant essential was to ascertain whether any of Grant's troops, as distinguished from Butler's, were on the south side of the James.

Early on the sixteenth Beauregard could not procure information; Lee could not act without it. To save Petersburg, the Confederate rear guard in front of Bermuda Hundred had in mid-morning to evacuate a second line. Troops of Johnson's division were able to reach Petersburg in time to support Wise and Hoke. In late afternoon they faced so heavy an assault that they abandoned another part of the works. During these stubborn exchanges, which continued into the night, army headquarters were transferred to the south side of the James. First Corps units were moved there to meet any new threat and to recover the Howlett Line. This put on the Southside a total of about 22,600 of Lee's troops and left north of the James Powell Hill's Third Corps, Kershaw's division of the First, and most of the cavalry—a total of approximately 21,000.

As night of June 16 approached, the unsettled question remained: It had not been possible to ascertain whether Butler alone, or Butler with large help from Grant, was attacking Petersburg. Near the end of the day's struggle, Beauregard reported the presence of Hancock's II Corps, but beyond that he confessed, "No satisfactory information yet received of Grant's crossing James River." That news had to be weighed. There was a chance that Grant was perpetrating a ruse and that he would strike at Richmond when he thought Lee's back was turned.[21]

The seventeenth of June brought new suspense to the Confederate capital and long hours of exciting adventure and gnawing uncertainty on the Southside. Veteran troops of the First Corps, under the calm and competent direction of Dick Anderson, had no difficulty in clearing Butler's X Corps from most of the Bermuda Hundred lines seized by the Federals when Beauregard had sent the defenders to Petersburg. A countermand had reached Pickett too late, and his troops rushed forward. Said the commanding general, "I believe that they will carry anything they are put against. We tried very hard to keep Pickett's men from capturing the breastworks of the enemy but couldn't do it."

Beauregard had a more difficult day. His first dispatch of the morning to the commanding general included in a new form the familiar proposal that Lee give him sufficient reinforcements to "take the offensive [and] thus get rid of the enemy here." Almost before the message was sent, the situation indicated that the enemy might "get rid" of Beauregard. An assault carried the Unionists into the works; 4 guns, 5 colors, and 600 prisoners were captured. Beauregard fought shrewdly and beat back repeated assaults, but he was nearing adversely the end of a desperate gamble. He telegraphed Lee: "We greatly need reinforcements to resist such large odds against us. The enemy must be dislodged or the city will fall."

All the reports of the morning and early afternoon confirmed the probability that a greater part of Grant's army had crossed the James. Powell Hill was ordered to march the Third Corps to Chafin's Bluff, whence he could move quickly to defend Richmond or cross the James and proceed to Petersburg. Kershaw's division, which had been waiting at Chafin's Bluff, was ordered to the Howlett Line. As a matter of military instruction, it was much to be regretted that virtually none of Lee's lieutenants witnessed this demonstration of his methods of sifting and interpreting his intelligence reports.

From Beauregard, about night, came a dispatch that was the more serious because it was not theatrical. Increasing numbers in his front would compel him that night to withdraw to a shorter line. "This I shall hold as long as practicable, but, without reinforcements, I may have to evacuate this city very shortly." This indicated more pressure than had been observed previously, and it appeared to Lee that Beauregard now genuinely needed further reinforcement. Kershaw therefore was directed to Petersburg at dawn. Powell Hill received orders to cross the pontoon bridge above Drewry's Bluff and await developments. No troops besides Lee's cavalry and the garrison at Richmond remained north of the James.[22]

The next few hours were decisive. Toward evening on the seventeenth the assaults on Beauregard had become more furious. Another section of the line was breached. A necessary counterattack by Matt Ransom's North Carolina brigade cost it many lives. By the time Ransom's men threw the Federals out of the salient they had taken, Beauregard was poised for a withdrawal to a new position that had been staked out by his capable chief engineer. Old Bory had the campfires piled high and the picket-line advanced. Then, under strictest injunction of silence, his men moved to the rear and went to work on the construction of a new inner line.

During the night a report by Rooney Lee of a Federal pontoon bridge across the James reached headquarters. This information removed the last doubt from Lee's mind. Grant evidently had shifted the entire infantry battle to the Southside. If his "left flank movement" had not succeeded north of the James, he would renew it where there would be no broad river to halt him. Regrouping of forces began immediately. Kershaw's orders stood: He was to proceed to Petersburg to reinforce Beauregard's weary men. Powell Hill was to follow Kershaw. On the Lynchburg front, Jubal Early was to push his offensive or, if that proved impossible, return to Petersburg. Army headquarters were to be moved to Petersburg. The secretary of war instructed all officers exercising separate commands in Virginia and North Carolina to receive their orders from General Lee.[23]

By these movements adequate reinforcements were assured the defenders of Petersburg. The night's labor on the new works had completed the exhaustion of Beauregard's troops. When they saw the glint of the morning sun on Kershaw's bayonets, they wept and cheered. As for Petersburg folk, their supreme hour came that afternoon, June 18, when Hill's corps marched through the city to take position on the line. The danger of sudden catastrophe passed.

For four reasons, the army's task now was vastly complicated. Because of the strength of Grant's position and the weight of his numbers, Lee, in the first place, could not afford to attack the Union entrenchments unless the necessity was desperate. At the same time, the army had to defend the approaches of Richmond as well as of Petersburg, and, third—cost what it might—the army must keep open lines of supply from the south. "If this cannot be done," Lee said, "I see no way of averting the terrible disaster that will ensue."[24] Finally, in the planning and execution of this difficult military course, the Confederates were crippled by lack of men and by loss of leaders. Many regiments had been reduced in size to companies, and brigades to regiments, and divisions to brigades.

One after another, between June 18 and July 30, these four obstacles to offensive strategy presented acute strategic problems. The first test came almost before the tired troops had begun to recover. On June 21–22 the launching of another cavalry raid, under Brigadier General James H. Wilson, was accompanied by an infantry demonstration against the Weldon Railroad near Petersburg. Wilson got away on an errand of mischief, but William Mahone plunged into a gap in the Union infantry force and took 1,600 prisoners. In this affair, Perry's Florida brigade particularly distinguished itself.

The next excitement was over Wilson's wide-ranging cavalry raid. After tearing up a long stretch of the Petersburg and Weldon, the raiders struck westward and did much damage to the Southside Railroad and still more to the Richmond and Danville. Wilson then wheeled and made for Reams's Station on the Weldon tracks, where he expected the Union lines to be extended. Hampton led his and Rooney Lee's divisions to Reams's where Mahone and Fitz Lee were waiting. Virtually surrounded, Wilson had to burn his wagons and cut his way out. This fine Confederate success yielded more than 1,000 prisoners and 13 guns; but the defeat of the raiders did not alter the fact that they had destroyed 60 miles of railways. This was the grimmest of all warnings that a superior Federal cavalry force at any time might interrupt and destroy communications on which the very existence of the army depended.[25]

The daily incidents of trench warfare at Petersburg soon showed how grievously the numerically inferior Confederate army was to suffer from attrition when it was chained down and unable to employ the offensive strategy that had won it many battles. Sharpshooting became costly and began to be demoralizing. "There is the chill of murder about the casualties of this month," said one brigadier in reporting the losses of July.[26] The constant danger of mortar fire added to the miseries of life.

After the first of July, mysterious and concealed activity at Elliott's Salient on the line of Bushrod Johnson's division indicated the enemy was mining. Countermining was begun, but nowhere could the Confederates break into the enemy's gallery. To reassure the troops, new works were constructed in rear and were nearing completion late in July. While the lines were agog with talk of shafts and tunnels, reports indicated Federal infantry being assembled on the Richmond front. Joe Kershaw and his division were sent back across the James, and on July 27–28 met what Grant had intended as a surprise diversionary attack to cover a new raid by Sheridan against the Virginia Central. In confused fighting Kershaw's men attacked successfully, but then had to retreat in greater haste than glory, with the loss of 300 prisoners and several colors. This affair at Deep Bottom prevented a raid by Sheridan, but at the same time, the demonstration compelled Lee to transfer so many troops that Grant thought the time ripe for a direct attack on Petersburg.[27]

On the morning of July 30, at dawn, the Confederate works at Elliott's Salient were blown high into the air by 8,000 pounds of powder. By the explosion at least 278 men were killed instantly or buried under hundreds of tons of earth, but the Federals who quickly rushed into the crater of the mine were slow and hesitant in assailing the breached line. The Confederates on either side of the crater, and to the south of it, rallied quickly and held their works. By 10 o'clock Mahone's division, admirably led, recovered most of the trenches the Federals had occupied. With 20 flags, perhaps 1,500 prisoners, and at least 3,500 Federals killed and wounded to offset their own gross losses of 1,500, the Confederates had won a unique victory. "It was the saddest affair I have witnessed in the war," said Grant. "Such opportunity for carrying fortifications I have never seen and do not expect again to have."[28]

To many a Confederate soldier, it has to be recorded, the Battle of the Crater, that hot thirtieth of July, connoted warfare of a more savage character because of the employment of Negroes against them. The change of mental attitude was startling. Of the Federals the usual remark had been, "They fit us, we fit them." Now it was different. The explosion of the mine was a "mean trick," the use of Negro troops an infamy. For the first time, said a hospital matron, she heard the wounded curse the enemy. It had been a desperate day in a cause daily more desperate.[29]

4. ATTRITION IN A CHANGED ARMY

An exchanged prisoner of war, reading in the Richmond papers of the Battle of the Crater, would have encountered so many unfamiliar names that he might have concluded that Lee had a new army. The trenches destroyed by the explosion were occupied by Elliott's South Carolina brigade; it had only come to Virginia in May. Nearby was Gracie's brigade, associated with none of the great contests of the old Army of Northern Virginia.

Wise's brigade, which participated gallantly in the action of July 30, had been absent for months from Virginia. All these troops were commanded by Major General B. R. Johnson. So unfamiliar was he that the public might have thought the initials incorrect, and the soldier Old Allegheny Johnson. At the instance of Beauregard, Bushrod Johnson was promoted to divisional rank after the fight at Drewry's Bluff.

What was true of the unfamiliarity with Johnson's division—the brigades of Henry Wise, Matt Ransom, Stephen Elliott, and Archibald Gracie—was true in large part of Hoke's division. Hagood's South Carolina brigade had come to Virginia during the emergency of Butler's attack. Thomas L. Clingman's North Carolina brigade had not fought as a unit of the Army of Northern Virginia until Cold Harbor. Kirkland's brigade was a familiar one that had suffered cruelly at Bristoe Station. Colquitt's brigade, the fourth unit of Hoke's division, had left Virginia after Chancellorsville to fight in Florida. It had been returned for the critical summer campaign. Thus two of the eight infantry divisions were in large part new to Lee's army. Of their eight brigade commanders, two only, Colquitt and Kirkland, had been schooled under the commanding general—and Colquitt had not shone in his last previous campaign in Virginia.

Still other officers of untested skill as brigade commanders had now to be promoted to fill vacancies that could not remain open. The list of brigades needing competent direction was long. No successor had been named to Abner Perrin, whose Alabama brigade had been Cadmus Wilcox's. Second, Rans Wright was absent by illness from a famous brigade that required a temporary commander of appropriate rank and prestige. Next, James L. Kemper had been exchanged as a prisoner of war but was so much weakened by the wound received at Gettysburg that he had been assigned to command the Virginia reserves. W. W. Kirkland had fallen at Cold Harbor with an injury that would involve long absence from his North Carolinians. In the same battle, George Doles lost his life and left one of the best brigades without a leader. A sixth vacancy had been caused by the death of Grumble Jones at Piedmont. The addition of scattered cavalry regiments to the army made a seventh nomination for brigade command desirable. An eighth and a ninth were necessary to fill the places of the promoted Hoke and the dead Micah Jenkins.

Some of these vacancies had been continued beyond the reorganization of June 4 because circumstances then had prompted delay or else because senior colonels were doing well enough to justify a trial before final decision was made. Most of the other cases were those of the tragic attrition that had been increasing rapidly since May. More frequent battles at close quarters had prompted officers to take more desperate personal risks when their men fought somewhat less well and the Federals fought better. Generals were being killed more rapidly than they could prudently be selected. Appointments had to be made when—but not until—reasonably well qualified men could be found. On occasion, brigades had to be entrusted to men of limited competence in the hope that the experience of the divisional commander and of the men themselves would make good the deficiencies of the new brigadiers.

One alleviating aspect was the new law for temporary appointments. The appointment to Rans Wright's brigade was a unique example of the operation of this law and of the swift attrition that was wrecking command. Captain Victor J. B. Girardey, who had served with high courage and marked capacity on Wright's staff, was transferred to the division and became a fixture on the staff of Mahone. In organizing and timing the attack of Mahone's division at the Crater, Girardey won the admiration of the entire army. As a reward he received a distinction never given any officer of Lee's command, promotion at a single jump from a captaincy to the temporary rank of brigadier general in command of Wright's Georgians. Girardey had every promise of being a brilliant officer, but before he had served a fortnight in the place of his absent former chief, he was killed.[30]

To Perrin's command, under the same act, Colonel J. C. C. Sanders of the 11th Alabama was promoted. A temporary commission went to William R. Terry, who had handled Kemper's brigade during its commander's captivity and invalidism. For the post of the wounded Kirkland, one of his stoutest colonels, William McRae of the 15th North Carolina, was advanced to the rank of temporary brigadier. Doles's brigade went to Colonel Philip Cook, a lawyer who had enlisted as a private in the 4th Georgia. Cook was a fighter who by long service was entitled to permanent rather than temporary rank as brigadier.

To Grumble Jones's weakened command Colonel Bradley T. Johnson was appointed as temporary brigadier. Why this able Marylander so long was denied advancement is among the Confederate mysteries. He was, to be sure, a lawyer and not a professional soldier, but many another lawyer of military skill less marked had been made a general officer. Stonewall Jackson several times had urged his promotion. The Maryland colonel probably had suffered from the typical émigré jealousies of officers from his own state. Now, at last, he received the distinction he long previously had earned. Another commission as brigadier, with similar assignment to the mounted arm, went to Colonel Martin W. Gary of South Carolina. A Harvard graduate and a lawyer already conspicuous in the politics of the Palmetto State, "Mart" Gary had led in re-equipping the Hampton Legion as mounted infantry. Recruitment and concentration of scattered units had added to the cavalry corps men enough to organize a small brigade, to which Gary was appointed as "permanent" general officer. He justified the appointment forthwith in a fight with Sheridan's raiders.

To Hoke's old brigade was assigned as brigadier the vigorous Colonel Archibald C. Godwin, who had commanded it at Rappahannock Bridge and fought there until overwhelmed. Now exchanged, Godwin was promoted to lead the troops with whom his record had been high. Promotion of the same sort went to Colonel John Bratton of the 6th South Carolina. This young physician had long been recommended for commission by Dick Anderson, but he had served in Micah Jenkins's brigade where promotion was slow. Now he had the brigade, still strong in numbers and indomitable in spirit.

In was improbable, of course, that all these men would succeed as brigade commanders. Not one of them had been a professional soldier. They simply seemed the logical appointees or those that appeared most likely to develop, or to escape failure. Outside the Army of Northern Virginia many general officers were available and awaiting assignment, but none was summoned to fill these latest vacancies. Lee doubtless reasoned that if they were qualified, positions would have been found for them in the armies that had dropped them.

In the fighting from Cold Harbor to the Crater, two names only besides that of the commanding general were found to possess new luster. One of these names was Wade Hampton's. Hampton lacked the glamour Stuart had in the eyes of the young troopers of 1862, but he appealed more strongly to the temper of 1864; Hampton had the respect of veterans. The operations in Spotsylvania, at Trevilian Station and afterward—these and all the minor clashes of reconnaissance and patrol had been handled without material blunder. Belief that the discretion of Hampton could be trusted led to his assignment on August 11 "to the command of the cavalry of this army." His division went to Calbraith Butler.

Equal with Hampton in distinction during May–June 1864 was William Mahone. Many officers who were competent, even conspicuous, at a particular rank in Confederate service, failed when given larger duties. Mahone reversed this. A brigadier of no shining reputation, he proved himself within three months one of the ablest divisional commanders the army ever had. He was a man never aroused to his full potentialities until he felt he had duties that challenged all he knew, all he could learn, all he could do. Small in person, he was so thin that when his wife heard he had received a flesh wound, she said, "Now I know it is serious, for William has no flesh whatever." Yet in action, said J. C. Haskell, there was about him a "cool promptness and dash which were peculiarly his own."[31]

Anderson's old division, which Mahone now led, seldom had been called to exceptional service, but Mahone made the men what Hood's and A. P. Hill's divisions had been at their best, the spearhead of attack. After the Battle of the Crater, Lee had Mahone's temporary commission as major general made permanent. Beyond doubt, Mahone was the military "discovery" of those summer days in front of Petersburg, precisely as John B. Gordon had been the "discovery" of the campaign in Spotsylvania.

The army had, from the time of the crossing of the James, what it never had counted in its personnel: A full general under the direction of the commanding general. For practical purposes, Beauregard became temporarily a corps commander, but because of his rank and prestige he enjoyed a privileged status. He was determined always that responsibility for major decisions should rest on the War Department. In directing the combat in front of Petersburg, before Lee's arrival, Old Bory was at his best. For the time his theatrical manner disappeared, not to be resumed until Lee was at hand. Beauregard had proved he could be useful, but he must be handled with some care; he showed himself in the contemporary vernacular most distinctly "touchy." Such men, if in high position, did not usually remain long with the Army of Northern Virginia.

Two other conditions on the half-immobilized front deserved consideration. The army itself was as much changed as its command. Many of the old, experienced units had been so reduced by casualties that they had lost their offensive power. Inexperienced and reluctant conscripts, in many instances, took the place of veteran volunteers. The infantry who remained in the trenches around Petersburg included a larger percentage of Carolinians than ever had been mustered in Lee's army—59 regiments and battalions in a total of 161. This most assuredly involved no loss of devotion or of valor, but it was to prove serious when some of these men, nostalgic and half-starved, heard that their homes were threatened by invaders who previously had not penetrated to the interior.

The other new condition was the absence of the Second Corps. In every heavy battle for two years past the Second Corps had borne its full part. Now it was gone. With it had moved not only the rifle-strength of 64 regiments and battalions, but also three division commanders who, in the Spotsylvania campaign, had much distinguished themselves. Any organization would be the weaker for the absence of three such men as Gordon, Ramseur, and Rodes, to say nothing of their new corps commander, Early.

In summary, then, that part of the Army of Northern Virginia in the Richmond-Petersburg area was weakened numerically, recruited uncertainly with less-experienced troops, and commanded by an officers' corps that included many incompetent regimental officers and not a few general officers of untested ability. The two new divisions were under the immediate direction of Beauregard, a general of full rank, whose relations with the administration and with Lee might involve difficulties. In succession to Stuart, there was every prospect that Wade Hampton might prove himself wholly qualified to command the cavalry. "Billy" Mahone was emerging as a division commander of great offensive skill. Grimly on the other side of the book of battle had to be written three stern entries: The army was being caged in the Petersburg trenches, the opposing odds were heavier, the absent Second Corps was engaged in a desperate gamble.

CHAPTER 33

The Darkening Autumn
of Command

1. JUBE EARLY GAMBLES AT LONG ODDS

In pursuing Hunter from Lynchburg on June 19, Jube Early's poorly organized cavalry were soon outrun. Early as well as Lee were disappointed that the raiders were so slightly punished. Both had been anxious to defeat and, if possible, destroy Hunter, who had burned V.M.I. and the home of ex-governor Letcher at Lexington and had countenanced much looting. After resting his men, Early proceeded into the Shenandoah Valley by way of Lexington. As Rodes passed through the town, he had the band of his leading regiment begin a dirge. To this music, some thousands of the men who had fought under Stonewall Jackson marched by his grave. It was his last review of them.[1]

Reaching Staunton, Early reorganized his forces. Robert Ransom and his cavalry that had been reporting to Breckinridge were now placed under Early's own command. Bradley Johnson was designated formally to head Grumble Jones's cavalry brigade. To give Breckinridge a force in keeping with his rank and abilities, Gordon's division was assigned to his command. The Kentuckian's other division was led by Brigadier General John Echols. Rodes's and Ramseur's divisions continued to report directly to Early. Altogether, the infantry, as reorganized, counted 10,000 men. Cavalry and artillery perhaps added 4,000.[2]

In Gordon's division there was a measure of almost vehement discontent. York's brigade combined the "discordant fragments" of the proud old Louisiana brigades of Hays and Stafford. Under Terry were the survivors of the Stonewall Brigade and other units of Allegheny Johnson's division. "Both officers and men object to their consolidation ...," wrote an inspector. "Strange officers command strange troops...." In this was a new challenge to John Gordon in making his troops believe themselves the special

739

instruments of victory. In Breckinridge's command was a problem of somewhat similar nature. Many of his soldiers had no desire to do battle beyond the mountains among which they lived. They would fight when the issue was joined but, left alone in a strange country, they would disappear mysteriously—to reappear, weeks later, at home.[3]

On June 28 the advance began. Early wrote Lee, "I hope to be able to do something for your relief and the success of our cause shortly." He was resolved to enter Maryland. Said Kyd Douglas afterward, "Jackson being dead, it is safe to say no other general in either army would have attempted it against such odds. . . . The audacity of Early's enterprise was its safety; no one . . . would believe his force was so small."[4] On July 3, Sigel's advance guard was struck and driven to Harper's Ferry. On July 6, without hesitation, Early led the Second Corps into Maryland for its third great adventure. The columns went over South Mountain and pressed eastward through Frederick. At 8:00 A.M., July 9, the van approached the Monocacy River and reported the presence of the enemy.

The day was young, and Old Jube decided to take his time and ascertain where he best could turn a position he did not wish to attack frontally. John McCausland showed the way with his cavalry brigade, fording the Monocacy and furiously assailing the Federal flank. This, Early said later, "solved the problem for me." He determined to throw Gordon's division across the river at the same ford and complete the turning movement McCausland had begun. Against the Federals' first line Gordon hurled his brigades, drove it back, stopped long enough to catch breath, and then charged and broke a second line. When a new line of Federals was seen advancing at the double-quick to a fence in front, the cry went up from the men, "Charge them! Charge them!" Said John Worsham, "It was useless for General Gordon to try to stop it now—nothing but a shot through each man could have done it. With a yell we were at the fence."

One volley scattered the Federals. From the opposite side of the river came the reassuring cheers of the two other divisions. Soon they, too, pushed over the Monocacy and joined the chase. It was, Worsham said, "the most exciting time I witnessed during the war." They captured between 600 and 700 men. The total loss of the enemy was nearly 1,300. Early's gross loss was under 700.[5]

Early hesitated in pushing after the enemy when he discovered the composition of the force that had contested the crossing of the Monocacy. It included—and this made every Confederate in the expedition attentive—reinforcements from the VI Corps, Army of the Potomac. Good news and bad that was! Whatever Early might or might not accomplish after the Battle of the Monocacy, he had achieved one of the objects the high command had in mind: He had forced Grant to detach troops from the Richmond-Petersburg area in order to defend Washington. Desirable as this was, it imposed greater caution on Early. He hoped to be able to attack and perhaps to capture Washington, but he was in no wise reckless. On July 10 he resumed his advance and sustained the reputation of the foot cavalry by marching his force thirty miles.[6]

The next day, July 11, was an historic date in American history. The Confederates might march straight to the defenses of Washington and, if they had the strength and the resolution, might storm them successfully. After the war men said that the charge on the third day at Gettysburg marked "the high-water mark" of the Confederacy, and in the just determination of military values, they were correct; but if proximity to White House, to Capitol, to Treasury be considered strategically the greatest advance, then the honor of it fell a year and a week after Pickett's charge to that strange, bitter, and devoted man, Jubal A. Early, former Commonwealth's attorney of Franklin County, Virginia.

He pressed the march as vigorously as he had on the tenth. When he and his staff rode past the sweating column, he told the troops he would take them into Washington that day. The men responded with their old yell, but the heat of the day was fast exhausting them. Early had to slacken the pace. When he came at last within sight of the city's heavy fortifications, he had to admit that an immediate attack was out of the question. The most he could do at the moment was to advance his skirmishers while he rested his men and studied the works. Investment was impossible; assault would be costly; but the fighting blood of Old Jube was up. If an attack could achieve results, he would make it.[7]

He ascertained that the whole of the VI Corps had arrived on the Washington front from Grant's army. In conferring on this news with his division commanders, he reminded them that a decision to fight or to move had to be made forthwith. Their counsel and Early's decision was to attack at earliest dawn the next morning unless some new development came. During the night of July 11–12 a message was received by Early from cavalryman Bradley Johnson, who was close to Baltimore. Johnson's information was that two corps had arrived from Grant's army to reinforce Washington. This was news to make Early hesitate. Orders consequently were sent the divisional leaders to delay the assault until daylight would show whether the defenses of the Federal capital were manned heavily.

As soon as Early could see in the soft summer dawn the far-spreading line of earthworks, he was at a vantage point and gazing at them with his binoculars. They were lined with troops. If the assault were successful, he had to tell himself, it would entail such losses that the remnant of his little army might not be able to escape. Should he fail in the assault, he almost certainly would lose his entire force. In either event, destruction of a Confederate army in front of Washington would have a fatally depressing effect on the South. Early saw no choice. The odds against him were too heavy. The plan must be abandoned![8]

The troops demonstrated and skirmished in front of Fort Stevens on the twelfth and beat off three "feeling out" advances by the enemy. That night they began their retreat to Virginia. "Major," said Early to Kyd Douglas just before the column slipped away, "we haven't taken Washington, but we've scared Abe Lincoln like hell!"

"Yes, General," Douglas answered, "but this afternoon when that Yankee line moved out against us, I think some other people were scared blue as hell's brimstone!"

"That's true," Early said, "but it won't appear in history."[9]

There were losses along with gains, and regrets as well as booty. Particularly cherished by Jube was $220,000 in cash he had levied on Hagerstown and Frederick, and the reports of his cavalry that they had destroyed numerous railroad and highway bridges. "Natural obstacles alone prevented our taking Washington," Dodson Ramseur wrote his wife. "The heat and dust were so great that our men could not possibly march further." Early himself was not greatly concerned over his failure to enter Washington, because he thought that was explicable. Lee was satisfied with the results and hopeful of still further gains from Early's presence on the frontier.[10]

In any review of the Battle of Monocacy, it would have been observed that most of the combat was the work of Gordon's single division. If it became a habit for Early to conduct his battles in this fashion, it might imply that he still was, in spirit, a division and not a corps or army commander. A general could not aspire to competence in army command if he thought only in terms of divisions and of divisional firepower. A second weakness of Early's operations was the lack of a consolidated command of his cavalry. Robert Ransom was incapacitated by illness. McCausland had several bold exploits to his credit; Bradley Johnson and Gilmore and Imboden had ridden far, burned bridges, and, in Johnson's case, threatened Baltimore. But their troopers were not—and without an able leader, a strong disciplinarian, could not be—a unified body of fighting men in the sense that Hampton's or Sheridan's troopers were. Early did not have the aptitude to improve his cavalry arm.

As soon as Early was back in Virginia, four Federal commanders— Sigel, Hunter, Averell, and Crook—gathered their forces to attack him. From Washington, Horatio G. Wright's VI Corps pursued. When Jube slipped away to the west, there followed a succession of skirmishes. The first affair of any importance was on July 20, when Ramseur was attacked suddenly by Averell near Stephenson's Depot. To the amazement of everyone, part of Hoke's trusted old brigade ran and spread confusion among Robert Johnston's troops. In the panic, 267 unwounded officers and men were captured. "I am greatly mortified at the result," Ramseur confessed to his wife. ". . . Newspaper editors and stay-at-home croakers will sit back in safe places and condemn me." Early felt that Ramseur had not taken "the proper precautions" in advancing, but beyond that he did not criticize his young lieutenant. The wound to the pride of the ambitious and devoted young Carolinian remained.[11]

Four days later, Ramseur had partial revenge in a sharp little action on the old battleground at Kernstown. There again a critic might have observed that the battle was fought by Echols's division which Breckinridge brilliantly led. The other divisions merely waited to join in the pursuit. Crook was routed with substantial losses, and the Confederate officers captured on the twentieth were recovered.[12]

Early now learned that during his advance to Washington, the homes of Alexander Hunter, a state senator, Colonel A. R. Boteler, and Colonel Edmund Lee, a kinsman of the commanding general, had been burned wantonly by the Federals. "I came to the conclusion," Early wrote afterward, "it was time to open the eyes of the people of the North to this enormity, by an example in the way of retaliation." John McCausland with his own and Bradley Johnson's brigade were started on July 29 for Chambersburg, Pennsylvania, which Early selected as the object of reprisal. McCausland's instructions were to demand $100,000 in gold or $500,000 in greenbacks for the indemnification of the persons whose property had been put to the torch by the Federals. If this indemnity was not forthcoming at once, McCausland was to reduce the town to ashes.

About 5:30 A.M., July 30, the Confederate cavalry brigades entered Chambersburg and presented their demand. The first member of the town council who was told of this was instant in answer: The citizens would not pay 5 cents. McCausland waited until 9 o'clock and then directed that the town be fired. His order provoked virtual mutiny on the part of some of his officers and men; he had to put Colonel William E. Peters of the 21st Virginia under arrest. As soon as the fires at Chambersburg were well ablaze, McCausland began his withdrawal toward the Potomac. He was prompt to relieve Colonel Peters of arrest, and doubtless was unaware of the many acts of robbery and violence charged against stragglers and thieves in his command. In his military autobiography Early wrote: "For this act I, alone, am responsible. . . . I see no reason to regret my conduct on this occasion."[13]

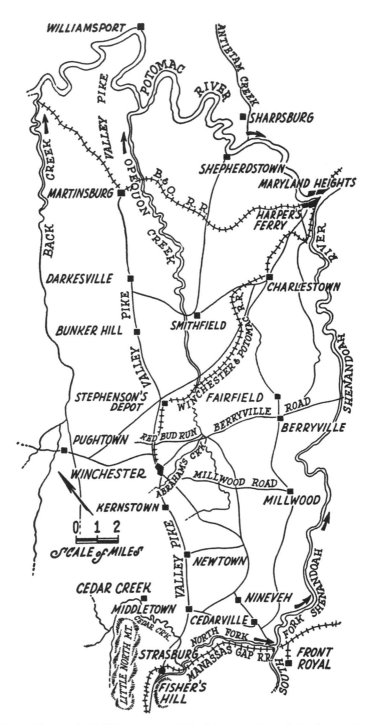

WILLIAMSPORT

POTOMAC RIVER

ANTIETAM CREEK

SHARPSBURG

VALLEY PIKE

SHEPHERDSTOWN

MARYLAND HEIGHTS

BACK CREEK

OPEQUON CREEK

B&O R.R.

MARTINSBURG

HARPER'S FERRY

DARKESVILLE

PIKE

SMITHFIELD

CHARLESTOWN

SHENANDOAH RIVER

BUNKER HILL

VALLEY

WINCHESTER & POTOMAC R.R.

STEPHENSON'S DEPOT

FAIRFIELD

ROAD

BERRYVILLE ROAD

PUGHTOWN

RED BUD RUN

BERRYVILLE

WINCHESTER

ABRAHAM'S CRK.

MILLWOOD ROAD

MILLWOOD

KERNSTOWN

0 1 2

SCALE of MILES

VALLEY PIKE

NEWTOWN

NINEVEH

SHENANDOAH

CEDAR CREEK

MIDDLETOWN

CEDAR CRK.

CEDARVILLE

NORTH FORK

SOUTH FORK

STRASBURG

MANASSAS GAP R.R.

FRONT ROYAL

LITTLE NORTH MT.

FISHER'S HILL

The lower Shenandoah Valley, scene of Early's operations, July–September 1864.

At the moment, Fate, as well as General W. W. Averell, seemed to pursue McCausland and Bradley Johnson on their return from Chambersburg. At Moorefield, in the belief that they were safe, the Confederate commanders relaxed their vigilance, with the familiar result. Averell descended on Johnson's camp in a surprise attack before daylight on August 7 and routed his brigade. McCausland's force was driven also. Averell reported that he captured 4 guns, 420 prisoners, and over 400 horses. Bradley Johnson himself was caught but was able to escape.[14]

The affair at Moorefield led to a violent denunciation of McCausland by Bradley Johnson. Johnson's account of the misbehavior of some of the troopers confirmed everything the residents of the burned Pennsylvania town were saying. He charged men of McCausland's brigade with infamous conduct: "Every crime in the catalogue of infamy has been committed, I believe, except murder and rape. . . . Pillage and sack of private dwellings took place hourly." Johnson sought a court of inquiry, but Early ignored this. He seemed powerless to control or to reorganize his cavalry. Painfully he was to discover that looting and robbery by a certain type of soldier are to him what traditionally the taste of human blood is to the tiger. Early was more than conservative when he said of the rout at Moorefield what he should have applied to the whole of the disgraceful Chambersburg raid: "This affair had a very damaging effect upon my cavalry for the rest of the campaign."[15]

Before McCausland and Johnson rejoined Early with their shamed and shattered men, a major change in the campaign had occurred. The Shenandoah Valley once more became a major theater of war. Lee had become convinced that Grant was dispatching other troops to aid Wright's VI Corps in assailing Early. On August 6, in conference with the President, Lee decided to send Kershaw's division of infantry and Fitz Lee's cavalry to assist the Second Corps. Under Dick Anderson, these troops at the outset were to operate in Early's behalf east of the Blue Ridge. To this region Lee was prepared to move still other units of his weakened army if it should develop that Grant was detaching heavily to the same quarter.

Old Jube needed Anderson and all additional reinforcement he could get, because news of the enemy's plans was ominous. Imboden reported on August 9 that a heavy Federal concentration was in progress at Harper's Ferry. His information was that the VI and XIX Corps, as well as Crook's troops, were being assembled and that they were under a new commander. Quickly the outposts learned that Early's adversary was Major General Phil Sheridan.[16]

With confident heart and probably in contemptuous spirit, Early determined to set the pace and occupy Sheridan by ceaseless maneuver. He began a succession of marches and demonstrations that puzzled Sheridan and created the impression of far greater force than the Confederates mustered. In this deception he was assisted by Anderson. Fitz Lee also gave skillful aid both in maneuver and in the attempted reorganization of Early's disorganized cavalry. It was manifest that relief had to be given Robert Ransom, whose illness kept him from field service. He was succeeded by one of Fitz Lee's former brigadiers, Lunsford L. Lomax. In surrendering his assignment, Ransom suggested many changes: Broad reorganization was necessary to bring Early's cavalry "to anything like a state of efficiency." Bragg forwarded these suggestions to Early, who, in the face of new warnings, did not take in hand any reorganization. Whatever was done in that essential had to be undertaken by Fitz Lee and Lomax. Early persisted—it is impossible to say why—in his curious neglect of his cavalry.[17]

During the first month of Early's maneuvering he did not gain a favorable impression of Sheridan. If it was his opponent's policy, said Early, "to convince me that he was not an energetic commander, his strategy was a complete success...." Early, in a word, became overconfident, a dangerous state of mind for any commander prior to actual test of his adversary. It was doubly hazardous for Early because after little more than a month he lost his infantry reinforcement. Anderson and Kershaw were ordered back to the Army of Northern Virginia. This loss did not curb Old Jubilee.

On September 18, Early had Gordon's division bivouacked at Bunker Hill. Rodes and Breckinridge were at Stephenson's Depot, and Ramseur one mile east of Winchester. Lomax's cavalry picketed the left, Fitz Lee the right. The strength of this force was reckoned by Early at 8,500 infantry, 2,900 cavalry, and 3 battalions of artillery—a total of about 12,150. In comparison, though Early did not know even the approximate figures, Sheridan could muster about 40,000 for the field, of whom more than 6,400 were cavalry.[18]

This strong Union army at length was moving. Standing on the defensive during August in obedience to Grant's orders, Sheridan had received heavy cavalry reinforcement while waiting. Now that he had reports of Kershaw's withdrawal, he determined to strike. Soon after dawn on September 19, Early learned that the Federals had forced the crossing of the Opequon on the Berryville road leading to Winchester. Immediately he ordered Gordon to support Ramseur. Then, as quickly as his horse could carry him there, Early rode to Ramseur's position east of Winchester. So plain were the indications of an attack that he directed his remaining infantry, that of Rodes and Breckinridge, to hurry to the ground where the young North Carolinian was standing in furious determination to wipe out the disgrace of his recent defeat at Stephenson's Depot.

Gordon led his men on the field about 10:00 A.M. Behind him, looking as much the god of war as ever, Robert Rodes advanced with three of his brigades. Almost before Gordon could be deployed on the extreme left, or Rodes could be placed between him and Ramseur, the attack opened on the line to which Ramseur skillfully had withdrawn. There was no mystery or finesse about this initial Federal advance. It manifestly was an effort to hold Ramseur in front while another column turned his left. Early's black eyes burned at the sight of this. He would meet it and show young Mr. Sheridan how the Army of Northern Virginia fought! Let Gordon and Rodes outflank the flankers and rout them.

Before Early's orders reached them, Gordon and Rodes themselves had decided to undertake this maneuver. Gordon proceeded at once to the front. Rodes turned away to observe his line, advancing under well-placed enemy fire. The fine black horse of the general—as familiar to the troops as Rodes himself—became restive. Rodes was trying to control the animal when a shell burst near him. A fragment struck the general on the head and knocked him from his horse. Although his heart beat feebly for a few minutes, he knew nothing. His troops had to go on without him. Presently, on the left flank, Rodes's absent brigade, Battle's, came up and attacked as ferociously as at Spotsylvania. Swiftly and with heavy loss the enemy was driven back.[19]

The repulse was sharp; the day appeared to have been won, though at heavy cost in the death of Rodes. The situation seemed even less dangerous as the minutes passed because of the arrival of Breckinridge, delayed repelling cavalry on the Opequon. Early held one of Breckinridge's brigades on the left and sent the remaining two to the right, now his weaker flank. Scarcely had the dispositions been made when the cavalry on the left was seen retiring in disorder before a powerful force of the enemy's mounted troops. Early brought Breckinridge back to the extreme left, where he was able to halt the enemy's advance. A simultaneous attack against the left, farther to the front, was repulsed also. Then noise accomplished what force had failed to do. As the men of Gordon, Rodes, and Ramseur heard the firing on their left flank, they became uneasy. In spite of all their officers could do, they began to make for the rear.

In growing confusion, Early fell back to a line of breastworks close to the town. With his old pugnacity and in the imperturbable manner of all his fighting he prepared to beat off the enemy, but soon he was attacked in front as well as on the left. Word was brought that the enemy was turning the right. Reluctantly Old Jube had to order a general withdrawal. The spirit of retreat was rising. Some of the troops were close to panic.[20]

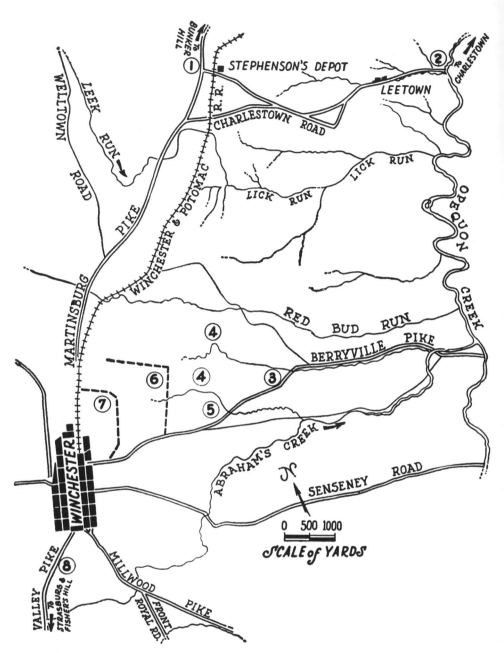

Confederate infantry positions, Third Battle of Winchester, September 19, 1864.
Encircled numerals indicate: (1) bivouac of Gordon and Rodes, night
of September 18–19; (2) Breckinridge's forenoon action; (3) Ramseur's first
position; (4) engaging position of Rodes and Gordon; (5) Ramseur's second
position; (6) Confederate position about 4:30 P.M.; (7) final Confederate line,
about 5:00 P.M.; (8) line of retreat to Fisher's Hill.

Soldiers who survived the onslaught now rallied south of the town. Then, rapidly, but not in rout, they retreated twenty miles to Fisher's Hill which, in Early's opinion, "was the only place where a stand could be made." He found that of his little army of 12,000, he had lost 3,611 of his infantry and artillerymen—1,818 of them captured—and probably 1,000 of his cavalry. This was almost 40 per cent of the force with which he had withstood Sheridan's advance. The command had suffered proportionately. Besides Rodes, who was irreplaceable at the moment, Early lost A. C. Godwin of Hoke's old brigade in circumstances that duplicated those of Rodes's death. Godwin seemed to have been promoted solely to be slain. He had held his commission forty days. Fitz Lee had been wounded seriously by a ball in the thigh—a most deplorable injury because it deprived Lomax of help in the reorganization of the cavalry.

Now, at Fisher's Hill, came another heavy loss of a different character: John C. Breckinridge received orders to return at once to his own Department of Southwest Virginia. Breckinridge had cooperated ably and heartily with Early and had fought at Winchester as a man who courted death. When Gordon protested that the Kentuckian was exposing himself needlessly, Breckinridge had said simply, "Well, General, there is little left for me if our cause is to fail." The departure of Breckinridge and his troops, after the grievous losses of Winchester, would have made Early's situation hopeless had he not received assurance of the early return of Kershaw. More cavalry was promised also.[21]

While awaiting these reinforcements, Early had to undertake reorganization. Little choice was his. With Rodes dead and Breckinridge gone, there were three men only in his army who could be regarded as sufficiently experienced to handle a division. Two of these were, of course, Gordon and Ramseur. The third was John Pegram. He had been commanding a brigade under Ramseur, but had led acceptably a division in the Army of Tennessee. Early gave Ramseur the division of Rodes. In command of Ramseur's men, Pegram was left as senior brigadier. To Gordon was transferred the forces previously called Breckinridge's division but styled Wharton's division during the time Breckinridge, as corps commander, had been directing both his division and Gordon's. This was the best arrangement that could be made. Ramseur's conduct at Winchester had been as brilliant as anything in his career and was full atonement for any charge of negligence in the affair at Stephenson's Depot. Gordon was never as happy under Early as he had been when Lee was in general command, but he was bold, intelligent, and capable of raising the morale of ill-disciplined or discouraged troops. Pegram was an experiment but probably a safe one.

At Fisher's Hill, which was near Strasburg, Early felt compelled to occupy a line almost four miles long—far too long for so small a force. In order to cover the front at all, while holding the Valley Pike, he dismounted Lomax's cavalry, which included the unstable, poorly disciplined units, and placed these troops, under their new commander, on his left. Late on the afternoon of September 22, Sheridan struck this exposed left, swept down it, took up the attack near the center, and forced a disorderly general retreat. The artillerists of the Second Corps had to cover this hurried withdrawal and, in doing so, held their ground too long. Twelve of the guns were taken, a serious loss, but in a realistic sense the minimum price that Early could have paid for escape. Casualties in the infantry and artillery were 1,235. Of these, almost 1,000 were prisoners or stragglers who did not return to the ranks.[22]

The most lamented individual casualty was the beloved and capable Sandie Pendleton, former A.A.G. to Jackson. In May 1864 this superb young officer had declined promotion to brigade command because he believed he was more useful on the staff. After service past reckoning, to Ewell and to Early, he fell while attempting to rally routed troops to form a line south of Fisher's Hill. He died the next day.[23]

The broken brigades reached Waynesboro, at the foot of the Blue Ridge, on September 28. En route they were cheered by the return of Kershaw, with 2,700 effectives. By October 5, Rosser's brigade of 600 cavalry arrived to reinforce Early. That indomitable lieutenant general, "bloody but unbowed," wrote later that on the arrival of these reinforcements, who "about made up my losses at Winchester and Fisher's Hill," he determined to take the offensive.[24] In a short time he undertook to do so, but, strategically, the chapter that began with the advance to Lynchburg in June had been ended.

Force and results considered, it was a chapter as full of honor as of disaster. Early had succeeded in drawing from the Army of the Potomac the whole of the VI Corps, which was an infantry force larger than his own total strength, had occupied Sheridan and one division of cavalry from James River, and had compelled the Federals to consolidate against him the troops of Crook and Averell who might have engaged in attacks on Confederate supply lines. This was a remarkable achievement for a command that at no stage of operations counted more than 13,200 infantry and about 3,700 cavalry—a force steadily and swiftly reduced.

The weight of these odds was not realized at army headquarters in Petersburg. Even when crediting Sheridan with fewer men than that officer commanded, Lee thought that Early's "reverses," as he termed them, could be "remedied." Said the commanding general, "One victory will put all things right." His chief criticism, voiced to Early, was that "you have operated more with divisions than with your concentrated strength." Lee perceived also, as Early did at length, that next to the heavy odds against which the Valley commander had fought, his defeats had been due to "the inefficiency of the greater part of" his cavalry. Early did not admit that this inefficiency was attributable to any failure of his to use a firm hand with his undisciplined troopers.[25]

The fullest of failure, with no allowance for the success of his diversion, was charged against Early. He had created many animosities by his snarling manner and his bitter sarcasms. Now his criticisms came home to him. Foremost among his adversaries was one of his former brigadiers, the governor of Virginia, William Smith. The charges of Smith were obvious—that Early had been surprised, that his tactics were poor, that he had lost guns. More serious was the allegation that the troops no longer believed Early "a safe commander." In a knowledge of the military limitations that had accompanied Extra Billy Smith's personal bravery, professional soldiers might laugh to see him in the role of critic. Before the Virginia people, with whom he was most popular, Smith's lack of standing as a professional soldier did not disqualify him. What he was saying, thousands were thinking. For the first time since the Army of Northern Virginia was reorganized by Lee after the Seven Days, public clamor was rising against one of his senior officers.[26]

2. "The Yankees Got Whipped and We Got Scared"

While Early was employing in the Shenandoah Valley the Second Corps, Kershaw's division, and Fitz Lee's cavalry, the Confederate army on the Richmond-Petersburg front consisted of five divisions of the First and Third Corps, Beauregard's command, and two divisions of cavalry. Most of these thin units had ceaseless trench duty and occasional hard fights in which they scarcely did more than hold off their adversary, who deliberately sought to exhaust them.

It was a grim story. On August 14 a strong demonstration was made against the eastern end of the Richmond defenses, where Charles Field of the First Corps commanded. In three days of small-scale fighting he was able to beat off the Federals; but during the fighting of the sixteenth, two brigades broke badly. "Not only the day but Richmond seemed to be gone," wrote Field.[27] While Lee was disentangling these units, his persistent opponent sought to seize the Weldon Railroad a few miles below Petersburg in the vicinity of Globe Tavern. In Lee's absence, direction of the defense was in the hands of Beauregard.

Old Bory sent Powell Hill against the Federals with two brigades of Heth and three of Mahone. The result on August 19 was a fine local success, and 2,700 prisoners were taken; but the enemy could not be dislodged immediately from the railroad. Two days later, Hill again undertook to regain the Petersburg and Weldon, by employing Mahone. That officer attacked furiously but in vain. Through a mistake on the part of Hill and Mahone, Hagood's brigade was caught inside an angle of the Union line and shattered. Hagood entered the action with 681 men; he brought out 274.[28]

This affair at Globe Tavern raised a question whether at the outset Beauregard had employed sufficient force. In the last stages of the fight there was room for disagreement concerning the reason for failure. Nobody could say that a particular commander had failed, or that any special move had been a mistake. Odds may of themselves have been an all-sufficient answer, but there had been a time when officers and men would have counted like odds as nothing more than a challenge. The operation, in a word, was disquieting.

Another test followed immediately. In a reconnaissance toward Reams's Station, four and a half miles south of Globe Tavern, Hampton found the II Corps loosely disposed while tearing up a section of the railroad. Lee decided to attack at Reams's Station in numbers adequate to the task. On August 24 the blow was struck. Heth and Wilcox attacked in front of the II Corps. Two of Wilcox's brigades were repulsed roughly, but Hampton slipped to the left of the Federals, dismounted his men, and assailed the exposed flank. The II Corps was routed. More than 2,100 prisoners were taken at a price that probably did not much exceed 720.

This Battle of Reams's Station could be accounted a Southern victory, but it did not recover the Petersburg and Weldon. Nothing would drive the Union troops away—and keep them away—except a bloody attack by more troops than Lee could afford to risk. Every aspect of the little battle and of every other engagement fought after the army left Spotsylvania underlined the solemn words Lee wrote Secretary Seddon the day before the fight at Reams's: "Without some increase of strength, I cannot see how we can escape the natural military consequences of the enemy's numerical superiority."[29]

Apart from a brilliant "cattle raid" by Hampton and Rosser on September 16—a raid that gave hungry Confederates 2,468 beeves—there came no action of importance on the Richmond-Petersburg front till Winchester and Fisher's Hill had been fought and lost. Then, on September 29, Grant delivered a surprise attack against Fort Harrison, below Chafin's Bluff on the James. The fort itself was held by so small a force that its loss was no disgrace. Success in holding the next heavy work to the north, Fort Gilmer, was vastly to the credit of the few defending troops. It was manifest that the loss of Fort Harrison threatened the rear of the works at Chafin's Bluff and thereby endangered the water gate to Richmond. Headquarters accordingly decided that the position must be retaken. Field's and Hoke's divisions and a brigade of Pickett's were sent to the Northside to deliver the attack. A division of cavalry was placed in support, and Porter Alexander given twenty-four additional guns.

These preparations were made under the eyes of the commanding general. With employment of less force, victories had been won in '62. Now, when the assault was delivered on September 29, nothing went well. Through some mistake, Tige Anderson advanced beyond his first objective and compelled Field to support him prematurely. Hoke's attack was not coordinated with that of the other division. After both were driven back, Lee called on Hoke's North Carolinians to make another charge. When this was repulsed, they tried a third time, only to fail so tragically that they did not halt until they were behind cover. Some of Hoke's regiments were wrecked. The 8th North Carolina, which carried only about 175 officers and men into the first charge, had at the close of the action 25 men under the command of a lieutenant, the surviving senior officer. There was no denying that the operation had been no credit to any of the participating commanders.

While the infantry was storming Fort Harrison, Hampton's cavalry struggled to hold a Federal advance on the right against the Southside Railroad, at Poplar Spring Church. Hampton drove the bluecoats wherever he met them, except for one contretemps. Colonel Joel R. Griffin of the 8th Georgia, replacing the ill James Dearing, commander of Beauregard's cavalry, lost his entire position. Hampton appraised the affair generally as "one of the handsomest I have seen," but—there was always a "but" now—the position wrested from Griffin was made by the Federals the basis for an extension of the front that Lee had sought to avoid. It was an extension that could not be met otherwise than at the direst risk.[30]

On October 7, under the direction of the commanding general, an effort was made to recover part of the line lost at Fort Harrison. Preparations were made with care. Everything went according to plan until it came Hoke's turn to charge. For reasons never explained, he failed to assault. The result was heavy loss for the other units and abandonment of the effort to recover the lost line. Nothing was said publicly concerning Hoke's responsibility for the failure; but not for the first time in this campaign had he failed to give his full cooperation in attack. The record was not inspiring. Hoke, as a division commander, manifestly was of the type that excels in individual performance, not in teamwork.[31]

To summarize the seven more important clashes during the period between the Battle of the Crater, July 30, and the abandonment of the effort to recover the works adjacent to Fort Harrison, this had been the performance of Lee's lieutenants:

Federal attack of August 14–16: Successfully repulsed by Charles Field, but marred by the break of two brigades.

Affair at Globe Tavern: A Confederate failure in the sense that the enemy seized and held the Petersburg and Weldon Railroad, though he lost more than 3,100 prisoners. The action raised a question whether Beauregard at the outset used sufficient force.

Battle of Reams's Station, August 24–25: A Confederate success, chiefly through Hampton's effort, without permanent gain.

Cattle raid of September 16: Distinctly to the credit of Hampton and Rosser.

Attempt to recover Fort Harrison, September 29: A failure both in coordination of attack and in outcome.

Engagement at Poplar Spring Church, September 29–October 1: Tactically a fine success for Hampton, Butler, and Rooney Lee, in spite of the break of Griffin's troopers; strategically a Union victory.

Assault on a section of the Richmond outer line, October 7: A repetition of the failure of September 29.

This was not a record of disgrace but it was a record far below the average achievement of the Confederate command at any comparable period in the Virginia campaigns fought under Lee—and it had been at heavy price in command. On August 16, the same day that Victor Girardy fell, Brigadier General John R. Chambliss was killed in fighting north of the James River. Thomas L. Clingman was wounded so severely in the leg, August 19, that his return to the army was doubtful. J. C. C. Sanders was mortally wounded on the twenty-first, two weeks after his appointment to lead Perrin's brigade. In September Brigadier General Goode Bryan resigned because of ill health. On the first of October fell John Dunovant, who had led Calbraith Butler's brigade of Hampton's cavalry division for slightly more than a month. Brigadier General John Gregg, he who had led the brilliant charge of May 6 in the Wilderness, was killed October 7. Add Godwin and Rodes killed in the Valley, and the number stricken off the list of active general officers during the two months past stood at nine.

There was another loss. With the command arrangements Beauregard had not been content. A deep grievance was the feeling that he, not Early, should have been given command in the Shenandoah Valley. Knowledge of Beauregard's dissatisfaction probably led Davis to arrange a transfer—a supervisory command, the Military Division of the West. He was glad to go, if not to assume his new duties. There probably was little regret at his departure. A change had come over the man who at Manassas had been anxious to get Joe Johnston off the field so he might have a free hand. Old Bory seemed to be developing a dislike for the responsibility of action. It may have had its origin in a feeling, scarcely conscious perhaps, that he had a reputation to maintain. If he was concerned over his fame, he manifestly was nearing the end of his usefulness. Every soldier is on the wane from the moment he begins to think more of reputation than of opportunity.

That could not be said of Jubal Early. He was unwilling to accept the defeats at Winchester and Fisher's Hill as the termination of the contest for the Shenandoah. In his camps near Staunton, after Sheridan had withdrawn northward, Early was meditating a new thrust at his adversary. In this he was encouraged by General Lee. Besides, reinforcements raised hopes. Kershaw and his division received a joyful welcome on their return to the Valley. Tom Rosser and his 600 men were regarded as a great accession; with Fitz Lee absent, wounded, Rosser assumed command of Lee's division. By Early's orders, he and Lomax soon challenged the enemy. On October 9, at Tom's Brook, near Fisher's Hill, they met the strong mounted divisions of George A. Custer and Wesley Merritt. The result was the rout of both Rosser and Lomax, with the loss of eleven guns and, Sheridan boasted, "everything else . . . carried on wheels."[32]

Early was not deterred by this minor disaster from pursuing his offensive. He found Sheridan on the north bank of Cedar Creek, where he waited in the hope that his opponent would retire or attack. Sheridan did neither. "I was now compelled," Early explained later, "to move back for want of provisions and forage, or attack the enemy in his position . . . , and I determined to attack."

Early shaped a flank operation in consequence of a reconnaissance by Gordon and Jed Hotchkiss. Gordon was to take the three divisions of the Second Corps and in the darkness march wide to the right, his objective Belle Grove farm, thought to be Sheridan's headquarters. Kershaw's division was to follow a shallower arc to strike the left of the force Gordon was to attack in front. Wharton's division, Breckinridge's old command, was to move down the Valley Pike and join in the attack. Rosser was to engage the enemy's cavalry opposite the Confederate left. Lomax's troopers were detached to loop far to the east to reach the enemy's rear. Rosser, Gordon, and Kershaw were to attack in that order at 5 o'clock, just before daylight, October 19.

It was an elaborate plan but it did not seem too ambitious for veteran troops. Everyone knew that some regiments did not have 50 per cent of their quota of officers, but this was accepted as a condition which could not be corrected and therefore should be disregarded. Most of the generals were confident; some were enthusiastic. Dodson Ramseur was full of excitement, and not solely because of the prospect of battle. An officer of the signal corps had delivered to him a somewhat mysterious message, "The crisis is over and all is well." This meant that his baby had been born, but whether it was a boy or girl, and how the mother fared, he did not know. He wrote a hurried note asking for details, closing it boyishly, "Oh Me! I want to see you so bad!"[33]

Before dawn Gordon with the entire Second Corps was in position, waiting in the moon-lit shadows. Early, who marched with Kershaw, came

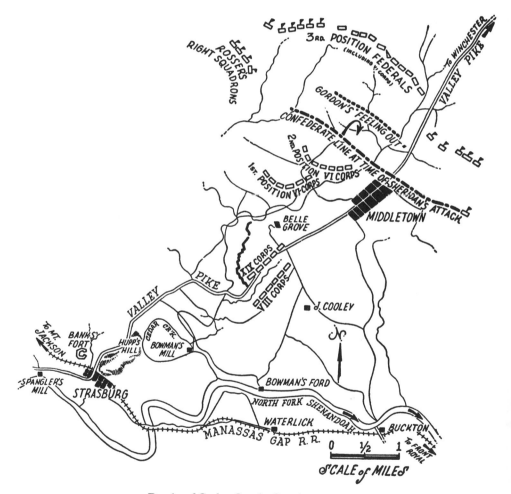

Battle of Cedar Creek, October 19, 1864.

within sight of the campfires of the sleeping enemy. It was a great hour for Jube, an hour of vengeance for Winchester and Fisher's Hill. He ordered Kershaw to cross Cedar Creek. From the left came the sound of Rosser's guns, from the right the rattle of Gordon's picket fire. Everything was proceeding according to plan and time-schedule! Early's black eyes must have kindled as he saw the Carolinians start forward. Their rush cleared the camp of the VIII Corps and carried them toward Belle Grove, where the XIX Corps was in confusion. Second Corps batteries galloped into place. There swelled from the rear of the Federals the furious fire of Gordon's men. Early rode triumphantly forward and met Gordon. The Georgian reported many prisoners and guns. Next he met Ramseur and Pegram, who told him they were facing the VI Corps and needed support. Early sent them Wharton. Ramseur was in the highest spirits. "I want to win this battle," he cried to Kyd Douglas, "for I must see my wife and baby!"[34]

The VI Corps now was rallying on what became known as the "second position" of the day. Units of the VIII and XIX fled beyond Middletown. General Wright's VI Corps men had lost most of their guns in the first Confederate onrush, and by 10 o'clock, as bright sun drove away the morning fog, had to fall back to the "third position" where Crook's troops and the XIX Corps were waiting the next turn of the battle. "His face," a staff officer wrote of Early, "became radiant with joy, and in his gladness he exclaimed, 'the sun of Middletown! The sun of Middletown!'" It was his Austerlitz.

"It is very well so far, General," said Gordon, "but we have one more blow to strike." Early did not appear to be impressed. "No use in that," he said; "they will all go directly!" Gordon answered, "This is the Sixth Corps, General. It will not go unless we drive it from the field." Early said only, "Yes, it will go too, directly."

Writing of this years afterward, Gordon said, "My heart went into my boots." Visions rose before him of the fatal halt on the first day of Gettysburg, of the hesitation to assault Grant's exposed flank on May 6 in the Wilderness. Gordon said no more. What was deep in the mind of Old Jube at the moment, history will never know. It must have seemed incredible to him that a Federal army that had lost 1,300 prisoners and eighteen guns would attempt a stand. It had been beaten; it should be in retreat; it soon would be.[35]

As the forenoon passed, Early's state of mind changed subtly and progressively from one of confidence to one of concern. His soldierly vigor was sapped by reports of his men turning back to plunder the enemy camps. The appearance of an increasing force of cavalry began to alarm him. At last, after hesitant delay and with manifest misgiving, he ordered Gordon to advance and drive the enemy from the third position. An initial repulse led Early to conclude that Gordon had abandoned the effort—in reality, Gordon saw this as a check only and was preparing to renew the assault—and he determined to suspend the offensive. "No orders came," said General Wharton, "and there we stood...." By successive stages, then, the triumphant Early who had acclaimed the "sun of Middletown" was reduced to confusion and perplexity of mind.

Sheridan had been absent from the battle and, at the first news of it, threw himself on his horse and started for Cedar Creek. At 4:30 P.M., while the Confederates stood idle, he launched a swift, oblique attack exactly where it could do most harm—on the left. So thinly held was this flank that the Federals quickly found a gap in Gordon's division. The left offered such resistance as it could, but collapsed quickly. Knowing their position hopeless, veteran troops started for Cedar Creek. When Kershaw's and Ramseur's divisions found that Gordon's men had given way, they, too, started for the rear. Panic began to show itself. Presently, through the efforts of every officer who could wield a sword or shout a command, a halt was made. It was not for long. Leaders began to fall. Dodson Ramseur, never more magnificent in battle, received a wound, which he ignored. When his horse went down under him, he changed to another. The second horse was shot. A moment later a bullet entered his right side and tore through both lungs. He was carried to the rear, but in his absence the temporary line sagged and broke.

This time there was no stopping the men. Tom Carter's artillery maintained its discipline and continued to cover the mad retreat. Early rode furiously about in an effort to stop the infantry, and swore that if he could get even 500 men to make a stand the day could be saved. Instead of a rally, there came a new alarm. Blue cavalry reached the Valley Pike in the rear. All the vehicles captured during the morning, some that belonged to the Confederates, and forty-three pieces of artillery, Union and Confederate, were taken. Failing in another rally, Early had to retreat to New Market.[36]

In his report Early convinced himself that the pillaging of the Federal camps was the reason he had not pursued his advantage during the forenoon of the nineteenth. Yet he was too intelligent a man and too experienced a soldier not to know that he had blundered ruinously in failing to press the attack against the Federals' third line. He showed this with curious naiveté. When he sent his report to Richmond by Jed Hotchkiss, the engineer entered in his journal that "General Early told me not to tell General Lee that we ought to have advanced in the morning at Middletown, for, said he, we ought to have done so." More bluntly, Jube told some of his officers, "The Yankees got whipped and we got scared."[37]

Neither then nor thereafter—such was his peculiar ineptitude for dealing with cavalry—did Early realize how he had invited disaster by his optimistic detachment of almost half his mounted troops to operate against the rear of an adversary he hoped to rout. He never once admitted that he might have given his army protection by keeping Lomax immediately on his flank. Through the detachment of Lomax, the fatal delay at Middletown, and a certain relaxation of grip after the action was joined, Early lost more than the 23 guns and 1,600 prisoners Sheridan captured. Irreplaceable veterans were lost by death and wounds. James Conner and Cullen Battle, brigadiers of much promise, were seriously wounded. Losses of regimental and company officers were so extensive that some commands were almost without leaders. Worst of all was the case of Dodson Ramseur. He had to be left in the hands of the enemy. At Sheridan's headquarters Union doctors labored with a Confederate surgeon in a futile effort to save him. A defeat was doubled in cost when it took that superb young combat officer.

The battle had not been without fine performance. All phases of the advance had been admirable. Many individual officers had outdone their previous valiant records. In the annals of the artillery of the Army of Northern Virginia nothing was finer than the manner in which Tom Carter's men had covered the retreat of the infantry. In the larger view, Early had put out of action between July 1 and October 20 the equivalent of a Federal corps or, roughly, as many Federals as he had infantry in any single engagement of the campaign. All this was against odds, not realized at the time, that often reached two and three quarters to one.

"It may be asked why with so small a force I made the attack," Early wrote of Cedar Creek. A letter from General Lee, he went on, "had expressed an earnest desire that a victory should be gained in the Valley if possible, and it could not be gained without fighting for it." That was bravely said, and truly said, but in the darkening autumn of the Confederacy it could not be stated in public. Early had retreated from Washington when it seemed within his grasp; he had been routed at Winchester, routed at Fisher's Hill, routed at Cedar Creek. That could only mean incompetence, mismanagement, and the loss of confidence of his officers and men. So ran the public indictment. Under it, a disappointed South tried and condemned Old Jube and clamored for his head. Few there were to say that Early was acting in accordance with orders and in unquestioning loyalty, personal as well as military, to the chief he so much admired and so little resembled.

CHAPTER 34

In a Ring of Iron

1. DISCIPLINE AND DESERTION

When the grievous news of Early's rout and Ramseur's death reached army headquarters, Lee had with him again his senior lieutenant to share the heavier burden the defeat in the Valley imposed. Longstreet returned the day Cedar Creek was fought. Although his right arm still was half-paralyzed, he had taught himself to write with his left hand and cherished some hope of ultimate recovery.[1] Long absence from the army had not destroyed the strategical complex he had developed during the Suffolk campaign. He was fertile in suggestion and vigorous in discipline from the hour he assumed command on the Northside.

Some of his wounded brigadiers and some of Hill's had come back to the line. McGowan, Kirkland, and Lane had resumed command in August. Archer had been exchanged. A few others came later, but there was no replacing such men as Stuart, Rodes, Ramseur, and some of the brigade commanders who had been killed after the Wilderness. "Alas," wrote war clerk Jones, when he set down the casualties of Third Winchester, "the chivalry have fallen!"[2]

In the hearts of some, hope was dying. Longstreet himself was losing faith in victory. Lee's lieutenants had followed the news of the appointment of their magnetic comrade John Hood to succeed Joe Johnston in command of the Army of Tennessee; and early in September they read that Hood had evacuated Atlanta. All men could see then that the Southern cause was losing in Georgia, and not in Georgia only. Lee had been compelled on October 4 to warn Secretary Seddon that Richmond might be captured. November brought the re-election of Lincoln and the assurance of a fight to the finish. Among the less determined a certain apathy was showing itself. From the trenches of Petersburg a young artillerist wrote, "Living cannot be called a fever here but rather a long catalepsy."[3]

If this were true among general officers, it was in the nature of the case

761

more widespread among regimental and company officers. Their ranks had been decimated; regiments often were commanded by captains and not infrequently by lieutenants. As conditions grew worse, the zeal, the ambition, the courage, even, of some company officers were dissipated. Decline in the alertness of command had its inevitable effect on discipline. June had marked the first clear evidence that the fighting edge of the army was being dulled by doubt. By mid-August the change of spirit in the ranks was discernible. Cadmus Wilcox probably stated the case precisely when his wrote his sister-in-law, "I sometimes of late think they are not quite so full of ardour as they were the first two years of the war."[4]

Probably the main reason in the early autumn for the wane in morale was that the stimulus of victory, which had been the specific for all the ills of the army, no longer could be applied. After the vain attempt to recapture the lines north of Fort Harrison, the Confederates took the offensive only when opportunity seemed large or necessity compelled. There was no great battle any day but a small battle every day. During these exchanges the Confederates could not hope to kill more opponents than the Federals themselves slew. The side numerically weaker of course had the heavier percentage of casualties. When the enemy was challenged, the odds usually were so adverse and the hardships so biting that Confederate morale was lowered, not raised.

An exception was the engagement of October 27. The Federals attempted to advance on both flanks. Longstreet repulsed them easily on the Northside by deciding correctly where the attack was to fall. Hampton's men on the Southside, with help from Heth and Mahone, drove off in confusion two Federal corps. It was a brilliant addition to Hampton's record, but bought at a price of personal anguish. In the action one of Hampton's sons, Preston, was mortally wounded. The other boy, Wade, galloped to his brother's side. When the general himself arrived, Preston was dying and Wade was gasping from a bullet that struck him while he was ministering to Preston. Afterward Hampton said that no son of his must ever be in his corps again. The younger Wade, on recovery, must join some other command. "The agony of that day—and the anxiety and the duties of the battlefield—it is all more than a mere man can bear."[5]

This notable action of October 27 was, to repeat, the exception. The infantry did not and could not leave the fortifications to taste the wine of stimulating success; rarely was there relief from the ghastly tedium of the trenches. In December the army received the last accession of strength it could hope to have. Kershaw's division, or what remained of it, left Early to rejoin its old corps north of the James. Gordon's and Pegram's troops were started from Waynesboro for Richmond by train. Both divisions had increased somewhat through the recall of detailed men, the return of convalescents, and the assignment of conscripts, but numbers of the drafted men already were deserting. When a deep snow in the Valley made it reasonably certain that Sheridan could not move, Rodes's division, under Bryan Grimes, was ordered back to the main army. By this movement, Early was left with no troops except Wharton's fragment of a division, a few batteries, and a little force of cavalry.[6]

On December 18 the telegraph clicked off the ominous intelligence that a powerful Federal fleet had left Hampton Roads, presumably for Wilmington.[7] It was imperative that Wilmington be defended. It was the only port into which blockade runners had a chance of bringing the supplies on which the life of the Confederacy depended. Hoke's division, in consequence, was detached from the Army of Northern Virginia. Its commander would return no more. Hoke had been a superlative colonel and an excellent, hard-hitting brigadier. As a division commander he had one defect only, but it might have been fatal—he could not or would not cooperate.

In terms of fighting strength, the loss of Hoke cost the army in the trenches the equivalent of 70 per cent of the infantry Lee had gained by the return of the survivors of Early's battles. Of men of all arms, presumably ready to fight, Lee had with him 51,776. Ewell's Richmond command added 5,358, some of whom were local defense troops and reservists. Meade commanded 83,826 and Butler 40,452. The Confederates were outnumbered more than two to one. In equipment, in subsistence, in regularity of supply, in everything that made for the health, comfort, and contentment of the troops, the advantage of the Federals was even greater.[8]

This was a gloomy calculation with which to end a fatal year. There had been nothing to renew the faith of the army in itself, nothing to give it hope for 1865, nothing to relieve the wretched exposure of the trenches. "Lee's Miserables," as they sometimes called themselves, knew in their hearts that they had won no shining victory since Chancellorsville. Faith was gone that the Confederates elsewhere could withstand the enemy. Hood had lost at Franklin and then at Nashville; Sherman had occupied Savannah; Fort Fisher at Wilmington had resisted successfully an attack, but a Confederate did not have to be a defeatist to admit that the enemy might come again and seal that last open port. In the face of this black prospect, the most determined soldiers refused to admit that the Southern cause would be destroyed. Others confessed privately that they did not see how the Confederacy could achieve its independence. Still others began to whisper that the end was near. Letters to the soldiers that expressed the confusion, misery, and despair on the home front fed these concerns.

Hunger deepened doubt. The notorious incapacity of the commissary was rendered daily worse by the wider Federal occupation of Southern territory and the inability of the railroads to deliver what food was available. In December there had been an acute shortage of meat. January witnessed still another crisis. The army's reserve of food was reduced to two days' short rations. February was to bring another time of hunger. "Taking these facts in connection with our paucity of numbers," Lee wrote the secretary of war, "you must not be surprised if calamity befalls us." This failure forced the retirement of chief commissary Northrop and the appointment of the able Brigadier General I. M. St. John. He improved the distribution of supplies; there remained the question whether enough could be brought to Virginia from the Carolinas to keep the army—both men and animals—from starvation.[9]

The result of weakened command, lack of victory, loss of hope, hunger, and alarm on the home front was desertion. After winter settled on the trenches in January, desertion literally multiplied. So many conscripts and even volunteers were leaving the ranks that rumors spread of impending desertion en masse. The nightly passage of men from the Southern to the Federal lines prompted a final, almost futile amnesty for the return of all deserters and a vain attempt by army commanders to stop the President's reprieves and pardons. "Hundreds of men are deserting nightly," Lee telegraphed the adjutant general on February 25, "and I cannot keep the army together unless examples are made." Over a period of ten days in February, for the entire army, 1,094 men disappeared. The greater part of these went home, rather than to the enemy, but they took arms with them and could defy the provost marshal's guard. By the beginning of March the Bureau of Conscription estimated that 100,000 deserters from the Southern armies were at large.[10]

The senior officers standing almost helpless in the face of desertion were themselves increasingly depleted in number. Governor Joe Brown of Georgia prevailed on Davis to detach Wofford and Rans Wright for service in their state. Many generals of brigade still were absent on account of wounds. Some were seriously sick. As of January 31, 1865, Longstreet, with thirteen brigades, had one major general and seven brigadiers absent. In the Second Corps, Rodes's division was without a regular leader; Early's old division was under a brigadier; one brigade was without a commander; two other brigadiers were on leave. The Third Corps was in better condition, with three only of its thirteen brigadiers absent. By the end of February the showing was worse. Of the ten major generals of infantry, only four were present. Five divisions were commanded by brigadiers. Of the thirty-nine brigade commanders, twenty-one were on duty. Seventeen brigades were under regimental officers.

Qualified men to fill some vacancies could not be found. Several of the weakest brigades were not supplied with new general officers because, in all probability, the unexpressed purpose of Lee was to unite them with other units. Longstreet urged a specific plan: Regimental vacancies should not be filled but made good by the consolidation of regiments; companies should be reduced to six per regiment, which would involve the least disruption of organization.[11] This plan was in itself an admission that most of the resources of command had been exhausted.

The personality of nearly all officers below corps command seemed to be submerged after the somber months of semi-siege. They had lost in the mud of the tangled trenches the glamour that had been theirs at Second Manassas or at Chancellorsville. Of those who retained their personality against this ugly background as the winter dragged wretchedly to its close, Longstreet stood out. He had gained the sturdy good health that always contributed to strengthen faith in him as a leader and as a fighting man. Although his loss of faith in victory became more pronounced, he neither voiced it nor permitted it to interfere with his duty. Of his division chiefs, Kershaw kept his fine, courageous spirit. Field was holding his division together with notable success. The other division of the First Corps, that of Pickett, had been employed as the mobile reserve of the army under the direct command of Lee. When Longstreet resumed command, Pickett guarded part of the outer defenses of Richmond. His case was somewhat mystifying. Although he was the senior major general of the army, Pickett was given no important detached command after his service at Petersburg in May 1864.

In the Second Corps, tragic change was ceaseless. Early had been left on the Waynesboro-Staunton front when the divisions of the corps were ordered back to Petersburg. Old Jube had little more than the equivalent of a brigade of infantry and a thin force of cavalry, under Lomax, to guard a wide area. Although defeated and discredited, Early held his head high and kept his tongue sharp. Public interest already had passed from him to John B. Gordon, who was acting commander of the Second Corps on the Richmond-Petersburg front and was gaining steadily in reputation. Gordon's temperament and his propinquity to Lee gave him a special place during the winter. He became Lee's principal confidant—as far as any man ever enjoyed that status.

Gordon's divisions were in the hands of men of measurable competence. Early's old division had been given to Ramseur and, after Ramseur moved over to command Rodes's division after that officer's death at Winchester, had passed to the command of its senior brigadier, John Pegram. This able young Virginian remained at that rank but exercised all the duties of a major general. Pegram had long been affianced to Hetty Cary of Baltimore, but his service in Tennessee and then his active duty with Lee and his wound had delayed the marriage. The day of their nuptials, January 19, 1865, was an event about which the Confederate capital talked excitedly. Eighteen days later John Pegram was killed in the trenches. His division passed temporarily to the recuperating James A. Walker.

Rodes's division, after the death of Ramseur at Cedar Creek, was under the direction of its senior brigadier, Bryan Grimes of North Carolina, who had succeeded previously to the command of Junius Daniel's brigade. On February 23, Grimes was made major general—the last officer of the Army of Northern Virginia to receive promotion to that rank. He was thirty-six and of quick and fiery temper, but in action showed judgment as well as skill and courage.

Gordon's division did not receive a new major general because Gordon presumably would return to his old command if Early again led the corps; meanwhile it was under Brigadier General Clement A. Evans. The division still contained unhappy and uncooperative remnants of famous old brigades that could not endure amicably the loss of their separate existence. William Terry's brigade included the fragments of thirteen Virginia regiments, among which were those of the Stonewall Brigade and other units of Jackson's Army of the Valley. In York's brigade were the survivors of no less than ten Louisiana regiments, including those of Dick Taylor's old brigade.

In spite of the progressive impairment of his health, Powell Hill kept the command of the Third Corps stable to the extent that all three of his division commanders were with their troops. Harry Heth had his wife with him in Petersburg and once came under the half-amused suspicion of the commanding general that he did not visit his lines as frequently as he should. Neither Lee nor Hill had to prod Mahone. Since Mahone's ambitions had been aroused by command of a division, his zeal had been complete and his service brilliant. Cadmus Wilcox was not happy. He thought often of transfer to the Trans-Mississippi Department so he could care for the widow and children of his recently deceased brother, Congressman John A. Wilcox of Texas. In this effort he failed, but dutifully he kept his troops in good condition; few divisions had a smaller number of absentees and deserters.[12]

There was, in addition, a fourth corps under Dick Anderson, though after Christmas 1864 it contained only four brigades—Elliott's, Gracie's, Matt Ransom's, and Wise's—and was in effect Beauregard's old command from the defenses of Charleston. Until Hoke was sent to Wilmington, his division also had been under Anderson. These forces had been assigned

Anderson after the departure of Beauregard and the return of Longstreet in order to preserve the separate status of the troops, assure their proper employment, and give Anderson a command in keeping with his rank. Dick Anderson himself was not in his old, easy mood. Ahead he could see the ruin of the Southern cause. He knew that his men had no faith in the future of the Confederacy and little spirit for the conflict that was certain to be renewed in a few weeks.[13]

The corps chiefs of artillery—Alexander on the Northside with Longstreet, Lindsay Walker on the Southside with Hill, Armistead Long in the Valley—discharged the active duties wisely and with little friction. After the excessive losses of guns in the Valley, there seemed no reason for retaining there, weaponless, so fine a combat officer as Tom Carter. With Braxton's and Cutshaw's battalions, he accordingly was brought back to the Richmond defenses and put in charge of the batteries of the Second Corps on that front. Stapleton Crutchfield, who had lost a leg at Chancellorsville, was able now to hobble about and was assigned to command the garrison at Chafin's Bluff and the heavy artillery battalion of the Richmond defenses. William J. Pegram, now a full colonel, continued with the Third Corps on the Petersburg line. In the same corps and with like rank were David McIntosh and William T. Poague. Because the cavalry needed more horses almost as badly as did the artillery, the officers of that service were gloomy and widely scattered. Lomax was to remain in the Valley, or near it, as long as he could. Tom Rosser was to return to the Richmond front in March.

In the events of the new year new brigade commanders had a share. Powell Hill had applied for Moxley Sorrel, Longstreet's A.A.G., to head the brigade of Rans Wright, sent to Georgia. Sorrel took command in November, and on February 7 went down with a chest wound that would incapacitate him for months. Another Georgia brigade, equally famous, also suffered a change. In succession to Wofford, also called to Georgia, was Dudley M. DuBose, former colonel of the 15th Georgia. George H. Steuart, exchanged prisoner of war, took Armistead's old brigade. Brigadier General J. J. Archer did not long survive his release from prison and resumption of command; Colonel William McComb of the 14th Tennessee was promoted to succeed him. The fragments of Bushrod Johnson's Tennessee brigade were consolidated with Archer's men. The brigade of the wounded Stephen Elliot was entrusted to Colonel William H. Wallace of the 18th South Carolina, who was made a brigadier in accordance with the act for temporary appointments. Colonel William H. Forney, 10th Alabama, was promoted and assigned to Sanders's brigade. James P. Simms, colonel of the 53rd Georgia, was named as successor to the resigned Goode Bryan. To Young M. Moody, colonel of the 43rd Alabama, was entrusted the brigade of Archibald Gracie, killed in the Petersburg trenches on December 3. Colonel W. F. Perry, who had commanded Law's old brigade for months, was appointed brigadier on March 16. Some of these were last-minute imperative appointments to assure direction of troops when open campaigning began. In more than one instance, perhaps, promotion was not made because the officer was assumed to be competent, but because other aspirants were manifestly, even notoriously unqualified. The springs of command had run dry.

Colonel Lindsay Walker received on March 1 the commission of brigadier general of artillery, which Long of the Second Corps and Alexander of the First already held. Of the cavalrymen, Colonel R. L. T. Beale of the 9th Virginia was advanced January 13 to the rank of brigadier and assigned formally to the brigade he had been leading ever since the death of John R. Chambliss.

Three other changes of a character more dramatic were made. Worn by hard service and outraged by unjust criticism, James A. Seddon insisted on resigning as secretary of war. On February 6, 1865, John C. Breckinridge succeeded him. Simultaneously, the position of the foremost Southern leader was changed. Because of discontent in the General Assembly of Virginia and in the Congress with the management of the war, the President somewhat reluctantly signed, on January 23, a bill for the appointment of a general-in-chief to command the military forces of the Confederate States. This avowedly was a last effort to utilize the abilities of Lee to the fullest. Had this order been interpreted by the Army of Northern Virginia as notice that Lee would cease to exercise direct control of his old troops, more harm than good would have been done. As it was understood that Lee would remain in command in Virginia and act elsewhere through the generals in the field, the enlargement of the duties of "Marse Robert" was to the men in the trenches little more than a matter of present pride and vague hope.

The third major change was full of tragedy. Near Waynesboro, on March 2, Jubal Early was attacked again by Sheridan in overwhelming strength. Early's small command was demoralized and in bad order. He had little more than 1,000 infantry and just 6 guns that could be moved; Tom Rosser collected about 100 cavalry to form a skirmish line. Early tried to make a stand long enough to evacuate his guns and supplies. It was not to be. The small force broke quickly; the enemy got in its rear. With about a score of companions, Early rode over the mountains in an effort to escape, and after much hardship reached Petersburg. He had left with a corps; he came back almost alone.[14]

Lee determined to send Jube back to the Valley, which Sheridan had by that time left, in the hope he would be able to collect and reorganize scattered troops. There was no thought, apparently, of restoring Early to the command of the Second Corps on the Petersburg front. Gordon was doing admirably. Lee must have reasoned, also, that Early's disasters would make him unacceptable to the troops. Failure overtook this considerate effort to keep Early in the service by employing him in the Valley. A desperate people and an embittered press were unwilling to have the defeated general retained in any position of military trust. So great was the clamor that Lee on March 30 had to relieve Early of command and send him home to await orders. To this fate had fallen Old Jube of Manassas and Williamsburg, of Cedar Mountain and Sharpsburg, of Salem Church and the Monocacy.

2. THE LAST ATTEMPTS AT GRAND STRATEGY

The miserable, wintry weeks of desertion and reorganization had witnessed desperate attempts by the Confederates to use the knife of strategy to cut the coils that were enveloping them. After the repulse of Butler's attack of December 23–26 on Fort Fisher, below Wilmington, the Federals returned to Hampton Roads, refitted, changed commanders, and steamed back. Fire from the fleet heavily damaged Fort Fisher on January 14. The next afternoon the fort with its armament and garrison fell. The defense had been conducted by Braxton Bragg, sent to Wilmington in advance, and by Robert Hoke and Chase Whiting and William Lamb, the immediate commander of the fort. Both Lamb and Whiting were wounded and captured. Whiting was sent to Fort Columbus, Governor's Island, whence he wrote a furious demand for an investigation of the conduct of Bragg, whom he blamed for the disaster. Whiting did not live to prosecute his charge or to witness the effect on the Southern cause of the loss of the fortifications he had built. Death from his wound ended on March 10 his strange, frustrated career.[15]

So desperate had the situation now become that the possibility of peace negotiations was seized upon eagerly. Francis P. Blair, Sr., had came to Richmond January 12; as mysteriously as he arrived, Blair left the city. Millions of Southerners hoped that he carried with him a draft of a peace treaty. It was manifest by the time of Blair's visit that Sherman would march northward from Savannah into South Carolina. If not resisted successfully there by the small force W. J. Hardee commanded at Charleston, Sherman could advance into North Carolina and into southern Virginia.

Were Lee's army to remain at Petersburg, facing Grant's troops, Sherman could destroy the last railroads that fed the army, and then he could take Lee in flank or rear.

Sherman must be stopped. That was imperative. By no possibility could "Lee's Miserables" contend against Grant and Sherman combined. Conner's brigade, which had been Kershaw's famous old command, accordingly was sent to South Carolina at the instance of Governor A. G. Magrath. Pending a decision whether additional infantry could be dispatched from Virginia, more cavalry had to be provided. Hampton believed that his crippled old division under Calbraith Butler could get mounts if it went back to South Carolina to seek them. Lee authorized the move, and regretfully, also, he authorized Hampton to leave the army and visit the Palmetto State and endeavor to stir the people.

This detachment of Butler on January 19 was the final instance in which the Army of Northern Virginia was weakened to strengthen the Confederate cause elsewhere. The release of one third of the cavalry seemed necessary and appeared to involve no heavier risks than had been taken half a dozen times; but the event was to show—as Lee himself saw afterward—that the departure of Hampton's division hastened the catastrophe.

Had it been possible to honor the departing Wade Hampton, he would have deserved the homage of massed regiments, dipping standards, and acclaiming hands. In all the high companionship of knightly men, none had exemplified more of character and courage and none had fewer mistakes charged against him. Untrained in arms and abhorring war, the South Carolina planter had proved himself the peer of any professional soldier commanding within the same bounds and opportunities. He may not have possessed military genius, but he had the nearest approach to it.

By the end of January, John M. Schofield, with heavy reinforcements, arrived at Wilmington and assumed direction of the Federal Department of North Carolina. Schofield was placed under the orders of Sherman, ominous confirmation of the fear that the stern man who had wasted Georgia would hasten up the Atlantic coast toward the dwindling army in the Petersburg trenches and on the bleak and muddy lines below Richmond.

As a consequence of Francis P. Blair's visit to the Confederate capital, on February 3 a conference was held in Hampton Roads between President Lincoln and Secretary of State William Seward on one side and, on the other, three Confederate representatives, Vice-President Alexander H. Stephens, Senator R. M. T. Hunter, and former Supreme Court Justice James A. Campbell. At the close of a single meeting the Southerners left and returned to Richmond. On the sixth President Davis announced formally that the Hampton Roads conference had failed because Mr. Lincoln "refused to enter into negotiations . . . or to permit us to have peace on any other basis than our unconditional submission to their rule. . . ."[16]

The disappointment came at a time of crisis in everything. Two days previously, Lee had been compelled to dissipate the last hope of the administration that he could hold his lines and still send substantial assistance to South Carolina. This could not be done, Lee said; Hardee or Beauregard or whoever commanded in the Palmetto State must oppose Sherman with such force as could be mustered there. No peace without surrender, no meat for men battling in wintry weather, no prospect of effective resistance to Sherman—in the face of all this the braver officers and men held together.

It was learned that Beauregard had resumed command in South Carolina. While he reported himself with fewer men than would constitute a strong brigade, Old Bory was fertile in suggesting what should be done with the troops of other leaders. With the fall of Wilmington, military chaos was threatened in North Carolina, and it was plain that command must be coordinated at once. Lee had to conclude that Beauregard, in the circumstances, was not "able to do much." Accordingly, in spite of the President's notorious dislike of Joseph E. Johnston, Lee as general-in-chief had Johnston given the direction of the Department of Tennessee and Georgia and of the Department of South Carolina, Georgia, and Florida. There was no time for finesse. Beauregard and his forces and Bragg's troops from Wilmington were directed to report to Johnston.[17]

Without hope of peace by negotiation, nothing remained for Lee's army except to resume the fight in the field, provided the men were willing to face the overmastering odds. By March, two possibilities of breaking the grip of the enemy were considered and, in time, were combined. One was for Johnston to hold off Sherman, beat the Federals if possible, and prevent a junction with Schofield. If Johnston failed in this, he was to move his own forces toward Virginia. The Army of Northern Virginia was to shake itself loose from Grant and march to join Johnston. The two Confederate armies were then to assail Sherman and, having defeated him, were to turn and attack Grant.

Johnston never had much faith in realization of the scheme because he knew the weakness of his troops, on whom Lee and the administration placed too much reliance, but the commander in North Carolina worked hard and honestly to checkmate his adversary. The enemy, Johnston soon concluded, was too strong and too advantageously placed to be attacked with any prospect of success. If junction was effected between Sherman and Schofield, "their march into Virginia," said Johnston on March 11, "cannot be prevented by me."

Concluding that Johnston's army could accomplish little, Lee studied a second plan that fitted into the first. Longstreet, Gordon, and Johnston had made the same general suggestion in different forms. It was, in effect, that Lee endeavor to hold Richmond and Petersburg, or Richmond only, with part of his forces and dispatch the rest to join Johnston for an attack on Sherman. Then the victorious army could move northward, relieve Richmond, and deal with Grant on terms less unequal. The main defect of the plan was patent: The Confederate lines on the Richmond-Petersburg front already were so lightly held that if any part of the defenders were detached, Grant could storm almost any sector he chose.[18]

Discussion produced at length, through the ingenuity of Gordon, a plan that seemed to overcome this objection. Gordon proposed that at a point he believed vulnerable, he assault the Federal line, break through, take a position in rear, and sweep down the Union works to force Grant to abandon the left of his line. Lee then would have a shorter front and consequently a greater density of force.[19] Perhaps it was indicative not only of the desperation but also of the distorted military thought of the Confederates that in planning this they should ignore the certainty of an immediate counterstroke by Grant. They assumed, apparently, that after the Confederates broke through, the Union commander submissively would disregard his own numerical superiority and docilely take up a shorter line. That was not Grant's way. He would blunder but he always would fight. At the moment he was thinking of Lee's retreat and the difficulty of overtaking him. Grant would have asked nothing better than that the Confederates assume the offensive.

In curious disregard of this, Lee authorized Gordon to develop his plan for storming the Federal lines and cutting off the Union left. Approval would depend in part on what happened in North Carolina, and in part on a new and most ominous factor, namely, the probable return of Sheridan's mounted troops to Grant's army. There was no reason why Sheridan's cavalry should remain in the Shenandoah Valley. He had destroyed all its barns and mills and stables; the Valley could supply no more food to the Confederate army. If Sheridan returned while Calbraith Butler's division was in Carolina to oppose the advancing Sherman and Schofield, the Confederate troopers of Fitz Lee and Rooney Lee would face odds that would be long and might be hopeless.

Events moved swiftly. On the night of March 23, after Gordon had explained to Lee what he intended to do, he was told to assemble his forces and make the assault on the morning of the twenty-fifth. The plan he had developed was to deliver a surprise attack before dawn at a point, Fort Stedman, where the opposing trenches were not more than 150 yards apart.

Men in three carefully chosen columns of 100 were to press through the enemy line, then make a rush for small forts behind the heavy main defenses. While fire from these forts was poured into the rear of the Federals, strong forces would rush through the break and advance up and down the trenches. Cavalry would push to the rear and destroy the enemy's lines of communication. Almost half the Confederate infantry on the Southside were to be thrown into the assault. On the twenty-fourth it was decided to bring Pickett's division from the Northside and use it also, if it could arrive in time. While the attack was being delivered, Longstreet was to demonstrate below Richmond.

All the preparations were made smoothly and with maximum secrecy. In the pre-dawn darkness, March 25, Gordon ordered the signal given. The Confederate pickets, who had crept forward, sprang silently upon the opposing pickets. Experienced axemen, with swift blows, hacked to pieces the sharpened timbers that protected the Union works. Behind them poured the three columns of 100, each man with a white band on his arm. After these troops surged the main body of the infantry.

Surprise scarcely could have been more nearly complete. Passageways were cut through the heavy obstructions. Everything worked to perfection. Gordon went with the troops into Fort Stedman, where he saw his men spread to left and right and observed a large number of sleepy, bewildered prisoners. It looked as if success would attend the operation on which hung the life of the Confederacy! Picked officers and men of Stribling's battalion of artillery turned the four guns of Fort Stedman on the enemy. Ordnance in an adjoining battery also was brought into service against the Federals. Never had fortune smiled more approvingly on John B. Gordon. What he wanted to hear now was the crash of guns from the small forts in the rear, the forts to which he had told those columns of 100 to press. If the guns in those earthworks would bring their fire to bear on the Union rear, the victory would be complete.[20]

Presently came couriers from the advance columns reporting that they could not find the forts they were seeking. There followed long, long minutes of uncertainty, confusion, and suspense. Then, gradually, a fine initial success became a reversed Battle of the Crater. Before they realized it, the Confederates were confined to Fort Stedman and a narrow front of trenches from which they could not advance. There was no prospect of reinforcements; Gordon had been warned that the arrival of Pickett was improbable. Grimly, at dawn, Gordon had to notify Lee that the rear forts had not been reached and that the advance had been halted.

Tenure of Stedman and the near-by captured line soon became intolerable. As it became light all the Federal batteries on a long stretch of line were hurling their projectiles into the fort and the adjacent work. In these works, open to the rear, Gordon's men were exposed helplessly. The Southern commander could see also, as morning light spread, that the enemy was massing troops in a cordon around Fort Stedman. An attack evidently would be made in a short time, and this could not be prevented by anything Gordon could do. John Gordon had learned the rewards of tenacity, and doubtless he would have died manfully, if the cause demanded the sacrifice, at the farthest traverse his troops had reached. That was not required of him. About 8:00 A.M. orders came from General Lee to evacuate the captured works.

There followed a scene that few of the Southern commanders liked to mention afterward. Every man in the ranks could see for himself that the return to the Confederate positions, across the open ground between the lines, would be a challenge of death. The bravest took the chance; the weak and the dispirited defied their commanders and chose surrender. When the broken divisions were back in their red trenches and able to estimate their losses, they found they had left behind in the Federal works and in the field between the lines probably 3,500 men. Of this total, approximately 1,900 were prisoners.

The action did not end with the return of the Confederates to their lines. An attack ordered by Meade against the picket lines in front of the II and VI Corps was successful and made the Confederate loss in prisoners that day heavier than in any day's action on Lee's front after the Bloody Angle. On the entire front, March 25, the Federal losses were 2,080 men. Gross Confederate casualties certainly reached 4,400 and perhaps 5,000. R. M. Stribling, who had taken his artillerists to Fort Stedman and served the guns there, had no illusions. "This attack," he wrote subsequently, "demonstrated that Lee's army had lost hope of final success, and the men were not willing to risk their lives in a hopeless endeavor. . . ."[21]

Gordon's responsibility for the greater part of the day's casualties was not appraised at the time and is not easy to determine now. His repulse was due, in part, to his failure to appreciate the severity of the artillery fire he had to encounter in the attack or while retiring in the event of repulse. Much of his heaviest loss was sustained when his men were recrossing the open field between the works. In his account of preparations for the attack, Gordon made singularly little reference to the artillery's part in the operation, and he seems not to have sought advice from Second Corps artillery commanders. Gordon's other serious mistake was in assuming that he could capture easily the "three small forts" in rear of Stedman. In fact very little was known of these forts, and there had been little chance that Gordon's men could find them in the dark. It seems strange that the engineers should not have known more of them; but perhaps Gordon, as in the case of the artillerists, may not have seen fit to consult with the engineer officers.

Gordon said later that the guides became lost in the rush of the advance columns and that the commanders had then been confused and unable to find the forts. With this he coupled the non-arrival of Pickett in support, though he had been warned that Pickett probably could not reach the scene in time to be of help.[22]

To none of this did the army command give thought after the failure of the attack. Nearer, fatal actualities absorbed every mind.

3. PICKETT AND PEGRAM: A CLOSING CONTRAST

Two days before the attack on Fort Stedman, Joe Johnston had telegraphed that Sherman and Schofield had formed a junction at Goldsboro, 120 miles from Petersburg. Johnston stated in fullest candor that his small command could not hinder Sherman's advance to a union with Grant. That had been one reason Gordon's assault had been set for the twenty-fifth. Now that Gordon had failed, every general officer and many a man of lesser rank sensed what Lee confided to the President on March 26: The time was at hand to evacuate Richmond and Petersburg and to unite with the forces in North Carolina.[23]

The one route to Johnston's lines, with railroad communication all the way, was via the Southside Railroad to Burkeville, and thence parallel to the Richmond and Danville to its terminus. Beyond Danville the army could use the Piedmont Railroad which led to Greensboro, North Carolina. All rail movement directly west from Petersburg and all delivery of supplies at Petersburg from the Southside Railroad manifestly depended on keeping the enemy from that line of track. Lee's army could not subsist many days if Grant seized the railroad beyond the extreme right of the Confederate line, which now rested on Hatcher's Run. Once Grant was astride the railroad, Petersburg was lost. Ipso facto, Richmond was. If, in addition, the Federal cavalry could swing far beyond the Confederate right and get across the roads that led to Danville. . . .

This must not be, but the threat now was imminent. Set free by Early's defeat at Waynesboro, Sheridan had reached, on March 19, White House on the Pamunkey. On the day of Fort Stedman, Fitz Lee sent word that Sheridan again was moving. The destination of this heavy mounted force could be none other than the Federal left. Sheridan therefore must be kept from the Southside Railroad until preparations to evacuate Petersburg had been completed.

To oppose Sheridan, who counted some 13,000 sabers, the Confeder-ates could employ Fitz Lee's division, Rooney Lee's, and Rosser's, if what remained of Rosser's forces could be termed a division. The strength of these units probably did not exceed 5,500. Butler was gone with his 2,200 men. Gone, too, was Hampton, whose leadership had offset odds on many a battlefield. The necessity that had compelled the dispatch of Hampton and Butler to the Carolinas might prove the decisive circumstance of the campaign; but there was no way of changing that. Fitz Lee must leave Gary's brigade on the left and bring the rest to the right. This would sup-plement by 900 the division of Rooney Lee, whose 2,500 must bear the heavier part of the fight. Fitz, as senior, would command all. To strengthen this force, a desperate, clumsy proposal made by Longstreet had been adopted: Infantry were to be used in place of cavalry. Pickett's division was to operate with Fitz Lee in protecting the right.[24]

On March 29, four days after the attempted breakthrough had failed, word came that Federal cavalry and infantry were moving south and west. Orders went out for an immediate concentration on the extreme right. During the night Pickett marched his troops across Hatcher's Run to the trenches farthest westward. The next morning, March 30, Pickett, Dick Anderson, and Heth met with the commanding general. Reports were that the enemy had reached Dinwiddie Court House, and had artillery as well as infantry and cavalry. Later came abundant evidence that Federal horse were spread widely to the south of Five Forks. All practical means of dealing with this advance by Sheridan were considered. Pickett seemed to have the best opportunity. He was told to take his three brigades, two of Anderson's, and six guns of William Pegram's and march to Five Forks, where Fitz Lee then was. Rooney Lee and Rosser were to report there as well. Pickett was to be in general command. From Five Forks he must advance in the direction of Dinwiddie Court House and assail the enemy. It was an order in the old spirit of the army—to disdain odds and attack.

This was an honor for Pickett but it carried a weight of responsibility. For-tune had not been kind to him since that great, bloody day at Gettysburg. His expedition in North Carolina had not been successful; the effort to cope with Butler's advance in May 1864 had put him in bed; the reputation of his famous division had been marred by the conscripts who no sooner reached the army than they tried to desert. Fame had passed him by. Now he must deal with Sheridan. A victory would be a triumph, but the roads were almost impassable, the men were hungry, the odds were frightful.

Soon after noon on the thirtieth General Lee rode grimly back to head-quarters near Petersburg. Pickett was his own commander now. It was 4:30 before his column, harassed by small bodies of cavalry, reached Five Forks,

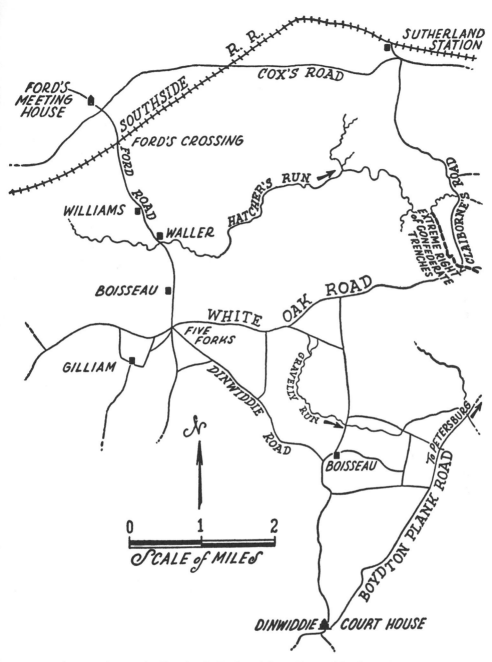

Approaches to the Southside Railroad from Dinwiddie Court House,
with references to the Battle of Five Forks, April 1, 1865.

a bare crossroads in the all-engulfing forest. There, as anticipated, Pickett found Fitz Lee. Rooney Lee and Rosser had not reached the rendezvous, and Pickett decided to wait until morning to continue his march. On March 31, with his cavalry reinforcement at hand, Pickett pressed his advance toward Dinwiddie Court House. His men were alert and full of fight; the spirit of the old army was apparently as stout as ever. After a day of sometimes sharp skirmishing with the blue cavalry, Pickett halted at dark within half a mile of the Court House.[25]

During the night he learned that Tom Munford's outposts on the left had captured two infantrymen from Warren's familiar V Corps. Pickett decided promptly that he should not remain in an advanced position. He had established that the Federal cavalry were in great strength at Dinwiddie Court House and had infantry support. He felt he should not expose his forces needlessly. It was better to take position where he could discharge his main duty, which was to protect the Confederate right flank and the approaches to the Southside Railroad. It was daybreak on the fateful first of April when the gray column began to move back northward through the mud. The enemy followed, but did not force a fight.

When Pickett reached Five Forks during the forenoon, he dispatched his wagons across the protecting shelter of Hatcher's Run and reported his movements and his needs to General Lee. He received a telegram from the commanding general: "Hold Five Forks at all hazards. Protect road to Ford's Depot and prevent Union forces from striking the Southside Railroad." Lee forbade a farther retreat for compelling reasons: If Five Forks was taken and the enemy reached the railroad, all would be lost. Again, if Pickett abandoned Five Forks, the Federals could get above the headwaters of Hatcher's Run and turn the Confederate right there. The position at Five Forks was weak, in itself, but strategically it was the most important in that sector. It had to be defended.[26]

Pickett wrote subsequently that he assumed his telegram concerning his withdrawal had been received at army headquarters, that reinforcements would be sent him, and that a diversion would be made in his behalf. On these assumptions, he may not have been vigilant or careful in deploying his troops to meet possible attack that day. Pickett put Rooney Lee's cavalry on the right. On his left he placed a regiment, and no more than a regiment, of Munford's troopers, to maintain contact with William P. Roberts's weak cavalry brigade, which in turn tenuously connected Pickett with the Confederate right-flank trenches held by Dick Anderson. Roberts's men were stout fighters but, like most of the regiments, they were lacking in field officers. A stronger brigade should have been in its place.

Between Roberts and Munford's regiment on the left and Rooney Lee's division on the right, and paralleling White Oak Road, Pickett deployed his infantry. With its left refused, Matt Ransom's brigade of Bushrod Johnson's division was on the extreme left. Wallace's brigade of the same division joined Ransom. Next, extending as far as the crossroads, was George H. Steuart's brigade. To his right was Terry. Beyond him as right-flank element was Corse's brigade. Corse had not fought at Gettysburg, but Terry's brigade had been Kemper's, and Steuart's had been Armistead's. The descent of those Virginia soldiers from their furious charge up Cemetery Ridge to their pathetic defense of a wooded crossroads was the epitome of their army's decline.

In rear of the infantry, the remaining units of Fitz Lee's division were posted along the road running to the railway. As a reserve, north of Hatcher's Run, were the two cavalry brigades of Dearing and McCausland, under Tom Rosser. The six guns of William Pegram were placed at intervals where the wooded country offered any field of fire. If these dispositions along White Oak Road were made with less care, and were followed by less than the usual field entrenchment, an explanation was offered, years afterward, by Fitz Lee: "We were not expecting any attack that afternoon, so far as I know." He believed that his men and Pickett's infantry could beat off any attack by Sheridan's cavalry. If Federal infantry left their lines to support Sheridan, then a corresponding force from Dick Anderson would be sent to Five Forks. Such was the reasoning of Fitz Lee as well as of Pickett.

These two officers failed to realize the significance of a fight that occurred to their left on March 31. To discourage any attempt by the Federals to penetrate the gap between Anderson's right and Pickett's left, Lee had directed Anderson to attack on his front. At first there had been hope for success, but it faded quickly for want of reinforcements. Gloomily, sullenly, the men of Anderson's command returned to their trenches. Losses were about 800. Reduced by that number, and with two of his brigades already assisting Pickett, Anderson manifestly was in no condition to give further aid to the right. Not realizing this, Pickett and Fitz Lee cherished the general belief that the commanding general somehow would contrive to achieve the "impossible," even though, in this case, the line was already stretched to the breaking point.[27]

Besides their overconfidence, and their lack of understanding of the dread immediacy of the crisis, it is probable that a third consideration, a most human one, led them to assume that "general precaution" sufficed. Cavalryman Tom Rosser has spent a day on the Nottoway River immediately before moving on March 30–31 to Five Forks. The shad had been running in the Nottoway, and with a borrowed seine Rosser had caught many of the fine fish. He brought them with him, and when his division was ordered north of Hatcher's Run as a reserve on April 1, he arranged for an afternoon shad-bake. In the assurance that this would provide a meal delectable at any time and incredible in the hungry days of bone-gnawing war, he invited Generals Pickett and Fitz Lee to his shad-bake. Neither man lost any time in preparing to keep the appointment.

Before Fitz Lee started for Rosser's headquarters, Tom Munford dashed up with a dispatch from Roberts's brigade on the extreme left. It reported that Roberts's troopers had been attacked by overpowering Federals to the east of Five Forks, and that the brigade had been split and driven off by the attack. If this information was correct, then Sheridan had reached White Oak Road and destroyed contact between Pickett's force and the right of the Confederate fortifications. The isolation of Pickett was a reality.

Fitz Lee was either impatiently hungry or uncritically skeptical. He said merely, "Well, Munford, I wish you would go over in person at once and see what this means and, if necessary, order up your division and let me hear from you." With that, the chief of cavalry went off. Munford saw Fitz and Pickett riding northward together in the direction of Hatcher's Run, some two miles distant, though he knew nothing of their destination or of their reason for being together. Their unannounced departure left Rooney Lee as senior officer, but he was far to the right, had no knowledge that his seniors had left the field, and no information of the skirmish on the left. Among the cavalrymen on the scene on the left, the senior was now Munford. The infantry, in the absence of Pickett, had Maryland Steuart as their commander. Pegram was the ranking artillerist. None, to repeat, knew that Pickett and Fitz Lee had quit the lines.[28]

The shad-bake was a social secret, but, as food was abundant, the affair was leisured and deliberate as every feast should be. If there was "something to drink" it probably was not shunned, but there was no evidence, then or thereafter, that any of the trio got drunk. Hours slipped pleasantly past. When two of Rosser's pickets came to report the enemy advancing on the roads they were guarding, there was little concern. All appeared to be quiet; the enemy evidently was approaching but he was not attacking. With any skirmishes that might be opened, the officers at the front could deal.

After 4 o'clock Pickett asked Rosser for a courier to take a message to Five Forks. The man set off with the dispatch and doubtless the conversation around Rosser's hospitable fire resumed. Soon there came from south of Hatcher's Run a burst of infantry fire. In plain view, on the other side of the stream, the generals saw the courier captured by the Federals. At the same time, a line of bluecoats crossed the road.

That ended the party. Pickett took horse and galloped across Hatcher's Run. He continued his pace until he came to a line of Fitz Lee's cavalrymen, under Munford, defending the road to Five Forks. They were retreating slowly before Federal infantry not 100 yards distant. "Hold them back till I can pass to Five Forks," Pickett called. Captain James Breckinridge, 3rd Virginia cavalry, heard Pickett's appeal and led a brief counterattack. It cost Breckinridge's life but probably saved Pickett's. The general threw himself forward on his horse, with his head on the farther side from the enemy, and ran the gantlet of several hundred yards of furious infantry fire.[29]

The battle that had occurred while the generals were eating shad was ending by this time. It had been as swift as it had been disastrous. Sheridan had eleven brigades of cavalry and Warren's V Corps of infantry. His full strength did not fall below 30,000 as against Pickett's 10,000. Sheridan demonstrated against the Confederate right while prodding forward the V Corps against the Confederate left. Deployment of the Federal infantry for the final attack was bold and unconcealed. Munford sent courier after courier to report to Pickett or Fitz Lee. Neither general was to be found; nobody knew whither either had ridden. The attack was irresistible on the left. Soon it rolled Ransom back on Wallace. When Pickett rode on the field, the retreating left was more than half a mile west of the original position. Corse's brigade held firmly together and was used to rally some of the fugitives. Rooney Lee beat off charges and, at dark, in good order, slipped away. Except for these stalwarts, those of Pickett's men who escaped from the field were reduced to panic and were pursued till night. The number captured by the V Corps was 3,244, and by the cavalry some 2,000, along with 11 flags and 4 guns. It probably was a more costly day than that of the attack on Fort Stedman, more costly than any since the Bloody Angle of the preceding year.[30]

To the artillerists it was a day of disaster not to be recorded solely in terms of four guns lost or of good soldiers captured. The chief of artillery on the field, Colonel William Pegram, had felt keenly the death of his magnificent brother John, the general of the family, on February 6. Harry Heth and Dick Anderson had asked for Willie Pegram's promotion to general officer and assignment to command an infantry brigade, and Powell Hill had endorsed the recommendation. It was returned, camp gossip had it, with the statement that "the artillery could not lose the services of so valuable an officer." It mattered little to the young artillerist. Harry Heth called Pegram "one of the few men who, I believe, was supremely happy when in battle. He was then in his element."

The frightful crash of Warren's opening volley had sent Pegram racing toward the assailed left. Soon he was among his gunners there. They were firing furiously but in perfect order at Federals who were not more than 30 to 50 yards in their front. He rode out between the guns. "Fire your canister low," he said to his men. A moment later he reeled and fell from his horse. "I'm mortally wounded; take me off the field," he cried. In time an ambulance was found and he was borne to the rear.

"I shall never forget that night of waiting," Pegram's adjutant, Gordon McCabe, wrote afterward. "I could only pray. He breathed heavily through the night, and passed into a stupor. I bound his wounds as well as I knew how and moistened his lips with water. Sunday morning he died as gently as possible."[31]

His cause was dying with him.

CHAPTER 35

The Last March

1. THE COLLAPSE OF COMMAND

The day of the Battle of Five Forks, April 1, was one of intensest anxiety on the front from which Pickett had been isolated. Nothing positive was known at the headquarters of Lee or of Powell Hill concerning Pickett's contest until late in the afternoon. Then it was apparent only that a reverse had been sustained. Dick Anderson was ordered to send the three remaining brigades of Bushrod Johnson's command to support the cavalry in defense of the Southside Railroad. By that movement, the three miles of line on the extreme Confederate right were, in effect, abandoned.

On receipt of the first news of Pickett's lost battle, Field's division of the First Corps was ordered to the Southside during the afternoon of April 1 to restore, if possible, the shattered right. Longstreet was directed to come in person with these troops. To all who knew of these instructions, the transfer of 4,600 men from the thinly held left was confession that the entire line south of the Appomattox was in danger of rupture even if it were not turned.[1]

Powell Hill sensed this as he went over this line, yard by yard, to see that abatis and *chevaux de frise* and all the other obstructions were in place. For the preceding year and more, Hill had received more than his share of the army's adversity. Few of his days after his promotion to corps command had been as brilliant as those of the year during which he had led the Light Division. At Gettysburg there had been a flash of splendor on the first of July, but after that Hill had a bystander's part in the drama. Bristoe Station, the stampede of Wilcox and Heth in the Wilderness, his own illness there and at Spotsylvania—all these must have been unhappy memories. The contests at Globe Tavern and Reams's Station had brought at least as much honor to Billy Mahone as to him. The Crater, too, had been Mahone's battle. Hill had the affection of his men; his magnetism and personality made him one of the most popular officers in the army. In rare instances, when he felt that his own punctilious observance of the military amenities was disregarded, he could be stiff, stern, bitter. The third senior officer of the army he was, and during Longstreet's absence, the second; but he may have felt what others often said privately—that as a corps commander he had not fulfilled expectations.

Ill health, like ill fortune, increasingly had been Hill's lot during 1864–65. After weeks of sickness he had procured leave in March. He hurried back to Petersburg with the approach of the crisis, and before his leave expired he resumed command, though his sickness clung to him. Now, as he sought sleep after his day of inspection, the guns were rumbling all along the line.

With the passing of the hours, the fire became more violent. Long before dawn, April 2, Hill was awakened by reports that the enemy had captured part of the line near Rives's Salient. He asked for any reports received during the night from Heth or Wilcox. Nothing had come; there was no further news of the break in the line. Hill mounted and rode rapidly to army headquarters. He went in at once to Lee, who was lying partly clothed on the bed. With little ceremony, the two began to discuss what could be done to hold the line. Abruptly, Colonel Venable broke into the room. Army wagons, he said, were being driven wildly along the road toward Petersburg. An officer occupying a hut far within the lines said that Federal skirmishers had driven him from it.[2]

Hill sprang up and hastened from the house: He must reach his troops at once and rally them. Venable and two couriers joined him. The four rode toward the enemy. Soon they had evidence of their own that Unionists already were inside the Confederate lines. Bullets began to whistle; bluecoats were swarming around the huts that had been used during the winter by Mahone's division. The only indication of the presence of any troops to oppose the Federals was the sight of an unemployed battalion of Southern artillery on a nearby hill. Venable was sent to place the guns where they could open on the enemy. Two Union infantrymen were captured by the party and sent to the rear under the guard of one of the couriers.

Accompanied now by only his chief courier, George Tucker, Hill continued across fields and through copses where Federals might be encountered at any minute. Soon Tucker spoke up: "Please excuse me, General, but where are you going?"

"Sergeant, I must go to the right as quickly as possible. We will go up this side of the branch to the woods, which will cover us until reaching the field in rear of General Heth's quarters. I hope to find the road clear at General Heth's." Tucker said nothing. The two silently crossed the Boydton Plank Road and followed the edge of the woodland for about a mile.

Not one person, Federal or Confederate, civilian or soldier, did they encounter. Hill must have felt this was but the luck of the moment. "Sergeant," he said, "should anything happen to me, you must go back to General Lee and report it."

On they went until they reached a field, beyond which, in a road, a mass of men was visible. Hill raised his field-glasses. "There they are," he said simply. Tucker asked, "Which way now, General?" Hill pointed to the woods that paralleled the Boydton road: "We must keep on to the right." They pushed ahead until they were within some 30 yards of the woods. Soon Tucker saw 6 or 8 Federals lurking among the trees. Two of them leveled their guns and took aim. Tucker flashed a quick glance at Hill at his side. "We must take them," said Hill, and he quickly drew his pistol.

"Stay there!" called Tucker. "I'll take them." Then he shouted to the Federals: "If you fire, you'll be swept to hell! Our men are here. Surrender!" "Surrender!" cried Hill in the same instant.

"I can't see it," one of the Federals said to his companion. "Let us shoot them." Two shots were fired. One went wild. The other struck the uplifted left hand of Hill, took off his thumb in the gauntlet, and entered his heart. Tucker dodged, reached out to catch the general's horse, and saw Hill on the ground, arms thrown out, motionless.[3]

A few hours later, Colonel William H. Palmer rode up to the Venable cottage near Petersburg and dismounted. His instructions from the commanding general were to break to Mrs. Hill the news of her husband's death, and then to move her and the two children across the Appomattox and out of the path of danger that day. At the door he heard from within a clear voice singing, a woman's voice. Hearing the footfall of her husband's chief of staff, Mrs. Hill turned her eyes to the doorway. The note of her music died in her throat. "The General is dead," she said in a strained, startled voice, "you would not be here unless he was dead."[4]

Worse than death seemed the ensuing events of that frightful second of April to other lieutenants of Lee. Ahead of Field's division, Longstreet arrived early at headquarters. With his unshakable calmness, as soon as Benning's brigade reached the flank he deployed it to protect the exposed right. In the absence of Heth, who was cut off from contact with the remainder of the Third Corps, Longstreet at Lee's instance assumed direction of such of Hill's troops as now began to collect behind their shattered lines.

By 9:00 A.M. the details of the catastrophe began to take form. The VI Corps had delivered at 4:40 A.M. an overpowering attack on Hill's front, shattered the line held by Heth's and Wilcox's divisions, and driven the Confederates to right and to left. The hope was that the shattered troops thrown westward could be united with those of Dick Anderson. Those of Hill's men driven to the left and rear of their captured fortifications were rallied on Fort Gregg and adjoining works. Still farther to the left, much of Gordon's first line had been stormed successfully at daylight, but his second line was intact. Gordon was proud that day and not a little harassed in mind, because his wife had just been delivered of a new baby; but at the front he was the same determined, competent, inspiring leader.[5]

No one now believed that more could be accomplished at Petersburg than to occupy the breaking line until nightfall. Then the whole of the Richmond-Petersburg front must be abandoned. The long-projected effort to unite with Johnston must be made. Dread notice of this necessity was telegraphed to Richmond. Mahone and Ewell on the Richmond front were to start their troops that evening by routes previously determined. The immediate objective was to be Amelia Court House, 39 miles southwest of Richmond and 36 northwest of Petersburg. This village was chosen because it was approximately equidistant from the major sectors and was on the railroad that would be the army's principal supply line on any retreat to join the forces in North Carolina.[6]

Even after such calamitous days as those of Five Forks and the second of April, the army was not to march into the night without one more demonstration of its old fighting prowess. This occurred at Fort Gregg, where the Confederates had to keep their grip until nightfall made possible an unassailed withdrawal. To lose Fort Gregg might put the battle in the streets of Petersburg. Come what might, the survivors of Nat Harris's brigade and of Wilcox's division must stay there and fight it out.

They did. Although the defenders of Fort Gregg probably numbered not more than 500, they beat off one assault, then another and another till count was lost. Wounded men loaded rifles and handed them to comrades behind the works. In the end, the few unwounded left in the fort fought hand-to-hand for 25 minutes on the parapet. The Federals had to charge themselves with 714 casualties in return for 57 Confederate dead and 159 prisoners, most of them wounded. Those Southerners who escaped received the assurance that their resistance had given Old Pete sufficient time to organize a thin, last-line defense for Petersburg. After the line was stabilized for the day, commanders were called to headquarters to hear the plan of the evacuation explained.[7]

On the extreme right, Dick Anderson learned that one object of the Federal advance against the Confederate right had been attained: The Southside Railroad had been reached. As Anderson could not recover the line or serve any good end by remaining where he was, he began the march westward prescribed by his instructions. At nightfall on April 2 he was beating off attacks by the pursuing Federal cavalry. Mahone was ready to leave the Howlett Line at Bermuda Hundred. From Drewry's Bluff and from the Northside the naval battalion, the infantry, and the heavy artillery were preparing to leave positions some of them had occupied for almost two years. The more difficult task would be taking from the Petersburg front the Second and Third Corps and Field's division, the field artillery, and, especially, the long, long wagon train.

Carefully, after 8:00 P.M., the guns were withdrawn. Artillerists brought out all the mobile ordnance except ten pieces and even took with them some of the mortars. Heavy weapons that had to be left were disabled. Field's division marched across the Appomattox in perfect order. Those units of the Third Corps that remained moved out as part of Longstreet's command. To Gordon was entrusted the rear guard. Across the James, in the absence of Longstreet, his comrade Ewell exercised general command. The remaining infantry of the First Corps were under Kershaw. All the other troops were entrusted to newly commissioned Major General Custis Lee. Stapleton Crutchfield, in charge of the heavy batteries on the James, led the gunners whose well-kept uniforms and smart red facings gave them the best appearance of the entire army. These troops crossed the James on the pontoon bridge below Richmond.[8]

The night was now far spent, but Richmond was in a frenzy. Everyone knew that evacuation had been ordered. The slums, the dives, the brothels, the bars had vomited into the streets all the city's thieves and wastrels and gamblers and harlots. The authorities were overwhelmed. Much liquor was consumed before guards could knock the barrels to pieces. Stores were broken into and looted. Soon fire succeeded the looting. Warehouses filled with tobacco had been set aflame by the provost marshal, under direction from the government, and flames from these buildings ignited others. By daylight a conflagration was sweeping the business district. All the departing Confederate soldiers could do was to behold and lament.[9]

Their Troy was falling, their cause was in its death throes, but some on the Richmond sector refused to admit the reality. Said Colonel Alexander Haskell, one of a great family of fighters, "The idea of subjugation never dawned upon us." A soldier who left the Northside wrote, "not one of us . . . despaired of the end we sought. . . . Not one word was said about a probable or personal surrender." In the dawn of April 3 such confidence was not general among troops who had been at grips with the enemy around Petersburg. Instead, every shade of woe and of despair was in the faces of those who had survived nine and a half months of sharpshooting and desperate combat. Theirs was a slow march, for more than 200 guns and 1,000 wagons had to be moved over the few roads available. The troops halted and started and stopped again endlessly. By the roadside they ate what was left of the rations they had brought with them.[10]

Some reserve supplies had been accumulated at Greensboro, Lynchburg, and Danville. It was toward Danville, at the terminus of the railroad from Richmond, that the army was moving. The Richmond and Danville was still in operation. Almost everyone in all the regiments had learned, in one way or another, that railway trains were carrying supplies to Amelia Court House, which the columns would reach on the fourth. Then, if all went well, the troops with replenished haversacks and cartridge boxes would march to join Johnston—"Little Joe," "The Gamecock." His name still had magic.

In this and like reflections the third of April ended. It had not been an easy day, nor a cheerful one, but it had not been disastrous. The enemy had not overtaken. Dick Anderson and the cavalry approached their crossing of the Appomattox before nightfall and awaited the main army. Pickett rejoined with fugitives who had escaped capture at Five Forks. A few hundred were the only survivors of the famous division. To Anderson's dark depression of spirit was added the unhappy news that almost every man of his two brigades "loaned" Pickett had been made prisoner on April 1.[11]

Those of Heth's and Wilcox's troops who had been driven west in the Federal breakthrough at Petersburg also reunited with the main army on the afternoon of the third. On the march Heth had his flank turned and approximately half his men fell into the hands of the enemy. Wrote the historian of Gregg's old brigade, "The Confederacy was considered as 'gone up,' and every man felt it his duty, as well as his privilege, to save himself. . . . So we moved on in disorder, keeping no regular column, no regular pace. . . . An indescribable sadness weighed upon us." Still, if Ewell succeeded in establishing junction with the main army, as Anderson, Pickett, and Heth had, a difficult convergence would be completed. The army of Northern Virginia might count then as many as 30,000 muskets.[12]

On April 4 the troops started early. Most of them were hungry, but officers said they would receive rations at Amelia Court House, their objective for the day. While the column marched, the familiar sound of skirmishing on the left was audible. Sheridan was catching up! But so long as the army could outmarch the Union infantry, Sheridan could not do great mischief. Longstreet's men could cope with him until Fitz Lee's troopers reached the flank.

At last the van approached the village of Amelia Court House. The columns were halted along the road. Hours passed. No rations were issued. Then army wagons were sent off under guard, which meant foraging, which was a confession that rations were not at hand. Although the commanding general had given orders for supplies to be sent to Amelia, they had not been delivered. Nobody knew why. All that could be said to the army was that General Lee had made an appeal to near-by farmers for food and fodder, and the wagons had gone to collect what the residents could spare.[13]

This information, spread swiftly through the ranks, brought to the surface the innate qualities of every man and tested what remained of discipline. One of the artillerists specified: "Many of [the men] wandered off in search of food, with no thought of deserting at all. Many others followed the example of the government and fled."[14] In those commands where discipline had not lost its compulsion, the fatal fourth of April merely was another day of hunger, unwelcome but endurable. The manner and activity of the ranking officers did not change. Theirs it was to encourage their men and to support the commanding general whose haggard face showed how heavily he appraised the failure to find supplies at Amelia. Lee knew that when he halted and sent out foraging parties, he lost his one-day lead.

A gray fifth of April and a slow spring drizzle added little to the misery of the troops. Rain was nothing; it was bread they must have. The railroad had brought none during the night. When the commissary wagons were hauled wearily back to camp, despair deepened. So little had been collected that it scarcely counted. The farmers had been visited previously by commissaries and quartermasters. Barns and storerooms were almost empty. Facing another day of acute hunger, the army must proceed down the railroad toward Burkeville in the hope of meeting one of the trains of provisions that had been ordered from Danville. If the enemy reached the railroad ahead of the column and severed connection with Danville, then . . .

Because the day's lead had been lost, they must outdistance the Union infantry. Everything that delayed the march must be left at Amelia. Artillery officers were instructed to reduce the number of guns and strengthen the remaining teams with horses released from the discarded batteries. The reserve caissons and ammunition sent to Amelia during the winter must be destroyed. Cavalry must protect flanks and trains. The long roll must be beaten at once. The choice was speed or doom.

In front was the cavalry screen of Rooney Lee's reliable command. Behind it marched Field, Mahone, and Pickett. The divisions of Heth and Wilcox followed. Then came Anderson's men. As they left Amelia, Ewell was arriving with the troops from the Richmond front. These last were held at Amelia while the strongest pressed forward to see whether the road to Burkeville was clear. The road ran seven miles to Jetersville, a station on the railway to Burkeville. Beyond Jetersville the highway to Burkeville rose slightly to a narrow watershed flanked by a woodland. The position was not one of great strength, but in the hands of the enemy it might prove troublesome. Lee and Longstreet rode forward to see what the woods con-

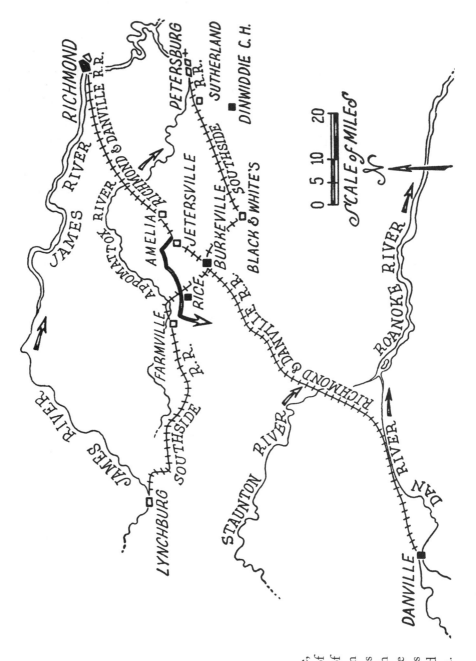

RICHMOND
JAMES RIVER
PETERSBURG
SUTHERLAND
DINWIDDIE C. H.
RICHMOND & DANVILLE R.R.
APPOMATTOX RIVER
AMELIA
JETERSVILLE
SOUTHSIDE
BURKEVILLE
BLACK & WHITE'S
RICE
FARMVILLE
SOUTHSIDE R. R.
RICHMOND & DANVILLE R.R.
STAUNTON RIVER
JAMES RIVER
LYNCHBURG
ROANOKE RIVER
DAN RIVER
DANVILLE
SCALE of MILES
0 5 10   20

Change of route,
April 5, 1865, of
the Army of
Northern
Virginia in its
effort to reach
Danville. The
heavy line shows
the projected
march.

cealed. The two generals, hearing the familiar crack-crack of skirmishers' exchange, continued past Jetersville until they met Rooney Lee. He had reconnoitered thoroughly. Dismounted Union cavalry undoubtedly were in front, he said. Infantry might be also. It certainly was approaching. The whole Federal army, said Rooney, appeared to be advancing on Burkeville.[15]

This might prove the most grievous intelligence of all! Grant's army, or part of it, was across Lee's line of retreat. A decision had now to be made whether the Southerners should or should not attempt to clear the road. This was a fateful question Lee evidently felt he should not leave to anyone else. As Longstreet waited silently and the soldiers spread themselves out by the roadside, the commanding general interrogated his son and studied the ground with his field-glasses. Finally Lee turned to Longstreet: The Federal position was too strong to be attacked. No farther advance could be made toward Danville by that route. The alternative—Lee did not say the last alternative—must be adopted. At Burkeville the Southside Railroad crossed the Richmond and Danville, which the retreating army had been following. Now, instead of continuing to move from northeast to southwest, the column must move westward to Farmville, on the Southside line. There the army might procure supplies sent down from Lynchburg. Revictualed, the troops then could strike southward again toward Danville.

From Jetersville to Farmville was twenty-three miles. If the army was to get ahead of its pursuers, it must keep the road all the remaining daylight hours and all night. This was the most cruel marching order the commanders had ever given the men in four years of fighting. Unless the columns reached Farmville and received food there before the arrival of the enemy, the proud Army of Northern Virginia would be helpless.[16]

Change in the route of march left a clear road for five and a half miles from Jetersville to Deatonsville. The bridge over Flat Creek collapsed, with maddening delay of all wheeled traffic. Infantry forded. Beyond Deatonsville the troops found themselves on the road the trains from Amelia Court House were using. Through a night that grew blacker as the hours passed, the men groped their way alongside an endless tangle of wagons. The experienced and resolute officers kept their men under control, but among the more discouraged and weaker units, command collapsed. Exhausted men staggered as if they were drunk. Nerves were so taut that panic spread wildly. A runaway horse started infantry fire. Troops thought they were being subjected to a night attack and fired into each other, killing and wounding an unascertained number of men.

Foraging parties were sent out in that unprosperous region "to bring in whatever they could lay hands on," in the words of Major McHenry Howard. It was a fruitless effort. Some of the detachments returned with nothing. Men of other foraging parties never caught up again. By daylight, officers were appalled to find to what degree brigades had dwindled by straggling. Some regiments almost had dissolved. Ewell's strength, which never had exceeded 6,000, already was cut in half. As these troops from the Richmond front were less inured to hardship than were the older combat divisions, they may have suffered more from straggling and exhaustion.

Even in the best commands fighting strength diminished hourly. The principal exceptions were the still-powerful divisions of Field and Mahone under Longstreet. They constituted the advance and had a road unencumbered by the wagons. Behind these two divisions were, in order, the fragments of the Third Corps, then Anderson, next Ewell, and, as rear guard, Gordon and the Second Corps. The infantry column thus was weakest in the center. Fitz Lee's cavalry were under orders to support the van and cover the rear. For tired teamster and for drowsing trooper, for gunner and for foot soldier, for every man in the army from general to youngest drummer, the decisive sixth of April was dawning.[7]

2. The Black Day of the Army

Through the hopeful dawn of a spring day that seemed to mock the miseries of man, the troops struggled on toward the Southside Railroad. This would be reached at Rice Station, seven miles southeast of Farmville. Of the enemy's approach to the railroad, little was known. It was now apparent that Sheridan had quit the rear and was operating parallel to Lee's left flank. Powerful Union infantry in rear, Sheridan able to strike the flank of a long column in motion—short of envelopment, a more dangerous situation scarcely could have existed for a starving army in full retreat!

At Lee's headquarters, this was realized. The anxious commander was as alert as ever. Some of his staff officers were conscious of all that was happening. Others were dazed by lack of sleep. Longstreet's advantage in moving at the head of the long, long column had given him some opportunities of rest. Mahone, Heth, and Wilcox, moving with the van, appear to have been masters of their minds. Gordon certainly was. The events of the day were to prove that the commanders who were losing their military judgment under the paralyzing strain were those who had been struggling all night to keep trains and guns and men moving.

The order of march toward Rice had placed Longstreet's wagons in rear of the First and Third Corps. Anderson and Ewell followed. Behind them were all the remaining vehicles with the column, protected by the rear guard, Gordon's Second Corps. Slowly, painfully, after Longstreet had gone ahead toward Rice, the other divisions toiled over the bad roads that led down to the two forks of Sayler's Creek. Continuously in this advance the infantry had to move out to the left, form line of battle, and repulse cavalry attacks. The energy of Sheridan's troopers seemed exhaustless. Driven off, they would find another road up which they could press an attack.

Lee had ridden ahead to expedite the march of Longstreet because it was imperative that the van make utmost speed. This left Ewell as ranking officer of all the troops in rear of Longstreet; but Ewell had no instructions to exercise command beyond that of the troops he had brought from Richmond. Whatever he did in any sudden emergency would be based on his seniority, which he always was slow to assert. His was as dolorous a part as any officer had in that tragic retreat. He who had commanded the old Second Corps on the road to Gettysburg now had 3,000 oddly assorted, half-despairing troops, some of them veterans, some of them clerks from closed government offices in smouldering Richmond.

About 11:00 A.M. Ewell found enemy cavalry stabbing viciously at the wagon train. Skirmishers were thrown out and the Federals repulsed. Wagons between Ewell and Gordon were started forward so that Gordon, as rear guard, would not have the whole length of the wagon train between him and Ewell in case the rear guard needed help from the troops ahead. For this passage of the wagons, Anderson's troops and then Ewell's halted by the roadside. After part of the trains had gone past, Ewell left the remainder between his rear and the van of Gordon's corps while he moved ahead to close on Anderson.

Then occurred the first of the mistakes that showed how exhaustion was destroying command. When Dick Anderson halted, he should have notified Mahone ahead of him; but by oversight or the mental paralysis of fatigue, Anderson failed to do this. Mahone, unaware of the halt in his rear, pushed on toward Rice Station. Across the gap thus created between Mahone and Anderson, the wagons began to roll. Federal cavalry observed them, rushed in, and set some of the vehicles on fire. This prolonged Anderson's halt until about 2:00 P.M. Then Anderson started again—only to be stopped once more by Federal cavalry in a strong position on his left front.[18]

His uncertainty was increased by a message from Gordon. The commander of the rear guard urged that the column push on as he was being pressed heavily. Seeking counsel and reinforcement, Anderson rode back through his column and found Ewell. Old Bald Head already had been informed of the presence of the enemy on Anderson's line of advance. He had directed that the wagons remaining behind him and in front of Gordon turn to the right and follow a road to a less exposed, lower crossing of

Sayler's Creek, two and a half miles north and west of the point where the Federals were in front of Anderson. In diverting the train, Ewell failed, precisely as Anderson had, to notify the next unit in the column. No staff officer or courier was posted at the road forks to tell Gordon that he must keep straight on to the southwest and close on Ewell, though the wagons had taken the right fork and started to the northwest.

The two bewildered and weary lieutenant generals, Ewell and Anderson, understood little of the terrain and scarcely knew where to expect the enemy next. This did not weaken Ewell's disposition, then as always, to help a comrade. Anderson thought that two divisions of cavalry were in his front, which he believed could be forced out of the way if he and Ewell united their commands and attacked. The alternative was to abandon the wagons and move to the right, through the woods, in hope of striking a road that would lead to Farmville. Ewell thought this the wiser course, but he suffered now from a weakness that had shown itself progressively after he had assumed corps command—he would not decide. He recommended the march through the woods, but left the decision to Anderson. His training as a soldier of Lee's prompted Anderson to undertake a direct attack to clear the road. In the preparations he directed, neither he nor his subordinates could display any zest. Initiative was gone. Dispirited men acted as if they were in a nightmare and could not make their muscles respond.

Ewell's troops had started their march up the road to support Anderson when, in an instant, the whole prospect changed. A messenger brought a report that staggered the two generals: The enemy was in large force in Ewell's rear and making ready to attack! It was true. Failure to notify Gordon of the change in the route of the wagons had brought acutest danger. Gordon had followed the wagons to the forks at which Ewell had diverted them to the northwest, and he had assumed, naturally, that their route was his, as it had been all day. Soon after he left the road toward Rice, the enemy closed on the troops from the Richmond front. Federals now faced Anderson from the southwest and Ewell from the east. The envelopment of both was threatened.[19]

At this intelligence, the exhausted Dick Anderson aroused himself. Ewell, said Anderson, would have all he could do to look after the rear; the attack on the flank must be met by Anderson's own troops. He rode off to rally his men. Ewell turned to his front, where Kershaw and Custis Lee feverishly were deploying for defense. On the left, young Lee had his local defense troops and his heavy artillerists. In his rear Ewell placed the naval battalion that had defended James River fortifications. On the right, stalwart still in their thin ranks, were the three brigades of Kershaw, brigades

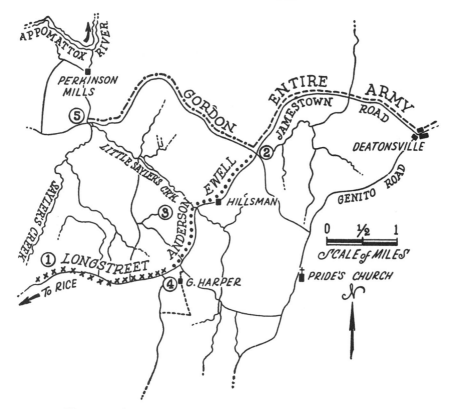

Vicinity of Sayler's Creek, scene of the battle of April 6, 1865.
The encircled numerals indicate: (1) line of Longstreet's march to Rice;
(2) forks of the Jamestown road where Gordon mistook the route of the wagon
train for that of the army and turned to the northwest; (3) scene of Ewell's stand
and surrender; (4) ground of Anderson's halt and vain attempt to cut his way
through; (5) Gordon's battleground.

that had been, in the day of the army's greatest prowess, those of Barksdale, Tom Cobb, and Paul Semmes.

Before this deployment was complete, Ewell did a curious thing. Although it was manifest that his men were soon to be subjected to attack, he rode off to see how Anderson's attempted breakthrough had succeeded. Old Bald Head had not been absent many minutes when the Union infantry began an assault. So long was the front that both of Ewell's flanks would be overlapped, but his men did not flinch. The Confederates, green clerks and four-year veterans, waited till the bluecoats were close and then poured into them a volley that had the ring and roar of Fredericksburg. Everywhere the Federals recoiled. The heavy artillerists, being less experienced, rushed out to grapple with the enemy. Their commander, Stapleton Crutchfield, went with them—led them probably—and fell dead with a bullet through his head. When his men returned to their position, shell tore them.

The Federals, by this time, began to turn James Simms's brigade, the right flank element of Kershaw. While this struggle waged uncertainly, Anderson sent word that the attack to clear the westward road had begun and might succeed if Ewell's men held on a little longer. Kershaw did his utmost to rally Simms's brigade. Every man in the thin Georgia regiments sought to fire faster. Humphreys's Mississippians gave their last ounce of energy to the battle. They were hanging on, with front engaged and right flank turned, when a cloud of men in blue appeared in rear of Simms.

Kershaw concluded that these troops must have beaten Anderson and now were enveloping the Confederates facing the rear. When Simms's Georgians saw themselves almost surrounded, they moved to their left and rear in the hope of escaping. Humphreys and Du Bose undertook the same maneuver. Kershaw gave such direction as he could on the confusing, fireswept field, but found his troops melting away. Federal cavalry, he told himself, were crowding the last field and wood by which his brigades might escape. The last alternative, then, had to be faced: Every man for himself! It was in vain. Kershaw, his staff, and practically all the survivors of his division were captured. So far as Kershaw could ascertain later, one man only slipped through the enveloping Federals. The same fate was Custis Lee's. His front broken, to save lives he knew would be wasted by further fighting, the son of the commanding general had to order his men to cease firing. Young Lee, his staff, and all his men, except perhaps a fleet-footed few, became Federal prisoners.[20]

This was not the full depth of the catastrophe. Ewell, who so strangely had left his own troops in order to witness the attack to the westward, had found Anderson and, at the side of the South Carolinian, awaited the opening of the attack. In minutes humiliating few, it failed. Anderson later reported in these brief, pathetic words: ". . . the troops seemed to be wholly broken down and disheartened. After a feeble effort to advance they gave way in confusion and with the exception of 150 or 200 men the whole of General Ewell's and my command were captured."

In reality, it was not quite that ruinous. Wise's and Bushrod Johnson's brigades, said Wise, "gained our road past the enemy." Almost all the other of Anderson's troops, with fifteen guns, were captured. Anderson himself rushed to the front and together with Johnson and a few others escaped through the woods on horseback. Pickett and two of his staff officers rallied a squad which fired bravely into the face of a charging cavalry squadron and delayed it long enough for the trio to outrun their pursuers.

When Anderson galloped off, Ewell turned back toward his command in the desperate hope of leading it through the woods to the north. He suddenly came on a strong line of enemy skirmishers. "This closed the only avenue of escape," he recorded, "as shells and even bullets were crossing each other from front and rear over my troops. . . . I surrendered myself and staff to a cavalry officer. . . ." He sent a note to Custis Lee to say he had surrendered, "and he had better do so too. . . ."

To this end came the man who had been Jackson's lieutenant and, in the mind of many, the successor to Stonewall. Ewell was shattered in spirit and, for the next day or two, scarcely responsible. "He was," said fellow-prisoner Eppa Hunton, "thoroughly whipped and seemed to be dreadfully demoralized." This wavering in the spirit of a courageous enfeebled man did not hurt his fame or mar the splendor of his soldiers' last fight. Kershaw said, "On no battlefield of the war have I felt a juster pride in the conduct of my command." Custis Lee was equally proud of his scratch division. Everyone had high praise for the naval battalion and the heavy artillery brigade from the Richmond defenses.[21]

The capture of Ewell's and Anderson's troops meant, in the eyes of the commanding general, the loss of two of his four corps. "General," said Lee to Pendleton, "that half of our army is destroyed." The other half escaped, though suffering heavy losses in a drama as strange as that of Ewell and Anderson. On Longstreet's arrival at Rice during the early forenoon with the van of the First Corps, he learned of the approach of enemy infantry. He deployed carefully, and at exposed points threw up light fieldworks. It was reported that a substantial Federal force had marched up the road toward Farmville, endangering two bridges over the Appomattox that must be saved, cost what they might, because the army's line of retreat might carry it to the north side of the river. Old Pete told Tom Rosser to follow and capture or destroy the venturesome Federals "if it took the last man of his command to do it."

At midday Rosser's command met a Union infantry force near the so-called High Bridge over the Appomattox. Some of Rosser's men dismounted to attack, but before the action had progressed far they were boldly charged by a Federal cavalry detachment. Taken by surprise, Rosser's men took shelter in a wood, formed there, and dashed out and overpowered the Union troopers. The Federal infantry then offered little resistance and surrendered en masse. Total prisoners numbered about 780. The cost was not light. The desperate front-line leadership shown by so many officers after the Wilderness fighting opened took in this Battle of High Bridge the lives of three Confederates of distinction—Brigadier General James Dearing, Colonel Reuben B. Boston of the 5th Virginia cavalry, and Major James W. Thomson of the horse artillery. Rosser was wounded once more, but was too busy to pay heed to his injured arm. When he returned to give Longstreet the details, he was carrying the saber and riding the fine black horse of the slain Federal commander.[22]

The fighting spirit of the cavalry was matched by the Second Corps in courageous defense. Virtually all the way from Amelia Court House to Sayler's Creek, fourteen miles, Gordon's men had been under attack. At intervals, behind any natural barrier, Gordon halted and held off the hard-hitting Union line until the wagons gained a mile or two. His artillery was employed effectively again and again. After Gordon turned from Ewell's route and followed the wagons northwestward, he found himself at a difficult crossing of Sayler's Creek. By 5 o'clock he was so desperately pressed that he feared he would lose all the wagons if he did not get help.

"So far I have been able to protect [the wagons]," he wrote in a note to Lee, "but without assistance can scarcely hope to do so much longer." The cavalry of Rooney Lee, which had covered Gordon's retreat, had been withdrawn. Gordon fought with no troops except his own. One assault he repulsed. After Ewell's troops were captured, Gordon's right was attacked from the south while his front was under heavy pressure and his left was threatened. His line broke in much confusion, but, west of the creek, Gordon rallied the survivors. Although his loss on that Flodden Field of the Confederacy was about 1,700, his had been a gallant fight.[23]

While Ewell and Anderson had been fighting their hopeless battle at the upper crossing of Sayler's Creek and Gordon at the lower, Longstreet had remained at Rice to cover the roads that led to the Appomattox bridges. After the disaster to Anderson and Ewell, Mahone's division had been moved by the commanding general to a hill west of and in full view of the scene of their surrender. There, in the late afternoon, occurred an incident that Mahone himself described: "At this spectacle General Lee straightened himself in his saddle, and, looking more the soldier than ever, exclaimed, as if talking to himself: 'My God! Has the army dissolved?' As quickly as I could control my voice I replied, 'No, General, here are troops ready to do their duty'; when, in a mellowed voice, he replied, 'Yes, General, there are some true men left. Will you please keep these people back?'" Fleeing men had crowded around Lee where he sat his horse holding aloft a Confederate battleflag. At Mahone's request Lee handed him the flag, with which, and with his own trusted men, Mahone drew a line behind which the fugitives rallied.[24]

Night scarcely brought relief. In other battles more men had been killed and wounded, but in no engagement had so large a part of the Army of Northern Virginia been destroyed. The day's casualties, which were between 7,000 and 8,000, represented probably one third of the men that had left Amelia Court House and Jetersville the previous day. Worst of all, time had been lost, the time bought by the agonizing night march of April 5–6. Union infantry now were on the heels of the Confederates. Sheridan had been on the flank all day. If he got ahead of the army . . .

3. THE ARMY SEES A RED WESTERN SKY

Whatever the dreadful possibilities of the morrow, headquarters on the night of April 6 had to collect the scattered fragments of broken commands and formulate plans. Anderson, Pickett, and Bushrod Johnson were somewhere in the woods. The few survivors of their commands, plus Wise's brigade, could be placed under Gordon. He and Longstreet now headed the two corps that remained. They could count six divisions, but four of these were wrecked. Field's and Mahone's alone were strong enough to make an all-day fight. As for route, manifestly the army could not strike immediately south. It must put the Appomattox between it and the enemy, and after that must describe a wider arc toward Danville or, if need be, westward toward the mountains.

To get the army across the river, Longstreet would continue on the road to Farmville. Mahone's division, Gordon, and the men who had escaped the day's defeats would cross the Appomattox at High Bridge and rejoin at Farmville. When the troops were on the north bank of the river, the bridges could be burned. In this way the lost day might be recovered. The Army of Northern Virginia might get one march ahead of the pursuers.

After darkness the march began. Hundreds of men separated from their commands wandered hopelessly along and crowded the road. Many lost heart that night and lay down by the roadside to die or to await helplessly the arrival of an enemy who, if he imprisoned, at least did not starve soldiers. The hardiest and most resolute kept on. They had firm assurance that rations were awaiting them at Farmville. Commissary I. M. St. John had seen General Lee and had hurried on to the railroad to be sure the cars from Lynchburg with bacon and meal were ready when the troops arrived.[25]

Longstreet's men had the worst of the marching conditions, on a crowded road deep in mud. Gordon to the north soon had the survivors of the Second Corps marching in their regular order by brigades. Though some of these brigades were smaller than a feeble regiment should have been, they did not throw off their discipline. At last—the night seemed a month—they crossed the Appomattox on a wagon bridge under the High Bridge of the Southside railway and pushed on toward Farmville where rations were awaiting them. The engineers assigned to burn the bridges awaited Mahone's order to do so, and when it did not come they sent to find him. On his belated order they set the lofty structure aflame, but could not get the wagon crossing vigorously afire before the enemy was upon them. Whether Mahone forgot to give the order earlier or assumed the engineers would act when he marched off, it is impossible to say.[26]

Plain speech and a picturesque political career had made Henry A. Wise a privileged character in the army. He had never hesitated to speak his mind to his superiors. Now, when he saw Lee on a little eminence where the weary commander was trying to rally stragglers, he made straight for the place. Lee gave him a good morning and asked the condition of his command. "Ready for dress parade," the quick-witted Wise answered, and with no further introduction he swore, "General Lee, these men shall not move another inch unless they have something more to eat than parched corn taken from starving mules!" Prompt was Lee's answer: "They deserve something to eat, sir," and he directed Wise to a nearby hill where rations from the cars at Farmville would be issued.[27]

The men of Wise's command and of Gordon's corps received two days' rations. Longstreet's men arriving in Farmville could draw their rations, move to the north bank of the river, and prepare them. A few hours might then be allowed for rest, for with the bridges destroyed the Appomattox would be impassable temporarily for the Federal infantry. The cavalry would be able to ford the stream, but they could be engaged and held. With good fortune, what was left of Lee's army might march toward Lynchburg and try, once again, to move toward a junction with the waiting troops of Joe Johnston.

This hope was reviving dimly as fires crackled and bacon fried, but soon there was an alarm: The enemy was advancing! Federals who had reached the wagon crossing at High Bridge had extinguished the fire and continued their pursuit with little delay. Mahone had not succeeded in pushing them back. Instead of enjoying a rest, the Confederates must make the north side of the river a battleground. Those who had finished their cooking could eat and fight. Others must leave their fires and take with them what they could snatch. Some thousands in the rear brigades, shuffling into Farmville, found the issue of rations halted and the trains gone. The best they could hope was that the cars might be run up toward Lynchburg and stopped again at a point on the Southside track that paralleled the road along which the army must renew its retreat.

Three and a half miles beyond Farmville the line of the Confederate retreat crossed that of the Federal advance from High Bridge. Mahone's division accordingly was posted at the road junction. When the Federals came they threatened a heavy attack, and Mahone had to fight to keep them at a distance. Gordon marched through the woods by the flank to cover the wagons against attack by the Federal cavalry. Fitz Lee's exhausted troopers met and repulsed one cavalry attack on the trains, but the danger remained essentially the same as on the sixth: The enemy would press hard from the rear while his cavalry tried to strike the left flank of the column from the south. Presumably, too, Federal infantry were marching south of Lee's army and parallel to it. If those strong blue columns, or even the blue cavalry, outmarched the Southerners, the only line of escape would be to the north—the direction opposite that of the desired movement to unite with Johnston.[28]

The retreat resumed, and in hundreds of instances strength failed many whose faith remained. An artillerist wrote, "Horses and mules dead or dying in the mud. . . . The constant marching and fighting without sleep or food are rapidly thinning the ranks of this grand old army. Men who have stood by their flags since the beginning of the war fall out of their ranks and are captured, simply because it is beyond their power of physical endurance to go any farther." This happened among some of the proudest units of the army. Until its stragglers rejoined, the Texas Brigade could engage but 130 rifles. One famished, ragged North Carolinian fell back and was overtaken by a squad of well-fed Union troops. "Surrender, surrender, we've got you!" they yelled. "Yes," said Johnny Reb as he dropped his gun, "you've got me, and the hell of a git you got!"

Gordon was to be moved forward to be the advance of the next day; Longstreet's corps would become rear guard. With nothing more encouraging than this in prospect, most of the men were too benumbed to do more than continue their torturing march. Their seniors were excited by two developments. During the late afternoon of the seventh efforts were made by the Federals to pass a flag of truce, but the fire had been too hot. About 9:00 P.M. another flag was presented opposite Mahone's lines and was received. A letter addressed to General Lee was handed over and hurried to field headquarters. The fact of the receipt of this letter and of the prompt dispatch of an answer became known to many officers during the night. Some of them correctly guessed what the letters concerned. Longstreet, but probably no one else, was shown the communication received from the Federal lines. He received it from Lee's hands, read it, and returned it with two words of comment—"Not yet."[29]

The other development that woeful seventh of April was without any precedent and technically was contrary to stern terms of Army Regulations. During the day several of the general officers talked of the plight of the army and of the black alternatives it faced. It could disperse and attempt to reassemble, or it could abandon all trains and cut its way out. To scatter through the countryside would subject the region to foraging and plunder by uncontrolled detachments that might never be brought together again. If the second alternative were adopted, the army's ammunition soon would be exhausted. There remained, then, no humane, practical alternative to the one thing no soldier had wished to consider or mention—immediate surrender. In that conviction, the officers felt that General Lee should be told that his generals believed the struggle hopeless and thought themselves unjustified in permitting more blood to be shed. Lee must be informed, also, that a desire to spare him the entire burden of decision prompted them to make their statement. General Pendleton was suggested as the person to lay the opinion of the officers before Lee. John B. Gordon, who had not shared in the conversation, suggested to Pendleton that Longstreet be informed before the matter was presented to Lee.

For some hours it seemed that the humiliating suggestion of surrender might be avoided. The morale of the army improved. The men were jaded but less despairing. The enemy was not troubling them; their march was unimpeded. Many began to predict they would reach Lynchburg. "Once there," they thought, their "safety seemed to be almost perfectly secured." Headquarters anticipated a harder struggle. Supplies had been ordered to Appomattox Station, twenty-five miles west of Farmville on the Southside Railroad. These must be secured before the enemy got them. Half dead though the troops might be, they must be kept on the road.[30]

Dick Anderson, George Pickett, and Bushrod Johnson still were with the army, but did not have commands that fitted their rank. To assign them to head other troops would entail the displacement of officers who had done their full duty and had not suffered defeat. To call on the three generals to remain with the army and have no part in its battles was humiliation. They accordingly were relieved and authorized to return home. If there was any implication in these orders that the three had been culpable in the loss of their troops—Pickett at Five Forks and the others at Sayler's Creek— their comrades-in-arms never knew it. Pickett nursed resentments for this treatment, or for what had happened at Gettysburg. Dick Anderson remained to the end the loyal lieutenant and in his final report voiced no protest. Johnson publicly said nothing. Wise's brigade and the other men from Johnson's division were assigned to Grimes's division of Gordon's corps. No fragment of infantry now remained outside the two corps in the determined hands of Longstreet and Gordon. Both were withstanding the strains of the agonizing week; both remained clear-headed.

During the forenoon Longstreet showed his old fighting spirit. Pendleton told him of the conference of the previous day, and asked if Longstreet would lay before Lee the conclusion of his officers. Instantly Old Pete reminded Pendleton of the article of war which provided the death penalty for proposing surrender. "If General Lee doesn't know when to surrender until I tell him," stormed Longstreet, "he will never know!" Pendleton found Lee resting on the ground beneath a large pine tree. Without a word, he permitted Pendleton to state his case. Then, firmly and probably with some sharpness, Lee answered that he still had too many brave men to think of surrendering. Lee's manner did not encourage argument or reiteration. "From his report of the conversation," Porter Alexander said of Pendleton, "he had met a decided snub. . . ."[31]

"The enemy left us to a quiet day's march on the 8th," Longstreet subsequently wrote, "nothing disturbing the rear-guard, and our left flank being but little annoyed. . . ." The excitement was in the ranks of the cavalry. If the commander of the mounted forces had been negligent at Five Forks, he was atoning now. Two miles behind Longstreet's troops, Fitz Lee was watching and calculating. He had no fight to wage at the moment because he was pursued by infantry alone. That fact was itself suspicious. It led him to conclude that Sheridan's divisions had left the rear and were moving parallel to the Southern infantry, in order to cut off supplies at Appomattox Station or to get across the Confederate line of advance. Fitz decided that he, too, should leave the rear and go to the front of the column. He determined to advance his whole force, other than a rear guard for the First Corps. Sheridan must be met quickly, and he must be met with every gun and saber the Confederates could command.[32]

To the west, in the late afternoon, when Gordon's van approached Appomattox Court House, a halt was called. General Pendleton was concerned for the surplus batteries that Lindsay Walker had been directed to move from Amelia ahead of the army. They were parked two miles ahead on the road to Appomattox Station. The gunners had repelled one cavalry attack, but Pendleton was fearful that without infantry support they would be overwhelmed. About 9:00 P.M. there was sound of artillery fire from the direction of Walker's camp, and then, suddenly, complete silence. Walker and his twenty-four guns must already have been captured.[33]

The abrupt cessation of the cannonade was not the sole omen of disaster. Another was in the heavens. After the last glint of the sun had faded, to the east there was redness near the earth. From the south came the same reflections, dim but unmistakable. Westward, too—hearts stood still at the sight!—the light of kindled campfires slowly spread. Only to the north was the darkness unrelieved by fiery notice that the enemy was waiting and almost had surrounded the army.

While the skies proclaimed this red warning, Longstreet, Gordon, and

Fitz Lee were conferring with the commanding general. Gordon and Fitz were told of the exchange of letters with General Grant. The letter which Longstreet had read and handed back to Lee with the comment "Not yet" had been a call by Grant for the surrender of the Army of Northern Virginia. Lee had replied that he did not take Grant's view of the hopelessness of further resistance, but reciprocated the desire to stop the flow of blood and therefore asked what terms Grant would offer. Grant replied: "Peace being my great desire, there is but one condition I would insist upon, namely, that the officers and men surrendered shall be disqualified for taking up arms against the government of the United States until properly exchanged." Lee had made this letter the occasion of a proposal to meet Grant, not to negotiate surrender of the army, but to consider how Grant's proposal "may affect the C.S. forces under my command and to tend to the restoration of peace."[34]

To this second letter from Lee, no answer had been received. In the light of this and in the face of the known military situation, Gordon and Fitz Lee and Longstreet were asked what they thought the army should do on the ninth. Discussion ranged from tactics of another battle to the future of the Southern people, but the decision was unequivocal—one more effort must be made to break through toward Lynchburg and then to turn southward.

The artillery must be reduced to two battalions. Only the ammunition wagons were to accompany the army. Fitz Lee would open the attack, supported by the Second Corps, and then he and Gordon would wheel to the left to cover the passage of the remaining guns and trains. Longstreet would close behind the trains and hold the position. If this succeeded, the army would fight on. In the event of failure, the end would have come. Fitz Lee made one request: He would like to be notified, before a surrender, in order that he and his men might leave the field and go to North Carolina to unite with Johnston, provided this could be done honorably and without compromising the general-in-chief. The request was granted; the conference ended. At 1:00 A.M. on the morrow, the ninth of April, the movement would begin. The old army would shake off its pursuers or perish on the field.[35]

4. APPOMATTOX: EXEUNT OMNES

At daybreak, Palm Sunday, half a mile west of Appomattox Court House, on the road to Lynchburg, Gordon boldly spread his men in line of battle. They numbered no more than 1,600 muskets of the 7,500 that had been in the soldiers' hands as recently as the first of March. On the right of Gordon's troops were the cavalry—Rooney Lee next the infantry, then Tom

Rosser and then Tom Munford. Fitz Lee was determined but he was not hopeful. He believed that his men could whip any mounted troops the Federals could bring against him. As an experienced soldier he knew that with his 2,400 men he could not break through strong Federal infantry. Privately he arranged with Gordon that if the Second Corps encountered infantry in its front, Gordon was to signal. Then Fitz would lead his cavalry off the field before a truce was declared.

As soon as it was light enough to see westward across the fields to the crossroads ahead, Federal earthworks were discernible. They were new and not heavy, the sort any soldiers might have thrown up during the night. Neither Fitz Lee nor Gordon could tell, at the distance and in the dim light, whether the men occasionally visible behind the field fortifications were dismounted troopers or the familiar blue infantry. After careful scrutiny, Gordon was satisfied that the Federals were cavalry and were Fitz Lee's prey. Young Lee was convinced that the Unionists were infantry and therefore meat for Gordon. They argued so long that Bryan Grimes, with all the zeal of a new major general, broke in. Somebody, he said, must attack and at once. "I will undertake it," Grimes volunteered.

"Well, drive them off!" answered Gordon. "You can take the other two divisions of the corps." Fitz Lee was ready to do his part, but he and his men believed the bluecoats at the crossroads were infantry and would mow down the attackers. A cavalryman of Beale's brigade observed, before the bugle sounded, "Old Company E will call the roll in Hell this morning."

At 5 o'clock the advance began in echelon on the right. It was a smart, well-ordered advance that would have evoked Stonewall Jackson's terse "Good, good!" The quaver of the rebel yell saluted the dawn. At the crossroads the breastworks were reached and swept. The uniform of the first fallen Federal showed to the relief of all that Gordon was correct. The defenders were dismounted cavalry who were sent hurrying to their horses. Two field guns were captured.[36]

Then Gordon wheeled by the left flank and formed a new line of battle facing south. The Lynchburg road was cleared and covered, as Lee had directed. Scarcely was Gordon in this new position than word came of Federals in a wood to his right and rear—and infantry at that, beyond all doubt infantry. Action swiftly followed report. These troops attacked Fitz Lee and drove him back on Gordon's flank. More distant Union regiments emerged from the wood and slipped to the east as if they intended to get between Gordon and Longstreet. Federal cavalry began to demonstrate against the left of Gordon's line. All this the enemy did smoothly and confidently and to the dismay of Gordon. He had Federal infantry to the west of him, the threat of infantry deployment to the east, and cavalry to the

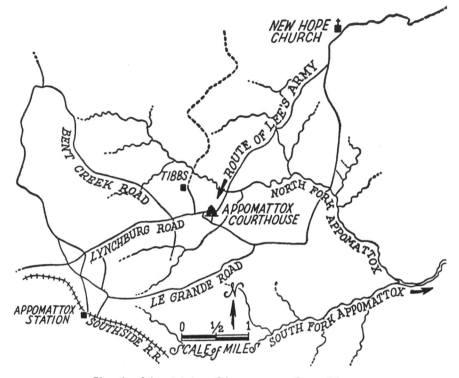

Sketch of the vicinity of Appomattox Court House.

southeast. Against such odds, he realized that the fight was hopeless. If John Gordon admitted that, his plight was almost past redemption, because in a black hour at Sharpsburg and in the madness of the Bloody Angle, his had been the voice of unshakable confidence.

Now, about 8 o'clock, Colonel Charles Venable rode up to ask how the contest was progressing. Never in his military career had Gordon been compelled to give such an answer as his honor demanded: "Tell General Lee I have fought my corps to a frazzle, and I fear I can do nothing unless I am heavily supported by Longstreet's corps." As Gordon stubbornly renewed his fight, Longstreet was closing the rear. Old Pete prepared to fight in front or in rear.[37]

Soon a courier brought Longstreet a message: The commanding general wished to see him at the front. Leaving Charles Field to guard the rear, Longstreet hurried toward the Court House. By the roadside, near a dying fire of fence rails, he saw Lee, Mahone, and a number of other officers. He observed that Lee had dressed most carefully, as if for a grand review, and wore sword, sash, and gold spurs. He looked vigorous, Longstreet thought. At closer range it was manifest that the commanding general was profoundly depressed.

As always, Lee's greeting was courteous but his preliminaries were brief: Venable had returned and brought the news that Gordon was under heavy attack by infantry and cavalry. The Second Corps could not break through. The army's subsistence stores doubtless had been lost on the railroad, which must be in the hands of the enemy. Gordon had asked help from the First Corps, but, said Lee, Longstreet doubtless would have his hands full in dealing with Meade, who was pressing the rear guard. It did not seem possible for the army to get along. What did Longstreet think? At such a time, Longstreet never wasted words. He asked whether the sacrifice of the army could in any way help the Southern cause elsewhere. "I think not," Lee answered.

"Then your situation speaks for itself."

At that answer, Lee looked unhappily aside and called to Little Billy Mahone. He gave Mahone the same résumé of the situation he had given Longstreet. After questioning Lee about the condition of the army, Mahone said he thought the army should surrender, and then he turned to Old Pete. Did not Longstreet agree? The corps commander had to say he did. Lee spoke to several others and to Porter Alexander, in particular, at some length. Then Longstreet saw his commander mount and ride to the rear to meet General Grant in accordance with Lee's request of the previous evening for an interview on general terms of peace.[38]

Longstreet was disturbed that nothing had been said about authorizing a truce. All the indications were that the Federals in the rear were preparing to attack. Field's veterans continued to fell trees and dig dirt in ignorance of the fact that their surrender might be under negotiation. Longstreet told no one. Presently a cavalry staff officer from the front hurried up to him: Fitz Lee, said the young man, had found a route by which the army could escape. Old Pete called lustily for a swift courier. Colonel John Haskell was at hand with a thoroughbred mare, famous in the army for her speed. Longstreet gave the message to Haskell and told him to overtake General Lee even if it cost the horse. Off hurried Haskell along the road Lee had followed. Longstreet waited. Outwardly he was composed. Inwardly, his fighting blood boiled. If there was a way out, as Fitz Lee said, he would take it in the event Lee could not get honorable terms. "I know my corps will follow me," he said. Before many minutes, another messenger rode up: General Fitz Lee regretted to report that he was mistaken; the route he had found was not one by which the army could escape. That intelligence was carried immediately to General Lee by Colonel John Fairfax.

Again there was a wait, a long wait, at Longstreet's headquarters. As Old Pete saw it, everything depended now on whether the commanding general had received at the hands of General Grant terms that could be accepted. If they were terms of degradation, then the army could do what Jeb Stuart said he had planned to do that June day in 1862 when he thought he might be trapped on the bank of the swollen Chickahominy: The army could "die game."

At length Haskell returned. He had met Fairfax on the road and knew of Fitz Lee's second message. In fact, Haskell reported, the commanding general had not credited the first one. "Fitz," the general had said, "has fooled himself." Lee, Haskell went on, said he had forgotten to notify Gordon that a truce would be asked. Would Longstreet inform Gordon of the situation so that the army would not be fighting in front while observing a truce in the rear? In all other respects, while Lee was between the lines, Longstreet was to use his own judgment. Longstreet listened, said little, and called for a staff officer to ride to Gordon with Lee's message.[39]

Gordon's few men were "fighting furiously in nearly every direction," to use their commander's words, when Longstreet's messenger arrived at the front. Gordon directed Colonel Green Peyton to ride out between the lines with a flag of truce and tell the Federal commander that "General Gordon has received notice from General Lee of a flag of truce, stopping the battle." Peyton returned quickly to report—it was a proud fact of history—that the Second Corps had no flag of truce. Gordon told him to take his handkerchief and tie that on a stick. Peyton confessed that he had no handkerchief. Tear up a shirt for the purpose, said Gordon. Peyton explained that neither he nor anyone else in the army had a white shirt. "Get something, sir; get something and go!" Gordon demanded.

Peyton secured a rag of some sort, and presently returned with a Union officer whose long, tawny hair fell almost to his shoulders. Gordon noted the length of the hair and the grace of the rider, who was handling a poor horse superbly. He introduced himself as General Custer, and said he bore a message from General Sheridan: "The General desires me to present to you his compliments, and to demand the immediate and unconditional surrender of all the troops under your command." Gordon's reply was polite but instant: "You will please, General, return my compliments to General Sheridan and say to him that I shall not surrender my command."

"He directs me to say to you, General, if there is any hesitation about your surrender, that he has you surrounded and can annihilate your command in an hour." Gordon was not to be shaken by threats. Nothing, he said, did he have to add to the simple message that General Lee had asked a truce. If Sheridan continued the fighting in the face of a flag of truce, the responsibility for the resultant bloodshed would be his. Custer was puzzled, and asked to be conducted to General Longstreet. Gordon assented, and sent him off under escort.

Almost immediately another flag of truce was advanced toward Gordon's line. Under it was Sheridan himself. Gordon rode out to meet his adversary. Sheridan was as anxious as Custer had been to receive the surrender of the army, but he was met with the same assurances. Sheridan then suggested that firing cease on both sides and that the two forces withdraw to agreed positions while they waited for a report of the outcome of the conference. Orders were dispatched immediately.⁴⁰

By the time Gordon and Sheridan suspended hostilities, Custer and his escort had reached the place on the roadside where Longstreet was awaiting Lee's return. The Federal—he was only twenty-five—walked up to Longstreet and called out in a voice audible to all: "I have come to demand your instant surrender. We are in position to crush you, and unless you surrender at once, we will destroy you." Longstreet blazed: "By what authority do you come into our lines? General Lee is in communication with General Grant. We certainly will not recognize any subordinate."

"Oh," answered Custer, "Sheridan and I are independent of Grant and we will destroy you if you don't surrender at once."

This was the spark to explode the wrath of Longstreet: "I suppose you know no better and have violated the decencies of military procedure because you know no better. But your ignorance will not save you if you do so again. Now, go and act as you and Sheridan choose, and I will teach you a lesson you won't forget! Now go!"—and he raised both hand and voice.

Custer said no more, and with his guard returned to his own lines, where the truce arranged by Gordon and Sheridan continued. Before the truce had been arranged, Gordon had given the agreed signal to Fitz Lee. That officer, Rosser, and Munford and the greater part of their cavalry had ridden off to escape surrender and to renew the campaign, as they hoped, with Johnston.⁴¹

Longstreet found the commanding general on the edge of a little orchard, waiting in the shade of an apple tree. Lee explained that he had gone to the rear to meet Grant and, instead, had received from a staff officer a letter in which the head of the Federal armies said he had no authority to treat for peace; the proposed meeting could do no good. Grant ended his letter with an expression of hope that no more blood would be shed. Lee then had been compelled to ask for a meeting in accordance with Grant's previous offer of terms of surrender. A truce had been requested by Lee and, after some delay, granted by General Meade, who had reached that part of the line. At Meade's suggestion, Lee had written another letter to Grant and dispatched it from the line near Appomattox Court House. He now was awaiting an answer.

Lee ended his account with an admission that he was afraid Grant's refusal to meet him was due to a knowledge that the plight of the Confederate army had worsened and that more severe terms could be imposed. Lee did not say so, but his dread was that his men would be marched off to Federal prisons. Longstreet answered that he knew the Federal general-in-chief well enough to feel that Grant would give such terms as, in reversed circumstances, the Confederate commander would demand. In his effort to reassure his chief, Longstreet saw that he was not succeeding and did not press the point. Lee was disposed to silence. Then, at 12:15, there arrived at the orchard under flag of truce a Union officer. Longstreet guessed his mission and turned again to Lee: "General, unless he offers us honorable terms, come back and let us fight it out!" As Lee prepared to leave for the interview with Grant, it seemed to Old Pete that the prospect of a fight had braced his chief.[42]

Three long hours passed, and more. The duration of the truce and the passage of so many white flags had spread wild rumor through the ranks. "We had been thinking it might come to that, sooner or later," wrote artillerist William Owen of the prospect of surrender, "but when the shock came it was terrible." Then there came a mutter along the road that led to the Confederate lines from Appomattox Court House. Men at the roadside saw a sight that startled some and made others blanch, and halted still others as if by a sudden, shouted command. General Lee was riding along the road. Behind him were a lieutenant colonel and a sergeant. Lee was flawlessly dressed. Traveller was perfectly caparisoned. On any other day the sight of Lee on the battlefield in that martial garb would have sent the rebel yell running through the ranks as it had at the Chancellor house that May noon in 1863. Now . . . it was different. Lee, supreme master of his emotions, was battling with tears. Late-comers caught the end of a disjointed answer to pleading inquiries from the men—"will all be paroled and go to your homes till exchanged."

Still the same question. "General, are we surrendered, are we surrendered?" His face gave the answer, but they followed him and thronged him and tried to touch him. They pressed about him till he reached the apple tree; they ringed the little orchard as closely as the guarding engineer detachment permitted. Later, when he and the staff rode to army headquarters a mile in the rear, many men still clung to the little cavalcade. There were soldierly avowals. "Blow, Gabriel, blow," shouted one agonized North Carolinian as he threw his musket from him. "My God, let him blow, I am ready to die!" Most of the surrendered troops were bewildered.

"Very little was said by men or officers. They sat, or lay on the ground in reflective mood, overcome by a flood of sad recollections."

During the late afternoon, commissary wagons entered the Confederate camps from the Union lines. Nothing except bread was issued to some commands that evening and to some, meat only, but whatever the food, it was devoured ravenously and gratefully. While this brought relief from the worst pangs of hunger, the pain of defeat and the humiliation of surrender scarcely were lessened. Bitter feelings deepened in the shadows of the spring afternoon. At length, as one officer phrased it, "the sun went down, and with it all the hopes of a people who, with prayers, and tears and blood, had striven to uphold that falling flag."[43]

The next day brought rain, more food, and the refreshment that came from the first untroubled sleep that some men had been allowed since April 3. There was nothing to do except to hope for more rations, to plan the journey home, and to wait for the issuance of paroles. Officers had much work in preparing and checking rolls. All officers of corps and divisional rank and all chiefs of staff bureaus were directed to prepare reports of the operations from Petersburg to the surrender. For arranging the details of the surrender with a like number of Federal officers, Lee designated Longstreet, Gordon, and Pendleton. In cordial spirit, the commissioners arranged readily for the formal surrender of arms, for the transfer of public property, for the departure of the Confederates under their own commanders, and for a variety of other matters.

Announcement of these terms was the first step in the effective reconstruction of the Union. Said cannoneer Ned Moore, "When we learned that we should be paroled, and go to our homes unmolested, the relief was unbounded. . . . The favorable and entirely unexpected terms of surrender wonderfully restored our souls. . . ." A South Carolinian elaborated: "I am forced to admit that the Federal officers and troops conducted themselves with singular propriety throughout this time," and Northern officers "came without parade, and departed without uncourteous reference to our misfortune."[44]

How few there were to respect this civility, the new muster-rolls tragically displayed. The four corps had been directed, first and last, by six lieutenant generals. Longstreet alone remained with the troops. Forty-seven men had fought under Lee as major generals. Thirteen had started the retreat from Petersburg. Seven were left now in command of troops. Lee's brigadiers had reached a total of 146. When "cease firing" was ordered, 22 of these men stood with the infantry. Not more than 85 colonels of infantry could be counted now; full organization called for upwards of 200. Organized, armed foot soldiers were reduced to 7,892. Cavalrymen had numbered perhaps 2,100 prior to the escape. Of all ranks and all branches of the armed service, equipped and weaponless, sick and able to fight, present or captured after April 8, the lists were to show 28,231.[45]

Formal surrender of the artillery was put first. The painful transfer of guns and animals, and the parole of the cannoneers, took place on April 11. Remaining cavalrymen of Rooney Lee's division laid down their swords the same day and then rode sadly off. The next morning the infantry were to go through the same last humiliation, that of surrendering arms, cartridge boxes, and flags. The Confederate commissioners had pleaded hard for permission to place the arms, accouterments, and standards on the ground in the camps; but to this General Grant would not consent, generous though he had been in every other particular. The surrender would be simple; it had to be actual, not symbolic.

The morning of April 12, the last day of the army's life, was chill and gray but without the rain that had fallen almost continuously since the surrender. After sunrise the column soon was formed. General officers mounted; regimental commanders took their stations; each man had his musket. The Stars and Bars were at their proper place midway of some regiments, but a few flagstaffs were without standards. Men had torn the bunting to bits or else hidden the banners. There were no bands. Without a beat of drum and in the silence of their black depression, the men started down the hill. At the front of the Second Corps, which headed the column, rode John B. Gordon. His was the same soldierly figure, but now his chin was on his breast, his eyes were downcast. Scarcely a career in the whole army had been more remarkable than his—from inexperienced captain to major general and corps commander.

In the order of march first place fittingly was given the Stonewall Brigade which, in its earliest days, Old Jack had acclaimed proudly the "First." Its 210 officers and men marched deliberately and without faltering up toward the village. Behind the men of Manassas moved the other brigades of Gordon's division. Shadows they were, but they represented most of the regiments of Jackson's old division—Lawton's fine Georgians, Dick Taylor's famous fighters of Middletown and Winchester, nearly all the other troops from Louisiana. Today each of the regiments occupied so little of the muddy road that they created a dramatic illusion. Their flags appeared to be massed. Federals who saw them coming to the Court House had to look a second time to be sure what it was they beheld: "The regimental battle-flags . . . crowded so thick, by thinning out of men, that the whole column seemed crowned with red."

Gordon's men were obeying in their last march the endlessly repeated command of Old Jack, the command heard on the way to Front Royal, and in Thoroughfare Gap, and along the forest road that led through the Wilderness to Hooker's flank—"Close up, men, close up!" As they closed now, they saw ahead, in line on the left and on the right of the road, two full Federal brigades. At the right of the line, the color guard carried the Stars and Stripes and the flag of the 1st Division of the V Corps. Under the colors was a little group of officers. The central figure was Brigadier General Joshua L. Chamberlain. He watched the column as it came nearer, and spoke a word to a man by his side. A bugle rang out above the shuffle of muddy feet. Instantly, regiment by regiment, as smartly as if on dress parade, the Union troops shifted from order arms to carry arms, the marching salute. Gordon heard the familiar sound of the shift and, half startled, looked up. His figure stiffened; he turned his horse to General Chamberlain; he brought down his sword in salute and, wheeling again to his own column, gave the command to carry arms. Salute answered salute. Said Chamberlain afterward, "On our part not a sound of trumpet more, nor roll of drums; not a cheer, nor word nor whisper of vain-glorying, . . . but an awed stillness rather, and breath-holding, as if it were the passing of the dead!"

The column moved on until the head of it reached the Federal left. There it halted and faced to the south. Officers dressed the line and took their post. Gordon and his few generals rode to the rear of the troops. At a word from officers, bayonets were fixed. A heavy pause ensued. Then, in a low voice, the last command was given to Jackson's foot cavalry. The men stepped forward four paces across the road and stacked their arms. Off came the cartridge boxes. In a moment these were hanging from the muskets. The color sergeants folded the regimental flags and laid them, too, on the stack. Silence held. They turned; they came back into the road, they marched ahead past the Court House. It was over.[46]

As fast as the divisions could—for waiting was torture—they moved up the road and repeated the ceremony. After Gordon came Rodes's old division of Early's. In the division of Grimes, formerly of Rodes, the brigade of Battle had been Rodes's at Seven Pines and at Sharpsburg. Cox's brigade, formerly Dodson Ramseur's, included the famous 1st Carolina, the "Bethel Regiment" that had shared the opening battle of the war in Virginia. It counted now 71 present. In Phil Cooke's brigade was the renowned 12th Georgia that had won the army's admiration at Front Royal and at Cedar Creek. The 12th now numbered 60 men. The most distinguished commanders of every brigade of the division were listed among the dead.

Early's division included the men who had been Garland's. Lewis's brigade had been Trimble's and Hoke's and Godwin's. The brigade of James A. Walker had a few of Dick Ewell's men of 1861. Pegram's brigade originally had been Elzey's and then Early's. A hundred names, a thousand memories the passing of the Second Corps recalled! Gordon was mindful of them all, and afterward he addressed them with overflowing eloquence.

While Gordon was speaking, Anderson's men were repeating the sad ceremony of surrender. Most of these units had not come to Virginia till the spring of 1864, but they included Wise's brigade, a part of which had been with Rodes at Seven Pines. Bushrod Johnson's division had borne much of the bitterest day-by-day fighting in the hideous red trenches of Petersburg.

To the village street moved the remnants of the Third Corps, under the command of that gallant, ill-fortuned gentleman Harry Heth. The men Heth surrendered included all the Tennesseans who in many battles far from home had acquitted themselves with honor. In John R. Cooke's brigade were the 118 survivors of the illustrious 27th North Carolina which, with the great old 3rd Arkansas, had stopped the Federal attack on the center at Sharpsburg. Wilcox's division was as close to Heth's in the last hour as it had been in the Wilderness that May night of 1864 when, it now was plain, the army was at the beginning of the end. Every one of Wilcox's brigades was renowned—Thomas's had fought through nearly the whole of the war; Lane's had been Branch's till Sharpsburg; McGowan's had been Gregg's; Scales's was Pender's. This fragment of a division, 2,681 men, included four of the brigades of A. P. Hill's famous old Light Division. Hill himself and four of the old brigadiers, Branch, Gregg, Pender, and Perrin, had been killed.

Mahone's division had at its head, in its last hour, the soldier who shared with Gordon and Hampton the highest distinction in the final year of the war. Mahone had grown with his duties. Scarcely with an exception, each of his battles had been better than the one that preceded it. Forney's brigade had been Cadmus Wilcox's pride; Weisiger's had been led for more than two years by Mahone himself. Nat Harris had raised most notably the standard of Posey's brigade, which once had been Featherston's. The wounded Moxley Sorrel's brigade had been Rans Wright's which had held on at Malvern Hill. Mahone's division had been Dick Anderson's that smoky day at Chancellorsville. Well the division had fought under Anderson, but never better than under Mahone.

Last, now, the great old First Corps! Of Kershaw's division, which had been McLaws's, only 805 surrendered. Their comrades were on the way to prison—the men who fought at Fredericksburg under Tom Cobb, and Barksdale's Mississippians who had waged the battle of the pontoons there, and McLaws's own fine Georgians. Pickett's men numbered 1,031, of whom 17 belonged to the 1st Virginia, a regiment with a history that ran back to the French and Indian War. Most of the soldiers of Pickett's division had lost their arms at Five Forks, or on the retreat or at Sayler's Creek. Those who formally laid down their weapons were merely "a little group," perhaps 60, but all the bloody grief of Gettysburg was typified by them— Pickett's exhortation, "Don't forget today that you are from Old Virginia," Armistead in the smoke with his hat on the point of his saber, Garnett wrapped in his overcoat, Cemetery Ridge red with Southern banners and with Southern blood.

Field's division was among the last to march between those silent blue lines. Except for Tige Anderson, it had none of the brigades of its earliest days, when part of it had been Whiting's and part David Jones's. The division's most renowned commander, John B. Hood, had left in the autumn of '63 and had himself suffered in body and in spirit as miserably as had any of his old veterans of Gaines' Mill, Second Manassas, Sharpsburg, the Wilderness. Evander Law had been transferred. Robert Toombs had resigned. John Gregg was dead. In the ranks still were some of Rock Benning's men who had stood opposite Burnside's Bridge on Antietam Creek that September afternoon in 1862. Of the Texas Brigade itself, perhaps the most renowned of all, 476 officers and men marched up the road and stacked rifles that had been heard in all the army's great battles except Chancellorsville. For absence from that action, they had made atonement at Chickamauga and in Tennessee. Their name, their deeds, with which the old 3rd Arkansas was associated, already had become a part of the tradition of their state.

The rear guard had surrendered the last cartridge, the last remnant of a bullet-torn flag. For the waning day there was such converse, friendly or bitter, as might be exchanged by lingering "paroled prisoners of war." Most Confederates were humiliated by their final defeat and half dazed from their long retreat. Such thought as they were able to fashion, when they started away, was of burned homes and fenceless farms, of a planting season without teams, of a hungry urban family and no wages with which to feed wife and children. With bitter thought honest exhortation was joined. "Go home, boys," said Bryan Grimes to Rodes's veterans, "and act like men, as you always have done during the war."[47]

Most precious of all were the words of Lee in his farewell order: "I need not tell the brave survivors of so many hard fought battles, who have remained steadfast to the last, that I have consented to this result from no distrust of them; but feeling that valor and devotion could accomplish nothing that could compensate for the loss that must have attended the continuance of the contest, I determined to avoid the useless sacrifice of those whose past services have endeared them to their countrymen. . . . You will take with you the satisfaction that proceeds from the consciousness of duty faithfully performed; and I earnestly pray that a Merciful God will extend to you His blessing and protection. With an unceasing admiration of your constancy and devotion to your Country, and with a grateful remembrance of your kind and generous consideration for myself, I bid you all an affectionate farewell."[48]

For the first day after the surrender, and for many another day, long and weary roads were theirs, and strange and sometimes winding; but the words of their leader they kept fresh in their hearts: "Consciousness of duty faithfully performed"—that was the consolation which became their reward, their pride, their bequest.

Notes

Abbreviations

CV—*Confederate Veteran*
Hotchkiss, *CMH* 3—Jedediah Hotchkiss, *Confederate Military History* (Vol. 3): *Virginia*
OR—U.S. War Department, *The War of the Rebellion: A Compilation of the Official Records of the Union and Confederate Armies,* and *Supplement.* Series I unless otherwise noted.
SHSP—*Southern Historical Society Papers*

Chapter 1: Opening Guns

1. *OR* 1, 266; Alfred Roman, *The Military Operations of General Beauregard* 1, 52ff., 64.
2. Beauregard graduated No. 2 in the class of 1838 at West Point.
3. *Richmond Dispatch,* May 1, 1861.
4. Roman, *Beauregard* 1, 66; *Richmond Dispatch, Richmond Examiner,* June 1, 1861; Sallie A. Putnam, *Richmond During the War,* 46.
5. Dunbar Rowland, ed., *Jefferson Davis, Constitutionalist* 5, 58.
6. *Richmond Examiner,* April 26, May 7, 1861.
7. *OR* 2, 894, 42; Roman, *Beauregard* 1, 66.
8. *OR* 2, 896, 901; J. E. Cooke, *Wearing of the Gray,* 83.
9. W. P. Snow, *Southern Generals* (1865 ed.), 212; Cooke, *Wearing of the Gray,* 83; *SHSP* 28, 287; *Richmond Whig,* July 26, 1861.
10. *OR* 2, 831, 879, 841, 846.
11. *OR* 2, 902.
12. *OR* 2, 907.
13. William Couper, *100 Years at V.M.I.* 1, 253; *OR* 2, 867ff.
14. *OR* 2, 868.
15. *OR* 2, 869; J. W. Thomason, *"Jeb" Stuart,* 63, 82, 83.
16. *OR* 2, 871–72, 877.
17. *OR* 2, 881, 896.
18. Yorktown and its environs were the principal defense. A small cooperating force was placed at Gloucester Point on the north bank of the river, opposite Yorktown.
19. *SHSP* 12, 105ff.
20. *Baltimore American,* April 23, *Richmond Dispatch,* April 26, 1861; Rowland, *Jefferson Davis* 8, 213.

21. *OR* 51:2, 36, 53; *OR* 2, 789–90, 865, 887, 884.

22. *OR* 2, 84, 95–96, 97, 82; Walter Clark, *North Carolina Regiments* 1, 88.

23. *Richmond Dispatch,* June 24, 1861.

24. *Richmond Dispatch,* July 4, 10, *Baltimore Sun,* June 27, 1861.

25. E. A. Pollard, *Lee and His Lieutenants,* 450; Clark, *North Carolina Regiments* 5, 645; 1, 125–26.

26. *Richmond Whig,* July 26, 1861; G. Moxley Sorrel, *Recollections of a Confederate Staff Officer,* 54. D. H. Hill and Jackson were brothers-in-law by Jackson's second marriage. Their wives were daughters of the first president of Davidson College, Robert Hall Morrison.

27. *OR* 2, 49, 51ff., 64ff.; Hotchkiss, *CMH* 3, 45.

28. Military record, Garnett Papers, Myrtle Cooper-Schwarz Collection; *Richmond Dispatch,* April 23, 1861; C. Vann Woodward, *Mary Chesnut's Civil War,* 176.

29. *OR* 2, 236–37.

30. Hotchkiss, *CMH* 3, 691.

31. Hotchkiss's notes, sketches, and tables of distances supplied virtually all the topographical data for this section and for much of what appears in later chapters on the operations of Jackson.

32. *OR* 2, 237–38, 242, 264, 256, 275.

33. *OR* 2, 257, 265, 260.

34. *OR* 2, 283, 262, 260, 258.

35. *OR* 2, 260, 262–63, 258–59, 266–67.

36. *OR* 2, 285–88; *Louisville Courier-Journal* clipping, n.d., S. M. Gaines, December 29, 1902, Garnett Papers.

37. Besides mention of 555 prisoners in Pegram's report, the only other detailed casualty list is that of the 23rd Virginia, which lost 32. The other units must have had at least 100 wounded and stragglers.

38. J. W. Gordon, August 14, 1861, Garnett Papers.

Chapter 2: Beauregard's Battlefield

1. Roman, *Beauregard* 1, 82.

2. Beauregard to Davis, June 12, Davis to Beauregard, June 13, 1861, Roman, *Beauregard* 1, 77–78.

3. *OR* 2, 943–44.

4. To L. T. Wigfall, July 8, 1861, Roman, *Beauregard* 1, 81–82.

5. Beauregard to Davis, July 11, Chesnut to Beauregard, July 16, 1861, Roman, *Beauregard* 1, 82–83, 85–87; *OR* 2, 504ff.

6. P. G. T. Beauregard, *Commentary on the Campaign and Battle of Manassas,* 30; *OR* 2, 472; J. E. Johnston, *Narrative of Military Operations,* 38.

7. Roman, *Beauregard* 1, 90.

8. *OR* 2, 440ff.; Roman, *Beauregard* 1, 92ff.; James Longstreet, *From Manassas to Appomattox,* 33ff.

9. *OR* 2, 478, 473.

10. *OR* 2, 486, 473, 474; Johnston, *Narrative,* 40–41.

11. Roughly 15,500 of 33,000. Smith's brigade is not included in the total, inasmuch as his men had not arrived.

12. *OR* 2, 486–87. Johnston's troops had been styled the Army of the Shenandoah; Beauregard had called his the Army of the Potomac. After the junction of the two, the latter name prevailed until supplanted the next year by the one that became even more renowned.
13. *OR* 2, 479–80. The defense made of these orders in 1886, after they had been criticized by General Johnston, will be found in Roman, *Beauregard* 1, 55ff. It is not apt to convince students.
14. *OR* 2, 518, 559, 474.
15. Roman, *Beauregard* 1, 447–48.
16. *OR* 2, 543, 565, 537, 487, 555.
17. *OR* 2, 488–89.
18. *OR* 2, 519, 491; E. Porter Alexander, *Military Memoirs of a Confederate*, 31.
19. *OR* 2, 474.
20. *OR* 2, 491, 536, 537, 543, 565; *OR* 51:2, 689.
21. Alexander, *Military Memoirs*, 34; Johnston, *Narrative*, 47.
22. *OR* 2, 475, 491, 543, 492.
23. *OR* 2, 475, 492; Johnston, *Narrative*, 48; *Battles and Leaders of the Civil War* 1, 248.
24. *OR* 2, 475.
25. *OR* 2, 493.
26. *OR* 2, 483, 347, 394, 402, 406, 407, 481, 494.
27. *OR* 2, 494–95.
28. *OR* 2, 495–96, 550, 547; *OR* 51:1, 29–30.
29. *OR* 2, 522, 476, 496.
30. *Richmond Whig*, November 20, 1861; Jubal A. Early, *Autobiographical Sketch and Narrative of the War Between the States*, 20ff.
31. *OR* 2, 476, 496, 556–57.

Chapter 3: Beauregard's Star Wanes

1. Johnston, *Narrative*, 52–53; *OR* 2, 476, 477, 497.
2. *OR* 2, 483; Early, *Autobiographical Sketch*, 25–26.
3. Longstreet, *Manassas to Appomattox*, 51–52; *OR* 2, 519, 544, 477, 497; Roman, *Beauregard* 1, 109.
4. Jefferson Davis, *The Rise and Fall of the Confederate Government* 1, 349; *OR* 2, 987; Alexander, *Military Memoirs*, 49.
5. Roman, *Beauregard* 1, 116; *OR* 2, 502, 503.
6. Johnston, *Narrative*, 59; Roman, *Beauregard* 1, 119.
7. *Richmond Dispatch*, July 31, 1861; *OR* 51:2, 215–16; *Richmond Examiner*, August 14, July 22, July 23, *Richmond Dispatch*, July 23, 1861.
8. *Charleston Mercury*, July 25, 1861; *Punch*, reprinted in *Richmond Examiner*, September 6, 1861.
9. Mary Anna Jackson, *Memoirs of Stonewall Jackson*, 178, 180; *SHSP* 19, 83, 302.
10. McHenry Howard, *Recollections of a Maryland Confederate Soldier and Staff Officer*, 35; Smith's diary in *CV* 7, 108; *Richmond Dispatch*, August 8, 1861.
11. *OR* 2, 476; *Richmond Dispatch*, August 8, *Richmond Examiner*, July 22, 1861.
12. John O. Casler, *Four Years in the Stonewall Brigade*, 25.
13. *OR* 2, 558; Pollard, *Lee and His Lieutenants*, 477; Cooke, *Wearing of the Gray*, 110ff.

14. *OR* 2, 474, 499; Thomas C. Caffey, *Battle-fields of the South,* 59.

15. Richard Taylor, *Destruction and Reconstruction: Personal Experiences of the Civil War,* 24; Putnam, *Richmond During the War,* 35–36; *SHSP* 22, 47ff.

16. *OR* 2, 476–77; *Richmond Whig,* August 3, 1861; E. P. Alexander in *SHSP* 9, 515.

17. *Richmond Dispatch,* July 15, 1861; *Dictionary of American Biography* 8, 213–14.

18. M. C. Butler in *Library of Southern Literature* 5, 2061ff.; *Richmond Dispatch,* May 29, 1861; Snow, *Southern Generals,* 472–73; Cooke, *Wearing of the Gray,* 61ff.

19. *OR* 2, 566–67.

20. Roman, *Beauregard* 1, 121–22, 123–24, 135; *Journal of the Congress of the Confederate States* 1, 305, 306; *OR* 2, 507–8; J. B. Jones, *A Rebel War Clerk's Diary* 1, 88.

21. For this controversy, see *OR* 5, 850, 877, 881, 903–4ff., 913, 920, 921, 945, 990; *OR* 51:2, 255, 272, 339, 345; Roman, *Beauregard* 1, 157, 161–62, 187ff.

22. *OR* 2, 484–504; *Richmond Dispatch,* October 23, 1861; *OR* 2, 508.

23. *OR* 2, 509, 512, 511–12; *Richmond Whig,* November 7, 1861.

24. Pollard, *Companions in Arms,* 248; *Richmond Examiner,* November 8, 1861.

25. *OR* 2, 515, 512–13, 513; Roman, *Beauregard* 1, 85–87.

26. *Journal C.S. Congress* 1, 645, 646, 654, 655, 656.

27. *OR* 5, 945; Roman, *Beauregard* 1, 189, 489, 491; *OR* 5, 1048; Jones, *War Clerk's Diary* 1, 107.

Chapter 4: *Johnston Passes a Dark Winter*

1. *OR* 5, 290ff.; *OR,* 51:2, 352–53; Johnston, *Narrative,* 80, 69.

2. Caffey, *Battle-fields of the South,* 305–6; Pollard, *Companions in Arms,* 409; Taylor, *Destruction and Reconstruction,* 42–44.

3. Marcus J. Wright, *General Officers of the Confederate Army,* 9–11.

4. Johnston, *Narrative,* 71–72.

5. IV *OR* 1, 605–8, 611; Rowland, *Jefferson Davis* 8, 257.

6. Woodward, *Mary Chesnut's Civil War,* contains many illuminating references to Benjamin. Also, Jones, *War Clerk's Diary* 1, 38, 71, 88, 89.

7. *OR* 5, 850, 877, 881, 903, 904–5, 906–8.

8. Johnston, *Narrative,* 78; *OR* 51:2, 402; *SHSP* 26, 150.

9. *OR* 5, 1011–12, 1015.

10. *OR* 5, 866, 881, 1027.

11. *OR* 5, 925, 389, 942–43, 965–66; *Richmond Dispatch,* November 4, 1861; Anna Jackson, *Stonewall Jackson,* 218.

12. *SHSP* 23, 124; *OR* 5, 1040–41, 1048, 1053.

13. *OR* 5, 1053.

14. *OR* 5, 1059–60, 1062, 1065, 1053.

15. *Richmond Whig,* April 26, 1873; Henry Kyd Douglas, *I Rode with Stonewall,* 26; *OR* 5, 1062–63.

16. *OR* 5, 1016–17, 974, 1037, 1045.

17. *SHSP* 44, 27; *Richmond Examiner,* Feb. 15, 26, 1862. The fullest and most hostile quotations from newspapers in every part of the South will be found in the *Charleston Mercury,* February 20–March 18.

18. Davis, *Confederate Government* 1, 462–63; Johnston, *Narrative,* 96.

19. Johnston, *Narrative,* 97.

20. *OR* 5, 1079, 1081.

21. *OR* 5, 1083; Johnston, *Narrative,* 101–2.
22. *OR* 5, 1087; Johnston, *Narrative,* 102.
23. Johnston, *Narrative,* 103, 98n; Early in Davis, *Confederate Government* 1, 468.
24. *OR* 5, 525–26, 537ff.; Rowland, *Jefferson Davis* 8, 187; *Richmond Examiner,* March 11, 1862.
25. *OR* 51:2, 1073–74; *OR* 5, 527–28.
26. Johnston, *Narrative,* 108; Jones, *War Clerk's Diary* 1, 142.
27. *OR* 11:3, 438.

Chapter 5: Challenge on the Peninsula

1. Johnston, *Narrative,* 111–12.
2. Johnston, *Narrative,* 114–16; G.W. Smith, *Confederate War Papers,* 41–43; Longstreet, *Manassas to Appomattox,* 66.
3. *Richmond Dispatch,* November 14, *Richmond Whig,* November 20, *Richmond Examiner,* November 22, 27, 1861; *OR* 51:2, 251; *OR* 2, 681, 686; *OR* 11:3, 450ff.
4. *OR* 11:3, 455–56, 461, 469, 473.
5. *OR* 11:3, 477, 485.
6. *OR* 11:3, 486ff.; *OR* 11:1, 337, 348.
7. D. S. Freeman, *Lee's Dispatches,* 10.
8. Sorrel, *Recollections,* 57–58.
9. *Richmond Dispatch,* September 25, 1861; *OR* 12:3, 832.
10. Sorrel, *Recollections,* 30.
11. IV *OR* 1, 182; *OR* 51:2, 310.
12. W. W. Blackford, *War Years with Jeb Stuart,* 47; Sorrel, *Recollections,* 41–42, 27; Pollard, *Companions in Arms,* 420; *SHSP* 28, 290–91; F. W. Dawson, *Reminiscences of Confederate Service, 1861–1865,* 130.
13. *OR* 4, 705, 662, 682; *OR* 5, 981.
14. IV *OR* 1, 1029; *Charleston Mercury,* February 15, March 31, April 3, 1862; IV *OR* 1, 1031, 1058–59, 1061–62, 1095ff.
15. Rowland, *Jefferson Davis* 9, 543; *SHSP* 28, 292, 10, 37; John Cheves Haskell, *The Haskell Memoirs,* 28.
16. Clark, *North Carolina Regiments* 2, 201–2; *OR* 11:3, 503.
17. Johnston, *Narrative,* 119; Alexander, *Military Memoirs,* 66.
18. *OR* 11:1, 275, 441ff.; Johnston, *Narrative,* 119–20.
19. Longstreet, *Manassas to Appomattox,* 72–73.
20. Johnston, *Narrative,* 120; Longstreet, *Manassas to Appomattox,* 72–73.
21. Longstreet, *Manassas to Appomattox,* 74; Johnston, *Narrative,* 120; *OR* 11:1, 275.
22. *OR* 11:1, 606, 607, 565, 602–3; *SHSP* 8, 285; Early, *Autobiographical Sketch,* 69.
23. *OR* 11:1, 603–7; Early, *Autobiographical Sketch,* 69.
24. Early, *Autobiographical Sketch,* 70–71; *OR* 11:1, 603, 610.
25. *OR* 11:1, 610.
26. *OR* 11:1, 603–4, 611; *SHSP* 8, 295.
27. *OR* 11:1, 568–69, 450, 448.
28. *OR* 11:1, 275, 276, 565–67.
29. *OR* 11:1, 607, 603, 604–5; Longstreet, *Manassas to Appomattox,* 78; Johnston, *Narrative,* 122.

30. OR 11:1, 275, 276, 627.
31. OR 11:1, 627, 629–30, 631, 618.
32. OR 11:1, 630; OR 11:3, 500.
33. John B. Hood, *Advance and Retreat*, 18–19.
34. Pollard, *Companions in Arms*, 673; Haskell, *Haskell Memoirs*, 16; OR 5, 1097.
35. Hood, *Advance and Retreat*, 21.
36. OR 51:2, 552–53.

Chapter 6: Seven Pines

1. OR 11:3, 499, 485, 503.
2. OR 11:3, 505, 507–8.
3. OR 11:3, 503, 500.
4. *Richmond Dispatch*, May 13, *Richmond Examiner*, May 13, 1862; OR 11:3, 517; *Battles and Leaders* 2, 206.
5. OR 11:1, 276; Johnston, *Narrative*, 128; *Battles and Leaders* 2, 208.
6. OR 11:3, 510–11; Davis, *Confederate Government* 2, 120; OR 11:3, 530.
7. Johnston, *Narrative*, 130–31; OR 11:3, 535.
8. OR 11:3, 543, 547.
9. OR 11:1, 681, 743.
10. Smith, *Confederate War Papers*, 146.
11. Smith, *Confederate War Papers*, 148–50.
12. OR 11:1, 943, 933.
13. Johnston, *Narrative*, 133–34; OR 11:1, 938; Alexander, *Military Memoirs*, 75.
14. *Richmond Dispatch*, July 8, August 20, September 28, November 6, 1861; OR 11:3, 524ff.; Caffey, *Battle-fields of the South*, 360.
15. *Battles and Leaders* 2, 241–42; Smith, *Confederate War Papers*, 164, 166.
16. Longstreet, *Manassas to Appomattox*, 91; OR 11:1, 942.
17. Smith, *Confederate War Papers*, 167, 170–71, 248–49; OR 11:1, 934.
18. Smith, *Confederate War Papers*, 167, 170; Davis, *Confederate Government* 2, 122; Alexander, *Military Memoirs*, 92.
19. OR 11:1, 934–35, 989ff.
20. *Battles and Leaders* 2, 229; *Richmond Examiner*, August 25, 1862; OR 11:1, 982.
21. OR 11:1, 943, 970ff.
22. OR 11:1, 961, 947ff., 945, 983, 987; Smith, *Confederate War Papers*, 204ff.
23. OR 11:1, 815–16, 838, 966, 953; Alexander, *Military Memoirs*, 89.
24. OR 11:1, 991–92, 941; *SHSP* 26, 144.
25. OR 11:1, 934–35, 940–41.
26. OR 11:1, 944–45, 993, 935.
27. Caffey, *Battle-fields of the South*, 254.
28. OR 11:1, 945.
29. OR 11:1, 980.
30. OR 11:1, 935; Smith, *Confederate War Papers*, 182.
31. Jones, *War Clerk's Diary* 1, 132; OR 11:1, 940, 935–39.
32. OR 11:1, 938.
33. OR 11:1, 563.
34. *OR Supplement* 2, 370–71.

35. *OR Supplement* 2, 371; *OR* 11:1, 938.
36. Smith, *Confederate War Papers,* 165ff.
37. *OR* 11:1, 986, 989.
38. Johnston, *Narrative,* 138–39; *SHSP* 18, 186–87; *Battles and Leaders* 2, 261.

Chapter 7: To Defend Richmond

1. *SHSP* 18, 181.
2. Freeman, *Lee's Dispatches,* 9.
3. *OR* 11:1, 976.
4. *SHSP* 10, 39; *OR* 11:3, 509ff., 608.
5. Freeman, *Lee's Dispatches,* 11.
6. Rowland, *Jefferson Davis* 9, 549; 10, 83; *OR* 11:3, 574.
7. *OR* 5, 777.
8. *OR* 5, 489, 490, 494, 1008, 1063.
9. June 4, 1862, H. B. McClellan mss., Confederate Memorial Institute.
10. *OR* 11:1, 1038.
11. *OR* 11:3, 590–91.
12. *OR* 11:1, 1044–45; *SHSP* 30, 346–48.
13. Cooke, *Wearing of the Gray,* 115ff., 141ff.
14. R. L. T. Beale, *History of the Ninth Virginia Cavalry,* 11.
15. Heros von Borcke, *Memoirs of the Confederate War for Independence* 1, 37; *OR* 11:1, 1036; G. W. Beale, *A Lieutenant of Cavalry in Lee's Army,* 24–25.
16. Cooke, *Wearing of the Gray,* 22ff.; Sorrel, *Recollections,* 29; *Richmond Dispatch,* November 7, 1861.
17. *OR* 11:1, 1036–37; Cooke, *Wearing of the Gray,* 176–77; G.W. Beale, *Lieutenant of Cavalry,* 27.
18. *OR* 11:1, 1037.
19. *OR* 11:1, 1038; R. L. T. Beale, *Ninth Virginia Cavalry,* 18; G.W. Beale, *Lieutenant of Cavalry,* 27; von Borcke, *Memoirs* 1, 39; H. B. McClellan, *The Life and Campaigns of J. E. B. Stuart,* 57.
20. McClellan, *Stuart,* 58; *OR* 11:1, 1038.
21. *OR* 11:1, 1038.
22. *OR* 11:1, 1038; Cooke, *Wearing of the Gray,* 179.
23. G. W. Beale, *Lieutenant of Cavalry,* 28; Cooke, *Wearing of the Gray,* 181.
24. Cooke, *Wearing of the Gray,* 182; G. W. Beale, *Lieutenant of Cavalry,* 28–29; von Borcke, *Memoirs* 1, 42; *OR* 11:1, 1039.
25. McClellan, *Stuart,* 61.
26. *OR* 11:1, 1038, 1039.
27. McClellan, *Stuart,* 62–63; Cooke, *Wearing of the Gray,* 186–87.
28. McClellan, *Stuart,* 64; G. W. Beale, *Lieutenant of Cavalry,* 30.
29. R. L. T. Beale, *Ninth Virginia Cavalry,* 20–21; G. W. Beale, *Lieutenant of Cavalry,* 30; McClellan, *Stuart,* 64–65; Cooke, *Wearing of the Gray,* 187; *OR* 11:1, 1017, 1039.
30. Alexander, *Military Memoirs,* 113–14; Thomason, *Stuart,* 153–55; McClellan, *Stuart,* 67.
31. Cooke, *Wearing of the Gray,* 180.

Chapter 8: Guarding the Valley

1. R. L. Dabney, *Life and Campaigns of Lieut.-Gen. Thomas J. Jackson,* 282; Anna Jackson, *Stonewall Jackson,* 212–13.
2. *SHSP* 19, 302; *Land We Love* 1, 310; Anna Jackson, *Stonewall Jackson,* 237.
3. *OR* 5, 1095.
4. Hunter H. McGuire in G. F. R. Henderson, *Stonewall Jackson and the American Civil War* 1, 230.
5. *SHSP* 19, 315, 302, 83; *SHSP* 9, 41; Casler, *Stonewall Brigade,* 92; Clark, *North Carolina Regiments* 1, 763; Caffey, *Battle-fields of the South,* 140–41; Howard, *Recollections,* 80.
6. Howard, *Recollections,* 78.
7. J. C. Wise, *The Long Arm of Lee* 1, 162–63.
8. *OR* 12:1, 380, 386; J. H. Worsham, *One of Jackson's Foot Cavalry,* 66.
9. *OR* 12:1, 383, 386, 381.
10. Worsham, *Jackson's Foot Cavalry,* 68.
11. Anna Jackson, *Stonewall Jackson,* 247; Taylor, *Destruction and Reconstruction,* 56.
12. William Allan, *History of the Campaign of Stonewall Jackson in the Shenandoah Valley of Virginia,* 163; Anna Jackson, *Stonewall Jackson,* 247. Actually the total of Federal killed, wounded, and missing was 590: *OR* 12:1, 346–47.
13. Casler, *Stonewall Brigade,* 66; Taylor, *Destruction and Reconstruction,* 79. Richard Garnett was a cousin of General Robert Garnett who had fallen at Carrick's Ford.
14. Anna Jackson, *Stonewall Jackson,* 249.
15. Jedediah Hotchkiss, *Make Me a Map of the Valley: The Civil War Journal of Stonewall Jackson's Topographer,* 5, 10.
16. Hotchkiss, *Journal,* 5; *OR* 12:3, 835; Allan, *Shenandoah Valley Campaign,* 171.
17. Howard, *Recollections,* 81, 87–88.
18. Clark, *North Carolina Regiments* 4, 446; Howard, *Recollections,* 83.
19. Hotchkiss, *Journal,* 20.
20. *OR* 12:1, 384.
21. Johnston's lost letter, dated April 8, can be reconstructed from Jackson's and Ewell's references in *OR* 12:3, 845, 848, 863.
22. *OR* 12:3, 848.
23. Howard, *Recollections,* 86; Hotchkiss, *Journal,* 28.
24. *OR* 12:1, 426; Hotchkiss, *Journal,* 27, 33; *OR* 12:3, 880.
25. *OR* 12:3, 871.
26. *OR* 12:3, 871.
27. *OR* 12:3, 872.
28. *OR* 12:3, 872.
29. Hotchkiss, *Journal,* 34–35; John A. Harman mss., Hotchkiss Papers, Library of Congress; *OR* 12:3, 861, 876.
30. Taylor, *Destruction and Reconstruction,* 37–38; Sorrel, *Recollections,* 56–57.
31. *OR* 51:2, 357; *Richmond Dispatch,* November 25, 1861; *OR* 5, 1089.
32. *SHSP* 7, 345; 20, 33; Taylor, *Destruction and Reconstruction.*
33. *OR* 12:3, 878.
34. *SHSP* 9, 364–65.
35. *OR* 12:3, 879, 881, 882.
36. *OR* 12:3, 884, 885; F. M. Myers, *The Comanches,* 37–38.

37. P. G. Hamlin, ed., *The Making of a Soldier: Letters of General R. S. Ewell,* 108.
38. Douglas, *I Rode with Stonewall,* 47–48; Howard, *Recollections,* 92, 99, 104; Henderson, *Stonewall Jackson* 1, 298–99.
39. *OR* 12:3, 891–92; Jackson mss., Confederate Memorial Institute.
40. *OR* 12:3, 891, 895.
41. *OR* 12:3, 894.

Chapter 9: Jackson Launches His Offensive

1. Hotchkiss, *Journal,* 36–37; Dabney, *Jackson,* 354.
2. *OR* 12:3, 893, 894.
3. Dabney, *Jackson,* 359; *OR* 12:3, 897.
4. Taylor, *Destruction and Reconstruction,* 49–50.
5. *OR* 12:3, 898, 896–97, 898, 897.
6. A. R. Lawton in Woodward, *Mary Chesnut's Civil War,* 499.
7. T. C. Johnson, *Robert Lewis Dabney,* 262, 270.
8. The authorization came from Johnston, to whom no doubt Lee had endorsed Jackson's telegram: Dabney Papers, Virginia State Library.
9. Hotchkiss, *Journal,* 48; *OR* 12:1, 702.
10. Taylor, *Destruction and Reconstruction,* 51–52; Dabney, *Jackson,* 365; Lucy R. Buck, *Diary of Lucy Rebecca Buck, 1861–1865,* 58.
11. *OR* 12:1, 556, 702, 725; Dabney, *Jackson,* 365–66.
12. Dabney, *Jackson,* 366–68; *OR* 12:1, 702, 557–58, 733–37; *SHSP* 24, 133; Allan, *Shenandoah Valley Campaign,* 210–11.
13. Dabney, *Jackson,* 368; Allan, *Shenandoah Valley Campaign,* 211; *OR* 12:1, 734; Taylor, *Destruction and Reconstruction,* 54.
14. *OR* 12:1, 703.
15. *OR* 12:1, 703
16. *OR* 12:1, 725–26, 703–4; Dabney, *Jackson,* 372–73; Taylor, *Destruction and Reconstruction,* 55.
17. *OR* 12:1, 726, 704.
18. E. A. Moore, *The Story of a Cannoneer Under Stonewall Jackson,* 56; Worsham, *Jackson's Foot Cavalry,* 84–85; J. B. Avirett, *The Memoirs of General Turner Ashby and His Compeers,* 196–97.
19. Dabney, *Jackson,* 375; *OR* 12:1, 726; Avirett, *Ashby,* 199.
20. *OR* 12:1, 735, 758.
21. Worsham, *Jackson's Foot Cavalry,* 86; *OR* 12:1, 758, 761.
22. Howard, *Recollections,* 110; Douglas, *I Rode with Stonewall,* 57–58.
23. Taylor, *Destruction and Reconstruction,* 58.
24. Dabney, *Jackson,* 379; Worsham, *Jackson's Foot Cavalry,* 87.
25. Hotchkiss, *CMH* 3, 242; Douglas, *I Rode with Stonewall,* 59; Taylor, *Destruction and Reconstruction,* 59; *OR* 12:1,706; Avirett, *Ashby,* 271; Dabney, *Jackson,* 381.
26. Dabney, *Jackson,* 381; *OR* 12:1, 709; *OR* 12:3, 901.
27. *OR* 12:1, 706–7, 710; Dabney, *Jackson,* 382; Anna Jackson, *Stonewall Jackson,* 265.
28. *OR* 12:1, 707, 730, 738, 708.
29. *OR* 12:3, 219, 266, 268; *OR* 12:1, 643.

Chapter 10: Victory in the Valley

1. Douglas, *I Rode with Stonewall*, 62–63; Hotchkiss, *Journal*, 49.
2. *SHSP* 40, 164–65.
3. Hotchkiss, *Journal*, 49.
4. *SHSP* 40, 166; Hotchkiss, *Journal*, 49–50.
5. *SHSP* 40, 168.
6. Hotchkiss, *Journal*, 50.
7. *OR* 12:1, 708; Hotchkiss, *Journal*, 50.
8. *OR* 12:3, 904; Taylor, *Destruction and Reconstruction*, 61.
9. *OR* 12:3, 904; Hotchkiss, *Journal*, 50–51; Taylor, *Destruction and Reconstruction*, 64–65; *OR* 12:1, 14.
10. *OR* 12:1, 708.
11. *OR* 12:1, 650; Douglas, *I Rode with Stonewall*, 71.
12. Hotchkiss, *Journal*, 51; *OR* 12:1, 731.
13. Hotchkiss, *Journal*, 51; Dabney, *Jackson*, 397.
14. Hotchkiss, *Journal*, 51; *OR* 12:1, 14.
15. Hotchkiss, *Journal*, 51–52.
16. *OR* 12:3, 906–7; Dabney, *Jackson*, 403–4. The evidence regarding these dispositions is in part inferential.
17. *OR* 12:3, 906; Hotchkiss, *Journal*, 52; Hotchkiss, *CMH* 3, 253.
18. *Charleston Mercury*, May 29, 1862; Douglas in A. K. McClure, ed., *Annals of the War*, 649; *OR* 12:3, 905, 906–7.
19. Taylor, *Destruction and Reconstruction*, 26.
20. *OR* 12:1, 712; Avirett, *Ashby*, 226.
21. *OR* 12:1, 712; Dabney, *Jackson*, 407–8.
22. Taylor, *Destruction and Reconstruction*, 72.
23. *OR* 12:1, 781, 732; Hotchkiss, *Journal*, 53. For Jackson, 13,000 infantry, plus 1,000 cavalry and 500 or 600 artillery seems a reasonable estimate.
24. *OR* 12:3, 907–8; Dabney statement (May 7, 1896), Hotchkiss Papers.
25. Hotchkiss, *Journal*, 53; S. J. C. Moore statement, Hotchkiss Papers; Douglas, *I Rode with Stonewall*, 85.
26. Dabney, Crutchfield statements (1896), Hotchkiss Papers.
27. Dabney, *Jackson*, 412–13; Allan, *Shenandoah Valley Campaign*, 270; *OR* 12:1, 713, 773.
28. *OR* 12:1, 714; Dabney, *Jackson*, 415.
29. *OR* 12:1, 712–13, 732, 781, 796.
30. *OR* 12:1, 782, 796, 714, 798.
31. Howard, *Recollections*, 124; *OR* 12:1: 818, 784.
32. *OR* 12:1, 714; Hotchkiss, *Journal*, 125–26; Dabney, *Jackson*, 419–21; Allan, *Shenandoah Valley Campaign*, 278.
33. *OR* 12:1, 740; Hotchkiss, *CMH* 3, 261.
34. *OR* 12:1, 740, 714, 760, 745, 747.
35. Hotchkiss, *CMH* 3, 261; *OR* 12:1, 798; Hotchkiss, *Journal*, 55.
36. *OR* 12:1, 741, 714, 729, 763, 786, 715.
37. *OR* 12:1, 693, 715, 802, 786; Taylor, *Destruction and Reconstruction*, 74–76.
38. *OR* 12:1, 742, 732, 715–16, 771; Dabney, *Jackson*, 425.
39. *OR* 12:1, 697, 691, 687, 690; Allan, *Shenandoah Valley Campaign*, 284.

40. *OR* 12:1, 716; Dabney, *Jackson*, 429–30; Anna Jackson, *Stonewall Jackson*, 283; Hotchkiss, *Journal*, 129.

41. Robert Stiles, *Four Years Under Marse Robert*, 245–46, on the authority of Hunter McGuire.

42. Taylor, *Destruction and Reconstruction*, 78–79.

43. *OR* 12:3, 908, 590, 594; Chilton mss., Museum of the Confederacy; Boteler in *SHSP* 40, 172–73; Robert E. Lee, *The Wartime Papers of R. E. Lee*, 193.

44. Hotchkiss, *Journal*, 57; *OR* 12:3, 913.

45. *OR* 12:1, 725.

46. Howard, *Recollections*, 130.

47. *OR* 12:1, 782.

48. *SHSP* 7, 530.

Chapter 11: Struggle for Richmond

1. *Battles and Leaders* 2, 296–97, 348.

2. Dabney memorandum (March 31, 1896), Hotchkiss Papers; C. S. Anderson, "Train Running for the Confederacy," *Railway and Locomotive Engineering* (August 1892), 287.

3. Dabney, *Jackson*, 435; Worsham, *Jackson's Foot Cavalry*, 97.

4. Dabney memorandum, Harman mss., Hotchkiss Papers; D. S. Freeman, *R. E. Lee* 2, 108.

5. Details and sources in D. S. Freeman, *R. E. Lee* 2, 110ff.

6. Dabney memorandum, Hotchkiss Papers.

7. Lee, *Wartime Papers*, 198–200; *OR* 11:1, 116–17.

8. Dabney memorandum (March 10, 1896), Hotchkiss Papers.

9. Dabney memorandum, Hotchkiss Papers; Davis Collection, Tulane University.

10. Dabney, *Jackson*, 440.

11. Dabney memorandum, Hotchkiss Papers; *OR* 11:2, 881; *OR* 11:3, 620.

12. *OR* 11:2, 756, 881–82, 834–35.

13. Dabney memorandum, Hotchkiss Papers; *OR* 11:2, 552, 562.

14. *OR* 11:2, 882, 886, 835.

15. *OR* 11:2, 882, 614, 553, 562; Dabney memorandum, Hotchkiss Papers.

16. *OR* 11:2, 860, 882, 835.

17. *OR* 11:2, 835–36, 491, 648, 899.

18. Total casualties came to some 1,475, of which 335 were in the 44th Georgia.

19. *OR* 11:2, 853–54.

20. *OR* 11:2, 836–37.

21. *OR* 11:2, 757.

22. *OR* 11:2, 624; Dabney, *Jackson*, 443.

23. *OR* 11:2, 615, 605–6, 492–93, 757.

24. *OR* 11:2, 553; Dabney memorandum, Hotchkiss Papers.

25. Dabney memorandum, Hotchkiss Papers; *OR* 11:2, 568, 606, 595, 570.

26. J. E. Cooke, *Outlines from the Outpost*, 50–51; Cooke, *Stonewall Jackson: A Military Biography*, 200.

27. *CV* 19, 78; Clark, *North Carolina Regiments* 1, 304; *OR* 11:2, 757, 595; Dabney, *Jackson*, 455.

28. Clark, *North Carolina Regiments* 4, 445; *OR* 11:2, 625–26.

29. Dabney, *Jackson*, 454; *OR* 11:2, 758.

30. *OR* 11:3, 238; *OR* 11:1, 51–60; Alexander, *Military Memoirs*, 131.
31. J. L. Brent, *Memoirs of the War Between the States*, 158–59.
32. *OR* 11:2, 662.
33. *OR* 11:2, 662.
34. Brent, *Memoirs*, 181; *OR* 11:2, 663.
35. *OR* 11:2, 789, 664.
36. *OR* 11:2, 675, 664.
37. *OR* 11:2, 726, 691, 717, 665, 687.
38. *OR* 11:2, 61, 431, 464, 477.

Chapter 12: Richmond Relieved

1. *OR* 11:2, 797, 789, 181, 185.
2. Dabney memorandum (April 22, 1896), Hotchkiss Papers; *OR* 12:1, 728.
3. J. E. B. Stuart Papers, Huntington Library.
4. *OR* 11:2, 789–90, 797, 495.
5. Brent, *Memoirs*, 191–92.
6. Dabney, *Jackson*, 464; *Battles and Leaders* 2, 387; *OR* 11:2, 653.
7. Dabney, *Jackson*, 465; *OR* 11:2, 655; Alexander, *Military Memoirs*, 148.
8. Alexander, *Military Memoirs*, 149–51; Dabney, *Jackson*, 465; *OR* 11:2, 627, 655.
9. *OR* 11:2, 557; Howard, *Recollections*, 148.
10. *OR* 11:2, 627, 557, 810, 566; Dabney, *Jackson*, 466–67; Alexander, *Military Memoirs*, 149–51.
11. *OR* 11:3, 392, 617.
12. *OR* 11:2, 907, 911; Clark, *North Carolina Regiments* 3, 163, 39; *Battles and Leaders* 2, 390.
13. Brent, *Memoirs*, 193–94; *OR* 11:2, 910, 908.
14. *OR* 11:2, 718, 666–67, 705, 707; Longstreet, *Manassas to Appomattox*, 139.
15. For the battle of June 30, variously known as Glendale, Frayser's Farm, and Riddell's Shop, see Freeman, *R. E. Lee* 2, 184ff.
16. *OR* 11:2, 790
17. *Battles and Leaders* 2, 391.
18. *OR* 11:2, 496, 667.
19. *OR* 11:2, 566.
20. *OR* 11:2, 675–77, 668, 691.
21. *OR* 11:2, 557, 496, 566, 811, 818.
22. *OR* 11:2, 274, 811–12.
23. *OR* 11:2, 818–19, 566.
24. *Battles and Leaders* 2, 391; *OR* 11:2, 496, 628, 669, 677.
25. *OR* 11:2, 562, 572, 653, 812; Longstreet, *Manassas to Appomattox*, 144.
26. *OR* 11:2, 628, 819, 691–92, 719.
27. *OR* 11:2, 819, 677–78, 566; Brent, *Memoirs*, 211.
28. *OR* 11:2, 669, 794, 814, 670, 749; Brent, *Memoirs*, 216.
29. *OR* 11:2, 729, 643, 634, 650.
30. *OR* 11:2, 795, 692, 719, 204

Chapter 13: Lessons of the Seven Days

1. Alexander, *Military Memoirs*, 171, 174.
2. *SHSP* 12, 105ff.; *OR* 11:3, 630.
3. Caffey, *Battle-fields of the South*, 373; Putnam, *Richmond During the War*, 148; *Charleston Mercury*, June 28, 1862; *SHSP* 28, 293; *OR* 11:3, 641.
4. *OR* 11:2, 660–74, 675–77, 684, 682, 679–80.
5. *OR* 15, 826, 880; *OR* 11:2, 674.
6. Putnam, *Richmond During the War*, 148; *OR* 11:2, 495, 818, 790.
7. *OR* 11:2, 629, 672, 495.
8. *OR* 2, 481, 476; *OR* 11:3, 484.
9. *OR* 51:2, 577–78; *OR* 11:3, 612–13
10. *OR* 11:2, 536; Susan P. Lee, *Memoirs of William Nelson Pendleton*, 194–95.
11. *OR* 11:2, 547.
12. Dabney memorandum (March 31, 1896), Hotchkiss Papers; *OR* 11:2, 555, 492, 496, 566–67; R. H. McKim, *A Soldier's Recollections*, 92.
13. Jones, *War Clerk's Diary* 1, 38–39; Raphael J. Moses, "Autobiography," Southern Historical Collection, University of North Carolina.
14. Woodward, *Mary Chesnut's Civil War*, 157; Jones, *War Clerk's Diary* 1, 40; *Richmond Dispatch*, July 24, 26, *Richmond Whig*, July 29, 1861.
15. Ulrich B. Phillips, ed., *The Correspondence of Robert Toombs, Alexander H. Stephens, and Howell Cobb*, 575, 577–78; Sorrel, *Recollections*, 53.
16. Phillips, *Correspondence of Toombs*, 594–95; Pleasant A. Stovall, *Robert Toombs, Statesman, Speaker, Soldier, Sage*, 243.
17. Stovall, *Robert Toombs*, 254–57, 601.
18. *OR* 11:2, 493, 496, 554, 558–59; John B. Gordon, *Reminiscences of the Civil War*, 67–68; *SHSP* 28, 292–93.
19. D. H. Hill, Jr., *Bethel to Sharpsburg* 2, 197ff.; *OR* 9, 496; *OR* 12:3, 917.
20. *OR* 11:2, 516–17; R.T.L. Beale, *Ninth Virginia Cavalry*, 26.
21. *OR* 11:2, 517–18.
22. *OR* 11:2, 518.
23. *OR* 11:2, 519–20.
24. Dabney, *Jackson*, 480–81; Alexander, *Military Memoirs*, 169.
25. *OR* 11:3, 657; *OR* 11:1, 1041.
26. *OR* 11:2, 515, 522.
27. W. N. McDonald, *The Laurel Brigade*, 196; Rosser mss., University of Virginia; *OR* 11:2, 532, 521.
28. *SHSP* 35, 57; *SHSP* 14, 11; *CV* 6, 270; *Richmond Examiner*, June 4, 1861.
29. *OR* 11:2, 837, 818–19, 983; *SHSP* 14, 12; Stiles, *Four Years Under Marse Robert*, 110.
30. *OR* 11:2, 763, 776, 758–59, 556.
31. *OR* 11:2, 776, 980.
32. *OR* 11:2, 838–39, 626.
33. Blackford, *War Years with Jeb Stuart*, 79, 82; *SHSP* 19, 311.
34. *Battles and Leaders* 2, 405, 389; Dabney, *Jackson*, 466–67; William Allan, *The Army of Northern Virginia in 1862*, 121.
35. *OR* 11:2, 552–53, 557; Henderson, *Stonewall Jackson* 2, 57.
36. Boteler in *SHSP* 40, 180–81.

37. *Richmond Examiner*, June 28, July 2, 8, 1862.
38. Sorrel, *Recollections*, 80–81; *Richmond Whig*, July 11, 1862; *OR* 11:3, 639–40; *OR* 51:2, 590–91.
39. Sorrel, *Recollections*, 81; Freeman, *Lee's Dispatches*, 39; *OR* 12:3, 919.
40. Taylor, *Destruction and Reconstruction*, 93.

Chapter 14: Facing a New Threat

1. Hotchkiss, *Journal*, 62.
2. Frank Paxton, *The Civil War Letters of General Frank "Bull" Paxton*, 49.
3. *OR* 12:3, 919.
4. John O. Casler, *Four Years in the Stonewall Brigade*, 101–2.
5. McDonald, *Laurel Brigade*, 75–76.
6. *OR* 12:3, 926; Freeman, *Lee's Dispatches*, 43.
7. Jackson letter book, Hotchkiss Papers; Garnett Papers.
8. Garnett Papers; *OR* 12:2, 182.
9. Howard, *Recollections*, 162.
10. *OR* 12:2, 214–15, 217, 181.
11. *OR* 12:3, 924, 922–23 ; John S. Mosby, *War Reminiscences*, 243–44.
12. *OR* 12:2, 21, 5, 23, 25; *OR* 12:3, 548.
13. *OR* 12:3, 553, 133, 547; *OR* 12:2, 153.
14. *OR* 12:2, 180–81, 226.
15. *OR* 12:2, 183, 215; Hotchkiss, *Journal*, 66; Howard, *Recollections*, 165.
16. Allan, *Army of Northern Virginia*, 165; *OR* 12:2, 223, 188, 215; Hotchkiss, *Journal*, 66.
17. *OR* 12:2, 228–29; Early, *Autobiographical Sketch*, 93–94.
18. *OR* 12:2, 229; Myers, *The Comanches*, 88; Early, *Autobiographical Sketch*, 94.
19. Howard, *Recollections*, 167; *OR* 12:2, 229–30; Early, *Autobiographical Sketch*, 95–96.
20. *OR* 12:2, 237–38, 230, 213–14; Early, *Autobiographical Sketch*, 96–97; Howard, *Recollections*, 169.
21. Moore, *Cannoneer Under Jackson*, 95.
22. Early, *Autobiographical Sketch*, 97; *OR* 12:2, 189, 226.
23. *OR* 12:2, 205, 289, 231, 219.
24. *OR* 12:2, 187, 231, 206; Dabney, *Jackson*, 501; Henderson, *Stonewall Jackson* 2, 95.
25. *OR* 12:2, 192, 222–23; Douglas, *I Rode with Stonewall*, 124.
26. *OR* 12:2, 184, 189, 215, 236.
27. *OR* 12:2, 184, 187, 226, 216, 239; Anna Jackson, *Stonewall Jackson*, 312.
28. *OR* 12:2, 184–85.
29. Dabney, *Jackson*, 505; *OR* 12:2, 184, 180, 139.
30. *OR* 12:2, 146–47.
31. *OR* 12:2, 185, 145; Dabney, *Jackson*, 507.
32. Howard, *Recollections*, 170–71; Anna Jackson, *Stonewall Jackson*, 312; *OR* 12:2, 178.
33. *OR* 12:2, 223; John Hampden Chamberlayne, *Ham Chamberlayne: Letters of an Artillery Officer*, 90.
34. *OR* 12:2, 10, 6.
35. *Richmond Examiner*, *Richmond Whig*, August 12, 1862; Freeman, *R. E. Lee* 2, 265ff.
36. *OR* 51:2, 593–94; *OR* 11:3, 671; *OR* 12:3, 930–31.
37. *OR* 51:2, 1075.
38. *OR* 12:2, 552.

39. *OR* 12:2, 726; Blackford, *War Years with Jeb Stuart*, 97–98; von Borcke, *Memoirs* 1, 105ff.
40. *OR* 12:2, 726; *OR* 12:3, 934, 940; Fitzhugh Lee, *General Lee*, 183.
41. *OR* 12:2, 580; Sorrel, *Recollections*, 94–95; Phillips, *Correspondence of Toombs*, 603–4.

Chapter 15: Return to Manassas

1. *OR* 12:2, 550, 547.
2. *OR* 12:2, 729, 726; Hotchkiss, *Journal*, 69.
3. *OR* 12:2, 727; McDonald, *Laurel Brigade*, 74.
4. *OR* 12:2, 731–32; *OR* 12:3, 941; von Borcke, *Memoirs* 1, 124; Douglas, *I Rode with Stonewall*, 133–34.
5. *OR* 12:2, 705–8; G. M. Neese, *Three Years in the Confederate Horse Artillery*, 101–2.
6. *OR* 12:2, 718–19, 605.
7. Hotchkiss, *Journal*, 71; Moore, *Cannoneer Under Jackson*, 99–100; *SHSP* 14, 209–10.
8. *OR* 12:2, 553–54; Freeman, *R. E. Lee* 2, 297ff.
9. *OR* 12:2, 650.
10. Allan, *Army of Northern Virginia*, 203; *OR* 12:2, 678; Hotchkiss, *Journal*, 71–72.
11. Allan, *Army of Northern Virginia*, 203; *OR* 12:2, 747; *Battles and Leaders* 2, 533; Dabney, *Jackson*, 517.
12. *OR* 12:2, 650.
13. *OR* 12:2, 734.
14. *OR* 12:2, 747–48, 650–51, 708; Blackford, *War Years with Jeb Stuart*, 112–15; Clark, *North Carolina Regiments* 2, 151.
15. *OR* 12:2, 670, 720–21, 643; Clark, *North Carolina Regiments* 2, 153.
16. Allan, *Army of Northern Virginia*, 215; Moore, *Cannoneer Under Jackson*, 103; *OR* 12:2, 656, 721; Blackford, *War Years with Jeb Stuart*, 115; Casler, *Stonewall Brigade*, 107.
17. *OR* 12:2, 540–41, 260; Moore, *Cannoneer Under Jackson*, 104–5.
18. *OR* 12:2, 656; Allan, *Army of Northern Virginia*, 216; Worsham, *Jackson's Foot Cavalry*, 121; Chamberlayne, *Letters*, 99.
19. *OR* 12:2, 644, 656, 670.
20. Hamlin, *Ewell Letters*, 125–26.
21. *OR* 12:2, 664, 656–57, 644–45.
22. Blackford, *War Years with Jeb Stuart*, 120–21; *OR* 12:2, 657, 710–11.
23. *OR* 12:2, 645, 658, 711; P. G. Hamlin, *Old Bald Head*, 129.
24. *OR* 12:2, 645, 38.
25. *OR* 12:2, 645, 652; Moore, *Cannoneer Under Jackson*, 114; Worsham, *Jackson's Foot Cavalry*, 130–31; Freeman, *R. E. Lee* 2, 318.
26. *OR* 12:2, 646, 735–36, 711–12, 687, 652, 680.
27. *OR* 12:2, 646, 687, 681; Douglas, *I Rode with Stonewall*, 138.
28. *SHSP* 13, 34; Early, *Autobiographical Sketch*, 124; Douglas, *I Rode with Stonewall*, 138; Chamberlayne, *Letters*, 100.
29. *OR* 12:2, 672, 681, 646; Withrow Papers, Washington and Lee University.
30. *Battles and Leaders* 2, 523; *OR* 12:2, 605.
31. Moore, *Cannoneer Under Jackson*, 119; *OR* 12:2, 671.
32. *OR* 12:2, 647; Douglas, *I Rode with Stonewall*, 140.
33. *OR* 12:2, 577–78; Worsham, *Jackson's Foot Cavalry*, 132; Allan, *Army of Northern Virginia*, 262ff.; Freeman, *R. E. Lee* 2, 331ff.

34. Freeman, *R. E. Lee* 2, 338; Jackson mss., Confederate Memorial Institute; *OR* 12:2, 682, 714; Hotchkiss, *Journal,* 77.
35. *OR* 12:2, 677, 715, 672, 813.
36. *OR* 12:2, 551.
37. Alexander, *Military Memoirs,* 219.

Chapter 16: Across the Potomac

1. *Charleston Mercury,* September 6, 1862.
2. Howard, *Recollections,* 180–81.
3. Hood, *Advance and Retreat,* 38–39.
4. Jackson mss., Confederate Memorial Institute.
5. *Richmond Dispatch,* August 20, 21, 1862; *OR* 19:2, 596, 597; Louise Haskell Daly, *Alexander Cheves Haskell: The Portrait of a Man,* 84.
6. Freeman, *R. E. Lee* 2, 352; Sorrel, *Recollections,* 103; W. M. Owen, *In Camp and Battle With the Washington Artillery of New Orleans,* 130.
7. Clark, *North Carolina Regiments* 2, 293, 296.
8. L. W. Hopkins, *From Bull Run to Appomattox,* 51; *OR* 19:2, 592.
9. Von Borcke, *Memoirs* 1, 185.
10. Freeman, *R. E. Lee* 2, 340; Douglas, *I Rode with Stonewall,* 147–49; Sorrel, *Recollections,* 97.
11. Douglas, *I Rode with Stonewall,* 149–50.
12. Von Borcke, *Memoirs* 1, 193–97; Blackford, *War Years with Jeb Stuart,* 140–42.
13. Worsham, *Jackson's Foot Cavalry,* 138; Moore, *Cannoneer Under Jackson,* 130ff.; J. F. J. Caldwell, *The History of Gregg's Brigade of South Carolinians,* 41.
14. Cooke, *Jackson,* 310; *OR* 19:2, 596, 602.
15. *OR* 19:2, 603, 592; *Battles and Leaders* 2, 606, 663; Longstreet, *Manassas to Appomattox,* 202–3.
16. *Land We Love* 4, 274, 275; *SHSP* 13, 420, 421.
17. Douglas, *I Rode with Stonewall,* 151–52.
18. Douglas, *I Rode with Stonewall,* 158; *OR* 19:2, 604.
19. Frank Moore, ed., *The Rebellion Record* 5, 444.
20. *OR* 19:1, 145, 839; William Allan Papers, Southern Historical Collection, University of North Carolina.
21. *OR* 19:1, 1019, 145; *Battles and Leaders* 2, 560.
22. *OR* 19:2, 595.
23. *OR* 19:1, 816, 140, 146; *Battles and Leaders* 2, 560; *SHSP* 39, 36; Allan Papers, Southern Historical Collection.
24. *OR* 19:1, 817.
25. Allan Papers, Southern Historical Collection.
26. *Battles and Leaders* 2, 561–62; *OR* 19:1, 1019–20.
27. *Battles and Leaders* 2, 562–64; *SHSP* 39, 35; *OR* 19:1, 1040.
28. *Battles and Leaders* 2, 564–66.
29. *OR* 19:1, 1020, 459, 215.
30. *OR* 19:1, 1020, 898, 903.
31. *OR* 19:1, 1020–21, 908–9, 922.
32. *OR* 19:1, 1021, 1034–36.

33. *OR* 19:1, 1021, 1022. Confederate losses were about 2,300, Federal losses 1,831.
34. *OR* 19:1, 852–53, 862.
35. *OR* 19:1, 853, 863; D. Augustus Dickert, *History of Kershaw's Brigade,* 148.
36. *OR* 19:1, 863, 854; Dickert, *Kershaw's Brigade,* 148.
37. *OR* 19:1, 853–54, 873, 818, 870.
38. *OR* 19:1, 854–55, 870–71, 873; von Borcke, *Memoirs* 1, 217–18.
39. *Battles and Leaders* 2, 571; *OR* 51:2, 618–19; Freeman, *R. E. Lee* 2, 371.

Chapter 17: Desperate Hours on the Antietam

1. *OR* 19:1, 953.
2. *OR* 19:1, 958, 953.
3. *OR* 19:1, 951.
4. *OR* 19:1, 914, 955.
5. *OR* 19:1, 955, 984; Allan, *Army of Northern Virginia,* 340; Early, *Autobiographical Sketch,* 137.
6. Douglas, *I Rode with Stonewall,* 162; *OR* 19:1, 529–30, 951.
7. *OR* 19:1, 951, 955, 960–61; von Borcke, *Memoirs,* 1, 224–25.
8. Caldwell, *Gregg's Brigade,* 43; Dickert, *Kershaw's Brigade,* 150.
9. *OR* 19:1, 967, 1007, 955.
10. *OR* 19:1, 147, 839.
11. Hood, *Advance and Retreat,* 42.
12. *OR* 19:1, 956.
13. Lee, *Memoirs of Pendleton,* 216; Hood, *Advance and Retreat,* 44.
14. Lee, *Memoirs of Pendleton,* 216; *OR* 19:1, 923; Hood, *Advance and Retreat,* 44; *SHSP* 8, 528.
15. *OR* 19:1, 909, 914–15, 858–59, 971.
16. Gordon, *Reminiscences,* 84.
17. *OR* 19:1, 1023, 1037–38; Alexander, *Military Memoirs,* 262.
18. *OR* 19:1, 1024, 849–50; Sorrel, *Recollections,* 105.
19. *OR* 19:1, 1024.
20. Clark, *North Carolina Regiments* 2, 436–37; Sorrel, *Recollections,* 107.
21. *OR* 19:1, 61.
22. *OR* 19:1, 886.
23. Stovall, *Robert Toombs,* 270.
24. *OR* 19:1, 890–91.
25. *OR* 19:1, 886, 1030, 897, 891.
26. *OR* 19:1, 988; Alexander, *Military Memoirs,* 266.
27. Daly, *Alexander Cheves Haskell,* 80.
28. *OR* 19:1, 891–92; *CV* 6, 28.
29. *OR* 19:1, 981; Daly, *Alexander Cheves Haskell,* 81–82.
30. Lee, *Memoirs of Pendleton,* 213; *OR* 19:1, 831–32.
31. *OR* 19:1, 832–34, 982; Lee, *Memoirs of Pendleton,* 214; Emily Mason, *Popular Life of Gen. Robert E. Lee,* 151; Douglas, *I Rode with Stonewall,* 184.
32. *OR* 19:1, 982, 834.
33. Chamberlayne, *Letters,* 116, 134; *OR* 19:1, 151.

Chapter 18: Rebuilding an Army

1. *Richmond Enquirer,* September 22, 24, *Charleston Mercury,* September 23, *Richmond Dispatch,* September 30, 1862.
2. IV *OR* 2, 198; *OR* 19:2, 643.
3. Sorrel, *Recollections,* 108; Owen, *Washington Artillery,* 157; *OR* 19:1, 841.
4. Lee, *Memoirs of Pendleton,* 230.
5. Walker in *Battles and Leaders* 2, 679; Hood, *Advance and Retreat,* 45. Walker has Jackson saying he will drive McClellan into the Potomac; surely he said the Antietam, not the Potomac.
6. Light Division letter book, New York Public Library; Jackson mss., Confederate Memorial Institute.
7. *OR* 19:2, 729–33.
8. *OR* 19:2, 643.
9. Anna Jackson, *Stonewall Jackson,* 349–50.
10. *OR* 19:1, 981.
11. IV *OR* 2, 97, 109.
12. IV *OR* 2, 110, 114.
13. IV *OR* 2, 205–7
14. Hood, *Advance and Retreat,* 38–39; *OR* 19:1, 923.
15. *OR* 19:2, 680, 681, 682.
16. Jackson letter book, Hotchkiss Papers; *OR* 19:1, 149, 821, 956.
17. *OR* 19:1, 915–16, 840, 1021, 1027; Gordon, *Reminiscences,* 88–91.
18. *OR* 19:1, 821, 969–71, 1017.
19. *OR* 19:2, 677, 678.
20. *OR* 19:2, 683–84.
21. *OR* 25:2, 645; Howard, *Recollections,* 180–81.
22. Eppa Hunton, *Autobiography of Eppa Hunton,* 81.
23. *OR* 19:1, 150; Jones, *War Clerk's Diary* 1, 241.
24. *OR* 19:1, 854, 758–59.
25. *OR* 19:1, 855–57, 148.
26. Chamberlayne, *Letters,* 134.
27. *OR* 19:1, 1021, 1027, 1033; Henry W. Thomas, *History of the Doles-Cook Brigade,* 68–69.
28. *OR* 21, 1030.
29. *OR* 19:1, 821, 897, 981.
30. *OR* 19:2, 597; *OR* 19:1, 1008.
31. *OR* 19:2, 55.
32. R. Channing Price, October 15, 1862, Price Papers, Southern Historical Collection, University of North Carolina.
33. Blackford, *War Years with Jeb Stuart,* 166.
34. *OR* 19:2, 57, 52; McClellan, *Stuart,* 141; Price, October 15, 1862, Price Papers.
35. Blackford, *War Years with Jeb Stuart,* 169–70.
36. *OR* 19:1, 53.
37. Blackford, *War Years with Jeb Stuart,* 179–80.
38. McClellan, *Stuart,* 155–56; Blackford, *War Years with Jeb Stuart,* 175.
39. McClellan, *Stuart,* 157–60; Blackford, *War Years with Jeb Stuart,* 175–78.

40. Price, October 15, 1862, Price Papers.
41. Blackford, *War Years with Jeb Stuart*, 168; *OR* 19:2, 54.

Chapter 19: Battle at Fredericksburg

1. *OR* 19:2, 414, 142–44. Stuart described the horse problem as "greased heel and sore tongue."
2. *Richmond Dispatch*, November 17, 1862.
3. Cooke, *Jackson*, 351–52; Douglas, *I Rode with Stonewall*, 198.
4. Hotchkiss, November 11, 1862, Hotchkiss Papers.
5. J. W. Jones, *Christ in Camp: Or, Religion in Lee's Army*, 283; Anna Jackson, *Stonewall Jackson*, 348, 358–59.
6. Cooke, *Jackson*, 354; *SHSP* 43, 24.
7. Anna Jackson, *Stonewall Jackson*, 360–61; Douglas, *I Rode with Stonewall*, 203.
8. Hotchkiss, *Journal*, 96; *SHSP* 43, 25.
9. *OR* 21, 86, 568–69; *OR* 19:2, 717.
10. *OR* 21, 1029, 1030, 1033, 539.
11. Clark, *North Carolina Regiments* 1, 27; 2, 295–96.
12. *Land We Love* 3, 183–97; *SHSP* 28, 294, 301.
13. William D. Pender, December 3, 1862, Pender Papers, Southern Historical Collection, University of North Carolina; *SHSP* 28, 299; *OR* 21, 569, 578; Allan, *Army of Northern Virginia*, 468.
14. *Dictionary of American Biography* 1, 607.
15. *OR* 21, 601–4, 578.
16. *OR* 21, 183; Owen, *Washington Artillery*, 180.
17. *OR* 21, 579, 569; *Battles and Leaders* 3, 75; Stiles, *Four Years Under Marse Robert*, 130.
18. *OR* 21, 645, 552.
19. *OR* 21, 569, 609, 579, 625; *OR* 51:2, 661.
20. *OR* 21, 643, 630, 641.
21. *OR* 21, 645, 653–54.
22. Francis E. Pierce, December 17, 1862, Pender Papers, Southern Historical Collection.
23. Hotchkiss, *Journal*, 100; *Battles and Leaders* 3, 75–76, 79.
24. *CV* 14, 66; Douglas, *I Rode with Stonewall*, 205; Clark, *North Carolina Regiments*, 2, 556.
25. Lee, *Wartime Papers*, 380; Sorrel, *Recollections*, 131.
26. Von Borcke, *Memoirs* 2, 113.
27. *OR* 21, 631, 553; von Borcke, *Memoirs* 2, 117ff.; Freeman, *R. E. Lee* 2, 457.
28. *OR* 21, 553, 631–32, 638, 649.
29. *OR* 21, 652–56; Caldwell, *Gregg's Brigade*, 59; Early, *Autobiography*, 172; *Battles and Leaders* 3, 140.
30. *OR* 21, 633; Moore, *Cannoneer Under Jackson*, 162–63; Anna Jackson, *Stonewall Jackson*, 369; Cooke, *Jackson*, 375.
31. *OR* 21, 647.
32. Owen, *Washington Artillery*, 184; *Battles and Leaders* 3, 91–92.
33. *OR* 21, 570, 580, 608.
34. *OR* 21, 608, 626; *CV* 7, 309.
35. *OR* 21, 580, 589, 625; *Land We Love* 1, 70.
36. *Battles and Leaders* 3, 81.

37. *OR* 21, 580, 589, 573–76; Dickert, *Kershaw's Brigade*, 188–89; Allan, *Army of Northern Virginia*, 503.
38. Moore, *Rebellion Record* 6, 100.
39. Caldwell, *Gregg's Brigade*, 61.
40. *OR* 21, 634.
41. *OR* 21, 643, 647, 666; Hood, *Advance and Retreat*, 49–50.
42. *OR* 21, 634, 666.
43. Hotchkiss, *Journal*, 101; Stiles, *Four Years Under Marse Robert*, 137.
44. *Richmond Whig*, December 24, 1862; *CV* 8, 538; *SHSP* 19, 309.
45. *SHSP* 43, 34.

Chapter 20: In Winter Quarters

1. Hood, *Advance and Retreat*, 50; *OR* 21, 555, 634, 577.
2. *OR* 21, 571, 634, 555.
3. *OR* 21, 48, 84ff., 91ff.; *Report of the Joint Committee on the Conduct of the War* 1 (1863), 653.
4. *Richmond Examiner*, December 15; *Richmond Dispatch*, December 15; *Charleston Mercury*, December 15; *Richmond Enquirer*, December 22, 1862.
5. *OR* 21, 562, 555–56, 571, 582. Federal losses, in comparison, were 12,653.
6. *OR* 21, 571, 547, 576, 667, 556.
7. *Land We Love* 1, 117.
8. *OR* 21, 547, 571; Hamlin, *Old Bald Head*, 130–31.
9. *OR* 21, 553, 555–56, 656, 646.
10. *OR* 21, 632, 667, 554, 672, 647.
11. *OR* 21, 556.
12. *OR* 21, 638, 648, 565–66, 643, 451.
13. *OR* 21, 645–46, 553, 632.
14. *OR* 21, 13ff., 69–91.
15. *OR* 21, 695; Channing Price, December 23, 1862, Price Papers, Southern Historical Collection, University of North Carolina.
16. *OR* 21, 731–32, 736–37; Price, January 20, 1863, Price Papers.
17. Price, January 20, 1863, Price Papers; *OR* 21, 733.
18. Price, January 20, 1863, Price Papers; *OR* 21, 732, 734–35; McClellan, *Stuart*, 202.
19. Hamlin, *Old Bald Head*, 133.
20. *CV* 11, 266; Blackford, *War Years with Jeb Stuart*, 16.
21. McDonald, *Laurel Brigade*, 109; *OR* 21, 747–48; *OR* 25:2, 604, 641, 654.
22. Hamlin, *Old Bald Head*, 131; Hamlin, *Ewell Letters*, 115–16.
23. Trimble, December 22, 1862, Jackson, January 1, 1863, Lee, January 2, Trimble mss., I. R. Trimble Collection; *OR* 25:2, 658; *OR* 21, 1099; Hotchkiss, *Journal*, 110.
24. Smith, *Confederate War Papers*, 255–56, 262–63.
25. *OR* 18, 59–60, 110; S. G. French, *Two Wars: An Autobiography*, 154.
26. Freeman, *Lee's Dispatches*, 69; *OR* 18, 819–20, 847, 851.
27. *OR* 18, 856, 861; Smith, *Confederate War Papers*, 338.
28. Smith, *Confederate War Papers*, 296–98, 300, 305–7.
29. Smith, *Confederate War Papers*, 307–16.
30. Smith, *Confederate War Papers*, 338.

Chapter 21: Facing a New Campaign

1. *OR* 21, 755.
2. Dickert, *Kershaw's Brigade*, 295–96; Worsham, *Jackson's Foot Cavalry*, 155–56; *OR* 51:2, 676.
3. *OR* 51:2, 175–76.
4. IV *OR* 1, 531, 594.
5. IV *OR* 2, 447–48.
6. D. S. Freeman, *The South to Posterity*, 65–66.
7. Lee, *Memoirs of Pendleton*, 246–47.
8. Blackford, *War Years with Jeb Stuart*, 44.
9. Blackford, *War Years with Jeb Stuart*, 204–5.
10. *OR* 19:2, 632, 646ff., 662.
11. *OR* 25:2, 614–19.
12. *OR* 25:2, 644–46.
13. *OR* 25:2, 728–30.
14. *SHSP* 38, 381.
15. Cooke, *Wearing of the Gray*, 139; Blackford, *War Years with Jeb Stuart*, 90.
16. Blackford, *War Years with Jeb Stuart*, 201; McClellan, *Stuart*, 217.
17. *SHSP* 38, 382–83; McClellan, *Stuart*, 210–11; Harry Gilmore, *Four Years in the Saddle*, 66–69.
18. *OR* 25:1, 63, 53; Gilmore, *Four Years in the Saddle*, 68–69.
19. *OR* 25:1, 59; *OR* 25:2, 675.
20. *OR* 18, 894–95.
21. *OR* 18, 57, 109–10, 905.
22. *OR* 18, 898, 903, 907–8, 184, 189, 931.
23. *OR* 18, 921–27, 933, 942.
24. *OR* 18, 970, 943, 931, 942, 969.
25. The principal exchanges are *OR* 18, 922, 924, 933, 934, 943–44, 950, 954.
26. French, *Two Wars*, 160–61.
27. *OR* 18, 304, 331, 334, 325–27, 336–37.
28. French, *Two Wars*, 163; *OR* 18, 325, 326–27.
29. Sorrel, *Recollections*, 146–47.
30. *OR* 51:2, 697.
31. *OR* 18, 1007, 211.
32. *OR* 18, 574, 674, 1031.
33. Hotchkiss, *Journal*, 101–2.
34. *CV* 20, 24; J. P. Smith, "Winter Quarters at Moss Neck," Hotchkiss Papers; *SHSP* 43, 37–39.
35. Blackford, *War Years with Jeb Stuart*, 200.
36. Douglas, *I Rode with Stonewall*, 213; Hotchkiss, *Journal*, 115.
37. Hotchkiss, *Journal*, 117, 125, 124.
38. Hotchkiss, *Journal*, 124, 125, 123.
39. Phillips, *Correspondence of Toombs*, 608.
40. Jackson letter book, Hotchkiss Papers; Woodward, *Mary Chesnut's Civil War*, 444.
41. William D. Pender, *The General to His Lady: The Civil War Letters of William Dorsey Pender to Fanny Pender*, 222.

42. *OR* 19:2, 731–33; *OR* 12:2, 214; Jackson mss., Confederate Memorial Institute.
43. *CV* 20, 24–26; Douglas, *I Rode with Stonewall*, 214–15; Anna Jackson, *Stonewall Jackson*, 396.
44. Hotchkiss, *Journal*, 124.
45. Hotchkiss, *Journal*, 116; Hunter McGuire and George L. Christian, *The Confederate Cause and Conduct in the War Between the States*, 213.
46. Paxton, *Civil War Letters*, 81; Anna Jackson, *Stonewall Jackson*, 409–13; Hotchkiss, *Journal*, 134.
47. Anna Jackson, *Stonewall Jackson*, 415–16.

Chapter 22: Jackson Gets His Greatest Orders

1. Hotchkiss, *Journal*, 136; *OR* 25:1, 1000.
2. Anna Jackson, *Stonewall Jackson*, 416.
3. *OR* 25:1, 939, 901, 1004.
4. *OR* 25:1, 1000, 796; *OR* 25:2, 759–60.
5. *SHSP* 7, 562.
6. Hotchkiss, *Journal*, 136–37.
7. *OR* 25:1, 939, 885, 1004, 850; Hotchkiss, *Journal*, 137; Sorrel, *Recollections*, 128; *OR* 25:2, 850, 862, 870.
8. Irvine Walker, *General Richard H. Anderson*, 133; *OR* 25:1, 824, 850.
9. *OR* 25:1, 824–25, 850, 940; *SHSP* 11, 137–38.
10. Freeman, *R. E. Lee* 2, 517.
11. Daly, *Alexander Cheves Haskell*, 99–100; *OR* 25:2, 764; Bryan Grimes, *Letters of Major-General Bryan Grimes to His Wife*, 28; *OR* 25:1, 850; *Land We Love* 1, 180.
12. Daly, *Alexander Cheves Haskell*, 100–101.
13. T. M. R. Talcott, "General Lee's Strategy at the Battle of Chancellorsville," *SHSP* 34, 16–18.
14. Dabney, *Jackson*, 675–76; Hotchkiss, *Journal*, 137.
15. Hotchkiss in Henderson, *Stonewall Jackson* 2, 432.
16. Alexander, *Military Memoirs*, 333.
17. Caldwell, *Gregg's Brigade*, 76.
18. *OR* 25:1, 940.
19. McGuire and Christian, *Confederate Cause*, 214; Thomas T. Munford mss., Duke University.
20. Fitzhugh Lee in *SHSP* 7, 572–73.
21. *OR* 25:1, 940; Munford mss., Duke University; Virginia State Library.
22. *OR* 25:1, 940–41, 1004, 915–16.
23. *Battles and Leaders* 3, 208.
24. *OR* 25:1, 941, 967, 974, 995.
25. *OR* 25:1, 941, 1004–5, 935, 890, 902, 916; R. E. Wilbourn in Cooke, *Jackson*, 416; *Battles and Leaders* 3, 233; Hotchkiss, *CMH* 3, 385.
26. From Chancellorsville westward to Wilderness Church, the newer Orange Plank Road overlay the old Turnpike, and local custom was divided on what to call this stretch of highway; here it will be called the Plank Road.
27. *SHSP* 8, 494; *Land We Love* 1, 181.
28. *SHSP* 6, 267; Cooke, *Jackson*, 419–20.
29. John Bigelow, Jr., *The Campaign of Chancellorsville*, 317; *Land We Love* 1, 181.

30. *SHSP* 6, 268–69; Hotchkiss, *Journal,* 138; Dabney, *Jackson,* 693–94. The fire was from the 18th North Carolina, Lane's brigade.
31. *SHSP* 6, 270; *CV* 13, 233; Hotchkiss, *Journal,* 138–39; *OR* 25:1, 885–86, 582.
32. *SHSP* 6, 270; *Battles and Leaders* 3, 212; Dabney, *Jackson,* 689; *Land We Love* 1, 181.
33. Cooke, *Jackson,* 427.
34. *SHSP* 6, 233–34; McGuire and Christian, *Confederate Cause,* 220–21.
35. *Battles and Leaders* 3, 213; McGuire and Christian, *Confederate Cause,* 221–22.
36. Dabney, *Jackson,* 695–96; McGuire and Christian, *Confederate Cause,* 223.

Chapter 23: Victory and Tragedy at Chancellorsville

1. Alexander, *Military Memoirs,* 342; McClellan, *Stuart,* 249.
2. *OR* 25:1, 891, 925; Alexander, *Military Memoirs,* 346.
3. *OR* 25:1, 891, 913, 902, 904, 935–36; Clark, *North Carolina Regiments* 1, 669.
4. *OR* 25:1, 902–3, 1005, 886.
5. *OR* 25:1, 1006, 1025–26; Caldwell, *Gregg's Brigade,* 80–81.
6. Bigelow, *Chancellorsville,* 353; *OR* 25:1, 943.
7. Alexander, *Military Memoirs,* 347–48; *OR* 25:1, 823, 938; *CV* 5, 288.
8. *OR* 25:1, 943, 996; Grimes, *Letters,* 31–32.
9. Bigelow, *Chancellorsville,* 357, 361; *OR* 25:1, 944, 996, 1014.
10. Alexander, *Military Memoirs,* 347; Bigelow, *Chancellorsville,* 375ff.; Freeman, *R. E. Lee* 2, 535ff.
11. Dabney, *Jackson,* 696, 707–8; *Battles and Leaders* 3, 213; McGuire and Christian, *Confederate Cause,* 223; Hotchkiss, *Journal,* 140.
12. Dabney, *Jackson,* 708–9; *OR* 25:2, 769; *Battles and Leaders* 3, 214.
13. *OR* 25:1, 1000–1001, 810; Early, *Autobiographical Sketch,* 198–99; Bigelow, *Chancellorsville,* 268.
14. Early, *Autobiographical Sketch,* 197; *OR* 25:1, 811.
15. Early, *Autobiographical Sketch,* 198–202; *OR* 25:1, 811–12.
16. *OR* 25:1, 812, 814, 1002; Early, *Autobiographical Sketch,* 202–3.
17. *Land We Love* 3, 448–49; *OR,* 25:1, 839.
18. *OR* 25:1, 839, 815; Early, *Autobiographical Sketch,* 205–6.
19. Early, *Autobiographical Sketch,* 208–9, 219–20; *Land We Love* 3, 450; *OR* 25:1, 839, 815–16; Owen, *Washington Artillery,* 218–19.
20. *OR* 25:1, 855; Wilcox mss., Library of Congress.
21. *OR* 25:1, 856–57.
22. *OR* 25:1, 857.
23. *OR* 25:2, 769–70; Early, *Autobiographical Sketch,* 220.
24. *OR* 25:1, 827.
25. Early, *Autobiographical Sketch,* 222–25; *OR* 25:1, 840–41.
26. Early, *Autobiographical Sketch,* 226–27; *OR* 25:1, 801, 827, 852; Alexander, *Military Memoirs,* 356.
27. *OR* 25:1, 802, 828, 852, 869; Early, *Autobiographical Sketch,* 228–29, 231, 233.
28. Dabney, *Jackson,* 709; McGuire and Christian, *Confederate Cause,* 224.
29. Hotchkiss, *Journal,* 140; Dabney, *Jackson,* 711.
30. Hotchkiss, *Journal,* 140; Dabney, *Jackson,* 711–13; McGuire and Christian, *Confederate Cause,* 225.

31. McGuire and Christian, *Confederate Cause,* 225–26; Hotchkiss, *Journal,* 141.
32. *OR* 25:1, 171; S. P. Bates, *The Battle of Chancellorsville,* 69; *Report of Joint Committee* 1 (1865), 125.
33. *Richmond Dispatch,* May 5, 8, *Richmond Sentinel,* May 9, *Richmond Whig,* May 8, 15, 1863.
34. Stiles, *Four Years Under Marse Robert,* 261; Freeman, *Lee's Dispatches,* 87–88; *OR* 51:2, 703.
35. *Land We Love* 3, 457–58.
36. *OR* 25:1, 803.
37. *OR* 25:1, 803.
38. Pender, *General to His Lady,* 235; Gordon, *Reminiscences,* 100–101.
39. *OR* 25:1, 803–4, 887–88, 823.
40. *OR* 25:1, 886, 1007, 810.
41. Dabney, *Jackson,* 715–16.
42. Dabney, *Jackson,* 715; Anna Jackson, *Stonewall Jackson,* 451; McGuire and Christian, *Confederate Cause,* 227.
43. Anna Jackson, *Stonewall Jackson,* 452–53; Dabney, *Jackson,* 717–19; McGuire and Christian, *Confederate Cause,* 227.
44. Freeman, *R. E. Lee* 2, 562; McGuire and Christian, *Confederate Cause,* 227; Dabney, *Jackson,* 719–21; Anna Jackson, *Stonewall Jackson,* 452–53.
45. Dabney, *Jackson,* 722–23; McGuire and Christian, *Confederate Cause,* 228; Anna Jackson, *Stonewall Jackson,* 456
46. McGuire and Christian, *Confederate Cause,* 228–29.

Chapter 24: Renewal and Reorganization

1. *Richmond Whig,* May 9, 1863.
2. *Richmond Dispatch,* May 12, *Richmond Sentinel,* May 19, 1863; Dabney, *Jackson,* 731–32; Anna Jackson, *Stonewall Jackson,* 462ff.
3. *OR* 25:2, 791, 793; Freeman, *R. E. Lee* 2, 524; *Richmond Examiner,* May 11, 1863.
4. R. E. Lee, Jr., *Recollections and Letters of General Robert E. Lee,* 94.
5. Hamlin, *Ewell Letters,* 118; Lee, *Memoirs of Pendleton,* 272, 276.
6. *OR* 25:2, 782.
7. *OR* 25:2, 811.
8. *OR* 25:2, 824–25; Hamlin, *Old Bald Head,* 78; Gordon, *Reminiscences,* 158.
9. Freeman, *Lee's Dispatches,* 91; *OR* 25:2, 810.
10. *Battles and Leaders* 3, 245.
11. A. P. Hill, May 24, 1863, Wilkins mss.; Wright, *General Officers,* 33; *OR* 25:2, 811.
12. Pender, *General to His Lady,* 235; Freeman, *Lee's Dispatches,* 99–100.
13. *OR* 25:2, 801–2, 774, 787.
14. Lee, *Memoirs of Pendleton,* 273.
15. *OR* 25:2, 810, 816.
16. Hotchkiss, *Journal,* 145–46; Lee, *Memoirs of Pendleton,* 277.
17. *OR* 25:2, 789.
18. Pender, *General to His Lady,* 238.
19. Freeman, *R. E. Lee* 3, 18ff.; Pender, *General to His Lady,* 242.
20. Von Borcke, *Memoirs* 2, 264–65.

21. Blackford, *War Years with Jeb Stuart*, 211–12; McClellan, *Stuart*, 261–62; von Borcke, *Memoirs* 2, 265–66.
22. *OR* 27:2, 680.
23. *OR* 27:2, 680, 727; Myers, *The Comanches, 183.*
24. McClellan, *Stuart*, 270–71; *Philadelphia Weekly Times*, June 26, 1880; *OR* 27:2, 681, 721–22.
25. McClellan, *Stuart*, 272–74, 277; *OR* 27:2, 755, 722, 749–50; Blackford, *War Years with Jeb Stuart*, 216.
26. *OR* 27:2, 546; McClellan, *Stuart*, 292–93.
27. *OR* 27:733–36.
28. McClellan, *Stuart*, 286–92; *OR* 27:2, 684, 729.
29. Pender, *General to His Lady*, 246.
30. *Richmond Examiner*, June 12, 1863.

Chapter 25: Across the Potomac Again

1. *OR* 27:2, 440, 460; Hotchkiss, *Journal*, 151–52.
2. Early, *Autobiographical Sketch*, 244–45; *OR* 27:2, 441, 450, 462–63, 477–78; McKim, *A Soldier's Recollections*, 146; Gilmore, *Four Years in the Saddle*, 87.
3. *OR* 27:2, 441, 500–501, 541, 508, 512; McKim, *A Soldier's Recollections*, 148–50; Hotchkiss, *Journal*, 152.
4. *OR* 27:3, 894; Hamlin, *Old Bald Head*, 140; Hotchkiss, *Journal*, 153; *OR* 27:2, 456, 442; Hotchkiss, June 15, 1863, Hotchkiss Papers.
5. *OR* 27:2, 547–50, 442–43, 305; *OR* 27:3, 914.
6. *OR* 27:3, 910; *OR* 27:2, 443; Hotchkiss, *Journal*, 155; Hamlin, *Ewell Letters*, 121.
7. *OR* 27:2, 443, 466–67; Early, *Autobiographical Sketch*, 256; Stiles, *Four Years Under Marse Robert*, 203–5.
8. Hotchkiss, *Journal*, 155; *OR* 27:2, 551.
9. *OR* 27:3, 943–44; Hotchkiss, *Journal*, 156; Casler, *Stonewall Brigade*, 173; Moore, *Cannoneer Under Jackson*, 185.
10. *OR* 27:2, 444, 607; *SHSP* 26, 122.
11. *OR* 27:2, 443; Moore, *Cannoneer Under Jackson*, 185.
12. *OR* 18, 959. This letter mentions the January 23 proposal, which must have been verbal.
13. Longstreet, *Manassas to Appomattox*, 327–28.
14. *Philadelphia Weekly Times*, July 27, 1879; *Battles and Leaders* 3, 244–45; Longstreet, *Manassas to Appomattox*, 329.
15. Longstreet in McClure, *Annals of the War*, 416–17; *Battles and Leaders* 3, 246–47; Longstreet, *Manassas to Appomattox*, 331; Freeman, *R. E. Lee* 3, 19.
16. McClure, *Annals*, 418; *OR* 27:2, 358, 316; Longstreet, *Manassas to Appomattox*, 359, 546.
17. Sorrel, *Recollections*, 147, 152, 155; Longstreet, *Manassas to Appomattox*, 333, 346–47; *OR* 27:2, 358; Arthur James Lyon Fremantle, *Three Months in the Southern States*, 243.
18. *Richmond Sentinel*, June 12, *Richmond Dispatch*, June 12, *Richmond Whig*, June 16, 1863.
19. *OR* 27:2, 692.
20. Charles Marshall, *An Aid-de-Camp of Lee*, 201; *OR* 27:2, 691; *OR* 27:3, 913, 915.
21. J. S. Mosby, *Stuart's Cavalry in the Gettysburg Campaign*, 76; McClellan, *Stuart*, 316–17; *OR* 27:3, 923.
22. Blackford, *War Years with Jeb Stuart*, 222; *OR* 27:2, 707.

23. McClellan, *Stuart*, 318–19; *OR* 27:3, 927–28.
24. *OR* 27:2, 692–93; McClellan, *Stuart*, 321.
25. *OR* 27:2, 693–94; McClellan, *Stuart*, 323–24; R. L. G. Beale, *Ninth Virginia Cavalry*, 78.
26. *OR* 27:3, 913; R. L. G. Beale, *Ninth Virginia Cavalry*, 80; *OR* 27:2, 694.
27. *OR* 27:2, 694–96; McClellan, *Stuart*, 326.
28. *OR* 27:2, 696, 707; McClellan, *Stuart*, 329.

Chapter 26: Two Days of Battle

1. *OR* 27:3, 859–60; *OR* 27:2, 293, 305, 613; Pender, *General to His Lady*, 247–48.
2. Pender, *General to His Lady*, 248, 250, 251; *Richmond Dispatch*, July 2, *Charleston Mercury*, June 23, 24, 1863.
3. *OR* 27:2, 317; Harry Heth, "Memoirs," *Civil War History* 8:3, 304; *SHSP* 4, 157.
4. *OR* 27:2, 317, 637–38, 646–49; *SHSP* 4, 158.
5. *OR* 27:2, 674, 317, 552, 444.
6. *OR* 27:2, 553–54, 444–45, 579–80.
7. *SHSP* 4, 158.
8. *OR* 27:2, 567, 317, 445, 468, 554–55, 638–39, 607.
9. *OR* 27:2, 444.
10. Gordon, *Reminiscences*, 155–57; Douglas, *I Rode with Stonewall*, 247.
11. Trimble in *SHSP* 26, 123–24.
12. *SHSP* 4, 255–56; *SHSP* 26, 123–24; *OR* 27:2, 469; Early, *Autobiographical Sketch*, 270; *SHSP* 33, 144–45; Walter H. Taylor, *Four Years with General Lee*, 95; *OR* 27:2, 318.
13. *OR* 27:2, 445, 555; *SHSP* 4, 256–57.
14. *SHSP* 4, 271–75; *OR* 27:2, 272, 318–19, 446.
15. *OR* 27:2, 446; Freeman, *R. E. Lee* 3, 80–82.
16. *OR* 27:2, 446.
17. *OR* 27:2, 538, 318; McClure, *Annals*, 414ff.; *Battles and Leaders* 3, 244ff.; Longstreet, *Manassas to Appomattox*, 358–59.
18. *OR* 27:2, 318; A. L. Long, *Memoirs of Robert E. Lee*, 277; *Battles and Leaders* 3, 340; McClure, *Annals*, 422; Longstreet, *Manassas to Appomattox*, 383–84.
19. S. R. Johnston Papers, Virginia Historical Society; McClure, *Annals*, 422; Hood, *Advance and Retreat*, 57; McLaws in *SHSP* 7, 68.
20. S. R. Johnston Papers, Virginia Historical Society; *SHSP* 7, 68.
21. Hood, *Advance and Retreat*, 57; *SHSP* 4, 274; McClure, *Annals*, 442.
22. McClure, *Annals*, 442; *OR* 27:2, 318; Dickert, *Kershaw's Brigade*, 235; *Battles and Leaders* 3, 319.
23. *SHSP* 7, 69–70; McClure, *Annals*, 423; *OR* 27:2, 318–19, 614.
24. *SHSP* 7, 70–72.
25. Hood, *Advance and Retreat*, 57–58; *SHSP* 7, 72; *OR* 27:2, 429.
26. *SHSP* 7, 72–73; Fitzgerald Ross, *A Visit to the Cities and Camps of the Confederate States*, 55; Alexander, *Military Memoirs*, 395–96; Hood, *Advance and Retreat*, 59; *Battles and Leaders* 3, 324–25; *OR* 27:2, 367–68; McClure, *Annals*, 424.
27. *OR* 27:2, 614, 618, 632–35; Alexander, *Military Memoirs*, 400; A. R. Wright, July 7, 1863, A. R. Wright Collection; C. M. Wilcox, c. 1866, Freeman, *R. E. Lee* 3, 555–56.
28. *OR* 27:2, 446–47, 504, 556; *SHSP* 26, 125; Long, *Memoirs of Lee*, 281.
29. *OR* 27:2, 504–5, 556, 480–81; McKim, *A Soldier's Recollections*, 196.

30. *OR* 27:2: 556, 588.
31. Taylor, *Four Years with Lee*, 99.
32. *OR* 27:2, 696–97; McClellan, *Stuart*, 330; Thomason, *Stuart*, 440.
33. *OR* 27:2, 447; Ross, *Cities and Camps*, 59.

Chapter 27: Gettysburg and Its Cost

1. *OR* 27:2, 477, 544, 568, 511, 447; McKim, *A Soldier's Recollections*, 203–4.
2. *OR* 27:2, 320, 359; McClure, *Annals*, 430, 428.
3. *OR* 27:2, 359; Longstreet, *Manassas to Appomattox*, 386, 388; Long, *Memoirs of Lee*, 288; Alexander, *Military Memoirs*, 416.
4. *OR* 27:2, 385, 320, 359; *Battles and Leaders* 3, 343; *SHSP* 4, 105; Alexander, *Military Memoirs*, 418; McClure, *Annals*, 432.
5. *SHSP* 4, 103–4; Owen, *Washington Artillery*, 248.
6. *OR* 27:2, 670, 666.
7. McClure, *Annals*, 430; *SHSP* 4, 104–5; Longstreet, *Manassas to Appomattox*, 391; Fremantle, *Three Months in the Southern States*, 263; Alexander, *Military Memoirs*, 421; Owen, *Washington Artillery*, 248.
8. *OR* 27:2, 239, 360; *SHSP* 4, 107; McClure, *Annals*, 430–31.
9. *SHSP* 4, 108; Alexander, *Military Memoirs*, 424; *SHSP* 32, 34.
10. *SHSP* 37, 148; D. E. Johnston, *The Story of a Confederate Boy in the Civil War*, 205–6; Clark, *North Carolina Regiments* 2, 365; *OR* 27:2, 360; *Battles and Leaders* 3, 345; *SHSP* 4, 108.
11. *Battles and Leaders* 3, 346; *OR* 27:2, 360; *SHSP* 9, 33; Alexander, *Military Memoirs*, 424–25.
12. Fremantle, *Three Months in the Southern States*, 265–66; *OR* 27:2, 360; Alexander, *Military Memoirs*, 425.
13. *Battles and Leaders* 3, 347; *OR* 27:2, 360.
14. Owen, *Washington Artillery*, 255.
15. Owen, *Washington Artillery*, 256; Fremantle, *Three Months in the Southern States*, 275.
16. *OR* 27:2, 323, 703.
17. *Charleston Mercury*, July 8, 30, *Richmond Enquirer*, July 7, 15, *Richmond Dispatch*, July 6, 10, *Richmond Examiner*, July 9, 14, 25, *Richmond Whig*, July 14, 1863.
18. *OR* 27:2, 318.
19. *OR* 27:2, 559.
20. Sorrel, *Recollections*, 157.
21. S. R. Johnston Papers, Virginia Historical Society.
22. Owen, *Washington Artillery*, 256.
23. Alexander, *Military Memoirs*, 419, 427.
24. *SHSP* 4, 103; Alexander, *Military Memoirs*, 431; *OR* 27:2, 352, 389.
25. Heth, "Memoirs," 304.
26. *OR* 27:2, 666; *SHSP* 9, 32–33.
27. Eppa Hunton, *Autobiography*, 98; McClure, *Annals*, 414–15.
28. *CV* 20, 379; *OR* 27:2, 310, 359; *SHSP* 4, 108; *CMH* 6, 436.
29. Clark, *North Carolina Regiments* 2, 362, 376–77; *OR* 27:2, 640–41.
30. W. C. Lee, October 21, L. G. Lewis, October 21, G. C. Wharton, September 5, 1893, Pender Papers, Southern Historical Collection.

31. Haskell, *Memoirs,* 49–50; Louise Wigfall Wright, *A Southern Girl in '61,* 142–43.
32. *OR* 27:3, 646.
33. Sorrel, *Recollections,* 267–68.
34. Freeman, *Lee's Dispatches,* 115–16.
35. Included here is Extra Billy Smith, who tendered his resignation on July 10 and received leave of absence.

Chapter 28: Challenges for Longstreet, Hill, and Stuart

1. *SHSP* 37, 94; *OR* 27:2, 708, 321, 316.
2. *OR* 27:3, 1068–69, 1075.
3. Rosser mss., University of Virgina.
4. McDonald, *Laurel Brigade,* 168–69; *OR* 29:2, 771–72, 779, 788.
5. Rosser mss., University of Virginia; Munford mss., Duke University.
6. *OR* 27:3, 1048, 1040, 1041.
7. *OR* 27:3, 1052.
8. *OR* 29:2, 641–42, 645–46; *OR* 51:2, 755; L. M. Blackford, August 12, 1863, Southern Historical Collection.
9. Stanley F. Horn, *The Army of Tennessee,* 239–40; Freeman, *R. E. Lee* 3, 162ff.; Longstreet, *Manassas to Appomattox,* 433–34.
10. *OR* 29:2, 699.
11. *OR* 29:2, 700–701, 702, 720, 706.
12. *OR* 29:2, 683, 706, 773, 713.
13. Longstreet, *Manassas to Appomattox,* 437.
14. Sorrel, *Recollections,* 180; *OR* 29:2, 713–14.
15. *OR* 29:2, 749.
16. *OR* 29:2, 731, 748, 750, 753–54, 766.
17. *OR* 30:4, 705–6; *OR* 30:2, 65–66; Longstreet, *Manassas to Appomattox,* 465.
18. Longstreet, *Manassas to Appomattox,* 466–68, 469–70n.
19. *OR* 29:1, 410–11; Caldwell, *Gregg's Brigade,* 115.
20. *OR* 29:1, 411, 426, 430; Clark, *North Carolina Regiments* 2, 440.
21. *OR* 29:1, 430, 433, 426.
22. *OR* 29:1, 426, 430–31, 427, 435; Clark, *North Carolina Regiments* 2, 440–41.
23. Clark, *North Carolina Regiments,* 2, 443, 441; *OR* 29:1, 432–33, 429.
24. Freeman, *R. E. Lee* 3, 183; *OR* 29:1, 427–28; Long, *Memoirs of Lee,* 331. The retiring Federal corps was the V, not the III.
25. *OR* 29:1, 439–40, 443; McClellan, *Stuart,* 380.
26. *OR* 29:1, 446–48, 453; Blackford, *War Years with Jeb Stuart,* 239–40; McClellan, *Stuart,* 390–92.
27. *OR* 29:1, 408, 411, 451–52; Blackford, *War Years with Jeb Stuart,* 241–42.
28. *OR* 29:1, 452.

Chapter 29: Tests and Trials of Winter

1. *OR* 29:1, 611–12, 631.
2. *OR* 29:1, 632, 633, 618, 621.

3. *OR* 29:1, 628, 610; Early, *Autobiographical Sketch,* 313–14.
4. *OR* 29:1, 611, 616; Lee, *Memoirs of Pendleton,* 305.
5. *OR* 29:1, 613, 623–24, 625–26.
6. *OR* 29:1, 827–28, 895, 831; Early, *Autobiographical Sketch,* 319.
7. *OR* 29:1, 832–33, 846–48, 856; Early, *Autobiographical Sketch,* 320–21.
8. Early, *Autobiographical Sketch,* 317; *OR* 29:1, 832, 834–35, 826, 829, 896.
9. *OR* 29:2, 517; George Meade, *Life and Letters of George Gordon Meade* 2, 157–58; *OR* 29:1, 17.
10. *OR* 29:1, 904.
11. Freeman, *R. E. Lee* 3, 204.
12. *OR* 29:2, 839ff.; *OR* 33, 1193.
13. *OR* 31:1, 217–18, 233.
14. Longstreet, *Manassas to Appomattox,* 488.
15. *OR* 31:3, 756, 757; *OR* 31:1, 491, 494.
16. *OR* 52:2, 564.
17. *OR* 31:3, 760; *OR* 31:1, 499–500, 462.
18. Woodward, *Mary Chesnut's Civil War,* 509.
19. *OR* 31:1, 497–98; *OR* 31:3, 881.
20. *OR* 31:1, 503–4, 470; McLaws, February 24, 1864, Ewell Papers, Library of Congress.
21. *OR* 31:1, 467–68, 469, 470, 505–6; *OR* 34:4, 692; McLaws Papers, Southern Historical Collection.
22. W. C. Oates, *The War Between the Union and the Confederacy,* 338; *OR* 31:1, 471–72; Sorrel, *Recollections,* 210.
23. Longstreet, *Manassas to Appomattox,* 524–25.
24. Longstreet, *Manassas to Appomattox,* 525.
25. *OR* 32:2, 790, 791–92, 818; *OR* 32:3, 627–28, 637–41, 641–42; Longstreet, *Manassas to Appomattox,* 546.
26. *OR* 32:3, 648, 655, 676, 656, 643, 736; Longstreet, *Manassas to Appomattox,* 547; *OR* 52:2, 649.
27. *OR* 32:2, 726, 802; *OR* 32:3, 583.
28. *OR* 32:3, 738.
29. *OR* 33, 1196.
30. *OR* 33, 1114.
31. *OR* 33, 1231, 1243, 1145, 1149ff.; A. B. Moore, *Conscription and Conflict in the Confederacy,* 308, 187.
32. *OR* 31:3, 701.
33. *OR* 35:1, 581; *OR* 42:3, 1165, 1167, 1169; *SHSP* 21, 144.
34. *OR* 29:2, 344; *OR* 29:1, 408–9; *OR* 33, 1085–86, 1172.
35. *OR* 33, 1124.
36. *OR* 29:1, 970.
37. *OR* 33, 7, 1061, 1067–68, 1167, 1168.
38. *OR* 33, 1166; *OR* 44, 1170.
39. *OR* 33, 1095–96, 1074–75; *OR* 29:1, 861; Hamlin, *Ewell Letters,* 123.
40. Mary C. Moffett, *Letters of General James Conner,* 116.
41. Hotchkiss, *Journal,* 200; Hamlin, *Old Bald Head,* 167–68.
42. Ramseur Papers, Southern Historical Collection.
43. *OR* 33, 141–42; Freeman, *R. E. Lee* 3, 218.
44. *OR* 33, 174, 178–79, 188.

45. *OR* 51:2, 857–58, 870, 874; Clark, *North Carolina Regiments* 5, 175.
46. *OR* 33, 1255, 1265–66, 1321; *OR* 32:3, 756.
47. *OR* 33, 1286; *OR* 32:3, 793; *OR* 31:1, 475, 473.
48. Freeman, *Lee's Dispatches*, 242.

Chapter 30: The Wilderness and Spotsylvania

1. Longstreet, *Manassas to Appomattox*, 553; Sorrel, *Recollections*, 228.
2. *CV* 21, 68.
3. *OR* 36:1, 1070; Howard, *Recollections*, 268; McClure, *Annals*, 487; *CV* 21, 68.
4. *OR* 36:1, 198; Alexander, *Military Memoirs*, 497.
5. *OR* 36:1, 1070, 1054.
6. *OR* 36:1, 1070.
7. *OR* 36:1, 1070, 1028; Gordon, *Reminiscences*, 238–39.
8. Heth, "Memoirs," 310; Alexander, *Military Memoirs*, 501; *OR* 51:2, 890; Clark, *North Carolina Regiments* 3, 118; *OR* 36:2, 952.
9. McClure, *Annals*, 494–95; Heth, "Memoirs," 311–12.
10. McClure, *Annals*, 495–96; Longstreet, *Manassas to Appomattox*, 571, 560–61; *Land We Love* 5, 484; *SHSP* 14, 525–26.
11. Clark, *North Carolina Regiments* 2, 665; *OR* 36:1, 1061, 1055; Haskell, *Memoirs*, 63; *SHSP* 14, 544.
12. Longstreet, *Manassas to Appomattox*, 561–62; *OR* 36:1, 1061–62, 1055; Sorrel, *Recollections*, 231–32.
13. *OR* 36:1, 1055; Longstreet, *Manassas to Appomattox*, 563.
14. Haskell, *Memoirs*, 65; *OR* 36:1, 1062, 1055; Moffett, *Letters of Conner*, 133.
15. Sorrel, *Recollections*, 238; Longstreet, *Manassas to Appomattox*, 565, 567; Haskell, *Memoirs*, 65; Alexander, *Military Memoirs*, 506; *OR* 36:1, 324, 1062; Stiles, *Four Years Under Marse Robert*, 247.
16. Haskell, *Memoirs*, 66; Dickert, *Kershaw's Brigade*, 353; *OR* 51:2, 893.
17. *OR* 36:1, 1077, 1071; Gordon, *Reminiscences*, 243–44, 255–56; Early, *Autobiographical Sketch*, 348.
18. Gordon, *Reminiscences*, 258, 250; *OR* 36:1, 1078.
19. Gordon, *Reminiscences*, 266–67; Neese, *Confederate Horse Artillery*, 262; *OR* 36:1, 218; Caldwell, *Gregg's Brigade*, 138.
20. *OR* 31:1, 505–6; *OR* 36:2, 955, 966, 967; Sorrel, *Recollections*, 238–39.
21. Early, *Autobiographical Sketch*, 350; *OR* 36:1, 1041; *OR* 36:2, 969, 970, 968; *OR* 51:2, 897.
22. *Papers of the Military Historical Society of Massachusetts* 4, 229; Caldwell, *Gregg's Brigade*, 135–36.
23. Alexander, *Military Memoirs*, 510–11; Haskell, *Memoirs*, 67; Dickert, *Kershaw's Brigade*, 357–58.
24. Alexander, *Military Memoirs*, 511–12; Haskell, *Memoirs*, 67–68; *OR* 36:1, 1056.
25. *OR* 36:1, 1071, 1056, 1093.
26. *OR* 36:1, 19.
27. *OR* 36:1, 1029; Early, *Autobiographical Sketch*, 354.
28. *OR* 36:1, 1071–72; *SHSP* 14, 527.
29. *OR* 36:1, 667–68, 1089, 1072, 1087.
30. Heth, "Memoirs," 313–14.

31. *OR* 36:1, 1044, 1086, 1079; Alexander, *Military Memoirs*, 518; *SHSP* 7, 535.

32. Howard, *Recollections*, 294, 301; *OR* 36:1, 1072, 1086, 1044, 1080; *SHSP* 33, 336–37; *SHSP* 21, 253, 240, 235–36.

33. *OR* 36:1, 1079; Gordon, *Reminiscences*, 277–78; Freeman, *R. E. Lee* 3, 319.

34. *OR* 36:1, 1072–73, 1082, 1092, 1094; Caldwell, *Gregg's Brigade*, 143; *Papers of the Military Historical Society of Massachusetts* 4, 269.

Chapter 31: Richmond Threatened

1. *OR* 36:1, 1027.

2. *OR* 36:2, 970–71; *OR* 36:1, 789–90, 812, 777; McClellan, *Stuart*, 410; *OR* 51:2, 909–10.

3. A. R. Venable to Fitz Lee, June 7, 1888; *OR* 51:2, 911–12; McClellan, *Stuart*, 411.

4. McClellan, *Stuart*, 412; Venable, June 7, 1888.

5. McClellan, *Stuart*, 412–14; *OR* 36:1, 817–18; Venable, June 7, 1888; *CV* 19, 531; *Battles and Leaders* 4, 194.

6. McClellan, *Stuart*, 414–16; Venable, June 7, 1888.

7. *SHSP* 7, 107–9; McClellan, *Stuart*, 416–17.

8. *SHSP* 7, 109; *OR* 36:1, 879; Cooke, *Wearing of the Gray*, 39; *OR* 33, 1257–58; *SHSP* 37, 68.

9. Neese, *Confederate Horse Artillery*, 268; Casler, *Stonewall Brigade*, 331.

10. *OR* 36:2, 955; Freeman, *Lee's Dispatches*, 182.

11. *OR* 36:2, 1001.

12. *SHSP* 33, 333; *OR* 36:1, 338, 1087; Meade, *Life and Letters* 2, 197.

13. *OR* 36:1, 1073, 1082–83; *SHSP* 14, 533.

14. Heth, "Memoirs," 312–13.

15. Early, *Autobiographical Sketch*, 348ff.; Gordon, *Reminiscences*, 258ff.; Freeman, *R. E. Lee* 3, 297n.; *OR* 36:1, 1071.

16. *SHSP* 33, 20–21, 24.

17. *SHSP* 14, 533.

18. Freeman, *R. E. Lee* 3, 331.

19. Roman, *Beauregard* 2, 193.

20. *OR* 51:2, 876, 880, 882, 886; *OR* 36:2, 950.

21. *OR* 36:2, 955–58; *OR* 51:2, 892–93.

22. *OR* 36:2, 255, 960, 965; *OR* 51:2, 895, 897.

23. *OR* 51:2, 895; *OR* 36:2, 255–56, 239, 251.

24. *OR* 51:2, 897–99, 894, 891; *OR* 36:2, 275, 972, 251, 240.

25. *OR* 36:2, 124, 240–42, 223, 172; *OR* 51:2, 901, 899.

26. *OR* 51:2, 973, 904, 906.

27. *OR* 36:2, 975, 242–43, 978, 979.

28. *OR* 36:2, 244, 979, 980; *OR* 51:2, 906–8.

29. *OR* 51:2, 915; *OR* 36:2, 36, 985.

30. *OR* 36:2, 986, 991–92; *OR* 51:2, 920, 921; Roman, *Beauregard* 2, 200.

31. *OR* 36:2, 924, 997; *OR* 51:2, 923–24, 927.

32. *SHSP* 25, 206–7; *OR* 36:2, 1024–25.

33. *OR* 36:2, 1004–6, 200–201, 1077, 1009; *OR* 51:2, 934–35.

34. *OR* 36:2, 200–204, 212–13, 237, 197; Owen, *Washington Artillery*, 318.

35. *OR* 36:2, 257–60, 210–11, 1026; *SHSP* 23, 190; *OR* 36:3, 312.

36. *OR* 36:3, 811; *OR* 51:2, 939; *OR* 36:2, 204.

Chapter 32: New Front, New Battles

1. *OR* 36:3, 815; *OR Supplement* 6, 729; Hotchkiss, *CMH* 3, 460.
2. *OR* 36:1, 1071, 1058, 918, 1030–31; *OR* 51:2, 957; *SHSP* 14, 535.
3. J. William Jones, *Personal Reminiscences . . . of Gen. Robert E. Lee*, 40.
4. Hotchkiss, *Journal*, 208; *OR* 36:1, 1074.
5. *OR* 36:1, 1031, 821; *OR* 36:3, 837–39, 849, 818–19; *OR* 51:2, 952–53; 964–65; Freeman, *Lee's Dispatches*, 209, 205.
6. *OR* 36:3, 851, 854, 850, 857; *OR* 51:2, 975; Early, *Autobiographical Sketch,* 362; Freeman, *Lee's Dispatches*, 207; Roman, *Beauregard* 2, 563.
7. *OR* 36:1, 998; *OR* 36:2, 40; *OR* 36:3, 320, 410, 858; Stiles, *Four Years Under Marse Robert,* 274; Clark, *North Carolina Regiments* 5, 198ff.
8. *OR* 36:1, 998–99, 1049.
9. *OR Supplement* 6, 729; Thomas, *Doles-Cook Brigade,* 47; *Battles and Leaders* 4, 217.
10. IV *OR* 3, 496.
11. *OR* 36:1, 1074; Hamlin, *Ewell Letters,* 127–30.
12. *OR* 37:1, 76ff.
13. *OR* 37:1, 95, 747, 758; *OR* 51:2, 905, 981–82; Freeman, *Lee's Dispatches,* 219.
14. *OR* 36:1, 1034, 1095; *OR* 37:1, 754.
15. *OR* 36:3, 884.
16. *OR* 36:2, 272, 289; *OR* 36:3, 884–85.
17. *OR* 36:1, 1095–96, 796–97, 809; Edward L. Wells, *Hampton and His Cavalry in '64,* 195–97.
18. *OR* 37:1, 346; *SHSP* 22, 326–27.
19. *OR* 40:2, 658, 650; *OR* 51:2, 1020; Early, *Autobiographical Sketch,* 374–77; *SHSP* 30, 279ff.
20. Freeman, *R. E. Lee* 3, 399, 404, 439; Freeman, *Lee's Dispatches,* 227–32; Roman, *Beauregard* 2, 230; *SHSP* 25, 13.
21. Freeman, *Lee's Dispatches,* 233, 245; Roman, *Beauregard* 2, 230, 232; *OR* 40:1, 168; *OR* 51:2, 1079.
22. Walter Harrison, *Pickett's Men,* 130–31; *OR* 51:2, 1019, 1079; *OR* 40:1, 522, 545; *OR* 40:2, 662–63; Roman, *Beauregard* 2, 234–35.
23. Roman, *Beauregard* 2, 232–33; Clark, *North Carolina Regiments* 3, 622; *OR* 51:2, 1080; *OR* 40:2, 667, 668, 654; Freeman, *Lee's Dispatches,* 249ff.
24. *OR* 40:2, 690.
25. *OR* 40:1, 750, 629–30; *SHSP* 2, 274–75; *SHSP* 19, 201ff.
26. *OR* 40:1, 767.
27. Alexander, *Military Memoirs,* 565ff.; *OR* 40:3, 777, 794; *OR* 40:1, 775, 778, 308–10, 16–17; Dickert, *Kershaw's Brigade,* 390.
28. *OR* 40:1, 788–89, 17, 134; Freeman, *R. E. Lee* 3, 469–77.
29. Phoebe Yates Pember, *A Southern Woman's Story,* 105–6.
30. *OR* 42:2, 1156–57, 210, 215, 301.
31. Sorrel, *Recollections,* 264; Haskell, *Memoirs,* 75.

Chapter 33: The Darkening Autumn of Command

1. *OR* 37:1, 766, 97; Clark, *North Carolina Regiments* 1, 275.
2. Early, *Autobiographical Sketch,* 385, 381.

3. *OR* 43:1, 609–10; *OR* 37:2, 591ff.
4. *OR* 51:2, 1028–29; Douglas, *I Rode with Stonewall,* 293–94.
5. Early, *Autobiographical Sketch,* 387–88; Gordon, *Reminiscences,* 310; Worsham, *Jackson's Foot Cavalry,* 238–39; *OR* 37:1, 202, 348.
6. *OR* 37:1, 347–48.
7. Hotchkiss, *Journal,* 215; *OR* 37:1, 348.
8. *OR* 37:1, 348; Early, *Autobiographical Sketch,* 392.
9. Douglas, *I Rode with Stonewall,* 296.
10. *OR* 37:1, 349, 346; Ramseur Papers, Southern Historical Collection; Early, *Autobiographical Sketch,* 349.
11. *OR* 37:1, 353, 327; *OR* 37:2, 599; Ramseur Papers, Southern Historical Collection; Early, *Autobiographical Sketch,* 397.
12. Early, *Autobiographical Sketch,* 399; *OR* 37:1, 347, 288–90.
13. Early, *Autobiographical Sketch,* 401, 404; *OR* 37:1, 337, 334–35; *SHSP* 31, 270.
14. *OR* 43:1, 494–95.
15. *OR* 43:1, 7–8, 994; Early, *Autobiographical Sketch,* 405.
16. *OR* 42:2, 1170–73; Early, *Autobiographical Sketch,* 406.
17. *OR* 43:1, 990, 992, 993, 1001, 1003–4.
18. Early, *Autobiographical Sketch,* 414–16, 419; *OR* 43:1, 1027, 60, 61.
19. Early, *Autobiographical Sketch,* 419–20, 421–22; *CV* 16, 269; *SHSP* 2, 26–27; *SHSP* 27, 5; *OR* 43:1, 555, 574.
20. *OR* 43:1, 555, 47; Early, *Autobiographical Sketch,* 425–26.
21. *OR* 43:1, 556; Clark, *North Carolina Regiments* 3, 421; *SHSP* 35, 143; Gordon, *Reminiscences,* 322.
22. Early, *Autobiographical Sketch,* 430; *OR* 43:1, 556.
23. Lee, *Memoirs of Pendleton,* 338, 368ff.; Early, *Autobiographical Sketch,* 431; Douglas, *I Rode with Stonewall,* 312–13.
24. Early, *Autobiographical Sketch,* 435.
25. *OR* 43:2, 880, 891; *OR* 43:1, 558–59.
26. *Richmond Enquirer,* September 22, 1864; *OR* 43:2, 894; *SHSP* 18, 255–56.
27. *SHSP* 14, 553.
28. *OR* 42:1, 940, 936.
29. *OR* 42:1, 940; *OR* 42:2, 1199–1200.
30. *OR* 42:1, 944ff., 979, 859, 947; Freeman, *R. E. Lee* 3, 503–4; Clark, *North Carolina Regiments* 1, 408.
31. Freeman, *R. E. Lee* 3, 507–10.
32. *OR* 43:2, 892; *OR* 43:1, 51, 613.
33. Early, *Autobiographical Sketch,* 438, 440–42; Ramseur Papers, Southern Historical Collection.
34. Gordon, *Reminiscences,* 337; Early, *Autobiographical Sketch,* 443–45; Douglas, *I Rode with Stonewall,* 317.
35. Gordon, *Reminiscences,* 359, 341–42; *OR* 43:1, 561.
36. *OR* 43:1, 561–62, 581–82; Early, *Autobiographical Sketch,* 440, 447, 449; Gordon, *Reminiscences,* 365, 361; *SHSP* 18, 257.
37. *OR* 43:1, 562–63; Hotchkiss, *Journal,* 241, 240.

Chapter 34: In a Ring of Iron

1. *OR* 42:3, 1140; Sorrel, *Recollections,* 265.
2. Jones, *War Clerk's Diary* 2, 288.
3. *OR* 42:3, 1134; Chamberlayne, *Letters,* 284.
4. Wilcox mss., Library of Congress.
5. Longstreet, *Manassas to Appomattox,* 576; Freeman, *R. E. Lee* 3, 513–14; Woodward, *Mary Chesnut's Civil War,* 665.
6. *OR* 43:1, 584, 586–87.
7. *OR* 42:3, 1278.
8. *OR* 42:1, 1362, 1358, 1114, 1123.
9. *OR* 46:2, 1035, 1040; *OR* 46:1, 380.
10. *OR* 46:2, 1228, 1229–30, 1258; *OR* 51:2, 1065.
11. *OR* 46:2, 1032–33.
12. Freeman, *R. E. Lee* 3, 530; Wilcox mss., Library of Congress; *OR* 46:2, 1173.
13. Anderson report, Lee Papers, Confederate Memorial Institute.
14. Early, *Autobiographical Sketch,* 462–64.
15. *OR* 46:1, 394ff., 441–42; *SHSP* 10, 350.
16. *Journal C.S. Congress* 7, 545.
17. *OR* 47:2, 1204, 1238; *OR* 53, 412–13; *OR* 46:2, 1242–45.
18. *OR* 47:2, 1271, 1297, 1373; Freeman, *R. E. Lee* 4, 12; Gordon, *Reminiscences,* 389.
19. Freeman, *R. E. Lee* 4, 14ff.
20. Gordon, *Reminiscences,* 407–10; *OR* 46:1, 317, 391.
21. Gordon, *Reminiscences,* 411; *OR* 46:1, 375, 51, 156; R. M. Stribling, *Gettysburg Campaign and Campaigns of 1864 and 1865 in Virginia,* 299.
22. Gordon, *Reminiscences,* 411.
23. *OR* 46:1, 1055; Freeman, *Lee's Dispatches,* 341ff.
24. *OR* 46:3, 391, 1357; *OR* 46:1, 390.
25. Harrison, *Pickett's Men,* 142–45.
26. Munford mss., Duke University; Harrison, *Pickett's Men,* 145; La Salle Corbell Pickett, *Pickett and His Men,* 386.
27. Harrison, *Pickett's Men,* 145; *OR* 46:1, 1299, 1300, 1288; Munford mss., Duke University; G. K. Warren, *Proceedings . . . of the Court of Inquiry . . . in the Case of Gouverneur K. Warren,* 376.
28. Rosser in *Philadelphia Weekly Times,* April 5, 1885; Rosser mss., University of Virginia; Munford mss., Duke University.
29. Munford mss., Duke University.
30. *OR* 46:1, 62, 1104–5, 1300, 836; Freeman, *R. E. Lee* 4, 31; Munford mss., Duke University.
31. *SHSP* 14, 17; Heth, "Memoirs," 320; Armistead C. Gordon, *Memories and Memorials of William Gordon McCabe* 1, 165–66, 169.

Chapter 35: The Last March

1. *OR* 46:1, 1288; *OR* 46:3, 1374; Longstreet, *Manassas to Appomattox,* 602.
2. *SHSP* 11, 565–66; *SHSP* 2, 302.
3. Venable in *SHSP* 12, 186; Tucker in *SHSP* 11, 566–68; *SHSP* 27, 33; *SHSP* 19, 184–85.

4. W. H. Palmer, June 25, 1905, W. H. Taylor Papers, Virginia State Library.

5. Longstreet, *Manassas to Appomattox,* 606, 608; *OR* 46:1, 903; Douglas, *I Rode with Stonewall,* 330–31.

6. *OR* 46:1, 1281; *SHSP* 38, 5.

7. Alexander, *Military Memoirs,* 592–93; *OR* 46:1, 1179.

8. *OR* 46:1, 1288, 1280; Walker, *Anderson,* 210–11; Howard, *Recollections,* 367–68.

9. Freeman, *R. E. Lee* 4, 162n.

10. Daly, *Alexander Cheeves Haskell,* 169; George Cary Eggleston, *A Rebel's Recollections,* 232; *OR* 46:1, 1281, 1283.

11. Walker, *Anderson,* 211; Harrison, *Pickett's Men,* 148.

12. Caldwell, *Gregg's Brigade,* 226; *OR* 46:1, 62.

13. Freeman, *R. E. Lee* 4, 509ff., 67.

14. Eggleston, *A Rebel's Recollections,* 244.

15. *OR* 46:1, 1265, 1281, 1294, 1296; Longstreet, *Manassas to Appomattox,* 610; Alexander, *Military Memoirs,* 595.

16. Longstreet, *Manassas to Appomattox,* 610; Latrobe mss., Virginia Historical Society.

17. *OR* 46:1, 1265, 1295, 1301–2; Stiles, *Four Years Under Marse Robert,* 326–28; Howard, *Recollections,* 376.

18. *OR* 46:1, 1294, 1265; Walker, *Anderson,* 211.

19. Walker, *Anderson,* 211; *OR* 46:1, 1294, 1265, 1297.

20. *OR* 46:1, 1297–98, 1294–95, 1284; Walker, *Anderson,* 211; Stiles, *Four Years Under Marse Robert,* 330–32; Howard, *Recollections,* 380–82; *SHSP* 25, 40ff.

21. Walker, *Anderson,* 211–12; *SHSP* 25, 18; Harrison, *Pickett's Men,* 154, 157; *OR* 46:1, 1295, 1284, 1297; Hunton, *Autobiography,* 125–26.

22. Lee, *Memoirs of Pendleton,* 401; Longstreet, *Manassas to Appomattox,* 612; *OR* 46:1, 1169, 1162, 1215, 1220, 1302; Myers, *The Comanches,* 376–78, 380; Owen, *Washington Artillery,* 377.

23. Gordon, *Reminiscences,* 429–30; Gordon report, Lee Papers, Confederate Memorial Institute.

24. Mahone in Longstreet, *Manassas to Appomattox,* 614–15.

25. Alexander, *Military Memoirs,* 597; St. John report, Lee Papers, Confederate Memorial Institute.

26. Owen, *Washington Artillery,* 377; *SHSP* 32, 71.

27. *SHSP* 25, 18–19.

28. Freeman, *R. E. Lee* 4, 100; *OR* 46:1, 1109, 1142, 1303.

29. Owen, *Washington Artillery,* 379; E. M. Boykin, *The Falling Flag,* 39; Freeman, *R. E. Lee* 4, 106ff.; Sorrel, *Recollections,* 297ff.; Longstreet, *Manassas to Appomattox,* 619.

30. Lee, *Memoirs of Pendleton,* 401–2; Gordon, *Reminiscences,* 433; Caldwell, *Gregg's Brigade,* 233.

31. *OR* 46:1, 1291; Longstreet, *Manassas to Appomattox,* 620; Lee, *Memoirs of Pendleton,* 402; Alexander, *Military Memoirs,* 600–601.

32. Longstreet, *Manassas to Appomattox,* 619–20; Fitz Lee letter, Lee Papers, Confederate Memorial Institute.

33. *OR* 46:1, 1282.

34. Gordon, *Reminiscences,* 435; *OR* 46:1, 56–57.

35. Gordon, *Reminiscences,* 435–36; *OR* 46:1, 1267, 1304.

36. *OR* 46:1, 1303–4; Grimes, *Letters,* 114–15; J. Armfield Franklin diary, Thomas Suter Collection; Clark, *North Carolina Regiments* 5, 260.

37. Gordon report, Lee Papers, Confederate Memorial Institute; Gordon, *Reminiscences,* 437–38.

38. Longstreet, *Manassas to Appomattox*, 624–25; Alexander, *Military Memoirs*, 603–5.

39. Longstreet, *Manassas to Appomattox*, 625–27; Haskell, *Memoirs*, 93–94.

40. Gordon, *Reminiscences*, 438–40.

41. Longstreet, *Manassas to Appomattox*, 627; Haskell, *Memoirs*, 94–95; *OR* 46:1, 1303.

42. Longstreet, *Manassas to Appomattox*, 627–28; Alexander, *Military Memoirs*, 609.

43. Owen, *Washington Artillery*, 382; Freeman, *R. E. Lee* 4, 144ff.; Grimes, *Letters*, 119; Clark, *North Carolina Regiments* 5, 262; Boykin, *The Falling Flag*, 61.

44. Moore, *Cannoneer Under Jackson*, 290; Caldwell, *Gregg's Brigade*, 242.

45. *OR* 46:1, 1279.

46. Joshua Chamberlain, *The Passing of the Armies*, 248, 258–61; Chamberlain in *SHSP* 32, 362.

47. Clark, *North Carolina Regiments* 1, 279.

48. Lee Papers, Confederate Memorial Institute.

Bibliography

Principal Manuscript Sources

William Allan Papers, Southern Historical Collection, University of North Carolina
R. H. Chilton mss., Museum of the Confederacy
R. L. Dabney mss., Hotchkiss Papers
R. L. Dabney Papers, Virginia State Library
George and Catherine Davis Collection, Tulane University
Richard S. Ewell Papers, Library of Congress
Richard B. Garnett Papers, Museum of the Confederacy
Robert S. Garnett Papers, Myrtle Cooper-Schwarz Collection
John A. Harman mss., Hotchkiss Papers
Jedediah Hotchkiss Papers, Library of Congress
Thomas J. Jackson letter book, Hotchkiss Papers
Thomas J. Jackson mss., Confederate Memorial Institute
S. R. Johnston Papers, Virginia Historical Society
Osmun Latrobe mss., Virginia Historical Society
Robert E. Lee Papers, Confederate Memorial Institute
Light Division letter book, New York Public Library
H. B. McClellan mss., Confederate Memorial Institute
Hunter H. McGuire Papers, Museum of the Confederacy
Lafayette McLaws Papers, Southern Historical Collection, University of North Carolina
Raphael J. Moses mss., Southern Historical Collection, University of North Carolina
Thomas T. Munford mss., Duke University
William Dorsey Pender Papers, Southern Historical Collection, University of North Carolina
R. Channing Price Papers, Southern Historical Collection, University of North Carolina
Stephen Dodson Ramseur Papers, Southern Historical Collection, University of North Carolina
Thomas L. Rosser mss., University of Virginia
J. E. B. Stuart Papers, Huntington Library
Walter H. Taylor Papers, Virginia State Library
Isaac R. Trimble mss., I. R. Trimble Collection
Cadmus M. Wilcox mss., Library of Congress
Withrow Papers, Washington and Lee University
Ambrose Ransom Wright mss., A. R. Wright Collection

Principal Biographical and General Works

Alexander, E. Porter. *Military Memoirs of a Confederate.* New York, 1907.

Allan, William. *History of the Campaign of Stonewall Jackson in the Shenandoah Valley of Virginia.* Philadelphia, 1880.

――――. *The Army of Northern Virginia in 1862.* Cambridge, Mass., 1892.

Avirett, J. B. *The Memoirs of General Turner Ashby and His Compeers.* Baltimore, 1867.

Bates, S. P. *The Battle of Chancellorsville.* Meadville, Pa., 1882.

Battles and Leaders of the Civil War. 4 vols. New York, 1887–88.

Beale, G. W. *A Lieutenant of Cavalry in Lee's Army.* Boston, 1918.

Beale, R. L. T. *History of the Ninth Virginia Cavalry.* Richmond, 1899.

Beauregard, P. G. T. *Commentary on the Campaign and Battle of Manassas.* New York, 1891.

Bigelow, John, Jr. *The Campaign of Chancellorsville.* New Haven, 1910.

Blackford, W. W. *War Years with Jeb Stuart.* New York, 1945.

Boykin, E. M. *The Falling Flag: Evacuation of Richmond, Retreat and Surrender at Appomattox.* New York, 1874.

Bradford, Gamaliel. *Confederate Portraits.* Boston, 1917.

Brent, J. L. *Memoirs of the War Between the States.* New Orleans, 1940.

Caffey, Thomas C. *Battle-fields of the South, From Bull Run to Fredericksburg.* New York, 1864.

Caldwell, J. F. J. *The History of Gregg's Brigade of South Carolinians.* Philadelphia, 1866.

Casler, John O. *Four Years in the Stonewall Brigade.* 2nd ed. Girard, Kansas, 1906.

Chamberlain, Joshua. *The Passing of the Armies.* New York, 1915.

Chamberlayne, John Hampden. *Ham Chamberlayne: Letters of an Artillery Officer.* Richmond, 1932.

Clark, Walter, ed. *Histories of the Several Regiments and Battalions from North Carolina in the Great War, 1861–65.* 5 vols. Raleigh, 1901.

Confederate Veteran. 40 vols. Nashville, 1893–1932.

Cooke, J. E. *Stonewall Jackson: A Military Biography.* New York, 1866.

――――. *Wearing of the Gray; Being Personal Portraits, Scenes, and Adventures of the War.* New York, 1867.

Couper, William. *100 Years at V.M.I.* 4 vols. Richmond, 1939.

Dabney, R. L. *Life and Campaigns of Lieut.-Gen. Thomas J. Jackson.* New York, 1866.

Daly, Louise Haskell. *Alexander Cheves Haskell: The Portrait of a Man.* Norwood, Mass., 1934.

Davis, Jefferson. *The Rise and Fall of the Confederate Government.* 2 vols. New York, 1881.

Dawson, F. W. *Reminiscences of Confederate Service.* Charleston, 1882.

Dickert, D. Augustus. *History of Kershaw's Brigade.* Newberry, S.C., 1899.

Douglas, Henry Kyd. *I Rode with Stonewall.* Chapel Hill, 1940.

Early, Jubal A. *Autobiographical Sketch and Narrative of the War Between the States.* Philadelphia, 1912.

Eggleston, George Cary. *A Rebel's Recollections.* New York, 1875.

Evans, Clement A., ed. *Confederate Military History.* 13 vols. Atlanta, 1899.

Freeman, D. S. *Lee's Dispatches.* New York, 1915.

――――. *R. E. Lee.* 4 vols. New York, 1934–35.

――――. *The South to Posterity: An Introduction to the Writing of Confederate History.* New York, 1939.

Fremantle, Arthur James Lyon. *Three Months in the Southern States.* New York, 1864.

French, S. G. *Two Wars: An Autobiography.* Nashville, 1901.

Gilmore, Harry. *Four Years in the Saddle.* New York, 1866.

Gordon, Armistead C. *Memories and Memorials of William Gordon McCabe.* 2 vols. Richmond, 1925

Gordon, John B. *Reminiscences of the Civil War.* New York, 1903.

Grimes, Bryan. *Letters of Major-General Bryan Grimes to His Wife.* Raleigh, 1883.

Hamlin, P. G. *Old Bald Head (R. S. Ewell).* Strasburg, Va., 1940.

———., ed. *The Making of a Soldier: Letters of General R. S. Ewell.* Richmond, 1935.

Harrison, Walter. *Pickett's Men.* New York, 1870.

Henderson, G. F. R. *Stonewall Jackson and the American Civil War.* 2 vols. New York, 1898.

Heth, Harry. "Memoirs," *Civil War History.* 8:3, 1962.

Hill, D. H., Jr. *Bethel to Sharpsburg.* 2 vols. Raleigh, 1926.

Hood, John B. *Advance and Retreat.* New Orleans, 1880.

Hopkins, L. W. *From Bull Run to Appomattox.* Baltimore, 1908.

Horn, Stanley F. *The Army of Tennessee.* Indianapolis, 1941.

Hotchkiss, Jedediah. *Make Me a Map of the Valley: The Civil War Journal of Stonewall Jackson's Topographer Jedediah Hotchkiss.* Ed. Archie P. McDonald. Dallas, 1973.

Howard, McHenry. *Recollections of a Maryland Confederate Soldier and Staff Officer.* Baltimore, 1914.

Hunton, Eppa. *Autobiography.* Richmond, 1933.

Jackson, Mary Anna. *Memoirs of Stonewall Jackson.* Louisville, 1895.

Johnston, D. E. *The Story of a Confederate Boy in the Civil War.* Portland, Ore., 1914.

Johnston, J. E. *Narrative of Military Operations During the Late War Between the States.* New York, 1872.

Jones, J. B. *A Rebel War Clerk's Diary.* 2 vols. Philadelphia, 1866.

Jones, J. W. *Christ in Camp: Or, Religion in Lee's Army.* Richmond, 1887.

Jones, J. William. *Personal Reminiscences, Anecdotes and Letters of General Robert E. Lee.* New York, 1874.

Journal of the Congress of the Confederate States, 1861–1865. 7 vols. Washington, 1904–5.

Land We Love, The. Charlotte, 1866–69.

Lee, Fitzhugh. *General Lee.* New York, 1894.

Lee, Robert E. *The Wartime Papers of R. E. Lee.* Eds. Clifford Dowdey and Louis H. Manarin. New York, 1961.

Lee, Susan P. *Memoirs of William Nelson Pendleton.* Philadelphia, 1893.

Long, A. L. *Memoirs of Robert E. Lee.* New York, 1886.

Longstreet, James. *From Manassas to Appomattox: Memoirs of the Civil War in America.* Philadelphia, 1896.

Marshall, Charles. *An Aid-de-Camp of Lee, Being the Papers of Colonel Charles Marshall.* Ed. Frederick Maurice. Boston, 1927.

Mason, Emily. *Popular Life of Gen. Robert E. Lee.* Baltimore, 1872.

McClellan, H. B. *The Life and Campaigns of J. E. B. Stuart.* Richmond, 1885.

McClure, A. K., ed. *Annals of the War, Written by Leading Participants North and South.* Philadelphia, 1879.

McDonald, W. N. *The Laurel Brigade.* Baltimore, 1907.

McGuire, Hunter, and George L. Christian. *The Confederate Cause and Conduct in the War Between the States.* Richmond, 1907.

McKim, R. H. *A Soldier's Recollections.* New York, 1910.

Meade, George. *The Life and Letters of George Gordon Meade.* 2 vols. New York, 1913.

Moffett, Mary C. *Letters of General James Conner, C.S.A.* Columbia, S.C., 1933.

Moore, A. B. *Conscription and Conflict in the Confederacy*. New York, 1924.

Moore, E. A. *The Story of a Cannoneer Under Stonewall Jackson*. New York, 1907.

Moore, Frank, ed. *The Rebellion Record*. 12 vols. New York, 1862–71.

Mosby, J. S. *Stuart's Cavalry in the Gettysburg Campaign*. New York, 1908.

————. *War Reminiscences*. Boston, 1887.

Myers, F. M. *The Comanches: A History of White's Battalion, Virginia Cavalry*. Baltimore, 1871.

Neese, G. M. *Three Years in the Confederate Horse Artillery*. Washington, 1911.

Oates, W. C. *The War Between the Union and the Confederacy*. Washington, 1905.

Owen, W. M. *In Camp and Battle with the Washington Artillery of New Orleans*. Boston, 1885.

Papers of the Military Historical Society of Massachusetts. 13 vols. Boston, 1895–1913.

Paxton, Frank. *The Civil War Letters of General Frank "Bull" Paxton*. Hillsboro, Texas, 1978.

Pember, Phoebe Yates. *A Southern Woman's Story*. New York, 1879.

Pender, William D. *The General to His Lady: The Civil War Letters of William Dorsey Pender to Fanny Pender*. Chapel Hill, 1962.

Phillips, Ulrich B., ed. *The Correspondence of Robert Toombs, Alexander H. Stephens, and Howell Cobb*. Washington, 1913.

Pickett, La Salle Corbell. *Pickett and His Men*. Atlanta, 1900.

Pollard, E. A. *Lee and His Lieutenants*. New York, 1867.

Putnam, Sallie A. *Richmond During the War*. New York, 1867.

Roman, Alfred. *The Military Operations of General Beauregard*. 2 vols. New York, 1884.

Ross, Fitzgerald. *A Visit to the Cities and Camps of the Confederate States*. London, 1865.

Rowland, Dunbar, ed. *Jefferson Davis, Constitutionalist: His Letters, Papers and Speeches*. 10 vols. Jackson, Miss., 1923.

Smith, G. W. *Confederate War Papers*. New York, 1884.

Snow, W. P. *Southern Generals*. New York, 1865.

Sorrel, G. Moxley. *Recollections of a Confederate Staff Officer*. Jackson, Tenn., 1958.

Southern Historical Society Papers. 52 vols. Richmond, 1876–1959.

Stiles, Robert. *Four Years Under Marse Robert*. Washington, 1903.

Stovall, Pleasant A. *Robert Toombs, Statesman, Speaker, Soldier, Sage*. New York, 1892.

Stribling, R. M. *Gettysburg Campaign and Campaigns of 1864 and 1865 in Virginia*. Petersburg, Va., 1905.

Taylor, Richard. *Destruction and Reconstruction: Personal Experiences of the Late War*. New York, 1879.

Taylor, Walter H. *Four Years with General Lee*. New York, 1877.

Thomas, Henry W. *History of the Doles-Cook Brigade*. Atlanta, 1903.

Thomason, J. W. *"Jeb" Stuart*. New York, 1930.

U.S. War Department. *The War of the Rebellion: A Compilation of the Official Records of the Union and Confederate Armies*. 128 parts in 70 vols. Washington 1880–1901. *Supplement*. Wilmington, 1994– .

Von Borcke, Heros. *Memoirs of the Confederate War for Independence*. 2 vols. London, 1866.

Walker, Irvine. *The Life of Lieutenant-General Richard Heron Anderson*. Charleston, 1917.

Wells, Edward L. *Hampton and His Cavalry in '64*. Richmond, 1899.

Wise, J. C. *The Long Arm of Lee, or the History of the Artillery Arm of the Army of Northern Virginia*. 2 vols. Lynchburg, 1915.

Woodward, C. Vann. *Mary Chesnut's Civil War*. New Haven, 1981.

Worsham, J. H. *One of Jackson's Foot Cavalry*. New York, 1912.

Wright, Louise Wigfall, *A Southern Girl in '61*. New York, 1905.

Wright, Marcus J. *General Officers of the Confederate Army*. New York, 1911.

Index

Richmond (*cont.*)
  fires in, 787, 793
  Longstreet's plan and, 548, 549
  in maps, 132, 154, 223
  Seven Days campaigns in defense of,
    see Seven Days battles
  Seven Pines and, 129–44
  Spotsylvania campaign and, 672, 673,
    675, 676
  Stuart's ride around McClellan,
    150–58, 159, 270, 390
  torpedoes used in defense of, 147
Richmond, Department of, 448
Richmond, Fredericksburg and Potomac
    Railroad (R. F. & P. Railroad), 101,
    123, 127, 399, 465, 496, 506, 672,
    687, 709
Richmond and Danville Railroad, 709,
    710, 731, 775, 788, 791
Richmond and Petersburg Railroad,
    701–3, 705, 706–7, 708, 709
Richmond Dispatch, 89, 371, 396, 418, 509,
    562
Richmond Enquirer, 371
Richmond Examiner, 52, 280, 418, 524,
    540, 598
Richmond Howitzers, 441, 678
Richmond Sentinel, 552
Richmond Whig, 89–90, 280, 509, 523,
    552
Rich Mountain, 61, 62, 65, 66, 67, 274
    in map, 63
Ricketts, Brig. Gen. James B., U.S.A.,
    291
Riddell's Shop, 246, 252
Ringgold, Ga., 641, 642
Ripley, Brig. Gen. Roswell S., C.S.A., 148,
    363, 379, 382, 386
    his early career, 148
    in Seven Days battles, 229, 258,
      261–62
    in Maryland, 346–49
    aids D. H. Hill at South Mountain,
      347, 348, 349, 386
    he is wounded, 376
River Road, 246, 250, 253, 271, 274
Rives's Salient, 784
Roanoke Island, 99

Roanoke River, 656
Roberts, Brig. Gen. William P., C.S.A.,
    778, 780
Robertson, Brig Gen. Beverly H., C.S.A.,
    286–87, 292, 297, 302, 309, 310,
    311, 344, 388, 431, 448, 555, 614
    his physical appearance, 286
    his early career, 286
    succeeds Ashby, 286–87
    at Second Manassas, 332
    transfer of, 532
    at Kelly's Ford, 536, 539
Robertson, Brig. Gen. Jerome B., C.S.A.,
    381, 382, 639–40, 659
    Longstreet's charges against, 643–44,
      645
    his transfer, 644
Robertson River, 292
Rockbridge Artillery, 187, 531
Rockville, Md., 558
Rodes, Maj. Gen. Robert Emmett, C.S.A.,
    87, 112, 143, 236, 516, 528, 530,
    531, 533, 534, 535, 541, 543, 546,
    547, 608, 652, 658, 698, 722, 739,
    763, 764, 766
    biographical sketch, 39
    his early career, 138
    at Seven Pines, 130, 131, 133, 135, 136,
      137, 138, 139, 141, 142, 236, 814
    Gordon leads his brigade, 253, 275
    aids D. H. Hill at South Mountain,
      347, 348, 349–50
    his position there, in map, 350
    at Sharpsburg, 363, 364, 366
    his position there, in map, 361
    at Chancellorsville, 466, 467, 469, 470,
      475, 476, 477, 478, 479–80,
      482–83, 486, 487, 489, 490, 491,
      492, 509, 510, 511, 514
    assumes command when Jackson is
      wounded, 482–83
    gives command over to Stuart, 486
    praise for his actions, 506, 511, 515
    his promotion, 511, 528
    at Brandy Station, 539
    orders given to, 546
    confers with Ewell before Gettysburg,
      547